GRAMMAR EXPRESS

For Self-Study and Classroom Use

Marjorie Fuchs

Margaret Bonner

To my Aunt Gerry, who loved words.—MF

To Aline and Luke.—MB

Grammar *Express*

Pearson Education, 10 Bank Street, White Plains, NY 10606

Vice president, director of publishing: Allen Ascher
Editorial director: Louisa Hellegers
Senior development manager: Penny Laporte
Senior development editor: Françoise Leffler
Vice president, director of design and production: Rhea Banker
Executive managing editor: Linda Moser
Production manager: Alana Zdinak
Senior production editor: Christine Lauricella
Senior manufacturing manager: Patrice Fraccio
Manufacturing supervisor: Edie Pullman
Photo research: Stacey Hunter
Cover design: Patricia Wosczyk
Text design: Patricia Wosczyk
Text composition: Preface, Inc.
Text art: Preface, Inc.
Photo credits: see p. xiii
Illustrators: see p. xiii
Cover image: © David Barnes, ICL 2000

Parts of *Grammar Express* are adapted from the intermediate
and high-intermediate levels of *Focus on Grammar,
Second Edition* © 2000.

ISBN: 0-201-52073-7

8 9 10—V011—12 11 10

Contents

iv

v

Appendices

About the Authors

Marjorie Fuchs has taught ESL at New York City Technical College and LaGuardia Community College of the City University of New York and EFL at the Sprach Studio Lingua Nova in Munich, Germany. She holds a Master's Degree in Applied English Linguistics and a Certificate in TESOL from the University of Wisconsin–Madison. She has authored or co-authored many widely used ESL textbooks, notably *On Your Way: Building Basic Skills in English, Crossroads, Top Twenty ESL Word Games: Beginning Vocabulary Development, Around the World: Pictures for Practice, Families: Ten Card Games for Language Learners, Focus on Grammar: An Intermediate Course for Reference and Practice, Focus on Grammar: A High-Intermediate Course for Reference and Practice,* and the workbooks to the *Longman Dictionary of American English,* the *Longman Photo Dictionary, The Oxford Picture Dictionary,* and *Focus on Grammar: Intermediate* and *High-Intermediate.*

Margaret Bonner has taught ESL at Hunter College and the Borough of Manhattan Community College of the City University of New York, at Taiwan National University in Taipei, and at Virginia Commonwealth University in Richmond. She holds a Master's Degree in Library Science from Columbia University, and she has done work towards a Ph.D. in English Literature at the Graduate Center of the City University of New York. She has contributed to a number of ESL and EFL projects, including *Making Connections, On Your Way,* and the Curriculum Renewal Project in Oman, where she wrote textbooks, workbooks, and teachers manuals for the national school system. She authored *Step into Writing: A Basic Writing Text,* and co-authored *Focus on Grammar: An Intermediate Course for Reference and Practice, Focus on Grammar: A High-Intermediate Course for Reference and Practice, Focus on Grammar: High-Intermediate Workbook,* and *The Oxford Picture Dictionary Intermediate Workbook.*

About the Book

Welcome to *Grammar Express*—the fast way to study and learn English grammar.

Grammar Express features

- Short, easy-to-use **four-page units**
- **Grammar points** presented and **contextualized** through cartoons, photos, and other illustrations
- Clear **Grammar Charts** showing the forms of the grammar point
- **Chart Checks** to help you use the grammar charts
- Clear **Grammar Explanations** and **Examples**
- **Usage Notes** telling you how English speakers use the grammar point
- **Be careful! Notes** showing typical mistakes students make
- **Pronunciation Notes** to help you pronounce words correctly
- A **variety of exercise types** to practice the grammar points
- **SelfTests** to check your progress
- **Appendices** with helpful lists and information
- An **Index** to help you quickly find grammar points
- An **Answer Key** so you can check your answers

UNITS

Grammar Express has 76 units. Each unit has four pages—two pages of grammar presentation and two pages of practice. Here's how a typical unit looks:

Presentation

The grammar point is presented in three steps.

1. Illustration

Each unit begins with an **illustration**—a cartoon, comic strip, photo with speech bubbles, newspaper headline—which introduces the grammar point in a real-life, real-language context. It also introduces the topic of the unit. *(For example, in Unit 8 the cartoon introduces the grammar point* used to, *and the unit topic, fashion.)*

A **Check Point** helps you think about the meaning of the grammar point in the illustration.

2. Charts

Grammar Charts show the forms of the grammar point. (*In Unit 8 you can see* used to *in statements, questions, and short answers.*)

Chart Checks ask questions about the grammar charts. They help you notice important information about the forms and uses of the grammar point you are studying.

An **Express Check** follows the Grammar Charts. This is a quick and easy way for you to try out the forms in the charts.

3. Notes

Grammar Notes present **Grammar Explanations** on the left and **Examples** on the right. Timelines show the meaning of verb forms. (*For example, in Unit 8 the timeline for* used to *shows that you can use it only for the past.*)

Usage Notes tell you how English speakers use the grammar point. (*In Unit 8 the Usage Note for* used to *explains that this form is more common in affirmative statements than in negative statements or questions.*)

Be careful! Notes point out typical mistakes that English students make. (*One of the Be careful! Notes in Unit 8 tells you not to confuse* used to *with* be used to *or* get used to.)

Pronunciation Notes tell you how to correctly pronounce the grammar point in everyday speech. These notes use easy pronunciation spellings.

Check it out! tells you where to look in the book (appendices or other units) to find more information about the grammar point.

Practice

Two pages of exercises give you practice in understanding and using the grammar point. A typical unit has four exercises.

Exercise 1

The first exercise is always a **"for recognition only"** exercise. This means that you will have to find or understand the grammar point, but you will not have to use it yet. (*For example, in Unit 8 you will read a short magazine article about fashion, and find and underline all the examples of* used to *which refer to past habits.*)

Exercises 2 and 3

In these exercises you actively practice the grammar point. There are a **variety of exercise types**, including multiple choice, fill-in-the-blanks, describing pictures, sentence combining, and asking and answering questions. The exercises always show the grammar point in a context that is related to the unit topic. (*In Unit 8, Exercise 2, you will complete sentences about fashion in the past while you describe pictures. In Exercise 3, you will use an old advertisement to ask and answer questions about sneakers.*)

Exercise 4

This is always an **editing** exercise. In this exercise, you will have to find and correct typical mistakes that students make when they use the grammar point.

TESTS

The 76 units of *Grammar Express* are divided into 15 parts. After each part you will find a **SelfTest**. These tests will help you review and see how well you have learned the material in the part. The **SelfTests** have multiple-choice questions similar to questions found on the TOEFL®, a test that is widely used for foreign students who want to attend college in the United States.

APPENDICES

In the back of the book, you will find 28 **Appendices** with useful information, such as lists of common irregular verbs, verbs followed by the gerund, verbs followed by the infinitive, and spelling and pronunciation rules.

ANSWER KEY

The **Answer Key** provides answers to the Check Points, Charts Checks, Express Checks, all the practice exercises, and the SelfTests.

Grammar Express can be used for self-study or in the classroom. Start with Unit 1 and work through the entire book, or choose the units you want to focus on. *Grammar Express* can help you reach your language goals quickly.

Your journey through English grammar can be an adventure of discovery. We hope you will enjoy traveling with *Grammar Express*.

All Aboard!!! . . .

Credits

Acknowledgments

Writing *Grammar Express* has been an exhilarating ride for us, the authors. The company of the following editors and colleagues has made the journey even more enjoyable. We are grateful to:

Françoise Leffler, our wonderful editor, for her dedication, her impeccable attention to detail, and, above all, for her sense of style and humor, which infuse the book. She's a pleasure to work with. *Mille mercis, Françoise!*

Louisa Hellegers, for her expert coordination of the many aspects of this project and for her readiness to go the extra mile. Despite an incredibly busy schedule that has her flying all over the world, she always had time for us.

Chris Lauricella, for expertly conducting the book through its various stages of production, and for keeping everything on track.

Rhea Banker and **Pat Wosczyk**, for an outstanding design: clear, user-friendly, and beautiful to look at.

Robyn Roth of Preface, Inc., for her intelligent and creative work in bringing together text and design.

Stacey Hunter and **Iris Bodre-Baez**, for their diligent work on several aspects of the project, notably photo research and obtaining permissions.

Diana Nott, for coming up with the perfect title.

We would also like to acknowledge the following reviewers for their careful reading of the manuscript and their thoughtful suggestions, many of which we incorporated into the book:

■ **Haydée Alvarado Santos**, University of Puerto Rico College of General Studies, Río Piedras Campus, Puerto Rico ■ **Frankie Dovel**, VESOL Coordinator, Orange County Public Schools, Orlando, Florida ■ **Marcia Edwards Hijaab**, Center for International Programs, Virginia Commonwealth University, Richmond, Virginia ■ **Steve Horowitz**, UESL Program, Central Washington University, Ellensberg, Washington ■ **Susan Jamieson**, International Programs, Bellevue Community College, Bellevue, Washington ■ **Martha McGaughey**, Language Training Institute, Englewood Cliffs, New Jersey, and New School ELSC, New York ■ **Angelita Moreno**, Instituto Cultural Brasil-Estados Unidos, Belo Horizonte MG, Brazil ■ **Gabriella Morvay**, CUNY Language Immersion Program, Bronx Community College, Bronx, New York ■ **Michaela Safadi**, South Gate Community Adult School, California ■ **Barbara Smith-Palinkas**, Assistant Director for Curriculum and Instruction, English Language Institute, University of South Florida, Tampa ■ **Cleide Silva**, Open House, Santos SP, Brazil ■ **Sávio Siqueira**, ACBEU, Salvador BA, Brazil ■ **Berrin Yildiz**, Dogus University Prep Program, Turkey.

Thanks to the following teachers for pointing us in the right direction with their valuable feedback during the developmental stages of this project:

■ **Belgún Akgeúk**, Private ATA High School, Turkey ■ **Marlene Almeida**, Wordshop, Belo Horizonte MG, Brazil ■ **Fatima Badry**, American University of Sharjah, Dubai, United Arab Emirates ■ **Ellen Balleisen**, CUNY Language Immersion Program, Bronx Community College, Bronx, New York ■ **Sheila Barbosa Fialho**, EPI, São José dos Campos SP, Brazil ■ **Matthew Bellman**, TCLC Language Academy, Nagoya, Japan ■ **Patricia Brenner**, University of Washington, Seattle, Washington ■ **Heloísa Burrowes Raposo**, Raposo English Center, Campos dos Goytacazes RJ, Brazil ■ **Fábio Delano Carneiro**, DEC, Fortaleza CE, Brazil ■ **Elton Carvalho**, Fundação Educacional do Distrito Federal, Brasília DF, Brazil ■ **Sergio J. Chiri**, Universidad Del Pacifico, Lima, Peru ■ **Judy A. Cleek**, Intensive English Program, Martin, Tennessee ■ **Jill Cook**, Zayed University, Dubai, United Arab Emirates ■ **Jason H. Davis**, CUNY Language Immersion Program, Bronx Community College, Bronx, New York ■ **Ricardo Delgado**, CCBEU, Belém PA, Brazil ■ **Beatriz B. Diaz**, Robert Morgan Voc. Tech., Miami, Florida ■ **Luiz Alberto Ferrari**, Colégio Barão de Mauá, Mauá SP, Brazil ■ **Patty Heiser**, University of Washington, Seattle, Washington ■ **Jung-Sinn Hyon**, Hunter College, New York, New York ■ **Amy Lewis**, Keio University, Tokyo, Japan ■ **Chao-Hung Lin**, Hunter College, New York, New York ■ **Maria Esther Linares de Pedemonte**, International Exams, Lima, Peru ■ **Joan McAuley**, CUNY Language Immersion Program, Bronx Community College, Bronx, New York ■ **Angelita Moreno**, Instituto Cultural Brasil-Estados Unidos, Belo Horizonte MG, Brazil ■ **Sandra Moreno Walter**, Masters, Sorocaba SP, Brazil ■ **Gabriella Morvay**, CUNY Language Immersion Program, Bronx Community College, Bronx, New York ■ **Marisa Nickle**, University of Washington, Seattle, Washington ■ **Martha Oval**, Orel Bilim Koleg, Ankara, Turkey ■ **Hyangmi Pae**, Hannam University, Segu Daegon, Korea ■ **Rosemary Palmer**, Bloomfield College, Bloomfield, New Jersey ■ **Stephen Russell**, Tokyo University of Foreign Studies, Tokyo, Japan ■ **John Ryder**, Kyoto Gakuen High School, Kyoto, Japan ■ **Maria Benedita Santos**, Casa Thomas Jefferson, Brasília DF, Brazil ■ **Cleide Silva**, Open House, Santos SP, Brazil ■ **Sávio Siqueira**, ACBEU, Salvador BA, Brazil ■ **Ricardo Augusto de Souza**, Wordshop, Belo Horizonte MG, Brazil ■ **Lee Spencer**, CUNY Language Immersion Program, Bronx Community College, Bronx, New York ■ **Ann Streeter**, Seattle Central Institute of English, Seattle, Washington ■ **Cláudia Suzano de Almeida**, Casa Thomas Jefferson, Brasília DF, Brazil ■ **Gerald Talandis, Jr.**, Toyama College of Foreign Languages, Toyama, Japan ■ **Lorena Trejo**, AU. Los Samanes, I. E. Henry Clay, Caracas, Venezuela ■ **Diane Triester**, University of Washington, Seattle, Washington ■ **Elkin Urrea**, Hunter College, New York, New York ■ ■ **Dr. Wilma B. Wilcox**, Southern Illinois University at Carbondale in Niigata, Japan ■ **Belkis Yanes**, AU. Los Samanes, I.E. Henry Clay, Caracas, Venezuela ■ **Shari Zisman**, CUNY Language Immersion Program, Bronx Community College, Bronx, New York

In addition we are grateful to the following institutions for helping us organize Focus Groups for teachers and students:

- **Bronx Community College**, Bronx, New York
- **Hunter College**, New York, New York
- **University of Washington**, Seattle, Washington

Finally, we would like to thank **Rick Smith** and **Luke Frances**, as always, for their help and support along the way. They made the journey and the stops, few and far between as they were, a lot more fun.

MF and MB

Present Progressive

Hundreds of fans **are waiting** for The Airheads to arrive.

Wow! The Airheads **are dropping** from the sky!

CHECK *POINT*

Check the best advertisement for this TV news show.

❏ It's happening now!

❏ It happens every day!

CHART CHECK 1

Check the correct answer.

The present progressive is made up of two parts:

❏ *be* + base form of verb

❏ *be* + base form of verb + *-ing*

Which part changes with different subjects?

❏ *be*

❏ base form of verb + *-ing*

AFFIRMATIVE STATEMENTS		
SUBJECT	**BE**	**BASE FORM OF VERB + -ING**
I	am 'm	
He/She/It	is 's	waiting.
We/You*/They	are 're	

NEGATIVE STATEMENTS			
SUBJECT	**BE**	**NOT**	**BASE FORM OF VERB + -ING**
I	am 'm		
He/She/It	is 's	not	waiting.
We/You/They	are 're		

*You is both singular and plural.

YES/NO QUESTIONS

BE	SUBJECT	BASE FORM + -ING
Am	I	
Is	she	**standing?**
Are	you	

SHORT ANSWERS

	AFFIRMATIVE			NEGATIVE	
Yes,	you	**are.**	**No,**	you	**aren't.**
	she	**is.**		she	**isn't.**
	I	**am.**		I	**'m not.**

WH- QUESTIONS

WH- WORD	BE	SUBJECT	BASE FORM + -ING
Why	**am**	I	
	is	she	**standing?**
Where	**are**	you	

EXPRESS CHECK

Complete these sentences with the present progressive form of the verbs in parentheses.

Why _____ you _____? They _____ still _____.
                        (leave)   (perform)

Grammar Explanations

Examples

1. Use the **present progressive** to describe something that is happening <u>right now</u>.

Now
Past ·········· **I'm standing** ··········► Future

- I'm **standing** outside the King Theater *right now*.
- As I'm **talking** to you, the fans **are gathering** in front of the theater.

2. Use the **present progressive** to describe something that is happening <u>these days</u>, even if it's not happening right now.

Now
Past ·········· *I'm studying guitar* ·········· ► Future

- The Airheads **are playing** at the King Theater *this week*.
- I'm **studying** guitar *this semester*.

3. USAGE NOTE: The **contracted form** is usually used in <u>speech</u> and in informal writing.

A: Bye, Jana, we**'re leaving** now.
B: Wait! I'm **coming** with you.

Check it out!

For different forms of negative contractions with *be*, see Appendix 24 on page 345.

For spelling rules for the present progressive, see Appendix 19 on page 343.

1

IDENTIFY • *Read this letter. Underline the present progressive verbs that describe something happening right now. Circle the present progressive verbs that describe things that are happening these days (but not necessarily right now).*

Dear Yev,

I(m working) very hard these days, but I have some good news. Right now,

I'm sitting at a desk in the Entertainment Section of the *Tribune*! Of course I'm

still taking journalism classes at night as well. The job is temporary—Joe Sims,

the regular reporter, is taking this month off to write a book. This week we're

preparing to interview your favorite group, the Airheads. In fact, at this very

moment they're flying into town by helicopter. They're performing at the King

Theater all week. How are you doing? Are you still writing music? Oops! The

crew is calling me. They're leaving for the theater now. Write soon!

Steph

2

COMPLETE • *Read this conversation. Complete it with the present progressive form of the verbs in parentheses. Use contractions whenever possible.*

BEV: Bye, Joe, I _____'m leaving_____ now.
　　　　　　　　　　　　1. (leave)

JOE: Where _____ you _____?
　　　　　　　　　　　　　　　　　　2. (go)

BEV: Running. Ann _____ downstairs.
　　　　　　　　　　3. (wait)

JOE: Great! Why don't you take the dog out with you?

BEV: Why don't *you* take him? It's your turn.

JOE: I can't. I _____ on my book.
　　　　　　　4. (work)

BEV: But you _____ anything right now. You _____ just
　　　　　　　5. (not do)

_____ there.
6. (sit)

JOE: That's not true. I _____ here, but I _____ also
　　　　　　　　　　7. (sit)

_____ about my work. Can't the dog run with you?
8. (think)

BEV: No, because afterwards we want to go to the Plaza. The Airheads

_____ there this week, and Ann wants to get their autographs.
9. (stay)

You know she's a big fan of theirs.

ASK & ANSWER • *Steph is interviewing the lead singer of the Airheads, Paul. Write questions using the words in parentheses. Give short answers.*

STEPH: Paul, <u>are you introducing any new songs on this tour?</u>
1. (introduce / any new songs on this tour?)

PAUL: <u>Yes, we are</u>. We're introducing some songs from our
2.
new album, *In the Air.*

STEPH: Your fans are so excited to see you after such a long time.

_____
3. (Why / tour / again?)

PAUL: We want to play for live audiences. We need that.

STEPH: _____
4. (What / work on / these days?)

PAUL: Some exciting new material. But we're not talking about it yet.

STEPH: _____
5. (Who / sing / with you now?)
She has a nice voice.

PAUL: Sylvia Sylva is singing some of the songs from the album.

STEPH: _____
6. (she / replace / Toti?)

PAUL: _____. Toti has a new baby, but she'll be back in
7.
a few months.

 EDIT • *Read this letter. Find and correct six mistakes in the use of the present progressive. The first mistake is already corrected.*

Dear Toti,
     'm writing
I ~~write~~ to you from my hotel room. Everyone else is sleep, but I sitting here and watching

the ocean. We're staying at the Plaza in Atlantic Beach, and the view is beautiful. The tour is

goes well. The audience is crazy about the new songs, but the fans is always asking for you.

How is the baby? She has a great voice. Do you teaching her to sing yet? Maybe both of you

will come along for the next tour!

                                         Sylvia

Simple Present Tense

Hank **is** always in a hurry and he **does** everything at once.

He **works** all the time—he never **relaxes**.

CHECK POINT

Check the best title for the cartoons.

❏ Hank at Work This Week

❏ Hank's Working Habits

CHART CHECK

Circle T (True) or F (False).

T F The form for *he/she/it* ends with *-s*.

T F Negative statements have *do not* or *does not* before the base form.

T F Questions have *do* or *does* after the subject.

AFFIRMATIVE STATEMENTS

SUBJECT	VERB
I/We/You*/They	**work**.
He/She/It	**works**.

NEGATIVE STATEMENTS

SUBJECT	*DO NOT*	BASE FORM
I/We/You/They	**do not**	**work**.
He/She/It	**does not**	

*You is both singular and plural.

YES/NO QUESTIONS

Do	SUBJECT	BASE FORM
Do	you	**work**?
Does	he	

SHORT ANSWERS

AFFIRMATIVE			NEGATIVE		
Yes,	I	**do**.	No,	I	**don't**.
	he	**does**.		he	**doesn't**.

WH- QUESTIONS			
WH- WORD	**DO**	**SUBJECT**	**BASE FORM**
Where When	**do**	you	**work**?
	does	he	

EXPRESS CHECK

Unscramble these words to complete the question.

rush • Why • he • does   _____ all the time?

Grammar Explanations

Examples

1. Use the **simple present tense** to talk about what <u>regularly happens</u>.

Now

Past ········X·····X·····X·····X·····X·····► Future

rush

- Some people **rush** through life.
- They **don't relax**.
- Other people **are** calm.
- They **don't feel** tense.

2. Use **adverbs of frequency** with the simple present tense to express <u>how often something happens</u>.

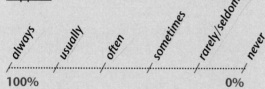

always usually often sometimes rarely/seldom never

/···········/···········/···········/···········/···········/
100%   0%

- She **never relaxes**.
- You **usually take** life easier.
- We **sometimes sleep** late.
- They **seldom take** a vacation.

▶ **BE CAREFUL!** Adverbs of frequency usually come before the main verb, but they go after the verb **be**.

- We **usually rush** around too much.
- We**'re often** stressed out.

3. Use the **simple present tense** to talk about <u>scientific facts</u>.

- Stress **causes** high blood pressure.
- Water **freezes** at 32°F.

Check it out!

For spelling rules for the third person singular *(he / she / it)* of the simple present tense, see Appendix 20 on page 343.

For pronunciation rules for the third person singular *(he / she / it)* of the simple present tense, see Appendix 27 on page 348.

1

IDENTIFY • *Read this part of a book review. Underline the simple present tense verbs. Circle the adverbs of frequency.*

Books   Section 10

CALM DOWN! By Dr. Sara Roads

In today's fast-paced world, we (never) escape stress. Stress (always) affects us psychologically, but according to Dr. Roads, author of the new bestseller, *Calm Down!*, it also affects us physically. For example, stress causes high blood pressure. Doctors (often) prescribe

medication for stress-related illnesses. Medicine usually lowers a patient's blood pressure. But, Dr. Roads claims, "You don't (always) need pills. Relaxation exercises are (sometimes) as effective as pills. For example, breathing exercises both relax you and lower your blood pressure. It only takes a few minutes!"

2

COMPLETE • *Megan and Greg have completely different types of personality (A and B). Read about one, write about the other.*

Type A: Megan

1. Megan **doesn't relax** easily.

2. She ___doesn't take___ time to enjoy the moment.

3. Megan and her boyfriend never **take** vacations.

4. She ___rush___ through the day.

5. She **is** nervous.

6. She **is** always in a hurry.

7. She **finishes** other people's sentences for them.

8. She ___worries___ a lot.

9. She ___doesn't have___ enough time to finish things.

10. Megan **has** high blood pressure due to stress.

Type B: Greg

• Greg _____relaxes_____ easily.

• He **takes** time to enjoy the moment.

• Greg and his girlfriend often ___take___ vacations.

• He **doesn't rush** through the day.

• He ___isn't___ nervous.

• He ___is___ never in a hurry.

• He ___doesn't finish___ other people's sentences for them.

• He **doesn't worry** a lot.

• He **has** enough time to finish things.

• Greg ___doesn't have___ high blood pressure due to stress.

ASK & ANSWER • *Todd is an accountant. Look at his schedule. Write questions and answers about his day.*

MONDAY NOVEMBER 18			
6:00–7:00	get up, exercise	**12:00–12:30**	lunch
8:00–9:00	work on reports	**12:30–5:00**	return phone calls
9:00–12:00	see clients	**5:30–7:00**	attend night school

1. When / get up?

<u>When does he get up?</u>   He gets up at 6:00.

2. exercise in the morning?

<u>Does he exercise in the morning?</u>   Yes, he does.

3. work on reports in the afternoon?

<u>Does he work on reports in the afternoon?</u>   <u>No, he doesn't.</u>

4. When / see clients?

<u>When does he see clients?</u>   <u>From 9:00 - 12:00</u>

5. take a lunch break?

<u>Does he take a lunch break?</u>   <u>Yes, he does</u>

6. What / do / from 12:30 to 5:00?

<u>What does he do from 12:30-5:00</u>   <u>He return phone calls.</u>

7. Where / go / at 5:30?

<u>Where does he go at 5:30?</u>   <u>He attend night school</u>

EDIT • *Read Todd's journal entry. Find and correct ten mistakes in the use of the simple present tense. The first mistake is already corrected.*

> never have   study   tells
> I'm so tired. I ~~have never~~ time to relax. I work all day and ~~studies~~ all night. My boss ~~tell~~
>   think
> me that I need a vacation. I agree, but I afraid to take one. Does my boss ~~thinks~~ that
>   don't
> the office can function without me? I ~~dont~~ want them to think I'm not necessary.
>   complains
> But my wife is unhappy too. She ~~complain~~ that she never sees me anymore. My
>   is
> schedule ~~are~~ crazy. I don't think I can keep this up much longer. I don't ~~wants~~ to quit
>   often
> night school, though. I think ~~often~~ that there has to be a better way.

Non-Action Verbs

CHECK *POINT*

Check the correct answer.

According to the fish, the worm

☐ has the flavor of chicken.

☐ acts like a chicken.

CHART CHECK

Circle T (True) or F (False).

T F Some verbs have both a non-action and an action meaning.

T F A verb used with a non-action meaning is not used in the progressive.

VERBS WITH NON-ACTION MEANINGS
I **want** to go fishing.
He **owns** a big boat.
The weather **seems** fine.
They **hate** fish.

VERBS WITH BOTH NON-ACTION AND ACTION MEANINGS	
NON-ACTION	**ACTION**
The fish **weighs** five pounds.	He**'s weighing** the fish now.
We **think** it's a good day for fishing.	We**'re thinking** about going.
This fish **tastes** delicious.	I**'m tasting** the fish now.
This food **smells** good.	The cook **is smelling** the food.

EXPRESS CHECK

Complete these sentences with the correct form of the verb **taste**.

I _____ the soup right now. It _____ salty.

10

Grammar Explanations

Examples

---

1. Many verbs <u>describe states or situations</u> instead of actions. These verbs are called **non-action verbs** (or stative verbs).

Most non-action verbs are <u>not</u> usually <u>used in the present progressive</u> even when they describe a situation that is happening right now.

- John **has** a boat.
  *(The verb **has** describes John's situation, not something he is doing.)*

- He **wants** fish for dinner.
  NOT ~~He is wanting fish for dinner.~~

---

2. Non-action verbs are usually verbs that:

   a. describe a **state of being**
      (be, feel)

   b. express **emotions**
      (hate, like, love)

   c. describe **mental states**
      (know, remember, believe, think [= believe], suppose, understand)

   d. show **possession**
      (have, own, possess, belong)

   e. describe **perceptions** and **senses**
      (hear, see, smell, taste, feel, notice, seem, look [= seem], appear, sound)

   f. describe **needs** and **preferences**
      (need, want, prefer)

   g. describe **measurements**
      (weigh, cost, contain)

- Jane **is** tired but happy.
- She **feels** good.

A: Do you **like** my new dress?
B: I **love** it!

- I **know** a lot of good recipes.
- Ari **remembers** your number.
- I **think** you're right.

- Cesar **has** a headache.
- Some students **own** microwaves.

- I **hear** the telephone.
- Dina **seems** tired.

- I **need** a pen.

- How much **does** it **cost**?

---

3. **BE CAREFUL!** Some verbs can have non-action and action meanings (*taste, smell, feel, look, think, have, weigh*).

NON-ACTION

- I **taste** garlic. Did you put some in here?
  (I notice garlic.)
- The soup **tastes** good. Try some.
  (The soup is good.)

ACTION

- I'm **tasting** the soup to see if it needs more salt.
  (I'm trying the soup.)

Check it out!

For a list of common non-action verbs, see Appendix 2 on page 337.

1   *IDENTIFY • Read this conversation. Underline all non-action verbs that describe a situation that is in progress. Circle all non-action verbs that describe a situation that is generally true.*

ALINE: This steak <u>tastes</u> delicious. Your salmon <u>looks</u> good too.

BEN: Here, I'm putting some on your plate. I <u>think</u> you'll like it.

ALINE: Mmm. I <u>like</u> it. Funny, I usually (don't like) fish.

BEN: Red (has) that effect on people.

ALINE: I <u>have</u> no idea what you're talking about. What <u>do</u> you mean?

BEN: Well, colors can change the way we (feel). For example, people often (feel) hungrier in a red room. I <u>notice</u> that you're looking right at the red wallpaper.

ALINE: And I certainly <u>feel</u> hungry right now. I'm eating half your salmon.

BEN: That's OK. I'm tasting your steak.

2   *CHOOSE • Complete this magazine article with the correct form of the verbs in parentheses.*

Lenny Kramer is in a sports store. He _____smells_____ flowers, but he isn't
                                           1. (smells / is smelling)
really paying attention to the aroma very much because he _____ at a
                                                         2. (looks / is looking)
pair of running shoes. They _____ a lot more than he usually pays, but
                                  3. (cost / are costing)
Lenny really, really _____ those shoes. He's the victim of "smart scents,"
                        4. (wants / is wanting)
aromas that stores use to make customers buy more.

Across town, Lenny's daughter Myra is taking a history test in a classroom
that was recently painted yellow. Although Myra _____ history, she
                                          5. (hates / is hating)
_____ to be doing well on this test. She _____ the new
6. (seems / is seeming)   **7.** (likes / is liking)
color of her classroom. She _____ that it's helping her on the test,
                        8. (doesn't suspect / isn't suspecting)
but it is. Scientists have shown that yellow improves both memory and concentration.

We now _____ that odors, colors, and sounds affect our moods and
                   9. (know / are knowing)
even our health. In fact, right now Lenny's wife, Cindy, _____ about
                                            10. (thinks / is thinking)
Lenny and Myra. She's sure that Lenny is spending too much on shoes and that
Myra is failing another history test. Cindy suffers from migraine headaches, but
she _____ a headache today. She's in the garden, and she
    11. (doesn't have / isn't having)
_____ birds and insect sounds. They always calm her down.
12. (hears / is hearing)

3 **COMPLETE •** *Read this conversation. Complete it with the correct form of the verbs in parentheses. Use the present progressive or the simple present tense.*

A: Hi, Ana. Mmm. Something _____smells_____ good! What's cooking?
1. (smell)

B: Fish soup. I _am teasting_ it to see if it _____needs_____ more garlic.
2. (taste)   **3.** (need)

_____do_____ you _____want_____ to try it?
4. (want)

A: Mmmm. It _____tastes_____ good, but I _____think_____ it needs salt.
5. (taste)   **6.** (think)

B: OK. I _am thinking_ about adding canned tomatoes too, even though it
7. (think)

_____is not_____ in the recipe.
8. (not be)

A: That _____sounds_____ like a good idea. But wait a minute. I _am looking_
9. (sound)   **10.** (look)

at the recipe, and it says you can add milk. How about that?

B: I _____don't know_____ if the milk _____is_____ fresh.
11. (not know)   **12.** (be)

A: I'll check. Hmm. I _am smelling_ it, but I _am not_ sure. Let's add
13. (smell)   **14.** (not be)

the tomatoes instead.

B: OK. I _____love_____ cooking! The whole house _____smells_____ great
15. (love)   **16.** (smell)

when you cook. And it always puts me in a good mood.

A: I _____know_____ what you _____mean_____. I _____feel_____ the
17. (know)   **18.** (mean)   **19.** (feel)

same way.

4 **EDIT •** *Read this journal entry. There are eight mistakes in the use of action and non-action verbs. Find and correct them. The first mistake is already corrected.*

March 16

Not a good day! I feel kind of depressed and I'm having *(have)* a headache. I'm needing *(I need)* to do

something right away to change my mood and get rid of this pain. Last week, I read an article

about how smells can affect mood and even health, so right now I smell *(am smelling)* an orange (for the

depression) and a green apple (for the headache). They smell nice, but I'm not thinking *(don't think)* that

I notice a difference in how I feel! I think I'm preferring *(prefer)* to eat something when I feel down.

But I worry that I'm weighing *(weight)* too much. So, at the moment I have *(am having)* a cup of peppermint tea with

lemon. The article says that the peppermint smell helps you eat less. Well, I don't know about

that! A chocolate ice cream sundae sounds pretty good right about now! It's seeming *(seems)* that

there are no easy solutions.

Present Progressive and Simple Present Tense

Cross-Cultural Confusion

Friends from different cultures often **have** different ideas about time.

Sometimes they **don't agree** about social distance, either.

CHECK *POINT*

Circle T (True) or F (False).

T **F** Karl is arriving late tonight.

T **F** In Sami's culture, people rarely stand close to each other.

CHART CHECK

Check the correct answers.

The present progressive has:

❏ one part

❏ two parts

The simple present tense has:

❏ one form

❏ two forms

PRESENT PROGRESSIVE			
SUBJECT	**BE**	**BASE FORM + -ING**	
I	am		
We/You*/They	are	arriving	now.
He/She/It	is		

*You is both singular and plural.

SIMPLE PRESENT TENSE			
SUBJECT		**VERB**	
I/We/You/They	never always	arrive	on time.
He/She/It		arrives	

14

EXPRESS CHECK

Complete the following charts with the verb **buy**.

PRESENT PROGRESSIVE			
SUBJECT	*BE*	**BASE FORM + *-ING***	
I			
You			flowers now.
He			

SIMPLE PRESENT TENSE			
SUBJECT		**VERB**	
I			
You	usually		chocolates.
He			

Grammar Explanations

Examples

1. Use the **present progressive** for things happening <u>right now</u>.

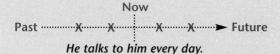

Now

He's talking to Taro.

Past ·········· X ──────▶ Future

Use the **simple present tense** to describe what <u>regularly</u> happens.

Now

Past ········· X ···· X ···┊··· X ···· X ──▶ Future

He talks to him every day.

- Sami **is talking** to Taro.
- At the moment, Taro **is speaking** English.

- Sami **talks** to Taro every day.
- Taro **speaks** Japanese at home.

2. Use the **present progressive** for things happening <u>these days</u>.

Now

Past ·········⌒·········· ──────▶ Future

We're studying.

- We**'re studying** in the U.S. *this month*.
- Laura**'s studying** in France *this year*.
- **Are** you **studying** hard *these days*?

3. **REMEMBER!** Most **non-action verbs** are <u>not usually used in the present progressive</u> even when they describe a situation that exists at the moment of speaking.

- Jane **wants** to go home right now.
  NOT ~~Jane is wanting to go home right now.~~

4. Use the **simple present tense** to talk about <u>scientific facts</u> and <u>physical laws</u>.

- Stress **causes** high blood pressure.
- Water **boils** at 100°C.

Check it out!

For a list of common non-action verbs, see Appendix 2 on page 337.

1

IDENTIFY • *Read these journal entries by Brian, a Canadian summer exchange student studying in Argentina. Circle all the verbs that describe what is happening now. Underline the verbs that describe what generally happens.*

June 28: I'm sitting in a seat 30,000 feet above the earth en route to Argentina! I usually have dinner at this time, but right now I have a headache from the excitement. My seatmate is eating my food. She looks happy.

June 30: It's 7:30. My host parents are still working. Carlos, my father, works at home. My little brother Ricardo is cute. He looks (and acts) a lot like Bobby. Right now, he's looking over my shoulder and trying to read my journal.

July 4: The weather is cold now. I usually spend the first weekend of July at the beach. Today I'm walking around in a heavy sweater.

August 6: I feel so tired tonight. Everyone else feels great in the evening because they take long naps in the afternoon.

2

COMPLETE • *Students are talking outside a classroom. Complete their conversations with the present progressive or the simple present tense of the verbs in parentheses.*

1. **LI-WU:** Hi, Paulo. What _____are_____ you _____doing_____?
   a. (do)

   PAULO: Oh, I _____ for class to begin.
   b. (wait)

   LI-WU: How are you? You _____ tired.
   c. (look)

   PAULO: I *am* a little tired. I _____ evenings this semester. Hey, is that your teacher over there?
   d. (work)

   LI-WU: Yes. She _____ to one of my classmates.
   e. (talk)

   PAULO: I wonder what's wrong. He _____ at her. He _____ embarrassed.
   f. (not look)
   g. (look)

   LI-WU: Oh. That _____ anything. In Taiwan it's not respectful to look directly at your teacher.
   h. (not mean)

2. **MORIKO:** Look, there's Miguel. He _____ to Luisa.
   a. (talk)

   NINA: Yes. They _____ a class together this semester.
   b. (take)

MORIKO: They _____ very close to each other. _____ you
c. (stand)

_____ they _____?
d. (think)   e. (date)

NINA: No. I _____ it _____
f. (not think)   g. (mean)

anything special. I _____ from Costa Rica,
h. (come)

and people there normally _____ that
i. (stand)

close to each other.

3. **RASHA:** There's Hans. Why _____ he

_____ so fast? Class _____
a. (walk)   b. (start)

at 9:00. He still _____ ten minutes!
c. (have)

CLAUDE: He always _____ fast. People from
d. (walk)

Switzerland often _____ to be in a hurry.
e. (appear)

4. **YOKO:** Isn't that Sergio and Luis? Why _____ they _____
a. (shake)

hands? They _____ each other.
b. (know)

JING: In Brazil, men _____ hands every
c. (shake)

time they _____.
d. (meet)

---

3 **EDIT** • *Read this student's journal. Find and correct eleven mistakes in the use of the present progressive or simple present tense. The first mistake is already corrected.*

           I'm sitting

It's 12:30 and ~~I sit~~ in the library right now. My classmates are eating lunch together,

                  never eat

but I'm not hungry yet. At home, we ~~eat never~~ this early. Today our journal topic is

culture shock. It's a good topic for me right now because I'm ~~being~~ pretty homesick.

                                 eat

I miss my old routine. At home we always ~~are eating~~ a big meal at 2:00 in the

                                     have

afternoon. Then we rest. But here in Toronto ~~I'm having~~ a 3:00 conversation class.

                                    asks

Every day, I almost fall asleep in class, and my teacher ~~ask~~ me, "Are you bored?" Of

                                 is always

course I'm not bored. I just need my afternoon nap! This class ~~always is~~ fun. This

                we are working

semester, ~~we work~~ on a project with video cameras. My team is filming groups of

                  analyzing

people in different cultures. We are ~~analyze~~ "social distance." That means how close to

                                        I am leaving

each other these people stand. According to my new watch, it's 12:55, so ~~I leave now~~

                                don't like

for my 1:00 class. Teachers here really ~~aren't liking~~ when you come late!

UNIT 5

Imperative

To do the Jab:
Bend your knees and
place your right foot in front,
like this. **Punch** with your
right fist.

CHECK POINT

Check the correct answer.

The woman in the photo is

❏ inviting someone to learn the Jab.

❏ giving instructions on how to do the Jab.

❏ ordering someone to do the Jab.

CHART CHECK

Check the correct answer.

Imperative sentences

❏ include a subject.

❏ don't include
a subject.

AFFIRMATIVE	
BASE FORM OF VERB	
Bend	your knees.
Punch	with your fists.

NEGATIVE		
	BASE FORM OF VERB	
Don't	**bend**	your knees.
	punch	with your fist.

EXPRESS CHECK

Use these verbs to complete the charts.

| touch | listen | stand |

AFFIRMATIVE	
BASE FORM OF VERB	
	to the music.
	your toes.
	straight.

NEGATIVE		
DON'T	**BASE FORM OF VERB**	
		to the music.
		your toes.
		straight.

Grammar Explanations

Examples

1. The **imperative** form of the verb is always the <u>base form</u>. It is the same whether it is directed to one or several people.

- Marla, please **get** ready.
- **Get** ready, guys!

2. The **subject** of an imperative statement is *you*. However, we <u>do not say or write *you*</u> in imperative sentences.

- **Stand up** straight.
  NOT ~~You stand up straight~~.

3. The imperative form has a number of **uses**. Use the imperative to:

- **a.** give **directions** and **instructions**

  - **Turn** left at the traffic light.

- **b.** give **orders** or **commands**

  - **Don't move!**

- **c.** make **requests** (Use *please* in addition to the imperative form.)

  - *Please* **read** this article.
  - **Read** this article, *please*.

- **d.** give **advice** or make **suggestions**

  - **Don't exercise** when you're sick.

- **e.** give **warnings**.

  - **Be** careful! **Don't trip!**

- **f.** **invite** someone

  - **Work out** with us tomorrow.

issue an invitation

MATCH • *Each imperative goes with a situation. Match the imperative with the correct situation.*

Imperative	Situation
_g_ **1.** Don't touch that!	**a.** Someone is visiting a friend.
_c_ **2.** Look both ways.	**b.** Someone is going out into the cold.
_b_ **3.** Dress warmly!	**c.** Someone is crossing a street.
_e_ **4.** Don't bend your knees.	**d.** Someone is taking an exam.
_d_ **5.** Mark each answer true or false.	**e.** Someone is exercising.
_a_ **6.** Come in. Make yourself at home.	**f.** Someone is tasting some food.
_f_ **7.** Try a little more pepper.	**g.** Something is hot.

MATCH • *You're going to give instructions for making a banana-strawberry smoothie. Match a verb from column A with a phrase from column B.*

Column A	Column B
Add	the ingredients until smooth.
Slice	six strawberries.
Wash	a banana.
Cut	orange juice into the blender.
Blend	the strawberries in half.
Pour	the fruit to the orange juice.

LABEL • *Now write the sentences in order under the correct pictures.*

1. _Slice a banana._

2. _wash six strawberries_

3. _cut the strawberries in half._

4. _pour orang juice into the blender_

5. _add the fruit to the orange juice_

6. _Blend the ingredients until smooth_

3 **CHOOSE & COMPLETE •** *Read this advertisement for a martial arts school. Complete it using the affirmative or negative imperative form of the verbs in the box.*

become	choose	decrease	increase	learn
miss	register	take	~~think~~	wait

MARTIAL ARTS ACADEMY

_____Don't think_____ that martial arts is only about physical training. A good
1.
martial arts program offers many other benefits as well. ____lern_____
2.
self-defense and more at the Martial Arts Academy:

♦ ____decrease_____ stress. Martial arts training helps you relax.
3.

♦ ____increase_____ concentration. Martial arts students focus better.
4.

♦ ____Become_____ fit. Strength and flexibility improve as you learn.
5.

We are offering an introductory trial membership. ____dont miss_____ this
6.
special opportunity. ____take_____ classes with Master Lorenzo Gibbons,
7.
a ninth-level Black Belt Master. ____choose_____
8.
classes from our convenient schedule.

____dont wait_____ ! ____Register_____ now
9. **10.**
for a two-week trial.

ONLY $20. ♦ **UNIFORM INCLUDED.**

4 **EDIT •** *Read part of a martial arts student's essay. Find and correct five mistakes in the use of the imperative. The first mistake is already corrected.*

For the Black Belt essay, Master Gibbons gave us this assignment:
          Write
~~You write~~ about something important to you. My topic is *The Right*
                                                              respect
Way, the rules of life for the martial arts. First, ~~respects~~
        help
other people—treat them the way you want them to treat you.
        do
Second, ~~helped~~ people in need. In other words, use your strength
       do   do
for others, not to use it just for your own good. Third, not lie
or steal. These are the most important rules to me.

SelfTest

Circle the letter of the correct answer to complete each sentence.

> **EXAMPLE:**
> Jennifer never _____ coffee.   **A** Ⓑ **C** **D**
> (A) drink   (C) is drinking
> (B) drinks   (D) was drinking

1. _____ ready for school? It's already 7:00.   **A** Ⓑ **C** **D**
   (A) Do you get   (C) You get
   (B) Are you getting   (D) You are getting

2. Nick _____ to Greece every year to visit his family.   **A** **B** **C** Ⓓ
   (A) is going   (C) go
   (B) he goes   (D) goes

3. Why _____? Class isn't over yet.   Ⓐ **B** **C** **D**
   (A) are you leaving   (C) do you leave
   (B) you are leaving   (D) you leaving

4. Something _____ good. Is that fresh bread in the oven?   Ⓐ **B** **C** **D**
   (A) smells   (C) smell
   (B) is smelling   (D) smelling

5. Which class _____ best?   **A** **B** **C** Ⓓ
   (A) are you liking   (C) you like
   (B) you are liking   (D) do you like

6. _____ loose clothes to exercise. You'll be more comfortable.   Ⓐ **B** **C** **D**
   (A) Wear   (C) Wears
   (B) Wearing   (D) You wear

7. Please _____ to class on time. We start at exactly 9:00.   **A** Ⓑ **C** **D**
   (A) we come   (C) you're coming
   (B) come   (D) comes

8. I _____ something outside. Are the doors locked?   **A** Ⓑ **C** **D**
   (A) 'm hearing   (C) hearing
   (B) hear   (D) hears

9. Walk! _____ run!   **A** **B** Ⓒ **D**
   (A) Not   (C) Don't
   (B) No   (D) You don't

10. —Do you like fish?   **A** Ⓑ **C** **D**
    —Yes, I _____.
    (A) am   (C) don't
    (B) do   (D) like

22

11. Harry works all the time. He _____.   Ⓐ B C D
    (A) never relaxes   (C) often relaxes
    (B) relaxes never   (D) relaxes sometimes

12. What _____ these days?   Ⓐ B C D
    (A) are you doing   (C) you are doing
    (B) do you do   (D) you do

13. The baby's so big! How much _____ now?   A B C Ⓓ
    (A) weigh   (C) is she weighing
    (B) she weighs   (D) does she weigh

14. —Are you taking an English class this semester?   A B C Ⓓ
    —Yes, I _____.
    (A) take   (C) do
    (B) am taking   (D) am

15. Water _____ at 212°F.   A Ⓑ C D
    (A) boil   (C) boiled
    (B) boils   (D) is boiling

SECTION TWO

Each sentence has four underlined words or phrases. The four underlined parts of the sentence are marked A, B, C, and D. Circle the letter of the one underlined word or phrase that is NOT CORRECT.

EXAMPLE:

Mike <u>usually</u> <u>drives</u> to school, but <u>today</u> he <u>walks</u>.   A B C Ⓓ
    A   B   C   D

16. Fran usually <u>is swimming</u> before <u>work</u>, but this morning she's <u>jogging</u>.   Ⓐ B C D
    swims
    A   B   C D

17. The wind is <u>blowing</u>, <u>it</u> <u>rains</u>, and the sky <u>looks</u> gray.   A B Ⓒ D
    rainging
               A   B   C   D

18. <u>Where</u> <u>you are</u> <u>working</u> these days <u>after school</u>?   A Ⓑ C D
    are
    A   B   C   D

19. The floor <u>is</u> wet, so <u>walk</u> slowly and <u>no</u> <u>fall down</u>!   A B Ⓒ D
    don't
    A   B   C   D

20. <u>Something</u> <u>is seeming</u> different—<u>are</u> you <u>wearing</u> a new perfume?   A Ⓑ C D
    seems
    A   B   C   D

21. We <u>always</u> <u>eat out</u> because we <u>hates</u> to <u>cook</u>.   A B Ⓒ D
    heat
    A   B   C   D

22. Luis <u>arrives usually</u> early, <u>but</u> <u>today</u> he's late.   Ⓐ B C D
    A   B C   D

23. I <u>need</u> my CD player if you <u>don't</u> <u>using</u> it <u>at the moment</u>.   A Ⓑ C D
    aren't
    A   B   C   D

24. I <u>never</u> <u>have</u> anything to write with <u>because</u> <u>I'm always lose</u> my pens.   A B C Ⓓ
    losing
    A   B   C   D

25. <u>Turn</u> left at the light, and <u>you</u> <u>don't</u> <u>forget</u> to signal!   A Ⓑ C D
    A   B   C   D

Simple Past Tense:
Affirmative Statements

CHECK POINT

Check the year these sentences appeared in a newspaper.

"Poet Albert Rimes lives in Belgium."

☑ 1989   ☐ 1999

"Poet Albert Rimes lived in Belgium most of his life."

☐ 1989   ☑ 1999

CHART CHECK

Check the correct answer.

How many forms does the past tense of **be** have?

☐ one   ☑ two

What do you add to the base form of regular verbs to form the past tense?

☑ -d or -ed   ☐ -t

THE SIMPLE PAST TENSE: *BE*		
SUBJECT	**BE**	
I/He/She/It	**was**	young in 1930.
We/You*/They	**were**	

You is both singular and plural.

THE SIMPLE PAST TENSE: REGULAR VERBS		
SUBJECT	**VERB**	
I/He/She/It/We/You/They	**moved**	fifty years ago.
	worked	

THE SIMPLE PAST TENSE: IRREGULAR VERBS		
SUBJECT	**VERB**	
I/He/She/It/We/You/They	**wrote**	poetry.
	became	famous.
	built	a monument.

EXPRESS CHECK

Complete the chart.

BASE FORM OF VERB	SIMPLE PAST TENSE
be	_____was_____ and _____were_____
come	_____came_____
save	_____saved_____

Grammar Explanations

Examples

1. Use the **simple past tense** to talk about things that are now <u>finished</u>. Past ·········X·········┊·············➤ Future Now *He was a poet.*	■ Albert Rimes **lived** in the twentieth century. ■ He **was** a poet. ■ He **wrote** poetry.
2. You can use the **simple past tense** with **time expressions** that refer to the past *(last week, by 1980, in the twentieth century, fifty years ago).*	■ *By 1930*, he **was** famous. ■ He **died** more than *ten years ago*.

3. The **simple past tense** of **regular verbs** is formed by adding *-d* or *-ed*.	**BASE FORM**		**SIMPLE PAST**
	live	→	lived
	join	→	joined
	play	→	played
▶ **BE CAREFUL!** There are often <u>spelling changes</u> when you add *-ed* to the verb.	study	→	studied
	hop	→	hopped
Many common verbs are **irregular**. Their past tense is not formed by adding *-d* or *-ed*.	be	→	**was/were**
	have	→	**had**
	get	→	**got**
	go	→	**went**

Check it out!

For spelling rules for the simple past tense of regular verbs, see Appendix 21 on page 344.

For pronunciation rules for the simple past tense of regular verbs, see Appendix 28 on page 348.

For a list of irregular verbs, see Appendix 1 on pages 336–337.

1 **IDENTIFY** • *Read about Japanese poet Matsuo Basho. Underline all the regular past tense verbs. Circle all the irregular past tense verbs.*

Matsuo Basho (wrote) more than 1,000 three-line poems, or "haiku." He chose topics from nature, daily life, and human emotions. He (became) one of Japan's most famous poets, and his work established haiku as an important art form.

Matsuo Basho (was) born near Kyoto in 1644. His father wanted him to become a samurai (warrior). Instead, Matsuo moved to Edo (present-day Tokyo) and studied poetry. By 1681, he (had) many students and admirers.

Basho's home burned down in 1682. Then, in 1683, his mother died. After these events, Basho (felt) restless. Starting in 1684, he traveled on foot and on horseback all over Japan. Sometimes his friends joined him, and they (wrote) poetry together. Travel (was) difficult in the seventeenth century, and Basho often (got) sick. He died in 1694, during a journey to Osaka. At that time he (had) 2,000 students.

2 **CHOOSE & COMPLETE** • *Read this biography of another poet, Emily Dickinson. Complete it using the simple past tense form of the verbs in the boxes.*

be	become	lead	leave	~~live~~	see	wear	write

Emily Dickinson, one of the most popular American poets,

_____lived_____ from 1830 to 1886. She _____wrote_____
      1.   **2.**

about love, nature, and time. These _____were_____ her
                                          3.

favorite themes. Dickinson _____led_____ an unusual life.
                                4.

After just one year of college, she _____became_____ a recluse—
                                          5.

she almost never _____left_____ her house in Amherst,
                       6.

Massachusetts. At home, she _____saw_____ no one except her
                                  7.

family, and she only _____wore_____ white.
                          8.

address   appear   happen   write

In addition to her poetry, Dickinson ____wrote____ many letters. Other
    9.
people always ____addressed____ the envelopes for her. During her lifetime only
    10.
seven of her 1,700 poems ____appeared____ in print—and this ____happened____
    11.   12.
without her knowledge or permission.

Now complete these lines from a poem by Emily Dickinson.

bite   ~~come~~   drink   eat   hop   see

A bird ____came____ down the walk:
    13.
He did not know I ____saw____;
    14.
He ____bit____ an angle-worm in halves
    15.
And ____ate____ the fellow raw.
    16.
And then he ____drank____ a dew
    17.
From a convenient grass,
And then ____hopped____ sidewise to the wall
    18.
To let a beetle pass.

3 **EDIT** • *Read part of a student's journal. Find and correct eight mistakes in the use of the
simple past tense. The first mistake is already corrected.*

                                                            enjoyed
       Today in class we read a poem by Robert Frost. I really ~~enjoy~~ it. It was about a
            chosed
person who ~~choosed~~ between two roads in a forest. Before he made his decision, he
spent
~~spents~~ a lot of time trying to decide which road to follow. Many people thought the
            was   took
person ~~were~~ Frost. In the end, he ~~take~~ the road that was less traveled on. He decided
                        changed
to be a poet. That decision ~~change~~ his life a lot.
                                            decided to come
       Sometimes I feel a little like Frost. Two years ago I ~~decide to come~~ to this
            was
country. That ~~were~~ the biggest decision of my life.

Simple Past Tense:
Negative Statements and Questions

THE DAILY NEWS

DID SHE CRASH???

—LAE, NEW GUINEA, JULY 2, 1937. Amelia Earhart's small plane left the island of Lae at exactly 12:00 midnight. She **was not** alone on the flight, but she and Fred Noonan, her navigator, were very tired. She reported her last position at 8:14 P.M. After that, she **did not make** radio contact again. Why **did** they **disappear**? **Were** they exhausted? **Did** they **run out** of gas? The U.S. Coast Guard started its search for the answer at 10:15 P.M.

CHECK POINT

Circle T (True), F (False), or ? (the article doesn't say).

T F (?)   The plane crashed.

T (F) ?   Earhart made radio contact after 8:14 P.M.

(T) F ?   Earhart had a navigator with her.

SIMPLE PAST TENSE: NEGATIVE STATEMENTS

CHART CHECK 1

Check the correct answers.

What word do you add to **be** to form a negative statement?

☐ *not*   ☐ *did not*

What do you add to other verbs to form a negative statement?

☐ *not*   ☐ *did not*

BE			
SUBJECT	**BE**	**NOT**	
I/He/She/It	**was**	**not**	here last year.
We/You*/They	**were**		

*You is both singular and plural.

CONTRACTIONS
was not = **wasn't**
were not = **weren't**

REGULAR AND IRREGULAR VERBS			
SUBJECT	**DID NOT**	**BASE FORM OF VERB**	
I/He/She/It We/You/They	**did not**	call fly	last night.

CONTRACTIONS
did not = **didn't**

SIMPLE PAST TENSE: QUESTIONS

CHART CHECK 2 →

Check the correct answer.

Which word(s) can begin *yes/no* questions with **be**?

☐ *was*

☐ *were*

☐ *did*

Which word(s) can begin *yes/no* questions with other verbs?

☐ *was*

☐ *were*

☐ *did*

YES/NO QUESTIONS: *BE*

BE	SUBJECT	
Was	she	here last year?
Were	they	

SHORT ANSWERS

AFFIRMATIVE			NEGATIVE		
Yes,	she	**was**.	No,	she	**wasn't**.
	they	**were**.		they	**weren't**.

WH- QUESTIONS: *BE*

WH- WORD	BE	SUBJECT	
Why	**was**	she	here last year?
	were	they	

YES/NO QUESTIONS: OTHER VERBS

DID	SUBJECT	BASE FORM	
Did	she	**fly**	to Mexico?

SHORT ANSWERS

AFFIRMATIVE	NEGATIVE
Yes, she **did**.	**No**, she **didn't**.

WH- QUESTIONS: OTHER VERBS

WH- WORD	DID	SUBJECT	BASE FORM
Why	**did**	it	**disappear**?

EXPRESS CHECK

Unscramble these words to form a question and an answer.

navigator • she • have • Did • a _____ *ncel* _____

fly • She • didn't • alone _____ *didnot* _____

Grammar Explanations

1. Use the **simple past tense** to make **negative statements** about actions or situations that are now <u>finished</u>.

Past ·······×···········┊···········→ Future
     wasn't alone   Now

2. Use the **simple past tense** to ask **questions** about actions or situations that are now <u>finished</u>.

Examples

- She **wasn't** alone.
- They **weren't** on an island.
- They **didn't find** the plane.
- He **didn't call** that night.

- **Was** she alone in the plane?
- Where **did** she **leave** from?

Check it out!

For questions about the subject, see Unit 24 on pages 102–103.

1 **READ** • *Look at some facts about Amelia Earhart.*

- She was born in the United States.
- She didn't complete college.
- She didn't keep her first airplane.
- She flew across the Atlantic Ocean.
- She received many awards.
- She married George Palmer Putnam.
- She didn't have any children.
- She wrote three books.

ANSWER • *Put a check in the correct box.*

		Yes	No
1.	Did she get many awards?	☑	☐
2.	Was she a college graduate?	☐	☑
3.	Was she an American citizen?	☑	☐
4.	Did she keep her first plane?	☐	☑
5.	Was she an author?	☑	☐
6.	Did she have a husband?	☑	☐
7.	Was she a parent?	☐	☑

2 **ASK & ANSWER** • *Use the cues to ask questions about Amelia Earhart. Then answer the questions with the information in the box.*

~~1928~~   1937   American   Columbia University   two years   New Guinea   three

1. When / she / cross the Atlantic Ocean?

   When did she cross the Atlantic Ocean? ____ In 1928. ____

2. Where / she / study?

   Where did she study ____ at Columbia U ____

3. How long / be / she / a social worker?

   How long was she social worker? ____ For 2 years. ____

4. Where / her last flight / leave from?

   Where did her last flight ——? ____ From New Guinea. ____

5. How many books / she / write?

   ____ did she ? ____ 3 ____

6. What / be / her nationality?

   ____ was ? ____ American ____

7. When / she / disappear?

   Whe did she ? ____ in 1937 ____

COMPLETE • *The magazine* Flying High *(FH) interviewed a young pilot. Complete the interview with the correct form of the verbs in parentheses and with short answers.*

FH: _____ Did _____ you always _____ want _____ to be a pilot?
1. (want)

SUE: _____ Yes _____, I _____ did _____. I saw a documentary about Amelia
2.
Earhart when I was six. She became my role model.

FH: _____ were _____ your parents happy with your decision?
3. (Be)

SUE: _____ No _____, they _____ weren't _____. They _____ didn't want _____ me to fly.
4. **5.** (not want)

FH: Why not? _____ did _____ they _____ feel _____ it was too dangerous?
6. (feel)

SUE: _____ Yes, _____, they _____ did _____. But I was very determined, and
7.
they _____ didn't keep _____ me from pursuing my dream.
8. (not keep)

FH: _____ Did _____ you ever _____ dream _____ of flying around the world?
9. (dream)

SUE: Of course. But I _____ didn't think _____ it would happen so soon.
10. (not think)

FH: _____ were _____ you alone on the flight?
11. (Be)

SUE: _____ No _____, I _____ wasn't _____. I had a co-pilot.
12.

FH: _____ was _____ it difficult to find a co-pilot for this flight?
13. (Be)

SUE: _____ No _____, it _____ wasn't _____. She's my roommate.
14.

EDIT • *Read this postcard. Find and correct six mistakes in the use of the simple past tense. The first mistake is already corrected.*

> receive
> Hi! Did you ~~received~~ my last letter? I didn't <u>knew</u> your   Know
>   did you
> new address so I sent it to your old one. When you
> move?
> <u>moved</u>? Did your roommate move with you? Right now
>
> I'm on board a plane flying to El Paso to visit Ana.
>   meet
> Did you <u>met</u> her at the conference last year? I wanted
>   didn't have
> to visit her in June, but <u>I no had</u> the time. At first I was
>
> going to drive from Los Angeles, but I decided to fly
>
> instead. This is only my third flight, but I love flying!
> didn't
> I <u>didnt</u> know flying could be so much fun! Hope to
>
> hear from you.   —M.

To: Sue Avila

1210 Bayview Place

Tampa, FL 33601

USA 24¢

UNIT 8

Used to

> Look at that! I **used to** wear baggy jeans!

CHECK POINT

Check the correct answer.

The man is thinking about

☐ a habit he has now.

☐ a habit he had in the past.

CHART CHECK 1

Circle T (True) or F (False).

T F   In affirmative statements, **used to** is used with all subjects.

AFFIRMATIVE STATEMENTS

SUBJECT	USED TO	BASE FORM OF VERB
I She They	**used to**	**wear** jeans.

NEGATIVE STATEMENTS

SUBJECT	DIDN'T USE TO	BASE FORM OF VERB
I She They	**didn't use to**	**wear** jeans.

CHART CHECK 2

Check the correct answer.

In questions, what form of **used to** is used?

☐ *did . . . used to*

☐ *did . . . use to*

YES/NO QUESTIONS

DID	SUBJECT	USE TO	BASE FORM
Did	you she they	**use to**	**wear** jeans?

SHORT ANSWERS

AFFIRMATIVE			NEGATIVE		
Yes,	I she they	**did.**	**No,**	I she they	**didn't.**

WH- QUESTIONS

WH- WORD	DID	SUBJECT	USE TO	BASE FORM
What	**did**	you she they	**use to**	**wear**?

EXPRESS CHECK

Circle the words to complete these sentences.

- He <u>used to / uses to</u> wear baggy jeans.

- Did you <u>use to / used to</u> shop for clothes with your friends?

- What did your parents use to <u>saying / say</u> about your clothes?

Grammar Explanations

Examples

---

1. Use ***used to*** + base form of the verb to talk about **past habits** or **past situations** that <u>no longer exist in the present</u>.

Now
Past ┈┈┈**x x x**┈┈┈┊┈┈┈┈┈┈┈┈┈➤ Future
  used to buy ┊

▶ **BE CAREFUL!** *Used to* always has a past meaning. There is <u>no present tense form</u>.

- Leo **used to buy** baggy jeans.
  (In the past, he often bought baggy jeans. He doesn't buy baggy jeans anymore.)

- In his youth, Leo **used to be** thin.
  NOT ~~Today Leo used to be thin.~~

---

2. We usually use ***used to*** in sentences that **contrast the past and the present**. We often emphasize this contrast by using time expressions such as ***now***, ***no longer***, and ***not anymore*** with the present tense.

- Jeans **used to come** only in blue. ***Now*** you can buy them in any color.

- They **used to live** in Genoa, but they ***no longer*** live there.

- She **used to wear** a size 6, but she does***n't anymore***.

---

3. **BE CAREFUL!** Form **questions** with ***did*** + ***use to***.

Form the **negative** with ***didn't*** + ***use to***.

USAGE NOTE: *Used to* is more common in affirmative statements than in negative statements or questions.

- **Did** you **use to** wear jeans?
  NOT ~~Did you used to wear jeans?~~

- They **didn't use to** come in different colors.
  NOT ~~They didn't used to come . . .~~

---

4. **BE CAREFUL!** Do not confuse ***used to*** + base form of the verb with the following expressions:

be used to *(be accustomed to)*

get used to *(get accustomed to)*

- I **used to wear** tight jeans.
  (It was my past habit to wear tight jeans.)

- I'**m used to wearing** tight jeans.
  (It is normal for me to wear tight jeans.)

- I **got used to wearing** tight jeans last year.
  (I got accustomed to wearing tight jeans.)

1   **IDENTIFY •** *Read this fashion article. Underline all the examples of* **used to** *that refer to a habit in the past.*

In many ways, fashion <u>used to be</u> much simpler. Women didn't <u>use to wear</u> pants to the office, and men's clothes never <u>used to come</u> in bright colors. People also <u>used to dress</u> in special ways for different situations. They didn't use blue jeans as business clothes or wear jogging suits when they traveled. Today you can go to the opera and find some women in evening gowns while others are in blue jeans. Even buying jeans <u>used to be</u> easier—they came only in blue denim. I'm still not used to buying green jeans and wearing them to work!

2   **CHOOSE & COMPLETE •** *Look at these pictures from an old magazine. Use the verbs in the box with* **used to**. *Write one sentence about each picture.*

| ~~be~~   carry   dance   dress   have   wear |

1. Women's skirts ___used to be___ long and formal.

2. All men _used to have_ long hair.

3. Children _used to dress_ like adults.

4. Men and women _used to dance_ at formal balls.

5. Women _used to wear_ many petticoats under their skirts.

6. Men _used to carry_ walking sticks.

3 **ASK & ANSWER** • Look at the information about sneakers from 1922. Complete the FAQs*. Use the correct form of **used to**.

STYLE	HIGH-TOP	LOW-TOP
MEN'S	98¢	89¢
WOMEN'S	38¢ WHITE	79¢
	95¢ BLACK	
BOYS' AND GIRLS'	85¢ SMALL	73¢ SMALL
	89¢ LARGE	79¢ LARGE
CHILDREN'S	–	65¢

1. **Q:** <u>Did sneakers use to come in many colors?</u>
   (sneakers / come in many colors?)

   A: <u>No. Only in white and black.</u>

2. **Q:** How many styles did they use to come in?

   A: <u>They use to come in two styles.</u>

3. **Q:** <u>How much did pair of men's high tops use to cost?</u>
   (How much / pair of men's high-tops / cost?)

   A: <u>They used to cost 98∅</u>

4. **Q:** What about women's sneakers? Did they use to cost the same as men's?

   A: <u>They used to cost 38¢ for white and 95 for black</u>

5. **Q:** What kind of sneakers did children use to wear?

   A: <u>They only used to be low-top.</u>

6. **Q:** How many sizes did there use to be for boys and girls?

   A: <u>They used to be small and large</u>

*FAQs = Frequently Asked Questions

4 **EDIT** • Read this student's journal. Find and correct five mistakes in the use of **used to**. The first mistake is already corrected.

>   use
> When I was younger, clothing didn't ~~used~~ to be a problem. All the girls at my
>
>   wear
> school used to <u>wore</u> the same uniform. I used to think that it took away from
>
> my freedom of choice. Now I can wear what I want, but clothes cost so much!
>
>   used
> Even blue jeans, today's "uniform," used to be cheaper. My mom <u>uses</u> to pay less
>
>   use
> than $20 for hers. I guess they didn't <u>used</u> to sell designer jeans back then.
>
> You know, I ~~was~~ used to be against school uniforms, but now I'm not so sure!

I was snowboarding.

CHECK *POINT*

Check the correct answer.

The girl in the hospital bed is giving her version of

❑ what she usually did in the past.

❑ what she was doing at the time of her accident.

CHART CHECK 1

Circle T (True) or F (False).

T F The past progressive is made up of the past tense of **be** + base form of the verb.

STATEMENTS

SUBJECT	BE	(NOT)	BASE FORM OF VERB + -ING
I/He/She/It	**was**	(not)	**jumping**. **falling**.
We/You*/They	**were**		

You is both singular and plural.

CHART CHECK 2

Check the correct answer.

In questions, the verb **be** comes:

❑ after the subject

❑ before the subject

YES/NO QUESTIONS

BE	SUBJECT	BASE FORM + -ING
Was	she	**jumping?** **falling?**
Were	you	

SHORT ANSWERS

AFFIRMATIVE		NEGATIVE	
Yes,	she **was**.	No,	she **wasn't**.
	we **were**.		we **weren't**.

WH- QUESTIONS

WH- WORD	BE	SUBJECT	BASE FORM + -ING
Where When	**was**	she	**jumping?** **falling?**
Why How long	**were**	you	

EXPRESS CHECK

Complete this conversation with the past progressive form of the verb **stay**.

A: Where _____ you _____?

B: I _____ at a resort in Colorado.

Grammar Explanations

Examples

---

1. Use the **past progressive** to describe an action that was <u>in progress at a specific time in the past</u>. The action began before the specific time and may or may not continue after the specific time.

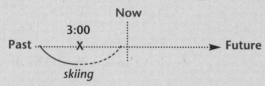

▶ **BE CAREFUL!** Non-action verbs are not usually used in the progressive.
(For a list of common non-action verbs, see Appendix 2 on page 337.)

A: What **were** you **doing** at 3:00?
B: We **were skiing**.
C: I **was eating** lunch at 3:00.

■ I **had** a headache last night.
   NOT ~~I was having a headache last night.~~

---

2. Use the **past progressive with** *while* to talk about <u>two actions in progress at the same time in the past</u>. Use the past progressive in both clauses.

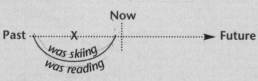

USAGE NOTE: In informal conversation, some people use *when* with the past progressive.

■ *While* he **was skiing**, I **was reading**.
                OR
■ I **was reading** *while* he **was skiing**.

■ Sorry, I **wasn't listening** *when* you **were talking**.

---

3. Use the **past progressive** to focus on the <u>duration</u> of an action, not its completion.

Use the **simple past tense** to focus on the <u>completion</u> of an action.

■ Sheila **was reading** a book last night.
   (We don't know if she finished the book.)

■ Sheila **read** a book last night.
   (She probably finished the book.)

1 **TRUE OR FALSE** • *Read each numbered sentence. Write T (True) or F (False) for the statement that follows. Write a question mark (?) if there is not enough information.*

1. While Tanya was watching the Winter Olympics on TV, Mikael was shoveling snow.

___F___ First Mikael finished shoveling snow. Then Tanya started watching TV.

2. In this photo, I was putting on my boots.

___F___ I was wearing boots in the photo.

3. At 5:00, they were drinking hot chocolate by the fire.

___T___ We don't know when they started drinking hot chocolate.

4. Last night, I was reading an article about skiing in Morocco.

___F___ I finished the article.

5. At 10:00, he drank a cup of coffee.

___T___ He finished the coffee.

6. It was snowing while she was taking the photograph.

___F___ First she took the photograph. Then it started to snow.

2 **DESCRIBE** • *Fritz and Karyn were at a ski café. Write about the picture. Use the past progressive.*

1. Fritz _____was wearing a hat._____
(wear / a hat)

2. Karyn _____wasn't wearing a hat._____
(wear / a hat)

3. They _____was sitting outside_____
(sit / outside)

4. It _____was snowing_____
(snow)

5. They _____was wearing sunglasses_____
(wear / sunglasses)

6. They _____
(wear / their gloves)

7. The waiter _____
(serve / drinks)

8. He _____
(serve / lunch)

9. Karyn _____
(smile)

10. She _____
(hold / a cell phone)

3 **COMPLETE** • Mountain Sports Magazine (MS) _interviewed the snowboarding champion, Rosie Happ (RH). Complete the interview with the correct form of the verbs in parentheses and with short answers._

MS: Congratulations! You just became a semi-finalist for the Olympic snowboarding team. _____**Were**_____ you _____**expecting**_____ to get this far in
1. (expect)
the competition?

RH: No, I _____**wasn't**_____. During the trials, I _____ from a
2. **3.** (recover)
bad cold. By the last day, I _____ very well. That's what
4. (not perform)
I thought, anyway.

MS: What _____ you _____ while you _____
5. (think) **6.** (wait)
for the announcement?

RH: Actually, I _____ about the competition at all. Some friends
7. (not think)
and I _____ a movie.
8. (watch)

MS: You're pretty new to this sport. Where _____ you _____
9. (snowboard)
at this time last year?

RH: In Switzerland. I _____ Barrett Christie and _____
10. (watch) **11.** (dream)
about being that good.

MS: _____ he _____ for the Olympics at that time?
12. (practice)

RH: Yes, he _____. And he was amazing.
13.

4 **EDIT** • _Read this journal entry. Find and correct eight mistakes in the use of the past progressive. The first mistake is already corrected._

> were
> Tonight, Sheila and I ~~was~~ looking at some photographs from my snowboarding trip with
> Fritz's family last year. By the end of the evening, we laughing like crazy. That was my first
> experience on a snowboard, so the pictures were pretty embarrassing. In one shot, I was came
> down the slope on my back. In another one, my board were falling out of the ski lift while I was
> riding up the slope. Fritz was taking that picture from the lift entrance. Good thing he not
> standing right under me! Where was I when Fritz was falling down the slope? I guess I wasn't
> carry my camera. It was amazing how fast Fritz's girlfriend, Karyn, learned that weekend.
> She was doing jumps by the second day. By that time, I spent a lot of time at the ski café.

UNIT 10

Past Progressive and Simple Past Tense

Did you see the accident?

Yeah ... The guy in the sports car was talking on his cell phone when he hit the other car.

CHECK **POINT**

Number these statements in the correct time order.

_____ There was a car accident.

_____ The driver of the sports car was on the phone.

CHART CHECK

Circle T (True) or F (False).

Use **while** to introduce

T F   a simple past tense action.

T F   a past progressive action.

PAST PROGRESSIVE AND SIMPLE PAST TENSE

PAST PROGRESSIVE	WHEN	SIMPLE PAST TENSE
He **was speeding**	when	the accident **happened**.

SIMPLE PAST TENSE AND PAST PROGRESSIVE

SIMPLE PAST TENSE	WHILE	PAST PROGRESSIVE
The accident **happened**	while	you **were driving**.

SIMPLE PAST TENSE AND SIMPLE PAST TENSE

SIMPLE PAST TENSE	WHEN	SIMPLE PAST TENSE
The police **came**	when	the accident **happened**.

PAST PROGRESSIVE AND PAST PROGRESSIVE

PAST PROGRESSIVE	WHILE	PAST PROGRESSIVE
They **were talking**	while	they **were driving**.

EXPRESS CHECK

Circle the correct words to complete these sentences.

• When / While the car crashed, he hit his head.

• How fast was he driving / did he drive when the accident occurred?

40

Grammar Explanations	**Examples**
1. Use the **past progressive with the simple past tense** to talk about <u>an action that was interrupted by another action</u>. Use the simple past tense for the interrupting action. 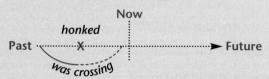 Use **when** to introduce the simple past tense action OR use **while** to introduce the past progressive action.	■ I **was crossing** the street when the driver **honked** his horn. ■ They **were driving** too fast when they **crashed**. ■ He was speeding **when** the light **turned** red. ■ **While** he **was speeding**, the light **turned** red.
2. **BE CAREFUL!** Notice the <u>difference in meaning</u> between these two different sentences. 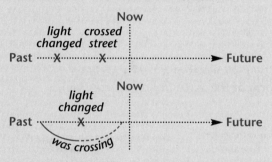	 ■ **When** the light **changed**, I **crossed** the street. *(First the light changed. Then I crossed the street.)* ■ **When** the light **changed**, I **was crossing** the street. *(First I was crossing the street. Then the light changed.)*
3. Use the **past progressive with while** to talk about <u>two actions in progress at the same time in the past</u>. Use the past progressive in both clauses. 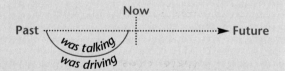	■ Lin **was talking** on the phone **while** he **was driving**. ■ They **weren't paying** attention **while** they **were crossing** the street.
4. The **time clause** (the part of the sentence beginning with **when** or **while**) can come at <u>the beginning or the end</u> of the sentence. The meaning is the same. Use a **comma** after the time clause when it comes at the <u>beginning</u> of the sentence.	■ **When you called,** I was leaving. ■ I was leaving **when you called**. ■ **While he was driving,** he was talking. ■ He was talking **while he was driving**.

1 **TRUE OR FALSE** • *Read each numbered sentence. Write T (True) or F (False) for the statement that follows.*

1. When our friends arrived, we ate lunch.

___T___ Our friends arrived before lunch.

2. While we were talking on the phone, I was driving to school.

___F___ We finished the conversation. Then I drove to school.

3. Lori heard about the accident while she was driving to work.

___T___ Lori knew about the accident by the time she got to work.

4. When they exited the freeway, it started to rain.

___F___ It was raining while they were on the freeway.

5. When Zoe got to school, her class was taking a test.

___T___ Zoe was late to class.

2 **COMPLETE** • *A police officer is interviewing two witnesses of a traffic accident. Complete the interview with the correct form of the verbs in parentheses and with short answers.*

OFFICER: _____Were_____ you _____standing_____ here when the accident
                                              1. (stand)
_____occurred_____?
        2. (occur)

WITNESS 1: Yes, we _____were_____. We ___were waiting___ at the bus stop
                     3.   **4.** (wait)
when we first ___noticed___ the car.
              5. (notice)

OFFICER: ___no was___ the car ___speeding___ when it
                              6. (speed)
_____got_____ to the intersection?
     7. (get)

WITNESS 1: Yes, it ___was___. It ___was going___ very fast when it
                   8.   **9.** (go)
___reached___ the corner.
   10. (reach)

WITNESS 2: No, it ___wasn't___! Those men ___were crossing___ against a red
                  11.   **12.** (cross)
light when the car ___hit___ them.
                   13. (hit)

OFFICER: ___Did___ the driver ___stop___ when he
                              14. (stop)
_____saw_____ the men?
   15. (see)

WITNESS 1: No, he ___didn't___. He ___was talking___ on his cell phone
                  16.   **17.** (talk)
while he ___was driving___. That's why he ___didn't stop___ in time.
         18. (drive)   **19.** (not stop)

WITNESS 2: But the men ___weren't paying___ attention while they ___were walking___.
                       20. (not pay)   **21.** (walk)

OFFICER: _____Was_____ it _____snowing_____ when the accident
22. (snow)

_____happened_____?
23. (happen)

WITNESS 2: Yes, it _____was_____. I'm sure of it. The roads were very slippery.
24.

WITNESS 1: No, it _____wasn't_____. The snow _____started_____ when the
25.   26. (start)

ambulance _____arrived_____.
27. (arrive)

3 **COMBINE** • *Read each pair of sentences. Combine them into one sentence using the simple past tense or the past progressive form of the verbs. Use a comma where necessary.*

1. Dana attended a party. The blizzard started.

When _the blizzard started, Dana was attending a party._

2. She drove home. She listened to her car radio.

While _she was driving, she listened to her radio._

3. She pulled over to the side of the road. The visibility got very bad.

She pulled over to the side of the road when _the visibility getting very bad._

4. She listened to the news. She heard about the accident.

She heard about the accident while _she was listening to the news_

5. It stopped snowing. She drove to the police station.

She drove to the police station when _it stopped snowing_

6. She talked to the police. She thought about her editorial for the morning paper.

While _she was talking to the police, she was thinking about her editorial for the morning paper_

4 **EDIT** • *Read part of the first draft of Dana's editorial. Find and correct five mistakes in the use of time clauses. The first mistake is already corrected.*

Yesterday, a man was talking on his cell phone while he was ~~drive~~ driving his car. Maybe
he was checking his daily planner while he was making his next appointment. He was
certainly not concentrating on the road when the light suddenly ~~was turning~~ turned red.
The two men in the street were ~~trying~~ tried to jump out of the way when they saw him,
but it was too late. No one was badly hurt, but that was just luck. Last year, the
City Council ~~weren't passing~~ didn't pass the "talking and driving law." We need that law!

SelfTest

Circle the letter of the correct answer to complete each sentence.

EXAMPLE:

Jennifer never _____ coffee.　　　　　　　　　　　　A Ⓑ C D
(A) drink　　　　　　　　　　(C) is drinking
(B) drinks　　　　　　　　　　(D) was drinking

---

1. Roger _____ me at 9:00 last night.　　　　　　　A B C D
   (A) called　　　　　　　　　　(C) used to called
   (B) calls　　　　　　　　　　(D) calling

2. Sara didn't hear the phone. She _____.　　　　　A B C D
   (A) sleeps　　　　　　　　　　(C) used to sleep
   (B) slept　　　　　　　　　　(D) was sleeping

3. There _____ a lot of people in the park yesterday.　A B C D
   (A) are　　　　　　　　　　(C) was
   (B) is　　　　　　　　　　(D) were

4. One day last March, I _____ a very strange letter.　A B C D
   (A) did get　　　　　　　　　　(C) used to get
   (B) got　　　　　　　　　　(D) was getting

5. Where _____ to school?　　　　　　　　　　A B C D
   (A) did you go　　　　　　　　　　(C) you go
   (B) you did go　　　　　　　　　　(D) you went

6. Claude didn't _____ in Canada.　　　　　　　A B C D
   (A) lived　　　　　　　　　　(C) used to live
   (B) use to live　　　　　　　　　　(D) used to living

7. Rick left class early because he _____ a headache.　A B C D
   (A) had　　　　　　　　　　(C) used to have
   (B) have　　　　　　　　　　(D) was having

8. As soon as the light turned red, she _____ the car.　A B C D
   (A) did stop　　　　　　　　　　(C) stops
   (B) stopped　　　　　　　　　　(D) was stopping

9. They _____ when the fire alarm rang.　　　　　A B C D
   (A) cook　　　　　　　　　　(C) was cooking
   (B) cooked　　　　　　　　　　(D) were cooking

10. Johnny _____ the paper when I interrupted him.　A B C D
    (A) read　　　　　　　　　　(C) was reading
    (B) reads　　　　　　　　　　(D) were reading

11. —Did you watch TV last night?

—_____ I was studying for a test.

(A) Yes, I did.   (C) No, I didn't.

(B) Yes, I was.   (D) No, I wasn't.

A B C D

12. I remember you. You _____ to go to school here.

(A) use   (C) were using

(B) used   (D) were used

A B C D

SECTION TWO

Each sentence has four underlined words or phrases. The four underlined parts of the sentence are marked A, B, C, and D. Circle the letter of the one underlined word or phrase that is NOT CORRECT.

> **EXAMPLE:**
>
> Mike <u>usually</u> <u>drives</u> to school, but <u>today</u> he <u>walks</u>.
>   A   B   C   D
>
> A B C (D)

13. <u>Why</u> <u>did</u> you <u>called</u> him <u>last week</u>?
   A B   C   D

A B C D

14. They <u>were</u> watching TV <u>while</u> I <u>were</u> <u>reading</u>.
     A   B   C   D

A B C D

15. What <u>are</u> you <u>doing</u> <u>last night</u> <u>at</u> 8:00?
      A   B   C   D

A B C D

16. The doctor <u>called</u> <u>this morning</u> <u>while</u> you <u>slept</u>.
         A   B   C   D

A B C D

17. It <u>was</u> <u>no</u> <u>raining</u> when the game <u>began</u>.
   A B   C   D

A B C D

18. Paul <u>was</u> <u>drying</u> the dishes <u>when</u> he <u>was dropping</u> the plate.
     A   B   C   D

A B C D

19. When Gloria <u>were</u> four, she <u>used to pretend</u> she <u>had</u> a horse.
          A   B   C   D

A B C D

20. What <u>do</u> you <u>use to</u> <u>do</u> when you <u>felt</u> afraid?
     A   B   C   D

A B C D

21. <u>As soon as</u> the alarm clock <u>rang</u>, she <u>woke up</u> and <u>was getting</u>
    A   B   C   D
out of bed.

A B C D

22. Once <u>when</u> I <u>was</u> ten, I <u>used to get</u> sick and <u>went</u> to the hospital.
       A   B   C   D

A B C D

23. <u>While</u> I <u>driving</u> home, I <u>turned on</u> the car radio and <u>heard</u> about
    A   B   C   D
the accident.

A B C D

24. What did you <u>do</u>, <u>while</u> you <u>were living</u> in Spain?
        A B C   D

A B C D

25. Pete and Andy <u>were</u> <u>driving</u> to work <u>when</u> they <u>were seeing</u>
          A   B   C   D
the accident.

A B C D

UNIT 11

Present Perfect:
Since and *For*

Come on!
You've **been** a pro
since 1994. Now
serve the ball!

Forget it!
You **haven't won** a
match **for weeks!**
Go home!

CHECK POINT

Circle T (True) or F (False).

T **F**   The man is still a professional
tennis player.

CHART CHECK 1

*Check the correct
answer.*

The present perfect is
made up of two parts:

❏ *have* + past tense

❏ *have* + past
participle

The regular form of
the past participle is:

❏ base form of
verb + *-d* or *-ed*

❏ base form of
verb + *-en*

STATEMENTS

SUBJECT	HAVE	(NOT)	PAST PARTICIPLE		SINCE/FOR
I/We/You*/They	**have**	**(not)**	**lived** **played** **been**†	here	***since*** May. ***for*** a long time.
He/She/It	**has**				

* *You is both singular and plural.*
† *Been is an irregular past participle. For a list of irregular verbs,
   see Appendix 1 on pages 336–337.*

YES/NO QUESTIONS

HAVE	SUBJECT	PAST PARTICIPLE		SINCE/FOR
Have	they	**lived** **played** **been**	here	***since*** May? ***for*** a long time?
Has	he			

SHORT ANSWERS

AFFIRMATIVE			NEGATIVE		
Yes,	they	**have.**	**No,**	they	**haven't.**
	he	**has.**		he	**hasn't.**

NOTE: For contractions with *have*, see Appendix 24 on page 346.

46

CHART CHECK 2

Check the correct answer.

For is used with:

☐ a point of time
☐ a length of time

	WH- QUESTIONS			
WH- WORD	**HAVE**	**SUBJECT**	**PAST PARTICIPLE**	
How long	**have**	they	**lived**	here?
	has	he	**been**	

SHORT ANSWERS

Since January.
For a few months.

EXPRESS CHECK

Look at the past participles. Check the correct column.

	Regular	Irregular		Regular	Irregular
driven	☐	☐	won	☐	☐
competed	☐	☐	tried	☐	☐

Grammar Explanations

Examples

1. Use the **present perfect** with *since* or *for* to talk about something that <u>began in the past and continues into the present</u> (and may continue into the future).

```
        1994           Now
        Past ·X·····················> Future
                   has been
```

- Martina Hingis **has been** a professional tennis player *since* 1994.

- She **has been** a professional tennis player *for* years.

  (She began her professional career years ago, and she is still a professional player.)

2. Use the present perfect with *since* **+ point in time** *(since 5:00, since Monday, since 1994)* to show <u>when something started</u>.

- She **has earned** millions of dollars *since 1994*.

3. *Since* can also introduce a **time clause**.

When the action in the time clause ended in the past, use the <u>simple past tense</u>.

When the action in the time clause began in the past but continues into the present, use the <u>present perfect</u>.

- Martina **has loved** sports *since she was a child*.

- She has won many tennis tournaments *since* she **moved** from Slovakia. *(She doesn't live there anymore.)*

- She has become extremely successful *since* she **has been** in Switzerland. *(She still lives in Switzerland.)*

4. Use the present perfect with *for* **+ length of time** *(for ten minutes, for two weeks, for years, for a long time)* to show <u>how long a present condition has lasted</u>.

- Martina's mother **has been** her coach *for many years*.

IDENTIFY • *Read about tennis star Martina Hingis. Underline all the verbs in the present perfect. Circle all the time expressions with* **since** *or* **for**.

Martina Hingis picked up her first tennis racket at the age of two. (Since then), she has become one of the greatest tennis players in the world. Born in Slovakia, she has lived in Switzerland for many years. She became the outdoor Swiss champion at age nine. Since then she has won many international competitions including Wimbledon, the U.S. Open, and the Australian Open.

For young stars like Martina, life has its difficulties. They are under constant pressure to win, and they don't have time to just hang out with classmates. In fact, Martina hasn't attended school since 1994, and she has been in the public spotlight for years. But she seems to be handling her success well. Since she turned professional, she has played tennis all over the world and has earned millions of dollars. She sees her life as normal because tennis has been the most important thing to her since she was a little girl.

COMPLETE & CHOOSE • *Read this magazine excerpt about a child genius. Complete it with the present perfect form of the verbs in parentheses. Choose between* **since** *and* **for**.

Thirteen-year-old Ronnie Segal _____ has loved _____ math _____ since _____ he
                  1. (love)   **2.** (since / for)

was a little boy. "I _____ interested in numbers _____
                3. (be)   **4.** (since / for)

nine years, five months, three weeks, and two days," says Ronnie. _____
                                           5. (Since / For)

the past year, Ronnie _____ graduate-level classes at the university.
                     6. (attend)

He _____ badly. _____ January he _____
      7. (not do)   **8.** (Since / For)   **9.** (take)

five exams and _____ a grade of less than 100 on any of them.
           10. (not get)

_____ Ronnie began classes, he _____ an average of
  11. (Since / For)   **12.** (meet)

1.324 people a month. And his future? Young Ronnie _____ about it
                                       13. (not think)

for years. He _____ _____ he was a little boy that he is
          14. (know)   **15.** (since / for)

going to become a famous sports announcer, get married, and have exactly 2.2 kids.

3 **ASK & ANSWER** • *Complete the interview about Martina Hingis. Use the words in parentheses to write questions. Then answer the questions with information from Exercise 1.*

1. (How long / she / play tennis?)

   Q: _How long has she played tennis?_

   A: _Since she was two._

2. (How long / she / live in Switzerland?)

   Q: _How long has she lived in switzerland_

   A: _for many years_

3. (she / win any competitions / since the outdoor Swiss championship?)

   Q: _Has she won any competition since the outdoor Swiss championship?_

   A: _yes she has_

4. (she / attend school / since 1994?)

   Q: _Has she attend school since 1994_

   A: _No_

5. (How much money / she / earn / since she began her career?)

   Q: _How much mony has she earnedsince she began her career?_

   A: _millons of_

6. (How long / tennis / be important to her?)

   Q: _How long tinnis been important to her?_

   A: _____

4 **EDIT** • *Read this student's paragraph. Find and correct seven mistakes in the use of the present perfect. The first mistake is already corrected.*

> have been
> For
> I ~~am~~ in Ms. Rodriguez's physical education class since two months. I enjoy it a lot
> missed
> and have only miss two classes since the beginning of the semester. I especially
> have not played
> like tennis, but since September we don't play because the weather has been too
> has
> cold. I also like volleyball, and my team has win two games since we ~~have~~ started to
> won
> compete with Lincoln High School. I'm looking forward to the next game.

Present Perfect:
Already and *Yet*

As you can see, the flu season **has already begun**. **Have** you **gotten** your flu shot **yet**? It's never too late!

FLU CHART

Well, almost never . . .

CHECK *POINT*

Circle T (True) or F (False).

T F The flu season will start soon.

CHART CHECK 1

Check the correct answer.

To say that something has happened before now,

☐ use *already*.

☐ use *yet*.

To say that something has <u>not</u> happened before now,

☐ use *already*.

☐ use *not . . . yet*.

AFFIRMATIVE STATEMENTS: *ALREADY*				
SUBJECT	**HAVE**	**ALREADY**	**PAST PARTICIPLE**	
They	have	*already*	**developed**	a new flu vaccine.
It	has		**saved**	many lives.

NEGATIVE STATEMENTS: *YET*					
SUBJECT	**HAVE NOT**	**PAST PARTICIPLE**			**YET**
They	**haven't**	**finished**	the interview		*yet*.
It	**hasn't**	**ended**			

CHART CHECK 2

Circle T (True) or F (False).

T F *Yet* is used in questions.

YES/NO QUESTIONS: *YET*				
HAVE	**SUBJECT**	**PAST PARTICIPLE**		**YET**
Have	they	**tested**	the new vaccine	*yet*?
Has	it	**gotten**	approval	

SHORT ANSWERS					
AFFIRMATIVE			**NEGATIVE**		
Yes,	they	**have.**	**No,**	they	**haven't.**
	it	**has.**		it	**hasn't.**

EXPRESS CHECK

Unscramble these words to form a question. Answer the question.

you • have • yet • lunch • had

_____Have you had lunch yet?_____?

_____No, I haven't_____

Grammar Explanations

1. We often use the **present perfect** with *already* to talk about things that <u>have happened before now</u>.

▶ **BE CAREFUL!** Do not use the present perfect with *already* when you mention a specific time in the past.

Already usually comes between *have* and the past participle.

Already can also come at the end of the clause.

2. Use the **present perfect** with *not yet* to talk about things that <u>have not happened before now</u>.

Notice that *yet* usually comes at the end of the clause.

Yet can also come between *have not* and the past participle.

3. We usually use *yet* **in questions** to find out if something has happened <u>before now</u>.

USAGE NOTE: Sometimes we use *already* **in a question** to express surprise that something happened sooner than expected.

Examples

A: Is your daughter going to get her flu shot?
B: She**'s** *already* **gotten** it.

DON'T SAY: ~~She's already gotten it last month~~.

■ Researchers **have** *already* **discovered** cures for many diseases.

■ They**'ve made** a lot of progress *already*.

■ They **haven't discovered** a cure for the common cold *yet*, but they hope to discover one in the future.

■ The flu season **hasn't arrived** *yet*.

■ They **haven't** *yet* **discovered** a cure for the common cold.

■ **Has** your son <u>gotten</u> his flu shot *yet*?
  got

■ **Has** he *already* **gotten** his flu shot? The flu season hasn't begun yet.

1 **MATCH** • *Each cause has a probable result. Match the cause with the appropriate result.*

Cause

   _e_   **1.** Tom has already gotten his flu shot, so he probably

         2. Dr. Meier has already finished his interview, so he

         3. Dr. Meier hasn't had lunch yet, so he

         4. Randy hasn't gotten his shot yet, so he

         5. Randy has already had lunch, so he

Result

a. is really hungry.

b. may get the flu.

c. has left the TV studio.

d. isn't very hungry.

e. won't get the flu this year.

2 **COMPLETE** • *Read these questions and answers from a magazine article. Complete them with the present perfect form of the verbs in parentheses plus* **already** *or* **yet.** *Use short answers.*

smallpox vaccine	tetanus vaccine	flu vaccine	polio vaccine	measles vaccine	world smallpox vaccination program	last case of smallpox	AIDS vaccine	cancer vaccine	malaria vaccine	common cold vaccine
1796	1880	1945	1954	1963	1966	1980	NOW			

Q: We plan to travel to the rain forest next year. ____Have____ they

    ____found____ a malaria vaccine ____yet____?
    1. (find)

A: ____No____, they ____haven't____. Talk to your doctor about ways to
                            2.

prevent this disease.

Q: My doctor told me I won't need another smallpox vaccination. I was surprised.

    _____ smallpox completely _____?
                                      3. (disappear)

A: _____, it _____.
                           4.

Q: They _____ vaccines against the flu. What about the common cold?
        5. (develop)

A: No. Because there are so many different cold viruses, they _____ to
                                              6. (not be able)

develop a vaccine _____.

Q: There has been so much cancer research. _____ anyone

    _____ a successful vaccine _____?
        7. (make)

A: _____ they _____. Researchers *have* made a lot of
                             8.

progress in recent years, however.

3

DESCRIBE • *Dr. Helmut Meier and his wife, Gisela, are planning a party. Look at their To Do lists and the pictures of their kitchen and dining room. Cross out the chores they have already done. Then write sentences about each item on their To Do lists.*

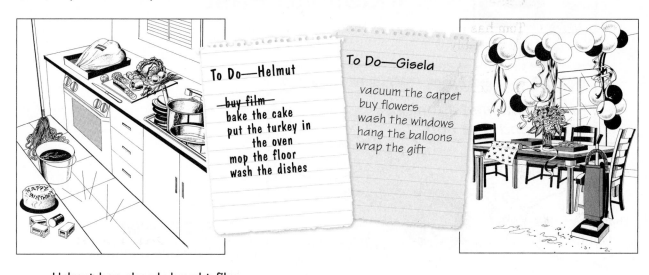

To Do—Helmut

~~buy film~~
bake the cake
put the turkey in
the oven
mop the floor
wash the dishes

To Do—Gisela

vacuum the carpet
buy flowers
wash the windows
hang the balloons
wrap the gift

1. Helmut has already bought film.

2. Gisela hasn't vacuumed the carpet yet.

3. _____

4. _____

5. _____

6. _____

7. _____

8. _____

9. _____

10. _____

4

EDIT • *Read this note from Gisela to Helmut. Find and correct six mistakes in the use of the present perfect with* **already** *and* **yet**. *The first mistake is already corrected.*

Helmut—I'm in a hurry. I haven't ~~went~~ ^(gone) shopping already, but I'll do it on the way home. Rita

have already had dinner and she's already had her bath. Have you call Mr. Jacobson yet?

He's called already three times today. His daughter has gotten her flu shot yet. Is it too

late? See you later.   G.

Present Perfect:
Indefinite Past

What's new on "Feldstein"?
Tune in Channel 4 tonight at 8:00 and find out!

I've recently **moved** in with my parents.

I've just **thought** of this crazy new idea!

Have you **ever met** anyone like us before?

I've **met** someone new. Again.

CHECK **POINT**

Check the correct answer.

The "Feldstein" cast is talking about things of importance to them

☑ now.

☐ in the past.

CHART CHECK 1

Circle T (True) or F (False).

T F You can use the present perfect without mentioning a specific time.

STATEMENTS				
SUBJECT	**HAVE**	**(NOT)**	**PAST PARTICIPLE**	
They	have	(not)	appeared	on TV.
It	has		been	

For a complete presentation of present perfect forms, see Unit 11, pages 46–47.

CHART CHECK 2

Check the correct answer.

Never and ***just*** come:

☑ before the past participle

☐ at the end of the statement

STATEMENTS WITH ADVERBS					
SUBJECT	**HAVE (NOT)**	**ADVERB**	**PAST PARTICIPLE**		**ADVERB**
They	have	*never*	appeared	on TV.	
It	has	*just* *recently*	been		
They	have (not)		appeared	on TV	*lately.*
It	has (not)		been		*recently.*

54

CHART CHECK 3

Circle T (True) or
F (False).

T **F** *Ever* has to be
used in *yes/no*
questions.

YES/NO QUESTIONS

Have	Subject	(*Ever*)	Past Participle
Have	they	*(ever)*	acted?
Has	she		won?

SHORT ANSWERS

Affirmative			Negative		
Yes,	they	have.	No,	they	haven't.
	she	has.		she	hasn't.

WH- QUESTIONS

Wh- Word	Have	Subject	Past Participle	
How often	have	they	acted	on this show?
Why	has	it	won	an award?

EXPRESS CHECK

Unscramble these words to form a question. Answer the question.

you • watched • Have • "The Simpsons" • ever

Have you ever watched the Simpsons? _Yes,_ _____

Grammar Explanations

1. Use the **present perfect** to talk about things that happened at an <u>indefinite time in the past</u>. You can use the present perfect when you don't know when something happened or when the specific time is not important.

2. You can use *ever* with the **present perfect** to <u>ask questions</u>. It means at *any time up until now*.

Use *never* to <u>answer negatively</u>.

3. Use the **present perfect** with *just*, *recently*, or *lately* to talk about events in the <u>very recent past</u>.

Usage Note: In <u>spoken American English</u> people often use *just* and *recently* with the simple past tense to talk about indefinite time.

▶ **Be careful!** Do not use *just*, *recently*, or *lately* with the present perfect and a specific past time expression.

Examples

- They**'ve won** several awards.
- I**'ve interviewed** the whole cast.
- She**'s been** in a Hollywood movie.
- I**'ve seen** his show many times.

A: **Have** you **won** an award?
OR
Have you *ever* **won** an award?
B: No, **I**'ve *never* **won** one.
OR
No, *never*.

- We've *just* **gotten** back from Los Angeles.
- I've *recently* **signed** a contract to write a book.
- He **hasn't had** time *lately*.

- We *just* **got** back from Los Angeles.

- I've *recently* **gotten** back from Los Angeles.
  Not ~~I've recently gotten back from Los Angeles last Monday.~~

1 **TRUE OR FALSE •** *Read each numbered sentence. Write T (True) or F (False) for the statement that follows.*

1. I've recently joined the show.

   __T__ I am a new cast member.

2. I have never been to Los Angeles.

   __F__ I went to Los Angeles a long time ago.

3. I've just finished Jimmy's book.

   __T__ I finished it a little while ago.

4. Have you ever seen this movie?

   __F__ I want to know when you saw the movie.

5. Arlene asks you, "Have you read any good books lately?"

   __F__ Arlene wants to know about a book you read last year.

6. She's visited New York several times.

   __F__ This is her first visit to New York.

7. She has become very popular.

   __T__ She is popular now.

2 **CHOOSE & COMPLETE •** *Read this script from a scene from "Feldstein." Complete it with the present perfect form of the verbs in the box. Some verbs are used more than once.*

have	make	stop	talk	travel	want

URSULA: This is a nice restaurant. _____Have_____ you _____had_____ the steak?
1.

JIMMY: No, but I _____ the spaghetti. I always have that. Actually
2.

I _____ eating meat. It's not that I love animals. I just hate
3.

plants. _____ you ever really _____ to a plant?
4.

They have absolutely nothing to say.

URSULA: Right. So, _____ you ever_____ to live outside
5.

of New York?

JIMMY: Outside of New York? Where's that? But seriously, I _____

never _____ to try another place. I love it here.
6.

URSULA: But _____ you ever _____ to a different city?
7.

JIMMY: No. Why should I do that? You like it here too, right?

URSULA: It's OK, but I _____ to other places too. It's a big world!
8.

JIMMY: I like it right here. Say, _____ you _____ plans
9.

for tomorrow night? How about dinner? Same time, same place . . .

3 **ASK & ANSWER** • *Complete the XYZ Network online interview with Jake Stewart, the actor who plays the part of Gizmo on Jimmy's show. Use the words in parentheses and the present perfect form of the verb.*

XYZ: Welcome to Live Studio, Jake. You've become very famous.

   <u>How many online interviews have you done?</u>
   1. (How many / online interviews / do?)

JAKE: None! _____. Very exciting!
   2. (never even / be / in a chat room)

XYZ: _____
   3. (How / change / as an actor?)

JAKE: I work with a group, so _____
   4. (become / a better team player lately)

XYZ: As a comic actor, _____
   5. (who / be / your role model?)

JAKE: Hard to say. _____
   6. (Charlie Chaplin / have / great influence on me)

XYZ: _____
   7. (What / be / your best moment on this show?)

JAKE: Well, you know, _____. That was fantastic.
   8. (Jimmy / just / win / the Emmy)

XYZ: All in all, _____
   9. (what / find / most rewarding about this experience?)

JAKE: Free coffee! No, really, _____
   10. (meet / some fantastic people on this show)

4 **EDIT** • *Read this message from an online message board. Find and correct seven mistakes in the use of the present perfect. The first mistake is already corrected.*

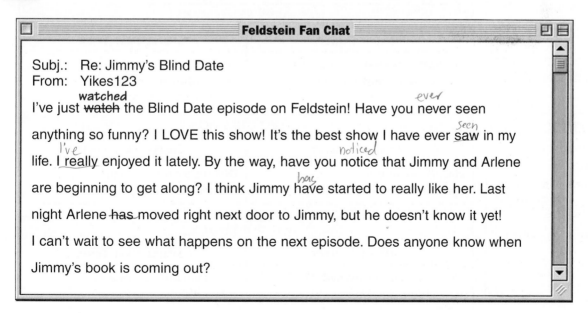

```
┌──────────────────── Feldstein Fan Chat ────────────────────┐
│                                                            │
│  Subj.:  Re: Jimmy's Blind Date                            │
│  From:  Yikes123                                           │
│          watched                    ever                   │
│  I've just w̶a̶t̶c̶h̶ the Blind Date episode on Feldstein! Have you never seen
│                                                    seen    │
│  anything so funny? I LOVE this show! It's the best show I have ever s̲aw in my
│       I've                    noticed                      │
│  life. I really enjoyed it lately. By the way, have you notice that Jimmy and Arlene
│                              has                           │
│  are beginning to get along? I think Jimmy have started to really like her. Last
│  night Arlene h̶a̶s̶ moved right next door to Jimmy, but he doesn't know it yet!
│  I can't wait to see what happens on the next episode. Does anyone know when
│  Jimmy's book is coming out?                               │
│                                                            │
└────────────────────────────────────────────────────────────┘
```

Present Perfect and Simple Past Tense

CHART CHECK 1

Check the correct answer.

Use **have** to form

☐ the simple past tense.

☐ the present perfect.

AFFIRMATIVE STATEMENTS

PRESENT PERFECT	SIMPLE PAST TENSE
She**'s owned** the business since 1996. They**'ve met** twice this month.	She **owned** the business from '96 to '98. They **met** twice last month.

NEGATIVE STATEMENTS

PRESENT PERFECT	SIMPLE PAST TENSE
She **hasn't owned** the business for long. They **haven't met** this month.	She **didn't own** the business for long. They **didn't meet** last month.

CHART CHECK 2

Check the correct answer.

Questions in the present perfect are formed with:

☐ **have** + base form of verb

☐ **have** + past participle

YES/NO QUESTIONS

PRESENT PERFECT	SIMPLE PAST TENSE
Has she **owned** it for long? **Have** they **met** this month?	**Did** she **own** it for long? **Did** they **meet** last month?

WH- QUESTIONS

PRESENT PERFECT	SIMPLE PAST TENSE
How long **has** she **owned** it? When **have** they **met** this month?	How long **did** she **own** it? When **did** they **meet** last month?

EXPRESS CHECK

Circle the correct words to complete these sentences.

They <u>have met / met</u> in 1989. They <u>have been / were</u> married since 1990.

Grammar Explanations

Examples

1. The **present perfect** is used to talk about things that started in the past, <u>continue up to the present</u>, and may continue into the future.

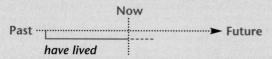

The **simple past tense** is used to talk about things that happened in the past and <u>have no connection to the present</u>.

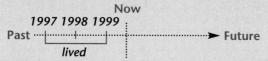

- They **have lived** apart for the past three years.
  (They started living apart three years ago, and they are still living apart.)

- They **lived** apart for three years.
  (They lived apart until 2000. They no longer live apart.)

2. The **present perfect** is used to talk about things that happened at <u>an unspecified time in the past</u>.

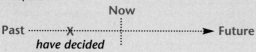

The **simple past tense** is used to talk about things that happened <u>at a specific past time</u>. The time is often stated.

- They **have decided** to travel back and forth.
  (We don't know exactly when they decided, or the time is not important.)

- They **lived** apart *in 1998*.
  (We know when they lived apart and can state the exact time.)

3. The **present perfect** is used to talk about things that have happened in a <u>period of time that is not finished</u>, such as ***today, this month, this year***.

The **simple past tense** is used to talk about things that happened in a <u>period of time that is finished</u>, such as ***yesterday, last month, last year***, and ***this morning*** when it is after 12 P.M.

- I**'ve had** three cups of coffee ***this morning***.
  (It's still this morning. I might have more.)

- I **had** three cups of coffee ***yesterday***.
  (Yesterday is finished.)

- I **had** three cups of coffee ***this morning***.
  (It's now 2 P.M. This morning is finished.)

IDENTIFY • *Read about Joe and Maria. Circle the verbs in the present perfect. Underline the simple past tense verbs.*

Many modern marriages are finding interesting solutions to difficult problems. Joe and Maria, for example, (have been) married since 1995. After their wedding, the couple <u>settled</u> down in Boston, where Maria opened an accounting business. Then in 1997 Joe lost his job. By that time, Maria's new business was booming, so they didn't consider moving. Joe never found a new job in Boston, but in 1998, he got a great offer on the other side of the country—in Los Angeles. The couple has lived apart ever since. How have they handled this "commuter marriage" up to now? Joe notes, "It certainly hasn't been easy. We've been geographically separated, but we've grown a lot closer emotionally. For that reason, it's been worth it."

TRUE OR FALSE • *Now write T (True) or F (False) for each statement.*

___F___ **1.** Joe and Maria are divorced.

_____ **2.** Maria started her own business in Boston.

_____ **3.** The couple used to live apart.

_____ **4.** In 1997, they thought about moving.

_____ **5.** The couple is now closer emotionally.

COMPLETE • *Joe is calling Maria. Complete their conversation with the correct form of the verbs in parentheses and with short answers. Choose between the present perfect and the simple past tense.*

JOE: Hi, honey. _____Did_____ you _____finish_____ that report yesterday?
                                                  1. (finish)

MARIA: ___No, I didn't___. I'm still writing it, and I _haven't stop_ worrying
                    2.   **3.** (not stop)
about it all week.

JOE: Besides that, how _____has_____ the week _____been_____ so far?
                                                          4. (be)

MARIA: OK, I guess. I'm a little tired. I only _____slept_____ a few hours last night.
                                                    5. (sleep)

JOE: It sounds like you _haven't gotten_ much rest this week. Listen—we
                              6. (not get)
___have seen___ each other only twice this month. I'll come tomorrow.
        7. (see)

MARIA: OK, but I still have to work. Last time I _didn't do_ any work.
                                                       8. (not do)

JOE: Right! And it ___didn't bother___ us at all, remember? Listen, why don't you
   9. (not bother)

   relax now? ___have___ you ___tried___ that special coffee yet?
                              10. (try)

MARIA: ___Yes, I have___. In fact, I ___have drank___ five cups today, and it's still
       11.   **12.** (drink)

   early. And yesterday I ___drank___ at least six. I'm really wired now.
                          13. (drink)   _full of energy_

JOE: Then have some herbal tea, and I'll see you tomorrow.

---

3 **ASK & ANSWER** • Lifestyle Magazine (LM) is interviewing Joe and Maria. Complete the interview using the words in parentheses and information from Exercise 1. Choose between the present perfect and the simple past tense.

LM: ___When did you get married?___
                                        1. (When / get married?)
JOE: ___We got married in 1995.___
                                        2.
LM: ___Did you live in Boston after that?___
                                        3. (live / in Boston after that?)
MARIA: ___Yes, we did.___
                                        4.
LM: _____
                                        5. (start your business / before your marriage?)
MARIA: _____
                                        6.
LM: _____
                                        7. (How long / own your own business?)
MARIA: _____
                                        8.
LM: _____
                                        9. (When / you / find your job in Los Angeles?)
JOE: _____
                                        10.
LM: _____
                                        11. (your commuter marriage / be very difficult?)
MARIA: _____!
                                        12.

---

4 **EDIT** • Read this entry from Maria's journal. Find and correct six mistakes in the use of the present perfect and the simple past tense. The first mistake is already corrected.

Thursday, December 28
             's been
It's 8:00 P.M. It ~~was~~ a hard week, and it's not over yet! I still have to finish that report. I've started

it last Monday, but so far, I've wrote only five pages. And it's due next week! Work was so difficult

lately. I've worked late every night this week. I'm tired, and I haven't gotten much sleep last night.

I miss Joe. I've seen him last weekend, but it seems like a long time ago.

Present Perfect Progressive

You've been **playing** with Patti the Platypus again!

Ty Warner **has been making** Beanie Babies since 1993, and people **have been collecting** them since then.

CHECK POINT

Check the correct sentence.

❑ Ty Warner doesn't make Beanie Babies anymore.

❑ People are still collecting Beanie Babies.

CHART CHECK 1

Circle T (True) or F (False).

T F The present perfect progressive always has the word **been**.

STATEMENTS						
SUBJECT	**HAVE**	**(NOT)**	**BEEN**	**BASE FORM OF VERB + -ING**		**SINCE/FOR**
I/We/You*/They	have	(not)	been	collecting making	toys them	*since* 1992. *for* a long time.
He/She/It	has					

*You is both singular and plural.

CHART CHECK 2

Check the correct answer.

In questions, which parts of the verb come after the subject?

❑ **have been**

❑ **been** + base form + **-ing**

YES/NO QUESTIONS					
HAVE	**SUBJECT**	**BEEN**	**BASE FORM + -ING**		**SINCE/FOR**
Have	you	been	collecting making	toys them	*since* 1992? *for* a long time?
Has	he				

SHORT ANSWERS					
AFFIRMATIVE			**NEGATIVE**		
Yes,	we	have.	No,	we	haven't.
	he	has.		he	hasn't.

WH- QUESTIONS					
WH- WORD	HAVE	SUBJECT	BEEN	BASE FORM + -ING	
How long	have	you	been	collecting making	toys? them?
	has	he			

EXPRESS CHECK

Complete these conversations.

A: How long _____ he been living here?

B: _____ a long time.

A: I've _____ collecting coins since last year.

B: Really? Have you been _____ foreign coins?

Grammar Explanations

Examples

1. Use the **present perfect progressive** to talk about things that started in the past and <u>continue up to the present</u>. The situation is usually not finished, and it will probably continue into the future. Now Past ···→ Future *have been collecting* **REMEMBER!** Non-action verbs are usually not used in the progressive.	■ **I've been collecting** Beanie Babies for four years. *(I started collecting them four years ago, and I'm still collecting them.)* ■ **I've owned** this doll for years. NOT ~~I've been owning~~ this doll for years.
2. Use the **present perfect progressive** to describe things that have <u>stopped very recently</u>. The action is not happening right now, but you <u>can still see the results</u> of the action.	■ The kids **have been playing** here. Their toys are all over the room. ■ It's **been raining**. The streets are still wet.

Check it out!

For a list of common non-action verbs, see Appendix 2 on page 337.

1

CHOOSE • *Read each numbered statement. Then circle the letter of the sentence (a) or (b) that best describes the information in the statement.*

1. Gina has been collecting stamps since high school.

   a. Gina stopped collecting stamps.

   (b.) Gina still collects stamps.

2. Enrico has been writing an article about toys.

   a. The article is finished.

   b. The article isn't finished yet.

3. They've been selling a lot of Pokémon toys.

   a. People are still buying Pokémon toys.

   b. The Pokémon fad is finished.

4. Enrico looked out the window and said, "It's been raining."

   a. It's definitely still raining.

   b. It's possible that it stopped raining a little while ago.

5. It's been raining since 6:00.

   a. It's still raining.

   b. It stopped raining a little while ago.

6. They've been playing for hours.

   a. They stopped playing.

   b. They're still playing.

2

COMPLETE • *Enrico Sanchez (ES) interviewed the manager of Toys and Us (TAU). Complete the interview with the present perfect progressive form of the verbs in parentheses. Use short answers when appropriate.*

ES: So, _____ have _____ you _____ been selling _____ a lot of toys this season?
                                          1. (sell)

TAU: _____ Yes, we have _____, Enrico. In fact, Pokémon toys and games _____
                2.   **3. (fly)**

out of the store. They're our most popular item right now.

ES: In case one of our viewers _____ on Mars, could you explain
                                        4. (live)

what Pokémon toys are?

TAU: Haha. I bet the company _____ Pokémon to Mars too. This product
                                       5. (send)

started out in Japan as a computer game. Since 1996, the characters

_____ in collectors' cards, board games—you name it.
      6. (appear)

ES: Why _____ this fad _____ people all over the world?
                                              7. (attract)

TAU: Well, my husband _____ these products for our children because
                              8. (choose)

the characters are cute and not violent. Maybe that's why.

ES: How about Power Rangers? _____ people _____ in
                                                              9. (stand)

line for them?

TAU: _____. People _____ for Power Rangers very
            10.   **11. (not ask)**

much anymore.

3 **DESCRIBE** • *Look at the two pictures of journalist Enrico Sanchez. Write sentences describing what has been going on. Use the present perfect progressive form of the verbs in parentheses. Choose between affirmative and negative forms.*

1. ___He's been doing research on new toys._____
   (do research on new toys)
2. _____
   (test the inline skates)
3. _____
   (shoot baskets)
4. _____
   (eat pizza)
5. _____
   (drink soda)
6. _____
   (build a racing car)
7. _____
   (play video games)
8. _____
   (send e-mail messages)

4 **EDIT** • *Read the thank-you note. Find and correct six mistakes in the use of the present perfect progressive. The first mistake is already corrected.*

Dear Aunt Toni,

Thank you very much for the Pokémon cards. My friend and I have been <del>play</del> playing
with them all day. So far, I am been winning. I really love Pokémon. My Mom been
buying the toys for us because she thinks they're cute too. All my friends were
collecting the cards for months now. Tonya loves the computer game you sent
too. She've been asking me to play with her, but I've been having too much fun
with my cards. How have you been? I've been thought about you a lot. I hope
you can come and visit us soon.

                                                    Love,

                                                    Patrick

Present Perfect and Present Perfect Progressive

That woman has no manners. She**'s been following** me all day. She**'s taken** 100 rolls of film and **written** 42 pages of notes. But she **hasn't** even **given** me a single peanut!

CHECK *POINT*

Circle T (True) or F (False).

The woman is finished

T F following the elephant.

T F taking 100 rolls of film.

CHART CHECK

Circle T (True) or F (False).

T F In some sentences you can use either the present perfect or the present perfect progressive.

PRESENT PERFECT
Elephants **have roamed** the earth for thousands of years.
I**'ve read** two books about elephants.
Dr. Owen **has written** many articles.
She**'s lived** in many countries.

PRESENT PERFECT PROGRESSIVE
Elephants **have been roaming** the earth for thousands of years.
I**'ve been reading** this book since Monday.
She**'s been writing** articles since 1990.
She**'s been living** in France for a year.

EXPRESS `CHECK`

Complete this conversation with the verb **eat** *and a short answer.*

A: He's been _____ all morning!

B: What _____ he _____ eating?

A: Peanuts. He _____ eaten five bags of peanuts!

B: _____ he eaten the whole supply?

A: _____, he _____. There are still ten bags left.

Grammar Explanations

Examples

1. The **present perfect** often shows that something is <u>finished</u>. It focuses on the <u>result</u> of the action.

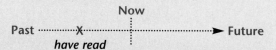

The **present perfect progressive** often shows that an activity is <u>unfinished</u>. It focuses on the <u>continuation</u> of an action.

- I**'ve read** a book about elephants.
  (I finished the book.)

- She**'s written** an article.
  (She finished the article.)

- I**'ve been reading** a book about elephants.
  (I'm still reading it.)

- She**'s been writing** an article.
  (She's still writing it.)

2. We often use the **present perfect** to talk about
  — <u>how much</u> someone has done.
  — <u>how many times</u> someone has done something.
  — <u>how many things</u> someone has done.

We often use the **present perfect progressive** to talk about <u>how long</u> something has been happening.

▶ **BE CAREFUL!** We usually do not use the present perfect progressive when we mention a <u>number</u> of completed events.

- I**'ve read** *a lot* about it.
- I**'ve been** to Africa *twice*.
- She**'s written** *three* articles.

- I**'ve been reading** books on elephants ***for two months***.

- I**'ve read** that book ***twice***.
  NOT ~~I've been reading that book twice.~~

3. Sometimes you can use either the **present perfect** OR the **present perfect progressive**. The meaning is basically the same. This is especially true when you use verbs such as ***live***, ***work***, ***study***, and ***teach*** with ***for*** or ***since***.

- She**'s studied** elephants ***for*** two years.
  OR
- She**'s been studying** elephants ***for*** two years.

  (In both cases, she started studying elephants two years ago and she is still studying them.)

1 **TRUE OR FALSE** • *Read each numbered sentence. Write T (True) or F (False) for the statement that follows.*

1. Professor Owen has been reading a book about elephants.

   __F__ She finished the book.

2. She's read a book about elephants.

   _____ She finished the book.

3. She's written a magazine article about the rain forest.

   _____ She finished the article.

4. She's been waiting for some supplies.

   _____ She received the supplies.

5. They've lived in Uganda since 1992.

   _____ They are still in Uganda.

6. They've been living in Uganda since 1992.

   _____ They still live in Uganda.

2 **CHOOSE** • *Here are some statements about Professor Owen's work. Circle the correct form of the verbs to complete these statements. In some cases, both forms are correct.*

1. Professor Owen is working on two articles for *National Wildlife Magazine*. She has written / has been writing these articles since Monday.

2. *National Wildlife Magazine* has published / has been publishing its annual report on the environment. It's an excellent report.

3. Five hundred and sixty African elephants have already died / have been dying this year.

4. Professor Owen has given / has been giving many talks about wildlife preservation in past lecture series.

5. She has spoken / has been speaking at our school many times.

6. Professor Owen was late for a meeting. When she arrived the chairperson said, "At last, you're here. We have waited / have been waiting for you."

7. Professor Owen has lived / has been living in England for the last two years.

8. She has worked / has been working with environmentalists in England and France.

9. Congress has created / has been creating a new study group to discuss the problem of endangered animals. The group has already met twice.

3 **COMPLETE** • *Read this entry from Dr. Owen's field journal about an elephant she calls Grandad. Use the present perfect or the present perfect progressive form of the verbs in parentheses.*

We ___**'ve been hearing**___ about Grandad since we arrived here in
1. (hear)

Amboseli Park. He is one of the last "tuskers." Two days ago, we finally saw him. His tusks

are more than seven feet long. I _____ never _____ anything like them.
2. (see)

Grandad _____ here for more than sixty years. He
3. (live)

_____ everything, and he _____
4. (experience)   **5.** (survive)

countless threats from human beings. Young men _____ their
6. (test)

courage against him, and poachers _____ him for his ivory.
7. (hunt)

His experience and courage _____ him so far.
8. (save)

For the last two days, he _____ slowly through the tall
9. (move)

grass. He _____ and _____.
10. (eat)   **11.** (rest)

Luckily, it _____ a lot this year, and even the biggest elephants
12. (rain)

_____ enough food and water.
13. (find)

4 **EDIT** • *Read this student's report. Find and correct six mistakes in the use of the present perfect and present perfect progressive. The first mistake is already corrected.*

> **living**
> Elephants and their ancestors have been ~~live~~ on this planet for 5 million years.
>
> Scientists have found their bones in many places, from Asia to North America.
>
> Present-day elephants has also survived in different kinds of environments, including
>
> very dry areas in Niger, grasslands in East Africa, and forests in West Africa.
>
> Because of their great size and strength, elephants have always fascinating
>
> humans. Our fascination has almost caused African elephants to become extinct. Poachers
>
> (illegal hunters) have already been killing hundreds of thousands of elephants for the
>
> ivory of their tusks. After 1989 it became illegal to sell ivory. Since then, the elephant
>
> population has been grown steadily. Recently several countries have been protecting
>
> elephants in national parks, and herds have became larger and healthier.

17 Past Perfect

> By the time I turned twelve, I **had** already **decided** on a career. I wanted to be paid to talk!

Talk-show host Oprah Winfrey with her TV audience.

CHECK **POINT**

Check the event that happened first.

❏ Oprah turned twelve.

❏ Oprah decided on a career.

CHART CHECK 1

Circle T (True) or F (False).

T F The past perfect uses *had* for all subjects.

STATEMENTS		
SUBJECT	**HAD (NOT)**	**PAST PARTICIPLE**	
I/He/She/We/You*/They	had (not)	**decided**	by then.
It		**been**	easy.

*You is both singular and plural.

CHART CHECK 2

Check the correct answer.

In past perfect questions, where does *had* go?

❏ before the subject
❏ after the subject

YES/NO QUESTIONS			
HAD	**SUBJECT**	**PAST PARTICIPLE**	
Had	she	**decided**	by then?
	it	**been**	easy?

SHORT ANSWERS					
AFFIRMATIVE			**NEGATIVE**		
Yes,	she	had.	No,	she	hadn't.
	it			it	

WH- QUESTIONS				
WH- WORD	**HAD**	**SUBJECT**	**PAST PARTICIPLE**	
Why	had	she	**decided**	to be a talk-show host?
		it	**been**	easy?

EXPRESS CHECK

Complete this conversation with the verb **arrive**.

A: Had she _____ by 9:00?

B: No, she _____ .

Grammar Explanations

Examples

1. Use the **past perfect** to show that something happened <u>before a specific time in the past</u>. 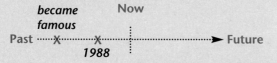	■ By 1988 Oprah Winfrey **had become** famous. ■ It was 1985. She **had** already **been** in a Hollywood film.
2. The **past perfect** always shows a <u>relationship with another past event</u>. Use the <u>past perfect for the earlier event</u>. Use the simple past tense for the later event. ▶ **Be careful!** In these sentences with **when**, notice the <u>difference in meaning</u> between the simple past tense and the past perfect.	■ In 1990 Oprah *invited* Matt on the show. He **had been** an author for two years. *(He was an author before 1990.)* ■ By the time Jill *got* home, "The Oprah Winfrey Show" **had finished**. ■ **When** the show ended, she **left**. *(First the show ended. Then she left.)* ■ **When** the show ended, she **had left**. *(First she left. Then the show ended.)*
3. *Already*, *yet*, *ever*, and *never* are often used with the past perfect to <u>emphasize the event which occurred first</u>.	■ I saw *The Color Purple* last night. I **had** *never* **seen** it before. ■ Jason **had** *already* **seen** it.
4. When the time relationship between two past events is clear, you can use the **simple past tense for both events**. The meaning is usually clear when you use *after*, *before*, or *as soon as* to connect the events.	■ *After* Oprah **had appeared** in *The Color Purple*, she **got** a part in another movie. OR ■ *After* Oprah **appeared** in *The Color Purple*, she **got** a part in another movie.
5. We often use the **past perfect** with *by* (a certain time).	■ *By 1966* Oprah **had decided** on a career.

1 **TRUE OR FALSE** • *Read each numbered sentence. Write T (True) or F (False) for the statement that follows.*

1. When I got home, "The Oprah Winfrey Show" started.

____F____ First the Oprah show started. Then I got home.

2. When I got home, "The Oprah Winfrey Show" had started.

____T____ First the Oprah show started. Then I got home.

3. Oprah's guest had lost 100 pounds when she interviewed him.

____T____ The guest lost the weight before the interview.

4. By the end of the show, I had fallen asleep.

____F____ I fell asleep after the show.

5. When I went to bed, I had turned off the radio.

____F____ I turned off the radio after I went to bed.

6. By midnight, I had finished the magazine article.

____T____ I finished the article before midnight.

2 **COMPLETE** • *Look at some important events in Oprah Winfrey's career. Then complete the sentences below. Use the past perfect with **already** or **not yet**.*

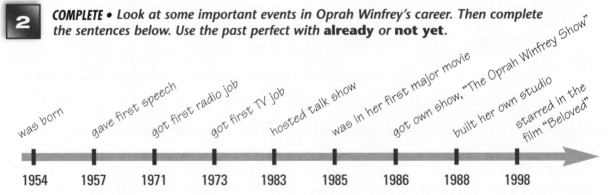

1. By 1958 Oprah ____had already given____ her first speech.

2. By 1971 she _____ her first TV job.

3. By 1972 she _____ her first radio job.

4. By 1972 she _____ in a major movie.

5. By 1985 she _____ her own TV show.

6. By 1986 she _____ in a major movie.

7. By 1987 she _____ her own studio.

8. By 2000 she _____ in the film *Beloved*.

3 **ASK & ANSWER** • *Look at this typical daily schedule for a TV talk-show host. Complete the questions about his schedule. Use the past perfect and give short answers.*

7:00 A.M.	Arrive at studio
8:00	Review day's schedule
11:00	Discuss future shows with assistant producers
2:00 P.M.	Hair and makeup
2:30	Meet the day's guests
3:00	Tape the show
4:30	Work out with trainer

1. It was 7:45. The host was on schedule.

   A: __Had he arrived__ at the studio yet?   **B:** __Yes, he had.__

2. At 7:30 the host was at his desk.

   A: _____ the day's schedule yet?   **B:** _____

3. At 10:55 he was having coffee.

   A: _____ the schedule by that time?   **B:** _____

4. It was 2:00. He was on his way to makeup.

   A: _____ the day's guests by then?   **B:** _____

5. At 4:00 he had a late lunch.

   A: _____ the show yet?   **B:** _____

6. He went to bed at 10:30.

   A: _____ with his trainer that day?   **B:** _____

4 **EDIT** • *Read this student's report. There are six mistakes in the use of the past perfect. Find and correct them. The first mistake is already corrected.*

Oprah Winfrey is an amazing person! By the time she was twelve, she ~~has~~ already had
decided on a career. Not long afterward, she got her first radio job. Although she hadn't
had
~~have~~ any experience, she became a news reporter. When she got her own TV talk show,
had
she ~~has~~ already acted in a major Hollywood movie. By the late 1980s "Oprah Winfrey"
had became a household word. Then in 1994 she decided to improve the quality of
talk-show themes. She also made a personal change. She had always had a weight
problem, but in 1995 TV viewers saw a new Winfrey. She had lost almost ninety
competed
pounds as a result of dieting and working out. She had also ~~compete~~ in a marathon.
She has really been an inspiration to many people.

UNIT 18 Past Perfect Progressive

By the time the last runner crossed the finish line, he **had been running** 7 hours, 16 minutes, and 24 seconds.

CHECK POINT

Circle T (True) or F (False).

T F The race is finished.

CHART CHECK

Check the correct answer.

What form of *be* does the past perfect progressive always use?

☐ *was* or *were*

☐ *is*, *am*, or *are*

☐ *been*

STATEMENTS

SUBJECT	HAD (NOT) BEEN	BASE FORM OF VERB + -ING	
I/He/She/It/We/You*/They	had (not) been	running working	all day.

*You is both singular and plural.

YES/NO QUESTIONS

HAD	SUBJECT	BEEN	BASE FORM + -ING	
Had	she	been	running working	all day?

SHORT ANSWERS

AFFIRMATIVE	NEGATIVE
Yes, she had.	No, she hadn't.

WH- QUESTIONS

WH- WORD	HAD	SUBJECT	BEEN	BASE FORM + -ING
How long Why	had	she	been	running? working?

EXPRESS CHECK

Complete this conversation with the past perfect progressive form of the verb **practice**.

A: How long _____ she _____ when she entered the race?

B: She _____ for more than two years.

A: _____ she _____ alone?

B: No, she _____ . She _____ with a partner.

Grammar Explanations

Examples

1. Use the **past perfect progressive** to talk about an action that was <u>in progress before a specific time in the past</u>. The progressive emphasizes the <u>continuation</u> of an action, not the end result.

REMEMBER! Non-action verbs are not usually used in the progressive.

■ It was 2:00 P.M. The runners **had been running** since 10:48 A.M.
■ I finally saw Rob at 4:00 P.M. **I had been waiting** for hours.
■ One runner fainted. She **hadn't been drinking** enough water.

■ It was 5:00 P.M. He **had had** a headache all day. NOT He ~~had been having~~ a headache all day.

2. The **past perfect progressive** always shows a <u>relationship with another past event</u>.

Use the past perfect progressive for the <u>earlier event</u>. Use the simple past tense for the later event.

■ She **had been practicing** for three years when she *entered* the race.
(First she practiced. Then she entered the race.)

3. We often use the **past perfect progressive** to <u>draw conclusions</u> about past events based on evidence.

■ She was out of breath. It was clear that she **had been running**.

■ The streets were wet. It **had been raining**.

4. **BE CAREFUL!** In these sentences with *when*, notice the <u>difference in meaning</u> between the past progressive and the past perfect progressive.

■ *When* the race started, it **was raining** and the streets were wet.
(It was still raining during the race.)

■ *When* the race started, it **had been raining** and the streets were wet.
(It wasn't raining during the race. It had already stopped.)

1

MATCH • *Each result has a cause. Match the result with the correct cause.*

Result	Cause
__b__ **1.** She was out of breath.	**a.** He had been reading.
_____ **2.** The ground was wet.	**b.** She had been running.
_____ **3.** Her eyes were red.	**c.** They had been watching the race.
_____ **4.** There was an open book on the couch.	**d.** She had been crying.
_____ **5.** There were empty cans on the floor.	**e.** It had been raining.
_____ **6.** The TV was on.	**f.** They had been drinking soda.

2

COMPLETE • *Read this story from a magazine article. Complete it with the past perfect progressive form of the verbs in parentheses.*

MARATHON RUNNING

BY BERNADINE MARTIN

On October 23, I ran the Boston Marathon with a partner, Marcia Davis. We ___**had been training**___
1. (train)
together since last year, and we

_____ to enter
2. (plan)
the race ever since we saw Oprah

in the Washington Marathon. The start of the race was dramatic. Up to that point, we

_____, but we were very serious when we lined up. I was so nervous
3. (joke and laugh)
I couldn't breathe. Marcia and I _____ on those same streets for a
4. (practice)
couple of weeks, so at the beginning we did well. By the time we got to Heartbreak Hill,

we _____ for almost four hours, and I really believed we could
5. (run)
finish. Then, halfway up the hill, Marcia stopped. She just couldn't run anymore.

We _____ to this race for so long that I didn't want to go on
6. (look forward)
alone, but Marcia wanted me to finish. When I got to the finish line, I saw Marcia. She

_____ for me for three hours. First we cried. Then we started talking
7. (wait)
about next year's marathon.

3 **CHOOSE & COMPLETE** • *The magazine* Runner's World (RW) *is interviewing marathon winner Paolo Esposito (PE). Complete the interview with the past perfect progressive form of the correct verbs from the box. Use short answers where appropriate.*

date	expect	live	~~practice~~	run

RW: You just won the marathon. ____Had you been practicing____ long for it?
1.

PE: ____Yes, I had____. For more than five years. First in Madrid,
2.

then in Rome.

RW: You tripped during the race. How long _____ when
3.

that happened?

PE: It was in the last hour. Luckily it didn't keep me from winning.

RW: I understand that you recently married your trainer, Emilia Leale. How long

_____ each other when you decided to get married?
4.

PE: About six months. We met in Rome and knew right away that we wanted to

be together.

RW: _____ in Rome for a long time when you met?
5.

PE: _____. In fact, I had just moved there.
6.

RW: When you crossed the finish line you looked very calm.

_____ to win?
7.

PE: _____! I was really surprised. And very happy.
8.

4 **EDIT** • *Read part of an entry from a runner's journal. Find and correct five mistakes in the use of the past perfect progressive. The first mistake is already corrected.*

> October 19,
>
> I just got back from the marathon! I'm tired but very happy. When I crossed the finish
>   had
> line, I ~~have~~ been running for four hours and twenty-five minutes. Jeremy was standing
>
> there. He had been waited for me the whole time. We were both soaking wet—I, because
>
> I had been sweating; he, because it has been raining just a little while before. I was so
>
> glad to see him. I had been look forward to this day for so long and hoping that I could
>
> finish the race in less than four and a half hours. When I got home, I called my parents.
>
> They had watching the marathon on TV and had actually seen me cross the finish line!

SelfTest

Circle the letter of the correct answer to complete each sentence.

EXAMPLE:

Jennifer never _____ coffee.   **A (B) C D**
(A) drink   (C) is drinking
(B) drinks   (D) was drinking

---

1. He _____ for the Olympics since 1998.   **A B C D**
   (A) practiced   (C) has been practicing
   (B) practices   (D) was practicing

2. We've known Sally _____ a long time.   **A B C D**
   (A) since   (C) while
   (B) by   (D) for

3. We've been living in Montreal since we _____.   **A B C D**
   (A) have graduated   (C) graduated
   (B) have been graduating   (D) graduate

4. They haven't _____ an AIDS vaccine.   **A B C D**
   (A) yet developed   (C) developed already
   (B) developed yet   (D) already develop

5. _____ you reserved your hotel room yet?   **A B C D**
   (A) Did   (C) Do
   (B) Have   (D) Has

6. She hasn't _____ very often.   **A B C D**
   (A) flew   (C) flown
   (B) flies   (D) flying

7. It _____ and the ground was still white.   **A B C D**
   (A) snows   (C) would snow
   (B) had been snowing   (D) has snowed

8. Tina _____ last week.   **A B C D**
   (A) has arrived   (C) has been arriving
   (B) arrived   (D) arrives

9. They _____ here for three years before they moved.   **A B C D**
   (A) live   (C) had lived
   (B) have lived   (D) have been living

10. The show has _____ won an award.   **A B C D**
    (A) just   (C) lately
    (B) ever   (D) yet

11. Professor Kidd _____ three books since 1999, and she's working
    on her fourth.
    (A) has been writing   (C) wrote
    (B) has written   (D) writes

A B C D

12. We _____ to buy that car yet.
    (A) haven't decided   (C) have decided
    (B) decided   (D) are deciding

A B C D

13. —Has Maria called yet?
    —Yes, she _____. But she didn't leave a message.
    (A) did   (C) hasn't
    (B) called   (D) has

A B C D

14. Since I _____ school, I haven't had much spare time.
    (A) begun   (C) have begun
    (B) began   (D) begin

A B C D

SECTION TWO

Each sentence has four underlined words or phrases. The four underlined parts of the sentence are marked A, B, C, and D. Circle the letter of the one underlined word or phrase that is NOT CORRECT.

> **EXAMPLE:**
> Mike <u>usually</u> <u>drives</u> to school, but <u>today</u> he <u>walks</u>.
>   A   B   C   D
>
> **A B C Ⓓ**

15. <u>When</u> she <u>was</u> younger, she <u>has</u> <u>played</u> tennis every day.
      A   B   C D

A B C D

16. It's <u>already</u> 10:00, but Teri <u>hasn't finished</u> her homework <u>already</u>.
    A B   C   D

A B C D

17. I've <u>been worrying</u> about you because you <u>haven't</u> <u>been seeming</u>
          A   B   C
    well <u>lately</u>.
       D

A B C D

18. <u>I've read</u> a good book <u>recently</u>, but I <u>haven't finished</u> it <u>yet</u>.
      A   B   C   D

A B C D

19. <u>Did</u> you written your paper, or <u>have</u> you <u>been</u> <u>watching</u> TV?
     A   B   C   D

A B C D

20. Karl <u>has</u> <u>been</u> <u>driving</u> <u>since</u> ten years.
        A   B   C   D

A B C D

21. We've <u>been</u> here <u>only</u> one day, but we've <u>been taking</u> three rolls of film.
       A B   C   D

A B C D

22. This hotel <u>has been</u> <u>already</u> in business <u>for</u> <u>fifty years</u>.
            A   B   C   D

A B C D

23. <u>How much</u> coffee <u>did</u> you <u>been drinking</u> <u>last night</u>?
      A   B   C   D

A B C D

24. <u>I've been studying</u> French <u>since</u> <u>I've</u> <u>started</u> high school.
           A   B   C   D

A B C D

25. Before she <u>became</u> a film star, she <u>has</u> <u>been</u> a stand-up comedian.
           A   B   C D

A B C D

Future:
Be going to and *Will*

Oh, no. It's **going to** rain! I'**ll get** all wet!

CHECK POINT

Check the main point of the cartoon.

☐ The man forgot his umbrella.

☐ The man is going to fall into the hole.

CHART CHECK 1

Check the correct answer.

How many forms does **be** have in **be going to**?

☐ one

☐ two

☐ three

STATEMENTS: *BE GOING TO*				
SUBJECT	**BE***	**(NOT) GOING TO**	**BASE FORM OF VERB**	
I	**am**			
He/She/It	**is**	**(not) going to**	**leave**	soon.
We/You†/They	**are**			

*For contractions with *be*, see Appendix 24 on page 345.
†*You* is both singular and plural.

CHART CHECK 2

Circle T (True) or F (False).

T F In questions, a form of **be** goes after the subject.

YES/NO QUESTIONS: *BE GOING TO*			
BE	**SUBJECT**	**GOING TO**	**BASE FORM**
Am	I		
Is	he	**going to**	**leave** soon?
Are	you		

SHORT ANSWERS					
AFFIRMATIVE			**NEGATIVE**		
	you	**are**.		you	**aren't**.
Yes,	he	**is**.	**No,**	he	**isn't**.
	I	**am**.		I	**'m not**.

WH- QUESTIONS: *BE GOING TO*				
WH- WORD	**BE**	**SUBJECT**	**GOING TO**	**BASE FORM**
When Why	**am**	I		
	is	he	**going to**	**leave**?
	are	you		

CHART CHECK 3

Circle T (True) or F (False).

T F The form of **will** is the same for all subjects.

STATEMENTS: *WILL*			
SUBJECT	**WILL* (NOT)**	**BASE FORM**	
I/He/She/It/We/You/They	will (not)	leave	soon.

*For contractions with *will*, see Appendix 24 on page 345.

YES/NO QUESTIONS: *WILL*			
WILL	**SUBJECT**	**BASE FORM**	
Will	he	leave	soon?

SHORT ANSWERS	
AFFIRMATIVE	**NEGATIVE**
Yes, he **will**.	**No**, he **won't**.

WH- QUESTIONS: *WILL*			
WH- WORD	**WILL**	**SUBJECT**	**BASE FORM**
When	will	he	leave?

EXPRESS CHECK

Unscramble these words to form two sentences.

to • rain • It's • going _____

an • get • I'll • umbrella _____

Grammar Explanations

Examples

1. You can use **be going to** or **will** to talk about future <u>plans</u> or <u>predictions</u>.

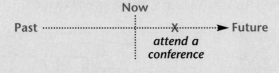

Past ···|······**X**·········▶ Future
Now
attend a conference

- Professor Vroom **is going to attend** a conference next week.
   OR
- Professor Vroom **will attend** a conference next week.

- I think it**'s going to be** very interesting.
   OR
- I think it**'ll be** very interesting.

2. Use **be going to** when there is <u>something in the present that leads to the prediction</u>.

Use **will** when you decide something at the <u>moment of speaking</u>.

- Look at those dark clouds! It**'s going to rain**. NOT Look at those dark clouds! ~~It'll rain~~.

- **A:** Professor Vroom is speaking at noon.
- **B:** Oh. I think I**'ll go** to his talk.

PRONUNCIATION NOTE
In informal speech, **going to** is often pronounced "gonna." Do not write *gonna*.

Check it out!

There are other ways to talk about the future. See Unit 20, pages 84–85.

1 **READ** • *Look at Professor Harry Vroom's e-mail message.*

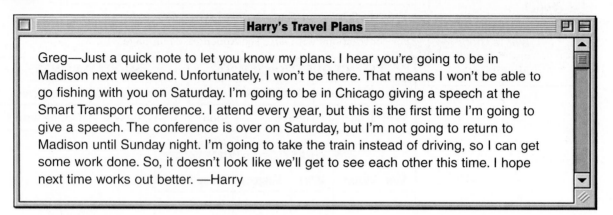

Harry's Travel Plans

Greg—Just a quick note to let you know my plans. I hear you're going to be in Madison next weekend. Unfortunately, I won't be there. That means I won't be able to go fishing with you on Saturday. I'm going to be in Chicago giving a speech at the Smart Transport conference. I attend every year, but this is the first time I'm going to give a speech. The conference is over on Saturday, but I'm not going to return to Madison until Sunday night. I'm going to take the train instead of driving, so I can get some work done. So, it doesn't look like we'll get to see each other this time. I hope next time works out better. —Harry

ANSWER • *Check all the things Harry Vroom is going to do next weekend.*

1. ☐ be in Madison   4. ☐ attend a conference   7. ☐ drive to Madison

2. ☑ be in Chicago   5. ☐ give a speech   8. ☐ see Greg

3. ☐ go fishing   6. ☐ return on Saturday

2 **DESCRIBE** • *Look at the pictures. They show events from a day in Professor Vroom's life. Write predictions or guesses. Use the words in the box and a form of* **be going to** *or* **not be going to**.

answer the phone   drive   give a speech   ~~rain~~   take a trip   watch TV

1. It's going to rain.

2. _____

3. _____

4. _____

5. _____

6. _____

COMPLETE • *After his speech, Professor Vroom answered questions from the audience. Complete the questions and answers. Use the words in parentheses and* **will** *or* **won't**.

WOMAN 1: My question is this, Professor Vroom: _____Will_____ the car of the

future _____run_____ on gasoline?
1. (run)

VROOM: No, it _____won't_____. It _____ probably
2.

_____ solar energy.
3. (use)

WOMAN 2: _____ we still _____ flat tires?
4. (get)

VROOM: No, we _____. By the year 2010, tires _____
5. **6.** (have)

a special seal so that they _____ themselves.
7. (repair)

MAN 1: In what other ways _____ cars _____ different?
8. (be)

VROOM: Well, instead of keys, cars _____ smart cards. These
9. (have)

_____ a lot like credit cards. They _____ doors
10. (look) **11.** (open)

and they _____ the seats, mirrors, and steering wheels. They
12. (adjust)

_____ even _____ the inside temperature.
13. (control)

MAN 1: _____ they _____ car thefts?
14. (prevent)

VROOM: Yes, they _____! Next question? That gentleman in the back.
15.

MAN 2: How much _____ these cars _____?
16. (cost)

VROOM: I don't know exactly, but they certainly _____ cheap.
17. (be)

 EDIT • *Read this e-mail message to Professor Vroom. Find and correct nine mistakes in the use of the future with* **will** *and* **be going to**. *The first mistake is already corrected.*

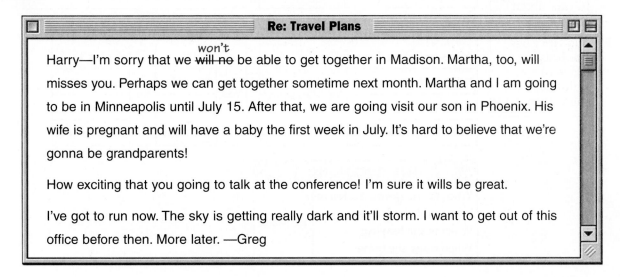

Re: Travel Plans

won't
Harry—I'm sorry that we ~~will no~~ be able to get together in Madison. Martha, too, will

misses you. Perhaps we can get together sometime next month. Martha and I am going

to be in Minneapolis until July 15. After that, we are going visit our son in Phoenix. His

wife is pregnant and will have a baby the first week in July. It's hard to believe that we're

gonna be grandparents!

How exciting that you going to talk at the conference! I'm sure it wills be great.

I've got to run now. The sky is getting really dark and it'll storm. I want to get out of this

office before then. More later. —Greg

Future: Contrast

Speech bubbles:
- Hurry up, sir. You**'re going to be** late. The shuttle **leaves** in five minutes.
- Don't worry. They **won't leave** without me. I'm the pilot!

CHECK *POINT*

Circle T (True) or F (False).

T F The shuttle to Mars has a scheduled departure.

T F The pilot is too late.

CHART CHECK

Circle T (True) or F (False).

T F There are several ways to talk about the future.

T F You can't use the present tense to talk about the future.

AFFIRMATIVE STATEMENTS	
We**'re going to leave**	
We**'ll leave**	for Mars soon.
We**'re leaving**	
We **leave**	

NEGATIVE STATEMENTS	
We **aren't going to leave**	
We **won't leave**	until 1:00.
We **aren't leaving**	
We **don't leave**	

YES/NO QUESTIONS	
Is she **going to leave**	
Will she **leave**	for Mars soon?
Is she **leaving**	
Does she **leave**	

SHORT ANSWERS			
	she **is.**		she **isn't.**
Yes,	she **will.**	No,	she **won't.**
	she **is.**		she **isn't.**
	she **does.**		she **doesn't.**

WH- QUESTIONS	
When **is** she **going to leave**	
When **will** she **leave**	for Mars?
When **is** she **leaving**	
When **does** she **leave**	

EXPRESS CHECK

Check the sentences that refer to the future.

☐ I'm leaving in five minutes.

☐ What time do you normally leave the office?

☐ Are you going to the conference in May?

☐ At the moment, I'm working on a report.

Grammar Explanations

1. Use **be going to**, **will**, the **present progressive**, and the **simple present tense** to talk about things in the future.

```
               Now
                │    fly
Past  ┈┈┈┈┈┈┈┈┈┈┼┈┈┈┈X┈┈┈┈┈┈▶ Future
               │ next week
```

2. **USAGE NOTES:** Sometimes only one form of the future is appropriate, but in many cases more than one form is possible.

　a. Use **be going to** or **will** to make predictions or guesses.

　b. Use **be going to** (not *will*) when something in the present leads to a prediction.

　c. Use **be going to**, **will**, or the **present progressive** to talk about future intentions or plans.

　d. We often use **will** when we decide something at the moment of speaking. We also use **will** to make offers.

　e. We often use the **present progressive** when we talk about future plans that have already been arranged. There is usually some reference to the future that shows that the event is not happening now.

　f. Use the **simple present tense** to talk about scheduled future events such as timetables, programs, and schedules.

Examples

■ I'm **going to fly** to Mars next week.

■ I'**ll fly** to Mars next week.

■ I'm **flying** to Mars next week.

■ I **fly** to Mars next week.

■ In a few years people **are going to fly** to Mars.
■ In a few years people **will fly** to Mars.

■ Look at that spaceship! It'**s going to land**!
　NOT It will land.

■ Dr. Green **is going to speak** tomorrow.
■ Dr. Green **will speak** tomorrow.
■ Dr. Green **is speaking** tomorrow.

A: Dr. Green is giving a talk tomorrow.
B: Oh! Maybe I'**ll go**.
A: Great! I'**ll get** you a ticket.

■ I'm **flying** to Mars *next week*. I've already gotten a ticket.

■ The shuttle to Mars **leaves** at 10:00 A.M. *tomorrow*.
■ We **land** at midnight.

IDENTIFY • *Professor Green is attending a conference this week. Read her conversation with Professor Russ. Underline all the verbs that refer to the future.*

RUSS: Ellen! It's nice to see you. <u>Are</u> you <u>presenting</u> a paper this week?

GREEN: Hi, Rick. Yes. In fact, my talk starts at two o'clock.

RUSS: Oh, maybe I'll go. What are you going to talk about? Robots?

GREEN: Yes. I'm focusing on personal robots for household work.

RUSS: I'd like one of those! Where's your son, by the way? Is he here with you?

GREEN: No. Tony stays in Denver with his grandparents in the summer. I'm going to visit him after the conference. So, what are you working on these days?

RUSS: I'm still with the Mars Association. In fact, we're going to be holding a news conference next month about the Mars shuttle launch.

GREEN: That's exciting. Maybe I'll see you there.

RUSS: Great. The conference begins at noon on the tenth.

 CHOOSE • *Circle the most appropriate words to complete these conversations.*

1. GREEN: Which project <u>do you work</u> / <u>(are you going to work)</u> on next?

   RUSS: I haven't decided for sure. Probably the Spacemobile.

2. RUSS: Look at those dark clouds!

   GREEN: Yes. It looks like <u>it's raining / it's going to rain</u> any minute.

3. GREEN: I'd better get back to my hotel room before the storm.

   RUSS: OK. <u>I'm seeing / I'll see</u> you later.

4. DESK: Professor Green, your son just called.

   GREEN: Oh, good. <u>I'll call / I'm calling</u> him back right away.

5. GREEN: Hi, honey. How's it going?

   TONY: Great. <u>I go / I'm going</u> fishing with Grandpa tomorrow.

6. GREEN: Have fun, but don't forget. You still have to finish that paper.

   TONY: I know, Mom. <u>I mail / I'm mailing</u> it tomorrow. I already have the envelope.

7. TONY: How's the conference?

   GREEN: Good. <u>I'm giving / I'll give</u> a talk this afternoon.

8. TONY: Good luck. When <u>are you / will you be</u> here?

   GREEN: Tomorrow. My plane <u>lands / will land</u> at 7:00, so <u>I see / I'll see</u> you about 8:00.

3

COMPLETE • *Read these conversations. Complete them with an appropriate form of the verbs in parentheses. (There is more than one correct answer for some items.)*

1. **A:** Hurry up! The shuttle _____leaves_____ in just a few minutes.
      (leave)

   B: Oh, I'm sure they _____ for us.
      (wait)

2. **A:** Look at those storm clouds! Do you think it _____?
      (rain)

   B: I don't know. I _____ the weather forecast.
      (check)

3. **A:** When _____ we _____ the shuttle?
      (board)

   B: We _____ first class, so we should be among the first
      (fly)
   to board.

4. **A:** Wow! This suitcase is heavy.

   B: I _____ it for you. Give it to me.
      (carry)

5. **A:** What time _____ we _____ on Mars?
      (land)

   B: According to the schedule, at 9:00 A.M., but I think we _____
      (be)
   a little late.

6. **A:** I'm hungry. I hope we _____ some food soon.
      (get)

   B: Me too. I _____ the seafood special. I ordered it
      (have)
   in advance.

7. **A:** Look! The flight attendant is getting ready to announce something.

   B: Great. That means we _____ boarding soon.
      (start)

4

EDIT • *Read this flight announcement on the shuttle to Mars. Find and correct seven mistakes in the use of the future. The first mistake is already corrected. (There is often more than one way to correct a mistake).*

"Good evening, ladies and gentlemen. This ~~will be~~ is your captain speaking. We be going

to leave the Earth's gravity field in about fifteen minutes. At that time, you are able

to unbuckle your seat belts and float around the cabin. Host robots take orders for

dinner soon. After these storm clouds, we are having a smooth trip. The shuttle

arrives on Mars tomorrow at 9:00. Tonight's temperature on the planet is a mild

minus 20 degrees Celsius. By tomorrow morning the temperature is 18 degrees, but it

is feeling more like 28 degrees. Enjoy your flight."

Future Time Clauses

When I grow up, I'm going to be a ballet dancer.

CHECK POINT

Check the correct answer.

☐ The child is talking about a present habit.

☐ The child is planning her future.

CHART CHECK

Circle T (True) or F (False).

T F The verb in the main clause is in the future.

T F The verb in the time clause is in the future.

STATEMENTS	
MAIN CLAUSE	**TIME CLAUSE**
I**'m going to be** a ballet dancer	*when* I **grow up**.
She**'ll join** a ballet company	*after* she **graduates**.

YES/NO QUESTIONS	
MAIN CLAUSE	**TIME CLAUSE**
Are you **going to be** a ballet dancer	*when* you **grow up**?
Will she **join** a ballet company	*after* she **graduates**?

SHORT ANSWERS			
AFFIRMATIVE		**NEGATIVE**	
Yes,	I **am**.	**No**,	I**'m not**.
	she **will**.		she **won't**.

WH- QUESTIONS		
MAIN CLAUSE		**TIME CLAUSE**
What	**are** you **going to be**	*when* you **grow up**?
	will she **do**	*after* she **graduates**?

EXPRESS CHECK

Unscramble these words to form a question and an answer.

be • What • grows up • she • when • will • she

_____

to • scientist • a • going • She's • be

_____

Grammar Explanations	**Examples**

1. When a sentence about future time has two clauses, the verb in the <u>main clause</u> is often in the **future** (*will* or *be going to*). The verb in the <u>time clause</u> is often in the **present tense**.

▶ **BE CAREFUL!** Do not use *will* or *be going to* in a future time clause.

The **time clause** can come at the beginning or the end of the sentence. The meaning is the same. Use a **comma** after the time clause when it comes at the <u>beginning</u>. Do not use a comma when it comes at the end.

main clause   time clause
■ He'**ll look** for a job *when* he **graduates**.

main clause   time clause
■ I'm going to work *after* I **graduate**.
NOT ~~after I will graduate~~.

■ ***Before she applies***, she'll visit schools.
OR
■ She'll visit schools ***before she applies***.
NOT ~~She'll visit schools, before she applies~~.

2. Here are some **common time expressions** you can use to begin future time clauses.

  a. *When*, *after*, and *as soon as* often introduce the <u>event that happens first</u>.

    Now
        graduate   look for a job
    Past ·········X···············X··········▶ Future

■ ***When*** I graduate, I'll look for a job.
■ ***After*** I graduate, I'll look for a job.
■ ***As soon as*** I graduate, I'll look for a job.
  (*First I'm going to graduate. Then I'll look for a job.*)

  b. *Before*, *until*, and *by the time* often introduce the <u>event that happens second</u>.

    Now
        finish school   get a job
    Past ·········X···············X··········▶ Future

■ ***Before*** I get a job, I'll finish school.
■ ***Until*** I get a job, I'll stay in school.
■ ***By the time*** I get a job, I'll be out of school.
  (*First I'll finish school. Then I'll get a job.*)

  c. *While* introduces an event that will happen <u>at the same time</u> as another event.

    Now
    Past ·········╱‾‾‾‾‾‾‾‾╲·········▶ Future
       look for a job
       continue to study

■ ***While*** I look for a job, I'll continue to study.
  (*I will look for a job and study during the same time period.*)

TRUE OR FALSE • *Read each numbered sentence. Write T (True) or F (False) for the statement that follows.*

1. Amber will open her own business when she finishes school.

   __F__ Amber will open her own business. Then she'll finish school.

2. Denzell won't quit until he finds another job.

   _____ Denzell will find another job. Then he'll quit.

3. Jake will retire as soon as he turns sixty.

   _____ Jake will retire. Then he'll turn sixty.

4. Marisa will call you when she gets home.

   _____ Marisa will get home. Then she'll call you.

5. While Li-jing is in school, she'll work part-time.

   _____ Li-jing will finish school. Then she'll get a part-time job.

6. By the time Marta gets her diploma, she'll be twenty-one.

   _____ Marta will turn twenty-one. Then she'll get her diploma.

2 **COMBINE** • *Read about Sandy and Jeff. Combine the sentences.*

1. Sandy and Jeff will get married. Then Sandy will graduate.

   __Sandy and Jeff will get married__ before __Sandy graduates.__

2. Jeff is going to get a raise. Then they are going to move to a larger apartment.

   _____ as soon as _____

3. They're going to move to a larger apartment. Then they're going to have a baby.

   After _____

4. They'll have their first child. Then Sandy will get a part-time job.

   _____ after _____

5. Their child will be two. Then Sandy will go back to work full-time.

   By the time _____

6. Sandy will work full-time. At the same time, Jeff will go to school.

   _____ while _____

7. Jeff will graduate. Then he'll find another job.

   _____ when _____

3 **COMPLETE** • *Look at this student's worksheet. Complete it with the correct form of the verbs in parentheses.*

GOAL PLANNING WORKSHEET

I. Write your major goal.

I ___'ll get_____ a job after I _____ .
(get)   (graduate)

II. List three benefits of achieving your goal.

1. When I _____ a job, I _____ more money.
(get)   (have)

2. When I _____ enough money, I _____ a used car.
(save)   (buy)

3. I _____ happier when I _____ employed.
(feel)   (be)

III. How will you reach your goal? Write down smaller goals.

1. As soon as I _____ in the morning, I _____ the
(get up)   (buy)
newspaper to look at the employment ads.

2. When I _____ to my friends, I _____ them if they
(speak)   (ask)
know of any jobs.

3. I _____ at the job notices board when I _____ to
(look)   (go)
the supermarket.

4. Before I _____ on an interview, I _____ my
(go)   (improve)
computer skills.

---

4 **EDIT** • *Read this dancer's journal entry. Find and correct seven mistakes in the use of future time clauses. The first mistake is already corrected. Don't forget to check for commas!*

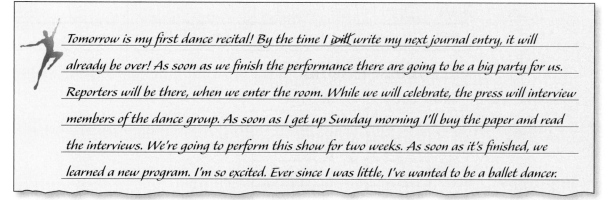

Tomorrow is my first dance recital! By the time I ~~will~~ write my next journal entry, it will

already be over! As soon as we finish the performance there are going to be a big party for us.

Reporters will be there, when we enter the room. While we will celebrate, the press will interview

members of the dance group. As soon as I get up Sunday morning I'll buy the paper and read

the interviews. We're going to perform this show for two weeks. As soon as it's finished, we

learned a new program. I'm so excited. Ever since I was little, I've wanted to be a ballet dancer.

Future Progressive

I'm sorry. I won't be here at 12:00. I'll **be** out **walking** the dog.

CHECK POINT

Check the correct answer.

When will Robo take the dog out for a walk?

☐ before 12:00

☐ at 12:00

☐ after 12:00

CHART CHECK

Circle T (True) or F (False).

T F You can form the future progressive with **be going to** or **will** plus **be** and the base form of the verb + **-ing**.

STATEMENTS

SUBJECT	BE (NOT) GOING TO/ WILL (NOT)	BE + BASE FORM + -ING	
I	am (not) going to		
He/She/It	is (not) going to	be working	tomorrow.
We/You/They	are (not) going to		
I/He/She/It/We/You/They	will (not)	be working	tomorrow.

YES/NO QUESTIONS

BE/WILL	SUBJECT	GOING TO	BE + BASE FORM + -ING	
Am	I			
Is	she	going to	be working	tomorrow?
Are	you			
Will	you		be working	tomorrow?

SHORT ANSWERS

AFFIRMATIVE		NEGATIVE	
Yes,	you **are**.	No,	you **aren't**.
	she **is**.		she **isn't**.
	I **am**.		I'm **not**.
	we **will**.		we **won't**.

WH- QUESTIONS				
WH- WORD	BE/WILL	SUBJECT	GOING TO	BE + BASE FORM + -ING
Where When	is	he	going to	be working?
	will	she		be working?

EXPRESS CHECK

Unscramble these words to form two questions. Answer the questions.

working • be • Will • tomorrow • you

_____?

_____.

you • be • What • doing • are • to • going

_____?

_____.

Grammar Explanations

Examples

1. Use the **future progressive** with *be going to* or *will* to talk about things that will be <u>in progress at a specific time in the future</u>.

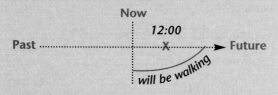

REMEMBER! Non-action verbs are not usually used in the progressive.

- Robo **is going to be walking** the dog at noon.

OR

- Robo **will be walking** the dog at noon.

- You**'re going to have** a headache tomorrow morning.
  NOT You're going to be having a headache tomorrow morning.

2. **USAGE NOTE:** We often use the future progressive to <u>hint that we would like someone to do us a favor</u>.

- **A:** **Will** you **be going** by the post office tomorrow?
- **B:** Yes. Do you need stamps?
- **A:** Yes. Could you get me some?

3. Remember that if the sentence has a **time clause**, use the <u>simple present tense</u> or <u>present progressive</u> in the time clause, not the future or future progressive.

- I**'ll be cooking** *while* the robot **is cleaning**.
  NOT I'll be cooking while the robot will be cleaning.

IDENTIFY • *Read this paragraph. Underline all the future progressive forms.*

Today we find most robots working in factories around the world. But what <u>will</u> robots of the future <u>be doing</u>? One Massachusetts Institute of Technology designer predicts that in just a few years, small, intelligent robots are going to be taking care of all the household chores. This is going to make life a lot easier. While one robot is cooking dinner, another one will be vacuuming the floor. But what about outside the home? Will robots be playing football or fighting wars? Scientists aren't sure. What is certain, however, is that robots will be playing a more and more significant role in our lives.

2 **COMPLETE** • *Read these conversations. Complete them with the future progressive form of the words in parentheses and with short answers.*

1. **STUDENT:** _____Will_____ you _____be having_____ office
   a. (Will / have)
   hours today? I'd like to talk to you about my robotics paper.

   TEACHER: _____Yes, I will_____. I _____ to lunch
   b.   **c.** (will / go)
   at 2:00. But stop in anytime before then.

2. **MRS. GEE:** When _____ you _____ the office?
   a. (be going to / leave)
   MR. GEE: At 2:00. Why? Do we need something?
   MRS. GEE: Would you mind picking up some milk? Robo forgot, and I

   _____ home until late.
   b. (won't / get)

3. **TONY:** Dad, what time _____ you _____
   a. (be going to / come)
   home today? I need some help with my science project.

   MR. GEE: I _____ Mia to the dentist after work, but
   b. (will / take)
   I'll be back by 4:00.

   TONY: _____ we _____ dinner before
   c. (Be going to / have)
   Mom comes home?

   MR. GEE: _____. You know we always wait for Mom.
   d.

4. **SALESMAN:** I'm calling from Robotronics Inc. I _____ your
   a. (be going to / visit)
   neighborhood soon to demonstrate our new robot.

   ROBO: I'm sorry. The Gee family _____ a new robot
   b. (won't / buy)
   for a while.

3 **COMPLETE** • *Look at Robo's and Robota's schedules for tomorrow. Complete the statements.*

Robo	
8:00	make breakfast
9:00	dust bedrooms
10:00	do laundry
12:00	make lunch
1:00	give Mr. Gee a massage
5:00	help Tony with homework
7:00	play chess with Tony

Robota	
8:00	pay bills
9:00	vacuum living room
10:00	repaint kitchen
12:00	recycle the garbage
1:00	shop for food
5:00	make dinner
7:00	walk the dog

1. While Robo _____*is making breakfast*_____, Robota _____*will be paying bills.*_____

2. Robo _____ the bedrooms while Robota _____

3. Robota _____ the kitchen while Robo _____

4. While Robo _____ lunch, Robota _____

5. Robo _____ a massage while Robota _____

6. Robota _____ dinner while Robo _____

7. While Robo _____ chess, Robota _____

4 **EDIT** • *Read this student's paragraph. Find and correct seven mistakes in the use of the future progressive. The first mistake is already corrected.*

In the future, robots will be ~~perform~~ *performing* more and more tasks for humans. This will be having both positive and negative effects. On the one hand, while robots will be doing the boring and dangerous jobs, humans will be devoting more time to interesting pursuits. In this way robots is going to be making life a lot easier for humans. On the other hand, the widespread use of robots is going create a lot of future unemployment. People will losing their jobs as robots fill their positions. And some robots could even become dangerous. I'm afraid that in the not-too-distant future, robots will be operating nuclear power stations! And before too long, robots are going to be fight in wars. Although, on second thought, that will be better than humans killing each other!

Future Perfect and Future Perfect Progressive

By February, he**'ll have been saving** for three years and I'll be rich!

By February, I**'ll have traded** Piggy for a shiny new Jaguar!

CHECK *POINT*

Check the correct answer.

☐ It's February.

☐ He hasn't been saving for three years yet.

CHART CHECK 1

Circle T (True) or F (False).

T F Both the future perfect and the future perfect progressive use **will have been**.

FUTURE PERFECT STATEMENTS		
SUBJECT	**WILL (NOT)**	**HAVE + PAST PARTICIPLE**
I/He/She/It/We/You*/They	**will (not)**	**have saved** enough money by then.

You is both singular and plural.

FUTURE PERFECT PROGRESSIVE STATEMENTS		
SUBJECT	**WILL (NOT)**	**HAVE BEEN + BASE FORM + -ING**
I/He/She/It/We/You/They	**will (not)**	**have been saving** for three years.

CHART CHECK 2

Circle T (True) or F (False).

T F Short answer forms are the same for the future perfect and the future perfect progressive.

FUTURE PERFECT *YES/NO* QUESTIONS		
WILL	**SUBJECT**	**HAVE + PAST PARTICIPLE**
Will	he	**have saved** enough by then?

SHORT ANSWERS	
AFFIRMATIVE	**NEGATIVE**
Yes, he **will**.	No, he **won't**.

FUTURE PERFECT PROGRESSIVE *YES/NO* QUESTIONS		
WILL	**SUBJECT**	**HAVE BEEN + BASE FORM + -ING**
Will	he	**have been saving** for long?

SHORT ANSWERS	
AFFIRMATIVE	**NEGATIVE**
Yes, he **will**.	No, he **won't**.

EXPRESS CHECK

Complete these sentences with the verb **drive**. *Use one word for each blank.*

- By June, I'll have been _____ my new car for a year.
- I'll have _____ 10,000 miles by then.

Grammar Explanations

Examples

---

1. When we use the **future perfect**, we imagine a certain point of time in the future, and we <u>look back at events that will be completed by that time.</u>

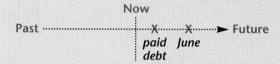

Use *by* + **time expression** to identify the point in time in the future.

Use *already* and *yet* to emphasize whether an event will have happened by a point in time.

- By June, he **will have paid** his debt.
- We **won't have saved** enough by then.

- *By June*, she**'ll have bought** a used car.
- She**'ll have looked** at a lot of cars *by then*.

- By May, he**'ll have *already*** saved $1,000.
- By May, he **won't have saved** $2,000 *yet*.

---

2. When we use the **future perfect progressive**, we imagine a certain point in the future, and we <u>look back on things already in progress.</u>

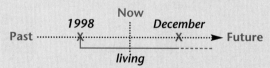

The **future perfect progressive** focuses on *how long* and often includes <u>the length of time.</u>

REMEMBER! Non-action verbs are not usually used in the progressive.

- We moved here in 1998. By next December we **will have been living** here for several years.

- We're moving to Paris next year. By 2005 we **will have been living** there for several years, and it should feel like home.

- You'll have been speaking French *for ten years* by then.

- By May, he**'ll have owned** his car for a year. NOT ~~he'll have been owning his car . . .~~

---

3. Use the future perfect or the future perfect progressive **with the simple present tense** to show <u>the order of events:</u>

FIRST EVENT: future perfect (progressive)

SECOND EVENT: simple present tense

Now
finish   start
dinner   to read   arrive
Past ········X·······X······X····➤ Future

- By the time you *arrive*, I**'ll have finished** dinner. NOT ~~By the time you will arrive,~~ I'll have finished dinner.

- By the time you *arrive*, I**'ll have been reading** for an hour.

1

TRUE OR FALSE • *Read each numbered sentence. Write T (True) or F (False) for the statement that follows.*

1. By this time tomorrow, I'll have decided which car to buy.

____T____ I haven't decided yet which car I'm going to buy.

2. We'll have already finished the grocery shopping by the time you get home.

_____ You will get home while we are shopping.

3. By next year, Mary will have been working at the newspaper for five years.

_____ Next year, Mary can celebrate her fifth anniversary at the newspaper.

4. By ten o'clock, she won't have finished writing her column yet.

_____ She will finish writing at ten o'clock.

5. We will have moved to a larger office by the year 2010.

_____ We will move to a larger office after the year 2010.

6. By next year, we'll have been publishing the newsletter for fifteen years.

_____ We started the newsletter less than fifteen years ago.

2

COMPLETE • *Look at the time line and complete the sentences about Tom and Linda's future accomplishments. Use the future perfect or the future perfect progressive form of the words in parentheses. Choose between affirmative and negative.*

| 2010 | 2011 | 2012 | 2013 | 2015 | 2017 | 2018 | 2022 |

1. By 2012, they ____'ll have bought____ a new car.
(buy)

2. By 2015, they ____'ll have been living____ in their own house for three years.
(live)

3. By Travis's first birthday, Tom _____.
(graduate)

4. By 2017, Tom _____ school for four years.
(attend)

5. By 2019, they _____ another car.
(buy)

6. They _____ their old car for eight years by then.
(drive)

7. By 2020, Linda _____ her business.
(open)

8. They _____ for two years by 2020.
(save)

9. By retirement, the couple _____ a lot.
(accomplish)

3 **COMPLETE** • *Read Linda Leone's (LL) interview with* **Teenage Couples Magazine** *(TC). Complete the interview with the correct form of the verbs in parentheses. Use the progressive form when possible. Use* **already** *or* **yet** *when appropriate.*

TC: You two are amazing! By the time you _____ get _____ married,
1. (get)

you _____ 'll have already planned _____ your whole life together!
2. (plan)

LL: Well, we've been dating since middle school. By the time we _____
3. (graduate)

from high school, we _____ about our marriage for a long time.
4. (think)

TC: When Travis _____ , Tom _____
5. (be born)   **6.** (not graduate)

from college _____ . How will you manage with Tom still in school?

LL: It won't be easy, but we've got a plan. Tom _____ most
7. (finish)

of his courses by then. He'll stay home with the baby during the day and go to

night school.

TC: By the time you _____ your tenth wedding anniversary,
8. (celebrate)

you _____ your business _____ .
9. (not start)

You have a lot of patience.

LL: Not really. I _____ years of practice on my job
10. (get)

by then. When I _____ the doors of Linda, Inc.,
11. (open)

I _____ a very experienced Web page designer.
12. (become)

TC: Well, good luck to you, and thanks for the interview.

4 **EDIT** • *Read this journal entry. Find and correct six mistakes in the use of the future perfect and the future perfect progressive. The first mistake is already corrected.*

> have been
> By August I'll ~~be~~ a word processor for ten years. And I'll earn almost the same salary for three
>
> years! That's why I've made a New Year's resolution to go back to school this year. First I'm
>
> going to write for school catalogs and start saving for tuition. By March, I'll have figure out
>
> how much tuition will cost. Then I'll start applying. By summer, I had received acceptance
>
> letters. In August, I'll talk to my boss about working part-time and going to school part-time.
>
> By that time, I'll have saved already enough to pay for a semester's tuition. By next New
>
> Year's Day, I'll have been study for one whole semester!

SelfTest

Circle the letter of the correct answer to complete each sentence.

EXAMPLE:
Jennifer never _____ coffee.   A Ⓑ C D
(A) drink   (C) is drinking
(B) drinks   (D) was drinking

1. It _____ tomorrow.   **A B C D**
    (A) rains   (C) 's going to rain
    (B) rained   (D) 's raining

2. The package will _____ on Monday.   **A B C D**
    (A) arrive   (C) arriving
    (B) arrives   (D) be going to arrive

3. Goodnight. I _____ you in the morning.   **A B C D**
    (A) 'll see   (C) 'm seeing
    (B) 'm going to see   (D) see

4. Hurry. The next bus _____ at 7:15.   **A B C D**
    (A) leave   (C) leaving
    (B) leaves   (D) will have been leaving

5. Bill will be _____ to Taipei tomorrow.   **A B C D**
    (A) flies   (C) fly
    (B) flying   (D) have flown

6. We _____ a new VCR soon.   **A B C D**
    (A) have owned   (C) 're owning
    (B) 'll own   (D) own

7. They'll be making copies while he _____ the report.   **A B C D**
    (A) finishes   (C) 'll finish
    (B) 'll be finishing   (D) 's been finishing

8. She'll _____ almost $1,000 by then.   **A B C D**
    (A) save   (C) have been saving
    (B) have saved   (D) be saving

9. By next year, Roger will _____ here for ten years.   **A B C D**
    (A) live   (C) have been living
    (B) be living   (D) be going to live

10. Will you buy an electric car when they _____ available?   **A B C D**
    (A) become   (C) are becoming
    (B) became   (D) will become

11. She'll have gotten married _____ June.   **A B C D**
    (A) already   (C) since
    (B) by   (D) until

12. Where _____ be living?   **A B C D**
    (A) they   (C) will they
    (B) they will   (D) are they

13. Look at those cars! They _____!   **A B C D**
    (A) will crash   (C) 're going to crash
    (B) will be crashing   (D) will have crashed

14. How _____ for college?   **A B C D**
    (A) should pay   (C) she pays
    (B) will she pay   (D) she's going to pay

SECTION TWO

Each sentence has four underlined words or phrases. The four underlined parts of the sentence are marked A, B, C, and D. Circle the letter of the one underlined word or phrase that is NOT CORRECT.

> **EXAMPLE:**
> Mike <u>usually</u> <u>drives</u> to school, but <u>today</u> he <u>walks</u>.   **A B C (D)**
>   A   B   C   D

15. <u>Will</u> you <u>been</u> <u>going</u> to the drugstore <u>tonight</u>?   **A B C D**
      A   B   C   D

16. The movie <u>starts</u> <u>at</u> 7:30, so I <u>think</u> I <u>go</u>.   **A B C D**
             A B   C D

17. We <u>are going</u> to <u>study</u> tonight <u>until</u> we <u>will finish</u> this chapter.   **A B C D**
        A   B   C   D

18. <u>By</u> April, I'll <u>have</u> been <u>driven</u> my new car <u>for</u> a year.   **A B C D**
     A   B   C   D

19. We'll <u>travel</u> <u>for</u> a couple of days, so you <u>won't</u> <u>be able to</u> call us.   **A B C D**
         A   B   C   D

20. Jan <u>finished</u> school <u>by</u> next summer, so <u>we're going</u> to <u>visit</u> her.   **A B C D**
         A   B   C   D

21. Which project <u>will</u> he <u>works</u> on <u>after</u> he <u>finishes</u> this job?   **A B C D**
             A   B   C   D

22. <u>By</u> January, he'<u>ll</u> have <u>yet</u> <u>saved</u> $1,000.   **A B C D**
     A   B   C D

23. Where <u>you will</u> <u>be</u> <u>staying</u> when you <u>go</u> to Morocco?   **A B C D**
          A   B C   D

24. I'<u>ll</u> <u>be studying</u> <u>while</u> Ana <u>will be</u> sleeping.   **A B C D**
     A   B   C   D

25. She <u>will not</u> <u>has</u> <u>graduated</u> <u>by</u> June.   **A B C D**
          A   B   C   D

UNIT 24

Wh- Questions:
Subject and Predicate

Check the correct answers.

The lawyer wants to know

❑ the events on the night of May 12th.

❑ the witness's profession.

❑ the names of people who saw the witness.

CHART CHECK 1

Circle T (True) or F (False).

T F *Wh-* questions about the subject have the same word order as statements.

QUESTIONS ABOUT THE SUBJECT

Wh- Word Subject	Verb	Predicate
Who	saw	you?

ANSWERS (STATEMENTS)

Subject	Verb	Predicate
He	saw	me.

CHART CHECK 2

Circle T (True) or F (False).

T F *Wh-* questions about the predicate have the same word order as statements.

T F Questions about the predicate can include a form of the verb *do*.

QUESTIONS ABOUT THE PREDICATE

Wh- Word Predicate	Auxiliary Verb	Subject	Verb
Who(m)	did	you	see?

ANSWERS (STATEMENTS)

Subject	Verb	Predicate
I	saw	him.

EXPRESS CHECK

Unscramble these words to form two questions.

night • happened • What • last _____?

do • did • What • next • you _____?

Grammar Explanations

Examples

1. Use *wh-* **questions** to <u>ask for specific information</u>. *Wh-* questions begin with question words such as *who*, *what*, *where*, *when*, *why*, *which*, *whose*, *how*, *how many*, *how much*, and *how long*.	■ **Who** did you see at Al's Grill? ■ **Why** did you go there? ■ **How many** people saw you there? ■ **How long** did you stay there?
2. When you are **asking about the subject** (usually the first part of the sentence), use a *wh-* question word in place of the subject. The <u>word order is the same as in a statement</u>.	<u>Someone</u> saw you. ↓ ■ **Who** saw you?
3. When you are **asking about the predicate** (usually the last part of the sentence), the question begins with a *wh-* word, but the <u>word order is the same as in a *yes/no* question</u>.	You saw <u>someone</u>. Did you see <u>someone</u>? 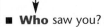 ■ **Who** did you see?

▶ **BE CAREFUL!** When you ask a *wh-* question about something in the predicate, you need either
 	
  a. a form of the verb *be*.
 	
          OR
 	
  b. a form of an **auxiliary** ("helping") verb such as *do*, *have*, *can*, *will*.
	■ Who **is** Harry Adams?
	■ Why **was** he at Al's Grill?
	
	■ Why **does** she want to testify?
	NOT ~~Why she wants to testify?~~

4. **USAGE NOTE:** In very formal English when asking about people in the predicate, *whom* is sometimes used instead of *who*. ▶ **BE CAREFUL!** If the main verb is a form of *be*, you cannot use *whom*.	VERY FORMAL ■ **Whom** did you see? INFORMAL ■ **Who** did you see? ■ **Who** *is* the next witness? NOT ~~Whom is the next witness?~~

1 **MATCH** • *Each question goes with an answer. Match each question with the correct answer.*

	Question		Answer
_f_	**1.** Who did you see?	**a.**	His wife saw me.
_____	**2.** Who saw you?	**b.**	She hit a car.
_____	**3.** What hit her?	**c.**	I gave the money to Harry.
_____	**4.** What did she hit?	**d.**	A car hit her.
_____	**5.** Which man did you give the money to?	**e.**	Harry gave me the money.
_____	**6.** Which man gave you the money?	**f.**	I saw the defendant.

2 **COMPLETE** • *Read this cross-examination. Complete it by writing the lawyer's questions.*

1. **LAWYER:** ___What time did you return home?___
  (What time / you / return home?)

  WITNESS: I returned home just before midnight.

2. **LAWYER:** _____
  (How / you / get home?)

  WITNESS: Someone gave me a lift.

3. **LAWYER:** _____
  (Who / give / you / a ride?)

  WITNESS: A friend from work.

4. **LAWYER:** _____
  (What / happen / next?)

  WITNESS: I opened my door and saw someone on my living room floor.

5. **LAWYER:** _____
  (Who / you / see?)

  WITNESS: Deborah Collins.

6. **LAWYER:** _____
  (Who / be / Deborah Collins?)

  WITNESS: She's my wife's boss. I mean she *was* my wife's boss. She's dead now.

7. **LAWYER:** _____
  (What / you / do?)

  WITNESS: I called the police.

8. **LAWYER:** _____
  (How many / people / call / you?)

  WITNESS: No one called me. Why?

3

ASK • *Read these statements. Then ask questions about the underlined words.*

1. <u>The witness</u> recognized Harry Adams.

   Who recognized Harry Adams?

2. The witness recognized <u>Harry Adams</u>.

   Who did the witness recognize?

3. Court begins <u>at 9:00 A.M.</u>

4. <u>Five</u> witnesses testified.

5. The jury found Adams guilty <u>because he didn't have an alibi</u>.

6. <u>Something horrible</u> happened.

7. The trial lasted <u>two weeks</u>.

8. <u>The judge</u> spoke to the jury.

9. Adams paid his lawyer <u>$2,000</u>.

10. The district attorney questioned <u>the restaurant manager</u>.

 4

EDIT • *Read this list of questions. There are six mistakes in the use of* **wh-** *questions. Find and correct them. The first mistake is already corrected.*

> ~~did~~
> What time ⌃the suspect return home?
>
> Who did see him? Were there
>   any witnesses?
>
> Whom was at home?
>
> Why did he call A. Smith?
>
> What did happen next?
>
> Where he did go?
>
> How much money he took with him?

Tag Questions

It's a nice day, **isn't it?**

CHECK *POINT*

Check the correct answer.

- ☐ The man is asking about the weather.
- ☐ The man is commenting on the weather.

WITH *BE* AS THE MAIN VERB

CHART CHECK

Circle T (True) or F (False).

T F If the statement is affirmative, the tag is affirmative.

T F If the statement has an auxiliary, use the same auxiliary in the tag.

T F If the statement does not have a form of ***be*** or an auxiliary, you need a form of ***do*** in the tag.

AFFIRMATIVE	NEGATIVE		NEGATIVE	AFFIRMATIVE
STATEMENT	TAG		STATEMENT	TAG
You're from L.A.*,	aren't you?		You're not from L.A.,	are you?

*L.A. = Los Angeles

WITH ALL AUXILIARY VERBS EXCEPT *DO*

AFFIRMATIVE	NEGATIVE		NEGATIVE	AFFIRMATIVE
STATEMENT	TAG		STATEMENT	TAG
You're moving,	aren't you?		You're not moving,	are you?
He's been here,	hasn't he?		He hasn't been here,	has he?
They can move,	can't they?		They can't move,	can they?

WITH *DO* AS AN AUXILIARY VERB

AFFIRMATIVE	NEGATIVE		NEGATIVE	AFFIRMATIVE
STATEMENT	TAG		STATEMENT	TAG
You live here,	don't you?		You don't live here,	do you?
They moved,	didn't they?		They didn't move,	did they?

EXPRESS CHECK

Unscramble these words to form a tag question.

actor • you • an • aren't • You're _____, _____?

Grammar Explanations	Examples

1. We often use **tag questions** to:

  a. <u>check information</u> we believe to be true

      OR

  b. <u>comment on a situation</u>

- Tom lives in L.A., **doesn't he?**
  (The speaker believes that Tom lives in L.A. and wants to check this information.)

- It's a nice day, **isn't it?**
  (The speaker is commenting on the weather.)

2. Tag questions have **a statement and a tag**. Forms of tag questions vary, but their meaning is always similar. The statement expresses an <u>assumption</u>. The tag means *Right?*

  a. If the statement verb is <u>affirmative</u>, the tag verb is <u>negative</u>.

  b. If the statement verb is <u>negative</u>, the tag verb is <u>affirmative</u>.

        statement   tag
- You're not from L.A., **are you?**
- You're Jack La Costa, **aren't you?**
- You don't drive much, **do you?**

    affirmative   negative
- You **work** on Fridays, **don't** you?

    negative   affirmative
- You **don't work** on Fridays, **do** you?

3. The **tag** always uses a form of <u>***be*** or an auxiliary verb</u> (***be***, ***have***, ***do***, or ***will***, or a modal such as ***can***, ***could***, or ***should***).

  USAGE NOTE: Notice the tag for ***I am***.

▶ **BE CAREFUL!** In the tag, only use <u>pronouns</u>.

  When the subject of the statement is ***this*** or ***that***, the subject of the tag is ***it***.

- It's a nice day, **isn't** it?
- You've lived here a long time, **haven't** you?
- You come from New York, **don't** you?
- You can drive, **can't** you?

- I'm next, **aren't** I?

- ***Tom*** works here, doesn't **he?**
  NOT Tom works here, ~~doesn't Tom?~~

- ***That's*** a good idea, isn't **it?**
  NOT That's a good idea, ~~isn't that?~~

4. When you use a tag question to **check information** or to **comment on a situation**, your <u>voice falls</u> on the tag. You expect the listener to agree or just show that he or she is listening.

  Tag questions can also be used to **get information**. As with *yes/no* questions, your <u>voice rises</u> at the end, and you expect to get an answer (*Yes* or *No*).

A: It's getting warmer, **isn't it?**
B: Yeah. Seems more like summer.

A: You're not moving, **are you?**
B: Yes. We're returning to L.A.
        OR
  No. We're staying here.

1   *IDENTIFY • Read this conversation. Underline all the tags.*

KAY: Hi, Tom. It's a nice day, <u>isn't it?</u>

TOM: Sure is. Not a cloud in the sky. How are you doing?

KAY: Good, thanks. You don't know of any vacant apartments, do you? My son is
looking for one.

TOM: He is? I thought he was staying with you.

KAY: Well, he really wants a place of his own. Do you know of anything?

TOM: As a matter of fact, I do. You know the Sobotas, don't you? Well, I just found out
that they're moving to New York next month.

KAY: They are? What kind of apartment do they have?

TOM: A one-bedroom.

KAY: It's not furnished, is it?

TOM: No. Why? He doesn't need a furnished apartment, does he?

KAY: Well, he doesn't have furniture. But I guess he can always rent some, can't he?

TOM: Why don't you give your son my number, and I'll give him some more information?

KAY: Will you? Thanks, Tom.

2   *MATCH • Each statement goes with a tag. Match each statement with the correct tag.*

	Statement	Tag
__i__	**1.** You've called the movers,	**a.** can't we?
_____	**2.** They're coming tomorrow,	**b.** do we?
_____	**3.** This isn't going to be cheap,	**c.** is he?
_____	**4.** You haven't finished packing,	**d.** isn't it?
_____	**5.** We don't need any more boxes,	**e.** are they?
_____	**6.** Paul is going to help us,	**f.** have you?
_____	**7.** We can put some things in storage,	**g.** isn't he?
_____	**8.** Jack isn't buying our bookcases,	**h.** is it?
_____	**9.** The movers aren't packing the books for us,	**i.** haven't you?
_____	**10.** Moving is hard,	**j.** aren't they?

3

COMPLETE • *A radio talk-show host is interviewing one of her guests, a Hollywood screenplay writer. Complete the interview with appropriate tags.*

HOST: You've lived in Hollywood for many years, <u> haven't you </u>?
1.

GUEST: Since I was eighteen and came here to write my first screenplay.

HOST: You didn't know anyone here at first, <u>   </u>?
2.

GUEST: No. And I didn't have a cent to my name. Just some ideas and a lot of hope. It

sounds crazy, <u>   </u>?
3.

HOST: But things have worked out for you, <u>   </u>?
4.

You're working on another screenplay now, <u>   </u>?
5.

GUEST: Yes. It's a comedy about some kids who become invisible.

HOST: Speaking of kids, you have some of your own, <u>   </u>?
6.

GUEST: Two boys and a girl—all very visible!

HOST: I know what you mean. Do you ever wish they were invisible?

GUEST: Now, that's an interesting thought, <u>   </u>?
7.

 4

EDIT • *Read this part of a movie script. Find and correct seven mistakes in the use of tag questions. The first mistake is already corrected.*

                                         hasn't

Ben: It's been a long time, Joe, ~~haven't~~ it?

Joe: That depends on what you mean by a long time, doesn't that?

Ben: What are you doing around here, anyway? It's dangerous.

Joe: I can take care of myself. I'm still alive, amn't I?

Ben: Yes, but you're still wanted by the police, are you?

Joe: Look, I need a place to stay. You have a place, don't you? Just for one night.

Ben: I have to think of my wife and kids. You can find someplace else, can you?

Joe: No. You've got to help me!

Ben: I've already helped you plenty. I went to jail for you, haven't I?

Joe: Yeah, OK, Ben. You remember what happened in Vegas, do you?

Ben: OK, OK. I can make a call.

Additions with *So, Too, Neither,* and *Not either*

HERALD SUN

Twins Separated at Birth Are Reunited!

Mark likes hunting, fishing, and Chinese food.
So does Gerald.

CHECK *POINT*

Check the correct answer.

☐ The men like different things.

☐ The men like the same things.

WITH *BE* AS THE MAIN VERB

CHART CHECK

Circle T (True) or F (False).

T F There is more than one way to make an addition.

T F Use **so** or **too** with negative statements.

T F When a statement does not have a form of **be** or an auxiliary verb, use a form of **do** in the addition.

AFFIRMATIVE		NEGATIVE	
STATEMENT	**ADDITION**	**STATEMENT**	**ADDITION**
Amy **is** a twin,	**and so is** Sue. **and** Sue **is too.**	Amy **isn't** very tall,	**and neither is** Sue. **and** Sue **isn't either.**

WITH ALL AUXILIARY VERBS EXCEPT *DO*

AFFIRMATIVE		NEGATIVE	
STATEMENT	**ADDITION**	**STATEMENT**	**ADDITION**
Amy **can** swim,	**and so can** Sue. **and** Sue **can too.**	Amy **can't** ski,	**and neither can** Sue. **and** Sue **can't either.**

WITH VERBS USING *DO* AS AN AUXILIARY VERB

AFFIRMATIVE		NEGATIVE	
STATEMENT	**ADDITION**	**STATEMENT**	**ADDITION**
Amy **likes** dogs,	**and so does** Sue. **and** Sue **does too.**	Amy **doesn't** like cats,	**and neither does** Sue. **and** Sue **doesn't either.**

EXPRESS CHECK

Unscramble these words to form additions.

is • Mark • and • neither   does • Gerald • so • and

Gerald isn't married, _____.   Mark fights fires, _____.

Grammar Explanations	Examples
1. Additions are phrases or short sentences that follow a statement. Use an addition to avoid repeating the information in the statement.	■ Gerald is a firefighter, **and so is Mark**. *(Gerald is a firefighter, and Mark is a firefighter.)*
2. Use **so** or **too** if the addition follows an <u>affirmative</u> statement. Use **neither** or **not either** if the addition follows a <u>negative</u> statement. ▶ **BE CAREFUL!** Notice the <u>word order</u> after **so** and **neither**. The verb comes before the subject.	■ Gerald **is** a firefighter, and **so is** Mark. OR ■ Gerald **is** a firefighter, and Mark **is too**. ■ Gerald **didn't** get married. **Neither did** Mark. OR ■ Gerald **didn't** get married. Mark **did*n't* either**. ■ So **is Mark**. NOT <s>So Mark is.</s> ■ Neither **did Mark**. NOT <s>Neither Mark did.</s>

3. Additions always use a form of <u>**be** or an auxiliary verb</u> (**be, have, do, will**, or a modal verb such as **can, could, should, would**).
 	
  a. If the statement uses a form of **be**, <u>use a form of **be**</u> in the addition too.
 	
  b. If the statement uses an auxiliary verb, <u>use the same auxiliary verb</u> in the addition.
 	
  c. If the statement has a verb that uses **do** as an auxiliary verb, <u>use the appropriate form of **do**</u> in the addition.
	
	■ I'**m** a twin, and so **is** my cousin.
	
	■ Gerald **had** quit his job, and so **had** Mark.
	■ I **can't** drive, and neither **can** my twin.
	
	■ Gerald **owns** a dog, and so **does** Mark.
	■ Gerald **bought** a jeep, and so **did** Mark.

4. In conversation, you can use short **responses** with **so, too, neither,** and **not either** to <u>agree</u> with another speaker. **USAGE NOTE:** In informal speech, people say **Me too** and **Me neither** to express similarity or agreement.	**A:** I have a twin sister. **B:** *So do I.* OR **I do *too*.** **A:** I don't have any brothers or sisters. **B:** *Neither do I.* OR **I don't *either*.** **A:** I'm left-handed. **B:** *Me too.* **A:** I've never heard of these twins. **B:** *Me neither.*

1 **TRUE OR FALSE •** *Read these short conversations between reunited twins. Write T (True) or F (False) for the statement that follows each conversation.*

1. **MARK:** I like Chinese food.
   GERALD: So do I.

   ___T___ Gerald likes Chinese food.

2. **ANDREA:** I don't want to go out.
   BARBARA: Neither do I.

   _____ Barbara wants to go out.

3. **JEAN:** I'm not hungry.
   JOAN: I'm not either.

   _____ Joan isn't hungry.

4. **AMY:** I've always felt lucky.
   KERRIE: So have I.

   _____ Kerrie has felt lucky.

5. **MIA:** I don't eat meat.
   BOB: I don't either.

   _____ Bob eats meat.

6. **JIM:** I have a headache.
   BILL: I do too.

   _____ Both Jim and Bill have headaches.

7. **NORA:** I can't swim.
   DINA: Me neither.

   _____ Dina can swim.

8. **CHET:** I shouldn't work so much.
   TODD: Neither should I.

   _____ Todd wants to work less.

9. **JASON:** I'd like to leave now.
   TYLER: Me too.

   _____ Tyler wants to leave.

2 **CHOOSE •** *Circle the correct words to complete this paragraph.*

Sometimes being a twin can cause trouble. In high school, I was in Mr. Jacobs's history class. Neither / So was my brother. One day we took a test. I got questions 18
1.
and 20 wrong. My brother did so / too. I didn't spell *Constantinople* correctly, and
2.
either / neither did he. The teacher was sure we had cheated. As a result, I got an F
3.
on the test, and so did / got my brother. We tried to convince Mr. Jacobs of our
4.
innocence, but he didn't believe us. The principal didn't either / too. We finally
5.
convinced them to give us another test. This time I got items 3 and 10 wrong.
Guess what? Neither / So did my brother. Our teacher was astounded. So / Too was
6.   **7.**
the principal. We weren't. We were just amused.

3 **COMPLETE** • *Marta and Carla are twins. They agree on everything. Complete their conversation with responses.*

MARTA: I'm so happy we finally found each other.

CARLA: So _____am I_____. I always felt like something was missing from my life.
                        1.

MARTA: So _____. I always knew I had a double somewhere out there.
                        2.

CARLA: I can't believe how similar we are.

MARTA: Neither _____. It's like always seeing myself in the mirror.
                        3.

CARLA: Not only do we look identical, but we like and dislike all the same things.

MARTA: Right. I hate lettuce.

CARLA: I _____. And I detest liver.
                    4.

MARTA: So _____. I *love* pizza, though.
                    5.

CARLA: So _____. But only with tomato and cheese. I don't like pepperoni.
                    6.

MARTA: Neither _____.
                        7.

CARLA: This is amazing! I wonder if our husbands have so much in common.

MARTA: Me _____!
                    8.

4 **EDIT** • *Read this student's composition. There are six mistakes in the use of sentence additions. Find and correct them. The first mistake is already corrected.*

> My Brother and I
>
> My brother is just a year older than I am. We have a lot of things in common.
>
>   is he
> First of all, we look alike. I am 5'10", and so ~~he is.~~ I have straight black hair and dark brown eyes, and so does he. We share many of the same interests too. I love to play soccer, and he too. Both of us swim every day, but I can't dive, and either can he.
>
> Sometimes being so similar has its problems. For example, last night I wanted the last piece of chocolate cake, and so does he. Often I won't feel like doing the dishes, and neither won't he. Worst of all, sometimes I'm interested in dating a certain schoolmate, and so he is. However, most of the time I feel our similarities are really nice. So does my brother.

SelfTest

Circle the letter of the correct answer to complete each sentence.

Example: Jennifer never _____ coffee. (A) drink (C) is drinking (B) drinks (D) was drinking	**A Ⓑ C D**

1. Where _____?

   (A) does she live   (C) she does live

   (B) she lives   (D) she lived

   A B C D

2. _____ lost this wallet?

   (A) Whom   (C) Who

   (B) Whose   (D) Who did

   A B C D

3. You're Cynthia, _____ you?

   (A) aren't   (C) didn't

   (B) are   (D) were

   A B C D

4. Laura loves soap operas, and _____.

   (A) Jane does too   (C) Jane loves too

   (B) so Jane does   (D) so loves Jane

   A B C D

5. I didn't like sports, and _____ my brother.

   (A) either did   (C) so did

   (B) neither does   (D) neither did

   A B C D

6. —That isn't Sam, is it?

   —No, _____. Sam's taller.

   (A) it is   (C) it wasn't

   (B) it doesn't   (D) it isn't

   A B C D

7. We didn't eat here last week, _____ we?

   (A) didn't   (C) do

   (B) haven't   (D) did

   A B C D

8. —Who _____ your bike?

   —Mike did.

   (A) did give you   (C) you gave

   (B) did you give   (D) gave you

   A B C D

9. —Who _____ at the party?

   —I saw Stefan.

   (A) saw you   (C) you saw

   (B) did you see   (D) you see

   A B C D

10. —I hate cabbage.
     —Me _____. I can't even look at it.   **A B C D**
     (A) too   (C) neither
     (B) either   (D) do too

11. _____ washing the dishes tonight?   **A B C D**
     (A) Whose   (C) Who are
     (B) Who's   (D) Who does

12. Liam was born in Ireland, and so _____ his brother.   **A B C D**
     (A) wasn't   (C) was
     (B) didn't   (D) did

SECTION TWO

Each sentence has four underlined words or phrases. The four underlined parts of the sentence are marked A, B, C, and D. Circle the letter of the one underlined word or phrase that is NOT CORRECT.

> **EXAMPLE:**
>
> Mike <u>usually</u> <u>drives</u> to school, but <u>today</u> he <u>walks</u>.   **A B C Ⓓ**
>   A   B   C   D

13. <u>This</u> is <u>a</u> good school, <u>wasn't</u> <u>it</u>?   **A B C D**
      A   B   C   D

14. <u>We</u> <u>went</u> to Stan's holiday party last year, <u>hadn't</u> <u>we</u>?   **A B C D**
      A   B   C   D

15. Kevin <u>has</u> always <u>been</u> a great student, <u>and so</u> <u>his brother has</u>.   **A B C D**
            A   B   C   D

16. My sister <u>has</u> never <u>gone</u> skiing, and <u>neither</u> <u>did</u> I.   **A B C D**
                A   B   C   D

17. Where <u>you worked</u> last year <u>when</u> you <u>were</u> <u>going</u> to school?   **A B C D**
              A   B   C   D

18. <u>That</u> sign is too small <u>to read</u>, <u>isn't</u> <u>that</u>?   **A B C D**
      A   B   C   D

19. English <u>isn't</u> an easy language <u>to learn</u>, <u>is</u> <u>it</u>.   **A B C D**
              A   B   C   D

20. My <u>parents</u> <u>are</u> both good cooks, <u>and</u> <u>me too</u>.   **A B C D**
          A   B   C   D

21. Tom and Fred <u>hadn't been</u> to Florida <u>before</u> then, <u>had</u> <u>he</u>?   **A B C D**
                   A   B   C   D

22. I'<u>m</u> <u>usually</u> right about the weather, <u>amn't</u> <u>I</u>?   **A B C D**
       A   B   C   D

23. <u>Paul</u> <u>likes</u> Italian food, <u>doesn't</u> <u>Paul</u>?   **A B C D**
      A   B   C   D

24. <u>Where</u> <u>did</u> they <u>went</u> <u>yesterday</u>?   **A B C D**
      A   B   C   D

25. <u>Why</u> <u>you</u> <u>call</u> me so <u>late</u> last night?   **A B C D**
      A   B   C   D

Ability:
Can, Could, Be able to

Can you **do** spreadsheets?

CHECK POINT

Circle T (True) or F (False).

T   F   The father wants to know if his daughter has permission to do spreadsheets.

CHART CHECK 1

Circle T (True) or F (False).

T   F   The form for ***can*** and ***could*** is the same for all subjects.

STATEMENTS: CAN/COULD

SUBJECT	CAN/COULD*	BASE FORM OF VERB	
I/He/She/It/We/You/They	can (not)	do	spreadsheets now.
	could (not)	use	a computer last year.

*Can and *could* are modals. They do not have *-s* in the third person singular.

YES/NO QUESTIONS: CAN/COULD

CAN/COULD	SUBJECT	BASE FORM	
Can	she	do	them?
Could	they	use	one?

SHORT ANSWERS

AFFIRMATIVE		NEGATIVE	
Yes,	she **can**.	No,	she **can't**.
	they **could**.		they **couldn't**.

WH- QUESTIONS: CAN/COULD

WH- WORD	CAN/COULD	SUBJECT	BASE FORM	
How well	can	she	do	spreadsheets?
	could	they	use	a computer?

CHART CHECK 2

Check the correct answer.

Which part of ***be able to*** changes for different subjects?

☐ ***be***   ☐ ***able to***

STATEMENTS: BE ABLE TO

SUBJECT	BE	ABLE TO	BASE FORM	
I	am			
He/She/It	is	(not) able to	do	spreadsheets.
We/You/They	are			

CHART CHECK 3

Check the correct answer.

In questions with **be able to**, what comes before the subject?

☐ a form of **be**

☐ a form of **able to**

YES/NO QUESTIONS: *BE ABLE TO*

BE	SUBJECT	ABLE TO	BASE FORM	
Are	you	able to	do	spreadsheets?
Is	she			

SHORT ANSWERS

	AFFIRMATIVE		NEGATIVE	
Yes,	I **am**.	No,	I'm **not**.	
	she **is**.		she **isn't**.	

WH- QUESTIONS: *BE ABLE TO*

WH- WORD	BE	SUBJECT	ABLE TO	BASE FORM	
How well	are	you	able to	do	spreadsheets?
	is	she			

EXPRESS CHECK

Complete these sentences with **can** *or* **be able to**. *Use one word for each blank.*

A: _____ she able _____ use a computer already?

B: Yes, she _____, and she _____ type and do spreadsheets too.

Grammar Explanations

Examples

1. Use **can** or **be able to** to talk about <u>ability in the present</u>. **USAGE NOTE:** In everyday speech, **can** is <u>more common</u> than **be able to** in the <u>present tense</u>.	■ She **can do** computer graphics. ■ She**'s able to do** computer graphics.
2. Use either **could** or **was/were able to** to talk about <u>ability (but not a specific achievement) in the past</u>. ▶ **BE CAREFUL!** Use only **was/were able to** to talk about <u>a specific achievement or a single event in the past</u>. Use either **could** or **was/were able to** in <u>negative sentences about past ability</u>.	■ Sami **could read** when he was four. ■ He **was able to use** a computer too. ■ He **was able to win** the Math Prize last year. NOT ~~He could win the Math Prize . . .~~ ■ I **couldn't win** the Math Prize last year. ■ I **wasn't able to do** one problem.
3. For forms and tenses <u>other than the present or past</u>, use **be able to**.	■ Jen wants **to be able to write** programs. *(infinitive)* ■ By June she **will be able to complete** her computer class. *(future)*

1 **IDENTIFY** • *Read part of an article about some talented young business people.*
Underline the words that express ability.

A surprising number of young people <u>have been able to create</u> successful Web-based businesses. One young entrepreneur is Sam Roberts. Sam could design Web pages when he was eight, but he got his break at twelve when a writer hired him to design a Web site. Sam's first business failed because he and his partner weren't able to get along. However, his new business, Webman, is up and running. Another young businessman, Jay

WEB BUSINESSES FOR FUN AND PROFIT

Leibowitz, was able to sell two software programs when he was fourteen. He made $30,000 on the deal and now Jay runs his own Web site. Dan Finley writes reviews of new software. He started his business at sixteen. A full-time college student, Dan can pay a staff of writers and still earn $500 a month. Although they all make money, all three started out to have fun at their hobby, not to make a profit.

COMPLETE • *Read each description. Complete it with a name from the article.*

1. _____Jay_____ sold software programs at the age of fourteen.

2. _____ didn't agree with his partner.

3. _____ earns money reviewing software.

4. _____ was able to design a Web page for a writer.

2 **COMPLETE** • *Read these paragraphs. Complete them with* **can**, **could**, *or* **be able to**.
Use **can** *or* **could** *when possible. Choose between affirmative and negative.*

1. Stefan is enjoying his computer class. Two weeks ago, he _____couldn't_____ even use the mouse, but now he _is able   to_ edit his homework. By next week, he _will be able to_ do research on the Internet.

2. Eleni misses her family in Greece. She _____couldn't_____ visit them for years, but they just got an e-mail account, so now they _____can_____ keep in touch daily.

3. I _cann't_ understand how to set up a presentation. The software instructions don't help. I think I'll take a professional development course. In a few months maybe I _will be able to_ make that presentation.

4. Mike and I _couldn't_ get along since we started this business. He ___cann't to__ work alone (he needs people), and I _____cann't__ work in a group (I have to work alone). I hope we _will be able to_ work out our problems soon.

3 **COMPLETE** • *Read this advertisement. Complete it with the appropriate form of* **can**, **could**, *or* **be able to** *plus the verbs in parentheses. Use* **can** *or* **could** *when possible.*

WILL B. HAPPY®
Professional Development Courses

Time Management   Presentations   Career Development   Teamwork

Think about your last presentation: _____Were_____ you ___able to prepare___ on time?
                                                                              1. (prepare)

_____ you _____ your ideas?
                          2. (communicate)

Will B. Happy® has helped others, and he _____ YOU!
                                                              3. (help)

"Before I took Will B. Happy's course, my work was always late because

I _____ a schedule. I also had big piles on my desk because I
        4. (follow)

_____ what was important. Now I _____ my time
      5. (decide)   **6.** (manage)

effectively. Next month, when my workload gets heavy, I _____ it
                                                                          7. (organize)

and do the important things first."
                                                          —*Scott Mathis, student*

"I didn't use to _____ in front of groups. Now I can!"
                          8. (speak)
                                                          —*Mary Zhang, sales manager*

4 **EDIT** • *Read this student's journal. Find and correct seven mistakes in expressing ability.*
The first mistake is already corrected.

> Today in my Will B. Happy Teamwork course, I learned about work styles—"Drivers" and
>   to
> "Enthusiasts." I'm a Driver, so I can make decisions, but I'm not able ᴧlisten to other
> people's ideas. The Enthusiast in our group can communicates well, but you can't
> depend on her. Now I understand what was happening in my business class last year,
> when I couldn't felt comfortable with my team. I thought that they all talked too much
> and didn't able to work efficiently. I could get an A for the course, but it was hard. I can
> do a lot more alone, but some jobs are too big for that. Our instructor says that soon
> the Drivers will able to listen and the Enthusiast could be more dependable.

Permission:
May, Can, Could,
Do you mind if . . .?

I think I have something in my eye. **Could** I **take** the test tomorrow?

CHECK *POINT*

Check the sentence that describes what's happening in the cartoon.

❒ The student wants to know if his eye will be better tomorrow.

❒ The student is asking the teacher to allow him to take the test tomorrow.

CHART CHECK 1

Check the correct answer.

Which modal is used in questions but NOT in short answers about permission?

❒ *may*

❒ *can*

❒ *could*

QUESTIONS: *MAY/CAN/COULD*			
MAY/CAN/COULD*	**SUBJECT**	**BASE FORM OF VERB**	
May **Can** **Could**	I/we/he/she/it/they	**start**	now?

*May, can, and *could* are modals. They do not have *-s* in the third person singular.

SHORT ANSWERS					
AFFIRMATIVE			**NEGATIVE**		
Yes,	you/he/she/it/they	**may.** **can.**	**No,**	you/he/she/it/they	**may not.** **can't.**

CHART CHECK 2

Circle T (True) or F (False).

T F After **Do you mind if . . . ?** the verb is the same for all subjects.

T F The answer **Not at all** gives permission.

QUESTIONS: *DO YOU MIND IF . . . ?*		
DO YOU MIND IF	**SUBJECT**	**VERB**
Do you mind if	I/we/they	**start?**
	he/she/it	**starts?**

SHORT ANSWERS	
AFFIRMATIVE	**NEGATIVE**
Not at all.	
No, I don't.	Yes, I do.

STATEMENTS: *MAY/CAN*		
SUBJECT	**MAY/CAN**	**BASE FORM**
I/He/She/It/We/You/They	may (not) can (not)	**start.**

EXPRESS CHECK

Circle the correct words to complete this conversation.

A: Do you mind if he <u>help / helps</u> me with my homework?

B: <u>Not at all / Yes I do</u>. He can <u>help / helps</u> you, but you should do most of the work.

Grammar Explanations	Examples
1. Use *may*, *could*, and *can* to <u>ask for permission</u>. **USAGE NOTE:** *May* is a little more <u>formal</u> than *can* and *could*. ▶ **BE CAREFUL!** Requests for permission always <u>refer to the present or the future</u>. When you use *could* to ask for permission, it is not past tense.	■ **May** I **call** you next Friday? ■ **Could** we **use** our dictionaries? ■ **Can** he **come** to class with me? ■ **May** I **leave** the room, Professor Lee? **A: Could** I take the test ***tomorrow***? **B:** Certainly. The test starts at 9:00 A.M.
2. We often say *please* when we ask for permission. Note the possible word orders.	■ **Could** I ask a question, ***please***? ■ **Could** I ***please*** ask a question?
3. Use *Do you mind if . . . ?* to ask for permission when your action might bother someone. ▶ **BE CAREFUL!** A <u>negative answer</u> to the question *Do you mind if . . . ?* <u>gives permission</u> to do something. It means, *It's OK. I don't mind.*	**A: Do you mind if** I clean up tomorrow? **B:** Yes, actually, I do mind. I hate to see a mess. **A: Do you mind if** I leave the room? **B: *Not at all***. *(You may leave the room.)*

4. Use *may* or *can* in <u>answers</u>. Do not use *could*.
 	
▶ **BE CAREFUL!** Do not contract *may not*.
 	
We often use **polite expressions** instead of modals to answer requests for permission.
	A: Could I borrow this pencil?
	B: Yes, of course you **can**.
	    NOT ~~Yes, you could.~~
	
	■ No, you **may not**.
	    NOT ~~No, you mayn't.~~
	
	A: Could I close the window?
	B: *Sure*.
	    Certainly.
	    Go ahead.
	    No, please don't. It's hot in here.

5. When people **refuse permission**, they often give <u>an apology and an explanation</u>. If the <u>rules are very clear</u>, someone may refuse without an apology or explanation.	**A:** Can I please have a little more time? **B: *I'm sorry, but the time is up***. **DRIVER:** Can I park here? **OFFICER: *No, you can't***.

1 **MATCH** • *Each request for permission goes with a response. Match each request with the correct response.*

Request	Response
__d__ 1. May we come in now?	a. No, you can't. It's a bus stop.
__f__ 2. Could I see your tickets, please?	b. Not at all. There's plenty of time.
__e__ 3. May I please speak to Harry?	c. Sure they can. We have room.
__c__ 4. Could they come with us?	d. Yes, you may. The test starts soon.
__g__ 5. Can I park here?	e. I'm sorry, he's not in.
__b__ 6. Do you mind if I have more tea?	f. Certainly. Here they are.

(above b: "a lot" written above "plenty")

2 **COMPLETE** • *Mr. Hamad is supervising a test. Complete his conversations with his students. Use a pronoun plus the correct form of the words in parentheses and short answers.*

AHMED: _____Could we come_____ into the test room now?
1. (Could / come)

MR. H: Yes, _____certainly_____. Please show your registration form
2.
as you come in.

SOFIA: My brother isn't taking the test. _do you mind he stay_ in the
3. (Do you mind / stay)
room with me?

MR. H: Yes, ___I mind___. Sorry, only people with tickets are
4.
permitted inside.

ROSA: ___May I use___ a pen to write my name on the test
5. (May / use)
booklet?

MR. H: No, ___you can not___. You must use a pencil. And everyone
6.
please remember, ___I can't start___ the test until I tell you to.
7. (can't / start)

ROSA: Jamie, _do you mind if I borrow_ this pencil? I only brought a pen.
8. (do you mind if / borrow)

JAMIE: _No I don't mind_. Take it. I brought a few.
9.

MR. H: OK, _may you open_ your test booklets and read the
10. (may / open)
instructions now.

JEAN: I'm late because my train broke down. ___Can I come___ in?
11. (Can / come)

MR. H: No, _you cannot_. We've already started the test.
12.

3

ASK • *Lucy and Carl are going to a concert. Read each situation. Write questions to ask for permission. Use the words in parentheses.*

1. Carl wants his friend Bob to come.

   CARL: I have an extra ticket. ___Do you mind if Bob comes?___
   (Do you mind if)

2. Carl wants to use Lucy's phone to call Bob.

   CARL: Great. I'll call him right now. _____
   (Could)

3. Carl wants to park in front of the stadium.

   CARL: We're going to the concert, Officer. _____
   (May)

4. Lucy, Bob, and Carl want to move up a few rows. Bob asks an usher.

   BOB: All those seats are empty. _____
   (Could)

5. Carl wants to tape the concert. Lucy asks the usher first.

   LUCY: My friend brought a tape recorder. _____
   (Can)

6. Lucy hates the music. She wants to leave.

   LUCY: This music is giving me a headache. _____
   (Do you mind if)

4

EDIT • *This exercise is similar to part of the TOEFL®. Find the mistake in each item and fill in the space that corresponds to the letter of the incorrect word or phrase. Then go one step beyond the TOEFL® and correct the mistake.*

1. Can he <u>~~comes~~</u> ^{come} on the train with me or <u>does</u> he <u>need</u> a ticket?   Ⓐ ●Ⓑ Ⓒ Ⓓ

A   B   C   D

2. <u>I'm sorry</u>, he <u>couldn't</u>. Only passengers <u>can</u> <u>board</u> the train.   Ⓐ Ⓑ Ⓒ Ⓓ

A   B   C   D

3. <u>Could</u> I <u>changed</u> seats with <u>you</u>? I'd like to <u>sit</u> next to my son.   Ⓐ Ⓑ Ⓒ Ⓓ

A   B   C   D

4. Yes, <u>you</u> <u>could</u>. <u>Go right ahead</u>. I'm <u>getting</u> off soon.   Ⓐ Ⓑ Ⓒ Ⓓ

A B   C   D

5. Mom, <u>may</u> <u>I</u> <u>to have</u> some candy? <u>I'm</u> hungry.   Ⓐ Ⓑ Ⓒ Ⓓ

A B C   D

6. No, you <u>mayn't</u>. <u>I'm sorry</u>, <u>but</u> you've <u>already</u> had enough candy.   Ⓐ Ⓑ Ⓒ Ⓓ

A   B   C   D

7. <u>Do</u> <u>you</u> mind <u>if</u> he <u>play</u> his computer game?   Ⓐ Ⓑ Ⓒ Ⓓ

A B   C   D

8. <u>Yes, I do</u>. He can <u>play</u> if he <u>wants</u>. It <u>won't</u> bother me.   Ⓐ Ⓑ Ⓒ Ⓓ

A   B   C   D

9. <u>I'm</u> still hungry. <u>Can</u> <u>we'll</u> <u>get</u> a sandwich soon?   Ⓐ Ⓑ Ⓒ Ⓓ

A   B C D

10. <u>Not at all</u>. <u>We</u> <u>can</u> <u>go</u> find the club car.   Ⓐ Ⓑ Ⓒ Ⓓ

A   B C D

Requests:
Will, Can, Would, Could,
Would you mind . . . ?

"Miss Fleming, would you mind dialling 911 for me?"

CHECK POINT

Check the correct answer.

The businessman is

☐ giving an order.

☐ asking someone to do something.

☐ asking for information.

NOTE: 911 is the emergency telephone number in the United States and Canada.

CHART CHECK 1

Circle T (True) or F (False).

T F You can use **would** and **could** in questions but NOT in short answers to requests.

QUESTIONS: *WILL/CAN/WOULD/COULD*			
WILL/CAN/ WOULD/COULD*	**SUBJECT**	**BASE FORM OF VERB**	
Will Can Would Could	you	**mail**	this for me?

*These words are modals. They do not have *-s* in the third person singular.

SHORT ANSWERS		
AFFIRMATIVE		**NEGATIVE**
Sure Certainly	(I **will**). (I **can**).	I'm sorry, but I **can't**.

QUESTIONS: *WOULD YOU MIND . . . ?*		
WOULD YOU MIND	**GERUND**	
Would you mind	mailing	this for me?

CHART CHECK 2

Check the correct answer.

Not at all means:

☐ *OK*   ☐ *no*

SHORT ANSWERS	
AFFIRMATIVE	**NEGATIVE**
No, not at all. I'd be glad to.	I'm sorry, but I **can't**.

EXPRESS CHECK

Complete this conversation.

A: _____ you mind filing these reports now?

B: _____, _____ at all.

A: Thanks. And _____ you answer the phone, please?

B: Sorry, but I _____. My hands are full.

Grammar Explanations

Examples

1. Use **will**, **can**, **would**, and **could** <u>to ask someone to do something</u>.

We often use **will** and **can** for <u>informal requests</u>.

We use **would** and **could** to make requests <u>more polite</u>.

> **SISTER:** **Will** you **answer** the phone?
> **Can** you **turn down** the TV?
>
> **BOSS:** **Would** you **type** this report?
> **Could** you **make** ten copies?

2. We also use **please** with **will**, **can**, **would**, and **could** to make the request <u>even more polite</u>. Note the word order.

> ■ **Could** you **please** close the door?
> OR
> ■ **Could** you close the door, **please**?

3. We also use **Would you mind** + gerund (without *please*) to make <u>polite requests</u>.

Note that a **negative answer** means that you <u>will do what the person requests</u>.

> **A:** **Would you mind waiting** for a few minutes? Mr. Caras is still at a meeting.
> **B:** **Not at all.**
> (OK. I'll do it.)

4. People usually expect us to say **yes** to polite requests. When we **cannot say yes**, we usually <u>apologize and give a reason</u>.

> **A:** **Could** you take this to Susan Lane's office for me?
> **B:** **I'm sorry, I can't.** I'm expecting an important phone call.

▶ **BE CAREFUL!** Do not use **would** or **could** to answer polite requests.

> **A:** I'm cold. **Would** you shut the window, please?
> **B:** **Certainly.**
> NOT ~~Yes, I would.~~

IDENTIFY • *Marcia has a new co-worker. Read their conversations. Underline all the polite requests.*

1. **MARCIA:** Hi. You must be the new office assistant. I'm Marcia Jones. Let me know if you need anything.

   LORNA: Thanks, Marcia. <u>Could you show me the coat closet?</u>

   MARCIA: Certainly. It's right over here.

2. **LORNA:** Marcia, <u>would you explain these instructions</u> for the fax machine?

   MARCIA: Sure. Just put your letter in here and dial the number.

3. **MARCIA:** I'm leaving for lunch. <u>Would you like to come?</u>

   LORNA: Thanks, but I can't right now. I'm really busy.

   MARCIA: Do you want a sandwich from the coffee shop?

   LORNA: That would be great. <u>Can you get me a tuna sandwich</u> and a soda?

   MARCIA: Sure. <u>Will you answer my phone</u> until I get back?

   LORNA: Certainly.

4. **MARCIA:** Lorna, <u>would you mind making some coffee?</u>

   LORNA: I'm sorry, but I can't do it now. I've got to finish this letter before 2:00.

 CHOOSE • *Lorna's roommate, Jana, is having problems today. Check the appropriate response to each of Jana's requests.*

1. Lorna, would you please drive me to class today? My car won't start.

   a. _____ Yes, I would.   **b.** _✓_ I'd be glad to.

2. Would you mind lending me five dollars? I'm getting paid tomorrow.

   a. _✓_ Not at all.   **b.** _____ Yes.

3. Lorna, can you take these books back to the library for me? I'm running late.

   a. _✓_ I'm late too. Sorry.   **b.** _____ No, I can't.

4. Could you lock the door on your way out? My hands are full.

   a. _____ Yes, I could.   **b.** _✓_ Sure.

5. Can you turn the radio down? I need to study for my math quiz this morning.

   a. _✓_ Certainly.   **b.** _____ Not at all.

6. Will you pick up some milk on the way home this afternoon?

   a. _____ No, I won't.   **b.** _✓_ Sorry. I'll be at work until 8:00.

3 **CHOOSE AND COMPLETE** • *Use the appropriate imperative from the box to complete these requests. Use **please** when possible, and make any necessary changes.*

Buy some cereal.	Call back later.	~~Close the window.~~
File these reports.	Shut the door.	Turn on the lights.

1. Can _____*you please close the window?*_____ It's freezing in here.

2. Could _____ I've finished reading them.

3. Would you mind _____ It's too dark in here.

4. Will _____ We don't have any left.

5. Could _____ Ms. Cho is on another call right now.

6. Would _____ There's too much noise in the hall!

4 **EDIT** • *Read these requests from Marcia's boss and Marcia's answers (in dark print). Find and correct six mistakes in making and responding to requests. The first mistake is already corrected.*

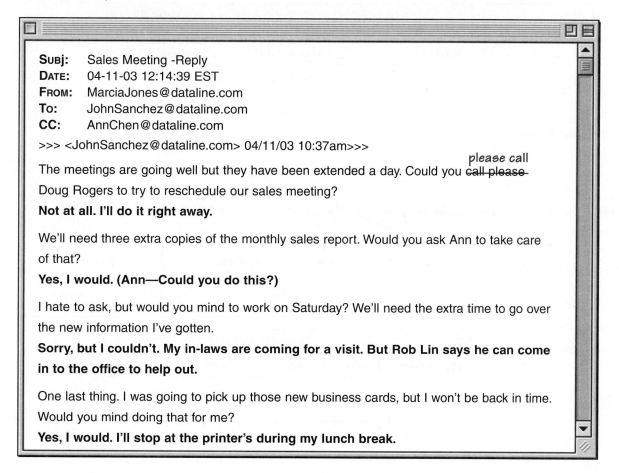

Subj: Sales Meeting -Reply
Date: 04-11-03 12:14:39 EST
From: MarciaJones@dataline.com
To: JohnSanchez@dataline.com
CC: AnnChen@dataline.com

>>> <JohnSanchez@dataline.com> 04/11/03 10:37am>>>

The meetings are going well but they have been extended a day. Could you ~~call please~~ *please call*
Doug Rogers to try to reschedule our sales meeting?
Not at all. I'll do it right away.

We'll need three extra copies of the monthly sales report. Would you ask Ann to take care
of that?
Yes, I would. (Ann—Could you do this?)

I hate to ask, but would you mind to work on Saturday? We'll need the extra time to go over
the new information I've gotten.
**Sorry, but I couldn't. My in-laws are coming for a visit. But Rob Lin says he can come
in to the office to help out.**

One last thing. I was going to pick up those new business cards, but I won't be back in time.
Would you mind doing that for me?
Yes, I would. I'll stop at the printer's during my lunch break.

Advice:
Should, Ought to, Had better

Check the correct answer.

☐ The interviewer is suggesting a
  type of job for the applicant.

☐ The interviewer is telling the
  applicant how to be successful.

CHART CHECK 1

*Circle T (True) or
F (False).*

T F The same form
of the verb
follows **should**,
ought to, and
had better.

	STATEMENTS: *SHOULD/OUGHT TO/HAD BETTER*		
SUBJECT	***SHOULD/OUGHT TO/ HAD BETTER***	**BASE FORM OF VERB**	
I/He/She/We/You/They	**should (not) ought to had better (not)**	**look**	for a new job.

*Should and *ought to* are modals. *Had better* is similar to a modal.
These forms do not have *-s* in the third person singular.

NOTE: For contractions of *should not* and *had better*, see Appendix 24 on page 346.

CHART CHECK 2

*Check the correct
answer.*

In questions about
advice, we usually use:

☐ *should*

☐ *ought to*

☐ *had better*

YES/NO QUESTIONS: *SHOULD*		
SHOULD	**SUBJECT**	**BASE FORM**
Should	I he	**look?**

SHORT ANSWERS					
AFFIRMATIVE			**NEGATIVE**		
Yes,	you he	**should.**	No,	you he	**shouldn't.**

WH- QUESTIONS: *SHOULD*				
WH- WORD	***SHOULD***	**SUBJECT**	**BASE FORM**	
Where	**should**	I he	**look**	for a new job?

EXPRESS CHECK

Complete this conversation.

A: They're looking for a cashier at McDonald's. _____ I apply for the job?

B: _____, you _____. You can get more money working at

the bookstore.

Grammar Explanations

Examples

1. Use *should* and *ought to* to say that <u>something is advisable</u>. **USAGE NOTE:** We do not usually use the negative of *ought to* in American English. We use *shouldn't* instead.	■ Mario **should find** a new job. ■ He **ought to read** the help wanted ads. ■ He **shouldn't quit** school. NOT COMMON ~~He ought not to quit.~~

2. Use *had better* for <u>urgent advice</u>—when you believe that something bad will happen if the person does not follow the advice. **USAGE NOTE:** We usually use the <u>contraction</u> for *had better*. The negative of *had better* is **had better not**. ▶ **BE CAREFUL!** *Had better* always refers to the <u>present</u> or the <u>future</u>, never to the past (even though it uses the word *had*).	■ You**'d better leave** now, *or you'll be late*. ■ You**'d better** apply for more than one job. NOT ~~You had better apply . . .~~ ■ You**'d better not** be late. NOT ~~You'd not better be late.~~ ■ We**'d better take** the bus *now*. ■ You**'d better call** them back *tomorrow*.

3. Use *should* for <u>questions</u>. We do not usually use *ought to* or *had better* for questions.	■ **Should** I **apply** for that job? ■ When **should** I **apply**?

4. It is usually considered impolite to give **advice to people of equal or higher status** (such as friends or bosses) unless they ask for it. When we give <u>unasked-for advice</u>, we often soften it with *maybe*, *perhaps*, or *I think*.	**FRIEND:** **Should** I **shake** hands with the interviewer? **YOU:** Yes, you **should**. **BOSS:** Where **should** I **take** our client to lunch? **YOU:** I think you **should go** to the Tuscan Grill. ■ Myra, *maybe* you **ought to apply** for this job.

PRONUNCIATION NOTE
Ought to is often pronounced "oughta" in informal speech. Do not write *oughta*.

1 **READ** • *Look at these job search tips.*

- You should tell all your friends that you are looking for a job.
- You'd better not quit your present job before you find a new one.
- You shouldn't tell your boss that you are looking for a new job.
- You ought to apply for several jobs at once.
- You shouldn't immediately ask an interviewer about job benefits.
- You should always give the interviewer accurate salary information.

ANSWER • *Check the things that are OK to do according to the tips.*

1. ☑ tell your friends about your job search
2. ☐ tell your boss about your job search
3. ☐ ask about job benefits right away
4. ☐ leave your job during your search
5. ☐ apply for several jobs at once
6. ☐ tell the interviewer your real salary

2 **CHOOSE** • *Read this advice for job seekers. Complete it with the correct words.*

Reader's Weekly Volume II, Issue 23

ADVICE FOR JOB SEEKERS

Want or need a new job? When's the best time to start looking? Right now! You _____'d better not_____ delay, or you'll start to feel "stuck."
1. (ought to / 'd better not)

These tips will help:

☛ A lot of people wait until after the holidays to look for a job. That means less competition for you right now. You _____shouldn't_____ wait!
2. (shouldn't / should)

☛ Too busy at work to schedule interviews? Early morning interviews have fewer interruptions. You _____should_____ ask for interviews before nine o'clock.
3. (should / 'd better not)

☛ If you are laid off, you _____shouldn't_____ take a lower-paying job just to get work. If your new salary is low, your employer won't appreciate your skills. If possible, you _____should_____ ask for a salary that matches your skills.
4. ('d better / shouldn't)
5. ('d better not / should)

☛ However, money isn't everything! You _____'d better not_____ take a position with a company you dislike, or you won't do a good job there.
6. (ought to / 'd better not)

☛ Don't talk about salary too soon. You _____'d better_____ wait—learn about the job and talk about your skills first.
7. ('d better / shouldn't)

COMPLETE • *Kim Yee's boss has invited him to dinner at his home. Complete Kim's conversation with his friend. Use* **should**, **ought to**, *or* **had better** *and the words in parentheses. Choose between affirmative and negative.*

KIM: _How should I dress?_____ In a suit?
          1. (How / dress?)

SCOTT: You don't have to wear a suit. _____'should' look neat_____,
                                              2. (look / neat)

but you can wear casual clothes.

KIM: _What time should we arrive____
          3. (What time / arrive?)

SCOTT: It's really important to be on time. Your boss and his wife are expecting you

at 7:00, so ___you had better not arrive after 7:15_. It's OK to be a little
              4. (arrive after 7:15)

late, but don't make them wait too long for you!

KIM: _Should we bring a gift___
          5. (bring a gift?)

SCOTT: Yes, but get something small. ___shouldn't buy an expensive gift_.
                                            6. (buy an expensive gift)

It would embarrass them.

KIM: _What should I buy___
          7. (What / buy?)

SCOTT: I think ___you had better get some flower_.
                    8. (get some flowers)

EDIT • *Read this letter. Find and correct six mistakes in expressing advice. The first mistake is already corrected.*

> Dear Son,
>
> We are so happy to hear about your new job. Congratulations! Just remember—you
> shouldn't ~~to~~ work too hard. The most important thing right now is your schoolwork.
> Maybe you only oughta work two days a week instead of three. Also, we think you'd
> better ask your boss for time off during exams. That way you'll have plenty of time to
> study. You would better give this a lot of careful thought, OK? Please take good care
> of yourself. You'd not better start skipping meals, and you definitely shouldn't worked
> at night. At your age, you will better get a good night's sleep. Do you need anything
> from home? Should we send any of your books? Let us know.
>
> With love,
>
> Mom and Dad

UNIT 31

Suggestions:
Could, Why don't . . . ?, Why not . . . ?, Let's, How about . . . ?

Let's Travel!

HOSTELLING INTERNATIONAL

Going to Germany?

Why not stay at a youth hostel?

How about a magnificent one like Altena Castle? Altena is also fun and cheap. So, **why don't** you **make** our castle your home?

Altena Castle, Germany

CHART CHECK 1

Check the correct answer.

The verb after **could**, **why don't**, **why not**, or **let's**

☐ changes for different subjects.

☐ does not change for different subjects.

COULD				
(MAYBE)	**SUBJECT**	**COULD***	**BASE FORM**	
(Maybe)	I/he/she/we/you/they	could	stay	in a castle.

*Could is a modal. It does not have -s in the third person singular.

WHY DON'T . . . ?				
WHY	**DON'T**	**SUBJECT**	**BASE FORM**	
Why	don't	I/we/you/they	stay	in a castle?
	doesn't	he/she		

WHY NOT . . . ?		
WHY NOT	**BASE FORM**	
Why not	stay	there?

LET'S		
LET'S (NOT)	**BASE FORM**	
Let's (not)	stay	there.

CHART CHECK 2

Circle T (True) or F (False).

T F Suggestions with **How about . . . ?** have only one form.

HOW ABOUT . . . ?		
HOW ABOUT	**GERUND/NOUN**	
How about	staying	in a castle?
	a castle?	

EXPRESS CHECK

Add the correct punctuation.

Let's take the train_____   Maybe we could take the train_____

Why not take the train_____   How about the train_____

Grammar Explanations	**Examples**
1. Use *Let's*, *(Maybe) . . . could*, *Why don't/ doesn't*, *Why not*, and *How about* to make <u>suggestions</u>.	**A: Let's take** a trip this summer. **B: Maybe** we **could go** to Germany. **A: Why don't** we **ask** Luke to go with us? **B:** Good idea. **Why doesn't** Tom **call** him tonight? **A: Why not call** him right now? **B: How about staying** at a youth hostel? **A: How about Altena Castle?**
▶ **BE CAREFUL!** When someone uses *Why not* and *Why don't/doesn't* to <u>make a suggestion</u>, these expressions are not information questions. The speaker does <u>not expect to receive information</u> from the listener.	SUGGESTION **A: Why don't** you **visit** Jill in Hong Kong? **B:** That's a good idea. INFORMATION QUESTION **A: Why don't** you **eat** meat? **B:** Because I'm a vegetarian.
2. *Let's* always <u>includes the speaker</u>. It means: *Here's a suggestion for you and me.*	■ **Let's go** to Hong Kong. *(I suggest that we go to Hong Kong.)*
3. Note the **different forms** to use with these expressions.	BASE FORM OF THE VERB ■ **Let's** *take* the train. ■ **Maybe** we **could** *take* the train. ■ **Why don't** we *take* the train? ■ **Why not** *take* the train? GERUND OR NOUN ■ **How about** *taking* the train? ■ **How about** *the train*?
4. Notice the **punctuation** at the end of each kind of suggestion.	STATEMENTS ■ **Let's** stay at a hostel. ■ **Maybe** we **could** stay at a hostel. QUESTIONS ■ **Why don't** we stay at a hostel? ■ **Why not** stay at a hostel? ■ **How about** staying at a hostel? ■ **How about** a hostel?

IDENTIFY • *Emily and Megan are visiting Hong Kong. Read their conversation. Underline all the suggestions.*

EMILY: <u>Why don't we go to the races?</u> I hear they're really exciting.

MEGAN: I'd like to, but I need to go shopping.

EMILY: Then let's go to the Temple Street Market tonight. We might even see some Chinese opera in the street while we're there.

MEGAN: That sounds like fun. If we do that, why not go to the races this afternoon?

EMILY: OK, but let's get something to eat first in one of those floating restaurants.

MEGAN: I don't think we'll have time. Maybe we could do that tomorrow. Right now, how about getting *dim sum* at the Kau Kee Restaurant next door? Then we could take the Star Ferry to Hong Kong Island and the racecourse.

EMILY: Sounds good. Here's an idea for tomorrow. Why not take one of those small boats—*kaido*—to Lantau Island? When we come back, we could have dinner at the Jumbo Palace.

MEGAN: Let's do that. It's a little expensive, but at least it floats!

 COMPLETE • *Read these conversations. Complete them with the appropriate expression in parentheses.*

1. **A:** I feel like having seafood for dinner, but we went to Tai Pak for seafood last night.

   B: _____ Why not _____ go again? The food's great, and so is the view.
   (Why not / Let's not)

2. **A:** I'm really tired. _____ resting before we go out?
   (Let's / How about)

   B: That's a good idea. I'm tired too.

3. **A:** I want to explore downtown Hong Kong.

   B: _____ take a minibus? We'll see a lot more that way.
   (Let's not / Why don't we)

4. **A:** A group of foreign students just checked in at the hostel.

   B: _____ ask them to join us for dinner.
   (How about / Maybe we could)

5. **A:** I still need to buy some souvenirs before we leave.

   B: _____ go shopping after dinner.
   (Let's / How about)

6. **A:** I don't want to go home tomorrow. I'm having a really good time here.

   B: So am I. _____ leave tomorrow.
   (Let's not / Why not)

3 **CHOOSE & COMPLETE** • *Read these conversations. Complete the suggestions with phrases from the box. Add pronouns and change the verbs as necessary. Punctuate correctly.*

take a trip together	try that new seafood place	~~buy tickets~~
go to the beach	buy another one	

1. **A:** There's an Oasis concert at the Hong Kong Convention Centre next weekend.

   B: We're near there now. Maybe ___we could buy tickets.___

2. **A:** It's going to be hot tomorrow.

   B: I know. How about _____

3. **A:** Sweaters are on sale. Maybe we could buy one for Brian's birthday.

   B: We got him a sweater last year. Let's not _____

4. **A:** I don't know what to do on spring vacation. I'm sick of staying in the dorm.

   B: Me too. Why don't _____

5. **A:** I'm hungry.

   B: Let's _____

4 **EDIT** • *Read these notes. Find and correct seven mistakes in the use of suggestions. The first one is already corrected. Don't forget to check punctuation.*

3:00

Emily

I'm going shopping. I'll be back at

5:00. Let's ~~eating~~ eat at 7:00. OK?

Megan

Megan   *4:00*

7:00 for dinner is fine.

How about go to a movie afterward.

See you later.

E.

Emily   *5:00*

I'm going to be too tired for a movie.

Maybe we could just hanging around

the hostel after dinner. Let's talk

about it later. I'm taking a nap.

M.

M—   *6:00*

Let's not eat at the same restaurant

tonight? Why don't we trying a new

place? How about Broadway Seafood.

I'll meet you downstairs at 7:00.

E.

UNIT 32

Preferences:
*Prefer, Would prefer,
Would rather*

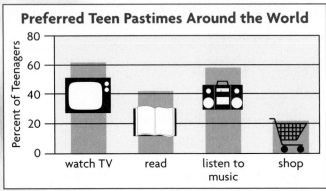

Preferred Teen Pastimes Around the World

Teenagers around the world **prefer watching** TV to all other leisure-time activities.

CHECK POINT

Check the main point of the bar graph.

☐ Teenagers like to watch TV, read books, and listen to music.

☐ Teenagers like to watch TV better than they like to do other things.

CHART CHECK 1

Check the correct answer.

Which word(s) can you use with all subjects?

☐ **prefer**

☐ **would prefer ('d prefer)**

STATEMENTS: *PREFER/WOULD PREFER*		
SUBJECT	**(WOULD) PREFER**	**NOUN/GERUND/INFINITIVE**
I/We/You*/They	**prefer**	**newspapers** (to magazines). **reading** newspapers (to reading books). **(not) to read** newspapers.
He/She	**prefers**	
I/He/She/We/You/They	**would prefer 'd prefer**	

You is both singular and plural.

CHART CHECK 2

Check the correct answer.

Which two forms of the verb can follow **prefer**?

☐ the base form or the gerund

☐ the gerund or the infinitive

YES/NO QUESTIONS: *PREFER/WOULD PREFER*			
DO/WOULD	**SUBJECT**	**PREFER**	**NOUN/GERUND/INFINITIVE**
Do	you/they	**prefer**	**newspapers**? **reading** newspapers? **to read** newspapers?
Does	he/she		
Would	you/they/he/she		

SHORT ANSWERS					
AFFIRMATIVE			**NEGATIVE**		
Yes,	I/we/they	**do.**	**No,**	I/we/they	**don't.**
	he/she	**does.**		he/she	**doesn't.**
	I/we/they/he/she	**would.**		I/we/they/he/she	**wouldn't.**

STATEMENTS: *WOULD RATHER*		
SUBJECT	**WOULD RATHER**	**BASE FORM OF VERB**
I/He/She/We/You/They	**would rather** **'d rather**	**read** newspapers (than read magazines). **(not) read** newspapers.

YES/NO QUESTIONS: *WOULD RATHER*			
WOULD	**SUBJECT**	**RATHER**	**BASE FORM**
Would	she	**rather**	**read?**

SHORT ANSWERS	
AFFIRMATIVE	**NEGATIVE**
Yes, she **would**.	**No**, she **wouldn't**. She**'d rather not**.

EXPRESS CHECK

Circle the correct words to complete this sentence.

I'd rather <u>read / to read</u> <u>than / to</u> shop, but Jo prefers <u>shop / shopping</u>.

Grammar Explanations	**Examples**
1. Use *prefer*, *would prefer*, and *would rather* to talk about <u>things that you like better</u> than other things.	■ We usually **prefer** *Italian food*. ■ I**'d prefer** *to have* Chinese food tonight. ■ I**'d rather** *cook* at home.
USAGE NOTE: We often use *prefer* for a <u>general</u> preference and *would prefer* or *would rather* for a preference in a <u>particular</u> situation.	■ Which **do** you **prefer**—chicken or shrimp? ■ **Would** you **prefer** chicken or shrimp tonight?

2. *Prefer* and *would prefer* may be followed by a <u>noun</u>, a <u>gerund</u>, or an <u>infinitive</u>.	■ I usually **prefer** the *newspaper*. `noun` ■ **Does** Bill **prefer** *reading* magazines? `gerund` ■ He**'d prefer** *to watch* TV. `infinitive`
Would rather can be followed by only the <u>base form of the verb</u>.	■ I**'d rather** *stay* home tonight. `base form`
USAGE NOTE: We often use *I'd rather not*, by itself, <u>to refuse</u> an offer, suggestion, or invitation.	**A:** Would you like to have some dessert? **B:** I**'d rather not**. I've had enough to eat.
▶ **BE CAREFUL!** The negative of *I'd rather* is *I'd rather not*.	■ I**'d rather not** have dessert. NOT ~~I wouldn't rather have dessert.~~

3. A **comparison with** *to* may follow *prefer/would prefer* + noun.	■ Lani **prefers** comedies *to* action movies. `noun` `noun`
A **comparison with** *to* may also follow *prefer/would prefer* + gerund.	■ I**'d prefer** visiting Lani *to* going to the party. `gerund` `gerund`
A **comparison with** *than* may follow *would rather* + base form of the verb.	■ I**'d rather** watch football *than* play it. `base form` `base form`

1 **TRUE OR FALSE** • *Julio ranked some activities from 1 to 8 according to his preferences (1 = his favorite). Look at his list. Then read each numbered sentence and write T (True) or F (False).*

Preferred Activities

___3___ listen to music

___5___ go swimming

___4___ go biking

___1___ watch TV

___8___ bake pies

___6___ play guitar

___7___ hike

___2___ read

___T___ **1.** He prefers listening to music to playing guitar.

_____ **2.** He'd rather hike than go swimming.

_____ **3.** He prefers swimming to biking.

_____ **4.** He'd rather not watch TV.

_____ **5.** He prefers baking pies to reading.

_____ **6.** He prefers watching TV to reading.

_____ **7.** He'd probably prefer a concert to a hike in the woods.

2 **CHOOSE & COMPLETE** • *Julio and Ana are discussing their evening plans. Complete their conversation. Use **would rather (not)** with one of the verbs in the box or by itself in short answers.*

have	cook	see	~~stay~~	go

ANA: Would you like to go to a movie tonight?

JULIO: _____**I'd rather stay**_____ home and watch TV.
                              1.

ANA: Sounds good. Maybe we could make dinner later.

JULIO: _____ tonight. I'm too tired.
                    2.

ANA: OK. _____ you _____ to
                                                              3.

a restaurant instead?

JULIO: Let's order out for some pizza.

ANA: How about a pepperoni pizza?

JULIO: _____. Pepperoni gives me heartburn.
                    4.

_____ mushrooms than pepperoni if that's OK.
        5.

ANA: No problem. Do you want to watch the Stephen King thriller at 8:00?

JULIO: _____. I don't like his movies.
                    6.

ANA: Well . . . there's a comedy on at 8:00 and a documentary at 8:30.

JULIO: _____ the comedy. I need a laugh.
                    7.

3 **COMPLETE •** *Read these conversations. Complete them with* **prefer**, **would prefer**, *or* **would rather**. *Use* **prefer** *to state general preferences. Complete the comparisons with* **to** *or* **than**.

1. **A:** We're going to Rome again next week. _____Would_____ you

   _____prefer_____ taking the train _____to_____ flying this time?

   B: You know me. I always _____ the plane _____ the train.

2. **A:** I _____ have the aisle seat _____ the window seat.

   B: That's fine with me. I _____ the window seat. That way I can look out.

3. **A:** Where would you like to stay? In a hotel or a *pensione*?

   B: Oh, I _____ to stay in a *pensione* this time. It's more personal.

4. **A:** I _____ eating in small *trattorias* _____ eating in

   big restaurants.

   B: Me too. They're less expensive and the food is always delicious.

5. **A:** Speaking of food, you make the best spaghetti with clam sauce in the world.

   B: Thanks, but I _____ order it in a restaurant _____

   make it at home!

6. **A:** When in Rome, _____ you _____ drinking tea or coffee?

   B: I definitely _____ coffee _____ tea. You know what

   they say, "When in Rome do as the Romans do!"

 4 **EDIT •** *Read Ana's report. Find and correct six mistakes in the use of* **prefer** *and* **would rather**. *The first mistake is already corrected.*

> For my study, I interviewed fifty men and women. There was no difference
> in men's and women's preferences for TV. I found that everyone prefers
> watching TV ~~than~~ to going to movies. Men and women both enjoy news programs
> and entertainment specials. However, men would rather watching adventure
> programs and science fiction, while women prefer soap operas. Men also like to
> watch all kinds of sports, but women would rather see game shows to sports.
> Reading preferences differ too. Men prefer to reading newspapers, while women
> would rather read magazines and books. When men read books, they prefer read
> nonfiction and adventure stories. Women are preferring novels.

SelfTest

Circle the letter of the correct answer to complete each sentence.

> **EXAMPLE:**
> Jennifer never _____ coffee.   **A (B) C D**
> (A) drink   (C) is drinking
> (B) drinks   (D) was drinking

1. —Would you shut the door, please?   **A B C D**
   —_____
   (A) Certainly.   (C) Yes, I could.
   (B) No, I can't.   (D) Yes, I would.

2. Why _____ a movie tonight?   **A B C D**
   (A) about seeing   (C) not seeing
   (B) don't we see   (D) we don't see

3. Marcia can't speak German yet, but after a few lessons   **A B C D**
   she _____ speak a little.
   (A) can   (C) is able to
   (B) could   (D) will be able to

4. In 1998, Tara Lipinski _____ win the gold medal in   **A B C D**
   figure skating at the Winter Olympics.
   (A) can   (C) will be able to
   (B) could   (D) was able to

5. I _____ make new friends since I moved here.   **A B C D**
   (A) can't   (C) haven't been able to
   (B) couldn't   (D) 'm not able to

6. She _____ better not arrive late.   **A B C D**
   (A) did   (C) 'd
   (B) has   (D) would

7. —Do you mind if I borrow a chair?   **A B C D**
   —_____ Do you need only one?
   (A) I'm sorry.   (C) Yes, I do.
   (B) Not at all.   (D) Yes, I would.

8. Would you mind _____ me tomorrow?   **A B C D**
   (A) call   (C) to call
   (B) calling   (D) if you call

9. I'd rather _____ the movie. I hear it's very good.   **A B C D**
   (A) watch   (C) watching
   (B) to watch   (D) not watch

10. You _____ miss the deadline or you'll have to pay a fee.   **A B C D**
(A) better not   (C) 'd better not
(B) 'd better   (D) had no better

11. _____ take the train instead of the bus? It's faster.   **A B C D**
(A) How about   (C) Why don't
(B) Let's   (D) Why not

12. May my sister _____ to class with me tomorrow?   **A B C D**
(A) come   (C) coming
(B) comes   (D) to come

13. I _____ have dessert. I'm trying to lose some weight.   **A B C D**
(A) 'd rather   (C) 'd prefer
(B) 'd rather not   (D) 'd prefer not

14. Jamie prefers working at home _____ working in an office.   **A B C D**
(A) more   (C) that
(B) than   (D) to

SECTION TWO

Each sentence has four underlined words or phrases. The four underlined parts of the sentence are marked A, B, C, and D. Circle the letter of the one underlined word or phrase that is NOT CORRECT.

> **EXAMPLE:**
> Mike <u>usually</u> <u>drives</u> to school, but <u>today</u> he <u>walks</u>.   **A B C Ⓓ**
>   A   B   C   D

15. <u>When</u> I was ten, I <u>could</u> swim, but I <u>wasn't</u> <u>able dive</u>.   **A B C D**
   A   B   C   D

16. Why <u>don't</u> we <u>have</u> dinner and then <u>go</u> see *Possible Dreams*<u>.</u>   **A B C D**
      A   B   C   D

17. You <u>drove</u> for seven hours today, so <u>maybe</u> you'd <u>not better</u> <u>drive</u> tonight.   **A B C D**
    A   B   C   D

18. <u>Will</u> you mind <u>bringing</u> your camera to the graduation party <u>tomorrow</u><u>?</u>   **A B C D**
   A   B   C D

19. Dad, <u>may</u> Jim <u>borrows</u> the car tomorrow or <u>does</u> Mom <u>need</u> it?   **A B C D**
       A   B   C   D

20. I <u>can't</u> <u>help</u> you, so <u>maybe</u> you should <u>to ask</u> Marta.   **A B C D**
     A   B   C   D

21. <u>Should</u> I <u>bring</u> flowers to Lisa's or <u>should</u> I <u>giving</u> her candy?   **A B C D**
   A   B   C   D

22. <u>Maybe</u> you <u>ought</u> <u>than</u> just <u>bring</u> flowers.   **A B C D**
   A   B   C   D

23. Silva <u>celebrated</u> <u>last year</u> because she <u>could</u> <u>win</u> the race.   **A B C D**
       A   B   C D

24. <u>It's</u> really late, so <u>let's</u> <u>we</u> <u>go</u> out to dinner tonight.   **A B C D**
   A   B C D

25. Why <u>would</u> you <u>rather</u> <u>stay</u> home <u>to</u> go out tonight?   **A B C D**
     A   B   C   D

Necessity:
Have (got) to and Must

CHECK **POINT**

Check the correct answer.

Using a seat belt is:

☐ a requirement

☐ a choice

You **must buckle** your seat belt. It's the law.

CHART CHECK 1

Circle T (True) or F (False).

T F We use **have got to** in affirmative and negative statements.

AFFIRMATIVE STATEMENTS: *HAVE (GOT) TO*

SUBJECT	*HAVE TO/ HAVE GOT TO*	*BASE FORM OF VERB*
I/We/You/They	**have (got) to**	**stop.**
He/She/It	**has (got) to**	

CONTRACTIONS

Have got to = **'ve got to**

Has got to = **'s got to**

NEGATIVE STATEMENTS: *HAVE TO*

SUBJECT	*DO NOT*	*HAVE TO*	*BASE FORM*
I/We/You/They	**don't**	**have to**	**stop.**
He/She/It	**doesn't**		

CHART CHECK 2

Check the correct answer.

In questions with **have to**, what comes before the subject?

☐ a form of **do**

☐ a form of **have to**

YES/NO QUESTIONS: *HAVE TO*

Do	SUBJECT	*HAVE TO*	*BASE FORM*
Do	we	**have to**	**stop?**
Does	he		

SHORT ANSWERS

AFFIRMATIVE			NEGATIVE		
Yes,	you	**do.**	**No,**	you	**don't.**
	he	**does.**		he	**doesn't.**

STATEMENTS: *MUST*

SUBJECT	*MUST* (*NOT*)	*BASE FORM*
I/He/She/It/We/You/They	**must (not)**	**stop.**

CONTRACTION

must not = **mustn't**

Must is a modal. It does not have -s in the third person singular.

EXPRESS CHECK

Complete this conversation. Use <u>one word</u> for each blank.

A: Why _____ she _____ _____ wear her seat belt?

B: It's the law. Everyone _____ wear a seat belt.

Grammar Explanations	Examples
1. Use *have to*, *have got to*, and *must* to express <u>necessity</u>.	
a. *Have to* is the most common expression in <u>everyday use</u>.	■ Everyone **has to pass** a road test before getting a driver's license.
b. *Have got to* often expresses strong feelings in <u>speaking</u> and <u>informal writing</u>.	■ He**'s got to drive** more slowly. I'm afraid he's going to have an accident.
c. *Must* is used in <u>writing</u> (forms, signs, notices).	■ You **must stop** completely at a stop sign.
Must is used in <u>spoken English</u>, when	
• the speaker is in a position of <u>power</u>.	■ Ling-ling, you **must clean** your room. *(mother talking to her young child)*
• there is <u>urgent necessity</u>.	■ You really **must talk** to your boss about a raise. *(friend talking to a friend)*
▶ **BE CAREFUL!** *Don't have to* and *must not* have <u>very different meanings</u>. *(See Unit 34.)*	■ You **don't have to stop** here. *(It isn't necessary to stop here.)* ■ You **must not stop** here. *(You can't stop here. It's not allowed.)*
2. Use the correct form of *have to* for <u>all tenses and forms</u>.	■ After his accident, Sal **had to take** a driver's improvement class. *(past tense)* ■ Sheila **has had to drive** to work for two years. *(present perfect)* ■ I**'ll have to drive** tomorrow. *(future)*
Use *have got to* and *must* only for the <u>present</u> or the <u>future</u>.	■ I**'ve got to wear** glasses all the time. ■ Everyone **must take** an eye test tomorrow.
3. Use *have to* for most <u>questions</u>. (We rarely use *have got to* or *must* for questions.)	■ **Does** Paul **have to drive**? ■ When **will** he **have to leave**?

PRONUNCIATION NOTE

In informal speech, *have to* is often pronounced "hafta" and *got to* is often pronounced "gotta." Do not write *hafta* or *gotta*.

1 **IDENTIFY** • *Read Ben Leonard's telephone conversation with a clerk from the California Department of Motor Vehicles (DMV). Underline the words that talk about necessity.*

DMV: Department of Motor Vehicles. May I help you?

BEN: I'm moving to California soon. <u>Will I have to get</u> a California license when I move?

DMV: Yes, you will. California residents <u>must have</u> a California driver's license.

BEN: When will <u>I have to get</u> my California license?

DMV: You <u>have to replace</u> your old license ten days after you become a resident. So come in and apply for your California license right after you get here.

BEN: Do <u>I have to take</u> any tests to exchange my Illinois license for a California license?

DMV: Since you already <u>have</u> an Illinois license, you won't <u>have to take</u> the road test. But you will <u>have to take</u> the written test.

BEN: How about the eye test?

DMV: Oh, everyone <u>has got to</u> take the eye test.

BEN: OK. Thanks a lot. <u>You've been</u> very helpful.

2 **COMPLETE** • *Read this conversation. Complete it with the correct form of **have to** or **have got to** and the verbs in parentheses. Use **have got to** and give short answers whenever possible.*

BEN: When _____ *do* _____ you _____ *have to use* _____ the car?
         1. (use)

ANN: I 've *to pick up* _____ Jim's school records pretty soon. Why?
      2. (pick up)

_____ you still _____ *change* _____ the oil?
          3. (change)

BEN: No, _____ . I did it early this morning. Oh, and
      4.

I bought some film.

ANN: Oh, you *didn't have to do* that. I bought three rolls yesterday.
      5. (not do)

BEN: We *have to take* lots of pictures on the trip.
      6. (take)

_____ Jim still _____ *have to pack* _____?
          7. (pack)

ANN: No, *he doesn't* . He finished and went to Sara's to say
      8.

goodbye. Why?

BEN: He *have to help* me clean out the car. It's full of his stuff.
      9. (help)

ANN: I'll call him again. It's hard for him to leave his friends.

I *have had to call* him to come home twice already.
      10. (call)

3 **CHOOSE & COMPLETE** • *Look at these signs. Use the verbs from the box to complete the sentences about things you* **must** *do and* **must not** *do.*

| turn | drive | ride | walk |

1. You _____*must not turn*_____ left.

2. You _____*must turn*_____ right.

3. You _____*must drive*_____ over 40 mph.

4. You _____*must not drive*_____ 60 mph.

5. Bicyclists _____*must ride*_____ on the right.

6. Pedestrians _____*must not walk*_____ on the right.

4 **EDIT** • *Read Jim's letter to Sara. Find and correct seven mistakes in expressing necessity. The first mistake is already corrected.*

> Dear Sara,
>
> How are you doing? We've been here about six weeks. It's strange living in the suburbs.
>
> There's no public transportation, so you've ~~get~~ *got* to drive everywhere. I had to signs up for driver's ed this semester so I can get my license by summertime. It's the law here that everyone musts wear a seat belt. I used to hate to buckle up, but with the traffic here, I have changed my mind. There are a lot of freeways, and you've gotta know how to change lanes with a lot of fast traffic. Even my Mom have had to get used to it. Dad works at home, so he hasn't has to do a lot of driving.
>
> Have you beaten those computer games yet? I'm having a lot of trouble with "Doom." You got to write to me and tell me how to get past the fifth level!
>
> Jim

UNIT 34

Choice: *Don't have to*
No Choice: *Must not*
and *Can't*

> No, we **don't have to stop** and **ask** for directions!

DRIVERS **MUST NOT PARK** IN THE CROSSWALK

CHECK *POINT*

Check the correct answer.

The driver can choose to

❏ park in the crosswalk.   ❏ stop to ask for directions.

CHART CHECK 1

Check the correct answer.

Which part of *do not have to* changes for different subjects?

❏ *do*   ❏ *have*

DON'T HAVE TO				
SUBJECT	DO NOT	HAVE TO	BASE FORM OF VERB	
I/We/You/They	don't	have to	stop	here.
He/She/It	doesn't		park	

CHART CHECK 2

Circle T (True) or F (False).

T F   The form of *must not* and *can't* changes for different subjects.

MUST NOT			
SUBJECT	MUST* NOT	BASE FORM	
I/He/She/It/We/You/They	must not	stop	here.

CAN'T			
SUBJECT	CAN'T*	BASE FORM	
I/He/She/It/We/You/They	can't	stop	here.

*These words are modals. They do not have *-s* in the third person singular.

146

EXPRESS CHECK

Unscramble these words to form two sentences.

stop • He • have • here • to • doesn't

_____

must • fast • You • not • drive • too

_____

Grammar Explanations	**Examples**
1. *Have to* and *must* have similar meanings. They both express the idea that something is <u>necessary or required</u>.	■ You **have to stop** at the stop sign. ■ You **must stop** at the stop sign.
Don't/Doesn't have to and *must not* have <u>very different meanings</u>.	
a. *Don't/Doesn't have to* expresses that something is <u>not necessary</u>. It means that there is another possibility. There is a **choice**.	■ You **don't have to drive**. I can do it. ■ He **doesn't have to turn** here. He can turn at the next intersection.
b. *Must not* expresses **prohibition**. It means that something is <u>not allowed</u> or is <u>against the law</u>. There is **no choice**.	■ You **must not use** the car without my permission. ■ You **must not drive** without a license. It's against the law.
2. *Must not* is used to express <u>prohibition in writing</u>, including official forms, signs, and notices.	■ You **must not use** your horn unnecessarily.
USAGE NOTE: In <u>spoken English</u>, we do not usually use *must not* when talking to or about another <u>adult</u>. We use *can't* instead.	■ We **can't park** here. It's a tow-away zone.
Sometimes people use *must not* to tell a <u>child</u> that there is no choice in a situation.	■ Jesse, you **mustn't take off** your seat belt while the car is moving.
3. You can use *not have to* for <u>all tenses and forms</u>.	■ You **don't have to drive**. *(present)* ■ She **won't have to renew** her license next year. *(future)* ■ We **haven't had to pay** a lot of parking fines this year. *(present perfect)* ■ They **didn't have to take** driver's education last year. Now it's required. *(simple past tense)*
Must not refers only to the <u>present</u> or the <u>future</u>.	■ Drivers **must not pass** on the right.

1 **IDENTIFY •** *Read this article. Underline the words that show that there is a choice about doing something. Circle the words that show that there is no choice.*

A New Alternative to Car Ownership

New drivers are usually excited about their new freedom: "My mom <u>doesn't have to drive</u> me everywhere anymore! I don't have to ask my friends for rides to school!" When you don't have your own car yet, any price seems worth paying. But once you buy a car, you (can't forget) your car payments and insurance premiums, or you won't be a driver for very long. You can't leave gas and maintenance out of the budget either. Car sharing offers an alternative to these problems, however. Members of car-sharing groups have a car when they need one for either short trips or vacations, but they don't have the high expenses of ownership. They pay very little to use a shared car, and they don't have to worry about maintaining the car or paying the insurance. Fees for short trips are only about $3.00 an hour plus $0.50 per mile. Groups do not have strict requirements either. Members must not have bad driving records or poor credit, and they must not return the cars in poor shape or they will pay extra.

2 **COMPLETE •** *Read this conversation. Complete it with* **can't** *or the correct form of* **not have to** *and the verb in parentheses.*

JIM: Austin _____doesn't have to sit_____ in a safety seat, but I do. It's not fair.
    1. (sit)

ANN: Jim, you really _____ like that in the car. Your father has
            2. (yell)

to concentrate on driving. Ben, turn left for the restaurant.

BEN: I _____ left. It's a one-way street. I'll go around the block.
        3. (turn)

ANN: There's the restaurant. Uh-oh. You _____ here. It's a bus stop.
                                    4. (park)

BEN: Maybe I'll park in that indoor garage. That way we _____
                                                    5. (worry)

about our stuff while we're eating. Remind me to buy gas after lunch.

ANN: We _____ gas, do we? The tank is still half full.
        6. (get)

BEN: I know. But we _____ gas for a long time. I'm not sure the
                    7. (buy)

gauge is working.

AUSTIN: You _____ that truck into the restaurant, Jim! It's too big.
                8. (bring)

JIM: Mom said OK. Anyway, I _____ to you. Let's eat!
                            9. (listen)

READ & COMPLETE • *Look at this sign at the Holiday Motel swimming pool. Complete each sentence with* **must not** *or* **don't have to** *and the correct form of the verb in parentheses.*

 Holiday Motel
Swimming Pool Rules and Regulations

Pool Hours 10:00 A.M.–10:00 P.M.

Children under 12 years NOT ALLOWED in pool without an adult.

Towels available at front desk.

NO
• ball playing
• radios
• diving
• glass bottles
• alcoholic beverages

---

1. Children under age 12 _____ must not swim _____ without an adult.
   (swim)

2. You _____ your own towel.
   (bring)

3. You _____ ball in or around the pool.
   (play)

4. You _____ into the pool.
   (dive)

5. Teenagers _____ with an adult.
   (be)

6. You _____ the pool at 8:00 P.M.
   (leave)

EDIT • *Read Austin's postcard to his friend. Find and correct five mistakes in expressing necessity. The first mistake is already corrected.*

Holiday Motel, Rte. 55

Hi, Janet!

We got to the motel late this evening because we got lost. But we were lucky—they kept our room so we ~~must not~~ **didn't have to** find another motel. Jimmy is really happy because he don't have to go to bed until after 10:00, when the swimming pool closes. We mustn't leave until 11:00 tomorrow (checkout time), so we can stay up later. Yosemite is only four hours away, so we won't had to drive the whole day tomorrow. It's going to be exciting. My parents say we absolutely must not to go out by ourselves because there are bears there. I'd love to see a bear (from the inside of the car). I'll send a postcard of one.   Austin

To: Janet Edwards

5500 Amherst Lane

Erie, PA 16506

Expectations:
Be supposed to

Oh no! **I was supposed to prepare** a speech!

He'd better hurry up with these pictures. **It's supposed to rain.**

Thank goodness **I'm not supposed to pay** for this photographer.

best man   bride's parents   maid of honor   bride   groom   groom's parents

CHECK *POINT*

Check the correct answers.

The groom's father is thinking about

❑ something he forgot to do.

❑ the usual way something is done at a wedding.

CHART CHECK

Circle T (True) or F (False).

T F You can use ***be supposed to*** in the simple present and simple past tenses.

STATEMENTS				
SUBJECT	**BE**	**(NOT) SUPPOSED TO**	**BASE FORM OF VERB**	
I	am was	(not) supposed to	stand be	here.
He/She/It	is was			
We/You*/They	are were			

*You is both singular and plural.

YES/NO QUESTIONS				
BE	**SUBJECT**	**SUPPOSED TO**	**BASE FORM**	
Am Was	I	supposed to	stand	here?
Is Was	he			
Are Were	you			

SHORT ANSWERS					
AFFIRMATIVE			**NEGATIVE**		
Yes,	you	are. were.	**No,**	you	aren't. weren't.
	he	is. was.		he	isn't. wasn't.
	I	am. was.		I	'm not. wasn't.

EXPRESS CHECK

Complete these sentences.

A: What _____ we supposed to wear yesterday?

B: Our suits. It _____ supposed to be a dress rehearsal.

A: Oops.

Grammar Explanations	Examples
1. Use *be supposed to* to talk about different kinds of <u>expectations</u>:	
a. rules and **usual ways** of doing things	■ The groom **is supposed to arrive** at the ceremony early. It's a custom.
b. predictions	■ It**'s not supposed to rain** tomorrow. I heard it on the radio.
c. hearsay (what everyone says)	■ The beach **is supposed to be** beautiful in August. Everyone says so.
d. plans or **arrangements**	■ The ceremony **isn't supposed to begin** yet.
2. Use *be supposed to* only in the **simple present** tense or in the **simple past** tense. Use the **simple present** tense to refer to both the <u>present</u> and the <u>future</u>. **USAGE NOTE:** The **simple past** tense often suggests that <u>something did not happen</u>.	■ The bride **is supposed to wear** white. ■ The ceremony **was supposed to begin** at 7:00. ■ It **wasn't supposed to rain**. ■ I**'m supposed to be** at the wedding rehearsal *tomorrow*. NOT ~~I will be supposed to be there tomorrow.~~ ■ Carl **was supposed to bring** flowers, *but* he forgot.

IDENTIFY • *Read this article and underline the phrases that express expectations.*

IT WASN'T SUPPOSED TO BE A BIG WEDDING

PROVIDENCE, JULY 19—The Stricklands wanted a quiet wedding—that's why they eloped to Block Island, off the Atlantic Coast of the United States. The island is quite small, so the Stricklands packed their bikes for the ferry trip. The weather was supposed to be lovely, and they had asked the mayor to marry them on a hill overlooking the ocean.

"When we got there, we found a crowd of cyclists admiring the view," laughed Beth.

When Bill kissed his bride, the audience burst into loud applause and rang their bicycle bells. "We weren't supposed to have fifty wedding guests, but we love cycling, and we're not sorry," Bill said.

While packing the next day, Beth left her wedding bouquet at the hotel. Minutes before the ferry was supposed to leave, Bill jumped on his bike, got the flowers, and made it back to the ferry on time. "Cyclists are supposed to stay fast and fit," he said.

TRUE OR FALSE • *Read the article again. Write T (True) or F (False) for each sentence.*

__F__ **1.** The Stricklands planned a big wedding.

_____ **2.** The weather forecaster predicted rain.

_____ **3.** The Stricklands invited fifty wedding guests.

_____ **4.** The ferry followed a schedule.

_____ **5.** People think that cyclists are in good shape.

COMPLETE • *Read these conversations. Complete them with a form of **be supposed to** and the verb in parentheses. Give short answers. Choose affirmative or negative.*

1. A: Netta, Gary called while you were out.

   B: _____Am_____ I _____supposed to call_____ him back?
                                            a. (call)

   A: _____No, you aren't_____. He'll call you this afternoon.
                     b.

2. A: The dress store called too. They delivered your wedding dress to your office.

   _____ they _____ that?
                                  a. (do)

   B: _____! That's why I stayed home today. They
               b.

   _____ it here.
         c. (deliver)

3. A: Let's get in line. The rehearsal _____ in a few minutes.
                             a. (start)

   B: We're bridesmaids. Where _____ we _____?
                                                   b. (stand)

4. A: Gary! You _____ here!
                                    a. (be)

  B: Why not?

  A: You _____ Netta until the ceremony. It's bad luck.
                          b. (see)

5. A: Sophie, could I borrow your handkerchief, please? I _____
                                                      a. (wear)

    something old, something new, something borrowed, and something blue. I don't

    have anything borrowed.

  B: It _____ today. Maybe I should lend you my
                    b. (rain)

    umbrella instead.

6. A: I hear Gary and Netta are going to Aruba on their honeymoon.

  B: Oh, that _____ a really nice island.
                        a. (be)

EDIT • Read Sophie's letter to a friend. Find and correct six mistakes in the use of be supposed to. The first mistake is already corrected.

Dear Kasha,

                             was

    I'm so sorry—I know I ~~am~~ supposed to write to you last week about my plans

to visit. I've been awfully busy. My friend Netta is getting married soon, and she's

asked me to be her maid of honor. She and Gary want a big wedding. They're

supposed to have about two hundred guests. I have a lot of responsibilities. I will be

supposed to give Netta a shower before the wedding (that's a party where everyone

brings presents for the bride). I am also suppose to help her choose the bridesmaids'

dresses. The best man's name is Jim. He'll help Gary get ready. I haven't met him

yet, but he's supposes to be very nice.

    I'd better say goodbye now. I supposed to leave for rehearsal five minutes ago.

                                       Love,

                                       Sophie

P.S. About my visit—I'm supposing to get some time off in July. Would that

    be convenient?

Future Possibility:
May, Might, Could

EUROPE'S WEATHER

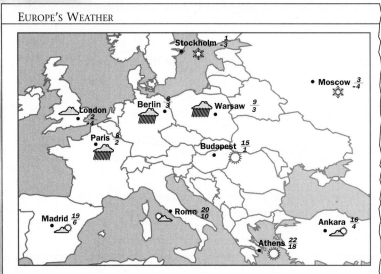

Temperatures in London **may drop** as much as eleven degrees by tomorrow morning. We **might** even **see** some snow flurries later on in the day. Winds **could reach** 40 mph.

CHECK *POINT*

Circle T (True) or F (False).

T F It's definitely going to snow in London tomorrow.

CHART CHECK 1

Circle T (True) or F (False).

T F *May*, *might*, and *could* have only one form for all subjects.

STATEMENTS

SUBJECT	MAY/MIGHT/COULD*	BASE FORM OF VERB	
I/He/She/It/We/You/They	may (not) might (not) could (not)	get	cold.

*These words are modals. They do not have -s in the third person singular.

CHART CHECK 2

Check the correct answer.

When do you use *may*, *might*, or *could* for future possibility?

☐ in questions
☐ in answers

YES/NO QUESTIONS

Are you going to fly to Paris?
Are you taking the train?

SHORT ANSWERS

I/We	may (not). might (not). could(n't).

WH- QUESTIONS

When are you **going** to Paris?

How long will you **be** there?

ANSWERS

| I/We | may <br> might <br> could | go | tomorrow. |
| | | be | there a week. |

EXPRESS CHECK

Complete this conversation with **might** *or* **might not**.

A: Are you going home after class?

B: I _____ . It's very possible. Why?

A: I _____ call you about the homework assignment. I don't understand it.

B: Maybe you should call Jean instead. I _____ understand it either.

Grammar Explanations	Examples
1. Use *may*, *might*, and *could* to talk about <u>future possibility</u>. ▶ **BE CAREFUL!** Notice the difference between *may be* and *maybe*. Both express possibility. *May be* is a <u>modal + verb</u>. It is always two words. *Maybe* is not a modal. It is an <u>adverb</u>. It is always one word, and it comes at the beginning of the sentence.	■ It **may be** windy later. ■ It **might get** cold. ■ It **could rain** tomorrow. ■ He **may be** late today. ■ **Maybe** he'll take the train. NOT <s>He'll maybe take the train.</s>
2. Use *may not* and *might not* to express the possibility that something <u>will not happen</u>. Use *couldn't* to say that something is <u>impossible</u>. ▶ **BE CAREFUL!** We usually <u>do not contract</u> *might not*, and we never contract *may not*.	■ There are a lot of clouds, but it **might not rain**. **A:** Why don't you ask John for a ride? **B:** I **couldn't do** that. He's too busy. ■ You **may not** need a coat. NOT <s>You mayn't need a coat.</s>
3. **Questions about possibility** usually are <u>not formed with *may, might,* or *could*</u>. Instead, they are formed with the future (*will, be going to,* the present progressive) or phrases such as *Do you think . . . ?* or *Is it possible that . . . ?* It's the **answers to these questions** that often have *may, might,* or *could*. In <u>short answers to *yes/no* questions</u>, use *may, might,* or *could* alone. **USAGE NOTE:** If a form of *be* is in the question, it is common to include *be* in the short answer.	**A:** When *will* it *start* snowing? **B:** It **might start** around lunch time. **A:** *Are* you *going to drive* to work? **B:** I **might take** the bus instead. **A:** When *are* you *leaving*? **B:** I **may leave** now. **A:** Will your office close early? **B:** It **might**. **A:** *Is* our train arriving late? **B:** It **might be**.

1 **IDENTIFY** • *Alice is a college student who works part time; Bill is her boyfriend. Read their conversation. Underline the words that express future possibility or impossibility.*

ALICE: I just heard that it <u>may snow</u> today. Are you going to drive to work?

BILL: No. I'll take the 7:30 train instead.

ALICE: I'll take the train with you. I have some work to do in the library.

BILL: Great. Why don't you cut your afternoon class and have lunch with me too?

ALICE: Oh, I couldn't do that. But let's meet at the train station at 6:00, OK?

BILL: I might have to work until 8:00 tonight. I'll call you and let you know.

ANSWER • *What will Alice and Bill do <u>together</u>? Check the appropriate box for each activity.*

	Certain	Possible	Impossible
1. Take the train at 7:30 A.M.	❐	❐	❐
2. Have lunch.	❐	❐	❐
3. Meet at the train station at 6:00 P.M.	❐	❐	❐

2 **COMPLETE** • *Alice is graduating from college with a degree in Early Childhood Education. Complete this paragraph from her diary. Choose the appropriate words in parentheses.*

I just got the notice from my school. I _____**'m going to**_____
                1. (might not / 'm going to)

graduate in June, but I still don't have any plans. Some day-care centers hire students

before they graduate, so I _____ apply for a job
         2. (could / couldn't)

now. Or I _____ apply to a graduate school and
      3. (might / might not)

get my master's degree. I'm just not sure though—these past two years have been

hard, and I _____ be ready to study for two more.
     4. (may / may not)

At least I <u>am</u> sure about my career: I _____
         5. ('m going to / might)

work with children. That's certain. I made an appointment to discuss my plans with my

teacher, Mrs. Humphrey, tomorrow. I _____ talk
       6. (maybe / may)

this over with her. She _____ have an idea about
      7. (won't / might)

what to do.

3 **DESCRIBE** • *Look at Alice's schedule for Monday. She put a question mark (?) next to each item she wasn't sure about. Write sentences about Alice's plans for Monday. Use* **may** *or* **might** *for things that are possible and* **be going to** *for things that are certain.*

MONDAY

call Bill at 9:00   go to work at 1:00

buy some notebooks before class ?   go shopping after work ?

go to meeting with Mrs. Humphrey at 11:00 take 7:00 train ?

have coffee with Sue after class ?   pick up pizza

---

1. Alice is going to call Bill at 9:00.

2. She may buy some notebooks before class.

3. _____

4. _____

5. _____

6. _____

7. _____

8. _____

4 **EDIT** • *Read this student's report about El Niño. Find and correct eight mistakes in expressing future possibility. The first mistake is already corrected.*

Every few years, the ocean near Peru becomes warmer. Called El Niño, this
variation in temperature ~~maybe~~ ^{may} cause weather changes all over the world.

The west coasts of North and South America might to have heavy rains. On

the other side of the Pacific, New Guinea might becomes very dry. Northern

areas could have warmer, wetter winters, and southern areas could become

much colder. These weather changes affect plants and animals. Some fish

mayn't survive in warmer waters. Droughts could causing crops to die, and

food may get very expensive. El Niño may happen every two years, or it

could not come for seven years. Will El Niños get worse in the future? They

could be. Pollution holds heat in the air, and it will increase the effects of

El Niño, but no one is sure yet.

UNIT 37

Assumptions:
May, Might, Could, Must, Have (got) to, Can't

Hhmm. You **must be** Gina Lemont.

Right again! This man **has got to be** a genius!

Gina Lemont

CHECK POINT

Check the correct answer.

The famous detective Sherlock Holmes is

❏ making a guess.

❏ talking about an obligation.

CHART CHECK 1

Circle T (True) or F (False).

T F The third-person singular modal does not end in -*s*.

STATEMENTS			
SUBJECT	**MODAL**	**BASE FORM OF VERB**	
I/He/She/It/We/You/They	may (not) might (not) could (not)	be	right.
	must (not) can't	work	there.

AFFIRMATIVE STATEMENTS: *HAVE (GOT) TO*			
SUBJECT	**HAVE (GOT) TO**	**BASE FORM**	
I/We/You/They	have (got) to	be	right.
He/She/It	has (got) to	work	there.

CHART CHECK 2

Circle T (True) or F (False).

T F All modals of assumptions are used in questions.

YES/NO QUESTIONS			
COULD	**SUBJECT**	**BASE FORM**	
Could	he	work	there?

NOTE: For contractions with *could not* and *cannot*, see Appendix 24 on page 346.

SHORT ANSWERS	
SUBJECT	**MODAL/** ***HAVE (GOT) TO***
He	must (not). may (not). might (not). could(n't). can't. has (got) to.

EXPRESS `CHECK`

Circle the correct words to complete this conversation.

A: I heard a sound coming from the basement. What <u>could / might</u> it be?

B: I'm not sure. It <u>can / might</u> be the cat. It <u>can / can't</u> be the dog. The dog's upstairs.

Grammar Explanations

Examples

1. We often make **assumptions**, or "best guesses," based on information we have about a present situation. The <u>modal</u> that we choose depends on <u>how certain</u> we are about our assumption.

100% certain

AFFIRMATIVE	NEGATIVE
must	**can't, couldn't**
have (got) to	**must not**
may	**may not**
might, could	**might not**

0% certain

2. When you are <u>almost 100 percent certain</u> that something is **possible**, use **must**, **have to**, or **have got to**.

USAGE NOTE: We use **have got to** in <u>informal</u> speech and writing, and we usually contract it.

When you are <u>less certain</u>, use **may**, **might**, or **could**.

Holmes is a brilliant detective.
ASSUMPTION
■ He **must solve** a lot of crimes.

■ He**'s got to be** a genius!

Watson knows a lot about medicine.
ASSUMPTION
■ He **might be** a doctor.

3. When you are <u>almost 100 percent certain</u> that something is **impossible**, use **can't** or **couldn't**.

When you are <u>slightly less certain</u>, use **must not**.

Use **may not** or **might not** when you are <u>less certain</u>.

▶ **BE CAREFUL!** *Have to* and *have got to* are not used to make negative assumptions.

■ He **can't be** dead! I think he's still breathing!

■ She **must not feel** well. She looks pale.

■ He **may not know** about the plan. His boss doesn't tell him everything.

■ It **can't be** true!
NOT It doesn't have to be true!

4. Use **could** in **questions**.

USAGE NOTE: We rarely use **might** and we never use **may** in questions about possibility.

■ Someone's coming. Who **could** it be?

RARE: **Might** he be at home?
NOT May he be at home?

5. In **short answers**, use **have (got) to** or a modal alone.

Use **be** in short answers to questions that include a form of **be**.

A: **Could** Ann know Marie?
B: She **has to**. They're neighbors.

A: **Is** Ron still with City Bank?
B: I'm not sure. He **might not be**.

1 **MATCH** • *Each fact goes with an assumption. Match each fact with the correct assumption.*

Fact   Assumption

_____f_____ **1.** Her last name is Lemont. She   **a.** must not be at home.

_____ **2.** He's only thirteen. He   **b.** must be married.

_____ **3.** Her eyes are red. She   **c.** has to be older than twenty.

_____ **4.** She's wearing a wedding ring. She   **d.** can't be married.

_____ **5.** His initials are M.B. He   **e.** might have allergies.

_____ **6.** The house is completely dark. They **f.** may be French.

_____ **7.** She has some gray hair. She   **g.** could be Marc Brunner.

2 **CHOOSE** • *Look at the picture and circle the correct words to complete this conversation.*

WATSON: Look! What's going on over there?

HOLMES: I don't know. It (could)/ couldn't be
  1.
  some kind of delivery.

WATSON: At this hour? It can't / must be
  2.
  almost midnight! Nothing's

  open now.

HOLMES: Hmm. 27 Carlisle Street. That

  can't / 's got to be the bank.
  3.

WATSON: It *is* the bank.

HOLMES: Can you see what that man is taking out of the carriage?

WATSON: It looks like a box. What do you suppose is in it?

HOLMES: I don't know, but it seems heavy. It could / must not contain gold.
  4.

WATSON: Look at that man in front of the bank. Could / Must he be the bank manager?
  5.

HOLMES: He might / might be.
  6.

WATSON: But why are they making this delivery at this time? This could / couldn't
  7.
  be normal.

HOLMES: The manager might not / must want people to know about it. He
  8.
  couldn't / may be worried about robbers.
  9.

3 **COMPLETE** • *Read Sherlock Holmes's conversation with a murder suspect. Complete it with the words in parentheses and a modal that shows the degree of certainty. (There may be more than one correct answer.)*

HOLMES: <u>You must be Gina Lemont.</u>
                   1. Almost certain (You / be / Gina Lemont)

LEMONT: _____. Who wants to know?
            2. Possible (I / be)

HOLMES: Sherlock Holmes. I hear something in the next room.

LEMONT: _____. I'm alone.
         3. Possible (It / be / the cat)

HOLMES: Alone? _____. There are two
           4. Almost certain (You / eat a lot)

plates on the table. _____ that
                  5. Possible (it / be)

you are mistaken?

LEMONT: No, _____. I was expecting
            6. Impossible (it / be)

someone, but he never came.

HOLMES: Does your cat smoke? I smell pipe tobacco.

LEMONT: _____
           7. Almost certain (It / come / from your own pipe)

_____
           8. Impossible (There / be / any other explanation)

HOLMES: Oh, _____. May we have
           9. Possible (there / be)

a look at this "cat"?

4 **EDIT** • *Read this student's reading journal for a mystery novel. Find and correct six mistakes in expressing assumptions. The first mistake is already corrected.*

The main character, Molly Smith, is a college ESL teacher. She is trying to find her dead
                                        be

grandparents' first home in the United States. It may ~~being~~ in a nearby town. The

townspeople there seem scared. They could be have a secret, or they must just hate

strangers. Molly has some old letters that might lead her to the place. They are in

Armenian, but one of her students mights translate them for her. They hafta be

important because the author mentions them right away. The letter must contain

family secrets. Who is the bad guy? It couldn't be the student because he wants to help.

It might to be the newspaper editor in the town.

UNIT 38

Advisability in the Past

I ought to have applied to college.

I could have become a doctor.

My parents might have encouraged me more.

I shouldn't have missed that opportunity.

I could have been rich and famous.

CHECK POINT

Check the correct answer.

The man

☐ is planning his future.

☐ regrets things in his past.

CHART CHECK 1

Circle T (True) or F (False).

T F You can add *not* to all modals that express past advisability or obligation.

STATEMENTS			
SUBJECT	**MODAL**	**HAVE**	**PAST PARTICIPLE**
I/He/She/We/You/They	should (not) ought (not) to could might	have	applied.

CHART CHECK 2

Circle T (True) or F (False).

T F In questions and short answers, we usually only use *should have*.

YES/NO QUESTIONS			
SHOULD	**SUBJECT**	**HAVE**	**PAST PARTICIPLE**
Should	he	have	applied?

SHORT ANSWERS	
AFFIRMATIVE	**NEGATIVE**
Yes, he should have.	No, he shouldn't have.

WH- QUESTIONS				
WH- WORD	**SHOULD**	**SUBJECT**	**HAVE**	**PAST PARTICIPLE**
When	should	he	have	applied?

CHART CHECK 3

Check the correct answer.

Which words are NOT usually contracted?

❏ *should have*

❏ *could have*

❏ *ought to have*

CONTRACTIONS		
should have	=	**should've**
could have	=	**could've**
might have	=	**might've**
should not have	=	**shouldn't have**

EXPRESS CHECK

Complete this conversation.

A: Should I _____ called you yesterday?

B: Yes, you _____. I waited all day for your call.

Grammar Explanations

Examples

1. Use *should have, ought to have, could have,* and *might have* to talk about things that were <u>advisable in the past</u>. These modals often express regret or blame.

- I **should've applied** to college.
  (I didn't apply to college, and I'm sorry.)
- I **ought to have taken** that job.
  (I didn't take the job. That was a mistake.)
- She **could've gone** to a better school.
  (She didn't go to a good school. Now she regrets her choice.)
- You **might've told** me.
  (You didn't tell me. That was wrong.)

2. *Should not have* and *ought not to have* are the only forms used in <u>negative statements</u>. *Should not have* is more common.

Should have is the most common form used in <u>questions</u>.

- He **shouldn't have missed** the exam.
- He **ought not to have missed** the exam.

- **Should he have called** the teacher?

PRONUNCIATION NOTE

In informal speech, *have* in <u>modal phrases</u> is often pronounced like the word *of* or *a.*
For example, *could have* sounds like "could of" or "coulda." Do not write *could of* or *coulda.*
Ought to is often pronounced like "oughta." Do not write *oughta.*

TRUE OR FALSE • *Read each numbered sentence. Write T (True) or F (False) for the statement that follows.*

1. I shouldn't have called him.

   __T__ I called him.

2. I should have told them what I thought.

   _____ I didn't tell them. Now I'm sorry.

3. He might have warned us about it.

   _____ He knew, but he didn't tell us.

4. Felicia could have been president.

   _____ Felicia is president.

5. I ought to have practiced more.

   _____ I didn't practice enough.

6. They shouldn't have lent him their car.

   _____ They lent him their car.

 COMPLETE • *Read this excerpt from a magazine article. Complete it with the correct form of the words in parentheses and a short answer. Choose between affirmative and negative.*

Regrets . . .

It's not unusual to feel regret about things in the past that you think you

___**should have done**___ and did not do—or the opposite, about things
1. (should / do)

you did do and feel you _____. In fact, we learn by
2. (should / do)

thinking about past mistakes. For example, a student who fails a test learns that

he or she _____ more and can improve on the
3. (should / study)

next test. Often, however, people spend too much time thinking about what they

_____ differently. Many regrets are simply not based
4. (could / do)

in fact. A mother regrets missing a football game in which her son's leg was

injured. "I _____," she keeps telling herself.
5. (ought to / go)

"I _____ home. I _____
6. (should / stay)   **7. (could / prevent)**

the injury. The officials _____ at least
8. (might / call)

_____ me as soon as it happened." Did she *really*
8. (might / call)

have the power to prevent her son's injury? _____ the

officials _____ her *before* looking at the injury? No, of
9. (Should / contact)

course, they _____. There is an Italian proverb that says,
10.

"When the ship has sunk, everyone knows how they _____ it."
11. (could / save)

It's easy to second guess about the past: The real challenge is to solve the problems

you face right now.

3 **REWRITE** • *Read Greta's regrets. Rewrite them using the modals in parentheses and choose between affirmative and negative.*

1. I didn't go to college. Now I'm unhappy with my job.

(should) ___I should have gone to college.___

2. I feel sick. I ate all the chocolate.

(should) _____

3. Christina didn't come over. She didn't even call.

(might) _____

4. I didn't have enough money to buy the shirt. Why didn't Ed offer to lend me some?

(could) _____

5. I jogged five miles yesterday, and now I'm exhausted.

(should) _____

6. The supermarket charged me for the plastic bags. They used to be free.

(should) _____

7. I didn't invite Cynthia to the party. Now she's angry at me.

(ought to) _____

8. Yesterday was my birthday, and my brother didn't send me a card. I'm hurt.

(might) _____

 4 **EDIT** • *Read this journal entry. Find and correct six mistakes in the use of modals. The first mistake is already corrected.*

December 15

About a week ago, Jennifer was late for work again, and Doug, our boss, told me he wanted to get

                                                  have

rid of her. I was really upset. Of course, Jennifer shouldn't ~~had~~ been late so often, but he might has

talked to her about the problem before he decided to let her go. Then he told me to make her job

difficult for her so that she would quit. I just pretended I didn't hear him. What a mistake!

I oughta have confronted him right away. Or I could at least have warned Jennifer. Anyway,

Jennifer is still here, but now I'm worried about my own job. Should I of told Doug's boss? I wonder.

Maybe I should handle things differently last week. The company should never has hired this guy.

UNIT 39

Speculations
about the Past

EASTER ISLAND: **Could** visitors from another planet **have built** these giant statues?

CHECK *POINT*

Check the correct answer.

The question under the photograph asks

❐ if it was possible that something happened.

❐ if people had permission to do something.

CHART CHECK 1

Circle T (True) or F (False).

T F The form of the modal does not change for different subjects.

	STATEMENTS			
SUBJECT	**MODAL/** *HAD TO*	**HAVE**	**PAST PARTICIPLE**	
I/He/She/We/You/They	**may (not)** **might (not)** **can't** **could (not)** **must (not)** **had to**	**have**	**seen**	the statues.

CHART CHECK 2

Check the correct answer.

Which modal can be used in both questions and short answers for speculations about the past?

❐ *can*

❐ *could*

❐ *might*

YES/NO QUESTIONS: *COULD*			
COULD	**SUBJECT**	**HAVE**	**PAST PARTICIPLE**
Could	he	**have**	**seen** aliens?

SHORT ANSWERS		
SUBJECT	**MODAL/** *HAD TO*	**HAVE**
He	**may (not)** **might (not)** **can't** **could (not)** **must (not)** **had to**	**have**.

EXPRESS **CHECK**

Circle the correct words to complete these sentences.

Could they <u>carved / have carved</u> the statues? They <u>might / might have</u>.

166

Grammar Explanations   ## Examples

1. We often **speculate**, or make "best guesses," about past situations based on the facts that we have. The <u>modal</u> that we choose depends on <u>how certain</u> we are about our speculations.

	100% certain	
AFFIRMATIVE		NEGATIVE
must have		**can't have**
had to have		**couldn't have**
may have		**must not have**
might have		**may not have**
could have		**might not have**
	0% certain	

2. When you are <u>almost 100 percent certain</u> that something was **possible**, use **must have** or **had to have**.

When you are <u>less certain</u>, use **may have**, **might have**, or **could have**.

The statues are very big.
SPECULATION
■ They **must have been** hard to move.

The islanders were able to carve the stone.
SPECULATION
■ The stone **may have been** quite soft.

3. When you are <u>almost 100 percent certain</u> that something was **impossible**, use **can't have** or **couldn't have**.

When you are <u>slightly less certain</u>, use **must not**.

Use **may not have** or **might not have** when you are <u>less certain</u>.

▶ **BE CAREFUL!** We do not usually use **had to have** for negative speculations.

■ The islanders **couldn't have moved** the stone! It was too heavy.

■ They **must not have moved** it without help.

■ The islanders **might not have moved** the statues over land. They could have used boats.

4. Use **could have** in **questions about possibility** or use questions without modals.

■ **Could** the islanders **have moved** the stone?
OR
■ Do you think they moved the stone?

5. Use **been** in **short answers** to questions that include a form of **be**.

Use only the **modal + have** in short answers to <u>questions with other verbs</u>.

A: **Could** von Däniken **have been** wrong?
OR
Was he wrong?
B: He certainly **could have been**.

A: Did the islanders **work** on their own?
B: They **could have**.

PRONUNCIATION NOTE
In informal speech, **have** in <u>modal phrases</u> is often pronounced like the word of.
For example, **must have** sounds like "must of." Do not write must of.

1 **MATCH** • *Each fact goes with a speculation. Match each fact with the correct speculation about author Erich von Däniken.*

Fact

___e___ **1.** The original title of *Chariots of the Gods?* was *Erinnerungen an die Zukunft.*

_____ **2.** Von Däniken visited every place he described in his book.

_____ **3.** In 1973, he wrote *In Search of Ancient Gods.*

_____ **4.** He doesn't have a degree in archaeology.

_____ **5.** Von Däniken's books sold millions of copies.

_____ **6.** As soon as von Däniken published his books, scientists attacked him.

Speculation

a. He must have traveled a lot.

b. They must not have believed his theories.

c. He could have learned about the subject on his own.

d. He must have made a lot of money.

e. He must have written it in German.

f. He might have written other books too.

2 **ANSWER** • *Some archaeology students are asking questions in class. Use the modals in parentheses to write short answers.*

1. A: Do you think the people on Easter Island built the giant statues themselves?

B: _____They could have_____. They had the knowledge and the tools.
                    (could)

2. A: Were many people impressed by von Däniken's theories?

B: _____. His books were read all over the world.
                    (must)

3. A: Von Däniken says that many ancient artifacts show pictures of astronauts. Could these pictures have illustrated anything closer to Earth?

B: _____. It's possible that the pictures show
                    (may)
people dressed in local costumes.

4. A: Was von Däniken upset by all the criticism he received?

B: _____. After all, it helped his book sales.
                    (might not)

5. A: Do you think von Däniken helped increase general interest in archaeology?

B: _____. Just look at the size of this class!
                    (must)

3 **COMPLETE** • *Read part of a review of Erich von Däniken's book* Chariots of the Gods? *Complete it with the verbs in parentheses.*

Who _____ **could have made** _____ the Easter Island statues? According
      1. (could / make)

to Erich von Däniken, our ancestors _____ these
      2. (could not / build)

structures on their own because their cultures were too primitive. His solution:

They _____ help from space visitors. When he
      3. (had to / get)

wrote his popular book, von Däniken _____ about
      4. (must not / know)

the Easter Island experiments that proved that the ancient islanders

_____ and _____ these
    5 (could / carve)   **6** (transport)

statues without any help from alien visitors. Not only that, the island's population

_____ much larger than von Däniken believes. One
      7. (might / be)

scientist speculates that as many as 20,000 people _____
                    8. (may / live)

on Easter Island—enough people to have done the job. Visitors from another planet?

A more logical answer is to think that our ancestors _____
                    9. (must / have)

great skill, intelligence, and strength to create these wonderful things.

4 **EDIT** • *Read part of a student's essay. Find and correct six mistakes in the use of modals for speculations about the past. The first mistake is already corrected.*

>   have been
> In 1927, Toribio Mexta Xesspe of Peru must ~~be~~ very surprised to see lines in the
> shapes of huge animals on the ground below his airplane. Created by the ancient
> Nazca culture, these forms are too big to recognize from the ground. However, at
> about 600 feet in the air the giant forms take
> shape. Without airplanes, how could an ancient
> culture had made them? What purpose could
> they have had? Author Erich von Däniken
> believes that the drawings might have mark a
> landing strip for the spacecraft of astronauts
> from another planet. Archaeologists, however,
> now believe that the ancient Nazcan civilization might develop flight.
> They could of built hot-air balloons and design the pictures from the air.

SelfTest

SECTION ONE

Circle the letter of the correct answer to complete each sentence.

> **EXAMPLE:**
> Jennifer never _____ coffee.   A (B) C D
> (A) drink   (C) is drinking
> (B) drinks   (D) was drinking

1. —Wasn't that Mehmet in class?   A B C D
   —It _____. Mehmet left school last week.
   (A) couldn't   (C) couldn't have been
   (B) could have been   (D) couldn't have

2. Frank watches all the Lakers games. He _____ to be one of   A B C D
   their biggest fans.
   (A) must   (C) couldn't
   (B) has got   (D) should have

3. Children under five years old _____ swim without an adult.   A B C D
   (A) don't have to   (C) have to
   (B) must not   (D) are supposed to

4. Where _____ we supposed to go for the test tomorrow?   A B C D
   (A) do   (C) will
   (B) are   (D) should

5. Bring your umbrella. It _____ later.   A B C D
   (A) might rain   (C) couldn't rain
   (B) rains   (D) might have rained

6. —Will your plane be late this afternoon?   A B C D
   —It _____. The airport was closed this morning.
   (A) couldn't be   (C) maybe
   (B) may be   (D) will

7. You _____ told Mark. You knew it was a secret.   A B C D
   (A) should have   (C) couldn't have
   (B) might have   (D) shouldn't have

8. They built this temple 3,000 years ago. This must _____   A B C D
   a great civilization.
   (A) has been   (C) was
   (B) have been   (D) not have been

9. Jan _____ to call Myra yesterday but he forgot.   A B C D
   (A) supposed   (C) supposes
   (B) is supposed   (D) was supposed

10. —Could Amy have been at home yesterday?
    —She _____. I really don't know.   A B C D
    (A) could have been   (C) had to have been
    (B) might be   (D) couldn't have

11. Chris _____ to clean up his room. It's a mess.   A B C D
    (A) have got   (C) must
    (B) has got   (D) got

12. I failed the test. I _____ studied harder.   A B C D
    (A) should have   (C) should
    (B) must have   (D) may

13. Lisa was in town recently. She might _____ me to say hello!   A B C D
    (A) call   (C) have called
    (B) has called   (D) be calling

SECTION TWO

Each sentence has four underlined words or phrases. The four underlined parts of the sentence are marked A, B, C, and D. Circle the letter of the one underlined word or phrase that is NOT CORRECT.

> **EXAMPLE:**
> Mike <u>usually</u> <u>drives</u> to school, but <u>today</u> he <u>walks</u>.   A B C (D)
>   A   B   C   D

14. Tom <u>didn't</u> <u>wave</u> to me, so he <u>must have known</u> I <u>was</u> here.   A B C D
        A   B   C   D

15. We'<u>d better</u> <u>hurry</u>, or the train <u>might</u> <u>leaves</u> without us.   A B C D
         A   B   C   D

16. His English <u>is</u> excellent, so he <u>had to</u> <u>has</u> <u>studied</u> hard.   A B C D
                A   B   C   D

17. We <u>ought to have</u> <u>look</u> at more cars <u>before</u> we <u>bought</u> ours.   A B C D
        A   B   C   D

18. You <u>gotta</u> <u>get</u> dressed <u>because</u> Sasha <u>may be</u> here soon.   A B C D
         A   B   C   D

19. You <u>have to</u> <u>buckle</u> your seat belt now or you <u>couldn't</u> <u>drive</u>. It's the law.   A B C D
         A   B   C   D

20. You <u>don't have to</u> <u>drive</u> faster <u>than</u> 65 mph or you <u>might</u> get a ticket.   A B C D
         A   B   C   D

21. Hardlie's <u>must</u> <u>has</u> <u>gone</u> out of business <u>recently</u>.   A B C D
               A   B   C   D

22. It <u>must</u> <u>rain</u> tonight, so I'<u>d better</u> <u>stay</u> home.   A B C D
        A   B   C   D

23. Jason <u>will be</u> <u>supposed</u> to be there <u>tomorrow</u>, but he <u>can't</u> attend.   A B C D
           A   B   C   D

24. It <u>must</u> <u>be</u> almost 11:00, so we really <u>hafta</u> <u>leave</u> now.   A B C D
        A   B   C   D

25. You <u>should of</u> <u>seen</u> that movie with us because it <u>may not</u> <u>be</u> here long.   A B C D
         A   B   C   D

feel well / health
feel good / happy

UNIT 40

Adjectives and Adverbs

The ad describes it **perfectly.**

Adjectives !
Describe noun or pronoun.
1/ non action verb.
1 - be main verb
2. seem - look - appear.
3. become - get
4- smell → adj
5- feel
6- taste → adj
7- sound → adj

Adverb
→ action verb
- look at
- hear

CHECK POINT

Check the correct answer.

The owner thinks the apartment is:

☐ perfect

☑ warm and cozy

CHART CHECK

Circle T (True) or F (False).

T F Adverbs often come before nouns.

T F Adjectives often come after action verbs.

T F Adverbs often end in **-ly**.

ADJECTIVES	ADVERBS
They are **quiet** tenants.	They work **quietly**.
It's a **fast** elevator.	It moves **very fast**.
The building seems **nice**.	She described it **nicely**.
It's absolutely **perfect**.	It's **absolutely** perfect.

The words dosent chang in adj or adv (don't add (ly))
–/ early
–/ fast
– / wrong
–/ late
–/ hard

EXPRESS CHECK

Complete these sentences with the correct form of the word **slow**.

A: It's a ___slow___ elevator. It moves very ___slowly___.

B: It's not ___slowly___. It just seems ___slow___.

172

Grammar Explanations

Examples

---

1. Use **adjectives** to describe <u>nouns</u> or <u>pronouns</u> (for people, places, and things).

Adjectives usually come immediately <u>before the noun</u> they describe.

Adjectives can also come <u>after non-action verbs</u> such as *be, look,* or *seem.*

noun   adjective   pron. adjective
■ The **houses** are *beautiful.* **They** are *new.*

adjective noun
■ This is a *small* **apartment**.

verb adjective
■ This apartment **seems** *small.*

---

2. Use **adverbs** to describe <u>verbs</u>, <u>adjectives</u>, and other <u>adverbs</u>.

Adverbs that describe adjectives and other adverbs usually come immediately <u>before</u> the word they describe.

verb   adverb
■ They **furnished** it *nicely.*

adverb adjective
■ It's an *extremely* **nice** house.

adverb adverb
■ They found it *very* **quickly**.

---

3. Use **adverbs of manner** to describe <u>action verbs</u>. These adverbs often answer *How?* questions. They come <u>after</u> the verb they describe.

▶ **BE CAREFUL!** Do not put an adverb of manner between the verb and its direct object.

■ It'**ll rent** *quickly.*
(Quickly *describes* <u>how fast</u> *it will rent.*)

verb   direct object
■ She'**ll rent** this apartment *quickly.*
NOT She'll rent quickly this apartment.

---

4. **Adverbs of manner** are often formed by <u>adding *-ly* to adjectives</u>.

▶ **BE CAREFUL!** Some adjectives also end in *-ly*—for example, *silly, friendly, lovely,* and *lonely.*

adjective
■ We need a **quick** decision.

lively
ugly

adverb
■ You should decide **quickly**.

adjective
■ It's a **lovely** apartment.

---

5. Some **common adverbs of manner** <u>do not end in *-ly*</u>.

a. The adverb form of *good* is **well**.

b. Some adverbs have the <u>same form as their related adjectives</u>, for example, **early, fast, wrong, late,** and **hard**.

▶ **BE CAREFUL!** *Lately* is not the adverb form of *late. Lately* means "recently." *Hardly* is not the adverb form of *hard. Hardly* means "almost not."

adjective   adverb
■ She's a **good** writer. She writes **well**.

ADJECTIVE	ADVERB
Bob was **late**.	Bob came **late**.
She's a **hard** worker.	She works **hard**.

■ She hasn't met any new people *lately.*

■ There's *hardly* enough time to prepare for her classes. Her part-time job takes up most of her time.

Check it out!

For a discussion of adverbs of frequency, see Unit 2, page 7.

1 **IDENTIFY** • *Read this notice about an apartment for rent. Underline the adjectives and circle the adverbs. Then draw an arrow from the adjective or adverb to the word it is describing.*

APT. FOR RENT

Students! Are you looking for a <u>special</u> place to live?
Come to 140 Grant Street, Apt. 4B. This apartment is
(absolutely) perfect for two <u>serious</u> students who are
looking for a <u>quiet</u> neighborhood, just 15 minutes from
campus. This (lovely) apartment is in a <u>new</u> building.
It is a <u>short</u> walk to the bus stop. The <u>express</u> bus goes
(directly) into town. At night the bus (hardly) makes any
stops at all. You can walk (safely) through the <u>wonderful</u>
parks on your way home. The rent is (very) <u>affordable</u>.
Call for an appointment: 555-5050.
Don't wait! This apartment will rent fast.

---

2 **COMPLETE** • *Many people went to see the apartment described in the notice above. Complete their comments about the apartment with the correct form of the words in parentheses.*

1. I'm very interested. I think the apartment is _____**extremely nice**_____ .
                                                 (extreme / nice)

2. I was expecting much bigger rooms. I was _terribly disappointed_ .
                                       (terrible / disappointed)

3. I thought the apartment would be hard to find, but it was _surprisingly easy_ .
                                       (surprising / easy)

4. I was happy to hear that the park is _extremely safe_ .
                                (extreme / safe)

5. It's a great place, and the price is reasonable. It will rent _incredibly fast_ .
                                               (incredible / fast)

6. The owner seems nice, but she talks _awfully slow_ .
                                      (awful / slow)

7. The notice said it was quiet, but I heard the neighbors _very clearly_ .
                                            (very / clear)

8. I heard them too. I thought their voices were _unusually loud_ .
                                      (unusual / loud)

9. All in all, it's an _exceptionally pleasant_ place.
                          (exceptional / pleasant)

3 **CHOOSE** • Complete Maggie's letter with the correct word in parentheses.

Dear Mom and Dad,

Life in New York is very ____exciting____. Luis and I weren't sure we'd like
1. (exciting / excitingly)

such a ____large____ city, but it's so interesting! Yesterday we saw a street
2. (large / largely)

musician near school. He played the violin so ____beautifully____ we couldn't believe he
3. (beautiful / beautifully)

wasn't in a big concert hall. You'd be surprised to see us. We walk ____happily____
4. (happy / happily)

down the ____busy____ streets, and the noise doesn't bother us at all! I'm sending
5. (busy / busily)

a photo of our apartment building. It looks ____nice____, doesn't it? It's so
6. (nice / nicely)

____quiet____ we can ____hardly____ believe it's in New York. Our next-
7. (quiet / quietly)   **8.** (hard / hardly)

door neighbor is very ____nice____. At first she seemed ____shy____,
9. (nice / nicely)   **10.** (shy / shyly)

but now we're ____good____ friends.
11. (good / well)

We hope you're both well. Please give our love to

everyone and write soon.

Love,

Maggie

4 **EDIT** • Read this student's journal entry. Find and
correct seven mistakes in the use of adjectives
and adverbs. The first mistake is already corrected.

	funny
○	Some apartment ads are so ~~funnily~~! One ad described a place as "~~warmly~~ warm and cozy." It was
	really hot and crowded, but the owner insisted that it suited me ~~perfect~~ Perfectly. I was trying very
	~~hardly~~ hard not to laugh while he was describing it, so I had to leave quickly. Another place I saw
	was supposed to be "nice and ~~cutely~~ cute." What a mess!! I left that place very ~~fastly~~ fast too. I'm not
	asking for the moon! I only want a small place in a clean building with friendly neighbors.
	I'm looking at another place tomorrow. The ad says, "Clean and bright. Small but convenient
	apartment on lovely, ~~quietly~~ quiet block." I wonder what that really means!

Participial Adjectives

NEW FRIENDS

> **Send me e-mail!**

> **Send me an online greeting!**

> **Send this to a friend!**

New to the Area

Screen Name: newgal@XYZ.com
Age & Gender: 20 year old Female
Location: Miami, FL
Looking for: Friends

Tired of doing things alone? Me too! 20 year old college student, new to the area, is **interested** in meeting **interesting** people for friendship and fun.

▶ **print/save**

CHECK *POINT*

Circle T (True) or F (False).

T F The writer of the ad says that she is an interesting person.

CHART CHECK

Circle T (True) or F (False).

T F There are two types of participial adjectives.

PARTICIPIAL ADJECTIVES	
-ING ADJECTIVES	**-ED ADJECTIVES**
He is **boring**. They had a **boring** date.	She is **bored**. They had a **bored** look on their faces.
She is **amusing**. They had an **amusing** date.	He is **amused**. They had an **amused** look on their faces.
The movie was **frightening**. They saw a **frightening** movie.	They were **frightened**. They had a **frightened** look on their faces.
The job is **tiring**. She has a **tiring** job.	She's **tired**. She has a **tired** sound to her voice.
The weekend was **relaxing**. He had a **relaxing** weekend.	He felt **relaxed**. He had a **relaxed** manner.

EXPRESS CHECK

Complete the chart.

-ING ADJECTIVES	-ED ADJECTIVES
exciting	
	interested
frightening	
	amused
tiring	

[Handwritten notes to the right of the chart:]

ing | *ed*
thing | Person
Person | animal.
The party sounds boring | we are bored
| amused

Grammar Explanations

1. Participial adjectives are adjectives that end with **-ing** or **-ed**. They usually describe feelings or reactions. The two forms have different meanings.

Examples

A: The last *Star Wars* movie was **amazing**!
B: I know. I was **amazed** by the special effects.

---

2. Participial adjectives that end in **-ing** describe someone or something that <u>causes</u> a feeling or reaction.

■ That actor is always **amusing**.
  (He causes amusement.)

■ These directions are **confusing**.
  (They cause confusion.)

---

3. Participial adjectives that end in **-ed** describe someone who <u>experiences</u> a feeling or reaction.

■ We were **amused** by that actor.
  (We felt amusement.)

■ I'm really **confused** by these directions.
  (I feel confusion.)

---

4. To the right are some <u>common participial adjective</u> pairs.

annoying	annoyed
boring	bored
depressing	depressed
embarrassing	embarrassed
exciting	excited
frightening	frightened
relaxing	relaxed
shocking	shocked
surprising	surprised

Check it out!

For a list of common participial adjectives, see Appendix 11 on page 339.

IDENTIFY • *Read this article. Underline all the -**ed** participial adjectives. Circle all the -**ing** participial adjectives.*

14 • SECTION 4 • LIFESTYLES

Not Personal Enough?

INTERNATIONAL WIRE SERVICES

In some countries, people who are interested in meeting others turn for help to personal ads in newspapers and magazines, and online. A surprising number of busy people view these ads as a practical way of increasing their social circle. "I've tried hard to meet people on my own," said one satisfied customer. "I was new in town and wanted to make friends fast. The personals provided me with a quick way of meeting many interesting people in a short period of time." Others are not so impressed. "I think it's kind of depressing when people need to resort to placing ads to make friends," observed one man. "A friend of mine tried the ads several times and was really disappointed with the results. It's just not personal enough."

 CHOOSE • *Read this conversation between Marta and Luis about their friend Alice. Circle the correct words to complete the conversation.*

MARTA: What's the matter with Alice?

LUIS: Who knows? She's always annoyed / annoying about something.
1.

MARTA: I know. I try to understand her, but this time I'm really puzzled / puzzling.
2.

LUIS: Really? What's so puzzled / puzzling this time?
3.

MARTA: I thought she was happy. She met an interested / interesting guy last week.
4.

LUIS: That's nice. Was she interested / interesting in him?
5.

MARTA: I thought she was. She said they saw a fascinated / fascinating movie together.
6.

LUIS: Well, maybe she was fascinated / fascinating by the movie but
7.
disappointed / disappointing with the guy.
8.

MARTA: I don't know. It's hard to tell with Alice. Her moods are always very
surprised / surprising.
9.

LUIS: I'm not surprised / surprising at all. That's just the way she is.
10.

3 COMPLETE • *Read this conversation between Alice and her date, Jake. Complete it with the correct form of the words in parentheses. Choose between **-ed** and **-ing** participial adjectives.*

ALICE: That was a very ___interesting___ movie. What did you think?
1. (interest)

JAKE: To be honest, I found it kind of ___boring___. I'm not that
2. (bore)
___interested___ in science fiction.
3. (interest)

ALICE: Really? I find it ___fascinating___. What kind of movies *do* you enjoy?
4. (fascinate)

JAKE: Mostly comedies. Have you seen *Home Again*?

ALICE: Yes, but I wasn't ___amused___ at all. In fact, I thought it was
5. (amuse)
___horrifying___. The story line was ___confusing___, and I couldn't
6. (horrify)   **7.** (confuse)
find any humor in the characters' problems. When I left the theater, I felt
kind of ___depressing___.
8. (depress)

JAKE: I'm ___amazed___ that you felt that way! I thought it was very
9. (amaze)
___amusing___.
10. (amuse)

ALICE: Well, I guess it's a matter of taste.

JAKE: Speaking of taste, would you like to get a bite to eat?

ALICE: Thanks, but it's late and I'm ___exhausted___.
11. (exhaust)

4 EDIT • *Read Alice's journal entry. Find and correct six mistakes in the use of participial adjectives. The first mistake is already corrected.*

> disappointed
> Just got home. I'm ~~disappointing~~ with the evening. At first I thought Jake was an
> interested guy, but tonight I felt somewhat bored with his company. We saw a very
> entertained movie, but Jake didn't like it. In fact, it seems like we have completely
> different tastes in things. After the movie, I tried to make conversation, but all I
> really wanted was to go home. So, I told him I was exhausting and didn't want to
> get home late. If he asks me out again—I'm not interesting. Trying to meet people
> can be very frustrated.

Adjectives and Adverbs:
Equatives

She rides **as fast as** he does. She controls her bike just **as well**. But her shoulders aren't **as wide** and her arms aren't **as long as** his. Why should she ride a bike designed for him?

TRAX—sized to fit *you*.

CHECK *POINT*

Check the things the boy and girl have in common.

❏ riding speed

❏ width of shoulders

❏ control of bike

❏ length of arms

CHART CHECK

Check the correct answers.

Which words are always used in equatives?

❏ *not*

❏ *as*

❏ an adjective or an adverb

ADJECTIVES: EQUATIVES					
	VERB* (NOT)	**AS**	**ADJECTIVE**	**AS**	
The girl			**fast**		the boy.
She	is		**good**		he is.
Her bike	isn't	**as**	**big**	**as**	his.
The girl's bike			**heavy**		the boy's.

*Non-action verbs like *be, look, seem.*

ADVERBS: EQUATIVES					
	VERB* (NOT)	**AS**	**ADVERB**	**AS**	
The girl			**fast**		the boy.
She	rides		**well**		he does.
Her bike	doesn't ride	**as**	**smoothly**	**as**	his.
The girl's bike			**consistently**		the boy's.

*Action verbs

180

EXPRESS CHECK

Complete these sentences with the equative form of the words in parentheses.

A: My old bike wasn't ___as expensive___ ___as___ my new one. Of course, it
      (expensive)

didn't perform ___as well as___ the new one.
           (well)

B: And it didn't look ___as good as___ the new one either.
              (good)

Grammar Explanations

| Examples |

1. You can use **equatives** (*as* + adjective + *as*) to compare <u>people, places, and things</u>.

- The Trax bike is **as expensive as** the Gordo. *(The Trax costs a lot of money. The Gordo costs the same amount of money.)*

- It's **not as light as** the Gordo, though. *(The two bikes are not the same weight.)*

Use *as* + adjective + *as* to compare people, places, and things that are <u>equal</u> in some way. Use *just* to emphasize the equality.

- This helmet is **as good as** yours.
- It's *just* **as expensive as** yours too.

Use *not as* + adjective + *as* to talk about people, places, and things that are <u>different</u> in some way.

- The new ad is **not as effective as** the old one.
- It is**n't as funny as** the old one either.

2. You can also use **equatives** (*as* + adverb + *as*) to compare <u>actions</u>.

- He rides **as fast as** she does. *(They ride equally fast.)*

- He doesn**'t** ride **as safely as** she does, though. *(They don't ride the same way. He rides safely, but she rides more safely.)*

Use *as* + adverb + *as* to talk about actions that are the <u>same or equal</u>. Use *just* to emphasize the <u>equality</u>.

- Kleen brightens **as thoroughly as** Brite.
- It removes stains *just* **as effectively as** Brite.

Use *not as* + adverb + *as* to talk about <u>actions</u> that are <u>not the same or equal</u>.

- Kleen does**n't** clean **as well as** Brite.

3. You do not always have to mention both parts of a comparison. Sometimes the meaning is clear from the context.

- Trax and Gordo are both great bikes, but Trax is**n't as light** (as Gordo).

- Jake and Christopher both ride fast, but Christopher does**n't ride as skillfully** (as Jake).

1 **IDENTIFY** • *Read this article on laundry detergents. Underline all the equatives with adjectives. Circle the equatives with adverbs.*

PRODUCT REVIEWS ✦ LAUNDRY DETERGENTS

So you were riding the trails this weekend, and you hit the dirt. Now your clothes look as bad as your bike. Never mind. They'll look as good as new next weekend. We checked out three major brands of detergent, and we can tell you which ones clean best and which ones don't remove trail stains as effectively as others.

Overall, Brite and Kleen aren't as expensive as Trend, but they didn't perform as well either. However, they were almost as good in particular categories. Trend removed both mud and grass stains effectively. Brite removed mud just as effectively as Trend, but it didn't remove grass stains as well. Kleen was effective on grass stains, but not on mud. Brite cleaned clothes as thoroughly as Kleen, but again, Brite and Kleen weren't as good as Trend in this category. On the other hand, Brite came out on top in brightening. Colors washed in Kleen and Trend just didn't look as bright as the ones washed in Brite.

---

2 **COMPLETE** • *Read these conversations. Complete them with equatives using the correct form of the words in parentheses.*

1. **TOMÁS:** _____Does_____ your new bike ___ride as comfortably as___ the old one?
   a. (ride / comfortable)

   DINA: It's great. The handlebars _____ and the handbrakes
   b. (not be / wide)

   _____ to reach. This bike was made for a small
   c. (not be / hard)

   person like me.

2. **HANS:** We need a name for this product. It should show that this detergent

   _____ the others but _____
   a. (clean / effective)   **b. (not be / unfriendly)**

   to the environment.

   EVA: I like "GreenKleen." It _____ other product names, and
   c. (sound / exciting)

   it _____ the message _____ theirs too.
   d. (express / clear)

3. **IN-SU:** The last group I rode with _____ a herd of
   a. (be / noisy)

   elephants. I prefer to ride alone, but I know it's dangerous.

   SUN-HI: Ride with me next weekend. I _____ a mouse.
   b. (pedal / quiet)

   I promise.

3 **COMPARE & COMPLETE** • *Read the chart comparing several models of bicycles. Complete the sentences with equatives using the correct form of the words in parentheses. Choose between affirmative and negative.*

Model	Price	Comfort	Braking speed, dry ground	Braking speed, wet ground	Shifting ease	On-road handling	Off-road handling
Trax	$999	◑	●	◑	●	◑	●
Huff	$550	●	◑	●	◑	●	◑
Gordo	$225	◑	○	○	◑	◑	○

Product Ratings ◆ Bicycles   **Key: Better ● → ◑ → ○ Worse**

1. The Gordo ___doesn't stop as quickly as___ the Trax and the Huff.
   (stop / quick)
2. On wet ground, the Huff _____ the Trax.
   (stop / slow)
3. The Gordo _____ the Trax and the Huff.
   (be / expensive)
4. The Trax _____ the Huff.
   (feel / comfortable)
5. The Trax _____ either.
   (be / cheap)
6. Even the Gordo _____ the Trax.
   (ride / comfortable)
7. On the road, the Gordo _____ the Trax.
   (handle / good)
8. Off the road, the Gordo and the Huff _____ the Trax.
   (handle / good)
9. The Gordo _____ the Huff.
   (shift / easy)

4 **EDIT** • *Read these bulletin board postings. Find and correct six mistakes in the use of equatives. The first mistake is already corrected.*

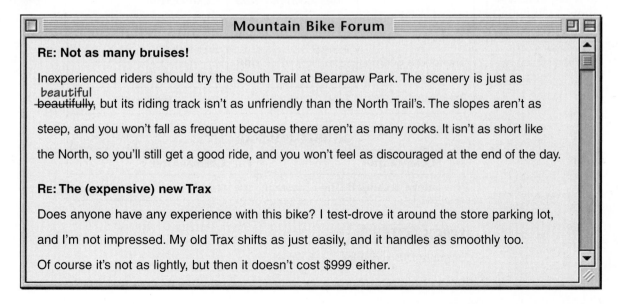

Mountain Bike Forum

RE: Not as many bruises!

Inexperienced riders should try the South Trail at Bearpaw Park. The scenery is just as
~~beautifully~~ beautiful, but its riding track isn't as unfriendly than the North Trail's. The slopes aren't as

steep, and you won't fall as frequent because there aren't as many rocks. It isn't as short like

the North, so you'll still get a good ride, and you won't feel as discouraged at the end of the day.

RE: The (expensive) new Trax

Does anyone have any experience with this bike? I test-drove it around the store parking lot,

and I'm not impressed. My old Trax shifts as just easily, and it handles as smoothly too.

Of course it's not as lightly, but then it doesn't cost $999 either.

Adjectives: Comparatives

CHECK POINT

Check the correct answer.

The new restaurant will be

☐ different from the old restaurant.

☐ the same as the old restaurant.

CHART CHECK

Circle T (True) or F (False).

T F The comparative adjective form always ends in *-er*.

T F You can use the same comparative adjective twice in a statement to show a change in a situation.

COMPARATIVES			
	COMPARATIVE	**THAN**	
The new restaurant is	brighter better	than	the old one.
	more comfortable less beautiful		

REPEATED COMPARATIVES			
	COMPARATIVE	**AND**	**COMPARATIVE**
The food is getting	better	and	better.
	worse		worse.
	more		more delicious.
	less		less interesting.

DOUBLE COMPARATIVES					
THE	**COMPARATIVE**		**THE**	**COMPARATIVE**	
The	more crowded	the restaurant,	the	slower	the service.

EXPRESS CHECK

Complete this sentence.

Mo's is bigger and _____ popular _____ Val's.

Grammar Explanations	**Examples**

1. Use the **comparative** form of adjectives to focus on a <u>difference</u> between people, places, and things.

- The new menu is **bigger than** the old menu.
- The new waiters are **more experienced than** the old waiters.

2. There is more than one way to **form the comparative of adjectives**.

a. For one-syllable adjectives and two-syllable adjectives ending in -y, use **adjective + -er**.

▶ **BE CAREFUL!** There are often <u>spelling changes</u> when you add **-er**.

▶ **BE CAREFUL!** Some adjectives have <u>irregular comparative</u> forms.

b. For most other adjectives of two or more syllables, use **more/less + adjective**.

c. For some adjectives, use either **-er** or **more/less**.

ADJECTIVE	COMPARATIVE
bright	**brighter**
friendly	**friendlier**
nice	**nicer**
big	**bigger**
pretty	**prettier**
good	**better**
bad	**worse**
comfortable	**more comfortable**
	less comfortable

- The Inn is **quieter** than Joe's.
- The Inn is **more quiet** than Joe's.

3. Use the comparative **with _than_** when you mention the things you are comparing.

- The apple pie is **better _than_** the cake.

Use the comparative **without _than_** when it is clear which things you are comparing.

- The new desserts are **better**.
  (The new desserts are better than the old desserts.)

4. Repeat the same comparative to talk about change—<u>an increase or a decrease</u>:
comparative adjective + **and** + **comparative adjective**

OR

more/less + and + more/less + adjective

- It's getting **harder and harder** to find an inexpensive restaurant.

- It's getting **more and more difficult**.
  (The difficulty is increasing.)

5. Use a double comparative to show <u>cause and effect</u>:

the + **comparative adjective** + **the** + **comparative adjective**

- **The shorter** the line, **the faster** the service.
  (When the line is shorter, the service is faster.)

Check it out!

For spelling rules for the comparative form of adjectives, see Appendix 22 on page 344.

For a list of irregular comparative adjectives, see Appendix 10 on page 339.

For a list of some adjectives that form the comparative in two ways, see Appendix 12 on page 339.

1 **TRUE OR FALSE** • *Look at these two restaurant ads. Then read the statements below, and decide if they are True (T) or False (F).*

Luigi's
Italian Restaurant

Family-style eating since 1990
Open Tuesday–Sunday, 12:00–9:00
EARLY-BIRD SPECIAL
(full dinner for $10.95 if ordered before 6:00)
No reservations necessary
No credit cards
875 Orange St.

Antonio's
Ristorante Italiano

Established in 1990
Relaxed dining in a romantic atmosphere
open seven days a week—dinner only
reservations suggested

all credit cards accepted

1273 Orange Street 453-3285
one free beverage with this ad

___F___ **1.** Luigi's is older than Antonio's.

_____ **2.** Antonio's is more romantic than Luigi's.

_____ **3.** Luigi's is probably less crowded.

_____ **4.** Antonio's seems cheaper than Luigi's.

_____ **5.** On Tuesdays, Luigi's has shorter business hours.

2 **COMPARE & COMPLETE** • *Look at part of Luigi's menu. Then complete the comparisons. Use the comparative form of the words in parentheses.*

> ♥ **Spaghetti Primavera** *(with lightly sautéed vegetables)* $6.95
> 🌶 **Spaghetti Arrabbiata** *(with hot chili peppers and tomatoes)* $7.85
> **Fettuccini Alfredo** *(with butter and heavy cream)* $8.29
> **Linguine Aglio e Olio** *(with garlic and oil)*....................................$5.67
> ♥ low fat, low salt 🌶 hot and spicy

1. The spaghetti primavera is _____cheaper than_____ the spaghetti arrabbiata.
(cheap)

2. The linguine aglio e olio is _____ the fettuccini Alfredo.
(expensive)

3. The spaghetti arrabbiata is _____ and
(hot)
_____ the linguine aglio e olio.
(spicy)

4. The fettuccini Alfredo is _____ the spaghetti primavera.
(fattening)

5. The spaghetti primavera is _____ the fettuccini Alfredo.
(healthy)

3 **COMPLETE** • *Read these comments about a restaurant. Complete them with the comparative form of the words in parentheses to show cause and effect or a change.*

1. **A:** I can't believe the size of this menu. It's going to take me forever to choose.

   B: _____The longer_____ the menu, ___the more difficult___ the choice.

           (long)   (difficult)

2. **A:** They say the food here is getting _____ and _____.

                                                                              (good)

   B: And _____ the food, _____ it is.

                   (good)   (expensive)

3. **A:** The service seems a little slow tonight.

   B: Yes, _____ the restaurant, _____ the service.

               (popular)   (slow)

4. **A:** The cigarette smoke here is getting _____ and _____.

                                                                            (bad)

   B: _____ the room, _____ my cough gets.

             (smoky)   (bad)

5. **A:** It's pretty loud in here.

   B: _____ the restaurant, _____ it is.

             (crowded)   (noisy)

6. **A:** They certainly give you a lot of food. I can't eat another bite.

   B: _____ the portions, _____ it is to finish.

             (big)   (hard)

7. **A:** Their desserts keep getting _____ and _____.

                                                             (delicious)

   B: And I keep getting _____ and _____!

                                                  (heavy)

4 **EDIT** • *Read this restaurant review. Find and correct eight mistakes in the use of the comparative of adjectives. The first mistake is already corrected.*

Dining Out

BY BRUCE NEWHART

Pete's Place has just reopened under new management. The dining room looks bigger, ~~more bright~~ **brighter**, and prettier as the old one. Although the food isn't better, it *is* just as good. The menu is more varied and less expensiver. Try one of their pasta dishes. You won't find a more fresher tomato sauce in town. And leave room for dessert. They just keep getting good and better.

The wait staff is friendly but not able to handle large numbers of people—the crowded the restaurant, the slower the service. At dinnertime the lines outside this popular eatery are getting longer and more long. Try lunchtime for a quieter and relaxeder meal.

Adjectives: Superlatives

To the **loveliest**
        Most original
Most vibrant
    Most exciting
Woman I know...

Who just happens to be my wife!

HAPPY VALENTINE'S DAY!

CHECK *POINT*

Check the correct answer.

The sender of this card thinks his wife is very:

❏ typical

❏ special

NOTE: Valentine's Day (February 14) is a holiday in the United States and Canada. Many people send cards to special people in their lives to tell them their feelings.

CHART CHECK

Check the correct answers.

Which word always goes before the superlative form of the adjective?

❏ *a* or *an*

❏ *the*   ❏ *most*

Which letters do you add to the end of a short adjective to form the superlative?

❏ *-er*   ❏ *-est*

Which words do you add before a long adjective to form the superlative?

❏ *more* or *less*

❏ *most* or *least*

SUPERLATIVES		
	SUPERLATIVE ADJECTIVE FORM	
You are	**the sweetest** **the funniest** **the best** **the most wonderful** **the least selfish**	person in the world.
That's	**the nicest** **the loveliest** **the worst** **the most amusing** **the least original**	card I've ever received.

EXPRESS CHECK

Complete the chart.

ADJECTIVE	SUPERLATIVE
nice	
beautiful	
warm	
happy	

Grammar Explanations

Examples

---

1. Use the **superlative** form of adjectives to single out people, places, and things from other people, places, and things.

- You are **the best** parents in the world.
- You are **the most wonderful** friend I've ever had.

---

2. There is more than one way to **form the superlative of adjectives**.

	ADJECTIVE	SUPERLATIVE

  a. For one-syllable or two-syllable adjectives ending in -*y*, use *the* + **adjective** + *-est*.

| | bright | **the brightest** |
| | friendly | **the friendliest** |

  ▶ **BE CAREFUL!** There are often spelling changes when you add *-est*.

	nice	**the nicest**
	big	**the biggest**
	pretty	**the prettiest**

  ▶ **BE CAREFUL!** Some adjectives have irregular superlative forms.

| | good | **the best** |
| | bad | **the worst** |

  b. For most other adjectives of two or more syllables, use *the most/the least* + **adjective**.

| | comfortable | **the most comfortable** |
| | | **the least comfortable** |

  ~~**c.** For some adjectives use either *the . . . -est* or *the most/the least*.~~

- My third hotel was **the quietest**. *or the most quiet.*
- My third hotel was **the most quiet**.

---

3. The superlative is often used **with expressions beginning with** *in* or *of*, such as *in the world* and *of all*.

- You're **the best** mother *in the world*.
- He's **the smartest** one *of us all*.

---

4. The superlative is sometimes **followed by a clause**. Often the clause uses the present perfect with *ever*.

- That's **the nicest** card *I've ever received*.
- You have **the loveliest** smile *I've ever seen*.

Check it out!

For spelling rules for the superlative form of adjectives, see Appendix 22 on page 344.

For a list of irregular superlative adjectives, see Appendix 10 on page 339.

For a list of some adjectives that form the superlative in two ways, see Appendix 12 on page 339.

1 **IDENTIFY •** *Read this Mother's Day card written by a young child. Underline all the superlative adjectives.*

cheep

This ____ is the cheepest
stor in the mall.

MOM

You are the best mother
in the whole wide world.
You are the smartest, the brightest, and
the funniest of all moms I've ever known.
You are the nicest mom I've ever had.
You are the most wonderful and definitely
the least mean.
No mom in the whole wide world is
better than you.
You are the greatest mother of all.
I love you very, very much!

Happy Mother's Day!

Love,
Erin

2 **COMPLETE & CHOOSE •** *Read these sentences from Valentine's Day cards. Complete them with the superlative form of the adjectives in parentheses and the expressions in the box.*

of all	in the school	of my life	in our family	~~in the world~~	of the year

1. You are so good to me. I am ____the luckiest____ person ____in the world____.
   (lucky)

2. The day we were married was ___the happiest___ day _of my life_.
   (happy)

3. You are a terrific teacher. You are ___The best___ teacher _in the school_.
   (good)

4. You make me feel warm even in ___cold out___ months _of the year_.
   (cold)

5. You are ___the nicest___ cousin _in our family_.
   (nice)

6. Grandma, you are ___the wisest___ person _of all_. Maybe that's
   (wise)
   why I love you the most. _morthe intelegent._

3 **DESCRIBE •** Look at these gift items. Write sentences about them. Use the superlative form of the words in parentheses.

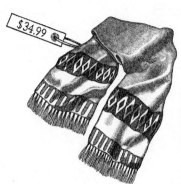

1. The book __is the least expensive gift.__
   (expensive)
2. The painting _the most unusual gift_
   (unusual)
3. The painting _the most practical_
   (practical)
4. The book _is the smallest gift_
   (small)
5. The painting _is the biggest gift_
   (big)
6. The scarf _is the most expensive gift_
   (expensive)
7. The toy _is the funniest gifts_
   (funny)

4 **EDIT •** Read this paragraph from a student's essay. Find and correct five mistakes in the use of superlative adjectives. The first mistake is already corrected.

Ramadan is the ~~seriousest~~ **most serious** time in Muslim culture. During Ramadan, we do not eat from sunup to sunset. This is difficult for everyone, but teenagers have the hardest time. Right after Ramadan is the Eid al-Fitr. This holiday lasts three days, and it's the most happiest time of the year. The morning of Eid, my family gets up early and goes to the mosque. After we greet our neighbors by saying "Eid Mubarek" (Happy Eid), we go home. We eat the big breakfast you have ever seen. Our parents give us gifts, usually new clothes and money. One year, Eid came around the time I graduated from high school. That year, I got the most beautiful clothes and the fatter envelope of money of all the children in my family. Eid Mela is part of Eid al-Fitr. On that day, we all go to a big park. Last year at Eid Mela, I had the better time of my life. I met my old high school friends, and we all ate junk food and showed off our new clothes.

Adverbs: Comparatives and Superlatives

*Come on, Bryant, try **harder**, man!*

*Watch Jordan. **The more** he plays, **the better** he looks.*

CHECK POINT

Circle T (True) or F (False).

T F   Jordan improves every time he plays.

CHART CHECK

Check the correct answer.

What do you add to long adverbs to form the comparative?

❏ *more* or *less*

❏ *-er* or *-est*

Which word do you always add to form the superlative?

❏ *most*

❏ *the*

COMPARATIVES				
	COMPARATIVE ADVERB FORM		**THAN**	
Jordan played	harder better		than	Bryant.
	more less	aggressively consistently		

SUPERLATIVES			
	SUPERLATIVE ADVERB FORM		
He threw	the fastest the best		of anyone in the game.
	the most the least	accurately frequently	

EXPRESS CHECK

Circle the correct words to complete these sentences.

Sims threw faster <u>than / of</u> Jones. He played <u>better / the best</u> of all.

192

Grammar Explanations

Examples

1. Use the **comparative form of adverbs** to focus on <u>differences</u> between actions.

Use the comparative **without** *than* when it is clear which things you are comparing.

- The Bulls played **better than** the Lakers.
- Jordan played **more skillfully than** O'Neal.

- He played **less aggressively**, though.

2. Use the **superlative form of adverbs** to <u>single out something about an action</u>.

We often use the superlative **with expressions beginning with** *of*, such as *of any player*.

- Bryant worked **the hardest**.

- He scored **the most frequently** *of any player* on the team.

3. There is more than one way to **form the comparative and superlative of adverbs**.

  a. For one-syllable adverbs, use **adverb + -er** or *the + **adverb + -est***.

  ▶ **BE CAREFUL!** Some adverbs have <u>irregular comparative and superlative</u> forms.

  b. For most adverbs of two or more syllables, use *more/less* + **adverb** or *the most/the least* + **adverb**.

  c. Some adverbs use either *more/less* or *-er* and *the most/the least* or *the . . . -est*.

ADVERB	COMPARATIVE	SUPERLATIVE
fast	**faster**	**the fastest**
hard	**harder**	**the hardest**
well	**better**	**the best**
badly	**worse**	**the worst**
skillfully	**more/less skillfully**	**the most/the least skillfully**
quickly	**more quickly quicker**	**the most quickly the quickest**

4. Repeat the same comparative to talk about change—<u>an increase or a decrease</u>:

comparative adverb + *and* + **comparative adverb**

OR

more/less + *and* + *more/less* + **adverb**

- Bryant is playing **better and better** as the season continues.
  (His performance keeps improving.)

- He is shooting **more and more accurately**.
  (His shooting keeps getting more accurate).

5. Use a double comparative to show <u>cause and effect</u>:

the + **comparative adverb** + *the* + **comparative adverb**

- **The harder** he played, **the better** he performed.
  (When he played harder, his performance improved.)

Check it out!

For a list of irregular comparisons of adverbs, see Appendix 10 on page 339.

1 **IDENTIFY •** *Read this feature story from the sports section of the newspaper. Underline all the comparative forms once. Underline all the superlative forms twice.*

Section 3 **Sports**

Golds Beat Silvers!

In the first soccer game of the season, the Golds beat the Silvers, 6 to 3. The Silver team played a truly fantastic game, but its defense is still weak. The Golds defended the ball much <u>more aggressively than</u> the Silver team did. Of course, Ace Jackson certainly helped win the game for the Golds. The Golds' star player was back on the field today to the delight of his many fans. He was hurt badly at the end of last season, but he has recovered quickly. Although he didn't play as well as people expected, he still handled the ball like the old Ace. He certainly handled it <u>the most skillfully</u> of anyone on the team. He controlled the ball the best, kicked the ball the farthest, and ran the fastest of any of the players on either team. He played hard and helped the Golds look good. In fact, the harder he played, the better the Golds performed. Watch Ace this season.

And watch the Silvers. They have a new coach, and they're training more seriously this year. I think we'll see them play better and better as the season progresses.

 2 **COMPLETE •** *Read this conversation between friends. Complete it with the comparative or superlative forms of the words in parentheses. Add* **the** *and* **than** *where necessary.*

BILLY: Did you hear about that new speed-reading course? It helps you read

_____faster_____ and _____better_____ .
   1. (fast)   **2.** (well)

MIGUEL: I don't believe it! The _____fastest_____ you read, the _____less_____
         3. (fast)   **4.** (little)

you understand.

BILLY: The ad says that after the course you'll read ten times _____
        5. (rapidly)

and understand five times more. And the best thing is that you won't have

to work any _____harder_____ .
    6. (hard)

MIGUEL: I'd like to see that. All through high school, I read _____ of
          7. (slowly)

any student in my class, but I also remembered details _____
          8. (clearly)

and _____ of any of my classmates.
   9. (long)

BILLY: Maybe you could read even _____ that and still remember
        10. (quickly)

details. That way, you'd have more time to go to the gym.

MIGUEL: Did you read the course description completely?

BILLY: I read it _____ I read most things.
     11. (completely)

3

CHOOSE & COMPLETE • *Look at the chart. Then complete the sentences with the comparative or superlative form of the words in the box. You will use some words more than once.*

| far | good | fast | bad | slow | high |

ATHLETE	BROAD JUMP	POLE VAULTING	5-MILE RUN
Cruz	14.3 feet	7 feet 3 inches	24 minutes
Smith	14.1 feet	7 feet 2 inches	28 minutes
Lin	15.2 feet	7 feet 8 inches	30 minutes
Storm	15.4 feet	8 feet 2 inches	22 minutes

1. Cruz jumped _____farther than_____ Smith.

2. Storm vaulted _____the highest_____ of all.

3. Lin ran _____.

4. Smith ran _____ Storm.

5. Storm jumped _____.

6. Cruz ran _____ Smith.

7. Storm vaulted _____ Smith.

8. All in all, Storm did _____.

9. All in all, Smith did _____.

4

EDIT • *Read this student's report about a basketball game. Find and correct seven mistakes in the use of adverbs. The first mistake is already corrected.*

Last night I watched the Lakers and the Bulls. Both teams played more

aggressively ᴧ I've ever seen them. In fact, they played the better of any game
than

I've watched this season. In the first half, Michael Jordan sprained his left ankle,

and Shaquille O'Neal was out of the game because of fouls. But they still didn't

start the second half any slower that the first. With Jordan out, Kukoc scored the

most frequenter of any player. He's been playing more and more better as the

season goes on. In fact, more he plays, the better he looks. The Bulls won 97 to

88. The Lakers seemed to get tired at the end. They played little and less

consistently as the game went on.

SelfTest

SECTION ONE

Circle the letter of the correct answer to complete each sentence.

> **EXAMPLE:**
> Jennifer never _____ coffee.   A Ⓑ C D
> (A) drink   (C) is drinking
> (B) drinks   (D) was drinking

1. I have _____ job in the world.   **A B C D**
    (A) a good   (C) the best
    (B) best   (D) the better

2. The apple pie smells _____!   **A B C D**
    (A) wonderful   (C) more wonderfully
    (B) wonderfully   (D) the most wonderfully

3. Our team didn't play _____ I expected. I was disappointed.   **A B C D**
    (A) as well as   (C) as badly as
    (B) well   (D) better

4. I passed my driver's test. It seemed much _____ this time.   **A B C D**
    (A) easy   (C) easiest
    (B) easier   (D) easily

5. The faster Tranh walks, _____.   **A B C D**
    (A) more tired   (C) the more tired he gets
    (B) he gets tired   (D) he gets more tired

6. Could you talk _____? I'm trying to work.   **A B C D**
    (A) more quietly   (C) more quiet
    (B) quieter than   (D) quiet

7. Lisa is staying home. Her cold is a lot _____ today.   **A B C D**
    (A) bad   (C) worst
    (B) worse   (D) the worst

8. Sorry we're late. Your house is much _____ than we thought.   **A B C D**
    (A) far   (C) farther
    (B) the farthest   (D) the farther

9. The movie was so _____ that we couldn't sleep last night.   **A B C D**
    (A) excitingly   (C) excite
    (B) excited   (D) exciting

10. Chris is working very _____ these days.   **A B C D**
    (A) hardly   (C) harder
    (B) hard   (D) hardest

11. Write the report first. It's more important _____ your other work.   **A B C D**
    (A) than   (C) from
    (B) as   (D) then

12. The lunch menu is very short. It's _____ than the dinner menu.   **A B C D**
    (A) varied   (C) less varied
    (B) more varied   (D) the least varied

13. Thank you! That's _____ I've ever received.   **A B C D**
    (A) the nicer gift   (C) nicest gift
    (B) a nice gift   (D) the nicest gift

14. It's getting more _____ to find a cheap apartment.   **A B C D**
    (A) hardly   (C) the most difficult
    (B) and more difficult   (D) and very difficult

SECTION TWO

Each sentence has four underlined words or phrases. The four underlined parts of the sentence are marked A, B, C, and D. Circle the letter of the one underlined word or phrase that is NOT CORRECT.

> **EXAMPLE:**
> Mike <u>usually</u> <u>drives</u> to school, but <u>today</u> he <u>walks</u>.   **A B C (D)**
>   A   B   C   D

15. <u>The harder</u> Sylvia <u>tries</u>, <u>less</u> she <u>succeeds</u>.   **A B C D**
     A   B C   D

16. This has been <u>the best</u> day <u>than</u> my <u>whole</u> life!   **A B C D**
               A   B   C   D

17. We're <u>always</u> <u>amazing</u> <u>by</u> John's <u>incredible</u> travel stories.   **A B C D**
          A   B   C   D

18. We took <u>a lot of</u> photos because she was <u>such</u> a <u>cutely</u> <u>little</u> baby.   **A B C D**
          A   B   C   D

19. Our <u>new</u> car is <u>hard</u> to drive <u>than</u> our <u>old</u> one.   **A B C D**
     A   B   C   D

20. Patrick doesn't <u>run quickly</u> <u>as</u> Lee, <u>but</u> he can run <u>farther</u>.   **A B C D**
           A   B C   D

21. You did <u>much</u> <u>more</u> <u>better</u> in the last test <u>than</u> in this one.   **A B C D**
        A   B   C   D

22. What's <u>the</u> <u>more</u> <u>popular</u> of all the <u>new</u> TV shows?   **A B C D**
       A   B   C   D

23. <u>The</u> <u>more</u> I practice the piano, the <u>most</u> <u>skilled</u> I get.   **A B C D**
   A   B   C   D

24. The garbage in the street <u>is</u> <u>more</u> <u>disgusted</u> <u>than</u> the potholes.   **A B C D**
                    A   B   C   D

25. Today seems <u>as</u> <u>hotter</u> <u>as</u> yesterday, but the humidity is <u>lower</u>.   **A B C D**
          A   B   C   D

Gerunds:
Subject and Object

I'm all out of breath again. I really need to quit **jogging**!

CHART CHECK

Check the correct answer.

What does the gerund end with?

❑ *-ed*

❑ *-ing*

What goes before the gerund to make it negative?

❑ *not*

❑ *don't* or *doesn't*

GERUND AS SUBJECT		
GERUND (SUBJECT)	**VERB**	**OBJECT**
Smoking	harms	your health.
Not smoking	makes	you healthier.

GERUND AS OBJECT		
SUBJECT	**VERB**	**GERUND (OBJECT)**
You	should quit	**smoking**.
My doctor	suggests	**not smoking**.

EXPRESS CHECK

Complete this conversation with the correct form of the verb **drink**.
Use the affirmative or negative.

A: _____ too much coffee isn't good for you.

B: I know. I quit _____ coffee last year.

A: My doctor suggested _____ soda either.

Grammar Explanations

1. A **gerund** (base form of verb + *-ing*) is a
<u>verb that functions like a noun</u>.

A gerund can be the **subject** of a sentence.

▶ **BE CAREFUL!** There are often <u>spelling changes</u>
when you add *-ing* to the base form of the verb.

Notice that a gerund is always <u>singular</u> and is
followed by the third-person-singular form of
the verb.

▶ **BE CAREFUL!** Don't confuse a gerund with the
progressive form of the verb.

Examples

■ **Drinking** too much coffee is bad for your health.

■ **Smoking** is also unhealthy.

| smoke | **smoking** |
| jog | **jogging** |

■ **Eating** junk food *makes* me sick.
■ **Inhaling** smoke *gives* me bronchitis.

gerund
■ **Drinking** coffee isn't healthy.

progressive form
■ He **is drinking** coffee right now.

---

2. A **gerund** can also be the **object** of
certain verbs.

To the right is a short list of <u>verbs that can be</u>
<u>followed by a gerund</u>.

■ I **enjoy** *exercising*.
■ I've **considered** *joining* a gym.

[handwritten: I] **admit** *[handwritten: telling the truth]*	**miss** *[handwritten: after those verbes]*
[handwritten: not do something] **avoid**	**practice** *[handwritten: we use gerund]*
consider	**quit**
[handwritten: don't...] **deny**	**resent**
enjoy	**suggest**
finish	**understand**

---

3. There are many common expressions with
go + **gerund**. These expressions usually
describe <u>activities</u>, such as *shopping, fishing,
skiing, swimming,* and *camping*.

■ We often **go** *swimming* in the lake.
■ Yesterday I **went** *shopping* for a new pair of
running shoes.

Check it out!

For more complete lists of common verbs that can be followed by the gerund,
see Appendix 3 on page 337 and Appendix 6 on page 338.

1 **IDENTIFY** • *Read part of an article from a health newsletter. Underline the words ending in **-ing** that are gerunds.*

YOUR HEALTH

<u>S</u>WIMMING is great exercise. It's healthy, fun, and relaxing. Because swimming is a "low-impact" sport, most people enjoy participating in this activity without fear of injury to their bones or muscles. Jogging, which is a "high-impact" activity, can at times be harmful. I know this from personal experience. Last year while I was jogging, I injured my right knee. I don't go jogging anymore. After a painful month of recovery, I stopped running and switched to water sports. I'm now considering joining a swimming team and competing in races.

2 **CHOOSE & COMPLETE** • *Read these statements about health issues. Complete them with the gerund form of the verbs in the box. Choose between affirmative and negative.*

increase	eat	do	walk	drink	~~smoke~~	swim	run	go

1. _____Smoking_____ is bad for your heart and lungs.

2. _____ too much fat and sugar is also unhealthy.

3. _____ enough water is bad for your general health.

4. Doctors suggest _____ the amount of fruits and vegetables in your diet.

5. Avoid _____ too many high-impact sports such as jogging and jumping rope.

6. Instead, consider _____ in a pool every day. It's an excellent low-impact activity.

7. Many health experts think that _____ is better than _____ because there is less stress on your body when your feet come into contact with the ground.

8. Some people are afraid of the doctor, but _____ for regular checkups is a mistake.

SUMMARIZE • *Read each numbered statement. Complete the following summary using the appropriate verb from the box and the gerund form of the verb in parentheses.*

| acknowledge | avoid | consider | deny | ~~enjoy~~ | go | quit |

1. **Tom:** Ann jogs, but I don't really like that kind of exercise.

    Summary: Tom doesn't ___enjoy jogging._____
                                        (jog)

2. **Marta:** Oh, no thanks. I don't smoke anymore.

    Summary: Marta _____
                                    (smoke)

3. **Chen:** I'm going to that new swimming pool. Would you like to go with me?

    Summary: Chen is going to _____
                                      (swim)

4. **Jim:** I smell smoke too. But don't look at me! I didn't have a cigarette!

    Summary: Jim _____
                                  (smoke)

5. **Ina:** I know I should exercise, but I don't want to. I guess you're right. I *am* lazy.

    Summary: Ina _____ lazy.
                                  (be)

6. **Phil:** No, thanks. The cake looks great, but I'm trying to stay away from sweets.

    Summary: Phil _____ sweets.
                                  (eat)

7. **Vilma:** I'm not sure, but I *may* go on a vacation.

    Summary: Vilma _____ a vacation.
                              (take)

 EDIT • *Read Jim's notes. Find and correct nine mistakes in the use of the gerund. The first mistake is already corrected.*

SMOKING
WAYS I CAN QUIT ~~SMOKE~~ CIGARETTES

Pick an exact date to quit smoke.

Stop smoking completely. (Cut down is harder than stopping all at once.)

Avoid to be around other smokers (at least at the beginning).

Start exercising daily. To exercise can reduce stress.

No drinking coffee may help too.

Imagine been a non-smoker. Positive mental images can help.

Consider to join a support group.

Don't delay to ask for help. Call Dr. Burns right away!

Keep trying and don't give up!

Gerunds after Prepositions

GET INVOLVED!

Interested **in improving** life on campus?

Tired **of hearing** complaints and not **finding** solutions?

Join the Student Council!

Next Meeting: Mon., March 25, 8:00 P.M., Main Auditorium

We look forward **to seeing** you there.

You CAN make a difference!

CHECK *POINT*

Circle T (True) or F (False).

The Student Council is looking for students who

T F want to make new friends.

T F want to improve life on campus.

T F like to complain.

CHART CHECK

Check the correct answers.

What part of speech is the word *to* in *look forward to*?

❑ part of the infinitive

❑ a preposition

What form of the verb follows a preposition?

❑ the base form

❑ the gerund

❑ the infinitive

	PREPOSITION	*(NOT)*	GERUND	
			GERUNDS AFTER PREPOSITIONS	
Do you have ideas	**for**		**improving**	life on campus?
We're good	**at**		**planning**	ahead.
You can help	**by**		**taking**	notes.
She believes	**in**	(not)	**compromising**.	
Are you tired	**of**		**hearing**	complaints?
Let's work	**instead of**		**complaining**.	
They insist	**on**	(not)	**coming**	to the meeting.
I look forward	**to**	(not)	**having to**	study next summer.

EXPRESS CHECK

Complete this conversation with the correct form of the verb **join**.

A: Are you happy about _____ the Student Council?

B: Sure. I'd been looking forward to _____ a group for a while.

Grammar Explanations

Examples

1. A **preposition** is a word such as *about*, *against*, *at*, *by*, *for*, *in*, *instead of*, *of*, *on*, *to*, *with*, and *without*. A preposition can be followed by a noun or a pronoun.

Because a **gerund** (base form of verb + *-ing*) acts as a noun, it <u>can follow a preposition</u> too.

noun
■ The council insists **on** *elections*.

pronoun
■ The council insists **on** *them*.

gerund
■ The council insists **on** *voting*.

2. Many **common expressions** are made up of a verb or an adjective followed by a preposition.

VERB + PREPOSITION	ADJECTIVE + PREPOSITION
advise **against**	afraid **of**
believe **in**	bored **with**
count **on**	excited **about**

These expressions can be <u>followed by a gerund</u>.

■ She **counts on** *going* to college.
■ He **is bored with** *working* in a store.

3. BE CAREFUL!

a. In the **expressions** to the right, *to* is a <u>preposition</u>, not part of an infinitive form. For this reason it can be <u>followed by the gerund</u>.

VERB + PREPOSITION	ADJECTIVE + PREPOSITION
look forward **to**	accustomed **to**
object **to**	opposed **to**
resort **to**	used **to**

■ I'm looking forward **to** *seeing* you.
   NOT I'm looking forward ~~to see you.~~

b. Do not confuse *used to* + **base form** of verb (for habits in the past) with *be/get used to* + **gerund** (meaning "be/get accustomed to").

■ I **used to take** the train.
   (It was my habit to take the train, but I no longer take the train.)

■ I'm **used to** *taking* the train.
   (I'm accustomed to taking the train.)

■ I'm **getting used to** *taking* the train.
   (I'm getting accustomed to taking the train.)

Check it out!

For a list of common verb plus preposition combinations, see Appendix 7 on page 338.
For a list of common adjective plus preposition combinations, see Appendix 8 on page 338.

1 **IDENTIFY** • *The Student Council wrote a letter to the college president. Read it and underline all the preposition + gerund combinations.*

> We, the members of the Student Council, would like to share with you the thoughts and concerns of the general student body. As you probably know, many students are complaining about life on campus. We are interested in meeting with you to discuss our ideas for dealing with these complaints.
>
> We know that you are tired of hearing students complain and that you are not used to working with the Student Council. However, if you really believe in giving new ideas a try, we hope you will think about speaking with our representatives soon. We look forward to hearing from you soon.

2 **CHOOSE & COMPLETE** • *Read these comments from the school newspaper. Complete the students' statements with the appropriate preposition from the box (you will use one of them several times) and the gerund form of the verb in parentheses.*

at   on   in   to   about   for

1. I don't have any plans for spring break, but I'm not concerned ____**about getting**____
   (get)
   bored. I can always take a walk or something.—*Jim Hsu*

2. What are my plans for spring break? I'm very interested _____
   (listen)
   to jazz. I'm going to attend the Spring Jazz Festival.—*Lisa Suarez*

3. My friends and I are driving to New Orleans. I'm excited _____,
   (go)
   but I'm nervous _____ at night.—*Emilia Leale*
   (drive)

4. I'm really looking forward _____ at home and just
   (stay)
   _____.—*Don Pitt*
   (relax)

5. I'm driving to Quebec. It's famous _____ great food. —*Eun Ko*
   (have)

6. I love languages, but I'm not good _____ them, so I'm studying for
   (learn)
   my Japanese class over the break. —*Claire Kaplan*

7. My friends and I are going camping, but my little brother insists _____
   (come)
   with us. A lot of fun that'll be!—*Omar Sisane*

8. My girlfriend plans _____ and _____ to the
   (read)   (go)
   movies, so I guess I'll read a lot and see a lot of movies.—*Tim Riley*

COMBINE • *Read these pairs of sentences about school life. Combine them with the prepositions in parentheses.*

1. You can't walk on campus late at night. You have to worry about your safety.

You can't walk on campus late at night without worrying about your safety.
(without)

2. We can make changes. We can tell the administration about our concerns.

_____
(by)

3. The administration can help. It can listen to our concerns.

_____
(by)

4. In some cases, students just complain. They don't make suggestions for improvements.

_____
(instead of)

5. Students get annoyed with some teachers. Some teachers come late to class.

_____
(for)

6. You can improve your grades. Study regularly.

_____
(by)

 EDIT • *Read this student's letter. Find and correct seven mistakes in the use of gerunds after prepositions. The first mistake is already corrected.*

Dear Brian,

    I have been attending Longtree College for a year. I'm very happy
      studying
about ~~study~~ here. At first, it was a little hard getting used to speak English

all the time, but now I feel very comfortable about communicate in my

second language.

    I just joined an international student group, and I'm excited with

meeting new people. Summer break is coming, and a few of us are planning

on do some traveling together. Before to join this group, I used to spend

holidays alone.

    Please write. I look forward to hear from you!

    K.

Infinitives
after Certain Verbs

ASK ANNIE

Dear Annie,

A month ago I met this great woman, Megan, and I **asked her to marry** me right away. She says things are "moving too fast," and she **wants me to think** about my proposal some more. I told her I **can't afford to wait** forever. Am I right? —*Impatient*

CHECK **POINT**

Check the correct answer.

❏ Megan wants more time to consider the marriage proposal.

❏ Megan thinks "Impatient" should consider his proposal more.

CHART CHECK

Circle T (True) or F (False).

T F   The infinitive = base form + **to**.

T F   The negative infinitive = **not** + infinitive.

T F   All verbs need an object before the infinitive.

STATEMENTS: WITHOUT AN OBJECT

SUBJECT	VERB	(NOT)	INFINITIVE	
They	decided agreed	(not)	to call to ask	Annie.

STATEMENTS: WITH AN OBJECT

SUBJECT	VERB	OBJECT	(NOT)	INFINITIVE	
They	urged advised	John him	(not)	to call to ask	her.

STATEMENTS: WITH AN OPTIONAL OBJECT

SUBJECT	VERB	(OBJECT)	INFINITIVE	
They	wanted needed	(John) (him)	to call to ask	her.

EXPRESS CHECK

Unscramble these words to form a sentence.

to • want • Annie • write • to • I _____

Grammar Explanations	Examples

1. Certain **verbs** can be followed by an **infinitive** (*to* + base form of the verb).

- I **want** *to get* married.
- I **asked** Annie *to help* me.

2. Some of these verbs are followed **directly by an infinitive**.

The verbs to the right can be followed directly by an infinitive.

- He **decided** *to write* to Annie.
- He **hoped** *to get* a quick reply.

agree	**plan**
begin	**refuse**
fail	**seem**

3. Some verbs need an **object** (noun or pronoun) **before the infinitive**.

The verbs to the right need an object before the infinitive.

- object
- I **invited** *Mary* **to celebrate** with us.

- object
- I **reminded** *her* **to come**.

advise	**tell**
encourage	**urge**
order	**warn**

4. Some verbs can be followed by either:

- **an infinitive**
  OR
- **an object** + **infinitive**

The verbs to the right can be followed either directly by an infinitive or by an object + infinitive.

- He **wants** *to leave*. He's tired.
  OR
- He **wants** *you to leave*. You're tired.

ask	**need**
expect	**want**
help	**would like**

5. Form a **negative infinitive** by placing *not* before the infinitive.

- Lee remembered **not** *to call* after 5:00.
  (Lee didn't call after 5:00.)

- Ana told me **not** *to go* to class.
  (Ana: "Don't go. The teacher is sick.")

▶ **BE CAREFUL!** A sentence with a negative infinitive can have a very different meaning from a sentence with a negative main verb.

- Van told me **not** *to give up*.
  (Van: "Don't give up.")

- Van **didn't tell** me to give up.
  (Van didn't say anything.)

Check it out!

For a list of common verbs followed directly by the infinitive, see Appendix 4 on page 338.

For a list of verbs followed by objects and the infinitive, see Appendix 5 on page 338.

For a list of verbs that can be followed either directly by an infinitive or by an object + infinitive, see Appendix 5 on page 338.

1 **IDENTIFY** • *Read Annie's response to "Impatient." Underline all the verb + infinitive and verb + object + infinitive combinations.*

Lifestyles 17

Dear Impatient,

Slow down! You <u>appear to be</u> in too much of a hurry. You've only known this person for a month and yet you asked her to marry you! What's the big rush? *Why* can't you afford to wait? Are you afraid that if she gets to know you better, she may decide not to tie the knot? I agree with your girlfriend. You need to consider things more carefully. You can't expect her (or yourself) to make such an important decision so quickly. If you don't want to regret a hasty decision, I advise you both to get to know each other better before you hurry to the altar. —Annie

2 **COMPLETE** • *Read this article. Complete it with the correct form of the verbs in parentheses. Use the simple present or the imperative form of the first verb.*

♥ Planning for Love →

Most people make careful plans when they _____decide to take_____ a vacation.
1. (decide / take)
Yet when they _____ a mate, they depend on luck.
2. (attempt / find)
Edward A. Dreyfus, Ph.D., _____ love to chance.
3. (warn / single people / not / leave)
He _____ his four-step plan when they search for a life partner.
4. (urge / them / use)
Remember: When you _____ you _____.
5. (fail / plan)   **6.** (plan / fail)
STEP ONE: Make a list. What kind of person do you _____?
7. (wish / meet)
Someone intelligent? Someone who loves sports? List everything.

STEP TWO: Make another list. What kind of person are you? _____
8. (Ask / two friends / read)
your list and comment on it. The two lists should match.

STEP THREE: Increase your chances. _____ in activities you like.
9. (Choose / participate)
STEP FOUR: Ask for introductions. Dr. Dreyfus _____
10. (advise / people / not / feel)
embarrassed to ask. Everyone _____ a matchmaker!
11. (want / be)

3

SUMMARIZE • Read each numbered statement. Complete the summary using the appropriate verb from the box followed by an infinitive or an object + infinitive.

agree	remind	would like	~~urge~~	invite	need	forget	encourage

1. **ANNIE:** I really think you should take things more slowly, Chet.

   SUMMARY: Annie <u>urged Chet to take things more slowly.</u>

2. **CARYN:** Tom, could you call me at 10:00?

   SUMMARY: Caryn _____

3. **KURT:** Emily, please remember to buy gas today.

   SUMMARY: Kurt _____

4. **JOHN:** We're going out for coffee, Marta. Would you like to join us?

   SUMMARY: John _____

5. **JASON:** OK, OK, Dad. I'll be home by 10:30 if that's what you want.

   SUMMARY: Jason _____

6. **JEFF:** Oh, no! It's 4:15. I didn't go to the 2:00 staff meeting!

   SUMMARY: Jeff _____

7. **MOM:** Come on, Lisa, don't be scared. Just try again.

   SUMMARY: Lisa's mother _____

8. **TERRY:** I'm using the car tonight. I'm taking Sue to the mall.

   SUMMARY: Terry _____

4

EDIT • Read this entry in a personal diary. Find and correct seven mistakes in the use of infinitives after certain verbs. The first mistake is already corrected.

>   to join
> Annie advised me ~~joining~~ a club or take a class, and I finally did it! I decided become
> a member of the school's Outdoor Adventure Club, and I went to my first meeting last night.
> I'm really excited about this. The club is planning a hiking trip next weekend. I definitely want
> to go rafting in the spring. At first I didn't want signing up, but the leader was so nice.
> He urged me to not miss this trip, so I put my name on the list. After the meeting, a group
> of people asked me to go out with them. We went to a coffee shop and talked for hours.
> Well, I hoped make some friends when I joined this club, but I didn't expect everyone being
> so friendly. I'm glad Annie persuaded me no to give up.

UNIT 49

Infinitives
after Certain Adjectives and Certain Nouns

It's **hard to find** good fries these days.

| CHECK | POINT |

Check the correct answer.

☐ Finding good fries is difficult.

☐ The man hardly eats anything but fries.

CHART CHECK

Check the correct answers.

The infinitive is formed with:

☐ *to* + base form of verb

☐ *to* + base form of verb + *-ing*

The infinitive follows:

☐ certain nouns and adjectives

☐ certain prepositions

INFINITIVES AFTER CERTAIN ADJECTIVES			
	ADJECTIVE	**INFINITIVE**	
It's	**hard**	**to find**	nutritious fast food.
We're	**eager**	**to hear**	about the new restaurant.
He seemed	**surprised**	**to learn**	the amount of fat in a burger.

INFINITIVES AFTER CERTAIN NOUNS			
	NOUN	**INFINITIVE**	
It's	**time**	**to go.**	
That's a high	**price**	**to pay.**	
Does he have	**permission**	**to stay**	out late?

EXPRESS CHECK

Unscramble these words to form two sentences.

convenient • It's • eat • fast • food • to _____.

pay • a • price • low • That's • to   _____.

Grammar Explanations

Examples

1. Certain **adjectives** can be followed by an **infinitive** (*to* + base form of the verb).

Many of these adjectives describe a <u>feeling</u> about the action in the infinitive.

Adjectives that express <u>praise or blame</u> are often followed by an infinitive.

Adjectives that show <u>the order of actions</u> are often followed by an infinitive.

      adjective infinitive
- They were **eager** *to try* the new taco.

- She was **glad** *to hear* that it was low in calories.

- I was **wrong** *to leave*.
- They were **brave** *to tell* him.

- We were **last** *to order*.
- When the check came, she was **first** *to leave* the restaurant.

2. We often use *It's* + **adjective** + **infinitive**.

When the action in the infinitive is done by a person, we often use *of* or *for* + **noun/pronoun**.

It's + **adjective** + **infinitive** is often used to make <u>general observations</u>.

     adjective infinitive
- **It's great** *to see* you again.

- It was **silly** *of Tom* to leave.
- It's **hard** *for us* to get here on time.

- **It's convenient** *to eat* fast food.
- **It's difficult** for students *to work* full time.

3. Certain **nouns** can be followed by an **infinitive**.

The **noun** + **infinitive** combination often expresses <u>advisability or necessity</u>.

    noun infinitive
- It's **time** *to take* a break.
- I have the **right** *to eat* what I want.
- They made a **decision** *to lose* weight.
- It's a high **price** *to pay*.
- He has **permission** *to stay* out late.

- Robin is the **person** *to ask* about that.
  (You should ask Robin about that.)

- I have a **test** *to study* for right now.
  (I must study for my test.)

Check it out!

For a list of common adjectives that can be followed by the infinitive, see Appendix 9 on page 338.

1

IDENTIFY • *Read this questionnaire. Underline all the adjective + infinitive and noun + infinitive combinations. Write* **A** *over the adjectives and* **N** *over the nouns.*

FAST-FOOD QUESTIONNAIRE

Please take a few <u>minutes to complete</u> this questionnaire about fast-food restaurants.
             N

Check (✓) all the answers that are appropriate for you.

1. How often are you <u>likely to eat</u> at a fast-food restaurant?
                    A

  ☐ 1–3 times a week   ☐ 4–6 times a week

  ☐ more than 6 times a week   ☐ never

2. In your opinion, fast food is:

  ☐ good to eat   ☐ a way to save time

  ☐ fun to order occasionally   ☐ unhealthy to have every day

3. Which statement best describes your feelings about the cost of fast food?

  ☐ It's a high price to pay for convenience.   ☐ You get a lot for just a little money.

4. Is it a good idea to include healthy choices in fast-food menus?

  ☐ Yes   ☐ No

2

COMPLETE • *Read these excerpts from letters to the editor of a college newspaper. Complete them with the correct form of the words in parentheses.*

Last year I stopped eating in the school cafeteria because the food was so bad and it

was such a grim ___place to have___ a meal. Yesterday I went back for
                 1. (place / have)

the first time. I was _____ Taco Bell there. Fast foods are
                  2. (delighted / find)

the _____! They're _____, and the
   3. (way / go)   **4.** (fun / eat)

cheerful atmosphere has made the cafeteria a _____ in. I'll be
                            5. (pleasure / eat)

eating lunch there every day from now on.—*L. Brenner*

It was a _____ fast-food chains to the campus. It's
      6. (mistake / bring)

_____ the exact same restaurants everywhere you go. The
  7. (outrageous / see)

food they serve isn't _____. It contains much too much sugar,
               8. (good / eat)

salt, and fat. For commuter students, it's _____ a healthy
                     9. (essential / have)

meal before evening class, and it's _____ off campus for
              10. (difficult / go)

dinner. We just don't have the time.—*B. Chen*

3 **CHOOSE & COMPLETE** • *Read these conversations between co-workers. Complete them with the words in parentheses and the infinitive form of a verb from the box.*

| get | cry | hear | keep | work | find | decide | wake up | show | ~~take~~ |

CHRIS: Hey, Dana. I've got to talk to you. Do you have _____*time to take*_____
1. (time)
a break?

DANA: Sure, Chris. What's wrong? You look like you're _____.
2. (ready)

CHRIS: Mr. Kay just asked me if I'd be _____ from 4:00 P.M.
3. (willing)
to midnight.

DANA: You have an early class. It's _____ early after
4. (hard)
working late.

CHRIS: Right. When I told him that he said, "I'm _____ that,
5. (suprised)
Chris. I thought you were _____ a promotion to
6. (eager)
shift manager."

DANA: It's _____ your grades up too. Did he give you
7. (important)
_____?
8. (time)

CHRIS: He just said, "OK. I'll ask Steve. We'll give *him* the _____
9. (chance)
his loyalty to the company."

DANA: Fast-food jobs are _____. Just concentrate on school.
10. (easy)

4 **EDIT** • *Read Mr. Kay's journal. Find and correct seven mistakes in the use of infinitives. The first mistake is already corrected.*

                                    to ask
Tonight I made the decision ~~asked~~ Chris to take the night shift. I
really thought she was going to be glad for getting the offer. She has
her own rent pay, and I know it's hard for she to meet all her
expenses. Looks like she was the wrong person I asked! The problem
was, she wasn't willing to said Yes or No, and I'm afraid I got a little
impatient. It was wrong of me to threaten to ask Steve. I could tell
that she was pretty upset to hear that. I'll think about giving her the
promotion anyway. She deserves getting a break.

Infinitives
with *Too* and *Enough*

"Son, your mother and I think that you are now old enough to get your own drink of water."

CHENEY

CHECK *POINT*

Circle T (True) or F (False).

T F The man's parents want the man to get them a drink of water.

T F The man wants his parents to get him a drink of water.

CHART CHECK

Check the correct answer.

Which word comes before the adjective or adverb?

❏ *too*

❏ *enough*

INFINITIVES WITH *TOO*

	Too	Adjective/ Adverb	(For + Noun/ Object Pronoun)	Infinitive	
We're (not)		**young**	(for people)	**to trust**.	
The teacher talked	too	**quickly**	(for me)	**to take**	notes.
It's (not)		**hard**	(for us)	**to decide**.	

INFINITIVES WITH *ENOUGH*

	Adjective/ Adverb	Enough	(For + Noun/ Object Pronoun)	Infinitive	
They're (not)	**old**		(for people)	**to trust**.	
She hasn't come	**often**	enough	(for me)	**to recognize**	her.
It's (not)	**easy**		(for us)	**to decide**.	

214

EXPRESS CHECK

Unscramble these words to form two sentences.

vote • She's • to • young • too _____

to • enough • old • We're • work _____

Grammar Explanations

Grammar Explanations	**Examples**
1. Use **too** + **adjective/adverb** + **infinitive** to give a <u>reason</u>.	■ I'm **too young** *to drive*. *(I'm not sixteen yet, so I can't drive.)* ■ She is**n't too young** *to drive*. *(She's over sixteen, so she can drive.)* ■ She arrived **too late** *to take* the test. *(She arrived twenty minutes after the test started, so she couldn't take the test.)* ■ She did**n't** arrive **too late** *to take* the test. *(She arrived only two minutes after the test started, so she could take the test.)*
2. You can also use **adjective/adverb** + **enough** + **infinitive** to give a <u>reason</u>.	■ I'm **old enough** *to go* into the army. *(I'm over eighteen, so I can go into the army.)* ■ He is**n't old enough** *to go* into the army. *(He isn't eighteen yet, so he can't go into the army.)* ■ I ran **fast enough** *to pass* the physical. *(I ran very fast, so I passed the physical.)* ■ She did**n't** run **fast enough** *to pass* the physical. *(She didn't run very fast, so she didn't pass the physical.)*
3. Notice that you don't need to use the infinitive when the meaning is clear from the context. ▶ **BE CAREFUL!** Note the <u>placement</u> of **too** and **enough**. **Too** comes <u>before</u> the adjective or adverb. **Enough** comes <u>after</u> the adjective or adverb.	■ I'm seventeen years old, and I can't vote yet. I'm **too young**. I'm not **old enough**. ■ She's **too old**. ■ I'm not **old enough**. NOT I'm not ~~enough old~~.
4. Sometimes we use **for** + **noun** or **for** + **object pronoun** before the infinitive.	■ We are too young **for people** *to trust* us. *(People don't trust us.)* ■ We are too young **for them** *to trust* us. *(They don't trust us.)*

1 **CHOOSE** • *People have different opinions about public issues. Read each numbered statement of opinion. Then circle the letter of the sentence (a) or (b) that best summarizes that opinion.*

1. Teenagers are responsible enough to stay out past 10:00 P.M.

    (a.) Teenagers should have permission to stay out past 10:00 P.M.

    b. Teenagers shouldn't have permission to stay out past 10:00 P.M.

2. Teenagers are too immature to vote.

    a. Teenagers should be able to vote.

    b. Teenagers shouldn't be able to vote.

3. Teenagers are responsible enough to use the Internet without censorship.

    a. Teenagers can use the Internet without censorship.

    b. Teenagers can't use the Internet without censorship.

4. Adults are too afraid of change to listen to children's ideas.

    a. Adults listen to children's ideas.

    b. Adults don't listen to children's ideas.

5. At age seventy, people are not too old to work.

    a. At age seventy, people can work.

    b. At age seventy, people can't work.

6. Sixteen-year-olds are not experienced enough to drive at night.

    a. Sixteen-year-olds can drive at night.

    b. Sixteen-year-olds can't drive at night.

2 **UNSCRAMBLE** • *Gina wants to drive to another city for a concert, but her mother thinks she's too young. Make sentences with the words in parentheses. Then write **G (Gina)** or **M (Mother)** to show whose opinion each sentence represents.*

1. You're too young to be out so late.   M

    (too / You're / young / to / out / be / so / late)

2. _____

    (get / It's / to / by ten / us / too / home / far / for)

3. _____

    (take care of / mature / myself / I'm / to / enough)

4. _____

    (dangerous / too / night / It's / to / drive / at)

5. _____

    (too / give / worry / I / much / to / permission / you)

6. _____

    (that / experienced / drive / aren't / far / enough / to / You)

3 **COMPLETE** • *Some teenagers are leaving a concert. Complete the sentences. Use the words in parentheses with the infinitive and* **too** *or* **enough**.

1. I couldn't hear that last song. The guitar was _____too loud for me to hear_____ the words.
(loud / me / hear)

2. Let's get tickets for the concert in Hampton. They're _____.
(cheap / us / afford)

3. I hope the concert hall is _____ all the fans!
(large / hold)

4. I hope my mother lets me go. This concert is going to be _____.
(good / me / miss)

5. Let's get a pizza at Sal's. The large ones are _____.
(big / share)

6. It's 9:30 already. It's _____ for pizza.
(late / stop)

7. I hate this curfew! I think we're _____ out past 10:00!
(old / stay)

8. Kyle didn't get out of work _____ tonight.
(early / come)

9. Van, I'm playing basketball tomorrow. Are you still _____ me?
(slow / beat)

10. Let's find out. But I want to walk. Your car isn't _____.
(safe / drive)

4 **EDIT** • *Read this student's journal entry. Find and correct eight mistakes in the use of infinitives with* **too** *or* **enough**. *The first mistake is already corrected.*

The Phish concert was awesome! Now I'm too excited ~~for sleeping~~ ^{to sleep}. That Mike Gordon can really sing. My voice isn't enough good to sing in the shower! After the concert we were really hungry, but it was to late to go for pizza. I HATE this stupid curfew! It's too weird understand. My friend Todd works and has to pay taxes, but the law says he's too young for staying out past 10:00! That's crazy enough to make me want to scream. That reminds me. I sure hope my mother changes her mind soon enough for I to buy a ticket to the Hampton concert. They sell out very quickly. Why doesn't she think I'm mature to drive fifty miles? I'll have to do it sometime! Well, I'd better try to get some sleep or I'll be too tired too get up in the morning.

Infinitives of Purpose

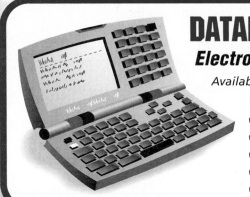

DATALATOR 534 F
Electronic Organizer $89.95

Available at all Lacy's Department Stores.

Use me
- ✔ **to look up** words
- ✔ **to store** names and phone numbers
- ✔ **to add** and **subtract**
- ✔ **to write down** ideas
- ✔ **to look** cool!

CHECK POINT

Check all the correct answers.

What can you use the Datalator as?

☐ an address book   ☐ a telephone   ☐ a dictionary   ☐ a note pad   ☐ a radio

CHART CHECK	AFFIRMATIVE	NEGATIVE
Circle T (True) or F (False).	I put his number in my organizer **(in order) to save** it.	I put his number in my organizer **in order not to lose** it.
T F There are two ways to form the affirmative infinitive of purpose.	I made a note **(in order) to remember** our date.	I made a note **in order not to forget** our date.
	I left at 9:00 **(in order) to arrive** early.	I left at 9:00 **in order not to arrive** late.
T F There are two ways to form the negative infinitive of purpose.	I ran **(in order) to catch** the bus.	I ran **in order not to miss** the bus.

EXPRESS CHECK

Unscramble these words to form two sentences.

store • addresses • use • I • an • organizer • to

_____

in order • I • not • set • oversleep • my • alarm clock • to

_____

Grammar Explanations

Examples

1. Use an **infinitive** (*to* + **base form** of the verb) to explain the purpose of an action. It often answers the question *Why?*

USAGE NOTE: In spoken English, you can answer the question *Why?* with an incomplete sentence beginning with *To*.

A: *Why* did you go to Lacy's?
B: I went there **to buy** one of those Datalators I saw in an ad.

A: *Why* did you go to Lacy's?
B: **To buy** an electronic organizer.

2. You can also use the longer form *in order to* + **base form** of the verb to explain a purpose.

USAGE NOTE: *To* + **base form** of the verb is more common in informal speech and writing.

■ I bought an organizer **in order to store** names and phone numbers.

■ I bought an organizer **to store** names and phone numbers.

3. Use *in order not to* + **base form** of the verb to express a negative purpose.

■ I use my Datalator **in order not to make** mistakes in pronunciation.
(I don't want to make mistakes.)

4. You can also use **noun/pronoun + infinitive** to express the purpose of an object.

■ I need an **organizer to help** me remember my schedule.

■ I need **it to help** me remember my schedule.

1 **IDENTIFY** • *Read this conversation. Underline all the infinitives that express a purpose.*

YOKO: It's 5:00. Aren't you going home?

LEE: No. I'm staying late <u>to finish</u> this report. What about you? Are you going straight home?

YOKO: No. I'm going to stop at the bank to get some cash. Then I'm going to Lacy's Department Store to take advantage of the sale they're having.

LEE: Oh, what are you going to get?

YOKO: One of those new electronic organizers they're advertising. I've been looking for something to help me with my work.

LEE: What's wrong with just a regular calculator?

YOKO: Nothing. But sometimes I have to convert other currencies to dollars.

LEE: What else are you going to use it for?

YOKO: Oh, to store important names and phone numbers and to balance my checkbook.

LEE: What did we do before they invented all these electronic gadgets?

YOKO: We made a lot of mistakes!

2 **ANSWER** • *Look at Yoko's list of things to do. Then write a phrase to answer each question.*

> **To Do**
> —Get gas
> —Make dental appointment
> —Buy batteries
> —Withdraw $100
> —Invite Rika and Taro to dinner
> —Buy milk and eggs

1. Why did she call Dr. Towbin's office? _To make a dental appointment._____

2. Why did she go to the bank? _____

3. Why did she call Mrs. Watanabe? _____

4. Why did she go to the supermarket? _____

5. Why did she go to the electronics store? _____

6. Why did she go to the service station? _____

3 **MATCH** • *For each action, find the correct purpose.*

Action	Purpose
g **1.** He enrolled in Chinese 101 because he	**a.** didn't want to get any phone calls.
b **2.** She took a bus because she	**b.** didn't want to be late.
___ **3.** She went to the store because she	**c.** wanted to store information.
___ **4.** We disconnected our phone because we	**d.** wanted to listen to the news.
___ **5.** He turned on the radio because he	**e.** didn't want to worry me.
___ **6.** He didn't tell me he was sick because he	**f.** needed to buy some dishes.
___ **7.** She bought a Datalator because she	**g.** wanted to learn the language.

REWRITE • *Combine the sentence parts above. Use the infinitive of purpose.*

1. He enrolled in Chinese 101 to learn the language. _____

2. She took a bus in order not to be late. _____

3. _____

4. _____

5. _____

6. _____

7. _____

4 **EDIT** • *Read Yoko's journal entry. Find and correct six mistakes in the use of the infinitive of purpose. The first mistake is already corrected.*

> to get
> I went to Dr. Towbin for getting my teeth cleaned today. While I was waiting, I used my
> Datalator to study for the TOEFL. Then I used it to helps me pronounce "novocaine" and
> "dental floss" for my appointment. After the dentist, I checked my schedule and saw
> "Rika and Taro, dinner, 7:30." I should use it in order to not forget appointments! Luckily,
> my recipes are already on the Datalator, so I used them for making a quick shopping
> list. When I got home, there was a note on my door—"Call bldg. super." I checked the
> Datalator dictionary to find "bldg. super." The "building superintendent" wanted to come
> up in order fix the doorbell! Rika, Taro, and I played with the Datalator all evening.
> You can program it for to play computer games too. I don't know how I lived without it!

Gerunds and Infinitives

CHART CHECK

Circle T (True) or F (False).

T F Some verbs can be followed by either the gerund or the infinitive.

T F The infinitive sometimes follows a preposition.

T F A gerund can be the subject of a sentence.

GERUNDS
Marta **enjoys going** to parties.
She **loves meeting** new people.
She **stopped buying** ice cream.
She's worried **about forgetting** people's names.
Meeting new people is fun.

INFINITIVES
Marta **wants to go** to parties.
She **loves to meet** new people.
She **stopped to buy** ice cream.
It's fun **to meet** new people.

EXPRESS CHECK

Complete these sentences with the correct form of the verbs **go** *or* **talk**.

• Phil wants _____ to the party.

• _____ to parties is exciting.

• Phil enjoys _____ about a lot of different things.

• It's fun _____ to new people.

Grammar Explanations	Examples
1. Some **verbs** are **followed by a gerund**.	■ Marta **enjoys** *meeting* people. ■ She **misses** *going* to parties.
2. Some **verbs** are **followed by an infinitive**.	■ Marta **wants** *to meet* people. ■ She**'d like** *to go* to parties.
3. Some **verbs** can be followed by either **a gerund or an infinitive**.	■ Marta **loves** *meeting* new people. OR ■ Marta **loves** *to meet* new people.
4. **BE CAREFUL!** A few verbs can be followed by either a gerund or an infinitive, but the **meanings are very different**.	■ Marta **stopped eating** ice cream. *(She doesn't eat ice cream anymore.)* ■ Marta **stopped to eat** ice cream. *(She stopped another activity in order to eat some ice cream.)* ■ Richard **remembered mailing** the invitation. *(First he mailed the invitation. Then he remembered that he did it.)* ■ Richard **remembered to mail** the invitation. *(First he remembered. Then he mailed the invitation. He didn't forget.)* ■ Marta **forgot meeting** Richard. *(Marta met Richard, but afterwards she didn't remember the event.)* ■ Marta **forgot to meet** Richard. *(Marta had plans to meet Richard, but she didn't meet him because she forgot about the plans.)*
5. A **gerund** is the only verb form that **can follow a preposition**.	preposition ■ Marta's worried **about** *forgetting* names.
6. To make **general statements**, you can use: • **gerund as subject** OR • *It's* + **adjective/noun + infinitive**	■ **Meeting** new people is fun. OR ■ **It's** fun **to meet** new people

Check it out!

For a list of common verbs followed by the gerund, see Appendix 3 on page 337.

For a list of common verbs followed by the infinitive, see Appendix 4 on page 338.

For a list of verbs that can be followed by the gerund or the infinitive, see Appendix 6 on page 338.

1 **TRUE OR FALSE** • *Read each numbered sentence. Write T (True) or F (False) for the statement that follows.*

1. Marta remembered meeting Mr. Jackson.

   __T__ Marta has already met Mr. Jackson.

2. Richard stopped smoking.

   _____ Richard doesn't smoke anymore.

3. She didn't remember to buy a cake for the party.

   _____ She bought a cake.

4. She stopped eating desserts.

   _____ She used to eat desserts.

5. Richard forgot to invite his boss to the party.

   _____ Richard invited his boss.

6. Richard forgot inviting his neighbor to the party.

   _____ Richard invited his neighbor.

7. Richard thinks giving a party is fun.

   _____ Richard thinks it's fun to give a party.

8. Marta likes going to parties.

   _____ Marta likes to go to parties.

2 **CHOOSE** • *Circle the correct words to complete these ideas from a book called* **Super Memory.***

1. Get into the habit of (repeating)/ to repeat things aloud.

2. Never rely on someone else's memory. Learn trusting / to trust your own.

3. It's easy forgetting / to forget what you don't want remembering / to remember.

4. Study immediately before going / to go to sleep. You'll remember a lot more.

5. Our memories are filled with things we never meant remembering / to remember.

6. Make it a habit to pass in front of your car every time you get out, and you'll never forget turning off / to turn off your headlights.

7. Playing / To play games is a fun way of improving / to improve your memory skills.

*SOURCE: Douglas J. Hermann, *Super Memory: A Quick Action Program for Memory Improvement* (Avenel, NJ: Wings Books, 1991).

3 SUMMARIZE • *Read each numbered statement or conversation. Complete the summary statement using a gerund or an infinitive.*

1. **ROGER:** Hi, Richard. I brought the soda. Where do you want me to put it?

   SUMMARY: Roger remembered <u>to bring the soda.</u>

2. **MARTA:** You're Natalya! We met last year at Richard's party! How have you been?

   SUMMARY: Marta remembers _____

3. **ROGER:** Don't look at *me*! I didn't spill grape juice on the couch!

   SUMMARY: Roger denied _____

4. **NATALYA:** I'm so glad Richard plays jazz at his parties. I listen to it a lot at home too.

   SUMMARY: Natalya enjoys _____

5. **LEV:** Would you like to go dancing some time?

   MARTA: Sure. I'd like that very much.

   SUMMARY: Lev suggested _____

   Marta agreed _____

6. **NATALYA:** Marta, can we give you a ride home?

   MARTA: Thanks, but I think I'll stay a little longer.

   SUMMARY: Natalya offered _____

   Marta decided _____

4 EDIT • *Read Marta's journal entry about Richard's party. Find and correct seven mistakes in the use of the gerund and infinitive. The first mistake is already corrected.*

>   *going*
>
> What a great party! I usually avoid ~~to go~~ to parties because it's such a problem for me to
>
> remember people's names. I'm so glad I read that book about improve your memory. The
>
> author suggested to do exercises, and they really helped. I stopped to worry about what
>
> people would think of me, and I tried to pay attention to what people were saying. As a
>
> result, I had a great time! I'm even planning going dancing with this guy Lev.
>
>   I have an English test tomorrow, so I should stop writing now and start studying.
>
> The book even had some good tips about study for an exam. I hope I remember using some
>
> of them tonight!

Make, Have, Let, Help, and *Get*

He'll never **let me take** that quiz again.

Oh, no! He's going to **make us stay** after class.

Jaime Escalante with two of his students.

CHECK POINT

Circle T (True) or F (False).

T F The teacher in the picture has very strict rules.

CHART CHECK

Circle T (True) or F (False).

T F *Make, have,* and *let* are always followed by the base form of the verb.

T F *Get* can be followed by either the base form of the verb or the infinitive.

T F *Help* can be followed by either the base form of the verb or the infinitive.

	MAKE, HAVE, LET, HELP				
SUBJECT	**MAKE/HAVE/ LET/HELP**		**OBJECT**	**BASE FORM OF VERB**	
The teachers	(don't)	make have let help	us students	do	homework.

	GET, HELP				
SUBJECT	**GET/HELP**		**OBJECT**	**INFINITIVE**	
The teachers	(don't)	get help	us students	to do	homework.

EXPRESS `CHECK`

Complete these sentences with the correct form of the verbs **correct** *or* **stay**.

A: Did the teacher get the students _____ their essays?

B: Yes. He had them _____ their essays in groups.

A: Do you think he'll make them _____ late again today?

B: I don't think so. But he'll let them _____ late if they need help.

Grammar Explanations

Examples

1. Use *make, have,* and *let* followed by **object + base form** of the verb to talk about things that someone can <u>require, cause, or permit another person to do</u>.	■ The teacher **makes** *his students do* homework every night. *(He requires them to do homework.)* ■ He **has** *them take* responsibility for their own learning. *(He causes them to take responsibility.)* ■ He **lets** *them choose* their own essay topics. *(He permits them to choose their own essay topics.)*
You can also use *make* to mean "cause to."	■ This will **make** *you become* a better student. *(This will cause you to become a better student.)*

2. *Help* can be followed by either: • **object + base form** of the verb 　　　　OR • **object + infinitive**. The meaning is the same. **USAGE NOTE:** *Help* + base form of the verb is more common.	■ She **helped** *me understand* the homework. 　　　　OR ■ She **helped** *me to understand* the homework.

3. *Get* has a similar meaning to *make* and *have,* but it is followed by **object + infinitive**, not the base form of the verb.	■ The teacher **got** *us to stay* a little later. NOT ~~The teacher got us stay a little later.~~ *(The teacher persuaded us to stay a little later.)* ■ She always **gets** *me to do* my best. *(She always persuades me to do my best.)*

1 **TRUE OR FALSE** • *Read each numbered sentence. Write T (True) or F (False) for the statement that follows.*

1. My teacher made me rewrite the report.

   __T__ I wrote the report again.

2. Ms. Trager let us use our dictionaries during the test.

   _____ We had to use our dictionaries.

3. Mr. Goldberg had us translate a short story.

   _____ We translated a short story.

4. Paulo helped Meng do her homework.

   _____ Paulo did Meng's homework for her.

5. Ms. Bates got the director to arrange a class trip.

   _____ The director arranged a class trip.

6. Professor Washington let us choose our own topic for our term paper.

   _____ We didn't choose our own topic.

 2 **CHOOSE** • *Circle the correct words to complete this article about Jaime Escalante.*

Miracle Teacher

When Jaime Escalante first arrived at Garfield High, the administration of this East L.A.* high school (let)/ made gangs of students roam the halls and spray the walls **1.** with graffiti. However, this math teacher from Bolivia believed in his U.S. students too much to help / let them run wild. He made / let them **2.** **3.** do massive amounts of homework, had / got **4.** them take daily quizzes, and even got / let **5.** them to fill out daily time cards. To develop team spirit, he got / made his students do **6.** football-like cheers before class. He knew they could succeed and would never let / get **7.** them drop out of class. Then he did the impossible. He had / let his students take **8.** the Advanced Placement Exam, a very difficult national test. When his students passed, the testing company suspected them of cheating. To prove their innocence, Escalante had / got them take the test again. **9.**
Again, everyone passed. How did Escalante work these miracles? In the words of a student, Escalante "let / made us feel **10.** powerful, that we could do anything."

*L.A. = Los Angeles

SUMMARIZE • Read each numbered statement. Complete the summary with the correct form of the verbs in parentheses. Choose between affirmative and negative forms.

1. **Ms. Allen:** Pablo, you can rewrite this composition, but only if you want to.

   Summary: She _____ didn't make Pablo rewrite _____ his composition.
   (make / rewrite)

2. **Ms. Allen:** I know you prefer working alone, Ana, but you really need to work in a

   group today.

   Summary: She _____ in a group.
   (make / work)

3. **Ms. Allen:** Listen, everyone! No dictionaries during the test, please. You should be

   able to guess the meaning from context.

   Summary: She _____ dictionaries.
   (let / use)

4. **Ms. Allen:** Fernando, could you do me a favor and clean the board before you leave?

   Summary: She _____ the board.
   (have / clean)

5. **Ms. Allen:** Jean-Paul, put the tip of your tongue between your teeth and say

   "th–, thorn." Yes! That's it!

   Summary: She _____ an English *th*.
   (get / pronounce)

6. **Ms. Allen:** Greta, please use English in class!

   Summary: She _____ in German.
   (let / speak)

7. **Ms. Allen:** Olga, you can take the test in the classroom. Just move your desk to

   a corner.

   Summary: She _____ the room.
   (make / leave)

4 **EDIT • Read this student's journal entry. Find and correct seven mistakes in the use of make, have, let, help,** *and* **get.** *The first mistake is already corrected.*

When I was a teenager, my parents never let me ~~to~~ play until I had finished all my

homework. They even made me helping my brothers with their homework before

I could have any fun. On the one hand, they certainly got me learn a lot. On the other

hand, they made me became too serious. I wish they had let me to have a little more

fun. When I become a parent, I want to have my child learns responsibility, but also

I would want to let he or she have fun. As Ben Franklin said, "All work and no play

makes Jack become a dull boy." I want to avoid that mistake.

SelfTest  IX

SECTION ONE

Circle the letter of the correct answer to complete each sentence.

> **EXAMPLE:**
> Jennifer never _____ coffee.
> (A) drink   (C) is drinking
> (B) drinks   (D) was drinking
>
> A (B) C D

1. Maria's going to stop _____ dinner, so she may be late.   **A B C D**
   (A) eating   (C) to eat
   (B) for eating   (D) eat

2. My glasses are in my book bag, but I don't remember _____   **A B C D**
   them there.
   (A) putting   (C) I put
   (B) to put   (D) put

3. I asked him _____, but he went anyway.   **A B C D**
   (A) not to go   (C) not going
   (B) to not go   (D) he doesn't go

4. _____ in a foreign country is sometimes difficult.   **A B C D**
   (A) I live   (C) Live
   (B) Living   (D) Lives

5. He's not used to _____ up so early.   **A B C D**
   (A) wake   (C) wakes
   (B) waken   (D) waking

6. We're eighteen, so we're _____ vote.   **A B C D**
   (A) too old to   (C) old enough to
   (B) young enough to   (D) old enough for

7. I don't think Tom enjoyed _____ me study for the test.   **A B C D**
   (A) helping   (C) helped
   (B) to help   (D) helps

8. I bought this new software _____ Chinese.   **A B C D**
   (A) for learning   (C) to learn
   (B) learning   (D) learned

9. We got a new card holder _____ lose our credit cards.   **A B C D**
   (A) in order not to   (C) not to
   (B) not   (D) for not

10. It isn't difficult _____ this textbook.   **A B C D**
    (A) understand   (C) for understanding
    (B) in order to understand   (D) to understand

11. Are you ready? It's time _____.   **A B C D**
    (A) for going   (C) going
    (B) to go   (D) go

12. I resented _____ that. He could have been more polite.   **A B C D**
    (A) he said   (C) his saying
    (B) he saying   (D) him to say

13. I talked to the students about working harder, but I couldn't _____   **A B C D**
    them to study.
    (A) make   (C) got
    (B) get   (D) let

14. My mother _____ do my homework or I can't go out.   **A B C D**
    (A) makes me   (C) gets me
    (B) helps me   (D) lets me

SECTION TWO

Each sentence has four underlined words or phrases. The four underlined parts of the sentence are marked A, B, C, and D. Circle the letter of the one underlined word or phrase that is NOT CORRECT.

> **EXAMPLE:**
>
> Mike <u>usually</u> <u>drives</u> to school, but <u>today</u> he <u>walks</u>.   **A B C (D)**
>   A   B   C   D

15. I <u>decided</u> <u>changing</u> jobs because my boss <u>makes</u> <u>me work</u> overtime.   **A B C D**
      A   B   C   D

16. Most students <u>appreciate</u> their <u>principal's</u> <u>try</u> to <u>improve</u> school conditions.   **A B C D**
           A   B   C   D

17. I <u>succeeded in</u> <u>to find</u> a job, so my parents <u>didn't make</u> me <u>go</u> to college.   **A B C D**
     A   B   C   D

18. <u>Get</u> more exercise <u>appears</u> <u>to be</u> the best way <u>to lose</u> weight.   **A B C D**
  A   B   C   D

19. <u>In order</u> <u>to not</u> <u>forget</u> things, I <u>put</u> a string around my finger.   **A B C D**
   A   B   C   D

20. Hans <u>is</u> only fourteen, but he <u>seems</u> <u>enough old</u> <u>to stay</u> out until ten.   **A B C D**
    A   B   C   D

21. I know you're <u>too busy</u> <u>to stay</u>, but I <u>look forward</u> <u>to see</u> you again.   **A B C D**
          A   B   C   D

22. I forgot <u>buying</u> gas, but I <u>got</u> to a gas station <u>before</u> I <u>ran out</u>.   **A B C D**
        A   B   C   D

23. <u>Getting</u> enough sleep <u>is</u> important <u>in order</u> <u>not fall</u> asleep in class.   **A B C D**
   A   B   C   D

24. <u>Let's stop</u> <u>to watch</u> so much TV so that we can <u>read</u> or <u>go out</u> instead.   **A B C D**
    A   B   C   D

25. I'm <u>trying</u> <u>to persuade</u> my sister <u>to drive</u>, but I can't get her <u>do</u> it.   **A B C D**
     A   B   C   D

Phrasal Verbs:
Inseparable

CHECK *POINT*

Check the correct answer.

Where does the woman
suggest eating?

❑ at home

❑ in a restaurant

❑ in a park

CHART CHECK

*Check the correct
answer.*

Where does the
particle go?

❑ before the direct
object

❑ after the direct
object

INSEPARABLE PHRASAL VERBS			
SUBJECT	**VERB**	**PARTICLE**	**DIRECT OBJECT**
They	came	back.	
	gave	up.	
	ate	out.	
	ran	into	his teacher.
	stuck	to	their decision.

EXPRESS CHECK

Unscramble these words to form two sentences.

into • We • Bob • ran

_____

out • was • He • eating

_____

Grammar Explanations	**Examples**
1. A **phrasal verb** (also called a <u>two-part</u> or <u>two-word verb</u>) consists of a **verb + particle**.	verb + particle ■ We often **eat out**.
2. Particles and prepositions look the same. However, particles are <u>part of the verb phrase</u>, and they often <u>change the meaning of the verb</u>.	verb + preposition ■ She **ran into** another runner because she wasn't paying attention. *(She collided with another runner.)* verb + particle ■ I **ran into** John at the supermarket. *(I met John by accident.)*
3. The verb and particle are usually common words, but their separate meanings may not help you guess the **meaning of the phrasal verb**. **USAGE NOTE:** Phrasal verbs are <u>very common</u> in everyday speech.	■ Please **go on**. I didn't mean to interrupt. *(Please continue.)* ■ We **got back** after dark. *(We returned after dark.)* ■ They **called off** the meeting. *(They canceled the meeting.)*
4. Most phrasal verbs are **transitive**. (They take direct objects). Some transitive phrasal verbs are **inseparable**. This means that both <u>noun and pronoun objects</u> always go <u>after the particle</u>. You cannot separate the verb from its particle.	direct object ■ You should **go after** *your goals*. direct object ■ She **ran into** *her friend* at the library. NOT She ~~ran her friend into~~ at the library. direct object ■ She **ran into** *her*. NOT She ~~ran her into~~.
5. Some phrasal verbs are used <u>in combination with certain prepositions</u>. These combinations are usually **inseparable**.	■ She **came up** *with* a brilliant idea. ■ I **dropped out** *of* school and got a job.

Check it out!

For a list of some common inseparable phrasal verbs, see Appendix 17 on pages 341–342.

To learn about separable phrasal verbs, see Unit 55, pages 236–237.

IDENTIFY • *Read this article. Circle all the phrasal verbs.*

The Art of Feng Shui

Ho Da-ming's new restaurant was failing. His customers rarely (came back). Why? Mr. Ho contacted a feng shui consultant to find out. Feng shui (meaning "wind and water") is the ancient Chinese art of placing things in the environment. According to this art, the arrangement of furniture, doors, and windows affects our health, wealth, and happiness. Mr. Ho was concerned about his business, but he didn't give up. Following the consultant's advice, he remodeled and redecorated his restaurant. His actions paid off. Soon business picked up and Mr. Ho became rich. "It was the best decision I ever made," he glows. And he isn't alone in his enthusiasm. Feng shui has caught on with modern architects and homeowners everywhere.

MATCH • *Write each phrasal verb from the article next to its meaning.*

Phrasal Verb	Meaning	Phrasal Verb	Meaning
1. _____	has become popular	4. _____	learn information
2. _____came back_____	returned	5. _____	quit
3. _____	were worthwhile	6. _____	improved

 CHOOSE • *Complete this student's journal entry by circling the correct particles.*

I just finished an article about feng shui. At the end, the author suggests sitting

(down) / up in your home and thinking about how your environment makes you feel.
   1.

So today when I got up / back from school, I tried it. I noticed that my apartment is
        2.

really quite dark and it makes me feel down. I think with the addition of some lights,

I'd cheer away / up considerably. I've come out / up with a few other ideas too.
     3.   **4.**

My apartment is small, but I think it will look more spacious if I just straighten out / up
                                                5.

more frequently. Hanging some more shelves for my books might work in / out well too.
                                                    6.

With just a few small changes, I could end out / up feeling happier in my own home.
                                           7.

It's certainly worth trying on / out!
               8.

3 **CHOOSE & COMPLETE** • *Read this article about the architect I. M. Pei. Complete it using the correct form of the phrasal verbs in the box.*

| come up with | give up | go back | go up | ~~grow up~~ | keep on | pay off | turn out |

Born in 1917, Ieoh Ming Pei (better known as I. M. Pei)

_____grew up_____ in Canton, China. When he was
     1.

seventeen, he went to the United States to learn about building.

As it _____, Pei became one of the most
          2.

famous architects of the twentieth century.

Pei is famous for his strong geometric forms. One of his

most controversial projects was his glass pyramid at the Louvre in Paris. The old museum

had a lot of problems, but no one wanted to destroy it. Pei had to _____
                                                                        3.

a solution. Many Parisians were shocked with his proposal for a 71-foot-high glass

pyramid. It _____ anyway, blending with the environment. Today
              4.

many people say that it is a good example of the principles of feng shui.

Pei _____ despite criticism. He strongly believed that "you have
       5.

to identify the important things and press for them, and not _____."
                                                                   6.

His determination _____. He continued to build structures that
                       7.

reflected the environment. Pei received many prizes for his work. He used some of the

prize money to start a scholarship fund for Chinese students to study architecture in

the United States and then to _____ to China to work as architects.
                                   8.

4 **EDIT** • *Read Bob's note to his roommate. Find and correct eight mistakes in the use of inseparable phrasal verbs. The first mistake is already corrected.*

Sorry the apartment is such a mess. I got ~~down~~ up late this morning and didn't have time to

straighten out. I'm going to the gym now to work off for an hour. I should get across before

you, and I'll clean up then. How about eating tonight out? Afterward, we can get together with

some of the guys and maybe see a movie. Or maybe we'll come over with a better idea. —Bob

Oh, —I ran Tom into at school. He'll drop off to see you later.

UNIT 55

Phrasal Verbs:
Separable

*Glove sticks to burr.
Burr sticks to fur.
Why? **Work** this **out**!*

*Uh-oh. I see another
weird invention coming.
George **is dreaming** it **up**
right now!*

Burr

CHECK **POINT**

Check the correct answer.

The dog thinks that

☐ George is dreaming.

☐ George is getting an idea for
an invention.

SEPARABLE PHRASAL VERBS

CHART CHECK

*Check the correct
answer.*

☐ Direct objects
that are nouns
can go before or
after the particle.

☐ Direct objects
that are pronouns
always go after
the particle.

NOT SEPARATED			
SUBJECT	**VERB**	**PARTICLE**	**DIRECT OBJECT**
He	dreamed	up	the idea.
	worked	out	the details.

SEPARATED			
SUBJECT	**VERB**	**DIRECT OBJECT**	**PARTICLE**
He	dreamed	the idea it	up.
	worked	the details them	out.

EXPRESS **CHECK**

Complete these sentences with the correct form of the words in parentheses.

Who _____? Did *you* _____?
      (dream up / that idea)   (dream up / it)

Grammar Explanations	**Examples**

1. A **phrasal verb** consists of a **verb + particle**.

verb + particle
■ She **set up** an experiment.

Particles look the same as prepositions, but they are <u>part of the verb phrase</u>. They often <u>change the meaning of the verb</u>.

verb + preposition
■ He **looked up** at the sky.
(He looked in the direction of the sky.)

verb + particle
■ He **looked up** the information on the Internet.
(He found the information on the Internet.)

The separate meanings of the verb and particle may be very different from the **meaning of the phrasal verb**.

■ They **turned down** my application.
(They rejected my application.)

2. Most phrasal verbs are transitive (they take direct objects). Most transitive phrasal verbs are **separable**.
This means the **direct object** can go:

a. <u>after</u> the particle
(verb and particle are <u>not separated</u>)
OR
b. <u>between</u> the verb and the particle
(verb and particle are <u>separated</u>)

verb + particle + direct object
■ I just **dreamed up** *a new idea*.
OR
verb + direct object + particle
■ I just **dreamed** *a new idea* **up**.

Notice that when the direct object is **in a long phrase**, it comes <u>after the particle</u>.

direct object
■ She **dreamed up** *an unusually complicated new device.*
NOT She ~~dreamed an unusually complicated new device up.~~

► **BE CAREFUL!** When the direct object is a <u>pronoun</u>, it **must** go <u>between the verb and the particle</u>.

■ She **dreamed** *it* **up**.
NOT She ~~dreamed up it.~~

3. With a small group of phrasal verbs, the verb and particle **must be separated**.

keep something **on**

■ **Keep** *your hat* **on**.
NOT ~~Keep on your hat.~~

talk someone **into**

■ She **talked** *her boss* **into** a raise.
NOT She ~~talked into her boss~~ a raise.

Check it out!
For a list of common separable phrasal verbs, see Appendix 17 on pages 341–342.
For a list of common phrasal verbs that must be separated, see Appendix 17 on pages 341–342.
For information about inseparable phrasal verbs, see Unit 54, pages 232–233.

1 **IDENTIFY** • *Read this article. Underline the phrasal verbs. Circle the direct objects.*

Eureka!

Did you know that two college dropouts thought up the idea of the first personal computer? What's more, they put it together in a garage. Inventions don't have to come out of fancy laboratories. Average people in classrooms, kitchens, and home workshops often dream up new and useful ideas.

The ability to think of something new seems like magic to many people, but in fact anyone can develop the qualities of an inventor. First, inventors follow their curiosity. The Swiss inventor George de Mestral wanted to find out the reason it was so hard to remove burrs from his dog's coat. His answer led to the idea for Velcro®, now used to fasten everything from sneakers to space suits. Second, inventors use imagination to put things together in new ways. Walter Morrison watched two men tossing a pie pan to each other and thought up the Frisbee®, one of the most popular toys in the world. Perhaps most important, successful inventors don't quit. They continuously look up information about their ideas and try new designs out until they succeed.

2 **CHOOSE & COMPLETE** • *Read about one of history's greatest inventors. Complete the information with the correct form of the appropriate phrasal verbs from the box.*

| fill up | keep away | bring about | ~~try out~~ | set up | carry out | pay back | pick up |

As a child, Thomas Alva Edison (1847–1931) _____tried out_____
   1.
almost anything he heard about—he even tried to hatch goose eggs
by sitting on them! Before he was twelve, he _____
   2.
his first laboratory using money he had earned himself.
He had hundreds of bottles, and he _____ them
_____ with chemicals for his experiments. He
   3.
labeled the bottles "poison" to _____ his family
_____. When he was fifteen, Edison _____ a new skill. He
   4.   5.
had saved a child's life, and the grateful father, a telegraph operator, _____

Edison _____ by teaching him telegraphy. After that, Edison was able to
   6.
work nights and _____ his experiments during the day.
   7.

In 1869, Edison fixed a piece of equipment for a company that supplied prices to gold brokers. This _____ his first useful invention—the stock ticker—
8.
for which he received $40,000. He was then able to spend all his time working on his new inventions. During his lifetime, Edison was issued 1,093 patents!

3 **COMPLETE** • *Read these conversations that take place in a school laboratory. Complete them with phrasal verbs and pronouns.*

1. **A:** Please **put on** your lab coats.

   B: Do we really have to _____put them on_____? It's hot in here.

2. **A:** I can't **figure out** this problem.

   B: I know what you mean. I can't _____ either.

3. **A:** Remember to **fill out** these forms.

   B: Can we _____ at home, or do we have to do it now?

4. **A:** Are you going to **hand out** the next assignment today?

   B: I _____ a few minutes ago. Weren't you here?

5. **A:** I can't get this to work. We'd better **do** the whole procedure **over**.

   B: We don't have time to _____. Class is over in ten minutes.

6. **A:** Are we supposed to **turn in** our lab reports today?

   B: No. Please _____ next week.

4 **EDIT** • *Read an inventor's notes. Find and correct seven mistakes in the use of phrasal verbs. The first mistake is already corrected.*

May 3 I dreamed ~~over~~ up a really good idea—a jar of paint with an applicator like the kind used for shoe
         polish. It can be used to touch on spots on a wall, when people don't want to paint a whole
         room. I know a manufacturer. I'll call up him and order several types so I can try them in.

July 3 I filled down an application for a patent and mailed it yesterday. I'll be able to set a strong and
         convincing demonstration of the product up soon.

August 30 I demonstrated the product at an exhibition for decorators. I wanted to point out that it's very
            neat to use, so I put white gloves for the demonstration. It went over very well.

SelfTest

Circle the letter of the correct answer to complete each sentence.

> **EXAMPLE:**
> Jennifer never _____ coffee.   A Ⓑ C D
> (A) drink   (C) is drinking
> (B) drinks   (D) was drinking

1. Come in. Please sit _____.   **A B C D**
   (A) down   (C) it down
   (B) down it   (D) up

2. Your mother called. She wants you to call her _____ tonight.   **A B C D**
   (A) in   (C) back
   (B) off   (D) over

3. Could you turn _____ the music so we can sleep?   **A B C D**
   (A) down   (C) over
   (B) away   (D) up

4. Please put _____ your lab coats before you leave the laboratory.   **A B C D**
   (A) off   (C) up
   (B) away   (D) in

5. Mark works so hard that he's sure to _____.   **A B C D**
   (A) give up   (C) turn over
   (B) work off   (D) get ahead

6. Kevin is going to _____ from vacation tomorrow.   **A B C D**
   (A) call back   (C) get back
   (B) give back   (D) get along

7. A lamp will _____ this corner nicely.   **A B C D**
   (A) turn on   (C) put up
   (B) blow up   (D) light up

8. Instead of arguing about the problem, let's _____.   **A B C D**
   (A) look it over   (C) take it away
   (B) charge it up   (D) talk it over

9. That's very original. How did you dream _____ that idea?   **A B C D**
   (A) about   (C) of
   (B) down   (D) up

10. That pot is hot. Don't pick _____!   **A B C D**
    (A) it up   (C) up
    (B) up it   (D) it

11. —It's cold outside. You need your jacket.
    —OK. I'll put _____.
    (A) it on   (C) on it
    (B) it over   (D) over it

    A B C D

12. She ran _____ on the way home.
    (A) him into   (C) into Jason
    (B) into   (D) Jason into

    A B C D

13. Slow down. I can't keep up _____ you!
    (A) of   (C) after
    (B) with   (D) to

    A B C D

SECTION TWO

Each sentence has four underlined words or phrases. The four underlined parts of the sentence are marked A, B, C, and D. Circle the letter of the one underlined word or phrase that is NOT CORRECT.

> **EXAMPLE:**
> Mike <u>usually</u> <u>drives</u> to school, but <u>today</u> he <u>walks</u>.
>   A   B   C   D
>
> **A B C Ⓓ**

14. Could we talk <u>over it</u> before you <u>turn</u> the whole <u>idea</u> <u>down</u>?
    A   B   C   D

    A B C D

15. I know I <u>let</u> <u>Andy</u> <u>down</u> when I forgot to pick his suit <u>out</u> from
    A   B   C   D
    the dry cleaner's.

    A B C D

16. I <u>ran into</u> <u>him</u> while I was <u>getting</u> <u>the bus off</u>.
    A   B   C   D

    A B C D

17. As soon as I <u>hand</u> <u>in</u> <u>my report</u>, I'm going to take all these books
    A   B   C
    <u>on</u> to the library.
    D

    A B C D

18. <u>We'd better</u> <u>get the bus on</u> now, or <u>we're</u> going to <u>miss it</u>.
    A   B   C   D

    A B C D

19. Instead of <u>calling</u> <u>off</u> the meeting, maybe we can just <u>put it</u> <u>over</u>
    A   B   C   D
    until next week.

    A B C D

20. If you don't use <u>out</u> the milk by Monday, please <u>throw</u> <u>it</u> <u>away</u>.
    A   B   C   D

    A B C D

21. Chet had to <u>cheer</u> <u>up her</u> after the company <u>turned down</u> <u>her application</u>.
    A   B   C   D

    A B C D

22. Do you want to <u>get up</u> by yourself, or would you <u>like</u> <u>me</u> to <u>wake up you</u>?
    A   B   C   D

    A B C D

23. Tom <u>asked</u> me to <u>pick</u> some stamps for <u>him</u> at the post office <u>up</u>.
    A   B   C   D

    A B C D

24. Did you <u>find</u> <u>out</u> how Jane <u>talked</u> <u>into Meg</u> working on Saturday?
    A   B   C   D

    A B C D

25. We <u>got</u> <u>over</u> well after we <u>found</u> <u>out</u> we were both from Chicago.
    A   B   C   D

    A B C D

UNIT 56 Nouns

ACROSS THE ATLANTIC ON A REED BOAT

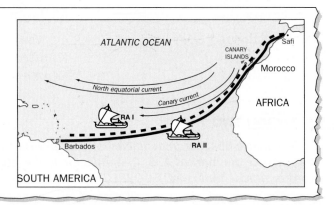

BARBADOS—**May** 17, 1970. Norwegian **explorer Thor Heyerdahl**, along with an international **crew**, has crossed the **Atlantic Ocean** on **Ra II**. The **reed boat**, modeled after those of the ancient **Egyptians**, made the **journey** in 57 **days**.

CHECK POINT

Check the correct answer.

The name of Heyerdahl's boat was: ☐ Ra II   ☐ Reed Boat

CHART CHECK 1

Circle T (True) or F (False).

T F Common nouns are written with capital letters.

PROPER NOUNS
Heyerdahl sailed **Ra II** across the **Atlantic**.

COMMON NOUNS
The **explorer** sailed his **boat** across the **ocean**.

CHART CHECK 2

Circle T (True) or F (False).

T F Count nouns can be plural.

T F Non-count nouns can be plural.

COUNT NOUNS				NON-COUNT NOUNS		
ARTICLE/ NUMBER	NOUN	VERB		NOUN	VERB	
A One	**sailor**	is	brave.	**Fire**	is	dangerous.
(The) Two	**sailors**	are		**Sailing**		

EXPRESS CHECK

Circle the correct words to complete these sentences.

The boats <u>was / were</u> made of reed. Crossing the ocean <u>was / were</u> hard.

Grammar Explanations	**Examples**

---

1. Proper nouns are the names of <u>particular people, places, and things</u>. To the right are some categories and examples of proper nouns.

<u>Capitalize</u> the first letter of most proper nouns. We <u>do not usually use an article</u> (*a/an* or *the*) with proper nouns.

Note that *the* is used with some nouns of places.

People	Heyerdahl, Egyptians
Places	Africa, Morocco, the Atlantic Ocean
Months	September, October
Days	Monday, Tuesday
Holidays	Easter, Passover, Ramadan
Languages	Arabic, Spanish

■ Heyerdal sailed across *the* **Atlantic Ocean**.

---

2. Common nouns refer to people, places, and things, but <u>not by their individual names</u>. For example, *explorer* is a common noun, but *Heyerdahl* is a proper noun.

People	explorer, sailor, builder
Places	continent, country, city
Things	pots, eggs, fish, honey

---

3. Common nouns are either count or non-count. **Count nouns** are things that you can <u>count separately</u>. They can be singular or plural. For example, you can say *a ship* or *three ships.* You can <u>use *a/an* or *the* before count nouns</u>.

Form the **plural** of most nouns by adding *-s* or *-es* to the noun. There are sometimes <u>spelling changes</u> when you form the plural.

▶ **BE CAREFUL!** Some nouns are <u>irregular</u>. They do not form the plural by adding *-s* or *-es*.

■ **a** sailor, **the** sailor, **two** sailors
■ **an** island, **the** island, **three** islands
■ **a** ship, **the** ship, **four** ships

ship	ships		potato	potato**es**
watch	watch**es**		country	countr**ies**

foot	**feet**		man	**men**
child	**children**		mouse	**mice**

---

4. Non-count nouns are things that you <u>cannot count separately</u>. For example, in English you can say *gold*, but you cannot say *a gold* or *two golds*. Non-count nouns usually have no plural forms. We usually <u>do not use *a/an* with non-count nouns</u>. To the right are some categories and examples of non-count nouns.

Some common non-count nouns do not fit into these categories. You must memorize nouns such as the ones to the right.

▶ **BE CAREFUL!** Non-count nouns take <u>singular</u> verbs and pronouns.

Abstract words	courage, education, time
Activities	exploring, sailing, farming
Fields of study	geography, history
Food	corn, chocolate, fish
Gases	air, oxygen, steam
Liquids	water, milk, coffee, gasoline
Materials	cotton, plastic, silk
Natural forces	cold, electricity, weather
Particles	dust, sand, sugar, salt, rice

advice	furniture	jewelry	money
clothing	garbage	luggage	news
equipment	homework	mail	work
food	information		

■ *Reed* **is** a good material for boats.
■ *It* **floats** in the heaviest storm.

Check it out!

For a list of some common irregular plural nouns, see Appendix 18 on page 343.

1 **IDENTIFY** • *Read this article about Thor Heyerdahl. Circle all the proper nouns. Underline once all the common count nouns. Underline twice the common non-count nouns.*

Was (Columbus) really the first explorer to discover the (Americas)? Thor (Heyerdahl) didn't think so. He believed that ancient people were able to build boats that could cross oceans. To test his ideas, he decided to build a copy of the reed boats that were pictured in ancient paintings and sail across the (Atlantic) from (North Africa) to Barbados. (Heyerdahl's) team also copied ancient (Middle Eastern) pots and filled them with food for their journey—dried fish, honey, oil, eggs, nuts, and fresh fruit. (Ra,) the expedition's boat, carried an international group including a (Norwegian), an (Egyptian), an (Italian), a (Mexican), and a (Chadian).

Who Really Discovered America?

The first trip failed, but everyone survived and wanted to try again. Departing on May 17, 1970, under the flag of the (United Nations), Ra II crossed the (Atlantic) in 57 days. The expedition proved that ancient civilizations had the skill to reach the (Americas) long before (Columbus).

2 **COMPLETE** • *Megan and Jason McKay are planning a hiking trip. Complete their conversation with the correct form of the words in parentheses.*

JASON: There ___**'s**___ still a lot of
        1. (be)
        ___**work**___ to do this evening.
        2. (work)
        We have to plan the food for the trip.

MEGAN: You're right. ___*food*___ certainly
        3. (Food)
        ___*is*___ important. I've been
        4. (be)
        reading this book about camping. There ___*are*___ some good
        5. (be)
        ___*ideas*___ in it.
        6. (idea)

JASON: Oh? What does it say?

MEGAN: We should bring a lot of ___*beans*___ and ___*rice*___.
        7. (bean)   **8.** (rice)

JASON: ___*Potatoes*___ ___*are*___ good on camping
        9. (Potato)   **10.** (be)
        ___*trips*___ too.
        11. (trip)

MEGAN: No, fresh ___*vegetables*___ ___*are*___ too heavy to carry. Maybe we
        12. (vegetable)   **13.** (be)
        can get some when we pass through a town.

JASON: _____is_____ the ___equipment___ ready? We should go over
14. (Be)   15. (equipment)

the checklist.

MEGAN: I did that. We need ___batteries___ for the radio.
16. (battery)

JASON: Why do we need a radio? I thought we were running away from civilization.

MEGAN: But the ___news___ never ___stops___. I still want to know
17. (news)   18. (stop)

what's happening.

JASON: That's OK with me. By the way, do we have enough warm ___clothing___?
19. (clothing)

It gets chilly in the mountains.

MEGAN: That's true. And the ___cold___ really ___bothers___ me at night.
20. (cold)   21. (bother)

JASON: But we have warm sleeping ___bags___.
22. (bag)

MEGAN: And we have each other!

EDIT • *Tina Arbeit sailed around the world alone on a small boat. Read her diary entries. There are fifteen mistakes in the use of nouns and subject–verb agreement. Find and correct them. The first two mistakes are already corrected.*

                                        Canary
October 27. I've been on the ~~canary~~ Islands for three days now. I'll start home when
            weather is
the ~~weathers are~~ better. I was so surprised when I picked up my ~~mails~~ today.
                                                              mail
                                            birthday
My family sent me some birthday presents. My ~~Birthday~~ is the 31st. I won't open

the gifts until then.
October
~~october~~ 29. I think the weather is getting worse. I heard ~~thunders~~ today, but there
                                              thunder
wasn't any rain. I stayed in bed with my cat, Typhoon. Every time it thundered,
Typhoon
~~typhoon~~ and I snuggled up closer under the covers. I started reading a ~~Novel~~,
                                                              novel
Brave New World.
                                              Columbus
October 30. I left the Canary Islands today—just like ~~columbus~~. There's a strong wind
                                        miles
and plenty of sunshine now. I went 250 ~~Miles~~.
                                  coffee
October 31. I'm 21 today! To celebrate, I drank some ~~coffees~~ for breakfast and I
                                              jewelry
opened my presents. I got some perfume and pretty silver ~~jewelries~~.
            electricity is
November 1. The ~~electricities are~~ very low. I'd better not use much until I get near
New York   water
~~new York~~. I'll need the radio then. It rained today, so I collected ~~waters~~ for cooking.

UNIT 57 Quantifiers *tells how many*

I'm glad I bought **a lot of batteries**.

Are there **any candles**?

I hope we have **enough chocolate**.

CHECK POINT

Check the correct answer.

The child wants to know if they have

☐ chocolate.

☐ a good supply of chocolate.

CHART CHECK

Circle T (True) or F (False).

- (T) F **A lot of** is used with both count and non-count nouns.

- T (F) **Several** is used with non-count nouns.

- (T) F **A few** is used with count nouns.

- (T) F **Any** is used in negative sentences.

QUANTIFIERS AND COUNT NOUNS		
	QUANTIFIER	**NOUN**
I have	some enough a lot of	batteries. cookies.
	a few several many	
I don't have	any enough a lot of many	

QUANTIFIERS AND NON-COUNT NOUNS		
	QUANTIFIER	**NOUN**
I have	some enough a lot of	candy. water.
	a little a great deal of much	
I don't have	any enough a lot of much	

EXPRESS CHECK

Complete this conversation with **much** *or* **many**.

A: We didn't buy ___*many*___ batteries.

B: Well, we didn't have ___*much*___ time before the storm.

A: That's true. We had ___*many*___ things to do.

246

Grammar Explanations	Examples
1. **Quantifiers** are expressions of quantity such as *a lot of* and *many*. They are used <u>before a noun</u>. Quantifiers can also be <u>used alone</u>, when it is clear what they refer to. Note that in *a lot of*, *of* is dropped.	■ We used *a lot of* water last summer. ■ There were *many* storms. **A:** How many **eggs** do we have? **B:** Not *a lot*, just *a few*.

2. Use *some*, *enough*, *a lot of*, and *any* with both <u>count and non-count nouns</u>.
 	
Use *any* in <u>questions</u> and in <u>negative sentences</u>.
 	
Use *some* when you make an <u>offer</u>.
	count non-count
	■ We have *some* **batteries** and *some* **gasoline**.
	
	         non-count count
	■ We have *enough* **water** and **eggs** for a week.
	
	          count non-count
	■ We have *a lot of* **beans** and **rice** left.
	
	       non-count count
	A: Do we have *any* **milk** or **teabags**?
	B: No, and we don't have *any* **coffee** or **paper plates** either.
	
	■ Would you like *some* **coffee**?

3. Use *a few*, *several*, and *many* with <u>plural count nouns</u> in <u>affirmative sentences</u>. Use *a little*, *a great deal of*, and *much* with <u>non-count nouns</u> in <u>affirmative sentences</u>. **USAGE NOTE:** In <u>affirmative sentences</u>, *many* is more formal than *a lot of*; *much* is very formal. ▶ **BE CAREFUL!** Don't confuse *a few* and *a little* with *few* and *little*. *Few* and *little* usually mean "not enough."	■ *A few* **people** got sick. ■ *Several* **children** went to the hospital. ■ *Many* **rescue workers** arrived. ■ They had *a little* **trouble** with the radio. ■ They threw away *a great deal of* **food**. ■ *Much* **planning** went into the rescue. MORE FORMAL: *Many* **people** agreed. LESS FORMAL: *A lot of* **people** agreed. VERY FORMAL: He showed *much* **courage**. LESS FORMAL: He showed *a lot of* **courage**. ■ They received *a little* **news** last night. *(not a lot, but probably enough)* ■ They received *little* **news** last night. *(probably not enough news)*
4. Use *many* with count nouns and *much* with non-count nouns in <u>questions</u> and <u>negative sentences</u>. **USAGE NOTE:** In <u>questions</u> and <u>negative sentences</u>, *many* and *much* are used in both formal and informal English.	**A:** How *many* **people** did you see? **B:** We **didn't** see *many*. **A:** How *much* **food** did they carry? **B:** Not *much*.

1 **IDENTIFY** • *Read this article about preparing for natural disasters. Underline the quantifiers + count nouns. Circle the quantifiers + non-count nouns.*

BE PREPARED

Are you ready? <u>Many people</u> don't realize that <u>some natural disasters</u> such as earthquakes can strike with (little warning). It may take <u>several days</u> for assistance to reach you. Prepare your disaster kit in advance! Here are a <u>few tips</u>.

⚡ Water may be unsafe to drink. Store (enough water) for <u>several days</u>. Each person needs a gallon per day for cooking and washing.

⚡ You will also need food for <u>several days</u>. It's a good idea to store <u>a lot of</u> of (canned meat, fruit, vegetables, and milk). However, also include <u>several kinds</u> of high-energy food, such as peanut butter and jelly. And don't forget (some "comfort food") like cookies and chocolate!

⚡ If you don't have (any electricity), you might not have (any heat) either. Keep <u>some blankets</u>, sleeping bags, and extra <u>clothes</u> for everyone.

⚡ Prepare a first aid kit with (some pain) relievers, <u>several sizes</u> of bandages, and an antiseptic.

⚡ The ATMs might not be working. Do you have (any cash?) You shouldn't keep (much money) in the house, but you should have a <u>lot of small bills</u>, and a <u>few larger bills</u> too.

---

2 **CHOOSE** • *Circle the correct words to complete this radio interview between* **This Morning** (TM) *and food psychologist Angie Welnitz* (AW).

TM: Dr. Welnitz, in a crisis, (a lot of) / much people crave chocolate. Does comfort food
1.
have (any) / many real benefit?
2.

AW: Yes, (Several) / A little types of food help give emotional balance. Chocolate gives an
3.
emotional lift because it contains (a great deal) of / many sugar, for example.
4.

TM: What about mashed potatoes? When I'm sad, I cook (a lot of) / much potatoes.
5.

AW: They remind you of childhood, when you felt safe. <u>Much</u> / (Many) traditional foods
6.
comfort us like this.

TM: I have a (few) / a little friends who eat comfort food to celebrate. Why?
7.

AW: We have (much) / many change in our lives today and a few / (few) ways to calm down.
8.   9.
Comfort food tells us, "Don't worry, (Some) / A little things are still the same."
10.

TM: We only have a few / (a little) time left. Tell us—what is *your* favorite comfort food?
11.

AW: Pistachio ice cream. I always feel better after I eat (a few) / few spoonfuls.
12.

3 **COMPLETE** • *Read these conversations. Complete them with the correct words.*

1. much, many, a few, a little

A: Hi, Barb. Did you and Jim lose _____*many*_____ trees in the storm?
 a.

B: Just one. And the house is OK. We only lost ____*a few*____ windows.
 b.
How about you?

A: We didn't have ____*many*____ problems either. We didn't have
 c.
____*much*____ time to shop before the storm, but thanks to the disaster kit,
 d.
we had ____*a few*____ candles and ____*a little*____ food on hand.
 e. **f.**

2. little, a little, a few, few

A: It's interesting to see what we used up from the disaster kit. I noticed we have
only ____*a little*____ hot chocolate left.
 a.

B: That's because ____*few*____ things taste better in a crisis. I bet there are
 b.
more than ____*a few*____ cans of spinach, though.
 c.

A: Six cans. I guess there's ____*little*____ reason to buy more of that.
 d.

B: We learned ____*a few*____ things about comfort foods during the storm,
 e.
didn't we?

4 **EDIT** • *Read this child's diary entry. Find and correct seven mistakes in the use of quantifiers. The first mistake is already corrected.*

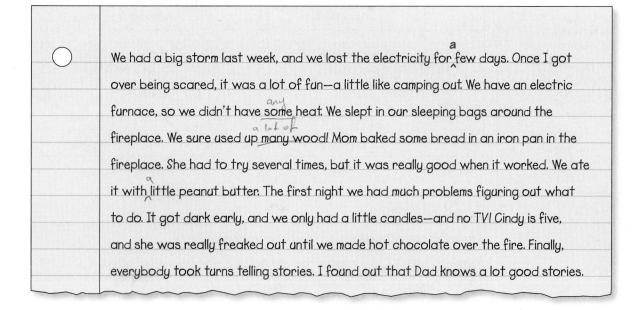

We had a big storm last week, and we lost the electricity for ^a few days. Once I got over being scared, it was a lot of fun—a little like camping out. We have an electric furnace, so we didn't have ~~some~~ ^{any} heat. We slept in our sleeping bags around the fireplace. We sure used up ^{a lot of} ~~many~~ wood! Mom baked some bread in an iron pan in the fireplace. She had to try several times, but it was really good when it worked. We ate it with ^a little peanut butter. The first night we had much problems figuring out what to do. It got dark early, and we only had a little candles—and no TV! Cindy is five, and she was really freaked out until we made hot chocolate over the fire. Finally, everybody took turns telling stories. I found out that Dad knows a lot good stories.

UNIT 58

Articles: Indefinite and Definite

An evil magician from **a** universe beyond ours is trying to conquer **the** Earth.

The magician is Zado. He has four helpers— and only YOU can destroy him!

SPACE DEFENDER

A NEW GAME FROM CEREBRO

CHECK POINT

Check the correct answer.

According to the ad for the video game:

☐ There is only one universe beyond ours.   ☑ There is only one Earth.

INDEFINITE *first time*   ## DEFINITE *second time*

<table>
<tr><th colspan="5">CHART CHECK</th></tr>
</table>

CHART CHECK

Circle T (True) or F (False).

T (F) **A/An** can be used with non-count nouns.

(T) F **The** can be used with singular and plural nouns.

✗ (T) F Use **the** when you mention a noun for the second time.

SINGULAR COUNT NOUNS

	A/An	Noun
Let's rent	a	video game.
It's	an	adventure.

SINGULAR COUNT NOUNS

	The	Noun	
Let's rent	the	game	by Cerebro.
It's		adventure	of Zado.

PLURAL COUNT NOUNS/ NON-COUNT NOUNS

	(Some)	Noun
Let's play	(some)	video games.
I won		gold.

Perfections and Jab

PLURAL COUNT NOUNS/ NON-COUNT NOUNS

	The	Noun	
Let's play	the	games	we rented.
It's		gold	Zado lost.

EXPRESS CHECK

Circle the correct articles to complete these sentences.

Cerebro has a / the new video game. A / The game is called *Space Defender*.

250

Grammar Explanations	**Examples**

1. We can use **nouns** in two ways:

a. A noun is **indefinite** (not specific) when either you or your listener <u>do not have a particular person, place, or thing in mind</u>.

A: Let's buy **a video game**.
B: Good idea. Which one should we buy?
(A and B are not talking about a specific game.)

b. A noun is **definite** (specific) when you and your listener <u>both know which person, place, or thing you mean</u>.

A: I bought **the new game** from Cerebro!
B: Great! Is it fun?
(A and B are both talking about a specific game.)

2. The **article** you use before a noun depends on <u>the kind of noun</u> (count or non-count) it is and on <u>how you are using the noun</u> (indefinite or definite).

a. Use the **indefinite article** *a/an* with <u>singular count nouns</u> that are **indefinite**.

A: I'm reading about **a magician**.
B: Oh, really? Which one?

Also use *a/an* for singular count nouns when you <u>classify</u> (say what something is).

A: What do you do for a living?
B: I'm **a pilot**. And you?

Use *a* before <u>consonant sounds</u>.
Use *an* before <u>vowel sounds</u>.

- *a* **m**agician, *a* **g**reat adventure
- *an* **e**vil magician, *an* **a**dventure

► **BE CAREFUL!** It is the <u>sound</u>, not the letter, that determines whether you use *a* or *an*.

- *a* **u**niverse (pronounced "yuniverse")
- *a* **h**ostile army (pronounced "hostile")
- *an* **h**onest warrior (pronounced—"ahnest")

b. Use **no article** or *some* with <u>plural count nouns</u> and with <u>non-count nouns</u> that are **indefinite**.

- There are **(some)** games on the shelf.
- I had to buy **(some)** medicine.

3. Use the **definite article** *the* with most nouns (<u>count and non-count, singular and plural</u>) that are **definite**.

A: *The* **magician** I told you about is on TV tonight.
B: Let's watch him!

Use *the* when:

a. a person, place, or thing is <u>unique</u>—there is only one.

- *The* **moon** is 250,000 miles away.
(The Earth has only one moon.)

b. the <u>context</u> makes it clear which person, place, or thing you mean.

A: *The* **music** was great.
B: I enjoyed it too.
(A and B are coming out of a concert.)

c. the noun is mentioned for the <u>second time</u> (it has already been identified).

- **A magician** is trying to conquer the Earth.
The **magician** is very powerful.

d. <u>a phrase or an adjective</u> such as *first, best, right, wrong,* or *only* identifies which one.

- Donkey Kong was *the first* **video game** with a story.

CHOOSE & DESCRIBE • *Read these conversations. Circle the letter of the statement that best describes each conversation.*

1. **CORA:** I'm bored. Let's rent a video game.
   FRED: OK.
   a. Fred knows which game Cora is going to rent.
   b. Fred and Cora aren't talking about a particular game.

2. **CORA:** Mom, where's the new video game?
   MOM: Sorry, I haven't seen it.
   a. Mom knows that Cora rented a new game.
   b. Mom doesn't know that Cora rented a new game.

3. **FRED:** I'll bet it's in the hall. You always drop your things there.
   CORA: I'll go look.
   a. There are several halls in Fred and Cora's house.
   b. There is only one hall in Fred and Cora's house.

4. **FRED:** Was I right?
   CORA: You weren't even close. It was on a chair in the kitchen.
   a. There is only one chair in the kitchen.
   b. There are several chairs in the kitchen.

5. **FRED:** Wow! Look at that! The graphics are awesome.
   CORA: So is the music.
   a. All video games have good graphics and music.
   b. The game Cora rented has good graphics and music.

6. **CORA:** This was fun. But why don't we rent a sports game next time?
   FRED: Good idea. I love sports games.
   a. Fred is talking about sports games in general.
   b. Fred is talking about a particular sports game.

 CHOOSE & COMPLETE • *Circle the correct articles to complete this paragraph.*

Board games are popular all over a / **the** world. Mah Jong is **an** / the example of
                                      1.   **2.**
a / an very old one. I had **an** / a uncle who had **an** / the old set from Singapore.
  3.   **4.**   **5.**
He kept a / **the** set in **the** / a beautiful box in a / **the** living room. He used to open
        6.   **7.**   **8.**
the / a box and tell me about **the** / a pieces. They were made of bamboo, and each
  9.   **10.**
one had **a** / the Chinese character on it. To me, they were **the** / a most fascinating
         11.   **12.**
things in a / **the** world.
            13.

3 **COMPLETE** • *Read each conversation. Complete it with the appropriate article* (*a, an,* or *the*).

1. **A:** _____A_____ car just pulled up. Are you expecting someone?

   B: No, I'm not. I wonder who it is.

2. **A:** Can we use _____the_____ car?

   B: OK, but bring it back by 11:00 o'clock.

3. **A:** Let's turn off _____the_____ game system before we leave.

   B: We don't have to. We can just leave it on *Pause.*

4. **A:** Do you have _____a_____ game system?

   B: Yes, I do. I just bought a Sega Genesis.

5. **A:** Do you see the video store? I was sure it was on Main Street.

   B: I think it's on _____a_____ side street, but I'm not sure which one.

6. **A:** There it is.

   B: Good. You can park right across _____the_____ street from the store.

7. **A:** Excuse me, do you have any new games?

   B: _____the_____ newest games are in the front of the store.

8. **A:** We'd better go. We've been here for _____an_____ hour.

   B: That was _____the_____ fastest hour I've ever spent.

9. **A:** Excuse me. I'd like to rent this game.

   B: Just take it to _____the_____ cashier. She's right over there.

4 **EDIT** • *Read this magazine article about video games. Find and correct nine mistakes in the use of articles. The first mistake is already corrected.*

The plumber
Once there was a plumber named Mario. ~~Plumber~~ had beautiful girlfriend. One day, a ape fell in love with the girlfriend and kidnapped her. The plumber chased ape to rescue his girlfriend.

This simple tale became *Donkey Kong,* a first video game with a story. It was invented by Sigeru Matsimoto, a artist with Nintendo, Inc. Matsimoto loved the video games, but he wanted to make them more interesting. He liked fairy tales, so he invented story similar to a famous fairy tale. Story was an immediate success, and Nintendo followed it with *The Mario Brothers.* The rest is video game history.

UNIT 59

Ø (No Article) and *The*

CHECK POINT

Check the correct answer.

Who is talking about roller coaster rides in general?

☐ the little girl ☐ the little boy

CHART CHECK

Check the correct answer.

You can use **Ø** (no article) for a noun that is:

☐ indefinite

☐ definite

You can use **Ø** for a count noun that is:

☐ singular

☐ plural

NO ARTICLE (INDEFINITE)
Ø + NON-COUNT NOUN
Do you like **cotton candy**?

Ø + PLURAL COUNT NOUN
Rides can be very exciting.

THE (DEFINITE)
***THE* + NON-COUNT NOUN**
The cotton candy in this park is great.

***THE* + PLURAL COUNT NOUN**
The rides in this park are exciting.

***THE* + SINGULAR COUNT NOUN**
The ride near the entrance is exciting.

EXPRESS CHECK

Circle **the** *or* **Ø** *(no article) to complete these sentences.*

A: Did you enjoy Ø / the roller coaster ride?

B: Yes, I love Ø / the roller coaster rides.

A: And did you try Ø / the cotton candy?

B: No. I don't like Ø / the cotton candy. It's always too sweet.

Grammar Explanations

1. We often use **Ø (no article)** before <u>non-count nouns</u> and <u>plural count nouns</u> that are **indefinite** (not specific).

Use **Ø** when you:

   a. have **no specific** person, place, or thing in mind.

   b. **classify** (say what something or someone is).

   c. make **general statements**.

Examples

A: What do you want to do tonight?
B: Let's stay home. We can listen to **music** or watch **videos**.

A: What's that?
B: It's **cotton candy**.
A: And what are those?
B: They're **tickets** for the roller coaster. I bought them while you were on the phone.

■ **Cotton candy** is very sweet.
   (cotton candy in general)

■ **Roller coasters** are popular.
   (roller coasters in general)

---

2. Use *the* with <u>non-count nouns</u> and <u>count nouns</u> (singular and plural) that are **definite**—when you are talking about a **specific or unique** person, place, or thing that you and your listener know about.

A: Can I taste *the* **cotton candy**?
B: Sure. Have as much as you'd like.

A: Where are *the* **tickets** for *the* **roller coaster**?
B: I put them in my pocket.

A: This is *the* **best roller coaster** in *the* **world**.

---

3. **BE CAREFUL!** <u>Singular count nouns cannot stand alone.</u> You must always use either an article, a pronoun, *one*, or a word such as *this, that, each,* or *every* before a singular count noun.

■ This is *a* delicious **candy bar**.
   NOT This is ~~delicious candy bar~~.

■ It's hard to eat just *one* **candy bar**, isn't it?
■ Give me *that* **candy bar**! You've had enough.
■ It's *my* **candy bar**.

1   **IDENTIFY • Read this announcement for a new amusement park. Underline all the common nouns that have no articles. Circle all the nouns with the.**

Grand Opening!

Do you enjoy amusement parks? Tomorrow, Blare Gardens will open to the public for the first time. The park features a wide variety of rides and games that will appeal to both adults and children. And of course an amusement park would not be complete without cotton candy and hot dogs. The food at Blare Gardens promises to be very good. Come early, bring the whole family, and be sure to stay for the fireworks display that takes place right after the sun sets. So check it out! You won't be disappointed.

2   **CHOOSE • Circle the correct words to complete this magazine article.**

Thrills and Chills

Why do people around the / Ø world flock to
1.
the / Ø amusement parks? The / Ø places like
2.   **3.**
Disney World and Coney Island offer the / Ø fun, relaxation, and escape from the / Ø
4.   **5.**
problems and boredom of everyday life. They offer the / Ø adults and children alike a
6.
chance to take the / Ø risks without the / Ø consequences. Thanks to advances in
7.   **8.**
the / Ø technology, the / Ø accidents in the / Ø amusement parks are now rare. You can
9.   **10.**   **11.**
go on the / Ø rides that look scary but are actually safe. You can scream and laugh as
12.
the / Ø roller coaster races down toward the / Ø ground and loops up to the / Ø sky
13.   **14.**   **15.**
again, leaving your cares and troubles behind.

Even though the / Ø roller coasters are the / Ø most
16.   **17.**
popular of all the / Ø rides, they are not for everyone. But
18.
don't worry. Today's amusement parks offer a lot more
than the / Ø thrills and chills. There are train rides
19.
through a replica of the / Ø rain forest. And there are
20.
the / Ø games with the / Ø prizes too. The / Ø hot dogs,
21.   **22.**   **23.**
ice cream, and cotton candy complete the / Ø picture of
24.
this perfect getaway for the / Ø whole family.
25.

3 **COMPLETE** • *Read this conversation about an amusement park. Complete the sentences with* **the** *where necessary. Use* **Ø** *if you don't need an article.*

A: I'm going to Blare Gardens next weekend. You work there. What's it like?

B: That depends. Do you like ___Ø___ scary rides? If you do, then you're going

1.
to love ___the___ rides at Blare Gardens.

2.

A: What's ___the___ most exciting ride there?

3.

B: The Python. I've seen people actually shaking with fear before they got on it.

A: Sounds like ___Ø___ fun. By the way, how's ___the___ food there? I

4. **5.**
hate ___Ø___ hot dogs.

6.

B: Then you might have a little problem. They sell ___Ø___ hot dogs and

7.
___Ø___ pizza, and that's about it. But do you like ___Ø___ music?

8. **9.**

A: I love it. I listen to ___Ø___ country music all the time. Why?

10.

B: ___the___ music at Blare Gardens is great. They have ___the___ best

11. **12.**
country music groups in ___the___ entire state.

13.

A: What exactly do you do there? Maybe we'll see you.

B: I dress like a cartoon character and guide people around ___the___ park.

14.

4 **EDIT** • *Read this postcard from Blare Gardens. Find and correct eight mistakes in the use of* **the** *and* **Ø** *(no article). The first mistake is already corrected.*

**Blare Gardens Amusement Park**

Hi! Blare Gardens is awesome! This
the
is best vacation we've ever gone on!
I love the rides here. I mean, I've been on the roller
coasters before, but nothing is like the one they've got
here! And food is great too. I usually don't eat the hot
dogs, but hot dogs here are great. So is pizza. Do you
like the amusement parks? If so, you've got to get your
family to come. The only problem is crowds here. People
have to wait to get into <u>everything</u>—even the
restrooms! See you soon. Nicky

To: Ryan Turner
31 Barcelona Dr.
Boulder, CO 80303

UNIT
60

Reflexive Pronouns and Reciprocal Pronouns

"I will not talk to myself, I will not talk to myself."

CHECK *POINT*

Circle T (True) or F (False).

T F The man is talking to
another person.

CHART CHECK

*Circle T (True) or
F (False).*

T F Singular
reflexive
pronouns end
in **-selves**.

T F Reciprocal
pronouns
always refer
to more than
one person.

REFLEXIVE PRONOUNS		
SUBJECT PRONOUN		**REFLEXIVE PRONOUN**
I		**myself.**
You		**yourself.**
He		**himself.**
She		**herself.**
It	looked at	**itself.**
We		**ourselves.**
You		**yourselves.**
They		**themselves.**

RECIPROCAL PRONOUNS		
SUBJECT PRONOUN		**RECIPROCAL PRONOUN**
We You They	looked at	**each other.** **one another.**

EXPRESS CHECK

Circle the correct words to complete this conversation.

A: Is someone in there with you, or are you talking to

<u>yourself / themselves</u>?

B: No one's here. I'm just talking to <u>one another / myself</u>.

Grammar Explanations	**Examples**
1. Use a **reflexive pronoun** when the <u>subject and object</u> of a sentence refer to the <u>same people or things</u>. In **imperative sentences** use: —***yourself*** when the <u>subject is singular</u> —***yourselves*** when the <u>subject is plural</u>	subject = object ■ **Sara** looked at ***herself*** in the mirror. *(Sara looked at her own face.)* ■ "Don't push ***yourself*** so hard, **Tom**," Sara said. ■ "Don't push ***yourselves*** so hard, **guys**," Sara said.
2. Use a **reflexive pronoun** to <u>emphasize a noun</u>. In this case, the reflexive pronoun usually follows the noun directly.	■ Tom was upset when he lost his job. The **job *itself*** wasn't important to him, but he needed the money.
3. ***By*** **+ a reflexive pronoun** means *alone* or *without any help*. ***Be*** **+ a reflexive pronoun** means *act in the usual way*.	■ Sara lives **by herself**. *(Sara lives alone.)* ■ We painted the house **by ourselves**. *(No one helped us.)* ■ Just **be yourself** at your interview. *(Act like you usually act.)* ■ He **wasn't himself** after he lost his job. *(He seemed different.)*
4. Use a **reciprocal pronoun** when the subject and the object of a sentence refer to the <u>same people</u> and these people have a <u>two-way relationship</u>. Use ***each other*** when the subject is <u>two people</u>. Use either ***one another*** or ***each other*** when the subject is <u>more than two people</u>. ▶ **BE CAREFUL!** Reciprocal pronouns and plural reflexive pronouns have <u>different meanings</u>.	subject = object ■ **Tom and Sara** met ***each other*** at work. *(Tom met Sara, and Sara met Tom.)* subject = object ■ **We all** told ***one another*** about our jobs. OR subject = object ■ **We all** told ***each other*** about our jobs. *(Each person exchanged information with every other person.)* ■ Fred and Jane talked to ***each other***. *(Fred talked to Jane, and Jane talked to Fred.)* ■ Fred and Jane talked to ***themselves***. *(Fred talked to himself, and Jane talked to herself.)*
5. **Reciprocal pronouns** have <u>possessive forms</u>: ***each other's***, ***one another's***.	■ Tom and Sara took ***each other's*** numbers. *(Tom took Sara's number. Sara took Tom's number.)*

Check it out!

For a list of verbs and expressions commonly used reflexively, see Appendix 16 on page 340.

IDENTIFY • *Read this article about self-talk. Underline the reflexive pronouns once and the reciprocal pronouns twice. Draw an arrow to the word that each pronoun refers to.*

SELF-TALK

Self-talk is the way we explain a problem to <u>ourselves</u>. It can affect the way we feel and how we act. Tom and Sara, for example, both lost their jobs when their company laid off a lot of people. Sara kept herself fit and spent time with friends. Tom gained ten pounds and spent all his time by himself. They were both unemployed, so the situation itself can't explain why they acted so differently from <u>each other</u>. The main difference was the way Tom and Sara explained the problem to themselves. Sara believed that she herself could change her situation. Tom saw himself as helpless. Later, everyone got their jobs back. When they all talked to one another back at the office, Tom grumbled, "They must have been desperate." Sara replied, "They finally realized they need us!"

CHOOSE • *Tom and Sara's company held an office party. Choose the correct reflexive or reciprocal pronouns to complete the conversations.*

1. **A:** Do you mind if we pour _____ourselves_____ something to drink?
   (myself / ourselves)

   B: Of course not. And there's food too. Please help _____.
   (yourselves / themselves)

2. **A:** That's the new head of Marketing. She's standing by _____.
   (herself / himself)

   B: Let's go and introduce _____.
   (himself / ourselves)

3. **A:** I'm nervous about my date with Niki. I cut _____ twice shaving.
   (myself / herself)

   B: You'll be fine. Just relax and be _____.
   (yourselves / yourself)

4. **A:** My boss and I always give _____ the same holiday gifts. Every year
   (ourselves / each other)
   I give him a book and he gives me a scarf.

   B: Funny. I always thought you bought _____ a lot of scarves.
   (yourself / himself)

5. **A:** The new software is so easy, it just seems to run by _____.
   (itself / myself)

   B: Really? In our department, we're still teaching _____ how to use it.
   (themselves / ourselves)

6. **A:** Did you and Armina go to Japan by _____ or with a tour group?
   (yourself / yourselves)

   B: With a group. We've all kept in touch with _____ since the trip.
   (one another / ourselves)

COMPLETE • *George Prudeau is a high school French teacher. Complete his talk to a group of new teachers. Use reflexive and reciprocal pronouns.*

I teach French, but the subject _____itself_____ isn't that important. I think my
                                        1.

experience applies to all subjects. Your first year may be hard, so teach

_____ to use positive self-talk and keep things simple. Remember that
       2.

a good teacher helps students learn by _____. Recently, John, one of my
                                               3.

students, was having trouble teaching _____ how to bake French bread.
                                             4.

I encouraged him to keep trying, and in the end he succeeded. As far as discipline

goes, I have just a few rules. I tell my students, "Keep _____ busy.
                                                                5.

Discuss the lessons, but don't interfere with _____'s work." Keep
                                                      6.

teaching materials simple too. I pride _____ on being able to teach
                                              7.

anywhere, even on a street corner. Finally, the salary for teachers is not great, but

you have a lot of freedom. I run my class by _____—just the way I want to.
                                                    8.

You will all have to decide for _____ if it's worth it. I can't afford to
                                      9.

travel to France, but I satisfy _____ with trips to Quebec!
                                     10.

EDIT • *Read this woman's diary. Find and correct seven mistakes in the use of reflexive and reciprocal pronouns. The first mistake is already corrected.*

> *I forgot to call Jan on his birthday. I reminded ~~me~~ all day, and then I forgot*
>   myself
>
> *anyway! I felt terrible. My sister Anna said, "Don't be so hard on yourselves,"*
>
> *but I didn't believe her. She prides her on remembering everything. Then*
>
> *I read an article on self-talk. It said that people can change the way they*
>
> *explain problems to theirselves. I realized that the way I talk to me is*
>
> *insulting—like the way our high school math teacher used to talk to us.*
>
> *I thought, Jan and I treat each other well. He forgave myself for my mistake*
>
> *right away, and I forgave him for forgetting our dinner date two weeks ago.*
>
> *Jan and I could forgive themselves, so I guess I can forgive myself.*

SelfTest

Circle the letter of the correct answer to complete each sentence. Choose Ø when no article is needed.

EXAMPLE:

Jennifer never _____ coffee.   A ⒝ C D
(A) drink   (C) is drinking
(B) drinks   (D) was drinking

---

1. I introduced _____ to Bill as soon as I saw him.   **A B C D**
   (A) himself   (C) myself
   (B) me   (D) each other

2. The job _____ isn't a problem. It's my boss.   **A B C D**
   (A) myself   (C) himself
   (B) itself   (D) it

3. The students exchange cards with _____ during the holidays.   **A B C D**
   (A) themselves   (C) each other's
   (B) ourselves   (D) one another

4. What a beautiful bracelet! Is it made of _____ gold?   **A B C D**
   (A) the   (C) Ø
   (B) some   (D) a

5. I bought _____ bottled water before the hurricane.   **A B C D**
   (A) a lot of   (C) twelve
   (B) a few   (D) many

6. How _____ eggs do you need for the cake?   **A B C D**
   (A) many   (C) Ø
   (B) much   (D) more

7. She was lonely because she had _____ friends at first.   **A B C D**
   (A) little   (C) few
   (B) a little   (D) a few

8. That's _____ best movie I've ever seen.   **A B C D**
   (A) a   (C) the
   (B) an   (D) Ø

9. Di's in _____ Europe on vacation.   **A B C D**
   (A) a   (C) Ø
   (B) an   (D) the

10. Freda's _____ astronaut. There are six of them on this mission.   **A B C D**
    (A) Ø   (C) an
    (B) a   (D) the

11. —I just rented _____ video.
    —Great! Which one?
    (A) the   (C) a
    (B) some   (D) any   **A B C D**

12. We don't have _____ fruit left. Could you buy some apples?   **A B C D**
    (A) much   (C) little
    (B) some   (D) many

SECTION TWO

Each sentence has four underlined words or phrases. The four underlined parts of the sentence are marked A, B, C, and D. Circle the letter of the one underlined word or phrase that is NOT CORRECT.

> **EXAMPLE:**
>   Mike <u>usually</u> <u>drives</u> to school, but <u>today</u> he <u>walks</u>.   **A B C Ⓓ**
>   A   B   C   D

13. There <u>are</u> <u>a lot of</u> <u>food</u> in the fridge, so help <u>yourself</u>.   **A B C D**
          A   B   C   D

14. Do <u>your</u> families <u>come</u> for <u>thanksgiving</u> or do you celebrate   **A B C D**
       A   B   C
    by <u>yourselves</u>?
       D

15. The <u>news</u> <u>are starting</u>, so let's watch <u>TV</u> in <u>the</u> living room.   **A B C D**
        A   B   C   D

16. Lee wants to open <u>his</u> business in <u>may</u> and <u>start</u> working   **A B C D**
                       A   B   C
    for <u>himself</u>.
        D

17. I <u>myself</u> don't eat chili, but it's <u>the most</u> popular <u>spice</u> in <u>a</u> world.   **A B C D**
       A   B   C   D

18. <u>A money</u> <u>isn't</u> everything—the job <u>itself</u> <u>has to</u> be interesting.   **A B C D**
       A   B   C   D

19. <u>Mathematics</u> <u>isn't</u> Todd's <u>best</u> subject, but he succeeds with <u>the</u>   **A B C D**
        A   B   C   D
    hard work.

20. <u>How</u> <u>many times</u> do <u>we</u> have before <u>the</u> movie starts?   **A B C D**
       A   B   C   D

21. <u>Smith</u> was <u>an</u> unpopular mayor, so he had <u>a few</u> friends in <u>politics</u>.   **A B C D**
       A   B   C   D

22. <u>We</u> have only <u>a few</u> milk left, so could you pick <u>some</u> up for <u>us</u>?   **A B C D**
       A   B   C   D

23. <u>We</u> didn't know <u>one another</u> names before <u>Maria</u> introduced <u>us</u>.   **A B C D**
       A   B   C   D

24. <u>Ben</u> has to save <u>a few</u> money so that he can go to <u>school</u> in <u>the</u> fall.   **A B C D**
       A   B   C   D

25. I met <u>an accountant</u> and <u>a lawyer</u> at <u>your party</u>, and <u>an accountant</u>   **A B C D**
             A   B   C   D
    said he'd help me.

UNIT 61

The Passive: Overview

The World Keeps Informed With Reader's Digest

Reader's Digest

Reader's Digest **was founded** in 1922.
Today it **is read** by people in every country in the world.
Shouldn't you be one of them? Subscribe today.

CHECK POINT

Check the information you can get from the ad.

☐ the name of the founder

☐ the number of years the magazine has existed

☐ the price of the magazine

CHART CHECK

Circle T (True) or F (False).

T F The object of an active sentence becomes the subject of the passive sentence.

T F Passive statements always have a form of the verb *be*.

T F Passive statements always have an object.

ACTIVE	PASSIVE
OBJECT	**SUBJECT**
Millions of people **buy** *it*.	*It* **is bought** by millions of people.
OBJECT	**SUBJECT**
Someone **published** *it* in 1922.	*It* **was published** in 1922.

PASSIVE STATEMENTS

SUBJECT	BE (NOT)	PAST PARTICIPLE	(BY + OBJECT)	
It	**is (not)**	**bought**	by millions of people.	
It	**was (not)**	**published**		in 1922.

YES/NO QUESTIONS

BE	SUBJECT	PAST PARTICIPLE	
Is	it	**sold**	in China?
Was			

SHORT ANSWERS

AFFIRMATIVE		NEGATIVE	
Yes, it	**is.**	No, it	**isn't.**
	was.		**wasn't.**

WH- QUESTIONS

WH- WORD	BE	SUBJECT	PAST PARTICIPLE
Where	**is**	it	**sold**?

EXPRESS CHECK

Complete this sentence with the passive form of the verb **print**.

How many copies of *Reader's Digest* _____ last year?

Grammar Notes

Examples

1. Active and **passive sentences** often have similar meanings but <u>different focuses</u>.	ACTIVE
	■ Millions of people **read** the magazine.
	   (*The focus is on the people.*)
	PASSIVE
	■ The magazine **is read** by millions of people.
	   (*The focus is on the magazine.*)

2. Form the **passive** with a form of *be* + **past participle**.	■ It **is written** in nineteen languages. ■ It **was published** in 1922. ■ It **has** just **been printed**.

3. Use the **passive** when:
 	
a. the <u>agent</u> (the person or thing doing the action) is <u>unknown or not important</u>.
 	
b. the identity of the <u>agent is clear from the context</u>.
 	
c. you want to <u>avoid mentioning the agent</u>.
	■ The magazine **was founded** in 1922.
	   (*I don't know who founded it.*)
	
	■ The magazine **is sold** at newsstands.
	   (*We can assume that the newsstand owners and employees sell it. We don't need to mention them.*)
	
	■ Some mistakes **were made** in that article.
	   (*I know who made the mistakes, but I don't want to blame the person who made them.*)

4. Use the **passive with** *by* if you mention <u>the agent</u>.
Mention the **agent** when:
 	
a. you introduce <u>necessary new information</u> about the agent.
 	
b. you want to give credit to someone who <u>created something</u>.
 	
c. the agent is <u>surprising</u>.
 	
▶ **BE CAREFUL!** In most cases, you do not need to mention an agent in passive sentences. Do not include an agent unnecessarily.
	■ The article **was written** *by a psychologist*.
	
	■ John Delgado is a famous sports writer. He **has** just **been hired** *by National Sports* to write a monthly column.
	   (*The name of John's employer is necessary new information.*)
	
	■ The article **was written** *by John Delgado*.
	
	■ Our windows **are washed** *by a robot*.
	
	■ The magazine **is published** once a week.
	   NOT The magazine is published ~~by the publisher~~ once a week.

1 **CHOOSE** • *Read these sentences and decide if they are* **Active (A)** *or* **Passive (P).**

_P_ 1. *Reader's Digest* was founded in 1922.

_____ 2. Millions of people read it.

_____ 3. A large-type edition is also printed.

_____ 4. They also record it.

_____ 5. *Reader's Digest* is published once a month.

_____ 6. It has been translated into many languages.

_____ 7. Many readers subscribe to the magazine.

_____ 8. It is sold at newsstands everywhere.

_____ 9. I read an interesting article in it.

_____ 10. The article was written by a famous scientist.

2 **READ & COMPLETE** • *Look at the chart. Then complete the sentences. Use the verb* **speak** *in the active or the passive form.*

LANGUAGE	NUMBER OF SPEAKERS (IN MILLIONS)
Arabic	246
Cantonese (China)	71
English	508
Ho (Bihar and Orissa States, India)	1
Japanese	126
Spanish	417
Swahili (Kenya, Tanzania, Uganda, Democratic Republic of Congo)	49
Tagalog (Philippines)	57

1. Japanese _is spoken by 126 million people_ .

2. One million people _speak Ho_ .

3. _____ by 57 million people.

4. Spanish _____ .

5. _____ Cantonese.

6. _____ 246 million people.

7. More than 500 million people _____ .

8. _____ in Uganda.

3 | **COMPLETE** • *Use the passive form of the verbs in the first set of parentheses to complete this report. Include the agent (from the second set of parentheses) only if absolutely necessary.*

Modern Reader Newsletter   TENTH ANNIVERSARY ISSUE

DID YOU KNOW...?

▶ *Modern Reader* __was founded by A. J. Thompson__ ten years ago.
        1. (found) (A. J. Thompson)

▶ At first it ___was printed___ only in English.
        2. (print) ~~(the printer)~~

▶ Today it _____ in three foreign-language editions.
        3. (publish) (the publisher)

▶ It _____ in more than ten countries.
        4. (read) (readers)

▶ Since 2000, twenty new employees _____.
        5. (hire) (our international offices)

▶ Back at home, ten new computers _____ last month.
        6. (purchase) (the company)

▶ They _____ to write our award-winning articles.
        7. (use) (our writers)

▶ *Modern Reader* _____ all over the world.
        8. (advertise) (advertisers)

▶ Our editorial staff _____ last month.
        9. (interview) (*Live at Ten TV*)

▶ The interview _____.
        10. (see) (millions of viewers)

---

4 | **EDIT** • *Read an editor's notes for a story for* **Modern Reader.** *Find and correct eight mistakes in the use of the passive. The first mistake is already corrected.*

                                                         are located

Two-thirds of Bolivia's five million people ~~locate~~ in the cool western highlands known as the Altiplano. For centuries, the grain quinoa has been grew in the mountains. Llamas raised for fur, meat, and transportation. And tin, Bolivia's richest natural resource, is mining by miners in the high Andes.

    The Oriente, another name for the eastern lowlands, is mostly tropical. Rice is the major food crop, and cows are raised for milk. Oil is also find there.

    Although Spanish is the official language, Native American languages are still spoken by people. Traditional textiles are woven by hand, and music played on reed pipes whose tone resembles the sound of the wind blowing over high plains in the Andes.

UNIT 62 — The **Passive** with Modals

Bill, something **has to be done** about Ed. He snores so loud he's going to knock us out of orbit!

zZzZzZ

I know, Carla. He **can be heard** back on Earth!

CHECK POINT

Check the correct answer.

According to Carla,

☐ Ed has to do something about his snoring.

☐ somebody has to do something about Ed's snoring.

CHART CHECK 1

Circle T (True) or F (False).

T F Passives with modals always use **be**.

T F You cannot talk about the future using the passive with modals.

STATEMENTS

SUBJECT	MODAL*	BE	PAST PARTICIPLE	
The crew	**will (not)** **should (not)**	be	replaced	next month.

SUBJECT	*HAVE (GOT) TO/* *BE GOING TO*	BE	PAST PARTICIPLE	
The crew	**has (got) to** **doesn't have to** **is (not) going to**	be	replaced	next month.

*Modals have only one form. They do not have -s in the third person singular.

CHART CHECK 2

Check the correct answer.

What comes before the subject in questions?

☐ **be**

☐ a modal or an auxiliary verb

YES/NO QUESTIONS

MODAL	SUBJECT	BE	PAST PARTICIPLE
Will **Should**	it	be	replaced?

SHORT ANSWERS

AFFIRMATIVE		NEGATIVE	
Yes, it	**will.** **should.**	No, it	**won't.** **shouldn't.**

YES/NO QUESTIONS				
AUXILIARY VERB	**SUBJECT**	**HAVE TO/ GOING TO**	**BE**	**PAST PARTICIPLE**
Does	it	have to	be	replaced?
Is		going to		

SHORT ANSWERS			
AFFIRMATIVE		**NEGATIVE**	
Yes, it	does.	No, it	doesn't.
	is.		isn't.

EXPRESS CHECK

Complete this conversation with the passive form of **will prepare**.

A: _____ food _____ on board?

B: No, it _____ . It _____ on Earth.

Grammar Explanations

1. To form the passive with a modal, use **modal + *be* + past participle**.

2. Use *will* or *be going to* with the passive to talk about the **future**.

3. Use *can* with the passive to express **present ability**.

Use *could* with the passive to express **past ability**.

4. Use *could*, *may*, *might*, and *can't* with the passive to express **future possibility** or **impossibility**.

5. Use *should*, *ought to*, *had better*, *have (got) to*, and *must* with the passive to express:

   a. advisability

   b. necessity

Examples

- The Space Shuttle *will be launched* soon.
- The launch *won't be postponed*.
- The crew *must be given* time off.
- Decisions *shouldn't be made* too quickly.

- It *will be launched* very soon.
  OR
- It's *going to be launched* very soon.

- The blastoff *can be seen* for miles.

- It *could be seen* very clearly last year.

- It *could be launched* very soon.
- French scientists *may be invited* to participate.
- Plants *might be grown* on board.
- It *can't be done*.

- The crew *should be prepared* to work hard.
- Crew members *ought to be given* a day off.
- Privacy *had better be respected*.

- Reports *have to be filed*.
- Everyone *must be consulted*.

1 **IDENTIFY** • *Read this article about the International Space Station* Unity. *Underline all the passives with modals.*

Living in Outer Space

Space Station *Unity* <u>will be completed</u> within the next decade, and international teams of astronauts will then be sharing close quarters for long periods of time. What can be done to improve living conditions in space? Here's what former astronauts suggest:

✴ FOOD It doesn't taste as good in zero gravity. Food should be made spicier to overcome those effects. International tastes must also be considered.

✴ CLOTHING Layered clothing could help astronauts stay comfortable. The top layer could be removed or added as temperatures vary.

✴ SLEEPING Because of weightlessness, sleep is often interrupted in space. Comfortable restraints must be provided to give a sense of stability.

✴ EMOTIONAL NEEDS People need "down time" in space just as they do on Earth. Time ought to be provided for relaxation and privacy.

2 **COMPLETE** • *Comet Magazine (CM) is interviewing aerospace engineer Dr. Bernard Kay (BK). Complete the interview with the passive form of the verbs in parentheses.*

CM: Dr. Kay, I'd like to ask how meals _____will be handled_____ in the Space Station.
1. (will / handle)
_____ food _____ on board or
2. (Be going to / prepare)
_____ from tubes?
3. (squeeze)

BK: Neither. Gourmet meals _____ on Earth and then they
4. (will / prepackage)
_____ on board.
5. (can / warm up)

CM: The Space Station will have an international crew. How _____
food _____ to suit everyone's taste?
6. (should / choose)

BK: An international menu _____. Food _____
7. (have to / offer)   **8.** (could / select)
from food preference forms that the crew members complete.

CM: _____ dishes _____ on board?
9. (Will / use)

BK: Probably. But utensils _____ to the plates so they won't fly
10. (had better / attach)
around! Meals _____ as pleasant as possible.
11. (ought to / make)

3 **CHOOSE & COMPLETE** • *Some scientists just completed a simulation of life on the Station. Complete their conversations with the modals in parentheses and the correct verbs from the box.*

| design | improve | keep | remove | ~~solve~~ |

KENT: These simulations showed that there are still some problems. I hope they

_____can be solved_____ before the real thing. For example, the temperature
       1. (can)

_____ at 68°, but I was uncomfortably warm most of the time.
       2. (should)

LYLE: The material for our clothing _____. Maybe clothing
                                         3. (ought to)

_____ in layers. A layer _____ if
       4. (could)   **5.** (can)

it's too warm.

| do | deliver | give | store |

HANS: I didn't like the food very much. We _____ more fresh food.
                                                6. (ought to)

HISA: Well, fresh fruits and vegetables _____ by the Shuttle regularly.
                                              7. (be going to)

HANS: What _____ with the trash? Space litter is already a problem.
              8. (will)

HISA: I'm sure it _____ on board and carried to Earth by the Shuttle.
                     9. (will)

4 **EDIT** • *Read an astronaut's journal notes. Find and correct seven mistakes in the use of the passive with modals. The first mistake is already corrected.*

> I used the sleeping restraints last night and slept a lot better. They ought to ~~make~~ ^be made^ more comfortable,
>
> though. I felt trapped. I just looked in the mirror. My face is puffy and my eyes are red. I'd better be
>
> gotten on the exercise bike right away. I can be misunderstanding when I look like this. Last night
>
> Max thought I was angry at him for turning on "Star Trek." Actually, I love that show. I might be given
>
> early lunch shift today. I hope they have more teriyaki. It's nice and spicy, and the sauce can actually
>
> been tasted, even at zero gravity. Some of it had better be fly in on the Shuttle pretty soon, or there
>
> might be some unhappy astronauts! Speaking of unhappy, last night Kristen called and told me she
>
> was planning to quit school. I think she could be talk out of it, but I'm afraid I'll get angry and yell if
>
> we discuss it. I might overheard by others. We need some privacy here!

The Passive Causative

CHECK POINT

Check the correct answer.

The guy wants to know if his girlfriend

☐ cut her own hair.

☐ went to a hair salon.

CHART CHECK

Circle T (True) or F (False).

T F The passive causative always has a form of the verb **be**.

T F You can form the passive causative with **have** or **get**.

T F The passive causative always needs an agent.

		STATEMENTS			
SUBJECT	*HAVE/GET*	**OBJECT**	**PAST PARTICIPLE**	**(BY + AGENT)**	
She	**has**	*her hair*	**cut**	by André	every month.
He	**has had**	*his beard*	**trimmed**		before.
I	**got**	*my nails*	**done**		at André's.
She	**is going to get**	*her ears*	**pierced**.		

		YES/NO QUESTIONS			
AUXILIARY VERB	**SUBJECT**	*HAVE/GET*	**OBJECT**	**PAST PARTICIPLE**	**(BY + AGENT)**
Does	she	**have**	*her hair*	**cut**	by André?
Has	he	**had**	*his beard*	**trimmed**?	
Did	you	**get**	*your nails*	**done**?	
Is	she	**going to get**	*her ears*	**pierced**?	

EXPRESS CHECK

Complete this conversation with the correct form of the verb **do**.

A: Where do you get your hair _____?

B: I don't get it _____. I _____ it myself.

Grammar Explanations	Examples
1. Use the **passive causative** to talk about <u>services that you arrange for someone to do for you</u>. ▶ **BE CAREFUL!** Do not confuse the simple past causative *(had something done)* with the past perfect in active sentences *(had done something)*.	■ I used to color my own hair, but now I **have** *it* **colored**. ■ I **get** *my nails* **done** by Marie. SIMPLE PAST CAUSATIVE ■ I **had** *it* **done** last week. *(Someone did it for me.)* PAST PERFECT ■ I **had done** *it* before. *(I did it myself.)*
2. Form the **passive causative** with the appropriate form of **have** or **get** + **object** + **past participle**. The passive causative can be used in <u>all tenses</u> and with <u>modals</u>.	■ I always **have** *my hair* **cut** by André. ■ I **haven't had** *it* **done** since June. ■ Last year I **got** *my coat* **cleaned** once. ■ Next week I**'m going to have** *my windows* **washed**. ■ I**'m getting** *them* **done** by Spotless. ■ I **had** *them* **washed** a long time ago. ■ You **should get** *the car* **checked**. ■ You **ought to have** *it* **done** soon.
3. Use **by** when it is necessary to mention the <u>person doing the service</u> (the agent). Do not mention the agent unnecessarily.	■ Lynne gets her hair done **by André**. ■ Where does Lynne **get her hair done**? NOT Where does Lynne get her hair done ~~by a hair stylist~~?

Check it out!

For more information about when to use an agent, see Unit 61, page 265.

1 **TRUE OR FALSE** • *Read each person's statement. Write T (True) or F (False) for the sentence that follows.*

1. **JAKE:** I'm going to get my hair cut tomorrow after work.

   __F__ Jake cuts his own hair.

2. **DEBRA:** I'm coloring my hair this afternoon.

   _____ Debra colors her own hair.

3. **AMBER:** I didn't pack any nail polish, because I had done my nails before the trip.

   _____ Amber did her own nails.

4. **JAKE:** I'm thinking of getting the floors waxed before the party.

   _____ Jake might hire someone to wax the floors.

5. **MARIE:** I had my apartment painted two months ago.

   _____ Marie painted her own apartment.

6. **TONY:** I'll wash the car this weekend.

   _____ Tony is going to wash the car himself.

2 **FIND OUT & REPORT** • *It's February 15. Look at the Santanas' calendar and write sentences about things they **had done** and things they **are going to have done**.*

FEBRUARY						
SUNDAY	**MONDAY**	**TUESDAY**	**WEDNESDAY**	**THURSDAY**	**FRIDAY**	**SATURDAY**
1	2	3	4	5	6	7 Deb–hairdresser
8	9	10	11	Jake– 12 barber	13 carpets	Amber– 14 dog groomer
Today's 15 date	windows 16	17	18	19	20 food and drinks	21 party!!
22	23	24	Amber– 25 ears pierced	26	27	28 family pictures

1. They / have / pictures / take ___They are going to have pictures taken.___

2. Debra / get / her hair / perm ___Debra got her hair permed.___

3. Amber / have / the dog / groom _____

4. They / get / the windows / wash _____

5. They / have / the carpets / clean _____

6. Amber / have / her ears / pierce _____

7. Jake / get / his hair / cut _____

8. They / have / food and drinks / deliver _____

CHOOSE & COMPLETE • *Debra and Jake are going to have a party. Complete the conversations with the passive causative of the appropriate verbs in the box.*

| dry clean | color | cut | paint | ~~shorten~~ | wash |

1. **DEBRA:** Your new dress is a little long. Why don't you __get it shortened__?

   AMBER: OK. They do alterations at the cleaners. I'll take it in tomorrow.

2. **DEBRA:** My blue dress has a small stain. I have to _____.

   AMBER: I can drop it off at the cleaners with my dress.

3. **JAKE:** The house is ready, except for the windows. They look pretty dirty.

   DEBRA: Don't worry. We _____ tomorrow.

4. **DEBRA:** Your hair is getting really long. I thought you were going to cut it.

   AMBER: I decided not to do it myself this time. I _____

   by André.

5. **DEBRA:** My hair's getting a lot of gray in it. Should I _____?

   JAKE: It looks fine to me, but it's up to you.

6. **GUEST:** The house looks beautiful. _____ you

   _____?

   JAKE: No, actually we did it ourselves last summer.

4 **EDIT** • *Read Amber's diary entry. Find and correct seven mistakes in the use of the passive causative. The first mistake is already corrected.*

February 21

The party was tonight. It went really well! The house looked great. Mom and Dad had the floors

waxed and all the windows ~~clean~~ cleaned professionally so everything sparkled. And of course we had the

whole house painted ourselves last summer. (I'll never forget *that*. It took us two weeks!) I wore my

new black dress that I have shortened by Bo, and I got cut my hair by André. He did a great job. There

were a lot of guests at the party. We had almost fifty people invited, and they almost all showed

up! The food was great too. Mom made most of the main dishes herself, but she had the rest of

the food prepare by a caterer. Mom and Dad hired a professional photographer, so at the end of the

party we all took our pictures. Dad's getting them back next week. I can't wait to see them!

SelfTest

Circle the letter of the correct answer to complete each sentence.

EXAMPLE:
Jennifer never _____ coffee.   A Ⓑ C D
(A) drink   (C) is drinking
(B) drinks   (D) was drinking

1. This book _____ written in 1999.   A B C D
   (A) is   (C) was
   (B) has   (D) were

2. Coffee is _____ in Colombia.   A B C D
   (A) grow   (C) been growing
   (B) grew   (D) grown

3. Millions of people _____ the movie.   A B C D
   (A) saw   (C) will be seen
   (B) were seen   (D) must be seen

4. The meeting won't _____.   A B C D
   (A) cancel   (C) been cancelled
   (B) be cancelled   (D) cancelled

5. Sally doesn't cut her own hair. She _____ at the salon.   A B C D
   (A) cuts it   (C) has it cut
   (B) has cut it   (D) gets it

6. That book was written _____ Maya Angelou. A B C D
   (A) at   (C) from
   (B) by   (D) of

7. The report _____ soon.   A B C D
   (A) publishes   (C) will be published
   (B) is published   (D) will publish

8. —When will the work be completed?   A B C D
   —It _____ be by June, but I'm not really sure.
   (A) has   (C) will
   (B) might   (D) won't

9. How often _____ your car serviced since you bought it?   A B C D
   (A) do you get   (C) had you gotten
   (B) did you get   (D) have you gotten

10. I have to get my picture _____ for my Web site.   A B C D
    (A) take   (C) taking
    (B) taken   (D) took

SECTION TWO

Each sentence has four underlined words or phrases. The four underlined parts of the sentence are marked A, B, C, and D. Circle the letter of the one underlined word or phrase that is NOT CORRECT.

EXAMPLE:

Mike <u>usually</u> <u>drives</u> to school, but <u>today</u> he <u>walks</u>.
     A   B   C   D   **A B C (D)**

11. Tomorrow <u>I'm getting</u> my car <u>serviced</u> <u>from</u> the mechanic that **A B C D**
    Jake <u>uses</u>.

12. The reports <u>were</u> <u>arrived</u> late, so I <u>had</u> <u>them sent</u> to you this morning. **A B C D**

13. Some mistakes <u>were</u> <u>made</u> in the brochure, but they might <u>corrected</u> **A B C D**
    before you <u>get</u> back.

14. You<u>'ll see</u> a copy before they<u>'re</u> <u>printed</u> <u>by the printer</u>. **A B C D**

15. A funny thing <u>was</u> happened when your <u>office</u> <u>was</u> <u>painted</u> yesterday. **A B C D**

16. <u>Will</u> your stay <u>be</u> <u>extended</u>, or will you <u>be returned</u> next week? **A B C D**

17. I used to <u>do</u> my own taxes, but now I <u>have</u> <u>done</u> <u>them</u> <u>by</u> an accountant. **A B C D**

18. Before a final decision <u>is reached</u>, the various possibilities <u>should</u> **A B C D**
    probably <u>discussed</u> <u>by</u> the whole team.

19. The house <u>painted</u> more than three years ago, but I'm not <u>going to</u> **A B C D**
    <u>have</u> <u>it done</u> again for a while.

20. We <u>didn't</u> <u>know</u> about the problem, so it <u>shouldn't</u> <u>be handled</u> in time. **A B C D**

21. A lot of crops <u>can't</u> be <u>grew</u> in the mountains because <u>it</u> <u>gets</u> too cold. **A B C D**

22. That pottery <u>was</u> <u>found</u> <u>by</u> an archaeologist while she <u>was worked</u> in **A B C D**
    this area.

23. <u>Does</u> the lightbulb <u>have to replaced</u> or is <u>it</u> still <u>working</u>? **A B C D**

24. <u>Have</u> you <u>had</u> your teeth <u>clean</u> yet <u>by</u> Dr. Ellin's new oral hygienist? **A B C D**

25. The last payment shouldn't <u>make</u> until all the work <u>has been</u> **A B C D**
    <u>completed</u> and carefully <u>checked</u>.

Factual Conditionals:
Present

Speech bubble: Sorry, Sir. If you **don't fit**, you **can't board**.

CHECK *POINT*

Circle T (True) or F (False).

T F The man may not be able to board the plane.

CHART CHECK

Circle T (True) or F (False).

T F The verbs in both clauses are in the present tense.

T F The *if* clause always comes first.

T F There is always a comma between the two clauses.

STATEMENTS		
IF CLAUSE		**RESULT CLAUSE**
If	it **snows,**	the airport **closes.**
	it's foggy,	planes **can't leave.**

STATEMENTS		
RESULT CLAUSE	**IF CLAUSE**	
The airport **closes**	if	it **snows.**
Planes **can't leave**		it's foggy.

YES/NO QUESTIONS		
RESULT CLAUSE	**IF CLAUSE**	
Does the airport **close**	if	it **snows?**
Can planes **leave**		it's foggy?

SHORT ANSWERS			
AFFIRMATIVE		**NEGATIVE**	
Yes,	it **does.**	No,	it **doesn't.**
	they **can.**		they **can't.**

WH- QUESTIONS	
RESULT CLAUSE	**IF CLAUSE**
Why **does** air **get** lighter	*if* it **expands?**

EXPRESS CHECK

Match the **if** *clauses with the result clauses.*

_____ 1. If you hate airplane food,

_____ 2. You might not be able to board

_____ 3. If people travel a long distance,

a. they often feel jet lag.

b. you can order a special meal.

c. if you don't check in at the gate.

Grammar Explanations

Examples

1. Use **present factual conditional** sentences to talk about <u>general truths</u> and <u>scientific facts</u>.

The *if* clause talks about the condition, and the result clause talks about what happens if the condition occurs.

Use the **simple present tense** in <u>both clauses</u>.

■ *If* it**'s** noon in Lima, it**'s** 6:00 P.M. in Rome.
    if clause   result clause

■ *If* air **expands**, it **becomes** lighter.
    if clause   result clause

2. You can also use **present factual conditional** sentences to talk about <u>habits</u> and <u>recurring events</u> (things that happen again and again).

Use the <u>simple present tense</u> or <u>present progressive</u> in the *if* clause. Use the <u>simple present tense</u> in the result clause.

■ *If* Bill **flies**, he **orders** a special meal.
    if clause   result clause

■ *If* I**'m traveling** far, I always **fly**.
    if clause   result clause

3. You can also use **modals** in the result clause.

■ If you practice your Chinese everyday, you *can* **improve** quickly.

■ You *might* **learn** more if you listen to Chinese tapes.

4. Use the **imperative** in the result clause to give <u>instructions, commands</u>, and <u>invitations</u> that depend on a certain condition.

■ If you want the seat to recline, **press** the button.

■ If the seat belt light is on, **don't leave** your seat.

■ If you come to Tokyo, **stay** with us.

5. You can **begin conditional sentences** with <u>the *if* clause or the result clause</u>. The meaning is the same.

Use a **comma** between the two clauses only when the *if* clause comes first.

■ **If the light goes on,** buckle your seat belt.
              OR

■ Buckle your seat belt **if the light goes on**.

IDENTIFY • *Read this article. In each factual conditional sentence, underline the result clause once. Underline the clause that expresses the condition twice.*

PASSENGERS' RIGHTS

If you run into problems on your journey, know your rights as a passenger. Often the airline company is required to compensate you for delays or damages. For example, the airline provides meals and hotel rooms if a flight is unduly delayed. However, the airline owes you a lot more if it caused the delay by overbooking. This can occur especially during holidays if airlines sell more tickets than there are seats. If all the passengers actually show up, then the flight is overbooked. Airlines usually award upgrades or additional free travel to passengers who volunteer to take a later flight. However, if no one volunteers, your flight may be delayed. In that case, the airline must repay you 100 percent of the cost of your ticket for a delay of up to four hours on an international flight. If the delay is more than four hours, you receive 200 percent of the cost of your ticket.

SUMMARIZE • *Read these conversations about Hong Kong. Summarize the advice with conditional sentences.*

1. **A:** I hate hot weather.
   B: The best time to go to Hong Kong is November or December.

   If you hate hot weather, the best time to go to Hong Kong is November or December.

2. **A:** I'm traveling with my children.
   B: Take them to Lai Chi Kok Amusement Park in Kowloon.

   _____

3. **A:** We need a moderately priced hotel.
   B: I suggest the Harbour View International House.

   _____

4. **A:** We like seafood.
   B: There are wonderful seafood restaurants on Lamma Island.

   _____

5. **A:** I'm fascinated by Chinese opera.
   B: You might like the street opera in the Shanghai Street Night Market.

   _____

6. **A:** I'd like to get a good view of Hong Kong.
   B: You should take the funicular to the Peak.

   _____

3 **COMBINE •** *Complete this interview between* **Careers** Magazine (CM) *and flight attendant* May Simka (MS). *Combine the sentences in parentheses to make a factual conditional sentence. Use the same order. Make necessary changes in capitalization and punctuation.*

CM: How long are you usually away?

MS: If I go to the Bahamas, I have a two-day layover.
　　　　1. (I go to the Bahamas. I have a two-day layover.)

CM: What do you do for two days?

MS: _____
　　　　2. (I spend a lot of time at the pool. I stay at a hotel.)

_____
　　　　3. (I stay with friends. I spend time with them.)

CM: Sounds nice.

MS: _____
　　　　4. (It's not so nice. I get a "Dracula.")

That's when you fly somewhere at midnight, spend four hours, and then fly back.

CM: Sounds like a tough job. Is it worth it?

MS: _____
　　　　5. (It's very rewarding. You don't mind hard work.)

CM: Who walks the dog and waters the plants when you're away?

MS: _____
　　　　6. (You have three roommates. You don't have trouble finding dogwalkers.)

CM: What's the best thing about this job?

MS: Free trips. _____
　　　　　　　　　7. (A flight has an empty seat. I ride for free!)

4 **EDIT •** *Read May's journal entry. Find and correct seven mistakes in the use of present factual conditionals. The first mistake is already corrected. Don't forget to check punctuation!*

> 　　　　　　　　　　　　　　　　　　　　　　　don't
> What a great weekend! If Lou and Teri aren't the best hosts in the world, I ~~won't~~ know who is.
>
> I've invited them to New York, but if you live in the Bahamas, you rarely want to leave. Tomorrow at
>
> midnight I fly round trip from New York to Pittsburgh. There's always a price to pay. If I get a free
>
> weekend in the islands I always get a "Dracula" afterwards. Oh, well. If I won't fall asleep, I can usually
>
> get a lot of reading done. Pat and Kim both flew to London yesterday. I hope someone can walk Frisky
>
> for me. Usually, if I'll be working, one of them is off. If Frisky is alone for a long time, he barked a lot.
>
> That disturbs the neighbors. Maybe I should just leave the TV on for him. He's always very calm, if
>
> the TV is on. Or maybe I'd better call Pat and ask her about her schedule. If it was 6:00 p.m. here in
>
> New York, it's 11:00 p.m. in London. That's not too late to call.

UNIT
65

Factual Conditionals:
Future

If Baker **raises** taxes, small businesses **will leave**.

CHECK *POINT*

Circle T (True) or F (False).

T F Baker is definitely going to raise taxes.

T F Small businesses are definitely going to leave.

CHART CHECK

Check the correct answer.

Use the simple present tense in

☐ the *if* clause.

☐ the result clause.

Use a comma between the two clauses

☐ when the *if* clause comes first.

☐ when the result clause comes first.

AFFIRMATIVE STATEMENTS	
IF CLAUSE: PRESENT	RESULT CLAUSE: FUTURE
If Baker **wins**,	he**'ll raise** taxes. he**'s going to fight** crime.

NEGATIVE STATEMENTS	
IF CLAUSE: PRESENT	RESULT CLAUSE: FUTURE
If he **doesn't lower** taxes,	businesses **won't return**.

YES/NO QUESTIONS	
RESULT CLAUSE: FUTURE	*IF* CLAUSE: PRESENT
Will he **lower** taxes **Is** he **going to fight** crime	*if* he **wins**?

SHORT ANSWERS			
AFFIRMATIVE		NEGATIVE	
Yes, he	will.	**No**, he	won't.
	is.		isn't.

282

WH- QUESTIONS	
RESULT CLAUSE: FUTURE	*IF* **CLAUSE: PRESENT**
What **will** he **do** **is** he **going to do**	*if* he **wins?**

EXPRESS `CHECK`

Unscramble these words to form a sentence. Add a comma if necessary.

fight • she • crime • she'll • If • wins

_____

Grammar Explanations

Examples

1. Use **future factual conditional** sentences to talk about what <u>will happen under certain conditions</u>. The *if* clause states the condition. The result clause states the result.

         if clause   result clause
■ *If* Baker **wins**, he**'ll raise** taxes.
  (It's a real possibility that Baker will win.)

Use the **simple present tense** in the *if* clause. Use the **future** with ***will*** or ***be going to*** in the result clause.

■ *If* Soto **wins**, she**'ll improve** housing.
■ *If* Soto **wins**, she**'s going to improve** housing.

You can also use a **modal** in the result clause.

■ If you want to vote, you ***must register***.
■ If you don't vote, you ***might regret*** it.

▶ **BE CAREFUL!** Even though the *if* clause refers to the future, use the <u>simple present tense</u>.

■ *If* she **wins**, she'll fight crime.
  NOT ~~If she will win . . .~~

2. You can **begin conditional sentences** with <u>the *if* clause or the result clause</u>. The meaning is the same.

■ **If you vote for Soto,** you won't regret it.
                    OR
■ You won't regret it **if you vote for Soto.**

Use a **comma** between the two clauses only when the *if* clause comes first

3. *If* and *unless* can both be used in conditional sentences, but their meanings are very different.

■ *If* you vote, you'll have a say in the future of our city.

Use *unless* to state a <u>negative condition</u>.

■ *Unless* you vote, you won't have a say in the future of our city.
                    OR

Unless often has the same meaning as *if . . . not*.

■ *If* you do**n't** vote, you won't have a say in the future of our city.

1 **MATCH** • *Each condition will have a result. Match the condition with the appropriate result.*

Condition	Result
__f__ **1.** If Soto wins, she	**a.** won't stay out of trouble.
_____ **2.** If she lowers taxes, business people	**b.** won't have a say in the government.
_____ **3.** If the education system improves, we	**c.** will have an educated work force.
_____ **4.** Unless young people have hope for the future, they	**d.** won't be able to vote.
_____ **5.** If crime decreases, this	**e.** will move their companies back to the city.
_____ **6.** Unless you register, you	**f.** will lower taxes.
_____ **7.** If you don't vote, you	**g.** will be a safer place to live.

2 **COMPLETE** • *Read this interview between* Politics Today (PT) *and mayoral candidate Daniel Baker* (DB). *Complete it with the correct form of the verbs in parentheses and* **if** *or* **unless**.

PT: What's the first thing you _____'ll do_____ _____if_____ you
    1. (do)   **2.** (if / unless)
_____ elected?
  3. (get)

DB: Well, it's been a long, hard campaign. _____ I _____,
                 4. (If / Unless)   **5.** (win)
I _____ a short vacation before I begin my new job.
  6. (take)

PT: Sounds good. Where to?

DB: Sorry, but I'd rather not say. _____ I _____ mayor,
                   7. (If / Unless)   **8.** (become)
I _____ to keep my personal life private. Even mayors need privacy.
  9. (try)

PT: I can understand that. Now, every election has a winner and a loser.

What _____ you _____ _____
                     10. (do)   **11.** (if / unless)
you _____?
  12. (lose)

DB: _____ I _____ this election, I _____ to be
   13. (If / Unless)   **14.** (lose)   **15.** (continue)
active in politics as a private citizen. _____ *both* parties
                           16. (If / Unless)
_____, this city _____ as great as it can be.
 17. (cooperate)   **18.** (not be)
Finally, _____ the people _____ me to office this time,
     19. (if / unless)   **20.** (not elect)
I _____ back in four years to try again!
  21. (be)

COMBINE • *Yuko Tamari is trying to decide whether to go to law school. She made a decision tree to help her decide. In the tree, arrows connect the conditions and the results. Write sentences about her decisions. Use future factual sentences.*

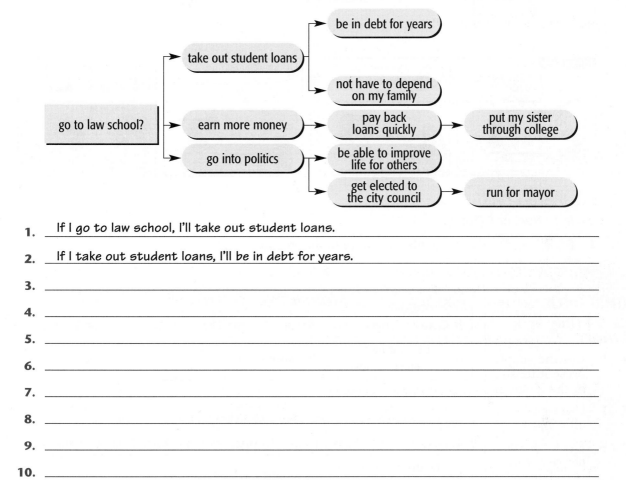

1. __If I go to law school, I'll take out student loans._____

2. __If I take out student loans, I'll be in debt for years._____

3. _____

4. _____

5. _____

6. _____

7. _____

8. _____

9. _____

10. _____

EDIT • *Read this journal entry. Find and correct six mistakes in the use of future factual conditionals. The first mistake is already corrected. Don't forget to check punctuation!*

Should I campaign for student council president? I'll have to decide soon if I ~~wanted~~ *want* to run. If I'll be

busy campaigning, I won't have much time to study. That's a problem, because I'm not going to get into

a good college if I get good grades this year. On the other hand, there's so much to do in this school,

and nothing is getting done if Todd Laker becomes president again. A lot of people know that. But

will I know what to do if I'll get the job? Never mind. I'll deal with that problem, if I win.

UNIT 66

Unreal Conditionals:
Present

CHECK *POINT*

Circle T (True) or F (False).

T F Schroeder, the piano player, wants to marry Lucy.

CHART CHECK

Circle T (True) or F (False).

T F Use the simple present tense in the *if* clause.

T F Use *were* for all subjects.

T F Use a comma between the two clauses when the result clause comes first.

AFFIRMATIVE STATEMENTS

IF CLAUSE: SIMPLE PAST	RESULT CLAUSE: *WOULD* + BASE FORM OF VERB
If he **loved** her, he **were*** in love,	he **would get** married.

*Note that *were* is used for all subjects with *be*.

NEGATIVE STATEMENTS

IF CLAUSE: SIMPLE PAST	RESULT CLAUSE: *WOULD* + BASE FORM OF VERB
If he **didn't love** her, he **weren't** in love,	he **would not get** married.

YES/NO QUESTIONS

RESULT CLAUSE		IF CLAUSE
Would I **get** married	**if**	I **loved** her? I **were** in love?

SHORT ANSWERS

AFFIRMATIVE	NEGATIVE
Yes, I **would**.	No, I **wouldn't**.

WH- QUESTIONS

RESULT CLAUSE		IF CLAUSE
What **would** you **do**	**if**	you **loved** her? you **were** in love?

NOTE: For contractions with *would*, see Appendix 24 on page 346.

EXPRESS CHECK

Circle the correct words to complete this question.

What <u>will / would</u> he do <u>if / when</u> he <u>was / were</u> a millionaire?

Grammar Explanations

Examples

1. Use **present unreal conditional** sentences to talk about <u>unreal, untrue, imagined, or impossible</u> conditions and their results.

The *if* clause presents the unreal condition. The result clause presents the unreal result of that condition.

if clause   result clause
■ *If* I **loved** him, I **would marry** him.
(But I don't love him, so I won't marry him.)

if clause   result clause
■ *If* I **had** more time, I **would travel**.
(But I don't have time, so I don't travel.)

2. Use the **simple past tense** in the *if* clause. Use *would* + **base form** of the verb in the result clause.

▶ **BE CAREFUL!**

   a. The *if* clause uses the simple past tense form, but the <u>meaning is not past</u>.

   b. <u>Don't use *would* in the *if* clause</u> in present unreal conditional sentences.

   c. Use *were* for <u>all subjects</u> when the verb in the *if* clause is a form of *be*.

   USAGE NOTE: You will sometimes hear native speakers use *was* in the *if* clause. However, many people think that this is <u>not correct</u>.

If clause   result clause
■ *If* they **had** money, they **wouldn't live** there.

■ *If* I **had** more money *now*, I would take a trip around the world.

■ *If* she **knew** the answer, she would tell you. NOT If she would know the answer . . .

■ *If* I **were** rich, I would travel around the world. NOT If I was rich . . .

3. You can also use a **modal** in the result clause.

■ If I had time, I *could* read more.

4. You can **begin conditional sentences** with <u>the *if* clause or the result clause</u>. The meaning is the same.

Use a **comma** between the two clauses only when the *if* clause comes first.

■ **If I had more money**, I would move.
OR
■ I would move **if I had more money**.

5. Statements beginning with *If I were you, . . .* are often used to <u>give advice</u>.

■ *If I were you*, I'd read "Peanuts." It's really funny.

1 **TRUE OR FALSE •** *Read each quotation from these "Peanuts" characters. Write T (True) or F (False) for the statement that follows.*

1. **SNOOPY:** If I were a human being, I wouldn't even *own* a dog!

   ___F___ Snoopy is a human being.

2. **LUCY** to **SNOOPY:** You wouldn't be so happy if you knew what was going to happen.

   _____ Snoopy is happy.

3. **LUCY** to **LINUS:** If I were you, I'd sleep underneath that tree.

   _____ Lucy is giving Linus advice.

4. **SNOOPY** to **WOODSTOCK:** What would you do if you had forty dollars?

   _____ Woodstock has forty dollars.

5. **SNOOPY:** If I ate one more snowflake, I'd turn into a blizzard.

   _____ Snoopy plans to eat another snowflake.

6. **LUCY:** If we were married, Schroeder, I'd come in every morning and dust your piano.

   _____ Lucy dusts Schroeder's piano.

2 **COMPLETE •** *Read part of an article about the comic strip "Peanuts." Complete it with the correct form of the verbs in parentheses.*

Peanuts

What makes "Peanuts" so popular? Of course, if it ___weren't___
1. (not be)
funny, people _____ it so much. But "Peanuts" provides
2. (not like)
more than just laughs. It addresses such universal themes as love, jealousy, loneliness, and
hope. If the characters _____ so real, we _____ with them.
3. (not be)   **4.** (couldn't / identify)
Take Lucy, for example. In love with the piano-playing Schroeder, Lucy complains, "If we

_____ married, and you _____ golf, I _____
5. (be)   **6.** (love)   **7.** (hate)
your golf clubs! If you _____ a sports car, I _____ your sports
8. (drive)   **9.** (hate)
car! If you _____ a bowler, I _____ your bowling ball." Without
10. (be)   **11.** (hate)
looking up from his piano or missing a beat, Schroeder asks, "So?" "I hate your piano!" shouts

Lucy as she kicks it out from under him. Recognizable behavior? In "Peanuts" we see ourselves

along with our weaknesses and hopes. But we don't have to analyze "Peanuts" to enjoy it.

If it _____ for comic strips like "Peanuts," our lives _____
12. (not be)   **13.** (might / be)
a little less fun.

3   **COMBINE** • *Read about these "Peanuts" characters. What would happen if their situations were different? Combine the two sentences into one, using the unreal present conditional.*

1. Schroeder ignores Lucy. She gets angry at him.

   If Schroeder didn't ignore Lucy, she wouldn't get angry at him.

2. Schroeder loves Beethoven. He plays his sonatas all the time.

   _____

3. Charlie Brown doesn't have enough friends. He feels lonely.

   _____

4. Sally doesn't know her teacher's name. She can't send her a card.

   _____

5. Linus is smart. He finds clever solutions to life's problems.

   _____

6. Woodstock and Snoopy have a close relationship. Woodstock confides in Snoopy.

   _____

7. Rerun's parents refuse to let him have a dog. He tries to borrow Charlie's dog.

   _____

8. Pig Pen doesn't take enough baths. He's filthy.

   _____

4   **EDIT** • *Read this boy's journal entry. Find and correct six mistakes in the use of the present unreal conditional. The first mistake is already corrected.*

I've got to stop staying up late reading "Peanuts"! If I weren't always so tired, I ~~will~~ would be able to stay awake in class. Whenever the teacher calls on me, I don't know what to say. Then I get really embarrassed because of that cute red-haired girl that I like. I would talk to her if I wouldn't be so shy. My friend Jason says, "If I was you, I'd ask her to a party," but I'm too afraid that if I asked her, she would have said no. After class, I played baseball. Nobody wanted me on their team. If I play better, I would get chosen sometimes. Life is hard! I can really understand that Charlie Brown character in "Peanuts." In fact, if I didn't laugh so hard while reading "Peanuts," I would cried!

UNIT 67

Unreal Conditionals:
Past

Best Bets for Holiday Viewing

It's a Wonderful Life

Rating: ★★★★ out of ★★★★

What would have happened if you had never been born? George Bailey's guardian angel, Clarence, shows George that **life in Bedford Falls would have been a lot different if George hadn't been there**. In the process, Clarence teaches us all how our lives touch those of others. Highly recommended for the whole family.

George (seated)
with his guardian angel

CHECK *POINT*

Circle T (True) or F (False).

T F George Bailey was never in Bedford Falls.

CHART CHECK

Check the correct answers.

Use the past perfect in

❑ the *if* clause.

❑ the result clause.

Use a comma between the two clauses when

❑ the *if* clause comes first.

❑ the result clause comes first.

STATEMENTS	
IF CLAUSE: **PAST PERFECT**	**RESULT CLAUSE:** **WOULD (NOT) HAVE + PAST PARTICIPLE**
If I **had (not) had** money,	I **would (not) have moved** away.

YES/NO QUESTIONS	
RESULT CLAUSE	**IF CLAUSE**
Would you **have left**	**if** you **had had** money?

SHORT ANSWERS	
AFFIRMATIVE	**NEGATIVE**
Yes, I **would have.**	**No**, I **wouldn't have.**

WH- QUESTIONS	
RESULT CLAUSE	**IF CLAUSE**
What **would** you **have done**	*if* you **had had** money?

CONTRACTIONS
would have = **would've**
would not have = **wouldn't have**

EXPRESS CHECK

Complete this sentence with the correct form of the verb **study**. *Add a comma if necessary.*

I _____ if I had known about the quiz today.

Grammar Explanations	**Examples**
1. Use **past unreal conditional** sentences to talk about past conditions and results that <u>never happened</u>. The *if* clause presents the unreal condition. The result clause presents the imagined result of that condition.	*if* clause · · · · · · · · · · · · · · result clause ■ *If* George **had died** young, he **wouldn't have had** children. *(But he didn't die young, so he had children.)* ■ *If* George **hadn't been born**, many people's lives **would have been** worse. *(But George was born, so their lives were better.)*
2. Use the **past perfect** in the *if* clause. Use *would have* + **past participle** in the result clause.	*if* clause · · · · · · · · · · · · · · result clause ■ *If* the film **had won** an Oscar, it **would have become** famous right away.
3. You can also use **modals** in the result clause.	■ If George had gone to college, he *might have become* an architect. ■ If George had become an architect, he *could have designed* bridges.
4. You can **begin conditional sentences** with <u>the *if* clause or the result clause</u>. The meaning is the same. Use a **comma** between the two clauses only when the *if* clause comes first.	■ **If he had won a million dollars,** he would have traveled to China. OR ■ He would have traveled to China **if he had won a million dollars**.
5. **Past unreal conditionals** are often used to <u>express regret</u> about what happened in the past.	■ *If* I **had known** Mary was in town, I **would have invited** her to the party. *(I regret that I didn't invite her.)*

1 **TRUE OR FALSE** • *Read each numbered sentence. Write T (True) or F (False) for the statement that follows.*

1. If I had had time, I would have watched *It's a Wonderful Life*.

   __T__ I didn't have time to watch *It's a Wonderful Life*.

2. I would have taped the movie if my VCR hadn't broken.

   _____ I taped the movie.

3. If Clarence hadn't been there, George might have killed himself.

   _____ Clarence was there.

4. George wouldn't have met Mary if he hadn't gone to his brother's graduation party.

   _____ George didn't go to the party.

5. George would have been happier if he had become an architect.

   _____ George became an architect.

6. The movie wouldn't have been so good if James Stewart hadn't played the part of George Bailey.

   _____ James Stewart played the part of George Bailey.

2 **COMPLETE** • *George is thinking about the past. Complete his thoughts with the correct form of the words in parentheses.*

1. I didn't go into business with my friend Sam. If I _____had gone_____ into
   (go)
   business with him, I ___would have become___ a success.
   (become)

2. I couldn't go into the army because I was deaf in one ear. I _____
   (go)
   into the army if I _____ my hearing in that ear.
   (not lose)

3. Mary and I weren't able to go on a honeymoon. We _____ away if
   (can / go)
   my father _____ sick.
   (not get)

4. Clarence showed me how the world would look without me. I _____
   (not know)
   that I was so important if Clarence _____ me.
   (not show)

5. My old boss once made a terrible mistake. If I _____ him, he
   (not help)
   _____ to jail.
   (can / go)

6. Mary _____ a happy life if she _____ me.
   (may / not lead)   (not marry)

7. Life here _____ really different if I _____.
   (be)   (not live)

REWRITE • *Read each true situation. Then write a past unreal conditional sentence to express how things could have been different.*

1. Clarence wasn't a first-class angel, so he didn't have much self-confidence.

   If Clarence had been a first-class angel, he would have had more self-confidence.

2. George was unhappy about his business. He yelled at his daughter on Christmas Eve.

   _____

3. Poor people could buy houses because George's business loaned them money.

   _____

4. Mr. Potter wasn't able to trick George, so George didn't sell Potter the business.

   _____

5. George's Uncle Billy lost $8,000. George got into trouble with the law.

   _____

6. George's friends didn't know about his troubles. They didn't help him right away.

   _____

7. George's friends collected money for him, so he didn't go to jail.

   _____

 EDIT • *Read Clarence's diary entry. Find and correct six mistakes in the use of the unreal conditional. The first mistake is already corrected. Remember to check punctuation!*

> Dear Diary,
>
> It's funny how things work out sometimes. If George ~~hasn't~~ ^{hadn't} wanted to jump off that bridge on Christmas Eve, I might never have getting an important job like saving him. And if he hadn't been so stubborn, I would never had thought of the idea of showing him life in Bedford Falls without him. One of the saddest things was seeing all those people who didn't have homes. If George gave up and sold his business to Mr. Potter, then Potter would have rented run-down apartments to all those people. But because of George, they now have good homes. By the time we were finished, George realized he really had a wonderful life. In fact, he will have gone to jail happily, if his friends hadn't given him the money he needed. Well, luckily they helped him out, and he didn't go to jail. And I got my wings and became a first-class angel!

Wish: Present and Past

Tiny Fairy Tales   THE THREE WISHES

The Three Wishes

One day a poor woodcutter was given three wishes by a tree elf. When his hungry wife heard the news, she said, "I **wish** I **had** some sausages." At once five sausages appeared on a plate. The woodcutter was furious about wasting a wish. "I **wish** those sausages **were hanging** from your nose," he shouted. At once the sausages hung from her nose. The two struggled to get them loose, but they could not. "I **wish** I **hadn't made** that wish," the woodcutter sighed. At once the sausages were on the plate again. The couple happily ate the sausages and wished for nothing more. ✳

49

CHECK *POINT*

Check the correct answer.

The woman wanted sausages

☐ that day.

☐ the day before.

CHART CHECK 1

Check the correct answer.

In wishes about the present, what verb tense follows *wish*?

☐ the simple present

☐ the simple past

WISHES ABOUT THE PRESENT			
MAIN CLAUSE	**WISH CLAUSE**		
She **wishes**	she	**had**	some food right now.
		were*	rich.

*Note that *were* is used for all subjects with *be*.

CHART CHECK 2

Check the correct answer.

In wishes about the past, what verb tense follows *wish*?

❑ the simple past
❑ the past perfect

WISHES ABOUT THE PAST			
MAIN CLAUSE	**WISH CLAUSE**		
He **wishes**	he	**had had**	food last night.
		had been	rich as a child.

EXPRESS CHECK

Complete these sentences with the correct forms of the verb **know***.*

- I wish I _____ a good story to tell in my next class.
- I wish I _____ more stories as a child.

Grammar Explanations	Examples
1. Use *wish* followed by a verb in the **simple past** tense to talk about <u>things that you want to be true now but that are not true</u>.	∎ He **wishes** he *had* a yacht. *(He doesn't have a yacht, but he wants one.)*
After *wish*, use *were* instead of *was*.	∎ Sometimes I **wish** I *were* a child again. NOT Sometimes I̶ ̶w̶i̶s̶h̶ ̶I̶ ̶w̶a̶s̶ a child again.
2. Use *wish* followed by the **past perfect** to express <u>regrets about events in the past</u>.	∎ They **wish** they *had moved* to the city. *(They didn't move to the city, and now they think that was a mistake.)*
3. Use *would* after *wish* to express a desire for someone or something to act in a different way. This often communicates <u>a complaint or a regret</u>.	∎ I **wish** you *would* **cook** breakfast. You have more time than I do. ∎ I **wish** she *would* **visit** more often. I really miss her.
Do not use *will* after *wish*.	NOT I̶ ̶w̶i̶s̶h̶ ̶s̶h̶e̶ ̶w̶i̶l̶l̶ ̶v̶i̶s̶i̶t̶ more often.
4. Use *could* or *could have* after *wish* to express <u>ability</u>.	∎ He **wishes** he *could* **earn** more money now. ∎ He **wishes** he *could have* **found** a better job when he was younger.
Do not use *can* after *wish*.	NOT H̶e̶ ̶w̶i̶s̶h̶e̶s̶ ̶h̶e̶ ̶c̶a̶n̶ ̶e̶a̶r̶n̶ more money.

TRUE OR FALSE • *Read each numbered sentence. Write T (True) or F (False) for the statement that follows.*

1. I wish I were a princess.

___T___ I'm not a princess.

2. I hated living in a big house as a child.

_____ I wish I had lived in a small house.

3. He wishes he could find a better job.

_____ He likes his job.

4. They couldn't take computer classes in college, so they are taking them now.

_____ They wish they could take computer classes.

5. Hal's wife plays computer games a lot. He wants her to stop.

_____ He wishes she wouldn't play computer games.

6. He wishes he had a lot of money.

_____ He doesn't have a lot of money.

 COMPLETE • *Read this article from a psychology magazine. Complete it with the correct form of the verbs in parentheses.*

PSYCHOLOGY FOR YOU   April 2000

WISHES AND SOLUTIONS

The old saying goes, "If wishes were horses, then beggars would ride." "I wish it _____**were**_____ that easy," says therapist Joel Grimes. "But we can't just wish
1. (be)

problems _____. We have to make our own solutions." According to him,
2. (will / go away)

complainers are really saying, "I wish I _____ a magical solution. I wish
3. (have)

I _____ with this myself." One client, for example, kept complaining,
4. (not have to / deal)

"I wish I _____ people, but my apartment is too small." Grimes urged her
5. (can / entertain)

to solve the problem. This year, she hosted a holiday open house, with people coming at

different times. She still wishes she _____ her whole family last year, but
6. (can / invite)

she learned she could solve her own problems. "At first clients get angry at me for not

handing them solutions," says Grimes. "But when they experience their own power, they

wish they _____ about it sooner."
7. (know)

3

REWRITE • *Joel Grimes's clients complain about things in the past and in the present. Rewrite their complaints as wishes.*

1. I didn't have time to read bedtime stories to my children.

   I wish I had had time to read bedtime stories to my children.

2. My husband won't ask for a raise.

   _____

3. My wife couldn't balance the checkbook last month.

   _____

4. My boyfriend is out of shape.

   _____

5. I'm too old to go back to school.

   _____

6. I can't stop smoking.

   _____

7. My son doesn't call me.

   _____

8. My parents didn't understand me.

   _____

 4

EDIT • *Read this journal entry. Find and correct five mistakes in the use of* **wish.** *The first mistake is already corrected.*

> were
> Today I told Dr. Grimes, "I wish there ~~was~~ a way to spend more time with my boyfriend,
> but we're both too busy." He just said, "If wishes were horses, beggars would ride." That's
> cute, but I wish I understand its meaning. Maybe it means that wishing won't solve
> problems. Well, that's why I went to see him!!! I wish he will tell me what to do right
> then and there, but he refused. Speaking of wishful thinking, I wish Todd and I could have
> spent the weekend together next week. My exams are over, but he has to fly to Denver to
> his job. If wishes were horses, I'd ride one to Denver. Hey! Todd is always saying, "I wish
> you would come with me sometimes." I guess I <u>can</u> go with him to Denver. Dr. Grimes must
> have meant that I can solve my own problems. Now I wish I haven't been so rude to him.

SelfTest

Circle the letter of the correct answer to complete each sentence.

EXAMPLE:

Jennifer never _____ coffee.   A (B) C D
(A) drink   (C) is drinking
(B) drinks   (D) was drinking

---

1. If you _____ a headache, you should take an aspirin.   A B C D
   (A) 'll have   (C) have
   (B) had   (D) are having

2. I wish we _____ a bigger house. This one is too small.   A B C D
   (A) have   (C) would have
   (B) had   (D) had had

3. _____ it rains very hard, the streets flood.   A B C D
   (A) If   (C) During
   (B) Always   (D) Unless

4. We'll be late unless we _____ now.   A B C D
   (A) leave   (C) had left
   (B) don't leave   (D) have left

5. What would Tom do if he _____ the truth?   A B C D
   (A) would know   (C) knows
   (B) has known   (D) knew

6. If I _____ you, I'd call and apologize.   A B C D
   (A) am   (C) were
   (B) would be   (D) was

7. If I _____ you were sick, I would have called sooner.   A B C D
   (A) have known   (C) would have known
   (B) had known   (D) know

8. If you want to go skiing in the South, _____ to Black Mountain.   A B C D
   (A) you go   (C) go
   (B) you'll go   (D) went

9. Jennifer has trouble with college math. She wishes she _____ more in high school.   A B C D
   (A) studies   (C) had studied
   (B) has studied   (D) studied

10. —If we invited you, would you come?
    —Of course I _____ .   **A B C D**
    (A) do   (C) would have
    (B) am   (D) would

11. Jake will win the election if he _____ harder.   **A B C D**
    (A) campaigns   (C) will campaign
    (B) would campaign   (D) campaigned

12. If you _____ told us about the bad service, we would have   **A B C D**
    eaten there.
    (A) didn't   (C) haven't
    (B) wouldn't have   (D) hadn't

SECTION TWO

Each sentence has four underlined words or phrases. The four underlined parts of the sentence are marked A, B, C, and D. Circle the letter of the one underlined word or phrase that is NOT CORRECT.

EXAMPLE:
Mike <u>usually</u> <u>drives</u> to school, but <u>today</u> he <u>walks</u>.   **A B C ⒟**
      A   B   C   D

---

13. <u>If</u> you <u>had been</u> here yesterday, you <u>would have</u> <u>see</u> Jean.   **A B C D**
     A   B   C   D

14. I <u>wish</u> our family <u>could of</u> <u>taken</u> vacations when we <u>were</u> younger.   **A B C D**
       A   B   C   D

15. Unless <u>we</u> work harder, we <u>will</u> <u>finish</u> on <u>time</u>.   **A B C D**
           A   B   C   D

16. <u>If</u> I <u>will have</u> to make a difficult decision<u>,</u> I always <u>discuss</u> it with   **A B C D**
     A   B   C   D
    my friends.

17. <u>If</u> Lara <u>is</u> older, she <u>would try</u> <u>to get</u> a job in California.   **A B C D**
     A   B   C   D

18. We <u>could had</u> <u>done</u> more <u>if</u> we <u>had had</u> more time.   **A B C D**
          A   B   C   D

19. We <u>ate</u> outside <u>tomorrow</u> <u>unless</u> it <u>rains</u>.   **A B C D**
       A   B   C   D

20. I <u>would</u> <u>take</u> the job <u>if</u> I <u>am</u> you.   **A B C D**
      A   B   C D

21. What <u>would</u> you <u>do</u> if you <u>will</u> <u>won</u> the lottery?   **A B C D**
         A   B   C D

22. <u>It's</u> hot, so you <u>will feel</u> better<u>,</u> if you <u>drink</u> more water.   **A B C D**
     A   B   C   D

23. If I <u>had set</u> my alarm clock, I <u>woulda</u> <u>gotten</u> up on time.   **A B C D**
        A B   C   D

24. <u>If</u> I have to <u>fly</u>, I <u>would get</u> very nervous, so I usually <u>drive</u>.   **A B C D**
     A   B   C   D

25. Lynn <u>wishes</u> she <u>had</u> a bigger apartment and <u>can</u> <u>buy</u> a car.   **A B C D**
         A   B   C D

Adjective Clauses with Subject Relative Pronouns

Bill, come meet the woman **who has changed** my life.

CHECK **POINT**

Circle T (True) or F (False).

T F The man is talking about the woman holding a report.

ADJECTIVE CLAUSE AFTER THE MAIN CLAUSE

CHART CHECK

Check the correct answers.

Adjective clauses describe:

❒ nouns

❒ verbs

Adjective clauses can go:

❒ before the main clause

❒ in the middle of the main clause

❒ after the main clause

MAIN CLAUSE	ADJECTIVE CLAUSE		
	SUBJECT RELATIVE PRONOUN	VERB	
That's my friend	*who*	lives	in Rome.

ADJECTIVE CLAUSE INSIDE THE MAIN CLAUSE

MAIN CLAUSE	ADJECTIVE CLAUSE			MAIN CLAUSE (CONT.)
	SUBJECT RELATIVE PRONOUN	VERB		
My friend	*who*	lives	in Rome	is a dancer.

EXPRESS CHECK

Unscramble these words to form a sentence.

the man • works • who • in the cafeteria • That's

_____

Grammar Explanations

Examples

---

1. Use **adjective clauses** to identify or give additional information about <u>nouns</u> or <u>indefinite pronouns</u> such as *someone*, *somebody*, *something*, *another*, and *other(s)*.

■ I know the woman **who lives there**.
(The adjective clause identifies the woman we are talking about.)

■ Rome is a city **which attracts tourists**.
(The adjective clause gives additional information about the city.)

The adjective clause <u>directly follows the noun (or pronoun)</u> it is identifying or describing.

■ Someone **who has a lot of friends** is lucky.
Not ~~Someone is lucky who has a lot of friends.~~

---

2. **Sentences with adjective clauses** can be seen as a combination of two sentences.

I have a friend. + He loves to shop. =
■ I have a friend **who loves to shop**.

My friend lives in Rome. + She paints. =
■ My friend **who lives in Rome** paints.

---

3. Adjective clauses are introduced by **relative pronouns**.

Subject relative pronouns are:

a. *who* or *that* for <u>people</u>
USAGE NOTE: *That* is less formal than *who*.

■ I have a **friend** *who* lives in Mexico.
■ I have a **friend** *that* lives in Mexico.

b. *which* or *that* for <u>places or things</u>
USAGE NOTE: *That* is less formal than *which*.

■ New York is a **city** *which* never sleeps.
■ New York is a **city** *that* never sleeps.

c. *whose* + **noun** for <u>people's possessions</u>

■ He's the **man** *whose* **dog** barks all day.

▶ **BE CAREFUL!** Do not use both a subject relative pronoun and a subject pronoun (*I, you, he, she, it, we, they*) in the same adjective clause.

■ Scott is someone **who loves sports**.
Not Scott is someone ~~who he loves sports~~.

---

4. Subject relative pronouns have the **same form** whether they refer to singular or plural nouns or to masculine or feminine nouns.

■ That's the **man** *who* lives next door.
■ That's the **woman** *who* lives next door.
■ Those are the **people** *who* live next door.

---

5. The **verb in the adjective clause** is singular if the subject relative pronoun refers to a singular noun. It is plural if it refers to a plural noun.

■ Ben is my **friend** *who* **lives** in Boston.
■ Al and Ed are my **friends** *who* **live** in Boston.

▶ **BE CAREFUL!** When *whose* + **noun** is the subject of an adjective clause, the verb agrees in number with the subject of the adjective clause.

■ Meg is a person *whose* **friends depend** on her.
Not Meg is a person ~~whose friends depends~~ on her.

1 **IDENTIFY** • *Read this paragraph about friendship. First circle the relative pronouns and underline the adjective clauses. Then draw an arrow from the relative pronoun to the noun or pronoun it describes.*

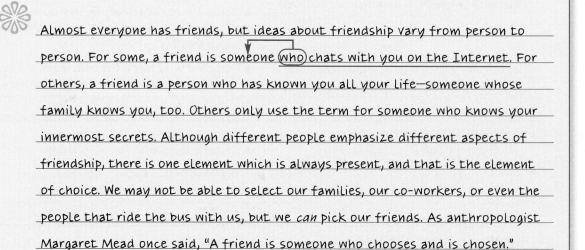

Almost everyone has friends, but ideas about friendship vary from person to person. For some, a friend is someone who chats with you on the Internet. For others, a friend is a person who has known you all your life—someone whose family knows you, too. Others only use the term for someone who knows your innermost secrets. Although different people emphasize different aspects of friendship, there is one element which is always present, and that is the element of choice. We may not be able to select our families, our co-workers, or even the people that ride the bus with us, but we *can* pick our friends. As anthropologist Margaret Mead once said, "A friend is someone who chooses and is chosen." It is this freedom of choice that makes friendship such a special relationship.

2 **COMPLETE** • *A U.S. magazine,* Psychology Today, *conducted a national survey on friendship. Here are some of the results. Complete each sentence with an appropriate relative pronoun and the correct form of the verb in parentheses.*

1. People _____who_____ _____have_____ moved a lot have fewer friends.
   (have)

2. People _____ _____ lived in the same place have more friends.
   (have)

3. The qualities _____ _____ most important in a friend are loyalty,
   (be)
   warmth, and the ability to keep secrets.

4. Someone _____ _____ a crisis turns to friends before family.
   (face)

5. Betrayal is the cause _____ _____ most often responsible for
   (be)
   ending a friendship.

6. Many people have friends _____ social or religious backgrounds _____
   (be)
   different from theirs.

7. Most people _____ friends _____ members of the opposite sex say
   (include)
   that these relationships are different from relationships with people of the same sex.

8. A survey _____ _____ in a magazine may not represent everyone.
   (appear)

9. Someone _____ _____ the magazine might have other ideas.
   (not read)

COMBINE • *Read each pair of sentences. Use a relative pronoun to combine them into one sentence.*

1. I have a friend. My friend lives in Mexico City.

I have a friend who lives in Mexico City.

2. Mexico City is an exciting city. The city attracts a lot of tourists.

_____

3. Marta has a brother. Her brother's name is Manuel.

_____

4. He works for a magazine. The magazine is very popular in Mexico.

_____

5. Manuel writes a column. The column deals with relationships.

_____

6. An article won a prize. The article discussed friendships.

_____

7. A person is lucky. That person has a lot of friends.

_____

 EDIT • *Read part of a student's essay. Find and correct six mistakes in the use of adjective clauses. The first mistake is already corrected.*

A writer once said that friends are born, not made. This means that we automatically become friends with people who ~~they~~ are compatible with us. I don't agree with this writer. Last summer, I made friends with some people who's completely different from me.

In July, I went to Mexico City to study Spanish for a month. In our group, there was a teacher which was much older than I am. We became really good friends. In my first week, I had a problem which was getting me down. Mexico City is a city who has a lot of distractions. As a result, I went out all the time, and I stopped going to my classes. Bob helped me get back into my studies. After the trip, I kept writing to Bob. He always writes stories that is interesting and encouraging. Next summer, he's leading another trip what sounds interesting. I hope I can go.

UNIT 70

Adjective Clauses with Object Relative Pronouns or *When* and *Where*

Minna,

Cracow is wonderful! Here's a picture of the main square with the café **where I spend all my time.** Can you find me with the new friend **that I made yesterday?** He's a writer, with gorgeous green eyes! I'm in love!

Vana

ADJECTIVE CLAUSE AFTER THE MAIN CLAUSE

CHART CHECK

Check the correct answer.

The verb in the adjective clause agrees with

☐ the noun in the main clause.

☐ the subject of the adjective clause.

Circle T (True) or F (False).

T F   The adjective clause always follows the main clause.

MAIN CLAUSE	ADJECTIVE CLAUSE		
	OBJECT RELATIVE PRONOUN	**SUBJECT**	**VERB**
He reads all the books	*that*	she	**writes**.

ADJECTIVE CLAUSE INSIDE THE MAIN CLAUSE

MAIN CLAUSE	ADJECTIVE CLAUSE			MAIN CLAUSE (CONT.)
	OBJECT RELATIVE PRONOUN	**SUBJECT**	**VERB**	
The book	*that*	they	**borrowed**	seems very interesting.

EXPRESS CHECK

Unscramble these words to form a sentence.

I • the • movies • all • he • directs • see • that

Grammar Explanations

Examples

1. A **relative pronoun** can be the **object** of an adjective clause. Notice that:

obj.
*Eva is a writer. + I saw **her** on TV. =*

a. The **object relative pronoun** comes <u>at the beginning</u> of the adjective clause.

obj.
■ Eva, ***who(m)* I saw on TV**, is a writer.

b. Object relative pronouns have the **same form** whether they refer to singular or plural nouns or to masculine or feminine nouns.

■ That's the **man *who(m)*** I met.
■ That's the **woman *who(m)*** I met.
■ Those are the **people *who(m)*** I met.

c. The **verb in the adjective clause** <u>agrees</u> <u>with the subject</u> of the adjective clause.

subj.   verb
■ I like the columns ***which* he writes**.
■ I like the column ***which* they write**.

▶ **BE CAREFUL!** Do not use both an object relative pronoun and an object pronoun (*me, you, him, her, it, us, them*) in the same adjective clause.

■ She is the writer **who I saw on TV**.
NOT She is the writer ~~who I saw her on TV.~~

NOTE: Object relative pronouns are often <u>left out</u>.

■ She is the writer **I saw on TV**.

2. Object relative pronouns are:

a. *whom, who,* or *that* for <u>people</u>
USAGE NOTE: *Whom* is very formal.
That is less formal than *who.*
<u>Leaving out the pronoun</u> is the least formal.

■ She's the writer ***whom* I met**.
■ She's the writer ***who* I met**.
■ She's the writer ***that* I met**.
■ She's the writer **I met**.

b. *which* or *that* for <u>things</u>
USAGE NOTE: *That* is less formal than *which.*

■ I read the book ***which* she wrote**.
■ I read the book ***that* she wrote**.
■ I read the book **she wrote**.

c. *whose* + **noun** for <u>people's possessions</u>

■ That's the author ***whose* book I read**.

3. A relative pronoun can be the **object of a preposition**.

USAGE NOTE: In **informal** speaking and writing, we put the <u>preposition at the end</u> of the clause, and we often leave out the relative pronoun.
In **formal** English, we put the <u>preposition at the</u> <u>beginning</u> of the clause. In this case, we use only **whom** and **which** (not *who* or *that*).

*He's the writer. + I work **for him**. =*
■ He's the writer ***that* I work *for***.
■ He's the writer **I work *for***.

■ He's the writer ***for whom* I work**.
■ That's the book ***about* *which* I told you**.

4. *Where* and *when* can also be used to introduce adjective clauses:

a. *Where* refers to a <u>place</u>.

*That's the library. + She works **there**. =*
■ That's the library ***where* she works**.

b. *When* or *that* refers to a <u>time</u>.

*I remember the day. + I met him **then**. =*
■ I remember the day ***when* I met him**.
■ I remember the day ***that* I met him**.

1   **IDENTIFY** • *Read this part of a book review. Underline all the adjective clauses with object relative pronouns. Circle the object relative pronouns, **when**, or **where**. Then draw a line from the circled word to the noun it refers to.*

Section 4   **BOOKS**

Lost in Translation: A Life in a New Language

At the age of nine, Eva Hoffman left Poland with her family. She was old enough to know what she was losing: Cracow, a city (that) she loved as one loves a person, the sun-baked villages where they had taken summer vacations, and the conversations and escapades with her friends. Disconnected from a city where life was lived intensely, her father would become overwhelmed by the transition to Canada. Eva would lose the parent whom she had watched in lively conversation with friends in Cracow cafés.

Eva Hoffman

And nothing could replace her friendship with the boy whose home she visited daily and whom she assumed she would someday marry. Worst of all, however, she would miss her language. For years, she would feel no connection to the English name of anything that she felt was important. *Lost in Translation: A Life in a New Language* (New York: Penguin, 1989) tells how Eva came to terms with her new identity and language. It's a story that readers will find fascinating and moving.

---

2   **COMPLETE** • *A school newspaper, the* Grover Bugle *(GB), interviewed a student, Maniya Suarez (MS). Complete the interview with relative pronouns, **when**, or **where**, and the correct form of the verbs in parentheses.*

 The Grover Bugle   VOLUME IX, ISSUE 20

GB: Maniya Suarez is a student _____ _who_ _____ many of you already
    1.
_____ _know_ _____ . Maniya, why did your family settle in Atlanta?
    2. (know)

MS: The cousin _____ we _____ with at first
    3.   **4.** (stay)
lives here. That's the reason we chose Atlanta.

Maniya Suarez

GB: What was the most difficult thing about going to school in the U.S.?

MS: The class in _____ I _____ the biggest problems at first
    5.   **6.** (have)
was English. It was hard to say the things _____ I _____ to.
        7.   **8.** (want)

GB: What is the biggest change _____ you _____ so far?
        9.   **10.** (experience)

MS: We used to live in a house _____ there _____ always
        11.   **12.** (be)
a lot of people. Here I live with my parents and two younger sisters _____
                                          13.
I _____ after school. I get a little lonely sometimes.
  14. (take care of)

COMBINE • *Read each pair of sentences. Use a relative pronoun, **when**, or **where** to combine them into one sentence.*

1. That's the house. I grew up in the house with my sister Emilia.

 That's the house that I grew up in with my sister Emilia.

2. The house was beautiful. We lived in the house.

_____

3. Emilia and I shared a room. We spent nights talking there.

_____

4. Across the hall, I had a good friend. I went to school with her.

_____

5. I took piano lessons from a woman. I met her in the bakery.

_____

6. I remember one summer. The whole family went to the lake then.

_____

7. Those were good times. I'll always miss them.

_____

 EDIT • *Read this student's essay. Find and correct nine mistakes in the use of adjective clauses with object relative pronouns. The first mistake is already corrected.*

>   where or in which
> Tai Dong is the small city in southeastern Taiwan ~~which~~ I grew up. My family
> moved there from Taipei the summer when I was born. The house in which I grew
> up in is on a main street in Tai Dong. My father sold tea, and my mother had a
> food stand in our front courtyard where she sold omelets early in the morning.
> A customer who I always chatted with him had a son my age. We were best friends.
> A cousin who his family I visited every summer lived with us. He was an
> apprentice which my father was teaching the tea business to. On the first floor of
> our house we had a huge kitchen in where we all gathered for dinner. It was a fun
> and noisy place. The bedrooms where the family slept was upstairs. My two brothers
> slept in one bedroom. I slept in one what I shared with my older sister. My younger
> sister shared a bedroom with another cousin which my family had adopted.

Adjective Clauses:
Identifying and Non-Identifying

Oops! This must be the picture file **he told me not to open!**

CHECK *POINT*

Circle T (True) or F (False).

T F There is only one picture file on the computer.

CHART CHECK

Check the correct answer.

Which type of adjective clause has commas around it?

☐ identifying

☐ non-identifying

Circle T (True) or F (False).

T F You can leave out a relative pronoun *only* when it is an <u>object</u> relative pronoun in an <u>identifying</u> adjective clause.

IDENTIFYING ADJECTIVE CLAUSES

	SUBJECT RELATIVE PRONOUN		
The computer	*which*	**is in the family room**	is broken.

	(OBJECT RELATIVE PRONOUN)		
The computer	*(which)*	**she bought last week**	is not working.

NON-IDENTIFYING ADJECTIVE CLAUSES

	SUBJECT RELATIVE PRONOUN		
The computer,	*which*	**is in the family room,**	is broken.

	OBJECT RELATIVE PRONOUN		
The computer,	*which*	**she bought last week,**	is not working.

EXPRESS CHECK

Cross out the relative pronouns when possible.

• I gave away my computer, which was only three years old.

• I bought a new one that had a lot more memory.

• It was the computer which we saw at E-Lectronics.

Grammar Explanations	**Examples**

1. Adjective clauses can be **identifying** or **non-identifying**.

a. Use an **identifying adjective clause** to identify which member of a group the sentence talks about.

- I have three phones. The phone **which is in the kitchen** is broken.
  (The adjective clause is necessary to identify which phone is meant.)

b. Use a **non-identifying adjective clause** to give additional information about the noun it refers to. The information is not necessary to identify the noun.

- I have only one phone. The phone, **which is in the kitchen,** is broken.
  (The adjective clause gives additional information, but it isn't needed to identify the phone.)

▶ **BE CAREFUL!** Do not use *that* to introduce a non-identifying adjective clause. Use *who* for people and *which* for places and things.

- Marie, **who** introduced us at the party, called me last night.
  NOT Marie, ~~that introduced us at the party,~~ . . .

2. In writing, a **non-identifying adjective clause** is separated from the rest of the sentence by **commas**.

- The switch, **which is on the back,** is off.
  (The machine has only one switch. It's on the back.)

In speaking, a non-identifying adjective clause is separated from the rest of the sentence by brief **pauses**.

- The switch *(pause)* **which is on the back** *(pause)* is off.
  (The machine has only one switch. It's on the back.)

Without commas or pauses, the clause is an **identifying adjective clause**, and the sentence has a very different meaning.

- The switch **which is on the back** is off.
  (The machine has more than one switch. This one is off.)

3. You **can leave out**:

a. **object relative pronouns** in identifying adjective clauses

- That's the computer *that* **I bought**.
- That's the computer **I bought**.

b. *when*

- I remember the day *when* **I met him**.
- I remember the day **I met him**.

USAGE NOTE: The most common spoken form is the one with no relative pronoun.

4. You **cannot leave out**:

a. **relative pronouns** in a non-identifying adjective clause

- She remembers Marc, *who* **she visited often**.
  NOT She remembers Marc, ~~she visited often~~.

b. *whose*

- That's the author *whose* **book I read**.
  NOT That's the author ~~book I read~~.

c. *where*

- That's the library *where* **I work**.
  NOT That's the library ~~I work~~.

TRUE OR FALSE • *Read each numbered sentence. Write T (True) or F (False) for the statement that follows.*

1. Use the computer which is in the living room.

   __F__ There is only one computer.

2. Press the red button, which is on the right.

   _____ There is probably only one red button.

3. My sister who fixes computers lives in Texas.

   _____ I have more than one sister.

4. My stereo, which worked yesterday, doesn't work today.

   _____ It's likely that I have another stereo I can use.

5. A cell phone which remembers numbers is very convenient.

   _____ All cell phones can remember numbers.

6. My roommate, who is afraid of computers, has never been on the Internet.

   _____ I probably have more than one roommate.

 ADD & CROSS OUT • *Read this article about technophobia. Add commas where necessary. Cross out the relative pronouns that can be left out.*

ˌtech · no ·ˈpho · bia *(noun)* a fear ~~that~~ some people have about using technology

If you have it, you're one of the 85 percent of people that this new "disease" has struck. Maybe you bought a phone on which you can program 25 numbers—then couldn't turn it on. Or perhaps you have just read that your new CD player, which you have finally learned how to use, will soon be replaced by DVD which you have never even heard of.

Some experts say that things have just gotten too complex. William Staples who authored a book on the electronic age tried to help a friend who had just bought a new stereo. The stereo which worked before wasn't working anymore. "On the front of the stereo receiver it literally had a couple of dozen buttons," says Staples. Donald Norman who has written about the effects of technology on people blames the designers of these devices, not the people who use them. "The best way to cure technophobia is to cure the reasons that cause it—that is, to design things that people can use and design things that won't break," claims Norman. Michael Dyrenfurth who teaches at the University of Missouri–Columbia believes we cause our own problems by buying technology that we just don't need. "Do we really need an electric toothbrush?" he asks. According to Dyrenfurth, important technology that we can't afford to run away from actually exists. To prosper, we have to overcome our technophobia and learn to use it.

3

COMBINE • Read these pairs of sentences. Combine them by changing the second sentence into an adjective clause. Use a relative pronoun only when necessary. Use commas for non-identifying adjective clauses.

1. I bought a cell phone. I can use it to send and receive e-mail.

   I bought a cell phone I can use to send and receive e-mail.

2. My new cell phone has become a necessary part of life. I only bought it a month ago.

   _____

3. I remember the day. I was afraid to use my new computer then.

   _____

4. Now, there are psychologists. They help technophobes use technology.

   _____

5. Dr. Michelle Weil wrote a book about "technostress." She is a psychologist.

   _____

6. I work in an office. In my office, the software changes frequently.

   _____

7. A lot of people suffer from technostress. Those people work in my office.

   _____

8. Some people dream of a job. They can do the job without technology.

   _____

 4

EDIT • Read this student's book report. Find and correct six mistakes in the use of identifying and non-identifying adjective clauses. The first mistake is already corrected.

I just read a book called *Technostress*, which was written by Dr. Michelle Weil.
Her co-author was Dr. Larry Rosen, that is her husband and also a psychologist.
According to the authors, everybody feels stress about technology. Our cell phones
and beepers, that we buy for emergencies, soon invade our privacy. Just because
they can, people contact us at places, where we are relaxing. Another problem is
having to learn too much too fast. Technological changes, used to come one at a
time, now overwhelm us. Dr. Weil suggests dealing with technostress using tips from
her latest book which can be purchased from her web site.

SelfTest

Circle the letter of the correct answer to complete each sentence. Choose Ø when no word is needed.

> **EXAMPLE:**
> Jennifer never _____ coffee.   **A Ⓑ C D**
> (A) drink   (C) is drinking
> (B) drinks   (D) was drinking

1. That's my friend _____ lives in Rio.   **A B C D**
   (A) which   (C) whom
   (B) who   (D) where

2. The plants which _____ in the living room need a lot of water. **A B C D**
   (A) are   (C) is
   (B) be   (D) am

3. She's the woman _____ sister babysits for us.   **A B C D**
   (A) who   (C) that's
   (B) which   (D) whose

4. That's the doctor for _____ Cliff works.   **A B C D**
   (A) that   (C) whom
   (B) which   (D) whose

5. Marie, _____ I met at the party, called me last night.   **A B C D**
   (A) that   (C) which
   (B) who   (D) whose

6. I remember Al, _____ rode the bus to school with.   **A B C D**
   (A) I   (C) which I
   (B) who I   (D) who

7. I used to enjoy the summer, _____ we had a big family picnic. **A B C D**
   (A) where   (C) which
   (B) when   (D) that

8. Take in the roll of film _____ Uncle Pete took at the reunion. **A B C D**
   (A) what   (C) Ø
   (B) with which   (D) whom

9. Please pay all the bills _____ are due this week.   **A B C D**
   (A) Ø   (C) when
   (B) that   (D) they

10. Let's try to agree on a time _____ we can all get together.   **A B C D**
    (A) which   (C) Ø
    (B) where   (D) at

11. Tell me about the city _____ you grew up.   **A B C D**
   (A) that   (C) which
   (B) where   (D) Ø

12. Annie found the souvenirs that _____ wanted at the gift shop.   **A B C D**
   (A) Ø   (C) she
   (B) where   (D) which

SECTION TWO

Each sentence has four underlined words or phrases. The four underlined parts of the sentence are marked A, B, C, and D. Circle the letter of the one underlined word or phrase that is NOT CORRECT.

> **EXAMPLE:**
>   Mike <u>usually</u> <u>drives</u> to school, but <u>today</u> he <u>walks</u>.   **A B C (D)**
>   **A**   **B**   **C**   **D**

13. After a week, <u>we</u> finally got to <u>Miami</u>, <u>that</u> my aunt <u>lives</u>.   **A B C D**
             A   **B**   **C**   **D**

14. My favorite uncle, <u>which</u> <u>lives</u> in Texas<u>,</u> <u>arrived</u> last night.   **A B C D**
                       A   **B**   **C**   **D**

15. Paulo is <u>someone</u> <u>who</u> <u>he</u> really <u>loves</u> soccer.   **A B C D**
            A   **B** **C**   **D**

16. One <u>singer</u> <u>who's</u> voice <u>I</u> like a lot <u>is</u> Madonna.   **A B C D**
       A   **B**   **C**   **D**

17. The <u>stories</u> <u>what</u> <u>I've told</u> you <u>are</u> all true.   **A B C D**
       A   **B**   **C**   **D**

18. I <u>enjoyed</u> reading the article <u>that</u> you <u>told</u> me about <u>it</u>.   **A B C D**
     A   **B**   **C**   **D**

19. She's read some <u>books</u> <u>that</u> <u>discusses</u> the time <u>when</u> this area   **A B C D**
                   A   **B**   **C**   **D**
   was undeveloped.

20. <u>San Francisco</u>, <u>that</u> <u>is</u> a beautiful city, <u>has</u> a population of six million.   **A B C D**
   A   **B** **C**   **D**

21. Do you know <u>whom</u> <u>wrote</u> the song <u>that</u> Al <u>was</u> singing last night?   **A B C D**
               A   **B**   **C**   **D**

22. My aunt's new <u>house</u> <u>is</u> next to a beautiful canal <u>in where</u> we <u>go</u>   **A B C D**
                 A   **B**   **C**   **D**
   swimming every day.

23. Van<u>,</u> <u>who with</u> I <u>went</u> to school, <u>has become</u> a famous writer.   **A B C D**
      A **B**   **C**   **D**

24. Do you remember <u>the</u> <u>night</u> <u>which</u> we ate at the restaurant <u>that</u>   **A B C D**
                   A **B**   **C**   **D**
   Bill owned?

25. Our neighbors, <u>who their</u> daughter <u>babysits</u> for us<u>,</u> <u>have</u> moved.   **A B C D**
                  A   **B**   **C** **D**

Direct and Indirect Speech: Imperatives

Dara! What are you doing?!

*I've been having trouble sleeping. The doctor told me **not to eat a heavy meal before bed**, so I'm having it now.*

CHECK *POINT*

Check the doctor's exact words.

❏ "Eat a heavy meal before bed."

❏ "Don't eat a heavy meal before bed."

❏ "Not to eat a heavy meal before bed."

CHART CHECK

Check the correct answer.

Which type of speech uses quotation marks?

❏ direct speech

❏ indirect speech

Circle T (True) or F (False).

T   F   Indirect imperatives always use the infinitive form of the verb (**to** + base form).

DIRECT SPEECH

SUBJECT	REPORTING VERB	DIRECT SPEECH
He	said,	"**Drink** milk." "**Don't drink** coffee."

INDIRECT SPEECH

SUBJECT	REPORTING VERB	NOUN/ PRONOUN	INDIRECT SPEECH
He	told	her	**to drink** milk. **not to drink** coffee.
	said		

EXPRESS **CHECK**

Circle the correct words to complete these sentences.

• The doctor told me <u>go / to go</u> to bed at the same time every night.

• She told me, "<u>Don't work / Not to work</u> in bed."

Grammar Explanations	**Examples**
1. **Direct speech** states <u>the exact words</u> a speaker used. In writing, use <u>quotation marks</u>. **Indirect speech** reports what a speaker said <u>without using the exact words</u>. There are <u>no quotation marks</u>.	■ **"Come early and bring your insurance card,"** said the doctor. ■ The doctor told her **to come early and bring her insurance card**.

2. The **reporting verb** (such as *say* or *tell*) is usually in the <u>simple past tense</u> for both direct and indirect speech. ▶ **BE CAREFUL!** Use *say* when the <u>listener is not mentioned</u>. Do not use *tell*.	DIRECT SPEECH ■ "Drink warm milk," he **said**. INDIRECT SPEECH ■ He **told** her to drink warm milk. ■ He **said** to call him in the morning. NOT He ~~told to call him~~ in the morning.

3. Direct speech imperatives use the base form of the verb. **Indirect speech imperatives** use the **infinitive** to report:

	DIRECT SPEECH	INDIRECT SPEECH
a. instructions	"**Come** early," he said.	He said **to come** early.
b. commands	"**Wait**."	He told me **to wait**.
c. requests	"Could you please **arrive** by 8:00?"	She asked him **to arrive** by 8:00.
d. invitations	"Could you **join** us for lunch?"	She invited me **to join** them for lunch.

4. Use a **negative infinitive** (*not* + infinitive) to report negative imperatives.

DIRECT SPEECH	INDIRECT SPEECH
"**Don't go**."	He told her **not to go**.

5. In **indirect speech**, make <u>changes to keep the speaker's original meaning</u>.

a. Change **pronouns** and **possessives**.	■ He said to Ann, "Tell **me your** problem." ■ He told Ann to tell **him her** problem.
b. Change **time phrases**.	■ "Call me **tomorrow**." ■ She said to call her **the next day**.
c. Change *this* and *here*.	■ "Sign **this** form **here**." ■ She told him to sign **that** form **there**.

Check it out!

For punctuation rules for direct speech, see Appendix 25 on page 347.

For a list of common reporting verbs, see Appendix 13 on page 340.

For a list of common time word changes in indirect speech, see Appendix 14 on page 340.

1 **IDENTIFY** • *Read this article about sleep disorders. Circle all the reporting verbs.*
Underline once all the direct imperatives. Underline twice all the indirect imperatives.

Tossing and Turning
BY CONNIE SUNG

Can't sleep? You're not alone. Millions of people are up tossing and turning instead of getting their zzzz's. Dr. Ray Thorpe, Director of the Sleep Disorders Clinic, (says), "Don't think that loss of sleep is just a minor inconvenience." During an interview he (told) me to think about what can happen if people drive when they're tired. Every year up to 200,000 car accidents are caused by drowsy drivers. Then he asked me to think about a recent industrial disaster. Chances are that it was caused at least in part by sleep deprivation.

Being an insomniac myself, I asked Dr. Thorpe for some suggestions. He told me to stop drinking coffee. He said to have a warm glass of milk instead. "A lot of old-fashioned remedies work. Have a high-carbohydrate snack like a banana before you go to bed," he said. But he advises patients not to eat a heavy meal before turning in for the night. What about exercise? "Regular exercise helps, but don't exercise too close to bedtime," he suggested. Finally, he told me not to despair. "Don't worry about not sleeping. It's the worst thing to do," he said. I don't know. After thinking about those industrial accidents, I doubt I'll be able to sleep at all!

2 **CHOOSE** • *Connie Sung visited Dr. Thorpe's sleep clinic. Complete her notes with the correct words in parentheses.*

Last week I visited the sleep clinic. Dr. Thorpe called and asked me ___to arrive___
1. (arrive / to arrive)

at 8:30 _____. He _____ me to bring _____
2. (tonight / that night)   **3.** (said / told)   **4.** (my / your)

nightshirt and toothbrush. I arrived on schedule. The technician, Juan Estrada,

invited me _____ TV in the lounge. He _____ to relax
5. (watch / to watch)   **6.** (said / told)

_____ while they got my room ready. An hour later, Juan came back and
7. (here / there)

got me ready to sleep. He attached electrodes to my body and hooked me up to a

machine. "Could you please _____?" I asked. The machine records brain
8. (explain / to explain)

activity. Juan instructed me _____ leave the bed until _____
9. (don't / not to)   **10.** (tomorrow / the next)

morning. To my surprise, I fell asleep right away. In the morning, Dr. Thorpe told me

that except for some leg movements during the night, I have healthy sleep patterns. He

advised me _____ some more exercise.
11. (get / to get)

REWRITE • *Read the advice that TV news commentator John Stossel gave viewers about the common and very dangerous problem of feeling sleepy when driving. Rewrite his advice in indirect speech.*

1. "Pull over and take a brief nap."   *He told them to pull over and take a brief nap.*

2. "Don't take a long nap."   *He said not to take a long nap.*

3. "Sing to yourselves." _____

4. "Turn your radio to an annoying station." _____

5. "Don't drink coffee." _____

6. "Open your window." _____

7. "Let cold air in." _____

8. "Be careful when you stop your car." _____

9. "Don't stop on a deserted roadside." _____

10. "Don't drink and drive." _____

 EDIT • *Read this student's journal entry. Find and correct fourteen mistakes in the use of indirect imperatives. The first mistake is already corrected. Remember to check punctuation!*

> In writing class today, Juan read one of his stories. It was wonderful. After class,
>
> the teacher invited me ^to^ read a story in class next week. However, I asked her no to call on
>
> me next week because I'm having trouble getting ideas. She said me not to worry, and
>
> she said to wait for two weeks. Then I talked to Juan, and I asked him tell me the source
>
> for your ideas. He said that they came from his dreams, and he told me keep a dream
>
> journal for ideas. He invited me "to read some of his journal." It was very interesting, so
>
> I asked him to give me some tips on remembering dreams. He said getting a good
>
> night's sleep because the longer dreams come after a long period of sleep. He also tell
>
> me to keep my journal by the bed and to write as soon as I wake up. He said to no move
>
> from the sleeping position. He also told me to don't think about the day at first. (If you
>
> think about your day, you might forget your dreams.) Most important—every night he
>
> tells himself that to remember his dreams tomorrow morning.

UNIT 73

Indirect Speech:
Statements (1)

CHECK POINT

Check the man's exact words.

❏ "It looks great on you!"   ❏ "It looked great on me!"

CHART CHECK

Check the correct answers.

What can change when you go from a direct to an indirect statement?

❏ the punctuation

❏ the word order in the statement

❏ the verb tense in the statement

❏ pronouns in the statement

DIRECT SPEECH		
SUBJECT	**REPORTING VERB**	**DIRECT STATEMENT**
She	said,	"I **like** the dress." "I **bought** it on sale." "I**'ve worn** it twice."

INDIRECT SPEECH				
SUBJECT	**REPORTING VERB**	**NOUN/ PRONOUN**	**INDIRECT STATEMENT**	
She	told	Jim me	**(that)**	she **liked** the dress. she **had bought** it on sale.
	said			she **had worn** it twice.

EXPRESS CHECK

Circle the correct words to complete this sentence.

She <u>said / told</u> the salesperson that she <u>is / was</u> going to buy the dress.

Grammar Explanations

Examples

1. An **indirect speech statement** reports what a speaker said <u>without using the exact words</u>. The word **that** can introduce the indirect statement.

DIRECT SPEECH
- **"It's a great dress,"** he said.

INDIRECT SPEECH
- He told her **that it was a great dress**.
- He told her **it was a great dress**.

▶ **BE CAREFUL!** Use **say** as the reporting verb when the <u>listener is not mentioned</u>. Do not use **tell**.

- He **said** that it was a great dress.
  NOT He ~~told that~~ it was a great dress.

---

2. When the **reporting verb** is in the **simple past tense**, the <u>verb in the indirect speech statement is often in a different tense</u> from the verb in the direct speech statement.

DIRECT SPEECH		INDIRECT SPEECH
Simple present	→	**Simple past**
Present progressive	→	**Past progressive**
Simple past	→	**Past perfect**
Present perfect	→	**Past perfect**

DIRECT SPEECH	INDIRECT SPEECH
He said, "It's great."	He said it **was** great.
"I'm leaving."	She said she **was leaving**.
"I made it."	He said that he **had made** it.
He said to her, "I've never lied."	He told her that he **had** never **lied**.

---

3. In indirect speech the **verb tense change** is **optional** when reporting:

a. something someone has **just said**

A: What did you just say?
B: I said I**'m** tired. OR I said I **was** tired.

b. something that is **still true**

- Rick said the bank **wants** a check.
- Rick said the bank **wanted** a check.

c. a **general truth** or **scientific law**

- She said that everyone **lies** sometime.
- She said that everyone **lied** sometime.

---

4. When the **reporting verb** is in the **present tense**, <u>do not change the verb tense</u> in indirect speech.

- **"I run** a mile every day."
- She **says** that she **runs** a mile every day.

---

5. **REMEMBER!** <u>Change</u> pronouns, time expressions, **this**, and **here** in indirect speech to <u>keep the speaker's original meaning</u>.

- Ann told Rick, "**I** bought **this** dress **here**."
- Ann told Rick that **she** had bought **that** dress **there**.

Check it out!

For a list of common reporting verbs, see Appendix 13 on page 340.

For a list of common time word changes in indirect speech, see Appendix 14 on page 340.

IDENTIFY • *Read this article about lying. Circle all the reporting verbs. Underline once all the direct statements. Underline twice all the indirect statements.*

THE TRUTH ABOUT LYING

BY JENNIFER MORALES

At 9:00 Rick Spivak's bank phoned and said that his credit card payment was late. "The check is in the mail," Rick replied quickly. At 11:45 Rick left for a 12:00 meeting across town. Arriving late, Rick told his client that traffic had been bad. That evening, Rick's fiancée wore a new dress. Rick hated it. "It looks just great on you," he said.

Three lies in one day! Yet Rick is just an ordinary guy. Each time, he told himself that sometimes the truth causes too many problems. He told himself that his fiancée was feeling good about her purchase. Why should he hurt her feelings?

Is telling lies a new trend? The majority of people in a recent survey said that people were more honest ten years ago. Nevertheless, lying wasn't really born yesterday. In the eighteenth century, the French philosopher Vauvenargues told the truth about lying when he wrote, "All men are born truthful and die liars."

COMPLETE • *Read this magazine article. Complete it with the correct words in parentheses.*

"Lying during a job interview is risky business," _____**said**_____ Marta Toledo,
                                                    1. (said / told)

director of a management consulting firm. "The truth always _____ a funny
                                                              2. (has / had)

way of coming out." Toledo tells the story of one woman applying for a job as an office

manager. The woman _____ the interviewer _____ she
                     3. (said / told)   **4.** (that / what)

_____ a B.A. degree. Actually, she was eight credits short. She also said
5. (has / had)

_____ _____ $30,000 at her last job. The truth was $5,000
     6. (I / she)   **7.** (made / had made)

less. When the interviewer called to check the information, the applicant's former boss

told her that the applicant _____. Another applicant, Gloria, reported that
                            8. (has lied / had lied)

she _____ her current job to advance her career. She got the new job.
     9. (is quitting / was quitting)

All went well until the company hired Pete, who had worked at Gloria's old company.

Pete eventually told his boss that his old company _____ Gloria.
                                                    10. (fired / had fired)

The new company fired her too, proving, once again, that it doesn't pay to lie.

REPORT • *Lisa and Ben are talking about Ben's job search. Use the verbs in parentheses to report their conversation. Make necessary changes in verbs and pronouns.*

1. **BEN:** I'm still looking for a job.

   (tell) _He told her he was still looking for a job._

2. **LISA:** I just heard about a job at a scientific research company.

   (say) _____

3. **BEN:** I majored in science at Florida State.

   (say) _____

4. **LISA:** They want someone with some experience as a programmer.

   (tell) _____

5. **BEN:** I work as a programmer for Data Systems.

   (tell) _____

6. **LISA:** They don't want a recent college graduate.

   (say) _____

7. **BEN:** I got my degree four years ago.

   (tell) _____

8. **LISA:** It sounds like the right job for you.

   (say) _____

 EDIT • *Read this student's essay. Find and correct ten mistakes in the use of indirect statements. The first mistake is already corrected.*

Once when I was a teenager, I went to my Aunt Leah's house. Aunt Leah collected
                                                    told
pottery, and when I got there, she ~~said~~ me that she wants to show me her new bowl.

She told she has just bought it. It was beautiful. When Aunt Leah went to answer the

door, I picked up the bowl. It slipped from my hands and smashed to pieces on the floor.

When Aunt Leah came back, I screamed and said what the cat had just broken your

new bowl. Aunt Leah got this funny look on her face and told me that it isn't important.

I didn't sleep at all that night, and the next morning, I called my aunt and confessed

that I have broken her bowl. She said I had known that all along. I promised that

I am going to buy her a new one someday. We still laugh about the story today.

Indirect Speech:
Statements (2)

CHECK POINT

Check the weather forecaster's exact words.

❏ "It would be windy."

❏ "It will be windy."

CHART CHECK

Check the modals that <u>do not change</u> when you go from direct to indirect speech.

❏ will

❏ ought to

❏ might

❏ must

❏ may

❏ should have

DIRECT SPEECH		
SUBJECT	**REPORTING VERB**	**DIRECT STATEMENT**
He	said,	"I'**ll leave** now." "I'**m going to drive**." "Traffic **may be** bad." "She **might move**." "He **can help**." "They **have to stay**." "You **must be** careful." "They **ought to buy** batteries." "We **should have left** sooner."

INDIRECT SPEECH				
SUBJECT	**REPORTING VERB**	**NOUN/ PRONOUN**	**INDIRECT STATEMENT**	
He	told	Jim me them	*(that)*	he **would leave** then. he **was going to drive**. traffic **might be** bad. she **might move**. he **could help**. they **had to stay**. I/we **had to be** careful. they **ought to buy** batteries.
	said			they **should have left** sooner.

EXPRESS CHECK

Read Jim's words. Check the sentence that correctly reports what he said.

JIM: "I may move soon."

☐ Jim said that I may move soon.　　☐ Jim said that he might move soon.

Grammar Explanations

Examples

---

1. As you learned in Unit 73, when the **reporting verb** is in the **simple past tense**, in the indirect speech statement the <u>verb tense often changes</u>.

Modals often change in indirect speech too.

DIRECT SPEECH		INDIRECT SPEECH
will	→	*would*
can	→	*could*
may	→	*might*
must	→	*had to*

DIRECT SPEECH	INDIRECT SPEECH
She said, "It**'s** windy."	She said it **was** windy.

DIRECT SPEECH	INDIRECT SPEECH
I said, "The winds **will be** strong."	I said the winds **would be** strong.
They told us, "You **can stay** with us."	They told us we **could stay** with them.
He said, "The storm **may last** all night."	He said that the storm **might last** all night.
She told us, "You **must leave**."	She told us we **had to leave**.

---

2. Some verbs do not change in indirect speech.

a. Do not change *should, could, might,* and *ought to* in indirect speech.

b. Do not change the **past perfect** in indirect speech.

c. Do not change verbs in **present and past unreal conditional** sentences in indirect speech.

d. Do not change **past modals** in indirect speech.

DIRECT SPEECH	INDIRECT SPEECH
"You **should listen** to the weather report," he told us.	He told us that we **should listen** to the weather report.
"I **had** just **moved** here a week before," she said.	She said she **had** just **moved** there a week before.
"If I **knew**, I **would tell** you."	Jim said if he **knew**, he **would tell** me.
"If I **had known**, I **would have told** you," said Jim.	He said if he **had known**, he **would have told** me.
"I **should have left**."	He said that he **should have left**.

---

3. REMEMBER! <u>Change</u> pronouns, time phrases, *here,* and *this* in indirect speech to <u>keep the speaker's original meaning</u>.

■ "I just got **here yesterday**."
■ Sam told me *he* had just gotten *there* **the day before**.

CHOOSE • *Read what someone reported about the weather forecast. Then check the sentence that shows the weather forecaster's exact words.*

1. She said it was going to be a terrible storm.
   - ☐ "It was a terrible storm."
   - ☑ "It's going to be a terrible storm."

2. She said the winds might reach 170 miles per hour.
   - ☐ "The winds may reach 170 miles per hour."
   - ☐ "The winds would reach 170 miles per hour."

3. She said there would be more rain the next day.
   - ☐ "There will be more rain the next day."
   - ☐ "There will be more rain tomorrow."

4. She told people that they should try to leave the area.
   - ☐ "You should have tried to leave the area."
   - ☐ "You should try to leave the area."

5. She said that they could expect a lot of damage.
   - ☐ "We can expect a lot of damage."
   - ☐ "We could expect a lot of damage."

"The Weather Watch" on Channel 5

REPORT • *You are in New York. Imagine you heard these rumors about a hurricane in Florida yesterday, and you are reporting them today. Use **They said** to report the rumors.*

1. "The hurricane will change direction tonight."

   They said that the hurricane would change direction last night.

2. "It's going to pass north of here."

   _____

3. "It may become a tropical storm when it lands here."

   _____

4. "They had to close some bridges yesterday because of high tides."

   _____

5. "They won't restore electricity until tomorrow."

   _____

6. "The schools here may be closed for a while."

   _____

7. "We ought to use bottled water for a few days."

   _____

REWRITE • *Read this interview with a meteorologist. Rewrite his answers as indirect speech. Change verb tenses when possible.*

1. **Q: A hurricane is just a bad storm, right?**

   A: To be a hurricane, a storm has to have winds of at least 74 miles per hour.

   He said that to be a hurricane, a storm had to have winds of at least 74 miles per hour.

2. **Q: We seem to be having more of these big storms.**

   A: It's true, and they will probably become more frequent.

   _____

3. **Q: Why is that?**

   A: The planet may be getting warmer, and that can cause more severe storms.

   _____

4. **Q: What went wrong after the last storm?**

   A: Emergency workers should have arrived much more quickly.

   _____

5. **Q: Is there an upside to all this?**

   A: The new satellites will help. If we didn't have them, we wouldn't be able to warn people.

   _____

EDIT • *Read Rita's e-mail to her friend Emily. Find and correct twelve mistakes in the use of indirect speech. The first mistake is already corrected.*

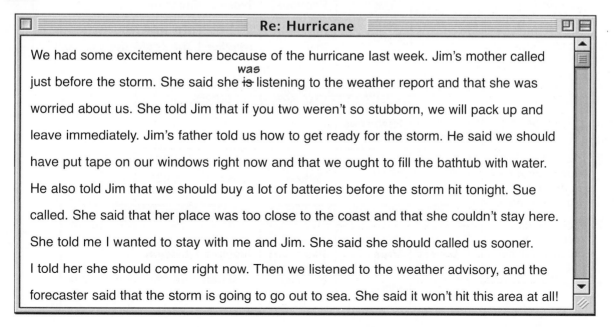

Re: Hurricane

We had some excitement here because of the hurricane last week. Jim's mother called
                                                  was
just before the storm. She said she ~~is~~ listening to the weather report and that she was
worried about us. She told Jim that if you two weren't so stubborn, we will pack up and
leave immediately. Jim's father told us how to get ready for the storm. He said we should
have put tape on our windows right now and that we ought to fill the bathtub with water.
He also told Jim that we should buy a lot of batteries before the storm hit tonight. Sue
called. She said that her place was too close to the coast and that she couldn't stay here.
She told me I wanted to stay with me and Jim. She said she should called us sooner.
I told her she should come right now. Then we listened to the weather advisory, and the
forecaster said that the storm is going to go out to sea. She said it won't hit this area at all!

Indirect Questions

Perhaps you didn't hear the question. Ms. Bentley asked **why you were still single**.

The Stress Interview

CHECK *POINT*

Check Ms. Bentley's exact words.

☐ "Why were you still single?"

☐ "Why are you still single?"

CHART CHECK 1

Circle T (True) or F (False).

T F You can leave out *if* or *whether* in indirect *yes/no* questions.

T F You do not use *do* to form indirect *yes/no* questions.

DIRECT SPEECH: *YES/NO* QUESTIONS

SUBJECT	REPORTING VERB	DIRECT QUESTION
He	asked,	"**Do you have** any experience?" "**Can you use** a computer?"

INDIRECT SPEECH: *YES/NO* QUESTIONS

SUBJECT	REPORTING VERB	(NOUN/ PRONOUN)	INDIRECT QUESTION	
He	asked	(Melissa) (her)	*if* *whether*	**she had** any experience. **she could use** a computer.

CHART CHECK 2

Circle T (True) or F (False).

T F An indirect question always ends in a question mark.

T F You do not use *do* to form indirect *wh-* questions.

DIRECT SPEECH: *WH-* QUESTIONS

SUBJECT	REPORTING VERB	DIRECT QUESTION
He	asked,	"**Who told you** about the job?" "**When do you want** to start?"

INDIRECT SPEECH: *WH-* QUESTIONS

SUBJECT	REPORTING VERB	(NOUN/ PRONOUN)	INDIRECT QUESTION
He	asked	(Melissa) (her)	*who* **had told her** about the job. *when* **she wanted** to start.

EXPRESS CHECK

Unscramble these words to complete the indirect question.

why • he • job • his • quit • had

He asked him _____

Grammar Explanations	Examples

1. Use *if*, *whether*, or *whether or not* to form **indirect *yes/no* questions**.

USAGE NOTE: *Whether* is more formal than *if*.

> DIRECT SPEECH
> ■ **"Can you type?"** she asked.
> INDIRECT SPEECH
> ■ She asked *if I could type*.
> ■ She asked *whether (or not) I could type*.

2. In **indirect *yes/no* questions**, the subject comes before the verb, the same as in statement word order.

Because of the statement word order, do not use *do, does*, or *did* to form indirect questions.

> DIRECT SPEECH
> ■ **"Can I start** tomorrow?"
> INDIRECT SPEECH
> ■ He asked *if he could start* tomorrow.
>   NOT He asked ~~could he start~~ tomorrow.
>
> DIRECT SPEECH
> ■ **"Does the job provide** benefits?"
> INDIRECT SPEECH
> ■ He asked *if the job provided* benefits.
>   NOT He asked ~~does the job provide~~ benefits.

3. Use **question words** to form **indirect *wh-* questions**.

> DIRECT SPEECH
> ■ **"Where is your office?"** I asked.
> INDIRECT SPEECH
> ■ I asked *where his office was*.

4. In **indirect *wh-* questions**, the subject also comes before the verb as in statements, and you do not use *do, does*, or *did*.

In **indirect *wh-* questions about the subject**, the question word is the subject and the verb follows as in statement word order.

> DIRECT SPEECH
> "**Why did you leave** your job?"
> INDIRECT SPEECH
> ■ She asked me *why I had left* my job.
>   NOT She asked me ~~why did I leave my job~~.
>
> DIRECT SPEECH
> ■ Bob asked, "**Who got** the job?"
> INDIRECT SPEECH
> ■ Bob asked *who had gotten* the job.

5. Indirect questions often end in a **period**, not a question mark.

> ■ I asked *why I didn't get the job*.
>   NOT I asked ~~why didn't I get the job?~~

Check it out! For a list of common verbs used to report questions, see Appendix 13 on page 340.

1

IDENTIFY • *Read this article about stress interviews. Underline all the indirect questions.*

The Stress Interview

A few weeks ago, Melissa Morrow had a stress interview, one which featured tough, tricky questions and negative evaluations. First, the interviewer asked <u>why she couldn't work under pressure</u>. Before she could answer, he asked who had written her application letter for her. Melissa was shocked, but she handled herself very well. She asked the interviewer whether he was going to ask her any serious questions. Then she left.

Companies give stress interviews in order to watch how candidates handle pressure. Suppose, for example, that there is an accident in a nuclear power plant. The plant's public relations officer must remain calm when reporters ask how the accident could have happened. Be aware, however, that in some countries, like the United States, certain questions are not allowed unless they are directly related to the job. If your interviewer asks how old you are, you can refuse to answer. The interviewer also should not ask whether you are married or how much money you owe. If you think a question is improper, ask how the question relates to the job. If it doesn't, you don't have to answer.

MATCH • *Check the direct questions that match the indirect questions in the article.*

☐ **1.** Can you work under pressure?

☑ **2.** Who wrote your application letter for you?

☐ **3.** Are you going to ask me any serious questions?

☐ **4.** Was there an accident in a nuclear power plant?

☐ **5.** How old are you?

☐ **6.** When were you married?

☐ **7.** Is the question improper?

2

REPORT • *Claire's friend Jaime wants to know all about her interview. Report his questions.*

1. "What kind of job is it?" _He asked what kind of job it was._____

2. "When is the interview?" _____

3. "Where's the company?" _____

4. "Do you need directions?" _____

5. "How long does it take to get there?" _____

6. "Are you going to drive?" _____

7. "Who's going to interview you?" _____

8. "When will they let you know?" _____

3 **REWRITE** • *These questions were asked at Claire's interview. Decide which ones Claire asked and which ones Pete, the manager, asked. Rewrite each question as indirect speech.*

1. "What type of training is available for the job?"

   Claire asked what type of training was available for the job.

2. "What kind of experience do you have?"

   Pete asked what kind of experience she had.

3. "Are you interviewing with other companies?"

   _____

4. "What will my responsibilities be?"

   _____

5. "How is job performance rewarded?"

   _____

6. "What was your starting salary at your last job?"

   _____

7. "Did you get along well with your last employer?"

   _____

8. "Do you hire many women?"

   _____

4 **EDIT** • *Read part of a memo an interviewer wrote. Find and correct eight mistakes in the use of indirect questions. The first mistake is already corrected. Check punctuation!*

Inter-Office Memo

I did some stress questioning in my interview with Carl Treng this morning. I asked

                              he couldn't

Mr. Treng why ~~couldn't he~~ work under pressure. I also asked him why did his

supervisor dislike him. Finally, I inquired when he would quit the job with our

company? Mr. Treng answered my questions calmly, and he had some excellent

questions of his own. He asked "if we expected changes on the job." He also wanted

to know how often do we evaluate employees. I was impressed when he asked why

did I decide to join this company. I think we should hire him.

UNIT 76 Embedded Questions

CHECK POINT

Check the questions the people have.

❏ Should we leave a tip?

❏ Was the service any good?

❏ Are these guys going to leave a tip?

❏ Is the service included?

CHART CHECK

Circle T (True) or F (False).

T F Embedded questions always end with a period.

T F You can use the infinitive after *whether* or a question word.

MAIN CLAUSE	EMBEDDED QUESTION
I'm not sure	*if* **I left** the right tip. *whether* **it was** enough.
Can you remember	*how much* **it was?** *where* **we ate?**
I don't know	*whether* **to tip.**
Do you know	*how much* **to tip?** *where* **to leave** the tip?

EXPRESS CHECK

Punctuate these sentences.

A: Do you know how much to tip_____

B: About 15%. But I'm not sure where to leave the tip_____

330

Grammar Explanations	Examples

1. In Unit 75 you learned to use **indirect questions** to report another person's words.

Indirect questions are a kind of **embedded question**—one that is <u>included in another sentence</u>. This unit discusses embedded questions <u>that do not report another person's words</u>.

DIRECT QUESTION	INDIRECT QUESTION
Should I tip?	He asked **if he should tip.**

EMBEDDED QUESTION
Do you know **whether I should tip?**

---

2. If the embedded question is **in a statement**, use a <u>period</u> at the end of the sentence. If the embedded question is **in a question**, use a <u>question mark</u> at the end of the sentence.

MAIN SENTENCE = STATEMENT
■ *I don't know* who our server is**.**
MAIN SENTENCE = QUESTION
■ *Do you know* who our server is**?**

---

3. We often **use embedded questions** to

a. <u>express something we do not know</u>.

b. <u>ask politely for information</u>.

USAGE NOTE: With strangers or in a formal situation, an embedded question is considered <u>more polite</u> than a direct question.

■ I wonder **why he didn't tip the mechanic.**

■ Can you tell me **if the tip is included?**

LESS FORMAL
■ Does our bill include a tip?
MORE POLITE
■ Can you tell me **if our bill includes a tip?**

---

4. Introduce **embedded *yes/no* questions** with *if, whether,* or *whether or not.*
USAGE NOTE: *Whether* is more <u>formal</u> than *if*.

Introduce **embedded *wh-* questions** with a <u>question word</u>.

You can also use the **infinitive** <u>after a question word or *whether*</u>.

▶ **BE CAREFUL!** Do not use the infinitive after *if* or *why*.

■ Do you know *if he tips?*
■ Do you know *whether (or not) he tips?*

■ Many tourists wonder *how much they should tip their restaurant server*.

■ Many tourists wonder *how much to tip*.
■ Some wonder *whether to tip* at all.

■ We wondered *why we should leave a tip.*
NOT We wondered ~~why to leave a tip~~.

---

5. BE CAREFUL! Use **statement word order** in all embedded questions.

<u>Do not leave out *if* or *whether*</u> in embedded *yes/no* questions.

<u>Do not use *do, does,* or *did*</u> in embedded questions.

■ Could you tell me *where they are*?
NOT Could you tell me ~~where are they~~?

■ Could you tell me *if it is* 6:00 yet?
NOT Could you tell me ~~is it 6:00 yet~~?

■ I don't know *when the pizza came*.
NOT I don't know ~~when did the pizza come~~.

Check it out!

For a list of common phrases introducing embedded questions, see Appendix 15 on page 340.

1 **IDENTIFY** • *Read this online ad for the book* **Tips on Tipping.** *Underline the embedded questions.*

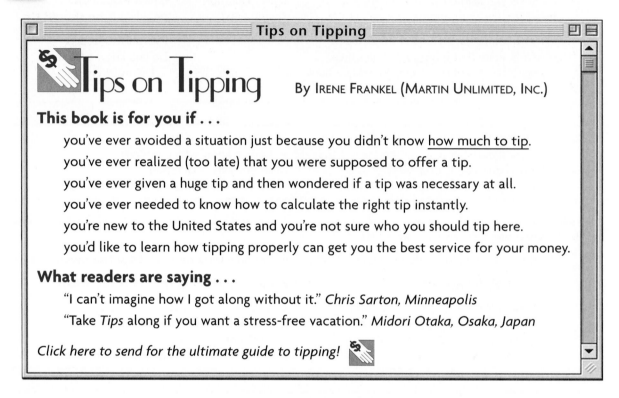

Tips on Tipping

$Tips on Tipping   By Irene Frankel (Martin Unlimited, Inc.)

This book is for you if . . .

you've ever avoided a situation just because you didn't know <u>how much to tip</u>.

you've ever realized (too late) that you were supposed to offer a tip.

you've ever given a huge tip and then wondered if a tip was necessary at all.

you've ever needed to know how to calculate the right tip instantly.

you're new to the United States and you're not sure who you should tip here.

you'd like to learn how tipping properly can get you the best service for your money.

What readers are saying . . .

"I can't imagine how I got along without it." *Chris Sarton, Minneapolis*

"Take *Tips* along if you want a stress-free vacation." *Midori Otaka, Osaka, Japan*

Click here to send for the ultimate guide to tipping!

2 **REWRITE** • *Complete these questions about tipping customs. Change the direct questions in parentheses to embedded questions. Use the infinitive whenever possible. Use correct punctuation.*

1. Can you tell me whether __to tip in Canada?_____
(Should I tip in Canada?)

2. I'm going to France. Please explain _____
(How can I tell if the tip is included in the bill?)

3. Can you tell me _____
(Why did service people in Iceland refuse my tips?)

4. I'm moving to Japan. I'd like to know _____
(How much should I tip airport porters?)

5. We're visiting Australia. Please tell us _____
(Who expects a tip and who doesn't?)

6. I'm vacationing in Norway. I'd like to know if _____
(Should I tip my ski instructor?)

7. I took a job in China. I need to know whether _____
(Is tipping still illegal there?)

8. In Germany the tip is included. I don't know whether _____
(Should I tip anyway?)

3 **CHOOSE & REWRITE** • *Two foreign exchange students are visiting Washington, D.C. Complete their conversations. Choose the appropriate questions from the box and change them to embedded questions. Remember to punctuate the sentences correctly.*

How much should we tip the taxi driver?	Where is the Smithsonian Museum?
Could we rent a car and drive?	What did they put in the sauce?
Where can we buy metro tickets?	~~Where is it?~~

1. **MARTA:** We're going to the Hotel Edison. Do you know <u>where it is?</u>
   DRIVER: Sure. Get in and I'll take you there.

2. **MIUKI:** *(whispering)* Do you know _____
   MARTA: According to the book, we're supposed to leave 10 to 15 percent. I've got it.

3. **MARTA:** Excuse me. Can you tell me _____
   OFFICER: Sure. Just turn right at the corner. You'll see it right away.

4. **MIUKI:** I'd like to take the metro to the zoo, but I don't know _____
   MARTA: Probably right in the station.

5. **MARTA:** I want to visit Williamsburg. Do you think _____
   MIUKI: Let's find out. That sounds like fun.

6. **MARTA:** This is delicious. Let's try to find out _____
   MIUKI: It tastes like ginger and garlic to me.

4 **EDIT** • *Read this entry from Marta's journal. Find and correct seven mistakes in the use of embedded questions. The first mistake is already corrected. Remember to check punctuation!*

When you live in a foreign country even a small occasion can be an adventure! Before my date
with Janek tonight, I didn't even know what ~~should I~~ **I should** wear! Jeans? A dress? John's Grill isn't a
fancy restaurant, but it was Janek's birthday and I wanted to make it a big occasion. Miuki was
very helpful, as always. I knew how to get to John's Grill, but I didn't know how long it was going
to take to get there? I left at 6:00, which should have given me plenty of time, but when I got
off the bus, I wasn't sure if to turn left or right. I asked a police officer where was John's, and
I was only a few minutes late. I had planned to take Janek out for a special dessert afterward,
but I couldn't remember how I to find the place Miuki had suggested, and Janek has been here
even less time than me. (Anyway, the desserts at John's turned out to be very good.) Then,
when we got the bill, I was wondering whether to tip or no. I had to ask Janek did he know.
Fortunately, he had read *Tips on Tipping*, so he told me to leave about 15%.

SelfTest

Circle the letter of the correct answer to complete each sentence.

EXAMPLE:

Jennifer never _____ coffee.

(A) drink   (C) is drinking

(B) drinks   (D) was drinking

A (B) C D

---

1. "You look beautiful in that dress."
   Last night she told me _____ beautiful in that dress.
   (A) you look   (C) I'll look
   (B) you looked   (D) I looked

   A B C D

2. We'd better find out _____ the train left.
   (A) if   (C) has
   (B) does   (D) did

   A B C D

3. —Should we turn left or go straight?
   —Hmm. I'm not sure which way _____.
   (A) do we turn   (C) should we turn
   (B) to turn   (D) it turned

   A B C D

4. "Why don't you join us for coffee, Don?"
   After the movie, we asked Don _____ us for coffee.
   (A) would he join   (C) to join
   (B) why he didn't join (D) for joining

   A B C D

5. "We must leave immediately!"
   When the fire alarm rang, our teacher said _____ leave immediately.
   (A) we had to   (C) not to
   (B) we have to   (D) he must

   A B C D

6. "Today is the happiest day of my life."
   At the reception last night, the groom said _____ the happiest day of his life.
   (A) today was   (C) yesterday was
   (B) that day is   (D) today is

   A B C D

7. I wonder who _____
   (A) our waiter is?   (C) our waiter is.
   (B) is our waiter.   (D) is our waiter?

   A B C D

8. "Please don't leave your boots in the hall."
   My mother is always telling me _____ boots in the hall.
   (A) not to leave my   (C) to not leave my
   (B) not to leave your (D) don't leave my

   A B C D

9. "Hi, Bob. Did you take the job?"   **A B C D**
   Bob's friend asked him _____ the job.
   (A) did he take   (C) if he had taken
   (B) did you take   (D) had he taken

10. "Weather patterns change."   **A B C D**
    Experts now say that weather patterns _____.
    (A) changed   (C) had changed
    (B) are changing   (D) change

SECTION TWO

*Each sentence has four underlined words or phrases. The four underlined parts
of the sentence are marked A, B, C, and D. Circle the letter of the one underlined
word or phrase that is NOT CORRECT.*

> **EXAMPLE:**
> Mike <u>usually</u> <u>drives</u> to school, but <u>today</u> he <u>walks</u>.   **A B C (D)**
>   A   B   C   D

11. The teacher <u>said</u> the class <u>that</u> hot air <u>rises</u> and cold air <u>sinks</u>.   **A B C D**
                 A   B   C   D

12. I <u>asked</u> Sean <u>how</u> <u>to pronounce</u> his name<u>?</u>   **A B C D**
       A   B   C   D

13. Gerry <u>called</u> last week and <u>said</u> <u>that</u> he needed the report right <u>now</u>.   **A B C D**
            A   B   C   D

14. Two days ago, the weather forecaster <u>warned</u> <u>us</u> <u>that</u> a tornado <u>is coming</u>. **A B C D**
                                          A   B   C   D

15. Sandy <u>called</u> from Miami during the storm and <u>said</u> <u>she</u> was swimming <u>here</u>. **A B C D**
            A   B   C   D

16. <u>Do you know</u> <u>if</u> <u>or not</u> <u>we</u> <u>need</u> to bring our passports?   **A B C D**
    A   B   C   D

17. She didn't know <u>if</u> to tip, so she <u>asked</u> me <u>what</u> <u>to do</u>.   **A B C D**
                    A   B   C   D

18. Ron <u>said</u> <u>that</u> he <u>wasn't</u> sure, but the storm <u>might stop</u> already.   **A B C D**
          A   B   C   D

19. <u>I'd like</u> lobster, but the menu <u>doesn't say</u> <u>how much</u> <u>does it cost</u>.   **A B C D**
    A   B   C   D

20. Lin <u>always</u> says <u>that</u> he <u>ran</u> a mile <u>every day</u> these days.   **A B C D**
          A   B   C   D

21. Could you tell me <u>when</u> the next train <u>leaves</u> and where <u>to buy</u> tickets<u>.</u>   **A B C D**
                      A   B   C   D

22. "<u>If</u> you can wait a few minutes<u>,</u> I <u>will give</u> you a ride<u>.</u> Rhoda said.   **A B C D**
     A   B   C   D

23. Jim <u>wants</u> to know <u>could you</u> call him and <u>tell</u> him where <u>to meet</u> you.   **A B C D**
          A   B   C   D

24. The dentist <u>said</u> <u>to brush</u> three times a day and <u>don't</u> <u>eat</u> candy.   **A B C D**
                A   B   C   D

25. At the interview they <u>asked</u> me when <u>can you</u> <u>start</u> work<u>.</u>   **A B C D**
                          A   B   C   D

Appendices

1 Irregular Verbs

Base Form	Simple Past	Past Participle	Base Form	Simple Past	Past Participle
arise	arose	arisen	grind	ground	ground
awake	awoke	awoken	grow	grew	grown
be	was/were	been	hang	hung	hung
beat	beat	beaten	have	had	had
become	became	become	hear	heard	heard
begin	began	begun	hide	hid	hidden
bend	bent	bent	hit	hit	hit
bet	bet	bet	hold	held	held
bite	bit	bitten	hurt	hurt	hurt
bleed	bled	bled	keep	kept	kept
blow	blew	blown	kneel	knelt	knelt
break	broke	broken	knit	knit/knitted	knit/knitted
bring	brought	brought	know	knew	known
build	built	built	lay	laid	laid
burn	burned/burnt	burned/burnt	lead	led	led
burst	burst	burst	leap	leapt	leapt
buy	bought	bought	leave	left	left
catch	caught	caught	lend	lent	lent
choose	chose	chosen	let	let	let
cling	clung	clung	lie (lie down)	lay	lain
come	came	come	light	lit/lighted	lit/lighted
cost	cost	cost	lose	lost	lost
creep	crept	crept	make	made	made
cut	cut	cut	mean	meant	meant
deal	dealt	dealt	meet	met	met
dig	dug	dug	pay	paid	paid
dive	dived/dove	dived	prove	proved	proved/proven
do	did	done	put	put	put
draw	drew	drawn	quit	quit	quit
dream	dreamed/dreamt	dreamed/dreamt	read /rid/	read /rɛd/	read /rɛd/
drink	drank	drunk	ride	rode	ridden
drive	drove	driven	ring	rang	rung
eat	ate	eaten	rise	rose	risen
fall	fell	fallen	run	ran	run
feed	fed	fed	say	said	said
feel	felt	felt	see	saw	seen
fight	fought	fought	seek	sought	sought
find	found	found	sell	sold	sold
fit	fit	fit	send	sent	sent
flee	fled	fled	set	set	set
fling	flung	flung	sew	sewed	sewn/sewed
fly	flew	flown	shake	shook	shaken
forbid	forbade/forbad	forbidden	shave	shaved	shaved/shaven
forget	forgot	forgotten	shine	shone	shone
forgive	forgave	forgiven	shoot	shot	shot
freeze	froze	frozen	show	showed	shown
get	got	gotten/got	shrink	shrank/shrunk	shrunk/shrunken
give	gave	given	shut	shut	shut
go	went	gone	sing	sang	sung

336

BASE FORM	SIMPLE PAST	PAST PARTICIPLE		BASE FORM	SIMPLE PAST	PAST PARTICIPLE
sink	sank	sunk		sweep	swept	swept
sit	sat	sat		swim	swam	swum
sleep	slept	slept		swing	swung	swung
slide	slid	slid		take	took	taken
speak	spoke	spoken		teach	taught	taught
speed	sped	sped		tear	tore	torn
spend	spent	spent		tell	told	told
spill	spilled/spilt	spilled/spilt		think	thought	thought
spin	spun	spun		throw	threw	thrown
spit	spit/spat	spat		understand	understood	understood
split	split	split		upset	upset	upset
spread	spread	spread		wake	woke	woken
spring	sprang	sprung		wear	wore	worn
stand	stood	stood		weave	wove	woven
steal	stole	stolen		weep	wept	wept
stick	stuck	stuck		win	won	won
sting	stung	stung		wind	wound	wound
stink	stank/stunk	stunk		withdraw	withdrew	withdrawn
strike	struck	struck		wring	wrung	wrung
swear	swore	sworn		write	wrote	written

 ## Common Non-action (Stative) Verbs

EMOTIONS	MENTAL STATES		WANTS AND PREFERENCES	APPEARANCE AND VALUE	POSSESSION AND RELATIONSHIP
admire	agree	know	hope	appear	belong
adore	assume	mean	need	be	contain
appreciate	believe	mind	prefer	cost	have
care	consider	presume	want	equal	own
detest	disagree	realize	wish	feel	possess
dislike	disbelieve	recognize		look	
doubt	estimate	remember	**PERCEPTION AND THE SENSES**	matter	
envy	expect	see (understand)	feel	represent	
fear	feel (believe)	suppose	hear	resemble	
hate	find	suspect	notice	seem	
like	guess	think (believe)	observe	signify	
love	hesitate	understand	perceive	smell	
regret	imagine	wonder	see	sound	
respect			smell	taste	
trust			taste	weigh	

 ## Common Verbs Followed by the Gerund (Base Form of Verb + -ing)

acknowledge	consider	endure	give up (stop)	miss	quit	resist
admit	delay	enjoy	imagine	postpone	recall	risk
advise	deny	escape	justify	practice	recommend	suggest
appreciate	detest	explain	keep (continue)	prevent	regret	support
avoid	discontinue	feel like	mention	prohibit	report	tolerate
can't help	discuss	finish	mind (object to)	propose	resent	understand
celebrate	dislike	forgive				

Common Verbs Followed by the Infinitive (*To* + Base Form of Verb)

afford	can('t) afford	expect	hurry	neglect	promise	volunteer
agree	can('t) wait	fail	intend	offer	refuse	wait
appear	choose	grow	learn	pay	request	want
arrange	consent	help	manage	plan	seem	wish
ask	decide	hesitate	mean	prepare	struggle	would like
attempt	deserve	hope	need	pretend	swear	yearn

 Verbs Followed by Objects and the Infinitive

advise	challenge	encourage	get	need*	persuade	require	want*
allow	choose*	expect*	help*	order	promise*	teach	warn
ask*	convince	forbid	hire	pay*	remind	tell	wish*
cause	enable	force	invite	permit	request*	urge	would like*

*These verbs can also be followed by the infinitive without an object (example: *ask to leave* or *ask someone to leave*).

 Common Verbs Followed by the Gerund or the Infinitive

begin	continue	hate	love	remember*	stop*
can't stand	forget*	like	prefer	start	try

*These verbs can be followed by either the gerund or the infinitive but there is a big difference in meaning.

 Common Verb + Preposition Combinations

admit to	believe in	count on	insist on	plan on	talk about
advise against	choose between/	deal with	look forward to	rely on	think about
apologize for	among	dream about/of	object to	resort to	wonder about
approve of	complain about	feel like/about	pay for	succeed in	worry about

 Common Adjective + Preposition Combinations

accustomed to	bored with/by	famous for	opposed to	sick of
afraid of	capable of	fed up with	pleased about	slow at
amazed at/by	careful of	fond of	ready for	sorry for/about
angry at	concerned about	glad about	responsible for	surprised at/about/by
ashamed of	content with	good at	sad about	terrible at
aware of	curious about	happy about	safe from	tired of
awful at	different from	interested in	satisfied with	used to
bad at	excited about	nervous about	shocked at/by	worried about

 Common Adjectives that Can Be Followed by the Infinitive*

afraid	anxious	depressed	disturbed	encouraged	happy	pleased	reluctant	surprised
alarmed	ashamed	determined	eager	excited	hesitant	proud	sad	touched
amazed	curious	disappointed	easy	fortunate	likely	ready	shocked	upset
angry	delighted	distressed	embarrassed	glad	lucky	relieved	sorry	willing

*Example: *I'm happy to hear that.*

Irregular Comparisons of Adjectives, Adverbs, and Quantifiers

ADJECTIVE	ADVERB	COMPARATIVE	SUPERLATIVE
bad	badly	worse *information*	worst
far	far	farther/further	farthest/furthest
good	well	better	best
little	little	less	least
many/a lot of	—	more	most
much*/a lot of	much*/a lot	more	most

Much is usually only used in questions and negative statements.

little   less   least

many   more   most
many   a lot of
much

 Common Participial Adjectives

-ed	-ing	-ed	-ing	-ed	-ing
alarmed	alarming	disturbed	disturbing	moved	moving *more*
amazed	amazing	embarrassed	embarrassing	paralyzed	paralyzing *most*
amused	amusing	entertained	entertaining	pleased	pleasing
annoyed	annoying	excited	exciting	relaxed	relaxing
astonished	astonishing	exhausted	exhausting	satisfied	satisfying
bored	boring	fascinated	fascinating	shocked	shocking
confused	confusing	frightened	frightening	surprised	surprising
depressed	depressing	horrified	horrifying	terrified	terrifying
disappointed	disappointing	inspired	inspiring	tired	tiring
disgusted	disgusting	interested	interesting	touched	touching
distressed	distressing	irritated	irritating	troubled	troubling

 Some Adjectives that Form the Comparative and Superlative in Two Ways

ADJECTIVE	COMPARATIVE	SUPERLATIVE
common	commoner / more common	commonest / most common
cruel	crueler / more cruel	cruelest / most cruel
deadly	deadlier / more deadly	deadliest / most deadly
friendly	friendlier / more friendly	friendliest / most friendly
handsome	handsomer / more handsome	handsomest / most handsome
happy	happier / more happy	happiest / most happy
likely	likelier / more likely	likeliest / most likely
lively	livelier / more lively	liveliest / most lively
lonely	lonelier / more lonely	loneliest / most lonely
lovely	lovelier / more lovely	loveliest / most lovely
narrow	narrower / more narrow	narrowest / most narrow
pleasant	pleasanter / more pleasant	pleasantest / most pleasant
polite	politer / more polite	politest / most polite
quiet	quieter / more quiet	quietest / most quiet
shallow	shallower / more shallow	shallowest / most shallow
sincere	sincerer / more sincere	sincerest / most sincere
stupid	stupider / more stupid	stupidest / most stupid
true	truer / more true	truest / most true

Common Reporting Verbs

STATEMENTS

acknowledge	claim	indicate	reply
add	complain	maintain	report
admit	conclude	mean	say
announce	confess	note	state
answer	declare	observe	suggest
argue	deny	promise	tell
assert	exclaim	remark	warn
believe	explain	repeat	write

INSTRUCTIONS, COMMANDS REQUESTS, AND INVITATIONS

advise	invite
ask	order
caution	say
command	tell
demand	urge
instruct	warn

QUESTIONS

ask
inquire
question
want to know
wonder

 Common Time Word Changes in Indirect Speech

DIRECT SPEECH		INDIRECT SPEECH
now	→	**then**
today	→	**that day**
tomorrow	→	**the next day** OR **the following day** OR **the day after**
yesterday	→	**the day before** OR **the previous day**
this week/month/year	→	**that week/month/year**
last week/month/year	→	**the week/month/year before**
next week/month/year	→	**the following week/month/year**

 Common Phrases Introducing Embedded Questions

I don't know . . .	I'd like to know . . .	Do you know . . . ?
I don't understand . . .	I want to understand . . .	Do you understand . . . ?
I wonder . . .	I'd like to find out . . .	Can you tell me . . . ?
I'm not sure . . .	We need to find out . . .	Could you explain . . . ?
I can't remember . . .	Let's ask . . .	Can you remember . . . ?
I can't imagine . . .		Would you show me . . . ?
It doesn't say . . .		Who knows . . . ?

 Verbs and Expressions Commonly Used Reflexively

amuse oneself	behave oneself	feel sorry for oneself	keep oneself	see oneself
ask oneself	believe in oneself	forgive oneself	kill oneself	take care of oneself
avail oneself of	blame oneself	give oneself	look after oneself	talk to oneself
be hard on oneself	cut oneself	help oneself	look at oneself	teach oneself
be oneself	deprive oneself of	hurt oneself	pride oneself on	tell oneself
be pleased with oneself	dry oneself	imagine oneself	push oneself	treat oneself
be proud of oneself	enjoy oneself	introduce oneself	remind oneself	wash oneself

(s.o. = someone s.t. = something)

NOTE 1: Inseparable phrasal verbs are shown with the object after the particle (*go after* s.t.).
Separable phrasal verbs are shown with the object between the verb and the particle (*call* s.o. *up*).
Verbs which <u>must be separated</u> are shown with an asterisk (*) (*do* s.t. *over*).

NOTE 2: Separable phrasal verbs can have the noun object either between the verb and the particle
or after the particle (*call Jan up* OR *call up Jan*). These verbs must, however, be separated when there
is a pronoun object (*call her up* NOT ~~call up her~~).

PHRASAL VERB	MEANING
ask s.o. **over**	*invite to one's home*
block s.t. **out**	*stop from passing through (light, noise)*
blow s.t. **out**	*stop burning by blowing*
blow s.t. **up**	*fill something with air (a balloon,*
	a water toy)
blow (s.t.) **up**	*(make s.t.) explode*
break down	*stop functioning*
break out	*occur suddenly*
bring s.t. **about**	*make something happen*
bring s.o. or s.t. **back**	*return someone or something*
bring s.o. **down**	*depress*
bring s.t. **out**	*introduce (a new product, a book)*
bring s.o. **up**	*raise (children)*
burn (s.t.) **down**	*burn completely*
call (s.o.) **back**	*return a phone call*
call s.t. **off**	*cancel*
call s.o. **up**	*telephone someone*
carry on s.t.	*continue*
carry s.t. **out**	*conduct*
catch on	*become popular*
cheer (s.o.) **up**	*(make someone) feel happier*
clean (s.o. or s.t.) **up**	*clean completely*
clear (s.t.) **up**	*make or become clear*
come about	*happen*
come along	*accompany*
come back	*return*
come in	*enter*
come off s.t.	*become unattached*
come out	*appear*
come up	*arise*
come up with s.t.	*invent*
cover s.t. **up**	*cover completely*
cross s.t. **out**	*draw a line through*
cut s.t. **down**	*bring down by cutting*
cut s.t. **off**	*1. stop the supply of something*
	2. remove by cutting
cut s.t. **out**	*remove by cutting*
do s.t. **over**	*do again*
dream s.t. **up**	*invent*
dress up	*put on special or formal clothes*
drink s.t. **up**	*drink completely*
drop by/in	*visit unexpectedly*

PHRASAL VERB	MEANING
drop s.o. or s.t. **off**	*take someone/something someplace*
drop out (**of** s.t.)	*quit*
eat out	*eat in a restaurant*
empty (s.t.) **out**	*empty completely*
end up	*1. do something unexpected*
	or unintended
	2. reach a final place or condition
fall off	*become detached*
figure s.o. or s.t. **out**	*understand (after thinking about)*
fill s.t. **in**	*complete with information*
fill s.t. **out**	*complete (a form, an application)*
fill (s.t.) **up**	*fill completely*
find (s.t.) **out**	*learn information*
follow (s.t.) **through**	*complete*
fool around	*be playful*
get s.t. **across**	*get people to understand an idea*
get ahead	*make progress, succeed*
get along	*relate well*
get back	*return*
get by	*survive*
get out (**of** s.t.)	*leave (a car, a taxi)*
get s.t. **out of** s.t.*	*benefit from*
get together	*meet*
get up	*rise from bed*
give s.t. **away**	*give without charging money*
give s.t. **back**	*return something*
give s.t. **out**	*distribute*
give (s.t.) **up**	*quit, abandon*
go after s.o. or s.t.	*pursue*
go along with s.t.	*1. support*
	2. be part of
go back	*return*
go off	*explode (a gun, fireworks, a rocket)*
go on	*continue*
go out	*leave*
go over	*succeed with an audience*
go up	*be built*
grow up	*become an adult*
hand s.t. **in**	*give some work to a boss or teacher*
hand s.t. **out**	*distribute*
hang up	*end a phone conversation*
hang s.t. **up**	*put on a hook or hanger*

(continued on next page)

PHRASAL VERB	MEANING
help (s.o.) **out**	*assist*
hold on	*wait, not hang up the phone*
keep (s.o. or s.t.) **away**	*(cause to) stay at a distance*
keep on	*continue*
keep s.t. **on***	*not remove (a piece of clothing or jewelry)*
keep up (with s.o. or s.t.)	*go as fast as*
lay s.o. **off**	*end someone's employment*
leave s.t. **on***	1. *not turn off (a light, a radio)*
	2. *not remove (a piece of clothing or jewelry)*
leave s.t. **out**	*omit*
let s.o. **down**	*disappoint*
let s.o. or s.t. **in**	*allow to enter*
let s.o. **off**	*allow to leave (a bus, a train, a car)*
let s.o. or s.t. **out**	*allow to leave*
lie down	*recline*
light (s.t.) **up**	*illuminate*
look out	*be careful*
look s.o. or s.t. **over**	*examine*
look s.t. **up**	*try to find in a book or on the Internet*
make s.t. **up**	*create*
pass s.t. **out**	*distribute*
pay s.o. or s.t. **back**	*repay*
pay off	*be worthwhile*
pick s.o. or s.t. **out**	1. *select*
	2. *identify*
pick up	*improve*
pick s.o. or s.t. **up**	1. *lift*
	2. *get (an idea, a new book, an interest)*
play around	*have fun*
point s.o. or s.t. **out**	*indicate*
put s.t. **away**	*put something in an appropriate place*
put s.t. **back**	*return something to its original place*
put s.o. or s.t. **down**	*stop holding*
put s.t. **off**	*postpone*
put s.t. **on**	*cover the body with a piece of clothing or jewelry*
put s.t. **together**	*assemble*
put s.t. **up**	*erect*
run **into** s.o.	*meet accidentally*
run **out** (of s.t.)	*not have enough of a supply*
see s.t. **through***	*complete*
set s.t. **off**	*cause to explode*
set s.t. **up**	1. *establish (a business, an organization)*
	2. *prepare for use*

PHRASAL VERB	MEANING
show s.o. or s.t. **off**	*display the best qualities*
show up	*appear*
shut s.t. **off**	*stop a machine or light*
sign up	*register*
sit down	*take a seat*
stand up	*rise*
start (s.t.) **over***	*start again*
stay up	*remain awake*
stick **with/to** s.o. or s.t.	*not quit, not leave*
straighten (s.t.) **up**	*make neat*
switch s.t. **on**	*start a machine or a light*
take s.t. **away/off**	*remove*
take s.t. **back**	*return*
take off	*depart (a plane)*
take s.o. **on**	*hire*
take s.t. **out**	*borrow from a library*
talk s.o. **into***	*persuade*
talk s.t. **over**	*discuss*
team up with s.o.	*start to work with*
tear s.t. **down**	*destroy*
tear s.t. **up**	*tear into small pieces*
think back on s.o. or s.t.	*remember*
think s.t. **over**	*consider*
think s.t. **up**	*invent*
throw s.t. **away/out**	*discard*
touch s.t. **up**	*improve by making small changes*
try s.t. **on**	*put clothing on to see if it fits*
try s.t. **out**	*find out if something works*
turn s.o. or s.t. **down**	1. *reject*
	2. *decrease the volume (a radio, a TV)*
turn s.t. **in**	*submit*
turn s.o. or s.t. **into**	*change from one form to another*
turn s.o. **off**	*(slang) destroy interest*
turn s.t. **off**	*stop a machine or light*
turn s.t. **on**	*start a machine or light*
turn out	*have a particular result*
turn up	*appear*
turn s.t. **up**	*raise the volume*
use s.t. **up**	*use completely, consume*
wake up	*arise after sleeping*
wake (s.o.) **up**	*awaken*
watch out	*be careful*
work s.t. **off**	*remove by work or activity*
work out	1. *be resolved*
	2. *exercise*
work s.t. **out**	*solve*
write s.t. **down**	*write on a piece of paper*
write s.t. **up**	*write in a finished form*

18 Some Common Irregular Plural Nouns

SINGULAR	PLURAL	SINGULAR	PLURAL	SINGULAR	PLURAL	SINGULAR	PLURAL
analysis	analyses	half	halves	man	men	mouse	mice
basis	bases	knife	knives	woman	women		
crisis	crises	leaf	leaves	child	children	deer	deer
hypothesis	hypotheses	life	lives			fish	fish
		loaf	loaves	foot	feet	sheep	sheep
		shelf	shelves	goose	geese		
		wife	wives	tooth	teeth	person	people

19 Spelling Rules for the Present Progressive

1. Add -ing to the base form of the verb.

   read   read*ing*
   stand   stand*ing*

2. If a verb ends in a silent -e, drop the final -e and add -ing.

   leave   lea*ving*
   take   ta*king*

3. In a one-syllable word, if the last three letters are a consonant-vowel-consonant combination (CVC), double the last consonant before adding -ing.

   C V C
   ↓ ↓ ↓
   s i t   sit*ting*

   C V C
   ↓ ↓ ↓
   r u n   run*ning*

However, do not double the last consonant in words that end in *w, x,* or *y.*

   sew   sew*ing*
   fix   fix*ing*
   enjoy   enjoy*ing*

4. In words of two or more syllables that end in a consonant-vowel-consonant combination, double the last consonant only if the last syllable is stressed.

   admit′   admit*ting*   (The last syllable is stressed, so you double the *-t.*)

   whis′per   whisper*ing*   (The last syllable is not stressed, so you don't double the *-r.*)

5. If a verb ends in -ie, change the *ie* to *y* before adding -ing.

   die   dy*ing*

20 Spelling Rules for the Simple Present Tense: Third-Person Singular *(he, she, it)*

1. Add -s for most verbs.

   work   work*s*
   buy   buy*s*
   ride   ride*s*
   return   return*s*

2. Add -es for words that end in -ch, -s, -sh, -x, or -z.

   watch   watch*es*
   pass   pass*es*
   rush   rush*es*
   relax   relax*es*
   buzz   buzz*es*

3. Change the *y* to *i* and add -es when the base form ends in a consonant + *y.*

   study   stud*ies*
   hurry   hurr*ies*
   dry   dr*ies*

   Do not change the *y* when the base form ends in a vowel + *y.* Add -s.

   play   play*s*
   enjoy   enjoy*s*

4. A few verbs have irregular forms.

   be   is
   do   does
   go   goes
   have   has

21 Spelling Rules for the Simple Past Tense of Regular Verbs

1. If the verb ends in a consonant, add -ed.

   return   return*ed*
   help   help*ed*

2. If the verb ends in -e, add -d.

   live   live*d*
   create   create*d*
   die   die*d*

3. In one-syllable words, if the verb ends in a consonant-vowel-consonant combination (CVC), double the final consonant and add -ed.

   C V C
   ↓ ↓ ↓
   h o p   hop*ped*

   C V C
   ↓ ↓ ↓
   r u b   rub*bed*

   However, do not double one-syllable words ending in -*w*, -*x*, or -*y*.

   bow   bow*ed*
   mix   mix*ed*
   play   play*ed*

4. In words of two or more syllables that end in a consonant-vowel-consonant combination, double the last consonant only if the last syllable is stressed.

   prefér   prefer*red*   (The last syllable is stressed, so you double the -*r*.)

   vísit   visit*ed*   (The last syllable is not stressed, so you don't double the *t*.)

5. If the verb ends in a consonant + *y*, change the *y* to *i* and add -ed.

   worry   worr*ied*
   carry   carr*ied*

6. If the verb ends in a vowel + *y*, add -ed. (Do not change the *y* to *i*.)

   play   play*ed*
   annoy   annoy*ed*
   Exceptions: pay—paid, lay—laid, say—said

22 Spelling Rules for the Comparative *(-er)* and Superlative *(-est)* of Adjectives

1. Add -*er* to one-syllable adjectives to form the comparative. Add -*est* to one-syllable adjectives to form the superlative.

   cheap   cheap*er*   cheap*est*
   bright   bright*er*   bright*est*

2. If the adjective ends in -e, add -*r* or -*st*.

   nice   nice*r*   nice*st*

3. If the adjective ends in a consonant + *y*, change *y* to *i* before you add -*er* or -*est*.

   pretty   prett*ier*   prett*iest*
   Exception: shy   shy*er*   shy*est*

4. If the adjective ends in a consonant-vowel-consonant combination (CVC), double the final consonant before adding -*er* or -*est*.

   C V C
   ↓ ↓ ↓
   b i g   big*ger*   big*gest*

   However, do not double the consonant in words ending in -*w* or -*y*.

   slow   slow*er*   slow*est*
   coy   coy*er*   coy*est*

23 Spelling Rules for Adverbs Ending in *–ly*

1. Add -*ly* to the corresponding adjective.

   nice   nice*ly*
   quiet   quiet*ly*
   beautiful   beautiful*ly*

2. If the adjective ends in a consonant + *y*, change the *y* to *i* before adding -*ly*.

   easy   eas*ily*

3. If the adjective ends in -le, drop the e and add -*y*.

   possible   possibl*y*

   However, do not drop the e for other adjectives ending in -e.

   extreme   extreme*ly*
   Exception: true   tru*ly*

4. If the adjective ends in -ic, add -*ally*.

   basic   basic*ally*
   fantastic   fantastic*ally*

Contractions with Verb Forms

1. SIMPLE PRESENT TENSE, PRESENT PROGRESSIVE, AND IMPERATIVE

Contractions with *Be*

I am	=	I'm
you are	=	you're
he is	=	he's
she is	=	she's
it is	=	it's
we are	=	we're
you are	=	you're
they are	=	they're

I am not	=	I'm not		
you are not	=	you're not	or	you aren't
he is not	=	he's not	or	he isn't
she is not	=	she's not	or	she isn't
it is not	=	it's not	or	it isn't
we are not	=	we're not	or	we aren't
you are not	=	you're not	or	you aren't
they are not	=	they're not	or	they aren't

Contractions with *Do*

| do not | = | don't |
| does not | = | doesn't |

SIMPLE PRESENT	PRESENT PROGRESSIVE
I'**m** a student.	I'**m studying** here.
He'**s** my teacher.	He'**s teaching** verbs.
We'**re** from Canada.	We'**re living** here.

SIMPLE PRESENT	PRESENT PROGRESSIVE
She'**s not** sick.	She'**s not reading**.
He **isn't** late.	He **isn't coming**.
We **aren't** twins.	We **aren't leaving**.
They'**re not** here.	They'**re not playing**.

SIMPLE PRESENT	IMPERATIVE
They **don't live** here.	**Don't run**!
It **doesn't snow** much.	

2. SIMPLE PAST TENSE AND PAST PROGRESSIVE

Contractions with *Be*

| was not | = | wasn't |
| were not | = | weren't |

Contractions with *Do*

| did not | = | didn't |

SIMPLE PAST	PAST PROGRESSIVE
He **wasn't** a poet.	He **wasn't singing**.
They **weren't** twins.	They **weren't sleeping**.
We **didn't** see her.	

3. FUTURE

Contractions with *Will*

I will	=	I'll
you will	=	you'll
he will	=	he'll
she will	=	she'll
it will	=	it'll
we will	=	we'll
you will	=	you'll
they will	=	they'll

| will not | = | won't |

FUTURE WITH *WILL*
I'**ll take** the train.
It'**ll be** faster that way.
We'**ll go** together.
He **won't come** with us.
They **won't miss** the train.

(continued on next page)

Contractions with *Be going to*

I am going to	=	**I'm going to**
you are going to	=	**you're going to**
he is going to	=	**he's going to**
she is going to	=	**she's going to**
it is going to	=	**it's going to**
we are going to	=	**we're going to**
you are going to	=	**you're going to**
they are going to	=	**they're going to**

FUTURE WITH *BE GOING TO*
I'm going to buy tickets tomorrow.
She**'s going to call** you.
It**'s going to rain** soon.
We**'re going to drive** to Boston.
They**'re going to crash**!

4. PRESENT PERFECT AND PRESENT PERFECT PROGRESSIVE

Contractions with *Have*

I have	=	**I've**
you have	=	**you've**
he has	=	**he's**
she has	=	**she's**
it has	=	**it's**
we have	=	**we've**
you have	=	**you've**
they have	=	**they've**
have not	=	**haven't**
has not	=	**hasn't**

You**'ve** already **read** that page.
We**'ve been writing** for an hour.
She**'s been** to Africa three times.
It**'s been raining** since yesterday.
We **haven't seen** any elephants yet.
They **haven't been living** here long.
She **hasn't taken** any photos today.

5. MODALS AND MODAL-LIKE EXPRESSIONS

cannot or can not	=	**can't**
could not	=	**couldn't**
should not	=	**shouldn't**
had better	=	**'d better**
would prefer	=	**'d prefer**
would not	=	**wouldn't**
would rather	=	**'d rather**

She **can't dance**.
We **shouldn't go**.
They**'d better decide**.
I**'d prefer** coffee.
She **wouldn't**.
I**'d rather take** the bus.

could have	=	**could've**
should have	=	**should've**
would have	=	**would've**
must have	=	**must've**
might have	=	**might've**

We **could've walked**.
We **might've arrived** late.

6. CONDITIONALS WITH *WOULD*

I would	=	**I'd**
you would	=	**you'd**
he would	=	**he'd**
she would	=	**she'd**
we would	=	**we'd**
you would	=	**you'd**
they would	=	**they'd**
would have	=	**would've**
would not	=	**wouldn't**

If I had time, **I'd travel**.
If you moved here, **you'd be** happy.
If she knew the answer, **she'd tell** you.
We'd buy a new car if we had the money.
If you invited them, **they'd come**.
If I had known, I **would've told** you.
I **wouldn't do** that if I were you.

25 Punctuation Rules for Direct Speech

Direct speech may either follow or come before the reporting verb. When direct speech follows the reporting verb,

    a. Put a comma after the reporting verb.

    b. Use opening quotation marks (") before the first word of the direct speech.

    c. Begin the quotation with a capital letter.

    d. Use the appropriate end punctuation for the direct speech. It may be a period (.), a question mark (?), or an exclamation point (!).

    e. Put closing quotation marks (") after the end punctuation of the quotation.

Examples: He said, "I had a good time."
               She asked, "Where's the party?"
               They shouted, "Be careful!"

When direct speech comes before the reporting verb,

    a. Begin the sentence with opening quotation marks (").

    b. Use the appropriate end punctuation for the direct speech. If the direct speech is a statement, use a comma (,). If the direct speech is a question, use a question mark (?). If the direct speech is an exclamation, use an exclamation point (!).

    c. Use closing quotation marks after the end punctuation for the direct speech (").

    d. Begin the reporting clause with a lower-case letter.

    e. Use a period at the end of the main sentence (.).

Examples: "I had a good time," he said.
               "Where's the party?" she asked.
               "Be careful!" they shouted.

 26 Pronunciation Table

VOWELS				CONSONANTS			
Symbol	**Key Word**	**Symbol**	**Key Word**	**Symbol**	**Key Word**	**Symbol**	**Key Word**
i	beat, feed	ə	banana, among	p	pack, happy	ʃ	ship, machine, station, special, discussion
ɪ	bit, did	ɚ	shirt, murder	b	back, rubber		
eɪ	date, paid	aɪ	bite, cry, buy, eye	t	tie	ʒ	measure, vision
ɛ	bet, bed			d	die	h	hot, who
æ	bat, bad	aʊ	about, how	k	came, key, quick	m	men
ɑ	box, odd, father	ɔɪ	voice, boy	g	game, guest	n	sun, know, pneumonia
ɔ	bought, dog	ɪr	beer	tʃ	church, nature, watch	ŋ	sung, ringing
oʊ	boat, road	ɛr	bare	dʒ	judge, general, major	w	wet, white
ʊ	book, good	ɑr	bar	f	fan, photograph	l	light, long
u	boot, food, student	ɔr	door	v	van	r	right, wrong
ʌ	but, mud, mother	ʊr	tour	θ	thing, breath	y	yes, use, music
				ð	then, breathe	t̬	butter, bottle
				s	sip, city, psychology		
				z	zip, please, goes		

STRESS
ˈ shows main stress.

Pronunciation Rules for the Simple Present Tense: Third-Person Singular *(he, she, it)*

1. The third person singular in the simple present tense always ends in the letter -s. There are, however, three different pronunciations for the final sound of the third person singular.

/s/	/z/	/ɪz/
talks	loves	dances

2. The final sound is pronounced /s/ after the voiceless sounds /p/, /t/, /k/, and /f/.

top	tops
get	gets
take	takes
laugh	laughs

3. The final sound is pronounced /z/ after the voiced sounds /b/, /d/, /g/, /v/, /ð/, /m/, /n/, /ŋ/, /l/, and /r/.

describe	describes
spend	spends
hug	hugs
live	lives
bathe	bathes
seem	seems
remain	remains
sing	sings
tell	tells
lower	lowers

4. The final sound is pronounced /z/ after all vowel sounds.

agree	agrees
try	tries
stay	stays
know	knows

5. The final sound is pronounced /ɪz/ after the sounds /s/, /z/, /ʃ/, /ʒ/, /tʃ/, and /dʒ/. /ɪz/ adds a syllable to the verb.

relax	relaxes
freeze	freezes
rush	rushes
massage	massages
watch	watches
judge	judges

6. *Do* and *say* have a change in vowel sound.

say	/sɛɪ/	says	/sɛz/
do	/du/	does	/dʌz/

Pronunciation Rules for the Simple Past Tense of Regular Verbs

1. The regular simple past always ends in the letter -d. There are, however, three different pronunciations for the final sound of the regular simple past.

/t/	/d/	/ɪd/
raced	lived	attended

2. The final sound is pronounced /t/ after the voiceless sounds /p/, /k/, /f/, /s/, /ʃ/, and /tʃ/.

hop	hopped
work	worked
laugh	laughed
address	addressed
publish	published
watch	watched

3. The final sound is pronounced /d/ after the voiced sounds /b/, /g/, /v/, /z/, /ʒ/, /dʒ/, /m/, /n/, /ŋ/, /l/, /r/, and /ð/.

rub	rubbed
hug	hugged
live	lived
surprise	surprised
massage	massaged
change	changed
rhyme	rhymed
return	returned
bang	banged
enroll	enrolled
appear	appeared
bathe	bathed

4. The final sound is pronounced /d/ after all vowel sounds.

agree	agreed
play	played
die	died
enjoy	enjoyed
row	rowed

5. The final sound is pronounced /ɪd/ after /t/ and /d/. /ɪd/ adds a syllable to the verb.

start	started
decide	decided

Index

Answer Key

NOTE: In this answer key, where the contracted form is given, the full form is also correct, and where the full form is given, the contracted form is also correct.

 Present Progressive

CHECK POINT

It's happening now!

CHART CHECK 1

be + base form of verb + *-ing*
be

CHART CHECK 2

F

EXPRESS CHECK

are . . . leaving
are . . . performing OR 're . . . performing

 I'm working very hard these days, but I have some good news. Right now, I'm sitting at a desk in the Entertainment Section of the *Tribune*! Of course I'm still taking journalism classes at night as well. The job is temporary—Joe Sims, the regular reporter, is taking this month off to write a book. This week we're preparing to interview your favorite group, the Airheads. In fact, at this very moment they're flying into town by helicopter. They're performing at the King Theater all week. How are you doing? Are you still writing music? Oops! The crew is calling me. They're leaving for the theater now. Write soon!

 2. are . . . going
3. is waiting OR 's waiting
4. 'm working
5. 're not doing OR aren't doing
6. 're . . . sitting
7. 'm sitting
8. 'm . . . thinking
9. are staying

 3. Why are you touring again?
4. What are you working on these days?
5. Who's singing with you now?
6. Is she replacing Toti?
7. No, she isn't. OR No, she's not.

I ~~write~~ **'m writing** to you from my hotel room. Everyone else is ~~sleep~~ **sleeping**, but I ~~sitting~~ **'m sitting** here and watching the ocean. We're staying at the Plaza in Atlantic Beach, and the view is beautiful. The tour is ~~goes~~ **going** well. The audience is crazy about the new songs, but the fans ~~is~~ **are** always asking for you. How is the baby? She has a great voice. ~~Do~~ **Are** you teaching her to sing yet? Maybe both of you will come along for the next tour!

 Simple Present Tense

CHECK POINT

Hank's Working Habits

CHART CHECK

T, T, F

EXPRESS CHECK

Why does he rush

 In today's fast-paced world, we never escape stress. Stress always affects us psychologically, but according to Dr. Roads, author of the new bestseller, *Calm Down!,* it also affects us physically. For example, stress causes high blood pressure. Doctors often prescribe medication for stress-related illnesses. Medicine usually lowers a patient's blood

(continued on next page)

pressure. But, Dr. Roads <u>claims</u>, "You <u>don't</u> always <u>need</u> pills. Relaxation exercises <u>are</u> sometimes as effective as pills. For example, breathing exercises both <u>relax</u> you and <u>lower</u> your blood pressure. It only <u>takes</u> a few minutes!"

3. take	**7.** doesn't finish
4. rushes	**8.** worries
5. isn't	**9.** doesn't have
6. is	**10.** doesn't have

3. Does he work on reports in the afternoon? No, he doesn't.
4. When does he see clients? He sees clients from 9:00 to 12:00.
5. Does he take a lunch break? Yes, he does.
6. What does he do from 12:30 to 5:00? He returns phone calls.
7. Where does he go at 5:30? He attends OR goes to night school.

I'm so tired. I ~~have never~~ ^{never have} time to relax.
I work all day and ~~studies~~ ^{study} all night. My boss ~~tell~~ ^{tells} me that I need a vacation. I agree, but I'm afraid to take one. Does my boss ~~thinks~~ ^{think} that the office can function without me? I ~~dont~~ ^{don't} want them to think I'm not necessary. But my wife is unhappy too. She ~~complain~~ ^{complains} that she never sees me anymore. My schedule ~~are~~ ^{is} crazy. I don't think I can keep this up much longer. I don't ~~wants~~ ^{want} to quit night school, though. I think ~~often~~ ^{often} that there has to be a better way.

UNIT 3 Non-Action Verbs

CHECK POINT
  has the flavor of chicken

CHART CHECK
  T, T

  'm tasting, tastes

ALINE: This steak <u>tastes</u> delicious. Your salmon <u>looks</u> good too.
BEN: Here, I'm putting some on your plate. I <u>think</u> you'll like it.
ALINE: Mmm. I <u>like</u> it. Funny, I usually don't like fish.
BEN: Red has that effect on people.
ALINE: I <u>have</u> no idea what you're talking about. What <u>do</u> you <u>mean</u>?
BEN: Well, colors can change the way we feel For example, people often feel hungrier in a red room. I <u>notice</u> that you're looking right at the red wallpaper.
ALINE: And I certainly <u>feel</u> hungry right now. I'm eating half your salmon.
BEN: That's OK. I'm tasting your steak.

2. is looking	**8.** doesn't suspect
3. cost	**9.** know
4. wants	**10.** is thinking
5. hates	**11.** doesn't have
6. seems	**12.** hears
7. likes	

2. 'm tasting	**11.** don't know
3. needs	**12.** is
4. Do . . . want	**13.** 'm smelling
5. tastes	**14.** 'm not
6. think	**15.** love
7. 'm thinking	**16.** smells
8. isn't	**17.** know
9. sounds	**18.** mean
10. 'm looking	**19.** feel

Not a good day! I feel kind of depressed and I ~~'m having~~ ^{have} a headache. I ~~'m needing~~ ^{need} to do something right away to change my mood and get rid of this pain. Last week, I read an article about how smells can affect mood and even health, so right now I ~~smell~~ ^{'m smelling} an

orange (for the depression) and a green

apple (for the headache). They smell nice,

but I'm not thinking that I notice a difference ~~'m not thinking~~ *don't think*

in how I feel! I think I'm preferring to eat ~~'m preferring~~ *prefer*

something when I feel down. But I worry

that I'm weighing too much. So, at the ~~'m weighing~~ *weigh*

moment I have a cup of peppermint tea with ~~have~~ *'m having*

lemon. The article says that the peppermint

smell helps you eat less. Well, I don't know

about that! A chocolate ice cream sundae

sounds pretty good right about now!

It's seeming that there are no easy solutions. ~~'s seeming~~ *seems*

Present Progressive and Simple Present Tense

CHECK POINT
  F, T

CHART CHECK
  two parts
  two forms

EXPRESS CHECK

PRESENT PROGRESSIVE			
SUBJECT	**BE**	**BASE FORM + -ING**	
I	am	buying	
You	are	buying	flowers now.
He	is	buying	

SIMPLE PRESENT TENSE			
SUBJECT		**VERB**	
I		buy	
You	usually	buy	chocolates.
He		buys	

 June 28: I'm sitting in a seat 30,000 feet above the earth en route to Argentina! I usually <u>have</u> dinner at this time, but right now I have a headache from the excitement. My seatmate is eating my food. She looks happy.

June 30: It's 7:30. My host parents are still working. Carlos, my father, <u>works</u> at home. My little brother Ricardo <u>is</u> cute. He <u>looks</u> (and <u>acts</u>) a lot like Bobby. Right now, he's looking over my shoulder and trying to read my journal.

July 4: The weather is cold now. I usually <u>spend</u> the first weekend of July at the beach. Today I'm walking around in a heavy sweater.

August 6: I feel so tired tonight. Everyone else <u>feels</u> great in the evening because they <u>take</u> long naps in the afternoon.

1. b. 'm waiting
  c. look
  d. 'm working
  e. 's talking
  f. isn't looking OR 's not looking
  g. looks
  h. doesn't mean
2. a. 's talking
  b. 're taking
  c. 're standing
  d. Do . . . think
  e. 're dating
  f. don't think
  g. means
  h. come
  i. stand
3. a. is . . . walking
  b. starts
  c. has
  d. walks
  e. appear
4. a. are . . . shaking
  b. know
  c. shake
  d. meet

It's 12:30 and I ~~sit~~ (**'m sitting**) in the library right now. My classmates are eating lunch together, but I'm not hungry yet. At home, we ~~eat never~~ (**never eat**) this early. Today our journal topic is culture shock. It's a good topic for me right now because I'm ~~being~~ pretty homesick. I miss my old routine. At home we always ~~are eating~~ (**eat**) a big meal at 2:00 in the afternoon. Then we rest. But here in Toronto ~~I'm having~~ (**I have**) a 3:00 conversation class. Every day, I almost fall asleep in class, and my teacher ~~ask~~ (**asks**) me, "Are you bored?" Of course I'm not bored. I just need my afternoon nap! This class ~~always is~~ (**is always**) fun. This semester, we ~~work~~ (**'re working**) on a project with video cameras. My team is filming groups of people in different cultures. We are ~~analyze~~ (**analyzing**) "social distance." That means how close to each other these people stand. According to my new watch, it's 12:55, so I ~~leave~~ (**'m leaving**) now for my 1:00 class. Teachers here really ~~aren't liking~~ (**don't like**) when you come late!

UNIT 5 Imperative

CHECK POINT

giving instructions on how to do the Jab

CHART CHECK

don't include a subject

EXPRESS CHECK

AFFIRMATIVE	
BASE FORM OF VERB	
Listen	to the music.
Touch	your toes.
Stand	straight.

NEGATIVE		
DON'T	**BASE FORM OF VERB**	
Don't	listen	to the music.
Don't	touch	your toes.
Don't	stand	straight.

1
2. c	**4.** e	**6.** a
3. b	**5.** d	**7.** f

2
2. Wash six strawberries.
3. Cut the strawberries in half.
4. Pour orange juice into the blender.
5. Add the fruit to the orange juice.
6. Blend the ingredients until smooth.

3
2. Learn	**7.** Take
3. Decrease	**8.** Choose
4. Increase	**9.** Don't wait
5. Become	**10.** Register
6. Don't miss	

4 For the Black Belt essay, Master Gibbons gave us this assignment: ~~You write~~ (**Write**) about something important to you. My topic is *The Right Way*, the rules of life for the martial arts. First, ~~respects~~ (**respect**) other people—treat them the way you want them to treat you. Second, ~~helped~~ (**help**) people in need. In other words, use your strength for others, ~~not to~~ (**don't**) use it just for your own good. Third, ~~no~~ (**don't**) lie or steal. These are the most important rules to me.

SelfTest

(Total = 100 points. Each item = 4 points.)

SECTION ONE

1. **B**	5. **D**	9. **C**	13. **D**
2. **D**	6. **A**	10. **B**	14. **D**
3. **A**	7. **B**	11. **A**	15. **B**
4. **A**	8. **B**	12. **A**	

SECTION TWO

(Correct answers are in parentheses.)

16. A (swims)   **21. C** (hate)
17. C (is raining)   **22. A** (usually arrives)
18. B (are you)   **23. B** (aren't OR are not)
19. C (don't)   **24. D** ('m always losing)
20. B (seems)   **25. B** (*delete* you)

UNIT 6 Simple Past Tense:
Affirmative Statements

CHECK POINT

1989
1999

CHART CHECK

two
–*d* or –*ed*

EXPRESS CHECK

was, were
came
saved

1 Matsuo Basho (wrote) more than 1,000 three-line poems, or "haiku." He (chose) topics from nature, daily life, and human emotions. He (became) one of Japan's most famous poets, and his work <u>established</u> haiku as an important art form.

Matsuo Basho (was) born near Kyoto in 1644. His father <u>wanted</u> him to become a samurai (warrior). Instead, Matsuo <u>moved</u> to Edo (present-day Tokyo) and <u>studied</u> poetry. By 1681, he (had) many students and admirers.

Basho's home <u>burned</u> down in 1682. Then, in 1683, his mother <u>died</u>. After these events, Basho (felt) restless. Starting in 1684, he <u>traveled</u> on foot and on horseback all over Japan. Sometimes his friends <u>joined</u> him, and they (wrote) poetry together. Travel (was) difficult in the seventeenth century, and Basho often (got) sick. He <u>died</u> in 1694, during a journey to Osaka. At that time he (had) 2,000 students.

2
2. wrote	**10.** addressed
3. were	**11.** appeared
4. led	**12.** happened
5. became	**14.** saw
6. left	**15.** bit
7. saw	**16.** ate
8. wore	**17.** drank
9. wrote	**18.** hopped

3 Today in class we read a poem by Robert
          enjoyed
Frost. I really ~~enjoy~~ it. It was about a person
      chose
who ~~choosed~~ between two roads in a forest.
           spent
Before he made his decision, he ~~spents~~ a lot
of time trying to decide which road to follow.
           was
Many people thought the person ~~were~~ Frost.
     took
In the end, he ~~take~~ the road that was less
traveled on. He decided to be a poet. That
       changed
decision ~~change~~ his life a lot.

Sometimes I feel a little like Frost.
        decided
Two years ago I ~~decide~~ to come to this
     was
country. That ~~were~~ the biggest decision of
my life.

UNIT 7 Simple Past Tense:
Negative Statements and Questions

CHECK POINT

?, F, T

CHART CHECK 1

not
did not

CHART CHECK 2

was, were
did

EXPRESS CHECK

Did she have a navigator?
She didn't fly alone.

1
2. No	**4.** No	**6.** Yes
3. Yes	**5.** Yes	**7.** No

2. Where did she study? (At) Columbia University.

3. How long was she a social worker? (For) two years.

4. Where did her last flight leave from? (From) New Guinea.

5. How many books did she write? Three.

6. What was her nationality? American.

7. When did she disappear? (In) 1937.

3. Were	**9.** Did . . . dream
4. No . . . weren't	**10.** didn't think
5. didn't want	**11.** Were
6. Did . . . feel	**12.** No . . . wasn't
7. Yes . . . did	**13.** Was
8. didn't keep	**14.** No . . . wasn't

receive
Hi! Did you ~~received~~ my last letter? I didn't
know
~~knew~~ your new address so I sent it to your
did you move
old one. When ~~you moved~~? Did your

roommate move with you? Right now I'm on

board a plane flying to El Paso to visit Ana.
meet
Did you ~~met~~ her at the conference last year?
didn't have
I wanted to visit her in June, but I ~~no had~~

the time. At first I was going to drive from

Los Angeles, but I decided to fly instead.

This is only my third flight, but I love flying!
didn't
I ~~didnt~~ know flying could be so much fun!

Hope to hear from you.

Used to

CHECK POINT

a habit he had in the past

CHART CHECK 1

T

CHART CHECK 2

did . . . use to

EXPRESS CHECK

used to
use to
say

In many ways, fashion <u>used to be</u> much

simpler. Women <u>didn't use to wear</u> pants to

the office, and men's clothes never <u>used to</u>

<u>come</u> in bright colors. People also <u>used to</u>

<u>dress</u> in special ways for different situations.

They didn't use blue jeans as business

clothes or wear jogging suits when they

traveled. Today you can go to the opera and

find some women in evening gowns while

others are in blue jeans. Even buying jeans

<u>used to be</u> easier—they only came in blue

denim. I'm still not used to buying green

jeans and wearing them to work!

2. used to have	**5.** used to wear
3. used to dress	**6.** used to carry
4. used to dance	

(Answers may vary slightly.)
2. They (only) used to come in two styles. (high-top and low-top)
3. How much did a pair of men's high-tops use to cost?
(They used to cost) 98¢.
4. No. Women's sneakers didn't use to cost the same as men's sneakers. Women's sneakers used to cost less than men's sneakers.
5. They (only) used to wear low-top sneakers.
6. There used to be (only) two sizes. (small and large)

use
When I was younger, clothing didn't ~~used~~ to

be a problem. All the girls at my school used
wear
to ~~wore~~ the same uniform. I used to think

that it took away from my freedom of choice.

Now I can wear what I want, but clothes

cost so much! Even blue jeans, today's
"uniform," used to be cheaper. My mom ~~uses~~ *used*
to pay less than $20 for hers. I guess they
didn't ~~used~~ *use* to sell designer jeans back then.
You know, I ~~was~~ used to be against school
uniforms, but now I'm not so sure!

UNIT 9 Past Progressive

CHECK POINT
what she was doing at the time of
her accident

CHART CHECK 1
F

CHART CHECK 2
before the subject

EXPRESS CHECK
A: were . . . staying
B: was staying

2. F   **5.** T
3. T   **6.** F
4. ?

3. were sitting outside.
4. wasn't snowing.
5. were wearing sunglasses.
6. weren't wearing gloves.
7. was serving drinks.
8. wasn't serving lunch.
9. wasn't smiling.
10. was holding a cell phone.

3. was recovering
4. wasn't performing
5. were . . . thinking
6. were waiting
7. wasn't thinking
8. were watching
9. were . . . snowboarding
10. was watching
11. (was) dreaming
12. Was . . . practicing
13. was

Tonight, Sheila and I ~~was~~ *were* looking at some
photographs from my snowboarding trip
with Fritz's family last year. By the end of
the evening, we *were* ^laughing like crazy. That
was my first experience on a snowboard, so
the pictures were pretty embarrassing. In
one shot, I was ~~came~~ *coming* down the slope on my
back. In another one, my board ~~were~~ *was* falling
out of the ski lift while I was riding up the
slope. Fritz ~~was taking~~ *took* that picture from the
lift entrance. Good thing he ~~not~~ *wasn't* standing
right under me! Where was I when Fritz
was falling down the slope? I guess I wasn't
~~carry~~ *carrying* my camera. It was amazing how fast
Fritz's girlfriend, Karyn, learned that
weekend. She was doing jumps by the
second day. By that time, I ~~spent~~ *was spending* a lot of
time at the ski café.

UNIT 10 Past Progressive and Simple Past Tense

CHECK POINT
2, 1

CHART CHECK
F, T

EXPRESS CHECK
When
was he driving

2. F   **4.** F
3. T   **5.** T

4. were waiting   **9.** was going
5. noticed   **10.** reached
6. Was . . . speeding **11.** wasn't
7. got   **12.** were crossing
8. was   **13.** hit

14. Did . . . stop
15. saw
16. didn't
17. was talking
18. was driving
19. didn't stop
20. weren't paying
21. were walking
22. Was . . . snowing
23. happened
24. was
25. wasn't
26. started
27. arrived

2. she was driving home, she listened to her car radio.
3. She pulled over to the side of the road . . . the visibility got very bad.
4. She heard about the accident . . . she was listening to the news.
5. She drove to the police station . . . it stopped snowing.
6. she was talking to the police, she was thinking about her editorial for the morning paper.

Yesterday, a man was talking on his cell
phone while he was ~~drive~~ ^{driving} his car. Maybe
he ^{was}‸checking his daily planner while he

was making his next appointment. He was

certainly not concentrating on the road
when the light suddenly ~~was turning~~ ^{turned} red.
The two men in the street ~~were trying~~ ^{tried} to

jump out of the way when they saw him, but

it was too late. No one was badly hurt, but

that was just luck. Last year, the City Council
~~weren't passing~~ ^{didn't pass} the "talking and driving

law." We need that law!

SelfTest

(Total = 100 points. Each item = 4 points.)

SECTION ONE

1. A	**4. B**	**7. A**	**10. C**
2. D	**5. A**	**8. B**	**11. C**
3. D	**6. B**	**9. D**	**12. B**

 TWO

(Correct answers are in parentheses.)

13. C (call)	**20. A** (did)
14. C (was)	**21. D** (got)
15. A (were)	**22. C** (got)
16. D (were sleeping)	**23. B** (was driving)
17. B (not)	**24. B** (*delete comma*)
18. D (dropped)	**25. D** (saw)
19. A (was)	

 Present Perfect:
Since and *For*

CHECK POINT
T

CHART CHECK 1
have + past participle
base form of verb + *–d* or *–ed*

CHART CHECK 2
a length of time

EXPRESS CHECK
driven: irregular
competed: regular
won: irregular
tried: regular

 Martina Hingis picked up her first tennis racket at the age of two. (Since then) she <u>has become</u> one of the greatest tennis players in the world. Born in Slovakia, she <u>has lived</u> in Switzerland (for many years.) She became the outdoor Swiss champion at age nine. (Since then) she <u>has won</u> many international competitions including Wimbledon, the U.S. Open, and the Australian Open.

For young stars like Martina, life has its difficulties. They are under constant pressure to win, and they don't have time to just hang out with classmates. In fact, Martina <u>hasn't attended</u> school (since 1994,) and she <u>has been</u> in the public spotlight (for years.) But she seems to be handling her success well. (Since she turned professional.)

she <u>has played</u> tennis all over the world
and <u>has earned</u> millions of dollars. She
sees her life as normal because tennis
<u>has been</u> the most important thing to her
(since she was a little girl).

3. 've been
4. for
5. For
6. has attended
7. hasn't done
8. Since
9. has taken
10. hasn't gotten
11. Since
12. has met
13. hasn't thought
14. 's known
15. since

2. How long has she lived in Switzerland?
(She has lived in Switzerland) for
many years.
3. Has she won any competitions since the
outdoor Swiss championship?
Yes, she has.
4. Has she attended school since 1994?
No, she hasn't.
5. How much money has she earned since
she began her career?
(She has earned) millions of dollars.
6. How long has tennis been important to her?
(Tennis has been important to her) since
she was a little girl.

I ~~am~~ in Ms. Rodriguez's physical education
(have been) / (for)
class ~~since~~ two months. I enjoy it a lot and
have only ~~miss~~ (missed) two classes since the
beginning of the semester. I especially like
tennis, but since September we ~~don't play~~ (haven't played)
because the weather ~~have~~ (has) been too cold. I
also like volleyball, and my team has ~~win~~ (won)
two games since we ~~have~~ started to compete
with Lincoln High School. I'm looking
forward to the next game.

UNIT 12 Present Perfect:
Already and *Yet*

CHECK POINT
F

CHART CHECK 1
use *already*
use *not ... yet*

CHART CHECK 2
T

EXPRESS CHECK
Have you had lunch yet?
Yes, I/we have. OR No, I/we haven't.

2. c
3. a
4. b
5. d

3. Has ... disappeared already OR yet
4. Yes ... has
5. have already developed
6. haven't been able ... yet
7. Has ... made ... yet
8. No ... haven't

3. Helmut has already baked the cake.
4. Gisela has already bought flowers.
5. Helmut hasn't put the turkey in the oven yet.
6. Gisela has already washed the windows.
7. Helmut has already mopped the floor.
8. Gisela has already hung the balloons.
9. Helmut hasn't washed the dishes yet.
10. Gisela hasn't wrapped the gifts yet.

I'm in a hurry. I haven't ~~went~~ (gone) shopping
~~already~~ (yet), but I'll do it on the way home. Rita
~~have~~ (has) already had dinner and she's already
had her bath. Have you ~~call~~ (called) Mr. Jacobson
yet? He's ~~called already~~ (already called) three times today.
His daughter ~~has~~ (hasn't) gotten her flu shot yet.
Is it too late? See you later.

UNIT 13 Present Perfect:
Indefinite Past

CHECK POINT

now

CHART CHECK 1

T

CHART CHECK 2

before the past participle

EXPRESS CHECK

Have you ever watched "The Simpsons"?
Yes, I/we have. OR No, I/we haven't.

2. F	4. F	6. F
3. T	5. F	7. T

2. 've had	6. 've . . . wanted
3. 've stopped	7. have . . . traveled
4. Have . . . talked	8. 've traveled
5. have . . . wanted	9. have . . . made

2. I've never even been in a chat room.
3. How have you changed as an actor?
4. I've become a better team player lately.
5. who has been your role model?
6. Charlie Chaplin has had great influence on me.
7. What has been your best moment on this show?
8. Jimmy has just won the Emmy.
9. what have you found most rewarding about this experience?
10. I've met some fantastic people on this show.

             watched
I've just ~~watch~~ the Blind Date episode on
            ever
Feldstein! Have you ~~never~~ seen anything so

funny? I LOVE this show! It's the best show
       seen   've
I have ever ~~saw~~ in my life. I really enjoyed
                noticed
it lately. By the way, have you ~~notice~~ that

Jimmy and Arlene are beginning to get
             has
along? I think Jimmy ~~have~~ started to really

like her. Last night Arlene ~~has~~ moved right

next door to Jimmy, but he doesn't know it
yet! I can't wait to see what happens on the
next episode. Does anyone know when
Jimmy's book is coming out?

UNIT 14 Present Perfect and
Simple Past Tense

CHECK POINT

T

CHART CHECK 1

the present perfect

CHART CHECK 2

have + past participle

EXPRESS CHECK

met, have been

Many modern marriages are finding
interesting solutions to difficult problems.
Joe and Maria, for example, (have been)
married since 1995. After their wedding, the
couple settled down in Boston, where Maria
opened an accounting business. Then in 1997
Joe lost his job. By that time, Maria's new
business was booming, so they didn't consider
moving. Joe never found a new job in Boston,
but in 1998, he got a great offer on the other
side of the country—in Los Angeles. The
couple (has lived) apart ever since. How
(have) they (handled) this "commuter marriage"
up to now? Joe notes, "It certainly
(hasn't been) easy. We (ve been) geographically
separated, but we (ve grown) a lot closer
emotionally. For that reason, it (s been)
worth it."

2. T	4. F
3. F	5. T

2

3. haven't stopped
4. has . . . been
5. slept
6. haven't gotten
7. 've seen OR have seen
8. didn't do
9. didn't bother
10. Have . . . tried OR Did . . . try
11. Yes, I have. OR Yes, I did.
12. 've drunk
13. drank

3

5. Did you start your business before your marriage?
6. No, I didn't.
7. How long have you owned your own business?
8. (I've owned my own business) since 1995/for *six* years.
9. When did you find your job in Los Angeles?
10. (I found my job in Los Angeles) in 1998/*three* years ago.
11. Has your commuter marriage been very difficult?
12. Yes, it has!

4

's been
It's 8:00 P.M. It ~~was~~ a hard week, and it's not

over yet! I still have to finish that report.
started
I ~~'ve started~~ it last Monday, but so far, I've
written
~~wrote~~ only five pages. And it's due next
has been
week! Work ~~was~~ so difficult lately. I've

worked late every night this week. I'm tired,
didn't get
and I ~~haven't gotten~~ much sleep last night.
saw
I miss Joe. I ~~'ve seen~~ him last weekend, but

it seems like a long time ago.

UNIT 15 Present Perfect Progressive

**CHECK** POINT

People are still collecting Beanie Babies.

CHART CHECK 1

T

CHART CHECK 2

been + base form + *-ing*

EXPRESS CHECK

A: has
B: For
A: been
B: collecting

1

| 2. b | 4. b | 6. b |
| 3. a | 5. a | |

2

3. have been flying
4. has been living
5. has been sending
6. have been appearing
7. has . . . been attracting
8. has been choosing
9. Have . . . been standing
10. No, they haven't.
11. haven't been asking

3

2. He hasn't been testing the inline skates.
3. He hasn't been shooting baskets.
4. He's been eating pizza.
5. He hasn't been drinking soda.
6. He's been building a racing car.
7. He's been playing video games.
8. He hasn't been sending e-mail messages.

4

Thank you very much for the Pokémon
playing
cards. My friend and I have been ~~play~~ with
've
them all day. So far, I ~~am~~ been winning.
has
I really love Pokémon. My Mom⹁been buying

the toys for us because she thinks they're
have been
cute too. All my friends ~~were~~ collecting the

cards for months now. Tonya loves the
She's
computer game you sent too. ~~She've~~ been

asking me to play with her, but I've been

having too much fun with my cards. How
thinking
have you been? I've been ~~thought~~ about you

a lot. I hope you can come and visit us soon.

Present Perfect and **Present Perfect Progressive**

CHECK POINT

F, T

CHART CHECK

T

EXPRESS CHECK

A: eating
B: has . . . been
A: has OR 's
B: Has
A: No . . . hasn't

2. T 4. F 6. T
3. T 5. T

2. has published
3. have already died
4. has given
5. has spoken
6. have been waiting
7. has lived OR has been living
8. has worked OR has been working
9. has created

2. 've . . . seen
3. has been living OR has lived
4. has experienced
5. has survived
6. have tested
7. have hunted
8. have saved
9. has been moving
10. has been eating
11. (has been) resting
12. has been raining OR has rained
13. have found OR have been finding

Elephants and their ancestors have been
living
~~live~~ on this planet for 5 million years.

Scientists have found their bones in many

places, from Asia to North America. Present-
have
day elephants ~~has~~ also survived in different

kinds of environments, including very dry

areas in Niger, grasslands in East Africa,

and forests in West Africa.

Because of their great size and strength,
fascinated
elephants have always ~~fascinating~~ humans.

Our fascination has almost caused African

elephants to become extinct. Poachers
killed
(illegal hunters) have already ~~been killing~~

hundreds of thousands of elephants for the

ivory of their tusks. After 1989 it became

illegal to sell ivory. Since then, the elephant
grown OR been growing
population has ~~been grown~~ steadily.

Recently several countries have been

protecting elephants in national parks, and
become
herds have ~~became~~ larger and healthier.

 Past Perfect

CHECK POINT

Oprah decided on a career.

CHART CHECK 1

T

CHART CHECK 2

before the subject

EXPRESS CHECK

A: arrived
B: hadn't

2. T 4. F 6. T
3. T 5. F

2. hadn't yet gotten
3. had already gotten
4. hadn't yet been
5. hadn't yet gotten
6. had already been
7. hadn't yet built
8. had already starred

3 **2.** Had he reviewed . . .   No, he hadn't.
     3. Had he reviewed . . .   Yes, he had.
     4. Had he met . . .   No, he hadn't.
     5. Had he taped . . .   Yes, he had.
     6. Had he worked out . . .   Yes, he had.

4 Oprah Winfrey is an amazing person! By the
time she was twelve, she ~~has~~ ^had^ already decided
on a career. Not long afterward, she got her
first radio job. Although she hadn't ~~have~~ ^had^ any
experience, she became a news reporter.
When she got her own TV talk show, she ~~has~~ ^had^
already acted in a major Hollywood movie.
By the late 1980s "Oprah Winfrey" had
~~became~~ ^become^ a household word. Then in 1994 she
decided to improve the quality of talk-show
themes. She also made a personal change.
She had always had a weight problem, but
in 1995 TV viewers saw a new Winfrey.
She had ~~losed~~ ^lost^ almost ninety pounds as a
result of dieting and working out. She had
also ~~compete~~ ^competed^ in a marathon. She has really
been an inspiration to many people.

Past Perfect Progressive

CHECK POINT
  T

CHART CHECK
  been

EXPRESS CHECK
  A: had . . . been practicing
  B: had been practicing
  A: Had . . . been practicing
  B: hadn't, had been practicing

1 **2.** e   **4.** a   **6.** c
     3. d   **5.** f

2 **2.** had been planning
     3. had been joking and laughing
     4. had been practicing
     5. had been running
     6. had been looking forward
     7. had been waiting

3 **3.** had you been running
     4. had you been dating
     5. Had you been living
     6. No, I OR we hadn't
     7. Had you been expecting
     8. No, I hadn't

4 I just got back from the marathon! I'm tired
but very happy. When I crossed the finish
line, I ~~have~~ ^had^ been running for four hours and
twenty-five minutes. Jeremy was standing
there. He had been ~~waited~~ ^waiting^ for me the whole
time. We were both soaking wet—I, because
I had been sweating; he, because it ~~has~~ ^had^ been
raining just a little while before. I was so
glad to see him. I had been ~~look~~ ^looking^ forward to
this day for so long and hoping that I could
finish the race in less than four and a half
hours. When I got home, I called my parents.
They had ^been^ ˄watching the marathon on TV and
had actually seen me cross the finish line!

SelfTest

(Total = 100 points. Each item = 4 points.)

SECTION ONE

1. **C**	5. **B**	9. **C**	12. **A**
2. **D**	6. **C**	10. **A**	13. **D**
3. **C**	7. **B**	11. **B**	14. **B**
4. **A**	8. **B**		

SECTION TWO

(Correct answers are in parentheses.)

15. **C** (*delete* has)
16. **D** (yet)
17. **C** (seemed)
18. **A** ('ve been reading)
19. **A** (Have)
20. **D** (for)
21. **D** (taken)
22. **B** (has already been in business OR for fifty years already)
23. **C** (drink)
24. **C** (*delete* 've)
25. **C** (had)

UNIT 19 — Future: *Be going to* and *Will*

CHECK POINT

The man is going to fall into the hole.

CHART CHECK 1

three

CHART CHECK 2

F

CHART CHECK 3

T

EXPRESS CHECK

It's going to rain.
I'll get an umbrella.

Items checked: 2, 4, 5

2. He's going to take a trip.
3. He's not going to drive. OR He isn't going to drive.
4. He's going to give a speech.
5. He's going to answer the phone.
6. He's not going to watch TV. OR He isn't going to watch TV.

3. 'll . . . use
4. Will . . . get
5. won't
6. will have
7. 'll repair
8. will . . . be
9. will have
10. will look
11. 'll open
12. 'll adjust

13. 'll . . . control
14. Will . . . prevent
15. will
16. will . . . cost
17. won't be

I'm sorry that we ~~will no~~ *won't* be able to get together in Madison. Martha, too, will ~~misses~~ *miss* you. Perhaps we can get together sometime next month. Martha and I ~~am~~ *are* going to be in Minneapolis until July 15. After that, we are going ^*to* visit our son in Phoenix. His wife is pregnant and ~~will~~ *is going to* have a baby the first week in July. It's hard to believe that we're ~~gonna~~ *going to* be grandparents! How exciting that you ^*are* OR *'re* going to talk at the conference! I'm sure it ~~wills~~ *will* be great.

I've got to run now. The sky is getting really dark and ~~it'll~~ *it's going to* storm. I want to get out of this office before then. More later.

UNIT 20 — Future: Contrast

CHECK POINT

T, F

CHART CHECK

T, F

EXPRESS CHECK

I'm leaving in five minutes.
Are you going to the conference in May?

RUSS: Ellen! It's nice to see you. <u>Are</u> you <u>presenting</u> a paper this week?
GREEN: Hi, Rick. Yes. In fact, my talk <u>starts</u> at two o'clock.
RUSS: Oh, maybe <u>I'll go</u>. What <u>are</u> you <u>going to talk</u> about? Robots?
GREEN: Yes. <u>I'm focusing</u> on personal robots for household work.

RUSS: I'd like one of those! Where's your
son, by the way? Is he here with you?

GREEN: No. Tony stays in Denver with his
grandparents in the summer.
I'm going to visit him after the
conference. So, what are you
working on these days?

RUSS: I'm still with the Mars Association.
In fact, we're going to be holding a
news conference next month about
the Mars shuttle launch.

GREEN: That's exciting. Maybe I'll see
you there.

RUSS: Great. The conference begins at
noon on the tenth.

2. it's going to rain
3. I'll see
4. I'll call
5. I'm going
6. I'm mailing
7. I'm giving
8. will you be, lands,
I'll see

1. 'll wait
2. 's going to rain, 'll check OR 'm going to
check
3. do . . . board OR will . . . board OR
are . . . going to board, 're flying
4. 'll carry
5. do . . . land OR are . . . going to land OR
will . . . land OR are . . . landing,
're going to be OR 'll be
6. 're going to get OR get OR 're getting
OR 'll get, 'm having OR 'm going to have
7. 're going to start OR 'll start OR start

4
"Good evening, ladies and gentlemen. This
~~will be~~ *is* your captain speaking. We ~~be~~ *are* going
to leave the Earth's gravity field in about
fifteen minutes. At that time, you ~~are~~ *will be* able to
unbuckle your seat belts and float around
the cabin. Host robots ₐ take orders for *are going to* OR *will*
dinner soon. After these storm clouds,
we ~~are having~~ *'re going to have* OR *'ll have* a smooth trip. The shuttle
arrives on Mars tomorrow at 9:00. Tonight's

temperature on the planet is a mild minus
20 degrees Celsius. By tomorrow morning the
temperature ~~is~~ *will be* 18 degrees, but it ~~is feeling~~ *'s going to feel* OR *'ll feel*
more like 28 degrees. Enjoy your flight."

Future Time Clauses

CHECK **POINT**
The child is planning her future.

CHART CHECK
T, F

EXPRESS CHECK
What will she be when she grows up?
She's going to be a scientist.

2. T
3. F
4. T
5. F
6. T

2. They are going to move to a larger
apartment . . . Jeff gets a raise.
3. . . . they move to a larger apartment,
they're going to have a baby.
4. Sandy will get a part-time job . . . they
have their first child.
5. . . . Sandy goes back to work full-time,
their child will be two.
6. Sandy will work full-time . . . Jeff goes to
school OR Jeff will go to school . . . Sandy
works full-time.
7. Jeff will find another job . . . he graduates.

I.
graduate
II.
1. get, 'll have OR 'm going to have
2. save, 'll buy OR 'm going to buy
3. 'll feel OR 'm going to feel, am
III.
1. get up, 'll buy OR 'm going to buy
2. speak, 'll ask OR 'm going to ask
3. 'll look OR 'm going to look, go
4. go, 'll improve OR 'm going to improve

4 Tomorrow is my first dance recital! By the time I ~~will~~ write my next journal entry, it will already be over! As soon as we finish the performance**,** there ~~are~~ [is] going to be a big party for us. Reporters will be there~~X~~ when we enter the room. While we ~~will~~ celebrate, the press will interview members of the dance group. As soon as I get up Sunday morning**,** I'll buy the paper and read the interviews. We're going to perform this show for two weeks. As soon as it's finished, we ~~learned~~ ['re going to learn OR 'll learn] a new program. I'm so excited. Ever since I was little, I've wanted to be a ballet dancer.

UNIT 22 Future Progressive

CHECK POINT

Before 12:00

CHART CHECK

T

EXPRESS CHECK

Will you be working tomorrow?
Yes, I will. OR No, I won't.
What are you going to be doing?
(Answers will vary.)

1 Today we find most robots working in factories around the world. But what <u>will</u> robots of the future <u>be doing</u>? One Massachusetts Institute of Technology designer predicts that in just a few years, small, intelligent robots <u>are going to be taking</u> care of all the household chores. This is going to make life a lot easier. While one robot is cooking dinner, another one <u>will be vacuuming</u> the floor. But what about outside the home? <u>Will</u> robots <u>be playing</u> <u>football</u> or <u>fighting</u> wars? Scientists aren't sure. What is certain, however, is that robots <u>will be playing</u> a more and more significant role in our lives.

2 1. **c.** 'll be going
2. **a.** are . . . going to be leaving
   b. won't be getting
3. **a.** are . . . going to be coming
   b. 'll be taking
   c. Are . . . going to be having
   d. No, we aren't. OR No, we're not.
4. **a.** 'm going to be visiting
   b. won't be buying

3 2. will be dusting OR is going to be dusting . . . is vacuuming OR vacuums the living room.
3. will be repainting OR is going to be repainting the kitchen . . . is doing OR does the laundry.
4. is making OR makes . . . will be recycling OR is going to be recycling the garbage.
5. will be giving OR is going to be giving Mr. Gee . . . is shopping OR shops for food.
6. will be making OR is going to be making . . . is helping OR helps Tony with homework.
7. is playing OR plays . . . will be walking OR is going to be walking the dog.

4 In the future, robots will be ~~perform~~ [performing] more and more tasks for humans. This will ~~be having~~ [have] both positive and negative effects. On the one hand, while robots ~~will be doing~~ [are doing OR do] the boring and dangerous jobs, humans will be devoting more time to interesting pursuits. In this way robots ~~is~~ [are] going to be making life a lot easier for humans. On the other hand, the widespread use of robots is going [to] create a lot of future unemployment. People will [be] losing their jobs as robots fill their positions. And some robots could even become dangerous.

I'm afraid that in the not-too-distant future,

robots will be operating nuclear power

stations! And before too long, robots are
           fighting
going to be ~~fight~~ in wars. Although, on

second thought, that will be better than

humans killing each other!

 Future Perfect and **Future Perfect Progressive**

CHECK POINT

He hasn't been saving for three years yet.

CHART CHECK 1

F

CHART CHECK 2

T

EXPRESS CHECK

driving, driven

2. F	**4.** F	**6.** T
3. T	**5.** F	

3. won't have graduated
4. will have attended OR will have been attending
5. won't have bought
6. 'll have been driving
7. won't have opened
8. 'll have been saving
9. will have accomplished

3. graduate
4. 'll have already been thinking
5. is born
6. won't have graduated . . . yet
7. will have already finished
8. celebrate
9. won't have started . . . yet
10. 'll have already been getting
11. open
12. 'll have already become

                                    have been
By August I'll ~~be~~ a word processor for
       have earned OR have been earning
ten years. And I'll ~~earn~~ almost the same

salary for three years! That's why I've made

a New Year's resolution to go back to school

this year. First I'm going to write for school

catalogs and start saving for tuition. By March,
           figured
I'll have ~~figure~~ out how much tuition will

cost. Then I'll start applying. By summer,
  'll have
I ~~had~~ received acceptance letters. In August,

I'll talk to my boss about working part-time

and going to school part-time. By that time,
            already saved
I'll have ~~saved already~~ enough to pay for a

semester's tuition. By next New Year's Day,
              studying
I'll have been ~~study~~ for one whole semester!

SelfTest

(Total = 100 points. Each item = 4 points.)

SECTION ONE

1. C	**5.** B	**9.** C	**13.** C
2. A	**6.** B	**10.** A	**14.** B
3. A	**7.** A	**11.** B	
4. B	**8.** B	**12.** C	

SECTION TWO

(Correct answers are in parentheses.)

15. B (be)
16. D (will go)
17. D (finish)
18. C (driving)
19. A (be traveling)
20. A (will finish OR is going to finish)
21. B (work OR be working)
22. C (already OR *delete* yet)
23. A (will you)
24. D (is)
25. B (have)

UNIT 24 *Wh-* Questions: Subject and Predicate

CHECK POINT

the events on the night of May 12th
the names of people who saw the witness

CHART CHECK 1

T

CHART CHECK 2

F, T

EXPRESS CHECK

What happened last night?
What did you do next?

2. a   **4.** b   **6.** e
3. d   **5.** c

2. How did you get home?
3. Who gave you a ride?
4. What happened next?
5. Who(m) did you see?
6. Who is Deborah Collins?
7. What did you do?
8. How many people called you?

3. What time (OR When) does court begin?
4. How many witnesses testified?
5. Why did the jury find Adams guilty?
6. What happened?
7. How long (OR How many weeks) did the trial last?
8. Who spoke to the jury?
9. How much did Adams pay his lawyer?
10. Who(m) did the district attorney question?

                    did
What time˄the suspect return home?
          saw
Who ~~did see~~ him? Were there any witnesses?
Who
~~Whom~~ was at home?

Why did he call A. Smith?
          happened
What ~~did happen~~ next?
          did he
Where ~~he did~~ go?
                    did he take
How much money ~~he took~~ with him?

UNIT 25 Tag Questions

CHECK POINT

The man is commenting on the weather.

CHART CHECK

F, T, T

EXPRESS CHECK

You're an actor, aren't you?

1
KAY: Hi, Tom. It's a nice day, <u>isn't it?</u>
TOM: Sure is. Not a cloud in the sky. How are you doing?
KAY: Good, thanks. You don't know of any vacant apartments, <u>do you?</u> My son is looking for one.
TOM: He is? I thought he was staying with you.
KAY: Well, he really wants a place of his own. Do you know of anything?
TOM: As a matter of fact, I do. You know the Sobotas, <u>don't you?</u> Well, I just found out that they're moving to New York next month.
KAY: They are? What kind of apartment do they have?
TOM: A one-bedroom.
KAY: It's not furnished, <u>is it?</u>
TOM: No. Why? He doesn't need a furnished apartment, <u>does he?</u>
KAY: Well, he doesn't have furniture. But I guess he can always rent some, <u>can't he?</u>
TOM: Why don't you give your son my number, and I'll give him some more information?
KAY: Will you? Thanks, Tom.

2. j   **5.** b   **8.** c
3. h   **6.** g   **9.** e
4. f   **7.** a   **10.** d

2. did you   **5.** aren't you
3. doesn't it   **6.** don't you
4. haven't they   **7.** isn't it

4
                              hasn't
BEN: It's been a long time, Joe, ~~haven't~~ it?

JOE: That depends on what you mean by a
                              it
long time, doesn't ~~that~~?

BEN: What are you doing around here, anyway? It's dangerous.

JOE: I can take care of myself. I'm still
alive, ~~amn't~~ *aren't* I?

BEN: Yes, but you're still wanted by the
police, ~~are~~ *aren't* you?

JOE: Look, I need a place to stay. You have a place, don't you? Just for one night.

BEN: I have to think of my wife and kids.
You can find someplace else, ~~can~~ *can't* you?

JOE: No. You've got to help me!

BEN:: I've already helped you plenty. I went
to jail for you, ~~haven't~~ *didn't* I?

JOE: Yeah, OK, Ben. You remember what
happened in Vegas, ~~do~~ *don't** you?

BEN: OK, OK. I can make a call.

*OR: You don't remember what happened in Vegas, do you?

---

26 **Additions** with *So, Too, Neither,* and *Not either*

CHECK POINT

The men like the same things.

CHART CHECK

T, F, T

EXPRESS CHECK

and neither is Mark
and so does Gerald

| 2. F | 4. T | 6. T | 8. T |
| 3. T | 5. F | 7. F | 9. T |

2
| 2. too | 4. did | 6. So |
| 3. neither | 5. either | 7. So |

3
| 2. did I | 4. do too | 6. do I | 8. too |
| 3. can I | 5. do I | 7. do I |

---

4 My brother is just a year older than I am. We have a lot of things in common.

First of all, we look alike. I am 5'10", and
so ~~he is~~ *is he*. I have straight black hair and dark brown eyes, and so does he. We share many of the same interests too. I love to play soccer,
and he˄ *does* too. Both of us swim every day, but
I can't dive, and ~~either~~ *neither* can he.

Sometimes, being so similar has its problems. For example, last night I wanted the
last piece of chocolate cake, and so ~~does~~ *did* he.
Often I won't feel like doing the dishes, and
neither ~~won't~~ *will* he. Worst of all, sometimes I'm interested in dating a certain schoolmate, and
so ~~he is~~ *is he*. However, most of the time I feel our similarities are really nice. So does my brother.

SelfTest

(Total = 100 points. Each item = 4 points.)

SECTION ONE

1. **A**	4. **A**	7. **D**	10. **A**
2. **C**	5. **D**	8. **D**	11. **B**
3. **A**	6. **D**	9. **B**	12. **C**

SECTION TWO

(Correct answers are in parentheses.)

13. **C** (isn't)
14. **C** (didn't)
15. **D** (has his brother)
16. **D** (have)
17. **A** (did you work OR were you working)
18. **D** (it)
19. **D** (?)
20. **D** (I am too OR so am I)
21. **D** (they)
22. **C** (aren't)
23. **D** (he)
24. **C** (go)
25. **A** (Why did you)

 27 **Ability:**
Can, Could, Be able to

CHECK POINT

F

CHART CHECK 1

T

CHART CHECK 2

be

CHART CHECK 3

a form of *be*

EXPRESS CHECK

A: Is . . . to
B: is . . . can

 1

A surprising number of young people <u>have been able to create</u> successful Web-based businesses. One young entrepreneur is Sam Roberts. Sam <u>could design</u> Web pages when he was eight, but he got his break at twelve when a writer hired him to design a Web site. Sam's first business failed because he and his partner <u>weren't able to get along</u>. However, his new business, Webman, is up and running. Another young businessman, Jay Leibowitz, <u>was able to sell</u> two software programs when he was fourteen. He made $30,000 on the deal and now Jay runs his own Web site. Dan Finley writes reviews of new software. He started his business at sixteen. A full-time college student, Dan <u>can pay</u> a staff of writers and still earn $500 a month. Although they all make money, all three started out to have fun at their hobby, not to make a profit.

2. Sam
3. Dan
4. Sam

 2
1. can, 'll be able to
2. hasn't been able to, can
3. can't, 'll be able to
4. haven't been able to, can't, can't, 'll be able to

3
2. Were . . . able to communicate
3. can help
4. couldn't follow

5. couldn't decide
6. can manage
7. 'll be able to organize
8. be able to speak

 4

Today in my Will B. Happy Teamwork course, I learned about work styles—"Drivers" and "Enthusiasts." I'm a Driver, so I can make decisions, but I'm not able ^to listen to other people's ideas. The Enthusiast in our group can ~~communicates~~ communicate well, but you can't depend on her. Now I understand what was happening in my business class last year, when I couldn't ~~felt~~ feel comfortable with my team. I thought that they all talked too much and ~~didn't~~ weren't able to work efficiently. I ~~could~~ was able to get an A for the course, but it was hard. I can do a lot more alone, but some jobs are too big for that. Our instructor says that soon the Drivers will ^be able to listen and the Enthusiast ~~could~~ will be able to be more dependable.

 28 **Permission:**
May, Can, Could,
Do you mind if . . .?

CHECK POINT

The student is asking the teacher to allow him to take the test tomorrow.

CHART CHECK 1

could

CHART CHECK 2

F, T

EXPRESS CHECK

A: helps
B: Not at all, help

 1
2. f   **4.** c   **6.** b
3. e   **5.** a

2
3. Do you mind if he stays
4. I do
5. May I use
6. you may not OR you can't
7. you can't start
8. do you mind if I borrow
9. Not at all OR No, I don't OR Go right ahead
10. you may open
11. Can I come
12. you can't

3 *(Answers may vary slightly.)*
2. Could I use your phone?
3. May I (OR we) park here?
4. Could we move up a few rows?
5. Can we (OR he) tape the concert?
6. Do you mind if I (OR we) leave?

4
2. B (can't)
3. B (change)
4. B (can)
5. C (have)
6. A (may not OR can't)
7. D (plays)
8. A (No, I don't OR Not at all)
9. C (we)
10. A (Yes, we can OR Sure OR Certainly)

UNIT 29
Requests: *Will, Can, Would, Could, Would you mind . . .?*

CHECK POINT
asking someone to do something

CHART CHECK 1
T

CHART CHECK 2
OK

EXPRESS CHECK
A: Would
B: No, not
A: will OR can OR would OR could
B: can't

1
1. MARCIA: Hi. You must be the new office assistant. I'm Marcia Jones. Let me know if you need anything.
   LORNA: Thanks, Marcia. <u>Could you show me the coat closet?</u>
   MARCIA: Certainly. It's right over here.
2. LORNA: Marcia, <u>would you explain these instructions for the fax machine?</u>
   MARCIA: Sure. Just put your letter in here and dial the number.
3. MARCIA: I'm leaving for lunch. Would you like to come?
   LORNA: Thanks, but I can't right now. I'm really busy.
   MARCIA: Do you want a sandwich from the coffee shop?
   LORNA: That would be great. <u>Can you get me a tuna sandwich and a soda?</u>
   MARCIA: Sure. <u>Will you answer my phone until I get back?</u>
   LORNA: Certainly.
4. MARCIA: Lorna, <u>would you mind making some coffee?</u>
   LORNA: I'm sorry, but I can't do it now. I've got to finish this letter before 2:00.

2
2. a 4. b 6. b
3. a 5. a

3
2. you file these reports?
3. turning on the lights?
4. you buy some cereal?
5. you call back later?
6. you shut the door OR you mind shutting the door?

4
The meetings are going well but they have been extended a day. Could you ~~call please~~ ^{please call} Doug Rogers to try to reschedule our sales meeting?
^{Certainly OR Of course OR Sure}
~~Not at all.~~ **I'll do it right away.**

We'll need three extra copies of the monthly sales report. Would you ask Ann to take care of that?
^{Certainly OR Of course OR Sure}
~~Yes, I would.~~ **(Ann—Could you do this?)**

(continued on next page)

I hate to ask, but would you mind ~~to work~~ *(working)*

on Saturday? We'll need the extra time to go

over the new information I've gotten.

Sorry, but I ~~couldn't~~ *(can't)*. My in-laws are

coming for a visit. But Rob Lin says he

can come in to the office to help out.

One last thing. I was going to pick up those

new business cards, but I won't be back in

time. Would you mind doing that for me?

Not at all OR *I'd be glad to*
~~Yes, I would.~~ I'll stop at the printer's

during my lunch break.

Advice:
*Should, Ought to,
Had better*

CHECK POINT

The interviewer is suggesting a type of job for
the applicant.

CHART CHECK 1

T

CHART CHECK 2

should

EXPRESS CHECK

A: Should
B: No . . . shouldn't

 Items checked: 1, 5, 6

2. shouldn't	**5.** should
3. should	**6.** 'd better not
4. shouldn't	**7.** 'd better

3
2. You should (OR You ought to) look neat
3. What time should I arrive?
4. you shouldn't (OR you'd better not) arrive after 7:15
5. Should I bring a gift?
6. You shouldn't (OR You'd better not) buy an expensive gift

7. What should I buy?
8. you should (OR ought to) get some flowers

4 We are so happy to hear about your new job.

Congratulations! Just remember—you

shouldn't ~~to~~ work too hard. The most

important thing right now is your schoolwork.
ought to
Maybe you only ~~oughta~~ work two days a

week instead of three. Also, we think you'd

better ask your boss for time off during

exams. That way you'll have plenty of time
'd
to study. You ~~would~~ better give this a lot of

careful thought, OK? Please take good care
better not
of yourself. You'd ~~not better~~ start skipping
work
meals, and you definitely shouldn't ~~worked~~
'd
at night. At your age, you ~~will~~ better get a

good night's sleep. Do you need anything

from home? Should we send any of your

books? Let us know.

Suggestions:
*Could, Why don't . . . ?,
Why not . . . ?, Let's,
How about . . . ?*

CHECK POINT

F

CHART CHECK 1

does not change for different subjects

CHART CHECK 2

F

EXPRESS CHECK

Let's take the train.
Maybe we could take the train.
Why not take the train?
How about the train?

1 EMILY: <u>Why don't we go to the races?</u> I hear they're really exciting.
MEGAN: I'd like to, but I need to go shopping.
EMILY: Then <u>let's go to the Temple Street Market tonight.</u> We might even see some Chinese opera in the street while we're there.
MEGAN: That sounds like fun. If we do that, <u>why not go to the races this afternoon?</u>
EMILY: OK, but <u>let's get something to eat first in one of those floating restaurants.</u>
MEGAN: I don't think we'll have time. <u>Maybe we could do that tomorrow.</u> Right now, <u>how about getting *dim sum* at the Kau Kee Restaurant next door?</u> Then <u>we could take the Star Ferry to Hong Kong Island and the racecourse.</u>
EMILY: Sounds good. Here's an idea for tomorrow. <u>Why not take one of those small boats—*kaido*—to Lantau Island?</u> When we come back, <u>we could have dinner at the Jumbo Palace.</u>
MEGAN: <u>Let's do that.</u> It's a little expensive, but at least it floats!

2
2. How about
3. Why don't we
4. Maybe we could
5. Let's
6. Let's not

3
2. going to the beach?
3. buy another one.
4. we take a trip together?
5. try that new seafood place.

4
Emily   3:00

I'm going shopping. I'll be back at 5:00. Let's ~~eating~~ *eat* at 7:00. OK?

Megan

Megan   4:00

7:00 for dinner is **fine**. How about ~~go~~ *going* to a movie afterward?

See you later.

E.

Emily   5:00

I'm going to be too tired for a movie. Maybe we could just ~~hanging~~ *hang* around the hostel after dinner. Let's talk about it later. I'm taking a nap.

M.

M—   6:00

Let's not eat at the same restaurant tonight. Why don't we ~~trying~~ *try* a new place? How about Broadway Seafood? I'll meet you downstairs at 7:00.

E.

UNIT 32 **Preferences:**
Prefer, Would prefer, Would rather

CHECK POINT
Teenagers like to watch TV better than they like to do other things.

CHART CHECK 1
would prefer ('d prefer)

CHART CHECK 2
the gerund or the infinitive

EXPRESS CHECK
read, than, shopping

1
2. F   4. F   6. T
3. F   5. F   7. T

2. I'd rather not cook
3. Would . . . rather go
4. I'd rather not
5. I'd rather have
6. I'd rather not
7. I'd rather see

1. prefer . . . to
2. 'd rather . . . than, prefer OR 'd prefer
3. 'd prefer
4. prefer . . . to
5. 'd rather . . . than
6. do . . . prefer . . . , prefer . . . to

For my study, I interviewed fifty men and women. There was no difference in men's and women's preferences for TV. I found that everyone prefers watching TV ~~than~~ ^{to} going to movies. Men and women both enjoy news programs and entertainment specials. However, men would rather ~~watching~~ ^{watch} adventure programs and science fiction, while women prefer soap operas. Men also like to watch all kinds of sports, but women would rather see game shows ~~to~~ ^{than} sports.

Reading preferences differ too. Men prefer ~~to reading~~ ^{to read OR reading} newspapers, while women would rather read magazines and books. When men read books, they prefer ~~read~~ ^{to read OR reading} nonfiction and adventure stories. Women ~~are preferring~~ ^{prefer} novels.

SelfTest

(Total = 100 points. Each item = 4 points.)

1. **A**	5. **C**	9. **A**	12. **A**
2. **B**	6. **C**	10. **C**	13. **B**
3. **D**	7. **B**	11. **D**	14. **D**
4. **D**	8. **B**		

(Correct answers are in parentheses.)

15. **D** (able to dive)	21. **D** (give)
16. **D** (?)	22. **C** (to)
17. **C** (better not)	23. **C** (was able to)
18. **A** (Would)	24. **C** (*delete* we)
19. **B** (borrow)	25. **D** (than)
20. **D** (ask)	

UNIT 33 **Necessity:** *Have (got) to* and *Must*

CHECK POINT

a requirement

CHART CHECK 1

F

CHART CHECK 2

a form of *do*

EXPRESS CHECK

A: does . . . have to
B: must

1

DMV: Department of Motor Vehicles. May I help you?

BEN: I'm moving to California soon. <u>Will I have to get</u> a California license when I move?

DMV: Yes, you <u>will</u>. California residents <u>must have</u> a California driver's license.

BEN: When <u>will I have to get</u> my California license?

DMV: You <u>have to replace</u> your old license ten days after you become a resident. So come in and apply for your California license right after you get there.

BEN: <u>Do I have to take</u> any tests to exchange my Illinois license for a California license?

DMV: Since you already have an Illinois license, you <u>won't have to take</u> the road test. But you <u>will have to take</u> the written test.

BEN: How about the eye test?

DMV: Oh, everyone <u>has got to take</u> the eye test.

BEN: OK. Thanks a lot. You've been very helpful.

2. 've to (OR 've got to) pick up
3. Do . . . have to change
4. I don't
5. didn't have to do
6. 've to (OR 've got to) take
7. Does . . . have to pack
8. he doesn't
9. 's got to (OR has to) help
10. 've had to call

 2. must turn   **5.** must ride
3. must drive   **6.** must not walk
4. must not drive

 How are you doing? We've been here about

six weeks. It's strange living in the suburbs.

There's no public transportation, so you've
got
~~get~~ to drive everywhere. I had to ~~signs~~ sign up

for driver's ed this semester so I can get my

license by summertime. It's the law here that
must
everyone ~~musts~~ wear a seat belt. I used to

hate to buckle up, but with the traffic here,

I have changed my mind. There are a lot of
got to
freeways, and you've ~~gotta~~ know how to

change lanes with a lot of fast traffic. Even my
has
Mom ~~have~~ had to get used to it. Dad works at
had
home, so he hasn't ~~has~~ to do a lot of driving.

Have you beaten those computer games

yet? I'm having a lot of trouble with "Doom."
've
You ‸got to write to me and tell me how to

get past the fifth level!

 Choice: *Don't have to*
No Choice: *Must not*
and *Can't*

 **POINT**
stop to ask for directions

CHART CHECK 1
do

CHART CHECK 2
F

EXPRESS
He doesn't have to stop here.
You must not drive too fast.

 New drivers are usually excited about their
new freedom: "My mom <u>doesn't have to drive</u>
me everywhere anymore! I <u>don't have to ask</u>
my friends for rides to school!" When you
don't have your own car yet, any price seems
worth paying. But once you buy a car, you
can't forget your car payments and insurance
premiums, or you won't be a driver for very
long. You can't leave gas and maintenance
out of the budget either. Car sharing offers
an alternative to these problems, however.
Members of car-sharing groups have a car
when they need one for either short trips
or vacations, but they don't have the high
expenses of ownership. They pay very little
to use a shared car, and they <u>don't have to</u>
<u>worry</u> about maintaining the car or paying
the insurance. Fees for short trips are only
about $3.00 an hour plus $0.50 per mile.
Groups do not have strict requirements
either. Members must not have bad
driving records or poor credit, and they
must not return the cars in poor shape or
they will pay extra.

 2. can't yell   **6.** don't have to get
3. can't turn   **7.** haven't had to buy
4. can't park   **8.** can't bring
5. don't have to worry **9.** don't have to listen

2. don't have to bring **5.** don't have to be
3. must not play   **6.** don't have to leave
4. must not dive

We got to the motel late this evening because

we got lost. But we were lucky—they kept
didn't have to
our room so we ~~must not~~ find another motel.

(continued on next page)

Jimmy is really happy because he ~~don't~~ *doesn't* have

to go to bed until after 10:00, when the

swimming pool closes. We ~~mustn't~~ *don't have to* leave

until 11:00 tomorrow (checkout time), so

we can stay up later. Yosemite is only four

hours away, so we won't ~~had~~ *have* to drive the

whole day tomorrow. It's going to be exciting.

My parents say we absolutely must not ~~to~~

go out by ourselves because there are bears

there. I'd love to see a bear (from the inside

of the car). I'll send a postcard of one.

 ## Expectations:
Be supposed to

 **POINT**

the usual way something is done at a wedding

CHART CHECK

T

EXPRESS CHECK

A: were
B: was

It <u>Wasn't Supposed to Be</u> a Big Wedding

Providence, July 19—The Stricklands
wanted a quiet wedding—that's why they
eloped to Block Island, off the Atlantic Coast
of the United States. The island is quite
small, so the Stricklands packed their bikes
for the ferry trip. The weather <u>was supposed
to be</u> lovely, and they had asked the mayor
to marry them on a hill overlooking
the ocean.

"When we got there, we found a crowd of
cyclists admiring the view," laughed Beth.

When Bill kissed his bride, the audience
burst into loud applause and rang their
bicycle bells. "We <u>weren't supposed to have</u>

fifty wedding guests, but we love cycling,
and we're not sorry," Bill said.

While packing the next day, Beth left
her wedding bouquet at the hotel. Minutes
before the ferry <u>was supposed to leave</u>, Bill
jumped on his bike, got the flowers, and
made it back to the ferry on time. "Cyclists
<u>are supposed to stay</u> fast and fit," he said.

2. F **3.** F **4.** T **5.** T

 2. a. Were . . . supposed to do
 b. No, they weren't
 c. were supposed to deliver
3. a. is supposed to start
 b. are . . . supposed to stand
4. a. aren't (OR 're not) supposed to be
 b. aren't (OR 're not) supposed to see
5. a. 'm supposed to wear
 b. 's supposed to rain
6. a. 's supposed to be

I'm so sorry—I know I ~~am~~ *was* supposed to write

to you last week about my plans to visit.

I've been awfully busy. My friend Netta is

getting married soon, and she's asked me to

be her maid of honor. She and Gary want a

big wedding. They're supposed to have

about two hundred guests. I have a lot of

responsibilities. I ~~will be~~ *am* supposed to give

Netta a shower before the wedding (that's a

party where everyone brings presents for the

bride). I am also ~~suppose~~ *supposed* to help her choose

the bridesmaids' dresses. The best man's name

is Jim. He'll help Gary get ready. I haven't

met him yet, but he's ~~supposes~~ *supposed* to be very nice.

I'd better say goodbye now. I *was* supposed

to leave for rehearsal five minutes ago.

P.S. About my visit—I'm ~~supposing~~ *supposed* to get some

time off in July. Would that be convenient?

UNIT 36 Future Possibility:
May, Might, Could

CHECK POINT

F

CHART CHECK 1

T

CHART CHECK 2

in answers

EXPRESS CHECK

B: might
A: might
B: might not

ALICE: I just heard that it <u>may snow</u> today. Are you going to drive to work?
BILL: No. I'll take the 7:30 train instead.
ALICE: I'll take the train with you. I have some work to do in the library.
BILL: Great. Why don't you cut your afternoon class and have lunch with me too?
ALICE: Oh, I <u>couldn't do</u> that. But let's meet at the train station at 6:00, OK?
BILL: I <u>might have to work</u> until 8:00 tonight. I'll call you and let you know.

1. Certain
2. Impossible
3. Possible

2. could	**4.** may not	**6.** may
3. might	**5.** 'm going to	**7.** might

3. She's going to a meeting with Mrs. Humphrey at 11:00.
4. She may (OR might) have coffee with Sue after class.
5. She's going to go to work at 1:00.
6. She may (OR might) go shopping after work.
7. She may (OR might) take the 7:00 train.
8. She's going to pick up pizza.

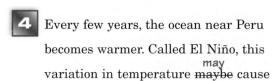

Every few years, the ocean near Peru

becomes warmer. Called El Niño, this

                  may
variation in temperature ~~maybe~~ cause

weather changes all over the world. The

west coasts of North and South America

might ~~to~~ have heavy rains. On the other side

                    become
of the Pacific, New Guinea might ~~becomes~~

very dry. Northern areas could have warmer,

wetter winters, and southern areas could

become much colder. These weather changes

                    may not
affect plants and animals. Some fish ~~mayn't~~

survive in warmer waters. Droughts could
    cause
~~causing~~ crops to die, and food may get very

expensive. El Niño may happen every two
         may OR might
years, or it ~~could~~ not come for seven years.

Will El Niños get worse in the future? They

could ~~be~~. Pollution holds heat in the air, and
may OR might OR could
it ~~will~~ increase the effects of El Niño, but no

one is sure yet.

UNIT 37 Assumptions:
May, Might, Could, Must, Have (got) to, Can't

CHECK POINT

making a guess

CHART CHECK 1

T

CHART CHECK 2

F

EXPRESS CHECK

A: could
B: might, can't

2. d	**4.** b	**6.** a
3. e	**5.** g	**7.** c

2. must	**6.** might be
3. 's got to	**7.** couldn't
4. could	**8.** might not
5. Could	**9.** may

3
2. I might (OR could) be
3. It could (OR might OR may) be the cat
4. You must eat a lot
5. Could it be
6. it can't (OR couldn't) be
7. It must come from your own pipe.
8. There can't (OR couldn't) be any other explanation.
9. there could (OR might OR may) be

4
The main character, Molly Smith, is a college ESL teacher. She is trying to find her dead grandparents' first home in the United States. It may ~~being~~ *be* in a nearby town.

The townspeople there seem scared. They could ~~be~~ have a secret, or they ~~must~~ *might OR may OR could* just hate strangers. Molly has some old letters that might lead her to the place. They are in Armenian, but one of her students ~~mights~~ *might* translate them for her. They ~~hafta~~ *have to* be important because the author mentions them right away. The letter must contain family secrets. Who is the bad guy? It couldn't be the student because he wants to help. It might ~~to~~ be the newspaper editor in the town.

UNIT 38 **Advisability** in the Past

CHECK **POINT**
regrets things in his past

CHART CHECK 1
F

CHART CHECK 2
T

CHART CHECK 3
ought to have

A: have
B: should have

 1
2. T   4. F   6. T
3. T   5. T

 2
2. shouldn't have done
3. should have studied
4. could have done
5. ought to have gone
6. shouldn't have stayed
7. could have prevented
8. might . . . have called
9. Should . . . have contacted
10. shouldn't have
11. could have saved

3
2. I shouldn't have eaten all the chocolate.
3. She might have called.
4. He could have offered to lend me some (money).
5. I shouldn't have jogged five miles yesterday.
6. They shouldn't have charged me (for the plastic bags).
7. I ought to have invited Cynthia (to the party).
8. He might have sent me a card.

4
About a week ago, Jennifer was late for work again, and Doug, our boss, told me he wanted to get rid of her. I was really upset. Of course, Jennifer shouldn't ~~had~~ *have* been late so often, but he might ~~has~~ *have* talked to her about the problem before he decided to let her go. Then he told me to make her job difficult for her so that she would quit.

I just pretended I didn't hear him. What a mistake! I ~~oughta~~ *ought to* have confronted him right away. Or I could at least have warned Jennifer. Anyway, Jennifer is still here, but now I'm worried about my own job. Should I ~~of~~ *have* told Doug's boss? I wonder.

Maybe I should ~~handle~~ *have handled* things differently last week. The company should never ~~has~~ *have* hired this guy.

Speculations about the Past

CHECK *POINT*

if it was possible that something happened

CHART CHECK 1

T

CHART CHECK 2

could

EXPRESS CHECK

have carved, might have

 1

2. a   4. c   6. b
3. f   5. d

 2

2. They must have been
3. They may have
4. He might not have been
5. He must have

 3

2. could not have built
3. had to have gotten
4. must not have known
5. could have carved
6. (could have) transported
7. might have been
8. may have lived
9. must have had

 4

In 1927, Toribio Mexta Xesspe of Peru must ~~be~~ *have been* very surprised to see lines in the shapes of huge animals on the ground below his airplane. Created by the ancient Nazca culture, these forms are too big to recognize from the ground. However, from about 600 feet in the air the giant forms take shape. Without airplanes, how could an ancient culture ~~had~~ *have* made them? What purpose could they have had? Author Erich von Däniken believes that the drawings might have ~~mark~~ *marked* a landing strip for the spacecraft of astronauts from another planet. Archaeologists, however, now believe that the ancient Nazcan civilization might ~~develop~~ *have developed* flight. They could ~~of~~ *have* built hot-air balloons and ~~design~~ *designed* the pictures from the air.

SelfTest

(Total = 100 points. Each item = 4 points.)

SECTION **ONE**

1. **C**	5. **A**	8. **B**	11. **B**
2. **B**	6. **B**	9. **D**	12. **A**
3. **B**	7. **D**	10. **A**	13. **C**
4. **B**			

SECTION **TWO**

(Correct answers are in parentheses.)

14. **C** (must not have known)
15. **D** (leave)
16. **C** (have)
17. **B** (looked)
18. **A** (have got to)
19. **C** (can't)
20. **A** (must not)
21. **B** (have)
22. **A** (may OR might OR could)
23. **A** (was OR is)
24. **C** (have to)
25. **A** (should have)

Adjectives and Adverbs

CHECK *POINT*

warm and cozy

CHART CHECK

F, F, T

EXPRESS CHECK

A: slow, slowly
B: slow, slow

1 Students! Are you looking for a <u>special</u> place to live? Come to 140 Grant street, Apt. 4B. This apartment is ⟨absolutely⟩<u>perfect</u> for two <u>serious</u> students who are looking for a <u>quiet</u> neighborhood, just 15 minutes from campus. This <u>lovely</u> apartment is in a <u>new</u> building. It is a <u>short</u> walk to the bus stop. The <u>express</u> bus goes ⟨directly⟩into town. At night the bus ⟨hardly⟩makes any stops at all. You can <u>walk</u> ⟨safely⟩through the <u>wonderful</u> parks on your way home. The rent is ⟨very⟩<u>affordable</u>.

Call for an appointment: 555-5050.

This apartment will rent⟨fast⟩.

2 **2.** terribly disappointed
3. surprisingly easy
4. extremely safe
5. incredibly fast
6. awfully slowly
7. very clearly
8. unusually loud
9. exceptionally pleasant

3 **2.** large   **7.** quiet
3. beautifully   **8.** hardly
4. happily   **9.** nice
5. busy   **10.** shy
6. nice   **11.** good

4 Some apartment ads are so ~~funnily~~ _funny_! One ad described a place as "~~warmly~~ _warm_ and cozy." It was really hot and crowded, but the owner insisted that it suited me ~~perfect~~ _perfectly_. I was trying very ~~hardly~~ _hard_ not to laugh while he was describing it, so I had to leave quickly. Another place I saw was supposed to be "nice and ~~cutely~~ _cute_."

What a mess!! I left that place very ~~fastly~~ _fast_ too. I'm not asking for the moon! I only want a small place in a clean building with friendly neighbors. I'm looking at another place tomorrow. The ad says, "Clean and bright. Small but convenient apartment on lovely, ~~quietly~~ _quiet_ block." I wonder what that really means!

UNIT 41 Participial Adjectives

CHECK POINT

F

CHART CHECK

T

EXPRESS CHECK

exciting	excited
interesting	interested
frightening	frightened
amusing	amused
tiring	tired

1 In some countries, people who are <u>interested</u> in meeting others turn for help to personal ads in newspapers and magazines, and online. A ⟨surprising⟩number of busy people view these ads as a practical way of increasing their social circle. "I've tried hard to meet people on my own," said one <u>satisfied</u> customer. "I was new in town and wanted to make friends fast. The personals provided me with a quick way of meeting many ⟨interesting⟩people in a short period of time." Others are not so <u>impressed</u>. "I think it's kind of ⟨depressing⟩when people need to resort to placing ads to make friends," observed one man. "A friend of mine tried the ads several times and was really <u>disappointed</u> with the results. It's just not personal enough."

2. puzzled
3. puzzling
4. interesting
5. interested
6. fascinating

7. fascinated
8. disappointed
9. surprising
10. surprised

2. boring
3. interested
4. fascinating
5. amused
6. horrifying

7. confusing
8. depressed
9. amazed
10. amusing
11. exhausted

 disappointed
Just got home. I'm ~~disappointing~~ with the

 interesting
evening. At first I thought Jake was an ~~interested~~ guy, but tonight I felt somewhat

 entertaining
bored with his company. We saw a very ~~entertained~~ movie, but Jake didn't like it.

In fact, it seems like we have completely

different tastes in things. After the movie,

I tried to make conversation, but all I really

wanted was to go home. So, I told him I was
 exhausted
~~exhausting~~ and didn't want to get home late.
 interested
If he asks me out again—I'm not ~~interesting~~.
 frustrating
Trying to meet people can be very ~~frustrated~~.

Adjectives and **Adverbs:**
Equatives

CHECK POINT

riding speed, control of bike

CHART CHECK

as, an adjective or an adverb

EXPRESS CHECK

A: as expensive as, as well as   **B:** as good as

So you were riding the trails this weekend, and you hit the dirt. Now your clothes look <u>as bad as</u> your bike. Never mind. They'll look <u>as good as</u> new next weekend. We checked out three major brands of detergent,

and we can tell you which ones clean best and which ones don't remove trail stains as effectively as others.

 Overall, Brite and Kleen aren't <u>as expensive as</u> Trend, but they didn't perform as well either. However, they were almost <u>as good</u> in particular categories. Trend removed both mud and grass stains effectively. Brite removed mud just as effectively as Trend, but it didn't remove grass stains as well. Kleen was effective on grass stains, but not on mud. Brite cleaned clothes as thoroughly as Kleen, but again, Brite and Kleen weren't <u>as good as</u> Trend in this category. On the other hand, Brite came out on top in brightening. Colors washed in Kleen and Trend just didn't look <u>as bright as</u> the ones washed in Brite.

1. **b.** aren't as wide
  c. aren't as hard
2. **a.** cleans as effectively as
  b. isn't as unfriendly
  c. sounds as exciting as
  d. expresses . . . as clearly as
3. **a.** was as noisy as
  b. (will) pedal as quietly as

2. doesn't stop as slowly as
3. isn't as expensive as
4. doesn't feel as comfortable as
5. isn't as cheap
6. rides as comfortably as
7. handles as well as
8. don't handle as well as
9. shifts as easily as

RE: Not as many bruises!

Inexperienced riders should try the South

Trail at Bearpaw Park. The scenery is just
 beautiful
as ~~beautifully,~~ but its riding track isn't as
 as
unfriendly ~~than~~ the North Trail's. The

slopes aren't as steep, and you won't fall
 frequently
as ~~frequent~~ because there aren't as many

(continued on next page)

                    as

rocks. It isn't as short ~~like~~ the North, so

you'll still get a good ride, and you won't

feel as discouraged at the end of the day.

RE: the (expensive) new Trax

Does anyone have any experience with

this bike? I test-drove it around the store

parking lot, and I'm not impressed. My old

          just as

Trax shifts ~~as just~~ easily, and it handles as

                light

smoothly too. Of course it's not as ~~lightly~~,

but then it doesn't cost $999 either.

 Adjectives: Comparatives

CHECK *POINT*

different from the old restaurant

CHART CHECK

F, T

EXPRESS **CHECK**

more . . . than

1 **2.** T   **3.** T   **4.** F   **5.** F

2
2. less expensive than OR isn't more
    expensive than
3. hotter . . . spicier than
4. more fattening than
5. healthier OR more healthy than

3
2. better . . . better,
    the better . . . the more expensive
3. the more popular . . . the slower
4. worse . . . worse, the smokier . . . the worse
5. The more crowded . . . the noisier
6. The bigger . . . the harder
7. more . . . more delicious, heavier . . . heavier

4 Pete's Place has just reopened under new

management. The dining room looks bigger,

  brighter   *than*

~~more bright~~, and prettier ~~as~~ the old one.

Although the food isn't better, it *is* just as

good. The menu is more varied and less

  expensive

~~expensiver~~. Try one of their pasta dishes.

You won't find a ~~more~~ fresher tomato sauce

in town. And leave room for dessert. They

        better

just keep getting ~~good~~ and better.

    The wait staff is friendly but not able to

                    more

handle large numbers of people—the crowded

the restaurant, the slower the service. At

dinnertime the lines outside this popular

                  longer

eatery are getting longer and ~~more long~~. Try

              more relaxed

lunchtime for a quieter and ~~relaxeder~~ meal.

 Adjectives: Superlatives

CHECK *POINT*

special

CHART CHECK

the, –est, most or *least*

EXPRESS **CHECK**

(the) nicest
(the) most beautiful
(the) warmest
(the) happiest

1 You are the best mother in the whole wide
world. You are the smartest, the brightest,
and the funniest of all moms I've ever
known. You are the nicest mom I've ever
had. You are the most wonderful and
definitely the least mean. No mom in the
whole wide world is better than you. You are
the greatest mother of all. I love you very,
very much! Happy Mother's Day!

2
2. the happiest . . . of my life
3. the best . . . in the school
4. the coldest . . . of the year
5. the nicest . . . in our family OR of all
6. the wisest . . . of all OR in our family

2. is the most unusual gift.
3. is the least practical gift.
4. is the smallest gift.
5. is the biggest gift.
6. is the most expensive gift.
7. is the funniest gift.

                                          most serious
Ramadan is the ~~seriousest~~ time in Muslim culture. During Ramadan, we do not eat from sunup to sunset. This is difficult for everyone, but teenagers have the hardest time. Right after Ramadan is the Eid al-Fitr. This holiday lasts three days, and it's the ~~most~~ happiest time of the year. The morning of Eid, my family gets up early and goes to the mosque. After we greet our neighbors by saying "Eid Mubarek" (Happy Eid), we go
                           biggest
home. We eat the ~~big~~ breakfast you have ever seen. Our parents give us gifts, usually new clothes and money. One year, Eid came around the time I graduated from high school. That year, I got the most beautiful
                      fattest
clothes and the ~~fatter~~ envelope of money of all the children in my family. Eid Mela is part of Eid al-Fitr. On that day, we all go to a big park. Last year at Eid Mela, I had the
best
~~better~~ time of my life. I met my old high school friends, and we all ate junk food and showed off our new clothes.

Adverbs: Comparatives and Superlatives

 **POINT**

T

CHART CHECK

more or *less, the*

EXPRESS CHECK

than, the best

In the first soccer game of the season, the Golds beat the Silvers, 6 to 3. The Silver team played a truly fantastic game, but its defense is still weak. The Golds defended the ball much <u>more aggressively than</u> the Silver team did. Of course, Ace Jackson certainly helped win the game for the Golds. The Golds' star player was back on the field today to the delight of his many fans. He was hurt badly at the end of last season, but he has recovered quickly. Although he didn't play as well as people expected, he still handled the ball like the old Ace. He certainly handled it <u>the most skillfully</u> of anyone on the team. He controlled the ball <u>the best</u>, kicked the ball <u>the farthest</u>, and ran <u>the fastest</u> of any of the players on either team. He played hard and helped the Golds look good. In fact, <u>the harder</u> he played, <u>the better</u> the Golds performed. Watch Ace this season.

And watch the Silvers. They have a new coach, and they're training <u>more seriously</u> this year. I think we'll see them play <u>better and better</u> as the season progresses.

2. better
3. faster
4. less
5. more rapidly
6. harder
7. the most slowly OR the slowest
8. the most clearly
9. the longest
10. more quickly than
11. more completely than

3. the most slowly OR the slowest
4. more slowly than OR slower than
5. the farthest
6. faster than
7. higher than
8. the best
9. the worst

4 Last night I watched the Lakers and the

Bulls. Both teams played more aggressively
~~than~~
^I've ever seen them. In fact, they played the
^best
~~better~~ of any game I've watched this season.

In the first half, Michael Jordan sprained his

left ankle, and Shaquille O'Neal was out of

the game because of fouls. But they still didn't
than
start the second half any slower ~~that~~ the first.

With Jordan out, Kukoc scored the most
frequently
~~frequenter~~ of any player. He's been playing
better and
~~more and more~~ better as the season goes on.
the
In fact, ^more he plays, the better he looks.

The Bulls won 97 to 88. The Lakers seemed
less
to get tired at the end. They played ~~little~~

and less consistently as the game went on.

SelfTest

(Total = 100 points. Each item = 4 points.)

SECTION ONE

1. **C**	5. **C**	9. **D**	12. **C**
2. **A**	6. **A**	10. **B**	13. **D**
3. **A**	7. **B**	11. **A**	14. **B**
4. **B**	8. **C**		

SECTION TWO

(Correct answers are in parentheses.)

15. **C** (the less)   21. **B** (*delete* more)
16. **C** (of)   22. **B** (most)
17. **B** (amazed)   23. **C** (more)
18. **C** (cute)   24. **C** (disgusting)
19. **B** (harder)   25. **B** (hot)
20. **A** (run as quickly)

 Gerunds:
Subject and Object

CHECK POINT

exercise

CHART CHECK

–ing, not

EXPRESS CHECK

A: Drinking
B: drinking
A: not drinking

1 Swimming is great exercise. It's healthy,
fun, and relaxing. Because swimming is a
"low-impact" sport, most people enjoy
participating in this activity without fear of
injury to their bones or muscles. Jogging,
which is a "high-impact" activity, can at
times be harmful. I know this from personal
experience. Last year while I was jogging,
I injured my right knee. I don't go jogging
anymore. After a painful month of recovery,
I stopped running and switched to water
sports. I'm now considering joining a
swimming team and competing in races.

2
2. Eating   6. swimming
3. Not drinking   7. walking, running
4. increasing   8. not going
5. doing

3
2. quit smoking
3. go swimming
4. denied OR denies smoking
5. acknowledges being
6. is avoiding eating
7. is considering taking

4
Smoking
Ways I Can Quit ~~Smoke~~ Cigarettes
smoking
Pick an exact date to quit ~~smoke~~.
Cutting
Stop smoking completely. (~~Cut~~ down is

harder than stopping all at once.)
being
Avoid ~~to be~~ around other smokers

(at least at the beginning).

Exercising
Start exercising daily. ~~To exercise~~ can

   reduce stress.
Not
~~No~~ drinking coffee may help too.
       being
Imagine ~~been~~ a non-smoker. Positive mental

   images can help.
       joining
Consider ~~to join~~ a support group.
          asking
Don't delay ~~to ask~~ for help. Call Dr. Burns

   right away!

Keep trying and don't give up!

47 Gerunds after Prepositions

CHECK POINT
   F, T, F

CHART CHECK
   a preposition, the gerund

EXPRESS CHECK
   A: joining
   B: joining

 We, the members of the Student Council, would like to share with you the thoughts and concerns of the general student body. As you probably know, many students are complaining about life on campus. We are interested in meeting with you to discuss our ideas for dealing with these complaints.
   We know that you are tired of hearing students complain and that you are not used to working with the Student Council. However, if you really believe in giving new ideas a try, we hope you will think about speaking with our representatives soon. We look forward to hearing from you soon.

 2. in listening
   3. about going, about driving
   4. to staying, relaxing
   5. for having
   6. at learning
   7. on coming
   8. on reading, (on) going

 2. We can make changes by telling the administration about our concerns.
   3. The administration can help by listening to our concerns.
   4. In some cases, students just complain instead of making suggestions for improvements.
   5. Students get annoyed with some teachers for coming late to class.
   6. You can improve your grades by studying regularly.

4 I have been attending Longtree College for
                                     studying
a year. I'm very happy about ~~study~~ here.

At first, it was a little hard getting used to
speaking
~~speak~~ English all the time, but now I feel
                         communicating
very comfortable about ~~communicate~~ in my

second language.

   I just joined an international student
                     about
group, and I'm excited ~~with~~ meeting new

people. Summer break is coming, and a few
                              doing
of us are planning on ~~do~~ some traveling
              joining
together. Before ~~to join~~ this group, I used to

spend holidays alone.
                                    hearing
   Please write. I look forward to ~~hear~~

from you!

48 Infinitives after Certain Verbs

CHECK POINT
   Megan thinks "Impatient" should consider his proposal more.

CHART CHECK
   F, T, F

EXPRESS CHECK
   I want to write to Annie.

1 Slow down! You <u>appear to be</u> in too much of a hurry. You've only known this person for a month and yet you <u>asked her to marry</u> you! What's the big rush? *Why* can't you <u>afford to wait</u>? Are you afraid that if she <u>gets to know</u> you better, she may <u>decide not to tie</u> the knot? I agree with your girlfriend. You <u>need to consider</u> things more carefully. You can't <u>expect her (or yourself) to make</u> such an important decision so quickly. If you don't <u>want to regret</u> a hasty decision, I <u>advise you both to get to know</u> each other better before you hurry to the altar.

2
2. attempt to find
3. warns single people not to leave
4. urges them to use
5. fail to plan
6. plan to fail
7. wish to meet
8. Ask two friends to read
9. Choose to participate
10. advises people not to feel
11. wants to be

3 *(Answers may vary slightly.)*
2. would like Tom to call her at 10:00.
3. reminded Emily to buy gas (today).
4. invited Marta to join them for coffee.
5. agreed to be home by 10:30.
6. forgot to go to the 2:00 staff meeting.
7. encouraged her to try again.
8. needs to use the car (tonight).

4 Annie advised me ~~joining~~ ^{to join} a club or take a

class, and I finally did it! I decided_∧^{to} become a

member of the school's Outdoor Adventure

Club, and I went to my first meeting last

night. I'm really excited about this. The club

is planning a hiking trip next weekend. I

definitely want to go rafting in the spring.

At first I didn't want ~~signing~~ ^{to sign} up, but the

leader was so nice. He urged me ~~to not~~ ^{not to} miss

this trip, so I put my name on the list. After

the meeting, a group of people asked me to

go out with them. We went to a coffee shop

and talked for hours. Well, I hoped_∧^{to} make

some friends when I joined this club, but

I didn't expect everyone ~~being~~ ^{to be} so friendly.

I'm glad Annie persuaded me ~~no~~ ^{not} to give up.

UNIT 49 **Infinitives** after Certain Adjectives and Certain Nouns

CHECK POINT
Finding good fries is difficult.

CHART CHECK
to + base form of verb
certain nouns and adjectives

EXPRESS CHECK
It's convenient to eat fast food.
That's a low price to pay.

1 Please take a few <u>minutes to complete</u>^N this questionnaire about fast-food restaurants. Check (✓) all the answers that are appropriate for you.
1. How often are you <u>likely to eat</u>^A at a fast-food restaurant?
   ❏ 1–3 times a week
   ❏ 4–6 times a week
   ❏ more than 6 times a week
   ❏ never
2. In your opinion, fast food is:
   ❏ <u>good to eat</u>^A
   ❏ a <u>way to save</u>^N time
   ❏ <u>fun to order</u>^A occasionally
   ❏ <u>unhealthy to have</u>^A every day
3. Which statement best describes your feelings about the cost of fast food?
   ❏ It's a high <u>price to pay</u>^N for convenience.
   ❏ You get a lot for just a little money.
4. Is it a good <u>idea to include</u>^N healthy choices in fast-food menus?
   ❏ Yes   ❏ No

2. delighted to find
3. way to go
4. fun to eat
5. pleasure to eat
6. mistake to bring
7. outrageous to see
8. good to eat
9. essential to have
10. difficult to go

3

2. ready to cry
3. willing to work
4. hard to wake up
5. surprised to hear
6. eager to get
7. important to keep
8. time to decide
9. chance to show
10. easy to find

4

Tonight I made the decision ~~asked~~ *to ask* Chris to take the night shift. I really thought she was going to be glad ~~for getting~~ *to get* the offer. She has her own rent ^*to* pay, and I know it's hard for ~~she~~ *her* to meet all her expenses. Looks like she was the wrong person ~~I asked~~ *to ask*! The problem was, she wasn't willing to ~~said~~ *say* Yes or No, and I'm afraid I got a little impatient. It was wrong of me to threaten to ask Steve. I could tell that she was pretty upset to hear that. I'll think about giving her the promotion anyway. She deserves ~~getting~~ *to get* a break.

Infinitives with *Too* and *Enough*

 **POINT**
F, T

CHART CHECK
too

EXPRESS CHECK
She's too young to vote.
We're old enough to work.

2. b
3. a
4. b
5. a
6. b

2. It's too far for us to get home by ten. **G**
3. I'm mature enough to take care of myself. **G**
4. It's too dangerous to drive at night. **M**
5. I worry too much to give you permission. **M**
6. You aren't experienced enough to drive that far. **M**

3

2. cheap enough for us to afford
3. large enough to hold
4. too good for me to miss
5. big enough to share
6. too late to stop
7. old enough to stay
8. early enough to come
9. too slow to beat
10. safe enough to drive

4

The Phish concert was awesome! Now I'm too excited ~~for sleeping~~ *to sleep*. That Mike Gordon can really sing. My voice isn't ~~enough good~~ *good enough* to sing in the shower! After the concert we were really hungry, but it was ~~to~~ *too* late to go for pizza. I HATE this stupid curfew! It's too weird ^*to* understand. My friend Todd works and has to pay taxes, but the law says he's too young ~~for staying~~ *to stay* out past 10:00! That's crazy enough to make me want to scream. That reminds me. I sure hope my mother changes her mind soon enough for ~~I~~ *me* to buy a ticket to the Hampton concert. They sell out very quickly. Why doesn't she think I'm mature ^*enough* to drive fifty miles? I'll have to do it sometime! Well, I'd better try to get some sleep or I'll be too tired ~~too~~ *to* get up in the morning.

Infinitives of Purpose

CHECK **POINT**

an address book, a dictionary, a note pad

CHART CHECK

T, F

EXPRESS CHECK

I use an organizer to store addresses.
I set my alarm clock in order not to oversleep.

 YOKO: It's 5:00. Aren't you going home?
LEE: No. I'm staying late <u>to finish</u> this report. What about you? Are you going straight home?
YOKO: No. I'm going to stop at the bank <u>to get</u> some cash. Then I'm going to Lacy's Department Store <u>to take</u> advantage of the sale they're having.
LEE: Oh, what are you going to get?
YOKO: One of those new electronic organizers they're advertising. I've been looking for something <u>to help</u> me with my work.
LEE: What's wrong with just a regular calculator?
YOKO: Nothing. But sometimes I have to convert other currencies to dollars.
LEE: What else are you going to use it for?
YOKO: Oh, <u>to store</u> important names and phone numbers and <u>to balance</u> my checkbook.
LEE: What did we do before they invented all these electronic gadgets?
YOKO: We made a lot of mistakes!

 2. To withdraw $100.
3. To invite Rika and Taro to dinner.
4. To buy milk and eggs.
5. To buy batteries.
6. To get gas.

 First Part:
3. f   **4.** a   **5.** d   **6.** e   **7.** c
Second Part:
3. She went to the store (in order) to buy some dishes.
4. We disconnected our phone in order not to get any phone calls.

5. He turned on the radio (in order) to listen to the news.
6. He didn't tell me he was sick in order not to worry me.
7. She bought a Datalator (in order) to store information.

 I went to Dr. Towbin <s>for getting</s> ^to get^ my teeth cleaned today. While I was waiting, I used my Datalator to study for the TOEFL. Then I used it to <s>helps</s> ^help^ me pronounce "novocaine" and "dental floss" for my appointment. After the dentist, I checked my schedule and saw "Rika and Taro, dinner, 7:30." I should use it in order <s>to not</s> ^not to^ forget appointments! Luckily, my recipes are already on the Datalator, so I used them <s>for making</s> ^to make^ a quick shopping list. When I got home, there was a note on my door—"Call bldg. super." I checked the Datalator dictionary to find "bldg. super." The "building superintendent" wanted to come up in order ^to^ fix the doorbell! Rika, Taro, and I played with the Datalator all evening. You can program it <s>for</s> to play computer games too. I don't know how I lived without it!

 Gerunds and **Infinitives**

CHECK **POINT**
F, T

CHART CHECK
T, F, T

EXPRESS CHECK
to go, Going, talking, to talk OR talking

 **2.** T   **4.** T   **6.** T   **8.** T
3. F   **5.** F   **7.** T

2. to trust
3. to forget, to remember
4. going
5. to remember
6. to turn off
7. Playing, improving

 (Answers may vary slightly.)
2. meeting Natalya last year (at Richard's party).
3. spilling grape juice (on the couch).
4. listening to jazz OR listening to Richard play jazz (at his parties).
5. going dancing (some time), to go (dancing some time).
6. to give Marta a ride home, to stay a little longer.

 What a great party! I usually avoid ~~to go~~ *going* to parties because it's such a problem for me to remember people's names. I'm so glad I read that book about ~~improve~~ *improving* your memory. The author suggested ~~to do~~ *doing* exercises, and they really helped. I stopped ~~to worry~~ *worrying* about what people would think of me, and I tried to pay attention to what people were saying. As a result, I had a great time! I'm even planning ~~going~~ *to go OR on going* dancing with this guy Lev.

I have an English test tomorrow, so I should stop writing now and start studying.

The book even had some good tips about ~~study~~ *studying* for an exam. I hope I remember ~~using~~ *to use* some of them tonight!

 Make, Have, Let, Help, and **Get**

 **POINT**
T

CHART CHECK
T, F, T

EXPRESS CHECK
A: to correct
B: correct
A: stay
B: stay

 2. F   **4.** F   **6.** F
3. T   **5.** T

2 **2.** let   **5.** got   **8.** had
3. made   **6.** made   **9.** had
4. had   **7.** let   **10.** made

3 **2.** made her work
3. didn't let them use (their) dictionaries
4. had him clean
5. got him to pronounce
6. didn't let her speak
7. didn't make her leave

4 When I was a teenager, my parents never let me ~~to~~ play until I had finished all my homework. They even made me ~~helping~~ *help* my brothers with their homework before I could have any fun. On the one hand, they certainly got me ~~_~~ *to* learn a lot. On the other hand, they made me ~~became~~ *become* too serious. I wish they had let me ~~to~~ have a little more fun. When I become a parent, I want to have my child ~~learns~~ *learn* responsibility, but also I would want to let ~~he or she~~ *him or her* have fun. As Ben Franklin said, "All work and no play makes Jack become a dull boy." I want to avoid that mistake.

SelfTest

(Total = 100 points. Each item = 4 points.)

SECTION ONE
1. C   **3. A**   **5. D**   **7. A**
2. A   **4. B**   **6. C**   **8. C**

9. A	**11. B**	**13. B**
10. D	**12. C**	**14. A**

SECTION TWO

(Correct answers are in parentheses.)

15. B (to change)	**21. D** (to seeing)
16. C (trying)	**22. A** (to buy)
17. B (finding)	**23. D** (not to fall)
18. A (Getting)	**24. B** (watching)
19. B (not to)	**25. D** (to do)
20. C (old enough)	

UNIT 54 Phrasal Verbs:
Inseparable

CHECK **POINT**

in a restaurant

CHART CHECK

before the direct object

EXPRESS CHECK

We ran into Bob.
He was eating out.

 1 Ho Da-ming's new restaurant was failing. His customers rarely (came back). Why? Mr. Ho contacted a feng shui consultant to (find out). Feng shui (meaning "wind and water") is the ancient Chinese art of placing things in the environment. According to this art, the arrangement of furniture, doors, and windows affects our health, wealth, and happiness. Mr. Ho was concerned about his business, but he didn't (give up). Following the consultant's advice, he remodeled and redecorated his restaurant. His actions (paid off). Soon business (picked up) and Mr. Ho became rich. "It was the best decision I ever made," he glows. And he isn't alone in his

enthusiasm. Feng shui (has caught on) with modern architects and homeowners everywhere.

1. has caught on	4. find out
2. came back	5. give up
3. paid off	6. picked up

2
2. back	6. out
3. up	7. up
4. up	8. out
5. up	

3
2. turned out	6. give up
3. come up with	7. paid off
4. went up	8. go back
5. kept on	

4 Sorry the apartment is such a mess. I got
up
~~down~~ late this morning and didn't have time
up
to straighten ~~out~~. I'm going to the gym now
out   back
to work ~~off~~ for an hour. I should get ~~across~~
before you, and I'll clean up then. How about
out tonight
eating ~~tonight out~~? Afterward, we can get
together with some of the guys and maybe
up
see a movie. Or maybe we'll come ~~over~~ with
a better idea.
into Tom
      Oh—I ran ~~Tom into~~ at school. He'll drop
by
~~off~~ to see you later.

UNIT 55 Phrasal Verbs: Separable

CHECK **POINT**

George is getting an idea for an invention.

CHART CHECK

Direct objects that are nouns can go before or after the particle.

EXPRESS CHECK

dreamed up that idea OR dreamed that idea up, dream it up

1 Did you know that two college dropouts <u>thought up</u> (the idea) of the first personal computer? What's more, they <u>put</u> (it) <u>together</u> in a garage. Inventions don't have to come out of fancy laboratories. Average people in classrooms, kitchens, and home workshops often <u>dream up</u> (new and useful ideas).

The ability to think of something new seems like magic to many people, but in fact anyone can develop the qualities of an inventor. First, inventors follow their curiosity. The Swiss inventor George de Mestral wanted to <u>find out</u> (the reason) it was so hard to remove burrs from his dog's coat. His answer led to the idea for Velcro®, now used to fasten everything from sneakers to space suits. Second, inventors use imagination to <u>put</u> (things) <u>together</u> in new ways. Walter Morrison watched two men tossing a pie pan to each other and <u>thought up</u> (the Frisbee®), one of the most popular toys in the world. Perhaps most important, successful inventors don't quit. They continuously <u>look up</u> (information) about their ideas and <u>try</u> (new designs) <u>out</u> until they succeed.

2
2. set up	**6.** paid . . . back
3. filled . . . up	**7.** carry out
4. keep . . . away	**8.** brought about
5. picked up	

3
2. figure it out	**5.** do it over
3. fill them out	**6.** turn them in
4. handed it out	

4

<u>May 3</u> I dreamed ~~over~~ ^{up} a really good idea—a jar of paint with an applicator like the kind used for shoe polish. It can be used to touch ^{up} ~~on~~ spots on a wall, when people don't want to paint a whole room. I know a manufacturer. I'll call ~~up him~~ ^{him up} and order several types, so I can try them ~~in~~ ^{out}.

<u>July 3</u> I filled ~~down~~ ^{out} an application for a patent and mailed it yesterday. I'll be able to set ˄ ^{up} a strong and convincing demonstration of the product ~~up~~ soon.

<u>August 30</u> I demonstrated the product at an exhibition for decorators. I wanted to point out that it's very neat to use, so I put ˄ ^{on} white gloves for the demonstration. It went over very well.

SelfTest

(Total = 100 points. Each item = 4 points.)

SECTION ONE

1. A	**5. D**	**8. D**	**11. A**
2. C	**6. C**	**9. D**	**12. C**
3. A	**7. D**	**10. A**	**13. B**
4. B			

SECTION TWO

(Correct answers are in parentheses.)

14. A (it over)
15. D (up)
16. D (off the bus)
17. D (back)
18. B (get on the bus)
19. D (off)
20. A (up)
21. B (her up)
22. D (wake you up)
23. D (pick some stamps up for him . . . OR pick up some stamps for him . . .)
24. D (Meg into)
25. B (along)

 UNIT 56 Nouns

CHECK POINT

Ra II

CHART CHECK 1

F

CHART CHECK 2

T, F

EXPRESS CHECK

were, was

 Was (Columbus) really the first <u>explorer</u> to discover the (Americas)? (Thor Heyerdahl) didn't think so. He believed that ancient <u>people</u> were able to build <u>boats</u> that could cross <u>oceans</u>. To test his <u>ideas</u>, he decided to build a <u>copy</u> of the <u>reed boats</u> that were pictured in ancient <u>paintings</u> and sail across the (Atlantic) from (North Africa) to (Barbados.) (Heyerdahl)'s <u>team</u> also copied ancient Middle Eastern <u>pots</u> and filled them with <u>food</u> for their <u>journey</u>—dried <u>fish</u>, <u>honey</u>, <u>oil</u>, <u>eggs</u>, <u>nuts</u>, and fresh <u>fruit</u>. (Ra), the <u>expedition</u>'s <u>boat</u>, carried an international <u>group</u> including a (Norwegian), an (Egyptian), an (Italian), a (Mexican), and a (Chadian).

The first <u>trip</u> failed, but everyone survived and wanted to try again. Departing on (May) 17, 1970, under the <u>flag</u> of the (United Nations) (Ra II) crossed the (Atlantic) in 57 <u>days</u>. The <u>expedition</u> proved that ancient <u>civilizations</u> had the <u>skill</u> to reach the (Americas) long before (Columbus.)

3. Food	**13.** are
4. is	**14.** Is
5. are	**15.** equipment
6. ideas	**16.** batteries
7. beans	**17.** news
8. rice	**18.** stops
9. Potatoes	**19.** clothing
10. are	**20.** cold
11. trips	**21.** bothers
12. vegetables	**22.** bags

 October 27. I've been on the ~~canary~~ Canary Islands

for three days now. I'll start home when
the ~~weathers are~~ weather is better. I was so surprised

when I picked up my ~~mails~~ mail today. My

family sent me some birthday presents.
My ~~Birthday~~ birthday is the 31st. I won't open the

gifts until then.
~~october~~ October 29. I think the weather is getting

worse. I heard ~~thunders~~ thunder today, but there

wasn't any rain. I stayed in bed with my

cat, Typhoon. Every time it thundered,
~~typhoon~~ Typhoon and I snuggled up closer under

the covers. I started reading a ~~Novel~~ novel,

Brave New World.

October 30. I left the Canary Islands
today—just like ~~columbus~~ Columbus. There's a

strong wind and plenty of sunshine now.
I went 250 ~~Miles~~ miles.

October 31. I'm 21 today! To celebrate,
I drank some ~~coffees~~ coffee for breakfast and

I opened my presents. I got some perfume
and pretty silver ~~jewelries~~ jewelry.
November 1. The ~~electricities are~~ electricity is very low.

I'd better not use much until I get near
~~new~~ New York. I'll need the radio then. It rained
today, so I collected ~~waters~~ water for cooking.

UNIT 57 Quantifiers

CHECK POINT

a good supply of chocolate

CHART CHECK

T, F, T, T

EXPRESS CHECK

A: many   **B:** much   **A:** many

1 Are you ready? <u>Many people</u> don't realize that <u>some natural disasters</u> such as

earthquakes can strike with⟨little warning⟩.
It may take <u>several days</u> for assistance to
reach you. Prepare your disaster kit in
advance! Here are <u>a few tips.</u>

• Water may be unsafe to drink. Store
⟨enough water⟩ for <u>several days</u>. Each
person needs a gallon per day for cooking
and washing.

• You will also need food for <u>several days</u>.
It's a good idea to store⟨a lot of canned
meat, fruit⟩, <u>vegetables</u>, and⟨milk⟩.
However, also include <u>several kinds</u> of high-
energy food, such as peanut butter and
jelly. And don't forget⟨some "comfort food"⟩
like cookies and chocolate!

• If you don't have⟨any electricity⟩, you
might not have⟨any heat⟩ either. Keep
<u>some blankets, sleeping bags,</u> and extra
<u>clothes</u> for everyone.

• Prepare a first aid kit with <u>some pain
relievers</u>, <u>several sizes</u> of bandages, and
an antiseptic.

• The ATM's might not be working. Do
you have⟨any cash⟩? You shouldn't keep
⟨much money⟩ in the house, but you should
have <u>a lot of small bills</u>, and <u>a few larger
bills</u> too.

2
2. any
3. Several
4. a great deal of
5. a lot of
6. Many
7. a few
8. much
9. few
10. Some
11. a little
12. a few

3
1. b. a few
c. many
d. much
e. a few
f. a little
2. a. a little
b. few
c. a few
d. little
e. a few

4
We had a big storm last week, and we lost
the electricity for ^*a* few days. Once I got over
being scared, it was a lot of fun—a little like

camping out. We have an electric furnace, so
we didn't have ~~some~~ *any* heat. We slept in our
sleeping bags around the fireplace. We sure
used up ~~many~~ *a lot of* wood! Mom baked some bread
in an iron pan in the fireplace. She had to
try several times, but it was really good
when it worked. We ate it with ^*a* little peanut
butter. The first night we had ~~much~~ *a lot of*
problems figuring out what to do. It got dark
early, and we only had a ~~little~~ *few* candles—and
no TV! Cindy is five, and she was really
freaked out until we made hot chocolate
over the fire. Finally, everybody took turns
telling stories. I found out that Dad knows
a lot ^*of* good stories.

UNIT 58 Articles: Indefinite and Definite

CHECK POINT
There is only one Earth.

CHART CHECK
F, T, T

EXPRESS CHECK
a, The

1
2. a
3. b
4. b
5. b
6. a

2
2. an
3. a
4. an
5. an
6. the
7. a
8. the
9. the
10. the
11. a
12. the
13. the

3
2. the
3. the
4. a
5. a
6. the
7. The
8. an, the
9. the

4 Once there was a plumber named Mario.
The plumber ~~Plumber~~ had *a* beautiful girlfriend. One day, *an* ~~a~~ ape fell in love with the girlfriend and kidnapped her. The plumber chased *the* ape to rescue his girlfriend.

This simple tale became *Donkey Kong,* *the* ~~a~~ first video game with a story. It was invented by Sigeru Matsimoto, *an* ~~a~~ artist with Nintendo, Inc. Matsimoto loved ~~the~~ video games, but he wanted to make them more interesting. He liked fairy tales, so he invented *a* story similar to a famous fairy tale. *The story* ~~Story~~ was an immediate success, and Nintendo followed it with *The Mario Brothers.* The rest is video game history.

UNIT 59 Ø (No Article) and *The*

CHECK POINT
the little girl

CHART CHECK
indefinite
plural

EXPRESS CHECK
A: the **B:** Ø **A:** the **B:** Ø

1 Do you enjoy amusement parks? Tomorrow, Blare Gardens will open to the public for the first time. The park features a wide variety of rides and games that will appeal to both adults and children. And of course an amusement park would not be complete without cotton candy and hot dogs. The food at Blare Gardens promises to be very good. Come early, bring the whole family, and be sure to stay for the fireworks display that

takes place right after the sun sets. So, check it out! You won't be disappointed.

2

2. Ø	10. Ø	18. the
3. Ø	11. Ø	19. Ø
4. Ø	12. Ø	20. the
5. the	13. the	21. Ø
6. Ø	14. the	22. Ø
7. Ø	15. the	23. Ø
8. Ø	16. Ø	24. the
9. Ø	17. the	25. the

3

2. the	7. Ø	11. The
3. the	8. Ø	12. the
4. Ø	9. Ø	13. the
5. the	10. Ø	14. the
6. Ø		

4 Hi! Blare Gardens is awesome! This is *the* best vacation we've ever gone on! I love the rides here. I mean, I've been on ~~the~~ roller coasters before, but nothing is like the one they've got here! And *the* food is great too. I usually don't eat ~~the~~ hot dogs, but *the* hot dogs here are great. So is *the* pizza. Do you like ~~the~~ amusement parks? If so, you've got to get your family to come. The only problem is *the* crowds here. People have to wait to get into *everything*— even the restrooms! See you soon.

UNIT 60 Reflexive Pronouns and Reciprocal Pronouns

CHECK POINT
F

CHART CHECK
F, T

EXPRESS CHECK
A: yourself
B: myself

Self-talk is the way we explain a problem to ourselves. It can affect the way we feel and how we act. Tom and Sara, for example, both lost their jobs when their company laid off a lot of people. Sara kept herself fit and spent time with friends. Tom gained ten pounds and spent all his time by himself. They were both unemployed, so the situation itself can't explain why they acted so differently from each other. The main difference was the way Tom and Sara explained the problem to themselves. Sara believed that she herself could change her situation. Tom saw himself as helpless. Later, everyone got their jobs back. When they all talked to one another back at the office, Tom grumbled, "They must have been desperate." Sara replied, "They finally realized they need us!"

1. yourselves
2. herself, ourselves
3. myself, yourself
4. each other, yourself
5. itself, ourselves
6. yourselves, one another

2. yourselves	7. myself
3. themselves	8. myself
4. himself	9. yourselves
5. yourselves	10. myself
6. each other	
OR one another	

 I forgot to call Jan on his birthday.
              myself
I reminded ~~me~~ all day, and then I forgot

anyway! I felt terrible. My sister Anna said,
              yourself
"Don't be so hard on ~~yourselves~~," but I didn't
              herself
believe her. She prides ~~her~~ on remembering

everything. Then I read an article on

self-talk. It said that people can change the
                            themselves
way they explain problems to ~~theirselves~~.
                            myself
I realized that the way I talk to ~~me~~ is

insulting—like the way our high school

math teacher used to talk to us. I thought,

Jan and I treat each other well. He forgave
      me
~~myself~~ for my mistake right away, and I

forgave him for forgetting our dinner date

two weeks ago. Jan and I could forgive
      each other
~~themselves~~, so I guess I can forgive myself.

SelfTest

(Total = 100 points. Each item = 4 points.)

SECTION ONE

1. **C**	4. **C**	7. **C**	10. **C**
2. **B**	5. **A**	8. **C**	11. **C**
3. **D**	6. **A**	9. **C**	12. **A**

SECTION TWO

(Correct answers are in parentheses.)

13. **A** (is)	19. **D** *(delete* the*)*
14. **C** (Thanksgiving)	20. **B** (much time)
15. **B** (is starting)	21. **C** (few)
16. **B** (May)	22. **B** (a little)
17. **D** (the)	23. **B** (one another's)
18. **A** *(delete* A *and*	24. **B** (a little)
capitalize Money)	25. **D** (the accountant)

 The Passive: Overview

CHECK POINT

the number of years the magazine has existed

CHART CHECK

T, T, F

EXPRESS CHECK

were printed

2. A	7. A
3. P	8. P
4. A	9. A
5. P	10. P
6. P	

2.
3. Tagalog is spoken
4. is spoken by 417 million people
5. Seventy-one million people speak
6. Arabic is spoken by
7. speak English
8. Swahili is spoken OR
   People speak Swahili

 3.
3. is published (~~the publisher~~)
4. is read (~~readers~~)
5. have been hired by our
   international offices
6. were purchased (~~the company~~)
7. are used (~~our writers~~)
8. is advertised (~~advertisers~~)
9. was interviewed by *Live at Ten TV*
10. was seen by millions of viewers

 4.
Two-thirds of Bolivia's five million people
      are located
~~locate~~ in the cool western highlands known

as the Altiplano. For centuries, the grain
                 grown
quinoa has been ~~grew~~ in the mountains.
          are
Llamas ʌ raised for fur, meat, and

transportation. And tin, Bolivia's richest
                              mined
natural resource, is ~~mining~~ ~~by miners~~ in

the high Andes.

   The Oriente, another name for the

eastern lowlands, is mostly tropical. Rice is

the major food crop, and cows are raised for
              found
milk. Oil is also ~~find~~ there.

   Although Spanish is the official language,

Native American languages are still spoken

~~by people~~. Traditional textiles are woven by
            is
hand, and music ʌ played on reed pipes whose

tone resembles the sound of the wind

blowing over high plains in the Andes.

UNIT 62 The Passive with Modals

CHECK POINT
somebody has to do something about
Ed's snoring

CHART CHECK 1
T, F

CHART CHECK 2
a modal or an auxiliary verb

EXPRESS CHECK
A: Will . . . be prepared
B: it won't, will be prepared

 1.
Space Station *Unity* <u>will be completed</u>
within the next decade, and international
teams of astronauts will then be sharing
close quarters for long periods of time. What
<u>can be done</u> to improve living conditions in
space? Here's what former astronauts
suggest:
- **FOOD** It doesn't taste as good in zero
  gravity. Food <u>should be made</u> spicier to
  overcome those effects. International
  tastes <u>must</u> also <u>be considered</u>.
- **CLOTHING** Layered clothing could help
  astronauts stay comfortable. The top
  layer <u>could be removed</u> or <u>added</u> as
  temperatures vary.
- **SLEEPING** Because of weightlessness,
  sleep is often interrupted in space.
  Comfortable restraints <u>must be provided</u>
  to give a sense of stability.
- **EMOTIONAL NEEDS** People need "down
  time" in space just as they do on Earth.
  Time <u>ought to be provided</u> for relaxation
  and privacy.

 2.
2. Is . . . going to be prepared
3. (is going to be) squeezed
4. will be prepackaged
5. can be warmed up

6. should . . . be chosen
7. has to be offered
8. could be selected
9. Will . . . be used
10. had better be attached
11. ought to be made

2. should be kept
3. ought to be improved
4. could be designed
5. can be removed
6. ought to be given
7. are going to be delivered
8. will be done
9. will be stored

I used the sleeping restraints last night and

slept a lot better. They ought to ~~make~~ _be made_ more

comfortable, though. I felt trapped. I just

looked in the mirror. My face is puffy and

my eyes are red. I'd better ~~be gotten~~ _get_ on

the exercise bike right away. I can be

~~misunderstanding~~ _misunderstood_ when I look like this.

Last night Max thought I was angry at him

for turning on "Star Trek." Actually, I love

that show. I might be given early lunch

shift today. I hope they have more teriyaki.

It's nice and spicy, and the sauce can actually

~~been~~ _be_ tasted, even at zero gravity. Some of it

had better be ~~fly~~ _flown_ in on the Shuttle pretty

soon, or there might be some unhappy

astronauts! Speaking of unhappy, last night

Kristen called and told me she was planning

to quit school. I think she could be ~~talk~~ _talked_ out

of it, but I'm afraid I'll get angry and yell if

we discuss it. I might _be_ overheard by others.

We need some privacy here!

UNIT 63 The Passive Causative

CHECK POINT
went to a hair salon

CHART CHECK
F, T, F

EXPRESS CHECK
A: done
B: done, do

2. T		4. T		6. T	
3. T		5. F			

3. Amber had the dog groomed.
4. They are going to get the windows washed.
5. They had the carpets cleaned.
6. Amber is going to have her ears pierced.
7. Jake got his hair cut.
8. They are going to have food and drinks delivered.

1. OR have it shortened
2. get (OR have) it dry cleaned
3. 're getting (OR having) them washed OR 're going to get (OR have) them washed
4. 'm getting (OR having) it cut OR 'm going to get (OR have) it cut
5. get (OR have) it colored
6. Did . . . get (OR have) it painted

The party was tonight. It went really well!

The house looked great. Mom and Dad had

the floors waxed and all the windows ~~clean~~ _cleaned_

professionally so everything sparkled. And

of course we ~~had the whole house painted~~ _painted the whole house_

ourselves last summer. (I'll never forget

that. It took us two weeks!) I wore my new

black dress that I ~~have~~ _had_ shortened by Bo, and

I ~~got cut my hair~~ _got my hair cut_ by André. He did a great

job. There were a lot of guests at the party.

We ~~had almost fifty people invited~~ _had invited OR invited almost fifty people_, and they

(continued on next page)

almost all showed up! The food was great
too. Mom made most of the main dishes
herself, but she had the rest of the food
~~prepare~~ *prepared* by a caterer. Mom and Dad hired a
professional photographer, so at the end of
the party we all ~~took our pictures~~ *had our pictures taken*. Dad's
getting them back next week. I can't wait
to see them!

SelfTest

(Total = 100 points. Each item = 4 points.)

SECTION ONE

1. **C**	4. **B**	7. **C**	9. **D**
2. **D**	5. **C**	8. **B**	10. **B**
3. **A**	6. **B**		

SECTION TWO

(Correct answers are in parentheses.)

11. **C** *(by)*
12. **A** *(delete were)*
13. **C** *(be corrected)*
14. **D** *(delete by the printer)*
15. **A** *(delete was)*
16. **D** *(return)*
17. **C** *(them done)*
18. **C** *(be discussed)*
19. **A** *(was painted)*
20. **C** *(couldn't OR wasn't able to)*
21. **B** *(grown)*
22. **D** *(was working)*
23. **B** *(have to be replaced)*
24. **C** *(cleaned)*
25. **A** *(be made)*

UNIT 64 Factual Conditionals: Present

CHECK POINT

T

CHART CHECK

T, F, F

EXPRESS CHECK

1. b   **2.** c   **3.** a

1

If you run into problems on your journey, know your rights as a passenger. Often the airline company is required to compensate you for delays or damages. For example, the airline provides meals and hotel rooms if a flight is unduly delayed. However, the airline owes you a lot more if it caused the delay by overbooking. This can occur especially during holidays if airlines sell more tickets than there are seats. If all the passengers actually show up, then the flight is overbooked. Airlines usually award upgrades or additional free travel to passengers who volunteer to take a later flight. However, if no one volunteers, your flight may be delayed. In that case, the airline must repay you 100 percent of the cost of your ticket for a delay of up to four hours on an international flight. If the delay is more than four hours, you receive 200 percent of the cost of your ticket.

2

1. OR The best time to go to Hong Kong is November or December if you hate hot weather.
2. If you're traveling with your children, take them to Lai Chi Kok Amusement Park in Kowloon. OR Take your children to Lai Chi Kok Amusement Park in Kowloon if you're traveling with them.
3. If you need a moderately priced hotel, I suggest the Harbour View International House. OR I suggest the Harbour View International House if you need a moderately priced hotel.
4. If you like seafood, there are wonderful seafood restaurants on Lamma Island. OR There are wonderful seafood restaurants on Lamma Island if you like seafood.
5. If you're fascinated by Chinese opera, you might like the street opera in the Shanghai Street Night Market. OR You might like the street opera in the

Shanghai Street Night Market if you're fascinated by Chinese opera.

6. If you'd like to get a good view of Hong Kong, you should take the funicular to the Peak. OR You should take the funicular to the Peak if you'd like to get a good view of Hong Kong.

 3

2. I spend a lot of time at the pool if I stay at a hotel.

3. If I stay with friends, I spend time with them.

4. It's not so nice if I get a "Dracula."

5. It's very rewarding if you don't mind hard work.

6. If you have three roommates, you don't have trouble finding dogwalkers.

7. If a flight has an empty seat, I ride for free.

4

What a great weekend! If Lou and Teri aren't the best hosts in the world, I ~~won't~~ *don't* know who is. I've invited them to New York, but if you live in the Bahamas, you rarely want to leave. Tomorrow at midnight I fly roundtrip from New York to Pittsburgh. There's always a price to pay. If I get a free weekend in the islands, I always get a "Dracula" afterwards. Oh, well. If I ~~won't~~ *don't* fall asleep, I can usually get a lot of reading done. Pat and Kim both flew to London yesterday. I hope someone can walk Frisky for me. Usually, if ~~I'll be~~ *I'm* working, one of them is off. If Frisky is alone for a long time, he ~~barked~~ *barks* a lot. That disturbs the neighbors. Maybe I should just leave the TV on for him. He's always very calm ✗ if the TV is on. Or maybe I'd better call Pat and ask her about her schedule. If it ~~was~~ *'s* 6:00 P.M. here in New York, it's 11:00 P.M. in London. That's not too late to call.

UNIT 65 Factual Conditionals: Future

CHECK POINT

F, F

CHART CHECK

the *if* clause

when the *if* clause comes first

EXPRESS CHECK

If she wins, she'll fight crime.

 1

2. e	4. a	6. d
3. c	5. g	7. b

 2

3. get
4. If
5. win
6. 'll take OR 'm going to take
7. If
8. become
9. 'll try OR 'm going to try
10. will . . . do OR are . . . going to do
11. if
12. lose
13. If
14. lose
15. 'll continue OR 'm going to continue
16. Unless
17. cooperate
18. won't be OR isn't going to be
19. if
20. don't elect
21. 'll be OR 'm going to be

 3

(possible answers)

3. If I take out student loans, I won't have to depend on my family, OR I won't have to depend on my family if I take out student loans.

4. If I go to law school, I'll earn more money. OR I'll earn more money if I go to law school.

5. If I earn more money, I'll be able to pay back my (student) loans quickly. OR I'll be able to pay back my (student) loans quickly if I earn more money.

6. If I pay back my loans quickly, I'll put my sister through college. OR I'll put my sister through college if I pay back my loans quickly.

7. If I go to law school, I'll go into politics. OR I'll go into politics if I go to law school.

8. If I go into politics, I'll be able to improve life for others. OR I'll be able to improve life for others if go into politics.

9. If I go into politics, I'll get elected to the city council. OR I'll get elected to the city council if I go into politics.

10. If I get elected to the city council, I'll run for mayor. OR I'll run for mayor if I get elected to the city council.

4 Should I campaign for student council president? I'll have to decide soon if I ~~wanted~~ ^{want} to run. If ~~I'll be~~ ^{I'm} busy campaigning, I won't have much time to study. That's a problem, because I'm not going to get into a good college ~~if~~ ^{unless*} I get good grades this year. On the other hand, there's so much to do in this school, and nothing ~~is getting~~ ^{will get OR is going to get} done if Todd Laker becomes president again. A lot of people know that. But will I know what to do if ~~I'll~~ ^I get the job? Never mind. I'll deal with that problem‸ if I win.

*OR if I *don't get*

66 Unreal Conditionals: Present

CHECK POINT
F

CHART CHECK
F, T, F

EXPRESS CHECK
would, if, were

2. T   4. F   6. F
3. T   5. F

2. wouldn't like
3. weren't

4. couldn't identify
5. were
6. loved
7. 'd hate OR would hate
8. drove
9. 'd hate OR would hate
10. were
11. 'd hate OR would hate
12. weren't
13. might be

2. If Schroeder didn't love Beethoven, he wouldn't play his sonatas all the time.
3. If Charlie Brown had enough friends, he wouldn't feel lonely.
4. If Sally knew her teacher's name, she could send her a card.
5. If Linus weren't smart, he wouldn't find clever solutions to life's problems.
6. If Woodstock and Snoopy didn't have a close relationship, Woodstock wouldn't confide in Snoopy.
7. If Rerun's parents didn't refuse to let him have a dog, he wouldn't try to borrow Charlie's dog.
8. If Pigpen took enough baths, he wouldn't be filthy.

4 I've got to stop staying up late reading "Peanuts"! If I weren't always so tired, I ~~will~~ ^{would} be able to stay awake in class. Whenever the teacher calls on me, I don't know what to say. Then I get really embarrassed because of that cute red-haired girl that I like. I would talk to her if I ~~wouldn't be~~ ^{weren't} so shy. My friend Jason says, "If I ~~was~~ ^{were} you, I'd ask her to a party," but I'm too afraid that if I asked her, she would ~~have said~~ ^{say} no. After class, I played baseball. Nobody wanted me on their team. If I ~~play~~ ^{played} better, I would get chosen sometimes. Life is hard! I can really understand that Charlie Brown character in "Peanuts." In fact, if I didn't laugh so hard while reading "Peanuts," I would ~~cried~~ ^{cry}!

Unreal Conditionals: Past

CHECK **POINT**

F

CHART CHECK

the *if* clause

the *if* clause comes first

EXPRESS CHECK

would have studied

 2. F 4. F 6. T
3. T 5. F

 2. could (OR would) have gone OR would have been able to go, hadn't lost
3. could have gone, hadn't gotten
4. wouldn't have known, hadn't shown
5. hadn't helped, could have gone
6. might not have led, hadn't married
7. would have been, hadn't lived

 (Answers may vary slightly)
1. OR Clarence would have had more self-confidence if he had been a first-class angel.
2. If George hadn't been unhappy about his business, he wouldn't have yelled at his daughter on Christmas Eve. OR George wouldn't have yelled at his daughter on Christmas Eve if he hadn't been unhappy about his business.
3. Poor people couldn't have bought (OR wouldn't have been able to buy) houses if George's business hadn't loaned them money. OR If George's business hadn't loaned them money, poor people couldn't have bought (OR wouldn't have been able to buy) houses.
4. If Mr. Potter had been able to trick George, George would have sold Potter the business. OR George would have sold Mr. Potter the business if Potter had been able to trick George.
5. If George's Uncle Billy hadn't lost $8,000, George wouldn't have gotten into trouble with the law. OR George wouldn't have gotten into trouble with the law if his Uncle Billy hadn't lost $8,000.

6. If George's friends had known about his troubles, they would have helped him right away. OR George's friends would have helped him right away if they had known about his troubles.
7. If George's friends hadn't collected money for him, he would have gone to jail. OR George would have gone to jail if his friends hadn't collected money for him.

 It's funny how things work out sometimes.
hadn't
If George ~~hasn't~~ wanted to jump off that

bridge on Christmas Eve, I might never
gotten
have ~~getting~~ an important job like saving

him. And if he hadn't been so stubborn,
have
I would never ~~had~~ thought of the idea of

showing him life in Bedford Falls without

him. One of the saddest things was seeing

all those people who didn't have homes.
had given up
If George ~~gave up~~ and sold his business to

Mr. Potter, then Potter would have rented

run-down apartments to all those people.

But because of George, they now have good

homes. By the time we were finished, George

realized he really had a wonderful life. In
would
fact, he ~~will~~ have gone to jail happily͓ if his

friends hadn't given him the money he

needed. Well, luckily they helped him out,

and he didn't go to jail. And I got my wings

and became a first-class angel!

 Wish: Present and Past

CHECK **POINT**

that day

CHART CHECK 1

the simple past

CHART CHECK 2

the past perfect

EXPRESS CHECK

knew, had known

 2. T   4. F   6. T
3. F   5. T

 2. would go away
3. had
4. didn't have to deal
5. could entertain
6. could have invited OR
   had been able to invite
7. had known

 2. I wish my husband would ask for a raise.
3. I wish my wife had been able to balance
   (OR could have balanced) the check book
   last month.
4. I wish my boyfriend weren't out of shape
   OR were in shape.
5. I wish I weren't too old to go back
   to school.
6. I wish I could stop (OR were able to stop)
   smoking
7. I wish my son called (OR would call) me.
8. I wish my parents had understood me.

 Today I told Dr. Grimes, "I wish there <u>was</u> a
              were

way to spend more time with my boyfriend,

but we're both too busy." He just said, "If

wishes were horses, beggars would ride."
           understood

That's cute, but I wish I <u>understand</u> its

meaning. Maybe it means that wishing

won't solve problems. Well, that's why
           had told

I went to see him!!! I wish he <u>will tell</u> me

what to do right then and there, but he

refused. Speaking of wishful thinking,
           spend

I wish Todd and I could <u>have spent</u> the

weekend together next week. My exams are

over, but he has to fly to Denver to his job.

If wishes were horses, I'd ride one to Denver.

Hey! Todd is always saying, "I wish you would

come with me sometimes." I guess I *can* go

with him to Denver. Dr. Grimes must have

meant that I can solve my own problems.
         hadn't

Now I wish I <u>haven't</u> been so rude to him.

SelfTest

(Total = 100 points. Each item = 4 points.)

SECTION ONE

1. **C**   4. **A**   7. **B**   10. **D**
2. **B**   5. **D**   8. **C**   11. **A**
3. **A**   6. **C**   9. **C**   12. **D**

SECTION TWO

(Correct answers are in parentheses.)

13. **D** (seen)   20. **D** (were)
14. **B** (could have)   21. **C** *(delete* will*)*
15. **B** (won't)   22. **C** *(delete comma)*
16. **B** (have)   23. **C** (would have)
17. **B** (were)   24. **C** (get)
18. **A** (could have)   25. **C** (could)
19. **A** ('ll eat OR
    are going to eat)

 Adjective Clauses with
Subject Relative Pronouns

CHECK POINT

F

CHART CHECK

nouns
in the middle of the main clause, after the
  main clause

EXPRESS CHECK

That's the man who works in the cafeteria.

Almost everyone has friends, but ideas about friendship vary from person to person. For some, a friend is someone (who) chats with you on the Internet. For others, a friend is a person (who) has known you all your life—someone (whose) family knows you, too. Others only use the term for someone (who) knows your innermost secrets. Although different people emphasize different aspects of friendship, there is one element (which) is always present, and that is the element of choice. We may not be able to select our families, our co-workers, or even the people (that) ride the bus with us, but we *can* pick our friends. As anthropologist Margaret Mead once said, "A friend is someone (who) chooses and is chosen." It is this freedom of choice (that) makes friendship such a special relationship.

1. OR that have
2. who (OR that) have
3. that (OR which) are
4. who (OR that) faces
5. that (OR which) is
6. whose . . . are
7. whose . . . include
8. that (OR which) appears OR appeared OR has appeared
9. who (OR that) doesn't read OR hasn't read

2. Mexico City is an exciting city that (OR which) attracts a lot of tourists.
3. Marta has a brother whose name is Manuel.
4. He works for a magazine that (OR which) is very popular in Mexico.
5. Manuel writes a column that (OR which) deals with relationships.
6. An article that (OR which) discussed friendships won a prize.
7. A person who (OR that) has a lot of friends is lucky.

 A writer once said that friends are born, not made. This means that we automatically become friends with people who ~~they~~ are compatible with us. I don't agree with this writer. Last summer, I made friends with some
were OR are
people who~~'s~~ completely different from me.

In July, I went to Mexico City to study Spanish for a month. In our group, there
who OR that
was a teacher ~~which~~ was much older than I am. We became really good friends. In my first week, I had a problem which was getting me down. Mexico City is a city
that OR which
~~who~~ has a lot of distractions. As a result, I went out all the time, and I stopped going to my classes. Bob helped me get back into my studies. After the trip, I kept writing
are
to Bob. He always writes stories that ~~is~~ interesting and encouraging. Next summer,
that OR which
he's leading another trip ~~what~~ sounds interesting. I hope I can go.

UNIT 70 Adjective Clauses with Object Relative Pronouns or *When* and *Where*

CHECK POINT
T

CHART CHECK
the subject of the adjective clause
F

EXPRESS CHECK
I see all the movies that he directs.

1 At the age of nine, Eva Hoffman left Poland with her family. She was old enough to know what she was losing: Cracow, a city (that) she loved as one loves a person, the sun-baked villages (where) they had taken summer vacations, and the conversations and escapades with her friends. Disconnected from a city (where) life was lived intensely, her father would become overwhelmed by the transition to Canada. Eva would lose the parent (whom) she had watched in lively conversation with friends in Cracow cafés. And nothing could replace her friendship with the boy (whose) home she visited daily, and (whom) she assumed she would someday marry. Worst of all, however, she would miss her language. For years, she would feel no connection to the English name of anything (that) she felt was important. *Lost in Translation: A Life in a New Language* (New York: Penguin, 1989) tells how Eva came to terms with her new identity and language. It's a story (that) readers will find fascinating and moving.

2
1. OR that
3. who OR whom OR that
4. stayed OR were staying
5. which
6. had
7. that OR which
8. wanted
9. that OR which
10. have experienced
11. where OR in which
12. were
13. who OR whom OR that
14. take care of

3
1. OR . . . in which I grew up . . .
2. The house that (OR which) we lived in was beautiful. OR The house in which we lived . . .
3. Emilia and I shared a room where (OR in which) we spent nights talking.

4. Across the hall I had a good friend who (OR whom OR that) I went to school with. OR . . . with whom I went to school.
5. I took piano lessons from a woman who (OR whom OR that) I met in the bakery.
6. I remember one summer when (OR that) the whole family went to the lake.
7. Those are good times that (OR which) I'll always miss.

4 Tai Dong is the small city in southeastern
where OR *in which* OR *that . . . in*
Taiwan ~~which~~ I grew up. My family moved there from Taipei the summer when I was born. The house in which I grew up ~~in~~* is on a main street in Tai Dong. My father sold tea, and my mother had a food stand in our front courtyard where she sold omelets early in the morning. A customer who I always chatted with ~~him~~ had a son my age. We were
whose
best friends. A cousin ~~who his~~ family I visited every summer lived with us. He was
who OR *whom* OR *that*
an apprentice ~~which~~ my father was teaching the tea business to. On the first floor of our
in which OR *where*
house we had a huge kitchen ~~in where~~ we all gathered for dinner. It was a fun and noisy place. The bedrooms where the family
were
slept ~~was~~ upstairs. My two brothers slept in
that OR *which*
one bedroom. I slept in one ~~what~~ I shared with my older sister. My younger sister shared a bedroom with another cousin
who OR *whom* OR *that*
~~which~~ my family had adopted.

*OR the house which (OR that) I grew up in

Adjective Clauses:
Identifying and
Non-Identifying

 **POINT**

F

CHART CHECK

non-identifying
T

EXPRESS CHECK

It was the computer ~~which~~ we saw at
E-Lectronics.

 2. T   **4.** F   **6.** F
3. T   **5.** F

 ˌtech • no • ˈpho • bia *(noun)* a fear ~~that~~
some people have about using technology

   If you have it, you're one of the 85 percent
of people ~~that~~ this new "disease" has struck.
Maybe you bought a phone on which you
can program 25 numbers—then couldn't
turn it on. Or perhaps you have just read
that your new CD player, which you have
finally learned how to use, will soon be
replaced by DVD, which you had never even
heard of.

   Some experts say that things have just
gotten too complex. William Staples, who
authored a book on the electronic age, tried
to help a friend who had just bought a new
stereo. The stereo, which worked before,
wasn't working anymore. "On the front of
the stereo receiver it literally had a couple
of dozen buttons," says Staples. Donald
Norman, who has written about the effects
of technology on people, blames the
designers of these devices, not the people

who use them. "The best way to cure
technophobia is to cure the reasons that
cause it—that is, to design things ~~that~~
people can use and design things that won't
break," claims Norman. Michael Dyrenfurth,
who teaches at the University of
Missouri–Columbia, believes we cause our
own problems by buying technology ~~that~~ we
just don't need. "Do we really need an
electric toothbrush?" he asks. According to
Dyrenfurth, important technology ~~that~~ we
can't afford to run away from actually exists.
To prosper, we have to overcome our
technophobia and learn to use it.

 2. My new cell phone, which I bought a
   month ago, has become a necessary part
   of life.
3. I remember the day when I was afraid to
   use my new computer.
4. Now, there are psychologists who (OR that)
   help technophobes use technology.
5. Dr. Michelle Weil, who is a psychologist,
   wrote a book about "technostress."
6. I work in an office where (OR in which)
   the software changes frequently.
7. A lot of people who work in my office
   suffer from technostress.
8. Some people dream of a job they can do
   without technology.

 I just read a book called *Technostress*, which
was written by Dr. Michelle Weil. Her
                                   who
co-author was Dr. Larry Rosen, ~~that~~ is her
husband and also a psychologist. According
to the authors, everybody feels stress about
technology. Our cell phones and beepers,
which
~~that~~ we buy for emergencies, soon invade
our privacy. Just because they can, people

(continued on next page)

contact us at places˯where we are relaxing.
Another problem is having to learn too
much too fast. Technological changes,˯used
to come one at a time, now overwhelm us.
Dr. Weil suggests dealing with technostress
using tips from her latest book, which can
be purchased from her web site.

SelfTest

(Total = 100 points. Each item = 4 points.)

SECTION ONE

1. **B**	4. **C**	7. **B**	10. **C**
2. **A**	5. **B**	8. **C**	11. **B**
3. **D**	6. **B**	9. **B**	12. **C**

SECTION TWO

(Correct answers are in parentheses.)

13. **C** (where)
14. **A** (who)
15. **C** *(delete* he)
16. **B** (whose)
17. **B** (that OR which OR *delete* what)
18. **D** *(delete* it)
19. **C** (discuss)
20. **B** (which)
21. **A** (who)
22. **C** (in which OR where)
23. **B** (with whom)
24. **C** (when OR that OR *delete* which)
25. **A** (whose)

 **Direct and Indirect
Speech:** Imperatives

CHECK *POINT*

"Don't eat a heavy meal before bed."

CHART CHECK

direct speech
T

EXPRESS **CHECK**

to go, Don't work

 Can't sleep? You're not alone. Millions of
people are up tossing and turning instead of
getting their zzzz's. Dr. Ray Thorpe, Director
of the Sleep Disorders Clinic, says, "Don't
think that loss of sleep is just a minor
inconvenience." During an interview he told
me to think about what can happen if people
drive when they're tired. Every year up to
200,000 car accidents are caused by drowsy
drivers. Then he asked me to think about a
recent industrial disaster. Chances are that
it was caused at least in part by sleep
deprivation.

    Being an insomniac myself, I asked
Dr. Thorpe for some suggestions. He told me
to stop drinking coffee. He said to have a
warm glass of milk instead. "A lot of old-
fashioned remedies work. Have a high-
carbohydrate snack like a banana before you
go to bed," he said. But he advises patients
not to eat a heavy meal before turning in for
the night. What about exercise? "Regular
exercise helps, but don't exercise too close to
bedtime," he suggested. Finally, he told me
not to despair. "Don't worry about not
sleeping. It's the worst thing to do," he said.
I don't know. After thinking about those
industrial accidents, I doubt I'll be able to
sleep at all!

2. that night	7. there
3. told	8. explain
4. my	9. not to
5. to watch	10. the next
6. said	11. to get

1. OR He said to pull over and take a
   brief nap.
2. OR He told them not to take a long nap.
3. He told them (OR He said) to sing to
   themselves.
4. He told them (OR He said) to turn their
   radios to an annoying station.
5. He told them (OR He said) not to
   drink coffee.

6. He told them (OR He said) to open their windows.

7. He told them (OR He said) to let cold air in.

8. He told them (OR He said) to be careful when they stop their cars.

9. He told them (OR He said) not to stop on a deserted roadside.

10. He told them (OR He said) not to drink and drive.

4 In writing class today, Juan read one of his stories. It was wonderful. After class, the teacher invited me ∧*to* read a story in class next week. However, I asked her ~~no~~ *not* to call on me next week because I'm having trouble getting ideas. She ~~said~~ *told* me not to worry, and she said to wait for two weeks. Then I talked to Juan, and I asked him ∧*to* tell me the source for ~~your~~ *his* ideas. He said that they came from his dreams, and he told me ∧*to* keep a dream journal for ideas. He invited me ×*to* read some of his journal.× It was very interesting, so I asked him to give me some tips on remembering dreams. He said ~~getting~~ *to get* a good night's sleep because the longer dreams come after a long period of sleep. He also ~~tell~~ *told* me to keep my journal by the bed and to write as soon as I wake up. He said ~~to no~~ *not to* move from the sleeping position. He also told me ~~to don't~~ *not to* think about the day at first. (If you think about your day, you might forget your dreams.) Most important—every night he tells himself ~~that~~ to remember his dreams ~~tomorrow~~ *the next* morning.

UNIT 73 Indirect Speech: Statements (1)

CHECK POINT

"It looks great on you!"

CHART CHECK

the punctuation
the verb tense in the statement
pronouns in the statement

EXPRESS CHECK

told, was

1 At 9:00 Rick Spivak's bank phoned and (said) that his credit card payment was late. "The check is in the mail," Rick (replied) quickly. At 11:45 Rick left for a 12:00 meeting across town. Arriving late, Rick (told) his client that traffic had been bad. That evening, Rick's fiancée wore a new dress. Rick hated it. "It looks just great on you," he (said)

Three lies in one day! Yet Rick is just an ordinary guy. Each time, he (told) himself that sometimes the truth causes too many problems. He (told) himself that his fiancée was feeling good about her purchase. Why should he hurt her feelings?

Is telling lies a new trend? The majority of people in a recent survey (said) that people were more honest ten years ago. Nevertheless, lying wasn't really born yesterday. In the eighteenth century, the French philosopher Vauvenargues told the truth about lying when he (wrote) "All men are born truthful and die liars."

2

2. has	**7.** had made
3. told	**8.** had lied
4. that	**9.** was quitting
5. had	**10.** had fired
6. she	

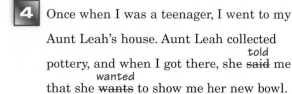

3

2. Lisa said (that) she had just heard about a job at a scientific research company.
3. Ben said (that) he had majored in science at Florida State.
4. Lisa told him (that) they wanted someone with some experience as a programmer.
5. Ben told her (that) he worked as a programmer for Data Systems.
6. Lisa said (that) they didn't want a recent college graduate.
7. Ben told her (that) he had gotten his degree four years ago OR before.
8. Lisa said (that) it sounded like the right job for him.

4

Once when I was a teenager, I went to my

Aunt Leah's house. Aunt Leah collected

pottery, and when I got there, she ~~said~~ me
                                    told

that she ~~wants~~ to show me her new bowl.
         wanted

She told ˄she ~~has~~ just bought it. It was
        me* *had*

beautiful. When Aunt Leah went to answer

the door, I picked up the bowl. It slipped

from my hands and smashed to pieces on

the floor. When Aunt Leah came back,

I screamed and said ~~what~~ the cat had just
                     that

broken ~~your~~ new bowl. Aunt Leah got this
        her

funny look on her face and told me that it

~~isn't~~ important. I didn't sleep at all that
wasn't

night, and the next morning, I called my

aunt and confessed that I ~~have~~ broken her
                           had

bowl. She said ~~I~~ had known that all along.
               she

I promised that I ~~am~~ going to buy her a
                   was

new one someday. We still laugh about the

story today.

*OR She said she . . .

Indirect Speech:
Statements (2)

CHECK POINT

"It will be windy."

CHART CHECK

ought to, might, should have

EXPRESS CHECK

Jim said that he might move soon.

2. "The winds may reach 170 miles per hour."
3. "There will be more rain tomorrow."
4. "You should try to leave the area."
5. "We can expect a lot of damage."

2. They said (that) it was going to pass north of there.
3. They said (that) it might become a tropical storm when it landed there.
4. They said (that) they had had to close some bridges the day before because of high tides.
5. They said (that) they wouldn't restore electricity until today.
6. They said (that) the schools there might be closed for a while.
7. They said (that) they ought to use bottled water for a few days.

2. He said (that) it was true, and (that) they would probably become more frequent.
3. He said (that) the planet might be getting warmer, and (that) that could cause more severe storms.
4. He said (that) emergency workers should have arrived much more quickly.
5. He said (that) the new satellites would help. He said (that) if they didn't have them, they wouldn't be able to warn people.

We had some excitement here because of

the hurricane last week. Jim's mother

called just before the storm. She said she ~~is~~
                                           was

listening to the weather report and that she

was worried about us. She told Jim that if

we
~~you~~ two weren't so stubborn, we ~~will~~ *would* pack

up and leave immediately. Jim's father told

us how to get ready for the storm. He said

we should ~~have~~ put tape on our windows
then
right ~~now~~ and that we ought to fill the

bathtub with water. He also told Jim that

we should buy a lot of batteries before the
that night
storm hit ~~tonight~~. Sue called. She said that

her place was too close to the coast and that
there *she*
she couldn't stay ~~here~~. She told me ~~I~~ wanted

to stay with me and Jim. She said she should
have
ₐcalled us sooner. I told her she should come
then
right ~~now~~. Then we listened to the weather

advisory, and the forecaster said that the
was
storm ~~is~~ going to go out to sea. She said it
wouldn't
~~won't~~ hit this area at all!

UNIT 75 Indirect Questions

CHECK POINT
"Why are you still single?"

CHART CHECK 1
F, T

CHART CHECK 2
F, T

EXPRESS CHECK
why he had quit his job.

 A few weeks ago, Melissa Morrow had a stress interview, one which featured tough, tricky questions and negative evaluations. First, the interviewer asked <u>why she couldn't work under pressure</u>. Before she could answer, he asked <u>who had written her application letter for her</u>. Melissa was shocked, but she

handled herself very well. She asked the interviewer <u>whether he was going to ask her any serious questions</u>. Then she left.

Companies give stress interviews in order to watch how candidates handle pressure. Suppose, for example, that there is an accident in a nuclear power plant. The plant's public relations officer must remain calm when reporters ask <u>how the accident could have happened</u>. Be aware, however, that in some countries, like the United States, certain questions are not allowed unless they are directly related to the job. If your interviewer asks <u>how old you are</u>, you can refuse to answer. The interviewer also should not ask <u>whether you are married</u> or <u>how much money you owe</u>. If you think a question is improper, ask <u>how the question relates to the job</u>. If it doesn't, you don't have to answer.

Items Checked: 2, 3, 5

2. He asked when the interview was.
3. He asked where the company was.
4. He asked if (OR whether) she needed directions.
5. He asked how long it took to get there.
6. He asked if (OR whether) she was going to drive.
7. He asked who was going to interview her.
8. He asked when they would let her know.

3. Pete asked if (OR whether) she was interviewing with other companies.
4. Claire asked what her responsibilities would be.
5. Claire asked how job performance was rewarded.
6. Pete asked what her starting salary at her last job had been OR had been at her last job.
7. Pete asked if (OR whether) she had gotten along well with her last employer.
8. Claire asked if (OR whether) they hired many women.

4 I did some stress questioning in my interview with Carl Treng this morning. I asked
Mr. Treng why ~~couldn't he~~ *he couldn't* work under pressure. I also asked him why ~~did~~ his supervisor ~~dislike~~ *disliked* him. Finally, I inquired when he would quit the job with our company. Mr. Treng answered my questions calmly, and he had some excellent questions of his own. He asked ✗if we expected changes on the job.✗ He also wanted to know how often ~~do~~* we evaluate employees. I was impressed when he asked why ~~did I decide~~ *I had decided* to join this company. I think we should hire him.

*OR *how often we evaluated*

Embedded Questions

CHECK POINT

Should we leave a tip?
Is the service included?

CHART CHECK

F, T

EXPRESS CHECK

A: ?   B: .

This book is for you if . . .

- you've ever avoided a situation just because you didn't know <u>how much to tip</u>.
- you've ever realized (too late) that you were supposed to offer a tip.
- you've ever given a huge tip and then wondered <u>if a tip was necessary at all</u>.

- you've ever needed to know <u>how to calculate the right tip instantly</u>.
- you're new to the United States and you're not sure <u>who you should tip here</u>.
- you'd like to learn <u>how tipping properly can get you the best service for your money</u>.

What readers are saying . . .

"I can't imagine <u>how I got along without it</u>."

"Take *Tips* along if you want a stress-free vacation."

2. how to tell if the tip is included in the bill.
3. why service people in Iceland refused my tips?
4. how much to tip airport porters.
5. who expects a tip and who doesn't.
6. I should tip my ski instructor.
7. tipping is still illegal there.
8. to tip anyway.

2. how much to tip (OR how much we should tip) the taxi driver?
3. where the Smithsonian Museum is?
4. where we can buy (OR where to buy) metro tickets.
5. we could rent a car and drive?
6. what they put in the sauce.

When you live in a foreign country even a small occasion can be an adventure! Before my date with Janek tonight, I didn't even know what ~~should I~~ *I should* OR *to* wear! Jeans? A dress? John's Grill isn't a fancy restaurant, but it was Janek's birthday and I wanted to make it a big occasion. Miuki was very helpful, as always. I knew how to get to John's Grill, but I didn't know how long it was going to take to get there. I left at 6:00, which should have given me plenty of time, but when I got off the bus, I wasn't sure ~~if~~ ^{whether} to

turn left or right. I asked a police officer

where ~~was John's~~ ^{John's was}, and I was only a few

minutes late. I had planned to take Janek

out for a special dessert afterward, but

I couldn't remember how ✗ to find the place

Miuki had suggested, and Janek has been

here even less time than me. (Anyway, the

desserts at John's turned out to be very

good.) Then, when we got the bill, I was

wondering whether to tip or ~~no~~ ^{not}. I had to ask

Janek ~~did he know~~ ^{if he knew}. Fortunately, he had read

Tips on Tipping, so he told me to leave

about 15%.

SelfTest

(Total = 100 points. Each item = 4 points.)

SECTION ONE

1. **D**	4. **C**	7. **C**	9. **C**
2. **A**	5. **A**	8. **A**	10. **D**
3. **B**	6. **C**		

SECTION TWO

(Correct answers are in parentheses.)

11. **A** (told OR said to)
12. **D** (.)
13. **D** (then)
14. **D** (was coming)
15. **D** (there)
16. **B** (whether or not OR if)
17. **A** (whether)
18. **D** (might have stopped)
19. **D** (it costs)
20. **C** (runs)
21. **D** (?)
22. **D** (, ")
23. **B** (if you could)
24. **C** (not to)
25. **B** (I could)

Clinical pharmacology
in dental practice

Dr Ante Bilič
liječnik - stomatolog

Clinical pharmacology in dental practice

SAM V. HOLROYD

D.D.S., M.S. (Pharmacology), M.S. (Periodontics), F.A.C.D.

Professor and Chairman, Department of Periodontics,
Washington University School of Dental Medicine,
St. Louis, Missouri

RICHARD L. WYNN

B.S., M.S., Ph.D.

Associate Professor and Chairman, Department of Pharmacology,
Baltimore College of Dental Surgery, Dental School,
University of Maryland, Baltimore, Maryland

With contributions by **Barbara Requa-Clark**

THIRD EDITION

Illustrated

The C. V. Mosby Company

ST. LOUIS • TORONTO • LONDON   1983

MOSBY

A TRADITION OF PUBLISHING EXCELLENCE

Editor: Darlene Warfel
Assistant editor: Melba Steube
Editing supervisor: Lin Dempsey Hallgren
Manuscript editors: Diane Ackermann, Robert A. Kelly
Design: Kay M. Kramer
Production: Carolyn Biby

THIRD EDITION

The C.V. Mosby Company
11830 Westline Industrial Drive, St. Louis, Missouri 63141

Library of Congress Cataloging in Publication Data

Main entry under title:

Clinical pharmacology in dental practice.

    Bibliography: p.
    Includes index.
    1. Dental pharmacology. I. Holroyd, Samuel V.,
1931-   . II. Wynn, Richard L. III. Requa-
Clark, Barbara. [DNLM: 1. Dentistry. 2. Pharmacol-
ogy. QV 50 C641]
RK701.C64 1983   615'.1'0246176   82-12438
ISBN 0-8016-2242-5

GW/VH/VH 9 8 7 6 5 4 3 2 1   02/D/297

Contributors

MARK S. ARTHUR, A.B., D.M.D., M.S.

Director of Addictions Education, Assistant Professor, Department of Pharmacology, Baltimore College of Dental Surgery, Dental School, University of Maryland at Baltimore, Baltimore, Maryland; Career Teacher in Addictions, National Institute of Drug Abuse, Bethesda, Maryland

**RONALD D. BAKER, D.D.S.,
M.A.(Education), F.A.C.D.**

Professor and Chairman, Department of Oral and Maxillofacial Surgery, School of Dentistry, University of North Carolina, Chapel Hill, North Carolina; Consultant in Oral and Maxillofacial Surgery to the National Naval Dental Center, Bethesda, Maryland; Consultant in Oral and Maxillofacial Surgery to Naval Regional Medical Center, Camp Lejeune, North Carolina; Consultant to North Carolina Memorial Hospital, Chapel Hill, North Carolina; Consultant to Dorothea Dix State Psychiatric Hospital, Raleigh, North Carolina; Consultant to Veterans Administration Hospital, Fayetteville, North Carolina

KEITH W. BESLEY, D.D.S.

Captain, United States Navy Dental Corps, Naval Hospital, Rota, Spain

WILLIAM K. BOTTOMLEY, D.D.S., M.S.

Professor and Chairman, Department of Oral Diagnosis and Treatment Planning, Georgetown University School of Dentistry, Washington, D.C.

ALBERT T. BROWN, Ph.D.

Professor of Oral Biology, Department of Oral Biology, College of Dentistry, University of Kentucky, Lexington, Kentucky

HAROLD L. CROSSLEY, D.D.S., Ph.D.

Assistant Professor, Director of Preclinical Studies, Department of Pharmacology and Fixed Restorative Dentistry, Baltimore College of Dental Surgery, Dental School, University of Maryland at Baltimore, Baltimore, Maryland

**TOMMY W. GAGE, B.S., D.D.S.,
Ph.D., F.A.C.D.**

Professor and Chairman, Department of Pharmacology, Baylor College of Dentistry, Dallas, Texas

**SAM V. HOLROYD, D.D.S., M.S.
(Pharmacology), M.S. (Periodontics),
F.A.C.D.**

Professor and Chairman, Department of Periodontics, Washington University School of Dental Medicine, St. Louis, Missouri

JAMES L. MATHENY, Ph.D.

Professor, Department of Oral Biology, University of Kentucky, Albert B. Chandler Medical Center College of Dentistry, Lexington, Kentucky

NORBERT R. MYSLINSKI, Ph.D.

Associate Professor, Department of Physiology, Baltimore College of Dental Surgery, Dental School, University of Maryland, Baltimore, Maryland

EDWARD M. OSETEK, D.D.S., M.A., F.I.C.D.

Associate Professor of Endodontics, Director of Advanced and Continuing Education in Endodontics, Northwestern University Dental School, Chicago, Illinois

GEORGE B. PELLEU, Jr., A.A., B.S., M.S., Ph.D.

Chairman, Research Department, National Naval Dental Center, Bethesda, Maryland

BARBARA REQUA-CLARK, Pharm.D.

Associate Professor of Dentistry (Pharmacology), University of Missouri–Kansas City, School of Dentistry, Kansas City, Missouri

BARBARA F. ROTH-SCHECHTER, B.S., Ph.D.

Professeur Conv. Pharmacology, Université Louis Pasteur Laboratoire de Pharmacodynamie, Strasbourg, France

R.C. TERHUNE, D.M.D., M.S.D.

Captain, United States Navy Dental Crops, Kailua, Hawaii

RICHARD L. WYNN, B.S., M.S., Ph.D.

Associate Professor and Chairman, Department of Pharmacology, Baltimore College of Dental Surgery, Dental School, University of Maryland, Baltimore, Maryland

I was once asked why most authors and editors
dedicate their books to their wives and children.
I answered that I guessed that most people dedicate what they do
to those they love. Although this is surely true,
I now know another reason. The legion of pressures inherent
in producing a book are conducive to the development of a
demeanor not unlike that of a wounded rhinoceros.

And so, I dedicate this book to my wife

Davene

and to our children

Eveann, Melissa, and Samuel

for their patience and understanding
during their residence with a wounded
but recovering rhinoceros

SAM V. HOLROYD

This book is dedicated to my wife

Estelle

who supported my efforts throughout
the many years of this project.

RICHARD L. WYNN

Preface

Clinical Pharmacology in Dental Practice was conceived as a teaching text to apply the science of pharmacology to the art of dental practice. The basic approach and objectives of this revision therefore are the same as those of the previous editions, that is, to relate the acquired knowledge of pharmacology to the treatment of the patient. We have attempted to direct this information to the needs of both the student and the practitioner. With the dental student in mind, we have made a special effort to relate pharmacology to clinical dentistry. With the practitioner in mind, we have made an effort to provide a condensed and practical source for easy review and rapid reference.

We do not intend that this book be used as a substitute for a complete reference source. A number of excellent encyclopedic pharmacology texts are available for that purpose. The intention is that this book serve as a dentally oriented supplement to the more voluminous reference texts. In many areas nonclinical details and in-depth pharmacology have been avoided to be more concise in emphasizing material of practical importance. In some areas, however, such as in Chapter 35, "Dental Plaque and the Control of Plaque-Related Oral Disease," nonclinical details are stressed because the mechanisms of antiplaque agents all rely on the biochemical mechanisms of plaque formation. We hope that the balance between superficiality in some areas and in-depth details in other areas will be an advantage rather than a disadvantage to the dental student and clinician.

Although all major drug groups are discussed, the points of emphasis differ. In chapters concerning drugs that the dentist prescribes or employs, the emphasis has been placed on information that will allow the dentist to make the safest and most effective use of these agents. In discussing drugs that the dentist normally does not prescribe, we have emphasized how these drugs modify a patient's physiologic functions and how these modifications are reflected in the proper handling of patients in a dental practice. We emphasize that dental pharmacology cannot be limited to the drugs a dentist prescribes. A large percentage of dental patients are taking medically prescribed agents, and there are many new drug entities marketed each year to treat the medically compromised. No patient should be given dental treatment unless the dental practitioner is fully aware of the effect these drugs will have on the patient. Additionally, in consultation with medical colleagues it is essential that dentists have at least conversant knowledge of the drugs that physicians are prescribing for dental patients. Dentists who believe they can limit their knowledge of pharmacology to only drugs they prescribe or use not only deprive their patients of the safest and most effective pharmacologic management but also compromise the status of their profession.

In this edition the rapid advancement of basic science information to explain the mechanisms of many dentally prescribed drugs has necessitated more basic pharmacology than in previous editions. Thus in-depth information on prostaglandins, thromboxanes, prostacyclin, and the mechanisms of the relatively new class of analgesics, the nonsteroidal anti-inflammatory drugs, has been added. Throughout, however, we have continued in our effort to bring together basic science areas and clinical areas in a condensed and readable manner.

New chapters on prostaglandins, minerals, drugs used for gastrointestinal disorders, drug abuse, dental plaque and the control of plaque-related oral disease, and endodontic medicaments and irrigating solutions have been added. The chapter on antiseptics and disinfectants has been revised to discuss the locally acting medications, which include antimicrobials, hemostatics, and protectives. In addition, the explosion of pharmacologic information in the treatment of hypertension has necessitated a separate chapter on diuretics and antihypertensive drugs. Finally, a list of the 200 most commonly prescribed drugs has been added to Appendix A, so the dental practitioner taking a patient's health history may use this textbook as a reference source.

The contributors of *Clinical Pharmacology in Dental Practice* were chosen for their expertise, clarity in writing style, and ability to relate basic science to the clinical practice of dentistry. We wish to express our sincere appreciation to these teachers, researchers, and practitioners for their contributions,

without whose efforts this third edition would not have been possible. Also, we would like to express our most sincere gratitude to Dr. Daniel T. Watts and Dr. Frieda G. Rudo, who led us into the world of pharmacology; to Dr. George D. Selfridge, for his leadership, guidance, and support; to Mrs. Norma Halfpenny, who ensured that manuscripts were typed and deadlines were met; to the illustrators, Jerry Gadd and Leslie Lecroix, who took the time to stress quality of work; to Eveann Holroyd, for the development of the index, and to Melba Steube, who picked up the slack when needed.

Sam V. Holroyd
Richard L. Wynn

Contents

PART ONE

General pharmacology

CHAPTER 1

SAM V. HOLROYD
BARBARA REQUA-CLARK

Introduction

DEFINITIONS[1]

Pharmacology (Gr. *pharmakon*, "drug"; L. *-logia*, "study of," from Gr. *logos*, "discourse") is the study of drugs. The extensive scope of this discipline is obvious if one considers that a drug may be broadly defined as any chemical substance that affects biologic systems. For convenience of reference, pharmacology may be divided into pharmacodynamics, pharmacotherapeutics, and pharmacokinetics.

Pharmacodynamics is a basic medical science that deals with the biochemical and physiologic effects and mechanism of action of drugs.

Pharmacotherapeutics (Gr. *pharmakon*, "drug"; *therapeia*, "treatment") is applied or clinical pharmacology that is concerned with the use of drugs in the treatment and prevention of disease.

Pharmacokinetics is the study of how the body handles drugs: their absorption, distribution, metabolism, and excretion.

Pharmacy deals with the procurement, preparation, and dispensing of drugs.

Pharmacognosy (Gr. *pharmakon*, "drug"; *gnōsis*, "knowledge") is concerned with the identification of crude or naturally occurring drugs. When most drugs were of natural origin, the subject of pharmacognosy was usually termed *materia medica*.

Posology (Gr. *posos*, "how much"; L. *-logia*, "study of") is the study of dosage.

Toxicology is the study of poisons or the adverse effects of drugs.

HISTORY

Pharmacologic thought had its beginning when early humans began to wonder why the chewing of certain plant roots or leaves altered their awareness or functions. As experience in root and leaf chewing progressed into therapeutic berry picking and smoke smelling, the experiences were shared and spread. As time progressed, some individuals naturally became more astute in observing and remembering that plant products produced predictable effects. Thus the first pharmacologist was born. Clearly this humble beginning has evolved through the years into a huge industrial and academic community that is concerned with the study and development of drugs. Drugs that are evolved are then prescribed and dispensed through the practice of medicine, dentistry, and pharmacy.

The progress of pharmacology is marked by the accomplishments of many scientists. Specific historic milestones are discussed in the appropriate chapters that follow. One may refer to Krantz for condensed and interesting historic detail concerning various drugs and to Cutting's handbook[3] for a similar presentation in outline form. Kremer's textbook[4] contains a detailed account of the history of pharmacy.

PHARMACOLOGY AND DENTAL PRACTICE

The dentist must be concerned with at least two areas of drug use. First, for the drugs that are used therapeutically in dentistry, the dentist should be able to obtain the maximal advantage while producing minimal disadvantages. This will require a knowledge of what drugs can do therapeutically and of what adverse effects can be produced. Second, the prescriber should be aware of how drugs that may be prescribed for patients by their physicians or that they may administer themselves (over-the-counter drugs) may modify the physiology of the patient being treated. This modification may be insignificant, but on the other hand, it may contraindicate certain dental procedures, alter intended treatment, or change the approach to the patient. Knowledge about these agents should focus on the alterations they may cause in dental treatment or the adverse effect they may produce.

The dentist should never use a drug with which he or she is not familiar. Treatment of a patient should never begin until the nature of any drugs that the patient has taken are known. This requires more than a basic knowledge of pharmacology. No one can remember everything about all drugs. New drugs are so frequently developed that what is competent knowledge one year is not the next. Consequently, the practitioner's understanding of pharmacology must be expanded by ready referral to reference material. Knowing where to look for quick answers is very important, and a knowledge of certain publications in pharmacology is essential.

PUBLICATIONS IN PHARMACOLOGY

The periodic literature provides the clinician with reports of recent pharmacologic developments. This information when sufficiently documented becomes incorporated into textbooks, pharmacopeias, and clinical references. An up-to-date textbook of general pharmacology is a fundamental reference and should be a part of every clinician's library. Several helpful pharmacology texts are listed in the references.[1-7]

The United States Pharmacopeia (USP) has been issued every 5 years by the U.S. Pharmacopeial Convention, Inc., which is composed of representatives from schools of medicine and pharmacy, the American Medical Association (AMA), state medical societies, the American Pharmaceutical Association (APA), the American Chemical Society, and other scientific organizations and federal agencies. A Dental Advisory Committee to the USP was established in 1972. This compendium lists single-entity drugs* of established merit. It sets official chemical and physical standards that relate essentially to strength and purity. *The United States Pharmacopeia Dispensing Information* (USP-DI) has been published annually since 1980. It is a continuously reviewed and revised base of drug information intended for use by prescribers, dispensers, and consumers of medications. Each drug monograph discusses the agent's pharmacologic category, precautions to be considered, side effects, information for the patient, dosing information, and dosage forms. A second section of the USP-DI, "Advice for the Patient," presents information for the patient in nontechnical language. This section includes a brief discussion of each drug, its proper use, precautions while taking the drug, and

side effects; it is also available as a booklet, "About Your Medicines," for direct patient use.

The National Formulary (NF) has been issued every 5 years and published by the USP convention. Like the USP, it is also recognized by federal law and further establishes official standards for drugs not described in the USP. The inclusion of a drug in the NF is based on the extent of its use and its therapeutic value.

Beginning in 1980 the USP and the NF were published in one volume.[8] Expert medical opinion will determine the basis for inclusion in this compendium. The new edition includes all drugs from USP XIX and NF 14 as well as new drugs discovered before 1980. Standards set by the USP are enforced under federal law, notably the Federal Food, Drug, and Cosmetic Act. The importance of the USP and the NF in dental practice is indirect because they set manufacturing standards for drugs of known value and are not commonly used for clinical references.

The British Pharmacopoeia (BP) is the English equivalent of the USP and is official in Great Britain and Canada. An international pharmacopeia, *Pharmacopoeia Internationalis* (PhI) is issued by the World Health Organization.

AMA Drug Evaluations (AMA-DE),[9] formerly *New and Non-Official Remedies* (NNR) and *New Drugs* (ND), is prepared by the Department of Drugs of the AMA. This publication provides authoritative, unbiased information on all single-entity drugs introduced during the preceding 10 years and all single-entity drugs or mixtures commonly prescribed in the United States. Other drugs of unusual toxicity or special importance are evaluated, and pharmacologic action, uses, and adverse reaction are discussed. The principal importance of this publication in dentistry is that it will provide authoritative and unbiased information on all drugs of current medical use.

Accepted Dental Therapeutics (ADT),[10] formerly *Accepted Dental Remedies* (ADR), is a biennial publication of the Council on Dental Therapeutics (CDT) of the American Dental Association (ADA). Drugs of recognized value in dentistry that are labeled and advertised in accordance with the CDT are included. ADT is primarily a handbook of dental pharmacotherapeutics and is intended to assist the dental practitioner in selecting the appropriate drugs for the treatment of oral diseases. The "status" of drugs, as determined by the CDT, is presented. All dentists should have immediate access to this publication.

---

*Single-entity drugs are those containing only one active ingredient, whereas multiple-entity drugs are those containing more than one active ingredient.

Physician's Desk Reference (PDR)[11] is published annually by some 200 manufacturers whose products are listed. Product descriptions that cover clinically related pharmacology in some detail are prepared by the manufacturer. Almost all currently available single- or multiple-entity preparations are included. The special value of the PDR is twofold: (1) it is published annually and therefore includes relatively up-to-date information, and (2) it is cross-indexed to include the use of proprietary names. The latter facilitates reference when only the proprietary name of a drug is known. One disadvantage is that the drug products are arranged by manufacturer rather than by pharmacologic class. Also, because the information included in the PDR is supplied solely by the drug manufacturers, it may be biased.

Physicians Desk Reference for Nonprescription Drugs (PDR-ND) has been published annually since 1980. It discusses over-the-counter drugs. PDR-ND indexing and format are similar to the regular PDR and, similarly, information contained is provided by the manufacturers.

Facts and Comparisons[12] publishes a reference tool that lists drugs by their pharmacologic class. This book is published yearly or by subscription, which supplies monthly supplements. Most of the drugs available in the United States on prescription as well as many over-the-counter drugs are listed.

DRUG NOMENCLATURE[13-16]

Unfortunately, all drugs have more than one name. This fact perplexes the teacher, confuses the clinician, and irritates the student.

During the time that a compound is being investigated for possible clinical use, it is identified by a *chemical name* that conveys the chemical structure of the compound. For convenience, or if the structure is not yet known, a code number may be assigned to the compound by the investigating company or activity. If the chemical is determined to be therapeutically useful and is to be marketed commercially, the company gives the drug their *trade name (proprietary name)*. This trade name is registered as a trademark under federal trade-mark law and becomes the property of the registering company. The trade name is generally short and amenable to commercial promotion. *Brand name* has been used to mean trade or proprietary name; however, it technically is the name of the company marketing the product. At this point the product is usually patented under federal patent law,

which gives the company exclusive right to manufacture the drug for 17 years.

Before any drug can be marketed, it must be given a generic (nonproprietary) name. This becomes the "official" name of the drug and is the one used in the USP-NF. Although additional trade names may come, go, and accumulate, there is only one generic name and it seldom changes.

Generic names are selected by the U.S. Adopted Name (USAN) Council. This council is sponsored by the AMA, the APA, and the USP Convention, Inc. The council is made up of one member from the AMA, one from the APA, one from the USP Convention, one from the Food and Drug Administration (FDA), and one at-large member selected by the sponsors. The manufacturer of a new drug usually submits a proposal for a generic name to the council. The council considers recommendations by respective pharmaceutical manufacturers, the FDA, and other foreign and international agencies to select a generic name that will be simple and meaningful and will not conflict with other drug names. After the generic name is selected, it is published by the AMA Department of Drugs in the *Journal of the American Medical Association* (J.A.M.A.).

Examples of names for two products are as follows:

CHEMICAL NAME:	2-diethylamino-2,6-acetoxylidide
GENERIC NAME:	lidocaine
TRADE NAMES:	Xylocaine
	L-Caine
	Dolicaine
	Octocaine
CHEMICAL NAME:	*N*-acetyl-*p*-aminophenol
GENERIC NAME:	acetaminophen
TRADE NAMES:	Tylenol
	Tempra
	Nebs
	Datril
	Phenaphen
	Valadol
	Tapar

The problem in drug nomenclature really begins when the original manufacturer's exclusive rights to market a product expire. Other companies may now put their brands on the market under different trade names. Thus it becomes more difficult to determine the nature of a drug a patient is taking.

For 17 years there was only one lidocaine; this was Xylocaine. Now there are L-Caine, Dolicaine, and Octocaine. If a patient told the dentist that he was allergic to Octocaine, there is a strong probability that the dentist would not know that Octocaine was lidocaine. The problem with medically prescribed drugs is particularly acute because of the large number of drugs being used and the fact that most are marketed under two or more trade names. Unfortunately, when a patient tells the dentist that he is taking a drug prescribed by his physician, he usually identifies it by its trade name. As in the case of lidocaine, if the patient said he was taking chloramphenicol, this would mean much more to the dentist than if he said he was taking Amphicol or Mychel, which are trade names for chloramphenicol.

More confusion is caused by drug nomenclature when multiple-entity drugs are considered. Many names are added with the creation of new trade names for combination products. For example, the 1981 edition of the PDR lists more than 100 names for preparations containing chlorpheniramine maleate, 80 names for preparations containing guaifenesin, and more than 80 names for preparations containing iron.

There are two important disadvantages of trade names: (1) they make the problem of drug identification complex, and (2) if a practitioner writes a prescription using a trade name, in many states the pharmacist must dispense that particular product despite the fact that less expensive generic preparations may be available. Some state laws allow substitution of a generic equivalent unless the prescriber specifically forbids it. There may be an advantage to prescribing a specific proprietary brand, and this will be discussed later, but the disadvantage of the cost differential should be recognized by the practitioner.

There are some advantages to using trade names: (1) they are convenient and save time when writing prescriptions for multiple-entity drugs; for instance, if a preparation contains more than one ingredient, the use of the product's trade name will avoid the necessity of listing each ingredient and its amount separately in a prescription, (2) trade names are usually shorter and easier to remember than are generic names, and (3) the use of a trade name demands the product of a specific manufacturer in whose manufacturing practices the practitioner may have special confidence.

This raises an important question: Does "generic equivalence," as now determined, accurately indicate "therapeutic equivalence"? As previously noted, after a drug company's exclusive right to manufacture a product expires, other companies frequently produce and market it. The latter companies may add their trade names to the product or simply market the drug under its generic name. In either case they usually sell the drug at less than the original producer's prices. In recent years foreign products under generic names have been imported into the United States at relatively low prices. It has been contended that the basis of determining *generic equivalence* (chemical and physical standards as required by the USP-NF) does not necessarily establish therapeutic equivalence.[17]

In considering the question of prescribing by generic or trade name, it may be concluded that although most generic preparations are less expensive than trade preparations and are generally accepted to be as therapeutically effective, there are some instances in which generic preparations are not as effective as their trade name counterparts.[17,18]

Even though these conclusions may be enlightening, they unfortunately do not give the prescriber a complete basis for determining the merit of using generic names instead of trade names.

Although the advantages and disadvantages of using generic names in prescription writing may be argued, *there is no question that both student and practitioner must relate drug information to generic names, not trade names.* The Kefauver-Harris amendments (1962) to the Food, Drug, and Cosmetic Act require that all drug labels list the generic names and quantities of all ingredients. The generic name must also appear in all advertising and labeling wherever the trade name appears. Consequently, if one's knowledge about a drug is associated with its generic name, it is unnecessary to learn a large number of trade names.

Most frequently prescribed drugs

Appendix A lists the 200 drugs most frequently prescribed in 1980. They are listed alphabetically as prescribed—by either generic or trade name. The generic name(s) of the ingredients, the pharmacologic class of these agents, and the chapter in which they are discussed in the text are listed. By using this list as a reference source, the dentist can develop a more accurate medical history. Also, contraindications or cautions to dental treatment can be determined.

FEDERAL REGULATORY AGENCIES

The production, marketing, advertising, labeling, and prescribing of drugs are under certain controls imposed and enforced by the federal government. Following are the principal agencies involved.

Food and Drug Administration

The FDA of the Department of Health and Human Services determines what drugs can be marketed in the United States. It considers data relative to safety and effectiveness for drug entities, and physical and chemical standards for specific products. It requires quality control in U.S. manufacturing plants, determines what drugs must be sold by prescription only, and controls the labeling and advertising of prescription drugs. The legal authority of the FDA in these matters is the Food, Drug, and Cosmetic Act of 1938 and its amendments, which include the Durham-Humphrey Law of 1952 and the Kefauver-Harris Bill of 1962.

Federal Trade Commission

The Federal Trade Commission (FTC) is not a part of the Department of Health and Human Services. This independent commission has the responsibility to regulate trade practices and prohibit false advertising of foods, nonprescription drugs, and cosmetics. Its authority is granted by the Federal Trade Commission Act.

Drug Enforcement Administration

The Drug Enforcement Administration (DEA) of the Department of Justice administers the Controlled Substance Act of 1970, which replaced the Harrison Narcotic Act. It enforces the federal control of drugs considered to have a potential for abuse, such as narcotics, stimulants, and sedatives.

REFERENCES

1. Gilman, A.G., Goodman, L.S., and Gilman, A.: Goodman and Gilman's the pharmacological basis of therapeutics, ed. 2, New York, 1980, Macmillan Publishing Co., Inc.
2. Krantz, J.C.: Pharmacologic principles of medical practice: a textbook on pharmacology and therapeutics for students and practitioners of medicine, pharmacy, and dentistry, Baltimore, 1972, The Williams & Wilkins Co.
3. Csaky, T.Z.: Cutting's handbook of pharmacology, ed. 6, New York, 1978, Appleton-Century-Crofts.
4. Kremer, E.K., Kremer's and Urdan's history of pharmacy, ed. 4, Philadelphia, 1976, J.B. Lippincott Co.
5. Goth, A., and Shore, P.A.: Medical pharmacology: principles and concepts, ed. 10, St. Louis, 1981, The C.V. Mosby Co.
6. DiPalma, J.R., editor: Basic pharmacology in medicine, New York, 1976, McGraw-Hill Book Co.
7. Meyers, F.H., Jawetz, E., and Goldfein, A.: Review of medical pharmacology, ed. 7, Los Altos, Calif., 1980, Lange Medical Publications.
8. United States Pharmacopeia XX, National Formulary XV, ed. 20, Rockville, Md., 1979, The U.S. Pharmacopeial Convention, Inc.
9. American Medical Association Department of Drugs: AMA drug evaluations, ed. 4, Acton, Mass., 1980, Publishing Sciences Group, Inc.
10. American Dental Association Council on Dental Therapeutics: Accepted dental therapeutics, ed. 38, Chicago, 1979, The Association.
11. Physician's desk reference, ed. 35, Oradell, N.J., 1981, Medical Economics Co.
12. Kastrup, K., editor: Facts and comparisons, rev. ed., St. Louis, 1981, Facts and Comparisons, Inc.
13. Holroyd, S.V.: Pharmacotherapeutics in dental practice, HAVPERS 10486, Washington, D.C., 1969, Bureau of Naval Personnel.
14. Pettit, W.: Manual of pharmaceutical law, New York, 1957, Macmillan Publishing Co., Inc.
15. Martin, E.W., editor: Remington's pharmaceutical sciences, ed. 13, Easton, Pa., 1965, Mack Publishing Co.
16. American Medical Association Council on Drugs: New names, J.A.M.A. **206:**118-119, 1968.
17. Varley, A.B.: The generic inequivalence of drugs, J.A.M.A. **206:**1745-1748, 1968.
18. Mindel, J.A.: Bioavailability and generic prescribing, Surv. Ophthalmol. **21:**262-275, 1976.

General principles of drug action

Drugs are chemical substances that are used for the diagnosis, prevention, or treatment of disease and the prevention of pregnancy. Most drugs are differentiated from inert chemicals and chemicals necessary for the maintenance of life processes by their ability to act *selectively* in biologic systems to accomplish a desired effect. This selective action of drugs with regard to their use in diagnosing, preventing, and treating disease is the basis of *pharmacotherapeutics*.

Historically, drugs were found by random searching for active components among plants, animals, minerals, and the soil. Today the search for new drugs involves a different approach. Systematic screening techniques are used to discover therapeutic agents from natural sources. Also, the rise of organic synthetic chemistry in this century has witnessed the development of thousands of new synthetic drugs. *Screening tests* are necessary to determine if natural and synthetic compounds elicit biologic activity. Once activity is established for a compound, more exacting quantitative evaluations are performed in studies known as *biologic assays*. This type of assay compares the activity of a drug with that of a preparation eliciting similar activity at a known strength—commonly referred to as a *reference standard*. If the drug eventually becomes available in a pure form, it is also standardized by *chemical assay*.

Chemical modifications of the structure of parent compounds exhibiting known pharmacologic activity have resulted in the production of congeners, or analogs—many of which have become useful members of a variety of drug classes. Local anesthetics, antihistamines, cholinergic agents, the phenothiazine and benzodiazepine type of tranquilizers, and barbiturate hypnotics are some examples of these classes. The technique of modifying a chemical molecule for the purposes of producing more useful therapeutic agents evolved from studies of the relationship between chemical structure and biologic activity *(structure activity relationships)*. For example, the naturally occurring cholinergic agent acetylcholine is not a useful drug, since it is rapidly hydrolized by plasma enzymes. On the addition of a methyl group to the beta carbon atom to form acetyl-β-methylcholine (methacholine), the acetylcholine is transformed into a cholinergic compound resistant to plasma hydrolytic enzymes, as follows:

$$CH_3-N^+-CH_2-CH_2-O-C-CH_3$$

Acetylcholine

$$CH_3-N^+-CH_2-CH-O-C-CH_3$$

Methacholine

Another example of structure-activity relationships can be cited from the barbituric acid derivatives. Barbituric acid lacks central depressant activity, but the addition of carbon groups at the C_5 atom to form, among others, pentobarbital confers sedative-hypnotic properties to the molecule. Taken one step further, the replacement of the oxygen atom by sulfur at the C_2 atom results in thiopental, an ultra-short-acting, potent hypnotic.

O
H ‖
N — C   H
/   \   /
O = C²   ⁵C
\   /   \
N — C   H
H   ‖
O

Barbituric acid

O
H ‖
N — C   CH₂CH₃
/   \   /
O = C   C
\   /   \
N — C   CHCH₂CH₂CH₃
H   ‖ |
O   CH₃

Pentobarbital

O
H ‖
N — C   CH₂CH₃
/   \   /
S = C   C
\   /   \
N — C   CHCH₂CH₂CH₃
H   ‖ |
O   CH₃

Thiopental

CHARACTERIZATION OF DRUG ACTION

Drugs are classified according to their biochemical actions, their physiologic effects, or the organ system on which they exert their therapeutic action. For example, drugs are described as hypoglycemic agents, antihypertensive agents, central nervous system (CNS) stimulants, and so on.

All drugs exert some effect on biologic systems, and in most instances a given effect can be related to drug dosage in a quantitative fashion. If the dose of a drug is plotted on a logarithmic scale against intensity of effect, a sigmoid log dose-effect curve is obtained (Fig. 2-1). From this curve two important expressions of drug action can be demonstrated—*potency* and maximal effect, or *efficacy*.

Potency is indicated by the location of the curve along the log dose axis. For example, the curve, if shifted to the right, would indicate that higher doses of a drug are necessary to attain similar intensities of effect. A shift to the left would indicate that lower

doses of a drug are needed to attain the same intensities of effect. Different drugs eliciting similar effects can be compared in potency by comparing the dose that gives 50% of the total or maximal effect. The maximal effect would be the effect attained at a certain dose of a drug that cannot be further increased with higher doses of the drug. A drug requiring less of a dose to elicit a 50% maximal effect would be more potent than a drug requiring a greater dose.

Potency is a relative term when the action of two similar drugs is compared, and it merely indicates that the less potent drug must be administered in higher doses to attain the desired effect. The absolute potency of any drug matters little as long as its appropriate dose is utilized. A clinical example may be cited to describe potency. Both meperidine HCl and morphine HCl elicit similar effects therapeutically in that they induce analgesia in even the most severe types of pain. However, a dose of 80 to 100 mg meperidine HCl parenterally is required to elicit the equivalent analgesic response attained by 10 mg morphine HCl.

The log dose-effect curve in Fig. 2-1 also indicates a maximal intensity of effect, or efficacy, as shown by the plateau of the curve. The efficacy of any drug is a major descriptive characteristic indicating some degree of its action. For example, the efficacy of meperidine HCl and morphine HCl is about the same, since both drugs relieve severe pain. Other analgesics, however, such as propoxyphene HCl and salicylates, are less efficacious in that they relieve only mild to moderate pain. The dose of a drug required to produce a specific intensity of effect in an individual is regarded as the effective dose for that individual. If the percentage of individuals who respond to a drug is plotted as a function of logarithm dose, a dose-percent curve is obtained (Fig. 2-2). The dose-percent curve is not a dose-effect curve but is a means to express individual variability for a single effect. The dose of a drug required to produce a specified intensity of effect in 50% of individuals (or the dose at which 50% of individuals respond) is known as the median effective dose, or ED_{50}.

If a given dose of drug is administered to many individuals, variations in response and effect will occur among those individuals. These variations are caused by individual variations to the general factors that characterize the actions of all drugs and that determine the effective level of any therapeutic agent at its site of action. These factors are (1) the routes of

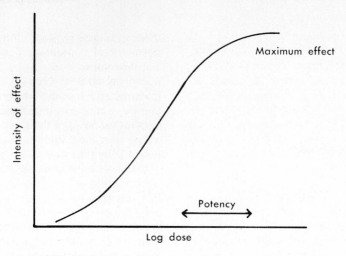

Fig. 2-1. Log dose-effect curve. A representative dose-effect curve indicating potency and efficacy.

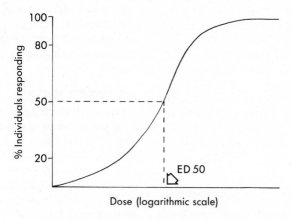

Fig. 2-2. Dose-percent curve. Dose at which 50% of individuals respond (median effective dose, ED_{50}) is illustrated.

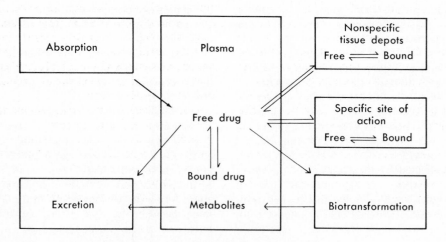

Fig. 2-3. Absorption and fate of a drug.

drug administration, (2) passage of drugs across body membranes, (3) absorption, (4) transport and distribution, (5) molecular mechanisms of action, (6) drug metabolism, and (7) excretion. These factors are depicted schematically in Fig. 2-3. An ideal goal in drug administration is to achieve adequate concentrations of the drug at sites of action in target tissues. The factors that influence the time course of drug action and also influence the amount of drug reaching these target sites are discussed.

ROUTES OF DRUG ADMINISTRATION

The route by which a drug is administered will affect the time required for the drug to enter the bloodstream. Since most drugs must be distributed throughout the body in the water phase of blood plasma before a response is elicited, the route of administration will affect the time of onset of drug action and to a lesser extent its duration of action. The routes of drug entry into a patient can be conveniently classified as *enteral* and *parenteral*. Enteral routes are those by which a drug is placed directly into the gastrointestinal tract from which absorption occurs across the enteric membranes, and this method includes oral and rectal administration. Parenteral administration bypasses the gastrointestinal tract and includes the routes of injection. Inhalation, topical administration, and the sublingual route are three additional routes by which drugs are administered.

Oral route

The simplest way to introduce a drug into the body is by the oral route, which allows the use of many different dose forms to attain desired results. Tablets, capsules, liquids, suspensions, and timed-release preparations are all conveniently given orally. It is the most frequently used route and is convenient for self-administration. The large absorbing area that the intestine presents is considered an advantage of this route. Oral administration is associated with a longer onset time of drug action compared with many parenteral routes, since absorption takes place relatively slowly. Many agents can cause stomach and intestinal irritation that results in nausea and vomiting. Other drugs such as certain penicillins and protein preparations (for example, insulin) are inactivated by gastrointestinal tract acidity or enzymes. One must remember that most drugs given orally are initially perfused into the hepatic portal circulation—a process that will

rapidly deactivate some drugs in the liver such as testosterone propionate. This process is called the first-pass effect.

The presence of food in the stomach slows drug absorption. Variability in the presence and absence of food, various pathologic conditions of the gastrointestinal tract, and the effect of gastric acidity and hepatic portal circulation make blood levels obtained after oral administration less predictable than levels obtained after parenteral administration.

Rectal route

Drugs may be given rectally by way of suppositories or creams. Agents that cause irritation when given orally may be better tolerated in the anal canal. Nausea and unconsciousness in the patient will not prevent the rectal administration of a drug. Both local effects and systemic absorption are obtained by this route. Most drugs, however, are not as well absorbed rectally as from the upper intestine, and absorption of many drugs is often irregular and incomplete.

Intravenous injection

The most rapid method of eliciting a drug response in a patient is by the intravenous route because the onset of drug action is immediate after intravenous injection. Of the several injectable routes available, this route can accommodate the largest volume of drug solution. Also, when compared with the oral route, a more predictable drug response can be obtained, since many of the factors affecting absorption have been eliminated. This is the route of choice for emergency administration of agents during crisis situations, for example, the injection of diazepam to counteract convulsions resulting from systemic toxicity of local anesthetics.[1] Constant plasma levels of drugs may be maintained by intravenous infusion. Intravenous injection is also a useful route to produce conscious sedation in apprehensive patients undergoing oral surgical procedures.

Disadvantages of this route include the occurrence of hazardous reactions because of high local concentrations of drugs that can result on injection. Also, drugs cannot be recalled once injected, whereas a stomach pump or emetic can be utilized to recall drugs after oral administration. Too rapid an injection rate may cause untoward effects on the circulation and respiration.

Intramuscular injection

Rapid absorption of drugs occurs after intramuscular injection because blood flow through skeletal muscle is high even while an individual is at rest (0.02 to 0.07 ml/min/gram tissue).[2] Large amounts of solution may be given by this route, and many irritating drugs are well tolerated, since less pain is associated with this route compared with subcutaneous injection. Intramuscular injection is an inconvenient method for repetitive drug administration. Injections are usually made in the deltoid region or gluteal mass underlying the upper outer quadrant of each buttock.

Subcutaneous injection

Although blood flow is poorer and absorption rates are said to be slower, it has been shown that the rate of subcutaneous absorption of certain drugs is as rapid as intramuscular absorption.[2] Solutions or suspensions of drugs are injected into subcutaneous aerolar tissue to gain access to the systemic circulation. However, irritating solutions are painful when injected subcutaneously, and sterile abscesses may develop as a result of irritation. Rates of drug absorption may be modified in subcutaneous regions by inducing peripheral vasoconstriction with cooling of the area or with the local application of epinephrine.

Intradermal injection

Drugs such as local anesthetics can be injected in small amounts into the epidermis of the skin. This technique provides an insensitive area through which longer needles can be passed without pain for much deeper injections.

Intrathecal injection

Spinal anesthesia is accomplished by injecting local anesthetic solutions into the spinal subarachnoid space. Some antiinfective drugs are also injected by this route to treat infections of the meninges.

Intraperitoneal injection

Injections may be made into the peritoneal cavity, where absorption of the drug occurs by way of the mesenteric veins. Because of dangers of infection and adhesions, however, this route is seldom employed clinically.

Inhalation

Gaseous, microcrystalline, and volatile drugs may be inhaled. They are then absorbed through the pulmonary endothelium at the alveoli to gain rapid access to the general circulation. Absorption can also take place through the mucous membranes of the respiratory tract. Drugs in solution may be atomized in an aerosol preparation and the fine droplets in the air inhaled.

Topical route

The topical route of drug administration includes application to the skin and other epithelial surfaces. Most drugs do not penetrate the intact skin, and this route is generally utilized for local drug effects. Systemic toxicities have occurred because of the absorption of highly lipid soluble agents such as organophosphate insecticides. Since absorption through the skin is proportional to the lipid solubility of a drug, lipid-insoluble agents and ions penetrate very slowly. Many potentially toxic drugs may be applied topically to the skin without worry of systemic side effects. For example, potent synthetic corticosteroids will relieve various localized skin disorders. Although some of the steroid drug may be absorbed systemically, plasma levels are insufficient to produce systemic effects. Drugs known to induce frequent allergic reactions such as penicillins should not be used topically because sensitization may occur.

Drugs are applied to the vagina and urethra for their local action. Certain drugs may reach the circulation through the mucous membranes at these sites. However, these routes are not utilized for this purpose. Drugs are applied intravaginally in the form of suppositories or creams and intraurethrally as suppositories or urethral inserts. Drugs applied into the ear and eye as solutions or suspensions are seldom absorbed systemically to any significant extent. In fact, some drugs that are extremely toxic systemically such as the organophosphate derivative echothiophate iodide may be safely administered in most patients as a local application to the eye.

Although drugs are applied topically to the nasal membranes in the form of solutions or sprays, on occasion the resulting effect is systemic. In fact, certain local anesthetics such as tetracaine achieve systemic blood levels after absorption through the pharyngeal mucous membranes that are similar to those after intravenous injection.[3]

Sublingual route

The mucous membranes of the oral cavity provide a convenient absorbing surface for the systemic administrations of drugs, which can be placed under the tongue (sublingual) or on other areas of the oral mucosa. Absorption of many drugs rapidly occurs into the systemic circulation, as exemplified by the fast onset of action of nitroglycerin sublingual tablets to treat anginal pain. Drugs that are susceptible to degradation by the gastrointestinal tract and even the liver, such as testosterone, are safely administered as sublingual tablets. The oral cavity provides an attractive topical drug administration route of which pharmacology has never fully taken advantage.

PASSAGE OF DRUGS ACROSS BODY MEMBRANES

The amounts of a drug moving across body membranes and the rates with which a drug moves have important implications in the time course of action and the variation in individual response. For a drug to be absorbed, transported and distributed to body tissues, metabolized, and subsequently eliminated from the body, it must traverse various membranes such as those of the blood capillaries, cellular membranes, and intracellular membranes. Although these membranes vary considerably in function, they share certain physicochemical characteristics that influence the passage of drugs and other chemical substances. Membranes are composed of lipids, proteins, and carbohydrates. Lipids comprise approximately 40% of the content of membranes; proteins, 50% to 60%; and carbohydrates, the remainder. The membrane lipids are a class of compounds called phospholipids, the presence of which makes the membrane relatively impermeable to ions and polar molecules. Membrane proteins act in a functional capacity as enzymes during transport processes and also make up the structural components of the membrane. Membrane carbohydrates consist of oligosaccharides, which are linked covalently to proteins to form complexes called glycoproteins or to lipids to form glycolipids. In the past it was believed that the chemical components of membranes were arranged into a bimolecular lipid sheet bordered on both sides by a monolayer of protein.[4] Biologic membranes have now been confirmed to be a dynamic mosaic of phospholipids, proteins, glycoproteins, and glycolipids.[5] The phospholipid molecules form the matrix of the mosaic and are oriented to form a fluid bimolecular layered structure with their hydrophobic ends shielded from the surrounding aqueous environment and their hydrophilic ends in contact with water. The proteins, glycoproteins, and glycolipids are embedded in and layered onto this fluid lipid bilayer with their hydrophilic groups on the membrane surface and their hydrophobic groups oriented into the membrane interior (Fig. 2-4). Studies on the membrane penetration of substances of varying molecular weights and sizes have also indicated the presence of a system of pores or membrane channels.

The physicochemical properties of drugs that influence their passage across biologic membranes are *lipid solubility, degree of ionization,* and *molecular size and shape*. The mechanism of drug transfer across biologic membranes is by passive transfer and specialized transport.

Passive transfer

Lipid-soluble substances move across the lipoprotein membrane by a passive transfer process of *simple diffusion*. In this process, drug molecules must dissolve in the membrane to penetrate through to the other side. The amount of drug dissolving in the membrane at any time is directly proportional to the concentration gradient and its degree of lipid solubility. Most drugs are partially ionized at physiologic pH, and only the nonionized species is soluble in lipid. Thus the degree of lipid solubility of the nonionized species will determine the total amount of drug being transferred. A steady state is achieved when the concentrations of the nonionized species is the same on both sides of the membrane.

Water-soluble molecules small enough to pass through the membrane channels (molecular radius of 30 Å for capillary membranes and 4 Å for other cell membranes) may be carried through the pores by the bulk flow of water.[6,7] This process of *filtration* through single cell membranes may occur with drugs of molecular weights of 200 or less. Drugs up to molecular weights of 60,000, however, can "filter" through capillary membranes.

Specialized transport

Certain substances, including low molecular weight ionized drug molecules, are transported across cell membranes by processes more complex than simple diffusion or filtration. *Active transport* is a process by which a substance is transported against a concentration gradient or electrochemical gradient and which is blocked by metabolic inhibitors. This action is mediated by transport "carriers" that furnish energy for transportation of the drug to regions of higher concentration.

The transport of some substances such as glucose into cells is also blocked by metabolic inhibitors. This type of transport, however, does not move

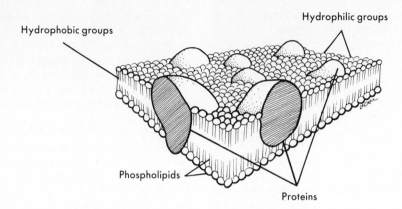

Hydrophobic groups

Hydrophilic groups

Phospholipids

Proteins

Fig. 2-4. Fluid mosaic model of membrane structure.

against a concentration gradient and is called *facilitated diffusion*. The process of pinocytosis (the ability of cells to engulf fluids) has been suggested to explain the passage of macromolecular substances into cells.

ABSORPTION

Absorption is the process by which drug molecules are transferred from the site of administration in the body to the circulating fluids. Since this process requires the drug to pass through biologic membranes, the *physicochemical factors* discussed earlier will influence the absorption rates of drugs. The *site of absorption* will also greatly affect the absorption rate. For example, one of the advantages of oral administration is attributable to the large absorbing area presented by the gastrointestinal mucosa. The route by which a drug is administered determines its site of absorption. *Drug solubility* is another important factor affecting absorption. Drugs in solution are more rapidly absorbed than are insoluble drugs.

Drug absorption with regard to their nature as weak electrolytes

Drugs that are weak electrolytes dissociate in solution as both a nonionized and an ionized form. The nonionized portion behaves as a nonpolar lipid-soluble compound, which readily traverses body membranes. The ionized portion, being less lipid soluble, will traverse these membranes with greater difficulty, if at all. The more the compound is ionized at membrane sites, the less the amount of absorption that occurs and vice versa.

The amount of ionization that any weak electrolyte

undergoes depends on the pH at the drug site in the tissues and its dissociation characteristics. The relationship to pH is as follows: for weak acids, the higher the pH, the greater degree of ionization; for weak bases, the lower the pH, the greater the ionization. The dissociation characteristics of a weak electrolyte are given by a dissociation constant (pKa), which is an indication of its tendency to ionize. The pKa of a compound is the same as the pH at which it will be half undissociated and half ionized. Aspirin has a pKa of 3.5. This means that at pH 3.5, aspirin is 50% ionized. Because aspirin is a weak acid, decreasing the pH below 3.5, as occurs in the stomach, decreases ionization to less than 50%, and increases the amount of nonionized aspirin absorbed. Conversely, increasing the pH above 3.5, as occurs in the intestine or if the gastric contents are alkalinized, increases the ionization of aspirin above 50% and subsequently decreases the amount absorbed.

Knowing the pKa of a drug, the clinician can calculate the extent to which it ionizes at any pH. For example, consider the ionization of weakly basic local anesthetics in the plasma. Assuming that the pKa of a typical local anesthetic is 8.4, at plasma pH 7.4:

$$pH = pKa + \log \frac{(\text{nonionized drug})}{(\text{ionized drug})}$$

$$7.4 = 8.4 + \log \frac{(\text{nonionized drug})}{(\text{ionized drug})}$$

$$\text{Antilog } (7.4 - 8.4) = \frac{(\text{nonionized drug})}{(\text{ionized drug})}$$

$$0.1 \text{ or } \frac{1}{10} = \frac{(\text{nonionized drug})}{(\text{ionized drug})}$$

Therefore at plasma pH the ratio of nonionized to ionized drug is 1:10, which means that 10% of the drug (nonionized) is available for passage through membranes from the plasma.

Although the calculations of the actual percentage of ionization at a known pH are of greater academic and research importance than of clinical significance, its theoretic basis has important implications for the rational utilization of drugs.

Oral absorption

Aside from those general factors previously mentioned that affect drug absorption, an important factor influencing absorption in the gastrointestinal tract is the dosage form of a drug. Unless administered as a solution, the absorption of a drug in the gastrointestinal tract involves its release from a dose form such as a tablet, capsule, or suspension. This release may involve the initial disruption of a tablet coating or capsule shell, the disintegration of the tablet or capsule contents, the dispersion of the concentrated drug particles, and the dissolution of the drug in gastrointestinal fluids. The process of drug absorption from a particular dose form is referred to as the *bioavailability* of the drug.

The dissolution rate is proportional to the surface area of the dissolving solid, and drugs such as griseofulvin (an antifungal) and spironolactone (a diuretic) are better absorbed in a microcrystalline state. The shape and crystal form of the drug particles also influence dissolution. Drugs such as steroids, barbiturates, and sulfonamides exist as several kinds of molecular arrangements within a crystal—a phenomenon known as polymorphism. These polymorphic forms of the drug differ in their rates of dissolution and subsequent absorption. The incorporation of water into drug crystals (hydrates) induces dissolution rates that differ from those of the original drug crystal. Pronounced differences in dissolution rates may also occur with salts and esters of original drug crystals. Different esters of erythromycin impart varying dissolution rates compared with the base compound, and the absorption rate is affected accordingly.

Absorption at injection sites

Absorption at various sites of injection depends on the solubility of the drug and the blood flow at the site. For example, drugs of low aqueous solubility such as the depot type of penicillins (procaine penicillin G suspension and benzathine peincillin G) are absorbed very slowly after IM injection. Absorption at injection sites is also affected by the dose form. For example, drugs in suspension are absorbed much more slowly than those in solution. This fact is utilized to decrease the absorption rate of certain insulin preparations by formulating them into suspensions.

Effects of food on drug absorption

Food influences the amounts of drug absorbed and the rate at which a drug is absorbed from the gastrointestinal tract by affecting blood flow and gastric emptying. The rate at which a drug is absorbed from the gastrointestinal tract into the venous capillary network is a function of the rate of blood flow through the capillaries. Different foods have been shown to affect this rate of blood flow. For example, a liquid glucose meal decreases flow, and a meal rich in protein increases flow. It has been shown that drugs such as griseofulvin, lithium citrate (used to treat manic-depression), propoxyphene (an analgesic), and propranolol (an antihypertensive) undergo increased absorption in the presence of certain foods.[8]

Foods that delay gastric emptying also delay the absorption of an orally administered drug. The entry of low-pH or high-fat solutes into the upper small intestine delay gastric emptying. Gastric emptying is also delayed by hot meals and solutions rich in fat and carbohydrate. Slow gastric emptying may also reduce the amount of drug absorbed because of the degradation of the drug in the acidic contents of the stomach. Drugs such as aspirin, penicillin, and acetaminophen undergo reduced and/or delayed absorption in the presence of food. As a rule of thumb, if food reduces or delays absorption of drugs, giving the drug at least 1 hour before meals will minimize this effect. If food enhances drug absorption, the drug is given with meals.

TRANSPORT AND DISTRIBUTION

For a drug to exert activity, it must be made available to its locus of action in the body, and distribution is the mechanism by which this is accomplished. Distribution is regarded as the passage of drugs into various body fluid compartments such as plasma, interstitial fluids, and intracellular fluids. The patterns of distribution in the body determine how rapidly a drug will elicit a desired response, the duration of the response, and in some cases whether a response will be elicited at all.

The primary purpose of drug distribution is to allow a drug to reach its site of action at specific tissue sites. Many drugs, however, are distributed to non-specific tissues, which serve as storage depots. Other drugs cannot be distributed in certain regions of the body. Still other drugs are redistributed from one tissue accumulation site to another.

Transport in plasma

After a drug is absorbed from its site of administration, it is transported to its site of action by the blood plasma. Therefore the biologic activity of a drug is usually related to its concentration in plasma. More specifically, drug activity is related to its concentration in *plasma water,* since a drug exists in this phase only in the free or *unbound state,* that is, not bound to plasma protein. This is the biologically active form of a drug.

The reversible binding of drugs to plasma proteins such as albumin and globulins is a well-known phenomenon that causes an unequal distribution of drugs in the body. Since only the unbound species is the biologically active form of a drug, that proportion of drug bound in the plasma does not contribute to intensity of drug action. In fact, the binding process is considered to be a site of drug loss or storage. This binding is reversible, and as the unbound drug disappears from plasma water to be distributed to tissue sites, a dynamic equilibrium results in a dissociation of bound to unbound drug—a process that results in an increased supply of unbound drug. In this way the plasma binding process prolongs drug activity. Without such a process, most drugs would have to be administered at very frequent intervals to be effective therapeutically.

The biologic half-life ($t_{\frac{1}{2}}$) of a drug is the time necessary for the body to eliminate half the peak quantity of drug present in the circulation. This is greatly affected by the extent of plasma protein binding. Drugs vary as to the extent of binding in the plasma, and most drugs used in medicine and dentistry do bind to some extent. Phenylbutazone, a nonsteroid anti-inflammatory agent, is bound to the extent of 98% of its therapeutic dose, whereas pentobarbital, a barbiturate hypnotic, is bound approximately 55%.

Plasma protein binding is characterized by the existence of a limited number of binding sites on albumin—the major plasma protein involved in drug binding. Two drugs having affinity for the same binding sites will compete with one another for binding.

If a drug is highly bound, the usual therapeutic dose may become toxic when followed by the administration of a drug that displaces it from its plasma protein storage sites.

Tissue distribution

Along with plasma transport drugs are simultaneously distributed to organ tissue sites. These sites are conveniently classified as *specific* or *nonspecific,* depending on whether the drug elicits therapeutic activity at the site in question. Tissue distribution from the plasma involves the passage of drugs across cell membranes—a process involving those factors discussed earlier for membranes in general. Tissue distribution of drugs also involves binding to intracellular components such as mucopolysaccharides, nucleoprotein, and phospholipids. Like plasma protein binding, binding to intracellular tissue components affects the $t_{\frac{1}{2}}$ of a drug. Without these tissue storage sites, many drugs would be rapidly metabolized and eliminated from the body, having little time to exert any effect. Some drugs show a greater affinity for tissue components than for plasma proteins, whereas other drugs prefer localization in one type of tissue rather than in another. For example, the tetracyclines have an unusual affinity for bone and enamel tissue. The antimalarial quinacrine binds selectively to nuclear material in liver and skeletal muscle cells. Guanethidine, a drug useful in treating hypertension, selectively binds to heart and skeletal muscle tissues. Thiopental, a barbiturate hypnotic, has a predisposition for adipose tissue. These ''affinity tissues'' may be sites of action or areas for transient storage.

Certain tissue sites of the body deserve special consideration in drug distribution. The passage of drugs into and out of the central nervous system involves transfer across the blood-brain barrier. This specialized limiting barrier consists of membranes of the capillary walls and surrounding glial cells. The passage of a drug through this barrier into the cerebrospinal fluid is related to its degree of lipid solubility and ionization. Thiopental, a highly lipid-soluble, nonionized drug, readily penetrates into the cerebrospinal fluid to induce sleep within seconds after intravenous injection. On the other hand, the less lipid-soluble barbiturate phenobarbital takes much longer to induce the same degree of narcosis. Lipid-insoluble drugs such as quaternary ammonium compounds pass a thousand times less rapidly into the cerebrospinal fluid than does thiopental.

Knowledge concerning the passage of chemical substances through the placenta is substantial. With respect to drug transfer, the placenta is considered to resemble the blood-brain barrier, and the majority of drugs are believed to cross by a process of simple diffusion in accordance with their degree of lipid solubility.[9,10] Thus nonionized drugs of high fat solubility such as anesthetics and barbiturate hypnotics cross the placenta readily and rapidly. Present evidence indicates that the fetus is probably exposed to all drugs taken by the mother.[11]

There are indications that the placenta may act as a selective membrane toward certain drugs passing into and out of fetal tissues. After intravenous injection of lidocaine, a large gradient existed between maternal and fetal blood levels, with higher levels of drug existing in fetal tissues for up to 40 minutes.[12] This gradient could not be explained by increased binding to fetal serum protein or transformation in the fetus to a more polar compound, which would prevent its passage out of the fetal tissues. Molecular drug characteristics other than lipid solubility may also influence transplacental transfer. Procaine has been shown to cross the placenta without difficulty but is detected in fetal venous blood only after the maternal injection of 4 mg/kg, whereas mepivacaine, another local anesthetic, can be detected in fetal blood after the injection of a much smaller dose. This phenomenon is explained by the fact that mepivacaine is resistant to enzyme attack in maternal blood, whereas procaine is readily hydrolyzed in maternal blood and is therefore less stable biologically.[13]

Redistribution

Redistribution of a drug from one organ tissue to another can greatly affect its duration of action. For example, if redistribution occurs between tissues at the site of action and nonspecific tissues, termination of the effect can result. The clinical example of thiopental may be cited. After a single IV dose of this hypnotic, plasma levels fall abruptly and subjects awake within 10 minutes. Subsequently, plasma levels decline slowly, and most of the drug localizes first in skeletal muscle, then in fat depots of the body. The rapid termination of the hypnotic action of this agent is caused by redistribution from the brain and other tissues to adipose tissue. Although a drug may be redistributed to other tissues after an action occurs, its eventual elimination from the body is dependent on biotransformation and excretion mechanisms.

MOLECULAR MECHANISMS OF DRUG ACTION

Most drugs elicit their effects by combining with macromolecular components of the body. Those drugs that do not interact with these components elicit their effects through physicochemical and other means. This section describes these mechanisms.

Drug-receptor interactions

The general concept of drug-receptor interactions is that drugs interact with specific macromolecular components of an organism to cause a modulation in function of that organism. Drugs do not impart a new function to the organism. These macromolecular components were proposed by Langley as long ago as 1878, and they were assumed to be capable of forming complexes with substances having proper chemical affinity.[14] These drug receptors have been characterized according to chemistry and function only over the last 2 decades.

The mechanism of drug action by receptor interaction is described according to the following. Drug (D) interacts with receptor (R) to form a drug receptor complex (DR) and results in an effect (E) with the drug-receptor combination being reversible. The following reaction equation describes this mechanism:

$$\text{Drug (D)} + \text{Receptor (R)} \underset{K_2}{\overset{K_1}{\rightleftharpoons}} DR \rightarrow \text{Effect (E)}$$

K_1 and K_2 are rate constants for the reversible combination of drug and receptor. This equation, however, does not adequately characterize most mechanisms of drug-receptor actions. Many of these actions are associated with enzymatic and regulatory processes that result in modulation of cell function only after a series of reactions, not just a single reaction of drug combining to receptor. The mechanism of digitalis that causes an increase in the force of contraction of the myocardium is cited as an example. The receptors for digitalis are sodium- and potassium-mediated adenosine triphosphatase (ATPase) proteins. These proteins ordinarily hydrolyze adenosine triphosphate (ATP) in the myocardial membrane to provide energy for the sodium pump. When bound to digitalis, however, no ATP is hydrolyzed and thus no energy is available for the sodium pump. Intracellular sodium increases and is exchanged for calcium. The increased calcium causes an increase in the force of contraction of the myocardial cells.

Most drug receptors are cellular proteins and are involved in transport processes, metabolic pathways, and regulatory pathways. Many of these proteins normally function to act as receptors for endogenous substances such as hormones, neurotransmitters (acetylcholine and norepinephrine), autocoids (kinins and prostaglandins), and the morphine-like neuropolypeptides (enkephalins and endorphins). The binding of drugs to receptors involves ionic, hydrogen, Van der Waals, and covalent bonds, and multiple bonding forces usually occur between reactive groups on the drug and receptor molecule. Covalent bonds are the strongest and usually result in a long duration of drug action.

When a drug combines with a receptor to cause a modulation in function, enhancement or inhibition of the organism results. Drugs are called *agonists* when they cause effects by directly altering the functional properties of the receptors with which they interact. Drugs can also cause effects by inhibiting the action of an agonist drug by competing for the agonist's binding sites on the receptor. These drugs usually have no intrinsic activity of their own and are called *antagonists*.

In the early part of this century, Clark[15] developed the concept that the intensity of drug response was directly related to the number of receptors occupied by the drug and that maximal effect results when all receptors are occupied by the drug. This concept is expressed by the reaction equation above. As previously mentioned, this is an oversimplification for many drug receptor actions, but it does help to describe the actions of antagonists. Although certain antagonists interact with receptors to inhibit the action of an agonist while initiating no effect themselves, the inhibition can be overcome by increasing the concentration of the agonist. This type of inhibition is termed competitive and occurs when the antagonist binds reversibly to a receptor. A noncompetitive antagonist prevents the agonist from producing effects, no matter what the concentration of the agonist, and usually results from the irreversible binding of the antagonist to the receptor.

Several decades ago, Nickerson[16] showed that maximal drug effects could be induced with certain drugs when only 1% of the available receptors were occupied. At the same time, Stephenson[17] also observed that a maximal effect could be produced by an agonist when only a small proportion of the receptors is occupied and that the response is not linearly proportional to the number of receptors occupied. These observations led to the concept of *spare receptors* in which a maximal effect can be achieved when a less than maximal fraction of receptors is occupied. Because a fraction of receptors are unoccupied, they are called the spares, or receptor reserve. This concept of spare receptors is explained when a drug-receptor interaction is only one event in a complex sequence of reactions, and a certain reaction occurring later in the pathway is rate limiting for the entire complex.

Physicochemical and other mechanisms

Some drugs affect the structure of essential macromolecules in membranes by affecting the solvent structure surrounding the molecule. This describes the volatile anesthetic gases that induce their effects through physicochemical rather than pure chemical means. Their diversity of structure suggests a nonspecific mechanism of action, and their relative potencies correlate well with their oil:water partition coefficient (Chapter 6). Another mechanism proposed for these compounds involves a physical combination with water molecules to form hydrate microcrystals called clathrates, the presence of which may alter the properties of nerve cell membranes to depress nerve function.[18]

Chelating agents are drugs that interact specifically with ions that are normally or abnormally found in the body. Also, antacids exert their actions by the chemical neutralization of gastric acid in the gastrointestinal tract (Chapter 27).

DRUG METABOLISM (BIOTRANSFORMATION)

Most drugs undergo metabolic transformation in the body. Metabolism, or biotransformation, is one of the factors that determine plasma and tissue levels of an active drug. A metabolic product is usually more polar and less lipid soluble than its parent compound. As a result, renal tubular reabsorption of the metabolite will be reduced, since this process favors lipid-soluble compounds. Also, specific secretory mechanisms in proximal renal tubules and parenchymal liver cells operate on highly polar compounds. Therefore kidney and biliary secretion of these polar compounds will be favored. Compared with their parent compounds, metabolites are less likely to bind to plasma or tissue macromolecules and to be stored in fat tissue.

Drug metabolism is an enzyme-dependent process that developed as an adaptation to terrestrial life. Unlike fish, terrestrial vertebrates are unable to excrete lipid-soluble compounds because renal tubular reabsorption favors their retention. Excretion of these substances is accomplished easily across gill membranes of fish into the surrounding water.[19] Although drug metabolism results in the formation of compounds of a more polar nature, it does not always result in the initial production of biologically inactive compounds. Enzymatic modification of a parent drug can be distinguished by three different patterns. First, an inactive parent drug may be transformed to an active compound, for example:

6-Mercaptopurine → 6-Mercaptopurine ribonucleotide
(inactive)   (active)

6-Mercaptopurine is useful as an antineoplastic agent but is inactive until converted to the corresponding ribonucleotide through conjugation in body tissues.[20] Also, parathion, a cholinesterase inhibitor, is inactive until converted to paraoxon by oxidative desulfuration in mammalian liver. When an agent is administered in its inactive form and subsequently converted to an active drug in tissues, the inactive species is referred to as a *prodrug*.

Second, an active parent drug may be converted to a second active compound, which is subsequently converted to an inactive product, for example:

Phenacetin
(active)

Acetaminophen
(active)

Acetaminophen
glucuronide
(inactive)

Phenacetin, a mild analgesic-antipyretic, is initially converted to acetaminophen, another analgesic-anti-

pyretic, through an oxidative mechanism. Acetaminophen is then inactivated through the formation of a second metabolite.

Third, an inactive compound may be formed from an active parent drug, for example:

Pentobarbital
(active)

Pentobarbital alcohol
(inactive)

Pentobarbital, a barbiturate hypnotic, is converted to its inactive alcoholic derivative, which is subsequently transformed into other inactive products. Reactions of this third general type are the most common in drug biotransformation. Drug metabolism rates and pathways may vary, depending on the species. Most studies indicate, however, that drug biotransformation in laboratory animals (the most studied population) is similar to that in humans.

Conjugations

One way the body converts lipid-soluble drugs to more polar compounds is through the synthesis of a conjugated compound. This is achieved by the attachment of a molecule of an acid normally present in the body to the drug in question. Both the parent compound and those metabolites formed by other reactions can be conjugated—a process mediated by enzymes called *transferases*.

Glucuronic acid, a normally occurring substance in the body, may be transferred to any drug molecule possessing an appropriate functional group to accept it, for example:

UDPGA   **Acetaminophen**   **Acetaminophen glucuronide**

Uridine diphosphoglucuronic acid (UDPGA) serves as a donor of glucuronic acid to the phenolhydroxyl group of acetaminophen to form an ether glucuronide. Some other acceptor substances with which glucuronic acid will combine to form a conjugate include alcohols, aromatic amines, and carboxylic acids.

Other synthetic mechanisms of drug metabolism include the acetylation of aromatic amines, the synthesis of mercapturic acids and of sulfuric acid esters, glutamine conjugation, and methylation. Table 2-1 summarizes these synthetic mechanisms and indicates the type of compound that is detoxified by each mechanism and the activated compound responsible for the donation of the molecule with which a particular compound conjugates. The synthesis of conjugated compounds from drugs occurs primarily in the liver, but also in plasma and other tissues.

Liver microsomal drug-metabolizing system

The body is faced with a more difficult problem if a drug molecule lacks appropriate functional groups suitable for conjugation. An enzyme system located in the smooth-surfaced hepatic endoplasmic reticulum is responsible for the oxidative metabolism of many drugs. These enzymes are known as *microsomal enzymes,* since they are located in the microsomal fraction as prepared from liver homogenates. A variety of oxidative reactions occur in the hepatic microsomes. A common occurrence, however, is that most of the oxidations consist of the hydroxylation of substrate or the direct incorporation of oxygen into the substrate molecule.[21] The specific metabolic reactions include the following:

Aromatic ring and side-chain hydroxylation
N- and O-dealkylation
Sulfoxide formation
N-oxidation and N-hydroxylation
Deamination of primary and secondary amines

In addition to their presence in the liver, microsomal oxidative enzyme systems are also present in other organs such as the kidney and gastrointestinal epithelium.

The hepatic microsomal oxidative enzyme system is characterized by a requirement for reduced nicotinamide-adenine dinucleotide phosphate (NADPH) and molecular oxygen. The oxidative processes of drug metabolism also involve an electron transport chain. The oxidative mechanisms may be summarized. A drug substrate binds with oxidized cytochrome P-450 (so called because it absorbs light at 450 nm when exposed to carbon monoxide).[22] The resulting drug–cytochrome P-450 complex is reduced by the flavoprotein NADPH-cytochrome P-450 reductase, and the reduced complex then combines with molecular oxygen. A second electron and two hydrogen ions are acquired from a flavoprotein donor system, and the resulting products are oxidized drug and water. Oxidized cytochrome P-450 is subsequently regenerated (Fig. 2-5).

The rate of drug biotransformation appears to be related to the amounts of cytochrome P-450 present in the microsomes. In fact, there is a direct correla-

Table 2-1. Synthetic mechanisms of drug metabolism

Mechanism	Compounds detoxicated	Active donor compound
Glucuronic acid conjugation	Compounds having: Phenolic OH Alcoholic OH COOH Aromatic amines	Glucuronic acid as uridine diphosphoglucuronic acid (UDPGA)
Acetylation	Aromatic amines	Acetyl CoA
Mercapturic acid formation	Aromatic hydrocarbons Halogenated aromatic hydrocarbons Halogenated nitrobenzenes	Activated glutathione
Sulfuric acid ester formation	Aromatic OH Aliphatic OH	3'-Phosphoadenosine-5'-phosphosulfate (PAPS)
Glutamine conjugation	Aromatic acids	CoA derivative of the acid to be conjugated
Methylation	Compounds having: Two phenolic OH >NH — NH$_2$	S-Adenosylmethionine

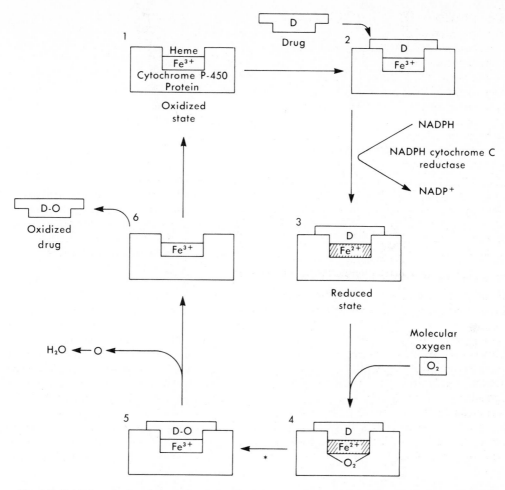

Fig. 2-5. Oxidation of a drug by cytochrome P-450. Cytochrome P-450 is a complex of protein and heme that contains an atom of iron initially in the ferric (Fe^{3+}) or oxidized state *(1)*. The cytochrome complex binds the drug *(2)*. The enzyme NADPH cytochrome C reductase, utilizing NADPH, reduces the heme iron to the ferrous form (Fe^{2+}) *(3)*, the form which then binds molecular oxygen *(4)*. One atom of the molecular oxygen then oxidizes the drug (D-O) and one forms water, with the cytochrome P-450 reverting to its oxidized form *(5)*. Oxidized drug is released *(6)*, and cytochrome P-450 is regenerated. The asterisk denotes the contribution of a second electron and two hydrogen ions from a flavoprotein donor system.

tion between the stimulation of drug oxidation by various substances and an increase in the amounts of cytochrome P-450.[23] Rates of biotransformation of drugs can vary sixfold or more between individuals, and these rates are genetically determined.

Other oxidations

Enzymes other than those of the hepatic microsomal system can mediate oxidative reactions of selected pharmacologic compounds. Alcohol is dehydrogenated by alcohol dehydrogenase to the corresponding aldehyde. Naturally occurring amines and a few drugs are oxidatively deaminated by monoamine and diamine oxidases located in the mitochondria of liver, kidney, and nervous tissue. Halogenated compounds (such as insecticides and industrial solvents) are dehalogenated by specific oxidative enzymes.

Hydrolysis

The hydrolysis of the local anesthetic procaine (an ester type of compound) by plasma cholinesterase is illustrative of this type of drug transformation:

$$\text{Procaine} \xrightarrow[\text{(+H}_2\text{O)}]{\text{Cholinesterase}} \text{p-Aminobenzoic acid} + \text{HOCH}_2\text{CH}_2\text{N(C}_2\text{H}_5)_2$$

Procaine: NH$_2$ — C$_6$H$_4$ — C(—OCH$_2$CH$_2$N(C$_2$H$_5$)$_2$)=O

p-Aminobenzoic acid: NH$_2$ — C$_6$H$_4$ — C(—OH)=O

Diethylaminoethanol: HOCH$_2$CH$_2$N(C$_2$H$_5$)$_2$

Drug metabolism by mechanisms of hydrolysis is limited to ester compounds. Hydrolytic enzymes such as cholinesterases are found in plasma and a variety of tissues.

Reduction

An example of this type of metabolic transformation is the reduction of chloral hydrate, a hypnotic agent, to trichloroethanol:

$$\text{Cl}_3\text{C} - \underset{\underset{\text{OH}}{|}}{\overset{\overset{\text{H}}{|}}{\text{C}}} - \text{OH} \rightarrow \text{Cl}_3\text{C} - \underset{\underset{\text{H}}{|}}{\overset{\overset{\text{H}}{|}}{\text{C}}} - \text{OH}$$

Alcohol dehydrogenase, found in the nonmicrosomal portion of hepatic cells, catalyzes this reduction of chloral hydrate. Another common reduction reaction is the nitro reduction of the antibiotic chloramphenicol. This reductive reaction is mediated by enzymes found in hepatic microsomes.

Clinical aspects of hepatic microsomal enzyme drug metabolism

Microsomal enzyme activity is influenced by the administration of various drugs. The experimental drug SKF525-A (β-diethylaminoethyl-2,2-diphenylpentanoate) is a well-known inhibitor of microsomal enzymes in animals. Clinically, coumarin anticoagulants inhibit the metabolic inactivation of tolbutamide and phenytoin through an effect on microsomal enzymes. The simultaneous administration of the anticoagulant with the former drug resulted in a hypoglycemic crisis, whereas administration with the latter drug resulted in toxic manifestations.[24,25]

It is a well-known fact that the activities of hepatic microsomal oxidative enzymes are decidedly increased when animals are treated with various drugs. The increased enzymatic activity is caused by an increase in the concentration of enzyme protein—a phenomenon referred to as *enzyme induction*.[23] These stimulatory effects of drugs on microsomal enzymes also have been found to occur in humans. The administration of 30 mg phenobarbital 3 times every 24 hours decreased the anticoagulant response to bishydroxycoumarin in hospitalized patients.[26] This effect was attributable to the stimulatory effects of phenobarbital on the hepatic microsomal enzymatic metabolism of the anticoagulant.[27]

Griseofulvin (an antifungal agent) was observed to stimulate the hepatic microsomal metabolism of the anticoagulant warfarin, and simultaneous therapy with the two drugs resulted in a decreased anticoagulant response.[28] Phenobarbital stimulates the metabolism of phenytoin and griseofulvin, an action that results in decreased plasma levels of the two drugs.[27,29] Also, phenylbutazone has been observed to cause an increase in the metabolic deactivation of the analgesic aminopyrine through a similar mechanism.[30] Certain drugs can stimulate their own metabolism when administered over a long period of time to humans. Patients who become tolerant to the hypnotic effects of glutethimide are found to have an increased capacity to metabolize the drug.[23]

EXCRETION

Drugs may be excreted by any route in the body that has direct access to the environment. Renal excretion is the most important route. Extrarenal routes include the lungs, bile and gastrointestinal tracts, and in sweat, saliva, and milk excretion. Drugs may be excreted unchanged or as a more polar, less lipid-soluble metabolite. Body excretion mechanisms favor the elimination of the latter compounds.

Renal route

Elimination of substances in the kidney is dependent on glomerular filtration, active tubular secretion, and passive tubular diffusion. Molecules of unchanged drug or its metabolites are first filtered through the glomeruli and are concentrated in the renal tubular fluid. Many drugs are added to the amount in the glomerular filtrate by active secretion that transports the drug from the blood across renal tubular epithelial cells into renal tubular fluid. Penicillin, an organic acid, is excreted rapidly by glomerular filtration and tubular secretion.

With most drugs, passive tubular diffusion plays a part in regulating the amount of drug in the tubular fluid. This is a reabsorption process that favors non-ionized lipid-soluble compounds. On filtration of these compounds through the glomerulus into the tubular fluid, passive diffusion of the substance will occur into the plasma through the epithelial cell membranes that line the tubules. More ionized, less lipid-soluble metabolites are less able to penetrate these cell membranes by passive diffusion and are more likely to be retained in the tubular fluid to be eventually eliminated in the urine.

Most drugs are weakly ionized acids or bases, and urinary pH has an influence on the renal excretion rates of these compounds. When tubular urinary pH is more alkaline than plasma, weak acids are excreted more rapidly. When tubular urine is more acid, weak acids are excreted more slowly. With weak bases, the effects of urinary pH are the opposite. Thus in aspirin or barbiturate poisoning, greater quantities of these weakly acidic drugs can be eliminated by simply making the tubular urine more alkaline than plasma. This is often accomplished by injecting sodium bicarbonate intravenously.

Extrarenal routes

Gaseous and volatile liquids such as those used in general anesthesia are absorbed and excreted across pulmonary alveolar membranes by the process of simple diffusion. Some drugs taken orally such as paraldehyde may also be partially eliminated by way of the lungs.

Biliary excretion is the major route by which systemically absorbed drugs enter the gastrointestinal tract where elimination in the feces occurs, unless the drug is reabsorbed through the enteric membranes of the intestine. Many organic acids, which exist in an ionized state at physiologic pH, and charged quaternary ammonium compounds can be recovered in the bile. This is believed to occur through specific carrier-mediated transport mechanisms. On the other hand, substances such as insulin and sucrose passively dif-

fuse into the bile. Drugs such as erythromycin, estradiol, and testosterone have been shown to be excreted in bile in amounts greater than 10% of an administered dose in humans.[31]

Excretions of drugs in milk and sweat are considered minor routes of elimination. Drugs excreted in milk may be potential sources of undesired effects to the nursing infant. Drugs such as nicotinamide, quinine, and sulfanilamide have been recovered from human sweat after oral administration.

The fact that drugs could be excreted in saliva after systemic administration was suggested as long ago as 1932.[32] Since that time, a variety of drugs have been shown to be excreted in the saliva of animals and humans. Early studies reported the salivary excretion of penicillin and other antibiotics, salicylates, and barbiturates.[33-35] More recent studies have reported the salivary excretion of lithium, anticonvulsants of the phenytoin family, diazepam, newer penicillins and cephalosporins, and digoxin.[36] A list of drugs excreted in human saliva with their ratios of saliva:plasma concentration is given in Table 2-2. Saliva:plasma ratios of greater than 1 means more drug is present in saliva per unit volume than in plasma. A ratio less than 1 means the opposite.

Present evidence suggests that most drugs that are secreted in the salivary glands enter saliva by simple diffusion, and their passage depends mainly on the lipid solubility of the drug. Thus a drug with high lipid solubility at plasma and salivary pH will readily enter saliva from plasma. A few drugs having low lipid solubility have been shown to enter saliva, although these compounds do not follow the laws of simple diffusion.[37]

Drug levels in saliva can be used to monitor therapy with certain agents. For example, antiepileptic drug monitoring is essential for the rational treatment of the epilepsies, and the measurement of these drugs in plasma is now routine. Salivary concentrations of these drugs have been shown to be a reliable, noninvasive method of predicting plasma levels.[38] Another example is that of theophylline, a drug used to relieve asthmatic conditions. A constant ratio has been shown to exist between simultaneously obtained plasma and saliva theophylline concentrations in normal adults. In a subsequent study involving asthmatic children, plasma theophylline levels were predictable by multiplying the measured salivary theophylline level by the previously established plasma:saliva ratio.[39] Salicylate therapy has also been monitored us-

Table 2-2. Drugs excreted in saliva

Drug	Saliva:plasma ratio
Acetylsalicylic acid (Aspirin)	0.27
Amobarbital (Amytal)	0.36
Ampicillin	0.03
Antipyrine	0.92
Carbamazepine (Tegretol)	0.26
Cephalexin	0.30
Cloxacillin	0.30
Diazepam (Valium)	0.03
Lithium	3.0
Penicillin VK	0.1
Phenobarbital	0.4
Phenytoin (Dilantin)	0.1
Propranolol (Inderal)	2.0
Theophylline	1.5

ing experimentally determined drug levels in saliva.[40] The diagnosis of drug overdose may be possible by the experimental determination of salivary levels, since these levels have been shown to reliably reflect the plasma levels of many drugs.

CONSIDERATIONS IN DRUG ADMINISTRATION

Most of this chapter has been concerned with those factors that affect the availability of a drug to its site of action in the body and their relation to the time course of drug action and variation in individual drug response. The remaining discussion involves some factors that have considerations for drug administration.

Tolerance

Drug tolerance is defined as the need for increasingly larger doses of drug to obtain the effects observed with the original dose or conversely, when after repeated administration, a given dose of drug produces a decreasing effect. Tolerance is commonly acquired with narcotic analgesics, sedatives and hypnotics, and nitrate coronary vasodilators. When a patient becomes tolerant to one drug, a cross-tolerance may develop to the actions of pharmacologically related drugs. Increasing the drug dosage is one method utilized to overcome this condition. If tolerance to a drug exists, normal sensitivity to the drug effect can usually be reestablished by suspending the administration of the drug.

Pathologic state

The pathologic condition of a patient may influence the response to medication. Hyperthyroid patients are extremely sensitive to the therapeutic and toxic effects of epinephrine. Patients with intracranial pressure are unusually sensitive to the actions of morphine. Hepatic and renal disease will have much influence on the hepatic metabolism and renal excretion of drugs.

Age and weight

Age is only rarely considered in determining drug dosage for adults. Weight, however, is the usual basis for determining drug dosage, and optimum therapeutic doses are generally identified in terms of amount of drug per kilogram of body weight of the patient.

Children's dosage presents a special problem in therapeutics. Traditionally, a child's dose has been adjusted in accordance with formulas based on body weight or age. With many drugs, however, the manufacturer issues suggested pediatric dose schedules usually in terms of amount of drug per pound of body weight per 24 hours. This is particularly common with antibiotic agents. The following formulas have been suggested for dose calculation for infants and preschool children:

CLARK'S RULE

$$\frac{\text{Weight (lb)} \times \text{Adult dose}}{150} = \text{Infant dose}$$

FRIED'S RULE

$$\frac{\text{Age (mo)} \times \text{Adult dose}}{150} = \text{Infant dose}$$

Clark's rule is based on the child's weight; Fried's rule is based on the child's age. The former rule assumes that an average adult weight is 150 pounds, and the latter rule assumes that by the 150th month, a child has reached an age when an adult dose can be tolerated.

Two other formulas have been suggested to be used for children ranging from preschool to adolescent years.

YOUNG'S RULE

$$\frac{\text{Age (yr)} \times \text{Adult dose}}{\text{Age (yr)} + 12} = \text{Child dose}$$

COWLING'S RULE

$$\frac{\text{Age (at next birthday)} \times \text{Adult dose}}{24} = \text{Child dose}$$

Both of these formulas are based on the age of the child, and Young's rule seems to be the more popular of the two.

Since weight may vary according to different children and infants of the same age, and in many cases the dose based on age is underestimated, a better method for the estimation of a child or infant dose is based on body surface area.

$$\frac{\text{Surface area} \times \text{Adult dose}}{2.00} = \text{Child dose}$$

This formula assumes that the body surface area of a 6-foot, 175-pound adult is 200 square meters. Tables are available indicating the body surface area in square meters given the child's height and weight. At present it is believed that the pediatric doses based on the manufacturer's or prescriber's experience are much better than those calculated from any of the above rules.

The elderly are particularly sensitive to drug effects at doses that are well tolerated by younger patients. This is because of age-related changes in receptor site sensitivity, and the central nervous system (CNS) seems to be most sensitive in this regard. The use of any CNS agent such as sedatives, tranquilizers, or narcotic analgesics should be considered with caution. For example, a sensitivity of the elderly to diazepam, chlordiazepoxide, and other benzodiazepine-type tranquilizers has been reported.[41]

Age-related changes also cause decreases in drug absorption. For example, the rate and completeness of diazepam absorption have been shown to be decreased in the elderly. In addition, chlordiazepoxide is absorbed more slowly in the older age group.[42,43] Also there are age-related changes in drug-binding affinity for plasma proteins.[44] For a review of these effects see Hicks and Davis.[45]

Blood level curves and dosing regimens

Blood level curves of drugs are often used to determine optimal dosing regimens. Typical blood level curves for a drug administered orally and IV are shown in Fig. 2-6. The concentration of drug in blood (usually expressed as milligrams per 100 ml of blood) is plotted on a log scale, and time course is plotted on the x-axis. After IV administration, there is an initial rapid decrease of drug in the blood caused by distribution to tissue compartments, which is followed by a less rapid elimination phase. The blood level after oral administration is characterized by an initial in-

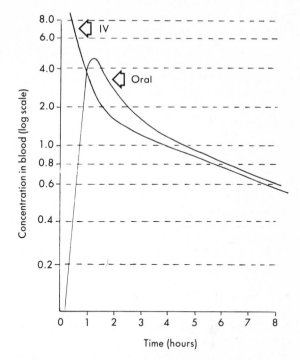

Fig. 2-6. Blood level curves for a single intravenous and oral dose of drug.

crease because of absorption from the gastrointestinal tract and followed by an elimination phase similar to that for IV administration. Blood level curves having two distribution phases, such as that depicted in Fig. 2-6 for IV administration, are known as two-compartment open systems, a discussion of which is beyond the scope of this chapter.

Parameters of importance to establishing dosing regimens can be calculated from blood level curves such as this. The slope (β) of the elimination phase can be obtained, and the $t_{\frac{1}{2}}$, defined for this purpose as the time required for the body to eliminate one-half the drug that it contains, can also be obtained. The relationship between $t_{\frac{1}{2}}$ and β is

$$t_{\frac{1}{2}} = \frac{0.693}{\beta}$$

where $t_{\frac{1}{2}}$ = hours and $\beta = ^{-1}$.

The elimination phases for IV and oral blood level curves in Fig. 2-6 are about the same, and β is observed to be 0.13. This figure was obtained by calculating the concentration of drug in blood (log axis) at any 1-hour interval within the elimination phase.

Using this figure, we determine that $t_{\frac{1}{2}} = 0.693/\beta = 0.693/0.13 = 5.33$ hr. Thus according to this blood level curve, it takes 5.33 hours for one-half the drug present to be eliminated. As a rule of thumb, the time required for almost complete elimination of a drug is equivalent to about four half-times. In the example, it would take about 21 hours (4×5.33) for the drug to be eliminated.

When a drug is given repeatedly, the rate of administration counterbalances the rate of elimination, and drug accumulation results. The amount of accumulation depends mainly on the time, the interval of dosing, and the rate at which the drug is eliminated. Since about four half-times are required for almost complete elimination of a drug, any dosage interval shorter than this will lead to some degree of accumulation. Fig. 2-7 is a blood level curve for an orally repeated administration of a drug. The solid line indicates the actual blood concentrations, and the dotted line represents the average concentration after each dosing interval. The drug has been administered in dosage intervals of $t_{\frac{1}{2}}$, and maximal accumulation has occurred after about four half-times. This means that the rate of drug elimination is equal to that of administration at this time. As a rule of thumb, any drug will acquire maximal accumulation for a given dose within four half-times, using a dosing schedule at intervals of $t_{\frac{1}{2}}$. It should be noted that maximal accumulation is not synonymous with maximal blood concentration, and blood concentrations vary according to the amount of drug administered at each dose and the dosing interval. Large repetitive doses given at intervals much shorter than $t_{\frac{1}{2}}$ will result in much higher blood levels than smaller doses given at intervals much longer than $t_{\frac{1}{2}}$.

Optimal therapeutic plasma levels for many classes of drugs have been established, and one goal of therapy is to ensure that dosing regimens provide these plasma levels. For example, the optimal therapeutic plasma levels for anticonvulsant drugs are shown in Table 2-3. These figures assume that any dosing schedule that provides less than, or more than, the optimal levels will be either ineffective or adversely effective. Thus the objective of a multiple-dose regimen is to maintain the patient's blood level within established maximal and minimal concentrations. Fig. 2-8 illustrates what would occur if dosing intervals were too short, too long, or ideal.

If the optimal therapeutic plasma levels are known

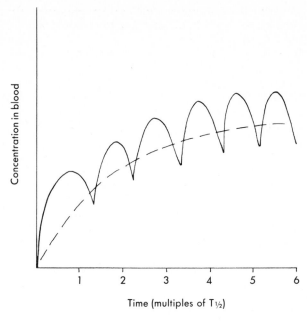

Fig. 2-7. Blood level curve for an oral repetitive dose of drug.

Table 2-3. Optimum therapeutic plasma levels for anticonvulsant drugs

Drug	Range (amount per ml)
Carbamazepine	4-10; 6-12 μg
Clonazepam	~30-60; 15-50 ng
Diazepam	>400-500; >600 ng
Ethosuximide	40-80; 40-100 μg
Phenobarbital	10-30; 10-25 μg
Phenytoin	10-20 μg
Primidone	5-10 μg
Valproic acid	~60-80; >50 μg

Reprinted from Notari, R.E.: Biopharmaceutics and pharmacokinetics: an introduction, ed. 3, 1980, by courtesy of Marcel Dekker, Inc.

for a particular drug, the size of the initial dose, the maintenance doses, and the dosing interval can be determined to provide these levels for a patient. The mathematics for these determinations are beyond the scope of this chapter but can be found in the text by Notari.[46]

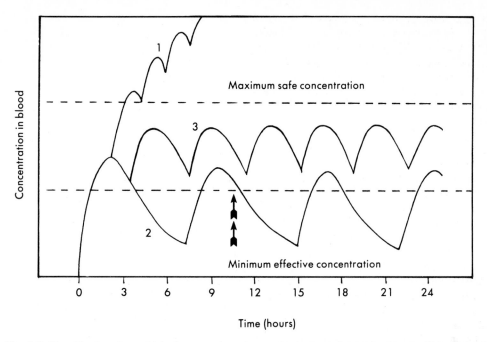

Fig. 2-8. The objective of a multiple-dosage regimen is to maintain the patient's blood level within maximal and minimal concentrations shown in the figure. Dosing interval is too short in curve 1, too long in curve 2, and ideal in curve 3. (Reprinted from Notari, R.E.: Biopharmaceutics and pharmacokinetics: an introduction, ed. 3, 1980, by courtesy of Marcel Dekker, Inc.)

REFERENCES

1. Feinstein, M.B., Lenard, W., and Mathias, J.: The antagonism of local anesthetic induced convulsions by the benzodiazepine derivative diazepam, Arch. Int. Pharmacodyn. Ther. **187**:144-154, 1970.
2. Goldstein, A., Aronow, L., and Kalman, S.M.: Principles of drug action: the basis of pharmacology, ed. 2, New York, 1974, John Wiley & Sons, Inc., p. 134.
3. Adriani, J., and Campbell, B.: Fatalities following topical application of local anesthetics to mucous membranes, J.A.M.A. **162**:1527-1530, 1956.
4. Robertson, J.D.: The ultrastructure of cell membranes and their derivatives, Biochem. Soc. Symp. **16**:3-43, 1959.
5. Singer, S.J., and Nicolson, G.L.: A fluid mosaic model of cell membranes, Science **175**:720-731, 1972.
6. Pappenheimer, J.R.: Passage of molecules through capillary walls, Physiol. Rev. **33**:387-423, 1953.
7. Solomon, A.K.: The permeability of red cells to water and ions, Ann. N.Y. Acad. Sci. **75**:175-181, 1958.
8. Welling, P.G.: Influence of food and diet on gastrointestinal drug absorption: a review, J. Pharmacokinet. Biopharm. **5**:291-334, 1977.
9. Ginsburg, J.: Placental drug transfer, Ann. Rev. Pharmacol. **11**:387-408, 1971.
10. Moya, F., and Thorndike, V.: Passage of drugs across the placenta, Am. J. Obstet. Gynecol. **84**:1778-1798, 1962.
11. Green, T.P., O'Dea, R.F., and Mirkin, B.L.: Determinants of drug disposition and effect in the fetus, Ann. Rev. Pharmacol. Toxicol. **19**:285-322, 1979.
12. Shnider, S.M., and Way, E.L.: The kinetics of transfer of lidocaine (Xylocaine[R]) across the human placenta, Anesthesiology **29**:944-950, 1968.
13. Usubiaga, J.E., et al.: Passage of procaine hydrochloride and para-aminobenzoic acid across the human placenta, Am. J. Obstet. Gynecol. **100**:918-923, 1968.
14. Langley, J.N.: On the mutual antagonism of atropine and pilocarpine, having special reference to their relations in the sub-maxillary gland of the cat, J. Physiol. **1**:339-369, 1878.
15. Clark, A.J.: General pharmacology. In Heffter, A., editor: Handbuch der experimentellen Pharmakologie, vol. 4, Berlin, 1937, Julius Springer-Verlag, p. 63.
16. Nickerson, M.: Receptor occupancy and tissue response, Nature (Lond.) **178**:697-698, 1956.
17. Stephenson, R.P.: A modification of receptor theory, Br. J. Pharmacol. Chemother. **11**:379-393, 1956.
18. Pauling, L.: A molecular theory of general anesthesia, Science **134**:15-21, 1961.
19. Brodie, B.B., and Maickel, R.P.: Comparative biochemistry of drug metabolism. In Brodie, B.B., and Erdös, E.G., editors: Metabolic factors controlling duration of drug action: proceedings of first international pharmacological meeting, vol. 6, New York, 1962, Macmillan Publishing Co., Inc., p. 299.

20. Allan, P.W., Schnebli, H.P., and Bennett, L.L., Jr.: Conversion of 6-mercaptopurine and 6-mercaptopurine ribonucleotide to 6-methylmercaptopurine ribonucleotide in human epidermoid carcinoma cells in culture, Biochim. Biophys. Acta **114:**647-650, 1966.
21. Gillette, J.R.: Biochemistry of drug oxidation and reduction by enzymes in hepatic endoplasmic reticulum. In Garattini, S., and Shore, P.A., editors: Advances in pharmacology, vol. 4, New York, 1966, Academic Press, Inc.
22. Omura, J., et al.: Function of cytochrome P-450 of microsomes, Fed. Proc. **24:**1181-1189, 1965.
23. Conney, A.H.: Pharmacological implications of microsomal enzyme induction, Pharmacol. Rev. **19:**317-366, 1967.
24. Hansen, J.M., Kristensen, M., Skovsted, L., and Christensen, L.K.: Dicumarol induced diphenylhydantoin intoxication, Lancet **2:**265-266, 1966.
25. Kristensen, M., and Hansen, J.M.: Potentiation of the tolbutamide effect of dicumarol, Diabetes **16:**211-214, 1967.
26. Corn, M., and Rockett, J.F.: Inhibition of bishydroxycoumarin activity by phenobarbital, Med. Ann. D.C. **34:**578-579, 1965.
27. Cucinell, S.A., et al.: Drug interactions in man: 1. Lowering effect of phenobarbital on plasma levels of bishydroxycoumarin (dicumarol) and diphenylhydantoin (Dilantin), Clin. Pharmacol. Ther. **6:**420-429, 1965.
28. Catalano, P.M., and Cullen, S.I.: Warfarin antagonism by griseofulvin, Clin. Res. **14:**266, 1966.
29. Busfield, D., et al.: An effect of phenobarbitone on blood-levels of griseofulvin in man, Lancet **2:**1042-1043, 1963.
30. Chen, W., et al.: Accelerated aminopyrine metabolism in human subjects pretreated with phenylbutazone, Life Sci. **1:**35-42, 1962.
31. Stowe, C.M., and Plaa, G.L.: Extrarenal excretion of drugs and chemicals, Ann. Rev. Pharmacol. **8:**337-356, 1968.
32. Amberson, W.R., and Hober, R.: The permeability of mammalian salivary glands for organic nonelectrolytes, J. Cell Physiol. **2:**201-221, 1932.
33. Adler-Hradecky, C., and Kelenty, B.: Salivary excretion and inactivation of some penicillins, Nature **198:**792-793, 1963.
34. Bener, I.B., Pressman, R.S., and Rashman, S.G.: Studies on excretion of antibiotics in human saliva, J. Am. Dent. Assoc. **46:**164-170, 1953.
35. Borzelleca, J.F., and Doyle, C.H.: Excretion of drugs in saliva: salicylate, barbiturate, sulfanilamide, J. Oral Ther. Pharmacol. **3:**104-111, 1966.
36. Matheny, J.L., and Wynn, R.L.: Drugs: salivary excretion and oral side effects. In Roth, G.I., and Calmes, R., editors: Oral biology, St. Louis, 1981, The C.V. Mosby Co., pp. 239-252.
37. Burgen, A.S.V.: The secretion of nonelectrolytes in the parotid saliva, J. Cell Physiol. **48:**113-138, 1956.
38. McAuliffe, J.J., et al.: Salivary levels of anticonvulsants: a practical approach to drug monitoring, Neurology **27:**409-413, 1977.
39. Levy, G., Ellis, E.F., and Koysooko, M.S.: Indirect plasma-theophylline monitoring in asthmatic children by determination of theophylline concentration in saliva, Pediatrics **53:**873-876, 1974.
40. Perez-Mateo, M., Erill, S., and Cabezas, R.: Blood and saliva salicylate measurement in the monitoring of salicylate therapy, Int. J. Clin. Pharmacol. **15:**113-115, 1977.
41. Boston Collaborative Drug Surveillance Program: Clinical depression of the central nervous system due to diazepam and chlordiazepoxide in relation to cigarette smoking and age, N. Engl. J. Med. **288:**277-280, 1973.
42. Garattini, S., et al.: The significance of measuring blood levels of benzodiazepines. In Davies, D.S., and Prichard, B.N.C., editors: Biological effects of drugs in relation to their plasma concentration, Baltimore, 1973, University Park Press, pp. 211-225.
43. Shader, R.I., et al.: Absorption and disposition of chlordiazepoxide in young and elderly male volunteers, J. Clin. Pharmacol. **17:**709-718, 1977.
44. Wallace, S., Whiting, B., and Runcie, J.: Factors effecting drug binding in plasma of elderly patients, Br. J. Clin. Pharmacol. **3:**327-330, 1976.
45. Hicks, R., and Davis, J.M.: Pharmacokinetics in geriatric psychopharmacology. In Psychopharmacology of aging, Flushing, N.Y., 1980, Spectrum Publications, Inc., pp. 169-212.
46. Notari, R.E.: Biopharmaceutics and clinical pharmacokinetics: an introduction, Ed. 3, New York, 1980, Marcel Dekker, Inc.

CHAPTER 3

RICHARD L. WYNN
BARBARA REQUA-CLARK

Adverse drug reactions

Although drugs act selectively in biologic systems to accomplish a desired effect, they lack absolute specificity in that they may act on many different organs or tissues. This lack of absolute specificity is the reason for undesirable or adverse drug reactions. No drug is free of producing some sort of adverse effect in a certain number of patients. This is a problem of importance that one must consider to practice dental therapeutics intelligently. It has been estimated that about 5% of the patients hospitalized annually in the United States are admitted because of adverse reactions to drugs,[1] with some hospitals reporting incidences as high as 20%.[2] Also, a minimum of 15% of hospitalized patients experience at least one adverse drug reaction.[3]

This chapter will summarize those principles of adverse drug effects that are fundamental to rational drug therapy. Definitions and classifications of adverse drug reactions are discussed and descriptions of selected clinical manifestations of those reactions are given. Also, fundamental principles of the toxicologic evaluation of drugs in lower animals and human beings are briefly discussed with regard to the evaluation of drug safety.

DEFINITIONS AND CLASSIFICATIONS OF ADVERSE DRUG REACTIONS

Unfortunately, every drug has more than one action. The actions that are clinically desirable are termed *therapeutic effects,* and the undesirable actions are termed *adverse effects.* The fundamental objective in pharmacotherapeutics is to select the drug and dosage that will give maximal therapeutic effects and minimal adverse effects.

The literature does not reflect consistency in definitions related to adverse drug effects. However, they can be classified into four general groups:

1. Toxic reactions
2. Allergic reactions
3. Idiosyncracies
4. Interference with natural defense mechanisms

Although toxicology can be broadly defined as the study of the adverse effects of chemicals on biologic systems, a more precise definition is needed. There is a distinction between toxic effects and other adverse reactions. *Toxic effects* are defined as adverse effects of an unexpected nature resulting from the direct action of the drug on the tissue or organ systems. This differentiates toxic reactions from allergic reactions, as allergic reactions require the production of other compounds to elicit a response.

The importance of distinguishing between various adverse drug effects is seen in the example of penicillin G. This drug has little or no effect on the tissue or organ systems and consequently is considered to have a low toxicity. However, the incidence of adverse reactions to penicillin G is high because of its allergic potential.

A *side effect* is often considered to be any undesirable effect. This is not a useful definition, however, since side effects and adverse reactions would thus be equivalent. In this text side effects are considered to be expected actions that occur in addition to the therapeutic effect. Side effects are generally predictable, mild reactions that must be accepted as being commonly present when a particular drug is used. In fact, given an adequate dose of a drug, side effects can occur in every patient. For example, the dryness of the mouth (xerostomia) that occurs with the use of anticholinergics for the treatment of ulcers is considered a side effect. Large doses of these agents can cause a glaucoma-like effect in some patients. Severity of this effect allows it to be categorized as a toxic effect. Obviously, the dividing line between a severe

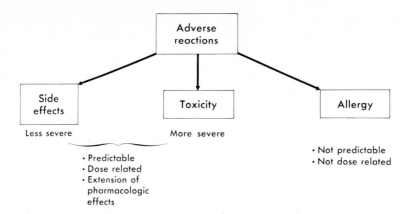

Fig. 3-1. Diagrammatic representation of the classification of adverse drug reactions. (From Requa, B.S., and Holroyd, S.V.: Applied pharmacology for the dental hygienist, St. Louis, 1982, The C.V. Mosby Co.)

side effect and a mild toxic effect is not distinct. Fig. 3-1 characterizes the types of adverse reactions with respect to predictability and dose dependency. Each of these adverse effects is described below.

CLINICAL MANIFESTATIONS OF ADVERSE DRUG REACTIONS
Toxic reactions

Toxic reactions occur as a result of exaggerated effects on target organs or tissues, effects on nontarget organs or tissues, effects on fetal development, local reactions, and drug interactions.

Exaggerated effects on target organs or tissues. These effects are considered to be an extension of the therapeutic effects produced in a sensitive patient or by an overdose of the drug. For example, patients given a therapeutic dose of an oral hypoglycemic agent for the treatment of diabetes have experienced exaggerated hypoglycemia.[4] The patient's blood sugar level may have dipped too low because of an unusual sensitivity to the drug or because the dose administered was too large. Occasionally, this type of drug reaction may result from the presence of a disease in the patient. Another example is a patient who has liver or kidney disease that may inhibit the termination of drug activity by interfering with either drug metabolism or excretion. This effect could prolong the action of the drug.

Effects on nontarget organs or tissues. The effects on nontarget organs or tissues is caused by nontherapeutic actions of a drug. They usually appear at higher doses or with more prolonged administration.

A reduction in the dose of the drug can generally terminate this adverse effect. For example, salicylism, which results from large doses of salicylates, is manifested as headache, dizziness, tinnitus, mental confusion, alterations in acid-base balance, hyperventilation, drowsiness, nausea, and vomiting. Note that these toxic reactions cause nontherapeutic actions in many tissues in the body. A preexisting disease may intensify the effect on nontarget organs. For example, the ulcerogenic potential of many drugs may be enhanced by a previous history of peptic ulcer disease. Also, congenital anomalies of body metabolism may alter a patient's reaction to many drugs—an area of study known as *pharmacogenetics.* For example, some drugs are capable of inducing hemolysis in red blood cells of subjects who have inadequate levels of reduced glutathione caused by a genetically inherited deficiency of glucose-6-phosphate dehydrogenase—the enzyme responsible for maintaining reduced glutathione levels in red blood cells. Hemolysis occurs because of the inadequate amounts of glutathione present to protect against oxidative destruction of cell constituents. Sulfonamides and the antimalarial primaquine are some of the drugs implicated in this effect.

Effects on fetal development (teratogenic effect). Karnofsky[5] has stated that "any drug administered at the proper dosage and proper stage of development to embryos of the proper species . . . will be effective in causing disturbances in embryonic development." The more drug studies that are conducted and reported, the closer to this statement the literature approaches. Although the human teratogenic effect associated with maternal rubella infection (German measles) and a few select drugs has been known for some time, the concern over the potential teratogenic effect of other drugs was not evident until the thalidomide disaster of 1962. This seemingly innocuous sedative, marketed without a prescription in Europe, was shown to be responsible for an incidence of about 20% of abnormal offspring from patients exposed to the drug during a certain critical stage of gestation. Fetal anomalies attributed to thalidomide included malformed or absent limbs or digits, cleft palate, malformed ears, and failure of closure of the spinal cord. A limited number of other drugs have now been shown to be teratogenic to the human fetus and include growth-inhibiting anticancer agents and a few steroid hormones.

Drugs used in dentistry such as penicillins, salicylates, sulfonamides, and vitamins have been shown to be teratogenic in a variety of animal species. The minor tranquilizer diazepam has been shown to be teratogenic in mice.[6] An association between ingestion of minor tranquilizers during pregnancy and increased risk of congenital anomalies in humans has been suggested by three recent studies.[7-9] One study showed that the rate of congenital anomalies was higher when meprobamate was prescribed during the first 6 weeks of pregnancy than when no drug was given.[7] For chlordiazepoxide the rate following exposure during the same period was also greater than the rates for other drugs. A second study reported an association of oral clefts with meprobamate and diazepam usage during pregnancy.[8] A third study showed that selected birth defects, including cleft lip, were associated with the use of diazepam by women during pregnancy.[9] The incorporation of tetracyclines into human fetal ossifying tissues results in irreversible staining of enamel, an action that can be considered teratogenic.

The information distributed about most drugs bears a statement that begins in a fashion similar to the following:
1. Safe use during pregnancy has not been established . . .
2. The possibility of fetal injury cannot be excluded . . .
3. Adequate animal reproduction studies to establish safe use have not been conducted . . .
4. Until more information is available . . .

The information about most drugs then concludes with a statement resembling the following:

1. . . . should not be prescribed for women of childbearing age unless, in the opinion of the physician, the potential benefits outweigh the possible risks.
2. . . . should not be administered until the potential benefits are weighed against the possible risks.
3. Possible teratogenic potential in women capable of bearing children should be carefully weighed against the benefits of therapy.

At some point a reference is occasionally made to the results of animal studies, if these are available.

The practical implications of the thalidomide disaster have served as an impetus to reduce the use of drugs during pregnancy and to monitor potential teratogenic agents by preclinical testing in animals. The importance of the teratogenic potential of drugs that could be used in dentistry can be clearly seen. The risk of any drug use by a pregnant woman must be considered in relationship to the benefit of those drugs. The benefits of any drug administered to a patient for a dental situation must be seriously considered, as many dental problems are elective (voluntary) in nature. Patients do not always indicate that they are pregnant, so it is important to ask them since drugs can be potential sources of problems, especially early in the pregnancy.

Local reactions. Local reactions are characterized by tissue irritation. Occasionally, injectable drugs can produce irritation, pain, and tissue necrosis at the site of injection. Topically applied agents can produce irritation or itching at the site of application. Gastrointestinal symptoms caused by the action on the stomach of drugs taken orally include nausea, vomiting, and dyspepsia.

Drug interactions. The influence of one drug on the effectiveness of another drug administered earlier, simultaneously, or later may result in an undesirable drug effect and in some cases toxic manifestations. These drug interactions are discussed in Chapter 33.

Allergic reactions

For drugs to produce an allergic reaction, they must act as an antigen and react with an antibody in a previously sensitized patient. These reactions are neither dose dependent nor predictable. For an allergic reaction to occur, an ingested drug must be metabolized to a reactive drug metabolite known as the hapten. This reactive drug metabolite can act as an antigen only after combining with high molecular weight compounds present in the body, such as protein. The antigen formed then stimulates the production of an antibody. Subsequent exposure to the drug (or more precisely its hapten) will cause the antigen formed after the administration of the drug to react with the antibody previously produced to elicit an antigen-antibody reaction. This reaction causes a series of biochemical and physiologic events that can be extremely serious. These events occur because the mediator substances released in the typical allergic reaction produce itching and bronchiolar constriction. These mediators, present in the body in an inactive form, become active when liberated. They include histamine, serotonin, and bradykinin. Antibodies to the drug antigen are formed during the sensitizing portion of the immune mechanism when the individual comes into initial contact with the antigen. The reaction part is seen when the sensitized individual is reexposed to the antigen. The various allergic reactions are described below.

Anaphylaxis. Anaphylaxis is an acute, life-threatening allergic reaction characterized by hypotension, bronchospasm, laryngeal edema, and cardiac arrhythmias. Symptoms most frequently appear after intravenous drug administration, although fatal anaphylaxis has sometimes occurred after a single oral dose of penicillin in highly sensitive individuals.[10,11]

Anaphylaxis occurs within 5 to 30 minutes after drug administration. Early symptoms include nausea, vomiting, and dyspnea, but the reaction can rapidly result in death. The reaction usually occurs during the institution of a new course of treatment with a drug to which there has been previous exposure. There may or may not have been allergic symptoms during earlier exposure to the drug. Some of the drugs used in dentistry that have produced fatal anaphylaxis include the penicillins, local anesthetics, and aspirin.[12] One to 10 deaths per 10 million injections of penicillin have been cited as attributable to anaphylaxis.[13] Unexpected anaphylaxis may occur during simple therapeutic procedures. For example, benzocaine has induced respiratory distress leading to the death of a patient who was medicated with a throat lozenge containing the drug.[14]

Serum sickness. Another allergic reaction, serum sickness, is produced by circulating antigen-antibody complexes. It is characterized by fever, rash, lymphadenopathy, arthritis, edema, and neuritis. Drugs that produce serum sickness include, among others, the penicillins, sulfonamides, phenytoin, and streptomycin.

Drug fever. Drug allergy may be manifested as a fever, particularly in association with treatment using penicillins, anticonvulsants, sulfonamides, and streptomycin. It is manifested by fever, leukocytosis, arthralgia, and dermatitis. A severe and sustained fever associated with small-vessel inflammation usually occurs.

Cytotoxic reactions. Allergic reactions to drugs may result in cellular damage because of a chemical reaction of the drug with the cell, making it susceptible to antibody-mediated cytotoxicity. Penicillin-induced hemolytic anemia is an example of this type of allergy. Large doses of penicillin cause the red blood cells to be altered by the penicillin haptens and combine with complementary antibodies. As a result, accelerated phagocytosis and lysis of the cells occur, causing increased red blood cell destruction and anemia. Cephalosporins and phenacetin have also caused immune hemolytic anemia.

Skin reactions. Drugs have been reported to produce almost every known cutaneous reaction. These include petechial, maculopapular, bullous, nodular, eczematous, urticarial, erythematous, or photosensitive eruptions. The occurrence of dermatitis in a patient receiving a pharmacologic agent should always raise the possibility of the presence of a drug allergy.

Idiosyncrasy

Idiosyncratic reactions are those that cannot be explained by any known pharmacologic or biochemical mechanisms. For example, barbiturates have caused excitement in some geriatric patients. Obstructive jaundice induced by phenothiazines is also considered to be an idiosyncrasy. Idiosyncratic reactions may involve allergic mechanisms since the obstructive jaundice condition is believed to result from hepatic sensitization.

Interference with natural defense mechanisms

Drug effects on nonspecific defense mechanisms can result in adverse reactions. Antibiotics have been shown to cause an overgrowth of the intestinal flora with nonphysiologic bacteria and fungi. Also, the long-term systemic administration of corticosteroids can result in a reduced resistance to infection.

TOXICOLOGIC EVALUATION OF DRUGS IN LOWER ANIMALS AND HUMAN BEINGS

Evaluations of the toxic effects of drugs are based on experiments with lower animals and clinical trials

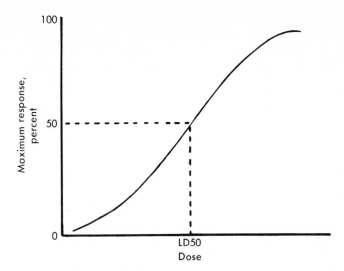

Fig. 3-2. Asymmetrical dose-response curve. Response is equivalent to death.

in human beings. The optimal situation is the ability to predict adverse drug reactions in humans from data acquired in animals. Unfortunately, many drug reactions occurring in humans are not manifested in animals or are difficult to observe. Species differences in the physiologic handling of the drug undoubtedly contribute to this problem. Also, many effects do not occur with enough frequency to be observed in the limited numbers of animals that are used for testing. The current animal tests used, however, are adequate in providing some fundamental information concerning the eventual safety of a drug in humans.

One of the first tests in evaluating the toxicity of any drug is to measure its LD_{50}. The term LD_{50} is that dose of a drug (usually expressed as milligrams per kilogram) that kills 50% of the treated animals. This is determined in a fashion similar to that for the ED_{50} (Chapter 2). If increasing doses of a drug are administered to groups of animals, the mortality of the groups will be a direct function of the dose administered, and a certain dose of the drug will be lethal to 50% of the animals. For example, Fig. 3-2 indicates the dose of a drug plotted against the percent maximal response of animals responding (response equivalent to death). An asymmetrical curve known as a *dose-response curve* is then obtained. The dose on the dose axis that corresponds to the 50% response level on the response axis can then be read directly from the curve. This figure is the LD_{50}.

Since all drugs are toxic at some dose, the LD_{50} is meaningless unless the ED_{50} is also known. For example, a drug having a lower ED_{50} (for example, 100 times less) than its congener may at first appear to be more useful, since it is the more potent of the two. However, if the LD_{50} of the drug is only twice its ED_{50}, and the LD_{50} of its congener is ten times its respective ED_{50}, the congener would be the more useful of the two. The original drug, even though more potent than its congener, is much more toxic. The ratio $LD_{50}:ED_{50}$ is known as the therapeutic index of a drug.

$$\text{Therapeutic index} = \frac{LD_{50}}{ED_{50}}$$

This is a useful figure that gives some measure as to how far a therapeutic dose may be exceeded before eliciting toxic effects. For the clinical situation a better measure would be "adverse-effect $dose_{50}/ED_{50}$," where a specific adverse effect is considered rather than the median lethal dose. It is difficult, however, to determine what the adverse-effect dose is in each case. Theoretically it would equal the dose of a drug that causes a specific adverse effect in 50% of the treated patients.

The LD_{50} and the therapeutic index as derived from animal studies are merely two measurements of many that are obtained for the evaluation of the safety of any drug. The following outline summarizes the various preclinical and clinical tests used to evaluate the safety of drugs:

1. Acute toxicity tests
2. Subacute (prolonged) toxicity tests

3. Chronic toxicity tests
4. Special studies
   a. Carcinogenicity
   b. Teratogenicity
   c. Mutagenicity
   d. Potentiation with other drugs
   e. Irritation
   f. Biotransformation
5. Clinical evaluation
   Phase I. Clinical pharmacology
   Phase II. Controlled evaluation phase
   Phase III. Broad trial phase

The preclinical tests are divided into three major phases—acute, subacute or prolonged, and chronic. It is during the acute phase that the LD_{50} is determined. For this phase single doses of the drug are administered usually on one occasion to two species, one of which is a rodent. Two routes of administration are used, with one being the intended clinical route.

The subacute phase generally consists of a duration of 2 to 13 weeks. The major purpose of this phase of testing is to determine in broad terms the dosages at which physiologic and specific toxicologic effects appear. Administration of the drug is generally by the intended clinical route, with rats and dogs being the usual species of choice. The doses given are based on the LD_{50} determined during the acute testing and usually consist of three levels. Evaluations are made of the state of health of the animals during the testing, and complete autopsies are performed.

Chronic tests are of necessity long in duration (90 days to 2 years). However, the methods are similar to the subacute testing, except that the testing may be carried through several generations of animals. The chronic tests sometimes reveal the need for specific tests requiring special procedures. Included are tests for carcinogenicity, teratogenicity, mutagenicity, drug potentiation, dermal irritation, and biotransformation characteristics of the compound.

Clinical trials performed for drug safety evaluation may also be divided into three phases. Phase I is a pilot study that uses small numbers of human volunteers. Initially, low doses of the drug that are gradually increased are used, and the toxic or exaggerated effects are monitored. Effects looked for are (1) those related to the desired pharmacologic effects but exaggerated at the recommended dose, (2) those resulting from actions on wrong target tissues, and (3) those unrelated to desired pharmacologic effects. If phase I produces the desired therapeutic effect without undesirable side effects, then the drug may be evaluated according to phase II. The drug is tested in limited numbers of hospitalized patients with the disease the drug is intended to treat. The test drug is compared to established drugs and placebo using a double-blind technique. Phase III testing is extended to large groups of outpatients to permit evaluation of the drug under conditions that may exist if the drug is marketed. If the drug proves to be safe and effective for its intended use, the FDA may approve the drug for marketing.

SUMMARY

One should note that drugs approved for therapeutic use are not necessarily free of adverse effects to the patient, since as previously mentioned, all drugs elicit some undesirable effects in a certain percentage of patients. With regard to those reactions that can be predicted from information obtained during safety evaluation studies in animals and humans, however, certain questions can be answered. For example, do the beneficial effects outweigh the adverse effects of the drug to the patient? If not, is the need for the drug in a particular clinical situation great enough to justify subsequent adverse effects to the patient? With regard to unpredictable drug effects, the competency of the clinician to recognize and to treat specific adverse drug reactions is an important factor that will help limit this problem. Finally, by being fully cognizant of the pharmacologic actions, therapeutic use, and adverse effects of each drug, dental and medical practitioners can begin to successfully control those consequences of drug therapy that result from both predictable and unpredictable adverse drug reactions.

REFERENCES

1. Azarnoff, D.L.: Application of metabolic data to the evaluation of drugs, J.A.M.A. **211:**1691, 1970.
2. Miller, L.C.: How good are our drugs? Am. J. Hosp. Pharm. **27:**367-374, 1970.
3. Report of the International Conference on Adverse Reactions Reporting Systems, Washington, D.C., 1971, National Academy of Sciences.
4. Sackner, M.A., and Balian, L.J.: Severe hypoglycemia after the ingestion of a sulfonylurea compound, Am. J. Med. **28:** 135-142, 1960.
5. Karnofsky, D.A.: Drugs as teratogens in animals and man, Ann. Rev. Pharmacol. **5:**447-472, 1965.
6. Miller, R.P., and Becker, B.A.: Teratogenicity of oral diazepam and diphenylhydantoin in mice, Toxicol. Appl. Pharmacol. **32:**53-61, 1975.

7. Milkovich, L., and van den Berg, B.J.: Effects of prenatal meprobamate and chlordiazepoxide hydrochloride on human embryonic and fetal development, N. Engl. J. Med. **291:**1268-1271, 1974.

8. Saxen, I.: Associations between oral clefts and drugs taken during pregnancy, Int. J. Epidemiol. **4:**37-44, March, 1975.

9. Safra, M.J., and Oakley, G.P.: Association between cleft lip with or without cleft palate and prenatal exposure to diazepam, Lancet **2:**478-540, 1975.

10. Maganzini, H.C.: Anaphylactoid reaction to penicillins V and G administered orally: report of two cases and brief review of the subject, N. Engl. J. Med. **256:**52-56, 1957.

11. Spark, R.P.: Fatal anaphylaxis due to oral penicillin, Am. J. Clin. Pathol. **56:**407-411, 1970.

12. Parker, C.W.: Drug allergy, N. Engl. J. Med. **292:**511-514, 1975.

13. Carr, E.A., Jr., and Aste, G.A.: Recent laboratory studies and clinical observations on hypersensitivity to drugs and use of drugs in allergy, Ann. Rev. Pharmacol. **1:**105-124, 1961.

14. Hesch, D.J.: Anaphylactic death from the use of a throat lozenge, J.A.M.A. **172:**12-15, 1960.

CHAPTER 4

SAM V. HOLROYD

BARBARA REQUA-CLARK

Prescription writing

Some years ago, prescription writing was a rather complex and pretentious art. Written in Latin and embellished by the hieroglyphics of the apothecaries' system of weights and measures, the prescription represented clinical virtuosity at its best. Early prescriptions described the compounding of a preparation from various and frequently numerous constituents. In more recent years, four changes have greatly simplified prescription writing:

1. The pharmaceutic industry currently provides drugs in the proper forms and dosages to fill most pharmacotherapeutic needs. Consequently, it is now seldom necessary to detail the compounding of a drug on a prescription form. It is only necessary to indicate the particular liquid, tablet, or capsule one wishes to prescribe, and the drug is dispensed by the pharmacist without the necessity of mixing the various ingredients of the preparation.
2. Prescriptions are no longer written in Latin (although currently used abbreviations are generally derived from the Latin).
3. The metric system of weights and measures has to a great extent replaced the more confusing apothecaries' system in prescription writing.
4. It is no longer considered unsophisticated to limit or eliminate the use of abbreviations in prescription writing.[1]

METRIC SYSTEM

Scientific calculations employ a base of 10. Consequently, the metric system, which is based on 10, is the language of scientific measurement. Metric units are employed in the USP-NF and should always be used in prescription writing.

The basic metric unit for the measurement of weight is the kilogram (kg). This unit is standardized as the mass of a metal cylinder kept at the International Bureau of Weights and Measures. The basic metric unit for volume is the liter (L), which was originally standardized as the volume of 1 kg of water at 4° C.

In 1964 the L was restandardized as 1 cubic decimeter, or 1000 cubic centimeters (cc).[2] Consequently, 1 milliliter (ml) is exactly equivalent to 1 cc. Since the various units of the metric system are based on multiples of 10, several prefixes that apply to units of both weight and volume can be used (Table 4-1).

Solid drugs are dispensed by weight (mg) and liquid drugs by volume (ml). It is rarely necessary to use units other than the milligram or the milliliter in prescription writing. Some practitioners learned and continue to use the apothecaries' system of weights and measures. Although this cumbersome system will in time be completely replaced by the metric system, one should be aware of its units. Table 4-2 shows the approximate equivalents of the metric and apothecaries' systems.

In summary, modern prescription writing is a simple procedure, usually requiring one of two units of metric measurement, the milligram (mg) or the milliliter (ml). In a few rare cases requiring the microgram (μg, mcg), it is best to spell this out rather than risk any confusion by abbreviating.

ABBREVIATIONS

Abbreviations are used in prescription writing to save time. They also make alteration of a prescription by the patient more difficult. In some cases they are necessary to get all the required information into the space available on the prescription form. Historically, abbreviations are of Latin and Greek terminology. Some that may be useful are shown in Table 4-3.

Unless a practitioner writes a large number of prescriptions daily, he saves little time using abbreviations. Since abbreviations are more likely to be misinterpreted by the pharmacist than are terms written in

Table 4-1. Metric weight and volume

Weight	Volume
*kilo*gram (kg) = 1,000 grams (gm)	liter (L) = 10 *deci*liters (dl) 100 *centi*liters (cl) 1,000 *milli*liters (ml) 1,000,000 *micro*liters (μl)
1 gram (gm) = 10 *deci*grams (dg) 100 *centi*grams (cg) 1,000 *milli*grams (mg) 1,000,000 *micro*grams (μg, mcg)	

Table 4-2. Approximate equivalents of metric and apothecaries' systems

Metric	Apothecary
Weight	
0.1 milligram (mg)	$^1/_{600}$ grain (gr)
0.5 mg	$^1/_{120}$ gr
1 mg	**$^1/_{60}$ gr**
30 mg	½ gr
60 mg	**1 gr**
100 mg	1½ gr
120 mg	2 gr
1 gram (gm)	**15 gr**
4 gm	1 dram (dr, ʒ)
30 gm	1 ounce (oz, ℥)
1 kilogram (kg)	2.2 pounds (lb)
Volume	
0.06 ml (cc)	1 minim (min, ♏)
1 ml	15 minims (min, ♏)
4 ml	1 fluidram (fl dr, fl ʒ)
15 ml	½ fluidounce (fl oz, fl ℥)
30 ml	1 fluidounce (fl oz, fl ℥)
500 ml	1 pint (pt)
1000 ml	1 quart (qt)

Table 4-3. Common abbreviations

Abbreviation	Latin or Greek	English
a. or ā	ante	before
aa or āā	ana	of each
a.c.	ante cibum	before food (meals)
ad lib.	ad libitum	as desired, as much as wanted
b.i.d.	bis in die	twice a day
c.	cibus	meal
c̄	cum	with
cap.	capsula	capsule
d.	dies	day
disp.	dispensa	dispense
gm		gram
gr		grain
gtt.	gutta	drop
h.	hora	hour
h.s.	hora somni	at bedtime ("hour of sleep")
no.	numero	number
non rep.	non repetatur	no refill, do not repeat
p̄	post	after
p.c.	post cibum	after food
p.o.	per os	by mouth
p.r.n.	pro re nata	as required, if needed
q.d.	quaque die	every day
q.h.	quaque hora	every hour
q.i.d.	quater in die	4 times a day
q.4h.	quaque quarta hora	every 4 hours
repet.	repetatur	to be repeated
s̄	sine	without
ss or s̄s̄	semis	one-half
sig.	signa	write (label)
stat.	statim	immediately (now)
tab.	tabella	tablet
t.i.d.	ter in die	3 times a day

full, the practitioner who uses them should ensure their clarity. This is of particular importance to the practitioner who does not write prescriptions with great frequency and may not be completely familiar with the use of abbreviations.

HOUSEHOLD MEASURES

Although the clinician will direct the pharmacist to dispense a liquid preparation in milliliters, it is generally necessary to convert this to a convenient household measurement in directions to the patient. For most drugs dispensed in dental practice, the teaspoon or tablespoon is sufficiently accurate (Table 4-4). The *teaspoon* holds about *5 ml* and the *tablespoon* about *15 ml*. When greater accuracy is required, the patient may need to use a graduated cylinder or medicine

Table 4-4. Common household equivalents

Household measure	Apothecary (approximate)	Metric
1 drop (gtt)	1 minim (min, ♏)	0.05 ml
1 teaspoonful (tsp)	1 fluidram (fl dr, fl ℨ)	5 ml
1 tablespoonful (tbsp)	½ fluidounce (fl oz, fl ℥)	14 ml

glass. A calibrated dropper is issued with most liquid preparations that require relatively exact measurements. One should be cautioned that the use of a medicine dropper is not particularly accurate if it is *not* calibrated. The size of a drop may vary considerably and depends on the specific gravity, temperature, and viscosity of the drug and on the diameter of the dropper's orifice.

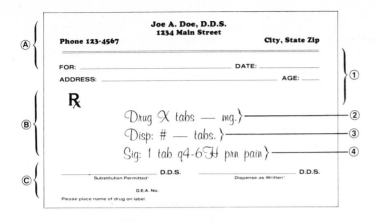

Fig. 4-1. Typical prescription blank. (Modified from Requa, B.S., and Holroyd, S.V.: Applied pharmacology for the dental hygienist, St. Louis, 1982, The C.V. Mosby Co.)

EXPLANATION OF LETTERS AND NUMBERS

Ⓐ - HEADING   ① - SUPERSCRIPTION
Ⓑ - BODY   ② - INSCRIPTION
Ⓒ - CLOSING   ③ - SUBSCRIPTION
                   ④ - TRANSCRIPTION

PARTS OF THE PRESCRIPTION

The parts of the prescription have been named and defined classically as follows:

SUPERSCRIPTION: Patient's name, address, and age; date; and the symbol ℞ (L. *recipe,* "[you] take" or "take thou of ").

INSCRIPTION: Name of drug, dosage form, and amount.

SUBSCRIPTION: Directions to the pharmacist.

TRANSCRIPTION (OR SIGNATURE): Directions to the patient.

The classic categorization serves no particularly useful purpose and is presented here only for reference. It is a more practical approach to consider the parts of a prescription to consist of the following information, which is shown in Fig. 4-1.

Heading

Name, address, and phone number of the prescriber.

Name, address, age, and phone number of the patient.

Date.

Body

The symbol "℞."

Name and dosage unit* or concentration (liquids) of the drug.

---

*"Dosage unit" refers to the size (mg) of the tablet or capsule.

Amount to be dispensed.

Directions to the patient.

Closing

Prescriber's signature.

Space for DEA number.

Refill instructions.

"Please place name of drug on label."

MECHANICS OF PRESCRIPTION WRITING

The prescription must serve two functions. First, it must tell the pharmacist the specific drug, dosage unit or concentration, and amount to be issued. Second, its directions to the patient, which will be transcribed to the packaged drug, must state precisely how the patient is to take the drug. Thus the essence of prescription writing is that the pharmacist knows exactly which preparation to dispense, and the patient has explicit written instructions for self-administration.

Heading

Printed on the top of the prescription form is the name, address, and phone number of the prescriber. Spaces for the date and the patient's name, address, age, and phone number are included. Identification of the prescriber is important in cases in which the pharmacist must contact the prescribing clinician.

The date is particularly important in that it allows the pharmacist to intercept prescriptions that may not have been filled at the time of writing. A patient may withhold filling a prescription until his problem intensifies, at which time a different pharmacotherapeutic regimen may be necessary. Under these conditions most pharmacists will either contact or refer the patient to the prescribing clinician. The age of the patient enables the pharmacist to double-check the dose.

Body

The first entry after the ℞ symbol must be the name of the drug being prescribed. This is followed by the size (mg) of the tablet or capsule desired. In the case of liquids, the name of the drug is followed by its concentration (mg/ml). The second entry is the quantity to be dispensed, that is, the number of capsules or tablets or milliliters of liquid. This should be preceded by *Dispense:* or *Disp:*

> ℞
> Codeine phosphate tablets, 32 mg
> Dispense: 8 (eight) tablets

or

> ℞
> Phenoxymethyl penicillin liquid, 125 mg/5 ml
> Dispense: 120 ml

In the case of tablets and capsules the word *dispense* is frequently replaced with the symbol for a number, #. When writing prescriptions for narcotics or other drugs that may require special control, it is wise to write out the number of tablets or capsules or put the number in Roman numerals in parentheses after the written number. This avoids the possibility of an intended 8 becoming 18 or 80 at the discretion of an enterprising patient. Directions to the patient now follow and are preceded by the abbreviation *Sig:* (L. *signa,* "write"). The directions to the patient must be completely clear and explicit, and should include the route, amount of medication, time, and frequency of administration. The statement "Use as directed" should not be used because the patient may not understand the clinician's oral directions or may forget the directions after leaving the office. Latin abbreviations that are used in writing the directions will be transcribed on the packaged drug in full and in English by the pharmacist. The completed body of the prescription then becomes the following:

> ℞
> Codeine phosphate tablets, 32 mg
> Dispense: 8 (eight) tablets, or 8 (VIII) tablets
> Sig: Take 2 tablets every 4 hours for pain

or, if abbreviations are used,

> ℞
> Codeine phosphate tabs., 32 mg
> Disp: 8 (eight) tabs., or # 8 (eight) tabs.
> Sig: 2 tabs. q.4h. for pain

Closing

Space for the prescriber's signature follows the body of the prescription. In this general area there should also be space for the prescriber's DEA number. Refill instructions may be included on the prescription.

It is good practice to place the name of the drug and the dosage unit on the packaged drug. Some states have laws that require pharmacists to routinely label all medications, but in any state a pharmacist is required to do so by having the statement "Please place name of drug on label" or "Label" printed on the prescription form. Placing the name of the drug on the package label is important for the following three reasons:

1. In case of overdose or adverse reactions, the drug's identity can be quickly obtained.
2. Other practitioners can identify drugs the patient is taking.
3. In most cases the patient has a right to know what drug he or she is taking.

It is good practice to write out the number of refills, since Arabic numbers can easily be changed, and a blank space can be filled in with any number. If no refill is desired, "No" should be written in the refill space to prevent forgery. Since dentists infrequently need to provide for refills, leaving a space for them may cause more problems. Refills can always be noted on the prescription even if no blank is provided.

Since the practice of printing the DEA number on the prescription blank increases the chances of stolen prescriptions being used, the DEA number should be written in for controlled substances (schedules II through V).

HINTS FOR PRESCRIPTION WRITING

Although these hints for prescription writing may seem self-evident, many prescribers fail to follow them, and errors result.

1. Write legibly in ink.
2. Use the metric system.
3. Avoid abbreviations.
4. Keep a copy of each prescription or transcribe the information to the patient's record.
5. Include complete information for the patient.
   a. Never use "Take as directed" unless a written instruction sheet is provided.
   b. Include the intended purpose, for example, "For relief of pain."
   c. Use precautions to remind a patient of a drug's side effects, for example, "Caution: sedation" or "Caution: May cause drowsiness."
   d. Add reminder phrases to increase the patient's compliance. Studies[3] have shown that over one half of patients fail to take medication properly. One example is to include, "Take until all are gone."

EXAMPLES OF PRESCRIPTIONS

The following are examples of the bodies of prescriptions that are frequently employed in dental practice.

EXAMPLE 1: Prescription for potassium penicillin G tablets as might be used in infections where the oral route is acceptable
Ŗ
K penicillin G tablets, 250 mg
Disp: 25
Sig: Take 1 tablet at bedtime and 1 hour before meals.

EXAMPLE 2: Example 1 using abbreviations
Ŗ
K penicillin G tabs., 250 mg
Disp: 25
Sig: 1 tab. h.s. and 1 h.a.c.

EXAMPLE 3: Prescription for a liquid preparation of potassium phenoxymethyl penicillin (penicillin V) as might be used for young children who are unable to swallow tablets
Ŗ
K penicillin V liquid, 125 mg/5 ml
Disp: 150 ml
Sig: 1 teaspoonful 1 h.a.c. and h.s.

EXAMPLE 4: Prescription for penicillin V tablets as might be used in patients with rheumatic heart disease who are appointed for procedures that would be expected to precipitate a bacteremia
Ŗ
Penicillin V tablets, 500 mg
Disp: 12
Sig: Take 4 tablets 30 to 60 minutes before appointment, and 1 tablet every 6 hours thereafter.

EXAMPLE 5: Prescription for a low adult dose of nystatin that might be employed in treating oral moniliasis (thrush)
Ŗ
Nystatin liquid, 100,000 U/ml
Disp: 180 ml
Sig: Swish 4 ml* in mouth for 2 minutes and then swallow q.6h.

EXAMPLE 6: Prescription for tetracycline hydrochloride capsules
Ŗ
Tetracycline HCl capsules, 250 mg
Disp: 25
Sig: Take 1 capsule every 6 hours.

EXAMPLE 7: Example 6 using abbreviations
Ŗ
Tetracycline HCl caps., 250 mg
Disp: 25
Sig: 1 cap. q.6h.

EXAMPLE 8: Prescription for diazepam that might be used in an adult for preoperative sedation.
Ŗ
Diazepam tablet, 5 mg
Disp: 5 (five)†
Sig: Take 1 tablet 1 hour before dental appointment. (Caution: sedation. Should be accompanied to dental office.)

EXAMPLE 9: Prescription for low adult dose of codeine sulfate to be taken with aspirin to add analgesic and antipyretic effects
Ŗ
Codeine sulfate tabs., 30 mg
Disp: 6 (six)
Sig: 1 tab. with 2 aspirin tabs. q.4h. p.r.n. pain (Caution: sedation)

EXAMPLE 10: Prescription for adult dose of meperidine HCl
Ŗ
Meperidine HCl tabs., 100 mg
Disp: 6 (six)
Sig: 1 tab. q.4h. p.r.n. pain (Caution: sedation)

DRUG LEGISLATION

The *Food and Drugs Act of 1906* was the first federal law to regulate interstate commerce in drugs. It was rewritten and reenacted to become the *Food, Drug, and Cosmetic Act of 1938*. This law and its subsequent amendments prohibit interstate commerce in drugs that have not been shown to be safe and effective. They further regulate labeling and packaging and establish standards of strength and purity. The enforcement of the Food, Drug, and Cosmetic Act is the responsibility of the FDA of the Department of Health and Human Services.

---

*The milliliter can be used in the directions here because the drug is dispensed with a dropper calibrated at 1 ml.
†Assumption that patient will need premedication for five appointments.

The *Durham-Humphrey Law of 1952* is a particularly important amendment to the Food, Drug, and Cosmetic Act because it requires that certain types of drugs be sold by prescription only. These preparations include certain habit-forming and addicting drugs and any other agents considered unsafe for lay use. The Durham-Humphrey Law requires that these drugs be labeled as follows: "Caution: Federal law prohibits dispensing without prescription." This law also prohibits the refilling of a prescription unless directions to the contrary are indicated on the prescription. This amendment allows the filling of prescriptions called in by telephone if the pharmacist promptly files a written record of the prescription.

The *Drug Amendments of 1962 (Kefauver-Harris Bill)* made some major changes in the Food, Drug, and Cosmetic Act. These amendments require that the manufacturer demonstrates both the drug's effectiveness and its safety before the drug can receive FDA approval for marketing. The manufacturers must follow stringent rules in preliminary testing and submit any reports of adverse effects and other relevant data on drugs already on the market to the FDA. In 1962 the amendments required that all drug labels and advertising list the generic name and quantity of all active ingredients. The advertising must briefly state the adverse effects, contraindications for use, and efficacy of a drug.[1]

The *Harrison Narcotic Act of 1914* and its amendments provided federal control over the importation, manufacture, production, compounding, selling, and dispensing of narcotic drugs. It required that all practitioners prescribing narcotics register with the Internal Revenue Service and receive a registration number. This law was administered by the Bureau of Narcotics of the U.S. Treasury Department.

The *Drug Abuse Control Amendments of 1965* required accounting for drugs with a potential for abuse: barbiturates, amphetamines, and any other depressants or stimulants that the U.S. Attorney General designates as having a potential for abuse. These amendments prohibited the refilling of a prescription for these drugs more than five times in 6 months after the date of the prescription.

The *Controlled Substance Act of 1970* replaced the Harrison Narcotic Act and the Drug Abuse Control Amendments to the federal Food, Drug, and Cosmetic Act. This new act is an extremely important one to the clinician. It sets current requirements for writing prescriptions for drugs frequently prescribed

in dental practice. The federal law divides the controlled substances into five schedules according to abuse potential. Individual states or local governments may legislate additional requirements concerning controlled substances. Whenever state and federal laws differ, the most stringent law must be followed. Drugs controlled by the federal law are divided into five schedules (Table 4-5) as follows.

Schedule I substances. Schedule I includes drugs with a high potential for abuse for which there is no accepted medical use in the United States. Examples include heroin, LDS, marijuana, peyote, mescaline, psilocybin, tetrahydrocannabinols (THC), and other hallucinogens. These substances cannot be prescribed but can be obtained for research purposes.

Schedule II substances. Schedule II includes drugs with a high potential for abuse (potential for severe psychic or physical dependence) for which there is a currently accepted medical use in the United States. Most of the narcotic drugs in this schedule had been categorized in the past as "class A narcotic drugs." Examples include narcotics such as opium, morphine, codeine alone, hydromorphone (Dilaudid), meperidine (Demerol), oxycodone (ingredient in Percodan, Percocet-5, Tylox), anileridine (Leritine), oxymorphone (Numorphan), levorphanol (Levo-Dromoran), and methadone (Dolophine); stimulants such as cocaine, most amphetamines including amphetamine (Benzedrine) and dextroamphetamine (Dexedrine), methylphenidate (Ritalin), and phenmetrazine (Preludin); and sedative-hypnotics such as amobarbital (Amytal), methaqualone (Quaalude, Parest, Sopor), pentobarbital (Nembutal), and secobarbital (Seconal).

Schedule III substances. Schedule III includes drugs with a lower potential for abuse than those in schedules I and II for which there is a currently accepted medical use in the United States. These drugs may lead to moderate or low physical dependence or high psychological dependence. They include those drugs formerly known as "class B narcotic drugs" plus a number of nonnarcotic agents. Examples include narcotics such as codeine mixtures like aspirin with codeine (Empirin with codeine), acetaminophen with codeine (Tylenol #3*, Phenaphen #3*), butalbital (Fiorinal #3),* and other narcotic mixtures including paregoric; stimulants such as benzphetamine (Didrex), chlorphentermine (Pre-Sate), clortermine

---

*The #3 is used as an example and designates the presence of 30 mg codeine. These products are also available in other strengths.

Table 4-5. Schedules of federally controlled substances

Schedule	Abuse potential	Examples	Comments	Handling
I	Highest	Heroin, LSD, marijuana, hallucinogens	No accepted medical use; illegal	Experimental or research use only
II	High	Morphine, meperidine, oxycodone, hydromorphone (Dilaudid), amphetamine, secobarbital, amobarbital	Formerly "class A narcotics"	Prescriber's written prescription only; no refills
III	Moderate	Codeine mixtures (Tylenol #3, Empirin #3), "weaker" stimulants and sedatives	Formerly "class B narcotics"	Prescriptions may be telephoned; no more than 5 refills in less than 6 months
IV	Less	Benzodiazepines (diazepam [Valium], dextropropoxyphene (Darvon), pentazocine (Talwin)	Mostly newly controlled drugs	
V	Least	Some codeine-containing cough syrups		Can be bought over the counter in some states

(Voranil), mazindol (Sanorex), and phendimetrazine (Plegine); and sedative-hypnotics such as butabarbital (Butisol), butalbital (ingredient in Fiorinal), glutethimide (Doriden), methyprylon (Noludar), and thiopental (Pentothal).

Schedule IV substances. Schedule IV includes drugs with a lower potential for abuse than those in schedule III for which there is a currently accepted medical use in the United States. Examples include sedative-hypnotic drugs such as chloral hydrate, chlordiazepoxide (Librium), chlorazepate (Tranxene), diazepam (Valium), ethchlorvynol (Placidyl), ethinamate (Valmid), flurazepam (Dalmane), meprobamate (Equanil, Miltown), methohexital (Brevital), oxazepam (Serax), paraldehyde, and phenobarbital; and stimulants such as diethylpropion (Tepanil, Tenuate), fenfluramine (Pondimin), pemoline (Cylert), and phentermine (Ionamin).

Schedule V substances. Schedule V includes drugs with a lower potential for abuse than those in schedule IV, for which there is a currently accepted medical use in the United States. Drugs in this category were previously known as "exempt narcotics."

• • •

Drug entities are continuously being evaluated and are moved from schedule to schedule as needed. One such drug, pentazocine (Talwin), previously unscheduled, has recently been added to schedule IV.

The *current requirements for prescribing controlled drugs,* as promulgated by the Controlled Substance Act of 1970, are as follows:

1. Any prescription for a controlled substance requires a DEA number (schedules II through V).
2. Schedule I drugs may not be prescribed because they have no medical use.
3. All schedule II through IV drugs and most schedule V drugs are *prescription drugs.*
4. Schedule II drugs must be written in the prescriber's handwriting, in ink, and cannot be refilled.
5. Schedule III and IV drugs may be telephoned to the pharmacist and may be refilled no more than five times in 6 months if so noted on the prescription.

An application for registration and assignment of a DEA number can be obtained by writing to the U.S. Department of Justice, Drug Enforcement Administration, P.O. Box 28083, Central Station, Washington, D.C. 20005. The prescriber should simultaneously apply to the state to obtain a Controlled Substances number.

REFERENCES
1. Holroyd, S.V.: Pharmacotherapeutics in dental practice (NAVPERS 10486), Washington, D.C., 1969, Bureau of Naval Personnel.
2. Conférence Générale des Poids et Mesures: Comptes rendus des séances de la 12ᵉ Conférence Générale des Poids et Mesures, Paris, 1964, Gauthier-Villars.

Pharmacology of the autonomic nervous system

Drugs affecting the autonomic nervous system play a major role in therapeutics as well as in the establishment of a basis for the mechanism of action of many drugs. These drugs differ widely in their pharmacologic applications, reflecting the diversity of control of the autonomic nervous system on body functions. Some drugs influence blood pressure and heart rate, whereas others may alter gastrointestinal tract motility or produce bronchodilation. The practical application of vasoconstrictors in local anesthetic solutions and of agents reducing salivary flow are familiar examples in dentistry. Antihypertensive drug action depends for the most part on alteration of autonomic control mechanisms both centrally and peripherally. The antipsychotic phenothiazines and antidepressants produce significant peripheral changes in autonomic activity even though their major activities take place within the CNS. The entire concept of chemical neurotransmitters and receptors is founded on the principles of the autonomic nervous system. Therefore dentists should have a working knowledge of autonomic pharmacology for use in dental therapy and be able to predict possible patient responses to medical treatment with drugs that have primary or secondary effects on autonomic function.

ORGANIZATION OF THE AUTONOMIC NERVOUS SYSTEM
Anatomic organization

The autonomic nervous system is divided into two divisions, the *sympathetic* and *parasympathetic,* distinguished by the location of their originating nerve cell bodies. Even though these cell bodies are located within the CNS and receive considerable CNS input, they must be regarded as peripheral in modes of action and drug reactions.[1] The first neuron of the efferent arm of fibers exiting from the CNS is termed *preganglionic*. This neuron then synapses with a second neuron to form the *autonomic ganglia*. The second neuron originating from the ganglionic synapse is termed *postganglionic* and terminates in the effector organ or tissue.

The sympathetic division originates with cell bodies that are located in the intermediolateral horn of the spinal cord and begin at the first thoracic through second or third lumbar vertebrae. Preganglionic fibers are sent out of the spinal column with the segmental spinal nerves. Many preganglionic fibers exiting from the cord leave the spinal nerves and almost immediately enter the *sympathetic chain* located along each side of the spinal column. Once a part of the sympathetic chain, preganglionic fibers may synapse with other cell bodies at the same segmental level or they may project up or down the sympathetic chain to synapse with cell bodies of different spinal segments. Some preganglionic fibers pass through the sympathetic chain without synapsing and enter into collateral ganglia. Preganglionic fibers synapse with those cell bodies that give origin to the postganglionic fibers. The postganglionic fibers then terminate at the effector organ or tissue site.[2]

A single sympathetic preganglionic fiber may form multiple synaptic junctions with numerous postganglionic neurons. The adrenal medulla also receives innervation from sympathetic preganglionic fibers. It functions much like a large sympathetic ganglion, with the glandular tissues of the medulla representing the postganglionic component. Discharge of the sympathetic division causes release of epinephrine from the adrenal medulla into the circulation. The high ratio of synaptic connections between preganglionic and postganglionic fibers and the release of epineph-

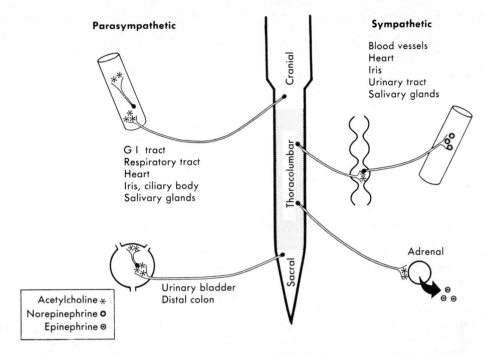

Parasympathetic

G I tract
Respiratory tract
Heart
Iris, ciliary body
Salivary glands

Urinary bladder
Distal colon

Acetylcholine ✳
Norepinephrine ⊙
Epinephrine ⊗

Cranial

Thoracolumbar

Sacral

Sympathetic

Blood vessels
Heart
Iris
Urinary tract
Salivary glands

Adrenal

Fig. 5-1. Divisions of the autonomic nervous system. (Courtesy R.L. Dorris, Baylor College of Dentistry, Dallas, Texas.)

rine into the circulation allow for a diffuse response from the sympathetic division.

The preganglionic fibers of the parasympathetic division originate with cell bodies in the nuclei of the third, seventh, ninth, and tenth cranial nerves as well as the first through fourth sacral spinal segments. Parasympathetic ganglia that give rise to postganglionic fibers are located on or in close proximity to the effector organ or tissue as opposed to a paravertebral chain of ganglia. There is, with certain exceptions, a much lower ratio of synaptic connections between preganglionic and postganglionic neurons; thus the response to parasympathetic discharge is not as pronounced or diffuse as that of the sympathetic division.[3] Fig. 5-1 illustrates the divisions of the autonomic nervous system.

Functional organization

The autonomic nervous system is concerned with the maintenance of a constant internal environment to provide for optimal cellular function and survival. This includes such functions as reflex vasodilation, where shifting of the blood supply helps to regulate body temperature. Blood glucose level, cardiac rate, water balance, and metabolism may be regulated through autonomic mechanisms. The sympathetic division is designed to cope with sudden emergencies, such as the fright and flight phenomenon. On the other hand, the parasympathetic division is concerned with the conservation of bodily processes. Reflex slowing of the heart rate is an example of parasympathetic activity.

The autonomic nervous system innervates almost all body tissues. Many receive innervation from both the sympathetic and the parasympathetic divisions. When this occurs, the functional capacity of the tissue is equal to the algebraic sum of the influences of the two divisions. Table 5-1 summarizes the response of the major tissue and organ systems to the autonomic nervous system.[4]

Neurotransmitters

To understand the function of the autonomic nervous system, as well as the manner in which drugs influence the system, it is necessary to have a basic knowledge of the concept of synaptic transmission.

Table 5-1. Response of major tissue and organ systems to autonomic nervous system

Organs or tissues (effector)	Parasympathetic division	Sympathetic division
Salivary	Vasodilation	Vasoconstriction
	Secretion (thin, high water content)	Secretion (viscid, low water content)
Heart	Cardiac slowing	Cardiac acceleration
	Coronary constriction (?)	Increase in force of contraction
		Coronary dilation (?)
Bronchial smooth muscle	Constriction	Relaxation
Iris of eye	Constriction	Dilation
	Accommodation, for near vision	Accommodation for distant vision
Adrenal medulla	—	Secretion of neurohumoral agents
Vessels of skeletal muscles	Dilation, if any	Dilation
Vessels of skin	Dilation, if any	Constriction
Intestines	Increase in peristalsis and secretions	Decrease in peristalsis and secretions
	Sphincters relax	Sphincter constriction
Liver	—	Glycogenolysis
Spleen capsule	—	Constriction

Nerves transmit bioelectric signals along their length by self-propagated impulses termed the *action potential*.[5] These signals are transmitted across nerve to nerve, or nerve to effector tissue, by chemical mediators termed *neurotransmitters*. Neurotransmitters are released by the nerve action potential to traverse the synaptic cleft and interact with the postsynaptic tissue. The specific membrane component that interacts with the neurotransmitter is the *receptor*. Receptors have been identified on both presynaptic and postsynaptic nerve terminals. The specificity of the neurotransmitter and the receptor dictates the effector tissue response.

It is well established that neurons of the autonomic nervous system contain the enzymes and metabolic processes necessary to synthesize neurotransmitters. Following or during synthesis, the transmitter substance is stored in numerous small vesicles located in the nerve terminal or synaptic varicosities along the neuron. The action potential releases Ca^{++}, which diffuses into the nerve terminal, causing the storage vesicle to fuse with the neuronal membrane and empty its contents into the synaptic cleft. The process of vesicle release of a transmitter is termed *exocytosis*. If sufficient transmitter is released to diffuse across the synaptic cleft, a receptor response will occur. The neurotransmitter-receptor interaction is short-lived, and the action is rapidly terminated by removal of the transmitter from the cleft. This process may involve enzymatic degradation, the diffusion of neurotransmitters into body fluids, or a specialized reuptake mechanism of the presynaptic neuronal membrane. Thus drugs can affect autonomic activity by altering any of the events of neurohumoral transmission: (1) synthesis, (2) storage, (3) release, (4) receptor interaction, or (5) disposition of the neurotransmitter.[6,7]

The chemical neurotransmitters of the autonomic nervous system are well known and accepted (Fig. 5-1). Acetylcholine is the specific chemical mediator at all autonomic ganglia and parasympathetic postganglionic synapses. It is also the transmitter substance of the neuromuscular junction in skeletal muscle. In the special case of the sweat glands, acetylcholine also mediates this sympathetic postganglionic action. The principal chemical mediator of the sympathetic postganglionic neuron is norepinephrine, whereas epinephrine is the major mediator released by the adrenal medulla. It has been traditional to classify the response produced by nerves on the basis of the chemical transmitter released at the synapse. Thus nerves releasing acetylcholine are termed *cholinergic* and those nerves releasing norepinephrine are termed *adrenergic*.

PHARMACOLOGY OF THE PARASYMPATHETIC DIVISION
Acetylcholine

Acetylcholine since its earliest identification has been confirmed as the neurotransmitter of both parasympathetic preganglionic and postganglionic neurons as well as the autonomic ganglia.[8] It is synthesized in the neuron from choline and acetylcoenzyme A (acetyl CoA) by the enzyme choline acetyltransferase as follows:

$$\text{Choline} + \text{Acetyl CoA} \xrightarrow{\text{Choline}\atop\text{acetyltransferase}} \text{Acetylcholine} + \text{CoA}$$

Acetylcholine is then stored in vesicles located in the presynaptic terminals of the various nerves.

An action potential traveling along the neuron causes the release of stored acetylcholine from the synaptic storage vesicles. A sufficient quantity of acetylcholine must be released to cross the synaptic cleft and initiate a response in the postsynaptic tissue. If the postsynaptic tissue is a postganglionic nerve, the usual consequence is depolarization, with generation of an action potential in that neuron. In the case of the postganglionic parasympathetic fibers, the postsynaptic tissue is an effector organ and the response will be that of the effector.[9]

The fact that some postsynaptic tissues respond to acetylcholine and not other mediators implies that acetylcholine must possess certain characteristics acceptable to the responding tissues. Therefore it must fit physically and chemically a specifically structured postsynaptic tissue component (the receptor) to be an effective mediator. It can be demonstrated that usual doses of atropine can block the action of acetylcholine at postganglionic endings but not at the neuromuscular junction. Other drugs have been used to illustrate similar stimulating or blocking effects at the various sites of action of acetylcholine. This information implies that different types of receptors may be located at the synapses for which acetylcholine has been identified as the mediator. Some of these receptors may be affected by one drug but not another. As an example, curare blocks the response of skeletal muscle to acetylcholine but does not block its effect on salivary glands. Other factors, such as the quantity of acetylcholine released, the size of the synaptic cleft, and the tissue penetrability of drugs, may also account for differences in receptor response to drugs at acetylcholine-mediated junctions.[10]

For acetylcholine to function as a physiologic neurotransmitter, its action must be reversible and terminate rapidly. The actions of acetylcholine are reversible since it is inactivated rapidly by the enzyme *acetylcholinesterase*. This enzyme is found associated with the synaptic tissues and can hydrolyze acetylcholine more rapidly than do other nonspecific plasma cholinesterases. The molecule is enzymatically hydrolyzed to inactive choline and acetic acid.[11]

Mechanism of action

The action of drugs affecting the parasympathetic division can be explained on the basis of the information presented about acetylcholine. Drugs resembling acetylcholine in chemical structure imitate effects similar to parasympathetic postganglionic activity. Such drugs are termed *cholinergic agonists,* and they possess the physical and chemical characteristics necessary to interact with the acetylcholine receptor. In addition, side chains or radicals may be added to alter the rate of enzymatic hydrolysis, thereby changing the duration of action and route of administration. Drugs are also available that selectively affect certain acetylcholine-mediated synapses but not others. It is possible to prolong the effects of acetylcholine with the use of drugs that are specific inhibitors of acetylcholinesterase, the *cholinesterase inhibitors*. Finally, the action of acetylcholine on the receptor can be blocked with the use of drugs termed *cholinergic blocking agents*. Drugs acting on the cholinergic receptor of the autonomic ganglia produce more widespread action either by a stimulating or blocking effect.

Cholinergic agonists

Choline esters. The natural prototype of the choline esters is acetylcholine. However, acetylcholine is not useful systemically as a therapeutic agent because of its rapid destruction by plasma esterases and its lack of a selective action. Since acetylcholine has a powerful parasympathetic stimulant action, efforts have been made to synthesize drugs of a similar chemical structure to that of acetylcholine but with a longer and more selective action. These efforts have met with limited success. Drugs in this category and their uses are shown in Table 5-2. All have the basic choline ester structure. As one can observe from the table, these drugs have their greatest usefulness in medicine.

The pharmacology of the choline esters reflects the actions of acetylcholine. The most noticeable effects are a fall in blood pressure attributable to generalized vasodilation, flushing of the skin, a slowing of the heart rate, and increased tone and activity of both the gastrointestinal and the urinary tracts. Topical application of the drugs to the eye causes miosis (constriction of the pupil) and a decrease in intraocular pres-

Table 5-2. Drugs of choline ester structure and their uses

Drug name	Medical use
Acetylcholine chloride (Miochol Intraocular)	Ophthalmology (to produce miosis)
Methacholine chloride	Infrequent use
Bethanechol chloride (Urecholine)	Postoperative abdominal distension and urinary retention
Carbachol (Isopto-Carbachol)	Ophthalmology (to produce miosis)

Table 5-3. Drugs with anticholinesterase activity and their uses

Anticholinesterase agent	Major use
Alkaloids	
Physostigmine salicylate (Antilirium)	Antidotal, anticurare action
Physostigmine (Isopto Eserine)	Miotic
Synthetic agents	
Neostigmine bromide (Prostigmin)	Myasthenia gravis, anticurare agent
Pyridostigmine bromide (Mestinon)	Anticurare agent, myasthenia gravis
Ambenonium chloride (Mytelase)	Myasthenia gravis
Demecarium bromide (Humorsol)	Glaucoma
Echothiophate iodide (Phospholine)	Glaucoma
Edrophonium chloride (Tensilon)	Diagnosis of myasthenia gravis, anticurare agent
Isofluorphate (Floropryl)	Glaucoma
Chemical agents	
Malathion	Insecticide
Parathion	Insecticide
Sarin	Chemical warfare agent
Tabun	Chemical warfare agent

sure. CNS effects are not observed with the usual therapeutic doses. Other manifestations of parasympathetic activity are observed in varying degrees, depending on the dose employed and the individual patient's sensitivity to the drug.

The side effects and toxic reactions associated with the use of the choline esters resemble those of a general stimulation of parasympathetic activity. Included in these reactions are excessive salivation, flushed skin, abdominal cramps with diarrhea, bradycardia, and a decrease in blood pressure. A cholinergic sympathetic response is associated with an increase in sweating. Larger doses may provoke serious cardiovascular problems and result in shock.

The choline esters have limited if any application in dental therapeutics. Attempts to use some of these drugs to promote salivation have been unsuccessful because of their widespread effect on various body systems. In case there should arise a situation in which a dentist would utilize these drugs, the contraindications to their use should be noted: (1) bronchial asthma, (2) hyperthyroidism, (3) mechanical obstruction of the gastrointestinal or urinary tract, (4) severe cardiac disease, (5) peptic ulcer, and (6) neostigmine therapy for myasthenia gravis. Antiarrhythmic drugs such as quinidine and procainamide have actions that could be antagonistic to these cholinergic drugs.[12]

Alkaloids. In addition to the synthetic choline esters, there are naturally occurring alkaloids that can stimulate the peripheral postsynaptic acetylcholine receptor. These drugs are muscarine, pilocarpine, and arecoline. The latter two can also stimulate the ganglia. Muscarine is useful as a research tool, and the action of acetylcholine at postganglionic parasympathetic sites is often referred to as a *muscarinic response*. Pilocarpine is the most useful of the alkaloids

in medicine being employed as a miotic and to treat glaucoma. It has been used with varying degrees of success to increase salivary flow. The usual adult dose is 5 mg given orally or by subcutaneous injection. If pilocarpine is used, the patient should be cautioned about the possibility of other parasympathetic effects such as sweating and visual disturbances. It should be pointed out that treatment of dry mouth may present a special management problem in that the lack of salivary flow may reflect a systemic disease that requires special care. Nicotine can produce either stimulation or blockade of the autonomic ganglia, depending on the dose used. The term *nicotinic response* is used to describe the stimulating action of acetylcholine on the ganglia as well as its action at the neuromuscular junction of skeletal muscle.[13,14]

Cholinesterase inhibitors

Prolongation of the effects of acetylcholine may be achieved by the use of drugs that inhibit the enzyme acetylcholinesterase. This may be accomplished with a rather large and heterogeneous group of agents, each with varying degrees of application. Table 5-3 lists drugs with anticholinesterase activity and their usual indications.

The anticholinesterase drugs may be divided into three categories based on the reversibility of their reaction with the esterase enzyme. Physostigmine and neostigmine are slowly reversible, whereas edrophonium is rapidly reversible. The chemical warfare agents and insecticides are essentially nonreversible and hence have a long duration of action.

The medically useful drugs in this group are employed in the treatment of glaucoma and myasthenia gravis, to improve muscle tone of the gastrointestinal tract and urinary bladder, or in anesthesia, to terminate the effects of curare-like neuromuscular blocking agents. Physostigmine is employed to manage the CNS anticholinergic side effects associated with atropine, the phenothiazines, the tricyclic antidepressants, and antihistamines. Several papers have appeared suggesting the use of physostigmine in cases of delirium associated with diazepam or lorazepam and now ketamine. Although physostigmine may possibly show some beneficial effects with these latter drugs, this should not be construed as a specific antidote for benzodiazepine toxicity—because one does not exist. It can be suggested that the synthetic anticholinesterase drugs would not produce a similar response because they are quaternary compounds and will not cross the blood-brain barrier.[15-17]

The side effects and toxic reactions associated with the use of anticholinesterase agents can be observed as a prolonged effect of acetylcholine. Such reactions include defecation, contracted pupils, sweating, excessive salivation, bronchial constriction, and skeletal muscle fasciculation. Undue exposure to the insecticides leads to reactions that may extend over a longer period of time, progressing to tremor, ataxia, hallucinations, respiratory paralysis, and death. Treatment requires the support of vital signs, artificial respiration, and atropine sulfate. The cholinesterase enzyme restorer pralidoxime chloride (2-PAM) (Protopam) is used in cases of organophosphate toxicity.[18]

It is important to note on the dental records whether a patient is taking one of these anticholinesterase agents, particularly neostigmine. There is the danger that use of atropine to reduce salivary flow could interfere with the cholinergic action of the drug. Since the choline esters and the anticholinesterase agents have little use in dentistry, dosages of these drugs have been omitted.

Cholinergic blocking drugs

The cholinergic blocking (anticholinergic) drugs consist of a large group of natural and synthetic agents competitively inhibiting the action of acetylcholine at parasympathetic postganglionic neuroeffector sites. Acetylcholine release is not prevented, but its interaction with the cholinergic receptor is blocked. Thus the cholinergic blocking drugs effectively prevent the action of acetylcholine on the eye, smooth muscle, glandular tissue, and heart. In the therapeutic dosages used by dentists little or no effect will be observed at the ganglia and neuromuscular junction.

The principal drugs in this category are atropine and scopolamine, which are naturally occurring belladonna alkaloids useful in dentistry as agents to control salivary secretion and as preanesthetic medication. Most of the synthetically prepared anticholinergic drugs have been designed to provide a longer duration of action and have a greater selectivity for action on the smooth muscle of the intestines.

The desirable clinical effects of the anticholinergics are mydriasis, antispasmodic effect, and reduction in gastric and salivary secretions, and related members are used for their antiparkinsonian benefits. Selected examples are presented in Table 5-4. Many are combined with a barbiturate or a tranquilizer to reduce either the patient's underlying psychic influence on gastrointestinal secretions or the influence of the CNS on parasympathetic activity. The rationale for such therapy is still under investigation.[19,20]

The pharmacologic actions of atropine and scopolamine are similar in many respects, as might be expected, since they differ from one another by only an oxygen atom. Atropine in the usual dose employed in dentistry does not show a CNS response, although in larger doses stimulation may occur. Scopolamine, however, has a depressant effect on the CNS, which accounts for its usefulness as a preanesthetic agent and perhaps its use in motion sickness in several over-the-counter preparations. Both drugs will reduce salivary flow and in larger doses block the cardiac-slowing effect of the vagus nerve, resulting in tachycardia. This latter effect is useful in preventing cardiac slowing during general anesthesia.[21]

Atropine, scopolamine, and the synthetic deriva-

Table 5-4. Some synthetic cholinergic blocking drugs and their uses

Drug name	Major use
Homatropine hydrobromide (Isopto Homatropine)	Mydriasis and cycloplegia
Methscopolamine bromide (Pamine)	Antispasmodic and antisecretory
Hexocyclium methylsulfate (Tral)	Antispasmodic
Cyclopentolate HCl (Cyclogyl)	Mydriasis and cycloplegia
Dicyclomine HCl (Bentyl)	Antispasmodic
Glycopyrrolate (Robinul)	Antispasmodic and antisecretory
Methantheline bromide (Banthine)	Antispasmodic and antisecretory
Propantheline bromide (Pro-Banthine)	Antispasmodic and antisecretory
Benzotropine mesylate (Cogentin)	Antiparkinsonian
Trihexyphenidyl HCl (Artane)	Antiparkinsonian

tives are also extremely useful in therapy and examination of the eye. These drugs produce dilation (mydriasis) and paralysis of accommodation for distance vision and light (cycloplegia). Such effects are generally long lasting and can also be manifested by larger systemic doses of the drugs.

The use of atropine and scopolamine in dentistry is limited to preanesthetic medication and reduction of salivary flow. Atropine sulfate may be used either orally or by injection to reduce salivation. Doses for adults range from 0.3 to 1 mg and should be given at least 1 or 2 hours before the dental procedure. Careful dosage adjustment is required in children because they are more responsive to the effects of these drugs.[22] After the use of atropine to reduce salivation, the patient should be warned that a dryness and burning of the throat will persist for a few hours. Additionally, vasodilation and flushing of the skin may occur, along with blurred vision. Perhaps some note of caution should be observed in those patients wearing contact lenses. Nursing mothers excrete atropine in their milk; therefore one must consider the real need for reduction of salivation in these patients to prevent a drug response in the infant. Scopolamine hydrobromide may also be used, but it is more useful in premedication for general anesthesia in doses of 0.3 to 0.6 mg for adults when given by injection.[23]

There are at least 50 or more different synthetic anticholinergic drugs designed to be an aid to peptic ulcer therapy and related disorders. Many of these agents have the side effect of reducing salivary flow; thus dentists have used this side effect to their advantage. Since so many of these agents exist, an example of only one will be used to illustrate how the antispasmodic drugs may be used. The ADT lists propantheline bromide (Pro-Banthine) as a possible selection.[24] Methantheline (Banthine) has also been used, but propantheline may cause fewer side effects. These drugs should be given orally at least 30 to 45 minutes preoperatively. The usual dose of propantheline for an adult is 7.5 to 15 mg, and occasionally 30 mg may be required. Since only single doses are employed, the incidence of side effects associated with more frequent use of such drugs may be avoided. However, even with a 15 mg oral dose, one patient was observed to have tachycardia. The practitioner must constantly keep in mind that each patient is an individual who is subject to varying responses to the usual dose of a drug. The dose used and the response should be noted on the patient's chart, so fewer side effects and greater therapeutic response may be attained by dosage adjustments at subsequent appointments. Another agent, glycopyrrolate (Robinul) has also been employed in oral doses to reduce salivary flow, but sufficient literature on its effectiveness is lacking.

Specific contraindications to the use of the anticholinergic agents include glaucoma, prostate hypertrophy (may cause urinary retention), and intestinal obstruction. Since these drugs affect the cardiovascular system, caution should be observed when using them in patients with severe cardiovascular problems.

Side effects are common with the anticholinergic drugs and include blurred vision, tachycardia, urinary retention, constipation, decreased salivation, sweating, and dry skin. Some of the effects can last several hours. Toxic reactions are most often associated with overdose or accidental poisoning and can include delirium, hallucinations, convulsions, and respiratory depression. Dry skin and elevation of body temperature also occur. Treatment of toxic reaction largely depends on the patient's symptoms. Vital signs should be controlled, and sponge baths may be given to lower body temperature.

The chief medical use of the atropine substitutes and belladonna preparations includes treatment of functional gastrointestinal disorders and peptic ulcer. In addition, these agents have been used to control secretions that occur with the common cold and in some cases of asthma. Drugs with anticholinergic effects are also used in treating parkinsonism and motion sickness. A thorough medical history will usually provide the information concerning which drug the patient is receiving. Additional anticholinergic drugs in these individuals may not be required to control their salivary flow.

Interaction with other medically useful drugs

Drugs in the cholinergic and anticholinergic categories have limited usefulness in dentistry. These drugs are more important to dentists because of the possible interactions with other categories of drugs that also have autonomic effects. The cholinergic and anticholinergic drugs are widely used in medicine and affect so many body systems that it is important to be able to recognize or anticipate synergistic and antagonistic drug reactions. Some of these reactions are clinically important and some may not be so clinically significant. Be that as it may, it is good practice to note these reactions so that patients achieve the intended therapeutic benefits of a drug.

The choline esters and anticholinesterases, when given together, potentiate cholinergic responses. Adrenergic drugs and atropine can antagonize the miotic effects of the cholinergics. Antihistamines are reported to reduce the activity of cholinesterase inhibitors and also produce dryness of the mouth similar to that of the anticholinergics.[25]

Anticholinergic drugs react with a wide assortment of other agents to produce a variety of responses. Those agents that can be considered to potentiate anticholinergic drugs include adrenergics, alphaprodine, meperidine, antihistamines, tricyclic antidepressants, corticosteroids, monoamine oxidase inhibitors (MAOIs), methylphenidate, the nitrates, tranquilizers, and urinary alkalinizers. Drugs that antagonize or inhibit anticholinergic actions include achlorhydria agents, urinary acidifiers, anticholinesterases, guanethidine, and reserpine. Levodopa, the latest drug developed for treatment of parkinsonism, may be potentiated by the anticholinergics. This list is far from exhaustive but should include most of the drugs commonly encountered in a day-to-day practice.[26]

PHARMACOLOGY OF THE SYMPATHETIC DIVISION
Norepinephrine and epinephrine

It is well established that norepinephrine and epinephrine are the chemical mediators of the sympathetic division of the autonomic nervous system. Norepinephrine is released by the sympathetic postganglionic neurons in response to a nerve impulse. Small amounts of norepinephrine are also released by the adrenal medulla, but the major neurotransmitter released by the adrenal gland is epinephrine. The ratio of epinephrine to norepinephrine release in the medulla is approximately 80:20 but can vary. Although norepinephrine release from the postganglionic neuron is usually thought of as acting on the innervated effector tissues, neurotransmitter release from the adrenal medulla is distributed in the circulatory system, reaching almost every portion of the body. Thus the sympathetic division is designed to meet local tissue needs as well as total body demands.[27] A third neurotransmitter related closely to norepinephrine is dopamine. It has more importance as a CNS mediator but has some peripheral activity as well. Collectively, these naturally occurring mediators may be termed catecholamines.

Adrenergic tissues (sympathetic) contain the necessary enzymes for the synthesis and storage of the catecholamines. Synthesis in the adrenergic neuron takes place along its length and is completed in the synaptic varicosity, whereas specialized chromaffin cells of the adrenal medulla contain the synthesis components. It is important to illustrate the steps in the synthesis process since drugs that alter the biosynthesis pathway are now used clinically. The synthesis pathway is as shown on p. 52.

In the adrenergic neuron, steps 1 through 2 occur in the axoplasm, step 3 in the storage vesicle, and step 4 almost exclusively in the adrenal medullary tissues. The synthesis is a continual dynamic process providing adequate stores of neurotransmitter availability. Reduction in norepinephrine neuronal levels signals the production of additional neurotransmitter by a feedback mechanism to the rate-limiting enzyme *tyrosine hydroxylase*.[28]

The release of the vesicular-stored norepinephrine occurs by a process analogous to acetylcholine release. A nerve impulse alters the permeability of the synaptic tissue to calcium. The calcium stimulus initiates the fusion of vesicular membrane with neuronal membrane and the emptying of the vesicular contents into the synaptic cleft. In this case stored ATP and protein are released with the norepinephrine.[29]

Adrenergic receptors

In 1948 Ahlquist[30] proposed the existence of two types of adrenergic receptors to explain the variations in tissue response associated with sympathetic stimu-

H   COOH

C — C — NH$_2$

H   H

HO

Tyrosine

↓ Tyrosine hydroxylase

H   COOH

C — C — NH$_2$

H   H

HO

HO

L-Dihydroxyphenylalanine (levodopa)

↓ Levodopa decarboxylase

H   H

C — C — NH$_2$

H   H

HO

HO

Dopamine

↓ Dopamine betahydroxylase

OH   H

C — C — NH$_2$

H   H

HO

HO

Norepinephrine

↓ Phenylethanolamine transferase

OH   H   CH$_3$

C — C — N

H   H   H

HO

HO

Epinephrine

lation. He proposed the receptors be termed *alpha* and *beta*. This concept presented the proposition that the "activation" of alpha receptors by an adrenergic drug produced one type of response and the "activation" of beta receptors caused a different response. His results demonstrated that epinephrine has an action on both receptor types but some greater selectivity for the alpha receptor. Isoproterenol, a synthetic catecholamine, acted principally on beta receptors.

Subsequently a family of adrenergic alpha and beta adrenergic receptors has been proposed and accepted. In 1967 Lands[31] provided evidence for the existence of two types of beta receptors, *beta*$_1$ and *beta*$_2$. Beta$_1$ receptors produced stimulation of the heart, causing both positive chronotropic and inotropic effects. Lipolysis is also promoted by beta$_1$ activation. The beta$_1$ receptor showed approximately equal affinity for both epinephrine and norepinephrine. The beta$_2$ receptor caused vasodilation in skeletal muscle and coronary muscles as well as bronchodilation. Beta$_2$ receptors showed a much higher affinity for epinephrine. Associated with the membrane-bound beta receptor is an enzyme, adenyl cyclase. Adenyl cyclase catalyzes the formation of cyclic adenosine monophosphate (cyclic AMP), which in turn activates many cellular actions and plays a prominent role in beta receptor–mediated functions. A presynaptic beta receptor has been suggested to function in the release of norepinephrine.[32]

Additionally, an alpha$_2$ receptor that regulated the feedback release mechanism of norepinephrine was suggested. Activation of the alpha$_2$ receptor inhibits the release of norepinephrine, thus regulating sympathetic tone (Fig. 5-2). Activation of the alpha$_1$ receptor causes vasoconstriction in vessels of the skin and mucosa and stimulation of glycogenolysis.[33]

Many tissues may have both alpha and beta receptors, with one type of receptor dominant. The response of the tissue to a specific adrenergic drug will depend principally on the majority of the receptor type present. It is most important to separate the actions of adrenergic drugs on receptors since their entire pharmacology is based on receptor selectivity and tissue receptor type. A summary of tissue responses and receptors is presented in Table 5-5.

The termination of action of norepinephrine, unlike that of acetylcholine, is not primarily dependent on rapid enzymatic hydrolysis. Instead the factor most responsible for the termination of action is a reuptake mechanism, the amine pump, in the sympa-

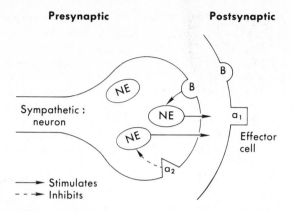

Presynaptic   **Postsynaptic**

Sympathetic : neuron

⟶ Stimulates
--- ⟶ Inhibits

Fig. 5-2. Simplified schematic view of an adrenergic nerve ending. When the nerve is stimulated, norepinephrine *(NE)* is released from its storage granules and enters the synaptic cleft to bind with alpha$_1$ (α_1) and beta (β) receptors on the effector cell (postsynaptic). In addition, a short feedback loop exists, in which NE binds to alpha$_2$ and beta receptors on the neuron (presynaptic), either to inhibit or to stimulate further release. (From Kaplan, N.M.: Systemic hypertension: therapy. In Braunwald, E., editor: Heart disease: a textbook of cardiovascular medicine, vol. 1, Philadelphia, 1980, W.B. Saunders Co.)

Table 5-5. Tissue receptors and responses

Organ	Receptor type	Response
Heart (sinoatrial node, atrioventricular node, atria, and ventricles)	Beta$_1$	Increase in heart rate, contractility, and conduction velocity
Bronchial smooth muscle	Beta$_2$	Bronchodilation to reduce airway resistance
Blood vessels (skin and mucosa)	Alpha$_1$	Vasoconstriction
Blood vessels (skeletal muscles)	Beta$_2$ and alpha$_1$	Vasoconstriction and vasodilation
Eye (radial muscle)	Alpha$_1$	Mydriasis (dilation of pupil)
Adipose tissue	Beta$_1$	Lipolysis
Salivary glands	Alpha	Viscous secretions

Data modified from Frishman, W., Am. Heart J. **97:**663, 1979, and Geffen, L.B., and Jarrott, B.: Cellular aspects of catecholaminergic neurons. In Brookhart, J.M., and Mountcastle, V.B.: Handbook of physiology, Sec. 1. The nervous system, Bethesda, Md., 1977, The American Physiological Society.

thetic postganglionic neuron. The norepinephrine taken up by the nerve is restored for future use. Thus the action of the biogenic amines may be longer lasting than acetylcholine.

Not all of the norepinephrine is inactivated by the reuptake process. At least two identifiable enzymes, monoamine oxidase (MAO) and catechol-*O*-methyltransferase (COMT), are involved in the metabolism of both epinephrine and norepinephrine. MAO, although found in many tissues, is thought to be responsible for metabolizing intraneuronal norepinephrine and thereby regulating its storage levels. COMT is involved in the metabolism of catecholamines extraneuronally. The end products of metabolism are excreted in the urine, where they can be readily measured.[34]

Mechanism of action

The complex synthesis and various receptor types allow for the development of a large group of drugs that act on the sympathetic division. Agents that mimic the action of sympathetic neurotransmitters are termed *adrenergic agonists*. These are further subdivided into *alpha agonists* and *beta agonists,* when it is known, receptor selectivity is specified, that is, beta$_1$ or beta$_2$. The indirect-acting adrenergic drugs cause release of stored norepinephrine to produce their effects. Some adrenergic drugs have mixed action, causing a direct effect as well as an indirect release. Specific adrenergic blocking drugs for the various receptors are also available. These include both the alpha and beta adrenergic antagonists. Many antihypertensive drugs interfere with storage and release of norepinephrine; methyldopa acts as an enzyme substrate in the synthesis pathway. Major antipsychotics block central dopamineric receptors, as well as peripheral autonomic receptors, as part of their action. The tricyclic antidepressants block the amine pump reuptake mechanism, whereas MAOIs increase the available norepinephrine stores by preventing metabolism. Thus the number of drugs that can influence the sympathetic division is larger and more complex when compared to the parasympathetic division.[35]

Adrenergic agonists
Epinephrine hydrochloride

The most useful and perhaps the best example of a drug that imitates the activity of sympathetic discharge is epinephrine. Its major effects are on the myocardium and smooth muscles of the blood vessels and lung. Therefore epinephrine acts as a direct cardiac stimulant. Both small and large doses of epinephrine cause an increase in strength of contraction, cardiac rate, cardiac output, and oxygen use.

The receptors located in the vessels of the skin, mucous membranes, and kidney are predominantly alpha, so epinephrine will cause vasoconstriction in these vessels. Receptors in those vessels located in skeletal muscle are for the most part beta, with some alpha. Therefore epinephrine will cause vasodilation in skeletal muscles. These two responses are extremely important in the regulation of blood pressure. Slow intravenous infusion of small doses of epinephrine will cause an increase in cardiac activity associated with a rise in systolic pressure but with a decrease in diastolic pressure because of the vasodilation occurring in skeletal muscles. Larger doses produce a rise in both systolic and diastolic pressures because the cutaneous alpha response predominates. Since the alpha response is of a shorter duration than the beta, a fall in pressure will be observed after the initial increase. The smooth muscles of the bronchi contain beta receptors and hence are relaxed by epinephrine. Alpha receptors located in the vascular smooth muscle of pulmonary arterioles respond with vasoconstriction to epinephrine. The net result is a reduction in resistance to air flow, which provides relief during asthmatic attacks.

The CNS effects attributed to epinephrine represent a manifestation of peripheral action of the drug. Epinephrine is fairly water soluble; thus it does not enter the brain to any significant extent. However, patients may have CNS-like effects, such as anxiety, weakness, apprehension, restlessness, and occasional tremor. The metabolic effects of epinephrine are seen in a rise in blood sugar levels and free fatty acids as readily available energy sources.

Epinephrine hydrochloride is available for use in the commercial form of Adrenalin. It is supplied in ampules of a 1:1000 aqueous solution for subcutaneous, intramuscular, or for extreme emergencies, intravenous injection. The most often used route of administration is the subcutaneous route, which allows the drug to be absorbed over a longer period of time. If given intravenously, 1 ml should be diluted to 10 ml with sterile water for injection and then given very slowly. The 1:100 dilution used for inhalation or topical application must not be confused with the injectable form because disastrous results might occur.

A topical solution, 1:1000, is also available for use as a hemostatic agent on bleeding gingival or pulpal tissues. Small quantities of the solution should be placed in a clean dappen dish for this purpose; cotton pledgets should not be saturated directly from the original container. Contaminants may cause premature deterioration of the epinephrine solution. All epinephrine should be stored in the original dark containers because light will also decompose the solution. The presence of a brownish color indicates an epinephrine solution that has lost its potency and should be discarded.[24]

Epinephrine is the drug of choice for acute asthmatic and allergic reactions. It may be injected subcutaneously, intramuscularly, or intravenously in doses of 0.2 to 0.5 ml of the 1:1000 aqueous solution. The drug is employed as a vasoconstrictor in local anesthetics. It is also employed as a cardiac stimulant in patients with cardiac arrest. Because the drug is a direct cardiac stimulant, it could cause ventricular fibrillation in certain cardiac emergencies. For this reason its use in patients with hemorrhagic, traumatic, or cardiogenic shock is not recommended. Epinephrine is contraindicated for use in certain types of glaucoma (congestive narrow angle) and for use with cyclopropane and halogenated hydrocarbon anesthetics. It should be used with caution in elderly people and in those with cardiovascular disease, hypertension, and hyperthyroidism. As with any drug, every situation must be evaluated on its own merits as to the safety and possible interaction with other drugs or disease processes.

Norepinephrine

The neurotransmitter agent released from the sympathetic postganglionic neurons is norepinephrine. Its action on alpha adrenergic receptors causes vasoconstriction in the cutaneous vessels, leading to an increase in peripheral resistance and an increase in both systolic and diastolic blood pressure. Baroreceptors are stimulated by the elevated pressure and cause a reflex firing of the vagus nerve, resulting in bradycardia. It does not relax bronchial smooth muscle since this is a beta$_2$ response. Alpha constriction of arterioles in the lungs will not provide sufficient reduction in airway resistance to be useful in asthma. The metabolic effects seen with epinephrine apparently do not occur with norepinephrine.

Norepinephrine bitartrate is available as the commercial product Levophed. It is intended to be used only in certain cases of hypotension associated with shock. It should not be part of the dental emergency kit because other adrenergic drugs are more suitable. It produces severe vasoconstriction in cutaneous vessels so that necrosis and tissue slough can occur. Therefore there can be little justification for its use in local anesthetic solutions.[23]

Toxic and side effects associated with the use of norepinephrine resemble those seen with epinephrine. Hypertension caused by norepinephrine is likely to be more severe, especially in the hyperthyroid patient. Contraindications to the use of norepinephrine are also similar to those for epinephrine.

Isoproterenol

Isoproterenol is a synthetic adrenergic derivative of epinephrine with action limited to the beta receptors. When injected, it acts as a direct cardiac stimulant, increasing both the rate and the strength of cardiac contraction. Since it stimulates only the beta receptor, a decrease in diastolic pressure is observed. It also decreases bronchial spasm by relaxation of the bronchial smooth muscle. Vasoconstriction of pulmonary vessels does not occur, since this represents an alpha response.

Isoproterenol hydrochloride is available commercially as Isuprel. Its primary use is in the treatment of bronchial asthma and heart block. Preparations include an inhalation product in a concentration of $1:400$. Sublingual tablets are supplied in 10 and 15 mg dosage forms, and a $1:5000$ (1 ml) ampule for injection is also available. Its side effects are similar to those of epinephrine, and like epinephrine and norepinephrine, it is not effective orally.

Dopamine

Dopamine is the immediate precursor of norepinephrine and has been shown to be an active catecholamine in the periphery. Its action as a neurotransmitter in the CNS is presented elsewhere in this text. Dopamine interacts with dopamine receptors as well as autonomic alpha and beta receptors. The dopaminergic receptors are located in renal, mesenteric, and coronary vessels. It acts via beta$_1$ receptors to stimulate heart rate, contractility, and cardiac output. Alpha receptor activation causes vasoconstriction with elevation of blood pressure.

Clinically, it is marked as the hydrochloride salt with the brand name of Intropin. It is indicated for use in shock associated with septic or myocardial etiol-

ogy. It is also used to treat acute heart failure associated with cardiovascular surgery or in refractory congestive heart failure unresponsive to the usual therapy. (See Chapters 20 and 21.) Dopamine is carefully administered intravenously with an infusion pump. Side effects resemble those of other catecholamines, including arrhythmias, local necrosis, gangrene in special circumstances, and angina pain. Drugs such as MAOIs may cause an increase in dopamine activity, whereas phenothiazines can negate dopamine action.[36]

Ephedrine

Ephedrine is a naturally occurring sympathomimetic agent with both direct and indirect effects. Unlike the previously mentioned drugs, it is effective when given orally and is used in numerous oral preparations intended for use in patients with bronchial asthma. Solutions of the drug have been used in ophthalmology to cause pupillary dilation (mydriasis). Since it has both alpha- and beta-stimulating effects, it is used in intranasal solutions to produce vasoconstriction for a localized decongestive effect. An isomer of ephedrine, pseudoephedrine, is also used effectively in the treatment of asthmatic and allergic disorders.[13]

Synthetic adrenergic drugs

Competition among pharmaceutical manufacturers has prompted the development of a large number of drugs having adrenergic properties. Each of these agents possesses the basic characteristic of vasoconstriction. Some are intended as nasal decongestants only; others are effective agents in combating hypotension. The use of one over the other is largely a matter of personal preference and familiarity.

Phenylephrine hydrochloride (Neo-Synephrine). Phenylephrine has vasoconstrictive properties that make it useful in the treatment of hypotension. It has also been employed as a vasoconstrictor in local anesthetics. Phenylephrine is not as potent as norepinephrine and can be used to elevate pressure without the danger of direct cardiac stimulation. It may be administered by injection or by mouth. Ophthalmic preparations provide excellent mydriasis.

Metaraminol bitartrate (Aramine). Metaraminol is a highly potent adrenergic agent used almost exclusively to treat severe hypotension. It also has cardiac-stimulant properties. Metaraminol is reported to be taken up by sympathetic nerve terminals in a manner similar to norepinephrine. In this way it has a mixed action. Its duration of action is longer than that of norepinephrine. As with all vasoconstrictors, one must exercise care when giving potent agents.

Mephentermine sulfate (Wyamine). Mephentermine is used as a vasoconstrictor to treat hypotension. It also has a mixed action. Dentists could select this agent either to place in their emergency drug kit for their use or to have on hand for use by medical personnel. It reportedly does not produce CNS-like stimulation as observed with other vasoconstrictors. The route of administration is either subcutaneous or intramuscular in a dosage range of 15 to 30 mg for adults.[37]

Miscellaneous drugs

Nasal decongestants. There appears to be an almost endless variety of adrenergic drugs that can be utilized for vasoconstriction. Symptomatic relief by the use of nasal decongestants reduces the swelling by vasoconstriction of vessels in the mucous membranes. Within a short time the congestion returns and the vasoconstrictor must be used again. If the recommended dosage schedules are not followed, a condition referred to as "congestion rebound" occurs. Vasodilation and congestion are then complicated by irritation and local tissue edema. Repeated use of stronger solutions, closely spaced dosages, and systemic absorption could provoke greater problems than congestion rebound. It should be emphasized that these agents provide only symptomatic relief. The following is a list of adrenergic drugs used as nasal decongestants: naphazoline HCl (Privine), tetrahydrozoline HCl (Tyzine), tuaminoheptane sulfate (Tuamine), oxymetazoline HCl (Afrin), xylometazoline HCl (Otrivin), phenylephrine HCl (Neo-Synephrine), cyclopentamine HCl (Clopane), and phenylpropanolamine HCl (Propadrine). The list is incomplete and is intended to be illustrative only.[18]

Bronchodilators. Epinephrine and isoproterenol are effective bronchodilators that have been used for years to treat asthmatic symptoms. These drugs are given both by inhalation and by injection. Ephedrine, a mixed-acting bronchodilator, has also been used as an effective oral bronchodilator. With the identification of beta$_2$ receptors and the desire to produce more selective bronchodilators without cardiovascular stimulating effects, selective beta$_2$ agonists are now available to treat asthma. The available drugs include metaproterenol (Alupent, Metaprel) and terbutaline (Brethine, Bricanyl). Terbutaline is more selective for the beta$_2$ receptor than metaproterenol; however, selectivity disappears with higher doses. Nevertheless, the drugs provide adequate bronchodilation without troublesome cardiovascular side effects. As is the case with theophylline, these drugs may act via the adenyl cyclase enzyme system. The principal side effects include skeletal muscle tremor, nervousness, and weakness. Metaproterenol is given orally or by inhalation; terbutaline is given orally or by subcutaneous injection.[38]

Amphetamines. The amphetamines are a group of drugs that have indirect adrenergic stimulant effects manifested by increases in blood pressure and reflex cardiac slowing. However, they are potent CNS stimulants. The more prominent members of this category of drugs include amphetamine sulfate (Benzedrine), dextroamphetamine sulfate (Dexedrine), and methamphetamine HCl (Desoxyn, Methedrine, or "speed"). The abuse potential associated with the use of this category of drugs has prompted their inclusion as controlled substances under the recent federal drug laws. Therefore prescriptions for these drugs must meet all the requirements for schedule II agents, that is, the same as the potent narcotic analgesics.

The use of these agents is limited in both medicine and dentistry. Medical uses have included treatment of mental depression, hyperkinesis, appetite control, and narcolepsy. The action of these agents in reducing appetite is still a matter of conjecture, since after a few days these drugs seem to loose their appetite-suppressant effects.

Prolonged use of these drugs may lead to such side effects as physical dependence, apprehension, wakefulness, and mental depression and may evoke suicidal tendencies. Toxic reactions associated with overdosage may result in cardiac irregularities, cardiovascular collapse, coma, and death.[39]

Vasoconstrictors and their use in local anesthetics

A general discussion of the use of vasoconstrictors in local anesthetic solutions is presented in Chapter 15. Further consideration of specific agents is given here. The following chemical structures depict the subtle molecular changes that occur among the most commonly employed agents. Although the changes in structure may seem small, the pharmacologic differences occurring as a result of the change are of extreme importance.

HO—⟨benzene ring⟩—CH—CH₂—NH with OH and CH₃

Epinephrine

HO—⟨benzene ring⟩—CH—CH₂—NH₂ with OH

Norepinephrine

HO—⟨benzene ring⟩—CH—CH₂—NH with OH and CH₃

Phenylephrine

HO—⟨benzene ring⟩—CH—CH—NH₂ with OH and CH₃

Levonordefrin

All of the commonly used vasoconstrictors in local anesthetics are of synthetic origin. Although norepinephrine and phenylephrine are listed in most texts as vasoconstrictors for local anesthesia, their use in this country is almost nil, and they will not be discussed further. Norepinephrine is used more frequently in European countries.

Pharmacologic activity

Epinephrine. Although the basic pharmacology of epinephrine has been discussed, its effect on cutaneous blood vessels should be mentioned again. Mucous membrane contains, for the most part, alpha receptors. The response to alpha stimulation is vasoconstriction; hence epinephrine can be used in concentrations smaller than those of other vasoconstrictors to give satisfactory results. Accidental intravascular injection may cause pronounced cardiac responses.

Levonordefrin. Levonordefrin, or α-methylnorepinephrine, is an effective vasoconstrictor for use in local anesthetic solutions. It is identified as the racemate of Cobefrin, but it is now more commonly used as the levo isomer, Neo-Cobefrin. Levonordefrin is stated to be less potent than epinephrine, but potency is used only to distinguish between the relative doses of drugs to produce a similar effect. The

concentration of levonordefrin found in local anesthetic solutions is 1:20,000 whereas epinephrine is 1:100,000. It should be expected that these two vasoconstrictors would produce similar actions. Methyldopa is an antihypertensive drug whose action is dependent on conversion to α-methylnorepinephrine in the CNS. Levonordefrin is a substrate for COMT rather than MAO.[40]

Absorption and excretion. All the vasoconstrictors used are absorbed systemically from the site of injection and are carried throughout all the body tissues. Accidental intravenous injection could result in alarming or hazardous consequences. Since the enzyme systems responsible for the metabolism of these drugs are similar, their rates of metabolism will be similar and the metabolites appear in the urine.

Commonly used concentrations. Vasoconstrictors are used in the following concentrations:

Epinephrine HCl	1:50,000 to 1:250,000; optimum—1:100,000
Norepinephrine bitartrate	1:30,000 to 1:50,000
Phenylephrine HCl	1:2000 to 1:2500
Levonordefrin HCl	1:20,000 to 1:30,000

Side effects and toxicity. Epinephrine hydrochloride, being the most commonly employed vasoconstrictor and the classic representative of the sympathetic nervous system, is perhaps the drug of choice used to describe side effects and toxic reactions to adrenergic vasoconstrictors. It should be noted that vasoconstrictors behave as desired except when excessive dosages are employed and accidental intravascular injections are made.[32]

Patients may demonstrate many sympathetic and CNS-like reactions to epinephrine. These sympathetic reactions may appear as side effects characterized by palpitation, tachycardia, hypertension, and headache. In addition, the patient may show anxiety, restlessness, and weakness, appear pale, and complain of dizziness. Many times these reactions may be wrongfully assigned to the local anesthetic, thereby creating future problems for the patient when more dental work is scheduled. Toxic reactions to vasoconstrictors are most often associated with dosages higher than those usually employed in dental local anesthetic solutions.[41]

Precautions in use. Over the years many controversies have arisen concerning the use of epinephrine or other vasoconstrictors in patients with hypertension, hyperthyroidism, and cardiovascular diseases. It is not uncommon for dentists to hear a word of caution from the patient's physician in regard to vasoconstrictors. All too often this is a problem in communication that could be resolved by the dentist's explaining to the physician about the strength and amount of vasoconstrictor employed.

In 1964 the *Journal of the American Dental Association*[42] carried a report of a joint conference by the ADA and the American Heart Association on problems with the patient who had cardiovascular disease and required dental treatment. The conference urged the careful cooperation of the physician and dentist in evaluating the use of both local anesthetics and vasoconstrictors. Vasoconstrictors are not contraindicated for the patient whose condition is diagnosed and controlled when they are used with careful aspiration and in optimal dosages. Premedication is suggested to help alleviate apprehension in these patients. Most information presented in the past years suggests the inclusion rather than the omission of vasoconstrictors so that a more profound and longer lasting anesthesia is possible. Fear, apprehension, and pain may be responsible for the patient elaborating more endogenous vasoconstrictor than the dentist would think about injecting.

There are a number of specific instances in which the vasoconstrictor should not be employed, such as in the hypertensive and hyperthyroid patient whose condition is uncontrolled. Epinephrine should be avoided in patients undergoing general anesthesia with cyclopropane or the halogenated hydrocarbons. These general anesthetic agents are capable of sensitizing the myocardium to epinephrine in such a way that cardiac arrhythmias and even fibrillation can occur.

Use for gingival retraction. There are numerous commercial preparations consisting of some type of string or cord impregnated with epinephrine or a racemic mixture of epinephrine isomers. Regardless of claims made by one over the other, these agents depend on the vasoconstrictive action of epinephrine on gingival blood vessels to bring about a retraction of tissue or hemorrhage control. The dentist should be aware that the concentrations of epinephrine in these preparations are relatively high and that systemic absorption does occur. Therefore these preparations may represent a potential source of danger in the cardiovascular and hyperthyroid patient. This also applies to the use of epinephrine-impregnated cords during general anesthesia with cyclopropane and the halogenated hydrocarbons. Wetting the gingival retraction cord with saliva in the floor of the mouth allows the epinephrine to be absorbed rapidly from this site for a systemic effect and could account for some arrhythmias or tachycardia observed in patients during general anesthesia.[43]

Adrenergic blocking drugs

There is a large group of drugs that have the capability of reducing or blocking sympathetic activity. Contrary to what might be expected, the development of drugs with the property of blocking alpha or beta adrenergic receptors confirmed that the two receptors were plausible. Most of these agents are used in the treatment of peripheral vascular disease, hypertension, and specific cardiac problems. Except for extremely rare instances, they are not suitable therapeutic agents for dentistry but are important in medical practice. Because catecholamines have been identified in the CNS, drugs are available that can also modify the psychic response in patients by means of interference with the metabolic inactivation of the catecholamines. These drugs also affect to some degree peripheral autonomic mechanisms and will be briefly mentioned.

Alpha adrenergic blocking drugs

The alpha adrenergic blocking drugs act by competitively inhibiting the action of catecholamines at the peripheral alpha receptor site. The first of the alpha blocking agents, phenoxybenzamine (Dibenzyline) and phentolamine (Regitine) were used in the therapy of peripheral vascular disease and in hypertension associated with the adrenal medullary tumor (pheochromocytoma). The ergot alkaloids also have alpha blocking properties and are used to control headaches thought to be of central vascular origin. Lack of specific alpha$_1$ receptor blocking properties has reduced the usefulness of these agents in hypertensive disease. However, prazosin (Minipress) is an alpha$_1$ blocking agent proving most useful in hypertensive disease. Its selectivity for the alpha$_1$ receptor ensures the alpha$_2$ feedback system remains intact, thereby reducing many undesirable side effects. These drugs are also discussed in Chapter 21. Other drugs with alpha adrenergic blocking action include the phenothiazines, the butyrophenones, and to a much lesser extent the tricyclic antidepressants.[44]

Other drugs modifying sympathetic response

The adrenergic neuronal blockers are distinguished from the adrenergic blocking agents in that the neuronal blockers prevent the discharge of stored transmitter. Circulating amines and those injected are not blocked. The principal drug employed for this purpose is guanethidine (Ismelin), the main use of which is in the treatment of hypertension. It is important to note the long-lasting effects of this drug even when therapy has been discontinued. Hypotension and weakness may accompany its use. Reserpine and its related alkaloids are also used to treat hypertension by a mechanism involving the depletion and blockage of catecholamine storage.

Beta adrenergic blocking drugs

The beta adrenergic blocking drugs have been in clinical use for more than a decade. Their action is one of competitively blocking the beta adrenergic receptor. Just as with the beta agonists, beta antagonists have been developed with a relative degree of selectivity for either the $beta_1$ or $beta_2$ receptors in the hope of reducing the troublesome side effect of bronchospasm. However, as the dosage of the more selective B_1 antagonists is increased, the selectivity seems to disappear. At present, four beta adrenergic blockers are in use in this country, propranolol (Inderal), metoprolol (Lopressor), nadolol (Corgard), and timolol (Timoptic). The latter agent is approved for use in glaucoma. Propranolol, the most common beta blocker in use today, is a major therapeutic agent for use in angina pectoris, hypertension, cardiac arrhythmias, pheochromocytoma, and prevention of migraine headache. Nadolol is approved for use in hypertension and angina, whereas metoprolol has only been approved for use in hypertension. Metoprolol is the only $beta_1$ selective antagonist in current clinical use.

The basic pharmacologic effects of the beta adrenergic blocking drugs is to prevent the action of catecholamines on the cardiovascular system. Both the chronotropic and inotropic actions are blocked. The reduction in blood pressure produced by these agents is related to their action on the heart as well as a possible reduction in renin production by the kidney. These and other actions on the heart are more thoroughly presented in the appropriate chapters related to cardiovascular and antihypertensive drugs. These drugs are contraindicated in patients with bronchospastic diseases.[45]

Ganglionic blocking drugs

Those drugs that have either a blocking or a stimulating effect on the autonomic ganglia have a limited usefulness in medicine. Nicotine, the alkaloid obtained from tobacco, is an interesting agent in that it can both stimulate and block the ganglia, depending on the doses used. Some of the sympathetic responses that a person feels after having stopped smoking and then beginning again are examples of its stimulating effects. The ganglionic blocking agents are used in the treatment of hypertension. These drugs include mecamylamine (Inversine) and trimethaphan (Arfonad). Both divisions of the autonomic nervous system show a peripheral response to the ganglionic blockers. One of the side effects associated with these drugs is dryness of the mouth.

Interactions with other drugs

The sympathetic-related drugs react in many ways with an exceptionally large number of other drugs. This is not only a reflection of the diffuse activity of the sympathetic amines but also that of so many other drugs having an indirect autonomic response.

The drugs that potentiate the activity of adrenergic stimulators include alcohol, antihistamines, cocaine, doxapram, ergot drugs, ganglionic blockers, and the xanthine group. Of course, adrenergic drugs are used together at times to potentiate decongestant effects. The halogenated anesthetics and cyclopropane increase the hazard of cardiac arrhythmias and should be avoided in combination with the adrenergic drugs. Digitalis is also associated with a predisposition to cardiac arrhythmias.

Three groups of drugs, the tricyclic antidepressants, the MAOIs, and the phenothiazines, may present special considerations concerning patients being treated with adrenergic agonists. Tricyclic antidepressants block the amine uptake pump mechanism, allowing for a longer contact with the adrenergic receptor. Because tricyclics cause cardiac arrhythmias as a side effect, the potential for additional effects is present when local anesthetics with a vasoconstrictor are used. The MAOIs prevent the intraneuronal catabolism of catecholamines, increasing the amount stored in nerve vesicles. Indirect-acting adrenergic agents such as tyramine trigger a greater release and the potential for a hypertensive crisis. There is little or no evidence to show that vasoconstrictors in local anesthetic solutions will cause a similar response. Phenothiazines are peripheral alpha receptor blocking agents. Thus epinephrine administered in therapeutic doses to patients receiving these drugs may cause hypotension. Since the alpha response to epinephrine is blocked, the beta vasodilatory effects predominate; this is commonly called epinephrine reversal.

The list of drugs that can interact with the adrenergic blocking drugs is extensive. Dentists would be wise to consult with the patient's physician if these drugs are being used. At the present no conclusive data are available regarding the potential hazards of vasoconstrictors in local anesthesia. However, beta adrenergic blockers should present less of a problem than alpha receptor blocking agents. Many of the drugs used in hypertensive disease will potentiate the hypotensive effects of adrenergic blockers. This interaction is used to the benefit of the patient.[25,26]

REFERENCES

1. Patton, H.D.: Higher control of autonomic outflows: the hypothalamus. In Ruch, T.D., and Patton, H.D., editors: Neurophysiology, Philadelphia, 1965, W.B. Saunders Co.
2. Truex, R.C., and Carpenter, M.S.: Strong and Elwyn's human neuroanatomy, Baltimore, 1964, The Williams & Wilkins Co.
3. Carisson, A., and Hillarp, N.A.: On the state of catecholamines of the adrenal medullary granules, Acta Physiol. Scand. **44:**163, 1958.
4. Guyton, A.C.: Textbook of medical physiology, ed. 6, Philadelphia, 1981, W.B. Saunders Co.
5. Hodgkin, A.L.: The conduction of the nerve impulse, Springfield, Ill., 1964, Charles C Thomas, Publisher.
6. Holman, M.E., and Hirst, G.D.S.: Junctional transmission in smooth muscle and the autonomic nervous system. In Brookhart, J.M., and Mountcastle, V.B., editors: Handbook of physiology: the nervous system, vol. 1, Bethesda, Md., 1977, American Physiological Society.
7. Cooper, J.R., Bloom, F.E., and Roth, R.H.: The biochemical basis of neuropharmacology, New York, 1970, Oxford University Press, Inc.
8. Loewi, O., and Navratil, E.: Über humorale Übertragbarkeit der Herznervenwirkung; über das Schicksal des Vagusstoffs, Pflueger's Arch. Ges. Physiol. **214:**678, 1926.
9. Collier, B.: Biochemistry and physiology of cholinergic transmission. In Brookhart, J.M., and Mountcastle, V.B., editors: Handbook of physiology: the nervous system, vol. 1, Bethesda, Md., 1977, American Physiological Society.
10. Paton, W.D.M.: Receptors as defined by their pharmacological properties. In Porter, R., and O'Connor, M., editors: Molecular properties of drug receptors, A Ciba Symposium, London, 1970, J. & A. Churchill, Ltd.
11. Davis, R., and Koelle, G.B.: Electron microscopic localization of acetylcholine esterase and nonspecific cholinesterases at the neuromuscular junction by the gold-thiocholine and gold-thioacetate acid methods, J. Cell. Biol. **34:**157, 1967.
12. Volle, R.L.: Cholinomimetic drugs. In DiPalma, J.R., editor: Drill's pharmacology in medicine, New York, 1971, McGraw-Hill Book Co.
13. Goth, A.: Medical pharmacology: principles and concepts, ed. 10, St. Louis, 1981, The C.V. Mosby Co.
14. Waser, P.G.: Chemistry and pharmacology of muscarine, muscarone and some related compounds, Pharmacol. Rev. **13:**465, 1961.
15. Nattel, S., Boyne, L., and Ruedy, J.: Physostigmine in coma due to drug overdose, Clin. Pharmacol. Ther. **25:**96, 1979.
16. Blitt, C.D., and Petly, W.C.: Reversal of lorazepam delirium by physostigmine, Anesth. Analg. **54:**697, 1975.
17. Toro-Matos, A., et al.: Physostigmine antagonizes ketamine, Anesth. Analg. **59:**764, 1980.
18. Polson, C.J., and Tattersall, R.N.: Clinical toxicology, ed. 2, Philadelphia, 1969, J.B. Lippincott Co.
19. Melmon, K.L., and Morelli, H.F., editors: Clinical pharmacology, ed. 2, New York, 1978, Macmillan, Inc.
20. Soine, T.O.: Autonomic blocking agents and related drugs. In Wilson, C.O., Gisvold, O., and Doerge, R.F., editors: Textbook of organic medicinal and pharmaceutical chemistry, Philadelphia, 1977, J.B. Lippincott Co.
21. Eger, E.I.: Atropine, scopolamine and related compounds, Anesthesiology **23:**365, 1962.
22. Kutscher, A.H., Zegarelli, E.V., and Hymon, G.A.: Pharmacotherapeutics of oral disease, New York, 1964, McGraw-Hill Book Co.
23. Jorgensen, N.B., and Hayden, J.: Premedication, local and general anesthesia in dentistry, Philadelphia, 1967, Lea & Febiger.
24. Accepted dental therapeutics, ed. 38, Chicago, 1979, American Dental Association.
25. Gage, T.W., and Radman, W.P.: Drug interactions—a professional responsibility, J. Am. Dent. Assoc. **84:**848, 1972.
26. The American Pharmaceutical Association: Evaluations of drug interactions, ed. 2 and supplement, Washington, D.C., 1976, The Association.
27. von Euler, U.S.: A specific sympathomimetic ergone in adrenergic nerve fibers (sympathin) and its relation to adrenaline and noradrenaline, Acta Physiol. Scand. **12:**73, 1946.
28. Blaschko, H.: Catecholamine release, Br. Med. Bull. **29:**105, May 1973.
29. Smith, A.D.: Mechanisms involved in the release of noradrenaline from sympathetic nerves, Br. Med. Bull. **29:**123, May 1973.
30. Ahlquist, R.P.: A study of the adrenotropic receptors, Am. J. Physiol. **153:**586, 1948.
31. Lands, A.M., et al.: Differentiation of receptor systems activated by sympathomimetic amines, Nature **214:**597, 1967.
32. Hoffman, B.B., and Lefkowitz, R.J.: Radioligand binding studies of adrenergic receptors: new insights into molecular and physiological regulation, Ann. Rev. Pharmacol. Toxicol. **20:**581, 1980.
33. Berthelson, S., and Pettinger, W.A.: A functional basis for classification of alpha-adrenergic receptors, Life Sci. **24:**79, 1977.
34. Sharman, D.F.: The catabolism of catecholamines, Br. Med. Bull. **29:**110, May 1973.
35. Weiner, N.: Norepinephrine, epinephrine and the sympathomimetic amines. In Gilman, A.G., Goodman, L.S., and Gilman, A., editors: Pharmacological basis of therapeutics, New York, 1980, MacMillan, Inc.
36. Goldberg, L.I., and Hsieh, Y.Y.: Clinical use of dopamine, Ration. Drug Ther. **11**(11):1, 1977.
37. DiPalma, J.R., editor: Basic pharmacology in medicine, New York, 1976, McGraw-Hill Book Co.
38. Holtzman, M.J., and Nadel, J.A.: Treatment of asthma and bronchoconstriction, Ration. Drug Ther. **15**(6):1981.

39. Ray, O.S.: Drugs, society and human behavior, ed. 2, St. Louis, 1978, The C.V. Mosby Co.

40. Ciarlone, A.E.: A brief review of some properties of alpha-methylnorepinephrine, J. Am. Dent. Assoc. **92:**748, 1976.

41. Holroyd, S.V., Watts, D.T., and Welch, J.T.: The use of epinephrine in local anesthetics for dental patients with cardiovascular diseases: a review of the literature, J. Oral Surg. **18:** 492, 1960.

42. Conference report: Management of dental problems in patients with cardiovascular disease, J. Am. Dent. Assoc. **68:**333, 1964.

43. Woycheshin, F.F.: An evaluation of the drugs used for gingival retraction, J. Prosth. Dent. **14:**769, 1964.

44. Davey, M.J.: Relevant features of the pharmacology of prazosin, J. Cardiovasc. Pharmacol. **2**(Suppl. 3):5287, 1980.

45. Davies, R.O., and McMahon, F.G.: The present status of beta blockers in clinical medicine, Ration. Drug. Ther. **14**(2):1, 1980.

PART TWO

Specific drug groups

General anesthetics

CHAPTER 6

TOMMY W. GAGE

General anesthetics are a class of drugs that are potent CNS depressants. They produce a reversible loss of consciousness and insensibility to painful stimuli. The cortex is the first CNS structure to be depressed, followed in order by the brain stem, spinal cord, and medulla. Protective reflexes are abolished by most of these agents, and with increasing doses, depression of respiration and many vital organ systems also occurs. For these reasons, the constant responsibility of the anesthesiologist throughout the anesthetic period is that of patient evaluation and monitoring of vital signs. General anesthesia is the result of the early efforts of general dentists who were seeking a suitable means of pain control for their patients. Since that time, general anesthesia has become a highly scientific and structured specialty.

A large number of general anesthetic agents have become available for use. Contemporary general anesthetic techniques employ a balanced combination of drugs for the total management of the patient, taking into account the patient's physical status as well as the preanesthetic and postanesthetic needs. Balanced techniques of anesthesia may involve the use of a preanesthetic narcotic and anxiolytic before induction with a rapidly acting intravenous barbiturate. The patient will then be maintained on combined inhalation anesthetics and a neuromuscular blocking drug for the operative period. In other cases, larger than usual doses of morphine are given intravenously with oxygen inhalation for certain types of cardiovascular surgery. Potent vasodilators are used in a hypotensive anesthesia technique to reduce blood loss. The combinations of drugs may seem endless, but all balanced anesthetic techniques are designed to provide maximal patient safety and optimal utility for the surgeon.[1]

Because of the variety of anesthetic agents and techniques employed, special training and complete knowledge of the pharmacology of each anesthetic is essential. The environment of the hospital operating room provides the optimal setting for general anesthesia, since the proper monitors for vital signs, resuscitative equipment, and trained anesthesia personnel are readily available. However, it should be noted that oral surgeons have used general anesthetics in their offices for many years with an excellent safety record. Indeed, dentists should have knowledge of general anesthesia because it is an indispensable tool for the total dental needs of special patients as well as for more extensive oral and maxillofacial surgery.[2]

HISTORY

Dentists have played a significant role in the recognition and use of drugs that could provide relief from pain. Although many drugs such as morphine and alcohol have been used to make surgery more comfortable, and Joseph Priestly is aptly given the credit for describing nitrous oxide, it took the concern of a dentist for his patient to bring the pain-relieving benefits of general anesthesia to the public eye. In December, 1844, Horace Wells, a dentist, observed a demonstration of the effects of nitrous oxide while attending a lecture. During the course of the program, Wells noted that one of the participants inhaling the gas had injured a leg without being aware of the associated pain. Wells was impressed with this observation and asked his associate, John Riggs, to remove one of his own teeth while he was under the effects of nitrous oxide. The extraction was completed without pain.

Wells persuaded a former dental partner and at that time Harvard University medical student, William

65

T.G. Morton, to arrange for a demonstration of the use of nitrous oxide. Wells obtained the necessary permission to demonstrate the gaseous agent before the Harvard University medical faculty. Unfortunately, the low potency of nitrous oxide was not known, and the anesthetic attempt failed.

In the months that followed, Morton, with the aid of C.T. Jackson, demonstrated the use of ether as an effective general anesthetic before the same Harvard University group. Later Howard W. Long, a Georgia physician, reported his earlier use of ether as an anesthetic for surgical procedures. A tragic conflict developed among these different individuals as each sought recognition for the introduction of general anesthesia. Wells committed suicide; however, as years passed, both the dental and medical professions have recognized his contribution.

It should also be pointed out that during this same period, a noted Scottish surgeon, James Y. Simpson, introduced the use of the volatile liquid chloroform for obstetric anesthesia in 1847.[3]

METHODS FOR ADMINISTERING ANESTHETIC AGENTS

The method employed for administering a general anesthetic agent is dictated by the choice of anesthetic agent. Ether and chloroform are volatile liquids at room temperature and were simply dropped onto a gauze-covered wire mask placed over the patient's face. As the liquid volatilized, its vapors mixed with the inspired air. This was a rather slow process and uncomfortable for the patient. Additionally, expiration of carbon dioxide and inspiration of adequate oxygen were uncontrollable. Towels were often draped around the open mask to increase the concentration of anesthetic vapors inhaled. Gas anesthetics are administered from storage cylinders through hoses, metered flow valves, and a face mask.

The demand for patient safety, explosion-free operating rooms, and a more suitable means of regulating volume flow of gases to the patient resulted in the development of sophisticated anesthetic machines. These units are usually self-contained packages consisting of metered flow valves, calibrated vaporizers for volatile anesthetic liquids, gas storage cylinders, a carbon dioxide absorber, and a breathing bag. These units are constructed in a variety of ways with the essential features including an adequate oxygen source that can be mixed with the anesthetic gas. This mixture can then flow through the vaporizer that

is adding the volatilized liquid anesthetic. The total anesthetic mixture is then delivered to the patient through a face mask. The system can be designed with a series of valves to allow rebreathing or nonrebreathing of gases. Excess carbon dioxide is removed by the absorber system. Some gases are explosive, requiring a closed-type system. The breathing bag serves as a reservoir for the anesthetic gas mixture, but more importantly, it provides a means for the artificial assistance of the patient's respiration. Most machines are equipped with an oxygen flush valve that allows for the rapid removal of anesthetic gases from the system while providing emergency oxygen to the patient.[4]

The intravenous route is commonly employed in dental offices and for the rapid induction of unconsciousness by the ultrashort-acting barbiturates. Also, muscle relaxants and other support-type drugs are given by this route during anesthesia. Whatever means is chosen, the more important factors to keep in mind would include the patient's comfort and safety and a patent airway. The competent use of anesthetic machines implies a knowledge of the equipment as well as specialized training.

THEORIES ON THE MECHANISMS OF ACTION

Many theories have been proposed in an effort to explain the mechanisms of action of the various general anesthetic agents, but unfortunately, none of them does so completely. It may seem relatively simple to say that these drugs are CNS depressants, but just how they depress the normal neuronal function is a matter complicated by lack of knowledge of the physiologic and biochemical events of arousal and unconsciousness. Adding further confusion is the wide variety of drugs that can be used as anesthetics, ranging from gases to steroidlike agents. Some of the more widely discussed theories of mechanisms of action follow:[5]

1. *Lipid or Meyer-Overton theory.* The lipid theory resulted from the combined efforts of Meyer[6] and Overton[7] and basically it relates the potency of anesthetic agents to their lipid solubility. Whereas certain effects of the anesthetics on the lipid neuronal tissues are related to their oil–water partition coefficient, this theory cannot explain the action of many other anesthetic agents.

2. *Inhibition of biochemical actions.* Numerous theories have been described relating the effects of

anesthetic agents to the utilization of oxygen by the cell. Early research suggested that anesthetics produced asphyxiation or antagonized the action of oxygen at the cell level. Quastel[8] sought to explain the role of barbiturate anesthetics by a decreased oxygen uptake. Greig[9] reported that chloroform inhibited respiration in the brain homogenates.

3. *Molecular theories.* At least two investigators, Miller and Pauling, have proposed mechanisms related to the effects anesthetics could have on water. Miller[10] suggested that the anesthetics cause the formation of "icebergs" around nerves that interfered with their function. Pauling[11] contends that certain inert anesthetic gases (xenon) produce minute crystals or "clathrates," which trap certain electrically charged groups of neuronal protein thus impeding neural transmission.

No attempt has been made to include every theory about how general anesthetics may act at the cellular level. No doubt this area of research will continue to provide provocative and interesting evidence for not only the action of drugs but also new information about arousal and unconsciousness. For the interested reader, a review reference is included.[5,12]

STAGES AND PLANES OF ANESTHESIA

In a relatively short time after the introduction of general anesthesia, anesthesiologists began to describe and identify the various levels of anesthetic depression. John Snow is credited with this early description, which was later amplified by Guedel[13] in 1920. Guedel's classification has become the standard for describing the various stages and planes of CNS depression. It is important to note that Guedel's system applied to the administration of ether by the open drop method in a nonpremedicated patient. Modern anesthetic techniques are such that many of these classic signs are not actually observed. It seems important to describe briefly the four stages, since reference to depth of anesthesia is still related to Guedel's system.

Stage I—Analgesia. This stage is characterized by the development of analgesia. The patient can still respond to command, and reflexes are present. This initial stage will terminate with the loss of consciousness. Some amnesia may also be evident.

Stage II—Delirium. This stage of anesthesia begins with unconsciousness and is associated with increased muscle tone. The patient moves and shows excitement. As the depth of anesthesia increases, the patient begins to relax and progresses to the next stage. This can be an uncomfortable time for the patient because vomiting and incontinence can occur. The ultrashort-acting barbiturates provide the modern anesthesiologist with a rapid means of inducing unconsciousness, thereby avoiding this stage.

Stage III—Surgical anesthesia. This is the stage associated with the majority of surgical procedures. Its onset is typically characterized by regular respiratory movements, muscular relaxation, and normal heart and pulse rates. Conjunctival and eyelid reflexes are absent. This stage is further divided into four planes that are differentiated on the basis of eye movements, depth of respiration, and muscular relaxation. Plane 3 is associated with decreased skeletal muscle tone and dilated pupils. The progression to plane 4 is characterized by intercostal paralysis, absences of all reflexes, and extreme muscle flaccidity. If the depth of anesthesia is allowed to increase, the patient will rapidly progress to the next stage.

Stage IV—Respiratory paralysis. This stage is characterized by complete cessation of respiration. If it is not reversed immediately, death of the patient occurs.

Modern anesthetic techniques now employ more rapidly acting agents than those associated with the signs of Guedel. Some of the signs associated with the early stages of anesthesia are less obvious, and the anesthesiologist must give undivided attention to the constant evaluation of anesthetic depth as measured by changes in the patient's reflexes, respiration, circulation, and muscular tone. The best depth of anesthesia is that which includes consideration for the patient's well-being in addition to the surgeon's requirements.

A more recent approach to measuring the stages of anesthesia is to consider phases as suggested by Flagg.[14]

Induction. Induction encompasses all the preparation and medication necessary for a patient up to the time the surgeon is ready to begin. Medication for preoperative sedation, adjunctive drugs to anesthesia, as well as those anesthetics required for induction of unconsciousness are included in this phase.

Maintenance phase. Maintenance begins with the patient at a depth of anesthesia sufficient to allow surgical manipulation and continues until completion of the procedure.

Recovery phase. The recovery phase begins with the termination of the surgical procedure and continues through the postoperative period until the patient is fully responsive to the environment.

These phases are more fully discussed by Bennett.[15] They are important to list because they demonstrate that modern general anesthesia is the result of a balanced combination of drugs and skill, all designed to provide the best care for the patient.

ANESTHETIC AGENTS

The general anesthetic agents are usually categorized according to their route of administration. The two principal classes are the inhalation agents and the intravenous agents. The inhalation type of general anesthetics may be divided into gases and volatile liquids. The volatile liquids are vaporized at or near room temperature and carried in gas form to the patient, usually in combination with nitrous oxide and oxygen. At least one drug, ketamine, can produce anesthesia when given intramuscularly.

Table 6-1 lists many of the drugs that have at one time or another been employed in general anesthesia. Nitrous oxide is the only gaseous agent of any importance in modern anesthetic techniques. Cyclopropane and ethylene are of historical interest only. Among the volatile liquids only halothane and enflurane (Ethrane) have any prominence, and the use of halothane is greatly diminished. The use of isoflurane will likely increase. The balance of the volatile anesthetics are presented for historical documentation, as most are used seldom, if at all. The intravenous agents are commonly used either for anesthetic induction or as single agents of anesthesia.

Inhalation anesthetics
Physical factors controlling inhalation anesthetics

A number of physical factors influence the ultimate anesthetic concentration in the brain. These factors include the partial pressure of the anesthetic(s) in the inspired gas, the concentration of anesthetic in the lungs at induction, the rate of uptake of anesthetic by the blood (blood/gas solubility), and the rate of uptake of anesthetic by the tissues (tissue/blood solubility). At the time of induction of anesthesia, the percentage of anesthetic gas in the lungs is nil, and the anesthetic is taken up rapidly as determined by rapid movement of the anesthetic from a high concentration (inspired air) to a low concentration (lung). The anesthetic is then carried to the blood and tissue by diffusion, moving from higher to lower concentrations.

If the anesthetic agent is poorly soluble in the blood, it will be transported rapidly to the tissues, hence a rapid induction. Conversely, if the anesthetic agent is highly soluble in blood, more of it will have to be dissolved in the blood before the concentration in the tissues can reach a desired level, hence a slow induction. Since the rate of uptake is initially very fast, an adequate volume flow and concentration of anesthetic are required at induction. Induction can be speeded by hyperventilation of the patient, thus increasing the rate at which the gases enter the lung. As the desired level of anesthesia is reached, the rate of exchange of anesthetic gases slows, and the concentration of the anesthetic in the inspired gas mixture is reduced to maintain the desired level.

Recovery from inhalation anesthesia is just the reverse. The anesthetic concentration of the inspired gas is reduced, and the gases diffuse from the tissues to the blood to the alveoli along the concentration gradient. If the anesthetic is highly soluble in body tissues, recovery will be slow. The fact that ether is highly soluble in blood whereas nitrous oxide is not correlates with their onset and duration of action.[16]

Minimum alveolar concentration

The specific dose of a general anesthetic is not given in a manner similar to that for other drugs. Instead, the term *minimum alveolar concentration* (MAC) has been used to compare the potency of the various general anesthetics. The concept of MAC was introduced in 1963 by Merkel and Eger[17] and has since gained universal acceptance as a standard of anesthetic potency. MAC is simply defined as the minimal alveolar concentration of an anesthetic, at 1 atmosphere, required to prevent 50% of a population (humans or animals) from responding to a supramaximal surgical stimulus by gross movement. This concept has proven to be invaluable in comparing the systemic effects of different inhalation anesthetic agents at equipotent doses. Potency is given as the reciprocal of the MAC.

It should be remembered that potency does not necessarily relate to the efficacy of a drug to produce a desired anesthetic response. The MAC of nitrous oxide has been given the value of 100. Halothane has an MAC value of 0.75 and methoxyflurane 0.16, whereas ether has a value of 1.92. The lower MAC value indicates a more potent anesthetic effect.

Pharmacologic effects

The general anesthetics are all CNS depressants. The development of analgesia, reduction in reflex ac-

Table 6-1. Classification of general anesthetics by route of administration

Inhalation agents		IV agents
Gases	**Volatile liquids**	**IV agents**
Nitrous oxide	Halogenated hydrocarbons	Neuroleptics
	Chloroform	Fentanyl with droperidol
Cyclopropane	Ethyl chloride	(Innovar)
	Trichloroethylene (Trilene, Trimar)	
Ethylene	Halothane (Fluothane)	Dissociative
		Ketamine (Ketalar, Ketaject)
	Halogenated ethers	
	Methoxyflurane (Penthrane)	Barbiturates
	Enflurane (Ethrane)	Methohexital sodium (Brevital)
	Isoflurane (Forane)	Thiamylal sodium (Surital)
		Thiopental sodium (Pentothal)
	Ethers	
	Diethyl ether (ether)	Narcotics
	Vinyl ether	Fentanyl (Sublimaze)
		Morphine

tions, and skeletal muscle relaxation is related to the degree of CNS depression. It is fortunate that the medulla is the least susceptible to depression because all the anesthetic agents are respiratory depressants. Nitrous oxide is unique in that it is not referred to as a respiratory depressant anesthetic except in hypoxic concentrations. The intravenous barbiturates are potent respiratory depressants, and dosage adjustment is more critical with these drugs.

Other body systems such as the cardiovascular system are also depressed by the general anesthetics. A number of general anesthetics also produce liver damage, limiting their usefulness. Included in this group are chloroform and the halogenated volatile anesthetics. Urine output is usually reduced, especially with procedures of long duration. The stress of general anesthesia can be accompanied by release of adrenocorticotropic hormone (ACTH), antidiuretic hormone, and sympathetic neurotransmitters.[18]

Gas anesthetics

Nitrous oxide. Nitrous oxide (N_2O) was first described by Joseph Priestly in 1771; its historic significance is thoroughly documented.[19] It is a colorless gas with little or no odor and is stored in blue cylinders at 750 psi.

As mentioned earlier, nitrous oxide is a low potency general anesthetic agent, and when used alone, it is unsatisfactory as a complete anesthetic. For induction of anesthesia a ratio of 85:15 nitrous oxide to oxygen

is required. The concentration is sustained only briefly, and the depth of anesthesia attained at a more desirable 65:35 ratio is insufficient for most surgery. Nitrous oxide is rarely used today as a sole induction agent. It is impossible to induce surgical anesthesia with nitrous oxide at 1 atmosphere without hypoxia. Even with 3 minutes of preoxygenation, there is a marked fall in actual oxygen saturation after only 2 minutes of 85% nitrous oxide. However, if anesthesia is first induced with a rapidly acting barbiturate and then nitrous oxide–oxygen administered with a low concentration of volatile anesthetic, a good quality of balanced anesthesia results.

Nitrous oxide is poorly soluble in blood and has a rapid onset of action as a result. Excretion of nitrous oxide is also rapid, and little if any metabolism occurs. During recovery, 100% oxygen is administered to prevent diffusion hypoxia. At the usual anesthetic concentrations the respiratory center response to carbon dioxide is not depressed. There is little change in the cardiovascular system during nitrous oxide anesthesia.

The adverse effects associated with the use of nitrous oxide are few and related to its poor quality as an anesthetic. Vomiting may occur in some patients, and there is no muscle relaxation. Toxicity is minimal as long as exposure is not prolonged. Nitrous oxide is more soluble than nitrogen in body tissues and will replace it in body cavities where nitrogen has accumulated.[20]

The use of nitrous oxide for sedation and analgesia in the dental office is discussed in Chapter 30.

Cyclopropane. Cyclopropane was introduced during the 1930s and is the most potent of the gas anesthetics. It is a gas at room temperature and is stored in gas cylinders. However, it is highly explosive and must be administered in a closed anesthetic system. Its chemical structure is as follows:

$$H_2C$$
$$\diagup\diagdown$$
$$H_2C - CH_2$$

Cyclopropane

Induction with cyclopropane occurs rapidly, in 2 or 3 minutes, resulting in complete surgical anesthesia and muscle relaxation without additional muscle relaxant medication. Excessive secretions can be controlled with an anticholinergic drug. Cyclopropane is rapidly absorbed and excreted through the lungs with very little metabolism.

The adverse effects associated with the use of cyclopropane include cardiac arrhythmias. Sympathetic nerve activity is increased, and the administration of exogenous catecholamines such as epinephrine or norepinephrine can induce serious cardiac arrhythmias. Because of increased bronchial constriction, patients with asthma are at risk with cyclopropane anesthesia. Although cyclopropane is a potent anesthetic, its use is limited because of the explosive hazard.

Ethylene. Ethylene ($CH_2 = CH_2$) is an unsaturated hydrocarbon that was first used for surgical anesthesia in 1923. Its popularity has declined over the years, and it has largely disappeared from use. Its explosiveness, lack of patient acceptability, and low potency have limited its usefulness.

Volatile anesthetics

The volatile general anesthetics are low boiling point liquids that volatilize easily at room temperature. Most of these agents are highly potent anesthetics and are relatively soluble in blood and fat. Vaporization is accomplished by special vaporizers attached to the anesthetic apparatus. There are three general classes of these agents: the ethers, the halogenated hydrocarbons, and the halogenated ethers.

Ethers

Diethyl ether. Ether ($CH_3CH_2 - O - CH_2CH_3$) has been the most popular volatile liquid anesthetic used since its discovery in the 1840s. Like most of the older liquid agents, its use has diminished and been replaced by the newer type of liquid anesthetics. Nevertheless, ether remains an interesting anesthetic agent.

Induction with ether is usually slow and uncomfortable for the patient. Its odor is objectionable, and irritation of mucous membranes produces secretions that have to be controlled with anticholinergic premedication. Ether is a complete anesthetic, providing analgesia and muscular relaxation for abdominal surgery. The cardiovascular system is depressed but is compensated by release of endogenous catecholamines from the adrenal medulla. As long as anesthetic concentrations are maintained, respiration is not depressed.

The principal disadvantages of ether include slow induction followed by slow recovery, objectionable odor, explosive hazard, and nausea and vomiting on recovery.

Ether is marketed in small copper-lined cans containing a 3% ethyl alcohol additive. The reason for this type of package is to minimize the formation of peroxides that are potentially explosive.

Halogenated hydrocarbons

Halothane (Fluothane). Halothane was introduced as a general anesthetic in the late 1950s and became widely used and accepted as a reliable anesthetic agent. Its chemical formula is $\dot{C}F_3 - CHClBr$; it has a fruity pleasant odor and is nonflammable and nonexplosive.

Induction is rapid at a 3% concentration, and patients are maintained with a concentration of 0.5% to 1.5% as needed. Recovery is also relatively rapid. The MAC for halothane is 0.75 with oxygen and 0.29 when combined with 70% nitrous oxide. Halothane is nonirritating to mucous membranes so that there is little increase in salivary or bronchial secretions, and it is considered an effective agent to use for asthmatic patients. However, it is a progressive respiratory depressant, reducing both tidal volume and alveolar ventilation. Therefore the depth of anesthesia must be carefully regulated. Pharyngeal and laryngeal reflexes are rapidly obtunded and bronchodilation occurs.[21]

The effects on the cardiovascular system are manifested in increased vagal activity, with cardiac slowing and peripheral vasodilation lowering the blood pressure. Halothane, unlike ether, does not cause the release of stored catecholamines. It will sensitize the myocardium to the cardiac stimulatory effects of injected epinephrine and norepinephrine, leading to serious cardiac arrhythmias such as ventricular fibrillation.

Halothane provides only moderate muscle relaxation, and muscle relaxants are required during surgery. Because the quality of pain relief is poor during recovery, supplemental analgesics are required. Kidney function is depressed, and uterine relaxation occurs.

One of the most common complaints regarding the use of halothane is suspected liver damage. In humans, halothane is reported to be no more or less hepatotoxic than any other inhalation anesthetic except chloroform even though it is commonly associated with postanesthetic hepatitis. It was once thought that the hepatocellular damage was related to an immunologic problem, but later evidence indicates the metabolites of halothane to be at fault. About 12% to 20% of halothane is metabolized in the liver. Certain conditions that favor the formation of reductive metabolic products are hepatic hypoxia, caused by either a reduced hepatic blood flow or a decreased arterial Po_2, and hepatic enzyme induction before or during exposure to halothane. Because of the evidence that suggests a causal relationship between halothane and postanesthetic hepatitis, many anesthesiologists choose another agent to avoid the controversy. Halothane is contraindicated in patients when a previous exposure to this agent or other halogenated anesthetic has been followed by evidence of liver toxicity.[22]

In summary, halothane has proved to be an effective and reliable general anesthetic. It can be used in almost every situation with the possible exception of obstetric anesthesia, in which uterine relaxation is a problem. Its adverse effects include cardiac arrhythmias when exogenous catecholamines are given, postoperative hepatic necrosis especially with multiple exposures, respiratory depression, and nausea and vomiting on recovery. It should be given in combination with oxygen or mixed with oxygen and nitrous oxide.[23]

Chloroform. Chloroform ($CHCl_3$) was introduced as a general anesthetic in 1847 in Great Britain, where its use was popular for a number of years. Induction with chloroform is rapid, and anesthesia is maintained by a 1% chloroform concentration. It is a more potent respiratory depressant than ether, and it is likely to produce hypotension during deep anesthesia. The known hepatotoxicity of this agent, the difficulty in regulation of anesthetic depth, plus the development of newer and safer anesthetics have diminished the use of chloroform. Currently it is of more historical than practical interest.

Ethyl chloride. Ethyl chloride (CH_3CH_2Cl) has been used as a general anesthetic agent but is no longer employed in this manner because of the occurrence of cardiac arrhythmias and liver toxicity. Its current usefulness is limited to that of a "spray-on" type of local anesthetic. Ethyl chloride is packaged in a small cylinder under pressure, and when released, it produces a form of cryoanesthesia of the skin by rapid evaporation and cooling. The depth of tissue anesthesia is small, and the duration is short. The principal adverse effects of this use include delayed healing and possible tissue slough if administered incorrectly.

Trichloroethylene (Trilene, Trimar). Trichloroethylene ($Cl_2C = CHCl$) is a volatile, nonflammable liquid with many properties similar to those of chloroform. Its dangers when used as a general anesthetic include cardiac arrhythmias and tachypnea. When exposed to soda lime, trichloroethylene decomposes to phosgene, hydrochloric acid, and dichloracetylene, all extremely toxic. Dichloracetylene, thought to be responsible for trigeminal nerve lesions with symptoms like those of tic douloureux, may be further degraded to phosgene and carbon monoxide. Care should be taken to avoid the use of trichloroethylene in anesthetic systems containing soda lime. Trichloroethylene has been used as an inhalation analgesic to control certain pain episodes such as tic douloureux. Its self-administration use carries with it the potential for drug abuse. Trichloroethylene has been used to supplement nitrous oxide anesthesia and provide pain relief during labor and childbirth.

Halogenated ethers

Methoxyflurane (Penthrane). Methoxyflurane is a volatile nonflammable liquid anesthetic with the chemical formula $Cl_2CH - CF_2 - OCH_3$. Concentrations of 1% to 3% produce general anesthesia with effective postoperative analgesia that frequently lasts until after the patient has regained consciousness, thereby reducing the need for supplemental analgesia. Muscle relaxation is perhaps better than with halothane, but succinylcholine or *d*-tubocurarine is necessary for good muscle relaxation. The MAC for methoxyflurane with oxygen is 0.16; it reduces to 0.07 in 70% nitrous oxide.

As is the case with halothane, methoxyflurane sensitizes the myocardium to the stimulant effects of injected catecholamines. Bradycardia and a decrease in blood pressure occur with anesthetic doses.

Methoxyflurane is metabolized in the liver, and certain of the metabolic products are believed to be associated with the neuropathy that sometimes occurs during methoxyflurane anesthesia. Cousins and Mazze[24] have suggested that vasopressin-resistant polyuric renal failure following methoxyflurane anesthesia may be the result of inorganic fluoride, a metabolite of methoxyflurane. For this reason, methoxyflurane is only used for short periods of time and in low concentrations. Its use is contraindicated in patients with a history of renal insufficiency or in combination with other nephrotoxic drugs. The effect appears to be dose related. For this reason a caution appears in the product information stating that methoxyflurane should not be administered to patients who have received the drug in the previous month. Additionally, its use should be avoided in patients with a previous history of jaundice occurring with other halogenated anesthetics.

Drug interactions appear to be prominent with methoxyflurane. The concurrent intravenous use of tetracycline with methoxyflurane has been implicated in renal toxicity. Other antibiotics may also be suspect, including gentamicin, kanamycin, the polymyxins, and amphotericin B. Enzyme-inducing drugs such as the barbiturates could increase the rate of metabolism, leading to an increase in the amount of toxic metabolites.[25]

As is the case with halothane, methoxyflurane is administered in combination with oxygen and nitrous oxide.

Enflurane (Ethrane). Enflurane is a halogenated ether anesthetic with a pleasant etheral smell. Its chemical structure is $CHF_2 — O — CF_2CFClH$. Induction concentrations of 2% to 4.5% produce a rapid pleasant induction and recovery, as it is relatively insoluble in blood. The MAC for enflurane with oxygen is 1.4; the use of nitrous oxide improves the MAC to 0.57. It provides moderate analgesia and sufficient muscle relaxation for surgery. Nondepolarizing muscle relaxants can be used in smaller doses compared to other anesthetics.

Enflurane is reported to be a more profound respiratory depressant than halothane, but the depression is partially overcome by surgical stimulation. Patients with pulmonary diseases can receive ethrane successfully. The myocardium is depressed and blood pressure is lowered. Reports on myocardial sensitization

to injected epinephrine vary, but it is generally believed that small amounts could be given. Infrequent cardiac arrhythmias occur with the use of enflurane during anesthesia.

A more prominent consideration in the use of enflurane is its activity in the CNS. Although it is a depressant, alterations in EEG activity resemble those associated with abnormal muscular twitching and jerking. Thus excessive motor activity may occur during anesthesia; decreasing the depth of anesthesia removes the muscular activity. Compared to the other halogenated anesthetics, little (2.4%) metabolism of enflurane occurs. Liver damage with repeated anesthetic exposures is uncommon. Absence of hepatotoxicity may be related to the small amount of metabolism. Enflurane also produces a transient depression of the immune response and kidney function.

Its characteristics of rapid induction and recovery, good muscle relaxation, and lack of hepatotoxicity has made enflurane one of the more popular anesthetic agents.[23,26,27]

Isoflurane (Forane). Isoflurane is a halogenated ether that is a structural isomer of enflurane. Its chemical formula is $CHF_2 — O — CHClCF_3$. Of the volatile inhalation anesthetics, isoflurane is the least soluble in blood, with a coefficient of 1.4, compared to 1.9 for enflurane and 2.3 for halothane. This physical factor allows for a rapid induction and recovery. The mildly pungent etheral smell limits the induction concentration to 1.5% to 3.5%; otherwise the patient may cough or hold his or her breath. The MAC for isoflurane in adults is 1.15 with oxygen and 0.5 when combined with 70% nitrous oxide.[28]

The effects of isoflurane on the various body systems is somewhat similar to other halogenated anesthetics, but only a small fraction is metabolized in the liver. This may be caused by its physical stability and rapid elimination from the body. As a result, liver toxicity does not appear to be a problem.[29] Isoflurane depresses respiration and decreases the respiratory response to increases in Pco_2. There is little or no depression of the myocardium when a decrease in peripheral resistance and lowering of arterial pressure occur. In comparison to other agents, larger amounts of injected epinephrine can be given; thus less sensitization of the myocardium occurs.[30] The amount of muscle relaxation produced with isoflurane is sufficient for most procedures, and potentiation of *d*-tubocurarine is similar to enflurane. As with other general anesthetics, renal blood flow and urine output are reduced. Nausea, vomiting, and shivering on recovery appear to be comparable to other anesthetics. Analgesic requirements after surgery are similar to halothane. One report, later proven to be incorrent, implicated isoflurane as a possible carcinogen in mice. The most undesirable feature is the potent respiratory depression and respiratory acidosis that can occur with deeper anesthesia. Isoflurane seems to have many advantages over the former halogenated ethers and should prove to be a very useful and popular agent for general anesthesia.

Intravenous anesthetics

The intravenous general anesthetics include the ultrashort-acting barbiturates and a nonbarbiturate dissociative anesthetic ketamine. The so-called neuroleptanalgesic combination of fentanyl and droperidol will also be included, although the exact position of this combination is hard to fix. The intravenous agents find their greatest usefulness in the rapid induction of unconsciousness so that delirium may be avoided.

Ultrashort-acting barbiturates

The ultrashort-acting barbiturates that are of current interest include methohexital sodium (Brevital) and thiopental sodium (Pentothal). Others such as thiamylal sodium (Surital) and hexobarbital sodium have been used less frequently in dental anesthesia. Although the basic pharmacology of the barbiturates is discussed in Chapter 7, there are certain pertinent facts about these drugs that need emphasis.

These drugs are ultrashort acting in that intravenous doses have a rapid onset of about 30 to 40 seconds. If repeated doses are given, as is often the case during anesthesia, the drug accumulates in body tissues, resulting in a prolonged recovery. This effect results from a redistribution of the drug from neural tissues to fat depots and muscle so that absolute recovery may take considerable time.

These drugs are sometimes employed as the sole anesthetic for short procedures, and if the degree of CNS depression is kept at or near anesthetic levels, the patient will respond to painful stimuli. No analgesia is observed. Doses necessary to reduce the pain stimulus response are very near apneic doses. For this reason the intravenous barbiturates function more effectively in smaller doses when used as part of a balanced anesthetic technique with local anesthesia.

A serious complication in the use of the intrave-

nous barbiturates occurs when the injected solution is accidentally given extravascularly or into an artery. If extravascular infiltration occurs, symptoms ranging from tissue tenderness to necrosis and sloughing can occur. Intra-arterial injection is an extremely dangerous situation. Arteriospasm associated with ischemia of the arm and fingers and severe pain may be observed. The injection should be stopped immediately. An injection of 1% procaine is used to relieve the pain and spasm. If the reaction progresses, it may be necessary in some cases to block the sympathetic response in the brachial plexus. In some cases heparin is given to prevent local thrombus formation, and an alpha adrenergic blocking agent such as phentolamine should be considered.[31]

Other complications with the ultrashort-acting barbiturates include laryngospasm and bronchospasm. In some patients hiccoughs, increased muscle activity, and delirium occur on recovery. Premedication with atropine has proved reasonably effective in reducing some of these recovery problems. Scopolamine and the opiates are also effective premedicants.[32]

The absolute contraindications to the use of these agents include an absence of suitable veins for administration, status asthmaticus, porphyria, and a known hypersensitivity. Adjustment of dosage and caution should be taken in patients with hepatic, renal, and cardiovascular impairment. Because these drugs are potent anesthetics, they should be administered by qualified individuals only, and resuscitative equipment should be readily available.[33]

Dissociative anesthesia

Ketamine (Ketalar, Ketaject). Ketamine is a newer type of anesthetic agent. It is not related chemically to the barbiturates or the narcotics. The anesthetic state it produces has been given the name *dissociative anesthesia*. Ketamine appears to disrupt association pathways in the brain and to depress both the reticular activating system and the limbic system. The mechanism of action remains to be described.

Ketamine hydrochloride

Ketamine may be given intravenously or intramuscularly with a rapid onset of action occurring by either route. Even intramuscular doses can produce unconsciousness within 1 or 2 minutes. After administration, there is a transient stimulation of both blood pressure and pulse rate that rapidly disappears. Pharyngeal and laryngeal reflexes remain unaffected with little respiratory change. Because excessive salivation is a common finding with ketamine, atropine is a necessary premedication. Muscle tone may increase during its use.

The principal drawback to the use of ketamine is the occurrence of delirium and hallucinations during recovery, most often in adults, older children, and drug abusers. Emergence reactions of this type may be minimized if visual and auditory stimuli are reduced during recovery. Small doses of the intravenous barbiturates and diazepam have been employed to control the recovery problems, but the success is variable.

Ketamine should be used by those experienced in anesthetic procedures. Specific contraindications include a history of cerebrovascular disease, hypertension, and hypersensitivity to the drug. Since protective reflexes are not obtunded, care should be taken not to stimulate the pharynx.[34]

Neurolept anesthesia

The term *neurolept analgesia* was coined by de Castro in 1958 to describe a so-called wakeful anesthetic state. It is induced by the administration of a combination of a neuroleptic drug and a narcotic type of analgesic. For all practical purposes the patient appears to be awake but is tranquil, catatonic, and free of pain. The proper placement of this type of pain and apprehension control is a puzzle, but reason should dictate their discussion with anesthetic agents.

A neuroleptic drug is one that is a major tranquilizer capable of inducing a catatonic state. It produces a placid and calm patient but has no analgesic effect. This drug also decreases the sensitivity of the patient to epinephrine and norepinephrine, inhibits learned behavioral activity, and is antiemetic. The particular neuroleptic drug used in this technique is the butyrophenone derivative droperidol (Inapsine). It is similar in many respects to the phenothiazine tranquilizers.

The narcotic agent employed in this type of anesthesia is known as fentanyl (Sublimaze). It is a potent CNS depressant and a derivative of meperidine. Fentanyl has all the properties of a narcotic, including analgesia and respiratory depression. It is a short-acting narcotic and will cause an increase in muscle tone.

The combination of fentanyl and droperidol is known as Innovar. This combination is usually given intravenously with a rapid onset of action. Although return to consciousness appears to be rapid, the effects of droperidol are long lasting, and complete recovery is slower. The adverse effects can be quite serious and are those that would normally be associated with the narcotics and major tranquilizers. Respiratory depression and CNS symptoms manifesting as extrapyramidal tremors have occurred. This combination of drugs should be used with great care, especially in patients with pulmonary insufficiency and parkinsonism. A "boardlike" chest reaction, associated with intercostal muscle paralysis and requiring ventilatory support, occurs in some patients. Fentanyl is becoming more popular as a sole agent for conscious sedation and anesthesia.[33]

ANESTHETIC HAZARDS

Surgical anesthesia administered with the goals of accurate patient monitoring, adequate muscular relaxation, and pain relief has become a safe procedure. However, it should be remembered that to produce anesthesia, potent CNS depressants are given in relatively high doses, and many combinations of drugs are employed in balanced anesthesia. Some of the possible interactions encountered are as follows:

1. Adrenergic blocking agents may mask the reflex stimulation of the adrenal medullary release of sympathetic neurotransmitters leading to hypotension.

2. Narcotics used in premedication reduce the amount of anesthetic required but could potentiate respiratory depression.

3. Anticholinergics, such as atropine, reduce the secretions associated with irritating anesthetics as well as block vagal slowing of the heart.

4. Cyclopropane, halothane, ethyl chloride, methoxyflurane, trichloroethylene, and chloroform sensitize the myocardium to the effects of epinephrine, norepinephrine, and isoproterenol. Serious cardiac arrhythmias may result. The newer agents may produce less sensitization.

5. Ether, enflurane, isoflurane, halothane, and methoxyflurane augment the neuromuscular blocking effects of tubocurarine, pancuronium, and gallamine, requiring a dose reduction.

6. The aminoglycoside antibiotics will potentiate

the effects of the neuromuscular blocking agents.[25]

A more recent concern regarding anesthetic hazards relates to the attending personnel rather than the patient. Current data seem to support the fact that waste anesthetic gases found to contaminate surgical suites are a potential health hazard. In a survey of operating room personnel, including dentists, an increase of spontaneous abortions in the wives of exposed dentists was noted. There was also a significant increase in liver disease in the exposed dentists. Other complaints included headache, fatigue, and irritability. There were other studies that also supported the hazard of exposure to trace anesthetic agents in the environment. In response to this survey and noting an increase in the use of inhalation agents in the dental office, the ADA appointed a special committee to study the potential hazard of trace anesthetic gases in the dental office.[35]

The report of the ADA Ad Hoc Committee on Trace Anesthetics as a Potential Health Hazard in Dentistry has been published. Such a report was welcomed because there was great concern for the continued safe use of inhalation agents in the dental office. In general, the committee concluded that current published data indicated that trace contamination could be a hazard, but it had reservations about bias in human studies and the reliability of transposing interpretation of animal data to humans. In addition, there was lack of evidence that nitrous oxide as a singular contaminant could produce many of the described hazards. A call for additional studies was requested. The National Institute of Occupational Safety and Health developed a document that defined risk and established standards for control and monitoring of trace anesthetic gases in 1977, but to my knowledge, they have not been implemented pending the collection of additional data.[36]

Many of the original hazards associated with exposure to trace anesthetics have been challenged concerning a cause-effect relationship. Evidence supporting an increase in spontaneous abortions in female operating room personnel is reasonably convincing.[37] Recently a published report concerning a study of dental professionals exposed to nitrous oxide indicated an increase in neurologic complaints. The rate of complaints was fourfold greater than for those who did not use nitrous oxide. However, the paper states that a direct cause-effect relationship could not be proven from the data, but the likelihood of such an effect still presents a hazard for dental personnel.[38]

In view of these facts, it would appear that as long as a chance for such a health hazard exists, every effort should be made to control contaminants in the dental operatory and operating room. This would involve checking equipment for leaks, avoiding spills, using scavenging devices, and monitoring to control the level of anesthetic gas contaminants.

REFERENCES

1. Stanley, T.H.: Narcotics as complete anesthetics. In Aldrete, J.A., and Stanley, T.H., editors: Trends in intravenous anesthesia, Chicago, 1980, Year Book Medical Publishers, Inc.
2. Driscoll, E.J.: ASOS anesthesia morbidity and mortality survey, ASOS Committee on Anesthesia, J. Oral Surg. **32:**733-738, 1975.
3. Thatcher, V.S.: History of anesthesia, Philadelphia, 1953, J.B. Lippincott Co.
4. Adriani, J.: The pharmacology of anesthetic drugs, ed. 5, Springfield, Ill., 1970, Charles C Thomas, Publisher.
5. Roth, S.H.: Physical mechanisms of anesthesia, Ann. Review Pharmacol. Toxicol. **19:**159, 1979.
6. Meyer, H.H.: Zur Theorie der Alkoholnarkose. I. Welche Eigenschaft der Anästhetika bedingt ihre narkotische Wirkung? Arch. Exp. Path. Pharmak. **42:**109, 1899.
7. Overton, E.: Studien über die Narkose zugleich ein Beitrag zur allgemeinen Pharmakologie, Jena, 1901, G. Fischer.
8. Quastel, J.H.: Biochemical aspects of narcosis, Curr. Res. Anesth. Analg. **31:**151, 1952.
9. Greig, M.E.: The site of action of narcotics on brain metabolism, J. Pharmacol. Exp. Ther. **87:**185, 1946.
10. Miller, S.L.: Effects of anesthetics on water structure, Fed. Proc. **27:**879, 1968.
11. Pauling, L.: A molecular theory of general anesthesia, Science **134:**15, 1961.
12. Wallace, W.D.: Effects of drugs on the electrical activity of the brain: anesthetics, Ann. Rev. Pharmacol. Toxicol. **16:**413-426, 1976.
13. Guedel, A.E.: Inhalational anesthesia: a fundamental guide, ed. 2, New York, 1951, Macmillan Publishing Co., Inc.
14. Flagg, P.J.: The art of anesthesia, ed. 7, Philadelphia, 1944, J.B. Lippincott Co.
15. Bennett, C.R.: Monheim's general anesthesia in dental practice, ed. 4, St. Louis, 1974, The C.V. Mosby Co.
16. Dripps, R.D., Eckenhoff, J.E., and Vandam, L.D.: Introduction to anesthesia: the principles of safe practice, ed. 5, Philadelphia, 1977, W.B. Saunders Co.
17. Merkel, G., and Eger, E.E., II: A comparative study of halothane and halopropane anesthesia, including a method for determining equipotency, Anesthesiology **24:**346, 1963.
18. Ngai, S.H.: Current concepts in anesthesiology: effects of anesthetics on various organs, N. Engl. J. Med. **302:**564, March 1980.
19. Schofield, R.E.: A scientific autobiography of Joseph Priestley (1733-1804), Cambridge, Mass., 1966, The M.I.T. Press, pp. 138-197.
20. Churchill-Davidson, H.C., editor: A practice of anaesthesia, Philadelphia, 1979, W.B. Saunders Co.

21. Saidman, J.L., et al.: Minimum alveolar concentration of methoxyflurane, halothane, ether, and cyclopropane in man: correlation with theories of anesthesia, Anesthesiology **28:** 994, 1967.

22. Subcommittee on the National Halothane Study of the Committee on Anesthesia, National Academy of Sciences–National Research Council: Summary of national halothane study, J.A.M.A. **197:**775, 1966.

23. Corbett, T.H.: Pharmacology and toxicology of halogenated anesthetics, Adv. Pharmacol. Chemother. **16:**195, 1979.

24. Cousins, M.J., and Mazze, R.I.: Methoxyflurane toxicity: a study of dose response in man, J.A.M.A. **225:**1611, 1973.

25. Evaluations of drug interactions, ed. 2, Washington, D.C., 1976, American Pharmaceutical Association.

26. VanStee, E.W.: Toxicology of inhalation anesthetics and metabolites, Ann. Rev. Pharmacol. Toxicol. **16:**67, 1976.

27. Hunter, A.R.: New drugs, ed. 12, Int. Anesthesiol. Clin. **16:** 1, 1978.

28. Stevens, W.C., et al.: Minimum alveolar concentrations (MAC) of isoflurane with and without nitrous oxide in patients of various ages, Anesthesiology **42:**197, 1975.

29. Holaday, D.A., et al.: Resistance of isoflurane to biotransformation in man, Anesthesiology **43:**325, 1975.

30. Johnston, R.R., Eger, E., II, and Wilson, C.: A comparative interaction of epinephrine with enflurane, isoflurane, and halothane in man, Anesth. Analg. **55:**709, 1976.

31. Buxton Hopkin, D.A.: Hazards and errors in anesthesia, New York, 1980, Springer-Verlag New York, Inc.

32. Dundee, J.W.: The influence of preanesthetic medication on thiopental and methohexital anesthesia, J. Oral Ther. **2:**388-389, 1966.

33. Dundee, J.W., and Wyant, G.M.: Intravenous anesthesia, London, 1974, Churchill Livingstone.

34. Hellinger, M.J.: Ketamine hydrochloride, a general anesthetic in oral surgery, J. Am. Dent. Assoc. **83:**349-351, 1971.

35. Cohen, E.N., et al.: A survey of anesthetic health hazards among dentists, J. Am. Dent. Assoc. **90:**1291-1296, 1975.

36. Ad Hoc Committee on Trace Anesthetics: Trace inhalation anesthetics in the dental office, J.A.D.A. **95:**749-792, 1977.

37. Spence, A.A.: Chronic exposure to trace concentrations of anesthetics. In Gray, T.C., Nunn, J.F., and Utting, J.E., editors: General anesthesia, ed. 4, London, 1980, Butterworth & Co.

38. Brodsky, J.B., et al.: Exposure to nitrous oxide and neurologic disease among dental professionals, Anesth. Analg. **60:**297, 1981.

CHAPTER 7

BARBARA REQUA-CLARK
SAM V. HOLROYD

Sedative-hypnotic drugs

The sedative-hypnotic drugs can produce varying degrees of CNS depression, from sedation to hypnosis, depending on the size of the dose administered. A small dose will produce a mild degree of CNS depression described as sedation (the reduction of activity and simple anxiety). A somewhat larger dose of the same drug will produce a greater CNS depression, resulting in hypnosis (sleep). Although agents may be promoted as either sedatives or hypnotics, the same drug may be either, depending on the dose.

Anyone who has practiced dentistry recognizes the value of having a relaxed patient. Often, but not always, a patient's anxiety is eliminated or sufficiently reduced by a calm, confident, and understanding attitude on the part of the dentist and assisting personnel. Patients approach dentistry with varying degrees of anxiety, ranging from complete calmness when anticipating extensive procedures to severe apprehension about the simplest of procedures. Although most patients experience emotions somewhere between these extremes, dentists should provide their patients with the most pleasant experience possible within the limits of safety. Inducing relaxation in a patient allows for more productive appointments with less nervous strain on both the patient and the dentist. For this reason and because orally administered sedative-hypnotic drugs are relatively safe, their use may be beneficial for reducing patient anxiety in many cases.

Working with a relaxed patient is not only a matter of pleasantness and convenience, but with some patients it may be a matter of life and death. McCarthy[1] has pointed out that sudden unexpected death is not uncommon, may even occur in people who appear to be in good health, and can be brought on by emotional stress. He states that this is strong justification for adequate pain and anxiety control for dental patients.

Before considering the sedative-hypnotic drugs, certain generalizations should be discussed. Although a precise degree of sedation can be obtained by IV titration and inhalation sedation, both require special training and experience by the practitioner. Therefore for many dentists oral sedation is the principal method of reducing anxiety in dental patients. This presents a most fundamental problem: sedation by orally administered drugs will not provide consistent or highly predictable results. As noted in Chapter 2, many factors influence the blood level obtained from orally administered drugs. Additionally, variations are seen in patient responses to similar blood levels. Because of the variations and lack of predictability from oral sedation, many practitioners continually switch from drug to drug, hoping to find the ultimate agent or dose that will provide ideal sedation. Neither the ultimate drug nor dosage is available so such searching usually is fruitless. The greatest consistency will be found in staying with one or two drugs, knowing these well, and knowing how they affect different types of patients. In the long run, this will yield greater benefit than ''jumping'' from drug to drug.[2]

The dose of a particular sedative used for a patient will depend on the degree of that patient's anxiety and the procedure to be performed. A sedative dose of these agents should not be expected to produce calmness in a patient undergoing dental treatment. It is designed to allow the patient to function as usual on a day-to-day basis but with less anxiety. A hypnotic dose was designed to provide a sufficient amount of drug to allow the patient to drift into sleep. Therefore a patient with apprehension about dentistry may re-

77

quire more than the usual sedative dose of the drug. Sedation of dental patients so that they are calm and cooperative about the dental procedure cannot necessarily be produced by the sedative dose of one of these drugs. Indeed, the hypnotic dose may be required more often than not to obtain the degree of patient relaxation desired.

One group of drugs used in the treatment of anxiety can be classed separately from the sedative-hypnotics as tranquilizers. The name *tranquilizer* refers to two quite different groups of agents—the minor tranquilizers, whose action is very similar to that of the sedative-hypnotics, and the major tranquilizers, which possess antipsychotic activity. The major tranquilizers or antipsychotic agents are useful in the treatment of psychoses, whereas the minor tranquilizers are useful in the treatment of anxiety or neuroses. In larger doses the minor tranquilizers produce more sedation and finally anesthesia, whereas the major tranquilizers can cause convulsions. The major tranquilizers are discussed in Chapter 8 and the minor tranquilizers in Chapter 9.

This chapter will deal with some of the sedative agents that can be used to allay anxiety—the barbiturates and the nonbarbiturates. Nitrous oxide, another agent that is useful in reducing apprehension, will be discussed in Chapters 6 and 30. The sedative-hypnotic agents can also be used for other purposes such as the treatment of insomnia.

BARBITURATES

The barbiturates are chemically related agents with similar pharmacologic effects. They differ mainly in their onset and duration of action. Since these agents have been used for years, the problems with their use have been well documented. Although nonbarbiturate sedative-hypnotics have been developed in an attempt to overcome the problem of barbiturate abuse, these agents seem to possess little, if any, clinical advantage over the barbiturates.

Chemistry

Diethylbarbituric acid, which has hypnotic action, was produced in 1904. Most of the clinically useful barbiturates are formed by the substitution of appropriate groups at the R_1 and R_2 sites shown below. Another modification can be made by replacing the carbon-2 (X = oxygen) with sulfur. This creates agents that are used intravenously.

Barbiturate nucleus

Mechanism of action

The barbiturates function by depressing the sensory cortex, motor function, and cerebellar function, causing either sedation or drowsiness. The mechanism by which these agents exert these actions occurs at the synapse by means of a delay of synaptic recovery. The barbiturates appear to affect polysynaptic pathways of the brain to a greater extent than monosynaptic pathways. In contrast, the benzodiazepine minor tranquilizers appear to function by presynaptic inhibition of the polysynaptic pathways. Both mechanisms produce sedation or hypnosis by either producing or enhancing gamma amino butyric acid (GABA).[1,2] The ability of the barbiturates to produce hypnosis appears to occur through its nonselective depression of synaptic potentials. At high enough blood levels, this property allows the barbiturates to be used as general anesthetics. In contrast, even at high blood levels, the benzodiazepines remain selective in their synaptic depression. This selectivity restricts the effect of the benzodiazepines to sedation; they do not produce general anesthesia as the barbiturates do.

Effect on the body

The barbiturates are usually used orally as hypnotics. They are given intravenously to control seizures or to induce general anesthesia. Because they are highly alkaline and consequently irritating, their parenteral use is limited to the intravenous route.

The more lipophilic barbiturates, such as the thiobarbiturates (thiopental, thiamylal), become quickly concentrated in the brain where they exert their pharmacologic effect. These drugs then redistribute from the brain, first to skeletal muscle and then to fat. It is this redistribution that is responsible for the ultrashort duration of action of methohexital and the thiobarbiturates. The less lipophilic barbiturates reach brain tissues more slowly and become rather uniformly distributed throughout the body. They cross the placenta and also appear in a nursing mother's milk.

Table 7-1. Classification, route of administration, and dosages of commonly used barbiturates

		Oral adult dose (mg)†	
Barbiturate	**Route of administration***	**Sedative (t.i.d. or q.i.d.)**	**Hypnotic (h.s.)**
Ultrashort acting (immediate onset)			
Methohexital	IV		
Thiamylal	IV		
Thiopental	IV		
Hexobarbital	O		250 to 500
Short acting (oral onset about 30 min; duration up to 3 hrs)			
Pentobarbital	O, R, IM, IV	20	100 to 200
Secobarbital	O, R, IM, IV	30 to 50	100 to 200
Intermediate acting (oral onset 40 to 60 min; duration 3 to 6 hrs)			
Amobarbital	O, R, IM, IV	25 to 50	100 to 200
Aprobarbital	O	40 to 80	40 to 160
Butabarbital	O	7.5 to 60	100 to 200
Butalbital	O	50 to 100	100 to 200
Long acting (oral onset 2 to 3 hrs; duration over 6 hrs)			
Phenobarbital	O	15 to 30	100 to 200
Talbutal	O	30	120

*O, Oral; R, rectal; IM, intramuscular; IV, intravenous.
†Children's dosages should be obtained from manufacturers' recommendations (PDR).

The thiobarbiturates are slowly metabolized by the liver. The short- and intermediate-acting barbiturates are more rapidly and almost completely metabolized by the liver. The long-acting barbiturates, such as phenobarbital and barbital, are excreted to a great extent (30% to 40%) as free drug in the urine. As a result of this, patients with liver damage may have an exaggerated response to the short-acting and intermediate-acting agents, and patients with renal impairment may have an accumulation of the long-acting agents.

Classification, administration, and dosage

The most practical clinical classification of the barbiturates is by duration of action. This classification of commonly used barbiturates, their routes of administration, and their sedative and hypnotic doses are shown in Table 7-1.

The distinction between a sedative and a hypnotic dose is not precise. Responses to barbiturates vary among different people. Additionally, the presence or absence of food in the stomach and the environment in which the drug is taken (dark, quiet room as opposed to the deck of a sinking ship) influence the sedative effect obtained. Greater sedation will occur when a barbiturate is taken by a small person with an empty stomach than if it is taken by a large individual with a full stomach. For example, a preoperative hypnotic dose may allow a child to doze as the appointment begins. As the dental drill is activated, the child awakens and attempts to climb out of the chair. When the procedure is accomplished, the child again sleeps. Consequently, stated doses should not be accepted as being absolute; they must be individualized.

Pharmacologic effects

The barbiturates are reversible depressants of all excitable tissues, especially those of the CNS.

CNS depression. Sedative and hypnotic doses are believed to act mainly at the level of the thalamus and ascending reticular activating system, and larger doses appear to act at all levels of the CNS.[3] Thus sufficiently large doses may depress cortical centers, motor functions, and medullary centers. These larger doses cause the depression of the inhibitory fibers of the CNS, resulting in disinhibition and euphoria. If excitation occurs at this point, it is caused by depression of the inhibitory pathways, resulting in less inhibition. The progression of effects with increasing doses of barbiturates can include:

Sedation
↓
Hypnosis
↓
General anesthesia
↓
Respiratory arrest

When a sufficient dose is administered, hypnosis can be produced. The administration of even higher doses can result in general anesthesia. Respiratory and cardiovascular depression, which is progressive during general anesthesia, prohibits the use of barbiturate anesthesia for other than short procedures. Cardiovascular depression may include both a reduction of cardiac output and peripheral vasodilation.

The final step is respiratory arrest. This progressive CNS depression parallels that caused by the general anesthetics (see Chapter 6).

Whether or not the barbiturates have antianxiety action is questionable. They are certainly inferior as antianxiety agents to the benzodiazepine minor tranquilizers.

Because the sedation caused by the barbiturates can impair mental and physical skills, a patient taking these agents should be warned against driving a car or operating dangerous equipment. The patient must also be warned against signing important papers. The patient should be accompanied to and from the dental office by a responsible individual.[4]

The CNS depression produced by the barbiturates is additive with other agents that produce this effect. For example, a patient who takes an alcoholic beverage and is prescribed a barbiturate will show additive sedation and respiratory depression.

Analgesia. Except in extremely large doses, the barbiturates have no significant analgesic effect and in fact are hyperalgesic. Even doses that produce general anesthesia do not block the reflex response to pain. Patients in pain may become agitated and even delirious if barbiturates are administered without an analgesic agent. Consequently, barbiturates should not be prescribed for patients in pain unless an analgesic is also prescribed. When a barbiturate is prescribed with an analgesic, the resulting relaxation may potentiate the effect of the analgesic. If an analgesic that produces sedation is used, the practitioner should remember that this sedation will be additive to that produced by the barbiturate.

Anticonvulsant effect. The barbiturates possess anticonvulsant action. The long-acting agents are most effective in preventing seizures. Agents such as

phenobarbital are routinely used in the treatment of epilepsy (see Chapter 14).

Adverse reactions

Sedative or hypnotic doses. In the usual therapeutic doses the barbiturates are relatively safe. However, one should be aware that CNS depression may be exaggerated in elderly and debilitated patients or those with liver or kidney impairment. This sedative effect is additive with that of other CNS depressants. In some patients, especially the elderly, the barbiturates can cause idiosyncratic excitement instead of sedation. This reaction is unpredictable. Rashes and nausea may occur. Although serious allergic reactions are rare, they have been reported.

Anesthetic doses. With larger doses of the barbiturates, concentrations attained in the blood can be lethal. Consequently, great care must be exercised to avoid compromising respiratory and cardiovascular function. Except for short duration of anesthesia, this is impossible. Coughing and laryngospasm have been reported rather frequently with intravenous use of the barbiturates. Large doses of the barbiturates may reversibly depress liver and kidney function, reduce gastrointestinal motility, and lower body temperature.

Acute poisoning. When prescribing the barbiturates, the practitioner must consider the possibility that acute poisoning can occur. Each year many deaths occur from overdoses of barbiturates. This usually results from the intentional ingestion of the barbiturate in a suicidal attempt. Although a lethal dose can only be approximated, moderately severe poisoning will follow the ingestion of 5 to 10 times the hypnotic dose and life is seriously threatened when over 15 times the hypnotic dose is consumed. However, if the individual is not discovered early, 8 to 10 times the hypnotic dose may be fatal. The cause of death when an overdose occurs is respiratory failure. The treatment includes conservative management and treatment of specific symptoms (Table 7-2).[5]

Chronic long-term use. Chronic use of the barbiturates can lead to physical and psychologic dependence. Long-term use produces a state similar to alcohol intoxication. The barbiturate addict becomes progressively depressed and is unable to function. Tolerance develops to most effects of the barbiturates but not to the lethal dose. There is cross-tolerance among the different barbiturates and between the barbiturates, the nonbarbiturate sedative-hypnotic agents, and general anesthetics.

Table 7-2. Treatment of barbiturate poisoning*

Do:
1. Observe continuously.
2. Maintain and support respiration.
3. Maintain body temperature and treat shock with blood, plasma substitutes, and vasopressors.
4. Maintain renal function and fluid intake with D_5W.
5. Increase excretion of drug by osmotic diuresis, alkaline diuresis, peritoneal dialysis, and hemodialysis.

Do not:
1. Use gastric lavage because it can lead to arrhythmias, aspiration, and respiratory arrest. This is controversial. Some recommend gastric lavage to remove ingested drug from the gastrointestinal tract.
2. Administer convulsant stimulants because they can cause convulsions or hyperpyrexia.
3. Give narcotic antagonists because they do not counteract the depression from barbiturates and some may even cause additive respiratory depression. This is not a problem with naloxone (Narcan).

*Adapted from Meyers, F.H., Jawetz, E., and Goldfien, A.: Review of medical pharmacology, ed. 7, Los Altos, Calif., 1980, Lange Medical Publications.

Contraindications and cautions

The use of barbiturates is absolutely contraindicated in patients with intermittent porphyria or a positive family history of porphyria. This is because the barbiturate can stimulate and increase the synthesis of porphyrins, which are already at an excessive level in this metabolic disease; an acute attack can result.

Drug interactions

Because the barbiturates are potent stimulators of liver microsomal enzyme production, they are involved in many drug interactions. These enzymes are responsible for the metabolism of many drugs. An increase in these enzymes can increase the rate of drug destruction and decrease the response to and duration of action. For example, an epileptic patient who is currently receiving phenytoin (Dilantin) is subsequently given phenobarbital. The phenobarbital stimulates the liver microsomal enzymes to destroy the phenytoin more rapidly, which could cause convulsions. This drug interaction requires repeated doses, usually a week of treatment, and is not significant with a single dose. Some barbiturate drug interactions are listed in Table 7-3.

Table 7-3. Barbiturate drug interactions

Interacting drug	Mechanism	Potential outcome
Alcohol, ethyl	Complex	CNS depression
Anticoagulants, oral	Induces hepatic enzymes	Decreased response to warfarin
Antidepressants, tricyclic (TCAs)	Increases metabolism of TCAs	Reduced effect of TCAs
Beta-adrenergic blocking agents	Increases metabolism	Reduced effect of beta-blocking agents
CNS depressants	Adds to CNS depression	CNS depression
Corticosteroids	Increases metabolism	Caution with asthmatics
Griseofulvin	Reduces absorption	Decreased plasma levels
Methoxyflurane	Stimulates increase in nephrotoxic metabolites	Two weeks should be allowed for induction to reverse
MAOIs	Decrease metabolism of barbiturates	CNS depression
Phenytoin	Increases phenytoin metabolism; phenobarbital competitively inhibits the metabolism of phenytoin	Reduced phenytoin effect; possible convulsions
Quinidine	Enhances metabolism of quinidine	Reduced antiarrhythmic effect
Sulfonamides	Compete with thiopental for plasma-protein binding	Less thiopental may be required for anesthesia
Tetracycline	Enhances metabolism of doxycycline	Reduced antibacterial effect

Uses

The uses of the barbiturates are determined by their duration of action (Table 7-1).

1. The ultrashort-acting agents are used intravenously for the induction of general anesthesia. For very brief procedures, they may be used alone. For more extensive procedures, they are used to induce stage III surgical anesthesia (see Chapter 6). Although this route can produce a precise degree of sedation, it requires extensive training and experience to properly use.

2. The short-acting agents can be used orally for their hypnotic or calming effect. These agents can be given preoperatively to allay anxiety. The hypnotic dose of pentobarbital or secobarbital is 100 to 200 mg orally, ingested 1 hour before an appointment. By taking one dose at bedtime, the patient will have a better night's sleep before a dental appointment. Physicians prescribe these agents for insomnia.

3. The intermediate-acting agents can also be prescribed to relieve anxiety before a dental appointment, although their effects will last longer than those of the short-acting agents. These agents are used for daytime sedation and the treatment of insomnia.

4. The long-acting barbiturates are used primarily for day-long sedation and the treatment of epilepsy (see Chapter 14).

NONBARBITURATE SEDATIVE-HYPNOTICS

During the last half of the nineteenth century the bromides and chloral hydrate began to replace opium, alcohol, and belladonna as drugs for the production of sedation. The barbiturates were introduced in 1904 and, until recently, remained the principal sedative-hypnotic drugs used in dental and medical practice. Today numerous nonbarbiturate sedatives of varying chemical structure are available.

The nonbarbiturate sedative-hypnotic drugs have essentially the same advantages and disadvantages as the barbiturates and in some cases are known to have additional undesirable features. Although the use of huge quantities of barbiturates over many years has largely elucidated their problems, the nonbarbiturate drugs are less well known. In general, the nonbarbiturates offer no advantage over the barbiturates. Preoperative sedation in dental practice can usually be adequately obtained with a properly selected dose of a short-acting benzodiazepine. Except for those rare patients in whom barbiturates are contraindicated,

few clear-cut indications exist for the use of the nonbarbiturate sedative-hypnotic drugs. Table 7-4 lists the nonbarbiturate sedative-hypnotics, their doses, and their duration of action. The most common agents will be discussed here.

Chloral hydrate

Chloral hydrate ($CCl_3CH[OH]_2$) is an inexpensive, orally effective sedative-hypnotic drug with a rapid onset (20 to 30 minutes) and a fairly short duration of action (about 4 hours). Therapeutic doses do not produce pronounced respiratory or cardiovascular depression. An exaggerated effect occurs in patients with advanced liver or kidney disease. Large doses or long-term use may produce peripheral vasodilation and hypotension with some degree of myocardial depression. Toxic doses may produce cardiac problems, especially in the cardiac patient. Gastric irritation with nausea and vomiting may occur; consequently, chloral hydrate should not be used in patients with ulcers or gastroenteritis. Gastric irritation can be minimized by taking chloral hydrate in diluted solutions with milk or food. The highly irritating effect of this drug on mucosa is illustrated by a report of laryngospasm in a child, which is believed to have been caused by the aspiration of chloral hydrate.[6] The disagreeable odor and taste of chloral hydrate can be partially masked in a flavored syrup or by using triclofos or chloral betaine, which produce chloral in the stomach. As with all the sedative-hypnotic agents, psychologic or physical dependence may follow the prolonged use of this drug.

Chloral hydrate is usually taken as a single hypnotic dose by mouth at bedtime. It usually does not suppress REM sleep, and on discontinuation, rebound increase in REM sleep does not occur. It has been used successfully in dentistry for the preoperative sedation of children[7] and can also be effective for adults. An effective oral dose for preoperative sedation in adults is about 1 gm (0.5 to 2 gm) given 30 minutes before the appointment. The oral or rectal sedative dose for children must be highly individualized, but the following guideline dosages have been recommended[8]:

Age	Approximate weight (lb)	Dose (mg)
6 months	15	100
1 year	20	150
3 years	30	200
5 years	40	300
7 years	50	400

Table 7-4. Nonbarbiturate sedative-hypnotics

Drug	Use in porphyria	Oral dose		Duration of action	Preparations* available
		Hypnotic	Sedative (t.i.d. or q.i.d.)		
Chloral derivatives					
Chloral hydrate (Noctec, Somnos)	Caution	500-2000 mg	250 mg	Short	C: 250, 500 mg Supp: various L: 500 mg/5 ml
Triclofos (Triclos)		1500 mg		Short	T: 750 mg L: 500 mg/5 ml
Chloral betaine (Beta-chlor)		870-1000 mg		Short	T: 870 (equals 500 mg chloral hydrate)
Paraldehyde		10-30 ml	5-10 ml	Short	L: 30 ml C: 1000
Carbamates					
Ethinamate (Valmid)	Avoid	500-1000 mg			C: 500 mg
Meprobamate (Equanil, Miltown)	No	800 mg	400 mg	Intermediate	T: 200, 400, 600 mg C: 200, 400 mg L: 200 mg/5 ml
Tybamate (Tybatran, Solacen)	No	500 mg			C: 125, 250, 350 mg
Ethchlorvynol (Placidyl)	No	500-1000 mg	100-200 mg (b.i.d. or t.i.d.)	Short	C: 200, 500, 750 mg
Piperidinediones					
Glutethimide (Doriden)	No	250-500 mg	125-250 mg	Intermediate	T: 125, 250, 500 mg C: 500 mg
Methyprylon (Noludar)	Avoid	300 mg	50-100 mg	Short	T: 50, 200 mg C: 300 mg
Methaqualone (Quaalude, Sopor, Parest, Somnafac)	Yes	150-300 mg	200-400 mg	Short	T: 75, 150, 300 mg C: 200, 400 mg

*C, Capsules; *Supp*, suppositories; *L*, liquid; *T*, tablets.

The disagreeable odor and taste of chloral hydrate are masked in a flavored syrup containing 500 mg/5 ml. It is also available in 250 and 500 mg capsules and 500 mg suppositories.

Chloral betaine

Chloral betaine (Beta-Chlor) was introduced in 1963 as a chemical complex of chloral hydrate and betaine. It produces essentially the same effectiveness and undesirable effects as chloral hydrate but is more expensive. It avoids the disagreeable taste of chloral hydrate. It is available as an 870 mg tablet, which is equivalent to 500 mg chloral hydrate. The usual oral dose for preoperative sedation in adults and children over 12 years of age is 870 mg. Chloral betaine has a slower onset than chloral hydrate and should be given 1 hour preoperatively.

Paraldehyde

Paraldehyde (polymer of acetaldehyde) is an inexpensive, orally effective sedative-hypnotic. It produces a rapid onset but a longer duration of action than chloral hydrate. Paraldehyde has a very disagreeable taste and odor. Since approximately 25% of the drug is exhaled, an extremely offensive breath causes limited patient acceptance. The drug not exhaled is metabolized by the liver; consequently, severe liver damage may exaggerate its effects. Gastric irritation can occur. Psychologic and physical dependence on paraldehyde can follow long-term use. Outdated paraldehyde is particularly toxic and should be discarded. The use of paraldehyde is greatly limited by patient acceptance, and it has no place in dental practice.

Ethinamate

Ethinamate (Valmid) produces a fast onset and short duration of action. Since its introduction in 1954, adverse reactions to ethinamate have been minimal. Excitement is occasionally seen in children, and gastrointestinal upset and skin rashes are sometimes observed. Thrombocytopenic purpura has been reported but is rare. Psychologic and physical dependence may follow long-term use. Teratogenic studies are insufficient to recommend its use in pregnant or nursing women. Ethinamate's short duration of action precludes its use as a daytime sedative.

It may be used as a preoperative sedative in dentistry. The usual oral dose of ethinamate for preoperative sedation in adults is 500 mg to 1 gm given 30 minutes before the procedure. It is available in 500 mg tablets. More effective agents, the benzodiazepines, are now available.

Ethchlorvynol

Ethchlorvynol (Placidyl) produces a rapid onset (15 to 30 minutes) and a short duration of action (5 hours). Its $t_{\frac{1}{2}}$ is 10 to 25 hours. Its use has been associated with a mintlike aftertaste, hypotension, gastric upset, dizziness, blurred vision, facial numbness, urticaria, and mild giddiness. Large doses have caused mental confusion and hallucinations. Syncope, prolonged hypnosis, and profound muscular weakness have been reported but are rare. Its therapeutic index is probably similar to the barbiturates. Treatment of acute poisoning from ethchlorvynol resembles that for barbiturate poisoning (Table 7-2).

Abusers have tremors, slurred speech, confusion, and sometimes toxic amblyopia. The withdrawal syndrome resembles delirium tremens and is especially severe in the elderly. Ethchlorvynol is contraindicated in patients with porphyria. Physical or psychologic dependence may follow prolonged use. Teratogenic studies are insufficient to recommend its use during pregnancy. Ethchlorvynol is used as a daytime sedative and as a mild hypnotic, but it has no particular indication in dental practice.

Glutethimide

Glutethimide (Doriden) is a sedative-hypnotic agent with marked anticholinergic effects including xerostomia. It is unpredictably absorbed from the gastrointestinal tract. Its use has been associated with "hangover," blurred vision, rash, headache, gastric irritation, and excitement. Blood dyscrasias, including aplastic anemia, can occur. It is contraindicated for patients with porphyria. With toxic doses, the antimuscarinic effects are pronounced. Tonic spasms and even convulsions are produced. It produces a withdrawal syndrome. This agent, because of its toxicity and lack of any advantages, has no justification for continued use.

Methyprylon

The hypnotic effect of methyprylon (Noludar) is indistinguishable from that of secobarbital. It is metabolized and conjugated to the glucuronide before excretion. Its $t_{\frac{1}{2}}$ is 4 hours. The adverse effects include "hangover," gastrointestinal distress, headache, and rash. Paradoxic excitement has been reported. Neutropenia and thrombocytopenia have occurred in patients taking methyprylon. Its potential for abuse and its withdrawal syndrome resemble those of the barbiturates.

Methaqualone

Methaqualone (Quāalude, Sopor, Parest, Somnafac) is a short-acting sedative-hypnotic agent. It possesses only one advantage over some other sedative-hypnotic agents: it can be used in patients with hereditary porphyria. Methaqualone's unwarranted reputation as an aphrodisiac has led to abuse of this agent. It has been associated with gastric upset, nausea, headache, and dry mouth. Peripheral neuropathy associated with numbness and tingling has been reported. Although the $t_{\frac{1}{2}}$ of this agent is short, "hangover" may occur. With a mild overdose, central depression similar to that caused by the barbiturates results, but with larger doses, convulsions can occur. The withdrawal syndrome can include grand mal convulsions. Because of this drug's potential for toxicity and lack of specific advantages, it has very limited use in dentistry.

SEDATIVE-ANALGESIC COMBINATIONS

Provision for concomitant sedation and analgesia is rational for three reasons: (1) sedation and pain relief are frequently required together, (2) sedatives potentiate analgesics, and (3) sedatives may induce excitement in patients experiencing uncontrolled pain. Both sedation and analgesia can be obtained from the narcotic drugs used singly, but it is not desirable to use a narcotic to add sedation to analgesia unless the analgesic potency of the narcotic is required. When analgesia can be adequately obtained with a nonnarcotic analgesic, these drugs and a sedative can be prescribed separately. Some fixed-dosage combinations of narcotic analgesic agents with sedative-hypnotic agents, such as Fiorinal, are discussed in Chapter 12. When more complete pain relief is required with sedation, a narcotic can be considered.

Meperidine-promethazine (Mepergan, Mepergan Fortis)

Meperidine (Demerol) is discussed in Chapter 12, and promethazine (Phenergan) is discussed in Chapter 15. Some studies have shown that the addition of promethazine allows the reduction of the required analgesic dose of meperidine by about one half. The smaller required dose of meperidine should reduce the narcotic side effects. Additionally, the sedation produced by promethazine adds to that provided by the meperidine. Although there is little doubt that significant analgesia and sedation can be obtained with this combination, definite evidence of advantages over larger doses of meperidine is lacking.

Adverse effects that might be expected with either constituent singly should be considered potential adverse effects of the combination. The most common possibilities are drowsiness, dizziness, xerostomia, and blurring of vision. The discussions of meperidine and promethazine should be consulted for other possible adverse effects.

The combination of meperidine and promethazine has been reported as useful for preoperative sedation in dentistry.[9] The adult oral dosage is 50 mg meperidine with either 12.5 or 25 mg promethazine every 4 to 6 hours. Table 12-4 lists the oral preparations (Mepergan and Mepergan Fortis).

SPECIAL CONSIDERATIONS

Certain generalizations should always be kept in mind relative to the use of sedative-hypnotic drugs.[4]

1. The practitioner should not rely exclusively on drugs to provide a calm and cooperative patient. The dentist's confident but relaxed manner and a pleasant, soothing office atmosphere are of great importance in relaxing an anxious patient. Drugs should not be substituted for patient education or for the proper psychologic approach to patient care.

2. When a sedative-hypnotic is required, the selection of the specific drug should be based on a knowledge of the advantages and disadvantages of the agents available and an understanding of the needs and contraindications that relate to the case at hand. In most instances a benzodiazepine (see Chapter 9) should be the drug of choice.

3. Regardless of the sedative-hypnotic selected, the following precautions pertain:
   a. Patients with immature or impaired elimination may experience exaggerated effects of medication. These individuals include the young, the elderly, the debilitated, and those with liver or kidney disease.
   b. CNS depression caused by all sedative-hypnotics will at least be additive with, and sometimes potentiate, depression with other CNS depressants that the patient may be taking. The patient should be made aware of this, particularly in regard to alcohol; over-the-counter sleep aids may also be a potential source of hazard.
   c. The patient should understand that the drug that the practitioner is prescribing may make it unsafe to perform acts requiring full alertness and muscular coordination, such as driving a car.

This is particularly important if the patient has not taken the drug previously and the response to it is consequently less predictable. The prescriber should be sure to inform the patient of this effect.

d. Psychic and physical dependence have been observed with all the sedative-hypnotic drugs. The dentist should consider all sedative-hypnotic drugs to have a potential for abuse and should limit their use accordingly. This is particularly important in regard to psychologically unstable individuals or those with a history of drug abuse because of the greater potential for addiction.

e. Suicide is commonly accomplished with depressant drugs. Consequently, the amount of the drug prescribed should be limited to that absolutely required to accomplish the therapeutic objective.

f. Newer drugs of this or any other group should not be administered to women of childbearing age if potential maternal or fetal dangers are not known. The nursing mother should also be given these drugs with caution. An exception would be a situation in which the clinical demands outweigh the risk; however, it is difficult to comprehend this situation.

g. Sedatives do not provide analgesia. In fact, the use of a sedative without adequate pain control may cause the patient to become highly excited and act irrationally. However, sedatives may potentiate the effect of an analgesic taken concomitantly.

REFERENCES
1. McCarthy, F.: Sudden, unexpected death in the dental office, J.A.D.A. **83**:1091, 1971.
2. Jastak, J.T., and Paravecchio, R.: An analysis of 1,331 sedations using inhalation, intravenous, or other techniques, J.A.D.A. **83**:1242-1249, 1975.
3. Cutting, W.C.: Handbook of pharmacology, ed. 4, New York, 1969, Appleton-Century-Crofts.
4. Pharmacotherapeutics in dental practice (NAVPERS 10486), Washington, D.C., 1969, U.S. Bureau of Naval Personnel.
5. Meyers, F.H., Jawetz, E., and Goldfien, A.: Review of medical pharmacology, ed. 3, Los Altos, Calif., 1972, Lange Medical Publications.
6. Granoff, D.M., McDaniel, D.B., and Borkowf, S.P.: Cardiorespiratory arrest following aspiration of chloral hydrate, Am. J. Dis. Child. **122**:170, 1971.
7. Robbins, M.B.: Chloral hydrate and promethazine as premedicants for the apprehensive child, J. Dent. Child. **34**:327, 1967.
8. Finn, S.B., et al.: Clinical pedodontics, ed. 3, Philadelphia, 1967, W.B. Saunders Co.
9. Small, E.W.: Preoperative sedation in dentistry, Dent. Clin. North Am. **14**:769, Oct., 1970.

CHAPTER 8

Psychotherapeutic drugs

BARBARA F. ROTH-SCHECHTER

Many drugs are known to have psychotropic activity; that is, they can affect mental activity. This chapter, however, deals exclusively with those agents that are presently employed in the management of major psychiatric disorders. The pharmacology of minor psychiatric disorders and various anxiety states is presented in Chapter 9. For information on psychotogenic drugs (drugs that *induce* psychosis-like behavior) the reader is referred to Chapter 34. The psychotherapeutic drugs will be presented according to their predominant clinical use. For this reason a brief description of the psychiatric illnesses treated with the drugs to be discussed is appropriate.

PSYCHIATRIC DISORDERS

Psychiatric disorders can be classified according to their known or suspected cause of origin and as such are one of two types: organic or functional.

Organic illnesses are defined as (1) those caused by or associated with acquired injuries or diseases that have damaged the brain (for example, tumor, trauma) and (2) those caused by congenital defects (for example, phenylketonuria). In contrast, functional psychiatric disorders by definition are at least partially of psychogenic origin and do not exhibit any clearly defined structural or biochemical abnormality in the brain. The four major classes of functional psychiatric illnesses are the psychoses, neuroses, psychophysiologic (somatic) disorders, and personality disorders.

Within the framework of this discussion, the psychoses and neuroses are of primary interest. During the past two decades major advances have been achieved in the pharmacologic treatment of these two classes of psychiatric disorders.

Psychoses can be termed the most violent type of psychiatric disorders. The two main types of psychoses are the schizophrenias and the affective disorders. A great variety of conditions exist under the heading of schizophrenia, and it is far beyond the scope of this discussion to describe the various forms of this disease. Suffice it to say that schizophrenia is a long-term psychosis characterized by extensive disturbance of the individual's personality function with an obvious loss of the perception of reality.

Affective disorders include the various types of depression, that is, the endogenous (involutional) and exogenous (reactive) depression, as well as the syndrome of manic depression. Endogenous depression is generally considered to be the more severe type of depression and is characterized by an onset apparently unrelated to external events and a high suicidal risk. Exogenous depression appears to be a psychotic reaction to a specific external event and seldom exhibits the severity of the endogenous type. Manic-depressive illness is a cyclic affective disorder characterized by alternating periods of mania (elation) and depression.

Neuroses, or psychoneurotic disorders, are the second major category of psychiatric disorders responsive to psychopharmacologic agents. Although less severe than psychosis, neurosis is a distinct psychiatric entity. It includes various forms of anxiety, phobia, and compulsiveness.

In summary, it must be emphasized that the classifications and definitions given in this introduction are oversimplified, but it is believed that the generally reported specific responses to different psychotherapeutic agents justify this approach. Furthermore, it is intended to aid the reader in the understanding and appreciation of the use of psychopharmacologic drugs. These agents will be presented under two main categories. The first group will include those drugs used in the treatment of psychoses, often referred to as major tranquilizers. The second group will deal with those drugs used to treat affective disorders. The discussion of minor tranquilizers in the management of various neuroses is discussed in Chapter 9.

DRUGS USED IN THE TREATMENT OF PSYCHOSES

Before the introduction of drugs for the management of psychiatric disorders, many physical treatment methods were discovered empirically. Some of these are still being used, alone or in combination with drug therapy, such as electroconvulsive therapy; others have been abandoned after a relatively short period of extensive use, such as physical shock treatment like sudden ducking and submersion of the mentally ill patient in water. Psychosurgery deserves mention because it appears to enjoy renewed interest. Although initially introduced as prefrontal lobotomy (section of the white matter in the plane of the coronal suture), it now has been refined into a highly specific surgical ablation of presumably behavior-controlling central structures. Undoubtedly, however, the introduction of specific psychopharmacologic drugs—not merely sedatives—has superseded many other types of treatment.

The first two psychopharmacologic drugs to be introduced into psychiatry, the phenothiazines and the *Rauwolfia* alkaloids, appeared almost simultaneously in Western medicine. Although extracts of *Rauwolfia serpentina* had been used extensively in Hindu medicine for a variety of diseases, including hypertension and insanity, it was not until 1954 that reserpine was reportedly used in Western medicine for the treatment of psychotic and hypertensive patients, respectively.[1,2] It soon became apparent that the phenothiazines were more effective and easier to control than the *Rauwolfia* compounds. For these reasons *Rauwolfia* alkaloids and their derivatives (reserpine, deserpidine, rescinnamine) are only occasionally used currently for the treatment of psychoses. The use of these drugs in the treatment of hypertension is discussed in Chapter 20.

By far the most widely used group of antipsychotic agents are the phenothiazines, followed by the butyrophenones and the thioxanthenes, the latter being chemically closely related to the phenothiazines. Furthermore, several other classes of heterocyclic compounds have been introduced recently, most notably

the indole compounds with molindone[3] as an example. These will be presented as a separate group following the discussion of the more well-known antipsychotic drugs.

Phenothiazines

Phenothiazine itself was used as early as 1934 as a urinary antiseptic and anthelmintic. Subsequently, many derivatives were synthesized, and the first important discovery was promethazine, which was found to be a powerful antihistamine with additional sedative effects. It was the sedative effect of promethazine that initiated attempts to improve on this central effect of phenothiazine derivatives, resulting in the synthesis of chlorpromazine. The French psychiatrist Laborit first observed the unique psychopharmacologic action of chlorpromazine: "There is no loss in consciousness, not any change in the patient's mentality but a slight tendency to sleep and above all disinterest for all that goes on around him."[4] Those psychiatrists who first used phenothiazine derivatives immediately noted that these effects were far superior to those of any drugs previously used in the treatment of schizophrenic disorders. The use of chlorpromazine quickly spread throughout the world, and its use paralleled a steady decrease in the number of hospitalized psychiatric patients.

Chemistry. Phenothiazine is void of any antipsychotic activity. Substitutions of pharmacologic significance are in positions $10(R^1)$ and $2(R^2)$. Substitutions at position 10 provide the basis for subclassification of the various antipsychotic phenothiazines. Chlorpromazine is the representative example of those phenothiazines that have an *aliphatic side chain (A)* substituted at the nitrogen in position 10. Members of this group are characterized by moderate extrapyramidal effects and an apparently higher rate of agranulocytosis than are members of the other groups of derivatives. The most potent phenothiazine derivatives are provided by members of the *piperazine side-chain substitutions (B)* (for example, trifluoperazine). These phenothiazines have a higher incidence of extrapyramidal side effects but have less sedative properties. An increase in antiemetic potency is generally obtained by the additional substitution by a halogen at position 2. The less toxic phenothiazines result from substitution by a *piperidine side chain (C)* whose members afford intermediate antipsychotic activity (Table 8-1). Generally, substitution in position

Table 8-1. Phenothiazine derivatives with antipsychotic activity

Substitution at R^1	Commonly available drugs of that group	Usual oral antipsychotic dose range (mg/24 hr)	Side effects		
			Frequent	Occasional	Rare
A—Aliphatic side chain	Chlorpromazine (Thorazine)	300-800	Oversedation Orthostatic hypotension Atropine-like effects*	Cholestatic jaundice Parkinsonism Akathisia Menstrual changes Dystonic reactions	Lenticular pigmentation ECG abnormalities Blood dyscrasias Photosensitivity
	Promazine (Sparine)	500-1000			
	Triflupromazine (Vesprin)	100-300			
B—Piperazine side chain	Acetophenazine (Tindal)	30-120	Parkinsonism Akathisia Atropine-like effects* Dystonic reactions	Photosensitivity Orthostatic hypotension Menstrual changes	Jaundice Blood dyscrasias Decreased libido Allergic reactions Sedation
	Fluphenazine HCl (Prolixin)	4-15			
	Trifluoperazine (Stelazine)	3-15			
C—Piperidine side chain	Mesoridazine (Serentil)	150-400	Oversedation Atropine-like effects* Orthostatic hypotension Weight gain	Parkinsonism Akathisia Photosensitivity Menstrual changes	Jaundice Blood dyscrasias Pigmentary retinopathy Dystonic reactions
	Piperacetazine (Quide)	25-150			
	Thioridazine (Mellaril)	100-500			

*Atropine-like (anticholinergic) effects include dry mouth, mydriasis, cycloplegia, urinary retention, tachycardia, decreased gastrointestinal motility.

2 of the ring results in increased antipsychotic activity. Depending on the type of substitution, this increased antipsychotic activity may or may not be accompanied by a simultaneous increase in antiemetic or side effects, or both. It is worthwhile to note that all antipsychotic phenothiazines have a 3-carbon bridge between ring and side chain nitrogen, whereas phenothiazines with predominantly antihistamine action have only 2 carbons in this position. (Antihistamines are described in Chapter 16.)

Absorption, metabolism, and excretion. All phenothiazines are well absorbed after oral as well as parenteral administration. Particularly after oral administration, a considerable proportion of the dose is removed into active enterohepatic circulation and is only slowly released into the general circulation. This is considered to be responsible for the long half-life of phenothiazines. For that reason sustained-release preparations of phenothiazines are of no advantage.

There is no specific and pharmacologically significant preferential tissue distribution of the phenothiazines. Hydroxylation followed by conjugation with glucuronic acid represents the major pathway of metabolism. In addition, numerous other metabolites

Phenothiazine

Phenothiazine derivatives

A. Aliphatic side chain (for example, chlorpromazine)

$$R^1 = -CH_2-CH_2-CH_2-N \begin{matrix} CH_3 \\ \\ CH_3 \end{matrix}$$

B. Piperazine side chain (for example, trifluoperazine)

$$R^1 = -CH_2-CH_2-CH_2-N \bigcirc N-CH_3$$

C. Piperidine side chain (for example, thioridazine)

$$R^1 = -CH_2-CH_2 \begin{matrix} \\ N \\ | \\ CH_3 \end{matrix}$$

have been postulated and some isolated. These are excreted in about equal proportions by way of the urine and feces. The important fact to appreciate, however, is that the ultimate half-life of a chronically administered phenothiazine is very long. For months after discontinuation of the drug, metabolites as well as free unchanged drug can be identified in the urine.

Addiction and tolerance. Although the phenothiazines are not addicting as defined in Chapter 34, rare and mild cases of physical dependence have been reported. Apparently, there is no development of central tolerance to their antipsychotic effect; however, some degree of tolerance to several of their side effects does occur. Psychologic dependence has not been observed with even long-term use, probably because of the lack of any euphoriant action of the phenothiazines.

Pharmacologic effects. The pharmacologic spectrum of phenothiazines is exceptionally wide and diverse.

Central effects of phenothiazines

1. The phenothiazines' main pharmacologic action is their antipsychotic effect that induces the "neuroleptic syndrome." This syndrome consists of a slowing of psychomotor activity in the agitated and disturbed patient, an emotional quieting with suppression of hallucinations and delusions, and loss of affect without loss of intellectual function.

2. Various degrees of sedation and drowsiness are effected by different phenothiazine derivatives. They are, however, to be differentiated from other sedatives in that phenothiazines will not induce anesthesia, even with large doses, and although drowsy, the patient can always be easily aroused under the influence of the drug. As mentioned earlier, there is no tolerance developed to the antipsychotic effect, but tolerance to the sedative action occurs within 1 to 2 weeks, the same time period necessary for the full antipsychotic effect to appear. Thus the combination of sedative and antipsychotic action of phenothiazines provides maximal initial benefit for the agitated and disturbed psychotic patient. The mechanism of action of the phenothiazines in producing their major pharmacologic effect is not understood. In addition to the observation of extrapyramidal stimulation (discussed later), extensive evidence has been accumulated to support the hypothesis that phenothiazines, and for that matter all antipsychotic drugs, interfere with the actions of dopamine as synaptic neurotransmitter in the brain.[5]

All other effects of the phenothiazines are either minor therapeutic or strictly side effects. Among the many phenothiazines marketed, no single phenothiazine is clearly superior to any other in its antipsychotic action. There are advantages and disadvantages with respect to side effects of each individual compound, and the consideration of the differential risk of all side effects remains a matter of clinical judgment. Chlorpromazine will be discussed here as the typical and most widely used phenothiazine.

3. The third, although minor, pharmacologic effect of therapeutic significance of chlorpromazine is an antiemetic action. This stems from specific depression of the chemotherapeutic trigger zone. Chlorpromazine is particularly potent in producing this effect at nonsedative doses. The antiemetic effect of phenothiazines has been found useful in controlling the nausea and vomiting that occurs during uremia, gastroenteritis, carcinomatosis, and drug-induced emesis. But because chlorpromazine acts by depressing the chemotherapeutic trigger zone, it is ineffective in controlling motion sickness or any other nausea caused by vestibular stimulation.

4. The hypothalamus is another central structure that is apparently uniformly depressed by chlorpromazine. This action manifests itself in a number of mostly undesirable side effects.

   a. The vasomotor center is depressed at relatively low doses; specifically, sympathetic outflow from the hypothalamus appears to be suppressed. Together with peripheral autonomic effects (discussed later), this action manifests itself as orthostatic hypotension.

   b. Temperature-regulating systems are disrupted, and a tendency toward poikilothermy can be observed. In case of environmental hypothermia, this effect combined with peripheral vasodilation can become detrimental.

   c. Release of pituitary gonadotropins is suppressed by chlorpromazine, which may cause delay in ovulation and menstruation in female patients, sometimes even induction of pseudopregnancy. The development of a certain degree of tolerance to this effect has been observed.

   d. Secretion of growth hormone, oxytocin, and adrenocorticotropic hormone (ACTH) is suppressed by chlorpromazine, but it remains to be unequivocally established whether adrenocortical secretion and thyroid activity are also reduced.

5. The medullary respiratory center is depressed only slightly at low doses of chlorpromazine, but this central depressive action has to be kept in mind when a sedative or other CNS depressant is administered to a patient who is receiving long-term phenothiazine therapy or at toxic doses of chlorpromazine.

6. Central motor effects can be either inhibitory or stimulatory.

    a. Skeletal muscular relaxation, which contributes to the neuroleptic syndrome, can be produced in other spastic conditions as well. It appears to be of central origin, possibly caused by depression of cerebral gamma motor systems.

    b. Chlorpromazine and other phenothiazines stimulate the extrapyramidal system, giving rise to the most common and most disagreeable series of side effects. There is considerable variation in individual susceptibility to the extrapyramidal syndrome, as well as between different types of antipsychotic drugs both with respect to onset and severity.[6] It has become customary to classify these extrapyramidal effects into five different syndromes. Simultaneously with the administration of the drug are known to appear the following: (1) an acute dystonia consisting of muscle spasms of the face, tongue, neck, and back; (2) an akathisia consisting of compulsive motor restlessness that can easily be confused with true anxiety; and (3) a parkinsonian syndrome indistinguishable from idiopathic parkinsonism, consisting of rigidity, bradykinesia, and resting tremor. Some of these undesirable side effects are responsive to antiparkinsonian therapy. Tardive dyskinesia (4) and the rabbit syndrome[7] (5) (perioral tremor) are late-appearing neurologic syndromes associated with the use of phenothiazines and other antipsychotic drugs. Tardive dyskinesia may occur after months or years, and it occurs more frequently in older patients. It consists of oral-facial dyskinesias as well as choreiform and purposeless, quick movements of the extremities. It may persist long after discontinuation of the antipsychotic, and at present no satisfactory treatment is known. In contrast, the antipsychotic-induced perioral tremor can be controlled by anticholinergic agents.

In dyskinetic patients, spasms of the muscles of mastication may be a phenothiazine-induced complication. The typical symptom is sudden and severe intermittent pain in the region of the temporomandibular joint. In an acute attack it becomes difficult to open or close the jaw, and unilateral or bilateral dislocation of the mandible may occur. Without any treatment the spasm will generally subside within several hours. Intravenous administration of amobarbital sodium or diphenhydramine hydrochloride, as well as oral administration of phenobarbital and methocarbamol, have been successful in relieving the acute spasm.

Peripheral effects of phenothiazines

1. Phenothiazine derivatives have extensive autonomic effects. Adrenergic receptors appear to be blocked by chlorpromazine, which augments the central sympatholytic effect mentioned earlier. The observable clinical manifestation is orthostatic hypotension with a compensatory tachycardia. Tolerance usually develops during the first weeks of medication.

There are mild anticholinergic side effects of chlorpromazine, primarily of the antimuscarinic type, that is, blurred vision, xerostomia, and constipation. Alone, the anticholinergic actions of phenothiazines are weak, but they can become of major significance when other anticholinergic medication is administered with phenothiazines.

2. Chlorpromazine can induce local anesthesia when injected proximally to a nerve, being twice as effective as meperidine, but this action is of no clinical value by itself.

3. Chlorpromazine is known to have a weak diuretic effect, which is thought to be caused by a decreased release of antidiuretic hormone, a direct action of chlorpromazine on the renal tubule, or a combination of both actions.

4. Phenothiazines have a direct negative inotropic effect on the heart. The main manifestation of chlorpromazine on the heart, however, is tachycardia, which is partially compensatory to the hypotensive action and partially caused by its atropine-like action.

5. Several other peripheral actions of chlorpromazine have been observed; they are believed to be either allergic and hypersensitivity reactions or long-term effects of unknown origin. Blood dyscrasias are known to occur, the most serious of which is agranulocytosis, which usually occurs within the first 6 to 8 weeks of medication. Although the occurrence is rare, the mortality is high (30%). Chlorpromazine-induced cholestatic jaundice is considered an allergic reaction, with most cases being benign and a return to normal liver function occurring on discontinuation of

the drug. A variety of skin eruptions has been associated with chlorpromazine medication, including urticarial, petechial, and edematous types. Photosensitivity reactions resembling severe sunburn, as well as blue-gray metallic discoloration of skin and eyes, are known to occur.

Drug interactions and overdose toxicity. In view of the actions of phenothiazines, it is not surprising that they interact in an additive or even potentiating fashion with all CNS depressants, such as barbiturates, alcohol, general anesthetics, and opiates. Chlorpromazine greatly enhances the respiratory depression produced by meperidine. For additive psychotherapeutic benefit, phenothiazines are often successfully combined with the tricyclic antidepressants. With this combination, however, the antihypertensive effect of guanethidine may be blocked. On the other hand, with all other antihypertensive drugs phenothiazines may act in an additive fashion, probably by their blockade of dopamine receptors. The same mechanism is thought to be responsible for the interaction of phenothiazines with levodopa, which results in a decreased antiparkinsonian effect. To control excessive extrapyramidal stimulation, phenothiazine therapy often has to be combined with antiparkinsonian medication of anticholinergic type. This combination is bound to exacerbate antimuscarinic peripheral effects such as xerostomia, urinary retention, bowel paralysis, and inhibition of sweating. Lastly, it should be emphasized that epinephrine should never be used for vasomotor collapse in a patient receiving phenothiazine medication because of the alpha-adrenergic blocking action of these drugs.

Acute overdose toxicity results from a combination of central and peripheral effects. It usually includes respiratory failure, convulsions or excessive extrapyramidal symptoms, cardiovascular collapse, and hypothermia. Chronic overdose toxicity generally manifests itself in exacerbation and intensification of most of the side effects described. A specific oral syndrome—primarily attributable to excessive anticholinergic action—can be described as dry mouth, diffuse redness of mucous membranes, loosened dentures, denture stomatitis, and black or white hairy tongue, all of which disappear on discontinuation of medication.

In general, the treatment of acute overdose toxicity is of a supportive and symptomatic nature to provide adequate respiration and circulation and to maintain body temperature. The treatment of chronic overdose toxicity consists of gradual withdrawal of the phenothiazine.

Therapeutic uses. Despite their wide spectrum of side effects, phenothiazines are relatively safe drugs. They have revolutionized mental hospitals and are the first line of defense against schizophrenia.[8] They also have been used, although with variable results, in the management of various neuroses and some character disorders. Treatment with phenothiazines is strictly on an individual basis. It should be appreciated that long-acting injectable phenothiazines are available with a duration of action of up to 4 to 6 weeks, thus allowing the effective control of chronic schizophrenia in patients who fail to take their oral medication regularly. Phenothiazines have been tried in the treatment of acute withdrawal from many abused CNS drugs. Although they seem of little use in the management of withdrawal from narcotics, they are being used successfully in the management of alcoholic hallucinosis. A second, minor therapeutic indication of chlorpromazine and other phenothiazines is as antiemetics, particularly in the control of vomiting induced by gastroenteritis or drugs, uremia, or carcinomatosis. Lastly, chlorpromazine has been used successfully in the control of intractable hiccoughs. For obvious reasons of additive interactions, phenothiazines are contraindicated in patients with myasthenia gravis, brain damage and epileptic disorders, cardiac disease, and hepatitis and in patients receiving antihypertensive therapy.

Butyrophenones

History. The first butyrophenone to be introduced for the treatment of psychoses was haloperidol. It was synthesized by Janssen[9] after an extensive synthetic program following the successful introduction of the analgesic meperidine. Haloperidol was made available for therapeutic use in 1960.

Chemistry. In contrast to other antipsychotic drugs, which tend to constitute more or less successful modifications of the basic phenothiazine structure, butyrophenones are chemically entirely different psychotherapeutic agents. The chemical formula of haloperidol is as follows:

Despite the structural dissimilarity, the butyrophenones resemble closely in their actions the piperazine phenothiazines. They also block the effects of dopamine and increase its turnover rate, which is believed to be their mechanism of action. The two members available in the United States are haloperidol and droperidol. This discussion will focus on the former, since it is by far the most widely used butyrophenone in the United States.

Absorption, metabolism, and excretion. At present, haloperidol is available for oral and parenteral administration. In human beings it has a long $t_{\frac{1}{2}}$ with persistence of the drug for several weeks after a single dose. Haloperidol concentrates in the liver; however, its primary pathway of excretion is by way of the kidney. Haloperidol has not been found to be addicting, but some degree of physical dependence may occur, manifesting itself in muscular discomfort and sleep disturbances after abrupt withdrawal of the drug.

Pharmacologic effects. The main pharmacologic action of haloperidol is its highly potent antipsychotic effect combined with a sedative and general CNS depressive action. This depression manifests itself in tiredness, lowering of blood pressure (apparently only of central origin), and a fall in body temperature. Both the sedative and the hypotensive effects of haloperidol are less severe than those of the phenothiazines. Furthermore, autonomic side effects are less pronounced than those of the phenothiazines. In low to medium therapeutic dose ranges, side effects of butyrophenones are restricted to extrapyramidal manifestations like parkinsonism and dystonic reactions. In high therapeutic dose ranges, side effects consist of blood dyscrasias, hypotension, and depression, all of which respond to a reduction in dosage. Hypersensitivity and allergic reactions have been observed only rarely. Like the phenothiazines, haloperidol has been found to induce all forms of the extrapyramidal syndromes with long-term administration.

Drug interactions. Butyrophenones potentiate the sedative effect of other CNS depressants such as barbiturates, general anesthetics, and analgesics. In high doses butyrophenones decrease the anticoagulant action of phenindione by stimulating its metabolism. They are contraindicated in any type of depressive state because of their potential to induce depression themselves.

Therapeutic uses. Butyrophenones are highly effective antipsychotic drugs, not only for the various forms of schizophrenia but also for the management of the manic phase of manic-depressive illness. In addition, they have been found to be effective in the treatment of Gilles de la Tourette's syndrome. Butyrophenones are preferred for use in patients with coronary or cerebrovascular disease because they produce less hypotension.

Thioxanthenes

Thioxanthenes are a less potent group of antipsychotic drugs when compared with the phenothiazines or butyrophenones. They are closely related chemically to the phenothiazines. Thioxanthenes have a lower incidence of adverse reactions than do the other antipsychotic drugs, consisting primarily of oversedation, but they are also considerably weaker antipsychotics. They have the same but weaker pharmacologic and toxicologic spectrum as the phenothiazines. Nevertheless, thioxanthenes have a definite place in the antipsychotic armamentarium for the management of certain schizoaffective disorders. In addition to chlorprothixene, thiothixene, and clopenthixol are available.

Diverse heterocyclic antipsychotics

Several highly effective antipsychotic drugs have become known recently that cannot be classified in the preceding categories. For convenience, and lack of sufficient information to justify separate headings, they are grouped together here. These drugs share the characteristics of being at least as powerful antipsychotics as the phenothiazines and having clearly less side effects. Therefore the various members are presented here in terms of the advantages and differences with the clear understanding that they are powerful antipsychotics.

Molindone is an indole derivative that is best known for the fact that it has considerably less alpha-adrenergic receptor blocking action, and therefore virtually no orthostatic hypotension is observed with this drug. It also is less sedative than the classic antipsychotics.

Loxapine is a piperazine-substituted tricyclic compound that seems to have less acute extrapyramidal side effects with minimal central antidopaminergic actions.

Sulpiride is an anisamide that is not yet available in the United States. It is considered to have virtually no sedative effects and reduced incidence of acute neurologic disturbances.

These drugs have not been used long enough for an appreciation of their full potential or full range and severity of side effects.

DRUGS USED IN THE TREATMENT OF DEPRESSION

Until the late 1950s, there was no widely accepted pharmacologic treatment for depression. Forms of mild depression were treated with psychotherapy, and severe depression was treated with electroconvulsive therapy. Although several drugs are now available for the treatment of depression, all of them share the same drawback: an onset of at least 1 to 2 weeks. Therefore in severe suicidal depression, electroconvulsive therapy still remains superior to any drug treatment presently available.

Tricyclic antidepressants (dibenzazepines)

Although the tricyclics were not the first antidepressive drugs developed, they now constitute one of the most widely used series of antidepressives. Many dibenzazepines had been synthesized as early as 1889, but they were not clinically investigated until the late 1950s. This can most probably be attributed to their close chemical and to some extent pharmacologic similarity to the phenothiazines, which resulted in overlooking them for their specific antidepressant action.

Chemistry. The close structural similarity between the tricyclic antidepressants and the phenothiazines can be appreciated by consideration of the illustrations at the top of the next column.

The replacement of the sulfur atom of chlorpromazine *(A)* by a $CH_2—CH_2$ bridge pharmacologically results in a change from an antipsychotic to an antidepressant agent, and pharmacokinetically prevents conjugation of this ring. Two different series of tricyclics are derived, depending on whether a nitrogen or carbon is in position 10 *(A-C)*. The two types of derivatives are the (1) iminodibenzyl compounds with imipramine (Presamine, Tofranil) *(B)* and (2) dibenzocycloheptenes with amitriptyline (Elavil, Triavil) *(C)* as their representative example. Their actions and side effects are sufficiently similar so that a discussion of the subtle differences of the two types of tricyclic antidepressants is not warranted. Suffice it to point out that the latter tricyclic derivatives exhibit sedative side effects more frequently than do the others. For convenience, pharmacodynamics and pharmacology of the dibenzazepines will be discussed in

A. Chlorpromazine

B. Imipramine

C. Amitriptyline

terms of imipramine, and differences will be emphasized only when necessary.

Absorption, metabolism, and excretion. Imipramine is rapidly and thoroughly absorbed into the general circulation, independent of the route of administration. The $t_{\frac{1}{2}}$ is surprisingly short in comparison with the long latency of onset of action of the drug (discussed later). Dibenzazepines are predominantly metabolized by hepatic ring hydroxylation, glucuronide conjugation, and demethylation. Metabolites and unchanged drug are excreted by way of the kidneys, amounting to a total of 70% of administered dose within the first 72 hours.

Pharmacologic effects. The therapeutically important action of imipramine is on the CNS and differs between normal and depressed individuals. Many of its central actions resemble those of the phenothiazines. Particularly in normal persons, imipramine produces mild sedation and fatigue accompanied by strong antimuscarinic (atropine-like) side effects as well as reduction of psychomotor activity, potentiation of CNS depressants, and hypothermia. In contrast, depressed patients respond to imipramine therapy with an elevation of mood and a feeling of well-being but without any euphoriant action. However, the onset of these actions in depressed patients is between 1 and 3 weeks. Tricyclic antidepressants should be given for 4 weeks before they are considered to be ineffective in the treatment of depression. Furthermore, depressed patients respond to imipramine therapy with increased mental and physical activity, together with a reduction in their morbid preoccupation with suicide. The primary effect of tricyclic antidepressants in depressed individuals has been described as a ''dulling of depressive ideation,'' but it may be accompanied by initial difficulty in concentration and thinking. In addition, euphoric stimulation and excitement have also been observed with tricyclics in a certain number of depressed patients.[10] The mechanism of action of the tricyclics, and for that matter of all antidepressants, is not understood. Contrary to the original catecholamine hypothesis of depression, which attributed the illness to a deficiency of monoamines at central synapses, present thinking assumes a hyperresponsive catecholaminergic system as the possible underlying cause of depression.[11] Chronic administration of tricyclic and atypical antidepressants (see below) as well as MAOIs has amply been shown to decrease the density of central beta-adrenergic receptor and 5-HT_2 binding sites.[12] Therefore antidepressant administration may result clinically in a desensitization of enhanced aminergic receptor function.[13] Lastly, the recent discovery of specific, saturable, high-affinity binding sites for ^{3}H-imipramine in human brain[14] may soon further our understanding of the mechanism of action of antidepressant drugs.

The medullary respiratory center is unaffected by therapeutic doses of imipramine, but respiratory depression has been observed after poisoning with imipramine and amitriptyline.

Adverse effects and drug interactions. Some tricyclic antidepressants have tremorigenic activity of central origin. It apparently is not attributable to extrapyramidal stimulation, and it therefore does not respond to antiparkinsonian medication. It consists of a fine tremor in the upper extremities and occurs in at least 10% of patients treated with the drug.

Primary peripheral effects of imipramine are on the autonomic nervous system. It has distinct anticholinergic effects, resulting in dry mouth, blurred vision, tachycardia, constipation, and urinary retention. Tolerance to these atropine-like effects tends to develop with continued use. Similarly to the phenothiazines,

imipramine initially produces orthostatic hypotension, and tolerance is acquired to this effect also.

The most serious peripheral side effect is from imipramine's cardiac toxicity. Myocardial infarction and precipitation of congestive heart failure during the course of treatment have occurred. Various arrhythmias and episodes of tachycardia have been attributed to imipramine's antimuscarinic effects.

Hypersensitivity reactions such as skin rashes, blood dyscrasias, and obstructive jaundice have rarely been observed with the use of tricyclic antidepressants.

Unlike the phenothiazines, tricyclic antidepressants potentiate the behavioral actions of amphetamines and other CNS stimulants. Simultaneous administration of imipramine and MAOIs has resulted in severe reactions consisting of signs and symptoms of severe atropine toxicity. It is generally agreed that at least a 1-week interval should be observed after the discontinuation of one drug and the initiation of the other type of drug. Similar precautions should be kept in mind when treating a patient who is receiving imipramine therapy with any anticholinergic drug. Imipramine-like compounds will potentiate the pressor effects of injected norepinephrine, apparently because of an interference with uptake mechanism of this amine. Probably for the same reason, tricyclics block the antihypertensive action of guanethidine.

Potentiation of the action of tricyclic antidepressants is known to result by various mechanisms. Plasma binding of tricyclics to albumin can be reduced by competition with phenytoin, phenylbutazone, aspirin, aminopyrine, and the phenothiazines. In addition, oral contraceptives and methylphenidate interfere with metabolism of tricyclics in the liver. On the other hand, the potency of tricyclics is reduced by the simultaneous administration of barbiturates and certain other sedatives that induce hepatic microsomal enzyme systems and thus increase tricyclic metabolism.

The short-term combination of phenothiazines and tricyclics has been employed successfully and safely in the treatment of severely anxious and agitated depressed individuals. Tricyclic antidepressants can also be well combined with electroconvulsive therapy; this may be of greatest advantage during the initial phase of drug therapy, in severe suicidal risks, since the onset of action of imipramine may be as long as several weeks. Because of the cardiac and autonomic side effects, tricyclic antidepressants are to be used cautiously in patients with cardiac disease, epilepsy, glaucoma, or prostatic hypertrophy.

Accidental poisoning with tricyclics has become more common, and such overdose can be lethal. Acute overdose toxicity consists of severe hypertension, cardiac arrhythmias, hyperpyrexia, convulsions, coma, and respiratory failure. Survivors may have permanent myocardial damage. Treatment is symptomatic and should be conservative in view of the known interactions with other central nervous system vasopressor agents. Physostigmine has been reported to be effective in treating severe poisoning by tricyclic antidepressants but must be used with caution.[15]

Tricyclic antidepressants have very rarely been found to produce psychic or physical dependence and certainly not the entire syndrome of addiction with central tolerance and the necessary increase in dose for an adequate antidepressant action. Slight withdrawal effects after abrupt discontinuation of the drug have been reported. Tolerance to many side effects, central as well as peripheral, develops with different time courses.

Therapeutic uses. Tricyclic antidepressants can be considered the initial pharmacologic approach to depression. This evaluation is based on a consideration of both the efficacy and the toxicity of all drugs used in the management of depression. The eventual effectiveness of the tricyclic agents approaches that of electroconvulsive therapy but has the additional advantage of preventing relapses and thus provides long-term control of this psychiatric disorder. Imipramine-like agents have been used with moderate success in the control of nocturnal enuresis in children.

Monoamine oxidase inhibitors

The heading of MAOIs includes a variety of drugs, all of which share in the ability to inhibit monoamine oxidase (MAO) and thus to block oxidative deamination of naturally occurring amines. With a few exceptions, these drugs inhibit MAO noncompetitively and irreversibly; that is, recovery from their action can occur only by synthesis of new enzyme, which is a matter of weeks. Long-term inhibition of MAO has been shown to result in the accumulation of norepinephrine, epinephrine, serotonin, dopamine, tyramine, or tryptamine in various tissues. The relationship between chronic MAO inhibition, the accumulation of these biogenic amines, and the therapeutic

usefulness of these drugs in psychiatry remains to be established. Currently, the most plausible hypothesis as to their antidepressive mechanism relates to their ability to reduce beta-adrenergic receptor density in brain.[12] However, one should keep in mind that MAOIs also inhibit many other enzyme systems such as dopamine-β-oxidase, several decarboxylases, and hepatic oxidative enzymes, as well as having numerous effects unrelated to enzyme inhibition.

Presently used MAOIs are nialamide (Niamid), which is a hydrazide; phenelzine (Nardil), which is a hydrazine derivative; tranylcypromine (Parnate); and pargyline (Eutonyl). Although chemically heterogeneous, MAOIs can be discussed as an entity as far as pharmacodynamics, their pharmacologic effects, and their uses are concerned.

Absorption, metabolism, and excretion. All currently available MAOIs are readily absorbed with either oral or parenteral administration. The metabolism of hydrazides and hydrazines apparently consists of cleavage resulting in inactivation. Tranylcypromine is partially metabolized to benzoic acid. Other unidentified metabolites and unchanged drugs are excreted primarily in the urine with a half-life of approximately 1 or 2 days.

Pharmacologic effects. The psychopharmacologic action of MAOIs is their ability to elevate the mood of depressed patients. (For a discussion of antihypertensive MAOIs, see Chapter 19.) This antidepressive action of MAOIs is described as euphoric stimulation and occurs in normal as well as depressed subjects. The onset of antidepressive action is slow, and usually several weeks are required for full benefit to become evident. Furthermore, MAOIs are very effective suppressors of REM sleep and thus have been used for the treatment of narcolepsy. When effective in the treatment of depression, they are known to correct any accompanying sleep disorders.

Adverse reactions and drug interactions. Frequent side effects of MAOIs consist of restlessness and insomnia, which in rare cases may lead to manic reactions and even hallucinations. The peripheral side effects of MAOIs are hypotension, dry mouth, nausea, constipation, and anorexia. Rare side effects may include paresthesia, skin rashes, and muscle spasms.

Knowing the many enzyme systems affected by MAOIs, one is not surprised that the actions of many different drugs are being modified by the presence of an MAOI. Since MAO metabolizes endogenous as well as exogenous amines, the action of any sympathomimetic amine administered is potentiated. In addition, since MAO is an intraneuronal enzyme, it is understandable that indirectly acting amines (tyramine, amphetamine) are potentiated to a greater extent than directly acting amines (norepinephrine, epinephrine). Many foods and beverages contain high levels of tyramine (cheeses, fish, beer). For this reason ingestion of such food poses the danger of precipitation of a hypertensive crisis in a patient receiving long-term MAOI therapy. In several cases intracranial bleeding, excessive fever, and death occurred because of this interaction.

Because of their general enzyme-inhibiting properties, mentioned earlier, MAOIs interfere with the detoxifying mechanism of many drugs. They are known to potentiate the CNS-depressing action of barbiturates, alcohol, and analgesics. The MAOIs also prolong and intensify the effect of tricyclic antidepressants as well as anticholinergic agents used in the treatment of parkinsonism.

Acute toxicity from overdosages is characterized by hallucinations, hyperreflexia, convulsions, hyperpyrexia, and hypertensive crisis more often than hypotensive collapse. Treatment has to be conservative and aimed at the maintenance of body temperature, respiration, blood pressure, and electrolyte balance. Treatment of choice of the hypertensive crisis is the administration of a short-acting alpha-adrenergic blocking agent such as phentolamine.

Therapeutic uses. It has been stated repeatedly that MAOIs are more successful in the treatment of exogenous rather than endogenous depression. However, the former is also known to respond much better to psychotherapy, and it appears that many successes attributed to MAOI therapy were primarily caused by an increased responsiveness to psychotherapy in the presence of the MAOI. On the other hand, MAOIs undoubtedly have euphoriant and antidepressive action, with tranylcypromine being the most effective and nialamide the least effective of the group. However, with their great potential for dietary and drug interactions as well as their own toxicity, combined with the availability of the tricyclic antidepressants, MAOIs are considered of limited usefulness for the treatment of depression. They are being reserved mainly for patients whose condition is refractory to any other form of treatment and for patients who are reliable enough to be trusted with a potentially highly toxic drug.

Lithium salts

As outlined earlier, manic-depressive illness constitutes one major segment of the affective disorders. It is characterized by the cyclic recurrence of mania alternating with depression (bipolar manic-depressive illness). Lithium carbonate is indicated for the treatment of the acute manic phase or for the prevention of recurrences of bipolar depression. It has been advocated as an alternative to tricyclics for the treatment of severe depression,[16] but this is not an FDA-approved indication.

Chemically, lithium is a monovalent cation and belongs in the group of alkali metals. It is used as lithium carbonate (Li_2CO_3) and is administered orally only.

After ingestion lithium is readily absorbed, with peak plasma levels being reached between 2 and 4 hours after administration. Lithium is apparently rather uniformly distributed throughout the body, since it has been identified in both cerebrospinal fluid and milk of lactating mothers. The main route of excretion is through the kidneys, and there it apparently is handled like sodium, since under conditions of lowered sodium intake, lithium excretion is reduced; thus the potential of lithium toxicity rises under those circumstances. No tolerance of any origin has been detected during the use of lithium in the treatment of psychiatric disorders.

The mechanism of action of lithium in unknown. It appears to act rather specifically, since it does not have any psychoactivity in normal individuals. Because 3 to 10 days of therapy are needed for lithium to become effective, a severely manic patient should be hospitalized and should receive phenothiazines with the lithium for the first few days. All experts agree that to assure safety and effectiveness, lithium serum concentrations should be monitored weekly and maintained below 1.5 mEq/L to avoid serious toxicity.

Side effects consist of polyuria, fine hand tremor, and mild thirst; in more severe cases they may extend to slurred speech, ataxia, nausea, vomiting, and diarrhea. Overdose toxicity is primarily manifested by CNS symptoms. Muscular rigidity, hyperactive deep reflexes, excessive tremor, and muscle fasciculations are observed, in addition to loss of consciousness and coma. Immediate cessation of medication is the treatment of choice. In severe cases intravenous administration of urea or mannitol may be used to enhance lithium excretion by osmotic diuresis. The drug is obviously contraindicated in patients with impaired renal function and should not be given to patients taking a restricted salt diet or diuretic therapy.

Atypical antidepressants

Several drugs should be mentioned as atypical antidepressants, although at this time none of them is available in the United States. These drugs share with the tricyclic antidepressants the ability to modify on chronic administration the density of central neurotransmitter binding sites. Mianserin is closest to the tricyclics because it is a tetracyclic, and it has been shown repeatedly to be a clinically effective antidepressant.[17] The greatest interest is currently focused on specific modifiers of central 5HT-receptors, and zimelidine should be mentioned as such, since it has been shown to be effective in depression.[18] Although there are a number of studies showing clinical effectiveness of iprindole, its status as an antidepressant has been questioned.[19]

PSYCHOTHERAPEUTIC AGENTS IN PEDIATRICS AND GERIATRICS

Before this chapter is closed, a brief discussion of differences in response to and problems with the use of psychotherapeutic agents in the very young patient and in the elderly is considered to be mandatory.

Use in pediatrics

Although the use of psychotherapeutic drugs is widespread in children, few well-controlled studies are available in pediatric psychopharmacology. This appears to stem from a combination of many factors. There is an increased difficulty in differentiating drug-induced changes from maturational changes. Also, children are more suggestible and dependent on their surroundings than are adults, thereby increasing possible placebo reactions. Nevertheless, most of the psychotherapeutic agents used in the adult are employed in children, although not always for the same purpose.

The phenothiazines, possibly because of their relatively long existence, are the most widely used drugs for the treatment of emotional disorders in children, not however, to treat mild or moderate neurotic behavior. In general, the phenothiazines are less potent in children than in adults. Similarly, side effects such as drowsiness, constipation, and skin reaction occur less frequently. With the exception of extrapyramidal dystonic reactions and seizure occurrence, children

can tolerate a larger amount of drug per kilogram of body weight than adults can.

The tricyclic antidepressants have been claimed to be of additional value for children with a large number of disturbances, such as hyperactivity, stammering, behavior problems, or poor learning, but at present only nocturnal enuresis has been established as a condition that is effectively treated by imipramine-like drugs. The most common side effects of imipramine in enuretic children are nervousness, sleep disorders, and mild gastrointestinal disturbances. Furthermore, adverse reactions rarely seen in adults include cardiac arrhythmias and agranulocytosis. Thus although imipramine appears to be effective in the treatment of enuresis in some children, it should be administered with the utmost care.[13]

The use of sedatives for the control of emotional disorders in children seems to be unjustified. Since they have no antipsychotic or antidepressant effect, they have been found to be inferior to placebo therapy.

Use in geriatrics

The use and effectiveness of any drug, and particularly the psychotherapeutic drugs, in geriatric patients is largely limited by their physical state. Also, the degree of variability found among individuals in their response to drugs is much larger in an older population. Changes in the rates of absorption, metabolism, and excretion as a function of pathophysiologic changes are the most obvious factors determining such variability. Generally, adverse effects of a given dose increase, whereas the primary effect remains the same or decreases. In any case the therapeutic index decreases. For this reason lower initial doses of psychotherapeutic drugs should be used in the older patient compared with doses in a young adult. The use of phenothiazines in geriatric psychopharmacology is primarily limited by two sets of side effects. Tardive dyskinesia has a considerably higher incidence in the elderly, and the autonomic side effects are of more problematic consequences. Hypotensive reactions and parasympatholytic effects on the gastrointestinal tract, the genitourinary system, and the eye are more severe than in young adult patients.

For the treatment of depression the use of tricyclic antidepressants in geriatrics has the same limitation as that of the phenothiazines. The toxic effects occur at a relatively lower dosage and with a higher incidence. Some authorities believe that, in the elderly, electroconvulsive therapy is to be preferred. There is uniform agreement that MAOI antidepressant therapy is to be used as a last resort only, since elderly individuals usually have to take other medication more frequently and are susceptible to dietary complications. Thus the potential of adverse drug interactions is greatly increased and does not justify the use of these drugs until all other possibilities have been explored.

In conclusion, use of psychotherapeutic agents in pediatric and geriatric patients should be guided by a more careful approach with anticipation of possible paradoxic reactions on the one hand and increased toxicity and complications on the other.

REFERENCES

1. Kline, N.S.: Use of *Rauwolfia serpentina Benth* in neuropsychiatric conditions, Ann. N.Y. Acad. Sci. **59:**107-132, 1954.
2. Wilkins, R.W.: Clinical usage of *Rauwolfia* alkaloids, including reserpine (Serpasil), Ann. N.Y. Acad. Sci. **59:**36-44, 1954.
3. Molindone: a new antipsychotic drug, The Medical Letter **17:**59-60, 1975.
4. Hordern, A.: Psychopharmacology: some historical considerations. In Joyce, C.R.B., editor: Psychopharmacology, London, 1968, Tavistock Publications.
5. Snyder, S.H., M'Pritchard, D., and Greenberg, D.A.: Neurotransmitter receptor finding in the brain. In Lipton, M.A., DiMascio, A., and Killam, K.F., editors: Psychopharmacology: a generation of progress, New York, 1978, Raven Press.
6. Baldessarini, R.J.: The ''neuroleptic'' antipsychotic drugs. II. Neurologic side-effects, Postgrad. Med. **65:**123-128, 1979.
7. Jus, K., et al.: Studies of the actions of certain pharmacological agents on tardive dyskinesia and on the rabbit syndrome, Int. J. Clin. Pharmacol. **9:**138-145, 1974.
8. Davis, J.M.: Overview: maintenance therapy in psychiatry. I. Schizophrenia, Am. J. Psychiatry **132:**1239-1245, 1975.
9. Janssen, P.A.J.: The pharmacology of haloperidol, Int. J. Neuropsychiatry **3:**S10-S18, 1967.
10. Bunney, W.E., Jr., Murphy, D.L., and Goodwin, F.K.: The ''switch process'' in manic-depressive illness, Arch. Gen. Psychiatry **27:**295-302, 1972.
11. Segal, D.S., Kuczenski, R., and Mandell, A.J.: Theoretical implications of drug-induced adaptive regulation for a biogenic amine hypothesis of affective disorder, Biol. Psychiatry **9:**147-159, 1974.
12. Peroutka, S.J., and Snyder, S.H.: Chronic antidepressant treatment lowers spiroperidol-labeled serotonin receptor binding, Science **210:**88-90, 1980.
13. Sulser, F., Vetulani, J., and Mobley, P.L.: Mode of action of antidepressant drugs, Biochem. Pharmacol. **27:**257-261, 1978.
14. Rehavi, M., et al.: Demonstration of specific high affinity binding sites for ^{3}H-imipramine in human brain, Life Sci. **26:**2273-2279, 1980.
15. Granacher, R.P., and Baldessarini, R.J.: Physostigmine in the acute anticholinergic syndrome associated with antidepressant and antiparkinson drugs, Arch. Gen. Psychiatry **32:**375-380, 1975.
16. Davis, J.M.: Overview: maintenance therapy in psychiatry. II. Affective disorders, Am. J. Psychiatry **133:**1-13, 1976.
17. Brodgen, R.N., et al.: Mianserin: a review of its pharmacological properties and therapeutic efficacy in depressive illness, Drugs **16:**273-301, 1978.
18. Georgotas, A., et al.: A clinical trial of zimelidine in depression, Psychopharm. Comm. **4:**71-77, 1980.
19. Zis, A.P., and Goodwin, F.K.: Novel antidepressants and the biogenic amine hypothesis of depression: the case of iprindole and mianserin, Arch. Gen. Psychiatry **36:**1097-1107, 1979.

Minor tranquilizers and centrally acting muscle relaxants

Drugs described in this chapter have the ability to relieve anxieties (minor tranquilizers) and to diminish skeletal muscle tone and involuntary movement by actions on the CNS (centrally acting muscle relaxants). Since many of the minor tranquilizers exert muscle relaxant actions in themselves, it is convenient to discuss the pharmacology of these two drug classes in a single chapter.

Both groups of drugs constitute a major portion of pharmaceuticals that are consumed by the public. In addition, the minor tranquilizers play an important therapeutic role as premedications for the anxious dental patient. Thus the drugs in this chapter will be discussed in terms of their use by the general public and in the practice of dentistry.

MINOR TRANQUILIZERS

Anxiety constitutes a major psychoneurotic disorder. Although less severe than psychosis, it is believed to have fundamental psychologic causes, but undoubtedly there are organic factors in addition to the functional ones. Anxiety is expressed by means of psychophysiologic mechanisms and thus manifests itself by a diverse group of signs and symptoms. There is a feeling of apprehension, panic, and fear coupled with and positively reinforced by muscular tension, restlessness, choking, palpitation, and excessive sweating and in the chronic form developing into irritability, fatigue, and insomnia.

In the practice of dentistry many forms of anxiety can be observed, ranging from a short episode of anxiety preceding a dental operative procedure to a full-blown neurosis. The symptomatology is usually the same as that just described and differs in severity only.

Antianxiety agents in general are ineffective against psychotic episodes but appear to have a definite antianxiety component. In addition, they usually have a wide spectrum of peripheral effects that contribute to and reinforce their antianxiety action. It must be appreciated that antianxiety agents constitute strictly symptomatic treatment; their use may alleviate the syndrome of anxiety temporarily but not cure the underlying psychopathologic defect. In dentistry these drugs have been employed for their ability to reduce tension and anxiety in the preoperative situation. Furthermore, they have been introduced as sedatives (intravenously) during dental procedures and thus promise to remain an important group of drugs in the hands of the dentist.

The three major chemical groups of antianxiety drugs or minor tranquilizers and their representatives are as follows:

Propanediols (propyl alcohol derivatives)
    Ethinamate (Valmid)*
    Meprobamate (Equanil, Miltown)
    Phenaglycodol (Ultran)
    Tybamate (Solacen)
Benzodiazepine derivatives
    Chlordiazepoxide (Libritabs, Librium)
    Clorazepate dipotassium (Tranxene)
    Diazepam (Valium)
    Flurazepam (Dalmane)
    Oxazepam (Serax)
Diphenylmethanes
    Benactyzine (Deprol)
    Buclizine (Softran)
    Diphenhydramine (Benadryl)†
    Hydroxyzine (Atarax, Vistaril)

Propanediols

Meprobamate and phenaglycodol are discussed as representatives of the propanediols.

---

*Discussed as a nonbarbiturate sedative in Chapter 7.
†Discussed as an antihistamine in Chapter 16.

Meprobamate

Meprobamate (Miltown, Equanil) is the most popular propanediol. It was developed to prolong the central muscle–relaxing action of mephenesin. Its assumed potential to relieve anxiety when used with a sedative component furthered its rapid acceptance. The structural formula of meprobamate is as follows:

$$H_2N-\overset{\overset{\displaystyle O}{\|}}{C}-OCH_2-\overset{\overset{\displaystyle C_3H_7}{|}}{\underset{\underset{\displaystyle CH_3}{|}}{C}}-CH_2O-\overset{\overset{\displaystyle O}{\|}}{C}-NH_2$$

Absorption, metabolism, and excretion. When administered orally, meprobamate is readily absorbed from the gastrointestinal tract and becomes uniformly distributed throughout the body. It is metabolized by oxidation, hydroxylation, and glucuronide conjugation. Excretion of unchanged and metabolized drug is by way of the urine. Prolonged use of meprobamate will cause central tolerance, compulsive use, and physical dependence. The last two characteristics are demonstrated by a withdrawal syndrome after abrupt discontinuation of the drug. Withdrawal resembles that observed after barbiturate withdrawal and consists of convulsions, psychotic behavior, and coma.

Pharmacologic effects. The difficulty is now appreciated of differentiating pharmacologically between meprobamate and the sedative barbiturates. Meprobamate clearly has sedative properties and anticonvulsant action, but with increasing dosage, relief of anxiety appears to be a more prominent effect rather than simple sedation. This relief of anxiety is accompanied by an increased reaction time and definite slowing of learning.

Meprobamate, like its predecessor mephenesin, has muscle-relaxing properties. The origin of this effect (central as opposed to peripheral) has not been established. Undoubtedly, the overall effect is beneficial for the anxious individual, since increased muscle tension always appears to be associated with anxiety.

Adverse reactions and drug interactions. In therapeutic doses meprobamate has a rather limited spectrum of side effects and is a relatively safe drug. However, it has occasionally been associated with the development of aplastic anemia and other hematologic disorders. Allergic reactions of a dermatologic nature have been reported. An unexplained hypotensive effect has been observed primarily in elderly patients.

Acute overdose toxicity from meprobamate is caused by excessive CNS depression and results in loss of consciousness, cardiovascular collapse, respiratory depression, and death. The treatment of choice is similar to that for barbiturate overdose, that is, primarily supportive and symptomatic.

The concomitant use of meprobamate with other CNS depressants must be carried out with caution. Interaction of meprobamate with them is determined by the duration of use of meprobamate, that is, whether central as well as pharmacodynamic tolerance has been induced. In the acute and subacute situation, other sedatives and hypnotics are potentiated by the simultaneous presence of meprobamate. In the chronic, tolerant situation, meprobamate could be expected to exhibit cross-tolerance with most of the nonopiate CNS depressants, including alcohol.

Uses, preparation, and dosages. Meprobamate is widely used for a great variety of anxiety states and as a daytime sedative or nighttime hypnotic. It is used in combination therapy with other muscle-relaxing medication and has been used in dentistry as an antianxiety agent. Meprobamate has been found to be particularly useful in conditioning the dental patient for the acceptance of a new prosthetic appliance.[1] The dosage in this study was 400 mg four times every 24 hours. Other studies have shown that meprobamate was effective in the management of the apprehensive dental patient with a dose schedule of 400 mg given the night before operative procedures.[2,3] A review of the use of meprobamate in dentistry for children is available to the reader.[4] In view of its wider margin of safety or favorable therapeutic index, it has been suggested that the use of meprobamate may be preferable to that of barbiturates in patients who are considered to be suicidal risks. It has also been used to relieve muscle spasm, but the question remaining is whether this effect is primarily attributable to direct muscle relaxation or the sedative effect. Meprobamate has also been used for the control of petit mal epilepsy. It is available in 200 and 400 mg tablets and as a 200 mg/5 ml suspension. The usual adult dose for anxiety is 400 mg every 6 to 8 hours.

Phenaglycodol

The pharmacologic properties and effectiveness of phenaglycodol are similar to those of meprobamate.

There have been few reports of significant adverse side effects and neither physical nor psychologic dependence has been reported. Drowsiness may occur after large doses.

Phenaglycodol is available in 300 mg capsules and 200 mg tablets. The usual adult dose for mild anxiety is 300 mg every 6 to 8 hours.

The benzodiazepines

The benzodiazepines are among the most widely used drugs in medicine. In 1974 over 80 million prescriptions for these minor tranquilizers were filled in United States retail pharmacies, with 59.3 million filled for diazepam (Valium), 19.5 million for chlordiazepoxide (Librium), and the remainder for flurazepam (Dalmane). Even today, diazepam and chlordiazepoxide account for approximately 75% of 100 million prescriptions written for sedatives and tranquilizers. These drugs are also popular for use in hospitalized patients. One study estimated that 30% of all patients hospitalized for medical reasons received diazepam and 32% received flurazepam.[5]

Chemistry. The benzodiazepines are so called because they are derivatives of the 1,4-benzodiazepine nucleus shown in Fig. 9-1. Chlordiazepoxide was the first of the derivatives synthesized by chemist Leo H. Sternbach and his associates at Roche Laboratories in 1955. The structures of chlordiazepoxide and the popular diazepam are shown in Fig. 9-2. Other derivatives that are currently available for use in the United States include oxazepam (Serax), flurazepam (Dalmane), clorazepate dipotassium (Tranxene), lorazepam (Ativan), prazepam (Verstran), and temazepam (Restoril). Chlordiazepoxide was shown in 1957 to elicit sedative, hypnotic, and anticonvulsant activity similar to that of meprobamate in animals. Trials in humans have since confirmed this compound to be a clinically useful antianxiety and anticonvulsant agent.

Because of the success of chlordiazepoxide, thousands of other benzodiazepine derivatives were screened for psychopharmacologic activity, as a result of which diazepam (Valium) was synthesized in 1959 and marketed in 1963. Although having actions similar to those of chlordiazepoxide, it was shown to be a more potent muscle relaxant and anticonvulsant in animals. Oxazepam (Serax) was found to be a pharmacologically active, hydroxylated, and demethylated end product of the metabolism of diazepam and was marketed in 1965. Subsition of a halogen at the ortho position (R_2) in the 5-phenyl ring of

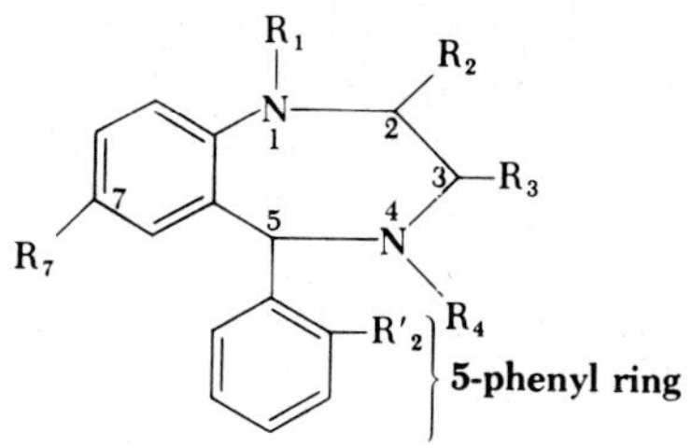

Fig. 9-1. 1,4-Benzodiazepine nucleus.

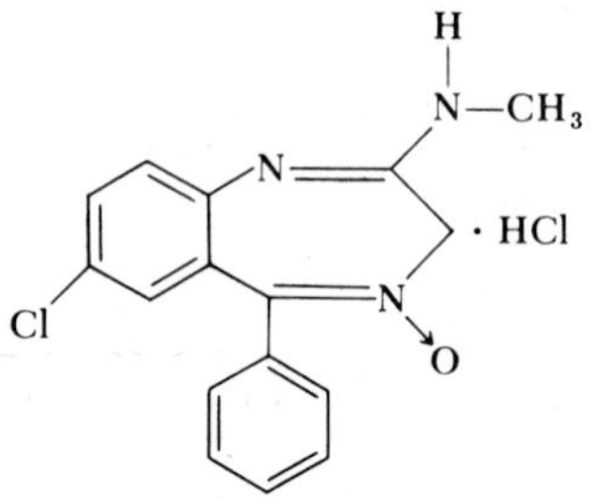

Chlordiazepoxide hydrochloride

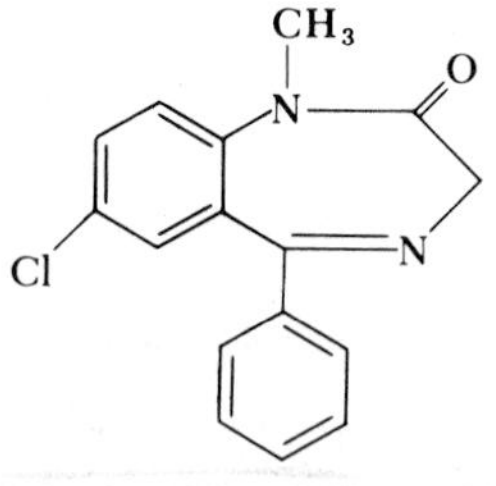

Diazepam

Fig. 9-2. Chemical structures of chlordiazepoxide and diazepam.

the benzodiazepine nucleus (Fig. 9-1) was shown to enhance the activity of these compounds.[6] Flurazepam (Dalmane) is such a derivative. This drug is used as a hypnotic agent and was marketed in 1970. Prazepam differs chemically from diazepam in that it has an N-1 cyclopropylmethyl side chain instead of an N-1 methyl group. Temazepam is the newest member of the benzodiazepines marketed in the United States and chemically is 3-hydroxydiazepam.

Some benzodiazepine derivatives include a nitro ($-NO_2$) group at position R_7. Nitrazepam (Mogadon) is one such derivative that is a useful hypnotic in most other areas of the world. The chlorine substitu-

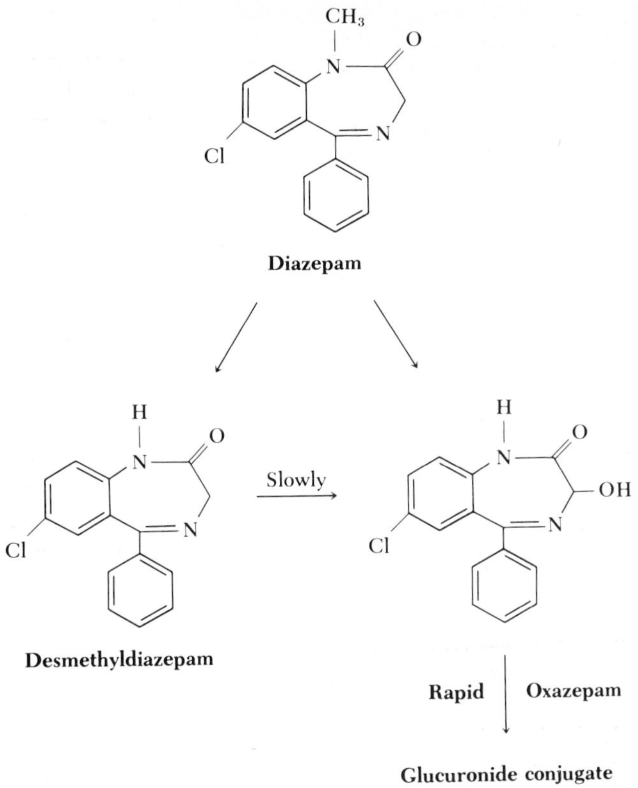

Fig. 9-3. Biotransformation of diazepam.

tion of oxazepam led to the discovery of lorazepam, which was found to be one of the most potent benzodiazepine derivatives available.[7]

Body handling. Chlordiazepoxide is available for clinical use as the water-soluble hydrochloride salt. It is well absorbed after oral administration. Parenterally, it is effective after intravenous administration but is absorbed slowly and erratically after intramuscular administration. The oral or intravenous route should be used to achieve reliable sedative effects. Peak blood concentrations are reached 4 hours after oral administration, and the $t_{\frac{1}{2}}$ varies considerably, that is, between 6 and 30 hours.[8] Biotransformation occurs in the liver, consisting of initial demethylation to form desmethylchlordiazepoxide, oxidative deamination to form demoxepam, and subsequent conjugation with glucuronic acid.[9] Both desmethylchlordiazepoxide and demoxepam are psychopharmacologically active, and repeated doses of chlordiazepoxide produce cumulative clinical effects because of the accumulation of these two metabolites.

Diazepam is water insoluble and relatively lipid soluble and is administered both orally and parenterally. Absorption is rapid and complete after oral administration, with peak blood levels occurring 2 hours after treatment.[10] Intramuscular absorption is slow and erratic and associated with a high incidence of pain.[11,12] Oral or intravenous routes are used to achieve reliable sedative effects. After a single oral or intravenous dose, diazepam rapidly distributes to all tissues, after which biotransformation occurs slowly, and it has a $t_{\frac{1}{2}}$ of 20 to 40 hours. Metabolism occurs in the liver with the formation of two active metabolites. Desmethyldiazepam is initially formed by removal of the N-1 methyl group, whereas the hydroxylation at the number 3 position of diazepam and removal of the N-1 methyl group yield oxazepam. The desmethyldiazepam is subsequently biotransformed extremely slowly, but the oxazepam is rapidly glucuronidated and excreted in the urine as the major urinary metabolite of diazepam (Fig. 9-3). Repeated administration of diazepam leads to accumulation of diazepam and desmethyldiazepam in the blood, and after termination of long-term administration, one or both compounds may be detected in the blood for a week or more.[10]

Oxazepam is available only as an oral preparation, and the completeness of oral absorption has not been determined. The $t_{\frac{1}{2}}$ of the drug is 3 to 21 hours, with no cumulative effects reported.[13] As mentioned earlier, oxazepam is rapidly metabolized to an inactive glucuronide conjugate with no metabolic intermediates identified to date. Flurazepam is available as a water-soluble dihydrochloride salt for oral administration only. It is rapidly metabolized to a psycho-pharmacologically active metabolite by removal of the N-1 side chain. This metabolite undergoes slow biotransformation and has a $t_{\frac{1}{2}}$ of 50 to 100 hours.[14] Since this metabolite can accumulate in the blood, repeated dosage of flurazepam produces cumulative effects as well as residual effects after termination of therapy. Clorazepate may be rapidly hydrolyzed to the N-1 demethylated analog of diazepam, desmethyldiazepam.[5] Desmethyldiazepam is slowly biotransformed, and long-lasting and cumulative effects can be anticipated during treatment with clorazepate. Clorazepate is supplied as an oral preparation of the water-soluble dipotassium and monopotassium salts.

Lorazepam is available as an oral preparation of the water-insoluble compound and as an injectable preparation (intravenous and intramuscular) in polyethylene glycol and propylene glycol. Lorazepam apparently does not yield pharmacologically active metabolites but is rapidly conjugated to the inactive glucuronide derivative. It has a $t_{\frac{1}{2}}$ of 14 to 20 hours after oral administration, resulting in a steady state blood level being reached in 2 to 3 days.[15] Accumulation occurs for a much shorter period than with other benzodiazepines. Prazepam is similar to clorazepate in pharmacokinetic profile since it is converted to desmethyldiazepam, although at a much slower rate. The desmethyldiazepam yielded after an oral dose of prazepam has a $t_{\frac{1}{2}}$ of 30 to 200 hours, and this metabolite accumulates in tissues. Prazepam is available only as an oral preparation.

Temazepam is metabolized to oxazepam in the body and subsequently conjugated to inactive compounds. After oral administration it has a $t_{\frac{1}{2}}$ of 10 hours.[16]

Pharmacologic effects. Pharmacologic effects of the benzodiazepines are mediated through the CNS. The various derivatives have qualitatively similar actions but vary in potency. These agents affect behavior, induce sleep, have anticonvulsant actions, and elicit relaxation of skeletal musculature.

Effects on behavior have been determined mainly through animal studies and may differ greatly from actual effects in humans. Behavioral effects in animals with appropriate doses of these drugs include a suppression of behavior motivated by punishment, a restoration of behavior suppressed by lack of reward, and an alteration of behavior accompanying stress and frustration. These animal effects are thought to be analogous to their clinical antianxiety effects. At high doses in animals the benzodiazepines will produce ataxia and other symptoms of nonspecific CNS depressions, which are considered to be side effects of these agents. These drugs also have the ability to reduce aggression and hostility in animals. In general, clinical effects on behavior by these drugs parallel their effects on animals, that is, anxiety reduction at small doses and drowsiness and other nonspecific CNS depression at larger doses. The physiologic mechanism of behavioral effects probably involves a selective depression of the limbic system activity at doses that do not depress the rest of the brain. More specifically, these agents probably depress electric activity arising from the amygdaloid nuclei within the limbic system.

Benzodiazepines have the ability to induce hypnosis in patients suffering from insomnia caused by anxiety. These drugs are routinely interchanged as tranquilizers or hypnotics.

Benzodiazepines, particularly diazepam, have strong anticonvulsant actions in animals and humans. They prevent or arrest generalized seizure activity produced by electric shock or analeptic agents. Diazepam has been shown to be an effective anticonvulsant for the prevention of local anesthetic–induced seizures.[17] The mechanism for anticonvulsant activity of these tranquilizers has not been established but may be similar to that for phenytoin. When an anatomic seizure focus exists, the benzodiazepines prevent propagation of seizures in surrounding tissue but have little effect on discharges at the focus itself. Diazepam and phenytoin have similar molecular conformation and might interact with similar receptor sites. Diazepam may be the drug of choice for protection against lidocaine-induced convulsions. DeJong and Heavner[17] reported that 0.25 mg/kg diazepam given intramuscularly increased the tolerance to intravenously administered lidocaine by two thirds in nonhuman primates and that 0.1 mg/kg given intravenously completely arrested lidocaine convulsions in these same species.

Chlordiazepoxide and diazepam can produce relaxation of skeletal musculature. Although the mechanism of this effect is unknown, it does occur within the CNS. Animal studies have shown that muscular relaxation by these drugs appears to require an intact spinal cord.[18] There probably is more than one site of action within the CNS, however, since diazepam can depress motor nerve and muscle function in healthy persons[19] and relax spastic musculature in patients with spinal cord transection.[20]

Our understanding of the mechanism of action of benzodiazepines at the molecular level has been radically altered since the discovery of high-affinity, saturable, and stereospecific binding sites for radioactively labeled benzodiazepines at synapses of the mammalian CNS.[21,22,23] Present understanding has advanced to the notion that there are heterogenous populations of benzodiazepine receptors that may mediate the different pharmacologic effects of the benzodiazepines. The presence of such benzodiazepine receptors in the CNS implies that endogenous substances are present that interact with the receptor under physiologic conditions. Several such putative endogenous ligands are under investigation.[24] In the near future one can certainly expect significant advances in the identification of endogenous ligands as well as in the search for pharmacologically more specific benzodiazepines.

Therapeutic doses of benzodiazepines have no adverse effect on the circulation and respiration, and very large doses of diazepam produce only minor degrees of cardiovascular and respiratory depression.[25] Transient episodes of bradycardia, hypotension, or apnea have occurred occasionally after rapid intravenous injection of diazepam. A recent study suggested that intravenously administered diazepam can dilate coronary blood vessels and enhance coronary blood flow.[26]

Use in general medicine. The benzodiazepines are useful in treating anxiety, insomnia, certain seizures, alcohol withdrawal, and some neuromuscular diseases. They also enjoy selected uses in anesthesia and surgery.

Neurotic anxiety is the most common indication for the use of benzodiazepines in general medicine. Anxiety is a major psychoneurotic disorder and describes a psychophysiologic response resembling fear. Manifestations of anxiety have been discussed earlier. The clinical efficacy of the benzodiazepines in treating neurotic anxiety is difficult to demonstrate. Most well-controlled clinical trials have compared the antianxiety effect of the benzodiazepines with those of placebo, barbiturates, and meprobamate. Benzodiazepines were definitely more effective than placebo in most studies and also more effective than barbiturates in that they produced less drowsiness with less frequency. It is questionable, however, whether these agents are superior to meprobamate.

If insomnia is a manifestation of anxiety, sleep will usually improve when chlordiazepoxide or diazepam is administered at bedtime with an antianxiety drug. Flurazepam is specifically indicated as a hypnotic, and 30 mg of the drug improves insomnia as effectively as the barbiturate hypnotics.[5] The benzodiazepines have two distinct advantages over the barbiturates as hypnotic agents. First, true addiction is rare, and second, the danger of serious poisoning after intentional overdosage is less.

Diazepam is effective when given intravenously in the treatment of grand mal, petit mal, and psychomotor and myoclonic seizures when intractable, repetitive seizures require parenteral therapy. The drug is usually administered through a large peripheral vein at 5 to 10 mg/min until seizure activity is controlled or until a total dose of approximately 0.5 mg/kg is reached. Orally administered diazepam is of little value as a prophylactic or maintenance anticonvulsant in the preceding seizure disorders.

Chlordiazepoxide has become a mainstay in the treatment for the alcohol-withdrawal syndrome.[27] Diazepam and oxazepam appear to be equally effective, but oxazepam cannot be given parenterally. In severe manifestations of withdrawal, 50 to 100 mg chlordiazepoxide or 5 to 20 mg diazepam is given orally and repeated hourly until adequate sedation is achieved. In the early stages of withdrawal intravenous therapy is preferable.

Benzodiazepines are used to control muscle spasticity that accompanies cerebral palsy, multiple sclerosis, parkinsonism, and cerebrovascular accidents. Diazepam is specifically utilized for relief of pain and spasm caused by back strain and disk lesions. Studies have suggested that diazepam is superior to other muscle relaxants such as methocarbamol, carisoprodol, and chlormezanone in this regard.[5]

Benzodiazepines enjoy a variety of uses in anesthesia and surgery. As premedicant sedatives admin-

istered before surgical procedures using general anesthesia, diazepam (10 mg orally) and chlordiazepoxide
(100 mg orally) have been shown to be effective.
Diazepam given intravenously at a dose of 10 to 20
mg effectively produces sedation and anterograde amnesia before cardioversion procedures. Similar doses
of diazepam are also used to facilitate gastroscopy,
sigmoidoscopy, and cystoscopy. Finally, parenterally
administered diazepam and chlordiazepoxide are suitable adjuncts to local and systemic analgesics given
during labor.

Lorazepam given intravenously or intramuscularly
at a dose of 2 to 4 mg effectively produces sedation
and relief of preoperative anxiety in surgical patients.
Profound anterograde amnesia lasting up to several
hours has been reported in a majority of patients after
intravenous injection of 4 mg of lorazepam.[28]

Dental use. In dentistry the benzodiazepines, particularly diazepam, have been employed for their
ability to reduce preoperative tension and anxiety.
Also, diazepam is popular as an intravenously administered sedative and amnesiac during dental procedures (Chapter 30). A double-blind trial of orally administered diazepam has shown the drug to be more
effective than placebo in allaying apprehension in
patients undergoing restorative procedures.[29] This
study also concluded that an initial treatment with the
assistance of diazepam will increase the likelihood of
subsequent successful treatment without it. The dose
of diazepam used in this study was one 5 mg tablet on
retiring, one tablet on arising, and one tablet 2 hours
before the dental appointment. Another study reported the use of diazepam in children undergoing
ear, nose, or throat surgery.[30] A dose of 0.2 mg/kg
was orally administered to 101 children 2 to 9 years of
age 2 hours before general anesthesia. The results
showed 47 children asleep after 2 hours, 35 drowsy
or calm, 7 apprehensive, 10 tearful, and 2 noisy. A
combination of diazepam (0.2 to 0.3 mg/lb) and
scopolamine (0.25 mg/lb) has been used successfully
as an oral premedication sedative for children who
fear injections.[31] Chlordiazepoxide was found to be
an effective premedicant for two adult patients who
underwent extensive restorative dental procedures.[32]
During the course of the treatment, 10 mg capsules
were prescribed four times every 24 hours.

Clorazepate dipotassium is a potentially effective
candidate for use as a sedative in dentistry. Two recent studies showed the drug to be superior to diazepam in the management of chronic anxiety. In the first
study a dose of 22.5 to 37.5 mg/24 hr gave excellent

overall responses in 25 out of 32 adult patients,
whereas diazepam produced excellent responses in
only 2 out of 31 patients.[33] In the second study clorazepate produced better effects than diazepam in the
management of anxiety and the feeling of muscular
tension.[34] A third study has confirmed that a long-
term dose of 22.5 to 45 mg/24 hr clorazepate was as
effective in relieving anxiety as a 15 to 30 mg/24 hr
dose of diazepam.[35]

Lorazepam has been shown to be an effective sedative for outpatient third molar surgery when administered intravenously at a dose of 0.05 mg/kg body
weight.[36]

Adverse effects. The most common side effect attributed to benzodiazepines is CNS depression manifested as fatigue, drowsiness, muscle weakness, and
ataxia. This side effect is more likely to occur in
elderly persons and less likely to occur in heavy
cigarette smokers.[37] In patients with liver cirrhosis a
two- to three-fold increase in $t_{\frac{1}{2}}$ of diazepam and
chlordiazepoxide has been observed,[38] implying a
significantly prolonged action of these benzodiazepines in such patients. Diazepam causes local pain in
many patients receiving it intravenously or intramuscularly. Phlebitis also results in a few patients after
intravenous diazepam administration. One study reported an incidence of phlebitis of 3.5% in patients
receiving the drug by the intravenous route.[39] Pain on
injection may be caused by precipitated particles of
drug or by the propylene glycol vehicle. Diazepam
also has been shown to decrease salivary secretions in
humans—a response that can be considered a side
effect. Basal and stimulated salivary secretion was inhibited 30 minutes after the oral administration of 10
mg diazepam and lasted up to 4 hours.[39]

The benzodiazepines can be abused, and they produce physiologic addiction if large doses are taken
over a long period of time. Their abuse and addiction
potential is less, however, than that of the other sedative-hypnotic agents such as barbiturates, glutethimide, methaqualone, and meprobamate. One of the
great advantages of benzodiazepines over the barbiturates is their wide range of "safe" dosage. Overdose
poisoning with these drugs has been rare and appears
to be difficult to achieve. Excessively large doses
have to be ingested to achieve respiratory and central
vasomotor depression.

Like all other antianxiety agents, benzodiazepines
interact in additive fashion with other CNS depressants, notably alcohol, barbiturates, and phenothiazines. As pointed out before, prolonged intake of

large doses of chlordiazepoxide will result in central tolerance. It is of significance that tolerance is observed to the sedative-hypnotic and anticonvulsant properties of the benzodiazepines but not to the anxiolytic (behavioral) actions.[40] There exists cross-tolerance between chlordiazepoxide and other CNS depressants. This is believed to be the underlying mechanism for the fact that chlordiazepoxide can substitute for ethyl alcohol, as indicated by its ability to relieve the symptoms of delirium tremens precipitated by acute alcohol withdrawal. All benzodiazepines can cause withdrawal reactions ranging from rebound insomnia following single nightly doses of some benzodiazepines to psychosis and convulsions. Other withdrawal effects such as tachycardia, sweating, nausea, tremor, and twitching have occurred following several weeks of using high levels of diazepam and chlordiazepoxide. There is general agreement that benzodiazepines should be stopped as early as possible, with tapering after prolonged use. Withdrawal symptoms can be treated either by reinstituting the drug or by substituting a barbiturate.[41]

Preparations and dosage. Chlordiazepoxide hydrochloride (Librium) is supplied as capsules (5, 10, and 25 mg) and tablets (5, 10, and 25 mg). A parenteral solution is also available. The usual oral dose for mild to moderate anxiety is 5 to 10 mg every 6 to 8 hours. Diazepam (Valium) is supplied as 2, 5, and 10 mg tablets and as an injectable preparation. The usual oral dose for the symptomatic relief of tension and anxiety states is 2 to 10 mg, two to four times every 24 hours. Oxazepam (Serax) is supplied as 10, 15, and 30 mg capsules and 15 mg tablets. The usual dose to treat mild to moderate anxiety is 10 to 15 mg three or four times every 24 hours. Flurazepam hydrochloride (Dalmane) is available in 15 and 30 mg capsules. The usual hypnotic dose is 30 mg before retiring.

Clorazepate dipotassium (Tranxene) is supplied as 3.75, 7.5, and 15 mg capsules and as 11.25 mg and 22.5 mg tablets. The usual dose to treat mild to moderate anxiety is 30 mg/24 hr in divided doses. Clorazepate monopotassium (Azene) is supplied as 3.25, 6.5, and 13 mg capsules. The usual dose for the symptomatic relief of anxiety is 26 mg daily in divided doses. Prazepam (Verstran) is supplied as a 10 mg tablet. It is indicated for the control of apprehension with a dose of 20 to 60 mg per day in a single bedtime dose or divided doses. Lorazepam (Ativan) is supplied as 0.5, 1, and 2 mg tablets and as injectable preparations of 2 and 4 mg/ml. A dose of 2 to 6 mg per day in divided doses is suggested to relieve anxiety. Temazepam (Restoril) is supplied as 15 and 30 mg capsules. It is indicated for the relief of insomnia at a dose of 15 or 30 mg at bedtime. Table 9-1 includes all of the benzodiazepines currently available in the United States.

The diphenylmethanes

The commonly used compounds of the diphenylmethane group are hydroxyzine (Atarax), benactyzine (Deprol), buclizine (Softran), and diphenhydramine (Benadryl). These compounds are clearly of minor effectiveness as antianxiety drugs, and their limited use does not justify extensive discussion here. Pharmacologically, these drugs are primarily antispasmodics and antihistamines. Hydroxyzine has had some use in dental practice and is discussed as a representative of the group.

Hydroxyzine (Atarax, Vistaril) has sedative, antihistaminic, antispasmodic, and antiemetic actions. It has been used clinically as a minor tranquilizer and in the management of anxiety-related allergies. It has been used in the treatment or prevention of nausea and vomiting, excluding that of pregnancy. Hydroxyzine has been used to allay anxiety, control nausea and vomiting, and reduce the narcotic requirement in preoperative and postoperative sedation. Since the intravenous route is no longer recommended, hydroxyzine should only be used orally or intramuscularly for preoperative sedation. The effect of therapy with hydroxyzine in controlling the behavior of 76 apprehensive and fearful pedodontic patients has been studied. The administration of 50 mg hydroxyzine 1 hour before the scheduled appointment was found to reduce significantly the behavioral difficulties exhibited by these patients.[42]

The most common side effect of hydroxyzine is drowsiness. Its overall toxicity appears to be low, and blood dyscrasias and adverse effects on the liver have not been reported.

Neither psychologic nor physical dependence has been attributed to hydroxyzine. However, caution should be exerted in prolonged administration to patients believed to be particularly susceptible to drug dependence. Fetal abnormalities have been caused by hydroxyzine in experimental animals, and clinical data are inadequate to establish that the drug is safe for humans during pregnancy. Consequently, its use during pregnancy is contraindicated. Hydroxyzine potentiates the effect of phenothiazines, opiates, barbiturates, and other CNS depressants.

Table 9-1. Benzodiazepines available in the United States

Generic name	Proprietary name	Dosage forms	Therapeutic use	Usual dose
Chlordiazepoxide	Libritabs	5, 10, 25 mg tabs	Anxiety	16-60 mg daily in divided doses
Chlordiazepoxide HCl	Librium capsules	5, 10, 25 mg caps	Anxiety	15-60 mg daily in divided doses
	Librium injectable	100 mg/5 ml	Anxiety; withdrawal symptoms of alcoholism; preoperative anxiety	50-100 mg IV per dose
	A-poxide capsules	5, 10, 25 mg caps	Anxiety	15-60 mg daily in divided doses
	SK-Lygen capsules	5, 10, 25 mg caps	Anxiety	15-60 mg daily in divided doses
Clorazepate dipotassium	Tranxene	3.75, 7.5, 15 mg caps; 11.25, 22.5 mg tabs	Anxiety	30 mg daily in divided doses
Clorazepate monopotassium	Azene	3.25, 6.5, 13 mg caps	Anxiety	26 mg daily in divided doses
Diazepam	Valium tablets	2, 5, 10 mg tabs	Anxiety; skeletal muscle relaxant	4-40 mg daily in divided doses
	Valium injectable	10 mg/2 ml ampul; 50 mg/10 ml vial; 10 mg/2 ml syringe	Anxiety; withdrawal symptoms of alcoholism; preoperative anxiety	2-20 mg I.V. per dose
Lorazepam	Ativan tablets	0.5, 1, 2, mg tabs	Anxiety	2-6 mg daily in divided doses
	Ativan injectable	2, 4 mg/ml vials; 2, 4 mg/ml syringes	Preoperative anxiety	2 mg I.V. or I.M. per dose
Oxazepam	Serax	10, 15, 30 mg caps; 15 mg tab	Anxiety	30-60 mg in daily doses
Prazepam	Verstran	10 mg tab	Anxiety	20-40 mg daily in divided doses
Temazepam	Restoril	15, 30 mg caps	Insomnia caused by anxiety	15-30 mg at bedtime
Flurazepam HCl	Dalmane	15, 30 mg caps	Insomnia caused by anxiety	30 mg at bedtime

Table 9-2. Centrally acting skeletal muscle relaxants

Generic name	Trade name	Oral dose (mg/24 hr)	NAS–NRC evaluation*
Carisoprodol	Rela, Soma	1000-1400	Possibly effective
Chlormezanone	Trancopal	300-400	No rating
Chlorphenesin	Maolate	1600-2400	No rating
Chlorzoxazone	Paraflex	1500-3000	Possibly effective
Mephenesin	Tolserol	3000-12,000	Possibly effective
Metaxalone	Skelaxin	2400-3200	Ineffective
Methocarbamol	Robaxin	4000-9000	Possibly effective
Orphenadrine	Disipal	150-300	Possibly effective

*From National Academy of Sciences–National Research Council: Drug efficacy study, Washington, D.C., 1969, National Academy of Sciences.

Hydroxyzine hydrochloride is available in 10, 25, 50, and 100 mg tablets, in 10 mg/5 ml syrup, and in parenteral solutions. Hydroxyzine pamoate is available in 25, 50, and 100 mg capsules and as a 25 mg/5 ml oral suspension. The usual adult oral dose of hydroxyzine for mild to moderate anxiety must be individualized and may vary from 25 to 100 mg every 6 to 8 hours.

CENTRALLY ACTING MUSCLE RELAXANTS

Drugs classified as centrally acting muscle relaxants exert effects on the CNS to cause skeletal muscle relaxation. A distinction between these agents and the curare-like neuromuscular blocking agents should be made. Neuromuscular blocking agents exert their effects on peripheral neuromuscular junctions, whereas the centrally acting agents depress spinal polysynaptic reflexes in the CNS. This group of drugs does not affect the neuromuscular junctions, the motor cortex, or the reticular formation like other drugs known to alter skeletal muscle function.

The list of indications for these drugs is long and includes skeletal muscle disorders such as muscle spasms, tetanus, sprains, spasms accompanying bursitis, slipped disk, multiple sclerosis, brain tumor, cerebrovascular accidents, and cerebral palsy. A sedative effect is exhibited to some degree by all the central muscle relaxants. Clinical testing indicates that for some of these drugs, sedative effects may predominate over selective muscle relaxant activity. For normal animals these agents can cause a decrease in skeletal muscle tone and in large doses cause transient flaccid paralysis and death from respiratory depression.

The side effects associated with these drugs are drowsiness, dizziness, headache, blurred vision, weakness, and ataxia. Nausea and vomiting are also observed after large oral doses.

Centrally acting muscle relaxants, when administered intravenously, have shown usefulness in treating acute muscle spasms and in producing muscle relaxation for certain orthopedic procedures. Orally administered muscle relaxants do not produce the flaccidity obtainable in humans with intravenous administration, and this is thought not to occur with clinically used oral doses. Thus until definitive studies show otherwise, it is reasonable to ascribe the beneficial effects of some of these drugs to their sedative actions.

A review of these drugs by the National Academy of Sciences–National Research Council (NAS–NRC) led to a rating of ineffective, effective, or possibly effective for each agent in treating skeletal muscle disorders.[43] This classification is adequate until further documentation is made for effectiveness. Table 9-2 provides this information.

Since this review by the NAS–NRC, two additional muscle relaxants have been approved for clinical use in the United States. Dantrolene is hailed for its advantage of having a direct muscle effect without CNS depression and is indicated mainly for muscle spasticity. However, because of its serious potential to cause hepatotoxicity, it enjoys only limited use. Baclofen is an analog of GABA and is extensively used in Europe in the treatment of spasticity caused by multiple sclerosis or other diseases of the spinal cord. It is anticipated that this drug will enjoy similar use in the United States.

In conclusion, some of these drugs are effective in reducing spasticity in neurologic disease or spinal cord injury, but their effectiveness in reducing muscle spasms under other conditions after oral administration is questionable.

REFERENCES

1. Wilson, H.D., and Parker, E.B.: Tranquilizing drugs as an aid to patient acceptance of dental prostheses, Dent. Surv. **34:**171-174, 1958.

2. Lefkowitz, W.: Use of meprobamate before operative procedures: a preliminary report, Ohio Dent. J. **32:**27-30, 1958.

3. Lund, L., and Anholm, J.M.: Clinical observations on the use of meprobamate in dental procedures, Oral Surg. **10:**1281-1286, 1957.

4. Kopel, H.M.: The use of ataraxics in dentistry for children, J. Dent. Child. **26:**14-24, 1959.

5. Greenblatt, D.J., and Shader, R.I.: Drug therapy: benzodiazepines, N. Engl. J. Med. **291:**1011-1015, 1974.

6. Sternback, L.H., et al.: Structure activity relationships of the 1,4-benzodiazepine series. In Burger A., editor: Drugs affecting the central nervous system, vol. 2, New York, 1968, Marcel Dekker, Inc.

7. Gluckman, M.L.: Pharmacology of 7-chloro-5-(o-chlorophenyl)-1,3-dihydro-3-hydroxy-2H-1,4-benzodiazepine-2-one (lorazepam: Wy 4036), Arzneim. Forsch. **21:**1049-1055, 1971.

8. Schwarts, M.A., Postma, E., and Gaut, Z.: Biological half-life of chlordiazepoxide and its metabolite, demoxepam, in man, J. Pharm. Sci. **60:**1500-1503, 1971.

9. Schwarts, M.A., and Postma, E.: Metabolic N-demethylation of chlordiazepoxide, J. Pharm. Sci. **55:**1358-1362, 1966.

10. Kaplan, S.A., Jack, M.L., and Alexander, K.: Pharmacokinetic profile of diazepam in man following single intravenous and oral and chronic oral administrations, J. Pharm. Sci. **62:**1789-1796, 1973.

11. Baird, E.S., and Hailey, D.M.: Plasma levels of diazepam and its major metabolite following intramuscular administration, Br. J. Anaesth. **45:**546-548, 1972.

12. Assaf, R.A.E., Dundee, J.W., and Gamble, J.A.S.: The influence of the route of administration on the clinical action of diazepam, Anaesthesia **30:**152-158, 1975.

13. Knowles, J.A., and Ruelius, H.W.: Absorption and excretion of oxazepam in humans: determination of the drug by gasliquid chromatography with electron capture detection, Arzneim. Forsch. **22:**687-692, 1972.

14. Kaplan, S.A., DeSilva, J.A.F., and Jack, M.L.: Blood level profile in man following chronic oral administration of flurazepam hydrochloride, J. Pharm. Sci. **62:**1932-1935, 1973.

15. Greenblatt, D.J., et al.: Single and multiple-dose kinetics on oral lorazepam in humans: the predictability of accumulation, J. Pharmacokinet. Biopharm. **7:**159-179, 1979.

16. Schwarz, H.J.: Pharmacokinetics and metabolism of temazepam in man and several animal species, Br. J. Clin. Pharmacol. **8:**23s-29s, 1979.

17. deJong, R.H., and Heavner, D.V.M.: Diazepam prevents and aborts lidocaine convulsions in monkeys, Anesthesiology **41:**226-230, 1974.

18. Przybyla, A.C., and Wang, S.C.: Locus of central depressant action of diazepam, J. Pharmacol. Exp. Ther. **163:**439-447, 1968.

19. Hopf, H.C., and Billman, F.: The effect of diazepam on motor nerves and skeletal muscle, Z. Neurol. **204:**255-262, 1973.

20. Cook, J.B., and Nathan, P.W.: On the site of action of diazepam in spasticity in man, J. Neurol. Sci. **5:**33-37, 1967.

21. Squires, R.F., and Braestrup, C.: Benzodiazepine receptors in rat brain, Nature **266:**732-734, 1977.

22. Möhler, H., and Okada, T.: Benzodiazepine receptor: demonstration in the central nervous system, Science **198:**849-851, 1977.

23. Bosmann, H.B., et al.: Diazepam receptor: specific binding of ^{3}H-diazepam and ^{3}H-flunitrazepam to rat brain subfractions, F.E.B.S. Letters **87:**199-203, 1978.

24. Skolnik, P., and Paul, S.M.: The mechanism(s) of action of the benzodiazepines, Medicinal Res. Rev. **1:**3-22, 1981.

25. Rao, S., Sherbaniuk, R.W., and Prasad, K.: Cardiopulmonary effects of diazepam, Clin. Pharmacol. Ther. **14:**182-189, 1973.

26. Ikram, H., Rubin, A.P., and Jewkes, R.F.: Effect of diazepam on myocardial blood flow of patients with and without coronary artery disease, Br. Heart J. **35:**626-630, 1973.

27. Greenblatt, D.J., and Greenblatt, M.: Which drug for alcohol withdrawal? J. Clin. Pharmacol. **12:**429-431, 1972.

28. Greenblatt, D.J., and Shader, R.I.: Prazepam and lorazepam, two new benzodiazepines. N. Engl. J. Med. **299:**1342-44, 1978.

29. Baird, E.S., and Curson, I.: Orally administered diazepam in conservative dentistry: a double blind trial, Br. Dent. J. **128:**25-27, 1970.

30. Boyd, J.D., and Manford, M.L.M.: Premedication in children, Br. J. Anaesth. **45:**501-506, 1973.

31. Root, B., and Loveland, J.P.: Pediatric premedication with diazepam or hydroxyzine: oral versus intramuscular route, Anesth. Analg. **52:**717-723, 1973.

32. Ahlin, J.H., and Steinberg, A.I.: Chlordiazepoxide HCl (Librium) as a premedicant for dental patients: a preliminary report, J. Dent. Med. **24:**39-41, 1969.

33. Feurst, S.I.: Clorazepate dipotassium, diazepam, and placebo in chronic anxiety, Curr. Ther. Res. **15:**449-459, 1973.

34. Norman, B.: Clinical and experimental comparison of diazepam, clorazepate, and placebo, Psychopharmacologia **40:**279-284, 1975.

35. Ricca, J.J.: Clorazepate dipotassium in anxiety: a clinical trial with diazepam and placebo controls, J. Clin. Pharmacol. **12:**286-290, 1972.

36. Barclay, J.K., Hunter, K.M., and Jones, H.: Diazepam and lorazepam compared as sedatives for outpatient third molar surgery, Br. J. Oral Surg. **18:**141-149, 1980.

37. Boston Collaborative Drug Surveillance Program: Clinical depression of the central nervous system due to diazepam and chlordiazepoxide in relation to cigarette smoking and age, N. Engl. J. Med. **288:**277-280, 1973.

38. Sellers, E.M., MacLeod, S.M., and Greenblatt, D.J.: Influence of disulfiram and disease on benzodiazepine disposition, Clin. Pharmacol. Ther. **21:**117, 1977.

39. Steiner, J.E., et al.: Effect of diazepam on human salivary secretion, Digestion **3:**262-268, 1970.

40. Tallman, J., et al.: Receptors for the age of anxiety: pharmacology of the benzodiazepines, Science **207:**274-281, 1980.

41. Medical Letter **22:**75-78, 1980.

42. Lang, L.L.: An elevation of the efficacy of hydroxyzine (Atarax, Vistaril) in controlling the behavior of child patients, J. Dent. Child. **32:**253-258, 1965.

43. National Academy of Sciences–National Research Council: Drug efficacy study, Washington, D.C., 1969, National Academy of Sciences.

CHAPTER 10

Nonnarcotic analgesics

BARBARA REQUA-CLARK
SAM V. HOLROYD

Pain control is of great importance in dental practice. It is often pain that brings the patient to the dentist. Conversely, fear of pain can be the factor that keeps the patient from seeking dental care at the appropriate time. Thus the dentist often works on the inflamed, hypersensitive tissues of a patient who suffers from mental fatigue after long endurance of pain.

Skillful use of drugs for the control of pain is therefore of major importance to the dentist and the patient.

PAIN AND ANALGESIC THERAPY

The sensation of pain is the means by which the body is made aware of the presence of tissue damage. For the person experiencing pain, it represents a protective reflex for self-preservation. Just as the touch of a hot object prompts one to quickly remove the hand, a painful dental abscess brings one to the dental office. For the dentist, pain represents a diagnostic symptom of an underlying pathologic condition. Although the relief of pain is an immediate objective, ultimate resolution can only be achieved by treatment of the underlying cause.

The treatment of pain differs considerably from other types of therapy because there are two components of pain, the perception and the reaction. Although individuals are surprisingly uniform in their perception of pain, they differ greatly in their reaction to it. Predisposition toward a greater reaction to pain has been associated with emotional instability, fatigue, youth, women, fear, and apprehension.[1] As a result, analgesic therapy must be selected for the individual. A level of discomfort that may not require drug treatment in one individual may require extreme therapy in another. Although approximately 15% of patients undergoing routine exodontia require no postoperative medication,[2,3] it is commonly reported that even the strongest analgesics will not completely control postoperative extraction pain in some individuals. For the same reason, the effectiveness of placebo treatment of dental pain cannot be ignored. As much as 80% of the effectiveness of any analgesic drug may be attributed to its placebo effect.[4] Thus to obtain maximal analgesic effectiveness, the practitioner should express confidence in the drug. The confidence that the patient has in the dentist will then be conveyed to the analgesic.

Pharmacologic relief from pain is accomplished by the use of anesthetics, which eliminate all modalities of sensibility, or by analgesics, which eliminate or reduce only pain sensations. The properties of analgesic drugs and their use in dental therapy will be considered here.

GENERAL CHARACTERISTICS

Nonnarcotic analgesics relieve pain without altering consciousness. Although they are ineffective for severe discomfort, most pain of dental origin can be controlled by these drugs. This is particularly important because the nonnarcotic analgesics are safer than narcotics, produce fewer side effects, and are not addicting.

Another difference between nonnarcotic and narcotic analgesics is their site of action. Nonnarcotic analgesics act principally at the peripheral nerve endings, whereas the action of narcotic analgesics is within the CNS. Nonnarcotic analgesics inhibit the synthesis of prostaglandins, which occurs at sites of tissue inflammation, and produce their analgesic and antiinflammatory effects peripherally. Their antipyretic effect is produced centrally.

As a result of the mechanism by which this group of drugs acts, two useful clinical considerations emerge. First, nonnarcotic analgesics are more effective if given before the pain and inflammation associated with prostaglandin synthesis occurs. Second, these analgesics are never completely effective because they do not affect the formation of the primary pain mediators such as bradykinin. Since dental disease is usually accompanied by inflammation, the common use of these drugs in dental therapy is well justified.

Nonnarcotic analgesics have the advantage that long-term use does not produce addiction or tolerance. Furthermore, the toxicity of these agents is lower than that of the narcotic analgesics. In general, however, the older nonnarcotic analgesics are effective only in the treatment of mild to moderate pain. Newer nonsteroidal antiinflammatory agents (NSAIAs) are currently being studied for use in the treatment of more severe pain. These agents may prove useful in the treatment of moderate to severe pain if the research is substantiated. Since it is clear that narcotic and nonnarcotic analgesics act at different sites by different mechanisms, their combination in analgesic therapy may be theoretically warranted.

The principal pharmacologic actions of this drug group include (1) analgesia, (2) antipyresis, and (3) antiinflammatory action. Of these actions the salicylates exhibit all three in therapeutically useful amounts, and the paraaminophenols exhibit only the first two, analgesia and antipyresis.

SALICYLATES

Extracts of willow bark containing the bitter glycoside salicin have been used since antiquity to reduce fever. The recognition and medical use of this natural product for its analgesic properties occurred in 1763.[5] After the isolation and identification of the active component, salicylic acid, acetylsalicylic acid (aspirin) was introduced into medical therapy in 1899. Since that time, numerous agents have been introduced with similar properties, yet none has achieved the widespread general use of aspirin. Salicylates other than aspirin are either too toxic for internal use (salicylic acid and methyl salicylate) or less effective than aspirin (sodium salicylate and salicylamide). A new salicylate, diflunisal, may prove to be the "better aspirin" for which investigators have searched. The chemical structure of aspirin is as follows:

Aspirin

Therapeutically useful salicylates and their importance are described below.

Salicylic acid—parent compound, toxic internally, topical fungicide, keratolytic agent

Sodium salicylate—internal use as an analgesic, less effective than aspirin, may be used in patients allergic to aspirin (asthmatic attack)

Methyl salicylate (oil of wintergreen)—external use as a counterirritant, flavoring in cooking

Salicylamide—internal use as an analgesic, less effective than aspirin, possibly less gastrointestinal irritation

Acetylsalicylic acid—widespread use as an analgesic, antipyretic, and antirheumatic

Diflunisal—an investigational salicylate, possibly better tolerated, effective at lower doses and with less frequent dosing; incidence of gastrointestinal pain and blood loss less than aspirin when given in equianalgesic doses; apparent therapeutic advantage over aspirin and perhaps other antiinflammatory agents; in therapeutic doses, does not affect either bleeding time or platelet adhesiveness

The pharmacologic effects of the salicylates are qualitatively similar. Since aspirin is the most widely employed drug in medical and dental practice, it will be discussed as being representative of the salicylates.

Acetylsalicylic acid (aspirin)
Mechanism of action

A common mechanism by which aspirin and other nonsteroidal antiinflammatory drugs exert their actions has been elucidated. The observations that have led to clarification of the mechanism of action of this group of drugs has resulted from a clearer definition of the role of the prostaglandins in the inflammatory response. Prostaglandins are lipids that are synthesized locally by inflammatory stimuli and exert biologic activity at the site of their production. The precursors for prostaglandin synthesis are the essential fatty acids such as arachidonic acid, which are found in all cell membranes in the phospholipid lecithin. Arachidonic acid is cyclized and oxygenated by the enzyme cyclooxygenase, producing unstable endoperoxides. The inflammatory stimulus activates or releases a phospholipase, which cleaves the essential fatty acid from membrane lecithin, thereby making it available for prostaglandin synthesis by the enzyme cyclooxygenase. Aspirin-like drugs inhibit the enzyme cyclooxygenase by acetylating a serine at its site of action.

Pharmacologic effects

Analgesia. The analgesic action of aspirin-like drugs is explained by synergism between prostaglandins and pain-producing substances such as bradykinin that are produced or released locally by the inflammatory process. In the presence of prostaglandin, which by itself is not a pain-producing substance, a subthreshold concentration of bradykinin becomes painful. Thus the inhibition of prostaglandin synthesis by aspirin-like drugs leads to analgesia by decreasing the sensitivity of pain fibers to the presence of pain-producing substances.

Antipyresis. The antipyretic action of aspirin-like drugs results from inhibition of prostaglandin synthesis in the hypothalamus (Chapter 11). Hypothalamic prostaglandin synthesis is produced by elevated blood levels of an endogenous leukocyte pyrogen, the release of which is stimulated by inflammation (e.g., bacterial endotoxins). Increased hypothalamic prostaglandin levels produce an increased body temperature. Therefore the inhibition of hypothalamic prostaglandin synthesis results in a return to more normal body temperature, even though infection and pyrogens may still be present. Heat is dissipated by augmenting both sweating and blood flow through the skin. Although aspirin-like drugs may reduce an elevated temperature, they have no effect on normal body temperature.

Antiinflammatory effects. The antiinflammatory effects of aspirin-like drugs are also derived from their ability to inhibit prostaglandin synthesis. The prostaglandins are potent vasodilator agents that also increase capillary permeability. Therefore aspirin therapy will lead to decreased redness and swelling of the inflamed area. Patients with rheumatic fever and other kinds of arthritis are often given large doses of aspirin (5 to 8 gm/24 hr) to provide symptomatic relief of joint pain associated with these inflammatory diseases.

It is undoubtedly an oversimplification to attribute all effects of aspirin-like drugs to their ability to inhibit prostaglandin synthesis. As more information is obtained on their biochemical effects, subtle pharmacologic differences that are seen between the various agents will be more accurately defined. However, all drugs considered in this chapter possess variable ability to inhibit prostaglandin synthesis, a property that offers one explanation for their actions.

The antiinflammatory effect of aspirin-like drugs is different from that of the antiinflammatory steroids. The steroids apparently act either to reduce local production of lymphocyte-derived products, the lymphokines, or to decrease release of lysosomal enzymes from polymorphonuclear leukocytes. In general, the antiinflammatory activity of aspirin is weaker than that of the steroids, but it is associated with fewer long-term adverse reactions.

Carbohydrate metabolism. The effect of salicylates on carbohydrate metabolism is complex. Some factors increase and others decrease the blood sugars. Large doses, through release of epinephrine, promote hyperglycemia and glycosuria by depleting glycogen stores. This effect is rarely if ever clinically significant.

Thyroid-stimulating effect. Long-term aspirin consumption will produce an elevated free thyroid hormone level in the blood, apparently by competitive displacement of the thyroid hormones from their plasma protein binding sites. The clinical importance is noted when laboratory testing is done for thyroid function.

Uricosuric effect. Large doses of aspirin (over 5 gm/24 hr) increase uric acid secretion and decrease plasma urate concentrations. Doses between 2 and 3 gm/24 hr usually do not alter the secretion of uric acid. Smaller doses of aspirin (1 to 2 gm/24 hr) may decrease the secretion of uric acid and elevate the plasma urate concentration. These small doses also annul the uricosuric effect of agents such as probenecid that are used to treat gout. Aspirin should therefore not be given to patients who are being treated for gout with uricosuric agents such as probenecid. Patients being treated for gout with allopurinol (Zyloprim), because of its different mechanism of action, may be given aspirin.

Platelet effects. Even at therapeutic doses, aspirin prolongs bleeding time. A dose of as little as 0.3 gm can alter the bleeding time of a normal patient for 4 to 7 days. The mechanism of this action is related to acetylation of platelet cyclooxygenase. It is recommended that aspirin therapy be stopped at least 1 week before extensive surgery so that the patient's platelets may return to normal. The therapeutic use of this effect of aspirin on blood clotting is currently being investigated for prophylaxis of coronary and cerebral thromboses.

Adverse effects

Gastrointestinal effects. Although aspirin is an extremely safe drug, troublesome and sometimes serious and fatal reactions occur. The most frequently observed adverse effect is gastrointestinal upset, which can generally be avoided if aspirin is taken with food or with a full glass of milk or water. The ingestion of a liquid antacid concomitantly can reduce gastric irritation. Gastrointestinal discomfort may be limited to simple dyspepsia (''heartburn''), nausea, and vomiting or may include gastrointestinal bleeding.

The adverse gastrointestinal effects are produced in several ways. In small doses, salicylates exert a local action. They break down the gastric mucosal barrier to back diffusion of hydrogen ion and reduce the protective mucus. They also reduce prostaglandin formation and impair platelet adhesiveness. These actions all contribute to aspirin's effect on the gastrointestinal mucosa, including increased occult blood loss. The slowly dissolving aspirin products produce the greatest effect. In large doses, aspirin can stimulate the chemoreceptor trigger zone, producing nausea and vomiting by a central mechanism. The blood loss produced by aspirin is exacerbated by the ingestion of alcohol.

The administration of aspirin causes a degree of increased gastric bleeding tendency in almost all individuals. Salicylate-induced gastric bleeding is painless and in most cases does not significantly affect the patient's health. However, in patients with upper gastrointestinal tract disease such as ulcers, gastritis, or hiatal hernia, it is wise to avoid aspirin completely. Conditions that predispose to nausea, vomiting, dyspepsia, or gastric ulceration should receive careful consideration before aspirin is prescribed. In the amounts present in most buffered aspirin preparations, the buffering agent does not produce a meaningful decrease in gastric acidity,[6] nor can it be relied on to reduce gastrointestinal upset.[7] Timed-release and enteric-coated aspirin offer no specific benefits and can contribute to erratic absorption.[6,8] The gastric effects of aspirin are reduced considerably when taken with plenty of water.[9] For the majority of patients, aspirin is unlikely to have such injurious gastric effects that it would be contraindicated.

Hypoprothrombinemia. Hypoprothrombinemia can result from doses well below the toxic level, particularly after long-term use. Aspirin is known to prolong the prothrombin time and inhibit platelet function. This is not likely to be clinically important except in patients with hemorrhagic diseases or those with peptic ulcers.

One should anticipate possible prothrombin deficiency in patients who have been receiving long-term aspirin therapy, such as patients with arthritis or rheumatic fever. Aspirin should also be expected to increase bleeding tendencies when taken with anticoagulants. When surgery is anticipated, prothrombin time and coagulation time measurements should be performed on these patients, particularly if petechiae are observed. Since aspirin interferes with the hepatic production of prothrombin by blocking the utilization of vitamin K, an acceptable prothrombin and coagulation time can usually be restored by administering vitamin K. Withholding aspirin should also restore prothrombin levels to normal. Any adjustment of prothrombin levels by the administration of vitamin K should be carried out in collaboration with the patient's physician.

Allergy. An infrequently observed untoward effect of aspirin therapy, but one that is potentially dangerous, is that of allergy. Many individuals, perhaps as many as 2 per 1000,[10] are allergic to salicylates. Allergic reactions to aspirin can be serious, and deaths have occurred. This reaction may be characterized by asthmatic symptoms, urticaria, angioneurotic edema, and anaphylactic shock. Many patients who exhibit allergic reactions to aspirin have a history of allergic disease, especially asthma. Middle-aged women are most frequently affected. Patients who have a history of allergic reactions, especially with asthma and nasal polyps, are likely to exhibit an asthmalike reaction to aspirin. The dentist should therefore use extreme caution in prescribing aspirin for patients with asthma and should ensure that a patient's medical history does not include indication of allergic reaction to salicylates. The dentist should be aware that many multiple-entity analgesic preparations include aspirin or other salicylates.

Toxicity

Signs and symptoms. When the toxic blood level for salicylate is exceeded, either by cumulation or by overdose, a wide variety of signs and symptoms ensue. A mild toxic reaction is termed *salicylism* and is characterized by tinnitus, headache, nausea, vomiting, dizziness, and dimness of vision. Gastrointestinal distress can often accompany salicyclate toxicity, and hemorrhagic phenomena can often be found. In more severe cases of salicylism, psychologic, circulatory, and respiratory changes may occur. The symptoms of salicylism usually disappear when the drug is withdrawn.

If the blood level of salicylate is sufficiently high, the signs and symptoms of salicylism proceed quickly and a serious toxic crisis exists. A concise and excellent description of the sequence of events in serious salicylate poisoning has been presented by Koch-Weser.[11] Briefly, this is the sequence: Hyperventilation causes a loss of blood carbon dioxide with a consequent increase in blood pH. The renal excretion of bicarbonate, sodium, and potassium in an attempt to bring the pH back toward normal (compensatory alkalosis) decreases the buffering capacity of the extracellular fluid. The system is then predisposed to respiratory and metabolic acidosis, which results from (1) depression of the respiratory center (carbon dioxide accumulation); (2) renal impairment from dehydration and hypotension (inorganic and metabolic acids accumulate); and (3) impaired carbohydrate metabolism that increases the production of metabolic acids, which the kidney, depressed by dehydration and hypotension, cannot adequately excrete. Severe acidosis and electrolyte imbalance are usually the causes of death.

These emergency situations generally occur as accidental poisonings in children, suicide attempts in adults, and therapeutically administered overdoses in infants, children, and severely debilitated adults. These reactions usually involve aspirin, but methyl salicylate liquid, which is commonly found in household flavorings, is often the agent causing accidental poisonings in children. Fatalities resulting from the accidental and intentional overdose of analgesics for 1965 and 1967, as reported to the National Center for Health Statistics, are presented in Table 10-1.

It is not realistic to believe that the statistics presented in Table 10-1 are complete or that they reflect fatalities from therapeutically administered overdose. However, they do illustrate the dangerous potential in salicylate poisoning. The lethal adult dose of aspirin is between 10 and 30 gm (30 to 100 of the 5-grain tablets).

The young child is highly susceptible to salicylate poisoning. An important clinical consideration in aspirin use is the fact that children, particularly debilitated children or those under 3 years of age, are highly susceptible to "therapeutic overdose." Craig and co-workers have stated that "in the preschool child more aspirin deaths are caused by faulty therapeutics than by accident."[12] They state that the child who is likely to be given aspirin is also more likely to have a less than desirable fluid intake and may be constipated, both of which conditions encourage the accumulation of salicylate.[12] When aspirin is prescribed for a child, one should ensure that (1) the dosage is accurately determined, (2) adequate fluid intake is maintained, and (3) the parent is cognizant of the dangers of salicyclate poisoning. The latter is of special importance because many parents consider aspirin to be almost completely innocuous. Childproof containers should be encouraged (although aspirin is packaged mainly in childproof containers, easy-open containers are commercially available for arthritic patients who reside in childless homes). The importance of proper education of the child about the dangers of medication and its differentiation from "candy" should be explained to the parent.

Treatment. The treatment of aspirin poisoning begins with inducing emesis or gastric lavage. Acti-

Table 10-1. Poisonings by analgesics in the United States (1965 and 1967)

Drug	Fatalities 1965		Fatalities 1967	
	Accidental	Suicide	Accidental	Suicide
Aspirin and salicylates	175	80	153	87
Morphine and derivatives	69	6	176	6
Other analgesics and soporific drugs	345	608	744	716

Data from Center for Health Statistics: Vital statistics of the United States. Volume 2. Mortality, Washington, D.C., 1965, 1967, U.S. Department of Health, Education and Welfare.

vated charcoal may be administered to adsorb the residual aspirin.

Severe toxic reactions require immediate hospitalization and the use of intravenous fluids to correct acidosis and electrolyte imbalance. Hyperthermia and dehydration are the first concerns. Bathing in tepid water and intravenous fluid administration must be promptly initiated. Alkaline diuresis should be maintained by the administration of sodium bicarbonate. Hypoglycemia and hypokalemia are treated symptomatically by the administration of glucose and potassium as required.

Since the severity of the reaction may be difficult to assess early, one should overestimate rather than underestimate the potential for severity. The responsibility of the dentist is to (1) be aware of the toxic potentiality of salicylates, particularly in regard to young patients, (2) counsel parents whose children are taking salicylates, (3) recognize a toxic reaction to salicylate early, (4) induce emesis, and (5) obtain immediate medical treatment, particularly in regard to instituting intravenous therapy.

Contraindications/cautions

Drug interactions. Table 10-2 lists some of the drug interactions with the salicylates, their mechanisms of action, and their potential clinical outcome. Their potential for clinical significance is rated from +++ (most) to + (least).

Warfarin. The most important drug interaction of the salicylates is that with the orally administered anticoagulants such as warfarin (Coumadin). The salicylates, like aspirin, have the ability to displace other drugs from plasma protein binding sites. Since

Table 10-2. Selected clinically significant drug interactions with salicylates

Drug	Level of significance*	Mechanism	Outcome
Alcohol, ethyl	++	Altered clotting produced by salicylates; gastrointestinal irritation produced by both	Increased gastrointestinal bleeding
Ammonium chloride	++	Acidified urine increases tubular reabsorption of salicyclate	Increased plasma salicylate
Antacids, oral	++	Alkalinized urine reduces tubular reabsorption of salicyclate	Reduced plasma salicyclate
Anticoagulants, oral	+++	Decrease prothrombin levels; may displace anticoagulant from plasma protein binding sites; produce gastrointestinal bleeding; interferes with platelet function	Gastrointestinal bleeding
Antidiabetic agents	++	Display an intrinsic hypoglycemic effect; displace sulfonylureas from plasma protein binding sites; interfere with renal tubular secretion	Enhanced hypoglycemia
Ascorbic acid (vitamin C)	+	Questionably produces acidic urine	Probably none
Corticosteroids	++	Increase glomerular filtration rate; decrease tubular reabsorption	Possible salicylate toxicity; gastrointestinal irritation
Methotrexate (MTX)	+++	Displaces MTX from plasma protein binding sites; blocks renal tubular secretion of MTX	Increased free plasma MTX levels
Probenecid	+++	Inhibits uricosuric activity; may share common binding site	Increased uric acid level
Phenytoin	+	Displaces phenytoin from plasma protein binding sites	Possible potentiation of phenytoin
Sulfinpyrazone	+++	Inhibits uricosuric activity	Increased uric acid level

Modified from Hansten, P.D.: Drug interactions, ed. 4, Philadelphia, 1979, Lea & Febiger.
*+, Least clinical significance; ++, moderate clinical significance; +++, most clinical significance.

warfarin is strongly bound to plasma protein binding sites, when aspirin is administered, it displaces warfarin from the sites. This increases the level of free or unbound (active) warfarin in the blood and amplifies its toxic effect. Blood levels in patients taking dicumarol or warfarin are carefully titrated to obtain a lowered prothrombin level. The prothrombin time in these individuals is approximately twice normal. Small changes in prothrombin time can result in clotting (decreased prothrombin time) or hemorrhage (increased prothrombin time). Administering salicylates to patients taking warfarin can dramatically increase the prothrombin time and promote gastrointestinal bleeding and hemorrhage. Patients receiving anticoagulant therapy should not be given aspirin or aspirin-containing products unless so directed by their physician. Some patients take warfarin and aspirin over a long period of time and then doses of each are carefully titrated. Aspirin itself also induces hypoprothrombinemia, causes a decrease in platelet adhesiveness, and produces gastrointestinal tract irritation and bleeding. These effects on bleeding can be exaggerated by warfarin.

Probenecid and sulfinpyrazone. The uricosuric agents probenecid (Benemid) and sulfinpyrazone (Anturane) are used in the treatment of gout. Aspirin, if given to a patient taking either of these medications, interferes with the excretion of uric acid. Aspirin has been reported to precipitate an acute attack of gout in a susceptible individual taking these medications.

Sulfonylureas. The sulfonylureas such as tolbutamide (Orinase) are occasionally used in the treatment of adult-onset diabetes mellitus. As with the anticoagulant agents, the oral hypoglycemic agents can be displaced from their plasma protein binding sites by the salicylates. Salicylates also interfere with the renal tubular secretion of the sulfonylureas. This drug interaction may enhance the hypoglycemic response to the sulfonylureas.

Methotrexate. The salicylates interact with methotrexate, which is used as a cancer chemotherapy agent or in the treatment of psoriasis. Methotrexate can be displaced by the salicylates from its plasma protein binding sites, leading to an increased concentration of free methotrexate. Salicylates also appear to block the renal excretion of methotrexate. Patients who take methotrexate should avoid aspirin. Administering salicylates to patients receiving methotrexate has produced fatal blood levels of methotrexate.

Pregnancy. There is no evidence that usual therapeutic doses of salicylates produce fetal damage.[13,14] Chronic ingestion of salicylates has produced babies with a low birth weight. There is a definite association between the ingestion of salicylates and perinatal mortality, anemia, prolonged gestation, hemorrhage, and complicated deliveries.[13,14] Prolonged, spontaneous labor and possible incomplete closure of the ductus arteriosis may also occur.

Glucose-6-phosphate dehydrogenase (G-6-PD) deficiency. G-6-PD deficiency is a relatively common inborn error of metabolism. Hemolysis can be produced by the administration of several drugs including aspirin. The incidence of G-6-PD deficiency has been estimated to be 13% in American black males[15] and it is also common in Orientals and persons of Mediterranean origin. Except in large doses, the administration of aspirin to these patients rarely causes hemolysis. Symptoms of hemolysis include abdominal or back pain, anemia, and hemoglobinuria.

• • •

Although aspirin is by no means a dangerous drug, long experience in its use has clearly defined those situations in which a hazard may be associated with its administration. A summary of these conditions appears in Table 10-3. The adverse effects of newer drugs discussed later in this chapter are less well known than those of aspirin. Consequently, one should not conclude from the less detailed consideration of their adverse effects that they are intrinsically safer than aspirin.

Administration, absorption, and metabolism

Aspirin is almost always administered orally. It is rapidly absorbed, partly from the stomach but mainly from the small intestine. A single oral dose produces an appreciable plasma concentration in less than 30 minutes with a peak blood level obtained in about 2 hours. Salicylate $t_{\frac{1}{2}}$ varies depending on the dose. In small doses the $t_{\frac{1}{2}}$ is between 2 and 3 hours. In large doses, because the enzymes that metabolize the drug become saturated, the $t_{\frac{1}{2}}$ is between 15 and 30 hours. The nonionized form of aspirin is the form that is absorbed. Increasing the pH by administering an antacid or buffering agent increases the nonionized form, which should reduce absorption, but it also increases the solubility thereby enhancing absorption. Any difference in the rate of absorption for unbuffered versus buffered aspirin probably has little therapeutic signif-

Table 10-3. Precautions and contraindications for the administration of aspirin

Disease or condition	Drug taken	Reason for precaution or contraindication
Peptic ulcer		Gastric irritant effect
Hemophilia		Gastric bleeding
Gout	Probenecid	Antagonizes uricosuric effect
Myocardial infarct	Warfarin	Displaces drug from protein-binding site, increasing its toxicity
Cancer, psoriasis	Methotrexate	
Asthma		High incidence of hypersensitivity reactions
Hypoprothrombinemia		Inhibition of platelet aggregation
Vitamin K deficiency		
Glucose-6-phosphate dehydrogenase deficiency		Hemolysis
Rheumatic fever		May be taking large quantities already
Pregnancy		Possible alteration of gestation period and labor

From Requa, B.S., and Holroyd, S.V.: Applied pharmacology for the dental hygienist, St. Louis, 1982, The C.V. Mosby Co.

icance since accumulation of the drug at receptor sites limits its therapeutic effect. Absorption of aspirin in the mouth is poor, and any effects obtained by topical administration are the result of that which is swallowed in the saliva. Topical application to the oral mucosa may produce painful ulceration. Although rectal absorption is slower, more incomplete, and more unreliable than that obtained orally, aspirin may be administered rectally in solution or suppositories when emesis precludes retention of oral medication.

Once absorbed, aspirin is rapidly hydrolyzed in the plasma to salicylic acid, which becomes unevenly distributed throughout the body. Relatively high concentrations are found in the lungs, liver, saliva, and kidney; lower levels are attained in muscle and brain. Salicylate crosses the placental barrier and also appears in the milk of lactating mothers.

The metabolic products of salicylate include salicyluric acid (the glysine conjugate), the ether or phenolic glucuronide, and the acyl or ester glucuronide. Small amounts are also metabolized to gentisic and genitsuric acid. These metabolic products formed principally in the liver are excreted by the kidney. Renal excretion, particularly that of free salicylate, is increased by alkalinization of the urine (as by administration of sodium bicarbonate) and by diuresis. Very little salicylate is excreted in the feces.

Uses

Aspirin is used as an analgesic for mild to moderate pain. It also has important uses in the control of fever (antipyretic effect) and in the treatment of rheumatic fever and arthritis (antiinflammatory and anti-rheumatic effects). In the past it has been used in the treatment of gout (uricosuric effect), but more effective agents are now available. The use of aspirin to prevent thromboses is still being investigated.

Dosage and preparations

The adult dosage of aspirin for pain and fever is 600 mg (two 5-grain tablets) every 4 hours. The analgesic-antipyretic dosage for children is 65 mg/kg/24 hr or 10 to 20 mg/kg every 6 hours (maximum 3.6 gm/24 hr) divided into four to six doses. Dosage for children should never exceed 60 mg (1 grain) per year of age five times a day, and administration to infants should never go beyond a few days.

Many types of preparations containing aspirin are available either by prescription or over the counter (Table 10-4). Some of these types are as follows:

1. Regular aspirin. A single-entity form of aspirin includes the commonly used 300 mg (5 grain) tablet and 75 mg (1¼ grain) flavored children's tablet. Many brand and generic products are available.

2. Enteric-coated aspirin (e.g., Ecotrin). Aspirin can be formulated with an enteric coating that dissolves in the intestine rather than the stomach. These products can give erratic absorption and unreliable blood levels. The time between administration and onset of action is too long to be useful in the treatment of the acute pain found in dentistry. Enteric-coated products may find limited use in the treatment of chronic arthritis.

3. Sustained-release aspirin (e.g., Measurin). Some aspirin-containing products are promoted for

Table 10-4. Composition of selected products containing aspirin

Type of aspirin	Selected brand names	Amount of aspirin (mg)	Other ingredients	Approximate amount
Regular	Bayer	325	None	
	Empirin	325		
	St. Joseph	325		
Enteric coated	Ecotrin	325	None	
Sustained release	Measurin	650	None	
Combinations				
Buffered tablets	Bufferin	324	Magnesium carbonate	100 mg
			Aluminum glycinate	50 mg
	Ascriptin	325	Magnesium-aluminum hydroxide	150 mg
Buffered solutions	Alka-Seltzer	325	Sodium bicarbonate	2 gm
			Citric acid	1 gm
Another analgesic	Empirin with codeine	325	Codeine	Various
	Excedrin Tablets	194	Caffeine	65 mg
			Salicylamide	130 mg
			Acetaminophen	100 mg
Sedative/antihistamine and another analgesic (some with caffeine)	Fiorinal*	200	Butalbital	50 mg
			Caffeine	40 mg
			Phenacetin	130 mg
	Equagesic*	250	Meprobamate	150 mg
			Ethoheptazine	75 mg
	Synalgos*	194	Promethazine	6.25 mg
			Phenacetin	162 mg
			Caffeine	30 mg
Caffeine	Anacin	400	Caffeine	32 mg

Modified from Requa, B.S., and Holroyd, S.V.: Applied pharmacology for the dental hygienist, St. Louis, 1982, The C.V. Mosby Co.
*Since several ingredients are combined, these products can be classified under several combinations.

their sustained or prolonged action. They also give erratic absorption and unpredictable blood levels. Regular aspirin tablets given in large doses can produce a long duration of action because of aspirin's variable $t_{\frac{1}{2}}$. Justification of the use of sustained-release aspirin is difficult.

4. Combinations

a. With antacid-buffering agent

(1) Buffered tablets (e.g., Bufferin). It has been claimed that compressed tablets containing a small amount of buffering agent decrease gastrointestinal irritation. The amount of antacid included in these tableted analgesic aspirin combinations is insufficient to affect gastric acidity substantially, and they have not been shown to reduce gastric irritation or acidity.

(2) Buffered solutions (e.g. Alka-Seltzer). Certain preparations contain enough buffering agent to produce a solution of aspirin when dissolved in water. These preparations reduce gastric irritation by adding enough buffering agent and by dissolving the aspirin, producing a solution. One problem with these prod-

ucts is the inclusion of substantial amounts of sodium in the form of sodium bicarbonate. An excess of sodium is contraindicated in patients with heart disease such as congestive heart failure or hypertension.

b. With another analgesic (e.g., Empirin and codeine). Aspirin is often combined with another nonnarcotic analgesic such as acetaminophen or a narcotic analgesic such as codeine. Recent evidence suggests a synergistic nephrotoxicity between aspirin and acetaminophen.[15a,15b] The combination of aspirin with a narcotic analgesic may produce greater analgesic effectiveness than the sum of the two (synergism).[16] However, some authors state that the two are only additive.[17]

c. With sedatives or antihistamines (e.g., Fiorinal or Equagesic). Sedatives or antihistamines can be combined with aspirin or other analgesics for use in certain situations. The effectiveness of this combination is related to the importance of anxiety in the perception of pain (anxiety lowers the pain threshold).

Prescribing a separate sedative agent may be more reliable, since the dose of the analgesic and the sedative can be varied independently. Furthermore, sedation may not be required throughout the entire period in which analgesia is desirable.

d. With caffeine (e.g., Anacin). No rationale currently has been proved for the inclusion of caffeine in analgesic preparations. One assumption may be that the CNS-stimulating effects of caffeine can improve the patient's mood and thereby increase the pain threshold. This belief has never been substantiated by clinical experimentation.

The worth of a particular combination can be determined by noting the ingredients contained in that preparation. Advertising claims for the success of many preparations are often poorly substantiated in clinical trials.

PARA-AMINOPHENOLS

The parent of the para-aminophenol group of drugs is acetanilid, which was introduced into medical practice in 1886 and was rapidly shown to be excessively toxic. Although acetanilid is not a para-aminophenol, it was found that a substantial fraction of it was converted to para-aminophenol derivatives. Subsequently, acetaminophen (paracetamol, N-acetyl para-aminophenol) and phenacetin (acetophenetidin) were introduced into therapy and found to be less toxic than acetanilid. Acetaminophen has become the accepted alternative to aspirin in its analgesic and antipyretic uses. Phenacetin is less favored because of its greater toxicity and is found only in drug mixtures. The chemical structures of these drugs are as follows:

Phenacetin   Acetaminophen

Administration, absorption, and metabolism

The para-aminophenols are rapidly and completely absorbed from the gastrointestinal tract, achieving a peak plasma level in 30 to 60 minutes. After therapeutic doses, acetaminophen is excreted with a $t_{\frac{1}{2}}$ of 1 to 4 hours. At concentrations achieved with acute in-

toxication, acetaminophen may be 20% to 50% bound to plasma proteins. Acetaminophen is metabolized by the liver microsomal enzymes to the glucuronide conjugate (60%), the sulphuric acid conjugate (35%), and cysteine. When large doses are ingested, a metabolite, N-acetyl-p-benzoquinone, is believed to be responsible for producing hepatotoxicity.

In the normal individual, 75% to 80% of phenacetin is metabolized to acetaminophen. Its peak concentration occurs in about 1 hour, and the acetaminophen produced from ingesting phenacetin peaks in 1 to 2 hours. There is a considerable first-pass effect. Phenacetin is converted to many other metabolites including para-phenetidin. Another metabolite and oxiding agent is responsible for the methemoglobinemia and hemolysis associated with phenacetin. Some individuals with a genetic deficiency are limited in their ability to metabolize phenacetin to acetaminophen. These patients convert a greater percentage of phenacetin to toxic metabolites responsible for the methemoglobinemia and hemolysis. Although the plasma levels of the conjugate forms of these drugs increases in the presence of kidney disease, there is little change in the levels of free phenacetin or acetaminophen.

Pharmacologic effects

The analgesic and antipyretic effects of acetaminophen and phenacetin are approximately the same as those of aspirin. However, the antiinflammatory activity of these drugs is less than that of aspirin and does not appear to be clinically significant. For this reason para-aminophenols are not used to treat arthritis. The ability of acetaminophen to inhibit prostaglandin synthesis in the brain is greater than its ability to inhibit prostaglandin synthesis in peripheral tissues.[18]

Therapeutic doses of acetaminophen or phenacetin have no effect on the cardiovascular or respiratory system. In contrast to aspirin, these drugs do not produce gastric bleeding, do not affect platelet adhesiveness,[19] and do not affect uric acid excretion. Acetaminophen enhances water transport in the kidney and has been used with some success in the treatment of diabetes insipidus.[20] Phenacetin given in 2 gm doses has been reported to produce a sedative effect less potent, but more unpleasant than 150 mg pentobarbital.[21] In the same study,[21] a 2 gm dose of acetaminophen could not be differentiated between aspirin or placebo.

Adverse effects

The principal toxic effects of the para-amino-phenols are (1) methemoglobinemia, (2) hemolytic anemia, (3) hepatic necrosis and (4) nephrotoxicity.

Methemoglobinemia. Methemoglobinemia is a condition that results from conversion of the iron in hemoglobin to an oxidized (ferric) state that cannot effectively carry oxygen.[22] The condition may occur spontaneously as a disease or from the effect of certain drugs. Symptoms include a dusky skin color with signs of anemia. Therapeutic doses of phenacetin convert 1% to 3% of the total hemoglobin to methemoglobin, and acetaminophen produces even less methemoglobin. Larger amounts of certain aniline metabolites formed may be responsible for this methemoglobinemia. Levels produced by these drugs are seldom of clinical significance. However, in the presence of preexisting methemoglobinemia, congenital deficiency of the ability to metabolize para-amino-phenols, or the presence of other drugs such as prilocaine (Citanest) that cause methemoglobinemia, the combined effect can be significant. The clinical signs of methemoglobinemia are cyanosis, dyspnea on exertion, and functional anemia. Over 30% of the blood hemoglobin must be converted before these signs appear. Unlike phenacetin, acetaminophen produces little or no methemoglobinemia.

Hemolytic anemia. Hemolytic anemia that occurs with para-aminophenols is most often associated with long-term ingestion. Hemolysis is caused by minor metabolites that oxidize glutathione in the red blood cell and thereby labilize the erythrocyte membrane to oxidative destruction. This shortens the red blood cell life span. *Acute* hemolytic anemia may occur in patients with glucose-6-phosphate dehydrogenase deficiency.[15] A similar reaction can occur in patients who are allergic to the para-aminophenols. In this case antigen-antibody complexes to the drug absorb onto the surface of the erythrocyte and lead to activation of complement and cell destruction. Allergy to aspirin does not confer allergy to the para-aminophenols.[23] Large doses of phenacetin but not acetaminophen have been reported to produce hemolytic anemia.[24] Clinical signs and symptoms of hemolytic anemia are abdominal or lower back pain, jaundice, hemoglobinuria, and anemia.

Hepatic necrosis. Hepatic necrosis may occur in adults after the ingestion of a single dose of 10 to 15 gm acetaminophen[25]; 25 gm or more is potentially fatal. Symptoms during the first 2 days after intoxica-tion are minor. Nausea, vomiting, anorexia, and abdominal pain may occur. Liver injury becomes manifest on the second to third day, with alterations in plasma enzyme levels (elevated transaminase and lactic hydrogenase), elevated bilirubin levels, and prolongation of prothrombin time. Hepatotoxicity may progress to encephalopathy, coma, and death. If the patient recovers, no residual hepatic abnormalities persist.

Treatment. The treatment of overdose toxicity should begin with gastric lavage if a drug has recently been ingested. Activated charcoal and magnesium or sodium sulfate solution may be beneficial. Transfusions may be needed in cases of acute hemolytic anemia.[27] In at least some studies, acetylcysteine, cysteamine,[28] or methionine[29] has reduced or even prevented liver damage if given within 10 hours of the ingestion of an overdose of acetaminophen. Conflicting reports may be based on treatment that began at a later time after ingestion.[30] Since acetylcysteine (Mucomyst) can be administered orally, it is now the drug of choice for treatment of acetaminophen overdose.

Nephrotoxicity. Nephrotoxicity has been associated with long-term consumption. The primary lesion appears to be a papillary necrosis with secondary interstitial nephritis. Although no single agent in the numerous preparations available can be identified as being specifically toxic, it is apparent that prolonged consumption of analgesics can lead to kidney disease.[26,26a] It is important that patients be convinced that daily intake of analgesics for long periods must be avoided. Since the use of analgesics in dental practice is rarely on other than a short-term basis, the possibility of nephrotoxicity does not present a significant problem in dental therapy.

CNS effects. For up to 3 to 4 days after long-term administration of phenacetin is ended, patients have noted restlessness and excitement.

Uses

Phenacetin and acetaminophen are employed as analgesics and antipyretics. Phenacetin is generally used in combination with other drugs such as aspirin and has had its greatest use as the *P* in APC (aspirin, phenacetin, and caffeine). Any advantage in reducing the aspirin content of a preparation by adding phenacetin has not been demonstrated. The use of phenacetin in modern medicine is questionable. It is inferior to aspirin and perhaps to acetaminophen in its analgesic and antipyretic properties, and it causes more methemoglobinemia and hemolytic anemia. Furthermore, phenacetin in combination analgesics contributes additively rather than synergistically so that there is little reason for its occurrence in multiple entity products.

Acetaminophen has gained popularity as an aspirin substitute. It is specifically valuable in patients who are allergic to aspirin or in whom aspirin-induced gastric irritation would present a special problem. Although this point is not well established, there is some indication that acetaminophen causes less alteration in acid-base balance than aspirin and consequently may present a reduced toxic potential in young children. It is not known to what degree the long-term use of acetaminophen might produce the renal lesions that have been attributed to its structural congener phenacetin. It has a greater propensity for producing hepatic necrosis when a large acute dose is ingested.

Dosage and preparations

Acetaminophen is available in many combinations and elixirs (Datril, Tempra, Tylenol). The usual adult dose is one (325, 500 mg) or two tablets or capsules. Not more than 4 gm in 24 hours should be ingested by adults. Various elixirs, drops, and chewable tablets that are convenient for administration to children are available. The concentration of the elixir is 120 mg/5 ml (1 teaspoonful); the drops contain 60 mg/0.6 ml. Acetaminophen should not be administered to young children (less than 3 years old) or for more than 10 days except on a prescriber's advice. The usual dosage for children is given in Table 10-5.

Single oral doses of 1000 mg acetaminophen have been reported to produce superior analgesia when compared with regular doses.[31] However, the potential toxicity of this dosage level has not been adequately investigated to determine if treatment with acetaminophen is sufficiently free of adverse effects to be routinely used at this higher dose.

NONSTEROIDAL ANTIINFLAMMATORY AGENTS (NSAIAs)

A continued search for agents that possess analgesic activity without the undesirable side effects of aspirin has resulted in the synthesis and testing of thousands of compounds. Although many of these tested drugs have been claimed to cause a lower incidence of gastrointestinal irritation than aspirin, none

is devoid of that characteristic. The available NSAIAs (Table 10-6) possess, although to varying degrees, many attributes that are similar to aspirin. They are effective in the same situations that aspirin is. They are all inhibitors of prostaglandin synthesis, platelet aggregation, and prothrombin synthesis. They are all analgesic, antipyretic, and antiinflammatory. All except the pyrazolones (Table 10-6) have the potential for cross-sensitivity with patients who exhibit an asthmalike reaction to aspirin. In general, they produce fetal abnormalities (increased incidence of dystocia) and delayed parturition (near term) and should be avoided during pregnancy or by nursing mothers. They are not addicting, and tolerance to these agents does not develop with repeated administration. No withdrawal syndrome can be induced even when the drug is abruptly withdrawn. Furthermore, as clinical experience with the use of these new drugs is gained, adverse reactions unique to these agents will become apparent. In some cases relatively new analgesics have found greater usefulness and a more rational application against inflammatory diseases such as arthritis than in the treatment of pain. Many of the antiinflammatory analgesics have been used in the treatment of dysmenorrhea.[32-34] Although several of these antiinflammatory analgesics have been clinically tested for use in oral surgery, at the present time their risks, both known and unknown, must be carefully weighed against their benefits to the dental patient.

Phenylpropionic acid derivatives

Three phenylpropionic acid derivatives are currently marketed in the United States: ibuprofen, fenoprofen, and naproxen (Table 10-6). Their mechanism of action appears to be related to inhibition of prostaglandin synthetase. These agents are both pharmacologically and therapeutically similar. Typical of the NSAIAs, they possess analgesic, antipyretic, and antiinflammatory properties. They are indicated for the symptomatic treatment of rheumatoid arthritis and osteoarthritis and mild to moderate pain such as dysmenorrhea, postextraction dental pain, and athletic injuries to the soft tissues.

The most frequent adverse reactions associated with the propionic acid derivatives are gastrointestinal upset and CNS effects such as dizziness, headaches, drowsiness, and tinnitus. The incidence of gastrointestinal problems is less than with equivalent doses of aspirin and indomethacin.

From 4% to 16% of patients taking propionic acid derivatives report epigastric pain. Nausea, vomiting, aphthous ulcerations of the buccal mucosa, burning tongue, dry mouth, diarrhea, and constipation have also been reported. Both hemorrhage and ulcer, either with or without bleeding, have occurred.

CNS effects frequently reported include dizziness, light-headedness, vertigo, and headache. Since they may produce drowsiness, patients should be cautioned about driving. From 3% to 9% of the patients

Table 10-5. Children's dosage of acetaminophen

Age of child (yr)	Amount of dose (mg)	Drops, 60 mg/ 0.6 ml (ml)	Elixir, 120 mg/5 ml (tsp)	Chewable tablets, 80 mg/tab (tabs)
Less than 1	60	0.6	½	—
1-3	60-120	0.6-1.2	½-1	—
3	120	1.2	1	1½
4-5	200	1.8	1½	2½
6-8	240	—	2	3
9-12	350	—	3	4

Table 10-6. Dosage and chemical classification of nonsteroidal antiinflammatory agents

Drug	Dosage (mg)		Safe interaction with warfarin† (Coumadin)
	Analgesic*	Arthritic	
Phenylpropionic acid derivatives			
Ibuprofen (Motrin)	400 q.4h. to q.6h.	300-600 t.i.d. or q.i.d.	No
Fenoprofen (Nalfon)	200 q.4h. to q.6h.	300-600 t.i.d. or q.i.d.	No
Naproxen (Naprosyn)	500 stat.; 250 q.6h. to q.8h.	250-375 b.i.d.	No
Naproxen sodium (Anaprox)	500 stat.; 275 q.6h.	275-550 b.i.d.	No
Ketoprofen‡			
Pyrazolones			
Phenylbutazone (Butazolidin)	—	100 t.i.d.	No
Oxyphenbutazone (Tandearil)	—	100 t.i.d.	No
Indoleacetic acid derivatives			
Indomethacin (Indocin)	—	25-50 t.i.d.	Yes
Sulindac (Clinoril)	—	150 b.i.d.	Yes
Pyrroleacetic acid derivatives			
Tolmetin (Tolectin)	—	400 t.i.d.	Yes
Zomepirac (Zomax)	100 q.4h. to q.6h.	—	Yes
Fenamic acid derivatives			
Meclofenamate (Meclomen)	—	50 to 100 q.i.d.	No
Mefenamic acid (Ponstel)	500 stat.; 250 q.6h.	—	No
Others			
Piroxicam (Feldene)	—	20 as single daily dose	?

*Those with analgesic doses listed are FDA approved for use as analgesics.

†*No,* do not use or use with caution; *Yes,* safe to use; *?,* unknown.

‡Not currently available in United States.

report dermatologic adverse reactions. Pruritus or rash is most frequently reported. Tinnitus is frequently reported. A metallic taste, decreased hearing, and ocular side effects have occurred.

Other adverse reactions include edema, arrhythmias, hematologic reactions, dysuria, myalgia, paresthesias, and alopecia. Hypersensitivity reactions include anaphylaxis, serum sickness, and lymphadenopathy.

The phenylpropionic acid derivatives are rapidly and almost completely absorbed with peak levels occurring in 1 to 2 hours (naproxen, 2 to 4 hours). Food interferes with the absorption of fenoprofen only. Divalent or trivalent cations (Ca^{++}, Al^{+++}) do not affect their absorption. All are highly protein bound, and their metabolites are excreted by the kidney. Naproxen's longer $t_{\frac{1}{2}}$ (13 hours) allows a twice-daily dosing schedule.

These agents have shown to be as effective as aspirin in the treatment of arthritis. Naproxen may be more effective for arthritis than either ibuprofen or fenoprofen.

The phenylpropionic acid derivatives, especially ibuprofen, have been shown to be superior to placebo, aspirin alone, and aspirin and propoxyphene in combination in the management of postoperative dental pain (oral surgery procedures).[35,36] The manufacturer's claim of superiority over codeine requires further substantiation. Administration of these agents prior to dental procedures may delay the onset of postoperative pain after third molar extraction.[37]

Indoleacetic acid derivatives

The indoleacetic acid derivatives currently consist of indomethacin (Indocin) and sulindac (Clinoril) (Table 10-6). Neither is currently approved for simple pain.

Indomethacin

Indomethacin, another NSAIA, possesses analgesic, antipyretic, and antiinflammatory activity approximately equivalent to that of aspirin. Its mechanism of action is probably related to its inhibition of the synthesis of prostaglandins. It has been used in the treatment of rheumatoid arthritis. However, because of the large number of adverse reactions, in some cases as high as 75%, its usage has become limited. Gastrointestinal adverse reactions similar to those caused by aspirin are frequently reported. Adverse CNS effects include headache, tinnitus, vertigo, and

confusion. Some more serious adverse reactions, such as blood dyscrasias have also been noted. At present, because of its toxicity and lack of advantage over other currently available NSAIAs, its use as a general analgesic is not warranted. Since it is a prostaglandin inhibitor, it is used in periodontal experiments when suppression of inflammation is desired. It is currently the first drug of choice to treat an acute gout attack.

Sulindac

Sulindac, a newer indoleacetic acid derivative, has fewer adverse reactions than indomethacin. It is useful in the treatment of rheumatoid arthritis because of its antiinflammatory action. It also has antipyretic and analgesic effects. Although reported with a lower incidence, adverse effects include gastrointestinal distress and bleeding, dizziness, headaches, tinnitis, and edema. Although sulindac would generally be preferred over indomethacin, other NSAIAs should also be considered for the treatment of arthritis.

Pyrroleacetic acid derivatives

These agents are quite similar to the indoleacetic acid derivatives. This group currently consists of tolmetin and zomepirac, the former used for arthritis and the latter solely indicated as an analgesic.

Tolmetin

Tolmetin (Tolectin) is another NSAIA with properties similar to the others in the group. Tolmetin is indicated for treatment of rheumatoid arthritis and osteoarthritis. Its mechanism involves reduction in the plasma levels of prostaglandin by inhibiting prostaglandin synthetase.

As with the other NSAIAs, tolmetin's primary adverse reaction is gastrointestinal. Other less frequent adverse effects related to the CNS include dizziness, tension, nervousness, and headache. Dermatologic manifestations include skin rash and pruritus. Cardiovascular adverse effects include peripheral edema secondary to sodium and water retention. Hematologic manifestations have also been reported. A few case histories of allergic reactions to tolmetin have been recently reported, ranging from urticaria to a true anaphylactic shock.[38-40]

Little is presently known about tolmetin's proper place in the treatment of dental pain because it is a relatively new drug and is presently used primarily in the treatment of rheumatoid arthritis and osteoarthritis. As tolmetin's usage increases and as more comparisons are done with other better known analgesics, its place in dental situations will become clear. Tolmetin can be used without difficulty by patients receiving warfarin anticoagulant therapy.

Zomepirac

Zomepirac (Zomax) is a relatively new, orally effective NSAIA. It is chemically related to tolmetin (Tolectin), (Table 10-6). Like the other NSAIAs, zomepirac exerts its effect by inhibiting prostaglandin synthetase, thereby preventing peripheral pain receptor stimulation by the prostaglandins.

As an analgesic, 100 mg of zomepirac was found to be more effective than placebo, 650 mg of aspirin, 2 tablets of APC, or 60 mg of codeine; 100 mg of zomepirac was also found to be equivalent to 60 mg of APC-codeine or to an oxycodone-APC combination.[41] Zomepirac's analgesic efficacy relative to morphine has yet to be firmly established. In oral doses of 100 to 200 mg, it may approximate 8 to 16 mg morphine given intramuscularly. Studies show, however, that zomepirac is more potent than most commonly used narcotic and nonnarcotic analgesic combinations for treating dental pain.[45-46]

The primary adverse reactions associated with zomepirac are gastrointestinal, such as nausea, dyspepsia, abdominal pain, gastrointestinal distress, constipation, diarrhea, and vomiting. CNS effects with a greater than 1% incidence include drowsiness, dizziness, and insomnia. Since the incidence of sedation with zomepirac is comparable to that with codeine,[47,48] patients should be warned about operating an automobile. In long-term studies, the incidence of lower urinary tract symptoms is greater with zomepirac than with aspirin.[49,50] Zomepirac in therapeutic doses prolongs bleeding time by reducing platelet adhesiveness.[51] This effect is reversed within 1 to 2 days after the drug is discontinued. This drug is contraindicated in patients who exhibit an asthmalike reaction to aspirin.

Although zomepirac is highly protein bound (98.5%), it does not interfere with the protein binding of warfarin (Coumadin). This makes zomepirac a useful analgesic for patients taking oral anticoagulant therapy.[52]

After oral administration, peak plasma concentrations are reached in about 1 hour. Its $t_{\frac{1}{2}}$ is about 4 hours. Some analgesia is obtained within ½ hour with maximal analgesia at 2 hours. Food, but not antacids, reduces the absorption of zomepirac. It is highly protein bound and is excreted by the kidney.

Its use in dentistry is for procedures in which mild to severe pain may be exhibited. For adults with mild pain, 50 mg every 4 to 6 hours is administered. For adults with moderate to severe pain, 100 mg every 4 to 6 hours produces its maximal analgesic effect. Its proper place as a dental analgesic will await the elucidation of less common serious adverse reactions such as blood dyscrasias or renal problems.

Fenamic acid derivatives

Currently the fenamic acid derivatives consist of mefenamic acid (Ponstel) and meclofenamate (Meclomen). Mefenamic acid is indicated for the treatment of pain and dysmenorrhea, and meclofenemate is used for rheumatoid arthritis and osteoarthritis.

Mefenamic acid

Mefenamic acid (Ponstel), like aspirin, is analgesic, antipyretic, and antiinflammatory. It is a potent inhibitor of prostaglandin synthesis. Its most common adverse reaction is gastrointestinal, including diarrhea and nausea. Sedation can occur, and patients should be cautioned against driving. Sometimes serious adverse reactions including autoimmune hemolytic anemia have been noted with long-term administration. It is indicated for moderate pain of less than 1 week duration or for dysmenorrhea. Since mefenamic acid is not superior to other better-known analgesics and has a potential for serious toxicity, it is difficult to justify its use in dental practice.

Meclofenamate

This fenamic acid derivative is indicated for the treatment of arthritis. Its effectiveness is approximately equivalent to aspirin with less tinnitis but more diarrhea. Its main adverse reaction is gastrointestinal including diarrhea, nausea, and vomiting. Edema, rash, headache, dizziness, and tinnitus have been reported. For acute pain and dysmenorrhea the initial dose is 500 mg, followed by 250 mg every 6 hours as needed (Table 10-6).

Pyrazolones

Two pyrazolones, phenylbutazone (Butazolidin) and oxyphenbutazone (Tandearil), possess antiinflammatory action and are used in the treatment of certain arthritic and inflammatory conditions. They have also been employed in the treatment of acute attacks of gout. Many adverse reactions have been reported with these agents, especially with prolonged use, including gastrointestinal distress, ulcerative stomatitis, xerostomia, and salivary gland enlargement.

Two adverse effects, agranulocytosis and aplastic anemia, although rare, are serious and have in rare cases proved fatal. These agents can cause patients with cardiac disease to retain fluids. A complete physical and laboratory test are required before therapy with these agents is begun. Because of their toxicity, these agents are recommended for use only when other agents are ineffective or for short-term use in acute conditions. They should not be used in dental practice.

SUMMARY

The drug of choice for mild to moderate pain is aspirin. Special caution must be exercised in regard to overdosage in children and in patients allergic to aspirin or susceptible to gastrointestinal distress. In cases in which aspirin is contraindicated or undesirable, acetaminophen is usually a good substitute. If aspirin or acetaminophen is inadequate for the relief of pain, the NSAIAs may be used. Their gastrointestinal and CNS effects must be considered. If more severe pain is encountered, the narcotic analgesic agents may be indicated (Chapter 12).

REFERENCES

1. Monheim, L.M.: Local anesthesia and pain control in dental practice, ed. 4, St. Louis, 1969, The C.V. Mosby Co.
2. Chilton, N.W., Lewandowski, A., and Cameroy, J.R.: Double-blind evaluation of a new analgesic agent in postextraction pain, Am. J. Med. Sci. **342**:704, 1961.
3. Popkes, D.L., and Folsom, T.C.: Comparative study of three analgesic agents used in oral surgical procedures, J. Oral Surg. **27**:950-954, 1969.
4. Wagner, W.A., and Hubbell, A.O.: Pain control with a mixture containing dextropropoxyphene hydrochloride, a mixture containing codeine phosphate and a placebo, J. Oral Surg. **17**:14, 1959.
5. Cutting, W.C.: Handbook of pharmacology, ed. 5, New York, 1972, Appleton-Century-Crofts.
6. Is all aspirin alike? Med. Lett. Drugs Ther. **16**:57-59, 1974.
7. DeKornfeld, T.J., Lasagna, L., and Frazier, T.M.: A comparative study of 5 proprietary analgesic compounds, J.A.M.A. **182**:1315, 1962.
8. Gastrointestinal disturbances with aspirin, Med. Lett. Drugs Ther. **7**:76, 1965.
9. Acetaminophen, Valadol, and analgesic renal injury, Med. Lett. Drugs Ther. **13**:74-76, 1971.
10. DiPalma, J.R., editor: Basic pharmacology in medicine, New York, 1976, McGraw-Hill Book Co.
11. Koch-Weser, J.: Harrison's principles of internal medicine, ed. 6, New York, 1970, McGraw-Hill Book Co.
12. Craig, J.O., Ferguson, I.C., and Syme, J.: Infants, toddlers, and aspirin, Br. Med. J. **5490**:757-761, 1966.
13. Collins, E., and Turner, G.: Maternal effects of regular salicylate ingestion in pregnancy, Lancet **2**:335-338, 1975.
14. Turner, G., and Collins, E.: Fetal effects of regular salicylate ingestion in pregnancy, Lancet **2**:338-339, 1975.
15. Glucose-6-phosphate dehydrogenase deficiency, Med. Lett. Drugs Ther. **17**:3-4, 1975.
15a. Goldberg, M.: Analgesic nephropathy in 1981: which drug is to blame? (editorial), JAMA **247**:64, 1982.
15b. Emkey, R.D., and Mills, J.A.: Aspirin and analgesic nephropathy, JAMA **247**:55, 1982.
16. Goodman, L.S., and Gilman, A.: The pharmacological basis of therapeutics, ed. 6, New York, 1980, Macmillan, Inc.
17. Neidle, E.A., Kroeger, D.C., and Yagiela, J.A.: Pharmacology and therapeutics for dentistry, St. Louis, 1980, The C.V. Mosby Co.
18. Ferreira, S.H., and Vane, J.R.: New aspects of the mode of action of nonsteroid anti-inflammatory drugs, Ann. Rev. Pharmacol. **14**:57-73, 1974.
19. Mielke, C.H., Jr., and Britten, A.F.H.: Use of aspirin or acetaminophen in hemophilia, N. Engl. J. Med. **282**:1270, 1970.
20. Nusynowitz, M.L., and Forsham, P.H.: The antidiuretic action of acetaminophen, Am. J. Med. Sci. **252**:429-435, 1966.
21. Eade, N.R., and Lasagna, L.: A comparison of acetophenetidin and acetaminophen. II. Subjective effects in healthy volunteers, J. Pharmacol. Exp. Ther. **155**:301-308, 1967.
22. Bodansky, O.: Methemoglobinemia and methemoglobin-producing compounds, Pharmacol. Rev. **3**:144-196, 1951.
23. Fein, B.T.: Aspirin shock associated with asthma and nasal polyps, Ann. Allergy **29**:598-601, 1971.
24. Hutchison, H.E., Jackson, J.M., and Cassidy, P.: Phenacetin-induced hemolytic anemia, Lancet **2**:1022, 1962.
25. Boyer, T.D., and Rouff, S.L.: Acetaminophen-induced hepatic necrosis and renal failure, J.A.M.A. **218**:440-441, 1971.
26. Phenacetin, Med. Lett. Drugs Ther. **6**:79, 1964.
27. Peterson, R.G., and Rumack, B.H.: Treating acute acetaminophen poisoning with acetylcysteine, J.A.M.A. **237**:2406, 1977.
28. Prescott, L.F., et al.: Cysteamine, methionine, and penicillamine in the treatment of paracetamol poisoning, Lancet **2**:109, 1976.
29. Crome, P., et al.: Oral methionine in the treatment of severe paracetamol (acetaminophen) overdose, Lancet **2**:829, 1976.
30. Douglas, A.P., Hamlyn, A.N., and James, O.: Controlled trial of cysteamine in the treatment of acute paracetamol (acetaminophen) poisoning, Lancet **1**:111, 1976.
31. Hopkinson, J.H., et al.: Acetaminophen (500 mg) versus acetaminophen (325 mg) for the relief of pain in episiotomy patients, Curr. Ther. Res. **16**:194-200, 1974.
32. Budoff, P.W.: Use of mefenamic acid in the treatment of primary dysmenorrhea, J.A.M.A. **241**:2713, 1979.
33. Henzl, M.R., et al.: The treatment of dysmenorrhea with naproxen sodium: a report on two independent double-blind trials, Am. J. Obstet. Gynecol. **127**:818, 1977.
34. Morrison, J.C., and Jennings, J.C.: Primary dysmenorrhea treated with indomethacin, South. Med. J. **22**:425, 1979.
35. Winter, L., et al.: Analgesic activity of ibuprofen (Motrin)

in postoperative oral surgical pain, Oral Surg. **45:**159, 1978.

36. Cooper, S.A., Needle, S., and Kruger, G.O.: Comparative analgesic potency of aspirin and ibuprofen, J. Oral Surg. **35:** 898, 1977.

37. Dionne, R.A., and Cooper, S.A.: Evaluation of preoperative ibuprofen for postoperative pain after removal of third molars, Oral Surg. **45:**851, 1978.

38. Acute allergic reaction to a nonsteroidal antiinflammatory agent, D.D.S. News **2**(7):26, 1981.

39. Restivo, C., and Paulus, H.E.: Anaphylaxis from tolmetin, J.A.M.A. **240:**246, 1978.

40. McCall, C.Y., and Cooper, J.W.: Tolmetin anaphylactoid reaction, J.A.M.A. **243:**1263, 1980.

41. Cooper, S.A.: Efficacy of zomepirac in oral surgical pain, J. Clin Pharmacol. **20**(4)(Pt. 2):230-242, 1980.

42. Forrest, W.H., Jr.: Orally administered zomepirac and parenterally administered morphine: comparison for the treatment of postoperative pain, J.A.M.A. **244:**2298-2302, 1980.

43. Wallenstein, S.L., et al.: Relative analgesic potency of oral zomepirac and intramuscular morphine in cancer patients with postoperative pain, J. Clin. Pharmacol. **20**(4)(Pt. 2):250-258, 1980.

44. Forrest, W.H.: Oral zomepirac and intramuscular morphine in postoperative pain, J. Clin. Pharmacol. **20**(4)(Pt. 2):259-260, 1980.

45. Cooper, S.A., and Sullivan, D.: Relative efficacy of zomepirac sodium compared with an APC/codeine combination (abstract), Clin. Pharmacol. Ther. **23**(1):111, 1978.

46. Stambaugh, J.E., and Sarajian, C.: Relative analgesic efficacy of zomepirac sodium as compared to oxycodone/APC combination in the treatment of cancer pain, Clin. Res. **26:**594a, 1978.

47. Mehlisch, D.R., et al.: Clinical comparison of Zomepirac with APC/codeine combination in the treatment of pain following oral surgery, J. Clin. Pharmacol. **20**(4)(Pt 2):271-278, 1980.

48. Mayer, T.G., and Ruoff, G.E.: Clinical evaluation of zomepirac in the treatment of acute orthopedic pain, J. Clin. Pharmacol. **20:**285, 1980.

49. Ruoff, G.E., Andelman, S.Y., and Cannella, J.J.: Long-term safety of zomepirac: a double-blind comparison with aspirin in patients with osteoarthritis, J. Clin. Pharmacol. **20:**377-384, 1980.

50. Honig, S.: Preliminary report: long-term safety of zomepirac, J. Clin. Pharmacol. **20:**392-396, 1980.

51. Zomepirac sodium: a new oral analgesic, Med. Lett. Drugs Ther. **23**(1):1-3, 1981.

52. Minn, F.L., and Zinny, M.: Zomepirac and warfarin: A clinical study to determine if interaction exists, J. Clin. Pharmacol. **20:**418-421, 1980.

Prostaglandins, thromboxanes, and prostacyclin

Prostaglandins and the broad spectrum of their biologic and pathologic activities were unknown until relatively recently. In 1930 Kurzrok and Lieb[1] observed that strips of human uterus could be made to relax or contract in the presence of human semen. Later in the 1930s both Goldblatt[2] and von Euler[3] found that seminal fluid contained vasodepressor and muscle-contracting activity. The active component of seminal fluid was subsequently identified as a lipidic substance. Von Euler termed this substance prostaglandin.

However, it was not until the 1960s when Bergström and Samuelsson[4] isolated and crystallized prostaglandin E_1 (PGE_1) and prostaglandin $F_{1\alpha}$ ($PGF_{1\alpha}$) that the structure of these compounds was shown to be comprised of a 20-carbon unsaturated carboxylic acid that contained a cyclopentane ring. It was not long before the structural similarity between prostaglandins and naturally occurring long-chain unsaturated fatty acids was recognized, and in 1964 independent studies by Bergström[5] and Van Dorp[6] showed the conversion of the 20-carbon unsaturated fatty acid, arachidonic acid, to prostaglandin E_2.

Since that time the structures of a large number of other prostaglandins isolated from virtually every body tissue have been determined; all have been shown to have a structure similar to that of PGE_1 and $PGF_{1\alpha}$, and all are derived from 20-carbon polyunsaturated essential and nonessential fatty acids. Not only are there a large number of structurally related prostaglandins, they have also been implicated to have a broad spectrum of biologic and pathologic roles in animals and humans. The proposed roles and functions of prostaglandins will be discussed later.

Recently two other classes of biologically active compounds have been discovered that like many of the prostaglandins are derived from arachidonic acid and possess a certain structural similarity to the prostaglandins. One of these classes consists of two compounds that have been collectively designated as the thromboxanes: thromboxane A_2 (TXA_2) and its degradation product, thromboxane B_2 (TXB_2),[7] whereas the other class consists of a single compound called prostacyclin (PGI_2).[8] Like the prostaglandins, the thromboxanes and prostacyclin have been implicated as being important in a large number of biologic processes.

In the last few years dozens of review articles and literally hundreds of scientific journal articles have been written concerning these three classes of compounds. Consequently, an in-depth treatment of this subject is well beyond the scope of a single chapter in this text. The purpose of this chapter, then, is to give an overview of the importance and diversity of the biologic and pathologic roles played by these three important classes of compounds, with emphasis on the prostaglandins.

SOURCE, STRUCTURE, AND NOMENCLATURE

The structures of all the prostaglandins that have been determined since their discovery in the early 1930s have two aspects in common:[7-12] (1) their basic structure is of the hypothetical 20-carbon parent compound, prostanoic acid, which is a 20-carbon unsaturated carboxylic acid containing a cyclopentane ring, and (2) they all are derived from 20-carbon essential or nonessential unsaturated fatty acids. It appears that in humans, the prostaglandins derived from arachidonic acid are the most abundant and perhaps the most important; consequently this discussion of prostaglandins will be for the most part restricted to those derived from this 20-carbon unsaturated fatty acid. The structures of arachidonic acid and prostanoic acid are shown below, and the major structural difference between them, in addition to the degree of unsaturation, is the occurrence of a cyclopentane ring in prostanoic acid that includes C_8, C_9, C_{10}, C_{11}, and C_{12}.

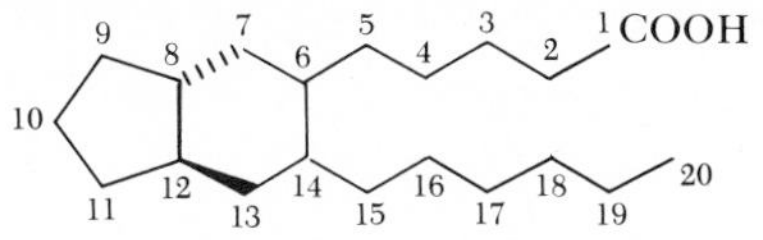

Prostanoic acid

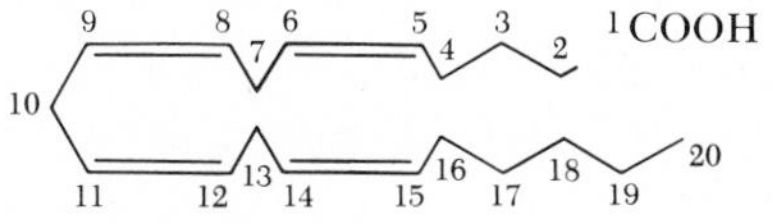

Arachidonic acid

All prostaglandins are designated in the nomenclature format PGX_n in which (1) *PG* stands for prostaglandin, (2) *X* designates a specific class of prostaglandins dependent on the types of functional groups on the cyclopentane ring of the parent compound, prostanoic acid, and (3) *n* refers to the number of double bonds found in the respective prostaglandin. For example, a prostaglandin of the E type with two double bonds would be designated as PGE_2, whereas prostaglandin of the E type with only a single double bond would be designated as PGE_1.

Fig. 11-1 shows the cyclopentane ring structure of important classes of prostaglandins derived from unsaturated fatty acids. These prostaglandins are divided into six separate groups designated A, B, C, D, E, and F. The structural differences among these groups of prostaglandins is dependent on which type of substitutions are on C_9 and C_{11} of the cyclopentane ring (Table 11-1). For example, prostaglandins of the D group have a carbonyl group on C_{11}, whereas prostaglandins of the E group have a hydroxyl group on C_{11}. All prostaglandins derived from arachidonic acid have two double bonds and hence are designated as PGA_2, PGB_2 . . . PGF_2, whereas those prostaglandins derived from other 20-carbon unsaturated fatty acids would have either one or three double bonds and would be designated as PGA_1, PGB_1 . . . PGF_1 or PGA_3, PGB_3 . . . PGF_3, respectively. Again, the prostaglandins containing two double bonds that are derived from arachidonic acid are probably the most abundant and important in humans, and the PGEs and PGFs, particularly PGE_2 and $PGF_{2\alpha}$, are

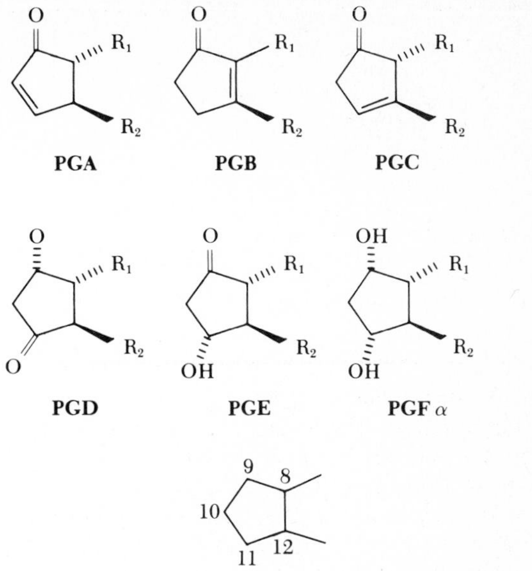

Fig. 11-1. Cyclopentane ring structures of the primary prostaglandins. ııı, Groups that lie behind the plane of the ring; ◄, groups that lie in front of the plane of the ring; —, groups that lie in plane of the ring.

Table 11-1. Substitutions on C_9 and C_{11}

	Substitutions	
Prostaglandin	C_9	C_{11}
PGA	=O	H
PGB	=O	2H
PGC	=O	H
PGD	H, OH	=O
PGE	=O	H, OH
PGF_α	H, OH	H, OH

probably the most important prostaglandins.[9-14] The structures of the PGEs and PGF_αs are shown in Fig. 11-2.

There are several important aspects that pertain to the relationship among prostaglandins, thromboxanes, and prostacyclin. Although 20-carbon unsaturated fatty acids other than arachidonate can serve as precursors of prostaglandin biosynthesis, only arachidonic acid can serve as a precursor for the production of thromboxanes and prostacyclin.[12,14] In addition, intermediates of arachidonic acid catabolism that are precursors for prostaglandin synthesis can alternatively be precursors for the synthesis of both thrombox-

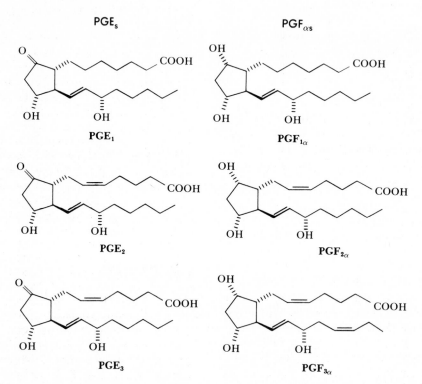

Fig. 11-2. Structures of the PGE and PGF$_\alpha$ prostaglandins. ⅠⅠⅠⅠ, Groups that lie behind the plane of the cyclopentane ring; ◄, groups that lie in front of the plane of the ring; —, groups that lie in the plane of the ring.

anes and prostacyclin.[12,14] These relationships will be discussed later in much greater detail. The structures of the two thromboxanes, TXA$_2$ and TXB$_2$, are shown below, as is the structure of PGI$_2$.

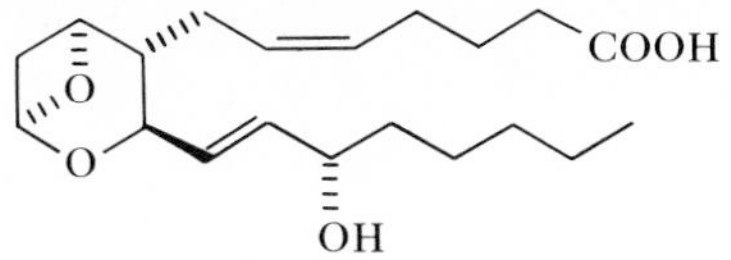

Thromboxane A$_2$ (TXA$_2$)

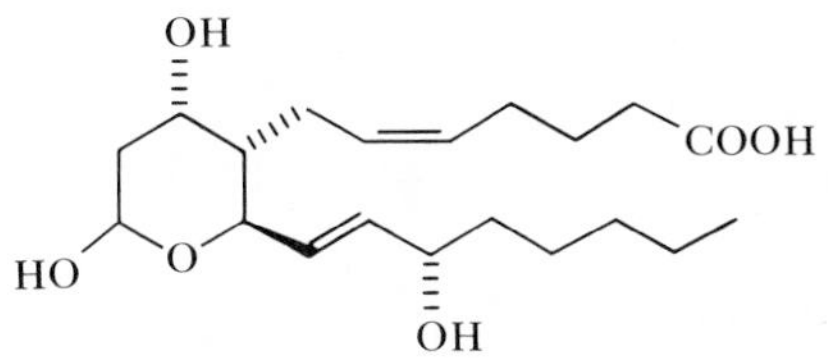

Thromboxane B$_2$ (TXB$_2$)

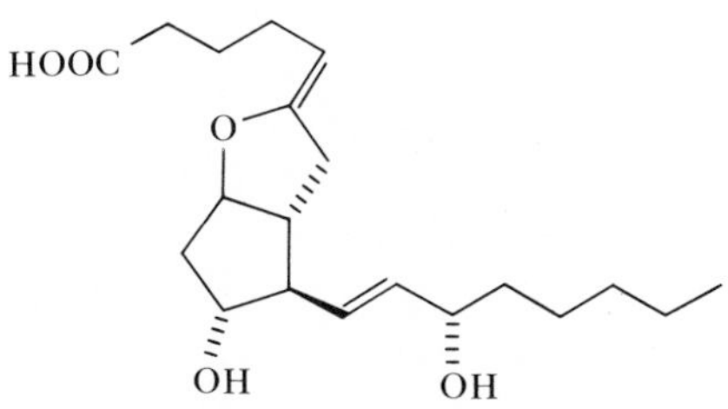

Prostacyclin (PGI$_2$)

The relationship of the structures of these two classes of compounds to the prostaglandins should be noted. TXA$_2$ differs structurally from the prostaglandins in that it contains an oxane rather than a cyclopentane ring, whereas prostacyclin contains a double heterocyclic ring structure in contrast to the single ring structures of the prostaglandins and thromboxanes.

BIOSYNTHESIS

As stated previously, arachidonic acid is the biosynthetic precursor of the most abundant prostaglandins, thromboxanes, and prostacyclin.[9-14] In humans there are three possible sources of arachidonic acid: (1) it can be derived from the diet, (2) it can be synthesized from the 18-carbon unsaturated fatty acid, linoleic acid, or (3) it can be released by hydrolytic cleavage from triglycerides or phospholipids of biomembranes and from other complex lipids such as arachidonate-containing cholesterol esters. Since lit-

tle free arachidonic acid is found in human tissues, its primary source is probably through its release from complex lipids. Since a great deal of prostaglandin biosynthesis probably takes place within or in close proximity to biologic membranes, much of the arachidonic acid used in prostaglandin, thromboxane, and prostacyclin synthesis is probably derived from the phospholipid content of these same biomembranes. One enzyme that can serve to release arachidonic acid from phospholipids is phospholipase A$_2$, which catalyzes the esterolytic release of the fatty acid acyl component from C$_2$ of the phosphoglyceride component of phospholipids.

In contrast to many other biologically active compounds, prostaglandins are not stored in large amounts in body tissues but rather are synthesized immediately before their release. In addition, prostaglandin biosynthesis is usually in response to a number of diverse physiologic, biochemical, mechanical, pharmacologic, and pathologic stimuli, many of which activate phospholipase A$_2$ activity. This increases free intracellular arachidonic acid to a level at which it can then function as a precursor for prostaglandin, thromboxane, and prostacyclin biosynthesis. It is probably fair to state that the rate-limiting step in prostaglandin biosynthesis is the dependency on phospholipase A$_2$ for arachidonic acid to be released from structural phospholipids.

Once arachidonic acid is released, the next event in prostaglandin, thromboxane, and prostacyclin biosynthesis is the metabolism of arachidonic acid by an enzyme complex called prostaglandin synthetase (fatty acid cyclooxygenase). Prostaglandin synthetase activity is found in all human tissues although its activity varies in different types of tissues. Because of the presence of prostaglandin synthetase, virtually all human tissues have the capacity to synthesize prostaglandins.

The collective reactions catalyzed by prostaglandin synthetase are shown in Fig. 11-3.[9-14] This enzyme complex first catalyzes the successive addition of two molecules of molecular oxygen (O$_2$) to arachidonic acid, giving a cyclic endoperoxide derivative called prostaglandin G$_2$ (PGG$_2$), which contains an oxygenated cyclopentane ring. PGG$_2$ is then converted into a second cyclic endoperoxide called prostaglandin H$_2$ (PGH$_2$). The conversion of PGG$_2$ to PGH$_2$ is dependent on the presence of glutathione in many instances, but in some cases compounds such as tryptophan can serve to replace the glutathione require-

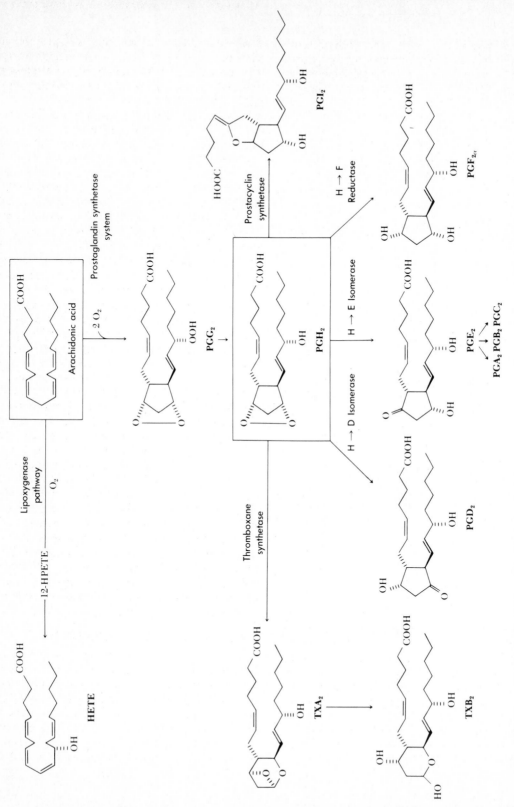

Fig. 11-3. Biosynthetic pathways for the production of the prostaglandins, thromboxanes, and prostacyclin. The lipoxygenase pathway, which is not discussed in the text, leads to the formation HETE, which is 12-hydroxy arachidonic acid.

ment. The importance of the cyclic endoperoxide PGH_2 is that it can serve as a precursor for the synthesis of not only prostaglandins but of the thromboxanes and prostacyclin as well.[12,14] In the case of prostaglandin synthesis, PGH_2 can serve as a substrate for three enzymes—PGH-PGE isomerase, PGH-PGD isomerase, and PGH-$PGF_{2\alpha}$ reductase—that function to convert PGH_2 to PGE_2, PGD_2, and $PGF_{2\alpha}$, respectively. The reducing equivalents for the PGH-$PGF_{2\alpha}$ reaction can be supplied by glutathione or reduced lipoic acid, and these three reactions that involve PGH_2 can take place nonenzymatically in vitro. PGE_2 can undergo further dehydration and isomerization reactions, which probably occur nonenzymatically and result in the production of the other three of the six primary prostaglandins, PGA_2, PGB_2, and PGC_2. PGEs and PGFs, especially PGE_2 and $PGF_{2\alpha}$, are the most abundant prostaglandins in human tissues and hence are probably the most biologically important.

In addition to serving as a precursor for prostaglandin biosynthesis, the endoperoxide PGH_2 can alternatively be converted to TXA_2 and TXB_2. PGH_2 is first converted to TXA_2 by the action of an enzyme called thromboxane synthetase. The product of the thromboxane synthetase reaction, TXA_2, can then be converted to a second thromboxane designated TXB_2. The pathway for thromboxane synthesis is also shown in Fig. 11-3.[12,14]

A third biologically important compound formed from PGH_2, in addition to prostaglandins and thromboxanes, is prostacyclin (PGI_2). PGH_2 can be converted to PGI_2 in many tissues by the action of the enzyme prostacyclin synthetase as shown in Fig. 11-3.[12,14] Although structurally different, prostaglandins, thromboxanes, and prostacyclins all have a broad spectrum of biologic activities, are derived from arachidonic acid, and are effective at extremely low, transient concentrations.

INHIBITORS OF BIOSYNTHESIS

One suggested role for the prostaglandins is that they are potent mediators of the inflammatory response, and this will be discussed in greater detail later. The observation that many nonsteroidal antiinflammatory drugs decrease the conversion of arachidonic acid into prostaglandins serves as evidence of the role of prostaglandins in the inflammatory process. Indeed it is now proposed that nonsteroidal antiinflammatory drugs, such as aspirin, phenylbutazone, indomethacin, zomepirac sodium,

ibuprofen, and acetaminophen, all decrease prostaglandin synthesis by inhibiting prostaglandin synthetase activity.[15,16,17] The ability of these nonsteroidal antiinflammatory agents to inhibit prostaglandin synthetase activity in vitro correlates to a great extent with the ability of these same compounds to alleviate experimentally induced inflammatory responses in animal models. Also, since prostaglandins have been proposed to have a role in temperature elevation, the ability of aspirin to lower elevated temperatures may result from its ability to decrease prostaglandin synthesis through inhibition of prostaglandin synthetase activity. In addition to nonsteroidal antiinflammatory agents, other classes of compounds such as long-chain unsaturated fatty acid analogues, phenelzine ring–containing compounds, and quinidine also inhibit prostaglandin synthesis, perhaps through inhibition of prostaglandin synthetase activity.

Since PGH_2 is also a precursor for the synthesis of thromboxanes and prostacyclin (Fig. 11-3) as well as the prostaglandins, any compound that serves to inhibit prostaglandin synthetase activity will also serve to decrease the production of the thromboxanes and prostacyclin. Certain classes of compounds, however, can selectively decrease the production of the thromboxanes and prostacyclin without appreciably affecting prostaglandin synthesis. For example, imidazole and related compounds along with certain analogues of the cyclic endoperoxides selectively inhibit thromboxane synthetase, thus preferentially decreasing synthesis of the thromboxanes.[13,14] In addition, certain lipid peroxides have been shown to selectively inhibit the production of PGI_2 in vitro.[13,14] Since the prostaglandins, the thromboxanes, and prostacyclin are involved in a broad spectrum of biologic as well as pathologic processes, the development of compounds that can selectively decrease the production of one of these three important classes of compounds without having adverse host side affects is of enormous potential therapeutic value.

BREAKDOWN AND EXCRETION

Prostaglandins, thromboxanes, and prostacyclin have two important characteristics in common: (1) they all exert their respective biologic and pathologic effects at extremely low concentrations, and (2) they have an extremely short half-life, usually less than 3 to 5 minutes. The reason for the short half-life, of these compounds is that they are rapidly broken down or catabolized, particularly in the liver and lungs, after synthesis and release into the circulatory system.[9-14] Once catabolism occurs, the end products are eliminated primarily in the urine.

The first step in the catabolism of the primary prostaglandins, PGEs and PGFs, is catalyzed by the enzyme prostaglandin dehydrogenase (PGDH), which oxidizes the hydroxyl group on C_{15} to the corresponding keto group. The 15 keto analogues of PGE and PGF then serve as substrates for an enzyme called prostaglandin Δ^{13} reductase (PGR), which saturates the double bond between C_{13} and C_{14}. The products of the PGR reaction then undergo a series of oxidative steps that occur primarily in the liver, collectively removing carbon atoms C_1 through C_4. The 16-carbon products of the oxidative reactions are then excreted in the urine. The metabolic events responsible for the catabolism of PGEs and PGFs are shown in Fig. 11-4.[12,14]

In the case of thromboxane catabolism, TXA_2 is first converted to TXB_2. The remainder of thromboxane breakdown then occurs by a single oxidation step that occurs mainly in the liver, which removes C_1 and C_2 from TXB_2. The product of the TXB_2 oxidation step, dinor TXB_2, is then excreted in the urine. The steps of thromboxane catabolism are also shown in Fig. 4.[12,14] The breakdown of prostacyclin has been studied in less detail. However, many prostacyclin metabolites such as those of the PGEs and PGFs have a keto group rather than a hydroxyl group on C_{15}. This indicates that a substantial fraction of prostacyclin may be metabolized by PGDH with the 15 keto product of the PGDH reaction being subsequently excreted in the urine. However, enzymes other than PGDH may also serve to oxidize the hydroxyl group on C_{15} of prostacyclin.

BIOLOGIC AND PATHOLOGIC ROLES

Prostaglandins have been implicated in a large number of both biologic and pathologic processes in animals and humans, and the action of these compounds is analogous to that of many hormones. However, prostaglandins cannot be categorized as a class of hormones since the term *hormone* is generally applied to compounds produced by the endocrine glands that are released into the circulatory system and travel to various tissues in which they exert their biologic effects. In contrast to hormones, which are produced primarily in the endocrine glands, prostaglandins are synthesized in virtually all types of tissues and in all probability exert their effects locally within these

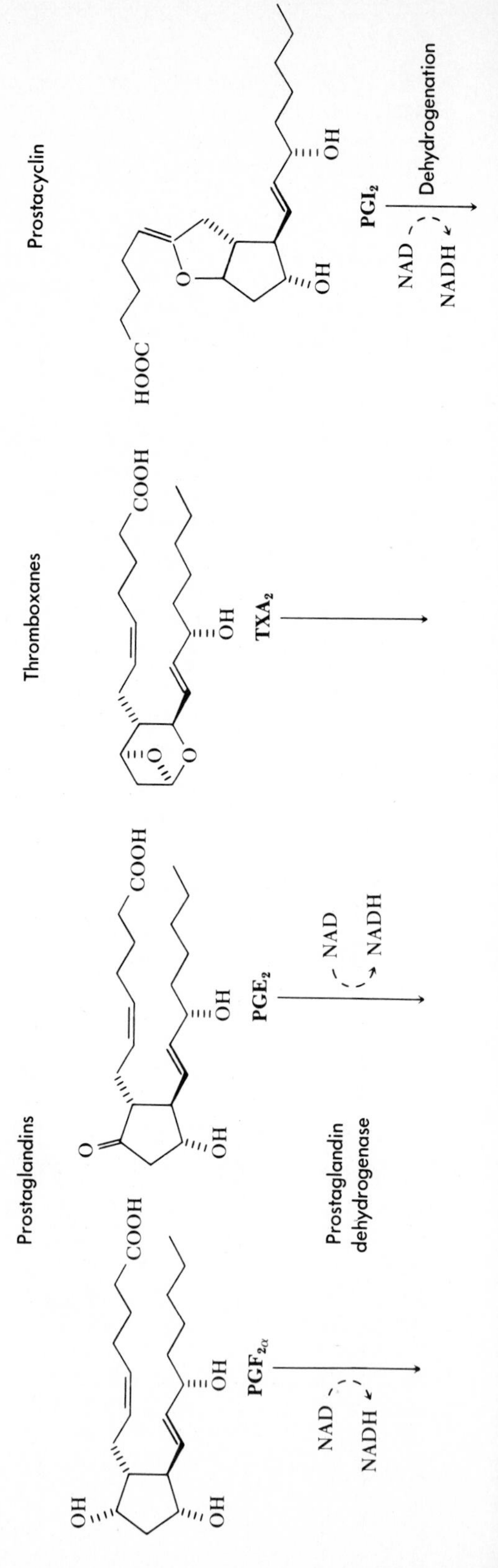

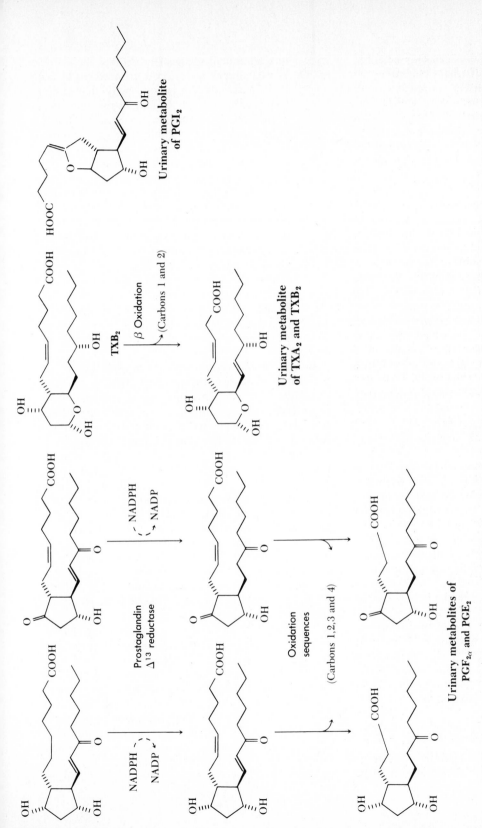

Fig. 11-4. Catabolism of the prostaglandins, thromboxanes, and prostacyclin. The dotted arrows indicate that pyridine nucleotides may be involved in the oxidative and reductive reactions shown above in certain tissues such as the skin.

same tissues. Thus prostaglandins can only be classified as local hormones at best. Perhaps the prostaglandins should be most appropriately classified as autocoids, a term derived from the Greek words *autos* (self) and *akos* (remedy). Autocoid compounds are not true hormones, yet they exert pronounced biologic and pharmacologic effects on a variety of tissues. For example, histamine, serotonin, angiotensin, and kallidin, in addition to the prostaglandins, are classified as autocoids.

A detailed discussion of the biologic and pathologic roles and effects of the prostaglandins are beyond the scope of this text since literally hundreds of journal articles, books, and monographs have dealt with this subject. However, some important characteristics concerning the prostaglandins in relation to their biochemical, pharmacologic, physiologic, and pathologic activities should be pointed out[9-14,18]:

1. Prostaglandins are synthesized in virtually all tissues from 20-carbon unsaturated fatty acids, particularly arachidonate, in response to a wide variety of stimuli, including stimuli of a hormonal nature.
2. They generally exert their effects at extremely low concentrations.
3. They have extremely short half-lives.
4. All of the prostaglandins have close structural similarity.
5. Different prostaglandins can have opposing or antagonistic biologic activity; for example, bronchial smooth muscle and uterine smooth muscle in nonpregnant animals are relaxed by PGE_2 but are contracted by $PGF_{2\alpha}$.
6. Certain single prostaglandins can exert opposing or antagonistic effects at different concentrations; for example, PGE_2 is a potentiator of blood platelet aggregation at low concentrations and an inhibitor of platelet aggregation at higher concentrations.
7. Prostaglandins can exert an effect on certain tissues in some mammalian species but not on others; for example, $PGF_{2\alpha}$ inhibits the release of progesterone from the ovaries of many subprimate species such as sheep, but it does not affect progesterone release from the ovaries of nonpregnant women.
8. Certain prostaglandins produce their respective biologic effects in all mammalian species; for example, PGEs cause a fall in blood pressure when they are administered intravenously into all animal species studied thus far.
9. Prostaglandins have a role in normal physiologic functions throughout body tissues but also participate in certain pathologic processes; for example, prostaglandins of the E series have a role in controlling gastric secretions but have also been implicated as mediators of the inflammatory response.
10. The primary prostaglandins are those of the PGE and PGF series since they are found at higher concentrations than other prostaglandins in practically all body tissues and have been implicated in more biologic and pathologic processes than other prostaglandins.
11. The prostaglandins may exert many of their affects through modulating the intracellular levels of cyclic nucleotides. This will be discussed in greater detail later in this chapter.

Table 11-2 lists a number but certainly not all of the biologic and pathologic effects of the prostaglandins.

In addition to prostaglandins, thromboxanes and prostacyclin also play roles in many diverse biologic processes.[12,14,18] For example, the administration of prostacyclin has been shown to increase renal blood flow and cause hypotension in animals and humans. Like the prostaglandins, the thromboxanes and prostacyclin are effective at extremely low concentrations and have extremely short half-lives. Perhaps the most interesting and most thoroughly studied biologic roles of the thromboxanes and prostacyclin are their opposing or antagonistic effects on platelet aggregation and vasodilation. TXA_2 is produced by the blood platelets themselves and is a potent stimulator of platelet aggregation, whereas prostacyclin is produced in the wall of the blood vessels and is a powerful inhibitor of platelet aggregation. In addition, TXA_2 is a potent constrictor of vascular smooth muscle, whereas prostacyclin is a potent vasodilator. The fact that TXA_2 induces platelet aggregation probably means that it plays an initiating role in hemostasis by causing the aggregation of blood platelets that then attach to the walls of damaged blood vessels. In contrast, the anti-platelet-aggregating activity of prostacyclin disallows the aggregation of platelets and hence probably prevents them from adhering to normal, healthy blood vessel walls. There is probably a normal balance between the activity of TXA_2 and prostacyclin. Undamaged blood vessels produce prostacyclin, which serves to counteract TXA_2-induced

Table 11-2. Selected systems, parameters, and effects proposed to be mediated by one or more of the prostaglandins

System	Parameter	Effect*
Reproductive	Uterine muscle tone	+ −
	Progesterone release	−
	Sperm transport	+
	Abortiofacient activity	+
Cardiovascular	Vascular muscle tone	+ −
	Cardiac output	+
	Blood pressure	+ −
Endocrine	ACTH release	+
	Growth hormone release	+
	Prolactin secretion	+
	Gonatropin secretion	+
	Leutenizing hormone release	+
	Thyrotropin release	+
	Insulin release	+
	Adrenocorticosteroid production	+
Respiratory	Bronchial muscle tone	+ −
	Tracheal muscle tone	+ −
Gastrointestinal	Longitudinal muscle tone	+
	Circular muscle tone	+ −
	Gastric acid secretion	−
	Pancreatic secretions	−
Blood	Platelet aggregation	+ −
	Erythropoiesis	+
	RBC fragility	+
Metabolism	Lipolysis	+ −
	Carbohydrate metabolism	+ −
	Bone resorption (Ca^{++})	+
Host defense system	Body temperature	+
	Inflammation	+

*Symbols: +, increase in the designated parameter; −, decrease; + −, prostaglandins are capable of causing opposing or antagonistic effects.

platelet aggregation followed by thrombus formation. However, when damage to the blood vessels occurs, prostacyclin synthetase activity, which serves to stop prostacyclin production, is decreased, thus allowing thromboxane-dependent platelet aggregation and thrombus formation to occur.

ANTAGONISTS OF PROSTAGLANDIN ACTIVITY

A number of compounds with diverse chemical structures have been shown to be antagonists of some of the biologic and pathologic activities shown by certain of the prostaglandins. It has already been mentioned that nonsteroidal antiinflammatory compounds such as indomethacin, phenylbutazone, aspirin, zomepirac sodium, ibuprofen, and acetaminophen probably exert some of their effects through decreasing prostaglandin biosynthesis via inhibition of prostaglandin synthetase activity.[12,14-17] Two other nonsteroid antiinflammatory compounds, flufenamic acid and meclofenamic acid, which also inhibit prostaglandin synthesis, can serve to inhibit the contraction of bronchial smooth muscle in response to $PGF_{2\alpha}$ but not its contraction in response to PGE_2. Phenylbutazone can also antagonize the response of bronchial smooth muscle to $PGF_{2\alpha}$, as can aspirin but to a lesser extent.

Other classes of compounds can also antagonize the ability of prostaglandins to contract smooth muscle. For example, 7-oxa-13-prostanoic acid is a prostaglandin analogue that is a potent inhibitor of PGE_1-induced and PGE_2-induced smooth muscle contraction in a variety of tissues. In addition, a dibenzo-oxazepine derivative called SC 19220 not only is an antagonist of gastrointestinal smooth muscle contraction in response to prostaglandins but also shows anticonvulsant and analgesic activity as well. Finally, polyphloretin phosphate (PPP) is also an antagonist of prostaglandin-induced smooth muscle contractions in numerous body tissues. However, the response of smooth muscle to all of these antagonists of prostaglandin-induced smooth muscle contraction varies from tissue to tissue.

Certain compounds can inhibit the synthesis of TXA_2 and thus impair thromboxane-induced platelet aggregation. Some of these compounds are imidazole, 1-methylimidazole, and 1-n-butylimidazole, which appear to impair TXA_2-induced platelet aggregation by directly inhibiting thromboxane synthetase. Aspirin and other nonsteroidal antiinflammatory compounds that inhibit prostaglandin synthetase also have a negative effect on thromboxane synthesis and have been shown to have anticlotting effects. These may be of value in the treatment of thromboembolic disorders.

PROSTAGLANDINS AND SECOND MESSENGERS

Certain hormones and other biologically active compounds exert their effects by stimulating cells to synthesize other compounds that have pronounced biologic activity themselves. These compounds, whose synthesis is stimulated by hormones and other biologically active compounds, are collectively called second messengers.[19] One important class of these second messengers is the cyclic nucleotides, cyclic AMP, and cyclic guanosine-3,5'monophosphate (cyclic GMP). It is well documented that cyclic AMP has a broad spectrum of biologic activity[19]:

1. Cyclic AMP modulates the activity of a class of enzymes called protein kinases, which in turn can direct metabolic processes such as glycogen synthesis, glycogen breakdown, and lipolytic activity.
2. It alters cellular permeability.
3. It causes muscle contraction or relaxation.
4. It signals the initiation of the synthesis of specific intracellular proteins.
5. It directs various secretory processes.

Compounds such as norepinephrine, glucagon, and insulin can modulate intracellular cyclic AMP levels by the following two mechanisms: (1) by binding to specific receptor sites on the cell surface and in the process causing an increase in membrane-associated adenylate cyclase activity, an enzyme that converts ATP to cyclic AMP and pyrophosphate, which results in an increase in the conversion of intracellular ATP to cyclic AMP, thus serving to elevate intracellular cyclic AMP levels, or (2) by binding to their respective receptor sites on the cell surfaces, initiating the release of membrane-associated adenylate cyclase into the cytoplasm, the compounds cause an increase in the rate of conversion of ATP to cyclic AMP. Similar mechanisms have been postulated to explain the ability of many of these same compounds to modulate intracellular cyclic GMP levels. Intracellular cyclic nucleotide levels may also be controlled through modulation of cyclic nucleotide 3'-5'-phosphodiesterases, which convert cyclic AMP and cyclic GMP to AMP and GMP, respectively.

Some of the broad spectrum of biologic and pathologic effects produced by the prostaglandins may be a result of their ability to increase or decrease the levels of intracellular cyclic nucleotides by modulating the activity of adenylate cyclase and cyclic nucleotide 3':5'-phosphodiesterase activity.* Indeed, cell surface receptor sites for PGE_1, PGE_2, and $PGF_{2\alpha}$ have been identified. In most tissues, prostaglandins have been shown to increase intracellular cyclic AMP levels by increasing adenylate cyclase activity. In

contrast, prostaglandins have been shown to decrease cyclic AMP levels in adipose tissues. In addition, cyclic AMP appears to stimulate prostaglandin biosynthesis in many tissues, thus indicating that a positive control mechanism may exist between prostaglandin biosynthesis and the adenylate cyclase system. It has also been shown that there is a positive correlation between prostaglandin levels and the intracellular concentration of cyclic GMP in certain tissues, although the significance of this is not as clear as the effect of prostaglandins on cyclic AMP synthesis. However, since cyclic GMP and cyclic AMP have been hypothesized to have opposing actions on certain cellular functions, a possible explanation for the opposite or antagonistic effects of certain prostaglandins on different tissues is that they preferentially increase or decrease the intracellular levels of either cyclic AMP or cyclic GMP. However, this is strictly conjecture. Although prostaglandins have been shown to effect the intracellular levels of cyclic nucleotides, there are in all likelihood other biochemical and physiologic mechanisms responsible for the wide range of biologic and pathologic activities of prostaglandins.

The opposing effects of TXA_2 and prostacyclin on platelet aggregation may also be explained by their ability to modulate the intracellular levels of cyclic nucleotides.[14,20] TXA_2 has been shown to inhibit adenylate cyclase activity in blood platelets and thereby lower the intracellular concentration of cyclic AMP, which coincides with increased platelet aggregating activity. In contrast, prostacyclin has been shown to stimulate adenylate cyclase activity and thus increase the cyclic AMP concentration within the platelets, which coincides with a marked decrease in platelet aggregation.

PREPARATIONS AND POTENTIAL USES

Since the prostaglandins, thromboxanes, and prostacyclin collectively possess such a broad spectrum of biologic activities, a great deal of interest has focused on the potential for the therapeutic uses of these three classes of compounds. Both PGE_2 and $PGF_{2\alpha}$ can stimulate contraction of the uterus in pregnant females and have been postulated to have an important role in human parturition. Preparations of both PGE_2 and PGF_2 have been used to induce labor and for abortive purposes. One of the preparations is called dinoprost tromethamine (Prostin F2 Alpha) and consists of a solution that contains $PGF_{2\alpha}$ (5.0 mg/ml)

---

*References 10, 11, 13, 14, 20, 21.

and has relatively widespread use as an abortiofacient.[22] A second preparation is called dinoprostone (Prostin E2), which comes in vaginal suppositories that contain 20 mg of PGE_2. Dinoprostone, like dinoprost thromethamine, is used to induce abortion and to evacuate the uterus in the management of missed abortion.[22] The prostaglandins are particularly useful for abortive purposes after the twelfth week of pregnancy, when surgical techniques offer certain disadvantages. The prostaglandins may be administered intravenously, intravaginally, or by intrauterine injection. The main side effects of prostaglandins administered for abortive purposes are diarrhea, nausea, and vomiting, and these particular side effects are more severe with $PGF_{2\alpha}$ than with PGE_2 preparations.

Other therapeutic uses of prostaglandins, in addition to their use of abortiofacients, have been studied.[14] The experimental use of PGE_2 has been studied in the treatment of bronchial asthma. Other prostaglandins as well as their analogues have been used to inhibit gastric secretion in humans and thus have potential importance in the treatment of ulcers. In addition, prostaglandin preparations have been used experimentally to treat cardiovascular, kidney, and circulatory disorders. Prostacyclin, like some of the prostaglandins, has also been shown to inhibit gastric secretion in humans and protect against platelet loss in animals. Although few preparations of prostaglandins are commercially available for therapeutic use at this time, the broad range of biologic activity of these compounds along with the high level of current interest being shown in their potential therapeutic value almost assures additional preparations and uses in the future.

PROSTAGLANDINS AND PERIODONTAL DISEASE

Prostaglandins are important to dentistry because they have been implicated in the pathogenesis of periodontal disease, which affects a large percentage of the adult population of the United States and is a major cause of tooth loss. Prostaglandins may play a role in what may be considered to be the two stages of periodontal disease: (1) inflammation of the gingiva, which results in erythema, edema, and an increase in gingival exudate, and (2) resorption of alveolar bone, which is generally followed by tooth loss.

The following experimental evidence and clinical observations support the hypothesis that prostaglandins, particularly those of the E and F series, are important mediators of the inflammatory response in both animals and humans[14,15,23]:

1. Nonsteroidal antiinflammatory drugs, such as aspirin and indomethacin, that inhibit prostaglandin synthesis also serve to reduce experimentally induced inflammation.
2. Rheumatoid synovial cells grown in tissue culture have been found to produce large amounts of prostaglandins.
3. When prostaglandins are injected directly into the joints of experimental animals, they produce an arthritic type of response.
4. Prostaglandins are pyrogenic when they are injected into cerebral ventricles.
5. Small amounts of prostaglandins injected intradermally markedly increase the pain sensitivity to other mediators of inflammation such as bradykinin and histamine.
6. Prostaglandins, when injected intradermally, are potent inducers of vasodilation.
7. Prostaglandins increase vascular permeability, which is greatly enhanced in the presence of histamine.
8. Platelets produce prostaglandins during aggregation.
9. Both neutrophils and macrophages produce prostaglandins during phagocytosis.
10. Prostaglandins are produced in both naturally occurring and experimentally produced fluids isolated from inflammatory sites.

Although the experimental evidence cited above does support the role of prostaglandins in inflammation, these data must be interpreted with caution in light of other observations that indicate that under certain circumstances prostaglandins may serve as inhibitors of the inflammatory response. For example, if prostaglandin synthesis in the lung is inhibited during anaphylactic challenge, an increase in the production of histamine and slow-reacting substance A (SRS-A) results, which suggests that prostaglandins may serve to decrease the synthesis of these two mediators of inflammation. In addition, prostaglandins have been shown to inhibit the release of lymphokines from activated lymphocytes.

If, indeed, prostaglandins are mediators of inflammation, their role(s) may occur much later than those of other mediators of inflammation such as histamine and bradykinin, since prostaglandins appear in fluids and exudates from 6 to 12 hours after tissue damage occurs. Consequently, prostaglandins may participate in the inflammatory response when tissue damage and destruction are most prominent.

Current evidence also supports the role of prostaglandins as mediators of the inflammatory response in oral soft tissues.[24,25]

1. Prostaglandins are found in the normal, healthy gingiva, but extracts obtained from the gingiva of patients with periodontal disease contained 10 times as much PGEs as that found in extracts obtained from normal, healthy gingiva.
2. PGE_1 is capable of initiating edema and erythema when it is injected intradermally into humans, and both of these conditions are seen in the early stages of periodontal disease.
3. PGE_1 has a toxic effect on human gingival fibroblasts.
4. PGEs and PGFs have been found to cause alterations in vascular permeability in both humans and animals.
5. PGE_1 can sensitize the permeability of the blood vessels to other mediators of inflammation such as histamine.
6. It is well known that polymorphonuclear leukocytes (PMNs) play a role in gingival inflammation and that during phagocytosis rabbit PMNs release relatively large amounts of PGE_1, which is chemotactic for PMNs. Thus additional PMNs could be attracted into the inflamed area and accelerate the progression of gingival inflammation.

Although still circumstantial, the evidence cited collectively points to a role of prostaglandins in the initial stage of periodontal disease.

The following experimental evidence also indicates that prostaglandins have a role in alveolar bone resorption, which eventually leads to tooth loss during periodontal disease.[24,25]

1. PGEs stimulate the accumulation of cyclic AMP in rat calvaria.
2. PGE_1 and PGE_2 are powerful stimulators of the resorption of cultured fetal rat long bones.
3. As stated previously, extracts obtained from the gingiva of patients with periodontal disease contained more PGEs than extracts prepared from normal, healthy gingiva.
4. Bone loss has been reported in the rat periodontium after repeated applications of PGE_1 to the gingiva.

5. Prostaglandins also induce resorption of the adult rat calvarium when they are injected over the bone surface.
6. PGEs can cause bone resorption in tissue culture.
7. The levels of PGE_2 found in an exudate obtained from a draining tooth abscess that had stimulated the resorption of alveolar bone were in the same concentration range as those that promoted maximum resorption of bone in tissue culture.
8. It has been shown that activation of complement in an organ culture system resulted in increased prostaglandin synthesis and the resorption of fetal rat bone.

Not only may prostaglandins play a role in alveolar bone resorption that takes place during periodontal disease, they may also prevent the synthesis of new bone since they can inhibit the incorporation of proline into collagen, thus serving to inhibit osteoblastic activity. Although current in vitro evidence is supportive of a role for prostaglandins in the destruction of both hard and soft tissues that occur during periodontal disease, the exact mechanisms by which they participate in the disease processes are purely speculative at this time.

REFERENCES

1. Kurzrok, R., and Lieb, C.C.: Biochemical studies of human semen. II. The action of semen on the human uterus, Proc. Soc. Exp. Biol. Med. **28:**268, 1930.
2. Goldblatt, N.W.: Properties of human seminal fluid, J. Physiol. **84:**208, 1935.
3. von Euler, U.S.: On the specific vasodilating and plain muscle stimulating substance from accessory genital glands in man and certain animals (prostiglandin and vesiglandin), J. Physiol. **86:**213, 1936.
4. Bergström, S., and Samuelsson, B.: The prostaglandins, Endeavour **27:**109, 1968.
5. Bergström, S., Danielsson, H., and Samuelsson, B.: The enzymatic formation of prostaglandin E_2 from arachidonic acid, Biochim. Biophys. Acta **90:**207, 1964.
6. Van Dorp, D.A., et al.: The biosynthesis of prostaglandins, Biochim. Biophys. Acta **90:**204, 1964.
7. Hamberg, M., Svensson, J., and Samuelsson, B.: Thromboxane: a new group of biologically active compounds derived from prostaglandin endoperoxides, Proc. Natl. Acad. Sci. **72:**2994, 1975.
8. Moncada, S., and Vane, J.R.: The discovery of prostacyclin: a fresh insight into arachidonic acid metabolism. In Kharasch, N., and Fried, J., editors: Biochemical aspects of prostaglandins and thromboxanes, New York, 1977, Academic Press, Inc.
9. Bergström, S., Carlson, L.A., and Weeks, J.R.: The prosta-

glandins: a family of biologically active lipids, Pharmacol. Rev. **20:**1, 1968.

10. Hinman, J.W.: Prostaglandins, Ann. Rev. Biochem. **41:**161, 1972.

11. Samuelsson, B., et al.: Prostaglandins, Ann. Rev. Biochem. **44:**669, 1975.

12. McGiff, J.C.: Prostaglandins, prostacyclin, and thromboxanes, Ann. Rev. Pharmacol. Toxicol. **21:**479, 1981.

13. Bowman, W.C., and Rand, M.J.: Textbook of pharmacology, ed. 2, Oxford, 1980, Blackwell Scientific Publications, Ltd.

14. Moncada, S., Flower, R.J., and Vane, J.R.: Prostaglandins, Prostacyclin, and Thromboxane A_2. In Gilman, A.G., Goodman, L.S., and Gilman, A., editors: The pharmacological basis of therapeutics, ed. 6, New York, 1980, Macmillan Publishing Co., Inc.

15. Trummel, C.L.: Antiinflammatory drugs. In Neidle, E.A., Donald, K.C., and Yagiela, J.A., editors: Pharmacology and therapeutics for dentistry, St. Louis, 1980, The C.V. Mosby Co.

16. Vane, J.R.: Inhibition of prostaglandin synthesis as a mechanism of action for aspirin-like drugs, Nature **231:**232, 1971.

17. Flower, R.J., and Vane, J.R.: Inhibition of prostaglandin synthesis, Biochem. Pharmacol. **23:**1439, 1974.

18. Weeks, J.R.: Prostaglandins, Ann. Rev. Pharmacol. **12:**317, 1972.

19. Sutherland, E.W., Robinson, G.A., and Butcher, R.W.: Some aspects of the biological role of adenosine 3',5'-monophosphate (cyclic AMP), Circulation **37:**279, 1968.

20. Samuelsson, B., et al.: Prostaglandins and thromboxanes: biochemical and physiological consideration, Adv. Prostaglandin Thromboxane Res. **4:**1, 1978.

21. Vapaatalo, H., and Parantainen, J.: Prostaglandins: their biological and pharmacological role, Med. Biol. **56:**163, 1978.

22. Rall, T.W., and Schleifer, L.S.: Oxytocin, prostaglandins, ergot alkaloids, and other agents. In Gilman, A.G., Goodman, L.S., and Gilman, A., editors: The pharmacological basis of therapeutics, ed. 6, New York, 1980, Macmillan Publishing Co., Inc.

23. Bonta, I.L., and Parnham, M.J.: Prostaglandins and chronic inflammation, Biochem. Pharmacol. **27:**1611, 1978.

24. Goodson, J.M.: The potential role of prostaglandin in the etiology of periodontal disease. In Kahn, R.H., and Lands, W.E.M., editors: Prostaglandins and cyclic AMP: biological actions and clinical implications, New York, 1973, Academic Press, Inc.

25. Bowles, R.D.: Implicated prostaglandins in periodontic disease, Dent. Student, **56:**68, February 1978.

CHAPTER 12

BARBARA REQUA-CLARK
SAM V. HOLROYD

Narcotic analgesics and antagonists

Narcotics are drugs that produce narcosis (stupor). Except for potency and duration of action, the differences among the narcotic analgesics are not great. Clinically important similarities among narcotic analgesics are that they all produce (1) potent analgesia, (2) addiction, (3) respiratory depression, (4) sedation, (5) emesis, and (6) constipation. Tolerance readily develops to the narcotics, and cross-tolerance as well as cross-addiction can be produced. Another common characteristic is that they are all antagonized by narcotic antagonists.

The narcotics are important in dental practice for pain that cannot be controlled by the less potent nonnarcotic drugs. Reynolds stated, "In order to control moderately severe pain, the use of narcotics is imperative. It is hard to understand how many dentists can practice without a federal narcotics license."[1]

Because of their addiction potential, the narcotics are subject to control under the Controlled Substance Act of 1970. They can be prescribed only by practitioners who register annually with the DEA, as described in Chapter 4.

CLASSIFICATION

The narcotic analgesics can be categorized into opium alkaloids, semisynthetic derivatives, and synthetic narcotics.

Opium alkaloids (Pantopon)
  Heroin (diacetylmorphine)
  Morphine
  Codeine (methylmorphine)
Semisynthetic derivatives
  Morphine
    Hydromorphone or dihydromorphinone (Dilaudid)
    Oxymorphone (Numorphan)
    Nalbuphine* (Nubain)
    Methyldihydromorphinone† (Metopon)
  Codeine
    Hydrocodone or dihydrocodeinone (Codone, Dicodid, in Hycodan,‡ Hycomine,‡ Vicodin‡)
    Dihydrocodeine (in Synalgos-DC‡)
    Oxycodone (in Percodan‡, Percocet‡, Tylox‡)
Synthetic narcotics
  Meperidine group
    Meperidine (Demerol)
    Ethoheptazine (Zactane)
    Alphaprodine (Nisentil)
    Anileridine (Leritine)
    Piminodine† (Alvodine)
    Fentanyl (Sublimaze)
    Diphenoxylate (in Lomotil‡)
    Loperamide (Imodium)
  Methadone group
    Methadone (Dolophine)
    Propoxyphene (Darvon)
  Morphinan group
    Levorphanol (Levo-Dromoran)
    Methorphan†
    Butorphanol tartrate* (Stadol)
  Benzomorphan group
    Pentazocine* (Talwin)
    Phenazocine† (Prinadol)

OPIUM ALKALOIDS

Opium is the dried juice obtained from the unripe seed capsules of the poppy plant *(Papaver somniferum)*. Approximately 25% of opium consists of alkaloids: 10% morphine, 0.5% codeine, 0.2% thebaine, 6% noscapine, 1% papaverine, and others. These alkaloids are either phenanthrene or benzylisoquinoline derivatives. The phenanthrene derivatives, including morphine and codeine, are analgesics that are addicting. The benzylisoquinoline derivatives (e.g.,

---

*Has antagonist properties.
†Not marketed in the United States.
‡Contains other active ingredients.

papaverine) are neither analgesics nor addicting but relax smooth muscle.

The prototype of the narcotic analgesic agents is morphine. It will be discussed in detail, and the other agents will be compared to it.

Morphine

Morphine was isolated in pure form from opium by Serturner in 1803. Although synthesized in 1952 by Gates and Tschudi, it is still commercially obtained from the natural source. The structure of morphine is as follows:

Mechanism of action

The narcotic analgesics act as agonists and bind with receptors present in the CNS. The potency of these agents is proportional to their affinity to these receptors. Endogenous substances such as enkephalins (methionine and leucine) and endorphins (alpha, beta, and gamma) normally act at these receptor sites. Beta endorphin is the most potent endogenous agonist yet identified.

Data suggest that the narcotic analgesics exert their effect by mimicking the actions of the enkephalins and endorphins. Their binding to the receptors results in reduced activity of adenylate cyclase in the nervous system, and cyclic AMP levels fall. Whether this effect produces the action of the narcotic analgesics is at the present time unknown.

Pharmacologic effects and adverse reactions

Unlike many drugs, the significant adverse effects of morphine do not relate to a direct damaging effect on hepatic, renal, or hematologic tissues. The principal adverse effects of morphine result from undesirable alterations of the function of several organ systems. Consequently, in this chapter the pharmacologic and adverse effects are considered together.

Analgesia and sedation. Morphine provides effective analgesia against severe pain. Although its exact mechanism is unknown, it may alter the release of certain central neurotransmitters, which alter the perception of painful stimuli. Patients who are given morphine describe the presence of pain, but it concerns them less. Morphine has a greater selectivity than many other drugs that act on the CNS. The narcotic analgesic agents produce a significant degree of analgesia with little impairment of other CNS functions.

Pain can be divided into its two components—the stimulation of the nerve generating an impulse and the interpretation of that impulse in the cerebral cortex. Although morphine's effect on the pain threshold is not uniform, an average dose will relieve clinical pain. Some authors state that both the sensation of pain and the patient's response to it are altered by morphine. Other authors conclude that the conduction of the nerve impulse is unaltered by morphine. If the pain does not produce fear or anxiety, the patient can more easily tolerate it.

Analgesic doses also produce sedation, which undoubtedly potentiates the analgesic effect. Some patients experience euphoria, especially if their pain is relieved. When pain is lacking, dysphoria can be produced in a few patients. Tolerance develops to the analgesic, sedative, and euphoric effects of morphine.

The potency of other narcotic analgesics is measured against morphine. Each agent is then placed into one of three categories—least, intermediate, and most potent (Table 12-1). Although most narcotics could relieve pain as severe as that relieved by morphine, the dose needed would produce an unacceptable number of adverse effects. For this reason, codeine is thought of as "weaker" than morphine.

Respiratory depression. Morphine sharply depresses the respiratory center in the medulla in a dose-related fashion. Equal respiratory depression is produced by equianalgesic doses (Table 12-1) of the narcotic analgesic agent. A reduced respiratory rate as well as a reduction in tidal volume occurs. The respiratory depression is secondary to a reduction in responsiveness of the respiratory center to carbon dioxide tension. The patient will breathe if commanded to do so, but not otherwise. Tolerance develops to this effect. Respiratory depression, the most common cause of death in an overdose, represents an important clinical consideration. The usual adult doses of morphine will have minimal effects on the respiration of healthy patients. In elderly or debilitated patients or those with severe pulmonary disease, therapeutic doses may produce a dangerous decrease in pul-

Table 12-1. Narcotic analgesics grouped by potency

Potency	Onset (min)	Peak (hr)	Duration (hr)	t½ (hr)	Intramuscular or subcutaneous dose (mg)	Oral dose (mg)	Preparations available
Greatest							
Morphine	20	½-1½	7	2-3	10.0	60.0	I: 2-15 mg/ml T: 10, 15, 30 mg L: 10 mg/5 ml
Heroin, diacetylmorphine (diamorphine)	5-10*	½	3-4		3.0	—	‡
Hydromorphone, dihydro-morphinone (Dilaudid)	15-30	½-½	4-5	4	1.5	7.5	T: 1, 2, 3, 4 mg S: 3 mg I: 1-4 mg/ml
Oxymorphone, dihydrohy-droxymorphinone (Numorphan)	5-10	½-1½	3-6	4-5	1.0-1.5	6.0	I§: 1, 1.5 mg/ml S: 5 mg
Levorphanol (Levo-Dromoran)	30*	1-1½	5-8	1.2	2.0-3.0	4.0	T: 2 mg I: 2 mg/ml
Methadone (Dolophine)	10-15	1-2	3-6	4-6	5.0-10.0	20.0	T: 5, 10, 40‖ mg I: 10 mg/ml
Phenazocine (Prinadol)	10-15	½-1	2-4		3.0	15.0	‡
Intermediate							
Meperidine (Demerol)	10-15	½-1	2-4	3-4	75.0-100.0	150.0-300.0	T: 50, 100 mg L: 50 mg/5 ml I: 50, 75, 100 mg/ml
Alphaprodine (Nisentil)	5-10	½	1-2		−10.0-60.0		I
Anileridine (Leritine)	15	½-1	2-3		25.0-50.0	50.0	T: 25 mg I: 25 mg/ml
Pentazocine† (Talwin)	15-13	1*	3	2-3	50.0	180.0	T: 50 mg I: 30 mg/ml
Oxycodone, dihydrohy-droxycodeinone (in Percodan, Percocet-5, Tylox)	15*	1*	4-5	4	10.0-15.0	30.0	T: ~5 mg¶
Hydrocodone, dihydroco-deine (Codone, Dicodid, in Vicodin and Hycodan)	15*	1*	4-6	4	5.0-10.0	30.0	T: ~5 mg¶
Butorphanol† (Stadol)	30	½-1	3-4		2.0	—	I: 1 mg/ml
Nalbuphine† (Nubain)	15	½-1	3-6	5	10.0	—	I: 10 mg/ml
Least							
Codeine, methylmorphine	15-30	1-1½	4-6	3-4	60.0-120.0	200.0	T: 8, 15, 32, 65 mg¶ I: 30, 60 mg/ml C: 16 mg¶
Dihydrocodeine (in Synal-gos-DC)	15*	1*	4-5	3-4	65.0		
Propoxyphene (Darvon)		2-2½		6-12	240		C

Modified from Requa, B.S., and Holroyd, S.V.: Applied pharmacology for the dental hygienist, St. Louis, 1982, The C.V. Mosby Co.
I, Injectible; *T,* tablets; *S,* suppository; *L,* liquid; *C,* capsules.
*Estimated.
†Has antagonist properties.
‡Not available in the United States.
§Injectible only.
‖For methadone maintenance programs.
¶Amount of narcotic ingredient. Preparation contains other active ingredients.

monary ventilation. The narcotic analgesics should be given with caution, if at all, to patients who may suffer hypotension, such as those in shock or with decreased blood volume. Patients with head injuries or delirium tremens are to be given these agents only with great care. Caution should also be exercised in administering these agents to patients with hepatic insufficiency. The narcotic analgesics may induce urinary retention in patients with prostatic hypertrophy or urethral stricture. The prescribed dose should be reduced in patients with myxedema, hypothyroidism, or Addison disease and patients who are receiving other CNS or respiratory depressants.[2] The use of narcotics in pregnant women should be avoided especially near term because of the respiratory depression that may be produced in the fetus.

Emesis and nausea. Analgesic doses of morphine tend to cause nausea and vomiting in many people. This is attributable to direct stimulation of the chemoreceptor trigger zone for emesis, which is located in the medulla.[3] This trigger zone is distinct from the vomiting center, which is depressed by morphine. After repeated doses, morphine depresses the vomiting center, and emesis is prevented. Since an ambulatory patient is more likely to experience nausea and vomiting, a vestibular component seems likely. This effect can be counteracted by the administration of a phenothiazine (Chapter 8).

Cough suppression. Although morphine depresses the cough center, antitussive effects can be obtained by less addicting drugs. Since the dose required to produce its antitussive effect is less than that required for analgesia, the antitussive effect can easily be obtained without producing any respiratory depression. Agents are available that possess no analgesic or respiratory depressant effects but possess some antitussive effect (e.g., dextromethorphan).

Gastrointestinal effects. Analgesic doses of morphine cause constipation by reducing gastrointestinal secretions and motility and increasing the muscle tone. The increase in tone produces spasms, which reduce the propulsive contractions throughout the intestines. This allows the fecal material to become dried. Also, the patient ignores the stimuli to defecate. These factors lead to constipation. Little tolerance develops to these effects. Although morphine's constipating effect may be useful in diarrhea, other narcotic agents are normally used for this purpose.

Renal effects. Morphine may cause urinary reten-

tion by increasing the smooth muscle tone of the bladder and ureter. It also produces an antidiuretic effect by stimulating the release of the antidiuretic hormone from the pituitary. Although analgesic doses do not pose a threat to the healthy patient, they may cause acute urinary retention in patients with prostatic hypertrophy or stricture of the urethra.[2]

Increased intracranial pressure. Morphine causes cerebral vasodilation, which appears to be secondary to respiratory depression. This results in an increase in intracranial and spinal fluid pressure. Consequently, morphine should not be used in patients with head injuries or where an increase in intracranial pressure may be already present. Since the presence of central depression and nausea are important in determining the extent of head injuries, the alteration of these factors by a drug cannot help but complicate the diagnosis.

CNS stimulation. Very high doses of morphine and its chemical relatives have produced convulsions by direct action on the cerebral cortex. Although relatively low doses of morphine may produce excitation in some animals (cats, lions, tigers, horses, cows, sheep, and goats), this generally does not present a therapeutic problem in humans.

Cardiovascular effects. Morphine depresses the vasomotor center and stimulates the vagus. These effects would generally not be clinically significant at the usual dosage levels, but higher doses may cause hypotension and bradycardia. Peripheral dilation may produce orthostatic hypotension.

Miosis. Morphine constricts the pupils. There is no tolerance to this effect, which serves as an important diagnostic sign in morphine overdose or morphine addiction.

Bronchiolar constriction. Morphine causes bronchiolar constriction. The effect is usually minor but may present a serious problem if used in a patient with respiratory disease.

Hepatic effects. Although these agents do not produce liver damage, high doses may constrict the biliary duct to cause biliary colic.

Uterus. Therapeutic doses of morphine may prolong labor.[4] It reduces the tone of a hyperactive uterus and also reduces the cooperation of the mother. These factors, in addition to the effect on fetal respiration, require that it be used with caution.

Skin. Morphine can produce cutaneous vasodilation, which can result in orthostatic hypotension. It also causes histamine release, resulting in sweating and pruritus especially at the site of injection.

Addiction

Morphine is highly addicting—a fact that represents an important limitation to its therapeutic use. Although patients with personality problems are more susceptible to addiction, others are also highly susceptible. This is a greater problem in medicine than in dentistry because the dental use of morphine is almost always of short duration. Despite this, the dentist should not minimize the importance of this problem. Every effort should be made to control pain with nonnarcotic analgesics or narcotics with the least addicting liability, such as codeine, before resorting to the use of morphine. The addiction potential of the narcotic analgesics is proportional to their analgesic potency. Morphine has both a high analgesic potency and addiction liability, whereas codeine is low in both.

The morphine addict may appear completely normal except for constipation and miosis, to which tolerance does not appreciably develop. A "withdrawal syndrome" is produced if the addict does not continue to receive morphine. This syndrome can be brought on almost immediately by the narcotic antagonists, which are discussed later. Symptoms of withdrawal range from depression to delirium and include lacrimation, perspiration, rhinorrhea, yawning, and progression to a restless sleep, which is followed by dilated pupils, gooseflesh, anorexia, irritability, tremor, nausea, vomiting, intestinal spasm, abdominal cramps, chills, tachycardia, and increased blood pressure.[3]

Overdose

As noted earlier, the principal danger in morphine overdose is respiratory depression. The diagnostic triad of overdose consists of coma, depressed respiration, and pinpoint pupils.

The treatment of choice is the use of a narcotic antagonist, such as naloxone (Narcan), which will bring prompt recovery. One must be aware that although adequate respiration will be quickly restored, this recovery can be associated with varying degrees of withdrawal symptoms in the addict. The latter in some cases may present greater hazards than does the pretreatment respiratory depression. Therefore narcotic antagonist use should be carefully monitored.

Allergic reactions. Allergic reactions to morphine are infrequent but can occur. They are often dermatologic in nature. Urticaria and wheals can occur at the site of injection secondary to histamine release. Although anaphylaxis secondary to these agents has been reported, its incidence is rare. When a patient gives a history of an allergy to a specific narcotic agent, a chemically unrelated agent should be used.

Administration, absorption, and metabolism. Although morphine is readily absorbed from the gastrointestinal tract, it is not very effective by this route because of the first-pass effect. This means that after the drug is absorbed from the gastrointestinal tract, it passes through the liver where a significant amount is metabolized. This significantly reduces the oral efficacy of morphine. Routes for abuse of morphine have been provided because it is also absorbed from the nasal mucosa (snuffing) and the lungs (smoking). Morphine is usually administered subcutaneously but is also administered intramuscularly or intravenously. The rate of absorption from subcutaneous or intramuscular routes may vary considerably because of differences in tissue circulation. Ordinarily the peak activity is seen in 45 to 90 minutes (Table 12-1). It is rapidly distributed to the tissues, particularly the kidney, lungs, liver, and spleen. The $t_{\frac{1}{2}}$ of morphine is approximately 3 hours.

Although approximately 33% of morphine is protein bound, it does not remain in the tissues long. It is metabolized by conjugation with glucuronic acid. Morphine is excreted mainly as the glucuronide and a small amount of unchanged drug by glomerular filtration.

Use, dosage, and preparations

Morphine, as the sulfate salt, is used parenterally for severe pain. The usual adult dose of 10 to 15 mg subcutaneously should cover severe pain of dental origin for 4 to 6 hours. For children, the dose is 0.1 to 0.2 mg/kg/dose, with the maximal dose being 15 mg.[2] Close observation should follow the use of morphine in a child. Parenteral solutions of morphine sulfate and oral preparations are available (Table 12-1).

Codeine

Codeine is the methoxy derivative of morphine. It differs from morphine by a methoxy group at the C_3 position *(arrow)*. Its structure is as follows:

Codeine

It is the most frequently used narcotic in dental practice and has the same pharmacologic actions as morphine but to a lesser degree. Tolerance and addiction to codeine develop more slowly than to morphine.

Pharmacologic effects

Whereas morphine is primarily used parenterally, codeine is quite effective orally. Codeine has less than one sixth the analgesic potency of morphine, and consequently it is not effective for more severe pain. Codeine is equivalent to morphine as an antitussive.

Adverse reactions

Just as codeine has the same therapeutic actions as morphine, its adverse effects are qualitatively similar although quantitatively different. Doses of codeine between 60 and 120 mg are likely to cause about as many troublesome effects as 10 mg morphine. Although most patients will be sedated to some degree by 30 to 60 mg codeine, euphoria is not likely to be seen at these doses. Little or no respiratory depression follows the usual analgesic doses of codeine (up to 60 mg). However, 120 mg is believed to produce respiratory depression that is approximately equal to that produced by 10 mg morphine.[3]

Emesis, nausea, and constipation may be seen with analgesic doses of codeine but will be less than that seen with morphine. Increased intracranial pressure is not likely to present a problem, unless doses are used that would also significantly depress respiration. Miosis and adverse renal, hepatic, cardiovascular, and bronchial effects are not likely to be seen with therapeutic doses of codeine. The excitatory effects of codeine may be greater than those of morphine, and convulsions have been seen in children. The amount of codeine present in the milk of nursing mothers taking therapeutic doses of codeine should not present a problem in the normal infant. Timing of the doses of codeine to avoid nursing time could further reduce the infant's dose.

Addiction

Codeine's addiction liability is much less than that associated with morphine. The short-term use of codeine, as would be employed in dental practice, usually does not present a problem.

Administration, absorption, and metabolism

Codeine is effectively absorbed orally and is usually administered by this route. Codeine is about two thirds as potent orally as parenterally. This is probably because of a diminished first-pass effect. Wide tissue distribution is obtained. Codeine is metabolized mainly to inactive metabolites in the liver. A small proportion is metabolized to morphine, which is subsequently conjugated and excreted in urine. The analgesic and other effects of codeine may be attributable to the morphine that is formed.

Use, dosage, and preparations

Codeine is used for mild to moderate pain. It is employed in dental practice for pain that cannot be controlled by nonnarcotic analgesics but that does not require the use of the more potent narcotics. It has additional use in medicine as an antitussive. It is almost always used orally, and the usual adult analgesic dosages are 15 to 60 mg (¼ to 1 grain) every 4 to 6 hours. Unless a patient has developed tolerance to narcotics, a maximal analgesic potency is generally obtained with 60 mg. This dosage will not equal that of 10 mg morphine. Increasing the dosage beyond 60 mg will prolong the duration of action and the number of adverse effects. For greater analgesic depth, the practitioner must use a more potent analgesic. A somewhat greater analgesic effect may be obtained by giving the drug subcutaneously.

Codeine sulfate and codeine phosphate are available as 15, 30, and 60 mg tablets and as 15, 30, and 60 mg/ml parenteral solutions (Table 12-1).

Codeine-containing combinations. Codeine is also available in various preparations with nonnarcotic analgesics, which add analgesic and antipyretic effects (Table 12-2). To estimate the value of the additive analgesic effect, one may assume that 30 mg codeine equals approximately 600 mg (10 grains) aspirin or acetaminophen. The addition of aspirin to codeine may be useful for two other reasons. First, it can provide antiinflammatory action. Second, the two work by different mechanisms. Some authors state that the nonnarcotic analgesics are synergistic with the codeine,[5] whereas other authors state that they are merely additive.[6] In either case, the nonnarcotic agent in that combination provides a substantial proportion of the analgesic effect for dental pain.[7] The optimal combination is a combination of the appropriate doses of each agent. For aspirin and acetaminophen, the optimal adult dose is at least 600 mg. When prescribing a codeine-containing combination product (Table 12-2), one must consider the optimal dose of each agent. Sometimes the administration of an additional tablet of aspirin or acetaminophen with the prescribed combination can accomplish this.

Aspirin and codeine (Empirin with codeine). The administration of this combination brings the antiinflammatory effect of aspirin to the centrally-acting narcotic, whether it is synergistic or additive. For pain of dental origin (inflammation) this combination is a good choice if there are no contraindications to the use of aspirin (e.g., coagulopathy).

Acetaminophen and codeine (Tylenol with codeine, Phenaphen with codeine). This combination can be effective for some dental pain. It does not provide the antiinflammatory effect that the combination with aspirin provides, but it can be used when aspirin is contraindicated.

Fiorinal with codeine. This combination (Table 12-2) provides the analgesia and antiinflammatory effects of aspirin while adding the sedative effects of butalbital, a barbiturate. It is indicated in the treatment of dental pain when a significant anxiety component exists.

Heroin

Heroin is produced by the acetylation of morphine. It is two to five times as potent as morphine as an analgesic. It is a highly euphoric and addicting drug. Although it has potent analgesic properties, its enormous addicting liability has precluded its therapeutic usefulness. Although it cannot be legally manufactured or imported into the United States, it is currently available in some European countries. There is some interest in using it for terminal intractable pain.

SEMISYNTHETIC DERIVATIVES OF MORPHINE OR CODEINE
Hydromorphone or dihydromorphinone

Hydromorphone (Dilaudid) is a more potent analgesic than morphine, and its tendency to produce adverse side effects is proportional. The analgesic ef-

Table 12-2. Composition of selected codeine-containing combinations

Drug*	Other ingredients	Amount (mg)
Empirin with codeine (#2, 3, 4)	Aspirin	325
Ascriptin with codeine (#2, 3)	Aspirin	325
	Magnesium aluminum hydroxide	150
Phenaphen with codeine (#2, 3, 4)	Acetaminophen	325
Tylenol with codeine (#1, 2, 3, 4)	Acetaminophen	300
Fiorinal with codeine (#1, 2, 3)	Butalbital	50
	Aspirin	200
	Phenacetin	130
	Caffeine	40

From Requa, B.S., and Holroyd, S.V.: Applied pharmacology for the dental hygienist, St. Louis, 1982, The C.V. Mosby Co.
*Drugs contain the following amounts of codeine according to the number listed: #1, 8 mg; #2, 15 mg; #3, 30 mg; #4, 60 mg.

fect and the typical narcotic side effects, including respiratory depression, of 2 mg of hydromorphone is approximately equal to that of 10 mg morphine (Table 12-1). Because of its rapid onset and short duration of action, its principal use is for acute pain of short duration. It is much better absorbed orally than morphine. The usual adult dose is 2 to 5 mg orally or 1 or 2 mg subcutaneously (Table 12-1).

Hydrocodone and dihydrocodeinone

Hydrocodone (Codone, Dicodid, in Vicodin*) has approximately the same analgesic potency as meperidine and a greater antitussive effect than codeine. Analgesic doses may depress respiration. Its addiction liability equals that of morphine. It is used as an antitussive and analgesic.

Oxymorphone

Oxymorphone (Numorphan) is similar to hydromorphone in that although it is more potent than morphine (eight to ten times), its undesirable effects are correspondingly high. It is extremely addicting and a potent respiratory depressant. The usual adult dose is 1 mg subcutaneously. It is available only for parenteral use.

*Contains other active ingredients.

Table 12-3. Composition of selected narcotic analgesic combinations

Drug	Narcotic analgesic	Amount (mg)	Other agents	Amount (mg)
Percodan	Oxycodone	~5	Aspirin	325
Percodan-Demi	Oxycodone	~2.5	Aspirin	325
Percocet-5	Oxycodone	5	Acetaminophen	325
Tylox	Oxycodone	~5	Acetaminophen	500
Mepergan	Meperidine	50	Promethazine	12.50
Mepergan Fortis	Meperidine	50	Promethazine	25
Demerol APAP	Meperidine	50	Acetaminophen	300
Synalgos-DC	Dihydrocodeine	16	Aspirin	356
			Phenacetin	162
			Promethazine	6.25
			Caffeine	30
Vicodin	Hydrocodone	5	Acetaminophen	500

From Requa, B.S., and Holroyd, S.V.: Applied pharmacology for the dental hygienist, St. Louis, 1982, The C.V. Mosby Co.

Oxycodone

Chemically, oxycodone is to codeine what oxymorphone is to morphine. Oxycodone is more potent and more addicting than codeine and produces proportionally more side effects. Like codeine, it retains from one half to two thirds of its effectiveness when taken by mouth. It is used in antitussive preparations and is available as an analgesic in four multiple entity products: Percodan, Percodan-Demi, Percocet-5, and Tylox (Table 12-3). These products are of intermediate potency and are now available as combinations formulated either with aspirin or acetaminophen.

Dihydrocodeine

Dihydrocodeine is the narcotic present in Synalgos-DC. This combination also includes APC and promethazine (Table 12-3). Dihydrocodeine is thought to be similar to, but possibly weaker than, codeine. The promethazine may account for this product's propensity to cause drowsiness. Based on a review by the NAS-NRC, the FDA has ruled this product "possibly effective" for the relief of moderate to moderately severe pain. Further investigation will be required to classify it as less than effective.

SYNTHETIC NARCOTICS
Meperidine and derivatives

Meperidine, alphaprodine, and anileridine are all phenylpiperidine derivatives and consequently are closely related chemically. Although they are related pharmacologically to the opiates, they are chemically different. All have the following structural nucleus and differ by the group at R_1 and R_2.

Phenylpiperidine nucleus

Ethoheptazine is included in this group because it is related to meperidine.

Meperidine

Meperidine (Demerol) is not infrequently used in dental practice. It is a phenylpiperidine with a CH_3 in the R_1 position and an H in the R_2 position. Although not as potent as morphine, it provides effective analgesia against moderately severe pain. Associated adverse effects are similar to but less than those of morphine; these include sedation, respiratory depression, and increased tone and secretions of the gastrointestinal tract. It produces less euphoria, bronchoconstriction, and constipation than morphine because it is less potent. Meperidine produces addiction, and tolerance develops. It is the most common narcotic abused by health professionals. Its overdose effects are counteracted by narcotic antagonists.

The most frequently observed side effects of meperidine are dizziness, nausea, vomiting, postural hypotension, sweating, and xerostomia. Reactions to overdose include tachycardia, excitement, disorientation, delirium, hallucinations, and convulsions. All precautions observed for morphine should be exercised with meperidine.

Meperidine is better absorbed than morphine because of its oral to parenteral effectiveness of approximately 50%. As with other narcotics, it is metabolized principally by the liver. Metabolites and some free drug are excreted in the urine.

The usual adult doses of meperidine (50 to 100 mg orally, subcutaneously, or intramuscularly) are effective against moderate to severe pain of dental origin. It is particularly valuable when used parenterally to obtain rapid analgesia and sedation. The 100 mg dose of meperidine approaches the analgesic potency of 10 mg morphine.

Meperidine is available in tablets, an elixir, and solutions for injection (Table 12-1). It is available in combination with acetaminophen or promethazine (Table 12-3). It may be prescribed in this way or taken separately with acetaminophen or aspirin. The use of meperidine with aspirin or acetaminophen increases the analgesic effect provided by meperidine and provides an antipyretic or antiinflammatory effect (aspirin). The sedating effect of the antihistamine promethazine is additive and may be potentiating. Consequently this combination may be useful when sedation is particularly important. However, one must be cautioned that promethazine and other phenothiazines can exaggerate the respiratory depression caused by meperidine and other narcotics. The promethazine may also act as an antiemetic agent.

Alphaprodine

Although alphaprodine was recently removed from the market because of its inappropriate use, it has been put on the market again. At least one death has been reported.[10] Shane and others[11] reported over 10,000 uses of alphaprodine, including 6 cases involving complications and 1 incident of apnea. Most recently a case of hypoxic encephalopathy resulting in deafness and blindness has been reported.[12]

Anileridine

In equivalent doses there are no distinctive differences between anileridine (Leritine) and meperidine. The usual adult dose is 25 to 50 mg every 6 hours orally, intramuscularly, or subcutaneously. It is available in tablets and as an injection (Table 12-2).

Ethoheptazine

Ethoheptazine (Zactane) is prepared synthetically and has a chemical structure similar to that of meperidine.

The only reported therapeutic effect of ethoheptazine is analgesia. Its relative analgesic potency is difficult to assess. When used alone, its potency is inferior to that of aspirin.[8] In fact, one study showed it to be less effective than a placebo.[9]

Adverse effects of therapeutic dosages of ethoheptazine are mild and similar to those associated with propoxyphene, principally dizziness and gastrointestinal disturbances. The FDA has listed it as "possibly effective" for relief of mild to moderate pain. It is used in combination with aspirin (Zactirin), APC (Zactirin Compound-100), or aspirin and meprobamate (Equagesic). Each of these preparations is probably only as useful as the other ingredients added to the ethoheptazine.

Methadone and derivatives

Methadone (Dolophine) is chemically distinct from both the opiates and the meperidine type of synthetics.

Methadone

It was synthesized in Germany during World War II and was shown to produce the same effects as morphine, including potent analgesia, respiratory depression, sedation, addiction, smooth muscle spasm, and miosis. Patients taking methadone exhibit the usual opiate side effects of constipation, nausea, vomiting, dizziness, xerostomia, and mental depression. Although methadone can be used to relieve severe pain, the fact that it prevents and alleviates the opiate withdrawal syndrome has led to its wide use as a narcotic substitute. Withdrawal from methadone appears to be accomplished more easily than from morphine, owing to its longer duration of action. Addicted patients are switched from heroin to methadone because it is orally active and has a longer duration of action when given in repeated doses. The patient can then be slowly withdrawn from or maintained on methadone (Chapter 34).

Methadone is absorbed orally and may also be used parenterally. It is metabolized chiefly by the liver, and metabolic products are eliminated in the feces and urine.

The usual adult analgesic dose of methadone for severe pain is 10 mg. This provides analgesia equivalent to 10 mg of morphine. Methadone is available in tablets and a parenteral solution (Table 12-1).

Propoxyphene

Propoxyphene (Darvon) is produced synthetically and has a chemical structure similar to that of the narcotic methadone.

Propoxyphene

The only therapeutic effect of propoxyphene is that of analgesia. Although it is sometimes said to equal codeine in analgesic potency or to have analgesic effects similar to those of codeine,[13] dental studies have found it to be slightly inferior to codeine with fewer side effects,[14] statistically less effective than codeine,[15] significantly inferior to aspirin,[16] equal to a placebo,[16,17] and inferior to a placebo.[18] Beaver[19] has stated that propoxyphene is superior to a placebo in doses of 65 mg or more but is of questionable efficacy in doses lower than 65 mg. He further states that propoxyphene is "certainly no more, and probably less, effective than the usually used doses of aspirin or APC." A study by Moertel and coworkers[9] found propoxyphene to be no more effective than a placebo. Miller reviewed 20 double-blind studies out of 243 articles on propoxyphene.[20] The studies showed that the analgesic effectiveness of propoxyphene was not superior to that of codeine or aspirin. Miller concluded that "factors other than intrinsic therapeutic value are responsible for the commercial success of propoxyphene."[20]

Adverse effects of therapeutic dosages of propoxyphene are mild and consist primarily of nausea, vomiting, abdominal pain, dizziness, headache, insomnia, and skin rashes. Although some cases of euphoria, tolerance, and psychologic and physical dependence have been reported, the addiction liability of propoxyphene is low. Despite this, drug abuse with propoxyphene appears to have attained significant proportions, and several hundred deaths annually have been attributed to this drug.

Severe overdosage may produce symptoms of inebriation, convulsions, respiratory depression, cyanosis, coma, circulatory failure, and death. The narcotic antagonist naloxone is the drug of choice to treat an overdose of propoxyphene. It counteracts the respiratory depression but not the CNS excitation, including tremors and convulsions. The antagonism between propoxyphene and the narcotic antagonists is not as complete as between other narcotics and the antagonists. CNS stimulants such as amphetamine or caffeine should not be used because fatal convulsions may be induced. Propoxyphene should not be prescribed for pregnant women, and its safety in children has not been established. It has produced withdrawal in neonates whose mothers used the drug.

Propoxyphene is rapidly absorbed orally and is given only by this route. Peak levels are obtained in 1 to 2 hours.[21] It cannot be used parenterally because of local irritation. It is metabolized primarily in the liver; metabolites and some active drug are excreted in the urine.

Propoxyphene hydrochloride is used against mild to moderate pain. The usual adult dosage is 65 mg every 6 to 8 hours, not to exceed 390 mg daily. Propoxyphene is frequently administered with aspirin, phenacetin, acetaminophen, or caffeine to provide an antipyretic effect and increase its analgesic potency. Some propoxyphene-containing preparations available are listed in Table 12-4.

Propoxyphene napsylate was approved for use when the patent for propoxyphene hydrochloride expired. Its purported advantage is its decreased water solubility. This allowed for the preparation of a liquid form and also discouraged the intravenous use by addicts. Although the pharmacologic effect of the napsylate salt is similar to that of the hydrochloride,[22] the difference in molecular weights means that 100 mg of the napsylate is equivalent to 65 mg of the hydrochloride. The usual adult oral dose of the napsylate salt is 100 mg three or four times daily not to exceed 600 mg. Table 12-4 lists available preparations.

Table 12-4. Selected preparations containing propoxyphene

Drug	Propoxyphene HCl (mg)	Propoxyphene napsylate (mg)	Aspirin (mg)	Phenacetin (P) or acetaminophen (A) (mg)	Caffeine (mg)
Darvon 32 mg*	32				
Darvon 65 mg*	65				
Darvon with A.S.A.	65		325		
Darvon Compound*	32		227	162 (P)	32
Darvon Compound-65*	65		227	162 (P)	32
Darvon-N 100 mg		100			
Darvon-N with A.S.A.		100	325		
Darvocet-N		50		325 (A)	
Darvocet-N 100*		100		650 (A)	
Darvon-N suspension		10 mg/ml			

From Requa, B.S., and Holroyd, S.V.: Applied pharmacology for the dental hygienist, St. Louis, 1982, The C.V. Mosby Co.
*Generics are available.

NARCOTIC AGONIST-ANTAGONISTS AND ANTAGONISTS

This group of drugs includes a wide variety of members along a continuum—from the mainly agonist pentazocine to the pure antagonist naloxone. In general, they can be divided into those agents used for their analgesic effect and those used for their action as antagonists (Table 12-5).

Their mechanism of action is relatively complex. The existence of at least three opioid receptors, mu (μ), kappa (κ), and sigma (σ), has been postulated.[23] Stimulation of the mu receptor produces supraspinal analgesia, respiratory depression, euphoria, and physical dependence. When the kappa receptor is stimulated, it induces spinal analgesia, miosis, and sedation. Its effect on respiration is not clear (it may depress respiration). The activation of sigma receptors is associated with dysphoria, hallucinations, and respiratory and vasomotor stimulation. The agonist-antagonists and the antagonists possess a different affinity for these receptors. It is thought that morphinelike drugs act primarily at the mu and less at the kappa receptors. Other agents such as nalorphine combine with the mu receptor and produce no effect (competitive antagonist) or only a small effect (partial agonist) while stimulating the kappa and sigma receptors. These drugs are termed agonist-antagonists. The pure antagonists such as naloxone antagonize all three sites—the mu, kappa, and sigma receptors. This explains why some agents can either antagonize morphine or produce morphinelike effects, depending on whether morphine is present or absent.

Agonist-antagonists

The development of the narcotic agonist-antagonist analgesics was based on the desire to develop an agent with strong analgesic properties but lacking addicting properties. With each new drug synthesized, this goal is becoming closer.

Pentazocine

Pentazocine was the first narcotic agonist-antagonist analgesic synthesized. Like all agonist-antagonists, its structure is similar to the narcotic analgesics. Its structure is as follows:

Pentazocine

Pharmacologic effects

CNS. The effect of pentazocine on the CNS is similar to that of the narcotic analgesic agents and includes analgesia, sedation, and respiratory depression. When given intramuscularly, pentazocine has about one third the analgesic potency of morphine (30 mg pentazocine equals 10 mg mor-

Table 12-5. Narcotic agonist-antagonist agents

Primary use	Agents
Antagonists	Levallorphan (Lorfan)
	Naloxone (Narcan)
	Nalorphine (Nalline)
	Naltrexone*
	Cyclazocine*
Analgesics	Pentazocine (Talwin)
	Butorphanol (Stadol)
	Nalbuphine (Nubain)
	Buprenorphine* (Temgesic)
	Propiram* (Dirame)

*Not marketed in the United States.

phine). It is about equipotent to codeine when administered orally (Table 12-1). Administered parenterally, a 20 mg dose of pentazocine produces about the same amount of respiratory depression as 10 mg of morphine. It is characteristic of the agonist-antagonists that increasing the dose of pentazocine does not produce an equivalent increase in respiratory depression as with morphine. Larger doses can produce a dysphoric or psychomimetic effect.

Gastrointestinal tract. In small doses pentazocine produces a morphinelike effect on the gastrointestinal tract. Increasing the dose does not result in a proportional increase in the gastrointestinal effect.

Cardiovascular system. The effect of pentazocine on the cardiovascular system is different from that of the narcotic agonists like morphine. Large doses can produce an increase in both blood pressure and heart rate. In the presence of cardiovascular disease, this can increase the work of the heart.

Adverse reactions. Pentazocine has many adverse reactions similar to those of morphine but usually less intense. It also has other adverse effects that are different from those of morphine. The most common adverse reactions are sedation, sweating, and dizziness or light-headedness. Nausea, vomiting, euphoria, and headache can occur. Less frequently, a wide variety of adverse effects can occur. Psychomimetic effects including anxiety, nightmares, and hallucinations, as well as dysphoria, have been reported. With large doses, respiratory depression associated with an increase in blood pressure and tachycardia can occur. Only naloxone antagonizes this respiratory depression. Repeated injections of pentazocine into the same location can produce severe sclerosis, fibrosis, ulceration, and hyperpigmentation.[24]

Abuse. Although not common, drug dependence on pentazocine can occur. Its potential for addiction is probably about equivalent to that of codeine or dextropropoxyphene. Most cases of drug dependency have occurred with parenteral use in persons prone to drug dependence. After repeated administration, physical dependence can be demonstrated because symptoms of withdrawal can be precipitated by naloxone. Even though withdrawal symptoms are similar to morphine withdrawal, they are milder in intensity. Because it is only a weak antagonist, pentazocine cannot reverse the respiratory depression secondary to morphine, but it can precipitate withdrawal in an addict.

Because pentazocine was not thought to have a significant potential for abuse, it was used indiscriminately by many prescribers. For that reason, many cases of pentazocine abuse have been reported. The combination of pentazocine and pyribenzamine became a popular mixture in the addict population. Pentazocine is now under schedule IV of the Controlled Substance Act. Methadone should not be substituted for pentazocine in the treatment of pentazocine addiction, but its dose should be slowly reduced.

Administration, absorption, and metabolism. Pentazocine is well absorbed orally and parenterally. When given intramuscularly, the peak effect is seen in 15 minutes to 1 hour. If taken orally, the drug peaks at about 2 hours. When taken by mouth, less than 20% of the drug enters the circulation because of the first-pass effect.[25]

Pentazocine is metabolized in the liver and excreted as the glucuronide by the kidneys. It passes the placental barrier. Since safe use during pregnancy has not been established, it should only be used when the risk-to-benefit ratio is favorable. Its administration to children younger than 12 years is not recommended because of a lack of clinical experience.

Use, dosage, and preparations. Pentazocine could be useful for dental pain when both codeine and the nonnarcotic analgesics are ineffective. The usual adult dose is 50 mg orally every 3 to 4 hours. This dose may be increased to 100 mg if needed, but the total daily dose should not exceed 600 mg.

Pentazocine, given by mouth, is about as potent as codeine, with 50 mg of pentazocine being equivalent to about 60 mg of codeine. Both agents can relieve more severe pain if given in larger doses, but more side effects are produced. It is available in both tablet and parenteral forms (Table 12-1).

Nalbuphine and butorphanol

Both nalbuphine (Nubain) and butorphanol (Stadol) are new narcotic agonist-antagonist analgesics recently introduced in the United States.

The structure of nalbuphine results from combining the narcotic oxymorphone with the narcotic antagonist naloxone. Chemically butorphanol is related to levorphanol. Both of these agents have something in common with pentazocine since all three are agonists-antagonists.

Pharmacologic effects. Although they are presently classed as intermediate in potency (Table 12-1), some sources think that nalbuphine and butorphanol are as potent as morphine. On a milligram per milligram basis, nalbuphine is approximately equal in potency to morphine, and butorphanol is about five times as potent as morphine.

Orally nalbuphine has approximately one fifth its intramuscular potency.[26] Nalbuphine is about one fourth as potent as nalorphine as an antagonist,[27] and butorphanol has approximately one fortieth the narcotic antagonist activity of naloxone.[28] Nalbuphine has about 10 times[26] and butophanol has about 30 times the narcotic antagonist potency of pentazocine.

Adverse reactions. Although the respiratory depressant effect of these agents is comparable at equi-analgesic doses (Table 12-1), the peak respiratory depressant effect is soon reached. Although two to three times the usual analgesic dose produces more respiratory depression than the usual dose, increasing the dose beyond that does not produce any additive respiratory depression. This larger dose does increase the duration of the respiratory depression. This is in marked contrast to morphine, which produces proportionally more respiratory depression as the dose is increased. The antagonist naloxone is effective against both of these agonist-antagonist narcotics.

The most common side effect associated with those agents is sedation. Sweating, nausea and vomiting, dizziness and vertigo, xerostomia, and headache have been frequently reported. The neuropsychiatric (psychomimetic) effects have been reported more frequently than with morphine and meperidine, but much less frequently than with pentazocine.

Administration, absorption, and metabolism. The onset of action of these agents is a few minutes when they are given intravenously and between 15 and 30 minutes when given intramuscularly.[28,29] The duration of action of nalbuphine is 3 to 6 hours, and that of butorphanol is 3 to 4 hours. The peak analgesic effect is about 30 minutes to 1 hour depending on the route of administration (Table 12-1).

Dosage and preparations. The usual dose of butorphanol is 2 mg every 3 to 4 hours, and the dosage of nalbuphine is 10 mg every 3 to 6 hours. Neither drug has been approved for use in persons less than 18 years of age nor is available in an oral dosage form.

Antagonists

Nalorphine, levallorphan, and naloxone are three agents currently available in the United States that are used as antagonists. These agents antagonize the respiratory depression produced by morphine and other narcotics. The respiratory depression caused by non-narcotic agents such as the barbiturates is not antagonized by these agents. Their chemical structures closely resemble those of the narcotic analgesics to which they are related.

Nalorphine and levallorphan

Nalorphine (Nalline) and levallorphan (Lorfan) possess both agonist and antagonist properties. When administered alone, they produce weak respiratory depression (agonist effect), but when administered to a patient who has respiratory depression caused by a narcotic analgesic, they reverse this depression (antagonist effect). Non-narcotic-induced respiratory depression could be deepened by these agents. For example, the respiratory depression induced by the barbiturates could be increased if these agents were administered. When given to a narcotic addict, these agents could precipitate the withdrawal syndrome. Since the duration of action of these agents may be shorter than that of a narcotic, their dose may need to be repeated if the respiration again becomes depressed.

Naloxone

Unlike nalorphine and levallorphan, naloxone (Narcan) is a pure antagonist with no agonist properties. It antagonizes the mu, kappa, and sigma receptors. When naloxone is given alone, it does not produce morphinelike effects. Naloxone is therefore the drug of choice in the treatment of respiratory depression from an unknown cause. If the respiratory depression is caused by a narcotic analgesic agent, it will be antagonized by any of the narcotic antagonists, but if the respiratory depression is caused by a barbiturate or other CNS depressant, naloxone will not cause any additive respiratory depression. In contrast to nalorphine and levallorphan, naloxone is effective in reversing the respiratory depression caused by pentazocine. It is also the drug of choice for reversing the respiratory depression secondary to the agonist-antagonists butorphanol and nalbuphine.

The initial adult dose of naloxone is 0.4 mg intravenously, intramuscularly, or subcutaneously. Effects should be observed within a few minutes. This dose may be repeated at 2- to 3-minute intervals. If significant improvement is not obtained after two or three doses, the respiratory depression is probably not associated with a narcotic overdose. Since the duration of action of the antagonist may be less than that of the narcotic causing the respiratory depression, it may be necessary to repeat the dose if the respiration becomes depressed again. Naloxone should be kept in the dental emergency kit in any dental office where narcotic analgesics are administered to patients or prescribed for them.

REFERENCES

1. Reynolds, D.C.: Pain control in the dental office, Dent. Clin. North Am. **15:**319, 1971.
2. American Medical Association Department of Drugs: AMA drug evaluations, ed. 4, Acton, Mass., 1980, Publishing Sciences Group, Inc.
3. Gilman, A.G., Goodman, L.S., and Gilman, A.: Goodman and Gilman's the pharmacological basis of therapeutics, ed. 6, New York, 1980, Macmillan Publishing Co., Inc.
4. Campbell, C., Phillips, O.C., and Frazier, T.M.: Analgesia during labor: a comparison of pentobarbital, meperidine and morphine, Obstet. Gynecol. **17:**714, 1961.
5. Pallasch, T.J.: Pharmacology for dental students and practitioners, Philadelphia, 1980, Lea & Febiger.
6. Neidle, E.A., Kroeger, D.C., and Yagiela, J.A.: Pharmacology and therapeutics for dentistry, St. Louis, 1980, The C.V. Mosby Co.
7. Cooper, S.A., and Beaver, W.T.: A model to evaluate mild analgesics in oral surgery outpatients, Clin. Pharmacol. Ther. **20:**241, 1976.
8. Non-narcotic analgesics, Med. Lett. Drugs. Ther. **8:**8, 1966.
9. Moertel, C.G., Ahmann, D.L., and Taylor, W.F.: A comparative evaluation of marketed analgesic drugs, N. Engl. J. Med. **286:**813, 1972.
10. Hine, C.H., and Pasi, A.: Fatality after use of alphaprodine in analgesia for dental surgery: report of a case, J. Am. Dent. Assoc. **84:**858, 1972.
11. Shane, S.M., Carrel, R., and Vandenberge, J.: Intravenous amnesia: an appraisal after seven years and 10,500 administration, Anesth. Progr. **21:**36, 1974.
12. Okuji, D.M.: Hypoxic encephalopathy after the administration of alphaprodine hydrochloride, J. Am. Dent. Assoc. **103:**50, 1981.
13. Gruber, C.M., Jr.: Codeine phosphate, propoxyphene HCl and placebo, J.A.M.A. **164:**966, 1957.
14. Koslin, A.J.: A single-blind comparison of codeine PO$_4$ and dextropropoxyphene HCl, Oral Surg. **12:**1203, 1959.
15. Chilton, N.W., Lewandowski, A., and Cameron, J.R.: Double-blind evaluation of a new analgesic agent in post-extraction pain, Am. J. Med. Sci. **242:**702, 1961.
16. Ahlstrom, U., and Lantz, B.: A comparison between dextropropoxyphene hydrochloride and acetyl salicyclic acid as analgesics after oral surgery, Odont. Rev. **19:**55, 1968.
17. Berdon, J.K., et al.: The effectiveness of dextropropoxyphene HCl in the control of pain after periodontal surgery, J. Periodontol. **36:**106, 1964.
18. Scopp, I.W., et al.: A double-blind clinical study of Dialog, Darvon and a placebo in the management of postoperative dental pain, J. Oral Ther. **4:**123, 1967.
19. Beaver, W.T.: Mild analgesics: a review of their clinical pharmacology, Am. J. Med. Sci. **250:**577, 1965.
20. Miller, R.R., Feingold, A., and Paxinos, J.: Propoxyphene hydrochloride, a critical review, J.A.M.A. **213:**996, 1970.
21. Miller, R.R.: Propoxyphene: a review. In Miller, R.R., and Greenblatt, D.J., editors: Drug therapy reviews, vol. 2, New York, 1979, Elsevier North-Holland, Inc.
22. Darvon and Darvon-N, Med. Lett. Drugs Ther. **14:**37, 1972.
23. Martin, W.R., et al.: The effects of morphine- and nalorphine-like drugs in non-dependent and morphine-dependent chronic spinal dog, J. Pharmacol. Exp. Ther. **197:**517-532, 1976.
24. Padilla, R.S., et al.: Cutaneous and nervous complications of pentazocine abuse, Arch. Dermatol. **115:**975, 1978.
25. Ehrnebo, M., Boreus, L., and Lonroth, U.: Bioavailability and first-pass metabolism of oral pentazocine in man, Clin. Pharmacol. Ther. **22:**888-892, 1977.
26. Beaver, W.T., and Feise, G.A.: A comparison of the analgesic effect of intramuscular nalbuphine and morphine in patients with postoperative pain, J. Pharmacol. Exp. Ther. **204:**487, 1978.
27. Jasinski, D.R., and Mansky, P.A.: Evaluation of nalbuphine for abuse potential, Clin. Pharmacol. Ther. **13:**78, 1972.
28. Kastrup, E.K., editor: Facts and comparisons, St. Louis, 1981, Facts and Comparisons, Inc.
29. Physician's Monograph. Nubain: Nalbuphine HCl, Garden City, N.Y., 1979, Endo Laboratories.

CHAPTER 13

RICHARD L. WYNN
BARBARA REQUA-CLARK

Central nervous system stimulants

CNS stimulants consist of a heterogeneous group of compounds that produce various degrees of stimulation, depending on the compound, the dose, and the occasion of its use. Agents such as pentylenetetrazol and nikethamide act mainly to stimulate respiration and to oppose the respiratory depressant actions of barbiturates. Because of their ability to overcome drug-induced respiratory depression and hypnosis, these drugs are termed *analeptics*. Other stimulants such as strychnine have selective stimulant actions on the spinal cord. In contrast, caffeine, amphetamines, and methylphenidate exert their primary actions on the cerebral cortex. In addition, the actions of some of these stimulants are not restricted to the CNS. For example, caffeine and two of its congeners, theophylline and theobromine, elicit various effects on other organ systems that have important therapeutic implications. This chapter discusses the CNS and other miscellaneous effects of these stimulant drugs.

As a general rule, dentists do not prescribe CNS stimulants. However, the increasing abuse of the amphetamines and cocaine and the ingestion of large quantities of caffeine in the form of coffee by the public cause an increase in the number of dental patients under the influence of these drugs. Also, since the effects of these drugs are not restricted to the CNS, the possibility of many drug interactions with these agents and the resulting change in the activity of other organs is raised.

In the past the CNS stimulants were widely used therapeutically, but only a limited few have any therapeutic usefulness today.

ANALEPTICS AND RESPIRATORY STIMULANTS

Drugs classified as analeptics and respiratory stimulants have been used to overcome severe intoxication by CNS depressants in the past. More recently, the use of these drugs in this situation has been discredited, and conservative measures are now being used for sedation overdoses. These agents have limited usefulness, but a few are occasionally indicated to stimulate respiration when a patient has pulmonary disease or to hasten recovery from a general anesthetic. If given in sufficient doses, each of these agents can produce generalized convulsions. Unfortunately, the margin of safety between the dose that stimulates respiration and that which produces convulsions is too narrow and unpredictable in nature. Analeptics and respiratory stimulants, along with their mechanisms of CNS stimulation and use, are listed in Table 13-1.

Pentylenetetrazol (Metrazol)

Pentylenetetrazol is a stimulant to the respiratory and cardiovascular systems and a CNS convulsant. The chemical structure of pentylenetetrazol is shown in Fig. 13-1. The drug causes an increase in respiration and blood pressure by the direct stimulation of the medullary respiratory and vasomotor centers. Convulsant activity occurs with higher doses because of activation of both the cerebrum and brain stem. Although the mechanism of pentylenetetrazol is unknown, there is evidence to support the theory of CNS excitatory effects caused by decreases in neuronal recovery time.

Pentylenetetrazol enjoys limited use as a diagnostic aid. It activates epileptogenic foci in epilepsy to characterize this cerebral disorder. As a convulsant in laboratory animals, it is used as a laboratory tool in the evaluation of potential anticonvulsant drugs. It has previously been used as a convulsant for shock therapy in involutional depression—a use superseded by electroconvulsive therapy. The drug has also been

Table 13-1. Analeptics and respiratory stimulants

Drug name		Mechanism	Use
Generic	Trade		
Pentylenetetrazol	Metrazol	Does not block inhibition; may act by enhancing excitation	Diagnostic aid in epilepsy; laboratory tool to study anticonvulsants
Ethamivan	Emivan	Same as above	Respiratory stimulant: antiquated use to counter CNS depressant drugs
Doxapram	Dopram	Same as above	Respiratory stimulant; analeptic to hasten postanesthetic recovery after general anesthesia
Nikethamide	Coramine	Same as above	Respiratory stimulant
Picrotoxin		Blocks presynaptic inhibition	None; antiquated use to counter CNS depressant drugs
Strychnine		Blocks postsynaptic inhibition	None; antiquated use as a tonic

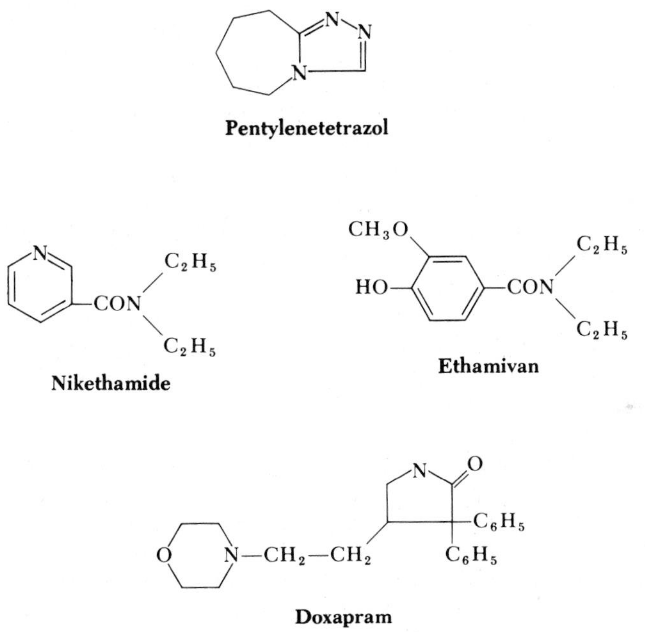

Pentylenetetrazol

Nikethamide

Ethamivan

Doxapram

Fig. 13-1. Structural formulas of some CNS stimulants.

used in the past to elevate the mood in chronically depressed patients and to relieve confusion and memory loss in geriatric patients. Any real benefit in this regard is questionable, however.

Pentylenetetrazol is not useful as an analeptic in drug-induced respiratory depression. The stimulant effect of the drug is brief and may be followed by a subsequent depression. Also, a narrow margin of safety exists between respiratory stimulation of drug-depressed respiration and convulsions. The drug is available as 100 mg tablets and as an elixir (100 mg/5 ml).

Nikethamide (Coramine)

Nikethamide is a derivative of the vitamin nicotinamide. Its chemical structure is shown in Fig. 13-1. The drug stimulates respiration at nonconvulsive doses and has been shown to stimulate morphine-induced respiratory depression. Larger doses produce convulsions that are indistinguishable from those produced by pentylenetetrazol. Nikethamide also exerts a CNS depressive action after its stimulant effect—an action that renders it useless as an analeptic agent. The drug has little effect on the cardiovascular system.

Clinically, nikethamide has been used as a respiratory stimulant to counter the effects of CNS depressant drugs. Nikethamide has been recommended for use as a respiratory stimulant in lung disease.[1]

Ethamivan (Emivan)

Ethamivan chemically resembles nikethamide but is more potent in its CNS stimulant action. Its chemical structure is shown in Fig. 13-1. It stimulates all levels of the cerebrospinal axis and stimulates the medullary respiratory centers in doses below those that cause convulsions. Like nikethamide it is recommended therapeutically as a respiratory stimulant, and its use in drug-induced respiratory depression has the same disadvantages that the other compounds have in such a situation. Ethamivan has been shown to be useful as a respiratory stimulant in hypoventilatory states.[2]

Doxapram (Dopram)

Doxapram is an effective respiratory stimulant and analeptic used to hasten arousal and the return of protective pharyngeal and laryngeal reflexes in the postanesthetic period after general anesthesia. The chemical structure of doxapram is shown in Fig. 13-1. The drug produces a significant increase in tidal volume and respiratory rate and is of short duration (5 to 12 minutes). Doxapram can also produce generalized CNS convulsions. Its margin of safety is sufficient, since the dose required to improve respiration is considerably below the dose needed to induce convulsions. Serious adverse effects have been produced by doxapram, including hypertension, tachycardia, arrhythmias, muscle rigidity, and vomiting.[3] Doxapram's short duration of action precludes its usefulness as a respiratory stimulant in drug-induced depression. Its untoward cardiovascular effects may be greatly increased in patients receiving sympathomimetic drugs or monoamine oxidase inhibitors.

Picrotoxin

Picrotoxin is a natural substance occurring in the seeds of the plant *Anamirta cocculus*. These seeds have been used to poison fish, hence the name *fish berries*.

Picrotoxin is a powerful stimulant to the CNS. The target cells are probably in the medulla, since convulsions produced by the drug persist after the removal of the cerebral hemispheres in laboratory animals. Tonic-clonic seizures occur with the drug, and respiratory volume is stimulated in the presence of drug-induced depression. Medullary stimulation of the respiratory and vasomotor centers accounts for the respiratory stimulation, hypertension, salivation, nausea, and vomiting that accompany use of the drug. The mechanism of convulsive activity is suggested to be a blockade of presynaptic inhibition.

The use of picrotoxin in the past has been limited to analepsis in drug-induced respiratory depression, particularly barbiturate overdosage. However, as has been stated before, the use of such an agent in this circumstance is controversial. It is no longer marketed in the United States.

Strychnine

Strychnine is a CNS convulsive agent of primarily toxicologic interest with no established therapeutic use. Strychnine is the alkaloidal component of nux vomica seeds of a tree native to India, *Strychnos nuxvomica*. This agent acts at all levels of the cerebrospinal axis, resulting in restlessness, increased respiration, muscle twitching, and convulsions. Opisthotonos and the initiation of tetanic convulsions by even the slightest sensory stimulus are the classic manifestations of its poisoning. The mechanism of strychnine is well known. The drug blocks postsynaptic inhibitory reflexes within the CNS, particularly in the spinal cord, allowing for the propagation of excitatory impulses throughout the complex interconnections in the cerebrospinal axis.[4] This mechanism explains why the stronger extensor muscles acting unopposed produce the characteristic posture of opisthotonos and why a variety of sensory stimuli elicit the characteristic seizures.

Strychnine was used for many years as a tonic—the tonic effect being the bitter taste, stimulation of the gastrointestinal tract, and an increase in tone of voluntary muscle. The latter two effects are difficult to achieve with therapeutic doses, however, and there remains no rational basis for the use of this drug in medicine.

Death from strychnine is usually caused by asphyxia from respiratory arrest during tetanic convulsions. Treatment of strychnine poisoning in the past has been aimed at blocking convulsions with intravenously administered barbiturates, an inhalant anesthetic, or a muscle relaxant, by the use of artificial respiration and oxygenation, and by minimizing sensory stimuli from the environment. Diazepam is superior to the intravenously administered barbiturates and today is considered the drug of choice to treat strychnine poisoning. Prompt control of convulsions by diazepam with little accompanying sedation affords distinct advantages over the more depressant barbiturates. Convulsions are terminated by 10 mg diazepam administered intravenously.[5] Doses are repeated as symptoms arise. The minimum lethal oral dose of strychnine is approximately 100 mg. There exists no official preparation of strychnine.

XANTHINES

Caffeine, theophylline, and theobromine are members of a class of compounds known as xanthines. These agents share several pharmacologic properties, but the extent of each of these properties varies with the different agents (Table 13-2).

Caffeine

Caffeine is the 1,3,7-trimethylxanthine and is the most widely ingested CNS stimulant by the public, since it is so readily accessible as a component in caffeinated beverages. The structures of the basic xanthine nucleus and caffeine are as follows:

Xanthine   1,3,7,-Trimethylxanthine (caffeine)

The pharmacologic effects of caffeine that are of therapeutic interest are those acting on the CNS. The drug increases mental alertness, decreases drowsiness, and provides for a clear flow of ideas.

Large doses of caffeine stimulate the medulla. This effect may have some therapeutic value when barbiturates depress the respiration. Large intravenous doses that produce CNS excitation are followed by depression. Effects other than on the CNS include

Table 13-2. Pharmacologic effects of the xanthines

Xanthine	CNS and respiratory stimulation	Diuretic effect	Bronchial relaxation	Cardiac stimulation
Caffeine	+++	+	+	+
Theophylline	++	+++	+++	+++
Theobromine	+	++	++	++

From THE PHARMACOLOGICAL BASIS OF THERAPEUTICS, 5th edition, Edited by Louis S. Goodman and Alfred Gilman. (Copyright © 1975 by Macmillan Publishing Co., Inc.)

bronchodilation, diuresis, increased gastric secretions, and cardiovascular effects. The drug increases the force of contraction of the myocardium to cause an increase in the cardiac output. There are mixed effects on blood pressure, with a decrease occurring because of peripheral dilation and an increase because of the myocardial stimulation. The resulting blood pressure is determined by the balance of these two effects.

Caffeine is used therapeutically to treat common headache in combination with analgesics such as aspirin and phenacetin (APC tablets) and to treat migraine headache in combination with the ergot alkaloid ergotamine. The rationale for the use of caffeine in headache remedies is the increase in cerebral vascular resistance that results from its ability to constrict the cerebral blood vessels. Its advantage over analgesics alone in the treatment of headache has not been established in controlled clinical trials. Caffeine is not an effective analeptic in severe drug-induced depression.

Side effects to the use of caffeine are nervousness, irritability, tremors, insomnia, and epigastric distress. Large doses (150 mg intramuscularly) will cause the respiratory stimulation mentioned earlier. Acute caffeine toxicity is manifested as CNS effects of restlessness, irritability, and generalized convulsions and as cardiovascular effects of tachycardia, hypertension, and circulatory failure. An excess of 10 gm is required to induce convulsions, but no fatalities have been reported after its use. Habituation to caffeine is a well-known phenomenon, and tolerance develops to the insomniac and alerting effects of the drug.[6] Withdrawal symptoms have been difficult to establish.

Caffeine is contraindicated in patients with a history of gastric ulcers. Caffeine should be used with caution in patients with coronary thrombosis, since it does increase cardiac work by stimulating the myocardium. In combination with nicotine (heavy smoking) and fatigue, caffeine has been known to cause paroxysmal atrial tachycardias. Caffeine has been implicated as a determining factor in myocardial infarction, and it may have mutagenic and teratogenic effects. Jick[7] reported a doubling of the incidence of myocardial infarction with the ingestion of 5 to 6 cups of coffee per day. A later study failed to confirm that association,[8] while Heyden[9] found no association between coffee usage and mortality. Caffeine induces chromosomal abnormalities and has potent mutagenic effects on microorganisms at concentrations much higher than those ingested by humans in the form of beverages or medications.[10] These effects do not appear to represent a genetic hazard in humans.[11] Weathersbee et al.[12] compared the intake of caffeine by mothers and fathers to the outcome of pregnancies. With an intake of over 600 mg by the woman, only 1 out of 16 (6.3%) pregnancies were uncomplicated. An intake of over 600 mg by the man also resulted in a 50% reduction in uncomplicated deliveries over those pregnancies in which neither parent consumed any caffeine. Minton et al.[13] have found an association between methylxanthine ingestion and the development of fibrocystic breast disease. Of the women who abstained from consumption of methylxanthines, 65% had a disappearance of all palpable nodules, yet only 4% of those who continued using methylxanthines had a resolution. There was a statistically significant reduction in the number of breast biopsies in women who abstained (35%) versus those who did not (96%). Heyden[14] takes issue with these conclusions. He does not believe there is any association between fibrocystic breast disease and coffee consumption.

It is important to remember that the ingestion of caffeine by the general population is usually in the form of coffee, tea, or cola beverages. Another source of caffeine ingestion is in products sold over the counter. These agents may be marketed as analgesics, diet suppressants, or awakening agents. Table 13-3 lists the amount of caffeine present in some preparations. By examining this table one can see that over-the-counter preparations as well as normally ingested caffeine-containing beverages contain substantial amounts of caffeine. The pharmacologic effects of this drug probably occur most frequently by ingestion of food or self-prescribed, over-the-counter products. Caffeine citrate is available in 65 mg tab-

Table 13-3. Caffeine content of commonly used agents

Agent	Caffeine content (mg)
Beverages (1 cup or glass)	
Brewed coffee	100-150
Instant coffee	50-100
Decaffeinated coffee	2-35
Tea	40-110
Cola drinks	35-60
OTC drugs* (1 dose)†	
Anacin‡	33
Excedrin‡	65
Cope‡	32
Tirend	100
Nodoz	100
Prolamine‡	140
Vivarin‡	200

*Over-the-counter drugs are those that can be purchased without prescription.
†Data from Van Tyle, W.K.: Internal analgesic products. In American Pharmaceutical Association: Handbook of nonprescription drugs, ed. 5, Washington, D.C., 1977, The Association.
‡These products contain other active ingredients.

lets, and caffeine and sodium benzoate are available as an intramuscular injection in ampules containing 0.25 gm/2 ml.

Theophylline and theobromine

Theophylline and theobromine are the 1,3-dimethylxanthine and 3,7-dimethylxanthine, respectively. Their chemical structures are as follows:

1,3-dimethylxanthine (theophylline)   3,7-dimethylxanthine (theobromine)

Theophylline and theobromine are weaker CNS stimulants than caffeine but have other useful properties that warrant discussion. The xanthine derivatives interfere with sodium reabsorption in the proximal renal tubules, resulting in a diuretic effect. Theophylline is the most potent and caffeine the least potent in this regard. The xanthines are also smooth muscle relaxants, with theophylline the most potent and caffeine the least potent. This action is direct and not mediated by autonomic mechanisms. As a result of smooth muscle relaxation, a therapeutically beneficial bronchodilating action is demonstrable in asthmatic patients, resulting in a concomitant decrease in airway resistance and respiratory effort.

Theophylline is the most potent and caffeine the least potent cardiac agent. A direct myocardial stimulating action of theophylline occurs, resulting in increased heart rate and force of contraction. This effect of theophylline is occasionally useful in treating acute congestive heart failure.

Although the exact mechanism of action of the methylxanthines is unknown, at least three actions of these agents may explain their effects: (1) translocation of intracellular calcium, (2) accumulation of cyclic nucleotides, and (3) adenosine receptor blockade. The antiadenosine action seems to be the favored mechanism at present. Other actions of the methylxanthines may be explained by their inhibition of prostaglandin synthesis and their reduction in the catecholamine levels in nonnervous tissues.

Theophylline is available as the free base but is generally used in combination with ethylene diamine and known as aminophylline. Aminophylline is available as tablets and elixir for oral administration, as a parenteral preparation, and as rectal suppositories and solution. Aminophylline is useful in the treatment of severe attacks of asthma—particularly status asthmaticus. It is also given over prolonged periods by mouth to reduce the number and severity of asthma attacks. A single dose of 0.25 gm is given three or four times every 24 hours. Theobromine is available as the free alkaloid and also as a variety of complexes, such as theobromine calcium salicylate (Theocalcin), theobromine sodium acetate, and theobromine salicylate.

SYMPATHOMIMETIC AMINES

Sympathomimetic amines include the amphetamines and other related agents, a few of which are shown in Table 13-4. They are potent CNS stimulants possessing significant pharmacologic effects on the cardiovascular system. Although many agents are available, they are all similar in pharmacologic effects. Amphetamine is considered the prototype.

Amphetamine is one of the most potent sympathomimetic amines in regard to CNS stimulation. A patient given a therapeutic dose of amphetamine will exhibit wakefulness, alertness, and a decrease in

Table 13-4. CNS-stimulating sympathomimetic amines

Generic name	Trade name
Amphetamine	Benzedrine
Dextroamphetamine	Dexedrine
Methamphetamine	Desoxyn, Methedrine
Phentermine	Ionamin
Chlorphentermine	Pre-Sate
Fenfluramine	Pondimin
Benzphetamine	Didrex
Phenmetrazine	Preludin
Diethylpropion	Tenuate, Tepanil
Methylphenidate	Ritalin

fatigue. The mood will be elevated and there will be an increase in ability to concentrate. A euphoric effect can be noticed as well as an increase in motor and speech activity. This euphoria predisposes these drugs to abuse. Physical performance is improved. Reactions that are common in the administration of amphetamine include the following: headache, confusion, dizziness, apprehension, dysphoria, and agitation. Orally administered amphetamine produces a rise in both systolic and diastolic blood pressures. The heart rate is usually reflexly slowed. There is little effect on the cardiac output.

Although amphetamines have been reported to be anorexic agents, the weight loss achieved in obese humans seems to be related to decrease in food intake. Even though this effect may occur in humans for a short period of time, tolerance develops rapidly. It is especially ineffective in treating patients whose obesity is related to overeating compelled by psychologic factors. Only by restriction of dietary intake can weight reduction be achieved. Higher doses can result in an analeptic effect. In humans the normal dosage of amphetamine does not cause an increase in respiration except when respiration is depressed by centrally acting agents. The use of amphetamines to counteract the effect of fatigue and lack of sleep has been generally known to the public. These agents tend to promote wakefulness and postpone sleep in patients who have been deprived of sleep. When the drug is withdrawn, the amount of sleep increases and rapid eye movement (REM) sleep is increased. Indiscriminant use of amphetamines can have adverse reactions.

With toxic doses of the amphetamines, dizziness, mental confusion, convulsions, and hallucinations can occur. Cardiovascular adverse reactions include palpatations, hypertension, and arrhythmia. Chronic toxicity, physical exhaustion and collapse, weight loss, insomnia, dermatitis, and psychotic episodes have been reported. Psychologic dependence can occur in users of amphetamines, but physical dependence is less completely established.

Frequent use of amphetamines results in tolerance, which can be impressive in addicts. When tolerance develops, a larger dose is needed to achieve the same effects. Toxic doses of amphetamines may induce auditory and visual hallucinations. Paranoid ideation and changes in affect may occur in association with a toxic overdose. Abrupt discontinuation of the sympathomimetic amines does not seem to produce any easily observable physiologic problems. Effects produced generally relate to prolonged sleep, fatigue, and an increased appetite as well as profound depression. Because the amphetamines suppress REM sleep, withdrawal from amphetamines results in an increase in REM sleep in a rebound fashion.

The use of amphetamines or their derivatives (Table 13-4) for obesity has been considered to be only minimally effective. Without caloric restriction these agents are totally ineffective in reducing weight. Because of the development of tolerance within a short period of time, long-term control of weight cannot be achieved without a change in basic eating habits. The lack of ability to separate the CNS-stimulating effects from the anorexic effects prohibits the use of these agents late in the day, when overeating is often prevalent. These agents may soon be more strictly monitored for this use, as they have been widely abused. Use of a constant dosage of amphetamines in the treatment of narcolepsy, a disease in which the patient falls asleep spontaneously, is warranted. Patients with this disease often can be maintained on a dosage that does not change with time. Tolerance does not seem to develop in these patients.

The use of the amphetamines or methylphenidate to treat hyperkinetic children has met with some success. The ability of these children to learn, as well as their behavior, is improved under treatment with the amphetamine-like agents. Their attention span is prolonged and restlessness decreases. These agents must be used for prolonged periods of time; tolerance does not develop.

Amphetamines have been used in the past to counteract the sedative action of antiepileptic agents, such as phenobarbital, on the CNS.

Certain precautions are taken with the use of amphetamines in patients with hypertension, cerebrovascular disease, hyperthyroidism, or cardiac disease. Because of their tendency to be abused, amphetamines should be prescribed with caution to emotionally unstable individuals.

Cocaine

Although cocaine is often listed as a local anesthetic, it has powerful CNS-stimulating activity. It produces restlessness, excitement, and talkativeness. There is a lessened sense of fatigue. The abuse of this agent is probably directly related to its CNS action. Its therapeutic use is now limited to its local anesthetic effect in the eye or as a topical agent on mucous membrane, but these uses have been supplanted by other agents in most instances. Cocaine is a popular drug of abuse, a discussion of which can be found in Chapter 34.

REFERENCES

1. Feinsilver, O.: The role of nikethamide as a respiratory stimulant in the management of pulmonary insufficiency, Curr. Ther. Res. **4:**165-177, 1962.
2. Rodman, T., et al.: Effect of ethamivan on alveolar ventilation in patients with chronic lung disease, N. Engl. J. Med. **267:**1279, 1962.
3. Wolfson, B., Siker, E.S., and Ciccarelli, H.E.: A double blind comparison of doxapram, ethamivan and methylphenidate, Am. J. Med. Sci. **249:**391-398, 1965.
4. Bradley, K., Easton, D.W., and Eccles, J.C.: An investigation of primary or direct inhibition, J. Physiol. (Lond.) **122:**474-488, 1953.
5. Jackson, G., et al.: Strychnine poisoning treated successfully with diazepam, Br. Med. J. **3:**519-520, 1971.
6. Colton, T., Gosselin, R.E., and Smith, R.P.: The tolerance of coffee drinkers to caffeine, Clin. Pharmacol. Ther. **9:**31-39, 1968.
7. Jick, J., et al.: Coffee and myocardial infarction, N. Engl. J. Med. **289:**63, 1973.
8. Hennekens, C.H., et al.: Coffee drinking and death due to coronary heart disease, N. Engl. J. Med. **294:**633, 1976.
9. Heyden, S., et al.: Coffee consumption and mortality, Arch. Intern. Med. **138:**1472, 1978.
10. Timson, J.: Caffeine, Mutat. Res. **47:**1, 1977.
11. Thayer, P.S., and Palm, P.E.: A current assessment of the mutagenic and teratogenic effects of caffeine, CRC Crit. Rev. Toxicol. **3:**345, 1975.
12. Weathersbee, P.S., Olsen, L.K., and Lodge, J.R.: Caffeine and pregnancy: a retrospective survey, Postgrad. Med. **62:**64, 1977.
13. Minton, J.P., et al.: Caffeine, cyclic nucleotides, and breast disease, Surgery **86:**105, 1979.
14. Heyden, S.: Coffee and fibrocystic breast disease, Surgery **88:**741, 1980.

CHAPTER 14

Anticonvulsant drugs

BARBARA REQUA-CLARK

EPILEPSY

Epilepsy is the most common cause of seizure disorders. Since approximately 1 person in every 200 has some form of epilepsy it is not unlikely that the dentist will be treating these patients. Anticonvulsant drugs can help between 70% to 80% of the patients with epilepsy. Since these drugs are used on a long-term basis, their long-term adverse reactions become important.

Epilepsy may be produced by brain tumors, cerebrovascular accidents, head trauma, hypoglycemia, hypocalcemia, overhydration, uremia, and intercranial infections, but in most forms of epilepsy no abnormality in the CNS can be demonstrated. This is termed idiopathic epilepsy. Seizure disorders generally occur with an abrupt onset of motor, sensory, psychic, or autonomic symptoms, sometimes with a decrease in consciousness. It is believed that these are associated with an excessive electric discharge in the brain. Table 14-1 classifies some of the more common types of seizures.

Tonic-clonic (grand mal) seizures

A grand mal seizure is heralded by an aura that is typical for each patient. This may be an unusual taste, smell, sensation in the stomach, or certain motor activity. After this aura, the patient loses consciousness and falls to the floor with a cry. Strong, tonic contractions of the skeletal muscles then occur. Dyspnea and cyanosis may be present. Following the tonic contractions, clonic movements of the body begin. Loss of bladder and bowel control, tongue biting, bruises, and frothing at the mouth occur at this point. After a short period of coma, the patient regains consciousness but may remain confused and disoriented. Sleep may then ensue. A dentist should be able to recognize a grand mal seizure because more than one half of all seizures are of this type, and its symptoms are more pronounced.

Absence (petit mal) seizures

Petit mal seizures consist of myoclonic jerking, akinetic seizures, and brief absences or blank spells without associated falling or body convulsions. This seizure type occurs most frequently in preadolescent children. Abnormal EEG patterns are present. Although there is momentary loss of consciousness, often neither the patient nor the parents are aware of it. Petit mal seizures present few management problems in the dental office.

Jacksonian seizures

During a jacksonian seizure, which may be motor, sensory, or autonomic in type, consciousness is not lost. The seizure may start in the corner of the mouth or in a limb as a localized clonic spasm, which then spreads in an orderly fashion. The patient may have the sensation of a smell or taste that is not present. This seizure may either remain localized or spread to a generalized seizure in which the patient loses consciousness.

Psychomotor seizures

A wide variety of seizures fall into the classification of psychomotor seizures. Compulsive behavior including incoherent speech, turning of the head and eyes, smacking of the lips, and writhing movements of the extremities may occur. Unconsciousness and amnesia are also common. An unusual EEG is frequently noted.

Status epilepticus

Status epilepticus is a condition in which severe, recurrent seizures occur without regaining of con-

Table 14-1. Types of epilepsy

Seizure type	Name(s)	Effect on consciousness	Symptoms
Partial (focal)			
Elementary symptomatology	Cortical focal; jacksonian	No impairment	Convulsions of a single muscle group or localized sensory disturbance
Complex symptomatology	Temporal lobe; psychomotor	Impairment (semiconsciousness)	Confused behavior, wide variety of manifestations, bizarre EEG
Generalized			
Absence	Petit mal	Unconsciousness	Abnormal EEG, some symmetric clonic motor activity
Tonic-clonic	Grand mal	Unconsciousness	Major convulsions, maximal tonic spasm of all body musculature followed by synchronous clonic jerking

sciousness between episodes. The patient's condition may progress to coma, hyperpyrexia, cyanosis, and death. This is an emergency situation, and treatment must be administered immediately.

Febrile convulsions

Some infants will exhibit convulsions in the presence of a high fever. These may be the first convulsions of an epileptic child.

DENTAL TREATMENT OF EPILEPTIC PATIENTS

The dentist should not treat a patient who has a history of seizures without reviewing the management of epileptic patients in the dental office. Familiarity with the following procedures for handling a patient with a history of grand mal epilepsy should be reviewed.

1. Handle the seizure patient properly.
   a. Chair. Position the patient to avoid furniture or equipment, preferably on the floor. Do not attempt to move the patient if a seizure has already begun. The chair should be lowered and tilted back. Since the attack is often preceded by an aura, the patient is often able to provide an early warning.
   b. Head. During the seizure tilt the patient's head to one side to prevent aspiration.
   c. Teeth. If the patient indicates that a grand mal seizure is about to begin, place a wrapped tongue blade or soft material between the teeth to prevent tongue biting. During a seizure it is nearly impossible to place anything in the mouth, and such attempts can produce additional trauma.
   d. Instruments. Remove all instruments and equipment from the patient's mouth. If an object is clasped between the teeth during a seizure, do not attempt to remove it until the seizure subsides.
2. Be aware that trauma can be incurred, including broken teeth or jaw or aspiration of teeth or equipment.
3. When taking the history, determine the degree of control of the epilepsy and the patient's compliance in using medication.
4. Avoid stressful situations or other stimuli (rhythmic light or sound) that could precipitate a seizure. An antianxiety agent may be useful for patients whose seizures are precipitated by stress. Occasionally, working with the patient's physician, the dentist may suggest that the patient's anticonvulsant medication be altered before exceptionally stressful dental situations.
5. Ensure that all office personnel are prepared for this emergency situation (seizures).

DRUG THERAPY

The potential problems with the disease epilepsy have been discussed. However, the drug therapy used to treat this disease can also cause adverse reactions. The anticonvulsant drugs are CNS depressants that can prevent epileptic seizures without causing excessive drowsiness. Although the exact mechanism of action of these agents is unknown, it is believed that their primary effect is to prevent the spread of abnormal electric discharges in the brain.

The anticonvulsant drug used in a specific patient depends on the type of seizures rather than their cause. For example, grand mal seizures are commonly treated with phenytoin and/or phenobarbital, whereas petit mal (absence) seizures are treated with ethosuximide or trimethadione (Table 14-2). The patient with a seizure disorder requires an individual regimen with a drug or combination of drugs tailored specifically to that patient.

Since the anticonvulsant agents are often continued for life, the chronic toxicity of these agents is an important consideration. The barbiturates are the most commonly prescribed agents for the treatment of epilepsy and will be discussed first.

Barbiturates

The barbiturates used in the treatment of epilepsy include phenobarbital, mephobarbital, and metharbital (Table 14-2). Both mephobarbital and primidone a barbiturate-like agent, are metabolized to phenobarbital. Since these agents have essentially the same actions, phenobarbital will be discussed as the prototype.

Phenobarbital

Phenobarbital is given alone for the treatment of a wide variety of seizure disorders or used in conjunction with phenytoin for the control of grand mal epilepsy. Because it is relatively safe and controls several types of seizures, it is often used initially. Phenobarbital is most effective in controlling seizures of grand mal epilepsy. It is less effective in the treatment of petit mal epilepsy and may even aggravate psychomotor epilepsy.

The most common adverse effect associated with phenobarbital is sedation. The drowsiness is usually transient because tolerance to the sedative effect, although not to the anticonvulsant effect, occurs with time. This CNS depression is additive with other CNS depressants. If a CNS depressant such as a narcotic analgesic, a sedative-hypnotic, or an antihistamine is administered, reduced doses should be used. In children the opposite effect is sometimes seen, and a child can become hyperactive.

Stomatitis. Stomatitis has been reported as an adverse reaction to the barbiturates. It is manifested by a patchy ulceration on the oral soft tissue and a positive Nikolsky sign (denudation of epidermis when rubbed) even in the absence of other body lesions.[1]

Toxic epidermal necrolysis.[2] The toxic necrolysis associated with the barbiturates is manifested by a scalded-skin appearance. The prodromal phase includes fever, malaise, irritability, and generalized body erythema.

With excessive doses, nystagmus and ataxia can occur. Rashes, probably allergic reactions, have been reported. Although the barbiturates are respiratory depressants, the usual therapeutic dose does not present a problem. If breathing difficulties do occur in a patient taking barbiturates, a barbiturate overdose must be suspected. Other effects and adverse reactions associated with the barbiturates are discussed in Chapter 7.

If a barbiturate is rapidly removed from an epileptic patient, convulsions may be precipitated. If reduction in dosage or withdrawal of a patient is desired, it should be accomplished very gradually.

Hydantoins

The most commonly used hydantoin is phenytoin (Dilantin), formerly called diphenylhydantoin (DPH). Since the effects and adverse reactions are similar for all the hydantoins, phenytoin will be discussed as the prototype.

Phenytoin

Phenytoin is used primarily for the treatment of grand mal epilepsy, either by itself or in combination with phenobarbital. It has also been used in the treatment of trigeminal neuralgia. Its mechanism of action is unknown but may be related to its prevention of the spread of abnormal electric activity.

CNS effects. The CNS side effects include ataxia, nystagmus, or slurred speech. These effects have caused the sufferer to be mistaken for an inebriated individual. Dermatologic reactions reported include erythematous, scarlatiniform, and morbilliform reactions, as well as hirsutism.

Gastrointestinal effects. Phenytoin sodium, because of its highly alkaline nature, can produce nausea and stomach pain. Taking it with meals can minimize this effect. Other drugs that can irritate the gastrointestinal tract should be used cautiously.

Other effects. Other adverse reactions include bone marrow depression, systemic lupus erythematosus, and lymphadenopathy. The Stevens-Johnson syndrome, also known as erythema multiforme exudativum, has been reported. Symptoms include fever, lethargy, and vesicular lesions on the skin and mucous membranes.

Gingival hyperplasia. The most common adverse reaction associated with the use of phenytoin is gingival hyperplasia. The incidence of this reaction varies greatly depending on the investigators; reported incidences have ranged from none to 84.5%. Angelopoulos and Goaz[4] found the incidence to be

Table 14-2. Drugs used in epilepsy

Drug	Type of seizure treated*	Adverse reactions
Barbiturates		
Phenobarbital (Luminal)	GTC, CF, F, A, M, Ak, Mixed, TL	Drowsiness, rash, ataxia
Mephobarbital (Mebaral)	GTC, A	Drowsiness, gastric distress, rash
Metharbital (Gemonil)	GTC, M, A, Mixed	Drowsiness, agitation
Hydantoins		
Phenytoin (Dilantin), formerly diphenylhydantoin (DPH)	GTC, TL	Drowsiness, gastric distress, gingival hyperplasia, rash, megaloblastic anemia, ataxia, diplopia, fever, hirsutism
Mephenytoin (Mesantoin)	GTC, CF, TL	Drowsiness, rash, blood dyscrasias
Ethotoin (Peganone)	GTC, TL	Drowsiness, rash, lymphadenopathy
Benzodiazepines		
Clonazepam (Clonopin)	A, M, Ak	Drowsiness, ataxia
Chlordiazepoxide (Librium)	Mixed	Drowsiness, ataxia
Diazepam (Valium)	M, ++, Mixed	Drowsiness, ataxia
Succinimides		
Ethosuximide (Zarontin)	A	Drowsiness, headache, rash, behavioral changes, blood dyscrasias
Methsuximide (Celontin)	A	Ataxia, drowsiness, headaches, anorexia, blood dyscrasias
Phensuximide (Milontin)	A	Dizziness, hematuria, nausea, rash
Oxazolidinediones		
Trimethadione (Tridione)	A	Severe dermatologic disorders, nephropathy, hepatitis, hair loss, congenital defects, blood dyscrasias
Paramethadione (Paradione)	A	Gastric distress, rash, photophobia, blood dyscrasias
Other agents		
Carbamazepine (Tegretol)	GTC, TL†, Mixed	Headache, drowsiness, feelings of inhibition, gait disturbances, nystagmus, nausea, aplastic anemia
Primidone‡ (Mysoline)	GTC, CF, TL	Gastric distress, nausea, vomiting, anorexia, dermatitis, drowsiness, blood dyscrasias
Acetazolamide (Diamox)§	A, GTC, Mixed, M	Drowsiness, facial and extremity paresthesia, fatigue, renal disorders, gastrointestinal disturbances
Phenacemide (Phenurone)	TL	Liver damage, psychotic behavior, nausea, rash
Bromide	GTC	Gastrointestinal disturbances, rash, neurologic aberrations
Meprobamate (Equanil, Miltown)	A, M	Drowsiness, ataxia
Dextroamphetamine (Dexedrine)	A, Ak	Nervousness, insomnia, anorexia
Valproic acid (Depakene)	A, M, GTC, CF, Ak	Nausea, vomiting, diarrhea, alopecia, weight gain, hypersalivation

*GTC, generalized tonic-clonic (grand mal) seizure; CF, cortical focal seizure; TL, temporal lobe (psychomotor) seizure; A, absence (petit mal) seizure; M, myoclonic spasms; F, febrile convulsions; Ak, akinetic convulsions; ++, Status epilepticus.
†Trigeminal neuralgia.
‡Metabolized to phenobarbital.
§Adjunctive treatment.

53% in a group of hospitalized patients taking phenytoin. The incidences most commonly quoted are 20% and 50%.

The hyperplasia is manifested as a progressive enlargement of the interproximal papillae, which may begin as soon as a few weeks or as long as a few years after initial drug therapy. There is excessive accumulation of fibroblasts and collagen fibers in the lesion.[5] In some cases the gingival enlargement is merely seen as nodular papillae. In other cases it has been noted to extend over the occlusal surfaces of the teeth and thus interfere with chewing.

The hyperplasia is more commonly located in the anterior portion of the oral cavity and occurs more often on the labial or buccal gingiva than on the lingual surface. Panuska and co-workers[6] found that, in order of severity, the affected areas of the mouth were the maxillary anterior facial, mandibular anterior facial, maxillary posterior facial, and mandibular posterior facial. Both normal and abnormal tissue may be found in the mouth of a patient with hyperplasia. Hyperplasia rarely occurs in edentulous areas.

The mechanism by which phenytoin produces gingival hyperplasia is unclear. There is some evidence that phenytoin directly affects soft tissue metabolism through an alteration in the activity of the adrenal glands.[7] It has also been postulated that hyperplasia is an allergic reaction to phenytoin. Some studies[8] have found that younger age groups are more likely to have hyperplasia than the adult population, but there is no racial or sexual predilection. An association between the dosage and duration of the medication and the degree of hyperplastic tissue has been noted,[6,9] but some authors do not believe these factors are related.[10] High concentrations of phenytoin are found in the saliva, and the effect on gingival tissues may be local. It may be caused by stimulation of growth or interference with its breakdown.

The relationship between gingival hyperplasia and good oral hygiene has been the subject of great debate in the literature.[10,11] Aas[12] found a statistically significant relationship between oral hygiene and the severity of gingival hyperplasia. Miscellaneous factors including malocclusion, caries, improper restorations, and other irritations may also have an effect on hyperplasia.[13]

The treatment for phenytoin hyperplasia includes the following modalities, none of which is curative:

1. Removal of the drug. Phenytoin may be replaced with another anticonvulsant drug. This must be done by the patient's physician. The benefits of this change must be weighed against the risk of less well-controlled epilepsy or a different type of toxic reaction caused by another agent.

2. Improved oral hygiene. Since several investigators have shown a relationship between the severity of the hyperplasia and oral health, meticulous oral hygiene is essential. Although this will usually decrease the rate of formation of the hyperplastic tissue, it will not totally prevent hyperplasia. Avoiding irritation from orthodontic bands or improperly placed restorations will also help to minimize the problem.

3. Surgery. When gingival hyperplasia interferes with plaque control, esthetics, or mastication, and oral hygiene has not succeeded in preventing overgrowth, surgical elimination is indicated. This occurs in approximately 30% of the affected patients. Surgery is not a final or permanent solution, since hyperplasia recurs in most cases and can progress to its original degree wtihin a relatively short period of time if the patient continues to receive phenytoin therapy.

4. Other drugs. Other drugs that have been tried for the treatment of gingival hyperplasia include ascorbic acid, antihistamines, diuretics, locally administered corticosteroids, and alkaline mouthwashes. Folic acid has been used to reverse the hyperplasia caused by phenytoin.[14] Its effectiveness is certainly questionable, as no statistical evidence was presented. None of these treatments has been shown to be successful.

Vitamin deficiency. Patients receiving long-term phenytoin therapy have decreased blood levels of vitamin D. After many years a few patients will show adult rickets with its defective bone development, decreased bone mass, and increased risk of pathologic fractures. A resorption or shortening of tooth roots, as occurs with hypoparathyroidism, can occur.[15]

Long-term administration of phenytoin can result in macrocytosis or megaloblastic anemia caused by folate deficiency. Dietary folate must be hydrolyzed before it can be absorbed. Phenytoin reduces the absorption of folate from the gastrointestinal tract. The administration of small amounts of folate can prevent this phenomenon. There is some suggestion that prolonged folate deficiency in children may lead to mental deficiency.

Teratogenicity. The congenital abnormality associated with phenytoin is called the fetal hydantoin syndrome. It includes craniofacial anomalies, limb defects, growth deficiency, and mental retardation. A variety of congenital abnormalities have been reported by Hanson.[16]

Other sedative-hypnotic agents and minor tranquilizers

All the sedative-hypnotic agents (Chapter 7) and minor tranquilizers (Chapter 9) have anticonvulsant action in high doses. Only the intermediate- and long-acting agents can be used therapeutically. Intravenous diazepam is the drug of choice (Table 14-3) for the treatment of status epilepticus.

Other anticonvulsants

Many other kinds of anticonvulsants are used in the treatment of seizures (Table 14-2). These drugs are generally used when agents such as phenobarbital and phenytoin are ineffective. Usually the side effects of these anticonvulsants are more severe than those of either phenobarbital or phenytoin.

Primidone

Primidone is chemically similar to the barbiturates and is used in situations in which phenobarbital or the other barbiturates are ineffective. Since it is metabolized to phenobarbital in the body, its actions and adverse effects are similar to those of phenobarbital. However, in contrast to the barbiturates, skin eruptions and blood dyscrasias have been reported in conjunction with its use. Reduction in the absorption of folic acid has been noted with primidone producing macrocythemia. Some patients taking this drug for a long period of time have complained of vague gingival pains.[3] The cause of this complaint is unclear.

Carbamazepine

Although carbamazepine has anticonvulsant action, its primary use is in the treatment of trigeminal and glossopharyngeal neuralgia. It appears to reduce synaptic transmission, as does phenytoin. Phenytoin is sometimes used instead or in conjunction with carbamazepine to control tic douloureux.

Trigeminal neuralgia or tic douloureux is an extremely severe facial pain caused by a lesion in the brain stem or trigeminal nerve root entry zone. It is often first seen in the dental office. Its onset is sudden and excruciating. Carbamazepine is the most successful drug used for its treatment. About two thirds[17] of patients can be successfully treated with this agent. The adverse effects associated with carbamazepine are varied and can be severe. Hematologic reactions include aplastic anemia, agranulocytosis, and thrombocytopenia. Hepatic, genitourinary, and renal side effects have been reported. CNS effects include drowsiness, dizziness, vertigo, and ataxia. The pa-

Table 14-3. Drugs of choice for seizures

Seizure type	Drugs	
	First choice	Alternatives
Absence (petit mal) or psychomotor	Ethosuximide (Zarontin)	Clonazepam (Clonopin) Trimethadione (Tridione) Valproic acid (Depakene)
Tonic-clonic	Phenytoin (Dilantin)	Phenobarbital (Luminal) Primidone (Mysoline) Carbamazepine (Tegretol) Valproic acid (Depakene)
Status epilepticus	Diazepam (Valium)	Phenytoin (Dilantin) Phenobarbital (Luminal)

tient should be cautioned about driving a car. Dermatologic adverse reactions include skin rashes, urticaria, and Stevens-Johnson syndrome. Nausea, vomiting, constipation, diarrhea, dry mouth and pharynx, glossitis, and stomatitis are gastrointestinal effects reported. Cardiovascular adverse effects include congestive heart failure and hypertension. Ophthalmic effects and musculoskeletal effects can occur. Carbamazepine is prescribed in an initial dose of 100 mg twice daily and increased in 100 mg increments every 12 hours until relief is obtained or side effects occur. The usual maintenance dose is between 200 and 800 mg daily. A reduction in maintenance dosage or termination of drug therapy should be attempted at least once every 3 months. Before the drug is administered, baseline laboratory tests should include platelet and reticulocyte count, serum iron level, complete blood count, urinalysis, and SMA-12 analysis. An ophthalmoscopy should be included. Blood counts should be repeated every week for 3 months, then every month for 2 or 3 years. Other tests should be repeated at regular intervals as long as the drug is administered.

Valproic acid

Valproic acid (Depakene) is a relatively new antiepileptic drug indicated in the treatment of absence seizures or as an adjunctive treatment of other seizure types if absence seizures are also present. Its primary use is in the treatment of seizures that are refractory to other agents. The most common adverse effect reported is gastrointestinal, including nausea, vomiting, diarrhea, and abdominal cramps. This can be minimized by taking the drug with food. Drowsiness is occasionally seen when this drug is taken alone but is not uncommon when administered concurrently with phenobarbital. Weight gain, alopecia, tremors, and excessive salivation have been reported. Alteration in platelet function can occur. It is teratogenic in animals. Higher blood levels of phenobarbital are attained when valproic acid is administered concurrently.

Trimethadione

Trimethadione (Tridione) is used to control absence seizures that do not respond to other agents. It is sometimes used in combination with other anticonvulsants. Its adverse effects include actions on gastrointestinal, central nervous, and hematopoietic systems. Hypersensitivity reactions include lymphadenopathy, rash, and exfoliative dermatitis. Bleeding gums have been reported.

Ethosuximide

Ethosuximide (Zarontin) is the drug of choice for the treatment of absence seizures. It is ineffective against psychomotor or grand mal seizures. Gastrointestinal irritation (nausea and vomiting) and CNS effects such as drowsiness and dizziness are commonly reported. Other behavioral effects such as agitation and aggressiveness, as well as the more serious reactions of Stevens-Johnson syndrome, systemic lupus erythematosus, and aplastic anemia have been noted. Swelling of the tongue and gum hypertrophy have been occasionally reported. Most patients require phenytoin concurrently.

NONSPECIFIC ADVERSE EFFECTS OF ANTICONVULSANT MEDICATION

Because seizure patients are often taking more than one medication simultaneously, it is sometimes impossible to ascertain the cause of reported adverse effects. The following alterations may occur in epileptic patients treated with several agents:

1. Thickening of the calvarium. Falconer and Davidson[18] studied sets of twins with only one member receiving anticonvulsant medication. Thickening of the cranial vault was found to be more common in the medicated twin. In a larger sample of institutionalized patients receiving anticonvulsants studied by Le Febvre,[19] definite cranial and facial changes were noted in one third of the group and possibly changes were noted in another one third.

2. Coarseness of facial features. Several authors have noted facial alterations in patients taking anticonvulsants.[18-20] A generalized thickening of the subcutaneous tissues, swelling of the lips, and a broadened nose have been reported. The significance of these findings is unknown, but long-term anticonvulsant therapy in children could have profound effects on the developing skull, craniofacial growth, position of teeth, and supporting bone.

The thickening of the calvarium and the coarseness of the facial features are hypothesized to be caused by a vitamin D deficiency. In these patients, cholecalciferol (D_3) is metabolized and excreted instead of being transformed into an active form.

3. Root abnormalities. Some evidence has been presented that the teeth are affected by anticonvulsant drugs. Richens and Rowe[21] have described a disturbance of calcium metabolism caused by anticonvulsant therapy. Harris and Goldhaber[15] have reported significant root abnormalities in 112 patients receiving anticonvulsant therapy.

4. Teratogenicity. The teratogenicity of the anticonvulsants is not fully known but varies from very likely for trimethadone to fairly likely for phenytoin and least likely for phenobarbital. The rate of congenital abnormalities in infants whose mother was taking anticonvulsant agents during her pregnancy is about two to three times the average. Anomalies encountered most frequently include cleft palate and lip and cardiac defects. Convulsions during the pregnancy as well as the anticonvulsant agents or other factors may also contribute to this rate.

REFERENCES

1. Lawson, B.F.: Severe stomatitis associated with barbiturate ingestion, J. Oral Med. **24:**13, 1969.
2. Giallorenzi, A.F., and Goldstein, B.H.: Acute (toxic) epidermal necrolysis: report of a case, Oral Surg. **40:**611, 1975.
3. Anticonvulsants. In American Dental Association Council on Dental Therapeutics: Accepted dental therapeutics, ed. 38, Chicago, 1979, The Association.
4. Angelopoulos, A.P., and Goaz, P.W. Incidence of diphenylhydantoin gingival hyperplasia, Oral Surg. **34:**898, 1972.
5. Hassell, T., Page, R.C., and Lindhe, J.: Histologic evidence for impaired growth control in diphenylhydantoin gingival overgrowth in man, Arch. Oral Biol. **23:**381, 1978.
6. Panuska, H.J., et al.: The effect of anticonvulsant drugs on the gingiva: a series of analyses of 1048 patients, J. Periodontol. **31:**336, 1960.
7. Werk, E.E., et al.: Cortisol production in epileptic patients treated with diphenylhydantoin, Clin. Pharmacol. Ther. **12:**698, 1971.
8. Livingston, S., and Livingston, H.L.: Diphenylhydantoin gingival hyperplasia, Am. J. Dis. Child. **117:**265, 1969.
9. Panuska, H.J., et al.: Effect of anticonvulsant drugs upon the gingiva: a series of analyses of 1048 patients, II., J. Periodontol. **32:**15, 1961.
10. Angelopoulos, A.P.: Diphenylhydantoin gingival hyperplasia:

a clinicopathological review. I. Incidence, clinical features and histopathology, J. Can. Dent. Assoc. **2:**103, 1975.

11. Ciancio, S.G., Yaffe, S.J., and Catz, C.C.: Gingival hyperplasia and diphenylhydantoin, J. Periodontol. **43:**411, 1972.

12. Aas, E.: Hyperplasia gingiva diphenylhydantoinea, Acta Odontol. Scand. **21**(suppl. 34):1, 1963.

13. Collins, J.M., and Fry, B.A.: Phenytoin gingival hyperplasia and chronic gingival irritation, Aust. Dent. J. **5:**165, 1960.

14. Reynolds, E.H.: Anticonvulsants, folic acid and epilepsy, Lancet **1:**1376, 1973.

15. Harris, M., and Goldhaber, P.: Root abnormalities in epileptics and the inhibition of parathyroid hormone induced bone resorption by diphenylhydantoin in tissue culture, Arch. Oral Biol. **19:**981, 1974.

16. Hanson, J.W., et al.: Risks to the offspring of women treated with hydantoin anticonvulsants, with emphasis on the fetal hydantoin syndrome, J. Pediatr. **89:**662-68, 1976.

17. Crill, W.: Carbamazepine, Ann. Intern. Med. **79:**79, 1973.

18. Falconer, M.A., and Davidson, S.: Coarse features in epilepsy as a consequence of anticonvulsant therapy: report of cases in two pairs of identical twins, Lancet **2:**1112, 1973.

19. Le Febvre, E.B., Haining, R.G., and Labbé, R.F.: Coarse facies, calvarial thickening and hyperphosphatasia associated with longterm anticonvulsant therapy, N. Engl. J. Med. **286:**1301, 1972.

20. Israel, H.: Abnormalities of bone and orofacial changes from anticonvulsant drugs, J. Public Health Dent. **34:**104, 1974.

21. Richens, A., and Rowe, D.J.F.: Disturbance of calcium metabolism by anticonvulsant drugs, Br. Med. J. **4:**73, 1970.

CHAPTER 15

Local anesthetics

SAM V. HOLROYD

BARBARA REQUA-CLARK

No drugs are employed more frequently in dental practice than are the local anesthetics. Their use has become so routine that one loses sight of the fact that these drugs have important systemic as well as local effects. It behooves the dentist to know the local anesthetic drugs well. Related clinical pharmacology should be reviewed at frequent intervals. The dentist should also exert leadership in giving direction to research and evolving a philosophy for use of the local anesthetic agents.

HISTORY

Discovery. Although primitive man undoubtedly observed the local anesthetic effect of chewing certain plants or leaves, clinical local anesthesia was established by three events: (1) the isolation of cocaine from the leaves of the coca plant (Niemann, 1860), (2) the topical use of cocaine in surgery of the eye (Köller, 1884), and (3) the use of cocaine for nerve block in surgery (Halsted, 1885).

The recognition that cocaine was highly toxic led to a search for local anesthetic agents of equal efficacy but greater safety. The synthesis of procaine by Einhorn in 1905 initiated a new era in local anesthesia.

Trends in local anesthesia for dentistry. Sometimes it helps to look back to see what lies ahead. If the first volume of *Accepted Dental Remedies* (ADR)* (1934) is examined, the reader will find that 2% procaine (Novocain) with epinephrine was considered to be the most effective local anesthetic for conduction anesthesia and 1% to 2% was considered most effective for infiltration anesthesia. ADR did not reflect any significant changes in dental local anes-

*Later renamed *Accepted Dental Therapeutics* (ADT).

thesia over the next several years. Butethamine (Monocaine) was added in the 1941 edition. The 1945 ADR indicated that procaine-epinephrine solutions continued to be the predominant local anesthetic in dentistry. The commercially available procaine solutions were 2%, except for a 2.2% solution with nordefrin (Cobefrin), 1:9000.

During the late 1940s there was a growing concern over the routine use of 4% procaine and mixtures of procaine and more powerful anesthetics such as tetracaine (Pontocaine), which had appeared commercially.[1] The combination of 2% procaine, 0.15% tetracaine, and 1:10,000 nordefrin was not accepted by ADR in 1945; however, it was accepted in 1950. Also in 1950 tetracaine was added to the listings, and commercial dental solutions of 4% procaine increased in number.

In 1952 lidocaine (Xylocaine) and another tetracaine combination, 2% procaine, 0.15% tetracaine, and 1:2500 phenylephrine, were added to ADR. By 1954 another tetracaine combination, 2% procaine, 0.15% tetracaine, and 1:30,000 levarterenol (Levophed), was accepted. Propoxycaine (Ravocaine) entered ADR in 1957. Since its potency is similar to that of tetracaine, a combination with 2% procaine followed, and the combination of 0.4% propoxycaine and 2% procaine with 1:10,000 nordefrin was added to ADR and in a second solution with 1:30,000 levarterenol. In 1958 metabutethamine (Unacaine), meprylcaine (Oracaine), and metabutoxycaine (Primacaine) were added, with a view toward shorter duration anesthesia. Levonordefrin (Neo-Cobefrin) was added in 1:20,000 concentration in 1959 as the vasoconstrictor in a 2% procaine–0.15% tetracaine combination. In 1961 chloroprocaine (Nesacaine), mepivacaine (Carbocaine), and isobucaine (Kincaine) were added to ADR. In 1962 chloroprocaine was removed and there were no additions. From 1962 to the present there have been additions of pyrocaine (Dynacaine) in 1964, dyclonine (Dyclone) in 1966, and prilocaine (Citanest) in 1967. Since 1967, metabutoxycaine (Primacaine), naepaine (Amylsine), meprylcaine (Oracaine), butethamine (Monocaine), and metabutethamine (Unocaine) have been deleted. At the present time ADT lists the following local anesthetic solutions for parenteral use: lidocaine, mepivacaine, prilocaine, procaine, tetracaine, propoxycaine, and bupivacaine; for surface application: benzocaine, chlorobutanol, lidocaine, butacaine, tetracaine, dyclonine, and cocaine.

Over the last 15 years we have seen the almost complete replacement of procaine by more potent local anesthetics. More recently, "short duration anesthesia," accomplished by increasing concentrations from 2% to 3% or 4% and elimination of the vasoconstrictor, has been promoted.

SAFETY OF DENTAL LOCAL ANESTHESIA

The history of local anesthetic safety can be considered as occurring in three eras, the first being the era of cocaine; the second, the era of procaine; and the third and present era, that of increased potency. The addicting properties and high toxicity of cocaine are well documented in the medical and dental literature for the years in which this anesthetic was in great use. The synthesis of procaine in 1905 led to the replacement of cocaine in dentistry by this nonaddicting and less toxic drug. The *Index to Dental Literature* reflects the early investigations of procaine (1906-1910), the enthusiasm for procaine (1911-1915), the taking over by procaine (1916-1920), and the obvious predominance of procaine anesthesia in dentistry by 1921. The movement toward more potent local anesthesia in dentistry was making itself felt by 1950. This brief introduction to the consideration of local anesthetic safety was necessary because the statistics on fatalities for any particular period reflected the dangers of the predominant anesthetics of the period. For instance, statistical studies conducted from 1930 to 1950 provided significant data relative to procaine toxicity but did not provide a basis for the security or lack of security in using lidocaine, mepivacaine, prilocaine, and other subsequently developed local anesthetic agents.

Mortality

The American Medical Association became concerned with deaths from local anesthesia in 1924 and appointed a committee to survey related fatalities. This committee reported 43 deaths from local anesthesia.[2] In 1928, 14 more deaths were reported.[3] A committee appointed by the Philadelphia Medical Society found 29 local anesthetic deaths in the Philadelphia area from 1935 to 1946,[4] and Dealy[5] reported 5 local anesthetic deaths at Queens General Hospital in New York from 1936 to 1941. It is difficult to assess the overall dangers in local anesthesia from such scattered reports; however, the lethal potential of local anesthetics is well illustrated. Adriani and Campbell[6] have stated, "Accurate statistics on the frequency of untoward reactions and fatalities due to local anesthetics are not available, because few such mishaps are reported." They indicated that 10 unreported deaths and numerous other nonfatal reactions have occurred at their hospital in a 15-year period. The 10 deaths reported by Adriani and Campbell occurred from the topical application of tetracaine. On the other hand, tetracaine was used 20,000 times in spinal anesthesia at this hospital during the same time period without a death. Other mortality reports attributable to topical application of local anesthetics seem to illustrate further the importance of the method of administration.[7-9] One may therefore conclude that medical statistics probably do not reflect the dangers or lack of dangers in using local anesthetics in dentistry. However, fatal allergic reactions, such as those reported by Criep and Ribeiro,[10] could occur as easily from dental use as from medical use.

Fortunately, five studies that provide a limited assessment of the dangers of local anesthesia in dentistry have been conducted. Seldin and Recant[11] surveyed the mortality files of New York City for the period 1943 to 1952. They found 2 deaths attributed to dental local anesthesia during the 10-year period, in which they estimate 90,000,000 local anesthesias (mostly procaine) must have been administered for dental purposes. Seldin[12] made a nationwide survey of anesthetic mortality in oral surgery for the period 1950 to 1956. A questionnaire was sent to each member of the American Society of Oral and Maxillofacial Surgeons. The 406 answers indicated that approximately 4,316,027 local anesthetics were admin-

Table 15-1. Local anesthetic deaths

Dates of survey	Total number of cases	Procedure	Mortality rate
1905-1950[7]	30,000	ENT (C)*	1:10,000
Before 1950[8]	39,299	ENT (C and T)	1.8:10,000
1948-1952[9]	58,700	Spinals (T)	3.7:10,000
	152,000	Regional and topical (P and C)	1.3:10,000
1943-1952[11]	90,000,000	Dental (P)	1:45,000,000
1950-1956[12]	4,316,027	Oral surgery (P)	1:1,438,000
During 1962[13]	71,874,000	Dental (L)	1:36,000,000
During 1965[14]	1,493,000	Oral Surgery (L)	1:1,493,000
During 1972[15]	1,853,750	Oral Surgery (L)	1:1,853,000

*Primary anesthetic: C, cocaine; L, lidocaine; P, procaine; T, tetracaine.

istered and 3 deaths occurred as a result of the anesthetic.

In the American Dental Association's *The 1962 Survey of Dental Practice,* an extrapolation of survey data from general practice found a death rate attributed to local anesthesia of 1:36,000,000.[13] Questionnaire surveys of oral surgical practices for 1965 by Driscoll[14] and for 1972 by the American Society of Oral and Maxillofacial Surgeons[15] found death rates of 1:1,493,000 and 1:1,853,000, respectively. Table 15-1 illustrates these statistics. Data concerning local anesthetic fatalities in medicine are shown for comparison.

Morbidity

Although anesthetic morbidity figures are highly subject to error, it would seem that dental local anesthesia is safer than medical local anesthesia. This is logical in view of the fact that in dentistry less anesthetic is generally used and the patient is usually in better overall health. Dental surgery also has fewer complications than most medical surgery.

It would also appear that local anesthetic mortality figures for general dentistry (approximately 1:40,000,000) are more favorable than for oral surgery (approximately 1:1,500,000). This probably results from the same factors that make the combined dental data more favorable than the medical data.

Although local anesthetic morbidity data are limited, it appears that dental local anesthesia is an extremely safe procedure. The dentist's commendable measures, including aspiration, minimizing dosage,

and attention to the patient's medical history, have been highly successful. Some will say that, "One death is one too many." We certainly agree but relate this germane case history. A dental patient went into anaphylactic shock 3 minutes after the injection of lidocaine. The dentist injected 0.5 ml 1:1000 epinephrine intramuscularly and administered oxygen. The patient quickly responded and survived without residual effects. Afterward a determination was made that the patient was allergic *not* to lidocaine but rather to a type of grass that was being mowed outside the dentist's office as the patient entered. If this patient had died, the death would have been a lidocaine statistic. The point being made is that *even if practitioners injected water, they would never obtain a zero morbidity figure.*

In spite of an excellent record of safety in dental local anesthesia, dentists must be aware of the potential dangers and not lessen their precautionary measures of *aspiration, minimizing dosage, and attention to the patient's medical history.* Lidocaine appears to have an excellent safety record, yet even with a good record serious and fatal reactions have occurred in dentistry[16-18] and medicine.[19-21] The toxicity and allergenicity of mepivacaine are approximately the same as those of lidocaine. Overall, dental local anesthesia can be considered to be remarkably safe.[22]

THE IDEAL LOCAL ANESTHETIC

A large number of chemical agents are capable of producing local anesthesia. However, not all are clinically acceptable. The basis of clinical acceptability is safety to the patient and adequacy of the anesthesia produced. Ideally, a local anesthetic would have the following properties[23]:

1. Potent local anesthesia
2. Reversible local anesthesia
3. Absence of local reactions
4. Absence of systemic reactions
5. Absence of allergic reactions
6. Rapid onset
7. Satisfactory duration
8. Adequate tissue penetration
9. Low cost
10. Stability in solution (long shelf-life)
11. Sterilization by autoclave
12. Ease of metabolism and excretion

The degree to which a particular agent approaches this ideal varies with the drug itself and also with the needs of a particular case.

CHEMISTRY

Most clinically acceptable local anesthetics consist of an aromatic nucleus (R_1) connected by an ester or amide linkage to an aliphatic chain containing a secondary or tertiary amino group.

With the exception of cocaine, the local anesthetics are synthetic and are formed by the attachment of various chemical groups to the aromatic nucleus, the aliphatic chain, or the amino group. The drugs thus formed are, almost without exception, white, generally odorless, viscid liquids or amorphous solids that are fat soluble but relatively insoluble in water. All are bases and form water-soluble stable salts with acids.

Properties of base and salt forms of local anesthetics. X, ester or amide.

Free base	Salt
1. Viscid liquids or amorphous solids	1. Crystalline solids
2. Fat soluble (lipophilic)	2. Water soluble (hydrophilic)
3. Unstable	3. Stable
4. Alkaline	4. Acidic
5. Uncharged, nonionized	5. Charged, cation (ionized)
6. Penetrates nerve tissue	6. Active form at site of action
7. Form present in tissue (pH 7.4)	7. Form present in dental cartridge (pH 4.5-6.0)

Esters of benzoic acid:

Cocaine

Esters of para-aminobenzoic acid:

Procaine

Amide derivatives of xylidine:

Lidocaine

Amide derivatives of toluidine:

Prilocaine

The first local anesthetics were esters of benzoic acid (cocaine) or para-aminobenzoic acid (procaine). Subsequently, more diverse chemical structures have evolved. A chemical classification of local anesthetics with an example of each is shown in Table 15-2.

Local anesthetic agents can be divided into three groups based on their potency and duration. The protein-binding capacity of these local anesthetics determines their durations—low degree of protein binding, short duration; high degree of protein binding, long duration.[24] The onset of action is determined by the ability of an agent to diffuse through the connective and nervous tissue. The onset of the amides and etidocaine is fast (2 to 4 minutes), whereas the onset of procaine and tetracaine is slow (10 to 20 minutes).[25]

DRUGS AVAILABLE

A large number of local anesthetics are available. Some have little or no dental use. These include proparacaine (Ophthaine), which is used for surface anesthesia in ophthalmology, and cyclomethycaine (Surfacaine), diperodon (Diothane), and pramoxine (Tronothane), which provide surface anesthesia of damaged skin and mucosa. Dimethisoquin (Quotane) is used for surface anesthesia. Dibucaine (Nupercaine), which is the most potent, toxic, and long-acting local anesthetic in current use,[26] is used for spinal and surface anesthesia. Although piperocaine (Metycaine), chloroprocaine (Nesacaine), and hexylcaine (Cylcaine) are all useful for infiltration and block anesthesia, they are seldom used in dentistry. Piperocaine and hexylcaine are also used topically, and the latter has additional use in spinal anesthesia.

Etidocaine (Duranest) is a long-acting local anesthetic used for infiltration, nerve blocks, and caudal anesthesia.

To emphasize agents of particular use in dentistry, the preceding local anesthetics will not be discussed further. The local anesthetics are shown in their respective chemical categories in Table 15-2. The drugs

Table 15-2. Chemical classification of local anesthetics*

Esters			Amides			
Of benzoic acid	Of meta-aminobenzoic acid	Of para-aminobenzoic acid (PABA)	Xylidine derivatives	Toluidine derivatives	Other	Other local anesthetics
Cocaine†	Cyclomethycaine	Butethamine (Mono-	Lidocaine (Xylocaine)	Prilocaine	Dibucaine	Chlorobutanol†
Meprylcaine	(Surfacaine)	caine)	Mepivacaine (Carbo-	(Citanest)	(Nupercaine)	Dyclonine†
Metabutethamine	Metabutoxycaine	Procaine (Novocain)	caine)			
Ethyl aminobenzoate†	(Primacaine)	Chloroprocaine	Pyrrocaine			
(Benzocaine)		(Nesacaine)	Etidocaine (Duranest)			
Butacaine† (Butyn)		Proparacaine (Oph-	Bupivacaine (Mar-			
Hexylcaine (Cyclaine)		thaine)	caine)			
Piperocaine (Metycaine)		Propoxycaine				
Tetracaine (Pontocaine)						

*From Requa-Clark, B.S., and Holroyd, S.V.: Applied pharmacology for the dental hygienist, St. Louis, 1982, The C.V. Mosby Co.
†Used only topically.

more commonly used in dental practice will be described in individual monographs after the general discussion of local anesthetics.

PHARMACOLOGIC EFFECTS

Peripheral nerve conduction. Reversible blockade of peripheral nerve conduction is the principal clinical function of local anesthetics. They inhibit the propagation of nerve impulses along fibers, at sensory endings, at myoneural junctions, and at synapses.[27] Local anesthetics exert their action by decreasing the rate of depolarization along the nerve membrane. Cellular depolarization therefore does not develop, and no action potential is propagated. The rate of repolarization remains constant. This is accomplished by effecting a decrease in sodium permeability at the nerve membrane. Since they do not penetrate the myelin sheath, local anesthetics affect myelinated fibers only at the nodes of Ranvier. Local anesthetics affect small, unmyelinated, or thinly myelinated fibers first and affect large or heavily myelinated fibers last. Consequently, the losses in the usual order are autonomics; sense of cold, warmth, pain, touch, pressure, and vibration; proprioception; and motor function.[28] Individual variation exists in the order in which functions are lost. With return of function, the order is reversed.

CNS effects. If the systemic blood level of a local anesthetic reaches a certain concentration, CNS effects, including clonic or tonic convulsions, can be observed. These effects represent the toxic reaction to a local anesthetic and are discussed under adverse effects.

Myocardial effects. The myocardium is depressed by high systemic doses of local anesthetics. Electrical excitability, conduction rate, and cardiac output are reduced. This is the basis for the use of procainamide and lidocaine as antiarrhythmic agents.

Smooth muscle effects. Smooth muscle is relaxed, possibly by the depression of sensory receptors.[29] This allows arteriolar dilation and a spasmolytic effect on intestinal and bronchial smooth muscle. This vasodilation may result in hypotension caused by smooth muscle relaxation. Although vasodilation with procaine requires the use of a vasoconstrictor for adequate dental local anesthesia, little or no vasodilation is seen with lidocaine, mepivacaine, and prilocaine.

Analgesic effects. Intravenous injection of a local anesthetic can increase the pain threshold. The rela-

tively narrow margin of safety has precluded the clinical use of intravenous injection of local anesthetic.

Anticonvulsant effects. In doses less than those that produce convulsions, some local anesthetics (lidocaine, procaine) demonstrate anticonvulsant activity. This action is a result of CNS depression.

ABSORPTION, DISTRIBUTION, AND METABOLISM

As soon as a local anesthetic is injected or absorbed topically, it begins to (1) establish anesthesia, (2) distribute through the tissues, and (3) enter the systemic circulation. Aside from the chemistry of the drug itself, the rate at which it leaves the site of administration and enters the circulation depends principally on the vascularity of the tissues injected and the presence or absence of a vasoconstrictor in the solution.

Greater vascularity, the absence of a vasoconstrictor, the application of heat or massage, and the presence of a spreading agent increase absorption. Less vascularity, the presence of a vasoconstrictor, and vasoconstriction induced by the application of cold decrease absorption.

The systemic blood concentration that is ultimately obtained depends on the amount of drug that enters the circulation per unit of time (total dose and rate of entry), the volume of distribution, and the rate at which the drug is broken down and eliminated. One should note at this point that the absorption of some drugs from topical application may be rapid. Investigators have shown that in dogs the blood level obtained from the application of tetracaine to mucous membrane closely simulates that of rapid intravenous injection.[6,30] This is of particular significance in view of the fact that tetracaine is one of the more toxic local anesthetics and is found in 2% concentration in topical sprays that are used in dentistry.

Once in the systemic circulation, local anesthetics permeate most tissues, particularly the liver, kidney, brain, heart, and lungs. They also cross the placenta.

In humans the ester types of local anesthetics, particularly procaine and chloroprocaine, are hydrolyzed by both plasma pseudocholinesterase and liver esterases. Procaine is hydrolyzed primarily to PABA and diethylaminoalcohol in plasma. The metabolite PABA is responsible for allergic reactions associated with the ester types of local anesthetic agents. About 0.03% of the population is unable to hydrolyze these esters because of the presence of an atypical form of pseudocholinesterase. This decreased ability to metabolize the esters is hereditary and results in an increase in systemic toxicity. Patients with a family history of this problem should not be given ester types of local anesthetic agents. Lidocaine and probably most other amide-type local anesthetics are metabolized principally in the liver. The entire metabolism of the xylidine derivatives occurs in the liver. Prilocaine, a toluidine derivative, although metabolized primarily in the liver, is also metabolized in plasma and in the kidney. Metabolites of both the ester and amide anesthetics and some of the unchanged drug are excreted in urine. The practitioner should be cautioned that severe liver disease will allow the systemic accumulation of local anesthetics, particularly the amides.

MECHANISM OF ACTION

Ionization factors. As previously noted, the local anesthetic free bases are fat-soluble (lipophilic) drugs. They are converted to their water-soluble (hydrophilic) hydrochloride salts to allow the preparation of an injectable solution. These solutions are stable and have a pH of 4.5 to 6.0. In solution an equilibrium is established between the ionized and nonionized forms of the local anesthetic drug. The proportion of the drug in ionized form depends, of course, on the pKa of the drug and the pH of the solution. At the usual solution pH of 6.0 or lower, most local anesthetics are almost completely in ionized form. The clinical importance of this fact is that only the nonionized free base form of the drug can readily penetrate tissue membranes. Consequently, local anesthesia can be obtained only if sufficient free base is available. The lower the pKa of the drug and the higher the pH of the solution or injected tissues, the more free base will be available.

Once the local anesthetic is injected, the buffering capacity and pH of the tissues (pH 7.4) tip the equilibrium in favor of free base formation. This conversion to free base allows greater tissue penetration of the local anesthetic. At physiologic tissue pH of 7.4, 20% of lidocaine (pKa 7.86) is in free base form (Fig. 15-1), whereas only 2% of procaine (pKa 8.92) exists as the free base. The presence of infection or inflammation in an injection site may lower the local tissue pH enough that there is a significant reduction in the concentration of free base. The amount of ionized local anesthetic present at the intracellular location depends on the pH of the tissues. Fig. 15-1 shows that more ionized local anesthetic is available at the normal tissue pH (7.35) than at the inflamed tissue pH of 6.5. Consequently, the depth of anesthesia is reduced.

The free base form of the local anesthetic is necessary for penetrating the nerve membrane. After penetration of the nerve fiber, an equilibrium is reached between the base form and the salt form, both of which have anesthetic action. The salt form acts from inside the cell membrane, whereas the base form acts on the outside, most likely at the same receptor.[31]

Action on the nerve fiber. Physiologically, a proportionally large number of negative ions (anions) accumulate on the inside of nerve fiber membranes, and a proportionally large number of positive ions (cations) accumulate on the outside of the membrane. Thus the resting nerve fiber is electronegative on the inside and electropositive on the outside (Fig. 15-2, *A*). A nerve impulse (nerve action potential) is a transient reversal of this polarity, which is propagated down the fiber like a wave. The resting membrane, only slightly permeable to sodium, is fully permeable to potassium. The high intracellular concentration of potassium is maintained by its attraction to negatively charged intracellular protein. In fact, at rest there is a negative electrical potential of approximately -90 mV across the membrane. On stimulation the membrane permeability to sodium rises and the membrane potential rises to the firing level of 50 to 60 mV.

Depolarization results from an increase in the permeability of an area of the fiber membrane to sodium ions. Since a much greater concentration of sodium exists on the outside of the membrane, a large influx of sodium ions enters the fiber to reverse the polarity (Fig. 15-2, *B*).

This depolarization travels the nerve fiber as an impulse. During the peak of the action there is a positive membrane potential of 40 mV. The fiber behind the traveling impulse is repolarized by the efflux of potassium ions and the influx of sodium ions along a concentration gradient (Fig. 15-2, *C*). To restore the normal concentration gradient a few sodium ions must be actively transported from the inside to the outside of the cell. This is the classic "sodium pump." This pump, driven by adenosine triphosphate (ATP) metabolism, may also transport potassium ions to the inside of the cell.[25]

Local anesthetics block nerve conduction by de-

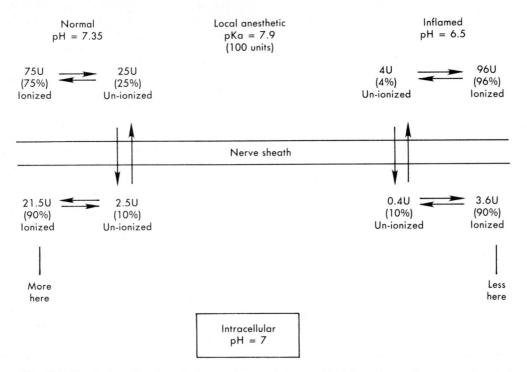

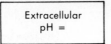

Fig. 15-1. Distribution of local anesthetic agent in normal tissue and in inflammation. More local anesthetic reaches its site of action (intracellular ionized) in the normal tissue than in the inflamed tissue.

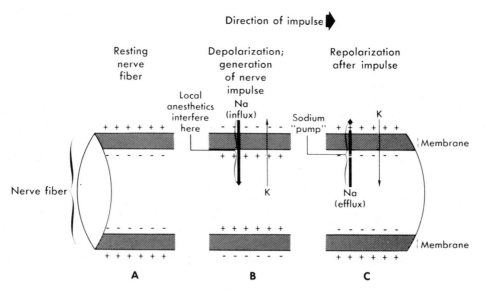

Fig. 15-2. Propagation of nerve impulse. (From Requa-Clark, B.S., and Holroyd, S.V.: Applied pharmacology for the dental hygienist, St. Louis, 1982, The C.V. Mosby Co.)

creasing the membrane permeability to sodium, thus interfering with the influx of sodium, which is essential for the depolarization of the fiber. In the past the action of the local anesthetics was thought to be related to calcium ions.[32] Now it is believed that the anesthetics block the sodium channels, thereby reducing membrane permeability to sodium.[25] The local anesthetics may inactivate these sodium channels either by enhancement of the normal inactivation process or by immobilizing the activation mechanism and inhibiting the normal inactivation.[31]

ANTIHISTAMINES AS LOCAL ANESTHETICS

Antihistamines have weak local anesthetic properties. The only clinical significance of this fact is that they may be useful when a patient is allergic to several types of local anesthetics, or in emergency cases in which the patient recalls a severe allergic reaction to an unknown local anesthetic.

Tripelennamine (Pyribenzamine) 1% and diphenhydramine hydrochloride (Benadryl) 1% have been injected as local anesthetics.[33] Both were found to provide satisfactory local anesthesia for tooth extraction. The average volume injected was 3 ml, and the maximal dose was 5 ml. The average duration of local anesthesia obtained with the antihistamines was about one half that obtained with 2% lidocaine with epinephrine 1:100,000. Another study compared 2% lidocaine with 1% diphenhydramine, both with 1:100,000 epinephrine.[34] The diphenhydramine solution had a slower onset, about one half the duration of action, and produced profound anesthesia in fewer patients. However, diphenhydramine provided profound or satisfactory anesthesia for the removal of 22 out of 25 partially embedded, carious, and malposed third molars without postanesthetic complications. The maximal dose of diphenhydramine used was 4 ml (40 mg). Roberts and Loveless[35] used diphenhydramine in conjunction with light intravenous conscious sedation to prepare three molar teeth. The patient had demonstrated an allergic reaction to the amides. A total of 90 mg was used during the 2-hour procedure. The preparation used was diphenhydramine 1% with epinephrine 1:100,000.

Fielding and Ligh[36] have reviewed the literature on the use of diphenhydramine as a local anesthetic. They consider it an alternative when allergies to the local anesthetics have been reported.

COMPOSITION OF ANESTHETIC SOLUTIONS

In addition to the anesthetic drug, local anesthetic solutions usually contain a vasoconstrictor (epinephrine, levonordefrin) and an antioxidant to preserve the vasoconstrictor (sodium bisulfite or sodium pyrosulfite). Antiseptics such as methylparaben are added to multiple-dose vials and sometimes to cartridges.

Vasoconstrictors in local anesthetics

Vasoconstrictors are included in local anesthetic solutions to (1) prolong and increase the depth of anesthesia by retaining the anesthetic in the area injected, (2) reduce the toxic effect of the drug by delaying its absorption into the general circulation, and (3) render the area of injection less hemorrhagic. A pharmacologic comparison of the various vasoconstrictors is presented in Chapter 5.

Eliminating the vasoconstrictor. Whenever a local anesthetic solution does not contain a vasoconstrictor, the anesthetic drug will be removed from the injection site and into systemic circulation faster than if the solution did contain a vasoconstrictor. This will provide a shorter duration of action and allow a more rapid buildup of a systemic blood level of the anesthetic. Any advantage gained by eliminating the vasoconstrictor (shorter duration and negated possible systemic effect of the vasoconstrictor) must be weighed against the potential for adverse effects. The latter will be determined by the nature, toxicity, and concentration of the anesthetic drug, the volume of drug required, and the size, age, and general health of the patient involved.

Concentration of the vasoconstrictor. How much vasoconstrictor is needed in a local anesthetic solution? A sufficient concentration should be present to allow anesthesia of adequate depth, duration, and safety. How much is this? On the point of safety, dentists have established an excellent safety record using 1:50,000 and 1:100,000 epinephrine or an equivalent concentration of levonordefrin with 2% procaine, lidocaine, and mepivacaine. The question then becomes: If adequate safety is obtained with 1:100,000 epinephrine, does one need the 1:50,000 concentration?

In 1963 Keesling and Hinds[37] carried out a double-blind study of various concentrations of epinephrine with 2% lidocaine in 119 subjects. They found that 2% lidocaine with 1:250,000 epinephrine was as effective in increasing the depth and duration of anesthesia as the solutions containing 1:50,000 or 1:100,000 epinephrine. Reeve stated in 1970, "There is no need at any time to use a concentration of epinephrine greater than 1:100,000 for dental anesthesia.[38] In spite of the fact that for years the dental profession used epinephrine in local anesthetic solutions at a concentration of 1:50,000, the use of 1:100,000 concentrations will provide an adequate prolongation of anesthesia and protection against rapid absorption.

There is no justification for the use of epinephrine in a concentration greater than 1:100,000 or even 1:200,000, except in those infrequent cases in which 1:50,000 is necessary to provide hemostasis.

Vasoconstrictors in patients with cardiovascular disease. During the 1930s and 1940s, statements were frequently made in the literature that vasoconstrictors should not be used in dental local anesthetics for patients with cardiovascular disease. The fear was that the vasoconstrictor might cause a rise in blood pressure that could not be tolerated by a patient with cardiovascular disease. Although these early fears were associated with a certain amount of logic, the effect of vasoconstrictors on the cardiovascular system in the quantities used in dental practice had not been adequately studied at that time. Additionally, physicians were accustomed then, as they are now, to think of epinephrine in terms of greater concentrations than are used in dentistry.

During the 1950s a number of studies demonstrated that the small amount of vasoconstrictor contained in dental local anesthetics had no effect on blood pressure. Notable here were the studies by McCarthy,[39] Wallace and coworkers,[40] Tainter and Winter,[41] Follmar and associates,[42] Salman and Schwartz,[43] Cheraskin and Prasertsuntarasai,[44-47] and Costich.[48] During the same period, Dick,[49] Follmar and associates,[42] and Mead[50] had indicated that discomfort after inadequate anesthesia would produce more endogenous epinephrine than that introduced in a local anesthetic solution. It is interesting to note that the *resting* adrenal medulla of a 70 kg man produces approximately 0.014 mg per minute epinephrine.[51] This equals the amount of epinephrine in 1.4 ml of a 1:100,000 solution. Under the stress of a dental appointment, this amount of endogenously produced epinephrine could increase tremendously.

The current status of vasoconstrictors in patients with cardiovascular disease is as follows:

1. A Working Conference of the American Dental Association and American Heart Association[52] has said,

> The concentration of vasoconstrictor normally used in dental local anesthetic solutions is not contraindicated in patients with cardiovascular disease when administered carefully and with preliminary aspiration. The following concentrations can be used: epinephrine, 1:50,000–1:250,000; levarterenol, 1:30,000; levonordefrin, 1:20,000; and phenylephrine 1:2,500.

2. The New York Heart Association[53] has stated,

> The dentist should have information from the physician about the nature and severity of the heart disease in the patient. He should also have knowledge of medication the patient is receiving, particularly such medication as might increase the activity of epinephrine. This knowledge is important because ordinary dental procedures may produce some emotional stress and cause cardiac disturbances that might be wrongly attributed to epinephrine.

3. As a guideline, the New York Heart Association recommends that for any one session no more than 0.2 mg (200 μg) epinephrine be administered for the healthy dental outpatient. This is the amount of epinephrine in 10 ml of a 1:50,000 solution or 20 ml of a 1:100,000 solution. The patient with organic heart disease should not receive more than 0.04 mg (40 μg) of epinephrine. Table 15-3 lists the maximal safe doses (MSD) for both the healthy and the cardiac patient for various vasoconstrictors. Note the relationship between the relative pressor potency and the MSD.

ADVERSE EFFECTS

Despite the enviable record of safety in dental local anesthesia, the practitioner must be aware of the potential for adverse reactions. Adriani[54] has said, "Few potentially hazardous drugs are used as thoughtlessly, as indiscriminately and with less knowledge of their pharmacology as are the local anesthetics." One must not consider local anesthesia as being without danger. A lack of caution will result in needless serious and fatal reactions. The treatment of adverse effects is discussed in Chapter 28.

Adverse reactions to local anesthetics can be local or systemic. Although these drugs can damage tissues locally,[55,56] this does not appear to present a signifi-

Table 15-3. Vasoconstrictors*

Drug	Concentration used in dentistry	Relative pressor potency	MSD† (normal adult)		MSD† (cardiac patient)		Approximate percentage of α/β activity
			mg	ml	mg	ml	
Epinephrine (Adrenalin Chloride)	1:100,000 (1 mg/100 ml)	1	0.2	20	0.04	4	50/50
Levonordefrin (Neo-Cobefrin)	1:20,000 (1 mg/20 ml)	1/5	0.5	20	0.2	8	75/25
Norepinephrine, levarterenol (Levophed)	1:30,000 (1 mg/30 ml)	3/5	0.34	10.2	0.14	4.2	90/10
Phenylephrine (Neo-Synephrine)	1:2500 (2 mg/5 ml)	1/20	4	10	1.6	4	99/1

*From Requa-Clark, B., and Holroyd, S.V.: Applied pharmacology for the dental hygienist, St. Louis, 1982, The C.V. Mosby Co.
†Maximal safe dose.

Table 15-4. Toxicity and maximal recommended doses of local anesthetics*

Drug	Toxicity		Absolute potency	Maximum recommended dose		Concentration used (%)	Approximate number of cartridges
	Absolute	Relative		mg	ml		
Procaine (Novocain)	1†	1†	1†	400	20	2	11.1
Lidocaine (Xylocaine, Octocaine)	1.5	1.5	2+	300	15	2	8.3
Mepivacaine (Carbocaine, Isocaine)	1.5	1.5	2+	300	15	2	8.3
				300	10	3	5.6
Prilocaine (Citanest)	1+	1+	2+	400	10	4	5.6
Tetracaine	10	1	10	30	20	0.15	11.1
Propoxycaine (Ravocaine)	10	2	10	30	7.5	0.4	4.2

*Modified from Bennett, C.R.: Monheim's local anesthesia and pain control in dental practice, ed. 6, St. Louis, 1978, The C.V. Mosby Co.
†Toxicity of procaine equals 1.

cant clinical problem in dentistry. Adverse systemic effects include toxic reactions, allergic reactions, and effects of the vasoconstrictor.

Toxic effects

As with any drug, toxic reactions to local anesthetics occur when a certain tissue concentration (toxic level) is exceeded. The particular concentration of a drug that causes a toxic reaction depends basically on the toxicity of the specific drug. Table 15-4 shows the relative toxicities of some local anesthetics of importance in dentistry. The blood level that will cause a toxic reaction varies somewhat among individuals and may also vary with time in the same individual. Children and elderly and debilitated patients may show toxic reactions at blood levels lower than those that are adverse in young healthy adults. The severity of the toxic effects is proportional to the toxicity of the drug and the blood level that exists.

Although the factors that determine the height of a particular blood level attained after the injection of a local anesthetic have been mentioned earlier, a more detailed consideration relative to toxicity should be made at this point.

1. *Nature of drug.* The rates at which currently used local anesthetics enter the circulation after submucosal injection are not significantly different. Although the ester-type drugs cause more vasodilation than do the amides, the clinical effects of vasodilation are usually counteracted by the inclusion of greater concentration of a vasoconstrictor. However, drugs such as tetracaine enter the circulation after topical application much more rapidly than does lidocaine.

2. *Concentration of drug.* Obviously, the higher the concentration of drug used the greater will be the amount of drug per unit of injected volume that will enter the systemic circulation.

3. *Route of injection.* The inadvertent intravenous injection of a local anesthetic is probably the most frequent reason for high systemic blood levels attained in dental practice—indicating how important it is to aspirate before injection.

4. *Vascularity of site.* Greater innate vascularity of an area or the presence of hyperemia as produced by inflammation or the application of heat will increase the rate of drug entry into systemic circulation. Vasoconstriction as produced by the application of cold will reduce systemic absorption.

5. *Presence of a vasoconstrictor.* The vasoconstrictor reduces systemic absorption. Adequate reduction in systemic absorption of the currently available local anesthetics is accomplished with 1:100,000 or even 1:200,000 epinephrine.

6. *Volume of distribution.* A dose of a local anesthetic administered to a 50-pound child will produce a higher blood-tissue concentration than if administered to a 150-pound adult.

7. *Rate of metabolism and elimination.* Infants, children, patients with liver or kidney disease, the debilitated, and the elderly will not metabolize or eliminate a drug as rapidly as other patients. This leads to increased systemic blood levels and potential for toxicity.

Systemic toxicity to local anesthetics is described as a descending stimulation of the CNS followed by depression of certain areas of the brain. It has been suggested that the entire effect of local anesthetics on the CNS is one of depression and that the phase of stimulation is the result of the depression of inhibitory neurons.[29,58] If the classic progression is observed, one might see the following:

1. Restlessness, apprehension, and tremors progressing to excitement and convulsions
2. Increasing blood pressure and pulse rate
3. Increasing respiratory rate
4. Respiratory and cardiovascular depression with loss of reflexes and consciousness

Depression, generally the cause of death, may appear without the initial stimulation. This pattern is characteristic of lidocaine toxicity.

On rare occasions, cardiovascular collapse and death have occurred after a low dose of infiltration anesthesia. Although the mechanism here is unknown, it is probably caused by cardiac arrest resulting from a direct effect on the pacemaker or sudden ventricular fibrillation.[37]

Allergic reactions

Allergic reactions to local anesthetics are uncommon. However, mild dermatologic reaction (urticaria or rashes), delayed reactions (serum sickness), or immediate reactions (anaphylaxis) may occur after the use of any local anesthetic. A carefully obtained medical history should disclose known sensitizations, but it is no assurance that an allergy does not exist. An allergy to any one drug will indicate that the patient is likely to be allergic to drugs with a similar chemical structure. The esters have a greater allergenic potential than do the amides. In fact, whether a true allergic reaction (antigen-antibody) can occur with the amides is still being debated. As a rule, use of the amides is safe in patients who are allergic to the ester type of drugs and vice versa. Cross-allergenicity does not appear to exist between lidocaine and mepivacaine. Consequently, they may usually be substituted for each other. However, some individuals are allergic to several anesthetics, and no substitute is an absolute guarantee that an allergic reaction will not occur.

Testing. The use of skin testing to ascertain the type of allergies a patient might have is unpredictable, since false positive and false negative results can occur. Only in a carefully controlled hospital setting should even trained persons attempt to challenge a patient's allergy to a local anesthetic. In one study of 20 patients with identified allergies to local anesthetics, no positive skin test and no change in vital signs were elicited by the administration of a local anesthetic.[58]

Methylparaben. Methylparaben, the antiseptic or preservative usually added to local anesthetic solutions, has the ability to cause allergies. For this reason a history of an allergic reaction to local anesthetics may mean that the patient is allergic to this preservative rather than the local anesthetic. A local anesthetic that does not contain methylparaben should be chosen for any patient with a history of allergies. The commonly used local anesthetics are now available without this preservative.

Vasoconstrictor. Some individuals may show signs and symptoms after the use of a local anesthetic that are believed to be caused by the vasoconstrictor. These reactions are most likely to follow inadvertent intravenous injection and include palpitation, apprehension, and tachycardia. They are usually mild and self-limiting. Differentiating these effects from a fear reaction is difficult if not impossible.

Precautions in topical anesthesia. Some local anesthetics are absorbed rapidly when applied topically to mucous membranes. To avoid toxic reactions from surface anesthesia, the practitioner should consider the following[22]:

1. Know the relative *toxicity* of the drug being used.
2. Know the *concentration* of the drug being used.
3. Use the *smallest volume* and the *lowest concentration* of the *least toxic* drug that will satisfy the clinical requirements.
4. Limit the *area of application* as much as possible.

The topical application of drugs is more likely to induce an allergic reaction than would oral or parenteral administration. Consequently, (1) highly allergenic drugs should never be used topically, and (2) the topical administration of parenterally useful drugs should be restricted as much as possible.

Drug interactions

CNS depressants potentiate the cardiac and respiratory depression of the local anesthetics. Both the ester-type local anesthetics and succinylcholine are metabolized by plasma pseudocholinesterase. Prolonged apnea could result from simultaneous administration of these drugs.

Induction of microsomal enzymes by the barbiturates could result in an increased metabolism of the amide-type local anesthetics. This could reduce the plasma levels of the agents.

Malignant hyperthermia

In genetically susceptible patients, malignant hyperthermia can result from the administration of certain drugs such as the amide local anesthetics. General anesthetic agents and neuromuscular blocking agents also can produce this effect in these patients. Symptoms include tachycardia, tachypnea, high fever, and cyanosis. Death is common. The amides are absolutely contraindicated in these patients. Ester-type agents can be safely used.

AGENTS FOR INJECTION

There are many local anesthetic agents available with similar pharmacologic and clinical effects and systemic toxicity. A few agents used frequently in the dental operatory will be discussed here. Table 15-5 lists the concentrations, duration, and chemical class of some of the local anesthetic agents.

Procaine. Procaine (Novocain) is a PABA ester. After its synthesis in 1905, it quickly replaced cocaine as the most frequently used local anesthetic in both medicine and dentistry. Procaine remained the principal local anesthetic in use until the late 1950s, when the amide type of drug gained popularity.

Procaine has a fast onset and a toxicity and potency of about half that of lidocaine. It causes marked local vasodilation and thus has a relatively short duration of action unless used with a vasoconstrictor. Rapid hydrolysis in plasma to PABA and diethylaminoethanol makes procaine one of the safest, if not the safest, local anesthetic known. Its metabolite, PABA, interferes with the antibacterial activity of the sulfonamides; consequently, it should not be used with these drugs.

Procaine is not effective topically but is used for infiltration, block, spinal, epidural, and caudal anesthesia. It is also used intravenously in the treatment of cardiac arrhythmias and seizures of status epilepticus.[26] It is also used as an antifibrillatory agent (procainamide) and is combined with penicillin to form procaine penicillin G. It is the drug of choice in the management of an arterial spasm produced by intra-arterial injection. The principal use of procaine hydrochloride in dentistry today is as a 2% solution combined with a more potent local anesthetic such as tetracaine or propoxycaine.

Lidocaine. Lidocaine (Xylocaine, Octocaine) is an amide derivative of xylidine. It was introduced in 1949 and quickly became an anesthetic of importance. It has to a great extent replaced procaine as the standard to which other local anesthetics are compared. It has a rapid onset, which is undoubtedly related to its tendency to spread well through the tis-

Table 15-5. Commonly available dental local anesthetics*

Local anesthetic	Concentration (%)	Vasoconstrictor	Concentration	Duration (hr)†	Chemical class
Procaine (Novocain)	2			1	Ester
	2	Epinephrine	1:50,000	1	
	4	Phenylephrine	1:2500	1	
Propoxycaine (available only mixed with 2% procaine) (Ravocaine)	0.4	Levonordefrin	1:20,000	2	Ester
	0.4	Levoarterenol	1:30,000	2	
Lidocaine (Xylocaine, Octocaine)	2			2	Amide
	2	Epinephrine	1:50,000	3	
	2	Epinephrine	1:100,000	3	
Mepivacaine (Carbocaine, Isocaine)	3			1	Amide
	2	Levonordefrin	1:20,000	3	
Prilocaine (Citanest, Citanest Forte)	4			1	Amide
	4	Epinephrine	1:200,000	3	
Pyrrocaine (Dynacaine)	2	Epinephrine	1:150,000	2	Amide
	2	Epinephrine	1:250,000	1	
Tetracaine (available with 2% procaine) (Pontocaine)	0.15	Levonordefrin	1:20,000	3+	Ester
	0.15	Levoarterenol	1:30,000	3+	
	0.15	Phenylephrine	1:2500	3+	
Bupivacaine (Marcaine)	0.5				Amide
	0.5	Epinephrine	1:200,000	3-10	
Etidocaine (Duranest)	0.5			3-10	Amide

*Modified from Bennett, C.R.: Monheim's local anesthesia and pain control in dental practice, ed. 6, St. Louis, 1978, The C.V. Mosby Co.
†Approximate.

sues. Lidocaine in 2% concentration provides profound anesthesia of long duration, especially if the solution contains a vasoconstrictor. Since lidocaine causes little or no local vasodilation, less vasoconstrictor is required than is necessary with procaine. It is twice as toxic as procaine (Table 15-5), but with proper care the doses required in dentistry cause few problems. There is no cross-allergenicity between lidocaine and the ester type of anesthetics, and apparently none between lidocaine and other available amines. Some patients appear to experience some sedation with lidocaine, and in toxic reactions one is likely to observe CNS depression initially rather than the CNS stimulation characteristic of other local anesthetics.

Lidocaine is used for topical, infiltration, block, spinal, epidural, and caudal anesthesia. It is also used intravenously to treat cardiac arrhythmias during surgery, to depress laryngeal and pharyngeal reflexes, to reduce the pruritus of jaundice and the pain caused by malignancy or burns, and to control the seizures of status epilepticus.[26]

In dentistry 2% lidocaine hydrochloride is used for infiltration and block anesthesia with 1:50,000 epinephrine and 1:100,000 epinephrine and also without a vasoconstrictor. Since vasodilation is produced by 2% lidocaine without vasoconstrictor, there are few clinical indications for such a product. It is used for topical anesthesia as a 5% ointment, a 10% spray, and a 2% viscous solution. Lidocaine with epinephrine provides a 1- to 1½-hour duration of pulpal anesthesia. Soft tissue anesthesia is maintained for 3 to 4 hours. The epinephrine concentration of 1:50,000 is used for hemostasis. Rebound vasodilation (beta effect) can be expected after the alpha effect (vasoconstriction) has occurred.

Mepivacaine. Mepivacaine (Carbocaine, Isocaine) is an amide derivative of xylidine. It was introduced in the late 1950s and has become an important local anesthetic. Its rate of onset, duration, potency, and toxicity are similar to lidocaine. There is no cross-allergenicity between mepivacaine and the ester type of local anesthetic and apparently none with the other currently available amines.

Mepivacaine is not effective topically but is used for infiltration, block, spinal, epidural, and caudal anesthesia. The usual dosage form in dentistry is a 2% solution with 1:20,000 levonordefrin (Neo-Cobefrin) as the vasoconstrictor. Since mepivacaine produces even less vasodilation than does lidocaine, it has been made available in a 3% solution without a vasoconstrictor. Caution should be exercised when increased concentrations of a local anesthetic are used to eliminate the vasoconstrictor. Except in unusual cases, the benefit of a shorter duration does not warrant eliminating the vasoconstrictor, especially if the concentration of the drug is increased. According to Reeve,[38] in regard to the elimination of the vasoconstrictor in patients with preexisting medical problems,

The excess concentration of a toxic anesthetic agent will do far more harm to the patient than the small concentration of 1:100,000 or less epinephrine used to prevent the rapid absorption of this drug into the circulating blood.

Prilocaine. Prilocaine (Citanest, Citanest Forte) is related chemically and pharmacologically to lidocaine and mepivacaine. A basic chemical difference, however, is that although lidocaine and mepivacaine are xylidine derivatives, prilocaine is a toluidine derivative. Prilocaine appears to be less potent and less toxic than lidocaine and has a slightly longer duration of action. It has been shown to produce satisfactory local anesthesia with low concentrations of epinephrine and without epinephrine. Although prilocaine toxicity has been said to be 60% of that of lidocaine,[60] several cases of methemoglobinemia have been reported after its use.

Large doses of prilocaine are metabolized to toluidine, which can induce the methemoglobinemia. A dose of 400 mg of prilocaine produces a methemoglobin level of 1%. Usually a 20% level is required to produce symptoms—cyanosis of the lips and mucous membranes and occasionally respiratory distress. Although the small doses required in dental practice are not likely to present a problem in healthy, nonpregnant adults, prilocaine should not be administered to infants or to patients with methemoglobinemia, anemia, hypoxia, heart failure,[26] or any other condition in which problems of oxygenation may be especially critical, such as in pregnancy. Methemoglobinemia can be reversed by the intravenous injection of 1% methylene blue (1 to 2 mg/kg). Patients receiving either of the para-aminophenols, acetaminophen or phenacetin, should not be given prilo-

caine because these agents all produce methemoglobinemia.

Prilocaine is used for infiltration, block, epidural, and caudal anesthesia. It is available in dental carpules as a 4% concentration with 1:200,000 epinephrine and also as a 4% solution without a vasoconstrictor. The use of increased concentrations of a drug without the use of a vasoconstrictor is open to considerable question.

Propoxycaine. Propoxycaine (Ravocaine) is another ester of PABA. In the late 1950s propoxycaine, like tetracaine, came to be used in combination with procaine. It is slightly less potent and less toxic than tetracaine and also has a long duration of action. Propoxycaine's rapid onset of action when injected and its lack of topical activity are its principal clinical differences from tetracaine.

Propoxycaine is used for infiltration and block anesthesia. Dental carpules contain 0.4% propoxycaine and 2% procaine with 1:20,000 levonordefrin or 1:30,000 levarterenol.

Pyrrocaine. Pyrrocaine (Dynacaine), like lidocaine and mepivacaine, is an amide derivative of xylidine. Its onset, potency, toxicity, and duration of action are similar to those of lidocaine and mepivacaine. It is available in carpules in 2% solutions with 1:150,000 and 1:250,000 epinephrine.

Tetracaine. Tetracaine (Pontocaine) is an ester of PABA. During the 1950s tetracaine obtained considerable use in combination with procaine for dental local anesthesia. This use decreased after the introduction of lidocaine and mepivacaine. Tetracaine has a slow onset and long duration and is generally estimated to have at least ten times the potency and toxicity of procaine. Topically, it is rapidly absorbed. In view of this drug's high toxicity and the rapidity with which it is absorbed from mucosal surfaces, great care must be exercised if it is used for topical anesthesia. A maximal dose of 20 mg is recommended for topical administration (1 ml of a 2% solution). As in the case of procaine and other PABA derivatives, tetracaine may reduce the effectiveness of concomitantly administered sulfonamides. It is used for topical, infiltration, block, caudal, and spinal anesthesia.

Carpules are available that contain 0.15% tetracaine and 2% procaine, with 1:20,000 levonordefrin, 1:30,000 levarterenol, or 1:2500 phenylephrine as the vasoconstrictor. Tetracaine is available in various sprays, solutions, and ointments for topical application. The concentration of tetracaine in most topical preparations is 2%.

Bupivacaine. Bupivacaine (Marcaine) is an amide-type local anesthetic related to lidocaine and mepivacaine. It is about four times more potent than the other amides (lidocaine and mepivacaine). Its vasodilating property is more than the other amides but less than procaine. Its major advantage is its prolonged duration of action. It is indicated in prolonged dental procedures in which pulpal anesthesia of greater than 1½ hours is needed or in which postoperative pain is expected. When it was compared to 2% lidocaine with epinephrine, the onset of 0.5% bupivacaine with epinephrine was slightly longer, but its duration was twice that of lidocaine.[61] It is to be available in dental cartridges, 0.5% and 0.75%, both with and without epinephrine. It should not be used in patients prone to self-mutilation. It has been used for infiltration, block, and peridural anesthesia.

Etidocaine. Etidocaine (Duranest) is another amide-type local anesthetic related to lidocaine and mepivacaine. It has a rapid onset of action and a duration of anesthesia comparable to that of bupivacaine. When Laskin[62] compared etidocaine with lidocaine (with both agents containing epinephrine), he found that the onset was similar and the duration was doubled with etidocaine. Although its place in dental practice has not yet been established, etidocaine has been used for infiltration, peripheral nerve blocks, and some types of epidural anesthesia.

TOPICAL ANESTHETICS

Lidocaine and tetracaine are effective topical anesthetics and have been discussed previously. The following drugs, except for cocaine, have a usefulness as surface anesthetics in dentistry. Cocaine is discussed for historic reasons and because it is still used to some extent in medical practice.

Cocaine. Cocaine, a naturally occurring ester of benzoic acid, was the first local anesthetic. It is potent and extremely toxic, and it is the only local anesthetic that causes definite vasoconstriction. Its effects on the CNS include excitement, tremors, tachycardia, and tachypnea. Because of its toxicity and possible addiction potential, it is no longer used parenterally. Cocaine is the subject of considerable drug abuse and is classified as a schedule II drug under the Controlled Substances Act. It is used topically in medical practice but has no application in dentistry.

Benzocaine. Benzocaine (ethyl *p*-aminobenzoate) is an ester of PABA. Because it lacks a basic nitrogen, it cannot be converted to a water-soluble form

for injection. It is poorly soluble, is poorly absorbed, and has a prolonged duration of action. It may interfere with the action of sulfonamides. Repeated use of benzocaine has resulted in local allergic reactions. It is available in many proprietary products promoted for a wide variety of conditions, from erupting teeth to hemorrhoids.

Dyclonine. Because dyclonine (Dyclone), a ketone, is chemically different from other local anesthetics, cross-sensitization with other local anesthetics does not occur. Its onset of action is slow (up to 10 minutes), but its duration is up to 1 hour. Its toxicity is low because of its poor solubility in water. It is not injected to the tissues and is available as a 0.5% solution.

CHOICE OF LOCAL ANESTHETIC

Each practitioner should choose a few local anesthetic solutions to use, depending on the duration of anesthesia desired. Below is a list of suggestions for anesthesia of various durations of action:

A. Less than 30 minutes
 1. Mepivacaine plain
B. Thirty to 60 minutes
 1. Lidocaine or mepivacaine with vasoconstrictor
 2. Propoxycaine/procaine with vasoconstrictor
C. Sixty to 90 minutes
 1. Prilocaine with vasoconstrictor
 2. Agents listed in B may be effective
D. Longer than 90 minutes
 1. Bupivacaine with vasoconstrictor
 2. Etidocaine with vasoconstrictor

DOSAGE

The amounts of local anesthetic and vasoconstrictor contained in a certain volume of solution can be calculated from the concentration of that solution in the following way.

Calculation of local anesthetic

To determine the amount of local anesthetic administered to the patient when the percentage concentration is known:

1. Express the percentage of solution as a fraction of 100, so that a 2% solution would be expressed as

$$\frac{2}{100}$$

Then add the units of gm/ml, so the 2% solution would be expressed as:

$$2\% \text{ lidocaine} = \frac{2 \text{ gm}}{100 \text{ ml}}$$

2. Convert grams to milligrams (1 gm = 1000 mg) and determine the number of grams contained in 1 ml:

$$\frac{2 \text{ gm}}{100 \text{ ml}} = \frac{2 \times 1000 \text{ mg}}{100 \text{ ml}} = \frac{2000 \text{ mg}}{100 \text{ ml}} = \frac{20 \text{ mg}}{1 \text{ ml}}$$

3. Multiply the concentration by the volume administered. For example, 1 carpule = 1.8 ml, so if 1 carpule of 2% lidocaine is administered:

$$\frac{20 \text{ mg}}{1 \text{ ml}} \times 1.8 \text{ ml} = 36 \text{ mg lidocaine}$$

Calculation of vasoconstrictor

1. Express ratio of concentration as a fraction with units of gm/ml:

$$\text{Epinephrine } 1:100,000 = \frac{1 \text{ gm}}{100,000 \text{ ml}}$$

2. Change grams to milligrams (1 gm = 1000 mg):

$$\frac{1 \text{ gm}}{100,000 \text{ ml}} = \frac{1000 \text{ mg}}{100,000 \text{ ml}} = \frac{1 \text{ mg}}{100 \text{ ml}} = \frac{0.01 \text{ mg}}{1 \text{ ml}}$$

3. Multiply the concentration by the volume administered. For example, 1 carpule = 1.8 ml, so if 1 carpule of 1:100,000 epinephrine is administered:

$$\frac{0.01 \text{ mg}}{1 \text{ ml}} \times 1.8 \text{ ml} = 0.018 \text{ mg}$$

Determination of maximal dosage

The following are maximal recommended doses for healthy adults. The objective is to use the minimal dose that will attain acceptable anesthesia.

The determination of a maximal safe dose can be calculated by first referring to Tables 15-3 and 15-4. Using the data in these tables, one can calculate the number of carpules of combined local anesthetic and vasoconstrictor that can be administered safely. For example, when administering lidocaine 2% with epinephrine 1:100,000, one can determine the limiting factor (agent that has a lower maximum safe dose) in the following way:

Lidocaine

$$\text{Maximal dose} = 300 \text{ mg}$$

$$2\% \text{ Lidocaine} = \frac{20 \text{ mg}}{1 \text{ ml}}$$

(See "Calculation of local anesthetic.")

20 mg × 1.8 ml = 36 mg/1 cartridge
300 mg ÷ 36 mg = 8.3 cartridges

Eight cartridges of 2% lidocaine can be used.

Epinephrine

$$\text{Maximal dose} = 0.2 \text{ mg}$$

$$\text{Epinephrine } 1:100,000 = \frac{0.01 \text{ mg}}{1 \text{ ml}}$$

(see "Calculation of vasoconstrictor")

$$\frac{0.01 \text{ mg}}{1 \text{ ml}} \times 1.8 \text{ ml} = 0.018 \text{ mg/1 cartridge}$$

0.2 mg ÷ 0.18 mg = 11.1

Eleven cartridges of 1:100,000 epinephrine can be used.

Therefore the limiting factor is lidocaine. This means that eight cartridges of 2% lidocaine with 1:100,000 epinephrine could be safely administered. These doses are the absolute maximal doses that can be administered to a healthy adult. For normal practice it is usually unnecessary to even approach these amounts. If two local anesthetic agents are administered, the sum of both agents should not exceed the lower MSD calculated.

REFERENCES

1. The other half of the picture (editorial), J. Am. Dent. Assoc. **32:**1031, 1945.
2. Mayer, E.: The toxic effects following the use of local anesthetics, J.A.M.A. **82:**876, 1924.
3. Mayer, E.: Fatalities from local anesthetics, J.A.M.A. **90:** 1928.
4. Ruth, H.D., Haugen, F.P., and Grove, D.D.: Anesthesia Study Commission, J.A.M.A. **135:**881, 1947.
5. Dealy, F.N.: Anesthetic deaths, 5-year report, Am. J. Surg. **60:**63, 1943.
6. Adriani, J., and Campbell, D.: Fatalities following topical application of local anesthetics to mucous membranes, J.A.M.A. **162:**1527, 1956.
7. Furstenberg, A.C., Wood, L.A., Magielski, J.E., and McMahon, G.F.: An evaluation of cocaine anesthesia: the perpetuation of equivocal concepts, Trans. Am. Acad. Ophthalmol. Otolaryngol. **56:**643, 1951.
8. Ireland, P.E., Ferguson, J.K.W., and Stark, E.J.: The clinical and experimental comparison of cocaine and pontocaine as topical anesthetics, Laryngoscope **61:**767, 1951.

9. Beecher, H.K., and Todd, D.P.: A study of the deaths associated with anesthesia and surgery: based on a study of 599,548 anesthesias in 10 institutions, 1948-1952, Am. Surg. **140:**2, 1954.

10. Criep, L.H., and Ribeiro, C.C.: Allergy to procaine hydrochloride with 3 fatalities, J.A.M.A. **151:**1185, 1953.

11. Seldin, H.M., and Recant, B.S.: Safety of anesthesia in the dental office, J. Oral Surg. **13:**199, 1955.

12. Seldin, H.M.: Survey of anesthetic fatalities in oral surgery and a review of the etiological factors in anesthetic deaths, J. Am. Dent. Soc. Anesth. **5:**6, 1958.

13. American Dental Association: The 1962 survey of dental practice. V. Some aspects of dental practice, J. Am. Dent. Assoc. **67:**158, 1963.

14. Driscoll, E.J.: Anesthesia morbidity and mortality in oral surgery, proceedings of the Conference on Anesthesia for the Ambulatory Patient, Chicago, 1966.

15. American Society of Oral Surgeons: ASOS anesthesia morbidity and mortality survey, J. Oral Surg. **32:**733, 1974.

16. Wigand, F.T.: Untoward reaction to lidocaine: report of a case, J. Oral Surg. **16:**334, 1958.

17. Morrissett, L.M.: Fatal anaphylactic reaction to lidocaine, U.S. Armed Forces Med. J. **8:**740, 1957.

18. Ningham, L.R., and Molherbe, P.H.: Xylocaine intoxication: a report of 3 recent cases, Dent. Abstr. **3:**143, 1958.

19. Medico-legal comment. Death after Xylocaine injection, Br. Med. J. **1:**280, 1952.

20. Hunter, A.R.: The toxicity of Xylocaine, Br. J. Anaesth. **23:**153, 1951.

21. Hanson, I.R., and Hingson, R.A.: Use of Xylocaine, new local anesthetic, in surgery, obstetrics and therapeutics, Anesth, Analg. **29:**136, 1950.

22. American Dental Association Council on Dental Therapeutics: Accepted dental therapeutics, ed. 37, Chicago, 1977, American Dental Association.

23. Pharmacotherapeutics in dental practice (NAVPERS 10486), Washington, D.C., 1969, U.S. Bureau of Naval Personnel.

24. Covino, B.G., and Giddon, D.B.: Pharmacology of local anesthetic agents, J. Dent. Res. **60:**1454-1459, 1981.

25. Covino, B.G.: Physiology and pharmacology of local anesthetic agents, Anesth. Prog. **28:**98-104, July/August 1981.

26. American Medical Association Council on Drugs: AMA drug evaluations—1973, Chicago, 1973, American Medical Association.

27. Krantz, J.C., Jr., and Carr, C.J.: The pharmacologic principles of medical practice, ed. 7, Baltimore, 1969, The Williams & Wilkins Co.

28. Adriani, J.: The clinical pharmacology of local anesthetics, J. Clin. Pharm. Exper. Ther. **1:**645, 1960.

29. Goodman, L.S., and Gilman, A.: The pharmacological basis of therapeutics, ed. 5, New York, 1975, Macmillan Publishing Co., Inc.

30. Campbell, D., and Adriani, J.: Absorption of local anesthetics, J.A.M.A. **168:**873, 1958.

31. Strichartz, G.R.: Current concepts of the mechanism of action of local anesthetics, J. Dent. Res. **60:**1460-1467, 1981.

32. Covino, B.G., and Vassalo, H.G.: Local anesthetics: mechanism of action and clinical use, New York, 1976, Grune & Stratton, Inc.

33. Meyer, R.A., and Jokubowski, W.: Use of tripelennamine and diphenhydramine as local anesthetics, J. Am. Dent. Assoc. **69:**112, 1964.

34. Welborn, J.F., and Kane, J.P.: Conduction anesthesia using diphenhydramine hydrochloride, J. Am. Dent. Assoc. **69:**706, 1964.

35. Roberts, E.W., and Loveless, H.: The utilization of diphenhydramine for production of local anesthesia: report of a case, Tex. Dent. J. **97**(8):13-15, 1979.

36. Fielding, A.F., and Ligh, R.: Benadryl as a local anesthetic, Penn. Dent. J. **44:**8-9, 1977.

37. Keesling, G.R., and Hinds, E.C.: Optimal concentration of epinephrine in lidocaine solutions, J. Am. Dent. Assoc. **66:**337, 1963.

38. Reeve, L.W.: Modern pharmacodynamic concepts of local anesthesia, Dent. Clin. North Am. **14:**783, 1970.

39. McCarthy, F.M.: Clinical study of blood pressure responses to epinephrine-containing local anesthetic solutions, J. Dent. Res. **36:**132, 1957.

40. Wallace, D.A., et al.: Gish, G.: Systemic effects of dental local anesthetic solutions, Oral Surg. **9:**1297, 1956.

41. Tainter, M.L., and Winter, L.: Some general considerations in evaluating local anesthetic solutions in patients, Anesthesiology **5:**470, 1944.

42. Follmar, K.E., et al.: The effects upon human blood pressure of representative local anesthetics and vasoconstrictors, Northwestern Univ. Bull. **54:**13, 1954.

43. Salman, I., and Schwartz, S.P.: Effects of vasoconstrictors used in local anesthetics in patients with diseases of the heart, J. Oral Surg. **13:**209, 1955.

44. Cheraskin, E., and Prasertsuntarasai, T.: Use of epinephrine with local anesthesia in hypertensive patients. I. Blood pressure and pulse rate observations in the waiting room, J. Am. Dent. Assoc. **55:**761, 1957.

45. Cheraskin, E., and Prasertsuntarasai, T.: Use of epinephrine with local anesthesia in hypertensive patients. II. Effect of sedation on blood pressure and pulse pressure and pulse rate in the waiting room, J. Am. Dent. Assoc. **56:**210, 1958.

46. Cheraskin, E., and Prasertsuntarasai, T.: Use of epinephrine with local anesthesia in hypertensive patients. III. Effect of epinephrine on blood pressure and pulse rate, J. Am. Dent. Assoc. **57:**507, 1958.

47. Cheraskin, E., and Prasertsuntarasai, T.: Use of epinephrine with local anesthesia in hypertensive patients. IV. Effect of tooth extraction on blood pressure and pulse rate, J. Am. Dent. Assoc. **58:**61, 1959.

48. Costich, E.P.: Study of inferior alveolar nerve block anesthesia in humans, comparing 2 per cent procaine plus 1:50,000 epinephrine, J. Dent. Res. **35:**695, 1956.

49. Dick, S.P.: Clinical toxicity of epinephrine anesthesia, Oral Surg. **6:**724, 1953.

50. Mead, S.V.: Use of epinephrine-containing anesthetic solutions in oral surgery, J. Oral Surg. **14:**79, 1956.

51. Guyton, A.C.: Textbook of medical physiology, ed. 4, Philadelphia, 1971, W.B. Saunders Co.

52. Working Conference of American Dental Association & American Heart Association on Management of Dental Problems in Patients with Cardiovascular Disease, J. Am. Dent. Assoc. **68:**333, 1964.

53. Special Committee of the N.Y. Heart Association, Inc.: Use of epinephrine in connection with procaine in dental procedures, J. Am. Dent. Assoc. **50:**108, 1955.

54. Adriani, J.: Local anesthetics. In Seminar Report, **I:**18, Fall, 1956, Philadelphia, Merck, Sharp & Dohme.

55. Costich, E.R.: The reaction of rat muscle to the constituents of procaine-epinephrine solutions in concentrations used for dental preparations, Oral Surg. **9:**205, 1956.

56. Brun, A.: Effect of procaine, Carbocaine and Xylocaine on cutaneous muscle in rabbits and mice, Acta Anaesth. Scand. **3**(2):59, 1959.

57. Bennett, C.R.: Monheim's local anesthesia and pain control in dental practice, ed. 6, St. Louis, 1978, The C.V. Mosby Co.

58. Sutherland, V.C.: A synopsis of pharmacology, ed. 2, Philadelphia, 1970, W.B. Saunders Co.

59. Barnard, D.P.: Evaluation of adverse reactions to local anesthetics: a survey of the literature and a report of a clinical investigation, J. Dent. Assoc. S. Afr. **31:**241, 1976.

60. Aström, A., and Persson, N.H.: Some pharmacological properties of *o*-methyl-α propylaminopropionanilide, a new local anesthetic, Br. J. Pharmacol. **16:**32, 1961.

61. Nespeca, J.A.: Clinical trials with bupivacaine in oral surgery, Oral Surg. **42:**301-7, 1976.

62. Laskin, J.L.: Use of etidocaine hydrochloride in oral surgery: a clinical study, J. Oral Surg. **36:**863-865, 1978.

Histamine
and antihistamines

HISTAMINE

Histamine is a rather ubiquitous biogenic amine. Although many of its actions are well known, its precise physiologic function and significance are not understood. It is for this reason that histamine is commonly classified as an autacoid with others such as serotonin, angiotensin, and bradykinin, that is, endogenous substances of intense pharmacologic activity whose role in the human body is not established.

Distribution, synthesis, and metabolism

Almost all mammalian tissues contain histamine or have the capacity to synthesize it. High concentrations are found in the intestinal mucosa, skin, and lungs, where histamine is primarily contained in mast cells.[1] Histamine is stored in the mast cell granule in physiologically inactive form. Current evidence indicates that histamine release correlates with degranulation of mast cells, is energy dependent, and requires the presence of calcium.[2] In blood, histamine is contained in basophils. In both of these "storage sites" histamine is bound to a heparin-protein complex. In the CNS, which is devoid of mast cells, histamine is most probably contained in synaptic vesicles, a finding that is consistent with the hypothesis of histamine possibly being a central transmitter.[3]

Synthesis of endogenous histamine is by way of decarboxylation of histidine by nonspecific L-amino acid decarboxylase (histidine decarboxylase), an inducible enzyme. Ingested histamine or that formed by bacteria in the gastrointestinal tract appears to be insignificant in maintaining body stores.

The two primary pathways of histamine metabolism are (1) to 1-methylhistamine by imidazole-methyltransferase (IMT) or (2) by diamine oxidase (DAO) to imidazole–acetic acid. These and additional metabolic products are excreted through the kidney.

The levels of both catabolic and anabolic enzyme systems of histamine vary considerably during different physiologic conditions, such as an increase in DAO activity during pregnancy, suggesting again a significant physiologic regulatory function of the autacoid in humans.

Pharmacologic actions

There are pronounced species differences in the actions of histamines. The following discussion deals with its actions in humans.

Histamine affects many organ systems but with different intensities and different sensitivities to drug action. Although the existence of more than one receptor for histamine had been postulated before,[4] only the synthesis of antagonists of specific histamine sites[5] made it possible to arrive at the presently accepted concept of histamine receptors. Accordingly, the actions of histamine are divided into those that are mediated by way of activation of the H_1 receptors, the H_2 receptors, or a combination of both.

1. Histamine is a powerful vasodilator and can cause extensive dilation of arterioles, venules, and precapillary sphincters. This effect is independent of innervation and apparently results from a direct effect on these tissues. This action of histamine can be blocked only by a combination of H_1 and H_2 histamine antagonists, and thus it is mediated by receptors of both H_1 and H_2 types.

2. Histamine will effect an increased permeability of capillaries and small veins[4] to the extent of releasing plasma proteins and fluid into extracellular space. These two main effects of histamine (vasodilation and increased capillary permeability) are primari-

ly responsible for initiating the most deleterious sequela of histamine—cardiovascular shock (discussed later).

3. Histamine has a direct stimulatory effect on nonvascular smooth muscle. In humans the most common effect observed is bronchoconstriction, which is particularly prominent in patients suffering from various pulmonary diseases. This action of histamine is easily antagonized by the long available "classic" antihistamines known to block H_1 receptors, and therefore it is considered to involve activation of the H_1 type of receptors exclusively.

4. Almost all exocrine glands are stimulated by histamine, but to various degrees. Histamine is a powerful stimulant of gastric secretion by a direct action on parietal and chief cells. This response to histamine can be effectively antagonized by antihistaminic drugs involving H_2 receptors, and thus stimulation of gastric secretion is considered to be the typical example of activation by way of a pure H_2 receptor.

5. Histamine stimulates cutaneous nerve endings, eliciting axon reflexes. Therefore histamine causes itching, when introduced into superficial layers of skin, and pain accompanied by itching, when introduced into deeper layers of skin. At the cellular level this is apparently also mediated by membrane permeability changes, which in this case result in depolarization and initiation of nerve impulses.

Histamine release

Many physiologic and pathophysiologic reactions as well as the administration of certain drugs will result in the release of endogenous histamine. The extent of release of histamine will determine the resulting pharmacologic actions, both in severity and spectrum. Although not always clinically significant, the fact should also be kept in mind that any mechanism resulting in the endogenous release of histamine from mast cells will simultaneously result in the release of heparin, which in turn may or may not affect blood-clotting time. At present, histamine release is known

to be calcium and temperature dependent and constitutes an active secretory process of exocytosis. Furthermore, it is probable that histamine secretion from mast cells and basophils is coupled to cyclic nucleotide metabolism.

When histamine's action is limited locally, that is, intradermal injection causes the well-known "triple response"[6]: a localized red spot caused by local dilation of arterioles, venules, and capillaries; a "flare" or red flush of irregular outline caused by dilatation of surrounding arterioles (by way of a local axon reflex mechanism); and a "wheal" formed by localized accumulation of edema fluid caused by increased permeability of surrounding fine blood vessels.

Undoubtedly histamine release occurs during antigen-antibody interactions and thus is associated with some allergic reactions. Whether histamine is the *sole* mediator in any of these reactions in humans is questionable and remains to be established. Histamine has been found to be released during the initial phase of inflammatory processes, but its role appears to be transient and incomplete and not essential for the development of the most characteristic changes that produce lasting tissue damage. Almost any agent or cause that results in tissue damage also liberates histamine,[7,8] including chemical, physical, thermal, or bacterial trauma.

Several drugs are known to release histamine from tissue stores. On the one hand there are "nonspecific" releasers that act by causing general tissue damage. These include, for example, surface-active agents like detergents. Interestingly, various plasma expanders (such as dextran) have also been found to release histamine in sufficient quantities to result in cardiovascular complications. The second group of drugs is of more common significance in their ability to release histamine. Their mechanism is not understood, and a wide variety of different drugs share the property. These include morphine, succinylcholine, dextrotubocurarine, epinephrine, some antibiotics, trimethaphan, and surprisingly enough, almost all

Histidine →(Histidine decarboxylase)→ **Histamine** $+CO_2$

antihistamine drugs involving the H_1 receptor. Thus some of the side effects encountered with any of these drugs are directly attributable to their histamine-releasing action, and the effects observed can reach anaphylactoid proportions.

A discussion of the pharmacologic actions of histamine—directly administered or endogenously released—would be incomplete without a brief description of the anaphylactic shock reaction and the symptoms of histamine toxicity. An acute anaphylactic shock reaction is likely to occur within minutes after contact with an antigenic protein or precipitating agent. As mentioned earlier, histamine's direct vasodilatory effect will result in a sharp fall in blood pressure, which is further intensified by the loss of fluid and plasma protein into extracellular space. This in turn will manifest itself in extensive edema formation. Thus circulation is greatly compromised by peripheral pooling of blood, together with an increased hematocrit. Subsequent decreased venous return and a compensatory tachycardia can easily lead to shock and cardiovascular collapse. The specific symptoms of an anaphylactic shock reaction may appear in the following order: apprehension, paresthesia, urticaria and edema, choking, cyanosis, cough, wheezing, fever, shock, loss of consciousness, coma, convulsions, and death.

Manifestations of an exogenously administered overdose of histamine are more exclusively caused by cardiovascular and pulmonary symptoms. There is profound immediate hypotension and possibly life-threatening bronchoconstriction. These symptoms are accompanied by the presence of intense headache, vomiting, and diarrhea.

The treatment of an acute allergic reaction like anaphylaxis is by physiologic antagonism rather than specific antihistaminic medication. Epinephrine is the drug of choice. Aminophylline also has bronchodilator activity and, for that reason, is used in the treatment of acute pulmonary edema as well as bronchial asthma. Steroids are used extensively as adjuncts in the management of allergic conditions to suppress any allergic inflammatory reactions. Further discussion of the treatment of an acute allergic reaction can be found in Chapter 28.

Inhibition of allergic release of histamine

Based on the knowledge of the importance of histamine release during various hypersensitivity and allergic reactions, a sound pharmacologic approach would be a selective inhibition of histamine release. This is accomplished by a new type of antiallergic drug exemplified by cromolyn (Aarane, Intal).[9]

This drug inhibits antigen-induced secretion of histamine and slow-reacting substance of anaphylaxis (SRS-A). It does not relax bronchial or other smooth muscle, nor does it interact with other bronchodilators. It blocks histamine release from pulmonary mast cells yet does not act on circulating basophils. Cromolyn constitutes an exclusively prophylactic therapy for bronchial asthma. Because of this clinical use and the fact that it is poorly absorbed when given orally, it is administered by inhalation via a special turboinhaler. Nasal sprays and ophthalmic solutions are also available, since its beneficial effect in allergic rhinitis is beyond doubt.[10] Side effects and toxicity of cromolyn appear to be minor, consisting mainly of irritation and congestion. Some rare cases of hypersensitivity to it have been reported. Thus it can be concluded that cromolyn constitutes an effective prophylactic drug in various forms of bronchial asthma and probably some other allergic reactions. Based on its known action of preventing the release of allergen-induced histamine, cromolyn clearly is not effective in the treatment of an asthmatic attack.

Clinical use

There are only minor clinical uses of histamine itself. More specific drugs with fewer side effects have replaced histamine as a diagnostic agent in assessment of achlorhydria and the determination of parietal cell mass. In particular, pentagastrin (Peptavlon) and to a lesser extent betazole (Histalog) are presently used to test for gastric secretory function. The use of pentagastrin obviates the simultaneous administration of an H_1 antagonist, and it rarely elicits allergic reactions.

Since intradermal histamine causes a "flare" that is mediated by axon reflexes, this test is administered to evaluate the integrity of sensory nerves in certain neurologic disorders.

It has been claimed that repeated administration of small doses of histamine will induce tolerance to the amine. Based on this premise, desensitization of allergic individuals has been attempted with histamine. Suffice it to say that, at present, the use of histamine for this purpose is highly controversial.

ANTIHISTAMINES

Although histamine was well described by Dale as early as 1911, it was 1937 by the time Bovet and his co-workers described the first compound with antihistaminic properties. These were identified by antagonism of histamine-induced contraction of smooth muscle and by a reduction of anaphylactic responses. The first clinically employed antihistamine was phenbenzamine (Antergan), soon to be followed by pyrilamine (Neo-Antergan), both of which are ethylenediamines. After minor modifications, diphenhydramine and tripelennamine were developed and introduced in the United States. Despite numerous attempts to improve on these initial compounds, they were incapable of blocking all actions of histamine, notably gastric acid secretion. Only with the discovery of the H_2 histamine blocking agents by Black and his colleagues[5] in 1972, a major breakthrough in antihistamine drugs was achieved. Presently, antihistamine drugs are subdivided depending on which histamine receptor they presumably occupy and thus what responses to histamine they prevent. Therefore they are classified as H_1 or H_2 receptor blocking agents, or simply as H_1 or H_2 antagonists. The two classes of antihistamine drugs will be discussed separately.

H_1 receptor antagonists

Chemistry. In simplified chemical terms all antihistamines involving H_1 histamine receptor sites can be looked on as structural analogs of histamine by showing the following same basic skeletal formula:

Histamine

Antihistamine

Depending on the substitution at X and type of —CH_2—CH_2—bridge, H_1 blockers are classified into five large groups. These are presented in Table 16-1 for a quick grasp of their chemical, pharmacokinetic, and gross pharmacologic differences.

Absorption, metabolism, and excretion. Generally, absorption, distribution, metabolism, and excretion of H_1 blocking drugs are relatively uncomplicated and of no significant specificity. After oral and parenteral administration, they are readily absorbed. Their onset varies between 15 and 60 minutes; the

duration of action of a single dose is between 3 and 12 hours, but some act much longer. Major metabolic pathways consist of hydroxylation followed by conjugation. Most of the metabolism takes place in the liver, but lung and kidney have been shown to metabolize at least some antihistamines. Most of the investigated antihistamines have been found to be excreted in the urine within 24 hours after one dose.

On long-term administration of H_1 antihistamines, a certain extent of tolerance develops to their sedative effect. This tolerance is apparently caused by a combination of developing central tolerance and an induction of drug-metabolizing enzymes in the liver.

Pharmacologic actions. The pharmacologic effects and therapeutic uses of H_1 antihistaminic drugs can most easily be classified into two groups: those resulting from blocking the action of histamine at the H_1 receptor sites and those actions resulting from direct effects independent of their antihistaminic properties.

In the former type of actions these drugs will block the effects of histamine on capillary permeability and on vascular, bronchial, and other types of smooth muscle. Their mechanism is by competitive blockade at the H_1 receptor site. H_1 antihistamines are most effective in preventing histamine-induced increased capillary permeability and edema formation. It is well established that in many species H_1 antihistamines can effectively antagonize the constricting action of histamine on respiratory smooth muscle. Yet they are not very effective in protecting against anaphylactic bronchospasm in humans, a condition in which apparently other autacoids are important. Histamine-induced hypotension is only partially inhibited by H_1 antihistaminic drugs, a combination of H_1 and H_2 antihistamines being much more effective. Apparently, for the action of histamine on the vascular tree, both H_1 and H_2 receptors are activated. H_1 blocking agents also block the stimulatory action of histamine on nerve endings and therefore are effective in suppressing the flare component of the triple responses and the itching associated with any histamine-mediated reaction.

The actions of H_1 antihistamines, other than those dependent on histamine blockade, are mostly of CNS origin. In many instances, particularly in dentistry, antihistamines are used for these actions, their "side effects." Antihistamines have depressant as well as stimulant action on the CNS. They are sedatives of varying effectiveness and are additive with the sedation produced by other CNS depressants. Develop-

Table 16-1. Chemical and pharmacotherapeutic properties of the various H$_1$ antihistamine groups

Group	Representative example	Usual adult dose (mg) and preparations available	Duration of action (hr)	Special properties	Other members of same group
Alkylamines $$R-C-CH_2-CH_2-N\begin{smallmatrix}R\\\\R\end{smallmatrix}$$	Chlorpheniramine (Chlor-Trimeton)	2-4 Tablets: 4, 8, 12	4-6	Low incidence of moderate sedation	Dexbrompheniramine (Dimetane) Triprolidine HCl (Actidil)
Ethanolamines $$R-O-CH_2-CH_2-N\begin{smallmatrix}R\\\\R\end{smallmatrix}$$	Diphenhydramine (Benadryl)	50 Capsules: 25, 50	4-6	High anti–motion sickness activity; high incidence of pronounced sedation	Dimenhydrinate (Dramamine) Carbinoxamine maleate (Clistin)
Ethylenediamine $$R-N-CH_2-CH_2-N\begin{smallmatrix}R\\\\R\end{smallmatrix}$$	Tripelennamine (Pyribenzamine)	50 Tablets: 25, 50 Sustained-release tablets: 100	4-6	Moderate incidence of pronounced sedation; gastrointestinal irritation	Pyrilamine (Neo-Antergan) Antazoline (Antistine) Methapyrilene (Histadyl, and as mixture: Co-Pyronil)
Piperazines	Chlorcyclizine HCl (Di-Paralene)	50 Tablets: 25, 50	8-12	Low incidence of moderate sedation	Meclizine (Bonine) Cyclizine (Marezine)
Phenothiazines	Promethazine (Phenergan)	25-50 Tablets: 12.5, 25, 50	4-6	Pronounced sedation; potential for all other phenothiazine side effects	Pyrathiazine HCl (Pyrrolazote) Trimeprazine tartrate (Temaril)

ment of tolerance to this effect has been pointed out before. Many H_1 antihistamines are used freely by the public as sleep medication. In addition, with prolonged use, the drugs induce various forms of oral symptoms, the most pronounced of which is xerostomia. The mechanism of this action is weak cholinergic blockade of muscarinic type.

Many but not all H_1 antihistamines have a pronounced anti–motion sickness action. Generally, these agents also effectively control nausea and vomiting from other labyrinthine disturbances. This central antiemetic action of H_1 antihistamines is the basis for their use in the control of postsurgical nausea in dentistry.

CNS stimulation does occur on rare occasions in adults with conventional doses. Children, however, show a high incidence (50%) of this response, which manifests itself in restlessness and excitement, possibly escalating into convulsions.

H_1 antihistamines have local anesthetic activity to varying degrees. It has been stated that they are more effective local anesthetics when applied topically on denuded skin rather than as an injection for nerve block.

Adverse effects and drug interactions. The most common side effect of the H_1 antihistamine drugs is excessive sedation, which may or may not be accompanied by dizziness, tinnitus, uncoordination, blurred vision, and fatigue. Not only may these effects be hazardous to the patient's effective daytime activities, but the patient will also be more sensitive to all other types of CNS depressant drugs. Undoubtedly a patient receiving H_1 antihistamine therapy will require less preoperative sedation than will an untreated individual.

The next most common side effects of antihistamines are gastrointestinal disturbances, such as anorexia, nausea, vomiting, constipation, and xerostomia, which can best be reduced by administering the drugs with meals.

H_1 antihistamines, as mentioned before, paradoxically are histamine releasers themselves. Allergic dermatitis is not an uncommon side effect. Other less frequent effects, apparently also from histamine release, are hypotension, palpitation, headaches, and tightness of the chest. Rare incidences of blood dyscrasias have been reported. Some antihistamines, particularly meclizine, cyclizine, and chlorcyclizine have been shown to have teratogenic effects in laboratory animals. Whether this response does occur in

humans and at what time course are not established. However, the potential hazard implicit in the use of these drugs in pregnant women should be appreciated.

Acute poisoning with H_1 antihistamine drugs has become relatively common because of their easy accessibility as over-the-counter drugs. Signs and symptoms are different in children than they are in adults, although in both cases they are caused by central actions of the drug. In smaller children the predominant effect is excitation manifested in hallucinations, excitement, uncoordination, and convulsions. Symptoms include fever, a flushed face, and fixed, dilated pupils. Death is caused by coma with cardiorespiratory collapse. In adults most commonly the convulsive phase is preceded by drowsiness. The ultimate phase is a postictal depression. In adults, fever and flushed face are rarely seen. Therapy is only symptomatic and supportive and depends exclusively on the correct diagnosis. In the case of convulsions, only short-acting barbiturates are indicated.

Therapeutic uses. Once again, therapeutic uses of these drugs can best be subdivided into those caused by H_1 antihistamine action and those by actions independent on blockade of histamine receptors.

Certain acute allergic reactions such as allergic rhinitis and seasonal hay fever can effectively be controlled by H_1 antihistamines. Contrary to many initial reports and rather widespread popular belief, these antihistamines are of rather limited value in the management of the common cold. The limited relief that they afford is primarily caused by their weak atropine-like action. Obviously, under those circumstances, sedation represents the most limiting side effect. Once again, H_1 antihistamines are not the drug of choice in an anaphylactic shock reaction; physiologic antagonists like epinephrine and certain xanthines are far superior. However, H_1 antihistamines are effective in relieving itching, edema, and erythema of an acute urticarial attack.

H_1 antihistamines, often in combination with corticosteroids, are sometimes useful in relieving the pain and swelling associated with certain allergic ulcers of the mouth. In this situation they are applied topically. The potential hazard of a sensitivity reaction to the antihistamine has to be weighed against the benefit of such treatment. Generally, however, these drugs are not highly allergenic.

The use of H_1 antihistamines in dentistry is primarily based on their actions independently of histamine blockade. They have been employed in preoperative sedation because of their sedative central action and antiemetic effects. Ethanolamines and promethazine are particularly useful for this purpose (Table 16-1). They are, however, less effective than the tranquilizers and barbiturates. Promethazine has also been used clinically with meperidine, as described in Chapter 12. H_1 antihistamines have also been substituted for local anesthetics, as described in Chapter 15.

Cimetidine

The H_1 antihistamines were once reported to control postoperative sequelae of dental surgery such as swelling, trismus, and pain.[11-14] Subsequently, well-controlled and double-blind studies did not find the antihistamines to be effective for this purpose.[15-18]

Many H_1 antihistamines, particularly diphenhydramine, dimenhydrinate, and cyclizine, are effectively used in the prevention and treatment of motion sickness. They also have been used in the control of postoperative vomiting or that induced by radiation. The use of some antihistamines in the control of nausea and vomiting of pregnancy is not considered completely safe because of their potential teratogenic action.

H_2 receptor antagonists

Chemistry. H_2 receptor antagonists have an obvious structural similarity consisting of the imidazole ring but differing in the side chains. They are polar, hydrophilic molecules, a fact that probably accounts for their lack of CNS effects. The first H_2 receptor antagonists introduced clinically were burimamide and metiamide. Both of them have been replaced, for reasons of poor absorption in the case of the former and of toxicity in the case of the latter compound. Cimetidine is presently the only H_2 receptor antagonist employed.[19,20]

Pharmacologic actions. The mechanism of cimetidine is by reversible, competitive blockade of those actions of histamine that are mediated by H_2 receptors, notably gastric acid secretion. It not only inhibits gastric acid secretion elicited by histamine infusion but also that evoked by pentagastrin or gastrin.

This inhibition manifests itself in a reduced volume of gastric juice secreted and in a reduced hydrogen ion concentration. Furthermore, cimetidine blocks all phases of physiologic secretion of gastric acid without affecting the rate of gastric emptying.

Therapeutic uses. Cimetidine is effective in the treatment of most cases of duodenal ulcer since it consistently lowers basal and nocturnal acid secretion as well as that stimulated by meals. With these actions pain is significantly reduced and healing is facilitated. Cimetidine has no effect on bowel motility and thus constitutes an advantageous drug for concomitant therapy with antacids and anticholinergic drugs. Evidence indicates that cimetidine is effective in reducing the rate of ulcer recurrence if given in maintenance therapy. Cimetidine is also indicated for the treatment of patients with Zollinger-Ellison syndrome and other hypersecretory states. Side effects of cimetidine can be considered minor and infrequent, consisting of dizziness, headache, and muscle pains. They rarely affect or limit the therapeutic usefulness of this drug.

REFERENCES

1. Riley, J.F., and West, G.G.: The occurrence of histamine in mast cells. In Eichler, O., and Farah, A., editors: Handbuch der experimentellen Pharmakologie. Histamine and antihistaminics, vol. 18/1, Berlin, 1966, Springer-Verlag.
2. McIntire, F.C.: Histamine and antihistamines. In Schacter, M., editor: International encyclopedia of pharmacology and therapeutics, vol. 1, Oxford, 1973, Pergamon Press, Ltd.
3. Schwartz, J.C.: Histaminergic mechanisms in brain, Ann. Rev. Pharmacol. Toxicol. **17:**325, 1977.
4. Ash, A.S.F., and Schild, H.O.: Receptors mediating some actions of histamine, Br. J. Pharmacol. Chemother. **27:**427, 1966.
5. Black, J.W., et al.: Definition and antagonism of histamine H_2 receptors, Nature **236:**385, 1972.
6. Lewis, T.: The blood vessels of the human skin and their responses, London, 1927, Shaw & Sons, Ltd.
7. Spector, W.G., and Willoughby, D.A.: Vasoactive amines in acute inflammation, Ann. N.Y. Acad. Sci. **116:**839, 1964.
8. Spector, W.G., and Willoughby, D.A.: The inflammatory response, Bac. Rev. **27:**117, 1964.
9. Cox, J.S.C., et al.: Disodium cromoglycate (Intal), Adv. Drug Res. **5:**115, 1970.
10. Toogood, J.H., et al.: Cromolyn-sodium therapy: predictors of response, Adv. Asthma Allergy **5:**2, 1978.
11. Silverman, R.E.: The use of antihistamines in oral surgery: a preliminary report, J. Oral Surg. **11:**231, 1953.
12. Silverman, R.E.: Further clinical observations on the use of antihistamines in oral surgery, J. Oral Surg. **12:**310, 1954.
13. Blinderman, J.J.: Control of edema, pain and trismus in oral surgery with an oral antihistamine, N.Y. J. Dent. **26:**231, 1956.

14. Macchia, A.F.: Antihistamines and their value in allaying postoperative distress in the removal of impacted teeth, Oral Surg. **10:**122, 1957.

15. Szmyd, L.: A clinical evaluation of an antihistaminic preparation in oral surgery, Oral Surg. **9:**928, 1956.

16. Keesling, G.R., and Hinds, E.E.: Clinical evaluation of antihistamines in oral surgery using the double unknown technic, J. Oral Surg. **15:**279, 1957.

17. Holland, M.R., and Jurgens, P.E.: The effectiveness of an antihistamine to reduce pain following oral surgical procedures, Oral Surg. **11:**138, 1958.

18. Snyder, B.S.: Effect of antihistaminic agents on inflammatory response after surgical trauma, J. Oral Surg. **18:**319, 1960.

19. Burland, W.L., and Simkins, M.A., editors: Proceedings of the second international symposium on histamine H_2-receptor antagonists: cimetidine, Excerpta Medica, Amsterdam, p. 7, 1977.

20. Fortran, J.S., and Grossman, M.I., editors: Third symposium on histamine H_2-receptor antagonists: clinical results with cimetidine, Gastroenterology **74:**7, 1978.

CHAPTER 17

Hormones*

NORBERT R. MYSLINSKI

Hormones are biologically active substances secreted by endocrine glands and transported by the blood to target organs. Endocrine glands include the pituitary, thyroid, parathyroids, pancreas, adrenals, gonads, and placenta. They help maintain homeostasis by regulating body functions and are controlled themselves by feedback systems. Drugs that affect the endocrine system include the active principles of the endocrine glands, synthetic hormone agonists and antagonists, and substances that influence the synthesis and secretion of hormones. The most important clinical application of these drugs is their use in replacement therapy, such as in the treatment of diabetes mellitus or myxedema. Additional applications include diagnostic procedures, contraception, and the treatment of glandular hyperfunction, cancer, and other systemic disorders.

MECHANISMS OF ACTION

Many peptide hormones, such as glucagon, calcitonin, parathyroid hormone, the trophic hormones of the anterior pituitary, the melanocyte-stimulating hormones, and some of the hypothalamic releasing hormones, work by a common mechanism. They produce their effects by interacting with specific receptor sites on the surface of the plasma membrane that are linked to the enzyme adenylate cyclase[1,2] (Fig. 17-1). Stimulation of adenylate cyclase increases the rate of synthesis of cyclic adenosine 3',5'-monophosphate *(cyclic AMP)*. Cyclic AMP acts as a "second messenger," which activates protein kinases to phosphorylate cellular constituents. These cellular constituents, in turn, alter the rates at which certain cellular processes proceed. In this way peptide hormones regulate such processes as protein synthesis, secretion, cell permeability, enzyme activation, and muscle contraction or relaxation.

The steroid hormones, such as the corticosteroids and sex hormones, act by a different mechanism. They attach to cellular receptors and are transported as a receptor-hormone complex to the nuclear chromatin. Here they stimulate the synthesis of particular proteins, which directly express information contained in the genetic apparatus.[3] Thyroid hormones are not steroids but possess a cellular mechanism similar to that of the steroids.[4]

Other hormones produce their effects by altering the uptake, release, or intracellular distribution of the calcium ion. Calcium and cyclic AMP often act with one another in the expression of hormonal effects.

PITUITARY HORMONES

The pituitary gland *(hypophysis)* is a small endocrine organ located at the base of the brain. It has been termed the "master" gland because of its regulatory effect on other endocrine glands and organs of the body. It secretes peptide hormones that regulate the thyroid, adrenal, and sex glands; the kidney and uterus; and growth. In addition to their regulatory effect, the pituitary hormones have a trophic effect that is necessary for the maintenance of many systems. For example, without the gonadotropins, the entire reproductive system fails; without growth hormone and thyrotropin, normal growth and development are impossible. The secretion of pituitary hormones is influenced by peripheral endocrine glands via hormonal feedback mechanisms, and by neurohumoral substances from the hypothalamus.

There are two parts to the pituitary gland, the anterior lobe *(adenohypophysis)* and the posterior lobe *(neurohypophysis)*.

---

*Hormones of the adrenal cortex are discussed in Chapter 18.

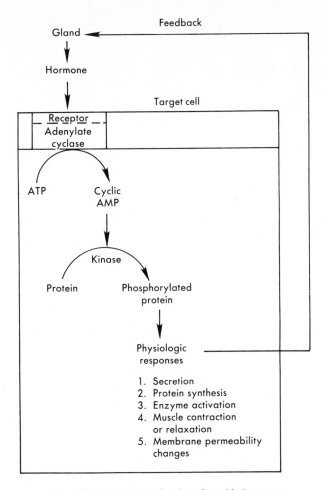

Fig. 17-1. Mechanism of action of peptide hormones.

Anterior pituitary hormones

The anterior lobe secretes *growth hormone* (GH), or somatotropin, *luteinizing hormone* (LH), *follicle-stimulating hormone* (FSH), *thyroid-stimulating hormone* (TSH), or thyrotropin, *adrenocorticotropic hormone* (ACTH), or corticotropin, and *prolactin.*

GH, also called *somatotropin,* causes an increase in the size and number of cells in most tissues of the body. It indirectly stimulates endochondral and periosteal bone growth by causing several proteins, collectively called *somatomedin,* to be formed in the liver and other tissues. Somatomedin in turn acts directly on the cartilage and bone to promote their growth.[5] GH also has metabolic effects that include increased rate of protein synthesis, increased mobili-

zation of fatty acids from adipose tissues, increased use of fatty acids for energy, and decreased rate of glucose utilization. It therefore increases body protein, decreases fat stores, and conserves carbohydrates. GH secretion increases in response to sleep, exercise, fasting, hypoglycemia, and excitement. An excess of GH during childhood produces *giantism;* after adolescence it causes *acromegaly.* A deficiency of GH causes *dwarfism.* Replacement therapy for dwarfism is the primary therapeutic use of GH.

Prolactin, in conjunction with other hormones, initiates and maintains lactation. Its concentration increases during pregnancy and reaches a maximum at term. This increase is required for the growth and development of the breast in preparation for breast-feeding. A few weeks after delivery the basal level of prolactin secretion returns to the nonpregnant level. Each time the mother nurses her baby, however, the suckling stimulus produces a tenfold or more increase in prolactin secretion from the pituitary. If nursing does not continue, the breasts lose their ability to produce milk. If nursing does continue, milk production can last for several years.

FSH is responsible for ovarian follicular growth and spermatogenesis. LH is important in the regulation of ovulation and androgen production. These gonadotropins are used therapeutically to stimulate ovulation in anovulatory females and to treat *cryptorchidism,* a condition in which the testes fail to descend.

TSH regulates the secretion of thyroid hormones and is used for the differential diagnosis of primary and secondary hypothyroidism. ACTH stimulates the adrenal cortex to secrete corticosteroids and is used to test the competency of hypophyseal-adrenal function. FSH, LH, TSH, ACTH, and adrenal hormones are discussed further in other sections of the text.

Other substances secreted by the anterior pituitary gland include beta and gamma *lipotropins,* which influence fat metabolism, alpha and beta *melanocyte-stimulating hormones* (MSH), which control skin pigmentation, and *endorphins* and *enkephalins,* which possess pharmacologic properties similar to those of opioids.

Hypothalamic-pituitary connection

The hypothalamus influences the anterior pituitary gland by means of neurohumoral substances, which are transported to the gland in the hypophyseal portal blood supply. These substances either stimulate or inhibit the synthesis and release of anterior pituitary hormones. The stimulation is an energy-requiring process possibly involving alterations in membrane permeability, calcium distribution, and cyclic nucleotide levels. There exist releasing substances for TSH, LH, FSH, GH, ACTH, MSH, and prolactin, as well as release-inhibiting substances for GH, MSH, and prolactin. Except for some diagnostic tests, clinical use of these substances is still experimental.

Posterior pituitary hormones

The posterior pituitary gland secretes *antidiuretic hormone* (ADH, vasopressin) and *oxytocin*.

ADH affects electrolyte balance by stimulating water reabsorption in the kidney collecting ducts. The main physiologic stimuli for ADH secretion are increased plasma osmolality and decreased extracellular volume. When the fluids of the body become highly concentrated, they stimulate the supraoptic nuclei of the hypothalamus that transmit impulses to the posterior pituitary to secrete ADH. ADH then increases the permeability of the kidney collecting ducts to water. As a result most of the water is reabsorbed from the tubular fluid, and electrolytes continue to be lost in the urine. This dilutes the extracellular fluids and returns them to normal.

Other stimuli for ADH secretion include pain, emotional stress, and an increase in the temperature of the blood perfusing the hypothalamus. ADH also has a number of nonrenal effects including a general pressor effect on all parts of the vasculature, including the coronary blood vessels. Preparations of ADH include vasopressin injection (Pitressin) and desmopressin acetate (DDAVP), which is administered intranasally. Therapeutically ADH is used to treat vasopressin-sensitive diabetes insipidus. The preparation of choice is desmopressin, which can produce local irritation and hypersensitivity when applied to the nasal mucosa. Other side effects include marked facial pallor and increased activity of the intestines and uterus. The most serious side effect is the pressor effect on coronary circulation, especially for those individuals with coronary artery disease.

Oxytocin controls uterine contractility. It stimulates both the frequency and the force of contraction of uterine smooth muscle, especially during the end of gestation. Oxytocin also controls mammary gland milk ejection. It contracts the myoepithelium of the breast, which forces milk from the alveolar channels into the ducts where it is easily available to the infant.

Oxytocin release is controlled by the paraventricular nucleus of the hypothalamus, which is stimulated by infant suckling. Therapeutically oxytocin is used to induce labor and control postpartum hemorrhage. Preparations include oxytocin injection (Pitocin), oxytocin nasal solution, and oxytocin citrate buccal tablets (Pitocin Citrate).

Pituitary deficiency *(hypopituitarism)* can produce a loss of secondary sex characteristics, decreased metabolism, dwarfism, diabetes insipidus, hypothyroidism, Addison's disease, loss of pigmentation, thinning and softening of the skin, decreased libido, and retarded dental development.[6] Hypersecretion of pituitary hormones can produce sexual precocity, goiter, Cushing's disease, acromegaly, and giantism.

THYROID HORMONES

Thyroxine (T_4) and *triiodothyronine* (T_3) are iodine-containing hormones synthesized and secreted by the thyroid gland. Both act on virtually every tissue and organ system of the body and are important for energy metabolism, growth, and development. Vulnerability to stress, altered drug response, and altered orofacial development are all possible manifestations of thyroid dysfunction.

Synthesis

The thyroid hormones are synthesized from iodine and tyrosine and stored as residues of thyroglobulin, a complex glycoprotein, until released. This process can be divided into four major steps: (1) the uptake of iodide by the gland, (2) the binding of iodide to tyrosine, (3) the coupling of the iodotyrosines, and (4) the secretion of the hormones.

The uptake of iodide ion is an energy-dependent active transport mechanism that can produce a glandular iodide concentration 20 to 100 times that of the plasma. A number of ions such as thiocyanate (SCN^-) and perchlorate (ClO_4^-) inhibit iodide uptake.[7]

After entering the gland, iodide is rapidly oxidized and then reacts with tyrosine molecules to form *monoiodotyrosine* (MIT) and *diiodotyrosine* (DIT). Molecules of MIT and DIT are coupled to form T_4 and the more potent T_3. On their release into the blood, both T_3 and T_4 are bound to plasma proteins, namely, *thyroxine-binding globulin* (TBG) and *thyroxine-binding prealbumin* (TBPA). Protein binding protects the hormones from metabolism and excretion, resulting in their long $t_{\frac{1}{2}}$ (6 to 7 days for T_4).

Only the unbound hormone, however, is free to produce a physiologic effect. The amount of binding can be influenced by certain drugs and a variety of pathologic and physiologic conditions. Pregnancy, for example, increases the amount of TBG and the percentage of hormone that is bound. Salicylates, dicumarol, and hepatic cirrhosis can all decrease the percentage of hormone bound to plasma protein.

Regulation

Thyroid function is regulated by TSH released from the anterior pituitary. TSH secretion, in turn, is controlled by the quantity of thyroid hormone in the circulation. Increasing thyroid hormones suppresses TSH secretion and therefore thyroid function; decreasing thyroid hormones enhances TSH secretion and thyroid function. TSH not only stimulates the uptake, synthesis, and release of thyroid hormones but also increases thyroid vascularity and produces hypertrophy of the thyroid cells.[8]

Actions

The actions of thyroid hormones include (1) effects on growth and development (2) calorigenic effects, and (3) metabolic effects. Most if not all of these effects are exerted through control of protein synthesis and enzymatic activity.

In animals, the dramatic effect of thyroxin on growth and development is best exemplified by its ability to transform a tadpole into a frog. In humans, the thyroid hormones affect a large number of tissues as is demonstrated by the extensive defects found in thyroid-deficient children. Probably the most important tissue affected in these individuals is in the nervous system, where myelinization and dendritic networks are defective.

The basal metabolic rate is increased by thyroid hormones especially in the heart, diaphragm, liver, and kidney. This calorigenic effect is important for increasing body temperature when exposed to the cold. Specific metabolic effects of thyroxine include increased intestinal absorption and hepatic synthesis of glucose and increased metabolism of carbohydrates and cholesterol. D-Thyroxine is sometimes used to lower the concentration of cholesterol in plasma.

Iodine

Normal thyroid function requires an adequate intake of iodine (approximately 125 μg per day). With-out it, normal amounts of hormone cannot be made, TSH is secreted in excess, and the thyroid hypertrophies. This thyroid hypertrophy is called *simple* or *nontoxic goiter*. Because iodine is not abundant in most foods, simple goiter is quite prevalent in some areas of the world. Marine life is the only food commonly eaten that is naturally rich in iodine. The introduction of iodized salt as a supplemental source of iodine has decreased the incidence of simple goiter in many countries.

Because of the compensatory adaptation of the thyroid to a lack of iodine, the hormonal activity in simple goiter is usually neither subnormal nor excessive *(euthyroid).*[9] However, if the gland continues to function under these stressful conditions for a prolonged period, it may undergo exhaustion, atrophy, and stop functioning, or it may convert into nodular goiter, which predisposes the patient to hyperthyroidism and thyroid carcinoma. Simple goiter resulting from iodine deficiency is treated with the appropriate dose of either a saturated solution of potassium iodide or Lugol's solution, containing 5% iodine and 10% potassium iodide.

Hypothyroidism

In the small child, thyroid hypofunction is referred to as *cretinism*. In the adult it is called *myxedema,* or simple hypothyroidism. The main characteristic is mental and physical retardation. Such patients are usually drowsy, weak, and listless and exhibit an expressionless, puffy face with edematous tongue and lips. Oral findings usually include delayed tooth eruption, malocclusion, and increased tendency to develop periodontal disease. The teeth are usually poorly shaped and carious. The gingiva is either inflamed or pale and enlarged. The cretin is often uncooperative and difficult to motivate for plaque control. Diagnostic radiographs and routine dental prophylaxis may require special assistance. Hypothyroid patients have a difficulty in withstanding stress and tend to be abnormally sensitive to all CNS depressants, especially the narcotic analgesics. If used, their dosages should be adjusted. Pregnant women with hypothyroidism tend to produce offspring with larger maxillary and mandibular teeth.[10]

Thyroid hypofunction is rationally and effectively treated by oral administration of exogenous thyroid hormones from animal thyroid glands. The following is a list of preparations used for thyroid hormone replacement therapy:

Levothyroxine sodium, (Synthroid)
Liothyronine sodium, (Cytomel)
Thyroglobulin, (Proloid)
Thyroid tablets, (Thyrar)
Thyroid

Hyperthyroidism

Diffuse toxic goiter (Graves' disease) and *toxic nodular goiter* (Plummer's disease) are the two forms of thyroid hyperfunction. Diffuse toxic goiter is characterized by a diffusely enlarged, highly vascular thyroid gland; is common in young adults; and is considered to be a disorder of the immune response. Toxic nodular goiter is characterized by nodules within the gland that spontaneously secrete excessive amounts of hormone while the rest of the glandular tissue is atrophied. It occurs primarily in older patients and usually arises from long-standing nontoxic goiter.

The adverse effects from excessive levels of circulating thyroid hormone, or *thyrotoxicosis*, include excessive production of heat, increased sympathetic activity, increased neuromuscular activity, increased sensitivity to pain, ophthalmopathy, *exophthalmos* (protruding eyes), and anxiety. Oral manifestations include accelerated tooth eruption, a marked loss of the alveolar process, diffuse demineralization of the jawbone, and rapidly progressing periodontal destruction.

The cardiovascular system is especially hyperactive because of a direct inotropic effect, an increased peripheral oxygen consumption, and an increased sensitivity to catecholamines.[4,11] Epinephrine is contraindicated in these patients. The potentiating effects of thyroid hormones and epinephrine on each other could result in severe cardiovascular problems, such as angina, arrhythmias, and hypertension. Adrenergic inhibiting drugs are therapeutically useful if such a condition does arise.

In addition to their increased sensitivity to pain, hyperthyroid individuals have an increased tolerance to CNS depressants. They may require higher than usual doses of sedatives, analgesics, and local anesthetics.

No treatment should be begun for any patient with a visible goiter, exophthalmos, or a history of taking antithyroid drugs until approval is obtained from the patient's physician. Medical management of the condition is important before any elective surgery is performed. Even in controlled patients who are considered to be euthyroid, stress should be kept at a minimum, preoperative sedation should be considered, and the practitioner should be alert for signs of significant imbalance in control (i.e., signs of overdosage of the controlling drug or signs of the disease itself).

The thyroid inhibitors used to treat hyperthyroidism can be classified into four categories:

1. Antithyroid drugs
2. Ionic inhibitors
3. Iodide
4. Radioactive iodine

Antithyroid drugs are the ones that the dental practitioner will most likely encounter. They interfere directly with the synthesis of thyroid hormones by inhibiting the iodination of tyrosine moities and the coupling of the iodotyrosines. Untoward reactions are relatively few, but the most serious is agranulocytosis, which can lead to poor wound healing, oral ulceronecrotic lesions, and oral infections. Paresthesia of facial areas and loss of taste are also seen. Not only are antithyroid drugs used over prolonged periods to bring a hyperactive thyroid to the euthyroid state, but they are also given before thyroidectomy to reduce the possibility of thyroid storm, a life-threatening acute form of thyrotoxicosis. Antithyroid drugs include propylthiouracil (Propacil) and methimazole (Tapazole).

Ionic inhibitors block the iodide transport mechanism. They include thiocyanate (SCN^-) and perchlorate (ClO_4^-). Iodide in high concentrations suppresses the thyroid in a still poorly understood manner. It may produce gingival pain, excessive salivation, and sialadenitis as side effects. Radioactive iodine is sequestered by the gland and results in localized destruction of thyroid tissue.

PARATHYROID HORMONE

Parathyroid hormone (PTH) is a polypeptide synthesized and secreted by the parathyroid glands. Its primary function is to maintain the extracellular concentration of calcium ion for optimal cellular and neuromuscular function. Plasma concentrations of calcium ion, in turn, regulate the secretion rate of PTH. When the concentration of ionized calcium is low, the secretion of PTH is stimulated along with amino acid uptake, nucleic acid and protein synthesis, and cytoplasmic growth of the gland. When the concentration of ionized calcium is high, the same functions are suppressed.

PTH helps to maintain plasma calcium at about 10

mg/100 ml by regulating the absorption of calcium from the gastrointestinal tract, the deposition and mobilization of calcium in bone, and the elimination of calcium. The most prominent effect is to promote the mobilization of calcium and phosphate from the stable, older portion of bone. This is accomplished by increasing the formation, activity, and $t_{\frac{1}{2}}$ of osteoclasts. PTH increases the intestinal absorption of calcium and phosphate, but vitamin D is more important in this regard. PTH increases the renal tubular reabsorption of calcium and the excretion of phosphate. It also decreases the elimination of calcium in saliva, sweat, and milk.

Hypocalcemia can be caused by a lack of PTH (*hypoparathyroidism*) or a lack of response to PTH by the target tissue (*pseudohypoparathyroidism*). Hypocalcemia can produce muscle spasms, tetany, paresthesia of the extremities, hair loss, brittle fingernails, cataracts, vascular spasms, enamel hypoplasia, hypodontia, root defects, and emotional disturbances.[12,13] Patients may also show a highly resistant form of oral candidiasis.

Hypercalcemia can be caused by *hyperparathyroidism*. In such cases calcium mobilized from bone is deposited in soft tissue, such as the heart, bronchi, kidneys, and stomach. Skeletal changes may also be seen on radiographs. Signs and symptoms of hyperparathyroidism include aches and pains in bones and joints, renal calculi caused by excessive calcium and phosphate in the urine, muscle weakness, and gastrointestinal disturbances. Salicylates are contraindicated because of the higher incidence of peptic ulcers in these patients. Dental manifestations include inflamed gingival tissues, alveolar breakdown, excessive tooth mobility, and recurrent gingival tumors.

PTH is rarely used therapeutically because of its antigenicity and unreliable biologic activity. It is, however, used for the diagnosis of certain calcium-related endocrine disorders.

CALCITONIN

Calcitonin is produced by the parafollicular cells of the thyroid gland. This production is regulated by plasma calcium levels. High calcium levels stimulate calcitonin production; low levels inhibit production. Calcitonin produces hypocalcemia and thus works opposite to PTH. It inhibits bone resorption by altering osteoclastic activity and enhances bone formation by stimulating osteoblastic activity. Despite these relationships, it is not known if calcitonin plays a significant physiologic role in calcium homeostasis.

Pharmacologically, calcitonin is used to decrease hypercalcemia in patients with hyperparathyroidism, vitamin D overdose, osteolytic bone metastases, and idiopathic hypercalcemia of infancy. It is also effective in *Paget's disease,* a bone-remodeling disorder in which bone resorption increases. Side effects seen with calcitonin are nausea, swelling, tenderness of the extremities, and urticaria.

PANCREATIC HORMONES

The two primary hormones secreted by the islets of Langerhans of the pancreas are *insulin* and *glucagon.* Insulin promotes fuel storage, whereas glucagon promotes fuel mobilization in the body.

Insulin

The synthesis of insulin begins with preproinsulin, which is converted to proinsulin in the endoplasmic reticulum of the islet's beta cells. Proinsulin is then transferred to the Golgi complex and then to storage granules, where it is converted to insulin. The finished hormone is then released by exocytosis.[14] The release of insulin is regulated by a number of factors, including the availability of food products, other hormones (especially gastrointestinal hormones), and neural stimuli. An elevated blood glucose level is the most important stimulus in humans.[15] The autonomic nervous system controls the basal rate of insulin secretion as well as influencing its rate of secretion during stress. Epinephrine and norepinephrine primarily decrease insulin secretion by stimulating the alpha-adrenergic receptors. Selective activation of $beta_2$-adrenergic receptors or muscarinic receptors produces the weaker effect of increasing insulin secretion.

Insulin promotes the conservation of energy by stimulating its storage in the form of glycogen (in muscle and liver cells) and triglyceride (in fat cells). This is accomplished by promoting glucose transport across cell membranes, stimulating glycogen production from glucose, inhibiting fat mobilization, stimulating protein synthesis, and inhibiting gluconeogenesis.

Diabetes mellitus

Diabetes mellitus results in almost all instances from inadequate secretion of insulin from the pancreas. It is primarily characterized by hyperglycemia and glycosuria. Other characteristics include hyperlipemia, azoturia, ketonemia, and, when the deficiency is severe, ketoacidosis.

Although there are a number of ways to classify this disease, the majority of patients can be said to have one of two forms. The first is *insulin-dependent* (previously termed juvenile-onset) *diabetes,* which usually develops in persons younger than 20 years and is associated with a complete lack of insulin secretion, rapid development, and severity of symptoms. The second is *insulin-independent* (previously termed maturity-onset) *diabetes,* which usually develops in persons older than 40 years, is associated with the ability of the pancreas to secrete some insulin, and involves a slower onset and less severe symptoms.

Patients usually experience general weakness, weight loss, polyphagia, polydipsia, and polyuria. Diabetics are more prone to periodontal disease.[16-18] This is probably because of increased levels of glucose in their gingival crevicular fluid.[19] Periodontoclasia secondary to diabetes mellitus is characterized by gingival inflammation and abscesses, bone loss, and mobile teeth that are painful on percussion.[20] Since mastication may be painful and difficult, these patients may practice poor nutrition and may need nutritional counseling and oral hygiene instructions.

Dental appointments should not interfere with meals and should involve minimal stress. In controlled diabetics, oral surgical procedures should be performed 1½ to 2 hours after the patient has eaten a normal breakfast and taken regular antidiabetic medication. Following surgery, the patient should receive an adequate caloric intake to prevent hypoglycemia. In uncontrolled diabetics, dental surgery should not be performed except for emergencies, and only after a consultation with a physician and under hospital conditions.[21,22]

Diabetics have fragile blood vessels and other vascular problems that result in delayed wound healing and a tendency to develop infections. Greater consideration should be given to antibiotic prophylaxis in these patients. Procedures such as subgingival curettage, which may injure soft tissue and bone, should be avoided unless the diabetic condition is well controlled.[21,23]

Drugs that may decrease insulin release or increase insulin requirements, such as epinephrine, glucocorticoids, or narcotic analgesics, should be used with caution in the diabetic patient. Caution should also be exercised with general anesthetics because of the possibility of acidosis.

Antidiabetic agents

Dietary control is still the cornerstone for all antidiabetic therapy. In addition, the patient may be taking insulin for replacement therapy or an oral antidiabetic agent.

Insulin

Insulin is usually administered by subcutaneous injection. The various preparations are prepared from beef or pork pancreas and differ primarily in their onset and duration of action. They can be divided into fast-, intermediate-, and long-acting preparations. They have onsets of approximately 1, 2, and 7 hours, respectively, and durations of approximately 10, 24, and 36 hours, respectively.

Fast-acting
    Insulin injection (Insulin)
    Prompt insulin zinc suspension (Semilente insulin)
Intermediate-acting
    Isophane Insulin Suspension (NPH insulin, Isophane insulin)
    Insulin zinc suspension (Lente insulin)
Long-acting
    Protamine zinc insulin suspension
    Extended insulin zinc suspension (Ultralente insulin)

The most common complication in the diabetic dental patient on insulin is a hypoglycemic reaction. This can be caused by an unintentional insulin overdosage *(insulin shock),* failure to eat, or unaccustomed exercise or stress. Symptoms that can be explained by an increased release of epinephrine from the adrenals include sweating, weakness, nausea, and tachycardia. Symptoms caused by glucose deprivation of the brain include headache, blurred vision, mental confusion, incoherent speech, and eventually coma, convulsions, and death. Treatment of hypoglycemic reactions in their early stages, when the patient is awake, includes fruit juice or soluble carbohydrates. When the patient is unconscious, treatment is with intravenous glucose or glucagon (these items should be readily available in the dental office for emergencies).[24]

It is often difficult clinically to distinguish insulin hypoglycemia from severe diabetic ketoacidosis. A few grams of sugar, however, added to diabetic acidosis will produce no harm. Insulin given to a hypoglycemic diabetic patient could result in death.

Oral antidiabetic agents

The *sulfonylureas* are the primary oral antidiabetic agents. Their effectiveness is based on their ability to stimulate the secretion of insulin from the beta cells.

They are indicated for insulin-independent diabetics who cannot be treated with diet alone and are unable or unwilling to take insulin. Side effects include blood dyscrasias, gastrointestinal disturbances, cutaneous reactions, and liver damage. Hypoglycemic reactions may occur and are most often seen in patients over 50 years of age with impaired hepatic or renal function. The same dental precautions are in order as for patients taking insulin. Drugs of interest to the dentist that may interact with the sulfonylureas to increase the risk of hypoglycemia include salicylates, sulfonamides, phenylbutazone, barbiturates, and alcohol. The following are the main antidiabetic sulfonylureas in increasing order of their duration of action:

Tolbutamide (Orinase)
Acetohexamide (Dymelor)
Tolazamide (Tolinase)
Chlorpropamide (Diabenese)

Glucagon

Glucagon is produced by the pancreatic alpha cells and promotes fuel mobilization. Its role is antagonistic to that of insulin. It increases hepatic glycogenolysis, gluconeogenesis, and lipolysis and decreases hepatic glycogenesis, protein synthesis, and lipogenesis. Its secretion is stimulated by a number of factors especially a decrease in plasma glucose concentration. Food intake therefore has opposite effects on insulin and glucagon. As a result of food intake, glucagon secretion decreases and insulin secretion increases, which serves to store fuels in liver, muscle, and adipose tissue. During starvation, glucagon secretion increases and insulin secretion decreases, which serves to break down fuels stored intracellularly to meet the energy needs of the brain and other tissues. Glucagon is also considered the hormone of injury since it stimulates the conversion of noncarbohydrates to glucose and thus provides the glucose necessary during infections or stress.[25] The only use for glucagon clinically is in the treatment of hypoglycemia.

FEMALE SEX HORMONES

The female sex hormones, *estrogen* and *progesterone,* are secreted primarily by the ovaries but also by the testes and placenta. They are largely responsible for producing the female sex characteristics, developing the reproductive system, and preparing it for conception. They also influence other tissues including the gingiva. For example, changes in sex hormone levels during the life of the female are related to the development of gingivitis at puberty *(puberty gingivitis),* during pregnancy *(pregnancy gingivitis),* and after menopause *(chronic desquamative gingivitis).*[26,27] Conscientious plaque control helps to minimize these conditions. Research has shown, however, that an increase in gingival inflammation can occur during pregnancy even when the amount of plaque decreases.[28]

Estrogen and progesterone levels vary daily. These changes are dependent on the gonadotrophic hormones FSH and LH. The interrelationship among these four hormones during the female sexual cycle is as follows: On day 1 of an average 28-day cycle, when the menstrual flow begins, the secretions of FSH and LH are beginning to increase. This release is caused by a reduction in the blood levels of estrogen and progesterone, which normally inhibit their release. In response to increased FSH, an ovarian egg matures, and the follicle in which it is contained grows in size and begins to produce and secrete estrogen. For reasons not entirely understood, on approximately day 12, the rate of secretion of FSH and LH increases markedly to cause a rapid swelling of the follicle that culminates in ovulation on day 14 of the average cycle. Following ovulation, LH causes the secretory cells of the follicle to develop into a corpus luteum that secretes large quantities of estrogen and progesterone. This causes a feedback decrease in the secretion of both FSH and LH. On approximately day 26 of the average cycle, the corpus luteum completely degenerates. The resultant decrease in estrogen and progesterone leads to menstruation and increased release of FSH and LH. The FSH initiates growth of new follicles to begin a new cycle.

Estrogens

In addition to their role in the female sexual cycle, estrogens are largely responsible for the changes that take place at puberty in girls. They promote the growth and development of the vagina, uterus, fallopian tubes, breasts, and axillary and pubic hair. They increase the deposition of fat in subcutaneous tissues and increase the retention of salt and water. They also cause increased osteoblastic activity and early fusion of the epiphyses.

The most potent endogenous estrogen is 17β-estradiol. The liver readily oxidizes it to estrone, which in turn can be hydrated to estriol. Synthetic estrogens are not as easily metabolized and can be administered orally. They are therefore used instead of the natural estrogens for therapy and contraception. Some representative examples are:

Diethylstilbestrol
Estradiol (Aquadiol)
Ethinyl Estradiol (Estinyl)
Conjugated Estrogens (Premarin)

In addition to their use as oral contraceptives, estrogens are used to treat menstrual disturbances (dysmenorrhea, dysfunctional uterine bleeding), osteoporosis, atrophic vaginitis, nondevelopment of the ovaries, hirsutism, cancer, and symptoms of menopause, particularly vasomotor instability (hot flashes, night sweats).

The most common side effect is nausea and vomiting. With continued treatment, tolerance develops and these symptoms usually disappear. Other side effects include uterine bleeding, vaginal discharge, edema, thrombophlebitis, weight gain, and hypertension. Estrogen therapy may also promote endometrial carcinoma in postmenopausal women. The incidence of vaginal and cervical carcinoma has been shown to increase in the female offspring of women given diethylstilbestrol (DES).[29] Other side effects are discussed in the section on oral contraceptives.

Antiestrogens

Antiestrogens are compounds that inhibit or modify the action of estrogens. Clomiphene citrate (Clomid) is one such drug used for the treatment of infertility in women. It prevents the feedback inhibition of gonadotropin release and induces ovulation in patients with anovular cycles. The formation of large and cystic ovaries is a frequent side effect.

Progestins

The corpus luteum is the primary source of progesterone during the normal female sexual cycle. Progesterone promotes secretory changes in the endometrium and prepares the uterus for implantation of the fertilized ovum. If implantation does not occur by the end of the menstrual cycle, progesterone secretion declines, and the onset of menstruation occurs. If implantation takes place, the developing trophoblast secretes chorionic gonadotropin, which sustains the corpus luteum, thus maintaining progesterone and estrogen levels and preventing menstruation. Other effects of progesterone include suppression of uterine contractility, proliferation of the acini of the mammary gland, and enhancement of

transplantation immunity to prevent immunologic rejection of the fetus.[30]

In addition to progesterone, which is given parenterally, there are many orally active *progestins,* or *progestational agents,* which have a longer duration of action. Some of the preparations available include:

Progesterone injection (Gesterol)
Progesterone suspension (Gesterol Aqueous)
Medroxyprogesterone acetate tablets (Provera)
Hydroxyprogesterone caproate injection (Delalutin)
Megestrol acetate (Magace)
Dydrogesterone (Duphaston)
Norethindrone (Micronor)

Uses of progestational agents include the treatment of endometriosis, dysmenorrhea, dysfunctional uterine bleeding, and premenstrual tension. The primary use is for oral contraception.

Oral contraception

Oral contraceptives contain estrogens and progestins, either alone or in combination. The combination preparation is the most common and about 99% effective. Preparations that contain a progestin alone (the "minipill") are slightly less effective, produce less regular menstrual cycles, but do not have most of the side effects of the combination preparation. The postcoital or "morning-after" pill contains DES alone. This preparation has serious side effects but is useful in emergencies such as rape or incest. Sequential preparations (estrogen is taken for 14 to 16 days and a combination is then taken for 5 or 6 days) have been taken off the market because of their low efficacy and greater incidence of endometrial tumors. The compounds most commonly found in oral contraceptives are the estrogens—ethinyl estradiol and mestranol—and the progestins—norgestrel, norethindrone, and norethynodrel.

The combination type of oral contraceptive is taken between days 5 and 25 of the menstrual cycle. It interferes with fertility by inhibiting the release of FSH and LH and therefore preventing ovluation. Early follicular FSH and midcycle FSH and LH increases are not seen. In addition, these contraceptive agents interfere with impregnation by altering the endometrium and the secretions of the cervix.

Two major side effects that have been attributed to oral contraceptives are their carcinogenicity and their tendency to produce thrombophlebitis and thromboembolism. The substantiation of these claims, however, is still controversial. The minor side effects of nausea, dizziness, headache, weight gain, and breast discomfort resemble those during early pregnancy and are mainly attributable to the estrogen in the preparation. These effects usually last only several weeks. Others include blood pressure elevation, liver damage, and gingival bleeding and inflammation.[31] Oral contraceptives are associated with a significant increase in the frequency of dry socket after extraction.[32,33] This risk can be minimized by performing extractions during days 23 through 28 of the tablet cycle. Contraindications for the use of oral contraceptives include thromboembolic disorders, significant dysfunction of the liver, known or suspected carcinoma of the breast or other estrogen-dependent neoplasm, and undiagnosed genital bleeding.

MALE SEX HORMONES

The main androgen, *testosterone,* is synthesized in the Leydig cells of the testes and to a minor degree in the ovaries and the adrenal cortex. This synthesis is controlled by the gonadotropin LH which in turn is controlled by a feedback mechanism from the testes. Testosterone has both androgenic and anabolic effects. It is responsible for the development and maintenance of secondary male sex characteristics and male sex organs. Its strong anabolic effects result in increased tissue protein and nitrogen retention in the body. Other effects include increased osteoblastic activity, epiphyseal closure, and an increased growth and secretion of the sebaceous glands, which may lead to infection and acne in some individuals. As in females, hormonal changes are believed to cause "puberty gingivitis." This condition is manifest in a gingiva that is enlarged and reddened and bleeds easily. Treatment includes subgingival debridement, restoration of faulty subgingival margins, and oral hygiene instruction. Persistent cases may be treated with corticosteroids, such as hydrocortisone acetate 2.5% ointment, or triamcinolone acetonide 0.1% (Kenalog in Orabase).

The primary use of androgenic steroids is in replacement therapy for hypogonadism, or androgen-deficient males. They are also used for their anabolic effects in both men and women, but this use, although of much wider potential application, is controversial. Other uses include the treatment of breast cancer, anemia, osteoporosis, menstrual disorders, suppression of lactation, and hypopituitarism. A possible future use of androgens is in combination with a progestin as a male oral contraceptive. This combination would decrease gonadotropin secretion and spermatogenesis while still maintaining secondary male traits.[34]

Preparations available can be divided into steroids that are used primarily for their androgenic effects and those used primarily for their anabolic effects. The androgenic steroids include the testosterone esters, methyltestosterone (Metandren), and fluoxymesterone (Halotestin). The anabolic steroids include methandrostenolone (Dianabol) and nandrolone decanoate (Deca-Durabolin).

The main side effect of androgens is virilism in the female. This includes hirsutism, acne, deepening of the voice, and menstrual irregularities. Other effects include salt and water retention and cholestatic jaundice. Buccal and sublingual preparations can cause stomatitis.

REFERENCES

1. Raacke, I.D.: Protein hormones and the eucaryotic genome: a general theory of hormone action, Perspect. Biol. Med. **21:** 139, 1977.
2. Catt, K.J., and Dufau, M.L.: Peptide hormone receptors, Annu. Rev. Physiol. **39:**529, 1977.
3. O'Malley, B.W., and Schrader, W.T.: The receptors of steroid hormones, Sci. Am. **234:**32, 1976.
4. Sterling, K.: Thyroid hormone action at the cell level, N. Engl. J. Med. **300:**117-123, 173-177, 1979.
5. Phillips, L.S., and Vassilopoulou-Sellin, R.: Somatomedins, N. Engl. J. Med. **302:**371-379, 1980.
6. Myllarniemi, S., Lenko, H.L., and Perheentupa, J.: Dental maturity in hypopituitarism, and dental response to substitution treatment, Scand. J. Dent. Res. **86:**307-12, 1978.
7. Wolff, J.: Transport of iodide and other anions in the thyroid gland, Physiol. Rev. **44:**45-90, 1964.
8. VanderLaan, W.P., and Storrie, V.M.: A survey of the factors controlling thyroid function, with special reference to newer views on antithyroid substance, Pharmacol. Rev. **7:** 301-334, 1955.
9. Ingbar, S.H.: Autoregulation of the thyroid response to iodide excess and depletion, Mayo Clin. Proc. **47:**814-823, 1972.
10. Garn, S.M., Osborne, R.H., and McCabe, K.D.: The effect of prenatal factors on crown dimensions, Am. J. Phys. Anthropol. **51:**665-678, 1979.
11. Buccino, R.A., et al.: Influence of thyroid state on the intrinsic contractile properties and energy stores of the myocardium, J. Clin. Invest. **46:**1669-1682, 1967.
12. Garfunkel, A.A., Pisanty, S., and Michaeli, Y.: Familial hypoparathyroidism, candidiasis and mental retardation: a histopathologic study of the dental structure, J. Oral Med. **34:** 13-17, 1979.
13. Jensen, S.B., Illum, F., and Dupont, E.: Nature and frequency of dental changes in idiopathic hypoparathyroidism and pseudohypoparathyroidism, Scand. J. Dent. Res. **89:**26-37, 1981.
14. Ostlund, R.E., Jr.: Contractile proteins and pancreatic beta-cell secretion, Diabetes **26:**245-252, 1977.

15. Hedeskov, C.J.: Mechanism of glucose-induced insulin secretion, Physiol. Rev. **60**:442-509, 1980.
16. Sznojder, N., et al.: Periodontal findings in diabetic and nondiabetic patients, J. Periodontol. **49**:445-448, 1978.
17. Cohen, D.W., et al.: Studies on periodontal patterns in diabetes mellitus, J. Periodont. Res. **4**(suppl.):35, 1969.
18. Belting, C.M., Hinicher, J.J., and Dummett, C.O.: Influence of diabetes mellitus on the severity of periodontal disease, J. Periodontal. **35**:476, 1964.
19. Kjellman, O.: The presence of glucose on gingival exudate and resting saliva of subjects with insulin-treated diabetes mellitus, Swed. Dent. J. **63**:11, 1970.
20. Gislen, G., Nilsson, K.O., and Matsson, L.: Gingival inflammation in diabetic children related to degree of metabolic control, Acta Odontol. Scand. **38**:241-246, 1980.
21. Martin, L.R., and Portera, J.J.: Dental awareness and management of the diabetic patient, J. Miss. Dent. Assoc. **36**:20-22, 24-25, 1979.
22. Lane, D.S.: Dental considerations of diabetes mellitus, Dent. Hyg. **53**:306-307, 1979.
23. Gottsegen, R.: Dental and oral considerations in diabetes mellitus, N.Y. State J. Med. **62**:289, 1962.
24. Seltzer, H.S.: Drug-induced hypoglycemia: a review based on 473 cases, Diabetes **21**:955-966, 1972.
25. Rayfield, E.J., et al.: Impaired carbohydrate metabolism during a mild viral illness, N. Engl. J. Med. **289**:618-620, 1973.
26. Lindhe, J., and Hugoson, A.: The influence of estrogen and progesterone on gingival exudation of regenerating dentogingival tissues, Paradontology **23**:16, 1969.
27. Lindhe, J., Attstroem, R., and Bjoern, A.: The influence of progestogen on gingival exudation during menstrual cycles: longitudinal study, J. Periodont. Res. **4**:97, 1969.
28. O'Neil, T.C.: Plasma female sex hormone levels and gingivitis in pregnancy, J. Periodontol. **50**:279-282, 1979.
29. Greenwald, P., et al.: Vaginal cancer after maternal treatment with synthetic estrogens, N. Engl. J. Med. **285**:390-392, 1971.
30. Siiteri, P.K., et al.: Progesterone and maintenance of pregnancy: is progesterone nature's immunosuppressant? Ann. N.Y. Acad. Sci. **286**:384-397, 1977.
31. Kalkwarf, K.L.: Effect of oral contraceptive therapy on gingival inflammation in humans, J. Periodontal. **49**:560-563, 1978.
32. Catellani, J.E.: Review of factors contributing to dry socket through enhanced fibrinolysis, J. Oral Surg. **37**:42-46, 1979.
33. Catellani, J.E., et al.: Effect of oral contraceptive cycle on dry socket (localized alveolar osteitis), J. Am. Dent. Assoc. **101**:777-780, 1980.
34. Ewing, L.L., and Robaire, B.: Endogenous antispermatogenic agents: prospects for male contraception, Ann. Rev. Pharmacol. Toxicol. **18**:167-187, 1978.

CHAPTER 18

JAMES L. MATHENY

Adrenocorticosteroids

A series of chemically similar compounds known as adrenocorticosteroids is synthesized in and released by the adrenal cortex. These compounds are categorized into two groups with respect to their predominant pharmacologic effects: glucocorticoids and mineralocorticoids. The glucocorticoids exert their major effect on carbohydrate metabolism, whereas the mineralocorticoids have more potent action on the renal tubules to increase sodium retention (see discussion of pharmacologic effects). It should be emphasized that with few exceptions the naturally occurring and synthetic corticosteroids exert some of both types of activity. Table 18-1 shows the relative glucocorticoid and mineralocorticoid potencies of some representative natural and synthetic steroids.

CHEMISTRY AND PREPARATIONS

The naturally occurring and synthetic corticosteroids have the same basic four-ring steroid structure. However, as shown in Fig. 18-1, minor substitutions and alterations in the basic structure can markedly alter the pharmacologic activity of these compounds. For example, the structures for cortisone (a glucocorticoid) and aldosterone (a mineralocorticoid) are shown. Also are shown the modifications of selected derivatives. For the most part, the alteration consists of a double bond between C_1 and C_2; and substitutions occur usually on C_6, C_9, C_{11}, C_{16}, C_{17}, or C_{21}. Many different preparations are available and are listed in Table 18-2 with dosages and routes of administration. The choice of a specific drug should be predicted on the symptom to be treated and the individual response. Preparations consisting of corticosteroids in combination with other drugs such as analgesics, antibacterial agents, or antifungal agents are available but are not recommended.[1] It is believed that because of the severity of the adverse effects of corticosteroids,

dosage should be individualized and closely monitored.

ABSORPTION, RATE, AND DISTRIBUTION

Natural and synthetic corticosteroids are absorbed rapidly and completely from the gastrointestinal tract following oral administration. Maximal plasma concentrations are reached within 2 hours, and hepatic degradation reduces plasma levels by approximately 15% within 8 hours. Drugs like the barbiturates, which promote activity of the liver microsomal drug metabolism enzymes, accelerate the destruction of corticosteroids, an effect that may indicate increased steroid dosage when concurrent therapy is necessary.

Rapid onset or prolonged action can be achieved by intravenous or intramuscular administration (respectively) of corticosteroids.

Local application of corticosteroids to the skin, synovial spaces, or conjunctival sac results in absorption for therapeutic effectiveness. However, if the area is large enough, systemic actions may occur.

The major portion of a corticosteroid dosage is transported in bound form (to protein) in plasma. The liver is the major site of metabolism, and reduction and oxidation to inactive metabolites are the predominant mechanisms.

Control of secretion

The adrenocorticosteroids are synthesized from cholesterol in the adrenal cortex in response to the actions of ACTH, or corticotropin, on the adrenal cortical cell membrane cyclic AMP system.[2,3] The release of ACTH from the adenohypophysis is controlled through two mechanisms: (1) nervous control and (2) corticosteroid negative feedback. Nervous control is exerted by corticotropin-regulating hormone (CRH), which is released from neuronal end-

Table 18-1. Glucocorticoid and mineralocorticoid potencies of selected corticosteroids

Generic name	Relative anti-inflammatory potency (gluco-corticoid effect)	Relative sodium retention (mineralo-corticoid effect)
Cortisone	0.8	0.8
Cortisol	1.0	1.0
Prednisone	2.5	0.8
Prednisolone	3.0	0.8
Methylprednisolone	4.0	0.0
Meprednisone	5.0	0.0
Triamcinolone	5.0	0.0
Dexamethasone	20.0	0.0
Betamethasone	30.0	0.0
Paramethasone	6.0	0.0
Desoxycorticosterone	0.0	10-25
Fludrocortisone	12.0	100.0
Aldosterone	0.2	250.0

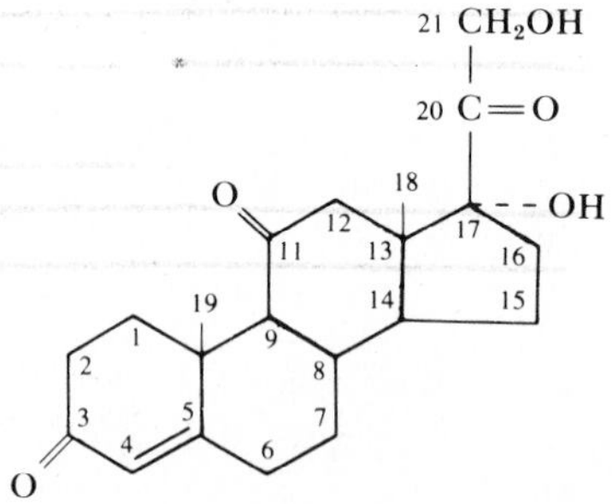

Cortisone 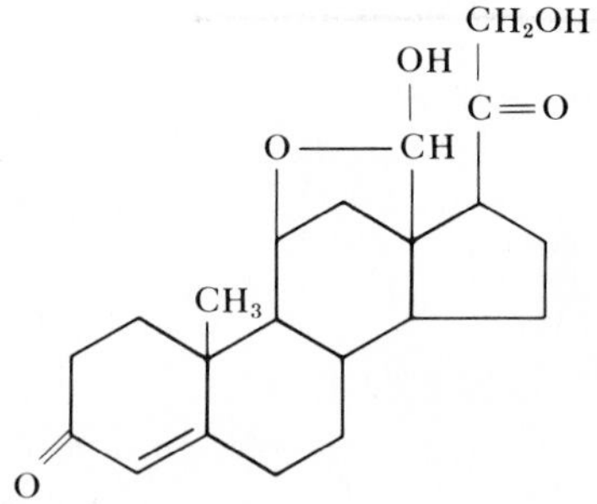   Aldosterone

Corticosteroid	Position and substitution				
	1-2	6	9	11	16
Hydrocortisone (cortisol)				OH	
Prednisone	Dbl bond				
Prednisolone	Dbl bond			OH	
Methylprednisolone	Dbl bond	CH_3		OH	
Meprednisone	Dbl bond				CH_3
Triamcinolone	Dbl bond		$F\alpha$	OH	$OH\alpha$
Dexamethasone	Dbl bond		$F\alpha$	OH	$CH_3\alpha$
Betamethasone	Dbl bond		$F\alpha$	OH	$CH_3\beta$
Paramethasone	Dbl bond	$F\alpha$		OH	$CH_3\alpha$
Fluprednisolone	Dbl bond	$F\alpha$		OH	

Fig. 18-1. Structural relationship of selected corticosteroids to cortisone.

Table 18-2. Corticosteroid preparations dosages and routes of administration

Generic name	Trade name	Dose (mg)	Route of administration
Cortisone	Cortone	50-100	Oral
		75-300	IM
Cortisol	Cortef, Acticort, Hydrocortone,	50-100	Oral
	Delacort (nonprescription)	100-500	IV
		100-250	IM
		5-75	Intraarticular, soft tissue, topical
Prednisone	Meticorten, Delta-Dome, Ora-	5-60	Oral
	sone, Deltasone, Sterapred		
Prednisolone	Meticortelone, Delta-Cortef, Meti-	5-60	Oral
	Derm, Sterane, Hydeltrasol	4-60	IM
		20-100	IV
		4-60	Intraarticular, soft tissue, topical
Methylprednisolone	Medrol, Depo-Medrol	10-20	Oral
		40-120	IM
		100-250	IV
		4-80	Intraarticular, soft tissue, topical
Meprednisone	Betapar	10-20	Oral
Triamcinolone	Aristocort, Kenacort, Kenalog,	4-48	Oral
	Aristospan	20-80	IM
		5-80	Intraarticular, soft tissue, topical
Dexamethasone	Decadron, Hexadrol	0.75-9	Oral
		8-16	IM
		0.2-6	Intraarticular, soft tissue
		0.4-0.6	Inhalation, topical
Betamethasone	Celestone	0.6-7.2	Oral
		6-12	IM
		0.75-6	Soft tissue, intraarticular, topical
Paramethasone	Haldrone, Stemex	2-4	Oral
Desoxycorticosterone	Doca, Percorten	1-3	IM
		125	Implantation
Fludrocortisone	Florinef	0.1	Oral
Fluprednisolone	Alphadrol	1.5-30	Oral
Halcinonide	Halog		Topical
Aldosterone			
Desonide	Tridesilon		Topical
Flumethasone	Locorten		Topical
Fluocinolone	Fluonid, Synalar, Synemol		Topical
Fluocinonide	Lidex, Topsyn		Topical
Fluorometholone	Oxylone		Topical
Flurandrenolide	Cordran		Topical

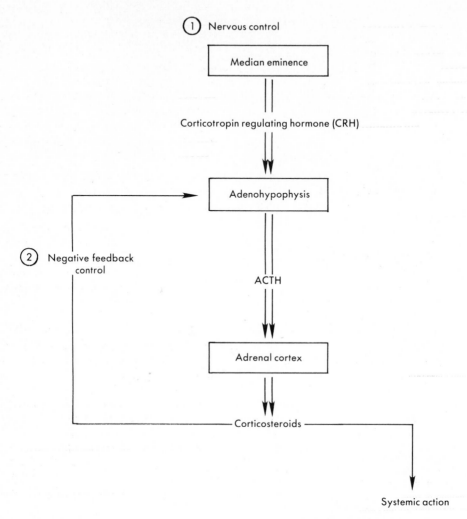

Fig. 18-2. Schematic diagram of the control of adrenocorticosteroid synthesis and release.

ings in the median eminence and is transported through the hypophyseal-portal vessels to the adenohypophysis. Negative feedback control is exerted by the corticosteroids, especially cortisol, through depression of the release and synthesis of ACTH by the adenohypophysis (Fig. 18-2).

Though ACTH does play a role in the control of the synthesis of the mineralocorticoid aldosterone; its secretion is chiefly controlled by the renin-angiotensin system of the kidney.

The adrenal glands secrete 15 to 30 mg of corticosteroids per day under basal conditions. The release of the corticosteroids occurs cyclically, and the highest blood levels appear from 4 AM to 8 AM in individuals maintaining a normal day and night activity schedule. The prevalent natural corticosteroids are cortisol, corticosterone, and aldosterone. Glucocorticoid output may increase as much as tenfold during periods of maximal stress.

MECHANISM OF ACTION

Like other steroid hormones, corticosteroids are thought to exert their effects by altering the rate of protein synthesis by reacting with specific receptor proteins in the cytoplasm of sensitive cells.[4] The steroid-receptor complex thus formed then enters the cell nucleus, binds to chromatin, and thus alters the genetic apparatus. Although this general mechanism has been demonstrated in several tissues, the exact steps that link these initial actions of the steroids to their ultimate metabolic effects have not been completely elucidated.[5]

PHARMACOLOGIC EFFECTS

For convenience, the pharmacologic effects of the adrenocorticosteroids will be discussed as being either glucocorticoid or mineralocorticoid. Again, however, it should be emphasized that most natural and synthetic drugs in this group exert both types of activity to some extent.

Glucocorticoids
Broad effects
- Affect carbohydrate metabolism and are antiinflammatory and antiallergenic
- Affect synthesis and activity of enzymes
- Affect membrane function and permeability
- Affect ribonucleic acid synthesis
Catabolic effects
- Increase gluconeogenesis
- Decrease utilization of glucose
- Inhibit protein synthesis
- Increase protein catabolism
  Decrease growth through negative nitrogen balance
  Impair wound healing
  Decrease resistance to infection
Mineralocorticoids
  Increase sodium retention
  Increase potassium depletion
- Lead to edema and hypertension if excessive
- Lead to dehydration and hypotension if insufficient

The glucocorticoids exhibit several metabolic effects. They enhance gluconeogenesis through breakdown of endogenous proteins to amino acids, which are then converted to glucose for storage in the liver or utilization; decrease the utilization of glucose (an antiinsulin effect) leading to hyperglycemia and increased glycogen storage; and increase lipolysis in

adipose tissue. Other effects of glucocorticoids include an antiinflammatory action, immunosuppression, an antiallergic action (see discussion of general therapeutic uses), effects on calcium metabolism and bone growth, effects on skeletal muscle contractility, CNS action, and suppression of steroid production by the adrenal cortex through the negative feedback mechanism previously mentioned (see discussion of adverse effects). The mineralocorticoids exert their major effect on electrolyte balance by acting on the distal tubules of the kidney to enhance the reabsorption of sodium and increase potassium and hydrogen excretion.

ABNORMALITIES OF ADRENOCORTICAL SECRETION
Hypoadrenalism: Addison's disease

Addison's disease results from failure of the adrenal cortices to produce adrenocortical hormones. Lack of aldosterone secretion decreases sodium reabsorption and allows excessive amounts of sodium chloride and water to be lost in the urine. Also, since potassium and hydrogen are not lost in exchange for sodium, hyperkalemia and acidosis occur. These changes lead to decreased extracellular fluid and plasma volume, increased red blood cell concentration, and decreased cardiac output, and the patient finally dies from shock.

The lack of cortisol (glucocorticoid) secretion leads to hypoglycemia between meals because of decreased gluconeogenesis and skeletal muscle weakness. Also, increased melanin pigmentation of mucous membranes is frequently seen, presumably because of the lack of cortisol negative feedback on the anterior pituitary, which secretes melanocyte-stimulating hormone. The causes and manifestations of adrenal insufficiency are:

Causes
  Atrophy of adrenal glands
  Destruction of adrenal glands
  Lack of ACTH
  Other (idiopathic)
Manifestations
  Weakness
  Hyperpigmentation
  Nausea
  Hypotension
  Weight loss
  Anorexia
  Hypoglycemia
  Hyperkalemia

Hyperadrenalism: Cushing's disease

Cushing's syndrome, or hyperadrenalism, can result from excess secretion of ACTH by the anterior pituitary or from hyperplasia of the adrenal cortex. Most of the abnormalities seen in this disease are attributable to the excess in cortisol secretion. A special characteristic of the disease is "buffalo" torso, which results from mobilization of fat from the lower part of the body with concomitant extra deposition of fat in the thoracic region. Other symptoms include edematous appearance of the face, "moon face," hyperglycemia, loss of and weakness of skeletal muscle, increased susceptibility to infection, osteoporosis, and purplish striae of the abdomen. In addition, the excess secretion of steroids with androgenic potency causes acne and hirsuitism. The causes of adrenal hyperfunction are:

Causes
- Hypersecretion of ACTH by pituitary
- Steroid therapy

Manifestations
- Round, puffy face
- Purple striae on abdomen
- Redistribution of fat (central obesity)
- Hypertension and edema
- Muscle atrophy
- Decreased resistance to infection
- Behavioral and personality changes
- Decreased wound healing
- Decreased growth
- Hirsutism
- Menstrual abnormalities
- Osteoporosis
- Arrhythmias caused by hypokalemia
- Thinning collagen

GENERAL THERAPEUTIC USES

Except for use as replacement therapy in cases of adrenocortical insufficiency, the corticosteroids should be reserved for use in treatment of life-threatening conditions or to treat severe disease symptoms that fail to respond to less drastic therapeutic measures because of the danger of inducing hypercorticism (Cushing's syndrome).

Most frequently, corticosteroids are used for their antiinflammatory and antiallergic actions (glucocorticoid effects). Several general statements can be made concerning corticosteroid therapy: (1) a single dose of corticosteroid, even a large dose, is unlikely to cause any adverse effect, (2) except where specific contraindications exist, a few days of corticosteroid therapy usually does not cause adverse effects unless extremely large doses are used, (3) prolonged therapy with doses resulting in higher than normal blood levels of corticosteroids increases the incidence and severity of adverse effects, (4) corticosteroid dosage should be individualized and evaluated frequently, (5) except in treatment of adrenal insufficiency, it should be recognized that corticosteroid therapy is only symptomatic treatment, and (6) abrupt withdrawal of corticosteroids following prolonged high-dosage therapy may result in severe adrenal insufficiency.

As mentioned previously, the glucocorticoids have been shown to be useful in the symptomatic treatment of disorders involving immune, inflammatory, or allergic responses. Although glucocorticoid therapy has been shown to be beneficial in treating immune responses such as graft rejection, there is no convincing evidence that they alter the titers of the circulating antibodies IgG or IgE.[8] Rather, they are now believed to act by suppression of the inflammatory response.[7,8,9]

The antiinflammatory action of glucocorticoids and ACTH involves their capacity to suppress or prevent the development of the gross signs of inflammation including local heat, redness, tenderness, and swelling. At the cellular and subcellular level, they inhibit edema formation, capillary dilatation and proliferation, fibrin deposition, migration of leukocytes to the inflamed area, phagocytic activity, fibroblast proliferation, collagen deposition, and scar formation. This antiinflammatory action occurs regardless of whether the cause of the inflammation is biologic, physical, or chemical.

The antiallergic action of corticosteroids is probably related to their antiinflammatory action. These drugs do not interfere with the antigen-antibody transactions that result in the release of histamine and other mediators of allergy, but they are believed to alter the inflammatory response to the agents released. Allergic reactions, acute hypersensitivity reactions, and anaphylactic reactions have been successfully treated with corticosteroids. Although, as stated above, these drugs do not alter the interaction of antigens with antibodies, there is some evidence to indicate that prolonged high-dosage therapy inhibits synthesis of new antibody—an action of benefit in autoimmune disease and certain hypersensitive states.[10] A listing of some disease states for which corticosteroid therapy has been shown to be useful follows.

Substitution therapy
  Acute and chronic adrenal insufficiency
  Congenital adrenal hyperplasia
  Adrenal insufficiency secondary to anterior pituitary insufficiency
Arthritis
  Rheumatoid arthritis
  Osteoarthritis
Rheumatic carditis
Renal diseases
  Nephrotic syndrome caused by systemic lupus erythematosus
  Other primary renal disease except renal amyloidosis
Collagen diseases
  Mixed connective disease syndrome
  Polymyositis
  Polyarteritis nodosa
  Granulomatous polyarteritis
  Systemic lupus erythematosus
Allergic diseases (Antiinflammatory effect)

DENTAL USES

As mentioned previously, the corticosteroids are effective in treating severe allergic reactions and thus should be included in the dental emergency kit.

In addition to the many other indications for corticosteroid therapy in medicine, there are several specific uses for these drugs in dentistry.[11,12]

In treatment of the oral ulcerative conditions, such as recurrent ulcerative stomatitis, the adrenocorticosteroids can be administered systemically, topically, or by a combination of these routes.[11,12] For topical use, one should choose a preparation that will remain on the ulcer as long as possible, thereby maximizing the therapeutic benefit. It should be emphasized that careful diagnosis should precede use of corticosteroids, since their use in treatment of herpetic ulcers is contraindicated because the infection may spread.

The use of corticosteroids in the treatment of hypersensitive cervical dentin, in pulp capping, or in pulpotomy procedures[13-15] is controversial. Although there is some evidence for a therapeutic antiinflammatory effect, there is evidence that, in cases of bacterial infection of the pulp, corticosteroids may increase the possibility of subsequent systemic infection.[16] Thus their use in these conditions is not recommended.

In addition to the previously mentioned uses for corticosteroids in dentistry, they have also been used to relieve the acute symptoms of rheumatoid arthritis or osteoarthritis of the temporomandibular joint[16] and to reduce edema, trismus, and pain following oral surgical procedures.[16,17] Intraarticular injection of corticosteroids as therapy for temporomandibular joint disorders requires special skill and is generally reserved for those cases that do not respond to more conservative forms of treatment. The use of corticosteroids to reduce postoperative symptoms caused by dental surgical procedures is controversial. Although some benefits have been reported, and side effects from short term dosage are unlikely, this use of corticosteroids is not generally recommended.

Osteoporosis of alveolar bone, degeneration of the fibers of the periodontal ligament, and increased inflammation of periodontal tissues following steroid therapy have been demonstrated in animals[18]; however, no increase in incidence or severity of periodontal disease has been shown in humans.[19]

ADVERSE EFFECTS

All corticosteroids have similar side effects, though some variation in degree of effect has been reported. For example, recent evidence[20] has indicated that some synthetic corticosteroids suppress the hypothalamic-pituitary-adrenal axis for longer periods of time than others. Betamethasone and dexamethasone may suppress the axis for more than 48 hours, whereas methylprednisolone and prednisolone suppress the axis for 24 to 36 hours. Thus it may be more desirable to control disease with the shorter-acting agents. Another method that has been used to avoid this side effect is "alternate day therapy," the administration of corticosteroids every other day. Another side effect that has been shown to vary in intensity with the specific compound used is myopathy. Triamcinolone and other fluorinated corticosteroids are reportedly more likely to produce this adverse effect.[20]

More important is the fact that all drugs in this group cause numerous adverse effects that are closely related to both dosage and duration of therapy. It should be noted, however, that most adverse effects of corticosteroid therapy disappear with reduction in dose or withdrawal of the drug.

Corticosteroids decrease the resistance to infections because they cause a general depression of the inflammatory response. Therefore minor or superficial infections may become systemic, quiescent infections may become active, and normally nonpathogenic organisms such as fungi may cause systemic disease. For this reason, corticosteroids should never be used for treatment of infections caused by herpes virus. Additionally, local and systemic symptoms of infections may be masked by corticosteroid therapy.

Long-term therapy with corticosteroids causes changes in physical appearance. These include redistribution of body fat with deposits in the upper back, cheeks, breasts, abdomen, buttocks, and thighs, that is, to the trunk of the body. Other changes include increased acne, hirsutism, purplish striae, and easy bruising.

CNS effects of corticosteroids range from mild irritability, euphoria, nervousness, and insomnia to severe depression or psychosis. In some patients these actions may be of significance and prevent such therapy.

Hyperglycemia may be aggravated or initiated by corticosteroid therapy. This adverse effect is usually not severe enough to prevent therapy but may require insulin therapy until corticosteroid doses can be reduced or terminated.

Because of their mineralocorticoid action, all corticosteroids have the potential to cause electrolyte imbalance and hypertension. Sodium retention and consequent edema are the underlying causes of hypertension. Another potentially troublesome electrolyte disturbance, hypokalemia, is also frequently seen with long-term corticosteroid therapy.

If corticosteroid therapy is continued for several months, most patients will exhibit signs of osteopenia. This is thought to be the result of reduced calcium absorption from the gastrointestinal tract with consequent hyperparathyroidism and reduced synthesis of collagen matrix by osteoblasts. Vitamin D or calcium therapy may be useful in cases of this type. Muscle weakness and atrophy occur in the majority of patients who receive suppressive doses of corticosteroids for several months. The hip girdle is usually altered first, and weakness is first noticed when climbing stairs and rising from chairs. An aggressive exercise program may be helpful in this situation if the dosage cannot be reduced.

Other side effects of corticosteroids include increased intraocular pressure, amenorrhea, and possibly aggravation of peptic ulcer.

Adrenal crisis

Acute adrenal insufficiency may occur in patients under treatment for Addison's disease who fail to increase their corticosteroid dose during stress or in patients with suppression of the hypothalamic-pituitary axis from ongoing corticosteroid therapy who abruptly discontinue their medications. An adrenal crisis can be precipitated by various stressful situations such as infection, surgery, trauma, or prolonged fasting. The symptoms of adrenal crisis include nausea with severe, often intractable vomiting and abdominal pain, fever, hypotension, lethargy or somnolence, hyperkalemia, hyponatremia, and acidosis.

Patients currently taking corticosteroids, and those who have taken significant courses of corticosteroids in the past year, should receive supplemental therapy during times of stress such as dental therapy. The exception to this general recommendation is the patient currently receiving a high dosage of corticosteroids. One should consult the patient's physician before initiating dental therapy. Generally, supplemental corticosteroid is begun the morning of treatment with gradual reduction following the procedure, depending on the situation. A more detailed discussion of this use of corticosteroids can be found elsewhere.[22]

REFERENCES

1. American Medical Association Council on Drugs: AMA drug evaluations, ed. 4, Acton, Mass., 1980, Publishing Sciences Group, Inc.
2. Haynes, R.C., Jr.: The activation of adrenal phosphorylase by the adrenocorticotropic hormone, J. Biol. Chem. **233:**1220-1222, 1958.
3. Haynes, R.C., Jr., Koritz, S.B., and Peron, F.G.: Influence of adenosine 3',5' monophosphate on corticoid production by rat adrenal glands, J. Biol. Chem. **234:**1421-1423, 1959.
4. Ballard, P.L., et al.: General presence of glucocorticoid receptors in mammalian tissues, Endocrinology **94:**998-1002, 1974.
5. Thompson, E.B., and Lippman, M.E.: Mechanism of action of glucocorticoids, Metabolism **23:**159-202, 1974.
6. Grieco, M.H., and Cushman, P., Jr.: Adrenal glucocorticoids after twenty years: a review of their clinically relevant consequences, J. Chronic Dis. **22:**637-711, 1970.
7. Cohen, J.J.: The effects of hydrocortisone on the immune response, Ann. Allergy **29:**358-361, 1971.
8. Weston, W.L., et al.: Differential suppressive effect of hydrocortisone on lymphocytes and mononuclear macrophages in delayed hypersensitivity of guinea pigs, J. Invest. Dermatol. **59:**345-358, 1972.
9. Balow, J.E., and Rosenthal, A.S.: Glucocorticoid suppression of macrophage migration inhibitory factor, J. Exp. Med. **137:**1031-1039, 1973.
10. Thorn, G.W.: Clinical considerations in systemic steroid therapy. In Thorn, G.W., editor: Steroid therapy, New York, 1974, Medcom Press.
11. American Dental Association Council on Dental Therapeutics: Accepted dental therapeutics, ed. 37, Chicago, 1977, American Dental Association, p. 227-232.
12. Eggleston, D.J., and Nally, F.: Hazards of systemic corticosteroid therapy, Oral Surg. **31:**590-594, 1971.
13. Bowers, G.M., and Elliott, J.R.: Topical use of prednisolone in periodontics, J. Periodontol. **35:**486-488, 1964.
14. Lawson, B.F., and Juff, T.W.: Desensitization of teeth with a

topically applied glucocorticoid drug: a preliminary study, J. Oral Ther. **2:**295-299, 1966.

15. Klotz, M.D., Gerstein, H., and Bahn, A.N.: Bacteremia after topical use of prednisolone in infected pulps, J. Am. Dent. Assoc. **71:**871-875, 1965.

16. Wenneberg, B., and Kopp, S.: Short term effect of intra-articular injections of a corticosteroid on temporomandibular joint pain and dysfunction, Swed. Dent. J. **2:**189-196, 1978.

17. Linenberg, W.B.: The clinical evaluation of dexamethasone in oral surgery, Oral Surg. **20:**6-28, 1965.

18. Messer, E.J., and Keller, J.J.: The use of intraoral dexamethasone after extractions of mandibular third molars, Oral Surg. **40:**594-598, 1975.

19. Glickman, I., Stone, I.C., and Chawla, T.N.: The effects of the systemic administration of cortisone upon the periodontium of white mice, J. Periodontol. **24:**161-166, 1953.

20. Krohn, S.: Effect of the administration of steroid hormones on the gingival tissues, J. Periodontol. **29:**300-306, 1958.

21. Hahn, B.H.: Arthritis and related disorders. In Costrini, N.V., and Thomson, W.M., editors: Manual of medical therapeutics, ed. 22, Boston, 1977, Little, Brown & Co.

22. Little, J.W., and Falace, D.A.: Dental management of the medically compromised patient, St. Louis, 1980, The C.V. Mosby Co.

CHAPTER 19

Antineoplastic drugs

WILLIAM K. BOTTOMLEY

Antineoplastic agents are medications that currently are used almost exclusively by physicians. However, even though dentists do not prescribe these drugs, they are frequently asked to evaluate and treat the oral sequelae that may be induced by their use. Therefore it is essential that the dentist be familiar with these agents, their mechanisms of action, and the management of their oral toxic manifestations.

USE OF ANTINEOPLASTIC AGENTS

Antineoplastic agents, sometimes referred to as *chemotherapeutics,* are used clinically to destroy and to suppress the growth and spread of malignant cells. In the past these agents were used when a neoplasm had not been controlled by either surgery or radiation or a combination of both approaches. Today, however, as a result of collective experiences and concerted clinical investigation, antineoplastic agents are employed at all levels of cancer treatment. In addition, they are considered to be the primary treatment for a number of malignancies, such as acute and chronic leukemia, choriocarcinoma, multiple myeloma, and Burkitt's lymphoma. When surgery and radiation are not curative, antineoplastic agents may provide a therapeutic means for cure, a longer remission or disease-free interval, decreased morbidity, and a resultant improved quality of life. The value of antineoplastics in reducing the size of neoplastic tumors before surgery or radiation therapy, or in ensuring a cure subsequent to these procedures, is gaining oncologic appreciation. Consequently, antineoplastics are being employed with increasing frequency.

A philosophy of therapy with antineoplastic agents that is receiving greater attention is to treat the disease very aggressively in the initial stages. Although this approach promises to be more effective in controlling and curing the disease process, the concomitant side effects, including adverse oral manifestations, can be anticipated to be more prominent.

MECHANISMS OF ACTION

The efficacy of antineoplastic agents is based primarily on their ability to interfere with the metabolism or the reproductive cycle of the tumor cells, thereby destroying them. The reproductive cycle of a cell is considered to consist of four stages (Fig. 19-1):

1. G_1 ("gap" 1), which is the postmitotic or pre–DNA synthesis phase
2. S, which is the period of DNA synthesis
3. G_2 ("gap" 2), which is the premitotic or post–DNA synthesis phase
4. M, which is the period of mitosis

Cells in a resting stage, or not in a process of cell division, are described as being in the G_0 stage. Cells enter the cycle from the G_0 stage. In some tumors a large proportion of the cells may be at the G_0 level.

Most antineoplastic agents are labeled either "cycle dependent," indicating that they are effective only at specific stages in the mitotic cycle, or "cycle independent," indicating that they are effective at all levels of the cycle. For example, the alkylating agents interfere with the malignant cells during all phases of the reproductive cycle as well as the resting stage (G_0) and are therefore classified as cycle independent.

Agents of widely different mechanisms of action are often employed together to inhibit the reproduction of neoplastic cells in all phases and to gain therapeutic advantage for the host. Mixtures of these agents may act synergistically, leading to enhanced

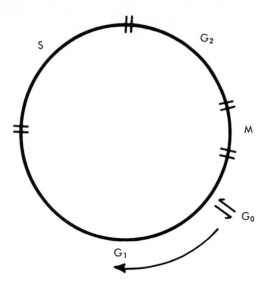

Fig. 19-1. Diagrammatic representation of the cell cycle.

Table 19-1. Major alkylating agents and their general uses as antineoplastics

Drug	Use
Nitrogen mustards	
Mechlorethamine (Mustargen)	Hodgkin's disease and other lymphomas
Cyclophosphamide (Cytoxan)	Lymphomas
Chlorambucil (Leukeran)	Chronic lymphocytic leukemia; primary macroglobulinemia
Melphalan (Alkeran)	Hodgkin's disease and other lymphomas
Nitrosoureas	
Carmustine (BiCNU)	
Lomustine (CeeNU)	
Semustine (Methyl-CeeNu)	Hodgkins' disease, other lymphomas, and myeloma
Busulfan (Myleran)	Chronic granulocytic leukemia

Table 19-2. Antimetabolites and their general uses as antineoplastics

Drug	Use
Folic acid analog	
Methotrexate (Amethopterin)	Acute lymphoblastic leukemia in children
Pyrimidine analogs	
Flourouracil (5-FU)	
Floxuridine (FUDR)	Carcinoma of the breast, gastrointestinal tract, ovary, cervix, and prostate
Cytosine arabinoside (Cytosar-U)	Induction of remission in acute leukemia in children and adults
Purine analogs	
Mercaptopurine (Purinethol)	Leukemia in children and adults
Thioguanine (TG)	Acute leukemia and induction of remissions in acute granulocytic leukemia

cytotoxicity with fewer side effects. This is the rationale for combination drug therapy.

CLASSIFICATION

Antineoplastic agents comprise several major groups of drugs.

Alkylating agents

The group of alkylating agents includes, among others, the nitrogen mustards such as mechlorethamine and cyclophosphamide, the nitrosoureas, and busulfan. Akyl radicals of these drugs react with DNA in all phases of the cell cycle, thereby preventing cell reproduction. They are most effective in chronic leukemias, lymphomas, myelomas, and carcinomas of the breast and ovary. Table 19-1 lists these alkylating agents and their general uses.

Antimetabolites

Agents representative of the antimetabolite group are mercaptopurine (Purinethol), methotrexate (Amethopterin), fluorouracil (5-FU), and cytosine arabinoside (Cytosar). They attack the cells in the S period of the reproduction cycle by interfering with the biosynthesis of the purine or pyrimidine bases. The antimetabolites have been used to treat the entire spectrum of cancers. Table 19-2 lists these antimetabolites and their general uses.

Other antineoplastics

Vinblastine (Velban) and vincristine (Oncovin) are naturally occurring plant alkaloids and comprise those agents that act by arresting cells in metaphase. Since they have little bone marrow toxicity, they are frequently used in combination regimens for the treatment of a wide variety of malignancies. Several of the antibiotics administered for antineoplastic therapy are dactinomycin (Actinomycin D), doxorubicin (Adriamycin), bleomycin sulfate (Blenoxane), and mitomycin (Mutamycin). These are effective in the treatment of a variety of solid tumors.

Adrenocorticosteroids, androgens, estrogens, and progestins are hormones found to be effective in specific neoplastic diseases. The steroids prednisone (Deltasone, Meticorten), prednisolone (Delta-Cortef, Meticortelone), cortisone acetate (Cortone), and cortisol (Cortef, Hydrocortone) are used alone or in combination therapy for acute leukemias. They interrupt the cell cycle at the G_1 stage. Dromostanolone proprionate (Drolban), fluoxymesterone (Halotestin), and testosterone (Oreton) are representative androgens whose primary use is for palliation in patients with inoperable carcinoma of the breast. The estrogens diethylstilbestrol (DES) and ethinyl estradiol (Estinyl) are considered as reliable palliative therapy in patients with carcinoma of the breast, especially in the postmenopausal patient.

L-Asparaginase is an enzyme found in *Escherichia coli* and when isolated is useful in the treatment of acute lymphoblastic leukemia. Cisplatin (Platinol) is a heavy metal complex of platinum. It has biochemical properties similar to the alkylating agents and is apparently cell-cycle nonspecific. Cisplatin is indicated in the treatment of metastatic testicular tumors and ovarian carcinoma. Table 19-3 lists these miscellaneous antineoplastics and their uses.

ADVERSE DRUG EFFECTS

Rapidly growing cells, such as neoplastic cells, are more susceptible to inhibition or destruction by antineoplastic agents. The most serious difficulty in antineoplastic therapy stems from the lack of selectivity between tumor tissue and normal tissue. Some normal cells exhibit a faster reproduction cycle than do slowly growing tumor cells. In an effort to eradicate a malignancy, certain normal cells are also destroyed, resulting in clinically expressed adverse effects. Since the cells of the gastrointestinal tract, bone marrow, and hair follicles are among the faster growing normal cells, the early clinical manifestations of side effects are associated with the loss of these cells.

The principal adverse effects are as follows:

1. There is a suppression of bone marrow activity resulting in leukopenia, thrombocytopenia, and ane-

Table 19-3. Miscellaneous antineoplastics and their uses

Antineoplastic	Use
Natural products	
Vinblastine (Velban)	Metastatic testicular tumor
Vincristine (Oncovin)	Hodgkin's disease and other lymphomas
Antibiotics	
Dactinomycin (Actinomycin D)	Wilm's tumor in children
Doxorubicin (Adriamycin)	Acute leukemias and malignant lymphomas
Bleomycin sulfate (Blenoxane)	Testicular carcinomas
Mitomycin (Mutamycin)	Gastric adenocarcinoma
Hormones	
Adrenocorticosteroids	Acute leukemias
Androgens and estrogens	Carcinoma of the breast
Progestins	Carcinoma of the endometrium
Other	
L-Asparaginase	Acute lymphoblastic leukemia
Cisplatin (Platinol)	Testicular tumors

mia. The degree of cytopenia that results depends on the drugs being employed, the condition of the bone marrow at the time of administration, and other contributing factors.

2. Gastrointestinal disturbances may occur, resulting from sloughing of the gastrointestinal mucosa. Clinically, these disturbances are expressed as nausea, stomatitis, vomiting, and hemorrhagic diarrhea.

3. Cutaneous reactions may occur infrequently, varying from mild erythema and maculopapular eruptions to exfoliative dermatitis and Stevens-Johnson syndrome. Alopecia is frequent, but the hair usually regrows when therapy is discontinued.

4. Hepatotoxicity occurs principally with the antimetabolites, for example, methotrexate, but it may occur with other agents as well.

5. Neurotoxic effects may develop, such as peripheral neuropathy, ileus, inappropriate ADH secretion, and convulsions, which are chiefly associated with vincristine or vinblastine administration.

6. Renal tubular impairment, occurring secondary to hyperuricemia, is caused by rapid cell destruction

and the release of nucleotides. For example, the treatment of leukemias and lymphomas often results in rapid tumor destruction with a consequent high uric acid level. Allopurinol (Zyloprim) is administered routinely before the initiation of a regimen of antineoplastic agents to prevent hyperuricemia.

7. Immune deficiency may occur, resulting in an enhanced susceptibility to infection and/or a second malignancy, since many antineoplastic agents have an immunosuppressant effect.

8. Inhibition of spermatogenesis and oogenesis is frequent, at least temporarily. Mutations within the germ cells may occur, and the menstrual cycle may also be inhibited. The patient can recover after discontinuation of the drug.

9. Adverse effects on oral tissue may develop. These are discussed below.

Oral considerations

Oral complaints precipitated by side effects of the antineoplastic agents are primarily those of discomfort, sensitivity of teeth and gums, pain, ulceration, gingival hemorrhage, dryness, and impaired taste sensation. Because of the complicated interaction of the antineoplastic agents with the body system, oral symptoms are best treated topically.

The most important therapeutic consideration is to attempt to prevent toxicity. When the decision has been made to institute antineoplastic therapy, appropriate maintenance of the oral cavity should receive priority attention. Plaque control instructions and their periodic reinforcement are essential to prevent or attenuate the anticipated oral complications. Commercial mouthwashes tend to dry the oral tissues and interfere with the delicate balance of the oral flora, and therefore they should be avoided. An alkaline saline rinse of warm water flavored with salt and sodium bicarbonate is a simple, effective remedy that can be used for oral flushing. A soft toothbrush will reduce the possibility of gingival or mucosal irritation or abrasion. Oral irrigating devices, if used, should be regulated to low pressure only to prevent initiating or exacerbating gingival hemorrhage. Gingival hemorrhage is an indication of some degree of ulceration of the crevicular lining. This should *not* be interpreted as a signal to discontinue brushing. Judicious brushing should be continued, or the local irritants produced by the unmolested plaque will promote the diseased state of the gingival crevice, resulting in increased hemorrhage and pain.

Candidiasis. Frequently, the altered oral environment allows the opportunistic overgrowth of *Candida albicans*. Since this is a predictable occurrence, nystatin (Mycostatin) therapy is often instituted simultaneously with the administration of antineoplastic agents. Rinses with 2 ml of an oral suspension of 100,000 unit/ml four times per 24 hours may be adequate to control the infection. If the oral candidiasis is persistent, an often efficacious therapeutic modality is to allow vaginal suppositories to slowly dissolve in the buccal vestibule, thereby allowing a constant supply of the antifungal agent to come in contact with the infectious agent.

Nystatin popsicles are a soothing and alternative method of delivering the antifungal agent to the oral tissue. These are made by placing 2 ml of the oral suspension in each receptacle of an ice cube tray, filling the container with water, and then freezing.

Xerostomia. Another side effect of antineoplastic agents is reduced salivary gland activity. Sequelae of this condition are sensitivity of the teeth and the mucous membranes. Frequent (e.g., every 2 hours) oral rinses with a 0.5% aqueous solution of sodium carboxymethylcellulose (Xero-Lube, Salivart) will often relieve these symptoms. Supportive therapy may also include allowing ice cubes to melt in the mouth. Discontinuing all caffeine-containing beverages, that is, coffee, tea, hot chocolate, and cola drinks, and increasing water intake will tend to improve salivary flow.

Ulcerations. Ulcerations of the oral mucous membranes occur most commonly with methotrexate, fluorouracil, dactinomycin (Actinomycin D), doxorubicin (Adriamycin), and bleomycin. However, any antineoplastic agent that significantly depresses the marrow can induce oral ulceration as a sequela to leukopenia. The characteristic oral lesion is a cratered ulceration with a wide, diffuse, erythematous border reflecting severely compromised host resistance to any tissue insult.

An effective regimen to bathe the tissues, guard against secondary infection, and control the *Candida* in the ulcerations is to use alternating rinses of 2 ml nystatin oral suspension, alkaline saline solution, and 0.5% providone-iodine solution, with 1-hour intervals between rinses.

Gingival hemorrhage. Constant, low-grade gingival hemorrhage frequently occurs when a thrombocytopenia develops as a result of either the disease process or the therapy. Periodontal packs may reduce the blood loss and mechanically contribute to local clotting. When the marrow is depressed to the degree that oral hemorrhage and ulcerations are not controllable on a local basis, systemic therapy may be necessary. The temporary discontinuation of the antineoplastic agents and transfusions of platelet packs will often quickly improve the oral health.

ELECTIVE DENTAL TREATMENT

Generally, elective dental procedures should not be performed when patients are receiving antineoplastic therapy, especially if the patient is experiencing acute adverse side effects. If possible, multiple extractions should be avoided. Before any extractions, the coagulation status of the patient should be carefully evaluated so that appropriate measures can be used at the time of surgery for anticipated complications. In a situation where a coagulopathy exists and an extraction is necessary, packing the socket with oxidized regenerated cellulose and suturing as indicated will tend to minimize postoperative difficulties.

Dental treatment of leukemic patients preferably should be performed during the remission phase.

There is a lack of consensus about antibiotic prophylactic coverage for required dental treatment on these patients. In support of antibiotic coverage is the observation that susceptibility to infection is increased in individuals who are receiving chemotherapy. On the other hand, the use of antibiotics may result in superinfection that may be difficult to manage. The decision about their use should be reached by mutual agreement with the referring physician.

REFERENCES
1. Holland, J.F., and Frei, E., III: Cancer medicine, Philadelphia, 1973, Lea & Febiger.
2. American Medical Association Council on Drugs: AMA drug evaluations, ed. 4, Acton, Mass., 1980, Publishing Sciences Group, Inc.
3. Cole, W.H.: Chemotherapy of cancer, Philadelphia, 1970, Lea & Febiger.
4. Ansfield, J.: Chemotherapy of malignant neoplasms, ed. 2, Springfield, Ill., 1973, Charles C Thomas, Publisher.
5. Greenwald, E.S.: Cancer chemotherapy, ed. 2, Flushing, N.Y., 1973, Medical Examination Publishing Co., Inc.
6. Carl, W., and Schaaf, N.G.: Proceedings: dental care for the cancer patient, J. Surg. Oncol. **6**(4):293-310, 1974.
7. Clinical oncology for medical students and physicians, ed. 4, Rochester, N.Y., 1974, University of Rochester School of Medicine and Dentistry.

CHAPTER 20

TOMMY W. GAGE

Diuretics and antihypertensive drugs

This chapter on diuretics and antihypertensive drugs discusses the wide variety of drugs now employed for the management of hypertension. The diuretics, even though a separate drug class, are actually among the most important and frequently used antihypertensives. Since not all diuretics are used for this purpose, their special indications are briefly discussed. The major portion of this chapter is devoted to the many antihypertensive drugs and those various sites and mechanisms of action that are known. Cardiovascular drugs that are employed for angina pectoris, heart failure, and other cardiac disorders are presented in Chapter 21.

HYPERTENSION

Hypertension, which affects some 35 million Americans, is the most common of all cardiovascular diseases.[1] Kaplan[2] has estimated that approximately 15 of every 100 adult dental patients may have hypertension. Half of these individuals may also be undiagnosed and untreated.[2] Hypertension is a major risk factor and the leading cause of death in cardiovascular disease. It does not usually produce any outward symptoms until some damage has occurred to the heart, kidney, brain, or retina. Persons with untreated hypertension are more likely to develop accelerated damage of these major organs. Fifty percent of people with untreated hypertension are reported to die of heart disease, 33% die of stroke, and 10% to 15% die of kidney failure. Fortunately, early detection of hypertension and treatment with appropriate drug therapy reduce the possibility of damage to vital organs and extend the lifetime of many patients.[3] The degree of hypertension may be divided into (1) mild (diastolic pressure 90 to 104 mm Hg), (2) moderate (diastolic pressure 105 to 114 mm Hg), and (3) severe (diastolic pressure 115 mm Hg or

above). Patients with diastolic pressures above 130 mm Hg are considered to be in hypertensive crisis.[4]

Hypertensive disease is generally divided into at least three categories based on cause or progression of the disease. The first group includes approximately 90% of the diagnosed hypertensive patients who have essential or primary hypertension. The exact cause of the hypertension of this category is unknown. However, evidence is growing that implicates an excessive dietary sodium intake as a cause. In addition, some investigators are studying the possibility of a genetic deficiency in the sodium-handling ability of the kidneys in offspring of parents with a history of hypertension. Such a cause and effect remains to be established, but the action of the diuretics in promoting sodium excretion lends validity to these concepts.[5]

The cause of the hypertension in the second category can be associated with a specific disease process. These processes include adrenal medullary tumor, or in women, the ingestion of estrogen as a component of birth control pills. The term *secondary hypertension* is used to describe this category, which accounts for about 10% of all hypertension. The third group of hypertensive patients are those with malignant hypertension. Blood pressures are high, and there is usually evidence of retinal and renal damage. Only a small number of patients are actually in this group, and some believe it to be a more severe progression of essential hypertension.[6]

PHILOSOPHY OF DRUG THERAPY

Drug therapy of hypertension is directed at those important factors influencing blood pressure, namely peripheral resistance and cardiac output. Other interrelated factors are shown in Fig. 20-1. The steps of active drug therapy usually begin as diastolic pres-

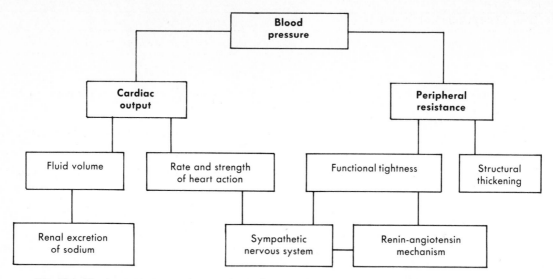

Fig. 20-1. Blood pressure depends on the output of the heart and the resistance to the flow of blood through the body, which in turn depend on the elements shown in this schema. The sympathetic nervous system can also activate the renin-angiotensin mechanism. (From Kaplan, N.M.: Am. Sci. **68:**537, 1980. Reprinted by permission of *American Scientist,* journal of Sigma Xi, The Scientific Research Society.)

sures range above 90 mm Hg. Initial therapy is normally begun with one of the thiazide diuretics and a weight control and sodium reduction diet. Other drugs are added as the situation dictates. Step 2 drugs usually include an adrenergic receptor blocking agent, such as propranolol or prazosin. Other step 2 drugs used in combination with the diuretics are the centrally acting antihypertensives, methyldopa and clonidine. Some patients may require the use of a vasodilator as a third step if additional control is needed. Step 4 therapy for the more difficult to control hypertension will see the addition of neuronal blocking drugs such as guanethidine. More recent therapy involves the use of captopril, an antagonist of the renin-angiotensin system. The exact combination of drugs eventually selected for a specific patient is determined by the response to the drugs in terms of reducing the hypertensive state as well as the complications associated with other disease processes. It is not unusual to discover that a dental patient may be taking five or even six different drugs for problems related to hypertension control. Therefore some basic knowledge of antihypertensive drugs is essential in evaluation of the hypertensive dental patient.[7]

DIURETICS
Review of renal physiology

The basic role of the kidney is to filter metabolic products from the plasma and to control sodium, potassium, and hydrogen ions and body water within rather narrow limits. The nephron is the functional unit of the kidney, consisting of a glomerular filtering membrane and the proximal tubule, Henle's loop, and the distal tubule across which ions are exchanged. The amount of sodium filtered is a function of the plasma concentration as well as the filtration pressure. The proximal tubule actively reabsorbs approximately 70% of the filtered sodium with chloride, water, and bicarbonate accompanying the reabsorption. The ascending limb of Henle's loop also reabsorbs a portion of the sodium ion remaining in the tubule but without the accompanying water. The distal tubule and the collecting ducts serve to make the final and critical adjustment of sodium ion reabsorption. Potassium and hydrogen ions are exchanged for sodium so that more sodium is reabsorbed for the body. Aldosterone, a hormone that increases sodium retention, has its effect on the distal tubule, which makes final volume adjustments. A disease process that would tend to reduce the efficiency of the kidney

Table 20-1. Classification of diuretics

Diuretics	Mechanism and site of action
Minor diuretics	
Mercurials	
Mercaptomerin (Thiomerin)	Inhibits active transport of chloride in the thick ascending
Merethoxylline procaine (Dicurin Procaine)	limb of Henle's loop
Carbonic anhydrase inhibitors	
Acetazolamide (Diamox)	Inhibits the enzyme carbonic anhydrase in the proximal
Ethoxzolamide (Cardrase)	tubules
Xanthines	
Theophylline ethylenediamine (aminophylline)	Increases glomerular filtration by improved renal bloodflow
Osmotics	
Mannitol (Osmitrol)	Decreases reabsorption in the proximal tubule and Henle's
Urea (Ureaphil)	loop
Glycerin (Glyrol, Osmoglyn)	
Major diuretics	
Thiazides	
Chlorothiazide (Diuril)	Inhibits reabsorption of sodium and chloride in thick ascend-
Hydrochlorothiazide (HydroDiuril, Esidrix)	ing limb of Henle's loop (renal cortex) and distal tubule
Many others	
Related nonthiazides	
Chlorthalidone (Hygroton)	Inhibits reabsorption of sodium and chloride in thick ascend-
Metolazone (Zaroxolyn)	ing limb of Henle's loop (renal cortex)
Loop diuretics	
Furosemide (Lasix)	Inhibits reabsorption of sodium and chloride in thick ascend-
Ethacrynic acid (Edecrin)	ing limb of Henle's loop (renal medulla)
Potassium-conserving diuretics	
Spironolactone (Aldactone)	Antagonizes aldosterone in distal tubule
Triamterene (Dyrenium)	Directly affects distal tubule to inhibit sodium reabsorption in exchange for potassium and hydrogen ions

to regulate ion exchange could lead to sodium retention and edema.[8]

Diuretics are an important group of drugs employed in the management of a variety of conditions in which edema is a prominent finding, including congestive heart failure, hypertension, cirrhosis of the liver, pregnancy, and some renal diseases. The basic effect of diuretic therapy is to increase the excretion of excess sodium ion, thereby reducing plasma volume and extracellular fluid accumulation. The reduction of blood volume is one means of reducing blood pressure. The diuretics can be classified into a minor and major category, depending on their relative importance in hypertension as shown in Table 20-1. Because of the large number of diuretics available, only selected examples of each category are presented.

Minor diuretics
Mercurials

The mercurial diuretics are among the oldest and most potent of the diuretic agents. At one time these agents were foremost in diuretic therapy, but they now have limited application. These agents inhibit the active transport of chloride ion in the ascending limb of Henle's loop. Sodium ion reabsorption is reduced, carrying with it excess water for excretion. However, refractivity to the mercurials develops after a short while, reducing their usefulness. The only mercurials still used are given intramuscularly or subcutaneously. Examples are mercaptomerin sodium (Thiomerin) and merethoxylline procaine (Dicurin Procaine). Side effects include stomatitis, cardiac and renal toxicity, gastric irritation, and hypochloremic alkalosis. The main usefulness of mercurial diuretics is to rapidly reduce edema in heart failure, renal diseases, or hepatic cirrhosis.[9]

Carbonic anhydrase inhibitors

The carbonic anhydrase inhibitors were used in combination with mercurial diuretics before the development of the thiazides. Their use has diminished, but they still have significant therapeutic value. The currently available drugs include acetazolamide (Diamox), ethoxzolamide (Cardrase), dichlorphenamide (Daranide), and methazolamide (Neptazane). Acetazolamide is the most frequently prescribed of this category. Like the thiazides, these drugs are structurally related to the sulfonamides.

The mechanism of action of these drugs is inhibition of the enzyme carbonic anhydrase, which catalyzes the reaction of water and carbon dioxide to carbonic acid:

$$CO_2 + H_2O \xrightarrow{\text{Carbonic anhydrase}} H^+ + HCO_3^-$$

The proximal tubule has now been identified as the major site of action, with minor activity in the distal tubule. As the carbonic anhydrase enzyme is inhibited, fewer hydrogen ions are available for exchange with sodium, and diuresis results. There is also an accompanying increase in potassium and bicarbonate loss. To minimize the loss of bicarbonate and the development of acidosis, the drugs are given on alternate days.

Adverse reactions to these diuretics are uncommon, but paresthesia of the face and extremities, drowsiness, and gastrointestinal effects have been known to occur. Because the drugs resemble the sulfonamides, a similar renal toxicity has been reported. Other adverse effects include hypersensitivity reactions and bone marrow depression.

The carbonic anhydrase inhibitors have been used to manage a variety of edematous states associated with cardiovascular diseases. However, they are not used specifically as diuretics now. Acetazolamide is currently used to reduce fluid accumulation in glaucoma and has been tried in epilepsy.

Osmotic and xanthine diuretics

The remainder of the minor group of diuretics include the osmotic nonelectrolytes mannitol, urea, and glycerin. These agents are highly filtered by the glomerulus and exert a solute-induced diuresis in the proximal tubule. They are used to reduce excess edema associated with neurosurgery or trauma to the CNS. The diuretic effects of the xanthines caffeine and theophylline are well known to coffee and tea drinkers. Theophylline ethylenediamine (aminophylline) is the most effective diuretic of this group. These agents are frequently combined with the mercurial diuretics to improve their efficacy. The action of theophylline in increasing cardiac output improves vascular flow to the kidney, with improved glomerular filtration.[10]

Major diuretics
Thiazides

The thiazide diuretics (benzothiadiazides) are the most important category of drugs for use in hypertension. It is estimated that the condition of approximately 40% to 70% of mildly hypertensive patients may be adequately managed with thiazides. This group of drugs evolved out of research designed to develop more potent diuretics similar to carbonic anhydrase inhibitors. They have a basic chemical resemblance to the sulfonamide type of drugs. The first thiazide diuretic marketed was chlorothiazide, and its success as a therapeutic agent stimulated the search and development of a large number of thiazide diuretics. Their principal pharmacologic effects are the same; they differ from one another in dose, duration, and onset of action. A number of thiazide diuretics and their single oral adult doses are listed in Table 20-2.

The mechanism of action of the thiazide diuretics at the cellular level is not established. However, the pharmacologic effects of diuresis and reduction of arterial blood pressure can be discussed. The diuretic

Table 20-2. Thiazide diuretics and single oral doses for an antihypertensive effect

Thiazide diuretic	Usual oral dose (adult)
Chlorothiazide (Diuril)	500 mg
Hydrochlorothiazide (HydroDiuril, Esidrix, Oretic)	50 mg
Benzthiazide (Exna)	50 mg
Hydroflumethiazide (Saluron, Diucardin)	50 mg
Bendroflumethiazide (Naturetin)	5 mg
Methyclothiazide (Enduron, Aquatensen)	5 mg
Trichlormethiazide (Naqua, Metahydrin)	4 mg
Cyclothiazide (Anhydron)	2 mg
Polythiazide (Renese)	2 mg

effect occurs as a result of the inhibition of Na^+ reabsorption in the distal tubule and the cortical ascending limb of Henle's loop. Chloride anion and water accompany the sodium ion, resulting in an increased urine volume. The inhibition of sodium reabsorption in the distal tubule occurs at a site different from that of the K^+ and Na^+ exchange. Because of an increased amount of sodium available for exchange with potassium in the distal tubule, more potassium is excreted than normal. For this reason, aldosterone antagonists are sometimes combined with a thiazide to conserve potassium. The properties of the thiazides to inhibit carbonic anhydrase are not important for diuresis.

The antihypertensive effect of the thiazides was not recognized until after their use as diuretics. The proposed reasons for the antihypertensive properties have oscillated back and forth between a reduced fluid volume and a direct effect on arterial smooth muscle. Part of the reason for this was that diazoxide, a thiazide-like compound without diuretic effects, was shown to lower blood pressure by a direct effect on vascular smooth muscle. However, evidence now presented attributes the antihypertensive action of the thiazides to a continual reduction in sodium and water. As such, there is a reduction in plasma volume and hence extracellular fluid volume. Volume reduction is associated with a reduction in cardiac output and peripheral resistance is lowered in response.[5]

All of the thiazide diuretics are absorbed well when given orally. Chlorothiazide is the most slowly absorbed and rapidly excreted. Hydrochlorothiazide is more rapidly absorbed, as is polythiazide, and they are also longer acting than chlorothiazide. The onset of action of the orally administered drugs is approximately 1 hour, with a duration lasting up to 24 hours or longer. The intravenously administered thiazides have a short duration of action. They are concentrated in the kidney, which is also the major organ concerned with the excretion of these drugs. Intervals of doses and duration of action are determined for the most part by the excretion rates of the various thiazides.

Adverse reactions associated with the thiazides are based on changes in plasma electrolytes. Their long-term use can lead to hypokalemia, and potassium chloride supplementation is often required to replace potassium ions. Hypokalemia can be of critical importance if thiazides and digitalis are combined since lowered serum potassium increases the toxicity of digitalis. Higher doses of thiazides can produce

anorexia with heartburn. This could be a source of confusion when thiazides are combined with digitalis therapy because these toxic symptoms are similar for both drugs. Thiazides also increase uric acid retention, producing a hyperuricemia that can adversely affect the gout patient. Thiazide therapy can produce hyperglycemia in certain individuals, but the cause is largely unknown. Other adverse reactions such as hypersensitivity-induced skin rashes may be observed. The increased toxicity of digitalis, gastric irritation occurring with potassium chloride supplements, potentiation of other antihypertensive agents, and hyperglycemia in patients taking oral antidiabetic agents are the most important drug interactions associated with thiazide use.[11]

Related nonthiazides

Chlorthalidone. Chlorthalidone (Hygroton) is a sulfonamide-type diuretic chemically unrelated to the thiazides but possessing the same basic pharmacologic effects. Quinethazone (Hydromox) and metolazone (Zaroxolyn) are other members of this type of diuretic. Uses and effects are similar to those of the thiazides.

Loop diuretics

Furosemide. Furosemide (Lasix) is a sulfonamide moiety containing a diuretic of high potency. Whereas some of its diuretic effects can be related to the inhibition of Na^{++} reabsorption in the distal tubule, its principal site of action is on the ascending limb of Henle's loop. The ascending limb functions as a countercurrent flow mechanism to conserve sodium and adjust the final urine concentration in the collecting tubules. Furosemide blocks this function, producing a rapid diuresis and dilute urine. Oral doses of 40 to 80 mg/24 hr are highly effective, and in an emergency, doses of 20 mg are given by intravenous or intramuscular injection.

The thiazides are better day-to-day antihypertensive drugs, but furosemide also has antihypertensive properties similar to those of the thiazides. It is employed as a single drug in hypertension, and like the thiazides it potentiates other antihypertensive drugs. Furosemide finds its greatest application in emergency edematous and hypertensive states. Adverse effects associated with furosemide are associated with serum electrolyte imbalance.

Ethacrynic acid. Ethacrynic acid (Edecrin) is a diuretic with a potency like that of furosemide. It differs from the thiazides and furosemide chemically in that no sulfonamide moiety is in the structure. The major site and type of pharmacologic action are the same as those of furosemide, with some effects on the proximal and distal tubular reabsorption mechanism. The principal indication for ethacrynic acid is severe edematous disease states, although there is some caution to be observed in patients with renal failure. Adverse effects resemble those for furosemide.

Potassium-conserving diuretics

There are a number of homeostatic mechanisms concerned with sodium ion regulation and volume of the circulatory system. One of the most important systems is that of the renin-angiotensin mechanism. Renin is released from the kidney in response to a decrease in blood flow through the kidney. Renin catalyzes the conversion of angiotensinogen to angiotensin I. Another enzyme acts to convert angiotensin I to angiotensin II, which can then act directly on the kidney, increasing sodium retention and vascular volume. Also, angiotensin can increase peripheral resistance. Both of these effects can elevate the blood pressure. Angiotensin II can also stimulate the adrenal cortex to produce aldosterone. Aldosterone increases sodium retention by the kidney, which in turn increases water retention and increases vascular fluid volume. This process results in a conservation of sodium at the expense of potassium. Theories on the etiology of hypertension are related to higher than normal levels of aldosterone or renin activity.

Spironolactone. Spironolactone (Aldactone) is structurally similar to the hormone aldosterone and exerts its diuretic effect by competitive antagonism of aldosterone on the distal tubule. The net effect is an increase in sodium ion excretion and conservation of potassium. Since this action takes place at a location different from that associated with the thiazides, spironolactone can be combined with the thiazides to conserve potassium and prevent hypokalemia in hypertensive diseases associated with elevated aldosterone plasma levels. A recent warning has appeared with the official package insert of a thiazide and spironolactone diuretic combination, implicating spironolactone as a tumorigen in rats. Consequently, there are certain limitations to the indications for the use of this type of therapy.

Triamterene. Triamterene (Dyrenium) is also a potassium-sparing diuretic with a mechanism of action related to a direct effect on the kidney. Sodium excre-

tion is enhanced and potassium retained. The general indications for its use are similar to those of spironolactone in supporting other diuretics in refractory cases of edema or hypertension.[12]

ANTIHYPERTENSIVE DRUGS

A large number of drugs are indicated for use in the symptomatic management of hypertensive diseases. A classification and selected examples are shown in Table 20-3. In general, the majority of these drugs act through either a central or a peripheral mechanism that diminishes sympathetic control of cardiovascular activity. The drugs are presented in the order described by the tabular listing.

Direct-acting vasodilators

Hydralazine

Hydralazine hydrochloride (Apresoline) exerts its antihypertensive effect by a direct vasodilator action on the smooth muscle of arterioles, resulting in a decrease in peripheral resistance. Accompanying the decrease in peripheral resistance is a reflex stimulation of heart rate and sympathetic activity. For this reason, hydralazine is usually considered a third-step drug in the management of hypertension. It is most useful in combination with a diuretic and a beta adrenergic receptor blocking agent. The diuretic is needed to reduce the fluid retention that can occur with the use of hydralazine only. The addition of a beta adrenergic blocker reduces the reflex increase in heart rate and sympathetic tone.

Hydralazine is normally given orally on a twice-daily basis. Doses above 400 mg have been associated with a reversible lupus erythematosus–like syndrome. If it is used as a single agent, cardiac arrhythmias and angina may occur. Other side effects include headache, dizziness, and postural hypotension. Side effects are reduced when hydralazine is combined with other antihypertensives, but caution should always be taken when other drugs are employed in dentistry that may also produce postural hypotension.[13]

Minoxidil

The newest direct-acting vasodilator marketed for use in hypertension is minoxidil (Loniten). It has an action similar to that of hydralazine but is indicated for use in severe hypertension when other therapy is unsuccessful. The drug is given orally in combination with a diuretic and a beta adrenergic receptor

Table 20-3. Sites of action of antihypertensive drugs

Antihypertensive drugs	Site of action

Direct-acting vasodilators
    Hydralazine (Apresoline)
    Minoxidil (Loniten)
    Diazoxide (Hyperstat I.V.)
    Sodium nitroprusside (Nipride)
	Directly affect vascular smooth muscle to reduce peripheral resistance

Neuronal blockers
    Guanethidine (Ismelin)
    Reserpine (Serpasil)
    Pargyline (Eutonyl)
	Blocks sympathetic neuron and norepinephrine release
	
	Inhibits monoamine oxidase enzyme

Centrally acting
    Methyldopa (Aldomet)
    Clonidine (Catapres)
	Acts in CNS to reduce sympathetic activity

Ganglionic blockers
    Mecamylamine (Inversine)
    Trimethaphan camsylate (Arfonad)
	Blocks action in autonomic ganglia

Adrenergic blockers
    Prazosin (Minipress)
    Phentolamine (Regitine)
    Phenoxybenzamine (Dibenzyline)
    Propranolol (Inderal)
    Metoprolol (Lopressor)
    Nadolol (Corgard)
	Blocks alpha receptor
	Blocks alpha receptor
	Blocks alpha receptor
	Blocks beta receptor
	Blocks beta receptor
	Blocks beta receptor

Other antihypertensives
    Metyrosine (Demser)
    Captopril (Capoten)
    Veratrum alkaloids
    Thiazide and other major diuretics
	Inhibits tyrosine hydroxylase
	Antagonizes renin-angiotensin system
	Sensitize baroreceptor reflex
	Deplete volume

blocking drug. Like hydralazine, minoxidil use is also associated with sympathetic activity and fluid retention. Oral doses must be given in small initial amounts and increased as patient response dictates. Adverse effects include increase sodium retention with edema, sinus tachycardia, hirsutism, and pericardial effusions.[14]

Other vasodilators

Two other vasodilator drugs with a direct vasodilator action on the vascular smooth muscle to reduce peripheral resistance are diazoxide (Hyperstat I.V.) and sodium nitroprusside (Nipride). Diazoxide is chemically similar to the thiazides but lacks diuretic activity. Both drugs are used in hypertensive crises, and when they are given intravenously, diazoxide and sodium nitroprusside have an onset of action within 2 to 3 minutes. The duration of sodium nitroprusside is extremely short, so a continuous infusion must be maintained. This limits its usefulness for a longer duration because the potential for cyanide toxicity increases. Sodium nitroprusside is also employed for controlled hypotension during surgical procedures. Side effects of diazoxide include hyperglycemia, whereas sodium nitroprusside is associated with renal and liver toxicity.[15,16]

Neuronal blockers
Guanethidine

Guanethidine (Ismelin) is an antihypertensive agent that blocks the release of norepinephrine from adrenergic nerve terminals by a direct effect on the neuron. Consequently, norepinephrine is not released in response to adrenergic stimulation. Additionally, the amount of norepinephrine normally stored in synaptic vesicles is reduced. Both of these mechanisms reduce the amount of norepinephrine available to interact with the receptor site, resulting in a reduced sympathetic tone and a decrease in blood pressure. Guanethidine has a rather long onset of action after oral doses (up to 3 days), and because guanethidine accumulates in the adrenergic nerve terminal, its effects are present for a long time (up to 2 weeks). The main indication for the use of guanethidine is in cases of resistant mild hypertension and severe hypertensive crisis. Patients taking guanethidine over a period of time tend to show sodium retention with edema. For this reason guanethidine is usually combined with a diuretic to minimize this response.

Patients taking guanethidine may show episodes of hypotension when they make sudden positional changes, such as that encountered on arising from the dental chair. Other side effects include diarrhea, interference with ejaculation, and cardiac problems in patients with marginal cardiac reserve. Muscle weakness may also be a complaint. A specific contraindication to the use of guanethidine is the presence of the adrenal medullary tumor pheochromocytoma. The action of guanethidine can be diminished by dextroamphetamine, chlorpromazine, and the tricyclic antidepressants. The effects of indirect-acting sympathomimetics are reduced in the presence of guanethidine. Cold remedies that contain direct-acting sympathomimetics in their formulation may produce a hypertensive episode as a result of increased sensitivity of the adrenergic receptor. Alcohol will potentiate the hypotensive effects of guanethidine.

Pargyline

The MAOI pargyline (Eutonyl) lowers blood pressure in certain cases. The central effects of pargyline are related to the inhibition of norepinephrine metabolism and do not account for the paradoxical lowering of blood pressure. At least one theory of its antihypertensive effects is related to a guanethidine-like response in inhibiting nerve impulse–induced release of norepinephrine. Pargyline has a limited usefulness in hypertension because of the many adverse reactions and drug interactions associated with the MAOI type of drugs. Also, better antihypertensive drugs are available, but it is occasionally used. The pharmacology of the MAOI drugs is discussed more fully in Chapter 8.

Rauwolfia

The therapeutic development of the rauwolfia alkaloids is similar to that of digitalis in that extracts of the *Rauwolfia serpentina* plant were used for years as a part of Hindu folk medicine. In the 1950s rauwolfia was recognized as a tranquilizer and subsequently as a drug that would lower blood pressure in a hypertensive patient. The principal alkaloid of rauwolfia is reserpine (Serpasil). Other alkaloids of rauwolfia or rauwolfia preparations include deserpidine (Harmonyl), rescinnamine (Moderil), alseroxylon (Rauwiloid), which is a whole-root extract, and a dried root preparation (Raudixin).

The mechanism of action of reserpine is to deplete norepinephrine by inhibiting the storage uptake mechanism in the adrenergic nerve terminal. Its central effects include an effect on 5-hydrotryptamine and a depletion of norepinephrine stores. Like other drugs in this group its CNS actions are not the major source of its antihypertensive effect. Reserpine, like guanethidine, has a cumulative effect, with a delayed onset of action and a prolonged duration. Reserpine is seldom useful as a single agent in controlling hypertension.

Adverse effects associated with the use of reserpine include diarrhea, bad dreams, sedation, and even psychic depression leading to suicidal tendencies. Reserpine causes an increase in gastric acid production, leading to gastrointestinal upset, and it can aggravate an already-present peptic ulcer. Reserpine will potentiate other depressant type of drugs, and an occasional extrapyramidal side effect may be observed.[13]

Centrally acting antihypertensives
Methyldopa

Methyldopa (Aldomet) is one of the most commonly encountered antihypertensive drugs. It is most effective when combined with a diuretic in second-step therapy. The mechanism by which methyldopa acts to reduce blood pressure is now better understood but lacks clarity. It is generally believed that methyldopa acts by stimulating alpha adrenergic receptors in the CNS. Activation of alpha adrenergic receptors is associated with reduced sympathetic activity. Methyldopa is incorporated into the scheme of norepinephrine synthesis, and as a result alpha-methylnorepinephrine is produced. Alpha-methylnorepinephrine replaces norepinephrine in the vesicular storage sites and is released by the nerve impulse. The released alpha-methylnorepinephrine can then stimulate the alpha receptors of the postjunctional tissues. The reduced sympathetic activity leads to a decrease in peripheral resistance. The vasoconstrictor levonordefrin found in local anesthetic preparations is also known as alpha-methylnorepinephrine.

Methyldopa can be given orally or intravenously, with effects lasting up to 24 hours. The adverse effects are similar to those associated with other antihypertensive agents and include postural hypotension, gastrointestinal upset, extrapyramidal tremors, vertigo, and psychic depression. Sedation is a common side effect. Excretory products of methyldopa can result in a positive direct Coombs test and interfere with the diagnosis of pheochromocytoma. Its use is contraindicated in patients with active liver disease. Methyldopa is useful in most hypertensive disease states and is of most benefit in those patients with renal damage.[17]

Clonidine

Introduced in 1974, clonidine hydrochloride (Catapres) is a more recently marketed centrally acting antihypertensive agent. It is effective in both moderate and severe hypertension. It is used in combination with a thiazide diuretic and hydralazine. Clonidine prevents tachycardia that results from hydralazine use and can substitute for a beta adrenergic receptor blocker. Propranolol and clonidine can be used together if they are not simultaneously and rapidly withdrawn from the patient.

Like methyldopa, clonidine reduces peripheral resistance through a CNS-mediated action that involves alpha receptors. However, clonidine has an action on both types of alpha receptors, in contrast to methyldopa. Clonidine appears to stimulate alpha postsynaptic receptors in the vasomotor centers, thus reducing outflow. On the hypothalamus, clonidine stimulates alpha$_2$ presynaptic receptors, blocking a feedback mechanism that normally maintains norepinephrine release. The net result is a reduction in sympathetic outflow. Thus clonidine reduces heart rate, cardiac output, and total peripheral resistance. Because of its alpha adrenergic agonist activity, intravenous doses produce a short-lived increase in peripheral resistance in comparison with the oral dose.[18]

Adverse effects of clonidine include sedation and dry mouth that may disappear after continued use.

Parotid gland swelling and pain have been noted in a small number of patients. Other oral side effects include an unpleasant taste. The most serious adverse effect occurs during a withdrawal in which a rapid elevation in blood pressure is noted. CNS depressants employed in dentistry may contribute to excessive postural hypotension when they are combined with clonidine use.[19]

Ganglionic blockers

The ganglionic blockers were among the first drugs used in the management of hypertensive disease. The currently available drugs for clinical use are mecamylamine (Inversine) and trimethaphan (Arfonad). Three other drugs in this same class are seldom if ever used today: hexamethonium, chlorisondamine, and trimethidinium.

The mechanism of action and pharmacologic effects of these agents are similar and can be discussed as a group. The ganglionic blockers act at the ganglia formed by the synapse of preganglionic and postganglionic autonomic neurons. These drugs act at the receptor site for acetylcholine that is located on the postganglionic fiber and essentially block ganglionic transmission. Therefore the tissue response will be related to the predominant action of either the sympathetic or parasympathetic division. In the arterioles and veins inhibition of sympathetic tone occurs with vasodilation and a reduction in blood pressure.

The blockade of parasympathetic effects accounts for most of the side effects of the ganglionic blockers. They include tachycardia, xerostomia, and a decreased amount of sweating. Among the most serious adverse effects is postural hypotension that can lead to syncope, and a patient who stands up following a long dental appointment could demonstrate such an effect. Other severe side effects include constipation, urinary retention, and paralytic ileus.

The use of these drugs has greatly diminished with the availability of more effective and less dangerous antihypertensive drugs. Mecamylamine is usually given orally to help support other drugs in hypertensive therapy. Trimethaphan is a rapid-acting agent that is used intravenously for severe hypertensive episodes.[17]

Adrenergic blockers

The most dramatic advance in antihypertensive drug therapy has been in the development of a large variety of drugs that block the action of the sympathetic nervous system by which it controls blood pressure. Since the proposal of specific receptors by Ahlquist,[20] attempts have been made to develop specific adrenergic receptor blocking drugs that directly influence blood pressure control. Indeed, specific drug-receptor interactions have been identified for both central and peripheral portions of the sympathetic nervous system. The CNS-acting agonists, clonidine and methyldopa, have been previously discussed. The emphasis in this section is on the peripheral blockade of specific receptors even though some of the beta adrenergic blockers do enter the CNS.

It is also well accepted that there are two basic receptor types of importance in the peripheral sympathetic nervous system that directly influence cardiovascular activity. One type is the alpha adrenergic receptor located in the vascular smooth muscle of arterioles. There are actually subtypes of alpha receptors termed alpha$_1$ and alpha$_2$. The alpha$_1$ receptors are located on postsynaptic effector tissue and are classically described as producing vasoconstriction, with an increase in peripheral resistance when they are stimulated by norepinephrine. Although alpha$_2$ receptors are located at many sites, they are also preganglionic in location, and stimulation inhibits feedback release of norepinephrine. The feedback mechanism is important in maintaining sympathetic tone; inhibition results in increased release of norepinephrine.

As is the case with alpha receptors, there are also two subtypes of beta adrenergic receptors as well as a preganglionic beta receptor. The subtypes of beta receptors are beta$_1$ and beta$_2$. Beta$_1$ receptors are found in heart tissue, and when they are stimulated, beta$_1$ receptors can increase heart rate, increase cardiac contractility, and accelerate atrioventricular conduction. Beta$_2$ receptors are found in bronchial and vascular smooth muscles. Activation results in bronchodilation in the lungs and vasodilation in skeletal muscle. Stimulation of presynaptic beta receptors causes release of norepinephrine. It is reasonable then to conclude that drugs with receptor blocking action could influence many cardiovascular parameters and be effective in control of hypertension. Even drugs with specific receptor selectivity could be chosen to minimize side effects. Fig. 20-2 is a composite illustration of the different receptor types.[13,21]

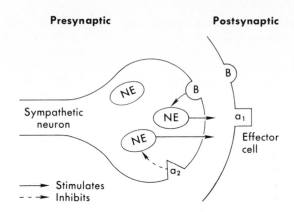

Fig. 20-2. Simplified schematic view of the adrenergic nerve ending showing that norepinephrine *(NE)* is released from its storage granules when the nerve is stimulated and enters the synaptic cleft to bind to alpha$_1$ (α_1) and beta receptors (β) on the effector cell (postsynaptic). In addition, a short feedback loop exists, in which NE binds to alpha$_2$ and beta receptors on the neuron (presynaptic), either to inhibit or to stimulate further release. (From Kaplan, N.M.: Systemic hypertension: therapy. In Braunwald, E., editor: Heart disease: a textbook of cardiovascular medicine, vol. 1, Philadelphia, 1980, W.B. Saunders Co.)

Alpha adrenergic blockers

The most therapeutically useful and beneficial alpha adrenergic receptor blocking drug is also the most recent to be marketed, prazosin (Minipress). It lowers blood pressure through peripheral vasodilation by a blocking action on the alpha$_1$ receptor. It does not have any effect on the alpha$_2$ receptor, which allows the normal feedback for norepinephrine release to remain functional. Thus many of the undesirable effects of alpha blockade, such as reflex tachycardia and renin release, are not seen with prazosin.[22]

Prazosin is indicated in moderate to severe hypertension, but because of fluid retention and increase in plasma volume, it has limited use as a single agent. It is most often combined with a diuretic and a beta-adrenergic receptor blocking agent. One of the major limitations to the use of prazosin is the first-dose phenomenon. Initial doses have been associated with a marked reduction in blood pressure, leading to troublesome postural hypotension. Thus initial doses must be quite low and gradually increased as patient response dictates. The most common adverse effects associated with prazosin use are postural hypotension, angina (when preexisting), and syncope when prazosin is combined with nitroglycerin. Other side effects include dryness of mouth, fluid retention, depression, nausea, and headaches.

The older alpha adrenergic receptor blocking agents phentolamine (Regitine) and phenoxybenzamine (Dibenzyline) block both alpha receptors. As the feedback loop is blocked, more norepinephrine is released, leading to undesirable effects such as increased cardiac output and reflex tachycardia. Because of this reason, the drugs now have limited application in the control of acute hypertensive episodes.[23]

Beta adrenergic blockers

The beta adrenergic receptor blocking drugs have become a vital group of drugs in the management of hypertensive disease, replacing many of the older drugs in the treatment regimen. Presently there are three approved for use: propranolol (Inderal), nadolol (Corgard), and metoprolol (Lopressor). Both propranolol and nadolol are nonselective beta blockers; that is, they block both beta$_1$ and beta$_2$ receptors. Metoprolol is reported to block only beta$_1$ receptors and is termed cardioselective. However, it still carries the caution of careful use in patients with severe bronchospastic disease because higher doses negate receptor selectivity.[24]

The exact mechanism of the antihypertensive effects of the beta adrenergic blockers is still unsettled because these drugs have such a wide range of activity. Among the explanations given for the hypotensive action are (1) a decrease in cardiac output, resulting from a slowing of heart rate and contractility, (2) a lowering of plasma renin levels, (3) an unexplained reduction in plasma volume and venous return, (4) a CNS action, and (5) a reduction in peripheral resistance, perhaps a result of a presynaptic blockade of norepinephrine release. Whatever the reason, these drugs, particularly propranolol, have proven to be effective antihypertensives.[25,26]

The beta adrenergic receptor blocking drugs are useful in all types of hypertensive diseases and can be combined with most of the other antihypertensive drugs. Nadolol has the longest duration of action and can be given on a once-daily basis. Doses for all the drugs need to be carefully adjusted to each patient's needs.

A number of adverse effects have been reported with use of the beta adrenergic blocking drugs. Many of the adverse effects are dose related. They include bradycardia, aggravation of heart failure, paresthesia of the hands, weakness, fatigue, gastrointestinal symptoms, and bronchospasm. Cardioselective agents may cause fewer problems of bronchospastic activity. Beta blockers can mask the signs of hypoglycemia in a patient with diabetes who is taking insulin or oral hypoglycemics. Specific contraindications include bronchial asthma, allergic rhinitis, cardiogenic shock, and MAOI-type drug therapy. Those patients requiring general anesthesia who are also taking propranolol require the expert management of an anesthesiologist since special reflex cardiovascular problems can be encountered. Sudden withdrawal of beta adrenergic blocker therapy is not recommended.[27]

Other antihypertensives

Captopril (Capoten) is the first of the antihypertensive drugs approved for use that can inhibit the renin-angiotensin system. Captopril is an inhibitor of the angiotensin-converting enzyme that catalyzes the reaction of angiotensin I to angiotensin II. Oral administration results in rapid onset. The decrease in blood pressure is associated with a decrease in peripheral resistance. Captopril can be combined with a diuretic or propranolol and is most effective in hypertension associated with high renin activity.

Adverse effects include neutropenia or a granulocytosis that requires careful monitoring in patients with impaired renal function or serious autoimmune disease. Other side effects reported are rash and pruritis, aphthous ulcers, transient loss of taste, and hypotension. Its contribution to antihypertensive therapy remains to be evaluated with more experience.[28-30]

The older group of veratrum alkaloid drugs once used in hypertensive diseases are now seldom employed. They acted mainly on the reflexes to sensitize the baroreceptors to changes in blood pressure. An interesting agent, metyrosine (Demser), which inhibits the enzyme tyrosine hydroxylase, is indicated for use in hypertension associated with pheochromocytoma. Inhibition of tyrosine hydroxylase results in a reduced availability of catecholamines.

Newer forms of drug therapy for the future management of hypertensive diseases will more than likely be directed at the cause rather than the symptomatic reduction of blood pressure. Research in this area includes a wide variety of approaches, such as dopamine agonists, calcium antagonists, and gamma-aminobutyric acid antagonists as well as involvement of the prostaglandins, the peptides with morphinelike activity, and the kinins. The dentist and dental student alike will be faced with a challenge of continual education to keep abreast of these remarkable advances in antihypertensive drug therapy.[31]

REFERENCES

1. Communication Division of the American Heart Association: Heart facts, Dallas, 1980, The Association.
2. Kaplan, N.M.: The hypertensive patient, paper presented at the meeting of the American Dental Association, New Orleans, October 1980.
3. Kaplan, N.M.: The control of hypertension: a therapeutic breakthrough, Am. Sci. **68:**537, 1980.
4. Gross, F.: The present status of the treatment of hypertension, Ration. Drug Ther. **14**(12), 1980.
5. Freis, E.D.: Salt in hypertension and the effects of diuretics, Ann. Rev. Pharmacol. Toxicol. **19:**13, 1979.
6. Marx, J.L.: Hypertension: a complex disease with complex causes, Science **194:**821, 1976.
7. Dollery, C.T.: Pharmacological basis for combination therapy of hypertension, Ann. Rev. Pharmacol. Toxicol. **17:**311, 1977.
8. Guyton, A.C.: Textbook of medical physiology ed. 6, Philadelphia, 1981, W.B. Saunders Co.
9. Goth, A.: Textbook of medical pharmacology, ed. 10, St. Louis, 1981, The C.V. Mosby Co.
10. Gilman, A.G., Goodman, L.S., and Gilman, A.: The pharmacological basis of therapeutics, ed. 6, New York, 1980, MacMillan Publishing Co., Inc.
11. Melmon, K.L., and Morrelli, H.F.: Clinical pharmacology: basic principles in therapeutics, ed. 2, New York, 1978, Macmillan Publishing Co., Inc.
12. Gross, F.: The present status of the treatment of hypertension, Ration. Drug Ther. **14**(12), 1980.
13. Kaplan, N.M.: System hypertension: therapy. In Braunwald, E., editor: Heart disease, vol. 1, Philadelphia, 1980, W.B. Saunders Co.
14. Okun, R.: New medications: 1981, Ann. Rev. Pharmacol. Toxicol. **21:**597, 1981.
15. Cohn, J.N., and Burke, L.P.: Nitroprusside, Ann. Intern. Med. **91:**752, 1979.
16. Thien, T.A., et al.: Diazoxide infusion in severe hypertension and hypertensive crisis, Clin. Pharmacol. Ther. **25:**795, 1979.
17. Frohlich, E.D.: Newer concepts in antihypertensive drugs. Prog. Cardiovasc. Dis. **20:**385, 1978.
18. Pettinger, W.A.: Pharmacology of Clonidine, J. Cardiovasc. Pharmacol. **2**(suppl. 1):821, 1980.
19. Houston, M.C.: Clonidine hydrochloride: review of pharmacologic and clinical aspects, Prog. Cardiovasc. Dis. **23:**337, 1981.
20. Ahlquist, R.P.: A study of adrenotropic receptors, Am. J. Physiol. **153:**586, 1948.
21. Frishman, W.: Clinical pharmacology of the new beta-adrenergic blocking drugs. Part 1. Pharmacodynamic and pharmacokinetic properties, Am. Heart J. **97:**663, 1979.
22. Davey, M.J.: Relevant features of the pharmacology of prazosin, J. Cardiovasc. Pharmacol. **2**(Suppl. 3):S287, 1980.
23. Graham, R.M., and Pettinger, W.A.: Drug therapy: prazosin, N. Engl. J. Med. **300:**232, 1979.
24. Scriabine, A.: β-Adrenoceptor blocking drugs in hypertension, Ann. Rev. Pharmacol. Toxicol. **19:**269, 1979.
25. Frishman, W., and Silverman, R.: Clinical pharmacology of the new beta-adrenergic blocking drugs. Part 2. Physiologic and metabolic effects, Am. Heart J. **97:**797, 1979.
26. Frishman, W.: Clinical pharmacology of the new beta-adrenergic blocking drugs. Part 9. Nadolol: a new long acting beta adrenoceptor blocking drug, Am. Heart. J. **99:**124, 1980.
27. Davies, R.O., and McMahon, F.G.: The present status of beta blockers in clinical medicine, Ration. Drug Ther. **14**(2), 1980.
28. Hollenberg, N.K.: Pharmacologic interruption of the renin-angiotensin system, Ann. Rev. Pharmacol. Toxicol. **19:**559, 1979.
29. Ferguson, R.K., and Vlasses, P.H.: Clinical pharmacology and therapeutic applications of the new oral angiotensin converting enzyme inhibitor, captopril. Am. Heart J. **101:**650, 1981.
30. Captopril approved for hypertension, F.D.A. Drug Bull. **11** (2), 1981.
31. Graham, R.M., and Campbell, W.B.: Speculative approaches in hypertension: concepts and drugs of the future. Fed. Proc. **40:**2291, 1981.

Other cardiovascular drugs

Cardiovascular disease is an inclusive term referring to a variety of diseases of the heart and blood vessels. These diseases include, among others, hypertension (high blood pressure), atherosclerosis, heart muscle disease, stroke, and congestive heart failure. Cardiovascular disease is the leading cause of death in the United States. It is estimated that as many as 40 million Americans have cardiovascular disease, and some 4 million experience angina or heart attack each year. With the development of cardiac care units, comprehensive drug therapy, and intensive screening for cardiovascular diseases, many patients are now living longer, more productive lives. Indeed, the use of surgical techniques for the correction of valvular defects and replacement of diseased coronary arteries has expanded greatly. These factors help to explain why cardiovascular disease affects such a large segment of the dental patient population.[1]

The numbers and varieties of drugs employed in the management of cardiovascular disease have expanded dramatically. In addition, most cardiovascular disease patients must continue to take selected combinations of these drugs throughout their lifetime. Many of these drugs have complex pharmacologic actions that can influence the treatment plan for the dental patient. Therefore a basic knowledge of the various drugs employed in cardiovascular therapy should provide dentists with more confidence in the skillful management of these patients and enable them to avoid potential drug interactions.

The cardiovascular drugs discussed in this chapter will include the cardiac glycoside, antiarrhythmic, antianginal, anticoagulant, and antihyperlipidemic agents. The antihypertensive drugs and diuretics are presented in Chapter 20.

CARDIAC GLYCOSIDES
Review of congestive heart failure

The function of the heart is to act as a pump to ensure an adequate circulation of blood to meet the oxygen and nutrient requirements of all body tissues. Circulation needs are variable, such as that dictated by exercise, and the heart must have enough myocardial reserve to meet this demand. Part of the myocardial reserve can be explained by the automatic neurohumoral and intrinsic mechanisms that result in an increased rate and contractility. The heart adjusts its cardiac output in relationship to the end diastolic volume. Increased ventricular filling lengthens and increases the tension of the cardiac muscle, thereby increasing the force of contraction (Starling's law) within physiologic limits. In a normal heart all of these compensatory mechanisms work together to ensure an adequate cardiac output and circulation.

The failing heart is characterized by an inefficient pumping mechanism with an inadequate cardiac output, resulting in a less than satisfactory circulation. Normal compensatory mechanisms usually involved in exercise must function even during reduced stress, and as a result the failing heart is compromised. A number of different forms of injury to the heart, that is, rheumatic heart disease, myocardial lesions, or arrhythmias, may contribute to heart failure. If heart failure is accompanied by an increased left ventricular filling pressure, increased hydrostatic pressure in the pulmonary capillaries can lead to pulmonary edema and congestion. If the failure occurs on the right side of the heart, systemic congestion occurs with edema in the extremities. Other organ systems such as the liver and kidney will respond to the reduced circulation in an adverse manner, further complicating the disorder. Both right and left ventricular failure may occur in the same patient. Patients with chronic congestive heart failure manifest symptoms of shortness of breath, an enlarged heart, and edema. Pulmonary congestion may require that the patient sleep on stacked pillows to ensure comfortable breathing. Congestive heart failure is the result of the failure of the myocardium to function as a pump and maintain an adequate circulation.[2]

Digitalis

The most important group of drugs in the treatment of congestive heart failure were first described by William Withering in 1785 and are called the cardiac or digitalis glycosides. The term *glycoside* is given to this group of drugs because the active molecular portion (the aglycone) is connected by a glycosidic linkage to a series of one to four sugar molecules. The aglycone portion of the molecule consists of a steroid structure with an attached lactone ring.

All of the glycosides have the same fundamental action on the heart. The sugar moiety is important in determining water solubility, which in turn accounts for the differences in potency, route of administration, onset and duration of action, and rate of excretion of the various glycosides. All of the medically useful glycosides are of botanical origin, coming from *Digitalis purpurea, D. lanata,* and *Strophanthus gratus,* the source of ouabain.

A large number of cardiac glycosides are available for clinical use. The two most widely prescribed are digitoxin (Crystodigin, Purodigin) and digoxin (Lanoxin). Powdered or whole digitalis leaf preparations (Digifortis, Pil-Digis) are not used as extensively as they once were. Other glycosides available but encountered less frequently include gitalin (Gitaligin), ouabain, lanatoside C (Cedilanid), and deslanoside (Cedilanid-D). Differences among the more important cardiac glycosides are shown in Table 21-1. The antiarrhythmic use of the glycosides is discussed later in this chapter.[3]

Pharmacologic effects. The principal effect of the cardiac glycosides on the failing heart is to increase the force of contraction of the myocardium, which is termed the *positive inotropic effect.* The improvement in contractile force makes the heart more efficient as a pump, increasing the stroke volume and cardiac output. As a result of this improved pumping action, other compensatory changes occur, such as a reduction in heart size with a decrease in heart rate and

venous pressure. All of these events occur provided there is still sufficient cardiac reserve present and cardiac function is not severely impaired. The action of digitalis is directly on the heart cell except for the decrease in rate, which is accounted for by an indirect vagal slowing. It should be pointed out that the positive inotropic effects of digitalis are seldom observed in a heart in which myocardial cell damage is the cause of failure.

In addition to the inotropic effect of digitalis on the myocardium, there are effects on the electrophysiologic properties of the heart that are dose dependent. These dose-dependent events are most significant when toxicity to digitalis occurs. Low doses of digitalis increase cardiac excitability, and high doses decrease excitability. Changes in conduction velocity are variable depending on the specific heart tissue, but some increase in conduction velocity is observed in the atria, with a decrease in the A-V nodal tissues. There is an increase in automaticity of the ventricles (chronotropic effect) and in ectopic pacemaker activity. This latter event becomes more evident with toxic doses.

Another effect of digitalis is the reduction in edema that occurs with its use. The diuresis that occurs is largely the result of an improved circulation and a decrease in venous pressure, causing an improved glomerular filtration rate. The net result is a more efficient kidney function that reduces the edematous fluid accumulation.[4]

Mechanism of action. The mechanism of action of the inotropic effect of digitalis is related to a complex interaction of the cell membrane pump regulating the distribution of Na^+ and K^+ ions across the cell membrane and the availability of Ca^{++} to trigger the excitation-contraction coupling mechanism. Cardiac glycosides have been shown to inhibit the Na^+,K^+-ATPase enzyme responsible for the energy-dependent transport of Na^+ and K^+ across the myocardial cell membrane. The reduced activity of the Na^+ pump results in an increase in intracellular Na^+ near the sarcolemma. This increase is believed to result in an increased availability of Ca^{++} through an interchange with the excess Na^+. The increase in available Ca^{++} enhances the contractile mechanism.[5]

Absorption, metabolism, and doses. The route of administration of the cardiac glycosides is usually determined by the urgency of the clinical situation. Since patients normally take digitalis on a lifetime basis, the oral route is preferred for the convenience

Table 21-1. Differences among more commonly used cardiac glycosides*

Preparation	Source	Routes	Oral onset	Duration	Oral maintenance dose per 24 hours
Digitalis leaf	*D. purpurea*	Oral	Slow	Long	100-200 mg
Digitoxin	*D. purpurea*	Oral, IV	Slow	Long	0.05-0.3 mg
Digoxin	*D. lanata*	Oral, IV	Fast	Medium	0.125-0.5 mg
Acetyldigitoxin	*D. lanata*	Oral	Medium	Medium	0.1-0.2 mg
Deslanoside	*D. lanata*	IV	IV only	Medium	
Ouabain	*Strophanthus gratus*	IV	IV only	Short	

Data modified from Dr. D.T. Watts, Richmond, Va.
*The previously mentioned glycosides gitalin and lanatoside C are not listed because they are infrequently used.

of self-administration. With the exception of ouabain, most of the cardiac glycosides are well absorbed when given orally. Digitoxin is the most efficiently absorbed, followed by digoxin. The whole leaf glycoside preparations are not as well absorbed, but they are sufficiently absorbed to be useful. With earlier commercial preparations, the bioavailability of marketed digoxin products presented some problems in therapy. A more recently implemented digoxin certification program has largely remedied this problem and at the same time modified older dosage schedules.[6]

A number of cardiac glycoside preparations are available for parenteral use. Pain and irritation on injection limit the intramuscular and subcutaneous routes of administration. The preferred but also the most critical route is intravenous. Both ouabain and digoxin are suitable for producing rapid plasma levels required for demanding clinical situations. After stabilization with parenteral doses, the patient can be switched to the oral route for more convenience in maintenance.

Digitoxin has the longest duration of action with the slowest onset. This may be accounted for by its high plasma protein binding affinity and its slower metabolism by the liver. Digoxin is not bound to plasma protein in as high a quantity and is excreted by the kidney largely unmetabolized. The presence of liver or kidney disease can influence the duration of action of these glycosides. A potent liver enzyme inducer such as phenobarbital could also alter the effects of digitoxin by speeding its metabolism.

The establishment of a dose of digitalis sufficient to provide symptomatic relief of congestive heart failure must be based on the individual patient's needs. Two basic means of providing adequate plasma levels

of the cardiac glycosides are employed. The classic dosage technique requires that an initial loading or digitalizing dose be started first. This initial dose is several times the maintenance dose and is necessary because of the slow tissue accumulation of the glycoside. Once the effective plasma level is established, daily maintenance doses can then be started based on the rate of elimination of the glycoside. Doses are just sufficient to replace the daily loss since the effects of repeated doses are cumulative.

Another dosage technique can be used provided the clinical situation is favorable. The patient is hospitalized, and the maintenance dose only is administered over several days until the cumulative drug effects are evident. This method is slower in establishing therapeutic levels but may avoid some of the toxic reactions associated with digitalization. These dosage techniques are suitable for patients who have not been taking digitalis. If the patient is taking digitalis and requires an additional amount of glycoside, careful use of smaller doses is required.[7]

Adverse effects. Dosage adjustment of the digitalis glycosides can be a problem because the margin of safety is low. Even slight changes in dosage, alterations in metabolism, or changes in rate of absorption can be sufficient to trigger toxic symptoms. These symptoms are similar for all the glycosides and are more evident in the long-term user. The signs of early toxicity to digitalis could be easily detected by the alert dental practitioner, and they would include anorexia (loss of appetite) and nausea and vomiting; copious salivation may also be evident. The importance of recognizing early toxicity is more fully appreciated when one realizes that a reduction in dosage is sufficient to reduce the toxicity. More serious cardiac irregularities develop with continued doses or with a too rapid initial loading. These reactions include arrhythmias that can progress to ventricular fibrillation. Neurologic signs of toxicity include headache, drowsiness, and visual disturbances. At least one neurologic sign of some significance to the dentist is pain in the lower face that resembles somewhat the pain associated with trigeminal neuralgia.

In the chronic heart failure patient, digitalis therapy is often combined with a diuretic, low-sodium diet, and limited exercise. Diuretics can produce hypokalemia, making the myocardium more sensitive to the toxic effects of digitalis. Weakness, faintness, and xerostomia may be observed in the patient. If liver damage results from a chronic congestive failure, drug metabolism may be reduced along with interference in normal coagulation processes.[8]

Drug interactions

The cardiac glycosides are commonly encountered drugs, and therefore drug interactions are likely. The effects of hypokalemia caused by diuretics have already been discussed. Amphotericin B may also lower potassium levels and could be a potential hazard. Other drugs employed by the dentist that are possible interactants include the barbiturates, which increase the metabolic activity of liver enzymes and increase the rate of digitoxin conversion to digoxin. The importance of this interaction seems to be minimal. Propantheline (Pro-Banthine), an anticholinergic agent occasionally employed to reduce salivary flow, may increase digoxin absorption in those patients taking slow-release digoxin preparations. Other drugs that can interfere with absorption of digitalis preparations include neomycin, kaolin-pectin, cholestyramine, and the nonabsorbable antacids. Also, when sympathomimetic drugs that cause beta adrenergic activity are used with digitalis, additive effects may result, including ectopic pacemaker activity.[9]

Chronic heart failure. Digitalis in combination with a low-sodium diet and rest is probably the most effective regimen in controlling congestive heart failure. However, chronic congestive heart failure generally requires the addition of vasodilator drugs to reduce the accompanying increase in peripheral resistance. These vasodilators include most of those employed in hypertension, such as direct-acting vasodilators and the nitrates used in angina pectoris therapy. Diuretics are also employed in acute congestive heart failure. More critical situations of failure may develop, requiring the use of other positive inotropic drugs

such as dopamine (Intropin) or the potent intravenously administered vasodilator sodium nitroprusside (Nipride).[10]

ANTIARRHYTHMIC AGENTS
Review of cardiac physiology

The function of the heart is dependent on rhythmic contractions of the cardiac muscle. The stimulus for contraction originates in specialized excitatory and conductive fibers that are a part of the cardiac muscle. The more rapid spontaneously depolarizing cells are found in the S-A node, or pacemaker, and have an inherent automaticity for depolarization. The wave of depolarization generated by the S-A node depolarizes the adjacent conductive tissues of the atrium, the A-V node, and finally the ventricular conducting fibers. Repolarization of these cardiac fibers to establish the resting membrane potential is associated with a period of refractoriness and additional depolarization. At the end of the refractory period, the cycle again repeats at a specified pacemaker rate.

The rate of cardiac contraction (beats per minute) is subject to regulation by the autonomic nervous system in response to demands by the organism. Vagal nerve (parasympathetic) stimulation causes a decrease in the S-A nodal rate and a decrease in A-V node excitability. This results in a slowing of the cardiac rate, and vigorous vagal stimulation can cause complete stoppage of the heart. The cardiac accelerator nerves (sympathetic) have the opposite effect; they increase S-A nodal rhythm and thereby increase the number of beats per minute.

Normal cardiac rhythm may be altered by disease or cardiac injury. The altered patterns of rhythm are referred to as cardiac arrhythmias. The causes of arrhythmias are related to many factors, such as the development of an ectopic pacemaker, blockage or alterations in the impulse-conducting systems, and abnormal pacemaker rhythms.[11] The types of cardiac arrhythmias are shown in Table 21-2.[12]

Drugs in current use

Quinidine. Quinidine, the dextroisomer of quinine, is one of the oldest and most commonly employed drugs in the treatment of cardiac arrhythmias. Quinidine is an alkaloid obtained from cinchona bark with pharmacologic actions similar to those of quinine. Its various salts are marketed as Quinaglute, Cardioquin, Quinidex, Quinora, and generic products. Its myocardial depressant action accounts for its

Table 21-2. Types of cardiac arrhythmias

Sinus bradycardia (less than 60 beats /min)	If uncomplicated by other disease, it may not be a problem; syncope may be common
Sinus tachycardia (more than 100 beats/min)	Gradual onset, if prolonged may be from cardiac disease and lead to cardiac failure
Sinus arrhythmia	Alternate changes in rate related to vagal tone
Wandering pacemaker	From shifting of pacemaker from S-A node to atria to A-V node; may be related to vagal tone
Premature contractions (impulses from any part of the heart evoking a beat)	May be from cardiac disease or drugs; importance and treatment depends on cause
Paroxysmal tachycardia (sudden rate increase because of ectopic pacemaker)	May be atrial, nodal, or ventricular; palpitations and heart failure may be observed; angina-like pain
Atrial flutter (rapid—200 to 300 beats/min)	Incomplete ventricular filling, ectopic atrial focus; syncope and weakness
Atrial fibrillation (rapid, irregular depolarization, 300 to 500 beats/min)	Decreased cardiac reserve; palpitations and thromboembolism
Ventricular fibrillation (rapid, uncoordinated beats, no pumping action)	Requires heroic defibrillatory treatment; sudden death
Pulse alternans (alterations in arterial pulse, small then large)	Requires diagnosis of various types of cardiac diseases

principal medical usefulness. Quinidine has both a direct and an indirect action on the heart. Its direct actions are characterized by a decrease in excitability, conduction velocity, and automaticity. The refractory period is increased, hence its ability to slow increased rates of cardiac rhythm. The indirect effects of quinidine are best described as atropine-like in that vagal influence on the myocardium is reduced. For quinidine to function as an effective antiarrhythmic agent, the clinician must adjust the dose so that the indirect effects do not complicate the cardiac condition.

Usual oral doses may cause nausea and vomiting. Hypersensitivity reactions occur rarely, the most serious being thrombocytopenia purpura, with a single case of oral hemorrhage reported.[13] Large doses of quinidine cause tinnitus, impaired hearing, and headache characterized as cinchonism. Intravenous or intramuscular doses can produce arterial hypotension and are seldom used. A paradoxical ventricular tachycardia can occur during the treatment of atrial flutter and fibrillation presumably as a result of its indirect action on A-V conduction. Specific contraindications to its use include complete A-V block and in cases of known hypersensitivity.[13]

Quinidine is used for the treatment and prevention of supraventricular tachyarrhythmias, ventricular tachycardia, and premature systoles. Quinidine sulfate is the preferred oral dosage form, and quinidine gluconate is used for intravenous injections. Drug in-

teractions with quinidine are more of a concern for the physician than the dentist. Other antiarrhythmics may show additive effects, and serum levels of digoxin are elevated with concurrent use. Anticoagulants and neuromuscular blocking agents are reported to show enhanced effects. Barbiturates and phenytoin use may reduce serum quinidine levels.

Procainamide. Procainamide is a derivative of the local anesthetic procaine, having an amide group instead of the ester linkage. It is marketed as procainamide hydrochloride (Pronestyl Hydrochloride). The response of cardiac muscle to procainamide is similar to that of quinidine. It can be used for the same types of arrhythmias as quinidine and serves as a valuable agent that can be given during emergencies associated with ventricular arrhythmias. Like quinidine it is effective when given orally or intravenously. Intravenous doses must be given slowly to avoid toxic reactions such as alarming increases in ventricular rate and central nervous system reactions of convulsions and hyperexcitability. Deaths have been reported with improper use. Oral doses may provoke nausea and vomiting, and hypersensitivity reactions may be observed. Long-term therapy is associated with a lupus erythematosus–like reaction. Procainamide is contraindicated in patients with complete or incomplete A-V nodal block.

Disopyramide. Disopyramide phosphate (Norpace) was introduced in 1978 for the treatment of ventricular arrhythmias. Its pharmacologic effects on the myocardium are similar to quinidine and procainamide. It has prominent anticholinergic activity, which may account for the side effects of dry mouth, blurred vision, constipation, and urinary retention. Other side effects include nausea, vomiting, and hypotension. The drug is presently approved for oral use only.[14]

Lidocaine. Lidocaine hydrochloride is a local anesthetic that is useful in the treatment of ventricular premature beats and tachycardia. It finds its greatest use in those patients recovering from cardiac surgery or myocardial infarctions. Its principal advantage is its short duration of action and, reportedly, a reduction in the amount of hypotension occurring with other antiarrhythmic drugs. It is given intravenously in a single dose of 1 mg/kg up to 100 mg. The patient is then maintained with infusions of 1 to 4 mg/min as required. Toxic reactions ranging from drowsiness and dizziness to convulsions can occur. Lidocaine hydrochloride solutions used to treat arrhythmias should not be confused with the dental anesthetic solution, since these preparations contain no epinephrine and are buffered differently.

Phenytoin. Phenytoin (Dilantin) is a commonly used antiepileptic agent that has been studied in recent years as a possible antiarrhythmic agent. It works best in arrhythmias associated with the ventricles and particularly if the arrhythmia is induced by digitalis. This drug has an action unlike that of quinidine and procainamide. Its action resembles that of lidocaine because it does not depress excitability or improve A-V conduction but does depress automaticity. Apparently, phenytoin exerts little effect on atrial arrhythmias, with the exception of paroxysmal atrial tachycardia associated with digitalis intoxication. Many clinicians believe that more studies are required before an adequate conclusion can be reached regarding its overall effectiveness. Toxic reactions associated with rapid intravenous injection of large doses of phenytoin include bradycardia, A-V nodal block, and ventricular standstill.[15]

Digitalis. The digitalis drugs, or cardiac glycosides as they are also known, are probably among the oldest of all drugs used in the treatment of cardiac disease. Although their principal use is related to the restoration of the failing heart in congestive heart disease, they are also employed in the treatment of supraventricular arrhythmias. Digitalis drugs reduce the automaticity of the atria and slow conduction through the A-V bundle, thereby reducing ventricular rate. Digitalis slows atrial flutter and fibrillation and terminates paroxysmal atrial tachycardia; however, the other antiarrhythmic agents quinidine, procainamide, and lidocaine must be used in combination with digitalis to produce the desired sinus rhythm. Dosages of digitalis for patients are based on individual requirements. There are numerous commercial forms of digitalis available, all of which have the same basic action on the myocardium.[16]

Propranolol. The beta adrenergic blocking agent propranolol hydrochloride (Inderal) is employed widely in a variety of cardiovascular diseases, including the control of catecholamine-induced arrhythmias. Its primary action is blocking the response of the $beta_1$ cardiac receptor to catecholamine action. Propranolol decreases automaticity of the myocardium and increases the refractory period. Current indications for use include digitalis-induced arrhythmias, paroxysmal atrial tachycardia, and anesthetic-induced arrhythmias.

Side effects occurring with the use of propranolol include bradycardia, a decreased cardiac output, slow conduction that can lead to congestive heart failure, bronchospasm, sleep disturbances, and diarrhea. Withdrawal of propranolol should be gradual and predetermined. Other beta blocking agents have not yet been approved for use in arrhythmias even though some are used experimentally.[17]

Verapamil. The most recent drug approved for use in cardiac arrhythmia therapy is the Ca^{++} channel blocking agent verapamil (Isoptin, Calan). Since Ca^{++} is such an important ion in the overall excitation-contraction coupling mechanism, an agent that reduces available Ca^{++} should be effective in arrhythmias. Verapamil appears to slow the S-A nodal discharge and A-V nodal conduction. Its principal indication for use is supraventricular arrhythmias. Adverse effects include prolonged hypotension, bradycardia, and A-V nodal block.[18]

Bretylium. Bretylium tosylate (Bretylol) has now been approved for use as an antiarrhythmic agent in severe refractory ventricular arrhythmias. It is used only after other antiarrhythmic therapy has failed. Bretylium has a direct effect on the myocardial cell membrane, but its principal action is the prevention of release of norepinephrine from sympathetic neurons. The drug is administered only by the parenteral route because oral doses are poorly absorbed. Adverse effects include a reduction in blood pressure, bradycardia, nausea, and vomiting. Sweating, nasal stuffiness, and diarrhea may also occur.[19]

Other antiarrhythmic agents. There are a number of other drugs that are used in treating cardiac arrhythmias. Their action is discussed briefly here, since their basic pharmacology and uses have been described in more detail in other chapters of this book.

Epinephrine and isoproterenol hydrochloride (Isuprel) are direct cardiac stimulants that increase automaticity and the force of contraction. Epinephrine can induce ventricular arrhythmias and angina pectoris when it is employed in the wrong cardiac disease. Isoproterenol is the drug of choice in complete heart block because it functions as a direct beta stimulant to the myocardium.

Anticholinergic drugs such as atropine are used to treat slow cardiac rates when ventricular pumping is so diminished as to cause serious hemodynamic changes. The action of atropine is that of reducing or blocking vagal slowing of the heart.[19]

A summary of the basic effects of the antiarrhythmic agents is given in Table 21-3.

ANTIANGINAL DRUGS

Angina pectoris is a common cardiovascular disease affecting a large segment of the population. It is characterized by pain or discomfort in the chest that frequently radiates to the left arm and shoulder. Pain may also be reported in the neck, back, and lower jaw. Lower jaw pain can be of such an intensity that it may be confused with a toothache. The cause of angina is related to a failure of the coronary arteries to supply a sufficient amount of oxygen to the myocardium on demand. It is easy to see why anginal pain can be precipitated by the stress induced by physical exercise. Emotional states that trigger cate-

cholamine release, such as the anxiety and stress of a dental appointment, could also provoke episodes of angina in certain patients. Coronary atherosclerosis is associated with angina and, if sufficiently severe, may dictate coronary artery surgical bypass rather than drug therapy. The basic effects of drugs in relieving the pain of angina are based on the use of vasodilators to improve coronary blood flow and agents that reduce the work load on the myocardium, thereby lowering the oxygen requirements of the myocardium. The drugs normally employed for angina therapy are classified as either vasodilators or beta adrenergic blocking drugs.

Vasodilators
  Nitrites
    Amyl nitrite
  Nitrates
    Nitroglycerin
    Nitroglycerin, topical (Nitro-Bid, Nitrol Ointment)
    Isosorbide dinitrate (Isordil, Isogard)
    Erythrityl tetranitrate (Cardilate)
    Pentaerythritol tetranitrate (Peritrate, Duotrate-45)
  Nonnitrate vasodilator
    Dipyridamole (Persantine)
Beta adrenergic blocking drugs
  Propranolol HCl (Inderal)
  Nadolol (Corgard)

Vasodilators
Nitrites and nitrates

The nitrites and nitrates are really different chemical classes of drugs, but because of basic pharmacologic effects, they can be discussed collectively. Often there is no distinction made between these terms. These drugs relax vascular smooth muscle with varia-

Table 21-3. Summary of the effects of antiarrhythmic drugs on the myocardium

Antiarrhythmic drug	Automaticity		Conduction velocity	Refractory period
	Atrium	Ventricle		
Quinidine	Decrease	Decrease	Decrease	Increase
Procainamide	Decrease	Decrease	Decrease	Increase
Lidocaine	No effect	Decrease	No effect	Decrease
Phenytoin	Decrease	Decrease	Increase	Decrease
Propranolol	Decrease	Decrease	Decrease	Increase
Digitalis	Decrease	Slight increase	Decrease	Atrium—increase; ventricle—decrease

tions in time of onset, potency, and duration of action. At one time these drugs were termed *coronary artery vasodilators,* and this was their presumed mechanism in the relief of angina. It is now recognized that they relax vascular smooth muscle throughout the body, reducing the work load (resistance) against which the heart has to pump. This would reduce the metabolic oxygen demand of the myocardium and hence bring about relief of pain.

Because these drugs produce vascular relaxation, hypotension and fainting are common side effects. Headache is also reported, and tolerance develops with long-term use of these drugs.

Amyl nitrite. Amyl nitrite is a highly volatile substance administered by inhalation only. It is the most rapidly acting of the antianginal drugs, producing effects in a few seconds. Its duration of action is only 3 to 5 minutes. It has no real advantages over nitroglycerin, and the odor is objectionable, especially in the closed atmosphere of a dental operatory. Because amyl nitrite is administered by inhalation, dosage regulation is variable and will affect the attending personnel as well as the patient. As a result, hypotension with fainting and headache is not uncommon. Amyl nitrite is packaged in thin glass ampules wrapped in gauze so that they may be easily and safely crushed with finger pressure.

Nitroglycerin (glyceryl trinitrate). Nitroglycerin is the most commonly employed drug and perhaps the drug of choice in angina therapy. It is administered sublingually and has a rapid onset of action. Its effects can last up to 30 minutes. An ointment form of nitroglycerin is also available for use, and when applied to the skin, it is absorbed for a therapeutic effect. Nitroglycerin is usually given in doses that range from 0.15 to 0.6 mg. Although this is a useful drug to have in the dental emergency drug locker, most dentists will probably find that angina patients keep nitroglycerin readily available for use. Failure of the patient to respond to 2 or 3 tablets of nitroglycerin within a few minutes indicates the need for emergency medical attention.[20]

Other nitrates. The other nitrates, isosorbide dinitrate and erythrityl tetranitrate, can also be given both orally and sublingually but are usually slower in their onset of action when compared with nitroglycerin. Pentaerythritol tetranitrate is a longer-acting nitrate that has been promoted for the prophylactic prevention of anginal attacks. There is little evidence that this drug or other similar long-acting nitrites are really effective in the prophylactic prevention of angina attacks. All of the nitrates are available under numerous trade names; only those more commonly known have been listed.

Nonnitrate vasodilator

Dipyridamole. Dipyridamole (Persantine) is an antianginal agent indicated for long-term prophylaxis. Although it has little effect on peripheral vessels, it improves coronary flow by dilation of the small resistance vessels of the coronary bed. At least part of the action of this drug is related to an accumulation of adenosine by inhibiting its uptake by other tissues. Adverse effects include dizziness, syncope, headache, and nausea.[21]

A large number of other types of drugs have been used at one time or another to treat angina or improve peripheral blood flow in atherosclerotic disease. The agents have included nicotinic acid, ethyl alcohol, the xanthines, and papaverine. Their efficacy still remains to be established.

Beta adrenergic blocking drugs

Two beta adrenergic blocking drugs are utilized in the management of angina but not the variant-type angina. These agents are propranolol (Inderal) and the longer-acting nadolol (Corgard). The action of these agents is related to the blockade of beta receptor response to catecholamines, thereby reducing the chronotropic and inotropic effects. This in turn would reduce the myocardial oxygen demand. The beta blocking agents are effective in exercise-induced angina and reduce the daily requirement for nitroglycerin. Nadolol is usually given in a once-a-day dose. The adverse effects of the beta adrenergic blockers include bradycardia, congestive heart failure, headache, dry mouth, blurred vision, and hallucinations.

ANTICOAGULANTS
Review of the clotting mechanism

Hemostasis is a defense mechanism designed to prevent the loss of blood from injury to a blood vessel. The leaking vessel is plugged by a complicated process of clot formation. The clotting mechanism is initiated when vascular injury releases a special tissue component known as thromboplastin. Thromboplastin in combination with factors V, VII, and X and calcium ions form the extrinsic prothrombin activator. The prothrombin activator is necessary for the conversion of prothrombin to thrombin. In turn, the action of thrombin on fibrinogen produces fibrin. Fibrin along with vascular spasm, platelets, and red blood cells form the final clot rapidly.

As long as the blood vessel remains smooth and intact, circulating blood will not clot. However, should internal injury to the vessel occur and a roughened surface develop, intravascular clotting will also occur. This process involves an intrinsic prothrombin activator consisting of a platelet factor, factors V and VIII through XII, and calcium ions. Once again the prothrombin activator is necessary for the conversion of prothrombin to thrombin. Thrombin enzymatically converts fibrinogen to fibrin, and thus there is clot formation. Intravascular clotting is a slower process, requiring several minutes for a clot to develop.

Many of the factors required in the clotting process are protein in nature and synthesized by normal metabolic processes. It is important to point out that factors VIII, IX, and X and prothrombin require vitamin K for synthesis in the liver. Therefore one of the mechanisms of anticoagulant drug action involves interference with vitamin K activity. The preceding clotting processes have been greatly simplified.[22]

Usefulness of anticoagulants

Although the clotting processes just mentioned appear simple, the exact mechanism of intravascular clotting still remains a difficult problem area. Suffice it to say, however, that intravascular clots do occur because of vascular diseases or changes in the blood. These clots, or thrombi, tend to break loose, forming emboli that can lodge in smaller vessels to the major organs such as the heart, brain, or lungs, thereby producing severe and fatal thromboembolic diseases. Anticoagulant therapy provides a way in which the incidence of intravascular clotting may be reduced and prevent life-threatening situations. However, one must keep in mind that anticoagulant therapy has to be adjusted to suit each patient's need. Constant supervision of the patient is required while the correct dosage and regimen for each situation are established. If the dose of anticoagulant is too large, hemorrhage may occur, or if the dose is too small, the danger of the embolism remains.

Drugs in current use

Heparin. Heparin is one of the most commonly employed anticoagulant agents. It is a sulfurated mucopolysaccharide consisting of glucosamine and glucuronic acid units in alternate linkages. Heparin acts as an antithromboplastin, preventing the enzymatic conversion of prothrombin to thrombin. It is given intravenously or subcutaneously and has a brief but rapid duration of action. Because it can be administered intravenously, it can have an immediate effect on clot formation. Since it cannot be used orally, its use is limited to hospital situations, and it is relatively expensive.

Adverse effects are associated with overdosage, leading to internal hemorrhage, and an occasional hypersensitivity reaction. Long-term use of heparin (6 months or longer) has caused osteoporosis. Overdosage of heparin can be effectively antagonized by protamine sulfate. Commercial heparin is obtained from beef and pork sources.

Coumarins. The coumarins are a group of chemically related drugs having a common mechanism of action; they are also referred to as the oral anticoagulants. In contrast to heparin, these agents are commonly given by the oral route, but because of absorption irregularities, dosage adjustment is complicated. These agents act as vitamin K antimetabolites, thereby interfering with the synthesis of factors VII, IX, and X and prothrombin. There is a delay in onset of action of coumarin until the usual plasma stores of these clotting agents are depleted. These agents are generally employed in long-term therapy because they are less expensive and more convenient to use than heparin.

Adverse effects with these agents are mostly related to overdosage and hemorrhage. Hemorrhage associated with overdose is managed by administering whole blood or vitamin K. Contraindications to the use of the coumarins would include any underlying disorder in which hemorrhage could result. Patient compliance and regular laboratory testing for anticoagulant effects are necessary to avoid serious problems.

A more important consideration is the potential drug-drug interactions that may either increase or decrease the effects of the oral anticoagulants. Although many drugs may interact with these agents, only a few are of major concern for the dentist. Drugs that can enhance the effects of the oral anticoagulants include the tetracyclines, salicylates, indomethacin, phenylbutazone, carbamazepine, and chloral hydrate. A potential for an enhanced effect exists with the newer nonsteroidal antiinflammatory analgesics, but evidence has yet to establish this fact. Phenobarbital, corticosteroids, ethchlorvynol, and glutethimide will decrease the effect of the coumarin anticoagulants. Because so many different drugs are potential interactants, it is advisable to double-check before prescribing for patients taking anticoagulants.[23]

The following is a list of the most commonly used, coumarin-like anticoagulants.

Bishydroxycoumarin (dicumarol)
Warfarin (Coumadin, Panwarfin)
Phenprocoumon (Liquamar)
Acenocoumarol (Sintrom)

Indandiones. The indandiones are a group of oral anticoagulants with an action similar to that of the coumarins. Medical use of the indandiones becomes a matter of judgment on the part of the physician as well as a consideration of side effects. Some of the indandione derivatives available for clinical use include phenindione (Danilone) and anisindione (Miradon).[24]

DRUGS FOR HYPERLIPIDEMIA

Drugs have been recommended for control of hyperlipidemia, one of the risk factors related to atherosclerosis. Therapy is directed toward lowering levels of cholesterol and other plasma lipids in those patients who have not responded to diet and are still at risk for the complications of atherosclerosis. It is advised that before any of these drugs are used, a definitive diagnosis as to the type of hyperlipidemia should be made. The long-term benefits of this type of therapy have not yet been established.[25]

Examples of lipid-lowering drugs include the bile-acid binding resins cholestyramine (Questran) and colestipol (Colestid). These drugs lower cholesterol but produce a variety of gastrointestinal problems. They may also interfere with absorption of some drugs. Clofibrate (Atromid-S) lowers triglyceride and cholesterol levels through a mechanism that involves inhibition of cholesterol synthesis. Other agents used include probucol (Lorelco), nicotinic acid, neomycin, sitosterols (Cytellin), and dextrothyroxine (Choloxin).[26]

REFERENCES

1. The American Heart Association: Heart facts, Dallas, 1981, The American Heart Association Communication Division.
2. Silber, E.N., and Katz, L.N.: Heart disease, New York, 1975, Macmillan Publishing Co., Inc.
3. Wilson, C.O., Gisvold, O., and Doerge, R.F.: Textbook of or-ganic medicinal and pharmaceutical chemistry, Philadelphia, 1977, J.B. Lippincott Co.
4. Selzer, A.: Drug therapy. In Selzer, A.: Principles of clinical cardiology, Philadelphia, 1975, W.B. Saunders Co.
5. Akera, T., and Brody, T.M.: The role of Na^+,K^+-ATPase in the inotropic action of digitalis, Pharmacol. Rev. **29**:187, 1977.
6. Revised digoxin dosage, FDA Drug Bull. **6**:31, Aug.-Oct., 1976.
7. Aviado, D.M.: The treatment of congestive heart failure. In Aviado, D.M., editor: Pharmacologic principles of medical practice, ed. 8, Baltimore, 1972, The Williams & Wilkins Co.
8. McCallum, C.A., and Harrison, J.B.: Pharmacological considerations in dental treatment for the patient with systemic disease, Dent. Clin. North Am. **14**:663-680, 1970.
9. Evaluations of drug interactions, ed. 2, Washington, D.C., 1976, The American Pharmaceutical Association.
10. Chatterjee, K., and Parmley, W.W.: Vasodilator therapy in chronic heart failure, Ann. Rev. Pharmacol. Toxicol. **20**:475, 1980.
11. Rushmer, R.F.: Cardiovascular dynamics, Philadelphia, 1970, W.B. Saunders Co.
12. Lyght, C.E., editor: The Merck manual, Rahway, N.J., 1968, Merck & Co., Inc.
13. Laskin, J.L.: Oral hemorrhage after the use of quinidine: report of a case, J. Am. Dent. Assoc. **88**:137, 1974.
14. Bigger, J.T., Jr., and Hoffman, B.F.: Antiarrhythmic drugs. In Gilman, A.G., Goodman, L.S., and Gilman, A., editors: The pharmacological basis of therapeutics, ed. 6, New York, 1980, Macmillan Publishing Co., Inc.
15. Melmon, K.L., and Morrelli, H.F.: Clinical pharmacology, ed. 2, New York, 1978, Macmillan Publishing Co., Inc.
16. Aronow, W.S.: The treatment of supraventricular tachyarrhythmias, Ration. Drug. Ther. **14**(8):1, 1980.
17. Davis, R.O., and McMahan, F.G.: The present status of beta blockers in clinical medicine, Ration. Drug. Ther. **14**(2):1, 1980.
18. Abramowicz, M., editor: Verapamil for arrhythmias, Med. Lett. Drugs Ther. **23**(6):29, 1981.
19. Braunwald, E., editor: Heart disease: a textbook of cardiovascular medicine, vol. 1, Philadelphia, 1980, W.B. Saunders Co.
20. Giles, T.D.: The current status of nitrites in the management of angina pectoris, Ration. Drug Ther. **15**(2):1, 1981.
21. Needleman, P., and Johnson, E.M., Jr.: Vasodilators and the treatment of angina. In Gilman, A.G., Goodman, L.S., and Gilman, A., editors: The Pharmacological Basis of Therapeutics, ed. 6, New York, 1980, Macmillan Publishing Co., Inc.
22. Guyton, A.C.: The textbook of medical physiology, ed. 6, Philadelphia, 1981, W.B. Saunders Co.
23. Hansten, P.D.: Drug interactions, ed. 4, Philadelphia, 1979, Lea & Febiger.
24. Coon, W.W.: Use of anticoagulant drugs. Ration. Drug Ther. **13**(10):1, 1979.
25. Cathcart-Rake, W.F., and Dujoune, C.A.: The treatment of hyperlipoproteinemias, Ration. Drug Ther. **13**(7):1, 1979.
26. Goth, A.: Medical pharmacology, ed. 10, St. Louis, 1981, The C.V. Mosby Co.

CHAPTER 22

BARBARA REQUA-CLARK
SAM V. HOLROYD

Antimicrobial agents

The control of infection is one of the most important problems in the dental office. An oral infection can rapidly spread and produce a severe illness or even become fatal. The prevention of postoperative dental infections requires attention to aseptic technique. The treatment requires a complete knowledge of the patient's medical history, the characteristics of infection, and the pharmacology of the antimicrobial agents available. Before discussing the individual antimicrobial agents the following terms will be defined:

antimicrobial agents Substances that kill or suppress the growth or multiplication or prevent the action of microorganisms.

antiinfective agents Substances that act against or tend to destroy infections. Like *antimicrobial,* this is a general term.

antibacterial agents Substances that destroy or suppress the growth or multiplication of bacteria.

antiviral agents Substances that destroy or suppress the growth or multiplication of viruses.

antifungal agents Substances that destroy or suppress the growth or multiplication of fungi.

antibiotic agents Chemical substances produced by microorganisms that have the capacity, in dilute solutions, to destroy or suppress the growth or multiplication of organisms or prevent their action.

The difference between the terms *antibiotic* and *synthetic antibacterial agents* is that the antibiotics are produced by microorganisms and the antibacterial agents are made in a laboratory.

The following terms are commonly used to describe the differences and similarities among the various antimicrobial agents.

spectrum The range of activity of a drug. An antibacterial agent may have a narrow spectrum; that is, it acts primarily against either gram-positive or gram-negative organisms. It may have a broad spectrum; that is, it is effective against a wide variety of organisms including both gram-positive and gram-negative bacteria as well as some viruses.

resistance The ability of a microorganism to be unaffected by an antimicrobial agent. *Natural* resistance occurs when an organism has always been resistant to the antimicrobial agent. *Acquired* resistance occurs when an organism that was previously sensitive to an antimicrobial agent develops resistance. Resistance can be acquired through natural selection of a spontaneous mutation. Genetic recombination, including conjugation, transformation, and transduction, can result in the passing on of resistance from one bacterial strain to another. The second strain becomes resistant to the same antibiotics as the first strain without having been exposed to the antibiotic.

bactericidal Having the ability to kill bacteria. This effect is irreversible; that is, if the bacteria are removed from the drug, they do not live.

bacteriostatic Having the ability to inhibit or retard the multiplication or growth of bacteria. This is a reversible process because the bacteria are able to grow and multiply when removed from the agent.

Some drugs may be bacteriostatic at low concentrations and bactericidal at high concentrations against the same or different microorganisms. Thus whether an antibacterial agent is labeled "bactericidal" or "bacteriostatic" depends on several variables, including the usual therapeutic concentration of that agent, the type of organism, and the mechanism of action of the agent. In patients with severely impaired defense mechanisms, a bactericidal agent would be preferred over a bacteriostatic agent because the body's ability to fight infection is compromised. Table 22-1 lists the most common antimicrobial agents and whether they usually are bactericidal or bacteriostatic.

blood level The concentration of the antibacterial agent present in the blood or serum. This level is an important index to drug dosage, since a certain concentration of the drug is required in the body fluids to inhibit or kill the microorganisms.

synergism Effect when a combination of two antibiotics is more rapidly bactericidal then either drug used alone. An example is the use of carbenicillin and gentamicin for the treatment of *Pseudomonas aeruginosa* septicemia. Combinations of antibiotics that are bactericidal (Table 22-1) generally are synergistic. Combinations of those that are bacteriostatic are merely additive.

antagonism Effect when the bactericidal rate for the combination of two drugs is less than that for either drug used alone. This is often exhibited when a bacteriostatic and a bactericidal agent are used in combination (Table 22-1).

245

Table 22-1. Classification of antibacterial agents—bactericidal or bacteriostatic

Drug	Bactericidal	Bacteriostatic
Penicillins	+	
Erythromycin		+*
Lincomycin/clindamycin		+*
Cephalosporins	+	
Tetracyclines		+
Chloramphenicol		+
Aminoglycosides	+	
Bacitracin	+	
Vancomycin	+	
Spectinomycin		+
Sulfonamides		+
Polymyxins	+	

Modified from Requa, B.S., and Holroyd, S.V.: Applied pharmacology for the dental hygienist, St. Louis, 1982, The C.V. Mosby Co.

*Erythromycin and lincomycin/clindamycin may be bactericidal against some organisms at some drug blood levels.

superinfection, suprainfection Infection caused by the proliferation of microorganisms that are different than those causing the original infection. When antibiotics disturb the normal flora of the body, this makes possible the emergence of organisms unaffected by or resistant to the antibiotic used. Superinfection is often caused by broad-spectrum antibiotics such as tetracycline. In this case a reduction in the number of gram-positive and gram-negative bacteria allows the overgrowth of the fungus *Candida albicans*.

Sometimes the pathogenic organisms emerging in a superinfection are more difficult to eradicate than the original organism. The fact that the practitioner can cause as well as eliminate infections emphasizes the importance of determining a definite need before these drugs are used.

INFECTION

Infection has been defined as "invasion of the body by pathogenic microorganisms and the reaction of the tissues to their presence and to the toxins generated by them."[1] One must remember that the simple presence of a pathogen does not constitute "invasion." The oral cavity is inhabited by many microorganisms, some of which are potentially pathogenic. The manifestation of infection as a disease state presupposes that the pathogen obtains an environment suitable for its growth and multiplication. The principal factors that determine the likelihood of a microorganism causing an infection are (1) virulence of the microorganism, (2) number of organisms present, and (3) resistance of the host. Host resistance should be considered as having both local and systemic components.

Locally, tissue trauma, inadequate wound closure, and lack of blood clot retention are important. Systemically, one is confronted with a number of conditions that decrease resistance to infection. These predisposing conditions occur in patients with diabetes, leukemia, Addison's disease, immunoglobulin deficiencies, malnutrition, agranulocytosis, and various other blood dyscrasias. Alcoholics, patients who have been taking adrenal steroids or immunosuppressive or cytotoxic drugs, and those debilitated for any reason also have a decreased resistance to infection.

A wide variety of microorganisms may cause infections of the oral structures. An excellent and condensed description of the normal oral flora, virulence and resistance factors, and the organisms involved in dental infections is presented by Burnett.[2] He concludes that most dental infections are caused by streptococci and staphylococci and will respond to antimicrobial agents with a predominately gram-positive spectrum. Kannangara and others[3] studied 61 cases of pyogenic dental infections. Of these cases, 74% had anaerobic infections of which 30% had *Bacteroides fragilis*. One third of these *Bacteroides* were resistant to penicillin, but all were susceptible to clindamycin.

Newer techniques have allowed the identification of anaerobic bacteria as the predominant organism in necrotic pulp. Sundquist[4] identified anaerobes as being more than 90% of the bacteria in necrotic pulp. The pulpal infection is often of a mixed flora—many including *Bacteroides melaninogenicus*.

Sabiston and others[5] identified anaerobic gram-negative rods including *B. melaninogenicus* and *Fusobacterium nucleatum* from two thirds of the cultures. It is now evident that the flora of the necrotic dental pulp is generally mixed, anaerobic, and similar to the flora of the gingival crevice, and it contains few groups of organisms. The flora of juvenile periodontitis consists of gram-negative capnophilic and anaerobic rods.[6,7] One organism frequently found was *Bacteroides ochraceus*. This organism has also been isolated from necrotic dental pulp.[4]

Acute necrotizing gingivitis is thought to be caused by a combination of anaerobic spirochetes, gram-negative anaerobes, and *F. nucleatum*.

INDICATIONS FOR ANTIMICROBIAL AGENTS

Considerable indecision exists relative to determining a need for antimicrobial agents. Although it is not within the scope or intent of this text to discuss indications in detail, some generalizations should be stated.

Therapeutic indications

All infections do not require antimicrobial therapy. Unfortunately, there is no simple rule that can be employed to give an immediate yes or no answer in regard to the need for therapy. The basic question is "Does this particular patient need the assistance of antimicrobial agents to resolve this particular infection?" The decision to use or not to use can be made only after considering all those factors that would indicate a need against those that obviate a need. The following should be evaluated:

1. *The patient.* One should never lose sight of the fact that the best defenses against pathogens are host responses. Properly functioning defense mechanisms in the healthy patient are of primary importance. The lack of these defenses, which may occur in conditions previously mentioned, must receive close attention. The presence or absence of systemic manifestations such as fever, malaise, and lymphadenopathy are indicators of how well the patient is doing without antimicrobial therapy.

2. *The infection.* The virulence and invasiveness of the etiologic microorganism are important in determining the acuteness, severity, and spreading tendency of the infection. Obviously, the acute, severe, rapidly spreading infection should generally be treated with antimicrobial agents. At the other end of the spectrum is the mild, localized infection where drainage can be established. Most cases are somewhere between these extremes. In these cases the decision can only be based on the clinician's capability to balance the patient's need for pharmacologic assistance against the potential toxicity of an antimicrobial agent.

Prophylactic indications

There are few situations in which a definite indication for prophylactic antibiotic coverage exists. One clear-cut indication is a history of rheumatic or congenital heart disease or the presence of a heart prosthesis. Since dental procedures may precipitate a bacteremia, prophylactic antibiotics must be given to prevent bacterial endocarditis. The prophylaxis against bacterial endocarditis is discussed in Appendix B. Other prophylactic uses of antimicrobial agents in dental practice are less clear.

Some clinicians suggest antibiotic prophylaxis for patients with total hip replacement.[8] An infection at the site of these prostheses can result in their rejection.[9] Jacobsen and Murray[10] suggest that many of these organisms isolated from infected hips were resistant to penicillin and that penicillinase-resistant penicillins, erythromycin, or clindamycin would be indicated based on these sensitivities. The organism most often isolated from the infected hips was *Staphylococcus aureus.*

In cases of compound mandibular fracture, the use of prophylactic antimicrobial agents has reduced the rate of infection.[11] Situations in which the need for prophylaxis is uncertain include Teflon implants and certain surgical procedures. A patient who has had coronary artery (bypass) surgery without complications and who has recovered does not need prophylactic antibiotic coverage.[12] Although dental studies concerning the value of prophylactic antibiotics are inconclusive, the failure of prophylactic antibiotic coverage to prevent postsurgical infections is well documented in the medical literature.[13] The following analysis concerns periodontic patients:

Most patients who undergo periodontal surgery are not going to develop a postoperative infection. Infections that do evolve might have been prevented by prophylactic antibiotics if the invading organism was susceptible to the particular drug selected. It is apparent from medical studies that some individuals who would not have developed a postoperative infection may do so if prophylactic antibiotics are used. The mechanism of this may be related to alterations in the normal flora which were induced by the antibiotic. Thus, in the final analysis, one must balance the infections he causes with antibiotics. If the medical literature on this subject accurately reflects the situation in periodontal surgery, the gains and losses in using antibiotics to prevent postsurgical infection are approximately equal. One's capacity to gain more than he loses from using antibiotics to prevent postsurgical infections is likely to be proportional to his ability to predict the likelihood of a postoperative infection in a particular case.[13]

In addition to specific prophylaxis against bacterial endocarditis, some patients with reduced defenses, as shown in Table 22-2, may require prophylactic antibiotics for some surgical or manipulative procedures.

Although there is some indication that prophylactic antibiotics may enhance healing and reduce postoperative discomfort,[13] this area of antibiotic use is strictly speculative. There is no evidence recommending such use.

Table 22-2. Diseases and drugs that decrease resistance to infection

Diseases	Drugs
Addison disease	Adrenal corticosteroids
Agranulocytosis	Cytotoxic drugs
Alcoholism	Immunosuppressive drugs
Blood dyscrasias	
Diabetes	
Immunoglobulin deficiency	
Leukemia	
Malnutrition	

From Requa, B.S., and Holroyd, S.V.: Applied pharmacology for the dental hygienist, St. Louis, 1982, The C.V. Mosby Co.

CULTURE AND SENSITIVITY TESTS

Ideally, all infections requiring antibiotic therapy would be cultured, and antibiotic sensitivity tests would be conducted. This is the only way in which one can reasonably ensure that a particular drug will kill or inhibit the growth of an infecting microorganism. In practice, this is difficult. These in vitro tests will not illustrate relative in vivo potency of the drugs, nor will they differentiate between bactericidal and bacteriostatic effects. They will only show which drugs adversely affect the growth of the microorganisms on the culture plate. This can generally be accepted as evidence that they will or will not adversely affect the microorganisms in vivo.

Culture

A sample from the infected site is taken and grown on culture media. After the pathogen is grown, sensitivity tests can be conducted. Since many dental infections are now thought to have an anaerobic component even though they are mixed, special precautions in obtaining and processing the sample are imperative.

Sensitivity

After the organism is identified, it is again grown on culture media and the effect of different antimicrobial agents on the organism is tested. One to 2 days are required before the results of this test are available. Although therapy is begun before this time, it may be changed after the results are available. One advantage of obtaining a culture and performing sensitivity tests is that an early correction of therapy is possible if the drug selected is ineffective against the microorganisms causing the infection. Another advantage is that pathogens grown on a culture before antibiotic therapy is begun can be more easily identified than after a therapeutic failure has occurred.

DURATION OF DOSAGE

An antimicrobial agent should be continued long enough to prohibit a regrowth of the causative microbe, but not so long as to induce toxic drug symptoms or alter the normal flora to the extent that superinfection results. It is generally agreed that the administration of antimicrobial drugs should continue for 48 hours after the symptoms of infection are absent. If beta-hemolytic streptococci are the causative organisms, antibiotic therapy, usually penicillin in this case, should be continued for at least 10 days. Antimicrobial therapy for osteomyelitis should be continued for at least 14 days after fever and tenderness are absent and drainage has ceased.[14] In patients with a depressed immune system or history of prolonged healing, antibiotic coverage usually needs to be continued longer than in the normal patient.[15]

BEGINNING OF SYSTEMIC ANTIMICROBIAL THERAPY

In 1932, Gerhard Domagk observed in Germany that the azo dye Prontosil protected mice against infection by streptococci. This milestone in medical history led to the development of the sulfonamides and marked the beginning of systemic antimicrobial therapy.

In 1940, Chain and co-workers[16] (England) made the following observation: "In recent years interest in chemotherapeutic effects has been almost exclusively focused on the sulfonamides and their derivatives. There are, however, other possibilities, notably those connected with naturally occurring substances."[16] Fleming (England) in 1928 observed that a mold produced a naturally occurring substance that inhibited the growth of certain bacteria.[17] He had named this substance "penicillin" and suggested that it might be useful for the application to infected wounds. In their classic paper Chain and co-workers reported in vivo animal studies that indicated the low toxicity and systemic antibacterial effectiveness of penicillin.[16] The excitement that had begun with the sulfonamides was being transferred to the "antibiotics." Today, as each new "therapeutic advancement in the treatment of infection" (antibiotic) is marketed, this excitement is again transferred.

MICROBIOLOGY OF ORAL INFECTIONS

The microbiology of oral infections is beyond the scope of this discussion, but several references are available.[18,3,19] The normal oral flora includes aerobic streptococci and the anaerobic species *Fusobacterium, Peptostreptococcus, Lactobacillus, Veillonella, Bacteroides, Actinomyces,* and *Corynebacterium.* Organisms from this list are often the pathogens in oral infections.

First, some general principles are presented. Not only are oral infections caused by the host's oral flora, but many studies show a predominance of anaerobic organisms. Reports of the number of infections contain at least one anaerobic agent have ranged from 0[20] to 100%.[21] Agents commonly reported as causing infections include aerobic staphylococci and streptococci. Also commonly implicated are species of anaerobic gram-positive rods: *Actinomyces, Arachnia, Eubacterium,* and *Lactobacillus;* gram-negative rods: *Bacteroides,* especially *B. melaninogenicus,* and *Fusobacterium;* gram-positive cocci: *Peptostreptococcus;* gram-negative cocci: *Veillonella;* gram-labile cocci: *Peptococcus;* and facultative gram-positive rods: *Actinomyces.*

Another general principle is that many oral infections are mixed, often including an aerobic gram-positive coccus and one or two anaerobic bacteria.

One of the most prevalent species of microorganisms in dental infections is *Bacteroides. B. melaninogenicus* is usually sensitive to penicillin, but *B. fragilis* is often resistant. Most of the other anaerobes are sensitive to penicillin. *Actinomyces israelii* requires high-dosage intravenous penicillin G. Sometimes an antibiotic may be effective in eradicating an oral infection even though in vitro tests show resistance. This is because the interplay between the organisms—aerobic and anaerobic—is altered if one or more of the microorganisms is eliminated.

Dental treatment

When antimicrobial agents are to be used in the treatment of dental infections, many factors must be considered. First, the normal flora must be taken into account. Although many organisms are present in the mouth, the gram-positive organisms predominate. This fact determines the antimicrobials that may be useful in the treatment of dental infections. The next thing that must be considered is the susceptibility of these microorganisms to the antimicrobial agents. When information about the normal oral flora and their susceptibility to antimicrobial agents is combined, a table can be generated that lists the antimicrobials used therapeutically in dentistry (Table 22-3). This table gives some of the common dental infections and the antimicrobial agents of first, second, and third choices. Note that penicillin and erythromycin are used most frequently and that only occasionally are other agents such as clindamycin, the cephalosporins, or tetracycline even considered. Table 22-4 lists the doses of those agents commonly used to treat dental infections.

ANTIBIOTICS EFFECTIVE PRIMARILY AGAINST GRAM-POSITIVE ORGANISMS
Penicillins

The penicillins can be divided into three major groups (Table 22-5). The first group contains penicillin G and V, the second group is composed of the penicillinase-resistant penicillins, and the third group includes the "wider"-spectrum penicillins. Because the penicillins have many properties in common, their similarities will be discussed first.

Source and chemistry

The mold *Penicillium notatum* and related species produce the naturally occurring penicillins. The semisynthetic penicillins are produced by chemically altering the naturally produced penicillins. All penicillins contain the nucleus 6-aminopenicillanic acid, which by itself has little antibacterial activity (Fig. 22-1). The addition of organic groups at the R position confers antibacterial activity to the compounds formed from 6-aminopenicillanic acid. These R groups create the various penicillins. The penicillins can be inactivated by any reaction that removes the R group or, in the case of penicillinase, breaks the beta lactam ring (B). Salts of the penicillins are made by reactions at the thiazolidine (T) carboxyl ($-COOH$) group (Fig. 22-1).

Although many naturally occurring penicillins have been produced, only penicillin G (benzylpenicillin) is clinically useful today. The various semisynthetic penicillins are formed by substituting other groups at the R position.

Administration and body handling

Penicillin can be administered either orally or parenterally but should not be applied topically because of its great allergenicity. When penicillin is administered orally, the amount absorbed depends on the type

Table 22-3. Antimicrobial use in dentistry

Use	Drug		
	First choice	**Second choice**	**Third choice**
Treatment of infections			
Soft tissue oral infections	Penicillin*	Erythromycin*	Tetracycline; cephalosporin
Osteomyelitis	Penicillin	Erythromycin	Cephalosporin; clindamycin
Specific infections			
Bacteroides fragilis	Clindamycin	Chloramphenicol	Metronidazole
Penicillinase-producing *Staphylococcus*	Dicloxacillin; cloxacillin	Cephalosporin; erythromycin	Clindamycin
Vincent infection	Penicillin	Tetracycline	Erythromycin
Candida albicans	Nystatin	Miconazole	Clotrimazole
Insensitive/resistant to penicillin G			
Gram-positive and -negative anaerobes	Clindamycin	Erythromycin	Cephalosporin; tetracycline
Mixed gram-positive and -negative	Amoxicillin	Tetracycline; cephalosporin	Sulfonamides
Prevention of bacterial endocarditis			
Rheumatic heart disease and most valvular damage	Penicillin	Erythromycin (tetracycline not indicated)	Cephalosporin
Valve prosthesis	Penicillin and streptomycin	Vancomycin	Erythromycin

From Requa, B.S., and Holroyd, S.V.: Applied pharmacology for the dental hygienist, St. Louis, 1982, The C.V. Mosby Co.
*Although either penicillin or erythromycin can be used for the treatment of oral infections, the choice is between the bactericidal penicillin, which has a propensity to produce allergic reactions, and the bacteriostatic erythromycin with less allergic potential.

Table 22-4. Oral dosage forms and doses of selected antibiotics used in dentistry

Drug	Usual adult dose*	Selected products†
Penicillin VK (Pen-Vee-K, V-Cillin K)	250-500 mg q.6h.	T: 125, 250, 500 mg L: 125, 250 mg/5 ml
Erythromycin (base—E-mycin, stearate—Erythrocin, ethylsuccinate—EES)	250-500 mg q.6h. (EES, 400 mg)	T/C: 125, 250, 500 mg (EES, 200, 400 mg) L: 125, 250 mg/5 ml (EES, 200, 400 mg/5 ml) D: 100 mg/1 ml (EES, 100 mg/2.5 ml)
Clindamycin (Cleocin)	150-300 mg q.6h.	C: 75, 150 mg L: 75 mg/5 ml
Cephalexin (Keflex)	250-500 mg q.6h.	C: 250, 500 mg T: 1000 mg L: 125, 250 mg/5 ml D: 100 mg/1 ml

*Higher doses may be required in more serious infections.
†*T,* tablets; *L,* liquid; *D,* drops; *C,* capsules.

Table 22-5. Penicillin subgroups

Narrow spectrum
  Penicillin G
  Penicillin V
Penicillinase resistant
  Methicillin
  Nafcillin
  Oxacillin
  Cloxacillin
  Dicloxacillin
  Floxacillin*
"Broader" or "wider" spectrum
  Ampicillin
  Hetacillin
  Bacampicillin
  Amoxicillin
  Cyclacillin
  Carbenicillin
  Ticarcillin
  Mezlocillin
  Piperacillin*

Modified from Requa, B.S., and Holroyd, S.V.: Applied pharmacology for the dental hygienist, ed. 1, St. Louis, 1982, The C.V. Mosby Co.
*Not marketed in the United States.

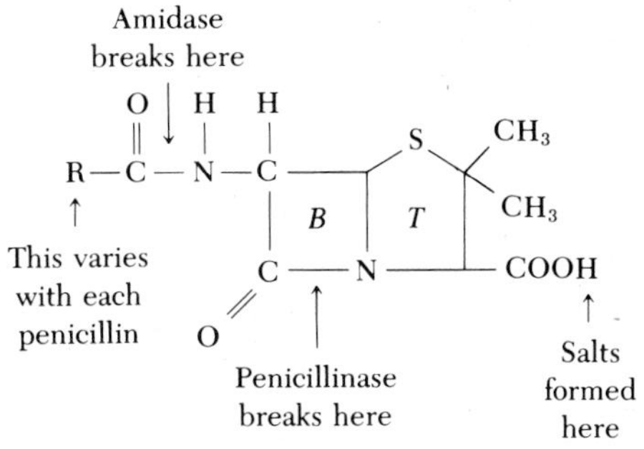

Fig. 22-1. Basic penicillin structure.

of penicillin given. The percentage can vary from 0% to 80% (Table 22-6). When the percentage absorbed is too low, as with methicillin, the penicillin is available only for injection. Note that penicillin V is better absorbed orally than penicillin G. The oral route provides the advantages of convenience and less likelihood of a life-threatening allergic reaction. The disadvantages of using the oral route rather than the parenteral route are as follows:

1. Blood levels are attained more slowly.
2. Gastric acid can produce some breakdown.
3. Blood levels are less predictable owing to variable absorption in the small intestine.
4. Patients may fail to take the medication correctly.

Since penicillin is degraded by the gastric fluid, it should be administered 1 hour before meals or 2 hours after meals. Certain acid-labile penicillins must be administered parenterally (Table 22-6).

After penicillin is absorbed, whether given orally or by injection, it is distributed throughout the body. Penetration is relatively poor into the CNS (cerebrospinal fluid), bone, and the synovial, pleural, and pericardial fluids. Although penicillin penetrates blood clots, it does not permeate pus to any significant extent.[22] Penicillin crosses the placental barrier, and a small amount appears to be excreted in the milk and saliva.

Although penicillin is metabolized by the liver, the rapid decrease in the blood level results from rapid renal clearance. About 90% is excreted by tubular secretion and 10% by glomerular filtration. In the presence of renal disease, high blood levels may result from failure to excrete the drug. The elimination $t_{\frac{1}{2}}$ of penicillin G is about 30 minutes in a normal adult, so that after less than 3 hours virtually no penicillin remains in the body.

Spectrum

Penicillin is a very potent bactericidal agent that acts by interfering with the synthesis of the bacterial cell wall (Table 22-7). It affects rapidly multiplying bacteria by inhibiting the transpeptidase enzyme responsible for the formation of the cross-linking of peptidoglycan polymers during the last stage of cell wall synthesis. It is inactive against dormant organisms. Its narrow spectrum of activity includes grampositive aerobic and facultative organisms (cocci: *Streptococcus* and *Staphylococcus;* rods: *Bacillus, Corynebacterium,* and *Clostridium;* spirochetes: *Treponema pallidum;* and certain gram-negative aerobic cocci: *Neisseria gonorrhoeae* and *N. meningitidis.* Penicillin is also effective against many anaerobes present in the oral cavity (diphtheroids, fusobacteria, peptostreptococci, *Actinomyces, Veillonella* and some *Bacteroides*).

The penicillinase-resistant penicillins (Table 22-5) are very effective against penicillinase-producing

Table 22-6. Properties of the penicillins

	Acid stable	Penicillinase-resistant	Extended spectrum	Route of administration	Percent (%) absorbed orally	Percent (%) protein bound	$t_\frac{1}{2}$ (hr)
Penicillin G							
Na,K (Pentids)	−	−	−	Oral, IM, IV	20-30	60	0.5
Procaine (Crysticillin)	−	−	−	IM	0	60	0.5
Benzathine (Bicillin)	−	−	−	IM	0	60	0.5
Penicillin VK (Pen-Vee-K, V-Cillin K)	+	−	−	Oral	75	75	0.5
Methicillin (Dimocillin, Staphcillin)	−	+	−	IM, IV	0	40	0.5
Nafcillin (Unipen)	+	+	−	Oral, IM, IV	10-15	90	0.5
Oxacillin (Prostaphlin, Resistopen)	+	+	−	Oral, IM, IV	20-30	90	0.5
Cloxacillin (Tegopen)	+	+	−	Oral	40-60	90	0.5
Dicloxacillin (Dynapen, Veracillin, Pathocil)	+	+	−	Oral	40-60	95	0.5
Ampicillin (Polycillin, Omnipen, Penbritin)	+	−	+	Oral, IM, IV	30-40	20	1.5
Bacampicillin (Spectrobid)	+	−	+	Oral	80	20	1.1
Hetacillin (Versapen)	+	−	+	Oral	80	20	0.3
Amoxicillin (Amoxil, Larotid)	+	−	+	Oral	80	20	1.0
Cyclacillin (Cyclapen-W)	+	−	+	Oral	80	20	0.5
Carbenicillin disodium (Geopen, Pyopen)	−	−	+	IM, IV	0	50	1.5
Carbenicillin indanyl (Geocillin)	+	−	+	Oral	80	50	1.5
Ticarcillin disodium (Ticar)	−	−	+	IM, IV	0	45	1.1
Mezlocillin (Mezlin)	−	−	+	IM, IV	0	30	0.9

Modified from Requa, B.S., and Holroyd, S.V.: Applied pharmacology for the dental hygienist, ed. 1, St. Louis, 1982, The C.V. Mosby Co.

Table 22-7. Mechanism and site of action of antimicrobial agents

Cell wall (No. 1 below)	Cytoplasm (No. 2 below)	Cytoplasmic membrane (No. 3 below)
Bacitracin Cephalosporins Penicillins Vancomycin	Aminoglycosides* Chloramphenicol* Erythromycin* Lincomycin/clindamycin* Spectinomycin† Sulfonamides‡ Tetracyclines†	Antifungals (nystatin, amphotericin B, griseofulvin, candicidin)

1. Inhibition of synthesis
2. Interference with metabolism
3. Interference with protective function and permeability

Modified from Requa, B.S., and Holroyd, S.V.: Applied pharmacology for the dental hygienist, ed. 1, St. Louis, 1982, The C.V. Mosby Co.
*Blocks protein synthesis by binding to 50S subunit.
†Blocks protein synthesis by binding to 30S subunit.
‡Antimetabolite.

Staphylococcus aureus. Their activity versus the agents that are sensitive to penicillin is *much less* than that of penicillin G or V.

The extended-spectrum penicillins (Table 22-5) are usually less active against organisms that are sensitive to penicillin G or V. They are not penicillinase resistant. Their extended or widened spectrum, depending on the agent, may include certain gram-negative bacilli *(Escherichia coli, Salmonella, Shigella, Proteus mirabilis, Haemophilus influenzae).* These agents may have the ability to penetrate the cell walls so that they can exert their bactericidal effect. Their spectrum of action includes that of the ampicillin-like group but also includes some species of *Pseudomonas* and *Proteus.* Certain ampicillin-resistant strains of *E. coli* and *H. influenzae* are sensitive to this group. The most recently developed members of this group also have activity versus species of *Klebsiella, Pseudomonas, Proteus,* and *Enterobacter.*

Resistance

Resistance to penicillin usually develops in a slow stepwise fashion. Staphylococci become resistant by producing penicillinases. These inactivate the penicillin moiety by cleaving the beta lactam ring (Fig. 22-1). Hospital environments notably have a large population of penicillinase-producing staphylococci. In increasing number of oral *Streptococcus viridans* strains that are currently sensitive to penicillin G and V are growing resistant.[23]

The antibacterial activity of penicillin is standardized in international units. One unit has the activity of 0.6 μg sodium penicillin G (1 mg sodium penicillin G = 1667 units). Because of the difference in molecular weights, the units vary somewaht. For example, 1 mg potassium penicillin G is equal to 1595 units, and therefore 400,000 units of penicillin is equivalent to approximately 250 mg. Penicillin G is usually measured in units, whereas other penicillins are expressed in milligrams.

Adverse reactions

The untoward reactions to the penicillins can be divided into toxic reactions and allergic or hypersensitivity-type reactions. Penicillin is the most common cause of drug allergies.

Toxicity. Because penicillin's toxicity is almost nonexistent, extremely large doses have been tolerated without adverse effects. For this reason there is a large margin of safety when penicillin is adminis-

tered. With massive intravenous doses, direct CNS irritation can result in depressed consciousness and myoclonic jerking movements (convulsions). Large doses of penicillin G have been associated with renal damage manifested as fever, eosinophilia, rashes, albuminuria, and a rise in blood urea nitrogen (BUN). Hemolytic anemia and bone marrow depression have also been induced by penicillin. The penicillinase-resistant penicillins are significantly more toxic than penicillin G. Gastrointestinal irritation can manifest itself as nausea with or without vomiting. The irritation caused by injection of penicillin can produce sterile abscesses if given intramuscularly or thrombophlebitis if given intravenously.

Allergy and hypersensitivity. An allergic reaction to penicillin presents the greatest danger of therapy. This reaction may be classified by the time for the onset of symptoms:

1. Immediate: Less than 30 minutes: includes anaphylaxis.
2. Accelerated: 2 to 48 hours; includes serum sickness and laryngeal edema.
3. Late: 3 or more days; includes rashes, oral lesions, and other symptoms.

These allergic types are described as follows:

1. Anaphylactic reaction. Anaphylactic shock, an acute allergic reaction, occurs within ½ hour after the administration of penicillin. It presents the most serious danger to patients. It is characterized by smooth muscle contraction (for example, bronchoconstriction), capillary dilation (shock), and urticaria caused by the release of histamine and bradykinin. If treatment does not begin immediately, death can result. The treatment of anaphylaxis is the immediate administration of parenteral epinephrine.
2. Delayed serum sickness. Serum sickness is manifested mildly as fever, skin rash, and eosinophilia or severely as arthritis, purpura, lymphadenopathy, splenomegaly, mental changes, abnormal electrocardiogram, and edema. It usually takes at least 6 days to develop and can occur during treatment or up to 2 weeks after treatment has ceased.
3. Rash. All types of skin rashes have been reported in association with the administration of penicillin. This type of reaction accounts for between 80% and 90% of allergic reactions to the penicillins. They are usually mild and self-limiting but can occasionally be severe. Even contact dermatitis has occurred as a result of topical exposure, for example, while preparing an injectable solution.
4. Oral lesions. Delayed reactions to penicillin can exhibit themselves in the oral cavity. These include severe stomatitis, furred tongue, black tongue, acute glossitis, and cheilosis. These oral lesions can occur most commonly with topical application but have been reported from other routes.
5. Other. Interstitial nephritis, hemolytic anemia, and eosinophilia occasionally reported during penicillin therapy are types of allergic reactions.

The extent and severity of an allergic reaction to penicillin are enormous. Some studies indicate that between 5% and 10% of patients receiving penicillin will have a reaction.[24] In one survey almost 8% of the patients receiving penicillin exhibited an allergic reaction.[25]

Testing. One way to decrease the incidence of penicillin allergy is to test for the presence of this reaction. Since the mechanism of the reaction to penicillin is complex, testing for this allergy is difficult. Penicilloyl-polylysine (PPL, Pre-Pen) and the "minor determinant mixture" (MDM) are mixed together for the skin test. Aqueous penicillin G can be used if the MDM is unavailable. This is important because the penicillin itself does not act as a haptene but rather is metabolized to potential haptenes.[26] Because this test can cause an anaphylactic reaction, it should be done only by an allergist in a controlled situation with emergency equipment and trained personnel available. The occurrence of false-positive and false-negative skin tests demonstrates that these tests are not completely dependable. Depending on the tests used, the reliability of a skin test varies from 19% to 76%.[27] But when PPL and MDM were used for skin testing, the results were more reliable.[28,29] In general a positive test forbodes a possible reaction and a negative test means that a serious reaction probably would not occur. A positive reaction to MDM points to an anaphylactic reaction with future exposure.

When reactions to penicillin occur, the consequences are often serious. It is estimated that the anaphylactic reaction occurs in between 0.004% and 0.04% of penicillin-treated patients,[30,31] with a mortality of between 9%[32] and 10%.[33] If statistics from other studies are projected, they indicate that 100 to 300 deaths caused by an allergic reaction to penicillin occur annually in the United States.[34,35] Although the chance of a serious allergic reaction to penicillin is greater after parenteral administration, anaphylactic shock and death after oral use have also been reported.[36-40] Atopic patients who have a history of other allergies are more likely to be allergic to penicillin.

Allergic reactions of any nature may be followed by more serious allergic reactions on subsequent exposure. Any history of an allergic reaction to penicillin contraindicates the use of this substance, and another antibiotic should be substituted. However, a negative history does not guarantee the lack of a penicillin allergy.

Uses

Penicillin is an important antibiotic in medical and dental practice. Its use in dentistry results from its bactericidal potency, lack of toxicity, and spectrum of action, which includes many organisms that cause dental infections. Table 22-3 demonstrates the number of dental infections for which penicillin is the drug of choice if patients are not allergic to it. Penicillin is also used for specific prophylactic indications. One study[41] showed that penicillin reduced trismus and swelling after third molar removal, but not pain, measured either subjectively or by the number of tablets taken. Before this can be recommended, the risk of side effects must be weighed against the potential advantage of administering the antibiotic. It is the agent of choice for the prophylaxis of bacterial endocarditis in nonallergic patients who have a history of rheumatic heart disease or valve damage (see Appendix B).

According to the 1979 edition of *Accepted Dental Therapeutics,* "The systemic use of penicillin is indicated in severe infections that are caused by penicillinase-sensitive organisms."[42] When a potent bactericidal agent is not needed, other antibiotics may be considered.

Penicillin G and V

Penicillin G, the prototype penicillin, is available as the sodium, potassium, procaine, or benzathine salt. These salts differ in their onset and duration of action and the plasma levels attained. Fig. 22-2 compares the blood levels obtained by the intravenous administration of the potassium salt and the intramuscular administration of the potassium, procaine, and benzathine salts. Note that the potassium salt given intravenously produces the most rapid and highest blood level, whereas the benzathine salt given intramuscularly produces a much lower and more sustained level. The potassium salt and the procaine salt given intramuscularly produce intermediate blood levels.

Given orally, penicillin G is poorly absorbed from the gastrointestinal tract. Only about one third of the penicillin is absorbed. If administered orally, penicillin G must be given in appropriately large doses to overcome this poor absorption. Penicillin G tablets are occasionally used on a daily basis as a continuous prophylaxis against bacterial endocarditis. For other forms of oral therapy, penicillin V is usually preferred.

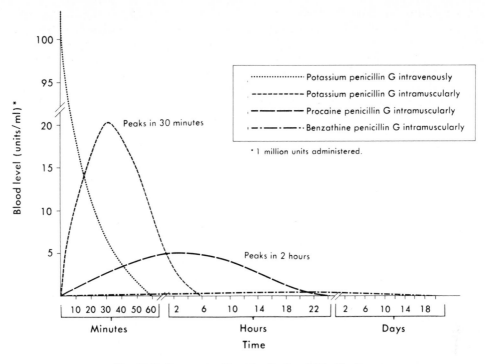

Fig. 22-2. Comparative blood levels of penicillin G salts.

Sodium and potassium penicillin G. The sodium and potassium salts of penicillin G are available for parenteral and oral use. They have identical antibacterial activity. In very high doses the sodium salt can be detrimental to patients with cardiac disease on low-sodium diets and the potassium salt can result in hyperkalemia in patients with renal failure. When these agents are administered parenterally, peak levels are rapidly obtained and lost. When given intravenously, they peak in 5 minutes (intramuscularly, 30 minutes) and last only a few hours. For severe infections very high doses of penicillin can be administered by the intravenous route. Because of poor oral absorption, potassium penicillin G is not usually administered orally. Occasionally, buffered potassium penicillin G is used orally when high blood levels are not required.

Procaine penicillin G. Procaine penicillin G has the same spectrum of action as sodium or potassium penicillin G. This less soluble salt has a slower rate of absorption when injected intramuscularly. The blood levels obtained with the procaine salt are lower and there is a slower onset and longer duration of ac-

tion than with the sodium or potassium salts (Fig. 22-2). Procaine penicillin G peaks in about 2 hours, and its duration is approximately 1 day. It may be used every 24 hours for prophylaxis of bacterial endocarditis.

Benzathine penicillin G. Benzathine penicillin G is a highly insoluble salt administered intramuscularly to provide an extended duration of action. It is slowly released from its injection site, thereby providing a low blood level for an extended period of time (Fig. 22-2). It is used only when low blood levels are acceptable. This dosage form is most commonly used for patients who have a history of rheumatic heart disease and are undergoing long-term prophylaxis of bacterial endocarditis. Given in usual doses, an intramuscular injection of benzathine penicillin G provides blood levels for 3 to 4 weeks. It is also available in combination with procaine penicillin G (Bicillin C-R) when an immediate blood level and sustained effect are desired. Allergic reactions to this salt present a greater problem because, owing to its insolubility and long duration of action, the drug is not as rapidly removed from the body.

Penicillin V. Penicillin V has a spectrum of action very similar to that of penicillin G. Given orally, penicillin V produces higher blood levels (approximately two to five times higher) than an equivalent amount of penicillin G. Given orally, about 65% of penicillin V is absorbed. Penicillin V has never been proved to be of greater therapeutic value than penicillin G given in higher doses. Because of the higher blood levels, penicillin V is used almost exclusively in the treatment and prevention of dental infections. The potassium salt of penicillin V (K penicillin V or penicillin VK) is more soluble than the free acid and therefore is better absorbed when taken orally. Table 22-3 lists some dental situations in which penicillin is the drug of first choice if the patient is not allergic to penicillin, and Table 22-4 lists the usual dose.

Penicillinase-resistant penicillins

Table 22-5 lists the penicillinase-resistant penicillins. These drugs, resistant to cleavage by penicillinase, should be reserved for use only against penicillinase-producing staphylococci. Compared to penicillin G, the penicillinase-resistant penicillins are less effective against penicillin G–sensitive organisms. They also produce more side effects such as gastrointestinal discomfort, bone marrow depression, and abnormal renal and hepatic function. Patients allergic to penicillin are also allergic to the penicillinase-resistant penicillins.

Except methicillin, which is acid labile, the penicillinase-resistant penicillins are stable enough to be administered orally. Since nafcillin is broken down by stomach acid more easily than cloxacillin, dicloxacillin, or oxacillin, it is not recommended for oral use. Cloxacillin and dicloxacillin are better absorbed than oxacillin (Table 22-6). Methacillin and nafcillin are even more resistant to penicillinase than the other members of this group. Floxacillin, which is not yet available in the United States, resembles cloxacillin. If an orally effective penicillinase-resistant penicillin is needed for the treatment of a penicillinase-producing staphylococci, either cloxacillin or dicloxacillin could be used. These agents are infrequently used in dentistry because of their very limited indication.

"Wider"- or "broader"-spectrum penicillins

The proliferation of this group of penicillins—the "wider"- or "broader"-spectrum penicillins—has necessitated dividing them into two groups—the ampicillin-like and the carbenicillin-like agents (Table 22-5). The ampicillin-like agents are similar in action and indications and will be discussed together.

Ampicillin-like agents. The ampicillin-like penicillins exert their antibacterial action like all the other penicillins—by inhibition of cell wall synthesis. The antibacterial spectrum of the members of this group are similar. Their spectrum of action includes that of penicillin G, but to a lesser extent, and some gram-negative bacilli including *E. coli, H. influenzae, P. mirabilis, Salmonella,* and *Shigella.* These agents may be able to penetrate the lipid coatings of these gram-negative organisms to exert their effect. They are not resistant to penicillinase.

Except for amoxicillin, the absorption of most of the other members of this group is decreased when administered with food. Both hetacillin and bacampicillin are metabolized in the body to ampicillin. They all have a similar spectrum of action. *H. influenzae* and *Streptococcus viridans* are usually extremely sensitive to the ampicillin-like penicillins. Although originally sensitive to ampicillin, a high percentage of *E. coli, P. mirabilis, Shigella,* and *Enterobacter,* as well as increasing numbers of *Salmonella,* are now resistant. They are also ineffective against *Pseudomonas, Serratia, Enterobacter, Acinetobacter,* indole-positive *Proteus,* and *Klebsiella.* These resistances have spawned the development the next group of penicillins—the carbenicillin-like agents. Because amoxicillin is better absorbed, it produces higher and more prolonged blood levels than does ampicillin, and it causes less diarrhea. When these agents are taken orally, peak blood levels are reached in 2 hours with a $t_{\frac{1}{2}}$ of 90 minutes. The adverse reactions of the wider-spectrum penicillins are similar to those of the penicillinase-resistant semisynthetic penicillins.

Ampicillin has a propensity to produce nonallergic rashes more frequently than other penicillins (7.7% compared with 2.7% with other penicillins).[43] It appears that these rashes are specific for ampicillin and do not indicate a true penicillin hypersensitivity[44]; they may be toxic in nature.[45-47] When ampicillin is administered to patients with mononucleosis, an extremely high percentage (95%) of them develop a rash.[48,49] The occurrence of this ampicillin-related rash is not considered a contraindication to future treatment with penicillins.[47]

As with all the penicillins, the major adverse reaction to the wider-spectrum penicillins is their allergenicity. Patients allergic to other penicillins are also likely to be allergic to the wider-spectrum penicillins. These agents should not be used as a substitute for penicillin G or V but should be reserved for specific gram-negative dental infections.

Carbenicillin-like agents. The carbenicillin-like agents also possess a wider spectrum of action than does penicillin G. For example, carbenicillin has activity against *Pseudomonas aeruginosa* and indole-positive *Proteus* as well as some ampicillin-resistant *H. influenzae* and *B. fragilis*. Depending on the agent within this group (Table 22-6), these agents can be active versus species of *Actinobacter, Citrobacter, Serratia,* and even *Klebsiella.* They are not penicillinase resistant and are used only parenterally for systemic effects (Table 22-6). Carbenicillin indanyl, an acid-stable ester of carbenicillin, can be used orally, not for systemic effects, but for the treatment of urinary tract infections. The adverse effects of the carbenicillin-like agents are similar to the other penicillins including hematologic effects—thrombocytopenia, leukopenia, neutropenia, and eosinophilia. Hemorrhagic manifestations with altered clotting and prothrombin time have been found in uremic patients. These drugs should be reserved for hospitalized patients with serious infections caused by *Pseudomonas, Proteus,* and *E. coli* strains resistant to ampicillin.[50] They are commonly combined with an aminoglycoside (gentamicin, tobramycin, amikacin) to act synergistically in the treatment of *Pseudomonas.* These agents are reserved for serious infections that require hospitalization. It would be unlikely that these agents would be used in an outpatient dental setting.

Erythromycin

Erythromycin is a macrolide antibiotic whose spectrum is similar to penicillin V.

Source and chemistry

In 1952, erythromycin was isolated from the bacterial strain *Streptomyces erythraeus.* Erythromycin is a high molecular weight organic base called a macrolide.

Body handling

Erythromycin is administered orally as the free base, various salt forms, or insoluble esters (Table 22-8). It is available in tablets and capsules, in oral

Table 22-8. Erythromycins

Drug	Route of administration
Erythromycin base (E-mycin)	Oral
Erythromycin stearate (Erythrocin stearate, Erypar)	Oral
Erythromycin ethylsuccinate (E.E.S. 400, Pediamycin)	Oral, IM
Erythromycin estolate (Ilosone)	Oral
Erythromycin lactobionate (Erythrocin piggyback)	IV
Erythromycin gluceptate (Ilotycin gluceptate)	IV

Modified from Requa, B.S., and Holroyd, S.V.: Applied pharmacology for the dental hygienist, St. Louis, 1982, The C.V. Mosby Co.

suspensions, and in intravenous and intramuscular forms. Because erythromycin is broken down in the gastric fluid, it is usually supplied as an enteric-coated tablet or an insoluble ester to reduce degradation by the stomach acid. It should be administered 2 hours before meals or several hours after meals. The peak blood level is usually attained in 1 to 4 hours after ingestion, depending on meals and time of digestion. Food reduces the absorption of erythromycin. The $t_{\frac{1}{2}}$ is 2 hours. Although different salts and esters provide variable blood levels, no therapeutic difference among them has been demonstrated.[51] Erythromycin is distributed to most body tissues, excreted in the bile, and partially reabsorbed through enterohepatic circulation. It is excreted in the urine and feces.

Activity and spectrum

Erythromycin is bacteriostatic in the usual therapeutic doses. It is believed to interfere with protein synthesis by inhibiting the enzyme peptidyl transferase at the 50S subunit of the ribosome. Clindamycin and chloramphenicol also bind at this 50S subunit. Since they all act at the same site one may inhibit the other if used concomitantly. Its antibacterial spectrum closely resembles that of penicillin; that is, it is primarily effective against gram-positive bacteria but also affects a few gram-negative bacteria. Certain strains of *Ricksettia, Chlamydia,* and *Actinomyces* are also sensitive to erythromycin. Erythromycin is the drug of first choice in the treatment of infections such as ₁*Mycoplasma pneumoniae* pneumonia, *Legionella pneumophila* infection, (Legionnaires' disease), diphtheria, pertussis, and some infections caused by *Chlamydia trachomatis.*[52] It is used as an alternative to penicillin in the treatment of group A streptococcal infections and some pneumococcal infections and as prophylaxis against bacterial endocarditis before dental procedures. Bacterial resistance can occur with erythromycin, and in some hospitals as many as 50% of the staphylococci are not inhibited by erythromycin.[53] Cross resistance between erythromycin and lincomycin is often seen.

Adverse reactions

The usual doses of erythromycin produce infrequent and generally mild adverse reactions that can include the following.

Gastrointestinal effects. The side effects most often associated with erythromycin administration are gastrointestinal and include stomatitis, abdominal cramps, nausea, vomiting, and diarrhea. These effects usually disappear when the drug is discontinued.

Cholestatic jaundice. Cholestatic jaundice and a change in liver function have been reported with erythromycin estolate. It also has been reported with the ethylsuccinate salt. Erythromycin base has not been associated with this reaction. Symptoms include nausea, vomiting, and abdominal cramps followed by jaundice and elevated liver enzyme levels. The mechanism of this adverse effect is believed to be a hypersensitivity reaction. It has occurred in some patients after a few days of treatment but usually follows 10 to 21 days of continual therapy.[54] After cessation of therapy, the symptoms disappear within a few days without residual effects. The estolate ester of erythromycin should not be given to patients with liver disease.

The FDA is currently attempting to remove the estolate from the market. FDA research claims 418 reports of hepatotoxicity from erythromycin and over 93% from the estolate salt. It is no more effective and may have more adverse effects than some other erythromycins.

Allergic reactions. Allergic reactions are infrequent and generally mild. Urticaria and rashes have been reported, but anaphylaxis and other serious reactions are rare.

Uses

Since erythromycin is active against essentially the same microorganisms as penicillin, it is useful in the treatment of the same infections. It is the drug of first choice against these infections in patients allergic to penicillin. As previously mentioned, erythromycin is active against most organisms that are likely to cause dental infections. It may be used in certain situations for the prophylaxis of rheumatic heart disease (see Appendix B). In one study[55] of patients receiving daily penicillin for prevention of bacterial endocarditis, up to 75% of the alpha hemolytic streptococci were resistant to penicillin. A major difference is that erythromycin is bacteriostatic rather than bactericidal, as is penicillin. This may be a factor in treating a compromised patient (Table 22-2). The various preparations of erythromycin are shown in Table 22-8.

The base (E-mycin), according to Fraser,[56] is the drug of choice when erythromycin is indicated. The absorption of the stearate is reduced with meals. The claims of a clinical advantage of other forms is not well documented. For pediatric use the ethylsuccinate is recommended. The usual dose of erythromycin is listed in Table 22-4.

Cephalosporins/cephamycins

The cephalosporins/cephamycin group of antibiotics, chemically related to the penicillins, is active against a wide variety of both gram-positive and gram-negative organisms. Of the cephalosporins/cephamycins listed in Table 22-9, only four, cephalexin, cephradine, cefadroxil, and cefaclor, are useful orally in the treatment of systemic infections. Because the cephalosporins have many properties in common, they will be discussed as a group.

Source and chemistry

The first source of the cephalosporins was *Cephalosporium acremonium,* isolated near a sewer outlet near Sardinia. Cephalosporin P was found to be elaborated by *Fusidium coccineum.* The cephamycins are derived from species of *Streptomyces.*

The structure of the cephalosporins is similar to that of the penicillins. The cephamycins, like cefoxitin, are similar to the cephalosporins. This group—the cephalosporins/cephamycins—will be referred to as the cephalosporins for simplicity. These com-

Table 22-9. Properties of the cephalosporin-like antibiotics

Drug	Route(s) of administration	Generation	Percentage protein bound (%)	$t_{\frac{1}{2}}$ (min)
Cephalexin (Keflex)	Oral	1st	5-20	30-70
Cephradine (Velosef, Anspor)	Oral, IM, IV	1st	0-20	45-120
Cefadroxil (Duricef)	Oral	1st	20	70-80
Cefaclor (Ceclor)	Oral		22-25	36-55
Cephaloglycin (Kafocin)	Oral	1st	0-30	90
Cephalothin (Keflin)	IM, IV	1st	50-80	25-60
Cephaloridine (Loridine)	IM, IV	1st	0-31	60-90
Cefazolin (Ancef, Kefzol)	IM, IV	1st	60-86	90-130
Cephapirin (Cefadyl)	IM, IV	1st	45-50	20-40
Cefamandole (Mandol)	IM, IV	2nd	56-78	30-60
Cefoxitin (Mefoxin)*	IM, IV	2nd	65-79	40-60
Cephacetrile	IM, IV			
Cefotaxime (Claforan)		3rd		
Moxalactam†		3rd		

Modified from Requa, B.S., and Holroyd, S.V.: Applied pharmacology for the dental hygienist, St. Louis, 1982, The C.V. Mosby Co.
*Cephamycin.
†Noncephalosporin, beta lactam.

pounds are relatively acid stable and highly resistant to penicillinase, but they are destroyed by cephalosporinase, an enzyme elaborated by some microorganisms. The different cephalosporins have varying resistance to this degradation.

Spectrum

The cephalosporins are bactericidal agents that are active against most gram-positive cocci and penicillinase-producing staphylococci and some gram-negative bacteria. The cephalosporins inhibit most *Salmonella* and *Klebsiella*, 60% of paracolon strains, 75% of *E. coli*, and 50% of *H. influenzae*.[57] *Enterobacter*, indole-positive *Proteus, Serratia*, methacillin-resistant *staphylococci*, and most *Pseudomonas* strains are unaffected. The generation of the cephalosporin (Table 22-9) designates the breadth of antimicrobial action with the first generation being less wide than the second, and with the third generation being the broadest in spectrum of action (cefotaxime).

Mechanism of action

The mechanism of action of the cephalosporins is similar to that of the penicillins: inhibition of cell wall synthesis (Table 22-7).

Body handling

The cephalosporins can be administered orally, intramuscularly, or intravenously, depending on the agent given. The agents that cannot be used orally are either too poorly absorbed or too rapidly excreted (cephaloglycin) to provide adequate blood levels for outpatient treatment of systemic infections. After absorption they are widely distributed throughout the tissues. The degree of protein binding varies among the different agents (Table 22-9). The cephalosporins are excreted in the urine with a $t_{\frac{1}{2}}$ that varies between 20 and 120 minutes (Table 22-9).

Adverse reactions

In general, the cephalosporins have a low incidence of adverse reactions and are well tolerated. The following reactions may occur.

Gastrointestinal effects. The most common adverse reaction associated with the cephalosporins is gastrointestinal, including diarrhea, nausea, vomiting, abdominal pain, anorexia, dyspepsia, and stomatitis.

Nephrotoxicity. Evidence suggests that the cephalosporins may produce nephrotoxic effects under certain conditions. Although some have suggested that this is a toxic reaction, it may be an allergic reaction. Cephaloridine is the most nephrotoxic cephalosporin.

Superinfection. As with all antibiotics, especially those with a broader spectrum of action, superinfection has been reported. Gram-negative organisms are often the culprits.

Local reaction. As with penicillin, the irritating nature of the cephalosporins can produce localized pain, induration, and swelling when given intramuscularly and abscess and thrombophlebitis when given intravenously.

Allergy. Various types of hypersensitivity reactions have been reported in approximately 5% of the patients receiving the cephalosporins. These reactions include fever, eosinophilia, serum sickness, rashes, and anaphylaxis. Large doses (12 gm) frequently (40%) produce a direct positive Coombs reaction. This can lead to a significant degree of hemolysis.

The incidence of hypersensitivity reactions to the cephalosporins is higher in patients who have a history of penicillin allergy. The degree of cross-sensitivity reported varies between 5% and 15%.[58] There appears to be little risk in administering a cephalosporin to a patient with a penicillin allergic history that was mild or in the distant past. Patients with severe, recent penicillin reactions should be given cephalosporins only with great caution, if at all. If patients who are allergic to penicillin are given a cephalosporin, they should be observed for ½ hour before dismissal from the office. Theoretically, since the cephalosporins and penicillin have a similar structure, cross-sensitivity could be expected.

Uses

The cephalosporins are indicated for infections that are sensitive to these agents but resistant to penicillin. They are especially useful in certain infections caused by gram-negative organisms such as *Klebsiella*. Their dental use is limited to the treatment of infections with sensitive organisms when other agents are ineffective or cannot be used. Their dose is listed in Table 22-4. They are not substitutes for penicillin V or erythromycin if these agents are effective. They may be used before dental treatment to prevent bacterial endocarditis in patients with a history of rheumatic heart disease when other agents cannot be used (see Appendix B).

Lincomycin and clindamycin

Lincomycin and clindamycin are bacteriostatic antibiotics effective primarily against gram-positive organisms and noted for their propensity to produce pseudomembraneous colitis.

Source and chemistry

Lincomycin (Lincocin) is elaborated from *Streptomyces lincolnensis* found in a soil sample from near Lincoln, Nebraska. Clindamycin (Cleocin) is produced by chemically modifying the lincomycin molecule. Lincomycin and clindamycin have similar structures that are distinctly different from those of other antibiotics. Because clindamycin is more active than lincomycin and causes fewer adverse reactions, the discussion of this group will be limited to clindamycin's properties.

Body handling

Clindamycin may be administered orally, intramuscularly, or intravenously. When taken orally, clindamycin is almost completely absorbed and reaches its peak concentration in 45 minutes with a $t_{\frac{1}{2}}$ of about 2.5 hours. Clindamycin is distributed throughout most body tissues, including bone, but not to the cerebrospinal fluid. It crosses the placental barrier. It is more than 90% bound to plasma proteins. Only about 10% of the active drug is eliminated in the urine. The rest is excreted as inactive metabolites in the urine and bile.

Spectrum

The antibacterial spectrum of clindamycin includes many gram-positive organisms and some gram-negative organisms. The antibacterial action results from interference with bacterial protein synthesis. These agents are bacteriostatic in most cases, although occasionally they are bactericidal at higher blood levels.

Clindamycin's activity, similar to erythromycin's, includes *Streptococcus pyogenes* and *viridans,* pneumococci, and *S. aureus.* In contrast to erythromycin, it is very active versus several anaerobes including *B. fragilis* and *B. melaninogenicus, Fusobacterium* species, *Peptostreptococcus* (anaerobic streptococci) and *Peptococcus* species, and *A. israelii.* It is interesting to compare this activity against anaerobic organisms isolated from the oral cavity or with agents isolated from oral infections (many anaerobes).

Bacterial resistance to clindamycin has not been

found to develop rapidly. Strains of bacteria that are resistant to clindamycin are often resistant to erythromycin also. An antagonistic relationship has been observed between clindamycin and erythromycin because of competition for the same binding site (50S subunit) on the bacteria. Consequently, these two drugs should not be administered simultaneously.

Adverse reactions

Gastrointestinal effects. The most commonly observed side effects of lincomycin and clindamycin are gastrointestinal, including diarrhea, nausea, vomiting, enterocolitis, and abdominal cramps. Glossitis and stomatitis have also been reported with these agents. The incidence of diarrhea has been reported to be between 5% and 20%, with one study reporting an incidence of 7% for clindamycin.[59]

A more serious consequence associated with these agents has been the development of pseudomembranous colitis (PMC) characterized by severe, persistent diarrhea and the passage of blood and mucus in the stool.[60,61] PMC, which can be fatal, is thought to be caused by a toxin produced by the bacterium *Clostridium difficile*.[62] It is associated not only with clindamycin and lincomycin but also with other antibiotics such as tetracycline,[63] erythromycin, penicillins, and cephalosporins.[64] The treatment of PMC includes discontinuation of the drug, oral administration of vancomycin (2 gm daily for 7 to 10 days)[65] or cholestyramine, and fluid and electrolyte replacement. Systemically administered corticosteroids have sometimes proven helpful. Narcotic-like agents such as diphenoxylate and atropine (Lomotil) may exacerbate the condition and should not be used. PMC may occur during treatment or may appear several weeks after the cessation of antibiotic therapy.

Superinfection. As with other antibiotics, superinfection by *C. albicans* is sometimes associated with the use of clindamycin.

Allergy. Skin rashes occur in about 10% of patients given clindamycin. Rarely, urticaria, angioneurotic edema, erythema multiforme, serum sickness, and anaphylaxis have occurred.

Other effects. Headache, dizziness, reversible hematologic effects, and abnormal liver function tests have been reported with these agents. Safety for use in pregnant women and newborns has not been established. Since lincomycin and clindamycin are rela-

tively new drugs, blood studies and liver function tests should be carried out in cases of prolonged use.

Uses

Although clindamycin is effective against many gram-positive organisms, other agents are available that are at least as effective as clindamycin and do not usually cause PMC. The indications for treatment with clindamycin are limited to a small number of infections caused by anaerobic organisms, especially *Bacteroides* species and some staphylococcal infections, when the patient is allergic to penicillin.[66] It is not an acceptable alternative to penicillin in treating acute oral infections when the patient is allergic to penicillin.[67]

Many oral infections have been shown to contain a predominance of anaerobic organisms.[68] Many of these anaerobes, such as *Bacteroides oralis; Peptostreptococcus, Fusobacterium,* and *Veillonella species;* and clostridia, are sensitive to 2 gm of oral penicillin G daily.[69] Only for *B. fragilis* (Table 22-3) is clindamycin the drug of choice. Also mixed-gram-positive and gram-negative anaerobic infections may be treated with clindamycin. It is important to emphasize that clindamycin should be used only when specifically indicated, not ever indiscriminately, and the patient should be informed of the potential for and appraised of the symptoms of PMC. The dose of clindamycin is listed in Table 22-4.

Vancomycin

Vancomycin is an antibiotic with a chemical structure only recently determined by x-ray analysis. It is unrelated to any other antibiotic currently marketed. Because it has minimal gastrointestinal absorption and causes irritation when used intramuscularly, it is administered only intravenously for a systemic effect.

It is bactericidal and active against many gram-positive cocci, including both staphylococci and streptococci. It acts by inhibition of bacterial cell wall synthesis. Resistance does not seem to develop readily, and cross-resistance with other antibiotics is not believed to occur.

Except when vancomycin is given in large doses, significant toxic reactions are infrequent. With large doses or prolonged therapy, some degree of ototoxicity and nephrotoxicity may occur. Permanent deafness and fatal uremia have resulted. Anaphylaxis and superinfection may occur rarely. Prolonged, repeated use can cause thrombophlebitis. The "red-neck syndrome," including chills, fever, and shock, can occur during intravenous administration. Occasionally, there may be rash, urticaria, chills, fever, and nausea. Vancomycin is useful in the prophylaxis of bacterial endocarditis for patients with a history of rheumatic heart disease who are allergic to penicillin and have prosthetic heart valve replacement (see Appendix B, Regimen B). It is also used orally—for its local effect—to treat PMC.

Vancomycin is considered here in more detail than it would ordinarily warrant in dentistry because of continued investigations concerning its topical use against oral lesions[70] and in preventing the formation of microplaque.[71] One study showed a reduction in caries only on the occlusal surface of the teeth treated with vancomycin[72]; another registered a decrease in caries in fissures and newly erupting teeth only.[73]

BROAD-SPECTRUM ANTIBIOTICS
Tetracyclines

The tetracycline antibiotics affect a wide range of microorganisms.

Source and chemistry

The first tetracycline was isolated from a *Streptomyces* strain in 1948. Since then, other tetracyclines have been derived from different species of *Streptomyces,* and the rest have been produced semisynthetically. The tetracyclines are closely related chemically and have similar structures. They are listed in Table 22-10.

Body handling

The tetracyclines are most commonly given by mouth. Absorption following oral administration varies but is fairly rapid. There is wide tissue distribution, and tetracyclines are secreted in the saliva and in the milk of lactating mothers. Tetracyclines are concentrated by the liver and excreted into the intestines via the bile. Enterohepatic circulation prolongs the action of the tetracyclines after they have been discontinued. The tetracyclines are stored in the dentine and enamel of unerupted teeth. They cross the placenta and enter the fetal circulation. The cord plasma level of tetracycline is 60% of the level in the mother's plasma. They are excreted by glomerular filtration into the urine. The amount of a particular tetracycline excreted unchanged depends on the agent.

The concomitant administration of foods with a high calcium content, such as dairy products, or antacids containing aluminum, calcium, or magnesium decreases the oral absorption of the tetracyclines. Apparently, the mechanism involves the chelation of tetracycline with the divalent or trivalent cations aluminum, calcium, and magnesium. Iron salts and sodium bicarbonate also reduce the absorption of the tetracyclines. An increase in gastric pH caused by the antacids might be another factor in decreasing the absorption of the tetracyclines.[74]

Spectrum

The tetracyclines are bacteriostatic and interfere with the synthesis of bacterial protein by binding at

Table 22-10. Properties of the tetracyclines

Drug	Route(s) administration	Usual adult dose (mg)	$t_{\frac{1}{2}}$ (hr)	Percent absorbed (%)	Percent protein bound (%)
Tetracycline (Achromycin, Panmycin)	Oral, IV	250-500 q.6h.	6-10	60-80	25-65
Chlortetracycline (Aureomycin)	Oral, IV	250-500 q.6h.	6-10	30	45-70
Oxytetracycline (Terramycin)	Oral, IV	250-500 q.6h.	6-10	60-80	20-40
Demeclocycline or demethyl chlortetracycline (Declomycin)	Oral	150-300 q.6h.	10-17	60-80	40-90
Methacycline (Rondomycin)	Oral	150 q.6h, or 300 q.12h.	10-17		80-90
Doxycycline (Vibramycin)	Oral, IV	100 q.12h. for 2 doses, then 100 q.d. or 50 q.12h.	14-25	95	60-95
Minocycline (Minocin, Vectrin)	Oral, IV	200 stat, then 100 q.12h.	11-20	100	55-75

Modified from Requa, B.S., and Holroyd, S.V.: Applied pharmacology for the dental hygienist, St. Louis, 1982, The C.V. Mosby Co.

the 30S subunit of bacterial ribosomes. At least two processes are required before the tetracycline can exert its effect. First, by passive diffusion, it penetrates the hydrophilic pores to enter the cell. Second, by active transport, it is pumped through the inner cytoplasmic membrane. Finally, it prevents the aminoacyl transfer RNA from getting to its acceptor sites on the messenger RNA. This blocks the addition of more aminoacids to the peptide chain. As broad-spectrum antibiotics, they are effective against a wide variety of gram-positive and gram-negative bacteria, rickettsiae, spirochetes *(Treponema pallidum),* some protozoa *(Entamoeba histolytica), Chlamydia,* and *Mycoplasma.* The tetracyclines differ in their spectrum of action, the percentage of drug absorbed, the amount metabolized, and the percentage excreted unchanged. Minocycline and doxycyclines are more active than is tetracycline against some organisms, especially the anaerobes. (The major differences among the various tetracyclines are their duration of action and methods of excretion.) Bacterial resistance develops slowly to the tetracyclines in a stepwise fashion; however, cross-resistance is probably complete. Resistant strains of staphylococci and pneumococci have been commonly noted.[42]

Adverse reactions

Although most adverse reactions to the tetracyclines occur infrequently, gastrointestinal distress is not uncommon.

Gastrointestinal effects. The gastrointestinal adverse effects include anorexia, nausea, vomiting, diarrhea, gastroenteritis, glossitis, stomatitis, xerostomia, and superinfection (moniliasis). The side effects are largely related to local irritation from alteration of the oral, gastric, and enteric flora, which can occur within 2 days. The stools can become softer and turn yellow-green in color. Doxycycline produces less change in the intestinal flora than does tetracycline.[75] If diarrhea occurs in a patient receiving tetracycline, the possibility of PMC (secondary to *C. difficile* overgrowth) must be ruled out. Ordinary diarrhea, in contrast to PMC, will not contain blood or mucus in the stools. Three types of infectious enteritis that have been associated with tetracycline therapy are staphylococcal enterocolitis, intestinal candidiasis, and PMC. Patients with ill-fitting dentures are likely to have candidiasis (moniliasis) associated with the areas of oral mucosa tissue breakdown. Patients taking tetracyclines have developed a yellowish

brown discoloration of the tongue. This can occur with either topical or systemic administration.

Hepatic toxicity. Hepatotoxicity occurs more frequently in patients receiving larger doses of parenteral tetracycline, usually more than 2 gm daily. It is more common in pregnant women, and deaths have been reported.[76] Of course, pregnant women should never be given tetracycline. Renal impairment leads to accumulation of tetracyclines and an increase in the likelihood of hepatic damage.

Renal toxicity. Toxic renal effects producing Fanconi's syndrome have been reported after the use of outdated and degraded tetracycline.[77] Old tetracycline should be discarded to prevent future use.

Kidney damage should be considered, especially with administration of larger doses and in patients who are predisposed to kidney disease. Since the nephrotoxic effect of the tetracyclines is additive with that of other drugs, tetracyclines should not be used concomitantly with other nephrotoxic drugs such as methoxyflurane (Penthrane).

Hematologic effects. Although hematologic changes are uncommon, hemolytic anemia, leukocytosis, and thrombocytopenic purpura have been reported after tetracycline therapy.

Effects on teeth and bones. Tetracycline is incorporated in calcifying structures. If tetracyclines are used during the period of enamel calcification, they can produce permanent discoloration of the teeth and enamel hypoplasia. The discoloration increases with a larger total amount of the drug given and with repeated courses of tetracycline. Consequently, they should not be used during the last half of pregnancy or in children up to 9 years of age. Tetracycline will affect the primary teeth if given to the mother during the last half of pregnancy or to the infant during the first 4 to 6 months of life. If tetracycline is administered between 2 months and 7 or 8 years of age, the permanent teeth will be affected. The mechanism involves the deposition of tetracycline in the enamel of the forming teeth. These stains are permanent and darken with age and exposure to light. They begin as a yellow fluorescence and progress with time to a brown color. This process is accelerated by exposure to light. The permanent discoloration ranges from light gray to yellow to tan. Oxytetracycline and tetracycline produce the least objectionable stains. With large doses of tetracyclines, a decrease in the growth rate of bones has been demonstrated in the fetus and in infants.

The treatment of tetracycline-stained teeth requires a careful technique to ensure minimal problems.[78] Heat plus 30% hydrogen peroxide (Superoxol) is applied to affected teeth to be treated, usually the anterior teeth.

Allergy. Anaphylactic and various dermatologic reactions to the tetracyclines have occasionally occurred, but the overall allergenicity of these drugs is low. Other effects attributable to a hypersensitivity reaction to tetracycline include glossitis and cheilosis. The mechanism of these effects may relate to alterations in flora. A patient who is allergic to one tetracycline is almost certain to be allergic to all tetracyclines.

Superinfection. With superinfection, resistant organisms multiply and may cause disease. One common situation, especially prevalent in the compromised host (Table 22-2), is an overgrowth of *C. albicans.*

Photosensitivity. Patients taking tetracyclines who are exposed to the sunlight sometimes react with an exaggerated sunburn, onycholysis, and nail pigmentation. Although the incidence seems to vary with the different tetracyclines, demeclocycline and doxycycline are more likely to produce this effect.

Drug interactions

Antacids. Antacids containing magnesium, calcium, or aluminum decrease the intestinal absorption by chelating with the tetracycline. If antacids are absolutely essential, at least 3 hours should be allowed after the tetracycline is administered before using them.

Oral anticoagulants. When given in large doses or with prolonged administration, tetracyclines can reduce the numbers of intestinal bacteria, which normally produce vitamin K. This may result in a decrease in the plasma prothrombin but is probably not clinically significant, even in patients undergoing therapy with anticoagulants such as warfarin (Coumadin).

Barbiturates. The barbiturates may enhance the metabolism of some tetracyclines. This could theoretically reduce the duration of action of the tetracyclines.

Iron. Orally administered iron impairs the absorption of various tetracyclines and should not be used concomitantly.

Methoxyflurane. A combination of methoxyflurane and tetracycline may produce additive nephrotoxic effects.

Uses

Although the tetracyclines are active against a wide variety of microorganisms, they are rarely the drug of choice for a specific infection. They have been used commonly to treat chlamydial and rickettsial infections and cholera, to prevent infections in patients with respiratory disease such as emphysema, and to prevent acne. Doxycycline has been shown to be effective in the prevention of traveler's diarrhea caused by *E. coli.*[79] It is given as follows: 200 mg as travel begins, then 100 mg every day.[80] Tetracycline is rarely the drug of first or alternative choice. It is indicated against infections only when the sensitivity tests indicate that a more potent or more specific antibiotic is ineffective or cannot be used. Tetracyclines should not be used for prophylaxis against bacterial endocarditis.

The tetracyclines have been used with mixed success to treat a wide variety of dental problems. If a tetracycline is used, doxycycline has been shown to be two to six times as active against anaerobic bacteria as tetracycline itself.[81]

The tetracyclines have been reported to be effective against recurrent aphthous stomatitis[82] and acute necrotizing ulcerative gingivitis (ANUG).[11] Graykowski and Kingman[83] found in a double-blind study that a suspension of tetracycline reduced the healing of recurrent aphthous ulceration. Although tetracyclines have been tried in the treatment of acute herpetic gingivostomatitis and periodontal abscesses, their success is largely testimonial. Scopp and others[84] suggest that tetracycline not be recommended for routine prophylactic use after periodontal surgery. Although often used as an adjunct to periodontal surgery, the clinical evidence that tetracycline significantly enhances the surgical outcome is lacking. Ciancio and others,[85] studying the effect of minocycline on gingival health, concluded that it was concentrated in the gingival crevicular fluid and reduced plaque scores. Its place in the treatment and prevention of periodontal disease is yet to be determined.

Chloramphenicol

Chloramphenicol (Chloromycetin) is a broad-spectrum, bacteriostatic antibiotic. Like erythromycin, lincomycin, and clindamycin, it inhibits bacterial protein synthesis by acting primarily on the 50S ribosomal unit (Table 22-7). It is active against a large number of gram-positive and gram-negative organisms, rickettsiae, and some chlamydiae. It is particularly active against *Salmonella typhi.*

Chloramphenicol has fallen into disuse primarily because of its serious adverse effects. Fatal blood dyscrasias including aplastic anemia, agranulocytosis, hypoplastic anemia, and thrombocytopenia have occurred even after short-term use. A non–dose-related bone marrow suppression has produced pancytopenia. Although the incidence is low (1:40,000), this condition is often fatal. In view of the seriousness and frequency of adverse reactions to chloramphenicol, it must be used against serious infections only when less dangerous antimicrobial agents are ineffective or cannot be used. Only in the treatment of life-threatening *H. influenzae* and *S. typhi* (typhoid fever) infections is chloramphenicol still the antibiotic of first choice. Its availability over the counter in some foreign countries should be noted. It is unlikely that any use for chloramphenicol in dentistry would be justified.

AMINOGLYCOSIDES

Table 22-11 lists the properties of the aminoglycoside antibiotics. Since there are many similarities among these agents, they will be discussed together.

These agents are poorly absorbed after oral administration and so must be administered by intramuscular or intravenous injection. After injection they are rapidly excreted by the normal kidney. Although they are bactericidal and have a broad antibacterial spectrum, their use is primarily in the treatment of aerobic gram-negative infections when other agents are ineffective. They have little action against gram-positive anaerobic or facultative bacteria. They appear to inhibit protein synthesis and to act directly on the 30S subunit of the ribosome.

Resistance can be produced rapidly by a mutation or by acquisition of a plasmid, which is genetic material located outside the chromosomal material. The plasmid can be transferred from one bacterial strain to another, thereby teaching resistance to antibiotics. An organism resistant to any agent on the list in Table 22-11 will almost always be resistant to those agents listed above it. For example, an organism resistant to gentamicin will also be resistant to kanamycin (listed above it) but might be sensitive to tobramycin (listed below it).

Adverse reactions

The adverse reactions of the aminoglycoside antibiotics seriously limit their use in clinical practice. Their major adverse effects include the following:

Ototoxicity. The aminoglycosides are toxic to the eighth cranial nerve, which can lead to auditory and vestibular disturbances. Patients may have difficulty in maintaining equilibrium and can develop vertigo. Hearing impairment and deafness, which can be permanent, have resulted from the administration of these agents. This side effect is more common in patients with renal failure because the drug accumulates in the body. The elderly are also more susceptible.

Table 22-11. Aminoglycosides

Drug	Route(s) of administration	Comments
Neomycin (Mycifradin)	Topical, IM, Oral	Used mostly topically
Streptomycin	IM	Used in combination for tuberculosis and prevention of bacterial endocarditis, tularemia, plague, and brucellosis
Kanamycin (Kantrex)	IM, IV, Oral	Used for severe gram-negative infections; others have mostly supplanted its use
Gentamicin (Garamycin)	IM, IV	Used for *Proteus, Pseudomonas, Serratia, Klebsiella, Enterobacter,* and other serious gram-negative infections
Tobramycin (Nebcin)	IM, IV	Used for *Pseudomonas aeruginosa* and other gram-negative infections resistant to gentamicin (combined with carbenicillin-like agent)
Amikacin (Amikin)	IM, IV	Used for organisms resistant to other aminoglycosides (reserve)

Modified from Requa, B.S., and Holroyd, S.V.: Applied pharmacology for the dental hygienist, St. Louis, 1982, The C.V. Mosby Co.

Nephrotoxicity. The aminoglycosides can cause kidney damage, especially when they accumulate in the body. It varies from 1% to 10% depending on the agent, trough levels, patient's age, and concomitant nephrotoxic drugs.

Neuromuscular blockade. The aminoglycosides act as weak neuromuscular blocking agents, potentially producing *apnea.* This is a problem if aminoglycosides are given in combination with general anesthetics or skeletal muscle relaxants—agents that are frequently used during surgical procedures.

Uses

The uses of the aminoglycosides are reserved for hospitalized patients with the serious gram-negative infections listed in Table 22-11. Their use in dentistry may be encountered in patients with prosthetic heart valves (Appendix B, Regimen B).

SPECTINOMYCIN

Spectinomycin (Trobicin) is related to the aminoglycoside antibiotics and is somewhat active against a number of gram-negative bacteria, although other antibiotics are more effective. It acts on the 30S subunit and is bacteriostatic. Its only indication is in the treatment of acute genital (urethral) and rectal gonorrhea in patients allergic to penicillin. It is usually administered as a single intramuscular dose of 2 gm. Disseminated gonococcal infections require multiple doses.

METRONIDAZOLE

Metronidazole (Flagyl) is trichomonocidal; that is, it kills *Trichomonas vaginalis.* It is also ambicidal and bactericidal for many anaerobes, most notably *Bacteroides* species. It is available orally as a tablet and in an intravenous solution for serious anaerobic bacteria.

Adverse reactions

The most common adverse effects are gastrointestinal, including nausea, anorexia, diarrhea, and epigastric pain. Headache, vomiting, and a metallic taste have been reported. Glossitis, stomatitis, and a furry tongue are side effects the dentist should note. These may be associated with moniliasis. Neurotoxic effects include paresthesias, urticaria, and dryness of the mouth. Also, dysuria and cystitis are side effects. A disulfiram-like reaction—nausea, flushing, vomit-

ing, or headache—can result if alcohol is ingested while the drug is being taken. The dentist should avoid prescribing or using any alcohol-containing products for these patients. If CNS effects occur, treatment should be discontinued. Because it is carcinogenic (rodents) and mutagenic (bacteria), it should be administered prudently. It is contraindicated during the first trimester of pregnancy.

Uses

It is the drug of choice in the treatment of *T. vaginalis* infection. It is also effective versus *Giardia lamblia* and some amebas. It is an alternative to clindamycin and chloramphenicol for the treatment of *B. fragilis* infection.[86] Its role in the treatment of dental infections will require more study, but it has been used for treatment of periodontal infections.[87] Rood and Murgatroyd[88] demonstrated its effectiveness in reducing the incidence of "dry socket" from 4% to 1%.

TOPICAL ANTIBIOTICS

The most commonly used topical antibiotics and their principal spectrum of action are shown in Table 22-12. Some products available are listed in Table 22-13. These agents are generally poorly absorbed orally, are not useful systemically because of their high degree of toxicity, and have a low degree of allergenicity. They are employed for periodontal dressings or superficial wounds. Because gentamicin has proved useful systemically, its topical use should be severely limited. Some topical antiinfectives are formulated using multiple antibiotics. One example is Neosporin, an agent containing polymyxin, neomycin, and bacitracin.

SYNTHETIC ANTIBACTERIAL AGENTS
Sulfonamides

Most of the sulfonamides currently on the market are derivatives of sulfanilamide. Strictly speaking, they cannot be classified as antibiotics because they are not produced by living organisms.

The demonstration that the antibacterial activity of the Prontosil molecule was associated with sulfanilamide led to the synthesis of a large number of related antibacterial sulfonamides. The earlier sulfonamides had low solubility in the urine, and the danger of crystallization in the kidney existed. Since the new sulfonamides are more soluble, they are less likely to precipitate in the kidney.

Table 22-12. Topical antibiotics

	Spectrum			
Drug	**Gram-positive organisms**	**Gram-negative organisms**	*Pseudomonas*	**Systemic toxicity**
Bacitracin	+			Nephrotoxicity
Polymyxin B		+		Nephrotoxicity, peripheral neuropathy
Neomycin	+	+		Nephrotoxicity, ototoxicity
Gentamicin	+	+	+	Nephrotoxicity, ototoxicity

From Requa, B.S., and Holroyd, S.V.: Applied pharmacology for the dental hygienist, St. Louis, 1982, The C.V. Mosby Co.

Table 22-13. Topical antiinfective agents (selected combinations of antibiotic ointments)

Trade name	Ingredients
Neosporin, Mycitracin, Triple Antibiotic	Polymyxin B, neomycin, bacitracin
Terramycin with Polymyxin B	Oxytetracycline, polymyxin B
Bacimycin	Bacitracin, neomycin
Spectrocin	Neomycin, gramicidin
Polysporin	Polymyxin B, bacitracin

From Requa, B.S., and Holroyd, S.V.: Applied pharmacology for the dental hygienist, St. Louis, 1982, The C.V. Mosby Co.

The introduction of many antibiotics limited the use of the sulfonamides. The introduction of trimethoprim-sulfamethoxazole, has greatly increased sulfonamide use.

Mechanism of action

The sulfonamides' structural similarity to para-aminobenzoic acid (PABA) is the basis for most of their antibacterial activity. Since many bacteria are unable to use preformed folic acid, an essential component of several enzyme systems, they must synthesize folic acid from PABA. Because of their structural similarity, the sulfonamides inhibit the bacterial enzyme that incorporates PABA into dihydropteroic acid, the precursor of folic acid.

Para-aminobenzoic acid (PABA)   Sulfanilamide

Thus, by competitive inhibition, adequate folic acid cannot be synthesized by the bacteria. Drugs that are metabolized to PABA, for example, the ester local anesthetics, could theoretically interfere with the action of the sulfonamides.

Spectrum

The sulfonamides are bacteriostatic against many gram-positive and some gram-negative bacteria. They are ineffective against *S. viridans* but are active against some *Chlamydia*.

The amount of the sulfonamide absorbed varies with the solubility. The readily absorbed sulfonamides are used for their systemic effects. Some sulfonamides that produce relatively low systemic blood levels but high urine concentrations are used for the treatment of urinary tract infections. Other relatively insoluble sulfonamides are used in the treatment of ulcerative colitis or before surgical procedures on the bowel. Since these sulfonamides are poorly absorbed, they have only a local effect on the gastrointestinal tract.

The sulfonamide that is absorbed distributes throughout the body, including the cerebrospinal fluid. The drug is metabolized by acetylation or conjugation to the glucuronide in the liver. Metabolites, some of which are less soluble, and some free drug are excreted in urine.

Adverse reactions

The most common adverse effect of the sulfonamides is an allergic reaction. This may be manifested as rash, urticaria, pruritus, fever, a fatal exfoliative dermatitis, or periarteritis nodosa. Other cutaneous allergic reactions include erythema nodosum, erythema multiforme, Stevens-Johnson syndrome, and epidermal necrolysis. These eruptions usually occur after 1 week of therapy. Cross-hypersensitivity can, but does not always, occur.

Other relatively common side effects include nausea, vomiting, abdominal discomfort, headache, and dizziness. Liver damage, depressed renal function, blood dyscrasias (agranulocytosis, thrombocytopenia, aplastic and hemolytic anemia), and precipitation of lupus erythematosus are seen less frequently.

The possibility of renal crystallization must always be kept in mind with the sulfonamides, particularly if the less soluble systemic agents are used or if renal function is not normal. Forcing fluids is generally advisable with these drugs.

Dental use

Even though sulfonamides have been reported to be effective in some dental infections,[98,99] almost without exception antibiotics are more effective and generally safer. Only in rare instances, when the antibiotics are ineffective or cannot be used, should sulfonamides be used against dental infections. Because of their high allergenicity, they should *not* be used topically on oral lesions. Patients with a history of rheumatic heart disease may be taking sulfadiazine for long-term prophylaxis of bacterial endocarditis (sulfadiazine 1 gm orally every day for a minimum of 5 years).

Trimethoprim-sulfamethoxazole

The combination of the drugs trimethoprim, an antibacterial and antimalarial agent, and sulfamethoxazole, a sulfonamide, represents an application of theoretical considerations. Since sulfamethoxazole inhibits the incorporation of PABA into folic acid, and trimethoprim inhibits the reduction of dihydrofolate to tetrahydrofolate, this combination inhibits two separate steps in the essential metabolic pathway of the bacteria, thus leading to a synergistic effect.

Trimethoprim-sulfamethoxazole (Bactrim, Septra), like the sulfonamides, is bacteriostatic against a wide variety of gram-positive bacteria and some gram-negative bacteria. Its adverse effects are also similar to those of the sulfonamides. About 75% of the adverse reactions associated with this combination involve the skin. Although rare, exfoliative dermatitis, Stevens-Johnson syndrome, and toxic epidermal necrolysis (Lyell's syndrome) have been reported. Adverse gastrointestinal effects include nausea, vomiting, diarrhea, glossitis, and stomatitis. CNS effects,

including headache, depression, and hallucinations, are other reported manifestations of toxicity. Hematologic reactions reported include megaloblastosis, thrombocytopenia, and leukopenia, as well as anemia, granulocytopenia, agranulocytosis, and coagulation disorders. Jaundice and renal damage can occasionally occur.

Trimethoprim-sulfamethoxazole is available in a fixed combination of 5:1, which, because of the body's handling of these two components, produces a 20:1 ratio in the plasma and tissues.

Its primary indication is in the treatment of selected urinary tract infections, certain cases of acute gonococcal urethritis, and selected respiratory and gastrointestinal infections. It is used extensively to treat acute otitis media in children often caused by *H. influenzae*.

Urinary tract antiseptics

Several antibacterial agents cannot be used to treat systemic infections, since therapeutic plasma concentrations are not reached in safe doses. But because they are concentrated in the kidney and urine, they can be used to treat urinary tract infections.

Methenamine

Methenamine is a urinary tract antiseptic that acts by the release of formaldehyde in an acid urine. It is orally absorbed and excreted in the urine. Since an acid pH (pH 5) promotes the production of formaldehyde, methenamine is administered with hippuric acid, mandelic acid, or cranberry juice. Gastrointestinal distress can occur with larger doses. Methenamine is available as methenamine mandelate (Mandelamine) or methenamine hippurate (Hiprex). Methenamine is useful for long-term suppressive therapy to prevent urinary tract infections in susceptible individuals.

Nitrofurantoin

Nitrofurantoin (Macrodantin) possesses a wide antibacterial spectrum including both gram-positive and gram-negative bacteria. It is bacteriostatic against many common urinary tract pathogens, including *Escherichia coli*. Many strains of *Klebsiella* and *Enterobacter* are resistant. It is rapidly absorbed from the gastrointestinal tract, but antibacterial plasma concentrations are not reached because the drug is rapidly excreted with a $t_{\frac{1}{2}}$ of less than 1 hour.

The most common adverse reactions are nausea, vomiting, and diarrhea, but taking the drug with food decreases these effects. The administration of the drug in a larger crystal size may cause less nausea. Hypersensitivity reactions include chills, fever, leukopenia, granulocytopenia, hemolytic anemia, cholestatic jaundice, and chronic active hepatitis. Other hypersensitivity reactions involving the lung include allergic pneumonitis and interstitial pulmonary fibrosis. Neurologic disorders observed include headache and a polyneuropathy with denervation and muscle atrophy. Nitrofurantoin's use is in the treatment or prevention of certain urinary tract infections, but is seldom as effective as antibiotics or sulfonamides for the treatment of these infections.

Nalidixic acid

Nalidixic acid (NegGram) is bactericidal to most of the gram-negative bacteria that cause urinary tract infections except *Pseudomonas*. Although resistance develops rapidly when tested, the population of resistant bacteria in the community does not seem to rise.[100] The compound is well absorbed orally and conjugated in the liver. It has a serum $t_{\frac{1}{2}}$ of 1½ hours and a urine $t_{\frac{1}{2}}$ of 6 hours.

Nalidixic acid, taken orally, may cause nausea, vomiting, and diarrhea. Allergic reactions reported include pruritus, urticaria, rashes, photosensitivity, eosinophilia, and fever. CNS effects include headache, drowsiness, vertigo, visual disturbances, and myalgia.

This drug is useful in the treatment of certain urinary tract infections, especially those caused by indole-positive *Proteus*.

Cinoxacin

Cinoxacin (Cinobac) is chemically related to nalidixic acid. Its spectrum includes aerobic gram-negative bacteria, such as *E. coli,* and species of *Klebsiella, Enterobacter,* and *Proteus*. It is indicated for the treatment of urinary tract infections in adults. Its side effects include gastrointestinal, CNS (insomnia and restlessness), and hypersensitivity reactions. Until more data are available, other agents are preferred for the treatment of urinary tract infections.

ANTITUBERCULOSIS AGENTS

The treatment of tuberculosis, a disease caused by the acid-fast bacterium *Mycobacterium tuberculosis*, is difficult for several reasons. First, patients with tuberculosis often have inadequate defense mechanisms. Second, the microorganisms develop resistant strains easily and have unusual metabolic characteristics, including long periods of inactivity. Finally, the drugs available are not bactericidal and because of their toxicity often cannot be used in sufficient doses.

The treatment of tuberculosis relies almost entirely on chemotherapy (Table 22-14). Because of the problem of resistance, at least two drugs are administered concurrently in all active cases. Isoniazid (INH, Nydrazid) and ethambutol (Myambutol) are combined for the treatment of mild pulmonary tuberculosis. When the pulmonary tuberculosis is severe, a three-drug combination including streptomycin or rifampin is employed. These therapeutic regimens are continued for at least 1½ years.

Certain tuberculin reactors (patients who are without evidence of systemic disease but have had a positive skin test) are treated with 300 mg of isoniazid daily for 1 year. The following tuberculin reactors are so treated:

1. Close contacts of patients with recently diagnosed tuberculosis
2. Those with x-ray findings that show no progression of disease
3. Those who converted (became positive) within the previous 2 years
4. Those at special risk (taking steroids, diabetic)
5. Those less than 35 years old

Some patients taking drugs that suppress the body's ability to fight infection, such as high-dose corticosteroids, are given isoniazid prophylactically as long as they are receiving steroids.

Isoniazid

Even though isoniazid is both bacteriostatic and bactericidal in vitro, its action in vivo is only against actively growing tubercle bacilli. "Resting" bacilli exposed to the drug are able to resume normal growth when the drug is removed. Resistant strains develop within a few weeks after the beginning of therapy.

The most important side effects of this drug are rash, fever, peripheral neuritis, and jaundice. Peripheral neuritis, occurring in up to 20% of untreated patients, can be prevented by the administration of pyridoxine (vitamin B_6) daily. Optic neuritis requires that vision be monitored. Other adverse reactions

Table 22-14. Antituberculosis agents

Drug	Usual dosage	Route of administration	Action	Side effects	Comments
Primary agents					
Isoniazid (INH)	300 mg/24 hr	Oral (IM available)	Bactericidal	Peripheral neuropathy, convulsions, rashes, hepatitis	Use pyridoxine 50-100 mg/24 hr to reduce peripheral neuropathy
Streptomycin	1 gm/24 hr for 60-90 days, then 1 gm 2 or 3 times/wk	IM	Bactericidal, bacteriostatic	Vestibular dysfunction, ototoxicity, nephrotoxicity, rashes, blood dyscrasias	Elderly more susceptible to toxic effects
Ethambutol (Myambutol)	25 mg/kg/24 hr for 2 months, then 15 mg/kg/24 hr	Oral (IV available)	Bacteriostatic	Optic neuritis, central scotomas, loss of green and red perception	Check vision
Rifampin (Rifadin)	600 mg/24 hr (single dose)	Oral	Bactericidal	Gastrointestinal irritation, fever, rash, mental confusion, blood dyscrasias	Turns urine, saliva, sweat, and feces red-orange
Secondary agents					
p-Aminosalicylic acid (PAS)	10-12 gm/24 hr	Oral	Bacteriostatic	Gastrointestinal disturbances, rash	
Ethionamide (Trecator)	500-750 mg/24 hr	Oral	Bacteriostatic	Similar to isoniazid	
Pyrazinamide (PZA)	25 mg/kg/24 hr	Oral	Bacteriostatic	Hepatic damage, uric acid retention	
Cycloserine (Seromycin)	750-1000 mg/24 hr	Oral	Bacteriostatic	Nausea, vomiting, peripheral neuritis	
Kanamycin (Kantrex)	0.5 gm/24 hr	IM	Bactericidal, bacteriostatic	Similar to streptomycin	
Viomycin	0.5 gm/24 hr	IM	Bacteriostatic	Renal and auditory damage	

From Requa, B.S., and Holroyd, S.V.: Applied pharmacology for the dental hygienist, St. Louis, 1982, The C.V. Mosby Co.

associated with the nervous system include mental abnormalities, excessive sedation, incoordination, dizziness, paresthesias, toxic encephalopathy, and convulsions. Severe and sometimes fatal hepatic injury with jaundice increases in incidence with age and may occur after cessation of therapy. Hypersensitivity reactions, including skin eruptions, fever, hematologic reactions, hepatitis, and arthritic symptoms have been noted. Dryness of the mouth, epigastric distress, urinary retention in men, methemoglobinemia, and tinnitus have also been reported. Isoniazid is used alone for prophylaxis against tuberculosis and in combination with other agents for the treatment of tuberculosis.

Ethambutol

Ethambutol (Myambutol) is a synthetic tuberculostatic agent effective against *Mycobacterium tuberculosis*. Resistance develops very slowly to this agent. The most important side effect is optic neuritis, resulting in a decrease in visual acuity and loss of ability to perceive the color green. Other side effects include rash, joint pain, gastrointestinal upset, malaise, headache, and dizziness. Ethambutol is used in combination with isoniazid and has replaced para-aminosalicyclic acid (PAS) because it has fewer side effects and better patient acceptance.

Streptomycin

Streptomycin, an aminoglycoside antibiotic, is both bacteriostatic and bactericidal for the tubercle bacillus in vitro, but in vivo it is merely suppressive. Random mutations result in some bacilli that are highly resistant to streptomycin. The longer therapy is continued, the more resistant strains will develop. Within 1 month, resistance is a problem in some patients. Mixing streptomycin with another drug will delay, but not prevent, the development of resistant strains. Streptomycin's primary use is in combination with other agents in the treatment of the most serious forms of tuberculosis—for example, meningitis.

Aminosalicylic acid

Aminosalicylic acid (para-aminosalicylic acid, PAS) is bacteriostatic, and large doses are required. The development of resistant strains requires at least 4 months. Adverse effects are reported in about 10% of those treated with PAS, and irritation of the gastrointestinal tract, resulting in anorexia, nausea, and diarrhea, is most common. The advent of ethambutol

and rifampin has reduced the importance of this drug in the treatment of tuberculosis.

Rifampin

Rifampin (Rifadin, Rimactane) inhibits the growth of most gram-positive and many gram-negative bacteria including *E. coli, Pseudomonas, Proteus,* and *Klebsiella*. It is inhibitory to the tubercle bacilli. Since the mycobacteria rapidly develop resistance to rifampin in a one-step process, it should not be used alone. Taken orally, it produces an orange-red color in the urine, feces, saliva, sputum, tears, and sweat. The most common adverse reactions include nausea and vomiting, rash, fever, a flu-like syndrome, and thrombocytopenia. Jaundice, a serious problem, hepatorenal syndrome, and gastrointestinal disturbances have been reported. Hypersensitivity reactions and hematologic effects cover a wide range of reactions to rifampin.

It is used in combination with other agents (isoniazid) in the treatment of tuberculosis or reserved for treatment failures. It also is used prophylactically in patients exposed to meningococcal disease. Its wide antimicrobial effectiveness portends future use.

ANTIFUNGAL AGENTS

Table 22-15 lists the most commonly used antifungal agents. Although several agents are available for the topical treatment of fungal infections, only nystatin (Mycostatin) is routinely used in dentistry.

Nystatin

Nystatin, a polyene antibiotic produced by *Streptomyces noursei,* is active against fungi and yeasts, particularly *C. albicans*. It is bound to a sterol moiety in the membranes of sensitive yeasts and fungi. This results in the formation of pores or channels, which results in a change in permeability allowing small molecules to leak out.[89] It is used topically against *C. albicans* infections (candidiasis or moniliasis) of the skin and mucous membranes. Absorption after topical or oral administration is negligible. Resistance does not usually occur in vivo. Allergic reactions have not been reported, but nausea, vomiting, and diarrhea may occur after oral use. Since nystatin has no effect on bacteria, superinfection is not a problem.

Although *C. albicans* is a usual inhabitant of the oral cavity, oral candidiasis (thrush) is most likely to occur in debilitated patients or in those taking broad-spectrum antibiotics or corticosteroids (Table 22-2).

Table 22-15. Antifungal agents

Drug	Route(s) of administration*	Indications	Adverse reactions
Nystatin (Mycostatin)	Oral, vaginal tablets, cream	Orally for intestinal candidiasis; topically for oral *Candida* infections	Rare
Amphotericin B (Fungizone)	IV, topical	Intravenously for systemic infections; topically for local infections	Renal damage, thrombophlebitis, fever
Candicidin (Vanobid)	Topical	For treatment of *C. albicans* infections	Rare
Griseofulvin (Fulvicin, Grifulvin V, Grisactin)	Oral	For long-term chronic dermatophytic infections (tinea, *Trichophyton* infections)	Gastrointestinal disturbance, renal damage, hepatotoxic effects
Flucytosine (5-FC, Ancobon)	Oral	Orally for systemic *Candida* or *Cryptococcus* infections	Nausea, vomiting, blood dyscrasias
Miconazole (Monistat 7, Micatin)	IV, topical	For systemic fungal infections and topically for athlete's foot and candidiasis	Phlebitis, pruritus, rash, nausea
Clotrimazole (Lotrimin)	Topical	For dermatologic use against *Candida* infections	Erythema, pruritus, urticaria

Modified from Requa, B.S., and Holroyd, S.V.: Applied pharmacology for the dental hygienist, St. Louis, 1982, The C.V. Mosby Co.
*Topical may be applied to the skin or mucous membranes (vaginally).

Thrush has been reported to occur during the use of tetracyclines for periodontal dressings but has not been associated with the similar use of bacitracin. Thrush has also been related to the prolonged use of topical corticosteroids in the treatment of oral lesions.[90]

For the treatment of oral candidiasis, nystatin is available in an aqueous suspension, an ointment, or an oral lozenge. The aqueous suspension is available as 100,000 units/ml and is dispensed in a 60 ml bottle containing a dropper calibrated for 1 ml. The recommended adult dose for oral infections is 4 to 6 ml four times a day until 48 hours after the signs of the infection have disappeared. The drug should be held in the mouth for 2 minutes before swallowing.

Nystatin is also available as an oral lozenge or vaginal tablet containing 100,000 units. In the treatment of oral candidiasis either of these forms can be placed in the mouth and allowed to dissolve four times a day. The flavored oral troche is preferred over the unflavored vaginal tablet in the treatment of oral infections but is available only in a dosage pack also containing vaginal tablets. The oral forms allow the drug to be in contact with the infection for a longer time. It is important that the patient understand how to use the medication prescribed. Some have recommended that treatment continue for at least 14 days and not be discontinued until two successive smears are negative.[91] The topical ointment containing nystatin may be used for localized lesions or applied directly to the denture before insertion in the mouth.

Amphotericin B

Amphotericin B, another polyene antibiotic, is effective against a wide range of fungi. It is used intravenously to treat systemic fungal infections such as blastomycosis, histoplasmosis, coccidioidomycosis, cryptococcosis, and disseminated candidiasis. Fatal cases of the later have been reported after tooth extraction.[92] Amphotericin B is not absorbed orally and is used topically against local *Candida* infections. Although it is combined with tetracycline in an oral preparation to suppress overgrowth of yeasts and fungi, there is no clinical evidence that this combination is necessary or effective.* However, the currently available topical preparations are not recommended for oral use.[93] A 2% concentration of amphotericin B in an adhesive paste (Orabase) or an adhesive powder formulation (Orahesive) has been reported to be useful in the treatment of mucous membrane lesions infected with *C. albicans*.[94,95]

Amphotericin B is toxic. Its parenteral use should be justified by a definitely established need for the drug. Patients treated parenterally with this drug must be kept under close clinical supervision, particularly

*The National Academy of Sciences–National Research Council has recently stated that this combination is ineffective as a fixed combination.

in regard to renal function. Over 80% of patients treated with amphotericin develop decreased renal function. Thrombopenia, chills, fever, anemia, vomiting, convulsions, headache, and flushing have been reported. Severe allergic reactions, including anaphylaxis and phlebitis, have also occurred. Although frequently reported, the proof of hepatic toxicity from amphotericin B is lacking. Topical application may cause local irritation, but it is otherwise well tolerated topically. Amphotericin B therapy requires hospitalization, at least for initiation of therapy. Adequate laboratory tests are required to monitor for toxicity.

Griseofulvin

Griseofulvin (Fulvicin U/F, Grifulvin V, Grisactin) is produced by *Penicillium griseofulvum dierckx*. It is used orally against several dermatophytic infections caused by *Trichophyton, Epidermophyton,* and *Microsporum.*

Side effects include headache, peripheral neuritis, lethargy, mental confusion, fatigue, syncope, vertigo, and blurred vision. Nausea, vomiting, diarrhea, and hepatotoxicity have also been noted. Other untoward reactions include hematologic effects, renal effects, serum-sickness syndrome, and angioedema. It is used for the treatment of myotic infections of the skin and nails caused by susceptible organisms (such as, ringworm or athlete's foot). Treatment varies between a minimum of 2 weeks to 1 year depending on the affected area. It has no application in dental practice.

Flucytosine

Flucytosine (Ancobon) is a synthetic antifungal agent related structurally to fluorouracil, a cytotoxic agent. It inhibits the multiplication of susceptible strains of fungi. Resistance frequently develops during therapy.[96] It has been used successfully in the treatment of some cases of mucocutaneous candidiasis.[97] It is rapidly absorbed from the gastrointestinal tract, with a peak level reached in 1-2 hours and a $t_{\frac{1}{2}}$ of 3 to 6 hours.

Adverse reactions include bone marrow depression resulting in anemia, leukopenia, and thrombocytopenia as well as gastrointestinal irritation resulting in nausea, vomiting, diarrhea, and enterocolitis.

Its use is primarily in combination with the more toxic amphotericin B. The development of resistant strains limits its more extensive use.

Imidazoles

Miconazole

Miconazole (Micatin, Monistat 7) is an imidazole with broad antifungal and some antibacterial action. It is used topically and by intravenous administration. It is effective against Tinea and cutaneous candidiasis. Applied topically, it can occasionally produce burning, itching, urticaria, and rash.

Clotrimazole

Clotrimazole (Lotrimin, Mycelex) is similar to miconazole in both structure and spectrum of action, such as against tinea and *C. albicans*. It is less effective than either miconazole or nystatin for candidiasis.

In at least one study, clotrimazole lozenges have been demonstrated to be effective in the treatment of oral candidiasis.[97] At the present time this antiinfective agent is available only in cream or solution form. Although the imidazoles have not yet been approved for oral infections, it is likely that they will be accepted in the future.

Other antifungal agents currently used for vaginal, systemic, or skin infections (Table 22-15), may be used in the future to treat *C. albicans* infections of the oral mucous membrane. Like clotrimazole, these agents are usually developed and tested for use against vaginal infections before they are marketed for oral mucous membrane use.

Ketoconazole

Ketoconazole (Nizoral) is an orally effective systemic antifungal agent with a low toxicity and a wide spectrum of action. It is related to miconazole and clotrimazole. This antifungal agent was approved by the FDA in 1981 because of its wide spectrum of action against many fungi and its effectiveness when taken orally. It constitutes a significant advancement in the treatment of fungal infections. It is indicated in the treatment of a wide variety of fungal infections, including chronic mucocutaneous candidiasis and oral thrush.

ANTIVIRAL AGENTS

The development of agents useful in the treatment of viral infections is difficult because viruses are obligate intracellular parasites (that is, they must live inside cells). Since the clinical symptoms of a viral infection often signal the last stage in the disease, eradication of the offending agent at this point would

Table 22-16. Antiviral agents

Drug	Indications	Route of administration
Amantadine (Symmetrel)	Influenza A virus, Parkinson disease and syndrome	Oral
Idoxuridine (IDU) (Stoxil, Dendrid)	Herpes simplex keratitis	Topical
Vidarabine (adenine arabinoside) (Vira A)	Herpes simplex virus encephalitis	IV, topical
Acyclovir (Zovirax)	Primary genital herpes	Topical

Modified from Requa, B.S. and Holroyd, S.V.: Applied pharmacology for the dental hygienist, St. Louis, 1982, The C.V. Mosby Co.

do little to change the disease process. The most common antiviral agents are listed in Table 22-16 and will be briefly discussed here.

Idoxuridine

Idoxuridine (IDU) (Dendrid, Herplex, Stoxil) exerts its activity primarily against the herpesvirus group. Herpes simplex is one of the most common viruses seen in dentistry. It produces a recurring lesion of the lip (herpes labialis), which begins as an area of erythema followed by vesicle formation. When the vesicles break, an encrusted ulceration remains that heals in about 1 week without treatment. Although idoxuridine has been used in the treatment of herpes labialis, it has met with little success, possibly because of the difficulty in penetrating the lesion.

Idoxuridine can be used topically or intravenously. Its primary clinical use has been in the treatment of herpes simplex keratitis.[101] It is not effective in herpes simplex type 2 (genital) infection, but herpetic stomatitis has been successfully treated with it.[102]

Vidarabine

Vidarabine (Vira-A) is effective when injected intravenously for the treatment of herpes simplex viral encephalitis. It can cause mild gastrointestinal adverse effects, some CNS reactions, rash, and an occasional hematologic abnormality. It is also used as an ophthalmic ointment specifically for the treatment of herpes simplex keratoconjunctivitis.

Amantadine

Amantadine (Symmetrel) is a synthetic antiviral agent structurally unrelated to any other antimicrobial agent. Studies have proven its effectiveness in preventing infection with different strains of influenza A virus.[103] This drug has the ability to prevent viral penetration of the host cell. It can also ameliorate clinical symptoms if given within 20 hours after the onset of illness.[104,105] It reduces symptoms and shortens the illness. It must be kept in mind that this drug is prophylactic against only one kind of virus: the influenza A virus. Its action on the brain is useful in the treatment of Parkinson's disease, a condition that results in involuntary tremors.

Acyclovir

Acyclovir (acycloguanosine, Zovirax) has been shown to be effective against the herpesvirus, including herpes simplex and varicella-zoster, and the Epstein-Barr virus. It is orally as well as topically effective. It has been well tolerated, and no adverse effects have been reported. This may be because it does not interfere with DNA synthesis in uninfected cells. Clinical research is currently continuing on many uses of acyclovir. This agent represents a real advance in the treatment of herpes. It is available as an ointment for topical use. Indications for its use at the present are limited, and only more controlled studies can elucidate its proper place in therapy.

REFERENCES

1. Dorland's illustrated medical dictionary, ed. 25, Philadelphia, 1974, W.B. Saunders Co.
2. Burnett, G.W.: The microbiology of dental infections, Dent. Clin. North Am. **14:**681, 1970.
3. Kannangara, D.W., Thadepalli, H., and McQuiter, J.L.: Bacteriology and treatment of dental infections, Oral Surg. **50:**103-109, 1980.
4. Sundquist, G.: Bacteriological studies of necrotic dental pulps, No. 7, Odontological dissertation, Umeå, 1976, Umeå University.
5. Sabiston, C.B., Gribsby, W.R., and Sergerstrom, N.: Bacterial study of pyogenic infections of dental origin, Oral Surg. **41:**430, 1976.
6. Slots, J.: The predominant cultivable organisms in juvenile periodontitis, Scand. J. Dent. Res. **84:**1-10, 1976.
7. Newman, M.G., and Socransky, S.S.: Predominant cultivable microbiota in periodontosis, J. Periodont. Res. **12:**120-128, 1977.

8. Rubin, R., Salvati, E.A., and Lewis, R.: Infected total hip replacement after dental procedures, Oral Surg. **41:**18, 1976.

9. Zallen, R.D., and Black, S.L.: Antibiotic therapy in oral and maxillofacial surgery, J. Oral Surg. **34:**349-51, 1976.

10. Jacobsen, P.L., and Murray, W.: Prophylactic coverage of dental patients with artificial joints: a retrospective analysis of 33 infections in hip prostheses, Oral Surg. **50:**130-133, 1980.

11. Zallen, R.D., and Curry, J.T.: A study of antibiotic usage in compound mandibular fractures, J. Oral Surg. **33:**431, 1975.

12. Kaplan, E.L., et al.: Prevention of bacterial endocarditis, American Heart Association Committee Report, Circulation **56:**139A-143A, 1977.

13. Holroyd, S.V.: Antibiotics in the practice of periodontics, J. Periodontol. **42:**584, 1971.

14. Med. Lett. Drug Ther. **9:**104, 1967.

15. Gabrielson, M.L., and Stroh, E.: Antibiotic efficacy in odontogenic infections, J. Oral Surg. **33:**607, 1975.

16. Chain, E., et al.: Penicillin as chemotherapeutic agent, Lancet **2:**226, 1940.

17. Krantz, J.C., Jr., and Carr, C.J.: The pharmacologic principles of medical practice, ed. 7, Baltimore, 1969, The Williams & Wilkins Co.

18. Linder, L.: Bacteriology of oral infections, Swed. Dent. J. **4:**3-7, 1980.

19. Greenberg, R.N., et al.: Microbiologic and antibiotic aspects of infections in the oral and maxillofacial region, J. Oral Surg. **37:**873-884, Dec. 1979.

20. Schuen, N.J., Panzer, J.D., and Atkinson, W.H.: A comparison of clindamycin and penicillin V in the treatment of oral infections, J. Oral Surg. **32:**503-505, 1974.

21. Burdon, K.L.: *Bacterium melaninogenicum* from normal and pathologic tissues, J. Infect. Dis. **42:**161-171, 1928.

22. Gabrielson, M.L., and Stroh, E.: Antibiotic efficacy in odontogenic infections, J. Oral Surg. **33:**607, 1975.

23. Druker, D.B., and Jolly, M.: Sensitivity of oral microorganisms to antibiotics, Br. Dent. J. **131:**442-44, 1971.

24. Feinberg, S.M.: Allergy from therapeutic products: incidence, importance, recognition, and prevention, J.A.M.A. **178:**815, 1961.

25. Smith, J.W., Johnson, J.E., and Cluff, L.E.: Studies on the epidemiology of adverse drug reactions. II. An evaluation of penicillin allergy, N. Engl. J. Med. **274:**998, 1966.

26. Pallasch, T.J.: The nature of penicillin antigenicity and effectiveness of various testing procedures for penicillin sensitization, J. Oral Ther. **3:**409, 1967.

27. Green, G.R., Rosenblum, A.H., and Sweet, L.C.: Evaluation of penicillin hypersensitivity: value of clinical history and skin testing with penicilloyl-polylysine and penicillin G, J. Allergy Clin. Immunol. **60:**339, 1977.

28. Herrell, W.E.: Skin testing for penicillin hypersensitivity, Clin. Med. **72:**12, 1972.

29. Adkinson, N.F., et al.: Routine use of penicillin skin testing on an inpatient service, N. Engl. J. Med. **283:**22, 1976.

30. Idsoe, O., et al.: Nature and extent of penicillin side reactions, with particular reference to fatalities from anaphylactic shock, Bull. W.H.O. **38:**159, 1968.

31. Rudolph, A.H., and Price, E.V.: Penicillin reactions among patients in venereal disease clinics: a national survey, J.A.M.A. **223:**499, 1973.

32. Welch, H., et al.: Severe reactions to antibiotics, Antibiot. Med. Clin. Ther. **4:**800, 1957.

33. Johnson, A.: Hypersensitivity to penicillin: a short review, Med. J. Aust. **2:**432, 1962.

34. Feinberg, S.M., and Feinberg, A.R.: Allergy to penicillin, J.A.M.A. **160:**778, 1956.

35. Welch, H., Lewis, C.N., and Putnam, L.E.: Acute anaphylactoid reactions attributable to penicillin, Antibiot. Chemother. **3:**891, 1953.

36. Batson, J.M.: Anaphylactoid reactions to oral administration of penicillin, N. Engl. J. Med. **262:**590, 1960.

37. Coates, W.H.: A case of anaphylactic shock following the administration of oral penicillin. Med. J. Aust. **50:**967, 1963.

38. Dunn, J.H.: Oral penicillin and anaphylactoid reactions, J.A.M.A. **202:**552, 1967.

39. Spark, R.P.: Fatal anaphylaxis due to oral penicillin, Am. J. Clin. Pathol. **56:**407, 1971.

40. Glauda, N.M., Henefer, E.P., and Super, S.: Nonfatal anaphylaxis caused by oral penicillin: report of case, J. Am. Dent. Assoc. **90:**159, 1975.

41. MacGregor, A.J., and Addy, A.: Value of penicillin in the prevention of pain, swelling, and trismus following the removal of ectopic mandibular third molars, Int. J. Oral Surg. **9:**166-172, 1980.

42. American Dental Association Council on Dental Therapeutics: Accepted dental therapeutics, ed. 39, Chicago, 1979, American Dental Association.

43. Shapiro, S., et al.: Drug rash with ampicillin and other penicillins, Lancet **2:**969, 1969.

44. Annotation: Ampicillin rashes, Lancet **2:**993, 1969.

45. Harris, J.R., et al.: Skin reactions to ampicillin, Br. Med. J. **1:**687, 1972.

46. Bass, J.W., et al.: Adverse effects of orally administered ampicillin, J. Pediatr. **83:**106, 1973.

47. Report of a collaborative study group: prospective study of ampicillin rash, Br. Med. J. **1:**7, 1973.

48. Pullen, H., Wright, N., and Murdoch, J.M.: Hypersensitivity reactions to antibacterial drugs in infectious mononucleosis, Lancet **2:**1176, 1967.

49. Brown, G.L., and Kanwar, B.S.: Drug rashes in glandular fever, Lancet **2:**1418, 1967.

50. Carbenicillin and other antibiotics for therapy of *Pseudomonas* infections, Med. Lett. Drugs Ther. **12:**101, 1970.

51. Billow, B.W., et al.: A clinical study of erythromycin: a comparative evaluation of several salts, Curr. Ther. Res. **6:**381, 1964.

52. Erythromycin, Med. Lett. Drugs Ther. **20:**94, 1978.

53. Sprunt, K., Leidy, G., and Redman, W.: Cross resistance between lincomycin and erythromycin in viridans streptococci, Pediatrics **46:**84, 1970.

54. Meade, R.H., III: Drug therapy reviews: antimicrobial spectrum, pharmacology and therapeutic use of erythromycin and its derivatives, Am. J. Hosp. Pharm. **36:**1185, 1979.

55. Stimmel, H.M., et al.: Penicillin-resistant alpha-hemolytic streptococci in children with heart disease who take penicillin daily, J. Dent. Child. **48:**29-32, 1981.

56. Fraser, D.E.: Selection of an oral erythromycin product, Am. J. Hosp. Pharm. **37:**1199, 1980.

57. Goodman, L.S., and Gilman, A.: The pharmacological basis of therapeutics, ed. 6, New York, 1980, Macmillan Publishing Co., Inc.

58. Mandell, G.L.: Cephaloridine, Ann. Intern. Med. **79:**561, 1973.

59. Swartzberg, K.E., Maresca, R.M., and Bennington, J.S.: Gastrointestinal side effects associated with clindamycin: 1000 consecutive patients, Arch. Intern. Med. **136:**876, 1976.

60. Cohen, L.E., McNeill, C.J., and Wells, R.F.: Clindamycin associated colitis, J.A.M.A. **223:**1379, 1973.

61. Wells, R.F., Cohen, L.E., and McNeill, C.J.: Clindamycin and pseudomembranous colitis (letter), Lancet **1:**66, 1974.

62. Bartlett, J.G., et al.: Antibiotic-associated pseudomembranous colitis due to toxin-producing clostridia, N. Engl. J. Med. **298:**531-4, 1978.

63. Tedesco, F.J., Stanely, R.J., and Alpers, D.H.: Diagnostic features of clindamycin-associated pseudomembranous colitis, N. Engl. J. Med. **290:**841, 1974.

64. Keighley, M.R.: Antibiotic-associated pseudomembranous colitis: pathogenesis and management, Drugs **20:**49-56, 1980.

65. Tedesco, F.J.: Clindamycin and colitis: a review, J. Infect. Dis. **135**(suppl):S95-8, 1977.

66. Antibiotic colitis: new cause, new treatment, Med. Lett. Drugs Ther. **21:**97-8, 1979.

67. LeFrock, J.L., et al.: The spectrum of colitis associated with lincomycin and clindamycin therapy, J. Infect. Dis. **131:**108-115, 1975.

68. Chow, A.W., et al.: Orofacial odontogenic infections, Ann. Intern. Med. **88:**392-402, 1978.

69. Olsen, R.E., Morello, J.A., and Kieff, E.D.: Antibiotic treatment of oral anaerobic infections, J. Oral Surg. **33:**619-21, 1976.

70. Scopp, I.W., et al.: Treatment of oral lesions with topically applied vancomycin hydrochloride, Oral Surg. **24:**703, 1967.

71. Mitchell, D.F., and Holmes, L.A.: Topical antibiotic control of dentogingival plaque, J. Periodontol. **36:**202, 1965.

72. Jordan, H.W., and DePaola, P.F.: Effect of prolonged topical application of vancomycin on human oral *Streptococcus mutans* populations, Arch. Oral Biol. **22:**193, 1977.

73. DePaola, P.F., Jordan, H.V., and Soparkar, P.M.: Inhibition of dental caries in school children by topically applied vancomycin, Arch. Oral Biol. **22:**187, 1977.

74. Barr, W.H., Adir, J., and Garrettson, L.: Decrease of tetracycline absorption in man by sodium bicarbonate, Clin. Pharmacol. Ther. **12:**779, 1971.

75. Hinton, N.A.: The effect of oral tetracycline HCl and doxycycline on the intestinal flora, Curr. Ther. Res. **12:**341-52, 1970.

76. Whalley, P.J., Adams, R.H., and Combes, B.: Tetracycline toxicity in pregnancy: liver and pancreatic dysfunction, J.A.M.A. **189:**357, 1964.

77. Cleveland, W.W., et al.: Acquired Fanconi syndrome following degraded tetracycline, J. Pediatr. **66:**333, 1965.

78. Corcoran, J.F., and Zillich, R.M.: Update on vital bleaching, J. Mich. Dent. Assoc. **61:**583-4, 1979.

79. Sack, D.A., et al.: Prophylactic doxycycline for traveler's diarrhea: results of a prospective double-blind study of Peace

80. Traveler's diarrhea, Med. Letter Drugs Ther. **21:**41, 1979.

81. Dornbusch, K.: Antibiotic susceptibility in oral bacteria, Swed. Dent. J. **4:**9-15, 1980.

82. Graykowski, E.A., et al.: Recurrent aphthous stomatitis: clinical, therapeutic, histopathologic, and hypersensitivity aspects, J.A.M.A. **196:**637, 1966.

83. Graykowski, E.A., and Kingman, A.: Double-blind trial of tetracycline in recurrent aphthous ulceration, J. Oral Path. **7:**376, 1978.

84. Scopp, I.W., et al.: Tetracyclines: double-blind clinical study to evaluate the clinical effectiveness in periodontal surgery, J. Periodontol. **48:**484, 1977.

85. Ciancio, S.G., Mather, M.L., and McMullen, J.A.: An evaluation of minocycline in patients with periodontal disease, J. Periodontol. **51:**530, 1980.

86. Metronidazole hydrochloride (Flagyl IV), Med. Lett. Drugs Ther. **23:**13-14, Feb. 20, 1981.

87. Loesche, W.J., et al.: Treatment of periodontal infections due to anaerobic bacteria with short-term treatment with metronidazole, J. Clin. Periodontol. **8:**29-44, 1981.

88. Rood, J.P., and Murgatroyd, J.: Metronidazole in the prevention of dry socket, Brit. J. Oral Surg. **17:**62-70, 1979-1980.

89. Hamilton-Miller, J.M.T.: Fungal sterols and the mode of action of the polyene antibiotics, Adv. Appl. Microbiol. **17:**109-134, 1974.

90. *Candida* infections, Med. Lett. Drugs Ther. **12:**29, 1970.

91. Lehner, T.: Candidal fungaemia following extraction of teeth and its relationship to systemic candidiasis, Br. Dent. J. **117:**253, 1964.

92. American Dental Association Council on Dental Therapeutics: Accepted dental therapeutics, ed. 35, Chicago, 1975, American Dental Association.

93. Kutscher, A.H., et al.: Amphotericin B in the treatment of oral monilial infections, Oral Surg. **17:**31, 1964.

94. Alban, J., and Grael, J.: Amphotericin B oral suspension in the treatment, Curr. Ther. Res. **12:**479, 1970.

95. Normark, S., and Schonebeck, J.: In vitro studies of 5-fluorocytosine resistance in *Candida albicans* and *Torulopsis glabrata*, Antimicrob. Agents Chemother. **2:**114, 1972.

96. Weissmann, G., and Sessa, G.: The action of polyene antibiotics on phospholipid-cholesterol structures, J. Biol. Chem. **242:**616, 1967.

97. Kirkpatrick, C.H., and Alling, D.W.: Treatment of chronic oral candidiasis with clotrimazole troches, N. Engl. J. Med. **299:**1201, 1978.

98. Cappuccio, J.P., and Dobbs, E.C.: Clinical evaluation of sulfadimethoxine, a long-acting antibacterial sulfonamide, in oral infections, J. Oral Surg. **18:**230, 1960.

99. Norris, J.P., and Becker, E.F.: A clinical comparison of sulfadimethoxine and penicillin in the endodontic management of acute dentoalveolar infection, J. Oral Ther. **1:**376, 1965.

100. Brumfitt, W., and Pursell, R.: Observations on bacterial sensitivities to nalidixic acid and critical comments on 6-centre survey, Postgrad. Med. J. **47:**16, 1971.

101. Maxwell, E.: Treatment of herpes keratitis with 5-iodo-2-

Corps volunteers in Morocco, Gastroenterology **76:**1368, 1979.

deoxyuridine (IDU): a clinical evaluation of 1500 cases, Am. J. Ophthalmol. **56:**571, 1963.

102. Jaffe, E.C., and Lehner, T.: Treatment of herpetic stomatitis with idoxuridine, Br. Dent. J. **125:**392, 1968.

103. Nafta, I., et al.: Administration of amatandine for the prevention of Hong Kong influenza, Bull. W.H.O. **42:**423, 1970.

104. Togo, Y., Hornick, R.B., and Dawkins, A.T.: Studies on induced influenza in man. I. Double-blind studies designed to assess prophylactic efficacy of amantadine hydrochloride against A2/Rockville/1/65 strain, J.A.M.A. **203:**1089, 1968.

105. Wingfield, W.L., Pollack, D., and Grunert, R.R.: Therapeutic efficacy of amantadine HCl and rimantadine HCl in naturally occurring influenza A2 respiratory illness in man, N. Engl. J. Med. **281:**579, 1969.

Locally acting medications: antimicrobials, hemostatics, and protectives

Antimicrobials, hemostatics, and protectives are locally applied agents that have wide application in dentistry. Antimicrobials are used for their disinfectant or antiseptic actions. *Disinfectants* and *antiseptics* are defined as chemical agents capable of killing or inhibiting the growth of pathogenic microorganisms. The primary distinction between them is that antiseptics are applied to living tissue and disinfectants to inanimate objects. Most disinfectants are destructive to tissues and cannot be used as antiseptics. In some special cases, however, a disinfectant may be used as an antiseptic. For example, disinfectants have been used as antiseptics in root canal treatment (Chapter 36). In such cases, the solution strength and exposure time will usually differ for the type of disinfectant or antiseptic used. The general term *germicide* is often used to denote a chemical agent capable of destroying microorganisms. The specific terms *bactericide, fungicide,* and *sporicide* describe the type of microorganism or its form affected by the agent. When a bacterial population has been reduced but not eradicated, the chemical agent responsible is called a *sanitizing agent.*

Hemostatics control excessive bleeding or hemorrhage from small blood vessels or capillaries. Protectives sooth and protect oral lesions. The indications, contraindications, mechanism of action, and toxicity of the available pharmacologic agents in these groups will be described in this chapter. Tables 23-1 and 23-2 list preparations and uses of antiseptics, disinfectants, hemostatics, and protectives.

ANTIMICROBIALS
Disinfectants

Because of the natural microbial status of the oral cavity, the achievement of a sterile intraoral environment, although desirable, is neither practical nor attainable. A more realistic goal would be to eliminate the possibility of introducing exogenous microorganisms into the oral cavity, for example, by sterilizing dental instruments before use. To do so, steam under pressure (121° C) is probably the most reliable method available; however, certain dental instruments may be damaged by heat, and therefore heat-sensitive instruments must be sterilized by employing disinfectants.

Ethylene oxide

Although the bactericidal properties of ethylene oxide were known as early as 1929, its use for this purpose did not begin until 1949. It is a gas at ordinary temperatures, liquefies at 10.8° C, and freezes at −111.3° C. It can be obtained either in the pure state as a liquid under pressure or mixed with carbon dioxide or fluorinated hydrocarbons to produce a nonflammable mixture.

Ethylene oxide is the most reliable substance available for gaseous sterilization. Its advantages are that in a gaseous state it is seldom damaging to materials, it is effective at room temperature, it is effective at low humidities, it leaves no residue, it is germicidal, and it is highly penetrative. The primary disadvantage is its slowness in action, but the time required for sterilization can be reduced to about 1 hour by increasing the temperature to 54° C or by using higher concentrations of gas. Proper ventilation should be employed to avoid direct inhalation of vapors. Other chemicals used as gaseous agents are propylene oxide, propiolactone, methyl bromide, ethylene glycol, formaldehyde, and ozone. The application of these gaseous agents in dentistry has not been fully explored.

Table 23-1. Antiseptics and disinfectants: preparations and uses

Generic name	Proprietary name	Preparation	Therapeutic use
Glutaraldehyde	Cidex 7	Aqueous solution	Disinfectant
	Sporicidin	Aqueous solution	Disinfectant
Phenol	Chloraseptic*	Gel, solution, lozenges	Antiseptic, Anesthetic
	Cepastat*	Spray, lozenges	Antiseptic, Anesthetic
	Anbesol	Gel, liquid	Topical Anesthetic
Eugenol	Eugenol	Solution	Cavity liner, anesthetic
Hexachlorophene	Gamophen antibacterial soap	Bar soap	Presurgical scrub
	Germa-medica MG	Solution	Presurgical scrub
	pHisohex	Solution	Presurgical scrub
Sodium hypochlorite	Hypogen	Solution	Root canal treatment
Povidone-iodine	Betadine	Solution, surgical scrub	Presrugical scrub
	Sana	Solution, surgical scrub	Presurgical scrub
Thimerosal	Merthiolate	Solution, tincture	Antiseptic
Benzalkonium chloride	Zephiran*	Solution	Antiseptic
Cetylpyridinium	Ceepryn*	Solution	Antiseptic
Hydrogen peroxide	Gly-oxide	Solution	Wound debridement
Carbamide Peroxide	PerioLav	Solution	Wound debridement
Chlorhexidine	Hibiclens antimicrobial Cleanser*		
	Hibistat germicidal hand rinse*		
	Hibitane tincture*	Solution	Presurgical scrub

*Not accepted by the Council on Dental Therapeutics, American Dental Association.

Table 23-2. Hemostatics and protectives: preparations and uses

Generic name	Proprietary name	Preparation	Therapeutic use
Epinephrine	Epinephrine	Solution, 1:500	Hemostatic, gingival retraction
Aluminum chloride	Gingi-Aid	Retraction cord solution (10%)	Hemostatic, gingival retraction
	Hemodent	Retraction cord, solution (25%)*	
Absorbable gelatin sponge	Gelfoam	Sponge, powder, dental packs	Hemostatic
Oxidized cellulose	Novocell	Pellets	Hemostatic
	Oxycel	Gauze, Cotton	Hemostatic
Oxidized regenerated cellulose	Surgical	Knitted Fabric Form	Hemostatic
Thrombin	Thrombostat	Powder	Hemostatic
Microfibrillar collagen hemostat	Avitene*	Powder	Hemostatic
Carboxymethyl cellulose sodium	Orabase	Paste	Protective, vehicle for medications

*Not accepted by the Council on Dental Therapeutics, American Dental Association.

Aldehydes

The aldehydes most frequently used as disinfectants are *formaldehyde* and *glutaraldehyde;* the more potent glutaraldehydes have greater potential for use in dentistry than formaldehyde. Both compounds are irritating to skin, producing necrosis and eschar formation with prolonged contact, and their use should be limited to sterilization of inanimate objects. Formaldehyde-containing cosmetics have been reported to produce contact dermatitis. The aldehydes are sporicidal when operatory instruments are immersed for periods of 10 to 18 hours. The ability of aldehydes to penetrate organic matter is enhanced by the addition of alcoholic compounds. Glutaraldehyde is available in a form that is "activated" by the addition of 0.3% sodium bicarbonate (Cidex). This alkaline solution of glutaraldehyde has a shelf life of only 14 to 21 days, which may be a disadvantage. Another glutaraldehyde-containing product, Sporicidin, reportedly has a shelf life of 30 days and kills spores more quickly than Cidex. The effectiveness of the aldehydes to kill human hepatitis virus is equivocal. Because of their irritative qualities, instruments bathed in these aldehyde preparations should be rinsed thoroughly before use in the oral cavity.

Antiseptics and disinfectants

Agents in this group may be classified as antiseptics or disinfectants, depending on their use in the dental operatory.

Phenols

The phenols exert their antibacterial effects by denaturing bacterial cell proteins. Phenol is considered the standard by which all other phenol-derived disinfectants are compared. It has the advantage of possessing bactericidal properties even in the presence of pus, saliva, blood, and other body fluids. Phenol is very irritating to living tissue and in high concentrations (5% to 10%) is limited to use on inanimate objects. Dilute (1.4%) solutions of phenol are used as a mouthwash or gargle for sore throat because phenol, as well as most phenolic compounds, possesses local anesthetic properties.

The Council on Dental Therapeutics (CDT) of the ADA does not recommend the use of phenolic compounds for disinfection of instruments or other surfaces in the operatory because of their inconsistent virucidal activity. Nor does the CDT include phenol-containing mouthwashes as acceptable for inclusion in *Accepted Dental Therapeutics* because of the lack of clinical evidence demonstrating antimicrobial efficacy in the oral cavity. Other phenolic compounds such as cresol and parachlorophenol are more potent and less toxic than phenol and are used as endodontic medicaments, which are discussed elsewhere.

Eugenol is a phenolic compound that shares local anesthetic, antiseptic, and irritative properties with other members of the phenolic group. It is often combined with zinc oxide as an interim restoration or as a base for extensive restorations. Its local anesthetic and rubefacient properties are most profound when used in over-the-counter preparations for relief of discomfort from "toothaches."

Hexachlorophene is another phenolic compound that gained popularity in the late 1950s and early 1960s. This antiseptic was shown to be highly effective against gram-positive microorganisms, particularly *Staphylococcus aureus,* and less effective in eliminating gram-negative species. Several reports published during the 1960 decade suggested that the hexachlorophene solutions (3%) being used by many hospitals to bathe newborns caused brain damage. The effectiveness of hexachlorophene in preventing staphylococcal infections in the nursery was supported by later findings that neonatal infections by gram-positive microorganisms increased when the use of these baths was curtailed. Today the use of hexachlorophene in the neonate has been largely eliminated. However, before dental surgery, preparations containing 2% hexachlorophene are used according to accepted presurgical scrub methods.

The phenolic compounds are also frequently used as cavity liners because of their antiseptic properties. Because the phenols will inhibit polymerization of certain autopolymerizing resin restorations, they are contraindicated as cavity liners in those cases.

Alcohols

The alcohols *ethanol* and *isopropanol* are frequently used as sanitizers in the operatory; that is, either ethanol (70%) or isopropanol (90%) in aqueous solutions is used to reduce the microbial population by wiping operatory equipment such as handpieces and chair controls between patients. However, in addition to the physical action of removing microorganisms, these alcohols possess bactericidal activity, a result of their ability to denature bacterial protein. These compounds are most effective the longer they remain in contact with the area to be disinfected. For this reason, the CDT does not recommend that these rapidly evaporating alcohols be used as disinfectants on dental instruments. These alcohols provide little, if any, effectiveness against microbial spores; however, they are often used in combination with aldehyde compounds to enhance their antimicrobial effectiveness. Both alcohols are very irritating to mucous membranes and abraded skin and may cause erythema on unabraded skin if left in contact for extended periods of time.

Halogens

Halogen compounds have been used for many years as antiseptics and disinfectants. *Iodine-* and *chlorine*-containing compounds exert their antimicrobial effects via oxidation of cellular constituents. However, their ability to inhibit key metabolic enzymes undoubtedly adds to their effectiveness. Both have been recommended by the CDT as suitable for disinfection of dental instruments. Inorganic forms of chlorine are mainly used as disinfectants or for water purification. Sodium hypochlorite (5%) is used as a root canal irrigant for its antibacterial qualities as well as its ability to debride the canal. It is very irritating to mucous membranes and should not remain in contact with these tissues for an extended period. Although chlorine-containing compounds are effective against many gram-positive and gram-negative bacteria, they are ineffective against *Mycobacterium tuberculosis* and do not easily penetrate dried or accumulated body secretions. Organic and inorganic forms of iodine penetrate these fluids to a greater extent than the chlorine compounds. Inorganic iodine tinctures used on mucous membranes and abraded skin have been reported to produce erythema, necrosis, and patient discomfort at the site of application. Organic iodine compounds (iodophors) have been produced that retain the bactericidal qualities of iodine but have reduced their tissue-irritative properties. Povidone-iodine, a complex of povidone and iodine, is designed to be a stable form of iodine that releases free iodine on contact with biologic materials. This organic complex has been used as an effective antibacterial surgical scrub for the patient and the operator. The reduced incidence of mucosal irritation has allowed its use as a preoperative antiseptic in the oral cavity and as an irrigant for the treatment of peri-

coronitis. The organic and inorganic forms of iodine may stain clothing and linens, and precautions should be taken to avoid this disadvantage.

Heavy metals

Heavy metal–containing preparations are weak antimicrobial agents. The two most prominent metals are *mercury,* either in an organic or inorganic form, and *silver* in the nitrate form. These compounds owe their antibacterial effects to their ability to combine with sulfhydryl groups on essential bacterial enzymes. Both can be very irritating to mucous membranes and can be toxic if ingested. Inorganic mercury-containing compounds are extremely toxic and are limited in their use. The organic forms of mercury such as thimerosal, merbromin, and nitromersol, although less irritating, are weakly bacteriostatic at best. None are effective against spore-forming bacteria and should not be relied on for instrument disinfection. The effectiveness of the mercurial compounds is also inhibited by organic material. Silver nitrate is the only commercially available silver-containing compound possessing antimicrobial properties. It exhibits concentration-dependent bactericidal activity in concentrations from 1%, for prophylaxis against gonococcal conjunctivitis, to 10%, for treatment of oral ulcerations (recurrent apthous and herpetic lesions). The latter use is undoubtedly not based on its antibacterial qualities, but its ability to act as an astringent and caustic to denervate sensory nerve endings, thereby providing some relief of discomfort to the patient. Silver nitrate produces a gray-black stain on contact with organic material or exposure to light.

Surface-active agents

Surface-active agents, or surfactants, are chemicals that possess both lipophilic and hydrophilic properties. These qualities allow the surfactants to concentrate at the bacterial cell surface and to cause disruption of the membrane. These compounds also lower surface tension and assist in the physical removal of bacterial forms. They exhibit weak, if any, antibacterial activity against acid-fast and spore-forming microorganisms. Their bactericidal activity is greatly reduced by the presence of pus, blood, sputum, or other body fluids. The surfactants are divided into two classes: those that carry a positive charge are called *cationic surface-active* agents, and those that possess a negative charge are called *anionic surface-active* agents. The two groups are incompatible with each other. The anionic surfactants are mainly effective against gram-positive microorganisms and include sodium lauryl sulfate and green soap. These are not considered bactericidal for disinfection purposes; they are used merely to enhance the physical removal of bacteria. The cationic forms include the quaternary ammonium compounds, such as benzalkonium chloride (Zephiran) and cetylpyridinium (Ceepryn). These agents are bactericidal against gram-positive and some gram-negative bacteria, with little or no effectiveness against tubercle bacilli, spore-forming microbes, and *Pseudomonas aeruginosa*. They do not readily penetrate organic matter. The cationic surfactants are inactivated by exposure to soaps and metallic ions; therefore any soap film remaining on the site to be disinfected should be rinsed with ethanol before wiping with the cationic compounds. Quaternary ammonium compounds are not recommended by the CDT for disinfection of instruments and environmental surfaces in dentistry. When used in high concentrations, these agents have been reported to be irritating to skin and mucous membranes with prolonged contact. Because of these limitations, the surface-active agents are used most often as detergents in conjunction with more efficacious antimicrobial agents.

Miscellaneous

Hydrogen peroxide either alone or in combination with glycerin (Gly-oxide) has been used as an antiseptic for conditions ranging from traumatic injuries to acute necrotizing ulcerative gingivitis. However, its antibacterial effects are feeble at best. Its value is in the effervescent evolution of oxygen caused by the hydrogen peroxide coming into contact with tissue catalase. The evolution of nascent oxygen helps to cleanse or debride the wound, thus enhancing the healing process. Some reports suggest that hydrogen peroxide kills anaerobic bacteria because of the oxygen released. The combination of hydrogen peroxide or carbamide peroxide (PerioLav) with glycerin enhances the stability of the product as well as the tenacity, tending to localize the peroxide in the area to be treated.

A relatively new antiseptic to be used in dentistry is chlorhexidine. This agent exerts its antibacterial action by disruption of the bacterial cell membrane.

Although chlorhexidine has not been approved for oral use in the United States, it is being used topically as a presurgical handwash in a concentration of 4% (Hibiclens). Experimentally, chlorhexidine has been used successfully to decrease plaque and to treat recurrent apthous ulcers.[1] Chlorhexidine exerts its bactericidal effects against many gram-positive and gram-negative microorganisms but is reportedly ineffective against *M. tuberculosis,* spores, and viruses. Chlorhexidine exhibits a residual antibacterial effect with repeated use, a property shared with hexachlorophene and povidone-iodine.

Although not accepted by the CDT, the controversial 9-aminoacridine persists in the literature as an antiseptic useful in the field of dentistry.[2] This compound exerts its bactericidal effects through inhibition of protein and DNA synthesis. It is not inactivated by organic matter, and it exhibits very low toxicity. It has been used for root canal irrigation as well as postoperative irrigation for control of dry socket. Its spectrum includes gram-positive and gram-negative bacteria, with the exception of *Pseudomonas aeruginosa.*

HEMOSTATICS

Hemostatic agents are defined as locally applied substances that are employed to arrest excessive bleeding or hemorrhage. These agents are intended for those instances in which bleeding occurs from small blood vessels or capillaries, and they are not intended for arrest of hemorrhage from the major blood vessels. The hemostatic agents are classified according to their mechanism of action: (1) *sympathomimetics* reduce bleeding by local vasoconstriction, (2) *styptics and astringents* arrest the flow of blood from small vessels by precipitating the tissue proteins in the immediate area, (3) *mechanical agents* act as matrices in which blood cells and/or fibrin can be entrapped, and (4) *thrombin,* a normal constituent of the blood coagulation scheme, combines with fibrinogen to form a clot.

Sympathomimetics

The sympathomimetic agents combine with the alpha receptors located in the smooth muscle walls of the arterioles to cause constriction, resulting in reduced blood flow and hemostasis. Epinephrine is the sympathomimetic most often used for this purpose. During the use of hydrophobic impression materials, control of gingival hemorrhage has been accomplished with any of the epinephrine-impregnated retraction cords currently available. Some retraction cords are impregnated with an 8% racemic mixture of epinephrine. Although the dextrorotatory form of epinephrine is about 15 times less active than the levorotatory form, this 8% concentration of racemic epinephrine represents a concentration of 1:25 of the levorotatory form. This highly concentrated form of epinephrine should be used with caution in any patient who exhibits a sensitivity to the drug or in whom sympathomimetics are contraindicated. Often a surgical procedure requires a reduction in blood flow to visualize the operatory field. In these instances, infiltration of a local anesthetic with 1:50,000 epinephrine should suffice to cause a marked reduction in blood flow. However, caution should be exercised in those surgical procedures that require adequate oxygenation of the tissue because sympathomimetic-induced vasoconstriction may produce local anoxia with resultant necrosis and sloughing of tissue. Common side effects of these hemostatic agents include generalized sympathetic stimulation characterized by tachycardia, increased blood pressure, and CNS stimulation characterized by tremors and irritability.

Styptics and astringents

Astringents, as mentioned previously, promote hemostasis by precipitating tissue proteins. A styptic is an astringent in a more concentrated and usually solid form. These agents are usually salts of heavy metals such as zinc chloride, aluminum chloride, or ferric subsulfate. Of these, aluminum chloride preparations seem to be the most reliable and devoid of side effects. Precipitation of tissue proteins results not only in hemostasis, but also in tissue shrinkage—a combination desirable for taking impressions with hydrophobic materials. In fact, gingival retraction for impressions should be attempted with these agents before retraction with epinephrine because the side effects of the latter are so prevalent. Although concentrated forms of aluminum chloride have been associated with tissue irritation and necrosis, accepted preparations used in dentistry (Table 23-2) do not exhibit this property.

Mechanical agents

Mechanical agents are usually reserved for those conditions of moderate bleeding when surgical intervention is not required and the area of hemorrhage is

too large for the two previous methods. The mechanical agents possess the added benefit of being absorbed within the surrounding tissue, allowing a more physiologic clot to form. Absorbable gelatin sponge (Gelfoam) provides a framework for fibrin strands released when the circulating platelets become entrapped in the matrix. The sponge is completely absorbed 4 to 6 weeks after placement. A solution of thrombin is often used in addition to gelatin sponge to enhance hemostasis. Oxidized cellulose (Oxycel) and oxidized regenerated cellulose (Surgicel) form an artificial clot as a result of the affinity of hemoglobin to cellulosic acid. Both are absorbed within 6 or 7 days after placement. The primary difference between the two forms is that oxidized cellulose interferes with epithelialization and therefore is contraindicated as a surface dressing. The regenerated form of cellulose does not retard epithelialization and may be used for surface dressing. Both have been reported to interfere with regeneration of bone and should not be used for packing in fractures.

Thrombin

Thrombin, a natural component of blood coagulation, is available in powder form of bovine origin. This hemostatic agent may be applied to areas of hemorrhage either alone or in conjunction with absorbable gelatin sponge. Thrombin is easily inactivated by an acid medium and is contraindicated with hemostatic preparations that release cellulosic acid. Parenteral administration of thrombin solutions is an absolute contraindication.

Microfibrillar collagen hemostat (Avitene) has been reported to be very effective as a postsurgical hemostatic agent in the oral cavity.[3,4] Its mechanism is similar to the other mechanical agents in that its fibrillar network attracts and adheres to circulating platelets. It is absorbed in 4 to 6 weeks. It does not interfere with epithelialization, nor does it retard regeneration of bone. Microfibrillar collagen hemostat is not currently accepted by the CDT for use in dentistry.

PROTECTIVES

Ulcerations of the oral mucosa can be an extremely painful consequence of trauma, disease, or nutritional deficiency. Patients may restrict their diets to avoid the discomfort associated with these lesions. In many cases, the ulcerations may take as long as 2 weeks to heal, and often patients are afflicted with frequent recurrences. Certain substances have an emollient or lipid-soluble property that allows them to remain in the aqueous environment of the oral cavity. These pharmacologic agents are called *protectives*. Sodium carboxymethylcellulose in an oil-soluble base (Orabase) is used as a paste to protect oral lesions and as a vehicle for antiinflammatory and local anesthetic preparations.

Though all of the pharmacologic agents previously discussed are topically applied and locally acting, each serves a distinct function, and each contributes significantly to the total spectrum of therapeutic agents available to the dental practitioner.

REFERENCES

1. Bassetti, C., and Kallenberger, A.: Influence of chlorhexidine rinsing on the healing of oral mucosa and osseus lesions, J. Clin. Periodontol. **7**:443-456, 1980.

2. Schmitz, J.P.: 9-Aminoacridine: its present status and current recommendations for use as a surgical and endodontic irrigant in dentistry, Oral Surg. **50**:273-276, 1980.
3. Evans, E.B.: Hemostasis in the mouth: avitene, a new local hemostatic agent, N.Y. State Dent. J. **44**:441-443, 1978.
4. Wirthlin, M.R., Vernino, A.R., and Hancock, E.B.: The use of a new topical hemostatic agent, J. Periodontol. **51**:225-227, 1980.

BIBLIOGRAPHY

Accepted dental therapeutics, ed. 38, Chicago, 1979, American Dental Association.

Boyd, R.F., and Hoerl, B.G.: Basic medical microbiology, ed. 2, Boston, 1981, Little, Brown, & Co.
Jawetz, E., Melnick, J.L., and Adelbert, E.H.: Review of medical microbiology, ed. 14, Los Altos, Calif., 1980, Lange Medical Publications.
Kruger, G.O.: Textbook of oral and maxillofacial surgery, ed. 5, St. Louis, 1979, The C.V. Mosby Co.
Physicians desk reference, ed. 35, Oradell, N.J., 1981, Medical Economics Co.

CHAPTER 24

Fluorides

R. C. TERHUNE

The effects of fluorides on biologic systems have been the subject of an ever-increasing amount of investigation since the fact was determined in the 1930s that small amounts of fluoride had a remarkable effect on the human dentition. There are presently enough textbooks, periodicals, and reports of clinical and laboratory research about the subject to fill a library. Nevertheless, despite all the accumulation of knowledge about fluorides, there is much remaining to be learned about their chemistry and mechanisms of action in biologic systems. Because of widely disseminated misinformation about fluorides, their effects on humans are still a subject of considerable controversy among many laymen. Although the beneficial effects of fluorides are widely recognized by scientists knowledgeable in the field, there is still disagreement about precise mechanisms of action and the value of various fluoride compounds.

It is extremely important for the dentist to have a good understanding of the action of fluorides on both the dentition and the remainder of the body. In addition to helping provide patients with the best possible preventive dental care, this information will enable the dentist to answer convincingly the inevitable questions posed by patients regarding the action and value of fluorides. Only by being highly knowledgeable on the subject of fluorides can the dentist properly evaluate and reply to the misinformation about their use and effects and be an effective spokesman for community fluoridation measures.

After a brief overall review of the occurrence, metabolism, and toxicity of fluorides, the bulk of the material in this chapter is devoted to the current status of fluoride therapy for dental diseases. Fluoridation of communal water supplies and some other methods of systemic application are examined first, followed by a discussion of the major approaches to topical fluoride therapy.

OCCURRENCE OF FLUORIDE

Fluorine (F) is the most electronegative chemical element and is so reactive that it is rarely, if ever, encountered in nature as elemental fluorine. Chemically combined in the form of fluoride, it is one of the most ubiquitous of all elements, being the seventeenth most common in the earth's crust.[1] Although the two principal sources of fluoride available to humans are the water they drink and the foods and drugs they consume, it is even present in the air they breathe. In short fluoride is everywhere and in everything humans take into their bodies.

Water derives its fluoride content primarily from its solvent action on the rocks and soil of the earth's crust. The fluoride content of soil tends to increase with depth. Fluoride occurs most commonly as fluorspar (CaF_2) but is also found in a wide variety of minerals such as apatite, the micas, hornblende, topaz, and cryolite, to name only a few. The amount of fluoride present in the water washing over these minerals depends on the solubility of the particular mineral present. In most cases the solubility is low. When fluoride compounds are dissolved in water, fluorine is mainly present as the fluoride ion F^-. Fluoride levels tend to be high in alkaline waters and in water with a relatively high temperature such as is associated with volcanic activity. Surface waters are generally low in fluoride, whereas underground waters may contain appreciable amounts because of their greater oppor-

☐ The opinions or assertions contained herein are the private ones of the writer and are not to be construed as official or as reflecting the views of the Navy Department or the naval service at large.

tunity to contact fluoride-containing minerals.

Virtually every food consumed by humans contains fluoride in at least trace amounts. Some foods such as tea and some varieties of fish have very high levels of fluoride. Plants used as food derive fluoride from soil and water, whereas animals used as food derive fluoride from plants and other animals they eat as well as from the water they consume. The fluoride content of food will also be influenced by the fluoride content of the water in which it is prepared. With the exception of drugs administered as anticariogenic agents and for treatment of skeletal disorders, most fluorides contained in drugs are in biologically inert forms and are thus unavailable for metabolism.

Considerable amounts of fluoride may enter the human environment as dusts and vapors. The dusts may be from surface soil containing large quantities of fluoride or from industrial processes. Vapors are entirely of industrial origin. The physiologic effects of these fluoride-containing dusts and vapors may result from swallowing as well as from inhalation. Deposition of dusts on plants and in water supplies will also increase human fluoride consumption.

Total consumption of fluoride will vary considerably in accordance with the fluoride content of the food and water an individual consumes, as previously discussed, and with the volume consumed. The average 1- to 3-year-old child consumes approximately 500 ml water a day and the adult, approximately 1 liter. If the water contains 1 ppm of fluoride, they will consume 0.5 mg and 1 mg fluoride a day, respectively, from their drinking water. Fluoride intake by adults from food exclusive of drinking water in some communities in the United States ranges from 0.34 mg to as much as 3.13 mg. [1]

FLUORIDE METABOLISM

As has been explained, fluoride ions may be ingested by means of food and water or inhaled as vapors or particulate matter in the air. Inhaled fluorides from dust or vapors are rapidly and almost completely absorbed into the bloodstream through the respiratory tract. Fluoride ingested in the dust is rapidly absorbed into the bloodstream from the alimentary tract, primarily from the stomach. The mechanism of fluoride absorption is one of simple diffusion across a semipermeable membrane. The fluoride that is in insoluble compounds or is not absorbed is eliminated in the feces. The presence of calcium, magnesium, or aluminum ions interferes with the absorption of fluoride in that they form insoluble compounds with it.

The mean plasma fluoride level in normal humans ranges from 0.14 to 0.19 ppm and is not elevated above this range in persons consuming water with up to 2.5 ppm fluoride. [2] Higher mean plasma levels are found when drinking water levels of fluoride are above 2.5 ppm. These water levels will also be reflected in a higher concentration of fluoride retained in hard tissues.

The fluoride content of soft tissue is approximately the same as that found in plasma. Fluoride is probably not incorporated into soft tissue structure itself (except perhaps for ectopic calcifications) but is present in the interstitial fluid. Fluoride is present in the hard tissues in the following descending order of concentration: cementum, bone, dentin, and enamel. It is incorporated in the mineral lattice of bones and teeth and may also be found at the hydroxyapatite crystal surfaces.

Fluoride is deposited in calcified tissues by the circulating blood and tissue fluids. Since bone is continually in a dynamic state of remodeling, fluoride will be released back into the blood by decalcification. As long as decalcification and recalcification stay in equilibrium, a state of fluoride equilibrium will exist. This will be manifested by the excretion of approximately the same amount of fluoride that is ingested. In children, who are undergoing bodily growth and the calcification of bones and teeth, less fluoride will be excreted than is ingested. If a person who has been ingesting water with a high level of fluoride moves to an area with water containing less fluoride, excess fluoride will be excreted because the plasma fluoride will decrease somewhat and exchangeable fluoride on the bone surface will be replaced by hydroxyl ions. The fluoride thus freed will be lost. On the other hand, the reverse process will be in effect for a person moving from an area with low amounts of fluoride in the water to an area with high amounts. That person will excrete less fluoride than is ingested. In both cases equilibrium will eventually be reached.

Most fluoride is excreted in the urine. Appreciable amounts are also excreted by sweat, with trace amounts being found in milk, saliva, and lacrimal fluid. The metabolic pathway of fluoride may be summarized briefly in Fig. 24-1.

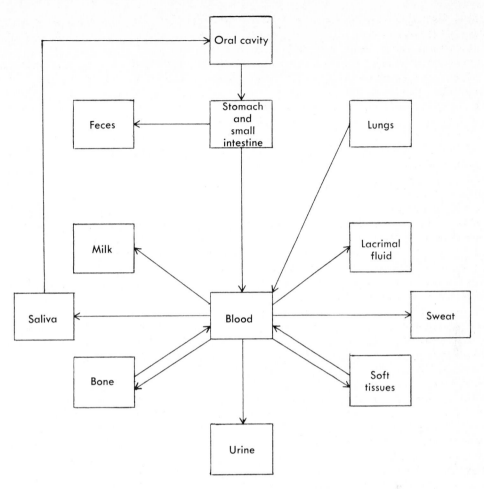

Fig. 24-1. Metabolic pathway of fluoride.

FLUORIDE TOXICITY

Before the recognition of the importance of fluorides in relation to dental disease, the ion was well known in the form of hydrofluoric acid, an agent used for etching glass, and as sodium fluoride, a common household insecticide and rodenticide. Unfortunately, its effect as a potent protoplasmic poison has colored its biologic appraisal over the years. A clear distinction must be made between the acute toxic effects resulting from a single massive dose of fluoride and the chronic toxic effects of small doses spread over an interval of time.

Acute fluoride poisoning is very rare, with only 435 cases being recorded worldwide in medical reports covering a period of 85 years.[3] These cases were primarily suicides, or accidents where fluoride compounds were mistakenly ingested. Sodium fluoride crystals are usually artificially colored blue so that they will not be mistaken for table salt. An acute lethal dose for a human being is approximately 5 gm fluoride as sodium fluoride.[3] The effects of large doses of fluoride are first manifested as irritation of the alimentary tract with nausea, vomiting, abdominal pain, and diarrhea. Excessive salivation, thirst, perspiration, and muscular spasms are also seen. Later, there may be depression of the respiratory, circulatory, and nervous systems, with such cases commonly having a fatal outcome in 2 or 3 days.[3] If large doses of fluoride are ingested, the stomach should be emptied as rapidly as possible and measures taken to reduce fluoride absorption. This can be accomplished by induced emesis and ingestion of milk or calcium salts, which will react with the fluoride ion to form relatively insoluble calcium fluoride.

Chronic fluoride toxicity may, depending on the dosage, be confined to minor physiologic alterations such as mottled enamel or result in a major crippling disease. It has been estimated that 10% to 15% of persons consuming water with 8 ppm fluoride will develop radiographically detectable osteosclerosis. To develop the crippling fluorosis found among some workers in the cryolite industry and in some areas of India, 20 to 80 mg fluoride must be ingested daily over a period of 10 to 20 years. [2] This would require a water fluoride level of 10 ppm or greater coupled with high water consumption. Excessive levels of fluoride are deposited in the skeleton over the years. The bones become heavy and irregular with multiple exostoses. There is often a reduced diameter of the spinal canal with compression of the cord. The vertebrae may become fused in numerous places, resulting in a so-called "poker back." Irregular bony deposits limit the movement of many other joints as well. Radiologically, affected bones appear very radiopaque with thickened cortexes and diminished medullary cavities. [3]

SYSTEMIC FLUORIDES AND DENTAL DISEASE
Chronic endemic dental fluorosis

The first relationship between fluoride and the dentition was established when the substance was discovered to be the cause of chronic endemic fluorosis, or mottled enamel. Although this condition was first described at the beginning of the twentieth century, [4] it was not until 1931 that the causative factor was determined to be fluoride. [5,6]

The mottling and staining of the enamel associated with chronic endemic dental fluorosis has been shown to be a hypoplastic defect resulting from a disturbance in the functioning of the ameloblasts during tooth development. Depending on the fluoride concentration in the drinking water, the condition has a wide variety of manifestations. These range from white spots or flecking of the enamel at concentrations up to 1.5 ppm to moderate and severe pitting and brownish staining of enamel at higher concentrations. It is com-

monly, but mistakenly, believed that erupted teeth can develop mottling when exposed to fluoride. The fact is that excessive fluoride affects the ameloblasts and therefore can cause mottling of the enamel *only* while the enamel is forming. Fluoride absorbed from topical contact or ingestion after eruption will not cause mottling.

Dental caries

Even before fluoride was discovered to be the causative agent for chronic endemic dental fluorosis, children with this defect were observed to have a lower than average caries prevalence. [7] In 1938, H. Trendley Dean [8] established that there was a greater percentage of caries-free children in areas with high levels of fluoride in the water than in areas with low amounts of fluoride. These findings suggested the possibility of reducing the prevalence of dental caries through adjustment of the fluoride content of public water supplies.

These findings and others demonstrated a generally inverse relationship between the amount of fluoride in a water supply and the dental caries experience of the children, with the amount of caries being as much as two or three times greater among children in some areas than in others. [9] A strikingly low caries prevalence was found in communities with water containing as little as 1 ppm fluoride. This concentration produced only sporadic findings of the mildest form of chronic endemic dental fluorosis. Thus it was concluded that significant inhibition of dental caries could be expected at fluoride concentrations not causing unesthetic enamel mottling.

Optimal fluoride level

The optimal fluoride level in a water supply should be one that will provide maximal protection against dental caries without producing adverse effects. This concentration has been established as approximately 1 ppm fluoride. The amount of fluoride consumed is a function not only of the amount of fluoride in the water supply but also of the mean annual air temperature. A high mean annual temperature will lead to a high fluoride intake because of the relatively large quantities of water consumed. Optimal fluoride levels therefore depend on climatic conditions. Based on safety standards and water consumption estimates, the U.S. Public Health Service has established recommended levels for fluoride concentrations in water

Table 24-1. Temperature ranges and recommended fluoride concentrations

Annual average of maximal daily temperatures (° F)	Fluoride concentrations (ppm)	
	Optimal	Acceptable range
50.0-53.7	1.2	0.9-1.7
53.8-58.3	1.1	0.8-1.5
58.4-63.8	1.0	0.8-1.3
63.9-70.6	0.9	0.7-1.2
70.7-79.2	0.8	0.7-1.0
79.3-90.5	0.7	0.6-0.8

Modified from U.S. Department of Health, Education, and Welfare, Public Health Service: Public Health Service drinking water standards, 1962, PHS Publication no. 956, Washington, D.C., 1962, U.S. Government Printing Office.

supplies for various mean annual air temperatures.[10] These levels are shown in Table 24-1. All water supplies whose fluoride levels have been adjusted should conform to these standards.

Mechanisms of protection

The mechanism by which fluoride imparts its protection against dental caries is not fully understood. It has been known for some time that the fluoride ion can replace the hydroxyl ion in the hydroxyapatite lattice in the inorganic portion of all calcified body tissues. This includes tooth enamel, dentin, and cementum, as well as bone and ectopic calcifications.[11] Because of its crystalline configuration, the fluoroapatite thus formed is less susceptible than hydroxyapatite to the attack of weak organic acids. Only a small portion of the hydroxyapatite is converted to fluoroapatite. The highest concentrations of 3000 to 4000 ppm fluoride are found at the crystal surface, whereas pure fluoroapatite has 38,000 ppm fluoride.[12]

In hard tissues, fluoride accumulates in proximity to circulating fluids; thus the fluoride level is greater in periosteal tissue than underlying bone, in dentin nearer the pulp, and in enamel near the surface.[12] The amount of these surface concentrations is directly proportional to the concentration of fluoride in the drinking water and the length of time the water was consumed. During the preeruptive maturation phase of tooth development, surface enamel continues to be bathed in fluoride-containing tissue fluid, thus accounting for the higher fluoride level found in surface enamel. The concentration of ionic fluoride in

the tissue fluid is closely related to the concentration found in the drinking water.[13] Only when there are very high concentrations in the water is the amount of fluoride in the deeper layers of enamel raised appreciably because the bulk of enamel mineralizes quickly. The critical times for fluoride incorporation are from shortly after birth until 2½ years of age for deciduous teeth and from 3 until 12 years for permanent teeth.

Since greater resistance to acid dissolution is one of the characteristics of fluoroapatite-rich enamel, and the surface enamel has the highest concentration, subsurface enamel would be more susceptible to initial demineralization. The commonly observed "white spot lesion" is subsurface enamel demineralization.

It has also been suggested that fluoride may inhibit caries by enzyme-inhibitory properties.[11,14,15] The inhibition of acidogenic bacterial enzyme systems can considerably reduce their acid production, but much higher concentrations of fluoride are required than are present in the saliva of persons drinking fluoridated water. It has been found, however, that the fluoride ion is concentrated in bacterial plaque. The degree of concentration may be of such magnitude as to inhibit acid production by many of the organisms in plaque. It has been demonstrated that the plaque taken from individuals consuming optimally fluoridated water undergoes a significantly smaller drop in pH when incubated with sucrose than does plaque from individuals consuming water with negligible concentrations of fluoride.[16] The increased fluoride levels found in plaque are thought to be from exogenous sources such as saliva, drinking water, or topical applications rather than from fluoride released from the enamel surface.[17,18]

The action of organic acids in removing calcium ions from the hydroxyapatite lattice renders it unstable. The presence of fluoride, on the other hand, causes the remaining dibasic phosphate (HPO_4) ions to reacquire calcium ions and thus promote crystal growth. In this way, the fluoride liberated by acid from the enamel or already present in the plaque would favor remineralization of the enamel and be antagonistic to demineralization.[19]

It may be that the combined effects of decreased enamel solubility, bacterial enzyme inhibition, and enhanced remineralization give fluoride its importance in preventive dentistry.

Fluoridation studies

Whatever the exact mechanism may be, the action of fluoride in caries reduction is well documented, both in areas where the substance is naturally present in the water at optimal or higher levels and in communities that have adjusted their water supplies to optimal levels. In January, 1945, Grand Rapids, Michigan, became one of the first cities to adjust its water supply to an optimal fluoride level.[20] Fifteen years later the number of decayed, missing, and filled teeth among 12- through 16-year-olds was from 47.9% to 63.2% lower than was found among the same age group at the beginning of the program. Seventeen and one-half years after controlled fluoridation had been instituted in Brantford, Ontario, the relationships shown in Table 24-2 were found among 16- and 17-year-olds residing there and in the neighboring cities of Stratford and Sarnia.[21]

Although most studies have been devoted to the effects of waterborne fluorides on children's permanent teeth, the benefits have been found to carry over into adults. Lifelong adult residents of communities with fluoridated water have been shown to have 50% to 60% fewer decayed, missing, and filled teeth than do their counterparts in communities with negligible amounts of fluoride in the water.[22,23]

It was generally accepted in the past that the protection imparted to the enamel by fluoride during tooth formation is not lost, regardless of whether fluoridated water is consumed after eruption. Investigators have observed, however, that with the cessation of fluoridation, there is an increase in the caries experience in children who had previously consumed fluoridated water.[24] It has also been shown that fluoride levels of surface enamel increase throughout life in individuals who drink water containing 1 ppm or more fluoride.[11] Since the caries-protective effect of

fluoride is exerted at the enamel surface, it would be logical to conclude that fluoride is beneficial not only during tooth formation but throughout life.

Malocclusion

Although the benefits of optimally fluoridated water supplies are well established in relationship to dental caries, their relationship to the prevalence of malocclusion is not so clear cut. The hypothesis has been advanced that the loss of tooth substance either through extraction or through destruction of mesiodistal contour because of caries results in loss of continuity of the dental arches, abnormal arch relationships, and subsequent malocclusion.[25] Malocclusion resulting from premature loss of deciduous teeth from caries is well documented. It would logically follow that the reduction in caries and tooth loss attendant on fluoridation would in turn reduce the prevalence of malocclusion. Some clinical studies have lent support to this hypothesis,[26-28] whereas others have detected no differences in the prevalence of malocclusion among children in fluoridated and nonfluoridated communities.[29-31]

Periodontal disease

Several studies have reported a possible relationship between water fluoride levels and periodontal health.[32-35] From their results it is generally conceded that neither the incidence nor the severity of gingivitis and periodontal disease in a community is influenced by the fluoride level of its water supply.

ALTERNATIVE METHODS OF SUPPLYING SYSTEMIC FLUORIDE

The value of optimal fluoride levels in the water supply is unquestioned by knowledgeable workers in the health professions.

Table 24-2. Results of controlled fluoridation among 16- and 17-year-olds in three communities in Ontario

	Brantford 1.00 ppm F (adjusted)	Stratford 1.0 ppm F (natural)	Sarnia negligible F
Percentage of individuals with caries-free teeth	11.8	12.8	0.41
Number of decayed, missing, and filled teeth per individual	4.74	4.19	10.44

Data from Brown, H.K., and Paplove, M.: J. Can. Dent. Assoc. **31:**505, 1965.

Nevertheless, there have been extremely vocal groups who have opposed this well-tested public health measure because of misinformation about its safety. This opposition continues in spite of epidemiologic studies and statistical analyses by independent investigators worldwide that reveal no differences in mortality rates, from all causes or from cancer, heart diseases, or any other specific diseases, between fluoridated and nonfluoridated communities.[36] Other groups question the effectiveness of fluoridation in spite of voluminous evidence to support it, while others oppose it because of political and moral convictions. Unfortunately, these groups have exerted influences vastly disproportionate to their numbers and have seriously impeded the universal fluoridation of communal water supplies. Currently, only 49% of the U.S. population consumes optimally fluoridated water.[37]

Even when all public water supplies are fluoridated, the significant proportion of the population who do not receive their water from public supplies will not directly benefit. It is obvious that other means must be utilized to provide the protective effects of systemic fluorides for those who are either (1) using public water supplies that are not fluoridated or (2) not using public water supplies and do not have their own source of naturally fluoridated water.

Many different methods of fluoride supplementation have been proposed and studied. Only a few of the more widely used and documented methods are discussed here. An extensive review of fluoride supplements has been made by Stookey,[14] and parts of his review are cited in this section.

Home fluoridators and bottled water

Home fluoridating units provide an optimally fluoridated water supply, but their very high cost severely limits their widespread use. Fluoridated bottled water contains a similar level of fluoride as a fluoridated water supply. The use of bottled water for drinking and cooking is increasing rapidly throughout the nation for reasons of taste and purity. The cost of fluoridated bottled water is nominal, being no more than that of plain bottled water. Therefore this is a highly effective home fluoridation method to recommend. The primary objection to both home fluoridators and bottled water other than cost is that only water consumed in the home will be fluoridated. If the children consume a large proportion of their daily water in-

take at school or elsewhere, they may not ingest enough fluoride for optimal benefit.

Fluoridated school water supplies.

Lack of a central water supply makes water fluoridation impractical for 23% of the United States population.[37] The proportion of the population not served by centralized water supplies is even higher in foreign countries. In some areas where fluoridation of the main water supply is not feasible, fluoridation of school water supplies has reduced the decayed, missing, and filled teeth of the children by as much as 39%.[38]

Although maximum benefits are derived from fluoridated water when it is consumed from birth, a significant amount of tooth calcification takes place after the child reaches school age. As discussed previously, there is also evidence to indicate a topical action of fluoridated water.

A limitation of school water fluoridation is that the children's consumption of water is intermittent. They attend school for only part of the day, 5 days a week, 9 to 10 months each year. To compensate for lack of continuous consumption, school water supplies have been adjusted to higher levels than those normally recommended. Water fluoride levels of up to 6.30 ppm have been used with little or no evidence of fluorosis resulting.[39]

Fluoride tablets

In areas where the public water supplies are sometimes not potable, a great deal of attention has been focused on fluoride tablets. Benefits equivalent to or greater than having the water fluoridated have been reported, with maximal caries reductions of up to 80% being found in both permanent and deciduous teeth.[40] In a review of 27 studies, only 5 showed a partially or entirely negative caries-reducing effect for fluoride tablets.[14]

Before fluoride supplements are prescribed, the fluoride content of the water supply should be known.

The daily fluoride allowance for children as recommended by the Council of Dental Therapeutics (CDT)[41] is contained in Table 24-3.

Tablets are available containing 1.00 and 0.50 mg fluoride in both chewable and nonchewable form. When writing a prescription, 2.2 mg of sodium fluoride yields 1.0 mg of fluoride. Chewable tablets are preferred since the topical effect obtained when they

Table 24-3. Daily fluoride supplementation for children

Age (years)	Fluoride in water supply		
	<0.3 ppm	0.3-0.7 ppm	>0.7 ppm
Birth-2	0.25 mg	0	0
2-3	0.50 mg	0.25 mg	0
3-14	1.00 mg	0.50 mg	0

are chewed is thought to be significant. For children requiring 0.25 mg of fluoride per day, fluoride drops should be prescribed. Most liquid preparations contain 0.25 mg of fluoride per drop. An alternative method of supplying fluoride for children under 2 years old is to add the daily fluoride allowance either in tablet or liquid form to 1 quart of water and to use this water for drinking, cooking, and formula preparation.

As a safety precaution, no more than 264 tablets (264 mg fluoride) should be prescribed at one time. Each package should bear the warning: CAUTION— *Store out of reach of children.*[41]

Much more information is needed about the metabolism of fluoride ingested in the form of tablets in relation to its effects on the dentition. Fluoride ingested in a single dose is rapidly absorbed and excreted in the urine with a very brief rise in the blood and tissue fluid level.[42,43] When the same amount of fluoride is given in three doses rather than a single large dose, about 50% less is excreted in the urine and much more is thus retained.[43] If much of the value of systemic fluoride is derived from bathing the developing tooth in tissue fluids containing elevated amounts of fluoride, a large number of small doses would appear to be more valuable than a single large dose.

The concentration of fluoride in human saliva is greatly increased after the administration of sodium fluoride tablets. Significantly higher salivary fluoride levels persist even after 24 hours.[44] These elevated salivary fluoride levels may contribute to the anticaries effect of fluoride tablets.

A number of other problems are inherent in the use of fluoride tablets. Although there is evidence to indicate the need for lifetime fluoride ingestion to obtain its optimal effects, it is unlikely that many individuals can be motivated to take tablets daily for their entire lives. Only the most highly motivated parents will see that their children take a tablet each day. A possible way of overcoming this problem is to use the tablets to fluoridate the water used in the home for cooking and drinking. (Dissolve 1 tablet, that is, 2.2 mg sodium fluoride, in 1 quart water.) The inconvenience of even this measure limits its use to those highly motivated toward good dental health.

Although fluoride tablets seem to be of value, evidence available to date would indicate that they are not an adequate substitute for water fluoridation.

Fluoride vitamins

The addition of sodium fluoride in therapeutic quantities does not appear to have any effect on the action of vitamin preparations and vice versa.[14] Fluoride-vitamin preparations have been shown to be highly effective in reducing dental caries attack in both deciduous and permanent teeth of children.[45] Fluoride-vitamin preparations are available in both drops and chewable tablets. Their recommended dosage is the same as given in Table 24-3.

An advantage of giving fluoride supplements combined with vitamins is the greater acceptability of these products. Parents are more likely to see that their children take vitamins prescribed for them than a fluoride tablet alone. This also points to the great disadvantage of this method of fluoride supplementation. Vitamins should never be prescribed indiscriminately. Therefore only the small group of children who require vitamin supplementation should receive fluoride in this manner.

Prenatal fluoride

Since the deciduous dentition and the permanent first molars undergo partial or complete calcification in utero, it could be reasoned that increased fluoride levels in the fetal circulation would be beneficial in reducing caries susceptibility in these teeth. Therefore increased fluoride ingestion by the mother, either from fluoridated water or prenatal fluoride supplements, would be thought to be of value.

The placenta acts as a barrier, protecting the fetus from sharp increases of fluoride concentration in the maternal circulation. However, there is evidence to indicate that some additional fluoride does pass the placenta because increasing the amount in water supplies leads to higher fluoride levels in fetal hard structures.[1] It is not known what levels of fluoride in the water are required to supply sufficient fluoride to the teeth in utero for significant caries protection. Clinical studies of fluoride's effects on the deciduous dentition calcified in utero have yielded conflicting evidence.[46,47] The currently available prenatal preparations that contain fluoride also contain minerals that, in animals, have been shown to interfere with the metabolic activity of fluorides, thus reducing the amount available to the fetus.[48]

Much further study of prenatal fluoride supplements is required before they should be routinely prescribed for expectant mothers residing in areas without appreciable fluoride in the water.

Fluoridated milk and salt

Fluoridated table salt and milk have been shown to be effective in lowering the incidence of dental caries in areas where the water is fluoride deficient, but to a lesser degree than fluoridated water.[14,49] These measures have aroused the greatest interest for use in areas lacking in communal water supplies and with low socioeconomic levels.

There are major problems attendant on both milk and salt fluoridation. For example, it is difficult to monitor all commercial milk processing plants to ensure a safe and effective fluoride level. The consumption of milk also varies greatly among children so that some would be likely to receive ineffectual amounts of fluoride, whereas others would receive too much. Since adults generally drink little milk, any posteruptive topical effect would be unavailable to them.

Much additional information is needed about the body's handling of fluoridated milk after ingestion before proper dosage levels can be determined. A similar problem exists with salt. Children ingest variable amounts of salt, usually not a great deal, and therefore it is difficult to regulate the intake. A program of supplementing table salt with 552.6 mg sodium fluoride per kilogram of salt (250 ppm fluoride) has yielded 40% reductions in the caries experience of 2- to 6-year-old children.[50]

Since it is believed that fluoride supplementation should be continued throughout life, a program of both salt and milk fluoridation has been proposed.[49] With this regimen children would be receiving the bulk of their fluoride through milk, and adults through salt. A great deal of additional information will be required before either part of this regimen should be instituted as a public health measure.

TOPICAL FLUORIDES

In addition to having anticariogenic properties when ingested during tooth formation, fluoride has been shown to exert an anticariogenic effect when applied topically to the erupted dentition. Like systemically administered fluorides, the mechanisms by which topically applied fluorides inhibit dental caries are incompletely understood. Recently, considerable interest has been aroused concerning the effects of topical fluorides on the supporting structures of the teeth. A growing body of laboratory and clinical evidence indicate that topical fluorides may play an important role in the prevention and treatment of periodontal disease.

A primary objective of topical fluoride therapy is to deposit maximal amounts of fluoride in the enamel as fluoroapatite, which is generally believed to impart caries resistance to the tooth. This may be in the form of a simple ionic exchange as represented by the following chemical reaction[51]:

$$\underset{\text{Hydroxyapatite}}{Ca_{10}(PO_4)_6(OH)_2} \xrightarrow{\overset{F^- \text{ in low}}{\text{concentration}}} \underset{\text{Fluoroapatite}}{Ca_{10}(PO_4)_6F_2} + 2(OH)^-$$

When high concentrations of fluoride are applied to enamel surfaces, the primary product is calcium fluoride.[51]

$$Ca_{10}(PO_4)_6(OH)_2 \xrightarrow{\overset{F^- \text{ in high}}{\text{concentration}}} CaF_2 + 6(PO_4)^{3-} + 2(OH)^-$$

After topical application the initially high surface fluoride levels are rapidly lost. First to go are unreacted fluoride ions, followed by calcium fluoride. Calcium fluoride is soluble in saliva so that surface deposits tend to dissolve or wash away. When calcium fluoride is deposited within enamel defects and fissures, it may remain for some time. This residual calcium fluoride may yield fluoride ions, which are then incorporated into the apatite crystal by direct replacement of the hydroxyl ions or by recrystallization (dissolution and reprecipitation of the apatite crystal incorporating fluoride rather than hydroxyl ions).[12]

In addition to the formation of fluoroapatite, the fluoride ions originating from the topical agent or released from calcium fluoride may interfere with the deposition and acid production of plaque.[52] Fluoride ions in low concentrations may also desorb both pellicle protein and bacteria from the enamel surface.[53]

Many different fluoride compounds have been evaluated with various methods of application. Some of the studies have yielded directly conflicting results, giving rise to considerable controversy among workers in the field as to the efficacy of some of the various compounds and techniques of application. The current status of only the more commonly used compounds and techniques of application are reviewed in this chapter.

Fluoride solutions
Sodium fluoride

The application of aqueous solutions of sodium fluoride is the oldest method of topical fluoride therapy. Although various application techniques and solution concentrations have been used, the procedure adopted by the CDT[41] has produced the most consistently beneficial results. It will reduce by 30% to 40% the incidence of new carious permanent teeth in children living in an area where the water supply is fluoride deficient.[14]

With the accepted procedure a series of four applications of a 2% sodium fluoride solution are made at 1-week intervals at 3, 7, 11, and 13 years of age. These ages were selected so that fluoride would be applied shortly after eruption of groups of teeth. The ages should be varied according to the eruption pattern of each individual patient. A prophylaxis is given before the first application in each series. The teeth are isolated and thoroughly wetted with the solution, which is allowed to dry for 4 minutes. No prophylaxis is given before the second, third, and fourth applications; however, its omission before the first application lessens the effectiveness of the treatment by one half.

The effectiveness of sodium fluoride in preventing caries in deciduous teeth, permanent teeth of children reared in fluoridated areas, and adult dentitions has not been investigated extensively. There is evidence to indicate that a 25% to 30% reduction in caries of deciduous teeth of children raised in a nonfluoridated area will result from sodium fluoride application.[14] Limited data do not indicate any benefits for the permanent teeth of children reared in a fluoridated area or for adults.[14]

The taste of sodium fluoride is not unpleasant, and since this compound is stable in solution, it does not have to be mixed for each patient. Very few dentists presently apply aqueous sodium fluoride because more convenient and effective compounds have been developed.

Stannous fluoride

The stannous fluoride application procedure, as originally developed,[54] calls for a single annual application of a freshly prepared 8% solution. This is preceded by a thorough prophylaxis, which includes carrying the pumice between the teeth with floss. The solution is applied to the teeth, which have been air dried and isolated, a quadrant or a half mouth at a time. The teeth are continually wetted for a period of 4 minutes. In patients whose caries susceptibility is high, applications of stannous fluoride every 6 months or even more frequently are recommended.

Stannous fluoride applied in the manner just described to the permanent teeth of children reared in nonfluoride areas has generally been shown to be more beneficial than sodium fluoride in reducing dental caries increments. It is also effective in reducing the caries increment in deciduous teeth of children reared in a nonfluoride area and in permanent teeth of children reared in fluoride areas. When applied in a 10% concentration, stannous fluoride has been shown to reduce the caries increment in adults.[14] The application of a 10% stannous fluoride solution for 15 or 30 seconds has yielded conflicting clinical results.[55-57]

Large amounts of calcium fluoride are formed when stannous fluoride is applied to sound enamel surfaces. Phosphate ions released by the calcium fluoride formation combine with the stannous tin to form insoluble tin-phosphate complexes.[58] Insoluble tin-phosphate complexes may also be formed when stannous fluoride is applied to precarious or carious enamel, which would give a caries-arrestment property in addition to a caries-preventive property.[59,60] This and the fact that stannous fluoride has an inhibitory effect on plaque formation that sodium fluoride does not[61] may account for the greater anticaries effect of stannous fluoride when compared with sodium fluoride.

The tin-phosphate complex imparts a light brown pigmentation to the carious or precarious areas that has caused objections from some patients and practitioners. This pigmentation is probably desirable, since it indicates the arrestment of a precarious or frankly carious lesion. The incidence and severity of this pigmentation is directly related to the caries activity and oral hygiene habits of the individual, with those exhibiting a high degree of caries activity and poor oral hygiene having the most pigmentation.[62] Very dark, objectionable stains, which are sometimes observed, result from the tin's forming a sulfide complex with the products of bacterial plaque.[59]

Although topical application of stannous fluoride will slow the progress of existing carious lesions,[63,64] the pigmented tin-phosphate complex is lost through washing and abrasion over a period of time, which indicates the necessity for repeated replacement of the stannous ion. The frequency of application of stannous fluoride therefore depends on the caries activity of the individual. Some may require treatment as often as every 3 or 4 months, whereas annual or semiannual treatment will suffice for others.

Stannous fluoride in a 10% solution has been successfully used as an indirect pulp-capping agent in both permanent and deciduous teeth. After a 3-month interval carious dentin treated with stannous fluoride has been found to be more radiopaque and harder than carious dentin treated with calcium hydroxide compounds.[65]

Stannous fluoride solutions have a highly unpleasant taste resulting from the presence of the tin ion. This taste is difficult to mask by flavoring agents. Aqueous solutions are unstable and should be freshly prepared for each patient. Solutions prepared with glycerin are reported to be stable and to have a prolonged shelf life. Commercially available products range in concentration from 0.4% to 30%.[41] The more highly concentrated forms should be diluted with distilled water before topical application. Once diluted, they should be used promptly.

Acidulated phosphate fluoride

Acidulated phosphate fluoride (APF) is currently available in solution or gel form with various flavors added. The solution is applied in the same manner as 8% stannous fluoride (4 minutes to dried and isolated teeth), whereas the gels are applied in either wax trays or custom-made mouthguard type of applicators.

In vitro and in vivo studies have shown that there is increased uptake of fluoride by the enamel when the fluoride solution has a low pH. The acidic solution dissolves the surface hydroxyapatite crystals of the enamel, thus freeing more calcium ions for reaction to calcium fluoride and subsequent recrystalliza-

tion as fluoroapatite.[51] Unfortunately, the dissolution of the surface enamel may overshadow the beneficial effects of increased fluoride uptake. The addition of phosphates to the acidulated fluoride solutions allows a high fluoride uptake without objectionable dissolution of the surface enamel.[66]

Acidulated phosphate fluorides have been shown to be effective in reducing new caries in the permanent teeth of children residing in a nonfluoride area. The more frequent the applications, the larger the caries reductions that result.[14,67] Daily applications of acidulated or neutral sodium fluoride gels by mouthguards have achieved caries reductions as high as 89% over a 21-month period.[68] Caries reductions of up to 63% were still evident 2 years after cessation of this treatment.[69] A thrice weekly application of APF gel to children residing in an area with optimally fluoridated water reduced the caries increment of their permanent teeth by 29%.[70]

Fluoride uptake by the enamel surface is much higher, and the fluoride penetrates the enamel much more deeply with APF solutions than with either sodium or stannous fluoride. There is also a significant reduction in the number of *Streptococcus mutans* from occlusal plaque samples after 8 to 10 daily applications of APF.[71] Although increased fluoride levels in enamel are undoubtedly beneficial in protecting against dental caries, it does not necessarily follow that higher and higher levels of fluoride in enamel will give correspondingly higher levels of caries protection, as evidenced by the similar caries reductions resulting from daily applications of both neutral and acidulated sodium fluoride.[68]

Acidulated phosphate fluorides taste acidic, but not disagreeably so. The addition of flavoring agents, although not affecting the clinical effectiveness of APF solutions, makes them pleasant tasting and highly acceptable to children. The solutions are stable and have a long shelf life so that they can be made up in bulk and not prepared for each patient.

Some properties of the three best known fluoride compounds are summarized in Table 24-4.

A topical application of APF followed by a topical application of stannous fluoride yields an enamel surface that is less porous and soluble than when either agent is used alone.[72,73] Whether or not this treatment technique will give an enhanced anticaries effect has not been determined clinically.

Table 24-4. Properties of three best known fluoride compounds

Properties	NaF	SnF$_2$	APF
Is effective in permanent teeth of children in nonfluoride areas?	Yes	Yes	Yes
Is effective in deciduous teeth in nonfluoride areas?	Yes	Yes	?
Is effective in fluoride areas?	No	Yes	?
Is effective in adults?	No	Yes	?
Requires a simple, one-appointment procedure?	No	Yes	Yes
Is stable in solution?	Yes	No	Yes
Has a pleasant taste?	Yes	No	Yes
Stains teeth?	No	Yes	No
Can arrest existing caries?	No	Yes	No

Other fluoride compounds

Numerous other fluoride compounds, such as aluminum fluoride, ammonium fluoride, and stannous hexafluorozirconate, have been developed and tested both clinically and in the laboratory. Although some of these compounds have shown considerable promise as anticariogenic agents, there is insufficient evidence at this time to indicate their use in either dental practice or public health programs.

Fluoride dentifrices

Numerous fluoride compounds have been incorporated in dentifrices with widely varying clinical effectiveness. The earliest fluoride dentifrices contained sodium fluoride. They proved to be of little value because the calcium carbonate or calcium phosphate in their abrasive systems yielded enough free calcium to inactivate the fluoride. Subsequently, many other fluoride compounds and abrasive systems have been used and manufacturers have made many claims, mostly unsubstantiated. There are currently two types of fluoride dentifrices that have undergone sufficient laboratory and clinical testing to be accepted by the CDT as being effective in reducing the incidence of new dental caries.[74] These are a sodium fluoride (NaF) dentifrice and four monofluorophosphate (MFP) dentifrices. The fluoride concentration in these dentifrices is NaF 0.22% and MFP 0.76%. These concentrations yield 1000 ppm of fluoride ion.[75]

A number of stannous fluoride dentifrices have been accepted by the CDT over the past 15 to 20 years. None of them are currently being marketed. Those stannous fluoride dentifrices currently available have not gained ADA acceptance.

The ionic fluoride in sodium fluoride and stannous fluoride dentifrices is very susceptible to incompatibility with abrasive agents, and covalently bound fluoride in MFP is more resistant.[75] Although many dentifrices have incorporated fluoride into their formulation, this does not mean they are effective anticaries agents since the fluoride may be inactivated. Results of carefully designed, long-term clinical testing should be required before any dentifrice is recommended to the patient as an effective caries-preventive agent.

Sodium monofluorophosphate dentifrices

Monofluorophosphate is different from other fluorides in that the fluoride is covalently bound rather than in ionic form. The fluoride ion is released in the mouth by hydrolysis and tends to form fluoroapatite.[76,77] Controlled clinical studies have shown that brushing with a sodium monofluorophosphate dentifrice reduces new caries in the range of 17% to 38% in both fluoridated and nonfluoridated communities.[41] Although their monofluorophosphate concentrations are the same, each of the four accepted dentifrices has a different abrasive system. They are calcium carbonate, calcium carbonate and silica, silica, and dicalcium phosphate dihydrate.[74]

Sodium fluoride dentifrice

The sodium fluoride dentifrice accepted by the CDT[74] has a silica abrasive system and is pH stabilized, which allows for more available fluoride than other formulations. Controlled clinical studies indicate caries reductions as high as 41%.[78]

Fluoride prophylaxis pastes

The caries-inhibitory effects produced by incorporating fluorides into dentifrices have suggested the value of adding them to prophylaxis pastes. Much higher concentrations of fluoride can be added to prophylaxis pastes than to dentifrices because these pastes are used so infrequently. As in the case of dentifrices, the ingredients of the prophylaxis pastes must be compatible with the fluoride used, or the fluoride will be inactivated and of no value.

All commonly used prophylaxis pastes are abrasive and remove significant amounts of enamel. This surface enamel is high in fluoride and gives caries protection to the tooth. The fluoride in a prophylaxis paste not only replaces the surface fluoride lost but raises the surface level slightly.[79] A nonfluoride prophylaxis, on the other hand, is of questionable cariostatic value to the patient.

Sodium fluoride prophylaxis paste

In the 1940s and 1950s sodium fluoride was added to prophylaxis pastes and clinically tested. The results, although generally encouraging, were highly inconsistent.[11] Little attention is presently being devoted to using this compound in a prophylaxis paste.

Stannous fluoride prophylaxis pastes

Semiannual prophylaxis with an 8.9% stannous fluoride–lava pumice paste has been shown to reduce the caries increment in permanent teeth of children in a nonfluoride community by 34%.[80] A similar caries reduction among children resulted from the same treatment in a natural fluoride area.[81] A 12% reduction in new carious surfaces was noted among U.S. naval personnel treated without regard to previous fluoridated water intake.[56] Another study has shown no caries-reducing effect from annual prophylaxis with a stannous fluoride–lava pumice paste.[82] There are currently no stannous fluoride prophylaxis pastes commercially available.

Acidulated phosphate fluoride prophylaxis pastes

Although acidulated sodium fluoride phosphate has been incorporated with various abrasives into pastes that are commercially marketed, there is meager clinical evidence to indicate their effectiveness as anticariogenic agents.

Multiple fluoride treatment

Although many of the previously described fluoride compounds and treatment techniques have been shown to have anticariogenic value, the stannous fluoride compounds have been used primarily in multiple treatment approaches. The anticariogenic effect of a stannous fluoride prophylaxis and topical application in children in fluoride and nonfluoride areas[80,81] as well as in adults[56] has been discussed. The inclusion of a topical application of stannous fluoride and daily use of a stannous fluoride dentifrice accepted by the ADA have demonstrated an additive effect for each element in reducing the increment of dental caries attack.[56,80,81] In addition to reducing the initiation of new carious lesions, multiple stannous

fluoride therapy has been shown to slow the progression of already existing carious lesions.[64] However, the stannous fluoride dentifrice used in all these studies is no longer marketed. The effectiveness of other types of fluoride dentifrices in a multiple-fluoride treatment regime are unknown.

Another multiple-treatment approach that has shown promising results is the application of APF gel containing 1.23% fluoride in custom trays at 4-month intervals coupled with weekly rinsing with a 0.2% sodium fluoride solution. The short-term exposure to high concentrations of fluoride in gel applicators may act on the enamel to retard demineralization. The long-term exposure to low concentrations of fluoride in the rinsing program may interfere with the enzymatic activity of the plaque and enhance remineralization of early enamel lesions.[83]

Self-treatment with topical fluorides

Traditionally, topical fluorides have been applied in a dental office by either dentists or trained auxiliary personnel. The cost of such a procedure, because of the professional work hours required and the need for dental treatment facilities, severely restricts the use of topical fluoride treatment in any public health program. To bring the benefits of topical fluoride treatment to more people at minimal cost, various methods in which the patients themselves apply the fluoride without special treatment facilities have been proposed and investigated.

Self-application of topical fluoride gel

The daily self-administration of a topical fluoride gel by means of a mouthguard type of applicator has been discussed.[68] Although the technique is of great value in a private dental practice, providing remarkable caries reductions, it is impractical for mass treatment programs. The initial cost of constructing mouthguards is considerable, and they would have to be replaced periodically because of loss, breakage, and changes in the dentition, especially in children.

Brushing the teeth with an APF gel alone has not been shown to reduce caries significantly. However, if the teeth are brushed with a nonfluoride prophylaxis paste before brushing with the gel, the caries increment has been reduced over 30%.[84]

Brushing with fluoride prophylaxis paste

In the three-phase stannous fluoride treatment previously discussed, the most time-consuming portion of the procedure is the prophylaxis. By having the patients perform their own prophylaxis in groups by means of supervised brushing with a fluoride prophylaxis paste, a great deal of time is saved and the requirement for a dental operatory is eliminated. The cariostatic effectiveness of this treatment technique using a lava pumice paste in conjunction with a topical application of aqueous stannous fluoride and daily use of a stannous fluoride dentifrice has been demonstrated among U.S. naval personnel.[85]

FLUORIDE MOUTHRINSES

Self-treatment with fluoride mouthrinses has gained widespread acceptance as a relatively easy and effective method of providing frequent topical fluoride applications to the teeth. There are two principal application techniques used. They are high concentration/low frequency programs and low concentration/high frequency programs.

The high concentration/low frequency program was designed for and is mainly applied in schools. In this program, a 0.2% solution of neutral sodium fluoride is used. The children rinse with 10 ml of the solution (5 ml for kindergartners) for 1 minute and then spit it out. This goes on once each week during the school year. More than a dozen clinical studies have shown 30% to 40% reductions in caries among children who have participated in such a program for over 2 years.[86] These programs are effective in both optimally fluoridated and fluoride-deficient communities. Currently, more than 8 million children are participating in school rinsing programs. The cost of these programs is low, approximately 50 cents per child per year.[86]

The high frequency/low concentration programs are designed for home use, especially for children who are caries active. There are three fluoride rinses employed in most daily home use programs. They are sodium fluoride 0.05%, APF 0.044%, and stannous fluoride 0.1%. Children are to rinse with 5 ml of these solutions for 1 minute, preferably at bedtime. Preschool children should not participate in such a program since they are more likely to swallow the solution than to spit it out. However, children 3 years of age and older living in a fluoride-deficient area could swallow the rinse solution in lieu of taking a fluoride tablet. A teaspoon (approximately 5 ml) of 0.05% sodium fluoride solution contains 1.0 mg of fluoride. Although a large number of mouthrinses

are accepted by the CDT,[41] only two preparations are available over the counter. These are a 0.05% sodium fluoride solution and a stannous fluoride tablet that, when dissolved in the prescribed amount of water, will yield a 0.1% solution.

The stannous fluoride rinse has been shown to be an especially effective anticaries agent. Daily use reduced caries by as much as 43% in areas where the water was optimally fluoridated.[87] Part of a stannous fluoride mouthrinse's effectiveness in reducing caries may stem from its antibacterial properties. When mouthrinses with equivalent fluoride ion concentrations of sodium fluoride and stannous fluoride were tested, the stannous fluoride had a significant antibacterial effect, but the sodium fluoride did not.[88] Stannous fluoride rinses interfere with the initial bacterial colonization of the tooth surface[89] and inhibit the drop in plaque pH after exposure to sucrose.[90] These effects are not found with sodium fluoride rinses. Although these antibacterial properties have been attributed to the tin ion, the fluoride ion must also be present because applications of stannous chloride were without antibacterial effect.[9 1]

Daily or periodic rinsing with a fluoride solution is a valuable adjunct to any caries prevention program. This treatment requires no professional supervision or facilities and is inexpensive. However, the presence in the home of mouthwashes with high fluoride concentrations may represent a potential hazard from a toxicity viewpoint. It is for this reason that the CDT limits its acceptance of sodium fluoride mouthrinses to those packaged to contain a maximum of 264 mg of sodium fluoride (120 mg of fluoride).[41] A 500 ml bottle of 0.05% sodium fluoride rinse will contain 100 mg of fluoride. Proper indoctrination of the patients and parents is mandatory for such a program.

Other fluoride vehicles

After all topical fluoride treatments, the initially high fluoride levels of the surface enamel are rapidly lost. Applying fluoride in a urethane lacquer preserves the high fluoride levels indefinitely in vitro. The adherent lacquer prolongs the time the fluoride ion is in contact with hydroxyapatite and thus leads to fluoroapatite formation. It also serves as a fluoride reservoir.[92] The two commercially prepared fluoride-containing varnishes are currently not marketed in the United States. In animal studies, a single application of these varnishes raised the surface enamel fluoride levels and reduced caries to an extent not significantly different from a single application of 1.23% APF gel.[93] In human studies, caries in children's teeth were reduced by 75% and, in contrast with other topical fluoride treatments, caries were greatly reduced in pits and fissures as well as on smooth and interproximal surfaces.[94,95]

A prophylaxis cup impregnated with either stannous fluoride or sodium fluoride increases the fluoride uptake of enamel when used in conjunction with fluoride-containing pastes at low pH.[96] The fluoride content of interproximal enamel has been increased by using fluoride-impregnated dental floss.[97]

The controlled intraoral release of fluoride is currently being tested. A pellet attached to the tooth surface will release fluoride at a constant, predetermined rate for up to 6 months. Release rates may range from 0.02 to 1.0 mg of fluoride per day. The release of 0.05 mg of fluoride per day produces a 30-fold increase in salivary fluoride levels and a 5-fold increase in plaque fluoride levels.[98]

Fluorides in restorative materials

Fluoride has been added to the flux of silicate cements to reduce enamel solubility at the margin of silicate restorations. The positive effect is well documented. In the hope of eliciting a similar effect from amalgam restorations, both sodium fluoride and stannous fluoride have been added to commercially available silver amalgam. Studies have shown that a concentration of 0.1% of either sodium or stannous fluoride does not significantly alter the amalgam's compressive strength, but higher concentrations decrease the strength. Sodium fluoride provides twice as much available fluoride as stannous fluoride does.[99] In vitro studies have shown that the depth and extent of demineralized enamel is significantly less around fluoride-containing amalgam restorations than is found around conventional amalgams subjected to the same environment.[100]

Sodium and stannous fluorides have been added to zinc oxide and eugenol cements in the hope of giving an anticariogenic effect to temporary restorations and cemented crowns and inlays. The increased fluoride uptake and decreased solubility of enamel adjacent to zinc oxide and eugenol cements with fluoride compare with that adjacent to silicate cements.[101] The microhardness and fluoride content of underlying dentin are also increased.[102]

Because of the low pH of the liquid used in mixing zinc oxyphosphate cements, these cements have a tendency to decalcify the tooth structure next to which they are placed. By addition of an equal amount of a 30% solution of stannous fluoride to a dehydrated cement liquid, a pronounced degree of solubility protection is imparted without any adverse effect on the compressive strength or setting time of the cement.[103] This solubility protection decreases after a period of time, however.

TOPICAL FLUORIDES AND PERIODONTAL DISEASE

Until recently, the only dental interest in fluoride therapy was directed toward its effect on dental caries, although considerable evidence pointed to an antibacterial mechanism in caries prevention. Since periodontal disease is also considered to be of bacterial origin, it would logically follow that fluorides might also have some effect on this disease. A growing volume of research is lending support to this hypothesis.

Stannous fluoride seems to be the fluoride compound that is most effective in combating periodontal disease. Use of a stannous fluoride dentifrice has been shown to reduce both plaque formation and gingivitis indices better than either a placebo or an MFP dentifrice.[104,105]

Daily rinsing with a stannous fluoride mouthrinse lowered plaque scores, wet weight of plaque, and the number of bacterial colony-forming units.[106] Daily rinsing with 0.1% stannous fluoride was significantly more effective in reducing plaque and gingival index scores than was daily use of a 0.05% sodium fluoride rinse.[107] Of even more potential significance is the action of fluorides on specific organisms such as *Bacteroides asaccharolyticus, Bacteroides melaninogenicus,* and *Actinomyces viscosus,* which have been implicated in destructive periodontal disease. Stannous fluoride has been shown to be extremely potent in acting against these organisms, whereas APF was significantly less effective, and sodium fluoride had little or no effect at all.[108] From these early research findings, it might be conjectured that stannous fluoride, professionally applied in a concentrated form and self-applied through daily use of dentifrices and/or mouthrinses, may be as important in controlling periodontal disease as it has been shown to be in controlling dental caries.

REFERENCES

1. Bell, M.E., et al.: The supply of fluorine to man. In Fluorides and human health, Geneva, 1970, World Health Organization, pp. 17-74.
2. Armstrong, W.D., et al.: Distribution of fluorides. In Fluorides and human health, Geneva, 1970, World Health Organization, pp. 93-139.
3. Bhussry, B.R., et al.: Toxic effects of larger doses of fluoride. In Fluorides and human health, Geneva, 1970, World Health Organization, pp. 225-271.
4. Eager, J.M.: Denti di chiaie (Chiaie teeth), Public Health Rep. 16:2576-2577, 1901.
5. Churchill, H.V.: The occurrence of fluoride in some waters of the United States, J. Indust. Engin. Chem. 23:996-998, 1931.
6. Smith, M.C., Lantz, E.M., and Smith, H.V.: The cause of mottled enamel, Science 74:244, 1931.
7. McKay, F.S.: The establishment of a definite relation between enamel that is defective in its structure as mottled enamel, and the liability to decay, Dent. Cosmos 71:747-755, 1929.
8. Dean, H.T.: Endemic fluorosis and its relations to dental caries, Public Health Rep. 53:1443-1452, 1938.
9. Dean, H.T., Arnold, F.A., and Elvove, E.: Domestic water and dental caries. V. Additional studies of the relation of fluoride domestic waters to dental caries experience in 4,425 white children aged 12 to 14 years, of 13 cities in 4 states, Public Health Rep. 57:1155-1179, 1942.
10. U.S. Department of Health, Education, and Welfare, Public Health Service: Public Health Service drinking water standards, 1962, PHS Publication no. 956, Washington, D.C., 1962, U.S. Government Printing Office.
11. Hodge, H.C., and Smith, F.A.: Biological effects of organic fluorides. In Simons, J.H., editor: Fluorine chemistry, vol. 4, New York, 1964, Academic Press Inc.
12. Brudevold, F.: Fluoride therapy. In Bernier, J.L., and Muhler, J.C., editors: Improving dental practice through preventive measures, ed. 3, St. Louis, 1976, The C.V. Mosby Co.
13. Gay, W.S., and Taves, D.R.: Relation between (F⁻) in drinking water and human plasma, International Association for Dental Research Program and Abstracts, no. 718, 1973.
14. Stookey, G.K.: Fluoride therapy. In Bernier, J.L., and Muhler, J.C., editors: Improving dental practice through preventive measures, ed. 2, St. Louis, 1970, The C.V. Mosby Co.
15. Jenkins, G.N.: In vitro studies using chemicals. In Harris, R.S., editor: Art and science of dental caries research, New York, 1968, Academic Press Inc.
16. Edgar, W.M., Jenkins, G.N., and Tatevossian, A.: The inhibitory action of fluoride on plaque bacteria, Br. Dent. J. 128:129-132, 1970.
17. Gron, P., Yao, K., and Spinelli, M.: A study of inorganic constituents in dental plaque, J. Dent. Res. 48:799-805, 1969.
18. Fitzgerald, D.B., and Fitzgerald, R.J.: Plaque acid production in hamsters pre-treated with fluoride, J. Dent. Res. 52:111-115, 1973.
19. Ingram, G.S., and Nash, P.F.: A mechanism for the anticaries action of fluoride, Caries Res. 14:298-303, 1980.
20. Arnold, F.A., et al.: Fifteenth year of the Grand Rapids fluoridation study, J. Am. Dent. Assoc. 65:780-785, 1962.
21. Brown, H.K., and Poplove, M.: Brantford-Sarnia-Stratford fluoridation caries study: final survey, 1963, J. Can. Dent. Assoc. 31:505, 1965.
22. Englander, H.R., and Wallace, D.A.: Effects of naturally fluoridated water on dental caries in adults, Public Health Rep. 77:887-893, 1962.
23. Russell, A.L., and Elvove, E.: Domestic water and dental caries. VII. A study of the fluoride–dental caries relationship in an adult population, Public Health Rep. 66:1389-1401, 1951.
24. Way, R.M.: The effect on dental caries of a change from a naturally fluoridated to a fluoride-free communal water, J. Dent. Child. 31:151-157, 1964.
25. Salzmann, J.A.: The effects of fluoride on the prevalence of malocclusion, J. Am. Coll. Dent. 35:82-91, 1968.
26. Ast, D.B., Allaway, V., and Draker, H.L.: The prevalence of malocclusion, related to dental caries and lost first permanent molars, in a fluoridated city and a fluoride-deficient city, Am. J. Orthod. 48:106-113, 1962.
27. Tank, G., and Storvick, C.A.: Caries experience of children one to six years old in two Oregon communities (Corvallis and Albany). II. Relation of fluoride to hypoplasia, malocclusion, and gingivitis, J. Am. Dent. Assoc. 70:100-104, 1965.
28. Erickson, D.M., and Graziano, F.W.: Prevalence of malocclusion in seventh grade children in two North Carolina cities, J. Am. Dent. Assoc. 73:124-127, 1966.
29. Pelton, W.J., and Elsasser, W.A.: Studies of dento-facial morphology. III. The role of dental caries in the etiology of malocclusion, J. Am. Dent. Assoc. 46:648-657, 1957.
30. Hill, I.N., Blayney, J.R., and Wolf, W.: The Evanston dental caries study. XIX. Prevalence of malocclusion of children in a fluoridated and control area, J. Dent. Res. 38:782-794, 1959.
31. Davis, W.R., McDonald, R.E., and Muhler, J.C.: The occlusion of children as related to water fluoride concentration and socioeconomic status (abstract), J. Dent. Res. 43:783-784, 1964.
32. Russell, A.L., and White, C.L.: Fluorides and periodontal health. In Muhler, J.C., and Hines, M.K., editors: Fluoride and dental health, Bloomington, Ind., 1959, Indiana University Press.
33. Englander, H.R., Kesel, R.G., and Gupta, O.P.: Effect of natural fluoridation on the periodontal health of adults: the Aurora-Rockford Illinois study. II., Am. J. Public Health 35:1233-1242, 1963.
34. Englander, H.R., and White, C.L.: Periodontal and oral hygiene status of teenagers in optimum and fluoride-deficient cities, J. Am. Dent. Assoc. 68:173-177, 1964.
35. Murray, J.J.: Gingivitis in 15-year-old children from high fluoride and low fluoride areas, Arch. Oral Biol. 14:951, 1969.
36. Newbrun, E.: Systemic fluorides: an overview, J. Can. Dent. Assoc. 46:31-37, 1980.
37. U.S. Department of Health, Education, and Welfare, Center for Disease Control: Fluoridation census, 1975, Atlanta, Ga., 1977, U.S. Government Printing Office.
38. Horowitz, H.S., Heifetz, S.B., and Law, F.E.: Effect of school water fluoridation on dental caries: final results in Elk

Lake, Pa., after 12 years, J. Am. Dent. Assoc. **84:**832, 1972.

39. Heifetz, S.B., and Horowitz, H.S.: Effect of school water fluoridation on dental caries: interim results in Seagrove, N.C., after four years, J. Am. Dent. Assoc. **88:**352-355, 1974.

40. Aasenden, R., and Peebles, T.C.: Effects of fluoride supplementation from birth on deciduous and permanent teeth, Arch. Oral Biol. **19:**321-326, 1974.

41. Accepted dental therapeutics, ed. 38, Chicago, 1979, American Dental Association.

42. Stookey, G.K., and Muhler, J.C.: Laboratory studies concerning fluoride metabolism using two different types of fluoride tablets, J. Dent. Child. **33:**90-100, 1966.

43. Muhler, J.C., et al.: Blood and urinary fluoride studies following the ingestion of single doses of fluoride, J. Oral Ther. Pharm. **2:**241-260, 1966.

44. Shannon, I.L., Feller, R.P., and Chauncey, H.H.: Fluoride in human parotid saliva, J. Dent. Res. **55:**506-509, 1976.

45. Hennon, D.K., Stookey, G.K., and Muhler, J.C.: The clinical anticariogenic effectiveness of supplementary fluoride-vitamin preparations—results at the end of four years, J. Dent. Child. **34:**439-443, 1967.

46. Blayney, J.R., and Hill, I.N.: Evanston dental caries study. XXIV. Prenatal fluorides—value of waterborne fluorides during pregnancy, J. Am. Dent. Assoc. **69:**291-294, 1964.

47. Katz, S., and Muhler, J.C.: Pre-natal and post-natal fluoride and dental caries experience in deciduous teeth, J. Am. Dent. Assoc. **76:**305-311, 1968.

48. Stookey, G.K., Hennon, D.K., and Muhler, J.C.: Skeletal retention and anticariogenic efficacy of fluoride when administered in the presence of a prenatal vitamin-mineral supplement, J. Dent. Res. **48:**1224-1230, 1969.

49. Marthaler, J.M.: The value in caries prevention of other methods of increasing fluoride ingestion, apart from fluoridated water, Int. Dent. J. **17:**606, 1967.

50. Toth, K.: Caries prevention in deciduous dentition using table salt fluoridation, J. Dent. Res. **52:**533-534, 1973.

51. Brudevold, F.: Interaction of fluoride with human enamel. In Symposium on chemistry and physiology of enamel, Ann Arbor, Mich., 1971, University of Michigan Press.

52. Tinanoff, N., and Weeks, D.B.: Current status of SnF_2 as an antiplaque agent, Pediatric Dent. **1:**199-204, 1979.

53. Rolla, G., and Melsen, B.: Desorption of protein and bacteria from hydroxyapatite by fluoride and monofluorophosphate, Caries Res. **9:**66-73, 1975.

54. Muhler, J.C.: Topical treatment of the teeth with stannous fluoride—single application technique, J. Dent. Child. **25:**306-309, 1958.

55. Mercer, V.N., and Muhler, J.C.: The effect of a 30 second topical SnF_2 treatment on dental caries reduction in children, J. Oral Ther. **1:**141-146, 1964.

56. Scola, F.P., and Ostrom, C.A.: Clinical evaluation of stannous fluoride when used as a constituent of a compatible prophylaxis paste, as a topical solution, and in a dentifrice in naval personnel. II. Report of findings after two years, J.A.D.A. **77:**594-597, 1968.

57. Horowitz, H.S., and Heifetz, S.B.: Evaluation of topical applications of stannous fluoride to teeth of children born and reared in a fluoridated community: final report, J. Dent. Child. **34:**355-361, 1969.

58. Wei, S.H.Y., and Forbes, W.C.: Electron microprobe investigations of stannous fluoride reactions with enamel surfaces, J. Dent. Res. **53:**51-56, 1974.

59. Muhler, J.C.: Stannous fluoride enamel pigmentation—evidence of a caries arrestment, J. Dent. Child. **27:**157-161, 1960.

60. Myers, H.M.: A hypothesis concerning the caries preventive mechanism of tin, J. Am. Dent. Assoc. **77:**1308, 1968.

61. Skjorland, K., Gjermo, P., and Rolla, G.: Effect of some polyvalent cations on plaque formation in vivo, Scand, J. Dent. Res. **86:**103-107, 1978.

62. Hyde, E.J., and Muhler, J.C.: Pigmentation of teeth treated with stannous fluoride and association with caries incidence and oral hygiene, J. Can. Dent. Assoc. **29:**514-520, 1963.

63. Mercer, V.N., and Muhler, J.C.: The clinical demonstration of caries arrestment following topical stannous fluoride treatment, J. Dent. Child. **32:**65-72, 1965.

64. Muhler, J.C., et al.: The arrestment of incipient dental caries in adults after the use of three different forms of SnF_2 therapy: results after 30 months, J.A.D.A. **75:**1402-1406, 1967.

65. Nordstrom, D.O., Wei, S.H.Y., and Johnson, R.: Use of stannous fluoride for indirect pulp capping, J. Am. Dent. Assoc. **88:**997-1003, 1974.

66. Brudevold, F., et al.: A study of acidulated fluoride solutions. I. In vitro effects on enamel, Arch. Oral Biol. **8:**167-177, 1963.

67. Horowitz, H.S., and Doyle, J.: The effect on dental caries of topically applied acidulated phosphate-fluoride: results after three years, J. Am. Dent. Assoc. **82:**359-365, 1971.

68. Englander, H.R., et al.: Clinical anticaries effect of repeated topical sodium fluoride applications by mouthpiece, J. Am. Dent. Assoc. **75:**638-644, 1967.

69. Englander, H.R., et al.: Residual anticaries effect of repeated sodium fluoride applications by mouthpieces, J. Am. Dent. Assoc. **78:**783-787, 1969.

70. Englander, H.R., et al.: Incremental rates of dental caries after repeated topical sodium fluoride applications in children with lifelong consumption of fluoridated water, J. Am. Dent. Assoc. **82:**354-358, 1971.

71. Loesche, W.J., et al.: Effect of topical acidulated phosphate fluoride on percentage of *Streptococcus mutans* and *Streptococcus sanguis* in plaque, Caries Res. **9:**139-155, 1975.

72. Shannon, I.L., and Edmonds, E.J.: Chemical alterations of enamel surfaces by single and sequential treatment with fluorides, J. Irish Dent. Assoc. **19:**135-139, 1973.

73. Wei, S.H.Y.: Effect of topical fluoride solutions on the enamel surface as studied by scanning electron microscopy, Caries Res. **9:**445-458, 1975.

74. Will the manufacturer of the best fluoride dentifrice please stand (editorial), J. Am. Dent. Assoc. **102:**958, 1981.

75. Forward, G.C.: Action and interaction of fluoride in dentifrices, Community Dent. Oral Epidemiol. **8:**257-266, 1980.

76. Gron, P., Brudevold, F., and Aasenden, R.: Monofluorophosphate interaction with hydroxyapatite and intact enamel, Caries Res. **5:**202-214, 1971.

77. Duff, E.J.: Orthophosphates. XV. A suggested mechanism for the inhibition of dental caries by monofluorophosphates, Caries Res. **7:**79-84, 1973.

78. Zacherl, W.A.: Clinical evaluation of a sodium fluoride-silica abrasive dentifrice, J. Dent. Res. **60:**557, 1981.

79. Stearns, R.I.: Incorporation of fluoride by human enamel. III. In vivo effects of nonfluoride and fluoride prophylactic pastes and APF gels, J. Dent. Res. **52:**30-35, 1973.

80. Bixler, D., and Muhler, J.C.: Effect on dental caries in children in a non-fluoride area of combined use of three agents containing stannous fluoride: a prophylactic paste, a solution, and a dentifrice. II. Results at the end of 24 and 36 months, J.A.D.A. **72:**392-396, 1966.

81. Gish, C.W., and Muhler, J.C.: Effect on dental caries in children in a natural fluoride area of combined use of three agents containing stannous fluoride: a prophylactic paste, a solution, and a dentifrice, J.A.D.A. **70:**914-920, 1965.

82. Horowitz, H.S., and Lucye, H.S.: A clinical study of stannous fluoride in a prophylaxis paste and as a solution, J. Oral Ther. Pharm. **3:**17, 1966.

83. Heifetz, S.B., et al.: Combined anticariogenic effect of fluoride gel trays and fluoride mouthrinsing in an optimally fluoridated community, Clin. Prevent. Dent. **1:**21-23, 1979.

84. Horowitz, H.S., Heifetz, S.B., McClendon, J., Uregas, A.R., Guimaraes, L.O.C., and Lopes, E.S.: Evaluation of self-administered prophylaxis and supervised toothbrushing with acidulated phosphate fluoride, Caries Res. **8:**39-51, 1974.

85. Scola, F.P.: Self-preparation stannous fluoride prophylactic technique in preventive dentistry: report after two years, J. Am. Dent. Assoc. **81:**1369, 1970.

86. Ripa, L.W.: Fluoride rinsing: what dentists should know, J. Am. Dent. Assoc. **102:**477-481, 1981.

87. Radike, A.W., Gish, C.W., Peterson, J.K., King, J.D., and Segreto, V.A.: Clinical evaluation of stannous fluoride as an anticaries mouthrinse, J. Am. Dent. Assoc. **86:**404-408, 1973.

88. Andres, C.J., Shaeffer, J.C., and Windeler, A.S., Jr.: Comparison of antibacterial properties of stannous fluoride and sodium fluoride mouthwashes, J. Dent. Res. **53:**457-460, 1974.

89. Kilian, M., et al.: Effects of fluoride on the initial colonization of teeth in vivo, Caries Res. **13:**319-329, 1979.

90. Svatun, B., and Attramodal, A.: The effect of stannous fluoride on human plaque acidogenicity in situ (Stephan curve), Acta Odontol. Scand. **36:**211-218, 1978.

91. Tinanoff, N., Brady, J.M., and Gross, A.: The effect of NaF and SnF$_2$ mouthrinses on bacterial colonization of tooth enamel: TEM and SEM studies, Caries Res. **10:**415-426, 1976.

92. Arends, J., and Schuthof, J.: Fluoride content in human enamel after fluoride application and washing—an in vitro study, Caries Res. **9:**363-372, 1975.

93. Gibbs, M., et al.: In vivo enamel fluoride uptake from and caries inhibition by topical fluoride agents, J. Dent. Res. **60:**770-775, 1981.

94. Stamm, J.W.: Fluoride uptake from topical sodium fluoride varnish measured by an in vivo enamel biopsy, J. Can. Dent. Assoc. **40:**501-505, 1974.

95. Kock, G., and Petersson, L.G.: Caries preventive effect of a fluoride containing varnish (Duraphat) after 1 year's study, Community Dent. Oral Epidemiol. **3:**262-266, 1975.

96. Stookey, G.K., and Stahlman, D.B.: Enhanced fluoride uptake in enamel with a fluoride-impregnated prophylactic cup, J. Dent. Res. **55:**333-341, 1976.

97. Chaet, R., and Wei, S.H.Y.: Enamel fluoride uptake from fluoride impregnated dental floss, International Association for Dental Research Program and Abstracts, No. 98, 1976.

98. National Institute of Dental Research: NIDR Research News, April, 1980.

99. Custer, F., and Cayle, T.: Mixed, spherical filling alloy amalgams, J. Mich. Dent. Assoc. **52:**93, 1970.

100. Heintze, V., and Marnstad, H.: Artificial caries-like lesions around conventional, fluoride-containing, and dispersed phase amalgams, Caries Res. **14:**414-421, 1980.

101. Swartz, M.L., Phillips, R.W., and Norman, R.D.: The effect of fluoride-containing zinc oxide–eugenol cements on solubility of enamel, J. Dent. Res. **49:**576-580, 1970.

102. Wolf, O., et al.: Effect of addition of CaFPO$_3$ to a zinc oxide-eugenol base liner on the microhardness and fluoride content of dentin, J. Dent. Res. **52:**467-471, 1973.

103. Gursin, H.V.: A study of the effect of stannous fluoride incorporated in dental cement, J. Oral Ther. **1:**630, 1965.

104. Ogard, B., Ghermo, P., and Rolla, G.: Plaque-inhibiting effect in orthodontic patients of a dentifrice containing stannous fluoride, Am. J. Orthod. **78:**266-272, 1980.

105. Bay, I., and Rolla, G.: Plaque inhibition and improved gingival condition by use of a stannous fluoride toothpaste, Scand. J. Dent. Res. **88:**313-315, 1980.

106. Tinanoff, N., et al.: Effect of stannous fluoride mouthrinse on dental plaque formation, J. Clin. Periodontol. **7:**232-241, 1980.

107. Leverett, D.H., McHugh, W.D., and Jensen, O.E.: The effect of daily mouthrinsing with stannous fluoride on dental plaque and gingivitis: four month results, J. Dent. Res. **60:**781-784, 1981.

108. Yoon, N.A.: The effect of fluoride on microorganisms implicated in periodontal disease, Thesis, Los Angeles, 1980, University of California at Los Angeles.

CHAPTER 25

Vitamins

RICHARD L. WYNN

The importance of nutrition in both general and dental health is well known. Dental practitioners must be concerned with the diagnosis and correction of deficiency states and should be aware of the relationships between nutrition and the growth and development of teeth, the prevention of dental caries, and the prevention and treatment of periodontal disease. For a discussion of general nutrition and its relationship to dental practice the reader is referred to the work of Nizel.[1] This chapter will deal with the more pharmacologic aspects of nutrition—the vitamins.

The vitamins are a group of low molecular weight organic compounds that are essential in small quantities for the maintenance of normal cellular metabolism and cell structure. Vitamins are classified into two large groups, *water-soluble* and *fat-soluble* vitamins. The water-soluble vitamins, except for vitamin C, function as components of coenzymes to aid in catalysis in a variety of enzyme reactions and are essential for the activity of a given enzyme. On a functional basis the water-soluble vitamins, except for vitamin C, may be subdivided into three classes: (1) those that primarily release energy from carbohydrates and fats (thiamine, pyridoxine, niacin, riboflavin, pantothenic acid, biotin), (2) those that among many other functions catalyze the formation of red blood cells (folic acid, vitamin B_{12}), and (3) those that have not been shown to be required in human nutrition (choline, inositol). Vitamin C does not function as a component of coenzymes but rather plays a role in biologic oxidation and reduction in cellular respirations.

In contrast to the water-soluble vitamins, the functions of the fat-soluble vitamins remain rather obscure. The fat-soluble vitamins are found in nature in association with lipid substances (such as vegetable oils) and include vitamins, A, D, E, and K. They do not appear to serve as components of coenzymes but function in other ways, requiring only trace amounts.

The water-soluble vitamins, except for vitamin C, are known as the *B complex vitamins* and a close interrelationship among these vitamins exists so that the deficiency of one will impair the utilization of the others. Also, there are many similarities in the signs and symptoms of deficiencies between individual B vitamins. This is probably because a deficiency of a particular member of the B complex is seldom produced. Rather, a diet deficient in one B vitamin is usually lacking in other B vitamins.

The vitamins are discussed individually with respect to their sources, chemical structures, requirements, physiologic and biochemical roles, and signs and symptoms of deficiencies. In addition, clinical considerations of the individual vitamins in dentistry and medicine are discussed.

WATER-SOLUBLE VITAMINS
Pyridoxine (vitamin B_6)

Pyridoxine is one of three different pyridine derivatives known as vitamin B_6, and its structure is shown below. The other two derivatives *pyridoxal* and *pyridoxamine* have similar chemical structures.

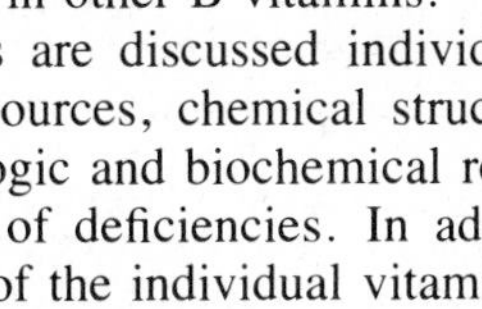

Pyridoxine

Vitamin B_6 is present in most foods of both plant and animal origin. Good sources of this vitamin include cereal grains, milk, meat, and certain vegetables. The recommended allowances for this vitamin are shown in Table 25-1, and approximately 2 mg daily are recommended for adults, with an additional 0.6 and 0.5 mg recommended during pregnancy and lactation, respectively. To exert physiologic activity, all three forms of vitamin B_6 are converted to pyridoxal phosphate in the body. Pyridoxal phosphate is the active coenzyme form of vitamin B_6 and participates in all metabolic reactions that require the vitamin.

The tuberculostatic drug isoniazid (isonicotinic acid hydrazide) inhibits the actions of vitamin B_6, and isoniazid-induced vitamin B_6 deficiency can be prevented by the administration of pyridoxine.[2]

Physiologic and biochemical role. Pyridoxal phosphate acts as a coenzyme for enzymes in a variety of metabolic transformations of amino acids, including transaminations and decarboxylations. An example of transamination involving pyridoxal phosphate is the conversion of alpha-ketoglutaric acid to L-glutamic acid, illustrated below. The pyridoxal phosphate is aminated to pyridoxamine phosphate by the donor amino acid and the pyridoxamine phosphate is subsequently deaminated by the acceptor alpha-ketoglutaric acid.

Decarboxylations requiring pyridoxal phosphate as a coenzyme include the decarboxylations of the amino acids tyrosine, arginine, and glutamine.

Clinical considerations. Vitamin B_6 deficiency is rare because of the widespread distribution of this vitamin in food. However, skin lesions about the eyes, nose, and mouth accompanied by stomatitis and glossitis can be produced by feeding a diet poor in vitamin B complex plus a vitamin B_6 antagonist 4-deoxypyridoxine. These lesions will clear rapidly after the administration of pyridoxine. The characteristics of vitamin B_6 deficiency resemble those of riboflavin, niacin, and thiamine deficiencies. These include angular cheilosis, stomatitis, dermatitis, and erythema of the nasolabial folds. The dorsal mucosa

Table 25-1. Recommended daily vitamin allowances

	Age (yr)	Water-soluble vitamins							Fat-soluble vitamins		
		B_6 (mg)	Thiamin (mg)	Riboflavin (mg)	Niacin (mg NE)*	B_{12} (μg)	Folic acid (μg)	C (mg)	A (μg RE)†	D (μg)‡	E (mg α-TE)§
Infants	0-0.5	0.3	0.3	0.4	6	0.5	30	35	420	10	3
	0.5-1.0	0.6	0.5	0.6	8	1.5	45	35	400	10	4
Children	1-3	0.9	0.7	0.8	9	2.0	100	45	400	10	5
	4-6	1.3	0.9	1.0	11	2.5	200	45	500	10	6
	7-10	1.6	1.2	1.4	16	3.0	300	45	700	10	7
Males	11-14	1.8	1.4	1.6	18	3.0	400	50	1000	10	8
	15-18	2.0	1.4	1.7	18	3.0	400	60	1000	10	10
	19-22	2.2	1.5	1.7	19	3.0	400	60	1000	7.5	10
	23-50	2.2	1.4	1.6	18	3.0	400	60	1000	5	10
	51+	2.2	1.2	1.4	16	3.0	400	60	1000	5	10
Females	11-14	1.8	1.1	1.3	15	3.0	400	50	800	10	8
	15-18	2.0	1.1	1.3	14	3.0	400	60	800	10	8
	19-22	2.0	1.1	1.3	14	3.0	400	60	800	7.5	8
	23-50	2.0	1.0	1.2	13	3.0	400	60	800	5	8
	51+	2.0	1.0	1.2	13	3.0	400	60	800	5	8
Pregnant		+0.6	+0.4	+0.3	+2	+1.0	+400	+20	+200	+5	+2
Lactating		+0.5	+0.5	+0.5	+5	+1.0	+100	+40	+400	+5	+3

Modified from Food and Nutrition Board, National Research Council, Washington, D.C., 1979, National Academy of Science.

*1 NE (niacin equivalent) is equal to 1 mg of niacin or 60 mg of dietary tryptophan.

†1 RE (retinol equivalent) is 1 μg retinol or 6 μg beta-carotene.

‡As cholecalciferol; 10 μg cholecalciferol is 400 IU vitamin D.

§1 α-TE (alpha-tocopherol equivalent) is 1 mg d-α-tocopherol.

Donor amino acid
L-Aspartic acid

$$HOOC-CH_2-CH-COOH$$
$$|$$
$$NH_2$$

Pyridoxal phosphate

L-Glutamic acid

$$HOOC-CH_2-CH_2-CH-COOH$$
$$|$$
$$NH_2$$

$$HOOC-CH_2-C-COOH$$
$$||$$
$$O$$

Pyridoxamine phosphate

$$HOOC-CH_2-CH_2-C-COOH$$
$$||$$
$$O$$

Oxaloacetic acid

Acceptor alpha-ketoglutaric acid

of the tongue seems to be unusually sensitive to single or mixed deficiencies of B vitamins. Specifically, a glossitis has been described resulting from pyridoxine deficiency in which the tongue surface was smooth, slightly edematous, painful, and purplish.[3]

A cariostatic effect of vitamin B_6 has been observed in rhesus monkeys, and it was attributed to the influence of the vitamin on protein metabolism of the microorganisms on the tooth.[4] Also, a higher incidence of caries in vitamin B_6–deficient rats has been observed.[5]

Vitamin B_6 can alter the therapeutic effectiveness of some selected drugs. For example, the administration of vitamin B_6 cancels the therapeutic and side effects of levodopa in the treatment of Parkinson's disease.[6,7] Industry, however, has produced and marketed a pyridoxine-free vitamin preparation (Larobec), which can be used to cover the needs of vitamins in patients receiving levodopa. The administration of vitamin B_6 enhances the therapeutic effectiveness of nicotinic acid in the treatment of schizophrenia.[8]

Estrogenic steroids can produce a state of vitamin B_6 deficiency in women. Specifically, 50% of women taking oral contraceptive agents containing estrogens experienced a deficiency in vitamin B_6.[9] The administration of 20 mg pyridoxine hydrochloride daily appeared necessary to prevent this deficiency. It is suggested that pyridoxine supplements be routinely taken by women who use oral contraceptive agents.

Preparations. Pyridoxine hydrochloride tablets are available in 5 to 500 mg. Pyridoxine hydrochloride injection is a sterile solution of pyridoxine hydrochloride in water containing 50 to 100 mg/ml.

Thiamine (vitamin B_1)

Thiamine, or vitamin B_1, is an essential water-soluble vitamin in humans. It is converted in the liver to its active coenzyme form, thiamine pyrophosphate (TPP). The chemical structure of TPP is as follows:

Thiamine pyrophosphate

Thiamine is present in foods of both animal and vegetable origin such as green vegetables, fish, meat, fruit, and milk. The highest levels are found in pork, whole grain, enriched cereal grains, and seeds of legumes such as peas. The vitamin tends to be destroyed if heated above 100° C. Thus significant amounts of the vitamin may be lost in foods by cooking too long above this temperature. The vitamin can also be leached out of foodstuffs being washed or boiled.

The requirement for thiamin is related to caloric intake. The recommended daily allowance is 0.5 mg/ 1000 cal with an additional 0.4 mg daily during the last two trimesters of pregnancy and 0.5 mg during lactation. It is suggested that the average adult have an intake of approximately 1.1 to 1.4 mg thiamine daily (Table 25-1).

Physiologic and biochemical role. TPP plays a principal role in intermediary metabolism. It is a coenzyme required for the oxidative decarboxylation of alpha-keto acids. For example, TPP is required for the oxidative decarboxylation of pyruvate to eventually form acetylcoenzyme A (acetyl-CoA); and in the oxidative decarboxylation of alpha-ketoglutarate to form succinylcoenzyme A. In this role TPP is sometimes referred to as *cocarboxylase.* TPP is also a coenzyme in the transketolation reactions that occur in the direct oxidative pathway of glucose metabolism (hexose monophosphate pathway). In these transketo-

$$\begin{array}{c} \text{D-Xylulose 5-phosphate} + \text{D-Ribose 5-phosphate} \\ \text{(5 carbon)} \qquad\qquad\qquad \text{(5 carbon)} \end{array} \quad \xrightleftharpoons[\text{(TPP) Mg}^{++}]{\text{Transketolase}}$$

$$\begin{array}{c} \text{D-Sedoheptulose 7-phosphate} + \text{Glyceraldehyde 3-phosphate} \\ \text{(7 carbon)} \qquad\qquad\qquad \text{(3 carbon)} \end{array}$$

lation reactions two-carbon fragments are transferred from one sugar to another. An illustration of a transketolation reaction is shown above.

Clinical considerations. A severe deficiency of thiamine leads to a condition known as beriberi. Characteristics of beriberi are peripheral neuritis, muscular weakness, paralysis of the limbs, enlargement of the heart, tachycardia, and edema. Gastrointestinal tract effects may also be present, including loss of appetite, intestinal atony, and constipation. The symptoms of mild thiamine deficiency are not nearly as characteristic as the preceding symptoms. They include tiredness and apathy, loss of appetite, moodiness and irritability, pain and paresthesias in the extremities, slight edema, decreased blood pressure, and a lowered body temperature. Possible oral manifestations of thiamine deficiency are burning tongue, loss of taste, and hyperesthesia of the oral mucosa. Thiamine deficiency is common in the more economically deprived areas of the world but uncommon in the United States and Europe.

Thiamine and other B vitamins may be effective in inhibiting bacterial growth in human saliva. One study has reported a significant reduction of *Staphylococcus aureus, S. albus,* and nonhemolytic group A *Streptococcus* when cultured from saliva that contained thiamine, riboflavin, and vitamin B_6.[10] Thiamine has also been shown to increase the fluoride retention effectively in rats exposed to daily fluoride supplements.[11]

Preparations. Thiamine hydrochloride tablets are available in sizes ranging from 5 to 500 mg. Thiamine hydrochloride injection is a sterile aqueous solution of the vitamin available in 50, 100, or 200 mg/ml. Thiamine hydrochloride is also available as an elixir containing 2.25 mg/5 ml.

Pantothenic acid

Pantothenic acid is another essential compound in addition to thiamine that is required for the oxidative decarboxylation of pyruvate to form acetyl-CoA. The structure of pantothenic acid is as follows:

Pantothenic acid

The active form of pantothenic acid is as a component of the more complex compound *coenzyme A.*

Pantothenic acid is a component of all living material, and egg yolk, liver, and yeast are excellent sources. Pantothenic acid is required by humans, other vertebrates, some bacteria, and some plants. No quantitative requirement has been established in humans for this substance. The Food and Nutrition Board of the National Research Council (NRC), however, has suggested that a daily intake of 5 to 10 mg pantothenic acid is likely to satisfy human requirements.[12]

Physiologic and biochemical role. Pantothenic acid is a constituent of coenzyme A, which is a required coenzyme in various metabolic reactions, some of which involve the transfer of acetyl (two-carbon) groups. As mentioned earlier, one of these reactions is catalyzed by the pyruvate dehydrogenase complex, which converts pyruvate to acetyl-CoA. Acetyl-CoA in turn serves as a central intermediate in the oxidation of carbohydrates, lipids, and some amino acids. Acetyl-CoA also serves as the biosynthetic building block in steroid biosynthesis (adrenal steroids, testosterone, estrogen) and fatty acid biosynthesis.

Coenzyme A is also involved in the decarboxylation of alpha-ketoglutarate to succinate in the Krebs tricarboxylic acid cycle (TCA cycle). This reaction produces succinyl-CoA as an intermediate. Finally, coenzyme A has an essential function in the metabolism of fatty acids.

Clinical considerations. Clinical deficiencies of pantothenic acid are extremely rare in humans. Deficiencies have been produced experimentally in humans using a pantothenic acid antagonist, however, which were characterized by fatigue, headache, malaise, nausea, abdominal pain, "burning" of hands and feet, and cramping of leg muscles.[13]

Preparations. Calcium pantothenate is available as tablets containing 10 to 250 mg.

Riboflavin (vitamin B₂)

Riboflavin (vitamin B_2) is a water-soluble vitamin composed of flavin and D-ribitol. It has the following structure:

Riboflavin

Riboflavin occurs abundantly in both plants and animals. However, dairy products and meats serve as the best source for this vitamin. Riboflavin is relatively stable to heat, and cooking will not cause appreciable loss of the vitamin from foodstuffs. It is destroyed by ultraviolet irradiation.

The requirements for this vitamin are related to energy expenditure with a minimal daily requirement established at 0.3 mg/1000 kcal. The FDA has set the adult daily minimal requirement of vitamin B_2 at 1.2 mg. The Food and Nutrition Board of the NRC, however, recommends a somewhat higher adult riboflavin allowance (Table 25-1).

Physiologic and biochemical role. Riboflavin carries out its functions in the body as a component of two flavoprotein coenzymes, riboflavin phosphate (flavin mononucleotide, FMN) and flavin adenine dinucleotide (FAD). Flavoprotein coenzymes in turn are proteins that act as electron acceptors and are involved in a variety of oxidation-reduction reactions.

These reactions include those within the electron transport chain of the mitochondria, which produce much of the cellular energy and also certain dehydrogenase reactions. In the mitochondrial electron transport chain, flavoproteins act as electron acceptors from the nicotinamide-containing electron carrier nicotinamide adenine dinucleotide (NADH). In other dehydrogenase reactions, flavoprotein dehydrogenases transfer electrons directly from a substrate to the electron transport chain. An example is succinate dehydrogenase in the TCA cycle.

The riboflavin-containing coenzyme FAD is also involved in the reduction of dihydrolipoic acid, which participates in the pyruvate decarboxylase complex mentioned previously. Thus riboflavin, as a constituent of FMN or FAD, has a fundamental role in metabolism by participating in various oxidation-reduction reactions involving carbohydrates, lipids, and electron transfer reactions.

Clinical considerations. Symptoms of riboflavin deficiency usually involve the lips, tongue, eyes, and skin. Angular stomatitis is an early and frequent finding. The lips may be either redder than usual or whitish because of desquamation. Ulceration may occur with painful fissuring at the corners of the mouth. Glossitis generally occurs, with the dorsum of the tongue becoming pebbly or granular; contact with food or drink may produce pain or a burning sensation on the tongue. In some instances the tongue may become magenta colored or purplish red. Vascularization of the cornea frequently occurs. In advanced cases, capillaries may invade the entire cornea, and there may be ulceration. Skin manifestations comprise a greasy, scaling inflammation about the nose, cheeks, and chin. Involvement of the scrotum and vulva is frequent. Other manifestations of riboflavin deficiency include anemia and neuropathy.

Riboflavin deficiency is most likely to be seen in alcoholics, economically deprived individuals, or patients with severe gastrointestinal disease, which cause loss of appetite, vomiting, and malabsorption syndromes. The manifestations of riboflavin deficiency are difficult to distinguish from other B vitamin deficiencies because of the similarities in syndromes.

Preparations. Riboflavin tablets are usually available in amounts ranging from 5 to 50 mg. Riboflavin injection contains 50 mg/ml.

Niacin (nicotinic acid) and niacinamide (nicotinamide)

Niacin (nicotinic acid) and niacinamide (nicotin-amide) are water-soluble organic compounds that have the ability to alleviate a deficiency syndrome known as pellagra (*pelle,* skin; *agra,* rough). The chemical structures of these compounds are as follows:

Niacin
(nicotinic acid)

Niacinamide
(nicotinamide)

Niacin, in the form of niacinamide, is a component of two coenzymes that participate in biologic oxida-tion-reduction reactions. These coenzymes are nico-tinamide adenine dinucleotide (NAD) and nicotin-amide adenine dinucleotide phosphate (NADP).

Good sources of this vitamin are lean metas, liver, and poultry. The requirement for niacin in the diet is somewhat dependent on caloric intake. It also prob-ably depends on the amount of protein in the diet be-cause tryptophan, an amino acid found in dietary protein, is metabolized to niacin in the body. It is esti-mated that approximately 60 mg tryptophan is con-verted to 1 mg niacin. Pellagra at one time was a com-mon disease in the southeastern United States among individuals subsisting on a diet exclusively of corn products because the protein in corn is extremely low in tryptophan. The minimal requirement of niacin, including that formed from tryptophan to prevent pellagra, is approximately 4.4 mg/1000 kcal. A mini-mal daily intake of between 9 and 13 mg is sug-gested to prevent pellagra. According to the Food and Nutrition Board of the NRC, the minimal daily re-quirement for niacin in the adult male is as great as 19 mg of niacin equivalent (Table 25-1).

Physiologic and biochemical role. The role of nia-cin is similar to that of riboflavin in that it plays a key role in metabolism by participating in a variety of oxidation-reduction reactions (the transfer of elec-trons). As a component of NAD and NADP, niacin is involved in the metabolism of carbohydrates and lip-ids as well as being involved in mitochondrial elec-tron transport. The nicotinamide portion of NAD and NADP participates directly in these oxidation-reduc-tion reactions because it has the ability to accept elec-trons as follows:

Oxidation-reduction of nicotinamide portion of NAD+
or NADP+

The lactate dehydrogenase reaction in which lactic acid is oxidized to pyruvic acid is an important reac-tion of carbohydrate metabolism, requiring NAD as a coenzyme. The lactate dehydrogenase reaction is a part of the anaerobic catabolism of glucose, and the reverse of this reaction (the conversion of lactic acid from pyruvate) is of primary significance in the pro-duction of lactic acid by oral microorganisms is that this will eventually cause demineralization of the tooth.

An important reaction in carbohydrate metabolism involving NADP is the glucose-6-phosphate dehy-drogenase reaction, in which glucose-6-phosphate is converted to 6-phosphogluconate. These reactions are only two of the numerous reactions in which either NAD or NADP serves as a coenzyme.

Clinical considerations. The clinical syndrome produced by niacin deficiency is called pellagra. Early symptoms appear as an erythematous cutaneous eruption on the back of the hands, glossitis, and stomatitis. In advanced stages pellagra can be diag-nosed by the classic "three D's"—dermatitis, diar-rhea, and dementia. The dermatitis consists of red-ness, thickening, and roughening of the skin followed by scaling desquamation and depigmentation. Diar-rhea is caused by atrophy of the gastrointestinal tract mucosal epithelium, followed by inflammation of the mucosal lining of the esophagus, stomach, and colon. The dementia results from regressive changes in the ganglion cells of the brain and tracts of the spinal cord.

Throughout the course of pellagra, symptoms are extremely evident in the oral cavity. A burning sensa-tion occurs throughout the oral mucosa. The lip and lateral margins of the tongue are initially reddened and swollen. In the later stages the entire dorsum be-comes red and swollen. In acute stages vascular hyperemia, proliferation, hypertrophy, atrophy, and extinction occur successively in the papillae.[2] Papil-lary loss may ultimately become complete, with the tongue surface becoming beefy red. Deep penetrating ulcers may appear on the tongue surface. In the gingiva desquamative epithelial degeneration may occur, exposing the tissue to infection, inflammation, and fibrinous exudation. Gingivitis caused by pellagra is characterized by ulcers in the interdental papillae and marginal gingiva. There is also excessive salivary secretion with enlargement of the salivary glands.[2]

Niacin deficiency most likely occurs in the poverty-stricken areas of the world because of inadequate intake. Deficiency may also arise from chronic alcoholism, gastrointestinal disturbances, pregnancy, hyperthyroidism, and infections.

Preparations. Niacin tablets (nicotinic acid) are usually available in 20, 25, 50, 100, and 500 mg amounts. Niacin injection is available in 50 or 100 mg/ml. Niacinamide tablets (nicotinamide) are available in 25, 50, 100, and 500 mg amounts. Niacinamide injection is available in concentrations of 100 or 200 mg/ml.

Biotin

Biotin was initially demonstrated to be an essential growth factor for yeast, and it was later shown that this substance could be isolated from both yeast and egg yolk. Its chemical structure was established in 1942, and shortly thereafter the vitamin was synthesized. Its chemical structure is as follows:

$$
\begin{array}{c}
\text{O} \\
\|\\
\text{C} \\
\diagup \quad \diagdown \\
\text{HN} \quad\quad \text{NH} \\
| \quad\quad\quad | \\
\text{HC}\!-\!\!-\!\!-\!\text{CH} \\
| \quad\quad\quad | \\
\text{H}_2\text{C} \quad\quad \text{CHCH}_2\text{CH}_2\text{CH}_2\text{CH}_2\text{COOH} \\
\diagdown \quad\quad \diagup \\
\text{S}
\end{array}
$$

Biotin

A deficiency of biotin can be induced by the feeding of large quantities of raw egg whites. Avidin, a glycoprotein component of egg white, has the ability to combine with biotin in the gastrointestinal tract to prevent its absorption. The avidin is denatured when the egg white is cooked, and the binding to biotin does not occur. Biotin is synthesized by the microflora of the intestinal tract. In fact, it has been demonstrated that the excretion of biotin in the feces exceeds its intake and is probably caused by the synthesis of the vitamin by the intestinal flora.

A deficiency in biotin is extremely rare but probably can be produced by concurrent administration of large amounts of raw egg white. A minimal daily requirement for this vitamin has yet to be established.

Physiologic and biochemical role. Biotin is a coenzyme required in metabolism in carbon dioxide fixation reactions (carboxylations). An important carboxylation reaction requiring biotin is the acetyl-CoA carboxylase reaction in which acetyl-CoA is carboxylated to form malonyl-CoA. This reaction is the first in a sequence of reactions giving rise to fatty acid biosynthesis.

Clinical considerations. A deficiency of biotin is extremely rare in humans. Experimentally induced biotin deficiency has produced a variety of symptoms. These include loss of appetite, mental depression, hyperesthesia of the skin, nausea, and malaise.

Preparations. There is no official preparation of biotin marketed in the United States.

Vitamin B$_{12}$ (cyanocobalamin)

Vitamin B$_{12}$, or cyanocobalamin, is a chemically complex substance that contains an extensively substituted pyrole ring system surrounding an atom of cobalt. The structure of this water-soluble vitamin is so complex as to be beyond the scope of this discussion. The structural formula of vitamin B$_{12}$ was elucidated by Hodgkin, a work of such importance as to warrant her receiving the Nobel prize in chemistry.[14] Vitamin B$_{12}$ contains a cyanide molecule attached to the cobalt, hence the name *cyano*cobalamin. There exists a chemical family of cobalamins, depending on what group replaces cyanide. The hydroxyl derivative is *hydroxocobalamin* (vitamin B$_{12a}$), the H$_2$O derivative is *aquocobalamin* (vitamin B$_{12b}$), the nitro derivative is *nitritocobalamin* (vitamin B$_{12c}$), the 5'-deoxyadenosyl derivative is *coenzyme B$_{12}$*, and the methyl derivative is methyl B$_{12}$. Vitamin B$_{12}$ is stable to heat at neutral pH but is readily destroyed by heat at an alkaline pH.

Foods of animal origin are good sources of the vitamin, with liver and kidney serving as the best sources and milk, cheese, and eggs serving as adequate sources.

Vitamin B$_{12}$ is not adequately absorbed from the gastrointestinal tract without the presence of a protein-binding factor (intrinsic factor) secreted by the gastric mucosa. The intrinsic factor is a glycoprotein formed and secreted by the parietal cells of the stomach, and it aids the mucosal absorption of B_{12} through a binding mechanism with the vitamin. Pernicious anemia is a conditional vitamin B_{12} deficiency disease caused by a lack of intrinsic factor in the gastric mucosa. Pernicious anemia can be treated by intramuscular injection of vitamin B_{12}, since adequate amounts of the vitamin are absorbed into the plasma by this route without the requirement of intrinsic factor.

A daily intake of 0.6 to 1.2 μg will sustain modest body stores of vitamin B_{12} in normal adults. The World Health Organization recommends a daily dietary intake for adults of 2 μg, after allowing for 60% to 80% absorption from food.[15] The Food and Nutrition Board of the NRC recommends a daily adult allowance of 3 μg vitamin B_{12} with an additional 1 μg during pregnancy and lactation (Table 25-1).

Physiologic and biochemical role. Vitamin B_{12} serves as a coenzyme for the hydrogen transfer and isomerization process required in the conversion of methylmalonyl-CoA to succinyl-CoA. Thus vitamin B_{12} is an important requirement for fat and carbohydrate metabolism, a reaction that occurs as follows:

$$CH_3 - CH - C \sim S - CoA \xrightarrow{\begin{array}{c} \text{Methylmalonyl-CoA} \\ \text{mutase} \end{array}}$$
$$|$$
$$COOH$$

Methylmalonyl-CoA　　　　**Coenzyme B_{12}**

$$HOOC - CH_2CH_2C \sim S - CoA$$

Succinyl-CoA

Vitamin B_{12} functions in this reaction in the form of the 5′-deoxyadenosyl derivative known as *coenzyme B_{12}*, or the *cobamide* coenzyme. Other reactions thought to require vitamin B_{12} as a coenzyme include the metabolism of the one-carbon group required in the synthesis of the bases for nucleic acids (for example, the methylation of uridine to form thymidine); transmethylation reactions, as in the biosynthesis of methionine; the synthesis of proteins in the microsomal system; and the synthesis of deoxyribonucleotides from ribonucleotides. The foregoing reactions have been suggested to require vitamin B_{12} to account for the clinical signs of deficiency. The involvement

of the vitamin in these reactions has yet to be definitely established, however.

Clinical considerations. The symptoms of vitamin B_{12} deficiency include inadequate hematopoiesis, gastrointestinal tract disturbances, inadequate myelin synthesis, and generalized debility. The lack of this vitamin affects those cells that are most actively dividing, such as those in the marrow and gastrointestinal tract. The erythroblasts do not undergo proper division and thus become megaloblasts. This results in a failure to maintain a normal level of red blood cells, resulting in anemia. Atropic changes occur in the alimentary canal. There is also myelin degeneration of the spinal cord. The patient suffers from weakness, numbness, and difficulty in walking, symptoms that fluctuate with remission and relapses. A distinctive lemon-yellow hue of the skin may occur.

The most common cause of vitamin B_{12} deficiency is pernicious anemia. This condition is thought to result from a defect in the stomach characterized by atrophic gastritis. As a result of the gastritis, intrinsic factor is not produced by the mucosal cells and thus vitamin B_{12} is not absorbed. Other causes of B_{12} deficiency include inadequate dietary intake and malabsorption syndromes caused by structural or functional damage to the stomach, where intrinsic factor is secreted, or to the ileum, where intrinsic factor functions to enhance vitamin B_{12} absorption.

Pernicious anemia results in a number of oral manifestations. Recurrent attacks of soreness and burning of the tongue occur before glossitis, at the peak of which the tongue is extremely painful and red. Atrophy of the filiform and fungiform papillae is a common occurrence. Involvement of the circumvallate papillae may cause diminution of taste. Painful, bright red lesions may occur in the buccal and pharyngeal mucosa and undersurface of the tongue.

Preparations. Cyanocobalamin injection (Rubramin) is an isotonic saline solution available in 1, 5, 10, and 30 ml vials for intramuscular injection containing 30, 50, 60, 100, or 1000 μg/ml.

Folic acid (pteroylglutamic acid)

Folic acid is a complex molecule consisting of glutamic acid, para-aminobenzoic acid (PABA), and pteridine and has the following chemical structure. Folic acid is sparingly soluble in water and is destroyed on heating in neutral or alkaline solutions.

Folic acid

Sources of folic acid include glandular meats such as liver, leafy vegetables (folic acid from Latin *folium,* leafy), and yeasts. The intestinal flora probably supplies some of the requirements for this vitamin. Protracted cooking or canning may destroy 50% to 95% of the folic acid content in foods.

The minimal daily human requirement of folic acid is approximately 5 μg in adults.[16] The World Health Organization recommends a dietary intake of 200 μg for adults, 50 μg for infants, 100 μg for children, and 400 μg during pregnancy and lactation. The Food and Nutrition Board of the NRC recommends a daily intake of 400 μg in adults (Table 25-1).

PABA, a component of the folic acid molecule, is essential in itself for certain microorganisms because of its incorporation into folic acid. The bacteriostatic agents, the sulfonamides, exert their mechanism of action by acting as antagonists to PABA and thus interfere with the folic acid biosynthesis in these microorganisms.

Physiologic and biochemical role. The biologically active form of folic acid is the reduced derivative tetrahydrofolic acid (THFA), formed enzymatically in the body. THFA functions primarily in the transfer and utilization of one-carbon groups, such as formyl (—CHO), formate (—COOH), hydroxymethyl (—CH$_2$OH), and methyl (CH$_3$). The transfer and utilization of one-carbon groups are important in relation to the metabolism of amino acids and nucleic acids and also in the formation of purine and pyrimidine bases. With the lack of folic acid, cells fail to complete mitosis and do not progress from metaphase to anaphase because of the absence of the biosynthesis of nucleoprotein.

Clinical considerations. Folic acid deficiency results in megaloblastic anemia, which is indistinguishable from that caused by vitamin B$_{12}$ deficiency. Other symptoms include weakness, weight loss, loss of skin pigmentation, and mental irritability. Oral manifestations include glossitis, angular chilosis, and gingivitis. The glossitis begins with swelling and pallor of the tongue, followed by desquamation of the papillae and accompanied by minute ulcers with fiery red borders. The angular chilosis and gingivitis resemble that seen with a deficiency of riboflavin.

Some of the causes of folic acid deficiency include inadequate diet, pregnancy, malabsorption syndromes, and chronic alcoholism. Folic acid deficiencies have been reported in association with anticonvulsant drug therapy.[17]

The administration of folic acid will cause a remission of the hematologic effects of pernicious anemia. Folic acid will not prevent the neurologic effects of vitamin B$_{12}$ deficiency.

Preparations. Folic acid tablets are available in strengths of 0.1, 0.25, 0.4, 0.8, and 1.0 mg. Folic acid injection is an aqueous solution of the sodium salt of folic acid available in 1, 2, and 10 ml ampules containing 5 mg/ml.

Choline and inositol

The presence of choline and inositol in foods such as meat, eggs, fish, and cereals led to their consideration as members of the B complex vitamins. However, neither choline nor inositol has been demonstrated to be required in the human diet. The chemical structures of choline and inositol (*myo*-inositol) are as follows:

Choline   *myo*-Inositol

Inositol is an isomer of glucose. Of several optically active forms of inositol, possibly only one, *myo*-inositol, is nutritionally active. It is estimated that the normal daily intake of choline is 250 to 600 mg and of inositol, about 1 gm.

Physiologic and biochemical role. Choline and inositol serve as lipotropic agents. These are agents that are necessary in the diet to prevent or correct fatty infiltration of the liver. In addition, choline serves as the precursor in the formation of acetylcholine, an important chemical mediator in the parasympathetic nervous system. Choline can also serve as a methyl donor in intermediary metabolism.

Clinical considerations. No deficiency symptoms for choline or inositol have been described for humans. A deficiency of choline in the rat results in both hemorrhagic kidney and fatty livers. Inositol deficiency in mice is characterized by spectacled eyes, alopecia, failure of lactation, and lack of growth. Inositol has been shown to be an essential component for the growth and survival of human cell lines in tissue culture.[18]

Ascorbic acid (vitamin C)

Ascorbic acid (vitamin C) chemically is a sugar acid that readily undergoes oxidation to form dehydroascorbic acid. The structures of ascorbic acid and its oxidation are as follows:

Ascorbic acid   Dehydroascorbic acid
(reduced form)   (oxidized form)

Because of its property of undergoing oxidation, ascorbic acid is an effective reducing agent.

Good sources of ascorbic acid are fresh fruits and vegetables, including citrus fruits, green vegetables, tomatoes, and berries. Because of its ability to be oxidized, ascorbic acid is readily destroyed by oxidation through cooking, and as much as 50% of the ascorbic acid content of foods can be lost in this manner. The recommended daily dietary allowance of the National Academy of Science–National Research Council (NAS-NRC) for ascorbic acid for the normal adult is 60 mg (Table 25-1).

Physiologic and biochemical role. The metabolic role of ascorbic acid is probably related to the fact that ascorbic acid and dehydroascorbic acid form a readily reversible oxidation-reduction system, and it is thought that this vitamin plays a role in biologic oxidation and reductions in cellular respirations. Ascorbic acid is oxidized by cytochrome C in the presence of cytochrome C oxidase. Dehydroascrobic acid can be reduced by glutathione. Also, ascorbic acid may function in maintaining SH-activated enzyme systems in their reduced form.

A specific requirement for ascorbic acid occurs in tyrosine metabolism. This vitamin acts as a reducing agent in the parahydroxyphenylpyruvic acid oxidase reaction, which converts parahydroxyphenylpyruvic acid (formed by tyrosine) to homogentisic acid. The role of ascorbic acid in the foregoing reaction is nonspecific, however, since other reducing agents can replace the vitamin in the oxidation of parahydroxyphenylpyruvic acid.

Ascorbic acid appears to be necessary for the reduction of folic acid to THFA in mammalian cells. THFA eventually functions in the transfer and utilization of one-carbon groups. Ascorbic acid also functions to catalyze the hydroxylation of proline to form the amino acid hydroxyproline. The subsequent distribution of the generated hydroxyproline occurs in collagen. Thus ascorbic acid plays a definite role in connective tissue metabolism in that it is required for the formation of collagen through the proline hydroxylation process.

The dramatic demonstration of the physiologic function of ascorbic acid is in the wound healing process. Scorbutic wounds (a deficiency of vitamin C) are characterized by a significant decrease in mature collagen fibrils associated with an accumulation of mucopolysaccharides or ground substance around a matrix of precollagenous fibers. Because of the absence of mature collagen, the tensile strength of the healing wound occurs, resulting in a normal healing process. The role of ascorbic acid in wound healing and collagen formation has been adequately reviewed.[19,20]

Clinical considerations. The manifestations of vitamin C deficiency occur because of the inability of the connective tissue to produce and maintain intercellular substances such as collagen, bone matrix, dentin, cartilage, and vascular endothelium. As a result of defective connective tissue formation, individuals with a vitamin C deficiency demonstrate alterations in bone formation tissue and in wound healing. The manifestations of defective connective tissue formation in vitamin C deficiency are listed in the outline below.

Alterations in wound healing, manifested as
  Lack of collagen
  Poor healing process
  Inadequate walling off of infections
Alterations in the integrity of capillary walls, manifested as hemorrhages in
  Skin
  Mucous membranes
  Muscles
  Lungs
  Joints
  Gingivae (spongy, edematous, inflamed)
Lack of formation of bone matrix, resulting in
  Disorganization of epiphyseal line
  Weakening of bones
  Pathologic fractures
  Resorption of alveolar bone with loosening and loss of teeth

Humans and other primates cannot synthesize vitamin C and must obtain it daily from their diet. Diets completely deficient in vitamin C are unusual, and there are few cases of serious vitamin C deficiency (scurvy). After a prolonged period of time without vitamin C (4 to 5 months), the following symptoms will occur in humans: weakness, anorexia, suppressed growth, anemia, lowered resistance to infection and fever, swollen and inflamed gums, loosened teeth, swollen wrist and ankle joints, petechial hemorrhages, fracture of ribs at costochondral junctions, and hemorrhaging caused by capillary fragility in joints, muscle, and intestine.

It was suggested, as long ago as 1942, that vitamin C could be therapeutically beneficial in preventing the common cold. Recently, Linus Pauling[21-25] produced a number of reviews of previous data by other investigators. He argued that these studies showed results that, if properly analyzed, indicated a substantial beneficial effect of vitamin C in preventing and treating the common cold. These studies suggested that daily ascorbic acid doses ranging from a few hundred milligrams up to several grams provided beneficial results in diminishing the incidence and severity of colds. Most recently, the clinical data relating to the efficacy of pharmacologic doses of ascorbic acid in relation to colds have been critically reviewed.[26] This review concluded that there is little evidence to suggest the effectiveness of ascorbic acid in preventing or treating the common cold and that the unrestricted use of ascorbic acid for these purposes should not be advocated on the basis of available evidence. Until the Pauling theory is subsequently verified or refuted by well-controlled experiments, it must be considered a hypothesis, at the very most.

Another hypothesis has been set forth by Cameron and Pauling[27] that large quantities of vitamin C may suppress neoplastic cellular proliferation, and they suggest that the use of ascorbic acid be investigated in cancer management including prophylaxis, supportive therapy, and palliative treatment in advanced terminal cancer.

Others have suggested that a prolonged marginal deficiency of vitamin C plays a contributory role in the initiation of periodontal disease.[28] This hypothesis probably stems from the fact that one of the manifestations of vitamin C deficiency is scorbutic gums (swollen, inflamed gingiva with loosening of the teeth). This hypothesis has not been substantiated by the findings of other investigators, however.[29,30] A deficiency of vitamin C may alter the local response to irritants and may lead to an increased severity of gingival disease.[31]

Ascorbic acid has been shown to interfere with the anticoagulation produced by heparin and dicumarol in animals.[32] Also, it has been reported that the vitamin caused a reduction in the desired prolongation of prothrombin time in a patient receiving warfarin.[33] Recently, it has been shown that vitamin C may inhibit the metabolism of drugs that undergo sulfate conjugation.[34]

Untoward effects have been reported with the use of vitamin C. A daily intake of 1 gm of the vitamin may produce diarrhea. Also, acidification of the urine by the vitamin may cause precipitation of oxalate stones in the urinary tract.

Preparations. Ascorbic acid tablets contain 25, 50, 100, 250, 500, or 1000 mg of the vitamin, and solutions for oral use are also available. Ascorbic acid injection is available containing 50, 100, 250, or 500 mg/ml. Orange or lemon juice contains approximately 0.5 mg/ml of the vitamin.

FAT-SOLUBLE VITAMINS
Vitamin A

Vitamin A is an essential fat-soluble compound necessary for normal growth as well as maintaining the health and integrity of certain epithelial tissues. Vitamin A occurs in a variety of chemical forms in nature, and the term *vitamin A* is used to represent these various forms. Vitamin A_1 (retinol) is found ex-

$$CH_3 \quad CH_3$$

Vitamin A₁ structure:

H₂C, C—CH=CH—C=CH—CH=CH—C=CHCH₂OH with CH₃ groups

Vitamin A₁ (retinol)

clusively in animal tissues and saltwater fishes. The structure of this compound is as shown below. Vitamin A₂ (3-dehydroretinol) contains an additional double bond in the ring structure and is found in the tissues of freshwater fishes. A group of substances known as carotenes are present in plants, and vitamin A may be derived from carotenes by the cleavage of these molecules. Beta carotene is oxidatively cleaved in humans to form two molecules of a form of vitamin A known as vitamin A₁ aldehyde (retinal). The carotenes are found in various pigmented fruits and in vegetables including carrots, pumpkins, sweet potatoes, apricots, and peaches.

The adult recommended daily dietary allowance for vitamin A is 800 to 1000 μg RE. One RE is equal to 1 μg retinol or 6 μg beta carotene. During pregnancy and lactation, an increased intake of from 200 to 400 μg RE of the vitamin is required (Table 25-1).

Vitamin A is essential for the maintenance of normal vision. Specifically, vitamin A is essential for the normal visual purple in the rod cells of the retina. Deficiency of the vitamin leads to impaired vision in dim light, called night blindness (nyctalopia). For a review of the actions of vitamin A on visual excitation, see Wald.[35] Vitamin A is also essential for the maintenance of certain epithelial surfaces, such as the mucous membranes of the eyes and the mucosa of the respiratory, gastrointestinal, and genitourinary tracts. A deficiency of vitamin A results in keratinization of mucosa, and keratinization of the corneal mucosa leads to impairment of vision, a condition called xerophthalmia. Irritation and inflammation may occur on the corneal mucosa, leading to softening, deformation, and destruction of the cornea, a condition called keratomalacia. Keratinization may also occur in the oral cavity and mucosa. In the respiratory tract, ciliated columnar epithelium may be replaced by stratified squamous epithelium. The normal

defense mechanism of cilia movement and mucus production is impaired, producing irritation and inflammation of these surfaces.

It has been suggested that vitamin A may play a significant role in the maintenance of the integrity and possibly the normal permeability of the cell membrane and the membranes of subcellular particles such as lysosomes and mitochondria.[36] Vitamin A deficiency decreases the activity of the osteoblasts and odontoblasts, thereby reducing the growth of bones and teeth. Excessive doses of the vitamin accelerate bone growth.

Since the human liver may store enough vitamin A to meet physiologic demands for as long as a year, a deficiency of the vitamin is usually rare. Deficiencies generally result from inadequate intake of the vitamin, malabsorption syndromes (especially disorders affecting fat absorption such as biliary tract disease), and severe liver disease.

Hypervitaminosis A is a toxic condition caused by excessive intake of the vitamin. Characteristics of the toxicity are itching skin, desquamation, coarse hair, painful subcutaneous swellings, gingivitis, hyperirritability, and limitation of motion. In infants, headache from increased intracranial pressure, gastrointestinal distress, jaundice, and hepatomegaly may occur. The margin of safety of vitamin A intake is large. Toxicity to the vitamin occurs in the adult only after the chronic daily ingestion of 50,000 μg RE.

Preparations. Vitamin A is either fish-liver oil or a solution of natural or synthetic vitamin A. Vitamin A capsules contain 1.5 to 15 mg retinal (5000 to 50,000 units) per capsule. Aquasol A (water-miscible vitamin A) is a concentrate of vitamin A dispersed in water and encapsulated.

Tretinoin (all *trans*-Retinoic acid; Retin-A), is available for topical use as a solution (0.05%), a cream (0.05% and 0.1%), and a gel (0.025% and

0.01%); it is also available in 0.05% saturated swabs. It is used for the treatment of acne and other skin diseases.

Vitamin D

The term *vitamin D* is used to refer to a group of closely related steroids produced by the action of ultraviolet light on certain provitamins. Vitamin D_3 (cholecalciferol) is produced in the skin of mammals from 7-dehydrocholesterol by the action of sunlight (irradiation). Vitamin D_2 (calciferol) is produced by the commercial irradiation of ergosterol. These reactions are as shown below. 7-Dehydrocholesterol occurs naturally in animal tissues and is synthesized from cholesterol in the skin and other peripheral tissues. Ergosterol occurs naturally in yeast and fungi. Vitamin D is generally used as the collective term for vitamins D_2 and D_3.

Vitamin D is required for normal mineralization of bone, and it is essential for the homeostatic regulation of plasma calcium concentration. Sources of vitamin D include food products of animal origin (eggs, cheese, milk, butter). The fish-liver oils are especially rich in vitamin D as well as vitamin A (cod-liver oil). Milk in the United States is fortified with vitamin D (as irradiated ergosterol), since the vitamin is intimately involved in calcium metabolism.

The recommended daily dietary allowance for this vitamin is 10 μg cholecalciferol (400 IU vitamin D) for a growing child. Recently an allowance for adults of between 5 and 7.5 μg cholecalciferol has been recommended. For pregnant or lactating women, an additional 5 μg of cholecalciferol has been recommended. Some of the daily requirement for vitamin D is obviously satisfied by exposure of the individual to sunlight.

Vitamin D promotes normal mineralization of bone by providing an adequate supply of calcium to bone by means of its action to stimulate the intestinal absorption of this ion. Vitamin D_3 itself does not cause the active transport of calcium from the intestine. Experiments have shown that it is an active metabolite of vitamin D_3 found in the kidney that is responsible for the calcium transport across the intestine and for its other effects.[37] Once formed in the skin or taken in the diet, vitamin D_3 is carried to the liver where it is hydroxylated in the number 25 position to form 25-hydroxyvitamin D_3 (25-OH-D_3). This hydroxylation occurs in the liver microsomal fraction. The 25-OH-D_3 is then transported to the kidney and converted to the physiologically active 1,25-dihydroxy-vitamin D_3 (1,25-$(OH)_2$-D_3 or 1,25-dihydroxy D_3). The active metabolite 1,25-dihydroxy D_3 may stimulate calcium transport through the intestine by

7-Dehydrocholesterol   Vitamin D_3

Ergosterol   Vitamin D_2 (calciferol)

inducing the formation of a calcium-binding protein in intestinal epithelial cells.[38]

The participation of vitamin D in the regulation of plasma calcium is by its action to promote mobilization of calcium from bone. The regulation of plasma calcium by this mechanism maintains those concentrations required for normal muscular and nervous function. Vitamin D, through its metabolite 1,25-dihydroxy D_3 also plays an integral part in the process of bone formation. It seems to be necessary for the initial calcification of bone matrix and probably exerts a prime action on the osteoblasts.

The actions of 1,25-dihydroxy D_3 are interrelated to parathyroid hormone (PTH). There is an increased formation of the D_3 hormone because of decreased plasma calcium—an effect mediated by way of PTH on the 1,25-dihydroxy D_3–forming mechanism in the kidney. The 1,25-dihydroxy D_3 together with PTH functions to mobilize calcium from previously formed bone. In addition, the 1,25-dihydroxy D_3 proceeds to the intestine where it functions directly to stimulate intestinal calcium absorption. These two phenomena result in the elevation of serum calcium to normal levels, which suppresses PTH secretion and hence 1,25-dihydroxy D_3 synthesis. Thus it has been suggested that 1,25-dihydroxy D_3 be regarded as a hormone derived from vitamin D_3 with the kidney as the endocrine organ and the intestine, bone, and possibly the kidney as target tissues. Increased formation of 1,25-dihydroxy D_3 is also mediated by decreased plasma phosphate (hypophosphatemia). The hormone also acts to stimulate the elevation of serum inorganic phosphate by enhancing the transport of the ion through the intestine. For a review of the mode of action of vitamin D, see DeLuca[39] or Haussler.[40]

In children, vitamin D deficiency results in *rickets,* whereas in the adult the disease state is *osteomalacia.* Rickets is characterized by a failure of mineralization of the osteoid matrix resulting in an excess of poorly mineralized osteoid tissue. The histologic characteristics of rickets include the failure of calcification of cartilage; overgrowth of cartilage; projection of masses of cartilage into the marrow cavity; disruption of osteochondral junctions; and weak, soft osteoid and cartilaginous tissues, which are easily bent, compressed, or fractured. The gross deformities of rickets include a squared appearance of the head caused by excess osteoid, collapse of the ribs and protrusion of the sternum (pigeon breast syndrome), curvature of the spine, and bowing of the legs. Bone pain and muscle weakness may also be present.

In osteomalacia the basic changes are similar to those of rickets. There is inadequate mineralization resulting in an excess of osteoid matrix. Because of the weakness of the bones, there are deformities of weight-bearing bones as well as pathologic fractures. Adults with this condition also suffer from bone pain and muscle weakness. Causes of vitamin D deficiency are dietary insufficiency and malabsorption syndromes.

Like vitamin A, vitamin D may be ingested excessively, resulting in hypervitaminosis D. Signs and symptoms of vitamin D toxicity are associated with hypercalcemia. Initial symptoms include weakness, fatigue, headache, nausea, vomiting, and diarrhea. Prolonged hypercalcemia may result in the calcification of blood vessels, heart, lungs, and kidney. Daily quantities of vitamin D in the order of magnitude of 2000 IU/kg body weight can be toxic to adults and children.

Preparations. Vitamin D preparations are available as fish-liver oils with or without vitamin A, multivitamin preparations containing vitamin D, preparations containing vitamin D and calcium salts, and preparations of vitamin D alone.

Vitamin E

Compounds possessing vitamin E activity are known chemically as tocopherols. There are three such tocopherols designated as alpha, beta, and gamma tocopherol. The structure of alpha tocopherol is as follows:

Vitamin E (α-tocopherol)

Vitamin E was originally isolated from wheatgerm oil, and alpha tocopherol is considered the most important vitamin E compound, since it elicits the greatest biologic activity in most bioassay systems. The metabolic role of vitamin E is not understood, although it appears that the vitamin functions as an antioxidant in mammalian tissues.

The best sources of vitamin E include vegetable

oils such as soybean, corn, and cottonseed oils; other sources include fresh greens and vegetables. It has been estimated that a daily intake of 10 to 30 mg of vitamin E will keep the vitamin E serum levels within normal range. The Food and Nutrition Board of the NRC recommends between 8 and 10 alpha tocopherol equivalents for adults per day.

As an antioxidant, vitamin E probably prevents (1) the oxidation of essential cell constituents and (2) the formation of toxic oxidation products. Its physiologic role is best defined, however, from symptoms that have been observed in deficiency states. It has been reported that resistance of erythrocytes to hemolysis in the presence of hydrogen peroxide was related to vitamin E intake so that a shortened red blood cell survival time was alleviated by administration of the vitamin.[41] It has been suggested that degenerative changes of skeletal muscle cells occur in humans during vitamin E deficiency.[42] Also, a deficiency of the vitamin has been shown to result in muscular dystrophy in monkeys.[43] There has been no clinical evidence to show any beneficial effect of the vitamin in the treatment of this disease, however. Vitamin E deficiency in male rats results in reproductive failure and sterility (degeneration of the germinal epithelium within testicular tissue). In the female rat a deficiency leads to fetal death and resorption. In humans vitamin E has been used for the treatment of sterility and habitual abortion, but there is no conclusive evidence that the vitamin provides any beneficial effect in these conditions.

Vitamin E is generally thought to have a low toxicity. Levels of vitamin E greatly in excess of the normal dietary requirements have been administered to human subjects with no apparent adverse effects.

Preparations. Vitamin E is a form of alpha tocopherol that includes the isomers of alpha tocopherol, alpha tocopheryl acetate, or alpha tocopheryl succinate. Vitamin E capsules (Aquasol E) contain 30 to 1000 IU of the vitamin.

Vitamin K

Vitamin K activity is elicited by at least two forms of the compound—vitamin K_1 (phylloquinone) and vitamin K_2 (the menaquinone series). The structures of these compounds are shown below.

Vitamin K_1 occurs in green vegetables such as alfalfa, cabbage, and spinach as well as egg yolk, soybean oil, and liver. The menaquinones (vitamin K_2) are synthesized by gram-positive bacteria, and microorganisms in the intestinal flora can provide some amounts of vitamin K to humans. Because of this source of supply, it is difficult to establish the requirement of this vitamin. Newborns do not have an established intestinal flora and are usually given a single dose of 1 mg vitamin K_1 at birth to prevent hemorrhagic disease.

Vitamin K is essential for the synthesis in the liver of prothrombin and for the blood-clotting factors VII, IX, and X. Prothrombin is the precursor of the active clotting agent thrombin, and the normal blood-clotting process does not occur without the presence of prothrombin and these clotting factors. Vitamin K deficiency is referred to as *hypoprothrombinemia,* and bleeding diathesis will result in the absence of the vitamin. Severe deficiency of vitamin K may result in

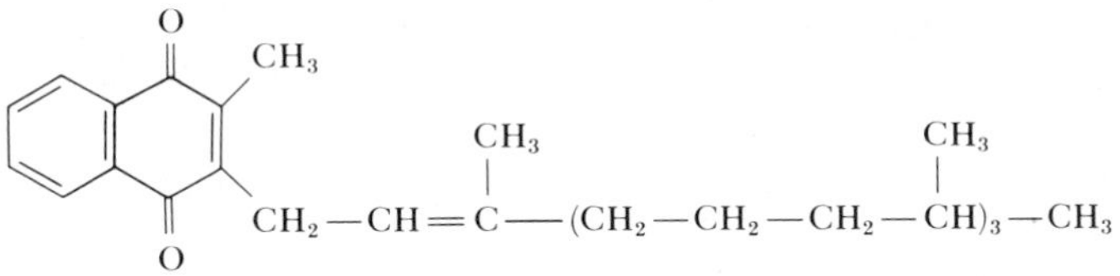

Vitamin K_1 (phylloquinone)

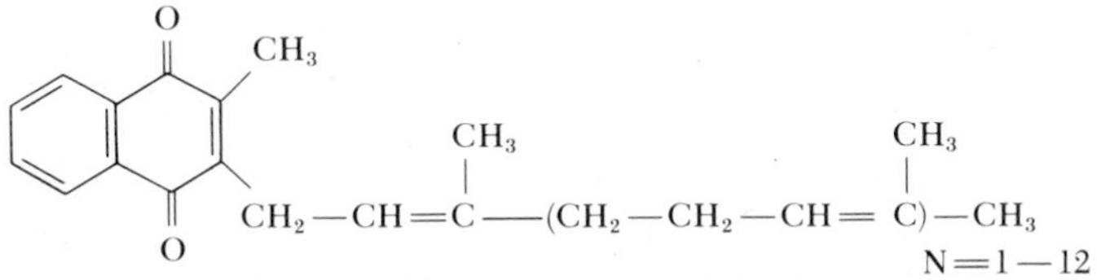

Vitamin K_2 (menaquinone series)

hemorrhage from the smallest trauma. Common sites of hemorrhage are operative wounds, skin (petechial bleeding), mucous membrane in the intestinal tract, and serosal surfaces.

The usual causes of vitamin K deficiency are malabsorption syndromes and inadequate intake. Other causes include hepatobiliary diseases in which there is an obstruction to the bile flow, causing inadequate absorption of the fat-soluble vitamin, alterations in the normal bacterial flora that synthesize the vitamin such as after prolonged antibiotic use, and inadequate reserves in the newborn because of marginal levels in the mother.

A number of synthetic quinone derivatives possess vitamin K activity, with menadione (vitamin K_3) being the most active of these compounds.

The natural vitamins K_1 and K_2 are nontoxic in massive doses, and menadione is relatively nontoxic. Menadione has been implicated in producing hemolytic anemia in the newborn and hemolysis in those individuals suffering from an erythrocytic deficiency of glucose-6-phosphate dehydrogenase.[44]

Preparations. Phytonadone (Mephyton, vitamin K_1) is available as 5 mg tablets and in ampules containing an emulsion of 2 or 10 mg/ml. Menadione (vitamin K_3) is available in tablets containing 2 or 10 mg and as an injectable preparation containing 2, 10, or 25 mg/ml. Menadione sodium bisulfite (Hykinone) is marketed in 5 mg tablets and in ampules containing 5 to 10 mg/ml.

REFERENCES

1. Nizel, A.E.: The science of nutrition and its application in clinical dentistry, ed. 2, Philadelphia, 1966, W.B. Saunders Co.
2. Umbreit, W.W.: Vitamin B_6 antagonists, Am. J. Clin. Nutr. **3**:291-297, 1955.
3. Dreizen, S.: Oral indications of the deficiency states, Postgrad. Med. **49**:97-102, 1971.
4. Rinehart, J.F., and Greenberg, L.D.: Vitamin B_6 deficiency in the rhesus monkey with particular reference to the occurrence of atherosclerosis, dental caries and hepatic cirrhosis, Am. J. Clin. Nutr. **4**:318, 1956.
5. Matsuda, T., and Toda, T.: Effects of vitamin B_6 on dental caries in rats, J. Dent. Res. **48**:1460-1464, 1967.
6. Duvoisin, R.C., Yahr, M.D., and Cote, L.D.: Pyridoxine reversal of L-dopa effects in parkinsonism, Trans. Am. Neurol. Assoc. **94**:81-84, 1969.
7. Cotzias, G.C.: Metabolic modification of some neurologic disorders, J.A.M.A. **210**:1255-1262, 1969.
8. Ananth, J.V., Ban, T.A., and Lehmann, H.E.: Potentiation of therapeutic effects of nicotinic acid by pyridoxine in chronic schizophrenics, Can. Psychiatr. Assoc. J. **18**:377-383, 1973.
9. Salkeld, R.M., Knorr, K., and Korner, W.F.: The effect of oral contraceptives on vitamin B_6 status, Clin. Chim. Acta **49**:195-199, 1973.
10. Balogh, K., Petrucz, K., and Angyal, J.: Inhibition of bacterial growth in human saliva, J. Dent. Res. **39**:886-891, 1960.
11. Stoohey, G.K.: Influence of thiamine on fluoride retention in the rat, J. Dent. Res. **53**:139, 1974.
12. Food and Nutrition Board, National Research Council: Recommended dietary allowances, ed. 8, Publication no. 2216, Washington, D.C., 1974, National Academy of Sciences.
13. Hodges, R.E., et al.: Human patnothenic acid deficiency produced by omega-methyl pantothenic acid, J. Clin. Invest. **38**:1421-1425, 1959.
14. Pratt, J.M.: Inorganic chemistry of vitamin B_{12}. New York, 1972, Academic Press, Inc.
15. FAO/WHO Expert Group: Requirements of ascorbic acid, vitamin D, vitamin B_{12}, folate and iron, World Health Organization Technical Report, Geneva, 1970, World Health Organization.
16. Herbert, V.: Nutritional requirements for vitamin B_{12} and folic acid, Am. J. Clin. Nutr. **21**:243-252, 1968.
17. Herbert, V., and Tisman, G.: Effects of deficiencies of folic acid and vitamin B_{12} on central nervous system function and development. In Gaull, G., editor: Biology of brain dysfunction, vol. 1, New York, 1973, Plenum Press, Inc.
18. Eagle, H., et al.: *Myo*-inositol as an essential growth factor for normal and malignant human cells in tissue culture, J. Biol. Chem. **226**:191-205, 1957.
19. Schwartz, P.L.: Ascorbic acid in wound healing—a review, J. Am. Diet. Assoc. **56**:497-503, 1970.
20. Gould, B.S.: The role of certain vitamins in collagen formation. In Gould, B.S., editor: Treatise on collagen, vol. 2, New York, 1968, Academic Press, Inc.
21. Cowan, D.W., Diehl, H.S., and Baker, A.B.: Vitamins for the prevention of colds, J.A.M.A. **120**:1268-1271, 1942.
22. Pauling, L.: Vitamin C and the common cold, San Francisco, 1970, W. H. Freeman & Co., Publishers.
23. Pauling, L.: Evolution and the need for ascorbic acid, Proc. Natl. Acad. Sci. U.S.A. **67**:1643-1648, 1970.
24. Pauling, L.: The significance of the evidence about ascorbic acid and the common cold, Proc. Natl. Acad. Sci. U.S.A. **68**:2678-2681, 1971.
25. Pauling, L.: Ascorbic acid and the common cold, Am. J. Clin. Nutr. **24**:1294-1299, 1971.
26. Dykes, M.H.M., and Meier, P.: Ascorbic acid and the common cold: evaluation of its efficacy and toxicity, J.A.M.A. **231**:1073-1079, 1975.
27. Cameron, E., and Pauling, L.: The orthomolecular treatment of cancer. I. The role of ascorbic acid in host resistance, Chem. Biol. Interact. **9**:273-283, 1974.
28. El-Ashry, G.M., Ringsdorf, W.M., and Cherashim, E.: Local and systemic influence in periodontal disease. II. Effect of prophylaxis and natural versus synthetic vitamin C upon gingivitis, J. Periodontol. **35**:250, 1964.
29. Glickman, L., and Dines, M.M.: Effect of increased ascorbic acid blood levels on the ascorbic level of treated and nontreated gingiva, J. Dent. Res. **42**:1152, 1963.
30. Shannon, I.L., and Gibson, W.A.: Intravenous ascorbic acid loading in subjects classified as to periodontal status, J. Dent. Res. **44**:355-361, 1965.

31. McBean, L., and Speckmann, E.W.: A review: the importance of nutrition in oral health, J. Am. Dent. Assoc. **89:**109-114, 1974.

32. Hayes, K.C., and Hegsted, D.M.: Toxicity of the vitamins. In Committee on food protection, food and nutrition board: Toxicants occurring naturally in foods, ed. 2, Washington, D.C., 1973, National Academy of Sciences.

33. Rosenthal, G.: Interaction of ascorbic acid and warfarin, J.A.M.A. **215:**1671, 1971.

34. Houston, J.B., and Levy, G.: Modification of drug biotransformation by vitamin C in man, Nature **225:**78-79, 1975.

35. Wald, G.: The molecular basis of visual excitation, Nature **219:**800-807, 1968.

36. Wasserman, R.H., and Corradino, R.A.: Metabolic role of vitamins A and D, Ann. Rev. Biochem. **40:**501-532, 1971.

37. Omdahl, J.L., and DeLuca, H.F.: Regulation of vitamin D metabolism and function, Physiol. Rev. **53:**327-372, 1973.

38. Taylor, A.N., and Wasserman, R.H.: Correlations between the vitamin D–induced calcium binding protein and intestinal absorption of calcium, Fed. Proc. **28:**1834-1838, 1969.

39. DeLuca, H.F.: Vitamin D: the vitamin and the hormone, Fed. Proc. **33:**2211-2219, 1974.

40. Haussler, M.R.: Vitamin D: mode of action and biomedical applications, Nutr. Rev. **32:**257-265, 1974.

41. Leonard, P.J., and Losowsky, M.S.: Relationship between plasma vitamin E level and peroxide hemolysis test in human subjects, Am. J. Clin. Nutr. **20:**795-798, 1967.

42. Mason, K.E.: Effects of nutritional deficiencies on muscle. In Bourne, G.H., editor: The structure and function of muscle, ed. 2, vol. 4, New York, 1973, Academic Press, Inc.

43. Dinning, J.S., and Day, P.L.: Vitamin E deficiency in the monkey, J. Exp. Med. **105:**395-402, 1957.

44. Zinkham, W.H., and Childs, B.: Effect of vitamin K and naphthalene metabolites on glutathione metabolism from normal newborns and patients with naphthalene hemolytic anemia, J. Dis. Child. **94:**420-423, 1957.

CHAPTER 26

ALBERT T. BROWN
JAMES L. MATHENY

Minerals

Minerals are inorganic elements that serve to support and sustain the life functions of organisms at all levels of the evolutionary scale from simple, procaryotic methane-producing eubacteria to higher, more complex mammalian species and humans. Generally speaking, minerals can be subdivided into two distinct types or classes. One of these classes of minerals is called either macrominerals or major minerals, and the other class is called either trace minerals or microminerals. The major difference between macrominerals and trace minerals is their daily dietary requirements. All macrominerals are required in the diet at levels in excess of 100 mg per day; trace minerals are required in the diet at levels much less than 100 mg per day. In addition, macrominerals are generally widely distributed in large amounts throughout the body; trace minerals occur in much smaller amounts. However, it must be stressed that both macrominerals and trace minerals participate in important biochemical and physiologic processes in both animals and humans. The following seven elements collectively comprise the macrominerals: calcium (Ca), phosphorous (P), magnesium (Mg), sodium (Na), potassium (K), chloride (Cl), and sulfur (S); and the following trace minerals have been established as playing important biologic roles in animals and humans: iron (Fe), zinc (Zn), iodine (I), molybdenum (Mo), selenium (Se), chromium (Cr), manganese (Mn), copper (Cu), and cobalt (Co). Fluoride is a trace mineral of importance for the maintenance of hard tissue structure, a discussion of which is presented in Chapter 24. Although macrominerals and trace minerals are involved in diverse, biologically important functions, they all have two important aspects in common: (1) All macrominerals and trace minerals must be supplied by dietary sources because they cannot be synthesized by organisms, as can components of other food groups such as nonessential amino acids, and (2) they cannot be broken down or catabolized to yield energy, as can other classes of nutrients such as carbohydrates, lipids, and proteins. Because of their major importance in performing a broad spectrum of biologic roles in animals and humans, entire books and hundreds of scientific journal articles have been written about each of the macrominerals and trace minerals. Therefore an in-depth discussion of each of these two classes of minerals is well beyond the scope of this text. Consequently, the purpose of this chapter is to give the reader an overview and an appreciation of the importance of the various minerals as related to their biologic roles in humans. For more detailed and specific information concerning the macrominerals and trace minerals, the reader is referred to other sources.[1-8]

REQUIREMENTS AND SOURCES

As previously stated, the dietary requirements for all macrominerals are 100 mg or more per day. However, as shown in Table 26-1, there is a broad range in the daily requirements of the various macrominerals. For example, the daily requirement of calcium for an adult male is between 800 and 1200 mg, whereas the daily requirement of potassium can be as high as 5625 mg per day. It is also important to stress that the daily dietary requirement of all of the macrominerals for various individuals is dependent on age and not, generally speaking, on sex (Table 26-1). Table 26-1 lists the seven macrominerals with their currently recommended daily dietary allowances and requirements.

Trace minerals, in contrast to macrominerals, are required in the diet at levels much less than 100 mg

Table 26-1. Safe and/or recommended daily allowances for macrominerals and trace minerals

| Mineral | Dietary allowance (mg) | | | |
| | Infant* | Child* | Adult | |
			Male*	Female*
Macromineral				
Calcium†	360-540	800	800-1200	800-1200
Phosphorus†	240-360	800	800-1200	800-1200
Magnesium†	50-70	150-350	300-450	300-450
Sodium	115-750	325-1350	1100-3300	1100-3300
Potassium	350-1275	550-2325	1875-5625	1875-5625
Chloride	275-1200	500-2100	1700-5100	1700-5100
Sulfur‡	—	—	—	—
Trace mineral				
Iron†	10-15	10-15	10-18	10-18
Zinc†	3-5	10	15	15
Iodine†	0.04-0.05	0.07-0.15	0.15	0.15
Molybdenum	0.03-0.08	0.05-0.15	0.15-0.50	0.15-0.50
Selenium	0.01-0.06	0.02-0.12	0.05-0.20	0.05-0.20
Chromium	0.01-0.06	0.02-0.08	0.05-0.20	0.05-0.20
Manganese	0.50-1.0	1.5-2.5	2.5-5.0	2.5-5.0
Copper	0.50-1.0	1.0-2.0	2.0-3.0	2.0-3.0
Cobalt§	—	—	—	—

*Ranges shown for amounts needed to fulfill recommended daily allowances are dependent on age. Generally speaking, as infants and children increase in age, daily dietary requirements for macrominerals and trace minerals increase, whereas in adults an increase in age generally means a decrease in daily recommended mineral requirements.

†Pregnant and lactating females have additional daily dietary requirements for calcium (400 mg), phosphorus (400 mg), magnesium (150 mg), iron (60 mg), zinc (10 mg), and iodine (50 μg).

‡Daily requirement of the sulfur-containing essential amino acid, methionine, must be fulfilled to have an adequate daily intake of sulfur. Sulfur is not utilized as the free mineral per se but rather through its incorporation into methionine. Hence its essential biologic roles are those of methionine.

§Recommended daily requirement for cobalt has not been established since it is required only in extremely small amounts and is found at adequate levels in virtually all foodstuffs.

per day. For example, the amount of iron, which is the trace mineral required at the highest level in the diet, is only 18 mg per day for adult males and females. As in the case of macrominerals, there is a broad range in the daily requirements of trace minerals. Whereas the daily recommended requirement of iron for adult males and females is 18 mg per day, the requirements for chromium and selenium are only 0.05 to 0.20 mg per day. Like the daily requirements for macrominerals, those for trace minerals are more dependent on age than on sex. The currently recommended daily safe dietary allowances for trace minerals are shown in Table 26-1.

The daily requirements of both macrominerals and trace minerals must be fulfilled by dietary intake be-

cause minerals are inorganic elements that cannot be biosynthesized, as can other classes of nutrients such as the nonessential amino acids, lipids, and carbohydrates. A number of dietary constituents are rich sources of macrominerals and trace minerals. However, no single dietary component is an adequate source of all of the macromineral requirements nor is a single dietary constituent an adequate source of all trace mineral requirements. For example, dairy products are an excellent source of the macromineral calcium, and grains and nuts are excellent sources of magnesium. In dietary sources of trace minerals, sea foods and iodized salt are adequate sources of iodine, and red meats and wine are excellent sources of iron. Because of the wide variation of mineral content in

Table 26-2. Food sources rich in macrominerals and trace minerals

Mineral	Food sources
Macromineral	
Calcium	Dairy products, dark green leafy vegetables, molasses, baked beans, dried legumes, dried figs, and nuts
Phosphorus	Meat, fish, poultry, eggs, milk, whole grain cereals, and vegetables
Magnesium	Whole grains, nuts, soybeans, and green, leafy vegetables
Sodium	Table salt, fish, sausages, cold cuts, cheese, eggs, milk, butter, and margarine
Potassium	Oatmeal, fish, coffee, prunes, bacon, dried fruits, and fruit juices
Chloride	Table salt, dairy products, and meat products
Sulfur	Meats, cereals, and eggs
Trace mineral	
Iron	Meats, wine, soybeans, molasses, dried peaches, and dried apricots
Zinc	Red meats, shellfish
Iodine	Seafoods, iodized salt
Molybdenum	Beef, kidney, cereals, and legumes
Selenium	All animal protein
Chromium*	Fats, meats, whole grains, brewer's yeast
Manganese	Nuts, seeds, whole grains, fruits, and vegetables
Copper	Liver, kidney, shell fish, dried fruits, and poultry
Cobalt*	All foodstuffs

*Chromium and cobalt deficiencies have not been reported in humans because virtually all foodstuffs contain adequate levels of these trace minerals.

different dietary constituents, an individual should consume a well-balanced diet to ensure an adequate intake of all macrominerals and trace minerals. Table 26-2 lists the macrominerals and trace minerals with food sources rich in the respective mineral content.

PHARMACOKINETICS
Absorption

Calcium, iron, potassium, magnesium, phosphate, and other ions are actively absorbed through the gastrointestinal mucosa. Normally, the monovalent ions are absorbed in large quantities, and the bivalent ions are absorbed in much smaller quantities. For some ions there are specific mechanisms that regulate absorption. For example, calcium absorption is greatly increased in the presence of the vitamin D derivative 1,25-dihydroxycholecalciferol and parathyroid hormone, and iron absorption is regulated according to the degree of saturation of circulating transferrin with iron.

Distribution

Most minerals are widely distributed throughout the body. However, for certain minerals there are specific transport processes for this distribution, and some minerals are sequestered preferentially in certain tissues. For example, iron is transported bound to transferrin and is stored, particularly in the liver, in combination with apoferritin as ferritin. Also large quantities of iron are associated with hemoglobin in red blood cells. Iodine is necessary for the production of thyroid hormone and is sequestered by the thyroid gland, whereas calcium, magnesium, and phosphorus are major structural components of hard tissues such as bone and teeth and are thus found there in large quantities. Circulating calcium levels are regulated through hormonal control by a dynamic process involving absorption and resorption of bone calcium. In addition, potassium is found at high intracellular concentrations in most tissues, and sodium is found primarily extracellularly.

Excretion

The kidneys, under hormonal control, play a major role in the maintenance of circulating levels of many minerals. The minerals enter the glomerular filtrate and are then reabsorbed to varying degrees from the renal tubules through active or passive transport processes.[6] In general, positive ions are transported through the tubular epithelium by active processes, whereas negative ions are usually transported passively as a result of electric differences developed across the membrane when positive ions are transported. For example, as sodium ions are transported out of the tubular fluid, the resulting electronegativity in the tubular fluid causes chloride ions to follow in the wake of the sodium ions. There are exceptions to this general rule; for example, phosphates or sulfates can be reabsorbed by active transport from the proximal tubules. Another exception can be illustrated by the secretion of potassium into the distal tubular fluid.

Excretion of minerals in the feces occurs through two major pathways. Ingested minerals that are not absorbed, generally components of insoluble salts, are passed in the feces. Also, minerals are transported from the blood back into the feces generally through passive mechanisms.

Other mechanisms for the excretion of minerals include sweating and salivation. The important minerals that are lost during excessive sweating are sodium and potassium. This loss can lead to severe electrolyte disturbances under certain conditions. The secretion of minerals in saliva is of prime importance in dentistry. The minerals present in saliva and gingival fluid play two major roles.[8,9] Calcium, phosphorus, and fluoride are especially important in maintenance of hard tissue structure, and these and other minerals play important roles in the metabolic processes of oral microorganisms. Detailed descriptions of the functions of salivary minerals in these processes can be found elsewhere.[9]

BIOCHEMICAL AND PHYSIOLOGIC ROLES

Not only do macrominerals and trace minerals occupy diverse locations on the periodic chart, they also perform a broad spectrum of biologically important roles and functions in both animals and humans. Generally speaking, the biologic roles fulfilled by macrominerals and trace minerals can be placed into one of four distinct groups, depending on the biochemical and physiologic functions within which the respective minerals participate. These four groups, as related to their functional roles for the macrominerals and trace minerals, are as follows:

1. Certain minerals serve as essential structural components of body tissues. Probably the most important of these minerals are the macrominerals calcium, phosphorus, and magnesium because they are essential structural components of bone, enamel, and cementum. The average adult body contains approximately 1250 gm of calcium, 840 gm of phosphorus, and 28 gm of magnesium, of which approximately 98%, 80%, and 70% of these amounts, respectively, are contained in body hard tissues, especially those of the skeletal system but also in enamel, cementum, and dentin. It should be noted that the calcium/phosphate ratio in the body is approximately 1.5:1.0, which indicates that a calcium/phosphate ratio in the diet of around 1:1 is desirable but not absolutely essential.

2. Macrominerals and trace minerals also serve as functional components of biologically important compounds that occur throughout the body. For example, iron is the functional component of hemoglobin, which is responsible for oxygen transport in higher organisms. In addition, iron is also the functional component of a number of cytochromes, which serve as electron carriers within the electron transport system that generates biologic energy (ATP) when coupled to oxidative phosphorylation. Other examples are that iodine is an essential functional component of the thyroid hormone, thyroxine, and cobalt is the essential functional component of vitamin B_{12}. Also of import is the fact that both macrominerals and trace minerals are essential for, and are participants in, the biochemical transformations catalyzed by many important enzymes. For example, the presence of magnesium is necessary for the reactions catalyzed by DNA and RNA polymerase enzymes, and the presence of zinc is required for the proteolytic reaction catalyzed by the enzyme carboxypeptidase. In addition, molybdenum is essential for xanthine oxidase activity, which catalyzes an important reaction during purine catabolism.

3. A third important biologic role for both macrominerals and trace minerals is that they are components of, and serve to maintain the structural integrity of, many biologically important substances throughout the body. Phosphorus, for example, is a structural component of both DNA and RNA and is also found in phospholipids, which are essential structural components of all biologic membranes. In addition, certain macrominerals and trace minerals serve to maintain the structural integrity of many enzymes throughout the body, and although they do not participate in the catalytic mechanism of the respective enzymes

Table 26-3. Biochemical and physiological functions of macrominerals

Macromineral	Biologic roles
Calcium	Structural component of hard tissues
	Bone
	Enamel
	Cementum
	Conversion of prothrombin to thrombin in blood clotting
	Muscle contraction
	Neurotransmitter release
	Regulation of sodium and potassium ion transport across membranes
	Enzymatic*
	Lipid breakdown
	Release of phosphate groups
	ATP breakdown
	Protein breakdown
	Glycogen breakdown
Phosphorus	Structural component of hard tissues
	Bone
	Enamel
	Cementum
	Component of high-energy phosphate bonds such as those found in ATP
	Structural component of many low molecular weight biologically active compounds, such as nucleosides, and monophosphate, diphosphate, and triphosphate, and metabolic intermediates
	Structural component of high molecular weight biologically important compounds such as DNA, RNA, phospholipids, and nucleoproteins
Magnesium	Structural component of hard tissues
	Bone
	Enamel
	Cementum
	Maintain structural integrity of ribosomes
	Binding RNA to ribosomes
	Enzymatic*
	DNA synthesis
	RNA synthesis
	High-energy phosphate bond formation
	Phosphate group transfer reactions
	DNA breakdown
	RNA breakdown
	Carbohydrate biosynthesis
	Carbohydrate breakdown

*Specific names of enzymes that require the presence of macrominerals for catalytic activity are not listed. However, overall metabolic processes within which respective enzymes participate are listed. For example, magnesium is required for the activity of glucokinase, which catalyzes the initial reaction of the glycolytic sequence and hence functions in carbohydrate breakdown or catabolism.

Table 26-3—cont'd

Macromineral	Biologic roles
Sodium	Maintenance functions
	Muscular irritability
	Nerve irritability
	Cell permeability
	Osmotic pressure
	Acid-base balance
	Water balance
	Gas transport
	Transport of amino acids and sugars across cell membranes
Potassium	Maintenance functions
	Muscular irritability
	Nerve irritability
	Osmotic pressure
	Acid-base balance
	Water balance
	Cell permeability
	Control of cardiac function
	Enzymatic*
	Glycogen breakdown and glycogen synthesis
Chloride	Maintenance functions
	Acid-base balance
	Water balance
	Osmotic pressure
	Carbon dioxide transport
	Potassium conservation
	Enzymatic*
	Starch breakdown in saliva
Sulfur	Component of sulfur-containing amino acids, especially essential amino acid, methionine, which is found in all body proteins, including enzymes and peptide hormones
	Lipid biosynthesis via S-adenosyl-methionine
	Component of glutathione, bile salts, and chrondroitin sulfate

per se, they are absolutely essential for enzymatic activity. Also, certain minerals serve to maintain the integrity of cellular structures such as membranes and subcellular organelles. The presence of magnesium, for example, is necessary to maintain the correct orientation of subunits in functional ribosomes.

4. Many minerals, particularly macrominerals, have important roles in directing, maintaining, and regulating biochemical and physiologically important processes throughout the body. For example, calcium is essential for the conversion of prothrombin to thrombin in the process of blood clotting and also plays an important role in muscle contraction and in the release of neurotransmitters such as acetylcholine. In addition, potassium is of primary importance in controlling cardiac function, and sodium, potassium, and chloride have important roles in maintaining water balance and osmotic pressure.

A detailed discussion of all of the important biochemical and physiologic roles of both the macrominerals and trace minerals is well beyond the scope and depth of this chapter. However, the reader is referred to Tables 26-3 and 26-4 for a more detailed listing of their biologic roles.

Table 26-4. Biochemical and physiologic functions of trace minerals

Trace mineral	Biologic roles
Iron	Oxygen transport as the functional component of hemoglobin and myoglobin
	Cellular respiration as the functional component of cytochromes
	Enzymatic*
	Hydrogen peroxide breakdown
	Cytochrome oxidation and reduction
	Purine breakdown
	Amino acid breakdown
	Amino acid biosynthesis
Zinc	Enzymatic*
	Carbon dioxide transport
	Alcohol metabolism
	Protein breakdown
	Carbohydrate biosynthesis
	Cleavage of phosphorylated compounds
Iodine	Thyroid hormones
Molybdenum	Enzymatic*
	Purine breakdown
	Alcohol metabolism
	Electron transport
Selenium	Enzymatic*
	Glutathione metabolism
Chromium	Proposed cofactor in the action of insulin
	Enzymatic*
	Carbohydrate metabolism
	Energy metabolism
	Fatty acid biosynthesis
	Cholesterol biosynthesis
Manganese	Enzymatic*
	Carbohydrate breakdown
	Carbohydrate biosynthesis
	Lipid biosynthesis
	Lipoprotein breakdown
	Amino acid biosynthesis
	Peptide breakdown
	Protein breakdown
	Mucopolysaccharide biosynthesis
Copper	Hemoglobin synthesis
	Enzymatic*
	Dihydroxyphenylalanine synthesis
	Vitamin C oxidation
	Cytochrome oxidation
Cobalt	Functional component of vitamin B_{12}
	Transport of carbon dioxide
	Metabolism of sulfur-containing amino acids

*Specific names of enzymes that require trace minerals for catalytic activity are not listed. However, overall metabolic processes within which respective enzymes participate are listed. For example, molybdenum is required for xanthine oxidase activity, which catalyzes an important reaction during purine breakdown.

SYMPTOMS OF EXCESS OR DEFICIENCY

Deficiencies of macrominerals can occur as a result of dietary deficiencies; however, they are usually secondary to existing disease states or may be caused by medications. There is some controversy concerning dietary calcium and osteopenia.[10] Conversely, deficiencies of the trace minerals are generally the result of dietary insufficiencies. The symptoms of mineral excess or deficiency in most cases are predictable, if one considers their normal physiologic role. Tables 26-5 and 26-6 are listings of the most frequently seen symptoms of mineral excess and deficiency. Thus only a few of the most frequently seen disturbances will be discussed.

Table 26-5. Symptoms of excess and deficient macromineral states

Macromineral	Excess	Deficiency

Calcium*	Hypercalcemia
	    Impaired kidney function
	    Renal stones
	    Calcification of soft tissues
	    Bone cysts
	    Osteoporosis
	    Apathy
	    Confusion
	    Cardiac arrhythmia
	Milk alkali syndrome
		Hypocalcemia
		    Tetany
		    Increased muscle and nerve irritability
		    Tremors
		    Convulsions
		    Rickets
		    Osteomalacia

Phosphorus†	Hyperphosphatemia
	    Childhood anemia
	    Necrosis of the mandible
	Inorganic phosphate poisoning
	    Symptoms associated with hypocalcemia
	    Gastrointestinal irritation
	    Cardiovascular failure
	    Hepatic necrosis
		Familial hypophosphatemia
		    Decreased ATP levels, erythrocytes
		    Hemolytic anemia
		    Impaired oxygenation of tissues
		Rickets
		Osteomalacia

Magnesium‡	Hypermagnesemia
	    Muscle weakness
	    Hypotension
	    Sedation
	    Confusion
	    Respiratory paralysis
	    Cardiac arrest
		Hypomagnesemia
		    Hypokalemia
		    Hypocalcemia
		    Symptoms of hypocalcemia
		    Skeletal and cardiac muscle changes
		Continued.

*Symptoms of calcium excess listed are reflected in elevated serum levels of calcium, which may be caused not only by excessive dietary intake of calcium but also by other physiologic factors or imbalances.

†Inorganic phosphate poisoning can be caused in both children and adults by consuming excess quantities of phosphate-containing laxatives. Hyperphosphatemia in children is caused by the fact that plasma levels of phosphate in growing children is higher than in adults. Phosphate deficiency is not generally caused by lack of dietary intake but rather by certain malabsorption syndromes such as familial hypophosphatemia.

‡Hypomagnesemia and hypermagnesemia generally are not caused by deficient or excessive magnesium intake. Hypomagnesemia can be caused by a number of conditions such as long-term diarrhea or after extensive hemodialysis. The common cause of hypermagnesemia is renal dysfunction.

§Sodium, potassium, and chloride deficiencies generally are not caused by insufficient dietary intake but rather by adverse physiologic conditions such as excessive diarrhea, vomiting, and sweating or by excessive use of diuretics. Sodium, potassium, and chloride excess can be a result of high dietary intake but can also be caused by other physiologic factors such as renal disease.

‖This condition of sulfur excess is caused by excessive use of topical sulfur-containing drugs.

Table 26-5. Symptoms of excess and deficient macromineral states—cont'd

Macromineral	Excess	Deficiency
Sodium§	Hypertension Cardiovascular disorders Edema	Decreased cardiac output Hypotension Dehydration Shock

Potassium§	Hyperkalemia
	  Muscle weakness
	  Cardiac dysfunction and arrest
		Hypokalemia
		  Neuromuscular dysfunction
		  Paralysis
		  Abnormal myocardial function

Chloride§ Sulfur‖	Hyperchloremia acidosis Dermatitis venenata	Hypochloremia alkalosis

Table 26-6. Symptoms of excess or deficient trace minerals states

Trace mineral	Excess	Deficiency
Iron	Hemochromatosis	Iron-deficiency anemia Small red blood cells deficient in hemoglobin
Zinc	Hypochromic anemia Subnormal growth Decreased wound healing	Thickening of skin (acrodermatitis enteropathica) Loss of hair Impaired taste

Iodine	Allergic reactions
	Brass taste
	Burning in mouth and throat
	Soreness of teeth and gums
	Increased salivation
	Skin lesions
	Inflammation of the pharynx, larynx, and tonsils
		Thyroid gland enlargement (goiter)
		Hypothyroidism
		  Fatigue
		  Muscle cramps
		  Paresthesias
		  Intolerance to cold
		Myxedema
		  Cretinism

Molybdenum	Connective tissue changes Weight loss Growth retardation	Decreased purine catabolism
Selenium*	Alkali disease and "blind staggers" in animals	White muscle disease (WMD) in animals Keshan disease Congestive cardiomyopathy
Chromium†	None adequately demonstrated	None adequately demonstrated
Manganese	Neurologic disturbances	Skeletal abnormalities Convulsions
Copper†‡§	None in adults	"Swayback" disease in animals Wilson's disease Anemia in children
Cobalt‖	Polycythemia Elevated hemoglobin Cyanosis Coma Death	Emaciation Wasting

*Although diets containing large amounts of selenium can cause selenium poisoning in both animals and humans, selenium deficiencies are generally seen only in animals (e.g., WMD). Selenium deficiency in humans is extremely rare and has been reported only in a selenium-deficient area in China.

†Both chromium and copper deficiencies are not seen in adult humans because requirements of these trace minerals are extremely small and adequate amounts are contained in almost all foodstuffs.

‡Some infants on virtually a total milk diet can develop anemia that requires a diet supplemented with both copper and iron to cure.

§Some adults can develop a copper deficiency caused by lack of production of ceruloplasmin, a blood plasma protein that binds and transports copper. This condition is known as Wilson's disease.

‖Cobalt deficiency has not been demonstrated in humans, only in ruminants.

As in absorption and metabolism, calcium and phosphorus excesses and deficiencies are related. Because of their major roles in hard tissue structure, changes are seen in these tissues when disturbances occur. Also, because of its role in muscle contraction, calcium excess or deficiency is manifested by changes in cardiac and skeletal muscle function. Calcium deficiency does not usually occur as a result of low dietary intake but most often results from vitamin D deficiency (Chapter 25).

Alterations in sodium and potassium levels mainly affect cardiovascular function. Excess dietary sodium has been implicated as a risk factor in the development and progression of cardiovascular diseases, especially hypertension. It should be noted that patients placed on low sodium diets should consider not only the sodium content of foods but also the sodium content of medicinals, especially those requiring no prescription for purchase. The most frequently seen potassium disturbance is deficiency from diuretic administration (see Chapter 20).

As mentioned earlier, alterations in levels of the trace minerals most frequently occur from differences in dietary intake levels, and the symptoms reflect their normal physiologic roles. This is clearly demonstrated by changes in the hematopoietic system caused by excesses or deficiencies of iron, zinc, or cobalt. Iron deficiency is the most common trace mineral disorder and results in anemia. Disorders of the other trace minerals are much less common. For example, selenium deficiency caused by dietary lack has only been shown in a selenium-deficient area of China,[11,12] and only one report details a possible deficiency in a patient receiving parenteral alimentation.[13]

PREPARATIONS AND USES

Several macrominerals, including calcium, magnesium, sodium, and potassium, are components of antacid or laxative preparations used for gastrointestinal disorders. These and other macrominerals, including potassium and chloride, are used in the treatment of fluid and electrolyte disturbances resulting from a wide variety of disorders ranging from renal disease to prolonged diarrhea and even including drug-induced disturbances. Sulfur is primarily used topically in the treatment of infectious cutaneous disorders, and there is no clinical use of elemental phosphorus. Preparations and uses of macrominerals are shown in Table 26-7.

Trace mineral deficiency is seen infrequently with the exception of iron deficiency. As shown in Table 26-8, both oral and parenteral preparations of iron are available. Deficiencies of selenium, copper, and cobalt are seen rarely; however, preparations of these trace minerals are used clinically to treat the disorders listed. Preparations containing zinc or manganese are used topically as antiseptics or astringents, whereas iodine is used in the treatment of thyroid dysfunction (see Chapter 17) and as a component of some expectorants. Chromium in its radioactive form is used as a diagnostic agent because it binds to red blood cells. It can, for example, be used to determine blood volume. There is no known clinical use for molybdenum and thus there are no preparations shown in Table 26-8.

Table 26-7. Preparations and uses of macrominerals

Macromineral	Preparations	Uses
Calcium	Calcium chloride, gluceptate gluconate, lactate, carbonate, phosphate, levulinate	Hypocalcemia, antacids
Phosphorus	White or yellow elemental phosphorus	Rodent poison
Magnesium	Magnesium citrate, sulfate, hydroxide, trisilicate	Hypomagnesemia, seizures associated with acute nephritis or eclampsia of pregnancy, laxatives, antacids
Sodium	Sodium bicarbonate, chloride, lactate, citrate, phosphate, alginate	Treatment of fluid and electrolyte disturbances, laxatives, antacids
Potassium	Potassium chloride, sodium tartrate	Hypokalemia, metabolic alkalosis, laxative
Chloride	Sodium chloride	Treatment of fluid and electrolyte disturbances
Sulfur	Sublimed, precipitated, or colloidal sulfur	Fungicide and parasiticide, with other keratolytics in treatment of cutaneous disorders

Table 26-8. Preparations and uses of trace minerals

Trace mineral	Preparations	Uses
Iron	Oral: ferrous salts Parenteral: iron dextran (Imferon)	Iron-deficiency anemia (microcytic anemia)
Zinc	Zinc sulfate, chloride, oxide, pyrithione	Astringents, antiperspirants, styptics, corrosives, mild antiseptics
Iodine	Iodine and potassium iodide (Lugol's solution) sodium iodide, potassium iodide	Hyperthyroidism, expectorants
Molybdenum	—	—
Selenium	Sodium selenite, selenium sulfide	Keshan disease, antiseborrheics
Chromium	Radioactive chromium (^{51}Cr)	Diagnostic agents
Manganese	Potassium permanganate	Local antiseptic, astringent
Copper	Copper sulfate	Hypocupremia
Cobalt	Cobaltous chloride	Normochromic, normocytic anemia associated with renal failure

REFERENCES

1. Nizel, A.E.: Nutrition in preventive dentistry science and practice, ed. 2, Philadelphia, 1981, W.B. Saunders Co.
2. Comar, C.L., and Bronner, F., editors: Mineral metabolism, 5 vols., New York, 1960-1969, Academic Press, Inc.
3. McGilvery, R.W.: Biochemistry, a functional approach, ed. 2, Philadelphia, 1979, W.B. Saunders Co.
4. West, E.S., et al.: Textbook of biochemistry, ed. 4, New York, 1966, Macmillan Publishing Co., Inc.
5. White, A., et al.: Principles of biochemistry, ed. 6, New York, 1978, McGraw-Hill Book Co.
6. Guyton, A.C.: Textbook of medical physiology, ed. 6, Philadelphia, 1981, W.B. Saunders Co.
7. Gilman, A.G., Goodman, L.S., and Gilman, A.: The pharmacological basis of therapeutics, ed. 6, New York, 1980, Macmillan Publishing Co., Inc.
8. Stiles, H.M., Loesche, W.J., and O'Brien, T.C.: Proceedings of a workshop at St. Simon, Ga., on microbial aspects of dental caries, sponsored by the National Caries Program, Washington, D.C., 1976, Information Retrieval, Inc.
9. Kleinberg, I., Ellison, S.A., and Mandel, I.D.: Proceedings of a workshop at State University of New York School of Dental Medicine, Stony Brook, on saliva and dental caries, sponsored by the National Caries Program, Washington, D.C., 1979, Information Retrieval, Inc.
10. Draper, H.H., and Scythes, C.A.: Calcium, phosphorus, and osteoporosis, Fed. Proc. **40:**2434-2438, 1981.
11. Keshan Disease Research Group of the Chinese Academy of Medical Sciences, Beijing: Epidemiologic studies on the etiologic relationship of selenium and Keshan disease, Chin. Med. J. (Engl.) **92:**477-482, 1979.
12. Keshan Disease Research Group of the Chinese Academy of Medical Sciences, Beijing: Observations on effect of sodium selenite in prevention of Keshan disease, Chin. Med. J. (Engl.) **92:**471-476, 1979.
13. Johnson, R.A., et al.: An occidental case of cardiomyopathy and selenium deficiency, N. Engl. J. Med. **304:**1210-1212, 1981.

Drugs used for gastrointestinal disorders

JAMES L. MATHENY

Every year millions of dollars are spent on prescription and nonprescription products to treat gastrointestinal disorders. Among these products, antacids are probably the most frequently used. Other types of drugs employed include laxatives and antidiarrheal drugs. The following discussion is intended to give the reader a general knowledge of the drugs available, their mechanisms of action, their side effects, and their interactions with other drugs that might be significant. For a more detailed coverage, the reader is referred to basic pharmacologic texts[1,2] or other texts that list specific products and preparations.[3,4]

ANTACIDS: ULCER THERAPY

Antacids, anticholinergics, and histamine H_2-receptor antagonists are useful in treating gastric distress. Acute gastritis is the most common type of gastric distress and is frequently termed "acid indigestion," "heart burn," "gas," "sour stomach," or "upset stomach." The symptoms usually include epigastric discomfort or a "burning" sensation, frequent belching, or flatulence following meals. Gastrointestinal ulceration is another type of gastric distress that responds to antacid therapy. Both of the disorders mentioned above result from the erosive effects of secreted acid and pepsin on the gastrointestinal lining.

Antacids

Gastric antacids are drugs that directly neutralize the hydrochloric acid secreted in the stomach. They do not fully neutralize the gastric contents (pH of 7.0) but raise the pH to 3 or 4. This of course, decreases the erosive effect of the acid and additionally inhibits the activity of pepsin. They are generally classified as systemic or nonsystemic, depending on the degree of systemic absorption from the gastrointestinal tract of the cation portion of the antacid molecule.

Sodium bicarbonate is the only systemic antacid. It is an effective antacid, acting rapidly to neutralize gastric acid. The major disadvantage of sodium bicarbonate is that the systemic absorption of sodium may cause alkalosis. For this reason this compound is not recommended, even though it is frequently used by the lay public.

Nonsystemic antacids, that is, those whose cationic portion is not absorbed systemically, are the preferred preparations. Although there are many prescription and nonprescription preparations available, there are only a few compounds that are used as the active ingredients in these preparations. These include calcium carbonate, aluminum salts, magnesium salts, and magnesium-aluminum hydroxide gels.

Calcium carbonate is a potent, fast-acting antacid with a long duration of action. It may be used safely in small doses for the treatment of occasional gastritis but is not recommended for chronic use. In addition to constipation, prolonged use of calcium carbonate may cause hypercalcemia[5] with subsequent neurologic and renal malfunction,[6,7] or the milk-alkali syndrome.[8] This syndrome results from ingestion of milk and calcium carbonate and is characterized by headache, nausea and vomiting, aching muscles, and weakness. Also, acid rebound (hypersecretion of acid 3 to 5 hours following dosage) has been shown to occur following single doses of calcium carbonate.[9,10,11]

Aluminum salts used as antacids include hydroxide, carbonate, phosphate, or aminoacetate. Aluminum hydroxide is the most potent of these but has less neutralizing capacity than calcium carbonate or sodium bicarbonate. The most common side effect of the aluminum antacids is constipation. Intestinal obstruction may occur in elderly patients. Constipation from the aluminum antacids can be counteracted by combining them with magnesium compounds or by administering laxatives concurrently. Though not proven, neurologic toxicity from systemic absorption of aluminum following long-term large-dose therapy has been postulated.[12] Since aluminum binds with phosphate in the gut and thus decreases phosphate absorption, aluminum compounds have been shown to be useful in patients with chronic renal failure who have hyperphosphatemia. This effect, however, may cause hypophosphatemia in others[13] manifested by anorexia, malaise, and muscle weakness.[14]

Several magnesium salts have antacid properties. The carbonate, hydroxide, and oxide salts are the most potent and have neutralizing ability less than calcium carbonate and greater than aluminum hydroxide. The trisilicate salt is less potent. The most common side effect of the magnesium antacids is osmotic diarrhea, which if prolonged can lead to systemic fluid and electrolyte disturbances.[7] The most severe toxic manifestation, hypermagnesemia, can occur because of absorption of magnesium chloride following hydrochloric acid neutralization in patients with renal disease who cannot adequately eliminate magnesium. The symptoms of hypermagnesemia include nausea, vomiting, hypotension, depressed reflexes, respiratory depression, and coma.[15,16] Again, magnesium and aluminum salts are frequently combined in products to avoid their gastrointestinal side effects.

Other ingredients that are used in some antacid preparations include simethicone, alginic acid, and oxethazaine. Simethicone, a gastric defoaming agent, allows easier elimination of gastric gas by belching or passing flatus. Alginic acid is used in chewable products because it reacts with sodium bicarbonate to form a highly viscous solution of sodium alginate. The patient is then instructed to drink water, which carries the viscous solution to the stomach. There it floats on the gastric contents so that, if esophageal reflux occurs, the esophageal mucosa does not come in contact with gastric acid.[17] The patient must remain in at least a semierect position for these products to be effective. Representative antacid preparations and their active ingredients are shown in Table 27-1.

Oxethazaine is a local anesthetic that is combined

in some antacid preparations recommended for ulcer therapy. Controversy exists over the effectiveness of these preparations as compared to antacids alone.[18,19]

Anticholinergics

Anticholinergic drugs such as propantheline (Pro-Banthine) are used as adjunctive therapy with antacids in treating peptic ulcers. They decrease gastrointestinal motility and secretions and thus prolong the action of antacids. The efficacy of this type of therapy for ulcer disease has been questioned,[20] but it is recommended for certain patients who do not respond to other types of therapy.[21] Generally, the benefit from anticholinergics in ulcer therapy seldom justifies the side effects they cause.

Histamine H$_2$-receptor antagonists

The H$_2$-histamine antagonists competitively block the release of gastric acid normally caused by histamine. Cimetidine (Tagamet), one compound in this group, has been shown to cause a significant decrease in gastric acid secretion[22] and to be effective in treating most ulcer patients.[23] Adverse reactions occurring with the use of cimetidine include gynecomastia, bradycardia, cholestatic hepatitis, sexual dysfunction, pancytopenia, confusion, hallucinations, and fever. Onset of these reactions may occur a few hours after dosage or may only appear after weeks of treatment.

Table 27-1. Representative antacid preparations

Trade name	Active ingredients
Alka-Seltzer	Sodium and potassium bicarbonate
Amphojel	Aluminum hydroxide
Basaljel	Aluminum carbonate and hydroxide
Chooz	Calcium carbonate, magnesium trisilicate
DiGel	Aluminum hydroxide, magnesium carbonate and hydroxide, simethicone
Gelusil	Aluminum hydroxide, magnesium hydroxide, simethicone
Maalox (Maalox Plus)	Aluminum and magnesium hydroxide, (simethicone)
Mylanta	Aluminum and magnesium hydroxide, simethicone
Rolaids	Dihydroxy aluminum sodium carbonate
Titralac	Calcium carbonate, glycine
Tums	Calcium carbonate

Drug interactions

Antacids alter the absorption of other drugs from the gastrointestinal tract. These interactions can usually be avoided by proper spacing of drug dosage. Antacids inhibit the absorption of several compounds by chemically combining to them. Drugs included in this group are tetracycline antibiotics,[24] digitalis preparations,[25] iron salts, chlorpromazine,[26] and indomethacin.[27] Conversely, levodopa absorption may be significantly increased if antacids are taken concurrently.[28] This occurs because alkalinization speeds gastric emptying, delivering more levodopa to the small intestine where it is absorbed.

LAXATIVES

As with antacids, the laxatives represent a multimillion dollar industry because they are widely used by the general population. Traditionally they are classified as bulk laxatives, lubricants, stimulants, stool softeners (emollients), or osmotic (saline) laxatives. Although there are rational therapeutic indications for laxatives, one should realize that these drugs are often abused because patients believe that "regular" bowel habits are essential.[29] There is wide variability in the number of bowel movements per day in normal individuals, ranging from three movements per day to three movements per week. Long-term use or short-term overdose of laxatives may lead to damage of the myenteric plexus of the colon[30,31] and atonic colon[32,33] with possible habituation to the laxative agent.

The rational uses for laxatives include their use in illnesses that cause short-term spastic or atonic constipation, postoperative use (such as after myocardial infarction to avoid stress), in preparation for diagnostic procedures (such as sigmoidoscopy, barium enema, or colonoscopy) or use following perianal operations (such as hemorrhoidectomy). Representative laxatives and their active ingredients are shown in Table 27-2.

Bulk laxatives

Bulk-forming laxatives are the preferred preparations for simple constipation because they act through the most physiologic mechanism. These compounds are natural or semisynthetic polysaccharides or cellulose derivatives that combine with the intestinal fluid to form gels, which increase peristalsis and thus facilitate the movement of the intestinal contents. The bulk-forming laxatives are relatively safe and are preferred if long-term therapy is indicated.[34] It should be noted that these compounds should not be administered concurrently with salicylates or digitalis preparations because absorption may be decreased. As with antacids, the timing of dosage becomes important.

Lubricants

The major lubricant laxative, mineral oil, is no longer recommended for use[35] because, when used over long periods, it may be absorbed and cause chronic bowel inflammation and perianal disorders.[36] Other digestible plant oils such as olive oil are effec-

Table 27-2. Representative laxative preparations

Trade name	Active ingredients			
	Stimulant	Bulk	Lubricant/emollient	Saline
Comfolax			Dioctyl sodium sulfosuccinate	
Dulcolax	Bisacodyl			
Ex-Lax	Phenolphthalein			
Feen-A-Mint	Phenolphthalein			
Fletcher's Castoria	Senna			
Haley's M-O			Mineral oil	Magnesium hydroxide
Hydrolose		Methylcellulose		
Milk of magnesia				Magnesium hydroxide
Mucilose		Psyllium		
Stimulax	Cascara		Dioctyl sodium sulfosuccinate	
Tonelax	Danthron			

tive and act to soften fecal contents by coating them and preventing colonic absorption of fecal water.

Stimulants

Laxatives in this group increase intestinal motility through local irritant actions on the intestinal mucosa or by actions on the neural plexus of the intestinal smooth muscle. The stimulant laxatives are potent and often cause undesirable effects such as cramping and excessive evacuation especially when abused. Although compounds in this group such as castor oil and bisacodyl are frequently used before radiologic examination of the gastrointestinal tract or before bowel surgery, they are not recommended for routine use for simple constipation.[36] In addition to the acute unpleasant side effects, these compounds can cause electrolyte and fluid deficiencies because of excessive cathartic activity. Other substances that have been used to stimulate intestinal motility include senna (Glysennid, Senokot), cascara, phenolphthalein, and danthron (Dorbane, Modane).

Stool softeners (emollients)

Dioctyl sodium sulfosuccinate (Colace) is the representative emollient laxative (wetting agent). It is an anionic detergent that softens the stool by net water accumulation in the intestine.[37] This action may involve inhibition of Na^+,K^+-ATPase, stimulation of adenyl cyclase, and a decrease in mucosal prostaglandin E_2.[38] Other stool softeners include dioctyl calcium sulfosuccinate (Surfak), dioctyl potassium sulfosuccinate (Kasof), and poloxalkol (Magcyl), which may be used if sodium is contraindicated. Although these compounds are claimed to be nontoxic, they should be limited to short-term use unless a physician is consulted.[36]

Osmotic (saline) laxatives

The sulfates or phosphates of magnesium or sodium are retained in the bowel and are thought to cause their laxative effect by osmotically holding water; however, this hypothesis is untested.[39] Controversy exists because magnesium stimulates the release of cholecystokinin,[40] which can then cause intraluminal accumulation of water and electrolytes.[41] As with magnesium-containing antacids, the magnesium laxatives should be used cautiously in patients with impaired renal function because some of the cation may be absorbed.[42]

As previously stated, the mechanism of action of sodium-containing laxatives has not been firmly established. The major toxicity of these drugs results from sodium absorption. Thus they should be avoided in patients on low-sodium regimens for other disorders.

ANTIDIARRHEALS

Available antidiarrheal agents are of three types: adsorbents, opiates, and antispasmodics. Representative antidiarrheal preparations and their active ingredients are shown in Table 27-3. Diarrhea is a symptom that may be caused by infection (bacterial, viral, fungal, or parasitic), poisoning, drugs, malabsorption, allergy, gastrointestinal lesions, neoplasms, or possibly psychogenic causes. The cause of persistent diarrhea should always be identified. Antidiarrheals are administered to avoid or correct fluid and electrolyte imbalances, which become a problem when diarrhea is persistent.

The adsorbents are the most frequently used type of antidiarrheal agents. The best agents of this type are those containing kaolin and pectin. These agents are useful in treating mild diarrhea. Bismuth-containing compounds and activated charcoal have been shown to be less effective than those containing kaolin and pectin. These compounds should be avoided, or dosage time should be considered, if they are used with antibiotics because they may adsorb the antibiotic, decreasing drug absorption and thus prolonging infection.[43]

The opiates are the most effective type of antidiarrheal agent. They act directly on the smooth muscle of the gut to produce spasm with decreased peristalsis. The major problem with the use of opiates is their dependence liability. For this reason, long-term use may be hazardous. The drugs of choice of this type, because of their lower addiction liability, are diphenoxylate (with atropine, Colonil, Lomotil) and loperamide (Imodium).[43]

The antispasmodic type of antidiarrheals should theoretically be ideal. However, these anticholinergic type of antispasmotics cannot usually be given in large enough doses without producing adverse side effects (such as anticholinergic effects other than on the gut). Compounds such as atropine and hyoscine are included in combination antidiarrheals but are present in subtherapeutic doses.

Cholestyramine (Questran) may be an effective

Table 27-3. Representative antidiarrheal preparations

	Active ingredients		
Trade name	Opiate	Adsorbent	Other
Amogel	Opium	Bismuth subgallate, kaolin, pectin	Zinc phenolsulfonate
Donnagel		Kaolin, pectin	Hyoscyamine, atropine, hyoscine
Kaopectate		Kaolin, pectin	
Lomotil, Colonil	Diphenoxylate		Atropine
Pepto-Bismol		Bismuth subsalicylate, calcium carbonate	
Rheaban		Activated attapulgite	

antidiarrheal when malabsorption of bile acids contributes to the condition. Two such situations are ileal resection[44] and the irritable bowel syndrome.[45]

REFERENCES

1. Goodman, L.S., and Gilman, A.: The pharmacological basis of therapeutics, ed. 5, New York, 1975, Macmillan Publishing Co., Inc.
2. DiPalma, J.R.: Drill's pharmacology in medicine, ed. 4, New York, 1971, McGraw-Hill Book Co.
3. APhA Project Staff: Handbook of nonprescription drugs, ed. 6, Washington, D.C., 1979, American Pharmaceutical Association.
4. Baker, C.E., et al.: Physicians desk reference for nonprescription drugs, ed. 2, Oradell, N.J., 1981, Medical Economics Co.
5. Stiel, J., et al.: Hypercalcemia in patients with peptic ulceration receiving large doses of calcium carbonate, Gastroenterology **53**:900-904, 1967.
6. Piper, D.W., and Heap, T.R.: Medical management of peptic ulcer with reference to anti-ulcer agents in other gastrointestinal diseases, Drugs **3**:366-403, 1972.
7. Fordtran, J.S.: Reduction of acidity by diet, antacids, and anticholinergic agents, In Sleisenger, M.H., and Fordtran, J.S., editors: Gastrointestinal disease: pathophysiology, diagnosis and management, Philadelphia, 1973, W.B. Saunders Co.
8. McMillan, D.E., and Freeman, R.B.: The milk-alkali syndrome: a study of the acute disorder with comments on the development of the chronic condition, Medicine **44**:485-501, 1965.
9. Reeder, D.D., et al.: Influence of hypercalcemia on gastric secretion and serum gastrin concentrations in man, Ann. Surg. **172**:540-546, 1970.
10. Levant, J.A., Walsh, J.H., and Isenberg, J.I.: Stimulation of gastric secretion and gastrin release by single oral doses of calcium carbonate in man, N. Engl. J. Med. **289**:555-558, 1973.
11. Fordtran, J.S., Acid rebound, N. Engl. J. Med. **279**:900-905, 1968.
12. Algrey, A.C., LeGendre, G.R., and Kaehny, W.D., The dialysis encephalopathy syndrome, N. Engl. J. Med. **294**:184-188, 1976.

13. National Institutes of Health: Antacids-adverse effects, J.A.M.A. **238**:1017-1018, 1977.
14. Morrissey, J.F., and Barreras, R.F.: Antacid therapy, N. Engl. J. Med. **290**:550-556, 1974.
15. Randall, R.E., et al.: Hypermagnesemia in renal failure: etiology and toxic manifestations, Ann. Intern. Med. **61**:73-88, 1964.
16. Goodwin, F.J., and Vince, F.P.: Hypermagnesaemic encephalopathy due to antacid ingestion occurring during regular dialysis treatment, Br. J. Urol. **42**:586-589, 1970.
17. Stanciu, C., and Bennet, J.R.: Alginate/antacid in the reduction of gastro-esophageal reflux, Lancet **1**:109-111, 1974.
18. Pontes, J.F., Richards, D.J., and Sartoretto, J.N.: Double-blind comparison of an oxethazaine-antacid combination (Oxaine M) against the antacid alone (Aludrox) in the treatment of duodenal ulcer pain, Curr. Ther. Res. Clin. Exp. **18**:315-323, 1975.
19. Garnett, W.R.: Antacid products. In Handbook of nonprescription drugs, ed. 6, Washington, D.C., 1979, American Pharmaceutical Association.
20. Meyer, J.H., et al.: Treatment of peptic ulcer disease: a symposium, West. J. Med. **126**:273-287, 1977.
21. Ivey, K.J.: Anticholinergics: do they work in peptic ulcer? Gastroenterology **68**:154-166, 1975.
22. Bodemar, G., and Walan, A.: Cimetidine in treatment of active duodenal and prepyloric ulcers, Lancet **2**:161-164, 1976.
23. Danilevicius, Z.: A new star: how brightly will it shine? J.A.M.A. **237**:2224, 1977.
24. Khalil, S.A., et al.: Effect of magnesium trisilicate and citric acid on bioavailability of tetracycline in man, Pharmazie **32**:519-522, 1977.
25. Brown, D.D., and Juhl, R.P.: Decreased bioavailability of digoxine due to antacids and kaolin-pectin, N. Engl. J. Med. **295**:1034-1037, 1976.
26. Fann, W.E., et al.: Effects of antacids on its gastrointestinal absorption, J. Clin. Pharmacol. **13**:388-390, 1973.
27. Galeazzi, R.L.: The effect of an antacid on the bioavailability of indomethacin, Eur. J. Clin. Pharmacol. **12**:65-68, 1977.
28. Rivera-Calimlim, L., et al.: Absorption and metabolism of l-dopa by the human stomach, Eur. J. Clin. Invest. **1**:313-320, 1971.

29. Connell, A.M., et al.: Variation of bowel habit in two population samples, Brit. Med. J. **2:**1095-1099, 1965.

30. Smith, B.: Effect of irritant purgatives on the myenteric plexus in man and the mouse, Gut **9:**139-143, 1968.

31. Rieman, J.F., and Zimmerman, W.: Ultrastructural studies of colonic nerve plexuses in chronic laxative abuse, Gastroenterology **74:**1085, 1978.

32. Rawson, M.D., Cathartic colon, Lancet **1:**1121-1124, 1966.

33. Thompson, W.G.: The irritable gut, Baltimore, 1978, University Park Press.

34. Rulter, K., and Maxwell, D.: Diseases of the alimentary system: constipation and laxative abuse, Br. Med. J. **2:**997-1000, 1976.

35. Thompson, W.G.: Laxatives: clinical pharmacology and rational use, Drugs **19:**49-58, 1980.

36. Darlington, R.C., and Curry, C.E., Jr.: Laxative products. In Handbook of nonprescription drugs, ed. 6, Washington, D.C., 1979, American Pharmaceutical Association.

37. Donowitz, M., and Binder, H.J.: Effect of dioctyl sodium sulfosuccinate on colonic fluid and electrolyte movement. Gastroenterology **69:**941-950, 1975.

38. Rachmilewitz, D., and Karmeli, F.: Effect of bisacodyl and dioctyl sodium sulfosuccinate on rat intestinal prostaglandin E_2 content, (Na + K)ATPase and adenyl cyclase activities, Gastroenterology **76:**1221a, 1979.

39. Binder, H.J., and Donowitz, M.: A new look at laxative action, Gastroenterology **69:**1001-1005, 1975.

40. Harvey, R.F., and Read, A.E.: Saline purgatives act by releasing cholecystokinin, Lancet **2:**185-187, 1973.

41. Mority, M., et al.: Effects of secretin and cholecystokinin on the transport of electrolyte and water in human jejunum, Gastroenterology **64:**76-89, 1973.

42. Godding, E.W.: Constipation and allied disorders, Pharmaceutical J. **216:**23, 1976.

43. Goth, A.: Drug effects on the gastrointestinal tract. In Goth, A., editor: Medical pharmacology: principles and concepts, ed. 10, St. Louis, 1981, The C.V. Mosby Co.

44. Hofmann, A.F., and Poley, J.R.: Cholestyramine treatment of diarrhea associated with ileal resection, N. Engl. J. Med. **281:**397-402, 1969.

45. Rowe, G.G.: Control of diarrhea by cholestyramine administration, Am. J. Med. Sci. **255:**84-88, 1968.

PART THREE   Special topics

CHAPTER 28

KEITH W. BESLEY

Emergency drugs

Emergency treatment is based on an accurate diagnosis of the problem and consists essentially of the maintenance of respiration and circulation. In dental emergencies the maintenance of these vital processes is generally accomplished by properly positioning the patient and delivering an adequate supply of oxygen (mechanical resuscitation). Drugs are usually only ancillary to these measures. It is impossible to maintain proper perspective on the subject of emergency drugs if it is divorced from diagnosis and the mechanical aspects of resuscitation. However, the intent of this chapter is a discussion of drugs and the emphasis is placed accordingly, with a review of the pharmacology, indication, and related physiology of several drugs that are useful in treating dental emergencies. The choice of drugs for a dental office emergency kit will depend on individual circumstances, experience, and personal preference.

The ultimate goal in any resuscitative effort is the maintenance of adequate tissue oxygenation. The practitioner must therefore assume that the essentials of airway management as well as support of respiration and circulation have been provided for before considering the use of drugs. The brain is unable to survive more than a few minutes under anaerobic conditions before irreversible changes take place. Although the heart and other organs are capable of metabolic adjustment in the form of anaerobic glycolysis, after a relatively short period of partial or complete lack of tissue perfusion and oxygenation, toxic products build up that may lead to an irreversible condition unless corrected. At this point mechanical means of ventilation and perfusion may not be enough, and chemical intervention becomes imperative. The time

□ The opinions or assertions contained herein are the private ones of the writer and are not to be construed as official or as reflecting the views of the Navy Department or the naval service at large.

for drug support depends on the type of emergency. For example, in complete cardiopulmonary arrest no more than 5 to 10 minutes will be tolerated, even when mechanical ventilation and perfusion are provided. On the other hand, a convulsion or airway obstruction may require only mechanical support.

In this chapter several drugs are listed initially that may be considered useful for dental office emergencies with the indicated uses, dosages, and routes of administration. A discussion of the individual drugs then follows. Table 28-1 at the end of the chapter summarizes diagnoses, signs, symptoms, and treatment.

The following list of emergency drugs with indications, adult dosages, and routes of administration is intended to act as a guide in setting up an emergency drug kit for most dental offices.

1. Epinephrine (Adrenalin)—1:1000
   Indications: anaphylaxis, cardiac arrest*
   Dose and route: 0.5 ml intravenously
2. Hydrocortisone sodium succinate (Solu-Cortef)—50 mg/ml
   Indications: cardiac arrest, anaphylaxis, acute adrenocortical insufficiency
   Dose and route: 2 ml intravenously, given slowly
3. Sodium bicarbonate—7.5%
   Indication: cardiac arrest
   Dose and route: 1 mEq intravenously initially, then half this every 10 minutes
4. Diphenhydramine (Benadryl)—10 mg/ml
   Indications: acute allergic reaction,† extrapyramidal reaction to phenothiazine
   Dose and route: 5 ml intravenously

*The most controversial aspect of emergency drugs is the use of vasopressors and particularly epinephrine. A safe statement when dealing with dental office emergencies is to say that there are only two instances in which epinephrine is indicated—cardiac arrest and anaphylactic shock.
†Response is delayed.

5. Aromatic spirits of ammonia—crush ampules
   Indications: syncope
   Dose and route: one ampule, by inhalation
6. Glyceryl trinitrate (nitroglycerin)—0.6 mg tablet
   Indication: angina pectoris
   Dose and route: one tablet sublingually
7. Morphine sulfate—15 mg/ml
   Indication: myocardial infarction
   Dose and route: 1 ml subcutaneously or intravenously
8. Phenylephrine hydrochloride (Neo-Synephrine Hydrochloride)—1:500
   Indications: toxic reaction to local anesthetic
   Dose and route: 1 to 2 ml intravenously
9. Dextrose in water—5%
   Indications: hypovolemia, intravenous route for drug administration
   Dose and route: 1000 ml intravenous drip
10. Diazepam (Valium)—5 mg/ml
    Indication: severe or prolonged convulsion as in toxic reaction to local anesthetic*
    Dose and route: 1 to 8 ml intravenously (titrated)
11. Naloxone hydrochloride (Narcan)—0.4 mg/ml
    Indication: narcotic depression
    Dose and route: 1 ml intravenously or intramuscularly
12. Isoproterenol hydrochloride aerosol—0.25%
    Indication: bronchospasm
    Dose and route: one or two inhalations
13. Physostigmine salicylate—1 mg/ml
    Indication: CNS depression following diazepam administration
    Dose and route: 0.5 to 2 ml intravenously (slow titration)

DISCUSSION OF INDIVIDUAL DRUGS

Epinephrine. The inclusion of epinephrine in a dental office emergency kit is mandatory for the treatment of cardiac arrest and overwhelming anaphylaxis. However, it must be emphasized that these extreme conditions are the *only* situations that would require its use in the dental office emergency. There are a few clinicians who maintain the mistaken belief that epinephrine is the drug of choice in shock or shocklike states. There are three principal reasons for disputing this belief. First, in shock from almost any cause there is decreased venous return to the heart because of peripheral venous pooling. Since the peripheral action of epinephrine is primarily on the arterial side, there is little gain in promoting peripheral vasoconstriction, which is already present because of the massive release of endogenous catecholamines (epinephrine and norepinephrine). At this point administration of epinephrine may further decrease venous

return and tissue perfusion. Second, a possible deleterious effect is an increase in selective ischemia that takes place in certain viscera such as the kidney. Here, as in peripheral vessels, the blood supply is constricted in a compensatory effort to increase blood flow to the more vital brain and heart tissues. Perpetuation of this condition could be undesirable. Third, the possible precipitation of ventricular fibrillation in the ischemic and irritable myocardium is an important factor.[1] This could be especially disastrous in the dental office where defibrillation equipment is usually not available. In early treatment of shock states the patient will benefit more from measures aimed at correction of the primary cause such as hypovolemia rather than misdirected attempts at pharmacologic correction.

The primary reason for using epinephrine in the case of cardiac arrest and severe anaphylaxis is direct (beta$_1$) stimulation of the myocardium. An additional benefit in severe anaphylactic reactions is that epinephrine acts as a physiologic antagonist to the results of massive histamine release such as bronchiolar constriction, which leads to decreased oxygen exchange.

It must be emphasized that the beneficial effects of epinephrine are depressed in the presence of acidosis that accompanies inadequate tissue perfusion.[2] It is therefore mandatory that the administration of epinephrine must be preceded by appropriate mechanical resuscitative measures such as external cardiac massage and support of respiration. Intravenous fluid administration should accompany the use of any vasopressor drug.[3] Epinephrine should not be added to a bicarbonate infusion because its effect may be altered. An alternative dose and route of administration are available when an endotracheal tube is in place. In this case 1 mg of epinephrine may be administered directly through the tube.

Sodium bicarbonate. Within a few minutes of cardiac arrest, metabolic acidosis reaches a critical level. Even when external cardiac massage is employed early, the buildup of lactic acid from hypoxic tissues requires compensatory measures. A safe rule of thumb is to administer 1 mEq/kg sodium bicarbonate intravenously, then one-half this dose every 10 minutes. No more than three or four ampules should be given before laboratory monitoring of acid-base balance is available. Critical acidosis may develop in any form of shock, but the process is seldom as rapid as in cardiac arrest unless the shock state is profound. The patient with severe chronic respiratory disease may develop acute acidosis from respiratory or circulatory

---

*Diazepam or barbiturates are not indicated in convulsion secondary to decreased cardiac output and cerebral anoxia. In this instance a neuromuscular blocking agent is the drug of choice.

failure. The usual manifestations are syncope, tachycardia, sweating, and tremors. In this case sodium bicarbonate is useful as adjunctive therapy. This is not to be confused with the acute asthmatic attack in which a drug such as isoproterenol is often employed to correct bronchiolar constriction. However, the dentist will normally be prepared for either of these eventualities by the patient's history.

Hydrocortisone sodium succinate. The concurrent use of cortisol sodium succinate with other measures in the treatment of cardiac arrest, anaphylactic shock, and acute adrenocortical insufficiency is based on two general actions of the drug: hemodynamic and antiinflammatory. The single 100 mg dose proposed here may result in potentiation of endogenous vasopressor drugs as well as protection against some of their toxic effects, and it may be given without fear of harmful side effects. This treatment is specific in acute adrenocortical insufficiency. The dentist is most likely to encounter this situation in patients receiving long-term steroid therapy or those who have been removed from such therapy within the past year. These patients may not respond normally to a stressful situation, since the effects of endogenous catecholamines will be minimized in the absence of sufficient steroid levels.

Although delayed, the antiinflammatory action of corticosteroid drugs may be beneficial in the severe anaphylactic reaction. Several mechanisms have been proposed. First, the corticosteroids may inhibit the regranulation of mast cells once they have discharged their histamine. The actions of histamine are discussed in another chapter. Second, stabilization of cell and lysosomal membranes is a possible mechanism. In conditions such as cardiac arrest and anaphylactic shock, cell injury is partly caused by tissue ischemia and acidosis, which results in the release of the hydrolytic lysosomes and further cell damage. Some of this may be prevented by the corticosteroids.

Diphenhydramine (Benadryl). Diphenhydramine has been included in this discussion because it is indicated in the allergic reactions, often appearing as urticaria and pruritus after drug administration. Allergic reactions may be accompanied by some degree of respiratory distress. Since the action of antihistamines is competition with histamine for tissue receptor sites, a rapid reversal of allergic symptoms cannot be expected. However, eventual improvement in the sequelae of histamine release such as bronchiolar constriction, capillary dilation, and edema may be expected. This delayed action is of little value in a se-

vere reaction and should not be relied on as primary therapy.

Diphenhydramine is often the drug of choice in the treatment of extrapyramidal reactions after the administration of phenothiazine drugs such as chlorpromazine (Thorazine), prochlorperazine (Compazine), promazine (Sparine), and trifluoperazine (Stelazine). These drugs are sometimes used by the dentist for premedication or as antiemetics. Symptoms of extrapyramidal reactions from phenothiazine may include restlessness, spasms of neck or back muscles, rolling back of the eyes, trismus, difficulty in swallowing, and parkinsonian type of movements. Not infrequently the patient is referred to the dentist for a spontaneous temporomandibular joint dislocation. Although it is seldom life threatening, the reaction can be a terrifying experience for the patient who is conscious but unable to control the abnormal muscular contractions. The intravenous administration of 2 to 5 ml diphenhydramine will reverse the majority of these symptoms in seconds or minutes. Although the response is usually rapid and dramatic, the fact should be pointed out that the reaction may recur in hours, days, or even several weeks. Therefore the patient should be so informed and observed even though phenothiazine therapy is discontinued. In the more severe reactions antiparkinsonian drugs may be required.

Aromatic spirits of ammonia. The signs, symptoms, and treatment of syncope are well known by every dentist. The typical beads of perspiration on the upper lip are seen fairly often and are automatically recognized as one of the signs of impending syncope. Also typical are the weak thready pulse, cold clammy skin, pallor, and dizzy feeling that may proceed to unconsciousness. Loss of normal vasomotor tonus produces pooling of blood peripherally so that the normal blood volume becomes insufficient. Thus the practice of placing the patient in a supine position and elevating his feet is, in effect, giving a transfusion of whole blood by utilizing the forces of gravity. However, it should be emphasized that the object is to return blood to the heart for circulation to the brain; consequently, the head should not be more than about 10 degrees lower than the rest of the body. Extreme Trendelenburg position may result in an artificially increased pressure in the carotid sinus with a reflex decrease in blood pressure.

Inhaled ammonia irritates trigeminal nerve sensory endings, with a resulting reflex stimulation of medullary respiratory and vasomotor centers. The administration of oxygen will aid in combating tissue anoxia.

Syncope is usually psychogenic and represents only a transient problem in normal individuals. However, in the cardiac patient even a short period of tissue ischemia may be serious. The dentist must be aware that the signs and symptoms of syncope may represent a progressive or more serious condition.

Glyceryl trinitrate. The use of glyceryl trinitrate (nitroglycerin) for the relief of anginal pain is common, but its mechanism of action is not completely clear. It has been assumed for some time that dilation of the coronary arteries produces relief from the pain of myocardial ischemia. There are more potent coronary vasodilators that do not afford the same relief from anginal pain. However, the clinical effectiveness of glyceryl trinitrate has made it the most frequently used medication for relief of angina pectoris.

In patients who suffer from frequent anginal attacks, glyceryl trinitrate may be administered before the stress of dental treatment is experienced. When this prophylactic use is being considered, the practitioner should remember that some decrease in blood pressure may occur because of peripheral vasodilation. This becomes more important in patients taking drugs that tend to produce orthostatic hypotension. *Rauwolfia* drugs (reserpine), methyldopa (Aldomet), and hydralazine (Apresoline) are some of the more commonly used antihypertensive drugs that tend to produce orthostatic hypotension.

When glyceryl trinitrate is placed in an emergency kit, it should be marked with the date, since the effective shelf life is about 6 months.

Angina pectoris is characterized by a usually stress-related, sudden onset of crushing chest pain that may radiate to the left arm, shoulder, neck, or mandible. Shocklike symptoms may also be present. The usual treatment consists of a 0.6 mg tablet held under the tongue with the patient in a semiprone or sitting position. Relief will normally be obtained within 2 or 3 minutes. Removal of the stressful situation, calm reassurance, and the administration of a high flow of oxygen are important aspects of the treatment. Failure to respond to this treatment is a sign of myocardial infarction. Persistent pain may require the administration of morphine. A physician should be consulted as soon as possible when myocardial infarction is suspected.

Some of the commercially prepared drug kits contain amyl nitrite in crush ampules, which is a more potent coronary dilator but is more likely to produce nausea and vomiting. A disadvantage of placing amyl nitrite in the kit is that although the crush ampule is yellow, it may be mistaken for the white ampule of ammonia. The accidental use of a vasodilator in syncope could lead to a more serious condition, especially in the patient with some degree of cardiac insufficiency.

Morphine sulfate. Morphine sulfate is administered to the patient with acute myocardial infarction for the relief of pain and to allay apprehension. Also, the central depression produced reduces the amount of cardiac work through a reduction in the release of endogenous catecholamines.[4] Peripheral hemodynamic effects tend to decrease myocardial oxygen requirements. The route of administration is usually subcutaneous, but intravenous injection is best if circulation is impaired.

Phenylephrine hydrochloride (Neo-Synephrine Hydrochloride). Phenylephrine hydrochloride is a vasopressor that acts directly on alpha adrenergic tissue receptors. Stimulation of these receptors produces primarily an increase in vascular resistance in the peripheral, gastrointestinal, and renal arterioles. The heart is stimulated *indirectly* through an increase in venous return with a resulting increased arterial pressure and reflex slowing of the heart rate.[4] The reason for the selection of phenylephrine as the vasopressor of choice is its lack of direct myocardial stimulation. This is of importance in the dental office emergency where, in the face of an undiagnosed cardiac arrhythmia or irritable myocardium, the possibility of contributing to or producing ventricular fibrillation must be minimized. The use of phenylephrine hydrochloride in cases of severe or prolonged depression after the administration of a local anesthetic has the advantage of positive action when it is needed yet minimizes the chance of deleterious effects. Vasopressors offering the same advantage are angiotensin amide (Hypertensin) and methoxamine hydroxide (Vasoxyl Hydroxide). If signs of significant peripheral vasoconstriction are present in addition to hypotension, an alpha adrenergic agent should not be used.

Many commercially available drug kits contain a vasopressor that acts on both alpha and beta adrenergic receptors. Here one of the actions is direct myocardial stimulation. This action is found in such drugs as norepinephrine, mephentermine (Wyamine), metaraminol (Aramine, Pressonex), and methamphetamine (Methedrine). It is my opinion that these drugs should not be used by the dentist in early treatment of dental office emergencies; their use should be relegated to a qualified physician when a proper diagnosis has been established.

5% dextrose in water. An intravenous route for drugs and fluid should be established in any serious dental office emergency. Most of the drugs used in an emergency situation are more effective if given intravenously. Fluid replacement is needed early in hypovolemia or peripheral vascular collapse. One of the ultimate results of shock in any form is a loss of intravascular fluid. Although the dentist is usually not directly responsible for the management of long-term fluid administration, he should at least initiate treatment in any emergency. There are some instances where this is imperative. Such is the case when vasopressors are employed.[3] On the other hand, there are instances where the rate of fluid administration should be minimal until adequate monitoring of vital signs, such as CVP, is available. This is true, for example, in the patient with congestive heart failure and in children.

Although there are instances where solutions such as Ringer's lactate, physiologic saline, plasma expanders, or whole blood are more appropriate, the type of solution given initially in an emergency is not as important as establishing an intravenous route. Five percent dextrose in water is compatible with all drugs and does not complicate acid-base balance problems.

Diazepam. In recent years diazepam (Valium) has become popular as an anticonvulsant. It has the advantages of relative safety if the dose is carefully titrated and of versatility as to route of administration in that it can be given either intravenously or intramuscularly. Except in high doses and for children or elderly patients, diazepam has little potential for cardiovascular or respiratory depression. This is a definite advantage when it is compared with the barbiturates or neuromuscular blocking agents. In this respect slow intravenous administration is best to titrate dosage for the individual response. The range may be from 2 to 40 mg; if it is given intramuscularly, 5 to 10 mg increments would be appropriate.

It should be emphasized that in the majority of cases convulsive episodes are usually self-limiting and require only supportive care in the form of protection of the patient from physical harm and, in some cases, the administration of positive pressure oxygen. This is especially true of convulsion secondary to decreased cardiac output and cerebral hypoxia. In this instance, anticonvulsants are contraindicated, and corrective measures should be directed toward tissue oxygenation. The most likely cause of a convulsive episode in the dental office is a toxic reaction to local anesthetic from overdose or idiosyncrasy. Here the problem is primarily one of central depression. Although the initial phase of the reaction may be manifested by stimulation in various forms, including convulsion, in dealing with lidocaine, the stimulation is actually caused by depression of central inhibitory centers.[5] The eventual or, in some cases, initial response is respiratory and circulatory depression. It is logical therefore to be conservative in the use of anticonvulsant drugs, which may enhance this central depression. On the other hand, a convulsion may occasionally be severe enough to be life threatening in the form of respiratory embarrassment and require drug intervention. Each dentist must decide for himself, before the occasion arises, when to intervene chemically and what drug to use.

The neuromuscular blocking agents, such as succinylcholine (Anectine), are potent anticonvulsants, but their use requires special skill and equipment concerned with support of respiration in the paralyzed patient. They are therefore not recommended for use in the dental office except by the trained specialist. The actions of these drugs are discussed in another chapter.

Naloxone hydrochloride (Narcan). Naloxone is a pure narcotic antagonist with little pharmacologic activity of its own. For this reason it has largely replaced nalorphine (Nalline) as an emergency kit narcotic antagonist. Its use in the reversal of narcotic depression is extremely safe with one major precaution: the duration of action may be shorter than that of the narcotic being antagonized. It is therefore imperative that the patient be constantly observed for signs of returning respiratory depression.

An initial adult dose of 0.4 mg (1 ml) is usually given intravenously but may be given subcutaneously or intramuscularly. Onset of action is approximately 2 minutes when the intravenous route is used but will be slightly slower for the intramuscular or subcutaneous route. Basic resuscitation should continue until an adequate response is noted. It may be necessary to repeat the initial dose if spontaneous respiration does not occur within a reasonable time period. It should be emphasized that naloxone hydrochloride is effective in reversing respiratory depression caused by opiate-derived drugs so that other causes must be considered when there is no response.

The mechanism of action is not firmly established, but it is likely that at least part of the effect is that of competitive antagonism whereby naloxone competes for receptor sites with the opioid.

Table 28-1. Summary of dental office emergencies

Diagnosis	Signs and symptoms	Treatment
Syncope	1. Pulse weak and slow 2. Skin pale, cold, and clammy 3. Dizziness or loss of consciousness	1. Supine position 2. 100% oxygen 3. Ammonia crush ampule

Toxic reaction to local anesthetic	1. Loss of central inhibitory centers
	  a. Apprehension, restlessness
	  b. Increase in blood pressure and respiratory rates, tachycardia
	  c. Convulsion
		1. Supine position
		2. Positive pressure oxygen
		3. In *severe* case; diazepam, 1-8 ml IV (titrated)

	2. Signs of central depression
	  a. Decreased level of consciousness
	  b. Decreased blood pressure and respiratory rate, bradycardia
		1. Continue to support respiration as necessary
		2. IV infusion of 5% dextrose in water
		3. Phenylephrine, 1 ml IV if severe or prolonged

Cardiac arrest	1. Sudden collapse 2. Absence of carotid pulse 3. Dilated pupils 4. Cold, pale extremities or cyanosis	1. Sharp blow to precordium; repeat if necessary 2. External cardiac massage 3. Positive pressure oxygen 4. Epinephrine, 0.5 ml IV; repeat as needed 3 to 8 minutes 5. IV infusion of 5% dextrose in water 6. Sodium bicarbonate, 10 ml per 5 minutes of arrest 7. Hydrocortisone sodium succinate, 2 ml IV (slowly)

Isoproterenol (Isuprel). Isoproterenol aerosol is indicated for the relief of acute bronchospasm associated with bronchial asthma or as an adjunct in the treatment of allergic reactions. The actions of isoproterenol are discussed in Chapter 5. Because of cardiac stimulation, isoproterenol should not be used in patients with known cardiac arrhythmias. Correct diagnosis is important to rule out dyspnea caused by problems such as airway obstruction. In this case auscultation of the chest will give sufficient evidence of the expiratory wheeze of bronchospasm. If a patient with a sudden onset of respiratory difficulty has received a general anesthetic agent, the most likely cause is laryngospasm, and it should be treated accordingly. In any case 100% oxygen should be administered.

Physostigmine salicylate (Antilirium). The intravenous use of diazepam for sedation is common in oral surgery and has become increasingly popular in other dental specialties as well as general dentistry. Although safe in well-controlled situations, diazepam may produce prolonged depression or even respiratory arrest and coma. This can occur with relatively small doses.[6] Reversal of these effects may be obtained with the use of physostigmine salicylate. The actions of physostigmine as an anticholinesterase are discussed in Chapter 5. The mechanism of action in reversing the adverse effects of diazepam is unknown at this time. Slow administration is the key to avoiding undesirable side effects such as bradycardia and hypersalivation. The dosage range is 0.5 to 2.0 mg intravenously; the drug should not be administered faster than 1 mg per minute. The initial dose should be 0.5 to 1 mg, and 15 minutes should elapse before additional medication is considered. A reduced dose is indicated if excessive sweating or nausea occurs. In oral surgery practice, diazepam is often combined with other drugs such as narcotics. In this instance naloxone hydrochloride should probably be administered first in the event of excessive or prolonged depression.

SUMMARY

Table 28-1 reviews some of the possible dental emergencies and suggested treatment. Some dentists have found it useful to make up cards for each major

Table 28-1—cont'd

Diagnosis	Signs and symptoms	Treatment

Allergic reaction
  1. Mild
 	
  2. Anaphylactic
	1. Urticaria
	2. Pruritus
	3. Tightness in chest
	4. Sudden collapse
	5. Fall in blood pressure, tachycardia
	6. Cardiac arrest
		1. Diphenhydramine, 5 ml IV or IM
		2. Epinephrine, 0.5 ml IV
		3. External cardiac massage and positive pressure oxygen as needed
		4. IV infusion of 5% dextrose in water
		5. Hydrocortisone sodium succinate, 2 ml IV (slowly)

Angina pectoris	1. Sudden, severe chest pain; may radiate to left arm, neck, or mandible 2. Extreme apprehension 3. Increased blood pressure, tachycardia	1. Sitting position 2. Oxygen 3. Nitroglycerin, 0.6 mg tablet sublingually 4. Reassurance
Myocardial infarction	1. Similar to angina but prolonged and no response to nitroglycerin 2. Arrhythmia	1. Sitting position 2. Oxygen 3. Morphine, 1 ml IM
Acute adrenal insufficiency	1. History of long-term steroid therapy 2. Weakness, syncope 3. Decreased blood pressure, tachycardia	1. Supine position 2. Oxygen 3. Hydrocortisone, 2 ml IV (slowly)
Extrapyramidal reaction (phenothiazines)	1. Restlessness 2. Eyes rolled back 3. Spasm of neck or back muscles (head extended) 4. Trismus 5. Difficulty in swallowing 6. Parkinsonian symptoms	1. Diphenhydramine, 5 ml IV
Respiratory depression (narcotics)	1. Shallow, slowed respirations 2. Tachycardia 3. Coma	1. Naloxone, 1 ml IV, IM, or SC
CNS depression (diazepam)	1. Prolonged or deep sedation (coma) 2. Respiratory depression, arrest	1. 100% oxygen 2. Physostigmine salicylate, 0.5-1.0 ml IV (slowly)
Bronchospasm	1. Dyspnea 2. Expiratory wheeze 3. Differentiate from obstruction or laryngospasm	1. Isoproterenol aerosol, 1 or 2 inhalations 2. 100% oxygen

emergency situation to include diagnosis, signs and symptoms, and treatment. It is convenient to place this card in a clear plastic bag with the drugs used in treatment of that particular condition.

REFERENCES

1. Goodman, L.S., and Gilman, A.: The pharmacological basis of therapeutics, ed. 6, New York, 1980, Macmillan Publishing Co., Inc.
2. Wood, W.B., Manley, E.S., Jr., and Woodbury, R.A.: Effects of CO_2-induced respiratory acidosis on depressor and pressor components of the dog's blood pressure response to epinephrine, J. Pharmacol. Exp. Ther. **139:**238-247, 1963.
3. Clauss, R.H., and Ray, J.E., III: Pharmacologic assistance to the failing circulation, Surg. Gynecol. Obstet. **126:**611-629, 1968.
4. DiPalma, J.R., editor: Drill's pharmacology in medicine, ed. 4, New York, 1971, McGraw-Hill Book Co., p. 364.
5. Monheim, L.M.: Local anesthesia and pain control in dental practice, St. Louis, 1969, The C.V. Mosby Co., p. 144.
6. Larson, G.F., Hurlbert, B.J., and Wingard, D.W.: Physostigmine reversal of diazepam-induced depression, Anesth. Analg. **56:**348-351, 1977.

CHAPTER 29

RICHARD L. WYNN

Pharmacology of intravenous sedation

Intravenous sedation is a useful technique in dentistry and utilizes those central nervous system (CNS) depressant drugs that have the actions of sedation, antianxiety, or tranquilization. Sedative drugs consist of a variety of pharmacologic agents from several drug groups, including the barbiturates, the nonbarbiturate sedative-hypnotics, the narcotic analgesics, the psychosedatives, and the minor tranquilizers. The intent of this chapter on the pharmacology of intravenous sedation is to review the degrees of CNS depression that can be induced by drugs, to classify the CNS depressants according to the degree of depression they produce, and to discuss the pharmacology of each individual agent used in intravenous sedation techniques. Some of the information presented in this chapter has been discussed in Chapter 9, which examines the general use of these sedative drugs. Some repetition is necessary, however, to relate this information to the intravenous use of drugs for sedation. Although not a sedative, ketamine is also discussed with respect to its pharmacology, since it is a useful agent in intravenous techniques. Clinical considerations of intravenous agents are mentioned only briefly and only in the context of their pharmacologic effects. For more detailed discussion on clinical uses of these intravenous agents in dentistry and on intravenous techniques in general, the reader is referred to Chapter 30 and to several review articles.[1-8]

DEGREES AND MECHANISMS OF CNS DEPRESSION

The depressant effects of drugs on the CNS are caused by actions on the reticular activating system (RAS), the medulla, and the cerebral cortex. The so-called reticular core within the CNS is composed of an intertwining net of small neurons coursing through portions of the medulla and midbrain. Within this network exists the RAS, which is a complex group of neuronal pathways extending into the hypothalamus and thalamus. Normal activity within the RAS maintains a conscious alert state by projection of ascending neuronal activity through the thalamus and into the cerebral cortex. Depression of the neuronal activity within the RAS results in sedation and hypnosis. Sedation is defined as a state of drowsiness or mental clouding, and for the purposes of this discussion will be considered synonymous with tranquilization or antianxiety. During sedation, intermittent periods of hypnosis may occur. Hypnosis is a depression of the CNS resembling normal sleep. The patient can be aroused, and there is no analgesia present.

The medullary areas of the brain function to control autonomic reflexes of the circulation, heart, and lungs. These reflex areas are known as the vital centers, because damage to them is usually fatal. *Respiratory depression* results from the direct depression of respiratory control within the medulla. Both the respiratory drive and the mechanisms responsible for the rhythmic character of respiratory movements are depressed. Depression of excitatory pathways within the cerebral cortex in addition to the depression of the RAS result in loss of consciousness. *General anesthesia* is traditionally defined as a loss of consciousness from which a patient cannot be aroused and is accompanied by analgesia. With the advent of the so-called dissociative anesthetics, however, general anesthesia can also be defined as that state in which a patient is insensitive to pain, has a blockage of noxious reflexes, and exhibits generalized muscle relaxation, with or without the loss of consciousness.

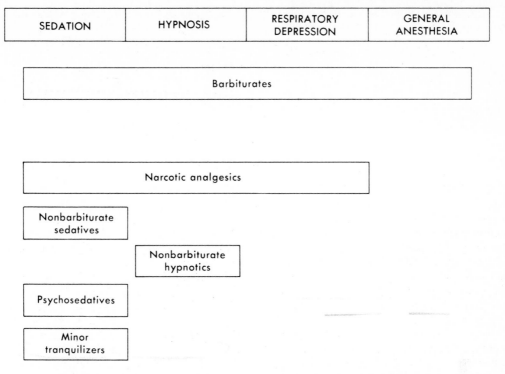

Fig. 29-1. Degree of CNS depression with usual therapeutic doses of depressant drugs.

CLASSIFICATION OF CNS DEPRESSANTS

The CNS depressants can be classified according to the degree of depression produced by therapeutic doses (Fig. 29-1). The actions of *barbiturates* range from sedation to general anesthesia, depending on the specific barbiturate. For example, phenobarbital induces sedation and some hypnosis at therapeutic doses. Respiratory depression or general anesthesia is uncommon with this drug except in cases of overdosage. Other barbiturates such as thiopental or methohexital, however, induce hypnosis, respiratory depression, and general anesthesia at therapeutic doses. The actions of the *narcotic analgesics* differ slightly from those of the barbiturates in that their depressant effects range from sedation to respiratory depression with therapeutic doses. The *nonbarbiturate sedatives* most commonly induce sedation with little hypnosis at therapeutic doses. The nonbarbiturate hypnotics produce hypnosis at therapeutic doses rather than sedation. The *psycho-*

sedatives and *minor tranquilizers* elicit sedative actions but have little hypnotic effects at therapeutic doses.

The nonbarbiturate sedatives include methyprylon (Noludar), chloral hydrate (Noctec), and ethchlorvynol (Placidyl). The nonbarbiturate hypnotics consist of methaqualone (Parest, Quaalude), glutethimide (Doriden), and ethinamate (Valmid). The nonbarbiturate sedatives and hypnotics are not available for intravenous administration and will not be included in this discussion.

Barbiturates

The barbiturates most useful in intravenous sedation include thiopental and methohexital. Thiopental is a sulfurated type of barbiturate and is considered to be the prototype of the intravenous anesthetics—those intravenous drugs inducing a true anesthesia. Methohexital is an oxybarbiturate, containing a methylated nitrogen atom on the ring structure. The chemical structures of thiopental and methohexital are as follows:

H N O
S
CH$_2$CH$_3$
N CHCH$_2$CH$_2$CH$_3$
H O
CH$_3$

Thiopental

H N O
O
CH$_2$CH=CH$_2$
N CHC≡CCH$_2$CH$_3$
CH$_3$ O

Methohexital

Both drugs are insoluble in water and are supplied for clinical use as the water-soluble sodium salt. Included in each preparation is sodium carbonate, which makes the solutions strongly alkaline (pH 11). On injection, the sodium carbonate is neutralized in the bloodstream, and the drugs revert back to their original chemical form from the sodium salts. Pentobarbital and secobarbital are also available for parenteral use and are effective as intravenous sedatives.

Barbiturates are general depressants to all tissues in the body, and the CNS is most sensitive to the depressant actions of these drugs. The barbiturates act on the RAS to depress the ascending neuronal conduction. Consciousness is not maintained, since there results a lack of ascending projection activity into the cerebral cortex. As a result, hypnosis ensues. With smaller doses some projection activity apparently remains, resulting in sedation rather than hypnosis. Doses of the barbiturates above the hypnotic dose will cause a true anesthesia, which is caused by the direct depression of excitatory pathways within the cerebral cortex in addition to the depression of the RAS.

Intravenous doses of thiopental, ranging from 2.0 to 3.5 mg/kg over a 15- to 30-second interval, will induce a general anesthesia. After induction supplemental doses may be given to maintain anesthesia, with the total dose not exceeding 1.0 gm. Intravenous doses of methohexital ranging from 1.0 to 1.4 mg/kg will induce general anesthesia. The duration of action of the intravenous barbiturates at these doses is extremely short—approximately 10 to 15 minutes—and

recovery may be accompanied by periods of restlessness.

Respiration must be carefully monitored when using these agents, because they are highly potent respiratory depressants. Respiratory effects of the barbiturates are a result of direct depressant actions on the medullary and pontine areas of respiratory control. Respiration is normally maintained by three physiologic influences: (1) a neurogenic control originating in the higher brain centers, which stimulates the medullary centers to drive respiration; (2) a chemical drive in which changes in blood pH and Pco$_2$ levels act on the medulla to control respiration; and (3) a hypoxic stimulus mediated by the chemoreceptors of the carotid and aortic bodies. Hypnotic doses of a barbiturate depress the neurogenic control of respiration so that control is dominated by the chemical drive, with the hypoxic drive still functional. Anesthetic doses diminish both the chemical and the hypoxic control. As intoxication doses increase, the chemical control is eventually inhibited with a shift in control of respiration to the hypoxic drive. At sufficiently high doses the hypoxic drive will also fail, and respiration will cease altogether. The margin between CNS depression and dangerous respiratory depression is sufficient to permit the barbiturates to be used as intravenous sedatives and anesthetics.

The effects of thiopental and methohexital on the cardiovascular system are mild and do not constitute a hazard in normal clinical practice. Myocardial contractility may be depressed by direct actions on the heart. Also, the medullary vasomotor center is depressed, resulting in a decreased heart rate. These drugs exert mixed effects on vascular resistance. Vascular resistance is usually decreased in the skin and increased in visceral tissues and in the CNS, resulting in an increase in total peripheral resistance. Studies with methohexital, however, have demonstrated that total peripheral resistance is most often decreased by this drug.[9]

Thiopental and methohexital rapidly penetrate all tissues because of their lipid solubility. This accounts for their rapid action, since they pass so rapidly into brain tissues. The rapid emergence from sleep after the intravenous administration of these two drugs is caused by a redistribution from the brain to other tissues. The rate at which various tissues take up the drugs is related to blood flow. Thus the brain and other visceral organs exhibit maximal concentrations within 30 seconds after administration. Soon, however, skeletal muscle becomes saturated, whereas fat depots accumulate the drugs several hours after administration. As the muscle and fat take up the drugs, plasma levels fall, and the drugs diffuse out of the brain. Consciousness is thus restored. Barbiturates may remain in the body fat for a period of days, which accounts for the cumulative effects of repeated doses of these drugs. Thiopental and methohexital are metabolized in the liver at a rate of 15% to 20% per hour.[10] The metabolic products result from oxidation by liver microsomal enzymes. In general, the metabolic products thus formed retain no hypnotic activity and are eliminated by way of the kidney.

Complications associated with the use of intravenous barbiturates include laryngospasms and muscle twitching. Methohexital has a greater incidence of muscle movements and causes hiccough on frequent occasions. The use of any barbiturate is absolutely contraindicated in patients with a medical history of acute intermittent porphyria. In this disease the porphyrins, the components of hemoglobin, are produced in excess. Barbiturates ordinarily stimulate specific enzymes to increase the production of porphyrins. In the case of porphyria, barbiturates will cause exacerbation of the disease process itself, and a fatal course is not uncommon. Most barbiturates are anticonvulsant in nature, and selected barbiturates are useful in the treatment of grand mal epilepsy.

Thiopental or methohexital should not be administered to patients who are taking other depressants or monoamine oxidase inhibitors (MAOIs), since serious drug interactions may occur. MAOIs are used for antidepression effects in some neurotic patients. Patients taking these drugs have experienced severe barbiturate intoxication after therapeutic doses of barbiturates.

Narcotic analgesics

Narcotic analgesics useful in intravenous sedation techniques include morphine, meperidine (Demerol), anileridine (Leritine), and fentanyl (Sublimaze).

Morphine. Morphine is a constituent of opium. A 3 to 15 mg intravenous dose of morphine produces euphoria, a sense of well-being. Drowsiness and mental clouding will occur with the drug and will last up to 2 hours. Respiration will be depressed in proportion to dose, with maximal depression occurring about 7 minutes after injection. No amnesia occurs with morphine, and there is little or no effect on the cardiovascular system when the drug is injected

slowly. Although theoretically useful, the drug is rarely if ever used for intravenous sedation techniques in dentistry. Morphine can be used parenterally for severe pain. A dose of 10 to 15 mg subcutaneously will obtund severe pain of dental origin for about 6 hours.

The following are the CNS effects after the administration of morphine. Analgesia occurs selectively by acting on the CNS at doses that do not induce sleep or affect other sensory pathways such as touch, hearing, or vision. Morphine induces hypnosis, which resembles normal sleep or that produced with small doses of barbiturates. Hypnotic effects of the drug are dose related and characterized by easy arousal. The probable mechanism is a depression of the RAS. The medullary respiratory center is extremely sensitive to morphine. Death from overdoses of the drug is caused by respiratory arrest. The mechanism of respiratory depression is a decrease in the sensitivity of the respiratory center to increases in P_{CO_2}. The vasomotor center may be depressed, resulting in a slowing of the heart and orthostatic hypotension.

Absorption of morphine is rapid after parenteral administration, and body distribution is favored in visceral tissues such as the lung, liver, kidney, and brain; it does not accumulate in fat tissues as the barbiturates do. Deactivation of the drug occurs through metabolism in the liver. Most of an administered dose is conjugated with glucuronic acid—a normal constituent of the body. A small amount of morphine is N-demethylated to normorphine. The drug is excreted by way of the kidney in the form of the glucuronic acid conjugate. Approximately 90% of an administered dose is excreted in 24 hours.

Morphine is contraindicated in patients suffering from biliary colic because of its ability to stimulate contractions within the bile duct. Patients suffering from severe asthma or chronic lung disease should not be given the drug because of its effect on respiration. The ability of morphine to cause constriction of the musculature of the bronchioles also contraindicates its use in the asthmatic patient. Morphine should be administered with caution in patients with conditions of hepatic insufficiency because the liver is the site of deactivation of the drug.

Meperidine (Demerol). Meperidine is a synthetic narcotic analgesic and does not occur naturally like morphine. Although it is pharmacologically similar to morphine, it is much less potent, and 60 to 80 mg meperidine are equal in analgesic potency to 10 mg morphine. Like morphine it produces analgesia and sedation-hypnosis. Also, its medullary effects are similar to those of morphine. It causes respiratory depression and depresses the vasomotor reflexes to cause slowing of the heart and orthostatic hypotension. Meperidine is well absorbed by all routes of administration. Metabolism occurs in the liver with the formation of the glucuronic acid conjugates of two oxidative metabolites of the drug. The conjugates are subsequently excreted in the urine.

Meperidine is an excellent agent with which to produce conscious sedation in the ambulant dental patient. When administered intravenously in small incremental doses, meperidine produces a calmed, somewhat euphoric patient while providing some degree of analgesia. Adult intravenous doses range between 50 and 100 mg. In most cases little or no respiratory depression is seen, and at this dose, dizziness is the most common complication. Postural hypotension may also occur if an erect posture is rapidly assumed. Meperidine should be administered with caution in patients medicated with the phenothiazine type of drugs, since enhancement of respiratory depression has been reported with these agents. Imipramine (Tofranil) and desipramine (Pertofrane) represent a group of antidepressant agents that are widely used in cases of endogenous depression. Both of these drugs have been shown to exert a dangerous supraadditive effect on meperidine-induced respiratory depression. MAOIs have produced deep coma in the past and extreme hypotension, resulting in a depression crisis when taken simultaneously with meperidine.[11,12]

Anileridine (Leritine). Anileridine is chemically related to meperidine. It is approximately two and one half times as potent as meperidine, having an adult intravenous sedative dose of 25 mg. It is similar to meperidine in its pharmacologic effects and duration of action.

Fentanyl (Sublimaze). Fentanyl is also chemically related to meperidine. The structure of this narcotic analgesic is as follows:

Fentanyl

It is the most potent of the narcotics used in intravenous sedation, being about 500 times more potent than meperidine and 150 times more potent than morphine. Its intravenous dose ranges from 0.05 to 0.2 mg. The drug has an immediate onset of action and a duration of 30 minutes and is the shortest acting narcotic analgesic available for use in intravenous sedation. Profound respiratory depression is a feature of fentanyl, and muscle rigidity has been described after its use. The muscle rigidity results in occasional "stiff chest syndrome," which has caused a reduction of chest wall compliance to make lung inflation difficult. Fentanyl has not been found to cause clinically significant cardiovascular depression, although it has a parasympathomimetic effect on the heart, accounting for bradycardia.

Fentanyl is metabolized by the liver microsomal enzyme systems to N-dealkylated and hydroxylated products. The scheme on p. 351 shows this metabolism.

Psychosedatives (phenothiazines)

Phenothiazines with important sedative actions include chlorpromazine, promethazine, and propiomazine. Phenothiazines affect the RAS and subcortical areas to cause drowsiness that is associated with easy arousal. They do not act on the cortex, like barbiturates or narcotic analgesics, and they do not block ascending neuronal projections in the RAS. Thus true hypnosis or general anesthesia is not produced by these drugs.

Phenothiazines are useful adjuncts for the control of fear and apprehension in many dental patients. Their contribution to intravenous sedation techniques is that they elicit psychomotor slowing and emotional quieting and allow the patient to be indifferent to environmental stimuli. These drugs elicit few side effects after the administration of single intravenous doses. Orthostatic hypotension is the most prevalent complication, and rare complications include respiratory depression and extrapyramidal reactions. Phenothiazines that are most useful in the production of conscious sedation include promethazine (Phenergan) and propiomazine (Largon) in intravenous doses of 25 to 50 mg and 10 to 20 mg, respectively. There is no overt effect on respiratory depression with small doses of the phenothiazines. Analgesia may or may not be demonstrated by the phenothiazines, depending on the compound. Chlorpromazine and other phenothiazines have consistent effects on the cardiovascular system, and they block the autonomic vaso-

Fentanyl metabolism

pressor tone of the peripheral vasculature. They cause direct relaxation of smooth muscle within the cardiovasculature to cause vasodilation. They also depress the contraction of the myocardium. The overall result of these three cardiovascular actions are hypotension and reflex tachycardia.

The phenothiazines are well absorbed by all routes of administration. They are also well distributed in tissues, and deactivation occurs through metabolism in the liver. The most common pathway of metabolic deactivation is the formation of glucuronic acid derivatives. Excretion occurs both in the urine and feces mostly as metabolites.

The use of phenothiazines is contraindicated in patients with myasthenia gravis because of their ability to cause relaxation of the skeletal musculature. Their use is also contraindicated in patients with epilepsy because of their ability to lower seizure thresholds within the CNS. Drug interactions between phenothiazines and CNS depressants are to be expected. These drugs will especially potentiate the respiratory depressant effects of meperidine, barbiturates, and morphine.

Minor tranquilizers (benzodiazepines)

Chlordiazepoxide (Librium) and diazepam (Valium) are the prototype drugs of a class of sedatives that differ chemically from other sedatives discussed so far. This class of sedatives is known as the benzodiazepines, which pharmacologically are classified as the minor tranquilizers.

Chlordiazepoxide as the prototype benzodiazepine has a definite sedative action, and produces tranquilizing effects that are indistinguishable from sedation. Chlordiazepoxide exhibits anticonvulsant effects in animals. The drug has been advocated as a central-acting skeletal muscle relaxant, since it has been shown to abolish spastic rigidity in animals. Chlordiazepoxide, although available parenterally, has not been used as an intravenous sedative in dentistry.

Diazepam differs from chlordiazepoxide in several aspects. It is a more potent anticonvulsant and muscle relaxant, its potency being approximately two and one half times that of chlordiazepoxide; it has a shorter duration of action when taken orally; and it will produce amnesia in many individuals when administered intravenously. When injected intravenously, diazepam will elicit a calming effect in the dental patient. In most cases the patient will also experience euphoria. Perhaps the most unique action of diazepam, as mentioned earlier, is in its amnesic properties. Approximately 50% of the patients experience retrograde amnesia in that they will not recall any of the events of the dental procedure. If amnesia is produced, its duration will be approximately 45 minutes. The intravenous dose useful for antianxiety and amnesic effects range from 2.5 to 15 mg. Diazepam has a complex metabolic fate, with the formation of the metabolic products probably occurring in the liver. Several metabolites appear in the urine and include the N-demethylated derivative, a hydroxylated compound, the N-demethylated hydroxylated compound (oxazepam), and the glucuronide conjugates.

Diazepam is an extremely safe drug with the doses used in intravenous sedation techniques. Perhaps the only complications are irritation at the injection site and postural hypotension. Diazepam has little if any effect on respiration or the cardiovascular system. The combination or concurrent use of diazepam with other drugs that the patient may be taking and that may produce additive or supraadditive effects should be avoided. These include barbiturates, phenothiazines, and the imipramine type of antidepressants such as imipramine (Tofranil) and amitriptyline (Elavil). Diazepam is suspected of having anticholinergic properties. Thus it is advised that the drug not be used in patients with glaucoma, since anticholinergic agents tend to enhance the glaucoma condition. In addition, diazepam should be used with caution in elderly patients, who are reportedly extremely sensitive to its effects.

Lorazepam (Ativan) is the most recent benzodiazepine approved for use as an intravenous sedative. Chemically it is a chloro derivative of oxazepam (refer to Chapter 9). Lorazepam is used orally as a sedative, hypnotic, and antianxiety agent, and parenterally for preoperative conscious sedation. Administration of 2 to 4 mg intravenously or intramuscularly in adults produces sedation, relief of preoperative anxiety, and in many cases an amnesic effect similar to that seen with diazepam. Advantages of lorazepam over diazepam seem to be a more rapid metabolic deactivation and less irritation at the injection site.

Neuroleptanalgesia and dissociative drugs

Neuroleptanalgesia is defined as a state of CNS depression with tranquilization and intense analgesia produced without the use of barbiturates or volatile anesthetics. Dissociative analgesia is defined as a state in which the patient is "dissociated" from his environment, resembling a state of catalepsy. In addition, amnesia and analgesia are present. If unconsciousness occurs in either case, the conditions are referred to as neuroleptanesthesia and dissociative anesthesia. Two drugs are required to produce the state of neuroleptanalgesia—a neuroleptic component and an analgesic component. Neurolepsis is a term applied to characterize a behavioral syndrome in animals and humans caused by these types of drugs. In experimental animals, this syndrome consists of the loss of voluntary movement, cataleptic immobility, and inhibition of learned conditional behavior.

All the neuroleptic drugs useful in neuroleptanalgesia chemically consist of a four-carbon chain linked to an amino group and at least one aromatic group such as a phenyl group. Also, a keto group (c=O) is required for high potency. Such a chemical structure is known as 4-phenylbutylamine or butyrophenone, the structure of which is as follows:

Butyrophenone

A butyrophenone derivative used in neuroleptanalgesia is haloperidol, an agent that exhibits much greater potency than butyrophenone itself. Another derivative is droperidol, which is approximately twice as potent a neuroleptic agent as haloperidol. Droperidol is the butyrophenone derivative most commonly used in neuroleptanalgesia at the present time. The structures of haloperidol and droperidol are as follows:

Haloperidol

Droperidol

The analgesic component of the neuroleptanalgesic technique is fentanyl. The pharmacology and use of fentanyl in intravenous sedation is discussed earlier and in Chapter 30.

Droperidol is classified pharmacologically as a major tranquilizer. It has an inhibitory effect on voluntary behavior and a significant antipsychotic effect in humans. Effects on the basal ganglia result in extrapyramidal dyskinesias, which are similar to those extrapyramidal effects caused by the phenothiazines. Droperidol inhibits the chemoreceptor trigger zone in the medulla to prevent emesis. In the presence of droperidol, function is well maintained in the RAS. Thus consciousness is maintained. The butyrophenones have little if any effect on the respiratory and circulatory (vasomotor) centers within the medulla. Droperidol is active within 5 minutes after injection, and its effects last between 6 and 12 hours.

Neuroleptanalgesia can be induced with a fixed 50:1 mixture of droperidol (2.5 mg/ml) and fentanyl (0.05 mg/ml) known as Innovar. Since droperidol has an extremely long duration of action (6 to 12 hours) compared with fentanyl (15 to 30 minutes), many clinicians believe it is unsafe to inject the two components as a fixed mixture. Thus the two agents are also available separately as Inapsine (droperidol, 2.5 mg/ml) and Sublimaze (fentanyl, 0.05 mg/ml). Clinical induction doses of Innovar result in a sedated but conscious patient with the following clinical symptoms. First, the patient appears resting, the eyes are closed, and the face is expressionless. The patient will talk clearly and rationally when spoken to. Second, the patient will be in an immobilized state with an absence of any voluntary muscle movement. Third, profound analgesia will be present. Fourth, amnesia most likely will occur, although it will not always be complete.

Side effects resulting from the administration of Innovar are caused by the actions of either the droperidol or fentanyl. Extrapyramidal effects of Parkinson's syndrome and dyskinesia are seen in a minority of patients. On rare occasions tetanus-like muscular contractions have been reported, which are caused by the droperidol. Other effects include muscular rigidity, hypotension, and respiratory depression, which are caused by the fentanyl.

Substances chemically related to hallucinogenic drugs such as lysergic acid diethylamide (LSD) have been proposed as anesthetics. The first of these, phencyclidine, caused unfortunate psychologic effects, including hallucinations. More recently a re-

lated drug, ketamine (Ketalar), was synthesized and used clinically. Chemically, ketamine differs from all other drugs used in intravenous sedation and has a structure as follows:

Ketamine

Ketamine is used either intravenously or intramuscularly in doses of 1 to 2 mg/kg and 4 to 6 mg/kg, respectively. When so used, it causes dissociative anesthesia because during induction the patient feels dissociated from the environment, including even his or her own extremities. Analgesia and amnesia occur. Muscle relaxation is poor, but respiration is not affected. Overall, the patient appears awake, with the eyes open but detached from external stimuli. The patient does not respond to painful stimuli and does not become hypnotic.

The site of action of ketamine in the brain is considered to be in the thalamus and cortex. The mechanism within these areas is unknown, however. The midbrain RAS is little affected. Also, there is no effect of the drug on medullary structures. Thus it has no sedative or hypnotic effects, since the RAS is spared, and it has no effect on respiration, since the medulla is spared.

Ketamine elevates arterial blood pressure and pulse rates in patients. The pressor effect is probably caused by an increase in cardiac output. Emergence phenomena are considered to be the most prevalent undesirable effect of ketamine. Vivid dreams are frequently noted by patients, some of which have been unpleasant, involving distortion of body image and temporal and spatial relationships. Diazepam and droperidol have been effective in preventing emergency phenomena.

Ketamine is not recommended for use in the adult patient or hypertensive patient. Muscular rigidity and heightened pharyngeal and laryngeal reflexes make oral procedures difficult. Actual operative time using ketamine is 30 to 50 minutes without supplemental doses, but the actual recovery times may be 2 to 3 hours.

REFERENCES

1. Foreman, P.A.: Pain control and patient management in dentistry—a review of current intravenous techniques, J. Am. Dent. Assoc. **80:**101-111, 1971.
2. Zauder, H.L., and Nichols, R.J.: Intravenous anesthesia, Clin. Anesth. **3:**317-358, 1969.
3. Trieger, N.: Intravenous sedation, Dent. Clin. North Am. **17:**249-261, 1973.
4. Dundee, J.: Comparative analysis of intravenous anesthetics, Anesthesiology **35:**137-148, 1971.
5. Kenney, W.M., and Rudo, F.G.: A review of intravenous sedation techniques in dentistry, J. Balto. Coll. Dent.-Surg. **29:**12-28, 1974.
6. Bennett, C.R.: Conscious sedation in dental practice, ed. 2, St. Louis, 1978, The C.V. Mosby Co.
7. Allen, G.D.: Dental anesthesia and analgesia, ed. 2, Baltimore, 1979, The Williams & Wilkins Co.
8. Wynn, R.L., and Kohn, M.W.: The pharmacology of intravenous sedation, Chicago, 1976, American Society of Oral Surgeons.
9. Bernhoff, A., Eklund, B., and Kaijser, L.: Cardiovascular effects of short-term anaesthesia with methohexitone and propanidid in normal subjects, Br. J. Anaesth. **44:**2-7, 1972.
10. Brand, L., et al.: Physiologic disposition of methohexital in man, Anesthesiology **24:**331-335, 1963.
11. Shee, J.C.: Dangerous potentiation of pethidine by iproniazid and its treatment, Br. Med. J. **2:**507-509, 1960.
12. Vigran, I.M.: Potentiation of meperidine by pargyline, J.A.M.A. **187:**953-954, 1964.

Parenteral sedation and nitrous oxide analgesia

Many experienced dental patients recognize the technologic progress made in their behalf, and consequently they have become more cooperative, appreciative, and less anxious patients. Most dental patients being treated in modern dental offices by aware, competent, and considerate dentists receive the benefits of comprehensive dental care in relative comfort with either oral or no sedation. There remain, however, a number of dental patients who, because of past experiences, hearsay, or their own psychologic being, approach dental appointments with varied degrees of apprehension, dread, or reluctance. To manage these patients effectively, the dentist needs to consider more predictable methods of sedation. To this end, agents and techniques of parenteral sedation as well as nitrous oxide analgesia will be considered. It is not intended that this chapter will prepare the dentist to accomplish parenteral sedation or nitrous oxide analgesia. The objective here is only to familiarize the reader with considerations relative to these techniques that will provide a sound basis for supervised training in their administration.

PSYCHOLOGICAL ASPECTS OF PATIENT MANAGEMENT

At the outset, the dentist's appreciation of the patient must be manifested by a careful consideration of the patient's needs relative to the procedure or procedures to be accomplished. The psyche cannot be separated from the physical human being. Consequently, both aspects of the patient demand very close attention. Many successful practitioners credit the major portion of the high esteem in which their patients hold them simply to the rapport that they have developed with each of them *personally*. Clearly, patient management requires the consideration of an indi-

vidual with a sincere appreciation of personal needs, desires, and fears. The dentist must have an empathy that is appreciated by the patient. With patient trust and confidence, in many instances one can achieve patient acceptance of unpleasant sensory situations that otherwise would cause severe, undesirable reactions.

The patient must be "examined" in his entirety, not just orally. The short discussion and observation period that this entails also serves as an ideal time to discuss what procedures the dentist plans and the conditions under which they will be accomplished. The patient needs to know what to expect, whether it be the type of preoperative sedation or steps in the procedure proper. The patient who is fully informed and thus properly prepared for the dentist's procedure will withstand it infinitely better than the one to whom it becomes a series of increasingly unpleasant surprises.

MEDICAL HISTORY

As the patient should be known to the dentist both orally and psychologically, so too should the patient's medical status be completely appreciated. No practitioner should consider the administration of any type of medication, or indeed even routine dental care, without full comprehension of the medical status of the patient. It is repeatedly emphasized that the advances of medical science have succeeded in increasing the life-span of patients who previously would not have survived. Many of these patients with extensive medical problems do not consider themselves as unusual because they have grown accustomed to living with their malady. Others are hesitant to volunteer information regarding their condition. There are many well-designed formats to elicit the information required to assess the current status of a patient or to determine if medical consultation may be indicated before dental therapy. It behooves each practitioner to choose the medical history form that may best be actively integrated into the practice.

The dentist should ensure that the history form that is used not only asks questions of general health but also provides space for listing medications that the patient is taking. This allows the dentist to avoid drug interactions. Specific examples of drug interaction are noted when individual drugs are discussed later. This consideration is set forth for emphasis because this is an area that formerly was given little attention in discussions of drug prescription, and it is one that is becoming increasingly complex and important.

In summary, the dentist has the responsibility to ascertain the patient's medical status, including current or recent past medications, and to assess these factors in light of the physical and psychologic needs of the patient.

LIMITATIONS OF ORAL SEDATION

The routine use of drugs for premedication has generally been accomplished by oral administration. By utilizing the recommended dosage and thoroughly understanding the properties of the drugs used, oral premedication has proved to be exceedingly safe. This has resulted from the standardization of doses in tablets or capsules that provide a wide range of safety for the normal adult. There are, of course, people who will be oversedated by the administration of 100 mg secobarbital orally; however, the curve of safety relative to dosage with these drugs is so skewed toward providing safety that a large proportion of the population will have sedative effects of less than the desired degree. In effect, the safety of oral medications is achieved by using standardized dosages, with a resulting compromise in the consistency of sedation achieved. In the instances in which adequate sedation is not attained, the dentist has not achieved the objective and has not properly prepared that patient for the procedure. To administer additional doses of oral medications to these patients when it becomes apparent that more sedation is in fact required will result in dosages beyond the standard. The premise of high degrees of safety is then lost. One must remember that once an oral medication is administered, the practitioner has lost all control of the effects of that dosage. Additionally, a protracted time period must be allowed to ensue before additional sedative effects are realized. Efficient office routine is thus disrupted.

There are certainly significant numbers of patients in daily practice who can be adequately premedicated with oral medication; however, the point to be realized is that standardized drug dosage yields widely variable results, not all of which can be considered as adequate sedation. In those patients in whom oral premedications have proved to be inadequate, in the severely anxious patient, in the obstructive child, and in the patient in pain, consideration should be given to the parenteral administration of premedicants.

INTRAMUSCULAR SEDATION

The intramuscular route of administration provides more certain absorption, a faster onset, and more predictable results than are obtained with oral sedation. The principal disadvantages of the intramuscular over the oral route are more complicated delivery, less patient acceptance, and greater cost. As with oral premedication, there is an inability to remove the drug if overdosage or overreaction occurs. In comparison with the intravenous route, intramuscular administration has a slower onset. Like the oral route, safe dosages still provide a range of sedative effects. The use of specific drugs in intramuscular sedation are discussed later.

INTRAVENOUS SEDATION

The principal disadvantage of intravenous sedation is that the potent drugs being used make mandatory the avoidance of excessive dosages with resultant untoward depression of the cardiovascular, respiratory, or central nervous systems. It is a hazardous procedure unless the clinician is adequately trained. He must be equipped and competent not only to administer the drugs but also to treat and control adverse reactions and complications.

Each member of the dental treatment team should be assigned specific responsibilities in the event of a medical emergency. There should be posted emergency call numbers, including rescue squad, ambulance service, emergency room, or nearby dentist or physician(s) who have agreed to be source persons in an emergency. Each office must be equipped with a discrete, mobile source of oxygen, airways, and an up-to-date emergency kit. It is axiomatic that drug usage in these instances must be known or prominently displayed and cannot be researched at the time of sedative difficulty. For these reasons, intravenous sedation is discussed in some detail.

The practice of intravenous administration of drugs, of recent interest in the United States, has long been accepted as routine in undergraduate teaching in Great Britain. Many practitioners regard intravenous sedation as involving more risks, being dangerous, or being in the realm of general anesthesia. It is, however, the most effective method of ensuring *predictable, adequate* premedication in *each* patient. By injection of the premedication drugs in small increments over an appropriate time span, with constant patient observation, each patient may be brought to that degree of sedation that ensures patient comfort and provides the necessary degree of cooperation to enable the operator to accomplish the planned procedures. This is the principle of *titration* to achieve the desired effect. Since the clinician has continuous control over the amount of drug given, it is not necessary to administer more than is required for adequate sedation. Essentially, in the oral and intramuscular routes, the whole drug dosage is administered at one time, whereas in intravenous administration, small increments allow minute-to-minute control over the level of sedation. Individual patient variance is thus eliminated as a factor of dosage. As previously noted, certain training requirements and precautions are required, of course, and a new set of potential complications evolve that the practitioner must be aware of and be prepared to avoid or treat.

Disadvantages

Initially, the introduction of intravenous sedation, as with any other newly introduced office technique, will require an increased expenditure of time. As facility increases and experience is gained, this disadvantage will be overcome, and indeed the time required for many procedures may be decreased because of patient cooperation thus secured.

The technique requires the placement of a needle into a vein. Although many people dread this experience, it is usually met with more acceptance than intraoral injections. Although intravenous sedation requires the concomitant use of local anesthesia, the patient is put into such a relaxed and at times amnesic state that the intraoral injection is not objectionable. Many times the patient will not remember the intraoral injection or have hazy recollections of its administration.

The utilization of parenteral sedative techniques does require the maintenance of sufficient quantities of various drugs in the office. Secure storage facilities are required, and an increased risk of forced entry must be assumed.

Although the foregoing are considerations, the overwhelming restriction imposed by this technique is that the operator must have knowledge of the procedures and the agents used and also comprehend fully the implications, restrictions, and complications of these agents. This is not the technique for the individual seeking an easy resolution to sedation problems. Intravenous sedation must be approached in a totally committed manner. There exists a sufficient body of knowledge in texts and the literature in all phases of sedation to provide the didactic background that is required. The true student and dedicated, conscientious practitioner must realize that one chapter, one text, or one "short course" is inadequate preparation for introducing this technique into a practice. Additional requirements in the realm of emergency drugs, equipment, their use, and even the venipuncture technique are not added burdens but represent facets of practice for which the dentist should already have prepared in consideration of emergencies in the dental office.

If the disadvantages presented seem overwhelming, a point has been made. This technique is demanding in regard to competence and attention to detail; however, many of its facets should already be within the expected standard of practice. Additionally, the advantages of the use of intravenous sedation are such that its use should have consideration in the daily practice of a significant number of practitioners.

Complications

As with all new techniques, the operator must become acquainted with a new set of complications. For the most part, complications are a result of lack of knowledge or inattention to detail.

Care must be taken at the time of drug infusion to prevent extravascular injection of the agent. This complication is the result of inattention and may be eliminated by developing good technique. The needle point must be carried a distance beyond vein entry to ensure intravascular drug administration. Before and during the injection, aspiration will easily determine the adequacy of the venous system in use. If inadvertent extravascular administration occurs, it may be treated by the infiltration of up to 10 ml of a 1% solution of procaine hydrochloride in the area. This provides the following functions:

1. It dilutes the agent injected.
2. It causes vasodilation and hence speeds the absorption of the agent. Note that lidocaine will not afford this function.
3. Barbiturates are highly alkaline. The procaine hydrochloride will tend to neutralize the alkalinity of the barbiturates and prevent tissue slough.

The most serious mechanical error is intraarterial injection. This, like the extravascular injection, is an error of technique. It may be prevented by palpation of the contemplated injection site before tourniquet placement, knowledge of the anatomy of the upper extremity, and close observation of hydrostatic pressures affecting the syringe at the time intravascular puncture has been achieved. The patient may complain of a severe radiating pain progressing distally from the puncture site, which is a result of vasospasm of the violated artery. The vasospasm of the artery may cause blanching of the skin in its peripheral distribution. Thrombus formation may subsequently occur, and, when it is extensive, gangrene may follow, and amputation may sometimes be necessary. The treatment of intraarterial injection may be divided into two phases:

1. *Immediate office treatment:* An attempt to maintain the needle in the artery should be made. If successful, 10 ml of 1% procaine hydrochloride is injected. This serves to dilute the agent (if one has been injected), relax the vasospasm, and ease the patient's pain.

2. *Consultation:* Depending on the results of the office therapy, consideration should be given to possible hospitalization and the performance of cervicothoracic ganglion (sympathetic interruption) blocks, or the administration of anticoagulants to the patient.

Perhaps the most common adverse sequela to intravenous utilization is the occurrence of thrombophlebitis. In these instances the vein will feel hard or ropelike along its path. This may be treated by resting the arm, elevating the arm, and applying hot soaks to the area.

The incidence of this complication may be dramatically reduced in many cases by dilution of the injected drug. This can be accomplished by injecting the drug into a flowing intravenous infusion. If the procedure is to be short, many experienced operators

do not think the inconvenience and additional cost of an intravenous infusion is necessary. Categorically it might be stated that the beginning sedationist should use such a system to provide prompt access for injection of emergency drugs, should this be needed. If the operator is, however, sedating with a direct intravenous injection, he may, by placing the drug in a larger syringe, aspirate blood from the system before injection and thus dilute the irritant chemical before injecting it into the vein. Added dilutions may also be accomplished. This is a method that has been used by members of our department for a number of years and has reduced the incidence of thrombophlebitis to nearly zero. It does, however, mandate the clinician to perform mental calculations at each aspiration to compensate for each dilution and to ensure knowledge of the actual administered drug dosage. The sedationist should also periodically review the FDA bulletins as well as the manufacturers' literature on drugs being used to check for any recommended changes in the method of drug administration. For example, two sedation techniques formerly described in the literature are no longer recommended because specific drugs in those regimens should no longer be used intravenously.

Respiratory or circulatory depression, or both, from overdosage should not occur in the well-managed sedative regimen; howver, the practitioner must be prepared to support respiration and circulation should overdepression occur.

Members of the dental staff should realize the medicolegal responsibility of ensuring that the patient and the responsible adult escort are both impressed with the patient's mental and physical limitations. The sedated patient *must* be accompanied home by a responsible adult. The patient and escort should know both the *degree* of restriction (i.e., not driving; avoiding stoves, stairs, or curbs; not making legal or business decisions) as well as the *length* of the restriction. It should be noted that many people who have been sedated for a dental procedure will leave the office with a "high" or a euphoric feeling but be mentally incompetent. These patients present great risk if they convince their escort that they indeed can perform such functions as driving themselves home. The doctor should realize that any postoperative instructions given to a sedated patient may be completely ignored; thus any special instructions should either be written or well understood by the patient in advance. The use of other drugs or self-administered agents (such as alcoholic beverages) should also be defined for the patient. Written instructions and a discussion with the patient before sedation, with the competent adult escort, or preferably with both parties, should ensure the safest transportation and care for the patient.

Precautions

Intravenous sedation must be accomplished by a strict aseptic technique. This involves a skin preparation usually accomplished with alcohol sponge wipedown. Today, a wide variety of prepackaged, sterile, disposable syringes, intravenous devices, and tubing is available, and their use is preferable for consistent maintenance of an aseptic routine.

The degree of patient monitoring necessary during drug administration and the operative procedure will vary directly with the degree of depression desired. With sedative techniques, pulse, respiration, and blood pressure monitoring should be adequate. There is an increasing variety of monitoring devices being made available to the profession. Depending on locale and practice, the acquisition of currently available devices may be advisable.

As with all procedures, a record should be maintained that at least indicates presedation vital signs, time and dosages of drugs administered, periodic vital signs, and a statement of the patient's progress and condition, including vital signs, when the procedure was concluded. Complete, accurate records are mandatory in this facet of dental practice.

Considerations in the performance of venipuncture

A detailed description of venipuncture technique is not within the purview of this text; however, a few significant points are vital enough to require emphasis.

Just as the dentist does not perform dental procedures without knowledge of the anatomy involved, so too the dentist should not accomplish venipuncture without a knowledge of the anatomical structures in the area and their relationships. Although a detailed consideration of anatomy will not be presented, it is important that the arterial pathways of the upper extremity be partially defined. The arm is supplied by the brachial artery, which divides into the radial and ulnar arteries at or slightly distal to the cubital fossa. Although the venous pathways of the forearm are variable, three main vessels proceed toward the el-

bow: the median, basilic, and cephalic veins. The median vein, as its name implies, courses between the other two vessels on the medial surface of the forearm and ends in the area of the cubital fossa by sending branches to the basilic and cephalic veins. The median-basilic vein is usually more prominent and appears as the most likely suitable vein in this area. Just deep to the median-basilic vein, however, lies the brachial artery, with only a fascial layer intervening. In light of previous discussions on intraarterial injections, it becomes apparent that this vein should be avoided despite its being a most attractive target.

The veins of the hand are located dorsally, a physiologic location to permit palmar action without impeding blood flow. When these veins are used for venipuncture, the patient may at times note some pain in the hand. This may be caused by the presence of arteriovenous shunts resulting in drug action initiating vasospasm of the arteries so affected.

In the distal forearm, arterial pathways seldom border as closely on venous drainage routes. Veins in the dorsal hand as well as the distal forearm constitute the main area of interest in intravenous sedation techniques.

Contraindications

There are three overriding considerations that form absolute contraindications to the intravenous sedative technique. The first of these concerns the uninformed and incompletely trained operator, which has already been discussed. The second deals with the facilities available. Before using this technique, the clinician must equip the office with a method of positive-pressure oxygen administration as well as a separate motor-driven suction apparatus. Additionally, the office suite must provide recovery space in which oxygen and suction are available. The office assistants must be trained as part of a team for the administration, intraoperative care, and recovery period observation. The third absolute contraindication consists of those systemic diseases and drug administration that compromise respiration or the cardiovascular system or that mandate the avoidance of specific drugs or procedures. The medical history and physical findings combined with the psychologic nature of the patient determine the feasibility of these techniques.

PREMEDICANTS AND TECHNIQUES

A definition of the uses and delineation of the disadvantages of a few specific agents that I consider to be of most value for office sedation follow. In this way it is hoped that the reader will achieve a useful appreciation of these agents rather than have a broad overview of the subject, which serves little practical purpose.

Barbiturates

The barbiturates are excellent agents for the relief of apprehension, but they do not have analgesic properties. Indeed Dundee and Wyant[1] note that small doses of barbiturates may cause exaggerated responses to painful stimuli. This facet of barbiturate usage has been recognized for many years and is responsible for the recommendation that barbiturates alone should not be used as sedative agents for patients in pain. When sedation is indicated for patients in pain, a suitable analgesic agent should thus be selected to offset the CNS effect of the barbiturate. As with any other combination therapy, the additive or possibly synergistic effects of the agents must be considered.

Indications for use

1. As a sole agent for preoperative sedation in pain-free patients and for procedures in which pain is not inherent or can be adequately controlled by local anesthesia
2. As a combination agent, providing the sedative effects in a barbiturate-analgesic (narcotic) technique

The barbiturates will depress the respiratory center, diminishing respiratory drive mechanisms, and hence cause a decreased respiratory minute volume. This effect is largely dose related. This becomes a consideration in the use of these drugs in patients with existing respiratory disease or compromise. Death from barbiturate overdosage is by way of profound respiratory depression. Concomitant use with many other drugs should be accomplished with a realization of possible interaction or synergism. The most common of these would be the phenothiazines, alcohol, reserpine, and the antihistamines. Drug abusers will require larger doses for sedation but will also show the depressant effects of the combination and will not usually exhibit tolerance to the respiratory depressant effects of these agents. The chronic marijuana user has peripheral vasodilation that is physiologically compensated for to result in little change in blood pressure. If barbiturate administration causes vasodilation in the compensating (constricted) vessels, profound hypotension may result that would be diffi-

cult to resolve. Patients may exhibit a cross-tolerance with other depressant agents. This may be caused by activation of increased degrees of liver enzyme function. Thus, the patient who imbibes alcohol freely may, in the absence of marked liver involvement, require larger drug doses to achieve sedative levels.

The histamine release that occurs after intravenous administration with these agents could cause asthmatics to be more likely to have a bronchospasm with these agents. This may be tragic; however, it may be minimized by injecting fractional doses slowly in an intravenous technique. This consideration should be seriously considered when choosing a sedative agent for the asthmatic patient. As anesthetic doses are approached, a hypotensive effect will be noted, caused in part by peripheral vasodilation. This effect will be greater in an upright position. One should not effect rapid changes in patient position because of the slow compensation of the peripheral vascular system. This is especially true at the end of a procedure if the patient has been treated in a reclining or semireclining position. Rapid elevation to a sitting position or allowing the patient to quickly stand might result in a sudden onset of postural hypotension and collapse. The patient with adrenal insufficiency that is not adequately managed by steroid replacement therapy, if challenged with barbiturates, will have prolonged sedative effects, hypotension, and pronounced respiratory depression. Barbiturates increase the rate of coumadin metabolism and thus must be used with care in patients taking these drugs. Any barbiturate is contraindicated in patients with porphyria. These agents will pass the placental barrier and also appear in the mother's milk. The young patient is moderately resistant to these agents and may require proportionally larger doses than the usual adult patient. The elderly patient is moderately more sensitive to these agents, and consideration should be given to a decreased or smaller dosage in these patients.

Contraindications and precautions

1. Definite contraindications
   a. Patients with an allergy to these agents
   b. Patients with already compromised respiratory function
   c. Patients with porphyria
2. Liver disease or dysfunction—smaller dosage adjustment or totally avoided in moderately affected patients

3. Concomitant drug therapy as it affects CNS, respiratory, or cardiovascular depression
4. Age
   a. Young—moderately resistant
   b. Elderly—moderately sensitive
5. Histamine release (asthmatic precaution)
6. Postural hypotension potential
7. Adrenal status
8. Pregnancy or lactation

Intramuscular use. If the patient is not experiencing pain, these drugs may be utilized alone as premedicants. At least 30 minutes should intervene after injection before operative procedures are instituted. Vital signs should be monitored, and a well-equipped emergency kit and oxygen should be available and familiar to the operator and the staff.

The dosage may be adjusted according to the procedure being contemplated, the degree of anxiety of the patient, and the patient's physical status. For example, a muscular adult athlete may be expected to require a somewhat proportionally larger dosage than a slightly built individual, with all other factors being equal; the alcoholic will usually require an increased dose, unless liver disease is present. Clinical judgment will effect more exact and suitable individualized dosages as experience is gained with the technique. Intramuscular techniques will usually provide a more positive and predictable sedative level than do oral medications, but they too result in a range of sedative effects. The technique is applicable when this range, more defined than with oral medication, is acceptable and desired by the operator and patient.

The intramuscular dosage of the barbiturate pentobarbital is as follows:

Pentobarbital (Nembutal) dosage: available in 50 mg/ml solution
Normal adult—50 to 150 mg intramuscularly
Children with normal height and weight relationships—1 to 2 mg/lb, up to 100 mg

Intravenous use. A convenient practice is to dilute 150 mg of pentobarbital (3 ml) with 7 ml sterile water for injection. This provides a 10 ml syringe, with each milliliter of solution containing 15 mg of the agent. An intravenous route is established, and 0.25 ml of the solution is first administered as a test dose. The patient is observed and the vital signs compared with preadministration values to detect significant untoward effects. If there are no such effects, an additional 3.75 to 4.75 ml of solution are administered, yielding a total injected dosage of 60 to 75 mg. This is

accomplished over 30 to 45 seconds while the dentist converses with the patient. At this point an additional 60 seconds are allowed to elapse to permit the assessment of the effects of the administered dosage. *In normal, healthy patients a 1-minute delay after injection of a quantity of these drugs may be expected to elicit nearly the full pharmacologic effect of that drug administration.* * Additional increments of 15 mg (1 ml) are then injected until a relaxed, cooperative patient is secured without excessive depression or until cortical symptoms of dizziness or tiredness are achieved. Before each increment, a 45- to 60-second delay is mandatory to prevent excessive depression, that is, to assess at all times the current status of the patient. As the patient approaches the desired sedative levels, clearly observable signs occur, including slurred speech, the patient stating that the room is revolving, difficulty in focusing, talkativeness, a happy, intoxicated state; in other words, the patient has become relaxed and no longer anxious. At any subsequent stage, additional increments may be added to maintain this level of sedation. One should appreciate that the dilution of the agent provides ease in administration of small additional fractions of the drug. Also, because the barbiturates are very alkaline in nature, dilution reduces the chemical insult to the vein, helping to prevent phlebitis. As in all intravenous administrations, care should be taken to avoid accidental intraarterial injection.

During administration, pulse and blood pressure should be checked periodically, with clinically significant depression calling for cessation of further drug injections. During the dental procedure the degree of sedation, the patient's reactions, and his vital signs may be used to monitor the depression of systems.

If thought is given to the dosages required to achieve sedation and to those dosages that are toxic, the difference, which represents the margin of error or conversely the degree of safety inherent with the drug, is wide enough so that pentobarbital may deserve consideration as the initial drug for the practitioner introducing intravenous technique into the practice. Goodman and Gilman state that although the lethal dose of barbiturates varies, ''severe poisoning is likely to occur when more than ten times [10X!] the

---

*Obviously, in sick or debilitated patients or those in shock, this generalization is not true. The management of these patients must be individualized, preferably in a hospital setting.

full hypnotic dose has been ingested at once.''[2] Clearly, these drugs, if not abused, provide a wide range of safety not found with other premedicants.

The duration of sedative effects may extend for 2 to 4 hours. This technique is ideal to allay apprehension and provide sedation for procedures that may be time consuming and unpleasant for the patient. Adequate local anesthesia is a requirement in view of former discussions relative to barbiturates and pain. If the procedure is manifestly painful or will entail postoperative pain, consideration should be given to the utilization of subsequently described techniques.

Narcotics

Although morphine remains the standard on which other narcotics are judged, its uses in dentistry remain minimal. In contrast, meperidine (Demerol) has found wide clinical acceptance. Meperidine tends to produce sleepiness but produces euphoria to only a slight degree. Like the barbiturates, meperidine will depress the respiratory center, and its effects last up to 4 hours. In usual analgesic doses, it has minimal effect on bronchial musculature. It may produce bronchospasm when given in larger doses. As with morphine, histamine release does cause concern with use in asthmatic patients. Meperidine has been used in smaller doses in treating patients with threatened status asthmaticus. If implicated in the precipitation of an asthmatic attack, the ill effects appear to be respiratory depression instead of actual bronchiolar constriction. Its use in asthmatic patients thus must be considered carefully with the possible consequences in mind. Meperidine has the potential to cause hypotension, although this primarily occurs in erect patients, with little such tendency in patients in the recumbent position. This tendency toward postural hypotension should be included as one of the precautionary notes when premedicated ambulatory patients are released.

Meperidine has an atropine-like effect, which may result in some degree of xerostomia. Like morphine the drug may cause the undesirable side effects of nausea, vomiting, and dizziness. It is primarily metabolized in the liver; hence liver disease will result in retardation of its destruction. Meperidine passes the placental barrier.

Respiratory depression secondary to overdose can be antagonized by nalorphine, 5 to 10 mg intravenously, with repeated doses as necessary but not to exceed 40 mg. Recently naloxone (Narcan) has found increasing clinical use as the narcotic antagonist of choice. It does not have the opiate-like effects of nalorphine and levallorphan and hence exerts little, if any, pharmacologic effects beyond pure narcotic antagonism. Intravenous administration will usually bring reversal of narcotic-induced effects within 2 minutes. The duration of action is up to 2 hours, which may be *less than* the depressant effects of the narcotic. Continued observation until narcotic effects have ceased and repeated antagonist administrations are thus the rule for the treatment of narcotic-induced respiratory depression. The adult dose of naloxone is 0.4 mg (1 ml) intravenously, repeated as necessary in 2- to 3-minute intervals, up to three doses. Each dental office in which narcotics are administered should have a narcotic antagonist readily available.

It is vital to be absolutely certain that meperidine is not administered to any patient who has been recently or is now taking an MAOI. The combination of meperidine and MAOI intake may result in delirium, convulsions, and possibly death. This drug has a moderate degree of safety, although not to the same degree as the barbiturates.

The intramuscular dosage of meperidine is as follows:

Meperidine (Demerol) dosage: available in 50 mg/ml solution
Normal adult—50 to 100 mg
Children with normal height and weight relationships—0.5 mg/lb

When used in intravenous techniques, this agent is titrated. Dosages may be less than or within the above noted ranges, depending on the sedation and depression obtained with the true sedative agent used.

Meperidine is seldom used alone as a premedicant drug, but rather it is used in combination with other agents. An intravenous technique that has received considerable recognition is the Jorgensen technique.[3] Many years ago Jorgensen combined the analgesic and sedative effects of meperidine with the sedative effects of pentobarbital. He also found that by administering the barbiturate first, the high incidence of nausea and vomiting with meperidine was eliminated. This produces a pleasant amnesic and analgesic state without the loss of consciousness. A significant advantage gained with the technique is that it tends to compress the time frame of reference for the patient so that a 2-hour appointment will seem like 30 minutes or less. The technique is as follows:

The patient should be made aware of the sequence of events at this appointment. He should be accompanied by a responsible person, one physically able to assist him, and should be aware of the physical and mental postoperative restrictions as noted previously. The supine position is preferable to avoid hypotensive episodes. Background distractions should be minimized, including instrument set-up, talking between staff, and excessive movement in the room. A syringe of pentobarbital with the solution having a concentration of 10 mg/ml pentobarbital is prepared. An intravenous route is established, and a test dose of approximately 3 mg pentobarbital is administered to observe any untoward reaction. In the absence of a reaction, 10 mg (1 ml) of the agent is subsequently injected every 30 seconds until a light stage of sedation is achieved. With the observance of the first sign of cortical depression, such as noted earlier, a stage has been reached that Jorgensen considers to be the "baseline." The dose required to reach this stage will vary from 20 to 200 mg. With added experience in the technique, a variable additional increment may be added for more effective sedation. This augmentation will be in the range of 10% to 15% above baseline dosage. The syringe is removed and replaced with a fresh syringe. All traces of the barbiturate must have been cleared from whatever infusion system is utilized, since meperidine and the barbiturates together form an insoluble precipitate. The fresh syringe contains 25 mg meperidine and 0.32 mg scopolamine, which have been diluted to form 5 ml of solution. The dilute solution permits slow infusion to achieve constant dose control. As these medications are injected, the patient's pulse is monitored, and at the first sign of depression the injection is terminated. For the person who has taken over 100 mg pentobarbital to reach the baseline, the entire contents of the second syringe will probably be required. This dosage is not exceeded.

The sedation procedure is now complete and will last more than 2 hours. The scopolamine will produce amnesia and decrease the patient's memory of the procedure.

The technique is not without its disadvantages. Obviously, approximately 10 minutes will be required to achieve the sedative stage. The duration of action of the drugs employed results in a long time span of effect. These two aspects make the technique less desirable for short procedures.

Tranquilizing drugs

Diazepam (Valium) is one of a group of tranquilizing drugs that has found ready acceptance as a premedicant in dental practice. Additionally, it provides muscular relaxation and a degree of amnesia. The amnesia produced by the drug is not retrograde in type; that is, amnesia for events immediately before the injection is not usually expected.[4,5] Amnesia does

follow the intravenous injection of diazepam closely. Driscoll and colleagues[6] studied the effects of intravenous diazepam sedation on patients having multiple extraction or on patients with impaction and treated on an outpatient basis. The total titration dose of diazepam averaged 19.04 mg for patients with impaction and 18.4 mg for patients having extraction. These dosages did not result in significant changes in cardiopulmonary function. They were responsible for producing amnesia in 53.9% of patients for the intraoral injection as tested on the day of surgery and in 70.6% for the injection procedure as measured at the postoperative visit. Gregg and coworkers[7] also showed that amnesia was attained without significant alteration of the level of consciousness or depression of the cardiopulmonary systems. They showed that amnesia of controlled stimuli was a direct function of dose. In this regard it was shown that body weight was a significant variable in determining the levels of amnesia. Their study showed a peak effect of amnesia at a 10-minute interval from intravenous administration with a return to placebo level depending on dosage per body weight. The amnesia seen with diazepam thus may be clinically variable; however, depending on the noted variables, amnesia may be expected to persist for up to 45 minutes, with more cognitive breakthrough occurring during the latter portion of that time period.

Diazepam is not analgesic, so adequate local anesthesia may also be required to accomplish most dental procedures. In those instances in which local anesthesia may be expected to be incomplete or inadequate, narcotics may be added to the intravenous sedative technique to provide greater patient comfort. Respiration is not depressed as with the barbiturates and narcotics. There is some evidence that respiratory function may be to a small degree more sensitive than the cardiovascular system, responding with slight respiratory depression.[8] If this characteristic is present, it is primarily caused by a decrease in tidal volume. Respiratory depression with the doses of diazepam administered for outpatient dental procedures has not been a constant finding.[9]

Increasing utilization of this agent as a primary sedative drug has been accompanied by more frequent reports of significant respiratory depression or even apnea.[10-13] The classic treatment of this depression, as with barbiturate overdose, is the maintenance and support of the respiratory system until such time that the ill effects are reversed by redistribution of the drug. Obviously, if a narcotic has also been administered, the depressant effects that might be attributed to it should be reversed with naloxone. Recently physostigmine, 1 to 4 mg in titrated doses, has been used in an attempt to reverse respiratory depression caused by diazepam administration. If this drug is placed in an emergency drug kit for such use, the pharmacology and toxicity of this agent should be well known to the operator. The cardiovascular system is not significantly affected,[14] although the relief of anxiety may result in some fall of blood pressure. The pulse rate may be unchanged, may decrease because of relief of anxiety or, as has been documented, may increase in the first 10 minutes after administration and subsequently return to normal rates.[7,14] The patient may manifest lightheadedness, dizziness, and ataxia. Diazepam should be avoided with patients in early pregnancy because its effects on the developing fetus are not yet fully realized. However, it is used in labor and delivery rooms with no significant cardiovascular or respiratory depression observable in neonates. Patients of advancing years may be somewhat more susceptible to the effects of this drug.

The metabolism of diazepam in the body is complex. It is known that after intravenous injection of diazepam there is a moderately rapid decline in the plasma concentration. The degree of this decline is dose related and corresponds to the clinical period of sedative and amnesia effects. The plasma level will again show an increased concentration 6 to 8 hours after administration, which is probably because of redistribution of the drug.[15] It does form the basis of what must be strongly emphasized to the patient—that activities even for the protracted period of 8 to 10 hours must be limited. In the postoperative period relative loss of sedative effects or light stages of euphoria, as often are seen with this drug, makes these precautions and patient warnings even more important. Coupled with slow detoxification and excretion, extending for as long as 7 days, a hypnotically active metabolite called desmethyldiazepam increases in concentration for a 50-hour period after intravenous administration, and then it, too, is slowly metabolized over several days.[8] Patients with closely repeated dosages of diazepam may thus be expected to have higher than anticipated plasma levels. One must remember that this agent will potentiate many other sedative drugs such as the barbiturates, antihypertensives, and narcotics. Ingestion of alcohol should be avoided during periods of diazepam administration. The protracted metabolism of the drug should be considered when patients are counseled in this regard. The drug's duration of action is less than that of those previously considered, yielding approximately 1 hour of sedation. It is thus an excellent agent to consider when relatively short periods of sedation are required.

The intramuscular dosage of diazepam is as follows:

Normal adult—10 mg
Children (according to SAAD[16])
    Age 4 to 6 years—5 mg
    Age 7 to 10 years—7.5 mg
    Age 11 to 14 years—10 mg

The foregoing may be followed as a general rule, with the final determination being made on the basis of the weight or surface area of the child.

Intravenous technique. Diazepam is packaged in a 2 ml, amber-colored ampule with each milliliter of solution containing 5 mg diazepam; it is also available in a multiple-dose vial of 10 ml. It should not be diluted before injection because it has some propensity to leave solution.

After mental and physical preparation of the patient, an intravenous route is established. Recent literature has suggested that small veins should be avoided. Past experience with the veins of the dorsum of the hand has evoked a "burning" response from the patient in the hand. It is recommended that the largest available suitable vein in the forearm or antecubital fossa be chosen for this injection. Additionally, the diazepam should be injected slowly to allow intravenous dilution of the drug, thus minimizing its irritating effects. Although the manufacturer does not recommend adding the drug to intravenous fluids, it is common practice to inject the agent slowly into a rapidly running intravenous infusion of 5% dextrose and water or Ringer's lactate solution. Administration in this manner may result in a cloudy-white solution suggestive of precipitation. This has not been shown to have any untoward or altered physical or pharmacologic effects, however. These precautions are to minimize the possibility of venous thrombosis or proximal phlebitis. As has been indicated earlier, these are the most common adverse sequelae to intravenous sedation.

Clinical experience with diazepam that has been administered properly has revealed a very low incidence of venous irritation. An initial dose of 2.5 mg

(0.5 ml) is slowly administered, followed by a 60-second period of observation. During this time period the patient is observed for signs of an unusual response to the agent. Additional increments are injected at a rate not to exceed 5 mg (1 ml) per minute. During the slow injection phase the patient is observed for signs of adequate sedation, which are similar to those noted earlier for the intravenous use of barbiturates. Adequate sedative effects can also be expected when Verrill's sign has been achieved.[17] This is observed by having the patient look straight ahead. The upper eyelid will begin to droop, and when it covers one half of the iris (eye is at "half-mast"), no more drug is administered. Although some people will be effectively sedated with low dosages of diazepam, Verrill's sign is seldom achieved unless dosages in excess of 10 mg are given in the normal adult patient. Depending on the patient, the patient's anxiety, the dentist's rapport with the patient, and the procedure itself, it will be found that 10 mg will provide adequate sedation in a large number of individuals, even though the aforementioned test point has not been reached. If one does proceed to "half-mast," no more than 20 mg should usually be administered to the routine dental outpatient. Even at 20 mg, however, there is a generous margin of safety with diazepam. Increments may be added during a procedure, within these guidelines, if they are required as the procedure progresses. The rapid decline of plasma levels coupled with delayed metabolism should induce caution as to the total dose administered during the course of one appointment. If a procedure has the potential for becoming protracted in time, perhaps another technique should be considered. With this agent the period of administration is sharply reduced from the Jorgensen technique. The efficient achievement of sedation combined with a short action makes the drug both practical and advantageous for short procedures.

The disadvantages of intravenous diazepam include a tendency for some patients to become talkative, especially when less drug is given than that required to achieve Verrill's sign. Additionally, there is a stringent requirement that patients who receive diazepam intravenously be accompanied by a responsible person and observe the noted restrictions for a lengthy postsedation period. This is especially true of diazepam because of its delayed metabolism and excretion and the commonly observed postoperative euphoria.

Combination of agents

Diazepam and meperidine. A slight modification of the intravenous diazepam administration and the Jorgensen technique affords advantages peculiar to both. In this technique for adults a 10 mg intravenous dose of diazepam is followed by 25 mg meperidine and 0.32 mg scopolamine. Added amnesia, relaxation, sedation, and analgesia are thus achieved. This combination offers advantages in the management of patients in pain at the inception of the procedure, for procedures that are in themselves painful, or in cases in which considerable postoperative pain is anticipated. There have been reports that indicate that a combination of diazepam and meperidine is responsible for significant alterations in blood gases. Respiratory depression can occur without clinical appreciation in the sedated patient. Dunsworth and associates,[18] while using diazepam and meperidine, showed an elevation in P_{CO_2} from 36.3 ± 3.6 mm Hg preoperatively to 40.3 ± 5.7 mm Hg at midsurgery and 39.2 ± 4.7 mm Hg in the 10- to 15-minute postoperative period. Dundee and Wyant state that "A combination of diazepam and an opiate produced a greater degree of respiratory depression than would be expected from the individual drugs."[19] It has been theorized that the two drugs competed for the same detoxification enzyme. The need for the narcotic with the attendant possibility of respiratory depression must be carefully assessed as regards the patient's physical and mental condition and the proposed therapy. As with all drug therapy, the benefits to be gained should be greater than the attendant risks.

Innovar. Innovar is a combination of a narcotic, fentanyl (Sublimaze), and a tranquilizer, droperidol (Inapsine), in a 1:50 ratio. Each milliliter of Innovar contains 0.05 mg fentanyl and 2.5 mg droperidol. The combination produces neuroleptanalgesia. This is a state of noticeable tranquilization and profound analgesia in which the patient, although conscious, is detached or mentally removed from his immediate surroundings. The patient will respond to commands, but when not so stimulated, he returns to a state of dissociation.

Fentanyl is a powerful narcotic with effects not unlike those of morphine. It differs significantly, however, in the following ways: The same analgesic effect is attained at approximately 1/100 the dose of morphine, its duration of action is significantly shorter, its effects on the cardiovascular system are more benign, it lacks emetic properties, and it does not cause histamine release. The latter action renders the agent suitable for use in asthmatic patients. Bradycardia, if produced by this agent, may be treated by the administration of atropine. Its main disadvantage relative to use in the routine dental outpatient is the great degree of respiratory depression it effects. Although this may be reversed with naloxone, respiration may have to be supported or controlled in the interim.

Droperidol is an active and highly potent tranquilizer with a significant antiemetic effect. Although it has minimal effect on the respiratory system, it can produce hypotension. It causes peripheral vascular dilation and reduction of the vasopressor effect of epinephrine. It will produce significant degrees of potentiation of other CNS depressants.

Innovar has found use in hospital anesthesia practice for diagnostic or surgical procedures where relief of pain and anxiety is required, for sedation with a low incidence of nausea or vomiting, or as an adjunctive agent in conjunction with local anesthesia. Skeletal muscle rigidity with thoracic ventilatory disruption may occur if the agent is administered too rapidly or in excessive amounts. This may be managed with muscle relaxants and controlled respirations. Patients who have received Innovar must be watched carefully. The respiratory depressant effect will last for a longer period of time than the perceived analgesic effect! Postoperative administration of depressant drugs must be limited and dosages reduced because of the profound potentiation mentioned earlier. Although Innovar has significant favorable qualities for use in a hospital environment, the possible adverse effects render it a drug to be used with extreme caution, if at all, by the general practitioner for outpatient premedication. The two agents combined in Innovar are now available separately, and their individual use might well be considered in conjunction with the preceding discussion.

Droperidol is available in 2 and 5 ml ampules with each milliliter having 2.5 mg of the drug. For preoperative sedation 1 to 2 ml may be administered; however, the possibility of hypotension with this agent should greatly minimize its use in the general dental practice. With its alpha adrenergic blocking effects, hypotension that results from the administration of this agent should *not* be treated with epinephrine. Such use may result in a paradoxical further drop in blood pressure. Considering the other sedative agents that are available, specific indications should exist for

the use of this agent over more routinely used drugs.

Fentanyl is available in 2 and 5 ml ampules, with each milliliter having 0.05 mg of the drug. Fentanyl has little hypnotic or sedative effect, but it is an excellent narcotic analgesic. It may be useful for controlling pain in the anxious patient, to supplement regional anesthesia during painful procedures, or in cases where postoperative pain may be expected.

As has been emphasized, the main disadvantage of this drug is its ability to cause severe respiratory depression. Apnea may be expected in doses in excess of 0.009 mg/kg.[20] Although this dosage would not be approached in supplementing sedation, with individual variation, it emphasizes the absolute need for a method of airway control with positive-pressure oxygen capability and narcotic antagonist availability. The duration of active analgesic effect is from 30 to 60 minutes when administered intravenously and from 1 to 2 hours when given intramuscularly. The onset of action is almost immediate with intravenous administration and within 10 minutes with intramuscular administration. As with the combination of these two agents, the respiratory depression will last longer than the analgesia obtained. Fentanyl should be used with caution in patients with respiratory disease as well as in those with liver and kidney disease.

The following dosages of fentanyl should be given*:

Normal adult—0.05 to 1.0 mg
   1 to 2 ml given intramuscularly 30 to 60 minutes before procedure or *slowly* intravenously just before procedure
Child—0.02 to 0.03 mg per 20 to 25 pounds

Diazepam and fentanyl. The combination of these two agents, each having a similar duration of action, has become increasingly popular. This combination will provide sedation and analgesia (narcosis) together with a variable postinjection amnesic state. For procedures of up to 1 hour, this provides an extremely satisfactory sedative technique. The patient quite frequently forgets the anesthetic injections as well as portions of the dental manipulations, even though he is conscious and may react appropriately to stimuli during those injections. The amnesia and added depression with the narcotic many times result in patients believing that their treatment was rendered with them totally asleep. This combination

---

*Dosage must be adjusted for the elderly, debilitated, or those receiving other depressant drugs.

also has the advantage of requiring minimal recovery time in the dental office before the patient can be released with an adult escort. At 1 hour after the injection, the vast majority of patients will be able to walk with only slight guidance. Although this is an advantage for the practitioner, it is important that postsedation euphoria is well understood by both patient and escort. In this regimen the doses of fentanyl, in quantities previously noted, are given first. There is certain logic in administering the more dangerous and potent agent first. In this manner any excessive depressant effects can more easily be recognized, and drug administration ceased, before an emergency ensues. The agent and its depressant effects may be reversed with naloxone if required. If the diazepam were to be given first, the reactions of the patient would be somewhat masked by the sedative effects of that agent and the fentanyl more difficult to titrate. After titration of the fentanyl to beginning signs of depression or sedation, as noted previously, the fentanyl is discontinued. Diazepam may then be slowly administered while verbal contact with the patient is maintained. The great majority of patients will require less than 20 mg of diazepam. Combined effects approaching a general anesthetic can be seen with much less than 20 mg of diazepam and 0.05 to 0.1 mg of fentanyl. As with all combination techniques, entrance into general anesthesia is much more likely than with single agent techniques. Practitioners just introducing intravenous sedation to their practice would be well advised to begin with conservative doses in single-agent techniques until a moderately successful experience level has been achieved. The initial patients chosen to introduce sedative techniques into a practice should not be those who are severe psychologic management problems. In addition, the practitioner should be aware of the high level of self-medication in today's society. Significant numbers of the population daily take some form of self-secured or prescription depressant drug. Thus the practitioner must be alert to sedative or depressant signs in patients that may occur with much less than the usual doses of sedative drugs.

NITROUS OXIDE ANALGESIA

The administration of nitrous oxide–oxygen inhalation analgesia in the dental office has undergone cyclic periods of enthusiasm and disfavor. Once again, this mode of sedation has become popular. The recent increase in its use is a result of continued use,

with evangelistic recommendation by a few devotees, increased awareness of the patient, improvements in medical aspects of dental education, and a perfection of equipment.

One old misunderstanding that still exists is that many people equate nitrous oxide with general anesthesia. Although nitrous oxide is used as a part of general anesthetic procedures, the inhalation sedative technique does not produce a state of general surgical anesthesia. The fact should be emphasized that when the anesthetic is properly administered, the patient remains conscious, and protective reflexes remain operational. The nitrous oxide–oxygen sedative technique may be adapted for use in a wide range of dental office procedures offering increased patient cooperation and comfort. Local anesthesia may not be required with this technique for many procedures in operative dentistry.

The following discussion of nitrous oxide analgesia should only be considered a basic familiarization that will facilitate and reinforce adequate supervised training in the use of this technique.

Nitrous oxide–oxygen sedation defined

As a consequence of training requirements during World War I, Guedel amplified the definitions then existing as to the stages of anesthesia. Although these best relate to an agent of slow progression, such as ether, exploration of a portion of these definitions becomes significant with this technique. Stage I of general anesthesia was defined as that time period and sequence of physiologic events lasting from the beginning of the anesthetic procedure until such time as the patient lost consciousness. Stage II represented a period of delirium with uncoordinated movements. After this the level of surgical anesthesia was reached at stage III. Stage III was subdivided further into planes of surgical anesthesia. Finally, the period from the cessation of respiration until cardiac failure was described as stage IV.

This chapter is restricted to dealing with a conscious patient so that attention is centered on stage I. This stage is of little interest in general anesthesia; however, it has become apparent that just as there are surgical levels within stage III, so too are there levels within stage I. Although these may be defined to some degree, an understanding of the physiologic effects in this stage is more important. Analgesia will be increased as the lower extent of the stage is approached and will reach 85% at the depths of this stage. Deeper into stage I, amnesia also progresses from minimal to nearly complete forgetfulness. The patient maintains contact with the operator until near unconsciousness. However, although the patient will follow directions while experiencing the midplane area; as the anesthesia state progresses, the patient may lose this response. Thus it can be seen that nearly complete amnesia and analgesia may take the patient close to that physiologic zone where one will pass into the excitement phase of stage II. Obviously, encroachment on this zone should be avoided. Progression of amnesia, analgesia, and relaxation may be achieved well into stage I, with only minimal decrease of protective reflexes. The important and significant consideration is that the area before and at the entrance into stage II be avoided.

Table 30-1 provides a means of defining the level of anesthesia, according to the scheme of stages of anesthesia, reached by a patient. It should be noted that in all of anesthesia, this progression is a continuum. The entrance into stage II is very slow with most gaseous anesthetics, but one can pass completely through stage II in a matter of seconds with ultrashort-acting barbiturates. The descriptions then provide observable signs that become a guide for maintaining a conscious sedative technique.

Advantages

As has been implied, the nitrous oxide–oxygen techniques has sufficient advantages to recommend its consideration in many dental care delivery systems. There is a rapid onset of sedative effects. Sensory changes are evident in less than 1 minute, and effective sedation is usually achieved in 3 or 4 minutes. This, of course, is in contrast to oral or intramuscular sedative techniques, in which a lengthy latent period is evident before sedation. Although intravenous sedative effects are quickly perceived, preparation and total administration time are greater than for nitrous oxide–oxygen sedation. Thus minimal preparation and a short time of onset are significant advantages of this technique. Additionally, of course, no intramuscular injection or venipuncture is required, which is appreciated by most people.

The technique allows for a very close control over the level of sedation achieved. In the conscious patient a change of the percentage of nitrous oxide administered results in rapid physiologic adjustment. Indeed, in patients with whom the technique is to be used for a series of procedures, the patient will learn to adjust the level to some degree by the amount of mouth breathing performed. This facility dispels fear of the procedure and provides ready acceptance, since the patient realizes that he has control over the technique and can quickly terminate its effects by total mouth breathing. In these instances in which the technique is used in a series of procedures, it often becomes apparent that as the patient's approval of and confidence in the technique are achieved, decreased percentages of nitrous oxide are required for later

Table 30-1. Signs of progression from sedation to anesthesia

Sign	Stage I (Guedel): consciousness to sedation	Stage II: excitement to anesthesia
Level of consciousness	Conscious; relaxed; decreasingly aware; responsive to verbal commands and painful stimuli; increasingly less responsive	Nonresponsive
Facial expression	Relaxed, at ease, dreamy, silly smile, detached look	Masklike, may have rigid stare
Eyes	Pupils normal, normal eyeball position; *eyelash* reflex present (a stroke of eyelash will cause contraction)	Pupils dilate, react to light, eccentric eyeballs; *eyelid* reflex lost (raise eyelid normally causes contraction of lid)
Respiration	Normal, smooth	Slow, irregular
Cardiovascular	Relatively normal pulse and blood pressure; depressed from preoperative level by (1) relief of anxiety, (2) use of depressant drugs in combination technique	Increased pulse rate; increased blood pressure (may also occur because of inadequate sedation: anxiety or pain)
Nausea	Rare	Possible
Analgesia	Increases as level deepens	
Amnesia	Increases as level deepens	

treatments. This placebo effect further increases the overall safety of the technique.

Recovery is rapidly effected with full return to presedative psychomotor capacity. Thus the need for the patient to be accompanied by an adult escort is usually eliminated. If the patient is administered prolonged periods of nitrous oxide sedation, it might be prudent to consider the desirability of the patient being escorted home. Residual effects, if any, certainly are minute when compared with intravenous sedation.

The technique is highly effective in the management of the young patient. Children of 5 to 10 years of age may actually tolerate nasal masks used in this technique better than adults, since they relate the mask to space masks and other games. Thus a game may be played with the child, effecting a smooth sedative procedure. Many adults with claustrophobic tendencies may be able to be treated with this technique by means of good chairside rapport.

The nitrous oxide–oxygen technique will not only offer comfort to the patient and increase acceptance of dental procedures but also will afford a more relaxed treatment administration; that is, the dentist should experience less tension and fatigue at the end of the office day.

Safety

As noted earlier, the following discussion is not intended to prepare the dentist to undertake nitrous oxide analgesia but to provide a basis for supervised training in this technique. Invariably, the complications that have occurred with the use of nitrous oxide–oxygen techniques have been the result of misuse or faulty installation of equipment. It remains the responsibility of the dentist to ensure that the installation or any subsequent alteration or repair of equipment is accomplished in such a manner as to provide proper administration of the bases. Obviously, an installation that crossed oxygen and nitrous oxide lines could be disastrous if 100% of nitrous oxide were given under the assumption that it were oxygen!

All cylinders are now colored in a standard manner. Nitrous oxide cylinders are blue, and oxygen cylinders are green. One may remember this easily by considering oxygen as the "good green gas." As systems may be of a central nature, wall mounted, or mobile, cylinders of varying sizes are available. The cylinders are additionally "pin coded" as an added measure of safety. This "pin index safety system," by providing matching pins in the apparatus' yoke and holes in the cylinders, prevents inadvertent mixing of cylinders and lines. Older machines in some manufacturers' designs have pins that can be loosened, and thus even this system is not infallible.

Combination with other sedative regimens will increase the potential danger of the patient entering a general anesthetic state. The dentist should appreciate the limits of each technique and select the appropriate technique for the patient in consideration of the procedures to be accomplished. If the dentist combines inhalation sedation with other modes of sedation, the dentist *must* be trained in and prepared for the eventuality that general anesthesia might be produced.

Contraindications

Since the nasal passages are utilized as passages for gaseous exchange, upper respiratory obstruction or coryza is an absolute contraindication for this technique. Other respiratory diseases must also be carefully evaluated, if present, since this technique requires a normally functioning respiratory system for safe administration.

Since patients experience euphoria or altered sensorium with nitrous oxide analgesia, emotional instability in a patient is an absolute contraindication to its use. It should be noted that this is not a unique consideration to nitrous oxide sedation but should be a consideration in other sedative techniques as well.

Systemic disease that renders a patient at risk for a particular procedure requires similar consideration relative to the analgesic technique. Use of nitrous oxide–oxygen in pregnant patients in the first trimester should also be avoided.

Pharmacology

Nitrous oxide is an inorganic, colorless, nonirritating gas that exhibits a faint sweet smell. It is 1.5 times heavier than air. Nitrous oxide is carried in solution in the plasma, being fifteen times more soluble than nitrogen. It undergoes no chemical change in the body and is eliminated unaltered mostly through the lungs, with small amounts through the skin, sweat, and urine.

The main physiologic effects of nitrous oxide are exerted on the CNS, hence the effects of analgesia and amnesia. Although there is sensory depression, auditory perception is not affected to the same degree. As a result, a tranquil, quiet environment is a requirement for nitrous oxide–oxygen analgesic procedures. The circulatory system is not significantly affected except that a peripheral vasodilation may occur. This property may facilitate venipuncture should an intravenous route be desired. The respiratory system is not affected significantly. Nitrous oxide does not stimulate secretions as some other inhalation agents do.

The degree of uptake in the lungs is in part a measure of the alveolar tension of that particular gas. Nitrous oxide quickly establishes an equilibrium between alveolar concentration and plasma concentration. Thus changes in the applied concentration of the agent result in rapid physiologic effectiveness. This, too, is the reason why a continuous flow of the agent should result in a more even level of sedation. This quick physiologic response based on the physical properties of the agent forms a part of the safety margin of the technique as well as being responsible for the rapid recovery. It does, however, provide a precautionary consideration at that time when the administration of nitrous oxide ceases.

During the administration of nitrous oxide, an equilibrium has been established between alveolar nitrous oxide and that dissolved in the blood. When nitrous oxide administration ceases, there will be relatively small amounts of nitrogen in the alveoli and the bloodstream as a result of displacement by the nitrous oxide. If at the end of a procedure the patient is permitted to breathe room air, nitrogen will begin to reenter the bloodstream. However, as was noted earlier, the nitrous oxide is more soluble in the blood than is nitrogen. Since the room air contains no nitrous oxide, the nitrous oxide will flood out of the bloodstream to establish a new equilibrium. Since the same quantity of blood will release more nitrous oxide into the alveoli than it can dissolve nitrogen, there will be a net increase in alveolar gas volume. This essentially causes a decreased concentration of oxygen. Thus the patient might be hypoxic even with the administration of over 20% oxygen. This process is known as diffusion hypoxia. By permitting the patient to breathe 100% oxygen for 4 to 5 minutes at the end of the sedative procedure, the nitrous oxide may be washed out of the bloodstream without hypoxia occurring.

Physical properties of the gases

It is important to realize that nitrous oxide, when compressed for medical utilization, forms a liquid that is in equilibrium with overlying gas. This equilibrium will remain, with nearly constant gauge pres-

sure being noted, until most of the liquid has been transformed into gas and utilized. At this point the gauge pressure will drop rapidly, and replacement of the cylinder is imminent. On the other hand, oxygen under pressure remains a gas in a compressed state. The gauge pressure falls more evenly, and gauge pressures more accurately reflect the amount of oxygen remaining.

Equipment

Numerous analgesia machines are currently available. With the decision to include nitrous oxide–oxygen analgesia in one's practice, a survey of the existing machines on the market is in order. A few generalizations can be made relative to the equipment in current use.

This brief discussion of the properties of nitrous oxide should have made the informed reader aware that this technique can be best managed by the utilization of moderate to high continuous flow of gases. Intermittent or demand flow machine usage may result in a bouncing-ball sedative course and has no overriding advantage to recommend this use.

Modern machines are equipped with flowmeters, whereby minute delivered volumes of oxygen and nitrous oxide can be determined. Most machines now in production have built-in safety systems that will prevent the delivery of nitrous oxide unless a suitable concentration of oxygen is also being delivered. This may vary with machines but should not be less than 25%. Some manufacturers build in alarm systems that also signal the loss of adequate oxygen pressures. Most machines are so built that even with normal oxygen pressures, oxygen flows of less than 25% are not possible. In addition, flow *rates* of more than 2.5 L/min of oxygen are automatically ensured on many machines. These are desirable safety features. The modern machines also offer direct instant oxygen flooding or flushing of the system as a facilitating means of applying oxygen in an emergency.

Although face masks have no place in dental analgesic regimens, they should be available for the application of positive pressure during emergency situations.

Nasal masks and cannulas are available for use with this technique. The cannula presents distinct disadvantages in that its diameter allows air dilution during inhalation, which may significantly alter applied concentrations of the agents. For example, if a 40% nitrous oxide–60% oxygen mixture is set on the flowmeters, the nitrous oxide concentration received would be much less if a nasal cannula were used. Essentially, the concentrations set on the machine are invalid if a nasal cannula is used with this technique. If the effects are diluted by room air intermingling to the point at which adequate sedation is not achieved, the dentist may abandon the technique. In these cases the technique is wrongfully rejected, since the actual cause of failure remains undetected. At the very least, utilization of the cannula makes the relation between flowmeter readings and sedative levels empirical.

The rebreathing or reservoir bag functions to permit a constant source of gases for the patient to breathe. It may also be used in conjunction with the face mask for positive-pressure oxygen administration.

Procedure

Before beginning the sedative procedures, the operator should ensure that the equipment is functioning properly. The procedure and sequence of events and sensations within the appointment should be explained to the patient. Because of the retention of hearing perception, background noise should be kept to an absolute minimum. Practitioners must remember that not only is the patient conscious, but an altered sensorium may cause a misunderstanding of remarks passed between staff members. Additionally, fanciful dreams occurring during the procedure may, on recovery, be interpreted as having actually occurred. Consequently, a female staff member must be in attendance when female patients are being treated. Aberrant sensations may lead to unfounded accusations unless this requirement is strictly adhered to.

The patient should neither come to the appointment in a fasting state nor should a large meal have been ingested in the past 3 hours. However, the incidence of nausea and vomiting is low with nitrous oxide–oxygen analgesia.

At the onset it should be appreciated that there is an individual variance of reaction to similar percentages and gas flows. Initially, a high flow rate of 8 to 10 L/min is used to begin the analgesic sequence. Commencing with 100% oxygen allows a gradual introduction of nitrous oxide as well as a washing out of nitrogen in the lungs, permitting a more efficient sedative induction. The nasal mask is adapted comfortably to the patient's face, and the patency and adequacy of gas flow are determined. The patient may have to be cautioned to maintain normal nasal breathing. Nitrous oxide can then be introduced at a level of 20%. The dentist should remember that at least 25% oxygen should be maintained during administration, and liter flow of oxygen should not be below 2.5 L/min. The concentration of nitrous oxide can be adjusted in increments of approximately 5% to achieve the proper level of sedation. The level of sedation may be evaluated as follows:

1. Perhaps the best indicator of the sedation level of the patient is the patient's response to questions. The patient may exhibit a slurred speech or a slow response, may often relate experiences of a feeling of well-being or of euphoria, and may remember the questioning but simply at that time not have the mental drive remaining to respond quickly.

2. The patient will be relaxed and cooperative. There will be almost no response to local anesthetic injections. The patient may remember the injection, but it is an unremarkable memory. If a series of injections are accomplished, the patient may remember them as a decreased number or even as one event. Inappropriate movement may be indicative of a patient too deep in stage I anesthesia.

3. The patient will maintain with ease an open-mouth position in the desired planes, whereas increased depth is associated with a tendency to close the mouth.

4. The eyes may be closed but opened easily by the operator. The pupils are normal in the desired planes of sedation but may become large in the plane approaching anesthesia. At that level the eyeballs may be eccentric or rolling.

5. In relative analgesia planes, respiration will be normal. The respiratory rate will decrease and become irregular as general anesthesia is approached.

6. The pulse rate and blood pressure are not suitable aids to determine the level of depression. While the patient is in the proper plane of analgesia there should be little change in pulse or blood pressure. Pain in this plane as well as an increasing depth may be the cause of increased pulse rate or a rise in blood pressure.

As nitrous oxide levels are varied or as the time of sedative induction increases, the patient will report subjective symptoms of the relative analgesia. The first symptoms related may be tingling sensations in the fingers, toes, lips, or tip of the tongue. These may become apparent at levels of 20% nitrous oxide. With increased concentrations the patient will state that he or she felt a warm wave of relaxation pass over and will develop an attitude of euphoria, sometimes with a feeling of detachment. Progression will also cause increased degrees of drowsiness. Above 50% nitrous oxide, the patient may have exaggerated dreams, requiring the precautions mentioned earlier.

In almost all instances, adequate relative analgesia can be achieved at applied concentrations of nitrous oxide of 50% or less. Even at 50%, care must be taken because more susceptible individuals may pass into early general anesthesia at this level.

Essentially then, by starting at 20% applied nitrous oxide and progressing, as required, in increments of approximately 5% increased concentrations, a relative analgesia state should be safely achieved in almost all patients before administration of 50% applied nitrous oxide. As the procedure continues, the rate of flow of the gases may be decreased, although at least 2.5 L/min oxygen should always be administered. At the end of the procedure, 5 to 8 L/min oxygen is administered for 4 or 5 minutes to avoid diffusion anoxia.

It is interesting and valuable for the dentist to question patients as to their subjective reactions under sedation. In addition to the features already mentioned, the patient will often indicate that the frame of time the procedure occupied in the patient's consciousness has been dramatically decreased. The operating time may appear to be one third or one half as long as it was in reality. By relating the subjective symptoms to the sedative course, the operator will gain added insight into the regimen of inhalation analgesia.

Nitrous oxide toxicity

In the past few years there has been an increasing concern regarding the potential ill effects on the dentist and the staff from the occupational exposure to nitrous oxide in the dental office.[21-24] Earlier and continued studies in the hospital operating room have shown a statistically significant increased degree of miscarriage, congenital malformations, and liver disease in those personnel exposed to anesthetic waste gases. In some studies there has been evidence to suggest that the wives of exposed male personnel in the operating room have an increased chance of having children with birth defects. Studies in the hospital environment cannot be directly applied to the dental office liability of exposure to nitrous oxide because the operating room has varying degrees of other anesthetic waste gas contamination not found in the dental

operatory. Studies in the dental literature have shown that there may be significant degrees of ambient nitrous oxide as a contaminant, causing occupational exposure in many dental offices. It should be further noted that this increases in degree with the amount of use of nitrous oxide in the office. Although not proven beyond a shadow of a doubt, it seems clear that there is a real potential for adverse physical and/or genetic effects on persons chronically exposed to nitrous oxide levels. Indeed the degree of exposure to nitrous oxide alone is potentially greater in the dental office than in the hospital operating room. This is because of the more-controlled air flow in the operating room as well as to the use of closed administration systems for general anesthesia versus the open administration system used for outpatient sedation. As a result of these findings, a concerted attempt should be made to reduce nitrous oxide concentrations in the dental office. The most effective method of accomplishing this reduction is by use of a scavenging system. These are available from a number of manufacturers. Essentially one tube system supplies the nitrous oxide–oxygen mixture to the patient. The nasal hood is modified to both collect gases expired into the hood and gather gases approximating the hood area. This tends to compensate for leakage around the hood secondary to the less than perfect fit and caused by the high gas flow. This "scavenged" gas is then exhausted through an independent tube system into a regular dental high volume–low pressure suction system. Although these devices add some degree of extra bulk and noise from the suction, they are extremely efficient in reducing the nitrous oxide level in the dental office. When using this system, the dentist must be assured that the waste gases are vented to the outside and not merely to another portion of the same building. Air conditioning in offices using nitrous oxide to any degree should be of a nonrecirculating type. If air is recirculated, any contamination will be simply shared equally by all members of the staff. The nitrous oxide lines, tanks, gauges, and machines should be checked periodically for leaks. Collection devices are becoming commercially available to monitor nitrous oxide levels in the dental office. It should be noted that single, short-term samples have not proven to be reliable in assessing the daily exposure rate. It is anticipated that the profession will be offered increased choices of ways to monitor nitrous oxide levels in the near future.

Although the level at which there is a potential for

ill effects is not known, there certainly should be an awareness of this and an attempt to reduce occupational exposure. Nitrous oxide provides an excellent service to the patient. Its use is certainly indicated and may be applied safely for both the patient and office staff if the previous precautions are taken.

Nitrous oxide abuse

The pleasant effects of nitrous oxide–oxygen sedation are graphically illustrated by the increasing reports of its abuse in the dental office.[25-28] Nitrous oxide myeloneuropathy has become a clinical syndrome associated with either recreational use of nitrous oxide or moderate to heavy patient use in a dental treatment center without scavenging devices or adequate ventilation, thus producing high ambiant levels of the agent. Although limited numbers of cases have been presented in the literature, larger numbers undoubtedly have either not been reported or have been misdiagnosed. There is a pattern that emerges in those cases that have been reported. Persons have reported a variable abuse from 2 to 3 hours per week up to 2 to 4 hours per day. There is also a variable length of time before the onset of symptoms. This has ranged from about 6 months to a number of years. In persons who deny abuse, the use of nitrous oxide in patient treatment in the office has been heavy. In these cases there also has been exposure for a period of months to years before the onset of symptoms. Clearly there is an individually differing susceptibility to nitrous oxide in which a threshold exposure must be reached before symptoms manifest themselves. The symptom complex results from neurologic involvement, which is speculated to be caused by an interference with the action of vitamin B_{12}. The patients have exhibited a variety of symptoms, including an ataxic or unsteady gait, sensory changes in the upper and lower extremities, and a lack of muscle coordination causing decreased manual dexterity. Persons have been diagnosed as having multiple sclerosis before the etiology was discovered. Almost invariably the symptom complex has resolved after eliminating exposure to nitrous oxide, with recovery taking several months.

To date there are no reports of dental patients being affected by this syndrome. Nitrous oxide sedation has provided a pleasant, positive dental treatment experience for untold numbers of patients who were previously difficult to treat. It is an exceptionally valuable adjunct in the administration of quality care com-

bined with concern for the patient as a whole. The abuse potential should not influence the dentist in deciding to provide this service to patients. The dentist should, however, recognize the abuse potential for oneself and one's staff and take such precautions as seem advisable in the treatment facility.

CONCLUSION

There are many varied, yet correct methods to achieve adequate preoperative sedation. The end result, however, is successful only if the patient has suffered no ill effects and an optimal environment for treatment has been provided. Comprehension, by reading texts and the literature, by participation in education courses, by detailed training and practice in proper sedative administration, and by attendance at professional meetings form the basis for intelligent, successful, and ethical application of any sedative technique. I hope that this chapter will be an additional aid in the preparation of the practitioner to control pain and anxiety in patients.

REFERENCES

1. Dundee, J.W., and Wyant, G.M.: Intravenous anaesthesia, London, 1974, Churchill Livingstone, pp. 64-65.
2. Goodman, L.S., and Gilman, A.: The pharmacological basis of therapeutics, ed. 6, New York, 1980, Macmillan Publishing Co., Inc., p. 359.
3. Jorgensen, N.B., and Hayden, J., Jr.: Sedation: local and general anesthesia in dentistry, ed. 3, Philadelphia, 1980, Lea & Febiger, pp. 48-50.
4. Clarke, P.R., et al.: The amnesic effect of diazepam (Valium), Br. J. Anaesth. **42**:690, 1971.
5. Pandit, S.K., Dundee, J.W., and Keilty, S.R.: Amnesic studies with intravenous premedication, Anaesthesia **26**:421, 1971.
6. Driscoll, E.J., Smilack, et al.: Sedation with intravenous diazepam, J. Oral Surg. **30**:332, 1972.
7. Gregg, J.M., et al.: The amnesic actions of diazepam, J. Oral Surg. **32**:651, 1974.
8. Dundee, J.W., and Wyant, G.M.: Intravenous anaesthesia, London, 1974, Churchill Livingstone, pp. 252, 257.
9. Schechter, H.O., and Cosentino, B.J.: Combinations of psychotherapeutic drugs and local anesthesia for dental procedures, J. Oral Surg. **28**:280, 1970.
10. Lopez, J.: Physostigmine reversal of diazepam-induced respiratory arrest: report of a case, J. Oral Surg. **39**:539, 1981.
11. Brauninger, G.R.M.: Respiratory arrest following intravenous Valium, Ann. Opthalmol. **6**:805, 1974.
12. Larson, G.F., Hurlbert, B.J., and Wingard, D.W.: Physostigmine reversal of diazepam-induced depression, Anesth. Analg. **56**:348, 1977.
13. Braunstein, G.M.: Apnea with maintenance of consciousness following intravenous diazepam, Anesth. Analg. **58**:52, 1979.
14. Dundee, J.W., and Wyant, G.M.: Intravenous anaesthesia, London, 1974, Churchill Livingstone, pp. 255-257.

15. Baird, E.S., and Hailey, D.H.: Delayed recovery from a sedative, Br. J. Anaesth. **44:**803, 1972.
16. Drummond-Jackson, S.L., editor: Intravenous anaesthesia, ed. 5, London, 1971, The Society for the Advancement of Anaesthesia in Dentistry, p. 244.
17. O'Neil, R., Verrill, P.J., and Aellig, W.H.: Intravenous diazepam in minor oral surgery, Br. Dent. J. **128:**15, 1970.
18. Dunsworth, A.R., et al.: Evaluation of cardiovascular and pulmonary changes during meperidine-diazepam anesthesia, J. Oral Surg. **33:**18, 1975.
19. Dundee, J.W., and Wyant, G.M.: Intravenous anaesthesia, London, 1974, Churchill Livingstone, p. 258.
20. Dundee, J.W., and Wyant, G.M.: Intravenous anaesthesia, London, 1974, Churchill Livingstone, p. 212.
21. Millard, R.L., and Corbett, T.H.: Nitrous oxide concentrations in the dental operatory, J. Oral Surg. **32:**593, 1974.
22. Campbell, R.L., et al.: Exposure to anesthetic waste gas in oral surgery, J. Oral Surg. **35:**625, 1977.
23. Whitcher, C., Zimmerman, D.C., and Piziali, R.L.: Control of occupational exposure to nitrous oxide in the oral surgery office, J. Oral Surg. **36:**431, 1978.
24. Scaramella, J., et al.: Nitrous oxide pollution levels in oral surgery offices, J. Oral Surg. **36:**441, 1978.
25. Layzer, R.B.: Myeloneuropathy after prolonged exposure to nitrous oxide. Lancet **9:**1227, 1978.
26. Gutmann, L., et al.: Nitrous oxide-induced myelopathy-neuropathy: potential for chronic misuse by dentists, J. Am. Dent. Assoc. **98:**58, 1979.
27. Paulson, G.W.: 'Recreational' misuse of nitrous oxide, J. Am. Dent. Assoc. **98:**410, 1979.
28. Gutmann, L., and Johnsen, D.: Nitrous oxide-induced myeloneuropathy: report of cases, J. Am. Dent. Assoc. **103:**293, 1981.

BIBLIOGRAPHY

Allen, G.D.: Dental anesthesia and analgesia, ed. 2, Baltimore, 1979, The Williams & Wilkins Co.
Langa, H.: Relative analgesia in dental practice: inhalation analgesia with nitrous oxide, ed. 2, Philadelphia, 1976, W.B. Saunders Co.
McCarthy, F.M.: Emergencies in dental practice: Prevention and treatment, ed. 3, Philadelphia, 1979, W.B. Saunders Co.

CHAPTER 31

WILLIAM K. BOTTOMLEY

Pharmacologic considerations in patients with systemic disease

The level of medical expertise continues to progress at an amazing rate. Sophisticated diagnostic procedures and therapeutic modalities allow successful treatment of disease processes that in some instances would have been hopeless only a few years ago. As a result the dental profession is confronted with a population surviving a multitude of systemic diseases largely because of the drug regimens prescribed for them.

Patients with systemic disease may be classified into three categories. One is those patients who have been diagnosed as having systemic disease that is being well controlled by medications. Another comprises patients who have diagnosed systemic disease that is not well controlled by medications. Either of these groups may be experiencing side effects to the medical therapy. The third category constitutes patients who have systemic disease and have not had it diagnosed. The possibility always exists that more than one system is affected, which may affect another system and complicate both the diagnosis and treatment.

A competent medical history, drug history, and thorough physical and clinical examination are the usual methods of diagnosing adverse medical conditions complicating the successful dental management of the patient. It is necessary to be familiar with the more commonly prescribed drugs, their expected side effects, and their possible interaction with other drugs, especially those that may be prescribed by the dentist. Working knowledge of the more prevalent clinical signs and symptoms of systemic diseases is essential in evaluating the general health status of the patient.

Admittedly, the physician is held accountable for the management of the patient's primary diagnosis, but once the dentist has any pharmacologic or, in a broad sense, psychogenic input with this patient, he shares the responsibility for maintaining the health status of the patient. It logically follows that a prudent course of action for the dentist in planning treatment for a patient with a systemic disease should include a consultation with the physician to arrive at a safe, successful pharmacotherapeutic approach in achieving total health care.

For purposes of organization in the following discussion, systemic disease is treated as disease of organ systems. The contents of this chapter necessitate the acceptance of a few basic premises. No discussion of therapeutics can be all-encompassing. The very nature of dosage regulation to allow for individual response to drugs dictates the use of generalizations. I have strived to make the following discourse function at all times as a practical and expedient reference.

In general, the drug regimen for a systemic disease can be predicted by allowing variances for individual response, dose-effectiveness of a drug, and degrees of severity of systemic debilitation. Representative examples of drugs most likely to be encountered in each systemic disease are discussed in respect to their effect on the oral cavity and dental treatment. When a drug interaction affects dosage requirements and one of the interacting drugs is withdrawn, dosage adjustments may be necessary. Therefore any possible interaction of these drugs with those the dentist might employ is given priority attention.

When a drug the dentist might institute is said to be contraindicated because of either interaction with drugs being employed for a systemic condition or because of potential deleterious side effects in a specific disease condition, it is implied that the drug would be given in prolonged or repeated doses.

375

In consonance with pharmacotherapeutic influences on the dental management of a patient with systemic disease, it is equally important to consider the effects of systemic diseases on dental procedures as well as the effect of dental treatment on systemic health problems.

CARDIOVASCULAR SYSTEM

The most common cause of death is cardiovascular disease. Consequently, drugs and medical conditions associated with disease of the cardiovascular system should be the most expected information elicited in the medical history.

Angina

Chest pain is recognized and interpreted by the patient on the basis of previous experience. Symptoms may include unexplained, periodic pain in the jaw and lower teeth. Angina is usually provoked by exhaustion, anxiety, or pain. The precautions of brief dental appointments scheduled early in the day, appropriate sedation, and adequate local anesthesia should be taken. Since angina may be aggravated by arrhythmias and hypertension, some medications, such as the beta-adrenergic blocking agents, may be considered to be effective for all three conditions.

Antianginals

Nitroglycerin (Angibid, Nitro-Bid, Nitroglyn, Nitrong, Nitrospan)
Erythrityl tetranitrate (Cardilate)
Pentaerythritol tetranitrate (Antora, Duotrate, Neo-Corovas, Pentryate, Peritrate, Steps, Tetrasule, Vaso-80 Unicelles; *with other components:* Cartrax, Corovas, Miltrate, Papavatral, Pentritol)
Isosorbide dinitrate (Isordil, Sorbitrate)
Atenolol (Tenormin)
Metoprolol tartrate (Lopressor)
Nadolol (Corgard)
Propranolol hydrochloride (Inderal)
Timolol maleate (Blocadren)
Verapamil (Isoptin, Calan)
Nifedipine (Procardia)
SIGNIFICANCE:
Used in management of angina pectoris.
Ask the patient to bring his medication to treat himself before stressful dental procedures. The dentist should maintain a minimal supply of sublingual nitroglycerin tablets ($1/150$ grain) for emergency use.

Adverse effects include a sudden fall in blood pressure and orthostatic hypotension. Halitosis is a side effect of isosorbide dinitrate.
Cimetidine may lead to an increase of blood concentration of propranolol, resulting in a lower resting sinus rate.
Verapamil decreases renal excretion of digoxin. The patient may display symptoms of digoxin toxicity, i.e., anorexia, visual disturbances, weakness, and apathy.

Antiarrhythmics

One result of chronic arrhythmia is congestive heart failure. The clinical signs of distended neck veins and cyanosis indicate the degree of severity of this condition. Conservative measures of short appointments, an upright sitting position, and sedation for anxiety are indicated. Oxygen support should be immediately available.
Digitalis (Digitora, Pil-Digis)
Digitoxin (Crystodigin, Digitaline Nativelle, Myodigin, Purodigin)
Digoxin (Davoxin, Lanoxin)
SIGNIFICANCE:
Used in the treatment of congestive heart failure and atrial fibrillation.
Barbiturates are contraindicated, since they may decrease the effects of these drugs.
Quinidine polygalacturonate (Cardioquin)
SIGNIFICANCE:
Used for prevention of cardiac arrhythmias.
An intravenous injection of epinephrine can precipitate a fibrillation in patients taking this drug.
Atenolol (Tenormin)
Metoprolol tartrate (Lopressor)
Nadolol (Corgard)
Propranolol hydrochloride (Inderal)
Timolol maleate (Blocadren)
Verapamil (Isoptin, Calan)
SIGNIFICANCE:
Used in the management of cardiac arrhythmias.
Side effects include orthostatic hypotension and hypoglycemia.
Procainamide hydrochloride (Pronestyl)
SIGNIFICANCE:
Used in the management of ventricular arrhythmias.
The neuromuscular blocking action of streptomycin, neomycin, kanamycin, and surgical muscle relaxants may be potentiated.

An intravenous injection of lidocaine (Xylocaine) may add to the neurologic effects of this drug, producing ventricular tachycardia and severe hypotension.

Antihypertensives

Hypertension may contribute to the development of congestive heart failure, coronary heart disease, stroke and progressive renal failure. This condition is treated with drugs that block sympathetic nerve conduction, diuretics, vasodilators, and angiotensin antagonists. The dentist should routinely take and record blood pressures of all patients since hypertension is usually asymptomatic.

Sympatholytics

Atenolol (Tenormin)
Metoprolol (Lopressor)
Nadolol (Corgard)
Propranolol hydrochloride (Inderal)
Timolol (Timoptic)
Prazosin (Minipress)
Clonidine (Catapres)
Reserpine (Butaserpine, Rau-Sed, Serpasil; *with other components:* Diupres, Diutensen-R, Eskaserp, Exna-R, Hydromox R, Hydropres, Metatensin, Naquival, Regroton, Renese-R, Salutensin, Solfo-Serpine, Unitensen-R)
Methyldopa (Aldomet)
Guanethidine sulfate (Ismelin)
SIGNIFICANCE:
Used in the treatment of hypertension.
Barbiturates may potentiate the hypotensive action.
Aspirin may contribute to the ulcerogenic effect of these drugs.
Side effects include dryness of the mouth, sore tongue, and orthostatic hypotension.

Diuretics

Spironolactone (Aldactone; *with hydrochlorothiazide:* Aldactazide)
Ethacrynic acid (Edecrin)
Acetazolamide (Diamox)
Furosemide (Lasix)
Chlorothiazide (Diuril; *with methyldopa:* Aldoclor)
Hydrochlorothiazide (Esidrix; *with other components:* Aldoril, Butizide, Dyazide, Esimil, Hydropres, Oretic, Ser-Ap-Es)
Triamterene (Dyrenium)

SIGNIFICANCE:
Used in the management of fluid retention and hypertension.
Aspirin may interfere with the diuretic action.
Side effects include dry mouth and increased thirst. This should alert the dentist to a possible electrolyte imbalance and potassium depletion.
Acetazolamide may produce facial paresthesia.
Symptoms of gout may occur. This could be manifested as a temporomandibular joint syndrome.
The possibility of orthostatic hypotension is enhanced.
Be alert for oral manifestations of diabetes mellitus from a possible diabetogenic effect of the diuretics.

Vasodilators

Hydralazine hydrochloride (Apresoline)
Minoxidil (Loniten)
SIGNIFICANCE:
Usually given with a beta-adrenergic blocker to minimize the reflex increase in heart rate and cardiac output.
Hydralazine may cause lupus reaction. Minoxidil can cause hypertrichosis, especially in women.

Angiotensin antagonists

Captopril (Capoten)
SIGNIFICANCE:
Usually reserved for treatment of hypertension refractory to other treatment.
Adverse effects include loss of taste, oral ulcerations caused by bone marrow depression, and renal damage.

SPECIFIC CONSIDERATIONS

The American Heart Association recommendations for the prevention of infective endocarditis in patients with congenital heart defects or a history of rheumatic fever are presented in Appendix B. The same regimen is recommended for outpatients with *heart prostheses.*

Patients with heart and other organ transplants

Ordinarily the dental management of these patients is intimately coordinated with the attending physician. However, if an emergency arises, the drug regimen for subacute bacterial endocarditis (SBE) prophylaxis may be instituted until the physician can be contacted.

The use of aspirin is contraindicated because of its ulcerogenic potential.

Patients with coronary bypasses

The current consensus is that the fact of a patient having had a bypass procedure does not dictate the necessity of prophylactic antibiotic coverage for dental treatment.

Patients with artificial joints

Based on the drug sensitivities of the most common organisms identified with hip prosthesis infections, the recommended drugs of choice for prophylactic treatment of dental patients with artificial joints are erythromycin, clindamycin, or a penase-resistant penicillin.

RESPIRATORY SYSTEM
Antituberculous preparations

Tuberculosis can be progressive, it is potentially fatal, and it may be transmitted to susceptible individuals. Therapy is directed toward preventing the development and transmission of the disease.

Isoniazid (Nydrazid, Triniad, Uniad; *with other components:* Niadox, Pasna Tri-Pack Granules)
SIGNIFICANCE:
Used in the treatment of active tuberculosis.
Epinephrine may enhance its neurovascular side effects.
Adverse effects include hepatotoxicity.

p-Aminosalicylic acid (PAS-C, Rezipas)
SIGNIFICANCE:
Potentiates the action of isoniazid.
Vitamin C increases the possibility of crystalluria.
Aspirin is contraindicated if aminosalicylic acid toxicity is suspected because of its additive effect.
Cardinal signs of toxicity are nausea and vomiting.

Ethambutol (Myambutol)
Streptomycin
Rifampin (Rifadin, Rimactane)
SIGNIFICANCE:
Used in combination therapy for tuberculosis.
Streptomycin may enhance the neuromuscular blockade action of surgical skeletal muscle relaxants.
Adverse effects of rifampin include leukopenia and jaundice.

Bronchial dilators

Episodic, reversible obstruction of the airway is associated with paroxysms of increased bronchial muscle activity and inflammatory reactions to allergens. Drug therapy is indicated to improve airflow.

Ephedrine hydrochloride (with other components: Amesec, Bron-Sed, Calcidrine, Co-Xan, Dainite, Duovent, KIE, Lufyllin-EPG, Mudrane, Quadrinal, Quelidrine, Tedral, Verequad)

Pseudoephedrine hydrochloride (Actifed, Bronchobid Duracap, Deconamine, Dimacol, Disophrol, Emprazil, Fedahist, Isoclor, Rondec, Sudafed)
SIGNIFICANCE:
Used in the treatment of bronchial asthma.
Asthmatic patients may be allergic to aspirin.
Side effects include dry mouth.

Antihistamines

Treatment of histamine-mediated responses are directed toward preventing the release or reducing the amount of histamine to minimize peripheral effects. Antihistamines antagonize the action of histamines by competing for receptor sites.

The three commonly used antihistamines listed represent only a small part of the large number of these drugs that are currently marketed.

Chlorpheniramine maleate (Teldrin; *with other components:* Allerest, Aristomin, Chlor-Trimeton Maleate, Colrex, Coricidin, Coriforte, Corilin, Co-Tylenol, Deconamine, Dehist, Demazin, Desa-Hist, Dextro-Tussin, Dor-C, Drinus, Duadacin, Extendryl, Fedahist, Histabid, Histaspan, Hycomine Compound, Isoclor, Napril, Narine, Narspan, Neotep, Nilcol, Nolamine, Novahistine, Oralen, Oraminic, Ornade, Pediacof, Quelidrine, Ryna-Tussadine, Sinodec, Sinovan, Sinulin, Tusquelin, Tussend, Tuss-Ornade, Tussi-Organidin, Wesmatic)

Pyrrobutamine phosphate (with other components: Co-Pyronil)

Brompheniramine maleate (Dimetane; *with other components:* Dimetapp, Drixoral)
SIGNIFICANCE:
Used for the symptomatic relief of allergenic states.
Barbiturates may cause additive depressant effects.
Side effects include dry mouth. If antihistamines are dispensed by the dentist, the patient should be cautioned that he may experience drowsiness; the drugs are potentiated by ethyl alcohol;

and antihistimines potentiate the effects of tricyclic antidepressants. (See discussion on neuromuscular system.)

SPECIFIC CONSIDERATIONS

Barbiturates, narcotics, and other central nervous system depressants should be used with caution in patients with emphysema to avoid respiratory embarrassment.

BONES AND JOINTS
Antiarthritics

Arthritis is commonly associated with joint pain of unknown cause, for example, rheumatoid arthritis and degenerative arthritis or osteoarthritis. The therapeutic goals are to reduce symptoms, maintain joint mobility, and prevent deformity.

Nonsteroidal antiinflammatory agents

Aspirin (many trade names)
Fenoprofen (Nalfon)
Ibuprofen (Motrin)
Indomethacin (Indocin)
Meclofenamate (Meclomen)
Mefenamic acid (Ponstel)
Naproxen (Naprosen)
Naproxen sodium (Anaprox)
Oxyphenbutazone (Oxalid, Tendearil)
Phenylbutazone (Azolid, Butazolidin)
Sulindac (Clinoril)
Tolmetin (Tolectin)
Zomepirac (Zomax)
SIGNIFICANCE:
   Effectiveness results from inhibition of prostaglandin synthesis.
   Used for the relief of pain and the reduction of inflammation in arthritis.
   May be useful as a nonaddictive analgesic for dysmenorrhea, postpartum pain, pain following oral surgery, and cancer pain.
   Adverse effects include gastric irritation, diarrhea, decreased platelet function resulting in a bleeding diathesis, and renal effects.
   Toxic effects may manifest as fever, sore throat, and lesions in the mouth (symptoms of blood dyscrasia).

Immunosuppressants

Azathioprine (Imuran)
Cyclophosphamide (Cytoxan)

Chelating agent

Penicillamine (Cuprimine)

Gold compounds

Aurothioglucose (Solganal)
Gold sodium thiomalate (Myochrysine)

Antimalarial agents

Chloroquine phosphate
Hydroxychloroquine sulfate (Plaquenil Sulfate)
SIGNIFICANCE:
   These drugs are reserved for severe refractory rheumatoid arthritis.
   Adverse and toxic effects are greater with the drugs and include oral ulcerations caused by blood dyscrasias.

GASTROINTESTINAL SYSTEM

The most common medical disorder of the gastrointestinal system is an acid peptic disorder. The therapeutic goal is to promote healing by reducing the active hydrochloric acid in the stomach and the duodenum. This is achieved by the administration of anticholinergics, antacids, H_2 receptor antagonists, or "coating" agents.

Antispasmodics and anticholinergics

Propantheline bromide (Pro-Banthine; *with phenobarbital:* Probital)
Belladonna (Prydon; *with other components:* B & O Supprettes, Barbidonna, Bar-Don, Belbarb, Belladenal, Bucladin, Butibel, Chardonna, Decholin-BB, Denol, Donnatal, Gourmase PB, Kinesed, Phen-O-Bel, Sidonna, Trac)
SIGNIFICANCE:
   Used in the treatment of peptic ulcer.
   Aspirin should be avoided because of its ulcerogenic contribution.
   Side effects include dry mouth.

Antacids

The following active ingredients are components of various brand-name preparations, which are listed in parentheses:
Aluminum hydroxide
Magnesium hydroxide
Calcium carbonate
Dihydroxyaluminum sodium carbonate
Magnesium trisilicate (Aludrox, Amphojel, Camalox, Creamalin, Delcid, Ducon, Gaviscon, Gelu-

sil, Maalox, Mylanta, Riopan, Rolaids, Titralac, Tricreamalate, Trisogel, Tums)

SIGNIFICANCE:

Used in the prevention and treatment of peptic ulcers.

They interfere with the absorption of tetracyclines.

Aspirin should be avoided in these patients because of its ulcerogenic potential.

Antacids containing aluminum may inhibit absorption of phosphorus and fluoride and increase the excretion of calcium, thereby promoting osteoporosis.

H_2 receptor antagonists

These drugs reduce the volume and concentration of gastric acid produced in the resting state and after stimulation by food and caffeine.

Cimetidine (Tagamet)

Ranitidine

SIGNIFICANCE:

Extremely effective for treatment of duodenal ulcers and esophageal reflux.

Adverse side effects include confusion, slurred speech, blood dyscrasias, and gynecomastia.

It interacts with propranol, resulting in a lower resting sinus rate. The dentist should be alert for orthostatic hypotension.

"Coating" agents

Sucralfate (Carafate)

SIGNIFICANCE:

Is not absorbed; therefore side effects are few and minor.

UROGENITAL SYSTEM
Ion-exchange resin

Sodium polystyrene sulfonate (Kayexalate)

SIGNIFICANCE:

Used in the treatment of hyperkalemia attributable to grossly impaired kidney function.

Potassium salts, such as K penicillins, should be avoided.

SPECIFIC CONSIDERATIONS

Vitamin C in large doses causes acidification of the urine, which could cause the precipitation of urate, oxalate, or cystine stones in the urinary tract. The dosage of potentially nephrotoxic antibiotics (tetracyclines, kanamycin, neomycin, cephaloridine) should be adjusted in patients with reduced renal function to prevent additional renal damage and damage to other organs. The blood concentration of the antibiotics can be reduced by increasing the interval between doses or by decreasing the individual doses.

EXAMPLE: tetracycline in reduced doses
1.00 gm/24 hr if BUN is 50 mg/100 ml
0.75 gm/24 hr if BUN is 75 mg/100 ml
0.50 gm/24 hr if BUN is 100 mg/ml

ENDOCRINE SYSTEM

Evidence of endocrine dysfunction visible to the dentist includes increased facial pigmentation, abnormal hair distribution, and oral tissue alterations.

Estrogens and progestins

Estropipate (Ogen)

Norethynodrel and mestranol (Enovid)

Norethindrone and mestranol (Norinyl, Ortho-Novum)

Norethindrone acetate and ethynyl estradiol (Norlestrin)

SIGNIFICANCE:

Used for contraception and occasionally in the treatment of acne.

Patients may demonstrate oral manifestations of pregnancy gingivitis.

Oral contraceptives can interfere with the absorption of folate, resulting in anemia.

Conjugated estrogens (Estratab, Femogen, Formatrix, Premarin, Trexinest)

SIGNIFICANCE:

Used in the treatment of hypermenorrhea, endometriosis, and osteoporosis.

These patients may display dry, atrophic, sensitive oral tissue.

Thyroid

Sodium levothyroxine (Letter, Levoid, Synthroid; *with other components:* Euthroid, S-P-T, Thyrolar)

Sodium liothyronine (Cytomel)

Thyroid globulin (Proloid)

SIGNIFICANCE:

Used as replacement therapy for diminished or absent thyroid function.

Barbiturates are preferred drugs for sedation.

Antithyroid

Isothiouracil sodium (Itrumil)

Methimazole (Tapazole)

SIGNIFICANCE:

Used in the treatment of hyperthyroidism.

Epinephrine injected intravascularly can precipitate a thyroid crisis.

Barbiturate preoperative sedation is recommended to relieve anxiety and stress.

Side effects include sore throat and loss of taste.

Corticoids

Dexamethasone (Decadron, Gammacorten, Hexadrol)

Prednisone (Delta-Dome, Deltasone; *with other components:* Arthralgen with Prednisone, Deltasmyl, Sterazolidin)

Meprednisone (Betapar)

Prednisolone (Ataraxoid, Delta-Cortef)

Triamcinolone (Aristocort, Kenacort; *with other components:* Aristomin)

Cortisone acetate (Cortone Acetate)

SIGNIFICANCE:

Used in the treatment of inflammatory and allergic conditions as immunosuppressive agents

Adjust dosage before stressful dental procedures (consult the patient's physician).

Aspirin is contraindicated because of the ulcerogenic contribution.

Oral manifestations of diabetes mellitus may be observed with prolonged corticoid therapy. (Diabetes mellitus is discussed under Metabolic system.)

Hypertension and mood swings are frequent side effects of protracted corticoid therapy.

THE BLOOD AND BLOOD-FORMING SYSTEMS

Anticoagulants

Anticoagulants do not dissolve blood clots. They interfere with the coagulation mechanism to prevent clot formation. The thromboembolytic agents streptokinase and urokinase stimulate body enzymes that dissolve blood clots.

Sodium warfarin (Coumadin, Panwarfin)

Bishydroxycoumarin (Dicumarol)

SIGNIFICANCE:

These are oral anticoagulants used by outpatients for the treatment of venous thrombosis and embolism.

Vitamin K (Synkayvite) is the antidote.

COMMON DRUGS THAT INCREASE THE ACTION OF ORAL ANTICOAGULANTS:

Acetaminophen (Anacin III, Nebs, Neopap, Temlo, Tempra, Tenlap, Tylenol; *with other components:* Arthralgen, Bancaps, Codalan, Coldene, Colrex, Dialog, Duacin, Esgic, Excedrin, Gaysal, Midrin, Ornex, Panitol, Parafon Forte, Percogesic, Prolaire-B, Scotgesic, Sinubid, Sinulin, Sinutab-II, Supac, T-Caps, Trind, Tussagesic, Vanquish)

Aspirin (Ecotrin, Empirin, Measurin; *with other components:* Alka-Seltzer, Anacin, A.S.A. Compound, Aspergum, Bufferin, Colban, Cope 1, Coricidin, Darvon Compound, Defensin, Dristan, Excedrin, Fizrin, 4-Way Cold Tablets, Midol, P-A-C, Sal-Fayne, Stanback, Trigesic)

Choline salicylate (Arthropan)

Salicylamide (*with other components:* Sal-Eze, Zarumin)

Cephaloridine (Loridine)

Diazepam (Valium)

Kanamycin (Kantrex)

Narcotic analgesics

Tetracyclines

COMMON DRUGS THAT DECREASE THE ACTION OF ORAL ANTICOAGULANTS:

Barbiturates (Amytal, Phenobarbital, Seconal)

Chlordiazepoxide (Librium)

Ethchlorvynol (Placidyl)

Glutethimide (Doriden)

Meprobamate (Equanil, Kesso-Bamate, Meprospan, Miltown; *with other components:* Bamadex, Deprol, Pathibamate)

Heparin sodium

SIGNIFICANCE:

This is an intramuscularly or subcutaneously administered anticoagulant.

Protamine sulfate, given intravenously is the antidote.

Since an increasing number of drugs are found to display varying interactions with different anticoagulants, it would be prudent for the physician to do frequent prothrombin times after the addition or withdrawal of *any* other drugs that are taken repeatedly by patients receiving anticoagulants.

Immunosuppressants

Azathioprine (Imuran)

Cyclophosphamide (Cytoxan)

Corticosteroids (See Endocrine system)

SIGNIFICANCE:

Used to suppress antibody formation and subsequent rejection in transplant patients.

Used singularly or in combination for the treatment of pemphigus and severe rheumatoid arthritis.

Consultation with the patient's physician should precede any dental treatment.

Antibiotic coverage prophylactically is recommended for all dental treatment.

Oral candidiasis should be anticipated.

Antineoplastic agents

Cisplatin (Platinol)
Busulfan (Myleran)
Mercaptopurine (Purinethol)
Cyclophosphamide (Cytoxan)
5-Fluorouracil (Efudex)
Chlorambucil (Leukeran)
Methotrexate
Cytarabine (Cytosar)
Corticosteroids (see Endocrine system)

SIGNIFICANCE:

Used primarily in the treatment of leukemias, lymphomas, and carcinoma.

Consultation with the patient's physician should precede any dental treatment.

Oral lesions may occur as a manifestation of the disease process or as a sequela of the drug therapy.

Oral candidiasis is a common sequela.

These patients may have an increased bleeding tendency.

Antibiotic coverage prophylactically is indicated because of the increased susceptibility to infection.

METABOLIC SYSTEM
Antidiabetic agents

Insulin
Chlorpropamide (Diabinese)
Tolbutamide (Orinase)
Acetohexamide (Dymelor)
Tolazamide (Tolinase)

SIGNIFICANCE:

Used in the treatment of diabetes mellitus. The sulfonylureas (acetohexamide, chlorpropamide, tolbutamide) and tolazamide increase the activity of the circulating insulin.

Sulfonylureas may prolong the effects of barbiturates.

Aspirin enhances the response to sulfonylureas and may precipitate a hypoglycemic coma.

Sulfonamides may potentiate the effects of the sulfonylureas.

Epinephrine increases insulin requirements and inhibits pancreatic insulin release.

Corticosteroids increase insulin requirements.

Infection increases insulin requirements. Therefore all precautions to prevent infection should be exercised.

Antigout agents

Elevated levels of uric acid in the blood, hyperuricemia, may result in deposition of urate crystals in joints. The clinical manifestations consist of severe arthritis and firm nodules on the ears (tophi). Therapy is directed toward reducing the inflammation, pain, and hyperuricemia.

Phenylbutazone (Azolid, Butazolidin)
Oxyphenbutazone (Oxalid, Tandearil)
Indomethacin (Indocin)
Allopurinol (Zyloprim)
Probenecid (Benemid)
Sulfinpyrazone (Anturane)
Ticrynafen (Selacryn)
Colchicine (*With other components:* Colbenemid, Salpacine)

SIGNIFICANCE:

Allopurinol interferes with the formation of uric acid.

Probenecid and sulfinpyrazone promote the urinary excretion of uric acid (uricosurics).

Colchicine, phenylbutazone, oxyphenbutazone, and indomethacin relieve the pain of acute attacks of gout.

Aspirin interferes with the action of probenecid, sulfinpyrazone, and ticrynafen.

When probenecid or ticrynafen is administered along with a penicillin or a cephalosporin, it increases the serum concentration of the antibiotic. This action is useful in the treatment of endocarditis and osteomyelitis.

Probenecid prolongs the action of the sulfonylureas (see Antidiabetic agents).

Sulfinpyrazone potentiates the action of the sulfonylureas and insulin.

The drugs classified as nonsteroidal antiinflammatory agents are frequently administered for the treatment of gout.

NEUROMUSCULAR SYSTEM
Tranquilizers (ataractics)

Tranquilizing drugs may be variously referred to as antipsychotic drugs, drugs for anxiety and insomnia, or major and minor tranquilizers. Because of the anticholinergic effects of the drugs and the disorders for which they are prescribed, the dental management of these patients requires more than routine attention.

Phenothiazines

Prochlorperazine maleate (Compazine; *with other components:* Combid, Eskatrol)

Thioridazine hydrochloride (Mellaril)

Trifluoperazine hydrochloride (Stelazine)

Chlorpromazine hydrochloride (Thorazine)

Propiomazine hydrochloride (*with other components:* Largon)

SIGNIFICANCE:

Used in the management of anxiety and tension. They potentiate other depressants.

Possible side effects include orthostatic hypotension, oral manifestations of a blood dyscrasia, dryness of the mouth, and uncontrolled movement of the muscles of the face, tongue, and jaw (extrapyramidal reactions).

Other tranquilizers

Diazepam (Valium)

Chlordiazepoxide hydrochloride (Librium)

Hydroxyzine hydrochloride (Atarax, Vistaril; *with other components:* Ataraxoid, Cartrax, Enarax, Marax)

Flurazepam hydrochloride (Dalmane)

Meprobamate (Equanil, Meprospan, Meprotabs; *with other components:* Deprol, Milpath)

Lorazepam (Ativan)

Oxazepam (Serax)

Temazepam (Restoril)

Clorazepate (Azene; Tranxene)

Prazepam (Verstran; Centrax)

SIGNIFICANCE:

Used in the management of tension, anxiety, and insomnia.

These drugs are potentiated by barbiturates, meperidine hydrochloride, MAOIs, and other antidepressants.

Side effects include dryness of mouth.

Diazepam is contraindicated in patients with acute narrow angle glaucoma.

The use of diazepam during pregnancy is contraindicated.

Antidepressants

Clinical signs of depression include a deterioration in personal appearance, minimal conversation, introverted personality, and poor oral hygiene. Depressed patients tend to demonstrate poor compliance. As a result of their mental status and the drug therapy for the condition, these patients require more frequent monitoring of their oral health.

MAOIs are considered the most effective antidepressants, but foods and drugs containing tyramine can cause a hypertensive crisis. Tricyclic antidepressants are therefore considered the drugs of choice for the treatment of severe depression. The tetracyclines, a new drug group, are promoted as being less anticholinergic than the tricyclics, with a quicker onset of action.

MAOIs

Isocarboxazid (Marplan)

Nialamide (Niamid)

Pargyline hydrochloride (Eutonyl)

Phenelzine sulfate (Nardil)

Tranylcypromine sulfate (Parnate)

SIGNIFICANCE:

Used in the treatment of depression.

An intravascular injection of epinephrine could precipitate a hypertensive crisis.

These drugs potentiate the effects of sedatives, hypnotics, and analgesics, especially increasing the CNS depressant effect of barbiturates, meperidine hydrochloride, and morphine.

Adverse effects include orthostatic hypertension, loss of appetite, and insomnia.

Tricyclic antidepressants

Amitriptyline hydrochloride (Elavil; *with other components:* Etrafon, Triavil)

Desipramine hydrochloride (Norpramin, Pertofrane)

Imipramine hydrochloride (Tofranil)

Nortriptyline hydrochloride (Aventyl Hydrochloride)

Protriptyline hydrochloride (Vivactil)

Doxepin hydrochloride (Sinequan)

SIGNIFICANCE:

Used in the treatment of depression.

An intravascular injection of epinephrine can precipitate an exaggerated hypertensive reaction.

Vitamin C and barbiturates can decrease the effects of these drugs.

Meperidine hydrochloride and antihistamines enhance the action of these drugs.

Adverse effects include dry mouth.

Tetracyclic antidepressants

Maprotiline hydrochloride (Ludiomil)

SIGNIFICANCE:

Essentially the same as the tricyclics.

Antimanics

Lithium carbonate (Eskalith, Lithane, Lithonate)
Lithium citrate (Lithonate-S)
SIGNIFICANCE:
Used to treat mania and manic-depressive disorders.
Adverse effects consist of dry mouth, tremors, edema, and confusion.

Antiparkinsonism drugs

Levodopa (Dopar, Larodopa)
Amantadine hydrochloride (Symmetrel)
Levodopa with *carbidopa* (Sinemet)
Bromocriptine mesylate (Parlodel)
SIGNIFICANCE:
Used to treat Parkinson's disease.
Adverse effects include orthostatic hypotension and dry mouth.

Anticonvulsants

Patients with convulsive disorders require special attention. Since fatigue and anxiety can contribute to the precipitation of seizures, these patients should be given short appointments in the morning, and treatment should be accomplished with anesthesia in a quiet environment.

Phenytoin, formerly termed diphenylhydantoin sodium (Dilantin)
SIGNIFICANCE:
Used in the control of grand mal seizures, in the treatment of cardiac arrhythmias, and in the treatment of neuralgias.
Stress and phenobarbital can decrease the effect of this drug.
Librium enhances the effect of Dilantin.
Side effects include gingival hyperplasia and oral manifestations of a blood dyscrasia, especially anemia.
It tends to depress serum folic acid and vitamin K levels.

Carbamazepine (Tegretol)
SIGNIFICANCE:
Used in the control of grand mal seizures and neuralgias.
Side effects include nausea and nystagmus.

Primidone (Mysoline)
Phenobarbital
SIGNIFICANCE:
Used to control seizures.
Side effects include gingival pain.

Clonazepam (Clonopin)
Valproic acid (Depakene)
Ethosuximide (Zarontin)
SIGNIFICANCE:
Used to control petit mal seizures.
Side effects include reduced salivation.

Parasympathomimetics

Pyridostigmine bromide (Mestinon)
Neostigmine bromide (Prostigmin)
SIGNIFICANCE:
Used in the symptomatic control of myasthenia gravis.
Promotes increased salivation.

Skeletal muscle relaxants—general

Carisoprodol (Rela, Soma)
Chlorzoxazone (*with acetaminophen:* Parafon Forte)
Orphenadrine (Disipal, Norflex; *with other components:* Estomul, Norgesic)
Methocarbamol (Robaxin)
SIGNIFICANCE:
Used in the treatment of muscle spasms, pain, and stiffness.
Other CNS depressants may enhance the effect of these drugs.
Robaxin should be used with caution in myasthenic patients receiving pyridostigmine bromide (Mestinon).
Orphenadrine may interact with Darvon, resulting in mental confusion, anxiety, and tremors.

Skeletal muscle relaxants—surgical

Succinylcholine chloride (Anectine, Sucostrin)
SIGNIFICANCE:
Used to produce muscle relaxation during operative procedures.
Kanamycin, neomycin, and streptomycin may enhance the effects of these drugs.

Sedatives

See Chapter 7.

Analgesics

See Chapters 9 and 10.

DISEASE STATES OF SPECIAL INTEREST

Asthma. Infection, allergies, and hypersensitivities are the primary causes of asthmatic attacks. The psychophysiologic stress of dental treatment may also provoke an attack. An asthmatic patient may have multiple allergies that have not been identified. Therefore the dentist should be judicious with the introduction of any medication to this patient, especially aspirin-containing drugs. A frequent side effect of antihistamines used to treat this condition is the reduction of salivary flow, which in turn adversely affects caries rate, periodontal status, tissue sensitivity, and the retention of complete dentures.

Emphysema. The reduced oxygenation of the blood resulting from pulmonary emphysema stimulates a compensatory erythrocytosis. Surgery on these patients should be preceded by an evaluation of the coagulation status. In severe emphysema a daily regimen of tetracycline is often prescribed as a prophylactic measure against a bacterial infection of the lungs. Tetracyclines tend to impair prothrombin utilization, thereby further promoting a potential bleeding diathesis.

Hypertension. In cases in which the numerical values of 90 mm Hg for diastolic pressure and 140 mm Hg for systolic pressure are exceeded on a consistent basis, the patient is considered to be hypertensive. In general, the higher the blood pressure is above the limits of normal the greater will be the potential of a cardiovascular accident. Elective dental treatment should be delayed until medical control of the blood pressure is demonstrated. Sedation with 5 mg diazepam (Valium) given 1 hour before the dental appointment may be indicated in cases in which anxiety is a complicating factor.

Congestive heart failure. The clinical signs of distended neck veins and cyanosis are indications of the degree of severity of congestive heart failure. Conservative measures of short appointments, an upright sitting position, and sedation for anxiety are indicated with this disease state. Oxygen support should be immediately available.

Myocardial infarction. Elective dental treatment should be delayed for at least 3 months after a myocardial infarction. These patients may be extremely anxious and intolerant of any pain. The same precautions should be applied in patients with this condition as in patients with angina. Anticoagulant therapy might be an additional complicating factor. If the clinical signs and symptoms of shortness of breath (SOB), intermittent chest pain, flushed face, and obvious obesity are present, a consultation with the patient's physician is indicated.

Anticoagulation. Therapy with anticoagulants always presents the threat of excessive bleeding with any procedure that may initiate some bleeding. However, at the controlled therapeutic level, routine dental procedures, including single extractions and subgingival curettage, may be accomplished without complications. Medications that either enhance the action of the anticoagulant or otherwise contribute an additional anticoagulant effect, for example, aspirin, should be avoided.

Rheumatic heart disease, congenital heart disease, and heart murmurs. With a history of any of these conditions, the primary dental concern is the increased susceptibility toward infective endocarditis. The cardiac status of the patient should be evaluated by the attending physician and a copy of the written consultation placed in the dental record. For any intervening dental treatment that will cause bleeding, the administration of antibiotics prophylactically is a judicious precaution. (See Appendix B.)

Pacemaker. There is a lack of consensus about the management of this condition. Precautions most usually implemented are avoiding the use of any electronic equipment, including vitalometers and the Cavitron, and using the prophylactic antibiotic regimen recommended for subacute bacterial endocarditis.

Prosthetic heart valves. There are two primary concerns regarding dental treatment for patients with heart valve prostheses: bacteremia and excessive bleeding. Outpatients should be covered with the prophylactic antibiotic regimen recommended for subacute bacterial endocarditis. A current prothrombin time should be requested since these patients are taking anticoagulants.

Hepatic failure. Clinical signs and symptoms that reflect the extent of hepatic failure are weakness, fatigability, jaundice, ascites, and ankle edema. The primary concern to the dentist is the impaired coagulation status caused by the development of a thrombocytopenia and a hypoprothrombinemia. The bleeding and prothrombin times should be evaluated before surgical treatment is initiated.

Hepatitis. The clinical signs and symptoms of jaundice, fever, malaise, and nausea indicate an acute viral hepatitis. Elective dental procedures should be delayed until the liver function tests have returned to normal. When it becomes necessary to treat a high-risk patient, the dentist should wear a face mask, glasses, and disposable gloves. The instruments should be washed with a 1% solution of sodium hypochlorite and then autoclaved.

Malabsorption syndrome. Oral signs and symptoms of glossitis, cheilosis, and anemia should suggest malnutrition, which may be caused by malabsorption. Laboratory tests for the levels of iron, vitamin B_{12}, and folates should be conducted before treatment is initiated. Treatment on an empirical basis may mask serious underlying physiologic defects.

Renal failure. During a period of acute renal failure, only emergency dental treatment should be entertained because of the multiple systemic complications and the high risk of an infection that may be difficult to control. Chronic or irreversible end-stage renal failure is treated by hemodialysis.

Dialysis. Complications influencing the dental management of a patient being treated by intermittent hemodialysis include an increased susceptibility to infection, a bleeding tendency caused by inadequate platelet factor III activity, the possibility of hypertension, a predisposition toward osteodystrophy complicated by secondary hyperparathyroidism, and a high rate of nonicteric viral hepatitis. Antibiotic coverage and close monitoring of the bleeding time are basic recommendations. Dental treatment is best accomplished in the morning of the day after dialysis.

Renal transplantation. The patient's host resistance to infection is depressed by immunosuppressive drug therapy. Aseptic necrosis of bone and impaired stress response are major sequelae of the steroid therapy employed. The periodontal status of these patients should be closely monitored because of the greater susceptibility to infection and the diabetogenic effect of the steroids. Treatment of the dialysis and renal transplant patient should be closely coordinated with the attending physician.

Seizure disorder. Anxiety generated by dental treatment or pain during the treatment caused by inadequate anesthesia may precipitate a seizure in patients taking anticonvulsant medication. A history of a recent seizure indicates poor therapeutic control. For best results the patient's appointment should be in the morning, when he is rested and shortly after he has taken his medication.

Stroke. All efforts should be directed toward keeping the patient calm, comfortable, and free of pain. Any event that effects a sudden, exaggerated rise in blood pressure has the potential of precipitating a cardiovascular accident. The patient should have a morning appointment when he is rested, premedication for anxiety should be given when indicated, and the operation should be performed with sufficient anesthesia.

Anemia. A deficiency of hemoglobin may be manifested orally by a loss of papillae on the tongue, a glossitis, and a generally pale color of all the mucous membranes. Constitutional symptoms of headache and fever may also be present. The patient should be referred to a physician for the diagnosis and treatment of the etiology of the anemia.

Leukemia. The malignant proliferation of immature white cells decreases the host resistance to infection and tends to crowd out the cells in the marrow that produce the red blood cells and platelets. Oral signs and symptoms include swollen gingivae, unprovoked bleeding, and secondary infection. Dental treatment should consist of conservative, supportive care directed toward improving oral comfort and preventing oral infections. It is imperative to maintain oral hygiene.

Thrombocytopenia. A deficiency in platelets may be manifested orally as ecchymotic areas and gingival bleeding. Referral for immediate diagnosis and therapy is essential. Any dental therapy that initiates bleeding could result in a life-threatening situation.

Hyperpituitarism. Acromegaly is the result of hyperfunction of eosinophil cells of the anterior pituitary after closure of the epiphyses. There is a general increase in size of the orofacial structures, which may lead to a provisional diagnosis of the condition. There is a high incidence of diabetes mellitus in acromegalics, which may be manifested as a poor response to oral healing and exacerbated periodontal disease.

Hypopituitarism. A deficiency of hormones produced by the anterior pituitary gland can affect the size, shape, and eruption rate of the teeth in children. These may be subtle changes but may constitute the first clinical evidence of hypopituitarism. In adults the hormonal deficiency affects the dependent glands and results in general constitutional symptoms.

Addison's disease. The diagnosis of adrenal insufficiency is based on the signs and symptoms of weakness, weight loss, low blood pressure, nausea, and vomiting. Pigmentation of the mucous membranes and a glossitis from malnutrition are oral signs of this condition. Elective dental treatment should be delayed until replacement steroid therapy is regulated.

Cushing's disease (syndrome). An excessive amount of adrenal cortical hormones, whether endogenous or exogenous, may result in hypertension, hirsutism, edema, thinning of the skin, elevated blood glucose level, and osteoporosis. Oral infections and periodontal disease may be more difficult to control. Candidiasis is more prevalent. Sedation and pain control are prime considerations for dental treatment, since there is no steroid reserve to respond to stress.

Pheochromocytoma. Oral candidiasis and headaches may be early dental complaints to indicate hypersecretion of epinephrine and norepinephrine caused by an adenoma of the adrenal medulla. Supporting evidence of hypertension, sweating, and tremors should prompt medical consultation.

Diabetes (mellitus). The primary dental concerns with the diabetic individual are a reduced host response to infection and a tendency toward candidiasis. In the adult who displays an unexplained exacerbation of periodontal disease and decreased salivary flow, undiagnosed or uncontrolled diabetes should be ruled out.

A patient with diagnosed diabetes who goes into a coma of clinically unrecognizable origin should be given a small amount of sugar (glucose) as a precautionary measure until medical attention is available.

Hyperparathyroidism. Dental radiographic findings of loss of the lamina dura and distortion of the normal trabecular pattern of the bone, producing a ground-glass appearance, are frequent indications of hyperparathyroidism. Immediate medical treatment should be instituted.

Hypoparathyroidism. Hypoparathyroidism may be manifested as recurrent oral candidiasis, circumoral paresthesia, and spasm of the facial muscles. The patient should be referred for medical treatment.

Hyperthyroidism. Only emergency dental treatment is indicated for patients with uncontrolled hyperthyroidism. Adequate sedation and pain control are necessary to prevent a hyperthyroid crisis. The classic clinical features are restlessness, sweating, tremors, and protruding eyes.

Hypothyroidism. An insidious hyposecretion of the thyroid may develop in adults, resulting in edema, increased weight, brittle hair, drowsiness, and an intolerance to cold. These features may appear in patients who are being given inadequate thyroid supplement. There are no contraindications for dental treatment, and the patient should be referred for medical correction of the condition.

Scleroderma. Tissues affected by scleroderma will display an extremely diminished response to injury or infection because of the compromised blood supply to the area. Radiographic findings of widened periodontal ligament spaces may be an early indication of diffuse scleroderma. Periodontal disease is particularly difficult to manage. Where facial masking is progressive, extraction of posterior teeth is recommended while there is mechanical accessibility.

Myasthenia gravis. Dental treatment may need to be modified because of the easy fatigability of the patient's head and neck muscles. The parasympathomimetic effects of the pharmacotherapy may increase salivary flow. If the border of a prosthesis encroaches on the parotid papilla, salivary drainage can be impeded because of impaired muscle action.

Ulcers (duodenal/gastric). Antacid medications and milk reduce the efficacy of tetracyclines. Oral signs of anemia may indicate a chronic blood loss or an iron deficiency due to inadequate acid in the stomach, as a result of the antacid medication, to convert ingested iron to the ferrous state for absorption.

Postradiation therapy. The primary adverse sequelae after radiation therapy are an inordinate risk of local infection caused by the compromised vascular supply to the area irradiated and xerostomia caused by inactivation of the salivary glands. Dental procedures that may result in bleeding require extended prophylactic antibiotic coverage. A 0.5% solution of sodium carboxymethyl cellulose will relieve the xerostomia. Candidiasis is a frequent occurrence in this condition.

Glaucoma. The use of antisialagogues is contraindicated because they tend to increase the pressure in the anterior chamber of the eye.

BIBLIOGRAPHY

American Medical Association Council on Drugs: AMA drug evaluations, ed. 4, Acton, Mass., 1980, Publishing Sciences Group, Inc.

Clin-Alert, Louisville, Ky., Science Editors, Inc.

American Dental Association Council on Dental Therapeutics: Accepted dental therapeutics, ed. 38, Chicago, 1979, American Dental Association.

Hansten, P.D.: Drug interactions, Philadelphia, 1971, Lea & Febiger.

The medical letter on drugs and therapeutics, New Rochelle, N.Y., The Medical Letter, Inc.

Penna, R.P.: A screening procedure for drug interactions, J. Am. Pharm. Assoc. **10:**66-67, 1970.

Physician's desk reference, ed. 36, Oradel, N.J., 1982, Medical Economics, Inc.

Pharmacologic management of certain common oral disease entities

To present treatment in its proper context, the introductory paragraph or paragraphs on each condition briefly review the occurrence, etiology, and principal signs and symptoms of the disease. No attempt is made to present complete diagnostic criteria. Sample prescriptions are included to facilitate the treatment procedure. (All doses are for adults unless otherwise indicated.)

ACTINIC CHANGES TO LIP

Long-term exposure of the lip to the elements may initiate irreversible tissue changes. The lower lip displays these changes more than the upper lip because of its more everted position. Sunscreen preparations serve to lubricate the lip and block out the solar radiation. A sunscreen with a high skin protection factor (SPF) of 10 to 15 is indicated to prevent lip damage especially where the normal skin pigmentation is minimal. The sunscreen should be applied 1 hour before sun exposure and replenished periodically.

Where keratotic changes have occurred on the vermilion border of the lip, aggressive treatment with 5-fluorouracil (FU) is recommended.[1] One percent 5-fluorouracil in a propylene glycol base is applied twice each day for 2 to 3 weeks.

Betamethasone valerate (Valisone) is used for relief of irritation caused by 5-fluorouracil. Healing is completed in 3 to 6 weeks after the 5-fluorouracil is discontinued.

℞ 5-Fluorouracil, 1%
Disp: 10 ml
Sig: Apply to lip twice daily.

℞ Betamethasone valerate cream, 0.1%
Disp: 5 gm
Sig: Apply to lip after meals and at bedtime.

ACUTE NECROTIZING ULCERATIVE GINGIVITIS

Acute necrotizing ulcerative gingivitis (ANUG) has been called *Vincent's infection, trench mouth*, and numerous other names. Although ANUG is less prevalent than it was in years past, it remains a disease of importance in dental practice. The etiology of ANUG appears to have both bacteriologic (spirochetes and fusiform bacilli) and predisposing (local irritants, physical and mental stress, debilitation) components. Basic to diagnosis is the typical pseudomembranous ulcer that begins at the tips of the interdental papillae. This painful spreading ulcer is usually associated with a distinctive odor and increased salivation. Systemic signs and symptoms are not necessarily present, but cervical lymphadenopathy, an elevated temperature, general malaise, nausea, and headache may be experienced.

The principal treatment of ANUG is *not* pharmacologic and includes the removal of irritants, the establishment of good oral hygiene, and a regimen of adequate rest and nutrition. However, certain drug categories should be discussed in regard to the treatment of ANUG.

Mouthwashes. Mouthwashes facilitate oral hygiene by their flushing action. For this reason they are useful during the treatment of ANUG. Hydrogen peroxide in a 1% to 1.5% solution or a physiologic saline solution may be used. The evidence is unconvincing that the oxygen-releasing agents are any more effective than saline rinses in home care of ANUG. The local effects of a dilute solution of an obtundent mouthwash, such as cetylpyridinium chloride (Cepacol), may be useful in some cases.

℞ Hydrogen peroxide, 3%
Disp: 8 oz
Sig: Dilute to half strength with warm water and rinse mouth every 2 hours.

Analgesics and antipyretics. In severe cases of ANUG, the mouth is very painful and the temperature is sometimes elevated. An antipyretic analgesic should be prescribed in these cases, and aspirin or acetaminophen (Tylenol) is usually adequate. Instructions to the patient to take two 5-grain aspirin or acetaminophen tablets every 4 hours if needed for pain is generally adequate. However, sometimes a prescription may be necessary even for these very commonly used drugs.

℞ Aspirin, 5 gr
Disp: 100 tablets
Sig: Take 2 tablets every 4 hours as needed for pain.

℞ Acetaminophen, 5 gr
Disp: 100 tablets
Sig: Take 2 tablets every 4 hours as needed for pain.

Food supplements. The oral tissues may be so painful in some cases of ANUG that eating becomes difficult. Certain commercially prepared food supplements (Meritene, Nutrament, Provimalt, Sustagen) may be used as meal substitutes if an adequate soft diet cannot be obtained or if the patient prefers the supplements. These food supplements provide required vitamins and minerals as well as the necessary carbohydrate, fat, and protein. There is no convincing evidence that the vitamin preparations are helpful in ANUG, but it is probably advisable to prescribe them in those cases where an inadequate vitamin intake has preceded the onset of the condition. In these cases any of a large number of multiple vitamin preparations should suffice.

℞ Meritene
Disp: 1 lb can
Sig: Take three servings daily. Prepare as indicated on can.

Antibiotics. There is no question that many antibiotics will improve the clinical course of ANUG. However, because of the rapid and dramatic recovery of patients with the condition after local treatment, antibiotics are infrequently required and their routine use is to be condemned. One should consider administering them only in severe cases where the patient's resistance to infection is low or there is evidence of significant systemic involvement. When antibiotics must be given, penicillin, erythromycin, and the tetracyclines are effective. Although clinical reports are lacking, lincomycin and clindamycin will also probably be effective. Patients with rheumatic or congenital heart disease should, of course, be premedicated with penicillin in accordance with the recommendations of the American Heart Association before debridement.

℞ Penicillin V tablets, 250 mg
Disp: 40 tablets
Sig: Take 1 tablet at bedtime and 1 hour before each meal.*

Topical caustics. Caustic drugs should not be used on the lesions of ANUG.

PRIMARY HERPETIC GINGIVOSTOMATITIS

Primary herpetic gingivostomatitis (primary herpes) is a common disease that is caused by the herpes simplex virus. It is principally a disease of infants and children and is frequently associated with pneumonia, meningitis, and upper respiratory infections. Primary herpes is seldom seen in adolescents or adults. The painful lesions may appear throughout the gingival, labial, buccal, palatal, glossal, and pharyngeal mucosa. They appear as depressed yellow-white ulcers circumscribed by an area of erythema. Systemic signs and symptoms that are generally associated with these lesions include high temperature, headache, refusal to take food, lymphadenopathy, and general malaise. The systemic reaction is usually less severe in adults than in children. In infants and young children, primary herpes can be dangerous because of the problems of dehydration, acidosis, contact spread to the hands and eyes, and visceral dissemination.

Therapeutic agents generally have little or no effect on the course of primary herpes, and treatment is essentially supportive. Drugs in the following groups are used.

Analgesics and antipyretics. Although the course of the primary herpes infection may be subclinical, many children experience a high temperature, which may reach 105° F but usually recedes shortly after the lesions appear. In view of the temperature and extremely painful nature of the lesions, an antipyretic analgesic such as aspirin or acetaminophen is indicated. One should note that in the use of aspirin and acetaminophen to control high temperature in chil-

---

*Dosage for treatment of ANUG when an antibiotic is indicated— not for subacute bacterial endocarditis prophylaxis.

dren, careful attention must be given to dosage. This is particularly true in primary herpes because the patient may be dehydrated. Fluid intake is often minimal in this disease because of the painful oral condition, and absorption of fluids may be hindered by a disturbance of gastrointestinal function. Sponging with tepid water frequently controls high temperatures effectively and thus allows minimal dosage with antipyretics. Dehydration and acidosis that may be associated with high temperatures in children can be dangerous and should receive prompt inpatient attention.

See earlier statement on analgesics and antipyretics.

Mouthwashes and topical obtundents. Mouthwashes, particularly those with local obtundent activity, may partially relieve the painful local symptoms of primary herpetic gingivostomatitis and thereby encourage the adequate intake of food and liquid. Viscous lidocaine, dyclonine hydrochloride in 0.5% aqueous solution, diphenhydramine (Benadryl), kaolin (Kaopectate), gentian violet, methylene blue, and combinations of these medications have been used topically to provide temporary symptomatic relief. We recommend the local anesthetics. The application of sodium carboxymethylcellulose paste (Orabase Emollient) to the lesions may also reduce the discomfort.

R Benadryl powder, 0.5% with dyclonine, 0.5% in physiologic saline
Disp: 8 oz
Sig: Rinse with 1 teaspoonful every 2 hours.

R Benadryl elixir, 12.5 mg/5 ml
Disp: 4 oz
Sig: Rinse with 1 teaspoonful for 2 minutes before each meal.

R Benadryl elixir, 12.5 mg/5 ml with Kaopectate, 50% mixture by volume
Disp: 8 oz
Sig: Rinse with 1 teaspoonful every 2 hours.

R Xylocaine viscous, 2%
Disp: 450 ml
Sig: Rinse with 1 tablespoonful every 4 hours.

Food supplements. In situations where a nutritious soft diet cannot be consistently obtained, the food supplements previously mentioned should be employed. If the soft diet is preferred, supplementation with a daily multiple vitamin and mineral preparation may be helpful, particularly in infants and children. Specific curative effects of individual vitamins are not established.

See earlier statement on food supplements.

Topical caustics. The results of the application of caustics such as silver nitrate, phenol, and trichloroacetic acid are not impressive, and their use is generally discouraged.

Corticosteroids. Since the etiologic agent in primary herpes is viral, the use of the adrenocorticosteroids may result in a serious and possibly fatal spread of the infection. Consequently, these drugs are *contraindicated* in primary herpes.

Antibiotics. Because of the viral nature of primary herpes, antibiotics are not considered helpful unless a secondary bacterial infection is present. However, some clinicians routinely start antibiotics in the severely affected infant or child.

See earlier statement on antibiotics.

RECURRENT HERPES LABIALIS

The lesions of recurrent herpes labialis, which are relatively common, are caused by the herpes simplex virus. The painful lesions occur at the vermilion border of the lip, where they may appear initially as an area of erythema followed by vesicle formation. Rupture of the vesicle leaves an encrusted ulceration. The lesions are usually single, last about 1 week, and heal without scarring. Elevated temperature and other signs and symptoms of systemic involvement associated with primary herpes are not usually seen with herpes labialis.

In treatment the practitioner is essentially concerned with the painful and unesthetic lip lesion. Many substances have been placed on these lesions to accelerate healing, but although numerous favorable reports have appeared, confirming studies have not been reported. The application of a lubricating agent seems to lessen the pain. Adrenocorticosteroid applications to cutaneous herpes simplex infections have been associated with serious disseminated infection with the herpes simplex virus.[2] Consequently, as in the case of primary herpes, the use of corticosteroids is contraindicated in herpes labialis.

Prophylactic measures. For patients in whom the recurrence has invariably been precipitated by exposure to the sun, the lesions may be prevented by applying a sunscreen with a high SPF. It should be applied to the area usually affected 1 hour before sun exposure for adequate absorption.

R Presun 15 sunscreen lotion
Disp: 4 fl oz
Sig: Apply to susceptible area 1 hour before sun exposure.

℞ Chap Stick sunblock 15 lip balm
Disp: 4 gm
Sig: Apply to lips 1 hour before sun exposure.

Antiviral agents. The topical application of 0.5% idoxuridine (Stoxil) ophthalmic ointment is not effective on lip lesions, probably because of the poor penetrability of the active ingredient. An antiviral agent approved for the treatment of occular herpes simplex (type I) is vidarabine (Vira-A). The 3% ophthalmic ointment of vidarabine applied to the area of anticipated recurrence may reduce severity and duration of symptoms.

℞ Vidarabine (Vira-A) ophthalmic ointment, 3%
Disp: 3.5 gm
Sig: Apply to lip four times a day.

Photochemical inactivation. Viruses can be inactivated by treatment with certain heterotricyclic dyes, for example 0.1% proflavine, and subsequent exposure to ordinary fluorescent light. Because of the possibility that this treatment might mutagenize cells into cancer cells, it is not recommended.

Vitamins. Water-soluble bioflavonoid–ascorbic acid complex, an essential constituent for normal capillary permeability and fragility, is valuable in reducing the signs and symptoms associated with recurrent herpes simplex (type I) virus infections.[3] As with all agents used, the therapy is more effective when instituted in the early prodromal stage of the disease process.

℞ Citrus bioflavonoids and ascorbic acid tablets (Peridin-C), 400 mg
Disp: 10 tablets
Sig: Take 2 tablets at once, then 1 tablet three times a day for 3 days.

An effective therapeutic regimen is a combination of a sunscreen prophylactically, then vidarabine topically, and citrus bioflavonoid–ascorbic acid systemically in the early prodromal stage.

RECURRENT APHTHOUS STOMATITIS

Recurrent aphthous stomatitis is a relatively common condition that is seen most frequently after 20 years of age. Investigative evidence indicated that a transitional L form of an alpha streptococcus was the etiologic agent; however, vaccinations against this organism proved ineffective.[4-7] Studies have disclosed an association between recurrent aphthae and deficiencies of vitamin B_{12}, folic acid, and iron.[8] Hematologic screening should precede the initiation

of vitamin therapy. The painful lesions of aphthous stomatitis are similar in appearance to those of primary herpes, but the associated systemic signs and symptoms are absent or much less severe. In some cases a low-grade fever, cervical lymphadenopathy, leukocytosis, and debilitation may occur.[9]

Symptomatic control by previously mentioned drugs is indicated: aspirin for pain and fever; obtundent mouthwashes for discomfort, particularly to allow the maintenance of an adequate diet; and food supplements where nutrition cannot be maintained otherwise.

Topical adrenal steroids have been beneficial in some cases.[3,10,11] However, in view of the problem of adrenocortical atrophy during steroid medication, the use of these drugs in recurrent aphthous stomatitis should be limited to short-term topical application in severe cases. A convenient form of steroid for intraoral application is 0.1% triamcinolone acetonide in a sodium carboxymethyl cellulose emollient paste (Kenalog in Orabase), which is to be applied two or three times daily. Since the use of steroids is contraindicated in fungal or viral lesions of the oral cavity, the practitioner must be certain of a diagnosis of an aphthous lesion. Relief from discomfort will be obtained in some cases if the emollient paste alone is applied to the lesions after meals and at bedtime.

Since the concentration of oral streptococci is thought to be a contributing factor in the recurrence of aphthae in susceptible persons, tetracycline medication has been employed. Graykowski, Barile, and Stanley[5] found the use of a tetracycline regimen helpful in about 70% of the cases studied. A suspension of 250 mg of tetracycline is held in the mouth for 2 minutes and then swallowed four times per 24 hours for 10 days. The patient should be instructed not to eat or drink for 1 hour after medication. The suspension is formed by mixing the contents of a 250 mg capsule of tetracycline in a teaspoonful of water.* The numerous tetracycline syrups do not seem to be effective, apparently because the syrup interferes with topical reaction of the medication.

The literature does not reflect any consistency in regard to the use of silver nitrate, smallpox and poliomyelitis vaccinations, antihistamines, gamma globulin, and vitamins in the treatment of recurrent aphthous stomatitis.

---

*The original suspension used by Graykowski is no longer available commercially.

℞ Kenalog in Orabase, 0.1%
Disp: 5 gm tube
Sig: Apply to lesion after each meal and at bedtime.

℞ Tetracycline capsules, 250 mg
Disp: 40 capsules
Sig: Suspend contents of 1 capsule in a teaspoonful of water.
    Rinse for 2 minutes four times a day and swallow.

For severe multiple aphthae and for *major aphthae,* which have been present for weeks or months, more aggressive treatment is indicated to control the ulcerative process. The topical and systemic employment of corticosteroids in a regimen of an initial large dose that is quickly tapered off is successful in clearing the lesions in a few days. An elixir of dexamethasone (Decadron) with a concentration of 0.5 mg/5 ml may be used in this manner.

℞ Dexamethasone elixir, 0.5 mg/5 ml
Disp: 200 ml
Sig: (Directions for taking elixir of dexamethasone)
    1. For 3 days, rinse with 1 tablespoonful four times a day and swallow. Then
    2. For 3 days, rinse with 1 teaspoonful four times a day and swallow. Then
    3. For 3 days, rinse with 1 teaspoonful four times a day and swallow every other time. Then
    4. Rinse with 1 teaspoonful four times a day and spit out. Discontinue medication when mouth becomes comfortable.
       When mouth discomfort recurs, begin treatment at step 3.

CANDIDIASIS (MONILIASIS)

Candidiasis is infection by the fungus (yeast) *Candida albicans.* Other species of *Candida* are infrequently pathogenic in humans. The infection of mucous membrane by *C. albicans* (thrush) is fairly common. The most frequent sites are the oral and vaginal mucosa; skin is less frequently involved. Visceral involvement is even less common and is generally associated with a strong predisposing component. The principal visceral involvement is aspiration pneumonia. Less frequently, hematogenous spread may involve the kidney, brain, meninges, heart, thyroid, pancreas, liver, and adrenals.[12]

Oral candidiasis. C. albicans is a normal inhabitant of the oral cavity. A disease state is manifested when the fungus is capable of unusually accelerated growth. Predisposing factors that increase the susceptibility to candidal overgrowth include (1) suppression of normal oral flora by antibacterial therapy (this is particularly important in the use of long-term or broad-spectrum antibiotics), (2) debilitation (may be caused by age or disease), (3) diabetes, (4) therapy with adrenal steroids, (5) antineoplastic therapy, (6) malnutrition, (7) pregnancy (increased incidence of vaginal candidiasis), and (8) infancy.

The diagnosis of oral candidiasis is based on the presence of the characteristic lesions plus a history of predisposition. Diagnosis can be confirmed by a microscopic study of smears taken from the lesions. The characteristic oral lesions of acute candidiasis are white, milk curd–like patches that adhere to the mucosa. Removal of the lesions leaves red areas or bleeding points.

Oral candidiasis in chronic form may be manifested as an angular cheilitis, a denture stomatitis, or hyperplastic candidiasis.[13] No systemic signs or symptoms are caused by oral candidiasis.

The treatment of oral candidiasis consists of the topical application of the antifungal drug nystatin (Mycostatin). When the aqueous suspension (100,000 U/ml) is used, the usual adult dosage is 2 ml four times per 24 hours. Zegarelli[14] has recommended a dose of up to 3 ml after each meal and before bedtime. The suspension should be swished in the mouth for 2 minutes before swallowing. Nystatin suspension is supplied in 60 ml bottles with a dropper calibrated at 1 ml. Cohen[13] has recommended the use of nystatin tablets. A tablet (500,000 units) is dissolved in the mouth four times per 24 hours. Nystatin vaginal tablets (100,000 units) may be used as lozenges. This modality supplies continuous therapy to the affected area, decreasing the duration of the clinical signs and symptoms. Regardless of whether the suspension or tablet is used, treatment should continue for at least 14 days and not be discontinued until two successive smears are negative[15] or at least until 48 hours after the signs of infection have disappeared. Treatment may require 4 to 6 weeks or longer to eliminate this rather tenacious infection. This is particularly true of chronic hyperplastic candidiasis.

℞ Nystatin oral suspension, 100,000 U/ml
Disp: 60 ml
Sig: Take 2 ml four times per 24 hours. Hold in mouth for 2 minutes and swallow.

℞ Nystatin vaginal tablets, 100,000 U/tablet
Disp: 30 tablets
Sig: Let tablet dissolve in mouth, three times per 24 hours.

Rinsing with the oral suspension of nystatin may be uncomfortable for patients with dry, sensitive oral mucosa, and the bitterness of the nystatin vaginal tablets may cause nausea. Both of these adverse side effects reduce patient compliance and consequently promote the persistence of the candidiasis. A synthetic imidazole, ketoconazole (Nizoral), for oral administration is effective against mucocutaneous candidiasis and is well tolerated as compared with amphotericin B.

Ŗ Ketoconazole tablets, 200 mg
Disp: 40 tablets
Sig: Take 1 or 2 tablets once daily at mealtime.

ANGULAR CHEILITIS/CHEILOSIS

Angular cheilitis (inflammation of the angles of the mouth) may be characterized by simple redness or may exhibit fissures, erosion, ulcers, and crusting. The area may be painless, may burn, or may be otherwise painful. Angular cheilitis may be caused by reduced vertical dimension with consequent accentuation of the commissural skin folds and drooling. It may also be caused by infection, allergic reactions, trauma, and nutritional deficiencies. In angular cheilitis from a nutritional deficiency (principally a lack of riboflavin), the lesion takes on a more "macerated" appearance and is generally given the more specific name, *angular cheilosis.*

The cause of angular cheilitis is usually multiple. Consequently, treatment must encompass all etiologic factors. Lesions from nutritional deficiency result principally from lack of riboflavin but are generally associated with multiple deficiencies. These lesions should be resolved by the establishment of adequate dietary intake. Temporary use of meal supplements or multiple vitamin preparations, particularly those heavy in the B-complex vitamins should be helpful. Allergy-induced angular cheilitis is rare and should be resolved by determining and eliminating the allergenic agent. Lesions induced by trauma, such as stretching and pulling during prolonged dental procedures, should heal without treatment after the traumatogenic component is removed. However, the traumatic angular lesion may become secondarily infected before complete healing obtains. Angular cheilitis caused by a reduced vertical dimension should be resolved by reestablishing an acceptable interocclusal distance. However, the cheilitis is frequently caused by both a loss of vertical dimension and infection.

Most cases of angular cheilitis that require pharmacologic management are caused by infection. The presence of infection by *C. albicans* or bacteria should be suspected in all cases of angular stomatitis that do not respond quickly to the removal of other etiologic components. Severe cases of angular cheilitis or any case that does not respond to other indicated procedures should be cultured to determine the presence of *C. albicans* or bacteria as etiologic agents. If *C. albicans* is a causative factor, the indicated treatment is the local application of nystatin ointment (100,000 U/gm) two to six times per 24 hours until at least 48 hours after the lesion has disappeared. Nystatin ointment is available in 30 gm tubes. If the infecting agent is bacterial rather than fungal, the lesion is likely to be resolved by keeping the area clean and by eliminating other etiologic factors. In cases where pharmacologic intervention is required to eliminate bacterial involvement, a bacitracin-neomycin preparation (Bacimycin Ointment: bacitracin 500 units, neomycin 23.5 mg/gm) may be applied three or four times per 24 hours. This ointment is available in 15 gm tubes. An alternative agent is 3% chlortetracycline ointment, applied three or four times per 24 hours. The 3% chlortetracycline preparation is available in 15 and 30 gm tubes. Some infections may be caused by a mixture of fungal and bacterial organisms. A preparation of nystatin-neomycin-triamcinolone acetonide (Mycolog) is effective in providing quick clinical improvement and symptomatic relief in mixed infections. Mycolog is available as an ointment in 15 and 20 gm tubes.

Ŗ Allbee with C capsules
Disp: 100 capsules
Sig: Take 1 capsule with each meal.

Ŗ Nystatin ointment, 100,000 U/gm
Disp: 30 gm
Sig: Apply to affected area after each meal and at bedtime.

Ŗ Bacimycin ointment
Disp: 15 gm
Sig: Apply to affected area after each meal and at bedtime.

Ŗ Chlortetracycline, 3% ointment
Disp: 15 gm
Sig: Apply to affected area after each meal and at bedtime.

Ŗ Mycolog ointment
Disp: 15 gm
Sig: Apply to affected area after each meal and at bedtime.

LICHEN PLANUS

Lichen planus is a relatively common skin disease that frequently involves mucous membranes. It is a disease of adults, with no sex predisposition. The etiology is unknown, but it is invariably precipitated by stress. Clinically, it has variable forms with the most characteristic being a white network on an erythematous base. The hyperkeratotic form is asymptomatic. The symptoms of oral erosive lichen planus vary in intensity from a slight sensitivity to acidic liquids and spicy foods to extreme discomfort with any contact of the affected area.

Treatment is directed toward improving the host response and the general nutritional state. Regimens of niacinamide plus vitamins B and C at 20 times the prophylactic dose for 4 weeks have been reported to be beneficial. The topical application of antiinflammatory agents improves the clinical symptoms. Ointments of 0.1% betamethasone valerate (Valisone) and 0.05% flurandrenolone (Cordran) are frequently employed. When these ointments are covered with Kenalog in Orabase, it prolongs their duration of action. Rinsing with an elixir of dexamethasone (Decadron) is a common treatment. In severe cases systemic steroids may be necessary to control the disease process. The same regimen recommended for major aphthae should be employed.

R Betamethasone valerate (Valisone) ointment, 0.1%
Disp: 15 gm tube
Sig: Apply to affected area after each meal and at bedtime.

R Flurandrenolone (Cordran) ointment, 0.05%
Disp: 15 gm tube
Sig: Apply to affected area after each meal and at bedtime.

R Kenalog in Orabase, 0.1%
Disp: 5 Gm tube
Sig: Coat the lesion after each meal and at bedtime.

R Dexamethasone (Decadron) elixir, 0.5 mg/5 ml
Disp: 100 ml
Sig: Rinse with 1 teaspoonful for 1 minute after each meal and at bedtime. Do not swallow.

BURNING TONGUE SYNDROME AND SYMPTOMATIC GEOGRAPHIC TONGUE

Either local irritants or systemic deficiencies or a combination of the two may result in sensitivity of the tongue. The ultimate treatment is based on the diagnosis, which in some instances requires a thorough medical evaluation to rule out nutritional deficiencies, malabsorption syndrome, endocrine disturbances, blood dyscrasias, secretory impairment, and allergic states.

Symptomatic relief may be achieved by rinsing with elixir of diphenhydramine hydrochloride (Benadryl). It coats the tissue temporarily, has mild topical anesthetic qualities, and if swallowed provides some sedation.

R Benadryl elixir, 12.5 mg/5 ml
Disp: 8 oz
Sig: Rinse with 1 teaspoonful for 2 minutes before each meal and swallow.

PERICORONITIS

Pericoronitis is the inflammation of tissues around the crown of a tooth. Although the term could be applied to any tooth, it generally refers to a common and painful inflammatory reaction around partially erupted lower third molars. In these teeth a flap of gingiva (operculum) covers part of the occlusal surface. The presence of food debris and bacteria between the operculum and tooth generates an inflammatory response. The swelling that results enlarges the operculum and frequently results in the development of periodontal pockets on one or more tooth surfaces. The edema thus enlarges the pocket area in which bacteria can grow and more debris can become entrapped.

Patients usually experience intermittent occurrences of mild inflammation and slight swelling of the soft tissues before more serious involvement. The component of infection that may be minimal initially can progress quickly to present a serious cellulitis.

When treatment is instituted early, only gentle debridement of the cul-de-sac areas by curet or saline irrigation may be required. The patient is usually instructed to continue warm saline rinses for a day or so. The problem will recur in most cases periodically until tooth eruption and/or degeneration or excision of the operculum has eliminated the debris-collecting area. If the full mouth treatment plan includes removal of the tooth involved, early extraction to avoid further episodes is desirable.

In the more severe cases of pericoronitis, debridement is still the primary treatment. However, other considerations must be made. Swelling may reach the point that the opposing maxillary third molar may traumatize the mandibular soft tissues. If the lower molar is ultimately to be removed, extraction of the opposing maxillary third molar is often helpful in alleviating the acute episode. Swelling may also interfere with opening and chewing. In these cases one must force fluids and ensure adequate nutritional intake. If this cannot be accomplished by the use of a soft diet, the nutritional supplements previously discussed should be employed to ensure adequate nutrition. Pain, induced by swelling and infection, will frequently require analgesics. Aspirin will be adequate in most cases, but more potent drugs will be required in some.

Infection will be resolved in most healthy patients by local and supportive treatment. However, the practitioner must be aware that infection associated with pericoronitis may abscess locally or may spread rapidly into alveolar bone and through fascial spaces. The following are rare but serious results: retropharyngeal, peritonsillar, masseter, and temporal space abscesses; laryngeal edema; Ludwig's angina, cavernous sinus thrombosis; and acute meningitis.[16] Consequently, indications that infection associated with pericoronitis are spreading in spite of local treatment, especially in elderly, debilitated, or otherwise unhealthy patients, should be treated vigorously with antibiotics. The selection of an antibiotic for cases of pericoronitis is based on the same principles discussed in Chapter 22.

R Penicillin V tablets, 250 mg
Disp: 40 tablets
Sig: Take 2 tablets at once followed by 1 tablet 1 hour before each meal and at bedtime.

ALVEOLAR OSTEITIS ("DRY SOCKET")

Alveolar osteitis occurs after 2% to 3% of all extractions.[17-19] It occurs predominately in lower molar areas, where the incidence may be much higher. The occurrence after the removal of impacted lower third molars has been reported to be as high as 25%.[20] The incidence of alveolar osteitis is increased by trauma, lack of aseptic techniques, and the presence of thick, relatively avascular bone.

Alveolar osteitis is caused by the loss or necrosis of the blood clot, resulting in unprotected bone within the extraction socket. The exposed bone is extremely painful, becomes to some degree necrotic, and is generally secondarily infected. The loss or necrosis of the original clot may result from its being rinsed out by the patient or may result from infection of, or inadequate blood supply to, the clot.

In addition to the absence of a clot or the presence of an ill-formed clot, the signs and symptoms include constant pain localized to or radiating from the site of a recent extraction and an associated foul odor. Swelling, elevated temperature, and lymphadenopathy indicate the presence of infection.

The treatment of alveolar osteitis consists essentially of (1) debriding the socket, usually with warm saline; (2) maintaining an antiseptic-analgesic pack in the socket until the osseous walls become covered by granulation tissue; (3) control of pain; (4) control of infection if present; and (5) supportive therapy, such as ensuring adequate rest, nutrition, and fluid intake.

Dressing. The socket dressing usually consists of a strip of gauze that contains obtundent and antiseptic agents. This dressing keeps debris out of the socket and provides analgesic and antiseptic effects. The dressings are placed after the socket has been carefully debrided. They are generally changed daily but may have to be changed two or three times a day to provide adequate pain relief. Although plain eugenol has been used effectively, several pastes and a wide variety of ingredients have been recommended for incorporation into the gauze. None of the more commonly recommended mixtures has any great advantage over the others. Some examples are (1) a paste containing equal parts of thymol iodide powder and benzocaine (3 gm), and Peruvian balsam (9 gm).[22] parts guaiacol and eugenol, (3) guaiacol (3 gm), benzocaine (3 gm), and Peruvian balsam (9 gm).[22]

Food supplements. The severe and often prolonged pain of alveolar osteitis may alter the patient's food intake to the point where dietary inadequacies develop that could conceivably delay recovery. Patient instruction in soft diets and/or the use of the food supplements previously mentioned should ensure adequate dietary intake.

See earlier statement on food supplements.

Analgesics. Both local (dressing) and systemic analgesics will be required in almost all cases of alveolar osteitis. Although aspirin may be adequate in some cases, more potent analgesics such as codeine will be frequently required.

R Codeine tablets, ½ gr
Disp: 12 tablets
Sig: Take 1 tablet with 2 aspirin tablets every 4 hours as needed for pain.

Antibiotics. Antibiotics that may be necessary when infection is associated with alveolar osteitis should be selected and prescribed as for other oral infections. One must be aware that what begins as an osteitis may progress to osteomyelitis. Consequently, the practitioner must recognize the presence of overt infection and institute early treatment. Thoma[23] has also pointed out the importance of a differential diagnosis between alveolar osteitis and osteomyelitis.

There is some indication that sulfonamide and

tetracycline cones placed in extraction sites may reduce the incidence of alveolar osteitis. In a recent, controlled double-blind study, Hall, Bildman, and Hand[24] found a statistically significant reduction in the incidence of "dry sockets," from 19% (control third-molar extractions) to 7% (tetracycline-treated extraction sites). In this study a 50 mg tetracycline hydrochloride tablet was dissolved in 1 ml tap water and absorbed in a gelatin sponge (Gelfoam), which was placed in the experimental extraction sites.

The favorable results reported from the local application of sulfonamides and tetracyclines in reducing the occurrence of alveolar osteitis do not justify their routine use. Aseptic technique, proper suturing when indicated, and minimal trauma in healthy patients should decrease the occurrence of alveolar osteitis. In cases where negative factors are present in third-molar extractions, such as broken aseptic technique, considerable trauma, and an unhealthy patient, the use of local tetracycline prophylaxis such as that reported by Hall, Bildman, and Hand[24] may be justified.

XEROSTOMIA

The condition of reduced salivary flow may result from a disease process, the treatment of disease, drug therapy, and the generalized decrease in secretions associated with aging. Sjögren's syndrome, salivary gland aplasia, and Mikulicz's disease are classic disease conditions that depress salivary gland activity. Radiation therapy in excess of 800 rads induces irreparable changes in the structure of the salivary glands, adversely affecting the amount and composition of the saliva. Antihistamines, tranquilizers, diuretics, and atropine-like drugs tend to decrease salivary production. Xerostomia is a frequent symptom in women after 40 years of age. Often it is associated with the hormonal and glandular changes observed with menopause. The etiology of the salivary discrepancy must be identified before effective, long-term therapy can be instituted.

The immediate symptoms can be relieved by the application of sodium carboxymethyl-cellulose. It is a nonirritating agent that moistens and lubricates the oral tissues and may be used for prolonged periods without adverse effects. Several flavored "artificial salivas" are available, such as Xero-lube, which contain phosphates, chlorides, and fluoride in addition to the sodium carboxymethylcellulose.

Ŗ Sodium carboxymethylcellulose, 0.5% aqueous solution
Disp: 8 oz
Sig: Use as a rinse as frequently as needed to relieve symptoms of dry mouth.

Ŗ Xero-lube
Disp: 6 oz
Sig: Use as a rinse as frequently as needed to relieve symptoms of dry mouth.

POSTIRRADIATION CARIES

The lack of proper oral plaque control and the qualitative and quantitative changes in saliva after radiation therapy to the dental region can produce an extremely accelerated rate of dental caries. This is characteristically manifested by generalized cervical decay within the first year after therapy. Recommended prophylactic and therapeutic measures include the institution of a meticulous oral hygiene program and the self-application of 1% sodium fluoride gel four times a day in a flexible bite guard. This regimen should be continued indefinitely.

Ŗ Fluoride gel, 1% sodium fluoride
Disp: 2 oz
Sig: Place 5 to 10 drops in bite guard and apply for 5 minutes four times a day.

ROOT SENSITIVITY

Hypersensitivity of exposed root surfaces is a common dental complaint. Pain in an area of exposed root may be precipitated by mechanically touching the area, by heat or cold, or by sweet or sour foods.

Root hypersensitivity may be caused by occlusal trauma or may result from the irritation of organic matter in exposed dentinal tubules.[16] Hypersensitive root surfaces not caused by occlusal trauma generally result from (1) exposure of roots by periodontal surgery, (2) extensive root planing, and/or (3) accumulation of tooth-accumulated materials (TAM) on exposed roots. In cases where occlusal trauma is the cause, occlusal adjustment is the treatment. The treatment of root sensitivities of other etiology can be highly frustrating. Basic to all treatment is ensuring that the root surface be kept free of TAM. This serves two purposes: (1) irritants are removed, and (2) direct contact by desensitizing agents is possible.

A wide variety of both simple and complex agents, including high concentrations of poppycock, have been painted, burnished, electroplated, tapped, poured, pushed, and brushed on sensitive roots. The consistency of results has not been terribly impressive. Treatments can be divided into those provided by the dentist and those instituted by the patient.

Agents applied by the dentist

No attempt is made to discuss the myriad of agents that have been used by the dentist to reduce root sensitivity. The following agents should be adequate for effective practice.

Glycerin. One of the most simple treatments for root hypersensitivity has been to burnish glycerin into the cleaned and dried sensitive area with a ball burnisher or orange-wood stick. The results are not highly predictable, and the mechanism of action is unknown. It is likely that any favorable effects result from the burnishing action rather than from any direct effect of the glycerin.

Sodium fluoride. Various mixtures of sodium fluoride have been applied to hypersensitive root areas. Although results have been neither consistent nor highly impressive, success has been obtained in some cases. There is no evidence that the more exotic mixtures of sodium fluoride are any more effective than straight 2% topical solution applied by cotton swab or placed in pumice for rubber cup application to clean, dry root surfaces.

Stannous fluoride. A number of stannous fluoride mixtures have also been applied to hypersensitive root areas. There is no evidence that the more exotic mixtures of stannous fluoride are any more effective than straight 10% topical solution applied by cotton swab or placed in pumice for rubber cup application to clean, dry root surfaces. The application of a 9% stannous fluoride paste should be equally effective or ineffective.

Adrenal steroids. Bowers and Elliott[25] evaluated the effectiveness of a prednisolone preparation against root hypersensitivity. This preparation had been used earlier to prevent sensitivity in cavity preparations.[26,27] They found that one or two applications of the following solution "appeared effective in the treatment of sensitivity due to incisal (occlusal) fractures, extensive occlusal adjustment or odontoplasty, periodontal surgery and post scaling and root planing procedures."[25]

Components	Percentages by weight
Parachlorophenol	25
Metacresyl acetate (Cresatin)	25
Gum camphor	49
Prednisolone	1

The solution was applied with a cotton pellet to clean, dry, sensitive areas. This prednisolone solution deteriorates rapidly and is not likely to be effective after 90 days. Sensitivity resulting from gingival recession was reduced but not as dramatically as in other cases. Although no side effects of the prednisolone solution were observed in this study, an effort should be made to limit systemic absorption by restricting the solution to tooth surfaces as much as possible.

Prichard[28] and others have used an ophthalmic solution of prednisolone (Metimyd) successfully. This 0.5% prednisolone solution is applied to clean, dry tooth surfaces. Each milliliter of this ophthalmic solution contains 5 mg prednisolone acetate, 100 mg sodium sulfacetamide, and preservatives. It is available in 5 ml bottles. The antibacterial action of sulfacetamide would have no purpose when this solution is used for desensitization. Although no studies are available, it might be equally effective and more rational to eliminate the unnecessary but active ingredient sulfacetamide by using an ophthalmic solution that contains 0.5% prednisolone as the only active ingredient. Such a solution is available (Optival) in 5 ml bottles.

The dentist should become familiar with the pharmacology and precautions related to adrenal steroids before their use. In view of the broad pharmacologic effects of systemically absorbed adrenal steroids, these drugs should not be used for root hypersensitivity unless contact with soft tissues can be minimized. This is not likely to be possible in cases of generalized hypersensitivity.

Agents applied by the patient

Home brushing of hypersensitive areas with concentrated sodium chloride solutions and 0.5% stannous fluoride have been recommended. The results are poorly documented. In cases where there is generalized tooth sensitivity, the self-application of 1% sodium fluoride gel for 5 minutes four times a day in a flexible bite guard has been beneficial.

Desensitizing toothpastes deserve some discussion. Many practitioners believe that optimal effects occur when office treatment is followed by the use of a desensitizing toothpaste. The degree of usefulness of these pastes is rather vague.

Hazen, Volpe, and King[29] conducted a double-blind clinical comparison of four dentifrices: (1)

0.76% sodium monofluorophosphate with insoluble sodium metaphosphate as the abrasive (pH 5.5); (2) a control having the ingredients of (1) minus the sodium monofluorophosphate; (3) a commercial dentifrice containing 1.4% formalin (pH 8.5); and (4) a commercial dentifrice containing 0.4% stannous fluoride with insoluble sodium metaphosphate as the abrasive (pH 4.8 to 5.2). Patients with chronic root sensitivity were randomly provided with one of the preceding dentifrices and instructed to brush in the usual manner at least twice daily. The patients were examined for root sensitivity after approximately 2 and 4 weeks. All dentifrices reduced tooth hypersensitivity after 4 weeks of use; however, only dentifrice (1) showed a statistically significant improvement over the control dentifrice.

Until further double-blind comparisons of desensitizing dentifrices are available, it is not possible to assess the practical superiority, if any, of special desensitizing dentifrices over regular dentifrices. Unquestionably, improved tooth cleaning is effective against root hypersensitivity regardless of the type of dentifrice used.

REFERENCES

1. Warnock, G.R., Fuller, R.P., and Pelleu, G.B.: Evaluation of 5-Fluorouracil in the treatment of actinic keratosis of the lip, Oral Surg. **52**:501-505, 1981.
2. Burket, L.W.: Oral medicine, ed. 5, Philadelphia, 1965, J.B. Lippincott Co., p. 109.
3. Terezhalmy, G., Bottomley, W.B., and Pelleu, G.B.: The use of water soluble bioflavonoid-ascorbic acid complex in the treatment of recurrent herpes labialis, Oral Surg. **45**:56-62, 1978.
4. Barile, M.F., et al.: L Form of bacteria isolated from recurrent aphthous stomatitis lesions, Oral Surg. **16**:1395-1402, 1963.
5. Graykowski, E.A., Barile, M.F., and Stanley, H.R.: Periadenitis aphthae: clinical and histopathologic aspects of lesions in a patient and of lesions produced in rabbit skin, J. Am. Dent. Assoc. **69**:118-126, 1964.
6. Stanley, H.R., Graykowski, E.A., and Barile, M.F.: The occurrence of microorganisms in microscopic sections of aphthous and nonaphthous lesions and other oral tissues, Oral Surg. **18**:335-341, 1964.
7. Graykowski, E.A., et al.: Recurrent aphthous stomatitis: clinical, therapeutic, histopathologic, and hypersensitivity aspects, J.A.M.A. **196**:637-644, 1966.
8. Wray, D., et al.: Recurrent aphthae: treatment with vitamin B$_{12}$, folic acid, and iron, Br. Med. J. **2**:490-493, 1975.
9. Ship, I.I., Merritt, A.D., and Stanley, H.R.: Recurrent aphthous ulcers, Am. J. Med. **32**:32-43, 1962.
10. Burket, L.W.: Oral medicine, ed. 5, Philadelphia, 1965, J.B. Lippincott Co., p. 117.
11. Browne, R.M., Fox, E.C., and Anderson, R.J.: Topical triamcinoline acetonide in recurrent aphthous stomatitis, Lancet **1**:565-567, 1968.
12. Braude, A.I.: Moniliasis (candidiasis). In Harrison's principles of internal medicine, ed. 6, New York, 1970, McGraw-Hill Book Co.
13. Cohen, L.: A synopsis of medicine in dentistry, Philadelphia, 1972, Lea & Febiger.
14. Zegarelli, E.V.: Therapeutic management of certain acute and chronic soft tissue diseases of the mouth, Dent. Clin. North Am. **14**:733-741, Oct., 1970.
15. Candida infections, Med. Lett. Drugs Ther. **12**:29, 1970.
16. Grant, D.A., Stern, I.B., and Everett, F.G.: Orban's periodontics, ed. 5, St. Louis, 1979, The C.V. Mosby Co.
17. Adkisson, S.R., and Harris, P.F.: Statistical study of alveolar osteitis, U.S. Armed Forces Med. J. **7**:1749, 1956.
18. Lehner, T.: Analysis of 100 cases of dry socket, Dent. Pract. **8**:275, 1958.
19. Hansen, E.H.: Alveolitis sicca dolorosa (dry socket): frequency of occurrence and treatment with trypsin, J. Oral Surg. **18**:409, 1960.
20. Quinley, J.F., Roger, R.Q., and Gores, R.J.: Dry socket after mandibular odontectomy and use of soluble tetracycline hydrochloride, Oral Surg. **13**:38, 1960.
21. Kruger, G.O.: Textbook of oral and maxillofacial surgery, ed. 5, St. Louis, 1979, The C.V. Mosby Co.
22. American Dental Association Council on Drugs: Accepted dental therapeutics 1971/72, Chicago, 1971, American Dental Association.
23. Thoma, K.H.: Oral surgery, ed. 5, vol. 1, St. Louis, 1969, The C.V. Mosby Co.
24. Hall, H.D., Bildman, B.S., and Hand, C.D.: Prevention of dry socket with local application of tetracycline, J. Oral Surg. **29**:35-37, 1971.
25. Bowers, G.M., and Elliott, J.R.: Topical use of prednisolone in periodontics, J. Periodontol. **35**:486, 1964.
26. Fry, A.E., Watkins, R.E., and Phatok, N.M.: Topical use of corticosteroids for the relief of pain sensitivity of dentin and pulp, Oral Surg. **13**:594, 1960.
27. Masteller, J.H.: Prednisolone for postoperative thermal sensitivity, J. Prosth. Dent. **12**:1176, 1962.
28. Prichard, J.F.: Advanced periodontal disease, Philadelphia, 1965, W.B. Saunders Co.
29. Hazen, S.P., Volpe, A.R., and King, W.J.: Comparative desensitizing effect of dentifrices containing sodium monofluorophosphate, stannous fluoride and formalin, Periodontics **6**:230-232, 1968.

CHAPTER 33

Drug interactions

RICHARD L. WYNN

BARBARA REQUA-CLARK

Drug interactions often result in undesired drug effects. This phenomenon is defined as the action of an administered drug on the effectiveness or toxicity of another drug administered earlier, simultaneously, or later. It is a problem of growing concern to the health professions and is directly related to increased incidence of multiple drug therapy. One study has shown that hospitalized patients received an average of 14 different medications during confinement.[1] Another study has observed that the incidence of drug interactions ranged from 4% to 5% when two drugs were used to 45% when more than two drugs were used.[2]

Dental professionals have more than just an academic interest in this drug problem. Much of the population receiving dental treatment is receiving concurrent drug therapy in the form of prescribed medication or as over-the-counter self-medication. Every dentist should be aware that medication prescribed may interact with other drugs to produce undesired effects in the patient. Also, a patient may already have drugs prescribed by a physician that interact with each other. Taking a complete medical history and familiarity with the pharmacologic actions, therapeutic uses, and side effects of individual drugs are usually sufficient for the dentist to predict the consequences of drug therapy. Often, however, unexpected drug interactions may occur to the surprise of the prescriber. Therefore a review of the current status of drug interactions in dentistry is necessary. This chapter discusses the mechanisms for drug interactions and those interactions that have occurred or could possibly occur through the use of dental drugs. A section on alcohol-drug interactions is also included because of the frequency of consumption of alcohol by many dental patients. In many cases, drug interactions in this chapter have been discussed in other chapters.

MECHANISMS

When two or more drugs interact, the result may be either enhancement or antagonism of pharmacologic effects. Drug enhancement or antagonism results when drug effects are additive or subtractive or when one drug influences one or more of the following aspects of the other: gastrointestinal absorption, plasma protein binding, tissue protein binding, biotransformation, renal excretion, action at receptor sites, and alteration of normal body constituents. The following examples illustrate these mechanisms of drug interactions.

Effects caused by similar pharmacologic actions. Drug interactions that result in enhanced activity are caused by combinations of drugs having similar actions. For example, the respiratory depression produced by narcotic analgesics is potentiated by other agents, such as phenothiazines, which in themselves cause respiratory depression. Also, potentiation of CNS depression can result with any combination of alcohol, barbiturates, antihistamines, or tranquilizers because of their similar actions.

Effects caused by opposing pharmacologic actions. Drugs having opposing actions when administered simultaneously may antagonize each other. For example, the cholinergic drug pilocarpine is used in the treatment of glaucoma, and the anticholinergic drug propantheline (Pro-Banthine) is used for the treatment of ulcers. In this example pilocarpine's effect on the eye (cholinergic) could be canceled by propantheline's opposite (anticholinergic) effect on the eye, even though they were indicated for separate diseases.

Gastrointestinal absorption. The absorption of a drug may be decreased if an inactive or insoluble derivative is formed in the gastrointestinal tract. Certain compounds such as antacids and ferrous sulfate contain divalent metal ions, such as calcium, magnesium, and ferrous iron, or trivalent ions, such as aluminum, which will impair the absorption of tetracyclines because of the formation of a metal-tetracycline complex. Certain drugs such as the anticholinergic drugs may decrease or delay drug absorption by reducing gastrointestinal motility. A change in the pH of the stomach or intestines can alter drug absorption. Because altering the pH influences the degree of ionization, the results are that acidic drugs are more readily absorbed in an acidic medium, and basic drugs are more readily absorbed in a basic medium.

Plasma protein binding. After drugs are absorbed into plasma, they become reversibly bound to the plasma proteins. The amount of this binding varies with the particular drug. The free drug exerts the pharmacologic effect of that agent, and the bound portion is biologically inactive. Since many weakly acidic drugs are bound to the same site in the plasma protein, one bound acidic drug can displace another bound acidic drug from the same plasma protein binding site. This increases the concentration in the plasma of the drug displaced and indirectly increases its pharmacologic effect and toxicity. For example, warfarin (Coumadin) is very highly bound, approximately 99%, to the plasma protein. If aspirin, a slightly acidic drug, is administered to a patient taking warfarin (Coumadin), the aspirin will displace the warfarin from the plasma protein binding sites. This can result in an increase in the free warfarin available and also an increase in its pharmacologic effect or toxicity. This toxicity can result in hemorrhage because more of the free drug is available to exert its pharmacologic effect. Conversely, warfarin can displace drugs to result in a toxicity of the drug displaced. For example, warfarin has produced hypoglycemia by displacing tolbutamide from plasma protein.[3] Because the coumarin-type anticoagulant agents are highly bound to plasma proteins, they have many drug interactions.

Tissue protein binding. Drugs may also be displaced from tissue protein by other drugs that have a greater binding affinity for the same binding sites. When the antimalarial agent pamaquine was administered to patients previously medicated with quinacrine, the pamaquine was displaced from tissue sites

and resulted in increased plasma concentrations.[4]

Biotransformation. The stimulation or inhibition of the metabolism of one drug by another are well-known mechanisms of drug interactions.[5]

Biotransformation of many drugs takes place in the microsomal enzymes located in the liver. A process known as enzyme induction can increase these enzymes in the microsomal fraction of the liver. This increase not only accelerates the metabolism of some other drugs but also accelerates the metabolism of the inducing drug. If a drug is more rapidly metabolized, its duration of action and intensity are decreased. It is of interest to note that if an inducing agent is being given a patient and another drug is titrated to the appropriate level, when the inducing agent is removed, that drug, which was properly titrated, may produce toxicity (excessive drug level). The most common drug that acts as an inducing agent is phenobarbital. Other sedatives such as glutethimide (Doriden) and ethchlorvynol (Placidyl) also have the ability to induce microsomal enzymes. An example of this reaction is phenobarbital and the anticoagulant warfarin (Coumadin). If a coumarin anticoagulant is given in the proper dosage and phenobarbital is added, the anticoagulant effect will be diminished, thereby prolonging the prothrombin time and potentially causing intravascular clotting.

Phenobarbital also stimulates the metabolism of zoxazolamine, hexobarbital, and bishydroxycoumarin by inducing the formation of microsomal enzymes responsible for their metabolism. This results in a decrease in activity of these compounds. Cholinesterase inhibitors enhance the actions of acetylcholine and some of its congeners by preventing the enzymatic hydrolysis of these agents. The enzyme MAO metabolizes drugs such as meperidine, chloral hydrate, some minor tranquilizers, sympathomimetic amines, barbiturates, and amphetamines. The inhibition of MAO by MAOIs could consequently enhance the actions of these drugs.

Renal excretion. Most drugs are excreted as metabolites by the kidney. If they are not bound to plasma proteins, they are filtered through the glomerulus (kidney) and then may be either secreted or reabsorbed by active transport or passively reabsorbed by diffusion. If a drug is not metabolized, or if an active metabolite is produced, the action of the drug is prolonged. The active transport systems in the kidney compete with one another. For example, penicillin and probenecid are actively secreted at the same site.

Therefore, the administration of probenecid prolongs the activity of penicillin given concomitantly.

The interaction involving passive reabsorption is related to the pH of the tubular fluid and the extent of ionization of the drugs in that fluid. Drugs that can alter the pH of the urine either increase or decrease the duration of action of the drugs being excreted. Weak acids are excreted more rapidly in an alkaline urine, and weak bases are excreted more rapidly in an acidic urine. In the case of an overdose, it would be helpful to increase the excretion rate of the drug.

Interactions at receptor sites. The autonomic nervous systems, adrenergic (sympathetic) and cholinergic (parasympathetic), possess sites for drug interactions. The neuromuscular junction also has synapses where drug interactions can occur. The neurotransmitter substances norepinephrine and acetylcholine and their deposition and inactivation can produce drug interactions. Interactions that affect the adrenergic (sympathetic) nervous system include interference with the metabolism of norepinephrine, the blocking of either the synaptic uptake or release mechanism, and action directly on the receptor.

The enzyme MAO normally destroys only a small amount of the norepinephrine produced at the synapse. MAOIs cause an accumulation of norepinephrine at the neuroeffector junction. Because certain sympathomimetic agents like amphetamines, ephedrine, and phenylpropanolamine produce their pressor effects indirectly, that is, by releasing norepinephrine, administration of these agents can result in severe hypertension in patients receiving MAOIs. Even tyramine, an agent found in some foods (cheeses and wines), can produce a hypertensive crisis if ingested by patients being treated with MAOIs.

The tricyclic antidepressants block the synaptic re-uptake of norepinephrine. The antihypertensive guanethidine must be taken up to exert its effect. Therefore the tricyclic antidepressants antagonize the antihypertensive effect of guanethidine.

Another antihypertensive agent, reserpine, depletes the stores of norepinephrine from the preganglionic neuron. In this case, those sympathomimetic agents that normally have their effect by releasing endogenous epinephrine would have a diminished effect (e.g., ephedrine).

Certain halogenated hydrocarbons that are used as general anesthetics, such as halothane, "sensitize" the heart muscle to the action of catecholamines.

Therefore, in the presence of these halogenated hydrocarbon anesthetics, the administration of epinephrine can result in arrhythmias.

In the parasympathetic nervous system, the anticholinergic drugs block the action of the cholinergic nervous system. Other agents, including the phenothiazines and the tricyclic antidepressants, which also possess anticholinergic activity, when used concomitantly with anticholinergics, can produce excessive anticholinergic activity. This can produce not only dry mouth but also constipation, tachycardia, urinary retention, and mydriasis.

At the neuromuscular junction some antibiotics, especially the aminoglycosides, and some general anesthetics can have a neuromuscular blocking effect. In the presence of a nondepolarizing neuromuscular blocking agent like tubocurarine, excessive muscular paralysis, including cessation of breathing, has been reported.

The depolarizing neuromuscular blocking agent succinylcholine is inactivated by hydrolysis by pseudocholinesterase present in the plasma. If patients are receiving anticholinesterase drugs, the duration of action of succinylcholine can be increased, and prolonged apnea can occur.

Body constituents. Alterations in body constituents by some drugs will affect the pharmacologic actions of others. Hypokalemia (lowered serum potassium levels) caused by thiazide diuretics will promote arrhythmias in the presence of digitalis.

ANTIBIOTIC COMBINATIONS

Some antibiotics when used in combination have a synergistic effect, or an effect that is more than additive. Also, antibiotics can be directly antagonistic and the effect of their combination can be less than that of one of the antibiotics used alone. In the treatment of enterococcal endocarditis, a combination of penicillin G and streptomycin has a synergistic effect. Another example of the synergistic effect of microbial agents is the combination of sulfonamides and trimethoprim. This is because these agents work by different mechanisms to produce folic acid. Some antibiotics when used together produce antagonistic results. An example is the combination of penicillin and tetracycline in the treatment of pneumococci. Antibiotics should not be used indiscriminately in combination without knowledge of the effects they might be producing: synergistic, antagonistic, or merely additive.

DENTAL DRUG INTERACTIONS

The following discussion of dental drug interactions includes those that are potentially most significant to the patient and that can be caused by drugs routinely prescribed in dentistry. For purposes of accuracy, differentiation is made between clinical reports and those interactions only observed in animal studies.

Drug interactions that may occur in dental practice are summarized in Tables 33-1 to 33-4. The interactions listed are those that have been reported to occur clinically by drugs used in dental practice. For simplicity and ease of reference, the interactions are described according to the resultant effects only. The reader is referred to the text for information concerning the mechanisms of these interactions.

Narcotic analgesics

In general, the CNS depression produced by morphine, meperidine, and codeine is enhanced by alcohol, sedatives, hypnotics, antihistamines, and other CNS depressants. Serious reactions have occurred clinically through the use of meperidine. The simultaneous administration of this drug with MAOIs has led to a deep coma and extreme hypotension, resulting in a depressor crisis.[6,7] This effect is believed to

be partially caused by an inhibition of meperidine degradation.[8]

Both the respiratory depression and the analgesia produced by narcotic analgesics can be enhanced by various drugs. For example, the phenothiazine derivatives including propiomazine, chlorpromazine, and promazine have dangerously exaggerated and prolonged the respiratory depression of meperidine.[9-11] The inherent hypotensive action of these phenothiazines is an additional complication to the sedative action of morphine and meperidine. Imipramine-like antidepressants exert a supraadditive effect on morphine- and meperidine-induced respiratory depression.[12] Phenothiazines are also able to reduce the dose of morphine required to produce a given level of analgesia.[13] Concomitant administration of meperidine with diazepam, amphetamines, or neostigmine results in an enhancement of its analgesic effect.[13-15] Phenobarbital has been shown to alter the metabolism of meperidine to result in a toxicity caused by the increased formation of normeperidine.[16]

The analgesic potency of codeine is enhanced by the simultaneous administration of aspirin, an effect that is clinically beneficial.[17] Also codeine will probably interact with the same drugs as described for

Table 33-1. Clinically significant dental drug interactions occurring with analgesics

Dental drug	Interacting drug	Resultant effect
Salicylates (Aspirin)	Coumarin anticoagulants	Enhanced anticoagulation; possible bleeding episodes
	Probenecid; phenylbutazone; sulfinpyrazone	Decreased uricosuria
	Sulfonylurea hypoglycemics	Enhanced hypoglycemia
	Methotrexate	Increased toxicity of methotrexate
	Corticosteroids	Ulcers
Acetaminophen	Anticoagulants	No significant effect
	Coumarin anticoagulants	Enhanced anticoagulation
Ibuprofen	Corticosteroids	Ulcers
Naproxen	Aspirin	Decreased effectiveness
Meperidine	MAOIs	Hypotension and coma
	Phenothiazines; imipramine antidepressants; furazolidone	Enhanced respiratory depression
	Diazepam; amphetamines; neostigmine	Enhanced analgesia
	Phenobarbital	Increased adverse effects
Morphine	Imipramine antidepressants; propranolol	Enhanced respiratory and CNS depression
	Phenothiazines	Enhanced analgesia
Codeine	Aspirin	Enhanced analgesia
Propoxyphene	Fenoprofen	Enhanced analgesia

morphine and meperidine since it is chemically similar in structure.

Animal studies have indicated some potential clinical interactions involving the narcotic agents. In rats the anticholinergic action of scopolamine potentiates the sedative action of morphine.[18] The combined action of atropine and morphine has been investigated in mice, and it was shown that the anticholinergic effects of atropine were enhanced by this narcotic.[19] The ganglionic blocker mecamylamine has potentiated the analgesia produced by morphine in rats.[20] Reserpine, however, caused a decrease in the anal-gesic effect of meperidine as shown by the increase in the analgesia ED_{50} for meperidine in reserpinized rats.[21] Preliminary reports indicate that the antibacterial furazolidone enhances meperidine depression in humans[22] and that the beta-blocking agent propranolol potentiated the CNS depression induced by morphine.[23] Addicting analgesics may enhance the response to oral anticoagulants.[24,25] Clinical significance of this effect has not been established, however, and it is unlikely that short-term administration of these drugs will have appreciable effects on oral anticoagulant response. Manufacturers' information

Table 33-2. Clinically significant dental drug interactions occurring with antibiotics

Dental drug	Interacting drug	Resulting effect
Penicillin	Tetracyclines, erythromycin	Inhibition of penicillin
	Probenecid, salicylates, sulfonamides	Enhanced effect of penicillin
	Oral anticoagulants	Hemorrhage
Erythromycin	Penicillin	Inhibition of penicillin
	Lincomycin, clindamycin	Antagonism
Tetracyclines	Antacids, dairy products, iron (oral)	Decreased absorption of tetracycline—decreased effect
	Penicillin	Inhibition of penicillin
	Oral anticoagulants	Hemorrhage
Cephalosporins	Probenecid, phenylbutazone	Enhanced effect of cephalosporin

Table 33-3. Clinically significant dental drug interactions occurring with sedatives and antianxiety agents

Dental drug	Interacting drug	Resulting effect
Barbiturates	MAOIs	Severe CNS depression
Phenobarbital	Coumarin anticoagulants	Decreased anticoagulation
	Phenytoin	Decreased effectiveness of phenytoin
	Aminopyrine; tricyclic antidepressants	Enhanced metabolism and renal excretion of these agents
	Griseofulvin	Oral absorption of griseofulvin inhibited
	Valproic acid	Enhanced effect of phenobarbital
Pentobarbital	Caffeine	Hypnotic effect inhibited
Secobarbital	Codeine	Enhanced hypnotic activity
Benzodiazepines (chlordiazepoxide, diazepam, clorazepate)	Tricyclic antidepressants	Increased toxicity of tricyclics
	MAOIs	Increased toxicity of MAOIs
	Antacids	Decreased oral absorption
	Disulfiram	Decreased plasma clearance of benzodiazepine
	Phenytoin	Enhanced phenytoin toxicity
Chloral hydrate	Coumarin anticoagulants	Decreased effectiveness of anticoagulant

Table 33-4. Clinically significant dental drug interactions occurring with sympathomimetics and miscellaneous drugs

Dental drug	Interacting drug	Resulting effect
Epinephrine	MAOIs; tricyclic antidepressants	Hypertension
	Beta adrenergic blockers (propranolol)	Hypertension and bradycardia
	Anticholinergics	Enhanced mydriases
	Oral hypoglycemics; insulin	Hyperglycemia
Norepinephrine	Guanethedine; methyldopa	Hypertension
	MAOIs; tricyclic antidepressants	Increased pressor response to norepinephrine
Atropine	Phenothiazines	Enhanced sedation
Diphenhydramine	Phenothiazines; anticholinergics (tri- hexyphenidyl, imipramine)	Acute dryness of mouth
Pyridoxine (vitamin B$_6$)	Levodopa	Inhibits antiparkinson action of levodopa
Ascorbic acid (vitamin C)	Coumarin anticoagulants	Decreased anticoagulation
Ascorbic acid	Aspirin	Decreased amounts of ascorbic acid in body tissues
Folic acid	Phenytoin	Decreased effectiveness of phenytoin

concerning propoxyphene has indicated that this analgesic may potentiate the toxic effect of the skeletal muscle relaxant orphenadrine. Symptoms of this interaction are reported to be mental confusion, anxiety, and tremors. It is interesting to note that these symptoms are those that occur during a hypoglycemic episode and that both propoxyphene and orphenadrine have been reported to induce hypoglycemic activity when given alone.[26,27] Propoxyphene has also been shown to elicit an additive analgesic action with fenoprofen when the two are administered simultaneously.[28]

Nonnarcotic analgesics

Bleeding episodes have occurred after the administration of salicylates to patients receiving anticoagulant therapy with the coumarin derivatives.[29] This reaction was probably caused by a decrease in blood prothrombin levels and subsequent increase in prothrombin time caused by the salicylates. Salicylates are also able to displace the coumarin type of anticoagulants from protein binding sites in plasma. This action results in increased peak plasma concentrations of the free (unbound) anticoagulant with a resultant decreased plasma half-life of the drug.[30]

Several other clinical interactions involving salicylates have been reported. The uricosuric action of both aspirin and probenecid was inhibited when the two drugs were administered simultaneously.[31] This action may result in an undesirable situation in patients suffering from gout. Like probenecid, sulfinpyrazone uricosuria is also inhibited by salicylates (both small and large doses). Both probenecid and sulfinpyrazone also inhibit the uricosuric effect of large doses of salicylates. Patients medicated with sulfinpyrazone should not take salicylates. The nonsteroidal antiinflammatory agent phenylbutazone has been observed to inhibit the uricosuric activity of aspirin.[32] Aspirin has reportedly caused hypoglycemic coma in diabetic patients receiving sulfonylurea hypoglycemic agents.[33] Plasma protein displacement of the sulfonylureas by aspirin or other salicylates appears to be the mechanism of this effect.[34] It has also been reported that administration of salicylates during a tapering of corticosteroid dosage in four patients resulted in an increased plasma level of unbound salicylates with concomitant salicylate intoxication in one of the patients.[35]

Another interaction between salicylates and corticosteroids occurs because of an additive ulcerogenic effect. These two drug families can cause gastrointestinal irritation and can exacerbate ulcers. Therefore their concomitant use should be avoided. The excretion of methotrexate appears to be blocked by the salicylates. Methotrexate, an antimetabolite, is used to treat various malignancies and severe psoriasis. Patients who are receiving methotrexate should be given aspirin only with caution, if at all.

Aluminum hydroxide, present in antacid preparations, reduces the peak plasma level of a salicylate, diflunisal, by 46%, presumably by decreasing the amount of drug absorbed from the gastrointestinal tract.[36] Salicylates have also been observed to displace phenytoin from plasma binding sites to result in an increased unbound plasma concentration of drug. The significance of this interaction has yet to be determined.[37]

Other actions of salicylates, although not observed clinically, may be of importance. Aspirin, indomethacin, ibuprofen, phenylbutazone, and other nonsteroidal antiinflammatory agents, when administered together, may cause enhanced irritation to the gastrointestinal tract. Any combination of these drugs may also cause enhancement of their ulcerogenic effects. Animal studies have indicated that acetazolamide, a specific inhibitor of carbonic anhydrase, enhances the oral absorption of salicylates to provide increased blood levels of these analgesics.[38] Apparently, acetazolamide lowers the gut pH, which favors absorption of the salicylates. In vitro studies indicate that salicylates may displace phenytoin, an antiepileptic agent, from plasma protein binding sites to result in a potentiation in the actions of the latter.[39] There is no clinical supporting evidence for this effect, however.[40] It has been noted that salicylates can cause as much as 50% decrease in sodium and chloride ion excretion in humans—an action that may antagonize thiazide diuretics.[41]

Although one report[42] stated that acetaminophen prolonged the prothrombin time in patients receiving oral anticoagulants, a second study found no significant effect.[43] In patients receiving warfarin (Coumadin), acetaminophen can be used as an analgesic.

The ulcerogenic effects of ibuprofen are enhanced when given simultaneously with other antiinflammatory agents such as corticosteroids and aspirin. Aspirin decreases the plasma levels of naproxen when administered concurrently. This results in a decrease in the therapeutic effectiveness of naproxen.[44] The prescriber should be aware that this interaction may occur with the other members of the nonsteroidal antiinflammatory family.[45] Probenecid has retarded naproxen plasma clearance by inhibiting naproxen glucuronide formation.[46] The clinical significance of this interaction has not yet been established.

Antibiotics

Various antibiotics are able to enhance the effect of simultaneously administered coumarin anticoagulants in humans. A mechanism suggested for this effect is the interference with vitamin K synthesis in

microorganisms of the gastrointestinal tract by antiinfective drugs.[47] Specifically, penicillin G has been reported to increase the prothrombin time response to oral anticoagulants.[25] Other agents likely to cause problems of this nature are tetracyclines. The intestinal absorption of some antibiotics in humans can be impaired by various agents. For example, antacids and milk that contain divalent and trivalent metal ions prevent absorption of tetracyclines.[48] According to one report, over 5% of the patients receiving tetracyclines also received such antacids.[49] The simultaneous administration of 40 mg ferrous sulfate with tetracycline resulted in a 50% to 90% lower serum level of this antibiotic.[50] Also, the concomitant administration of sodium bicarbonate reduces the absorption of oral tetracycline in humans. One suggested mechanism for this effect is the insolubility of the drug at higher pH in the stomach resulting from the bicarbonate.[51] Another report has suggested that the tetracycline capsule itself is responsible for the decrease in absorption because the capsule does not dissolve in neutral or basic solutions.[52] Lincomycin failed to clear up a severe dental infection because the absorption of the drug was inhibited by cyclamates that were inadvertently ingested with the drug.[53]

Tetracyclines and erythromycin effectively antagonize the antimicrobial activity of simultaneously administration of either of these two agents with penicillin to treat infection is contraindicated.[54–56] The mechanism of this effect probably results from the fact that penicillin is most effective against bacteria during the stage of rapid multiplication, and tetracyclines reduce this rapid rate of bacterial multiplication. There is some evidence to indicate an antagonism between lincomycin and erythromycin,[57] although a mechanism of action and clinical significance have yet to be established. Lincomycin and erythromycin have similar antimicrobial activity, and indications for their simultaneous use in dentistry should be rare, if at all. The possibility of antagonism is further reason to avoid any use of the two drugs together.

Some important clinical interactions have been observed with penicillins and cephalosporins. Probenecid produces increased plasma levels of unbound penicillin.[58] This action occurs by two mechanisms: the inhibition of the renal tubular secretion of penicillin and the displacement of penicillin from plasma protein binding sites. Also, salicylates, sulfonamides, and paraaminobenzoic acid have been shown in humans to displace penicillin from protein binding sites in the serum.[59] Both of these interactions of penicillin cause an enhancement of its antimicrobial activity in vivo. Probenecid and phenylbutazone interact with cephalosporins by competing for renal tubular secretion. This results in a decrease in the renal secretion of cephalosporins and an increase in the serum levels—most likely causing an increase in its antimicrobial action in the tissues.[60]

Sedatives and antianxiety agents

As a general rule, any combination of alcohol, barbiturates, antihistamines, and other CNS depressants should be considered with caution, since enhancement of sedation by one another will result. Severe barbiturate intoxication occurred in a patient treated with an MAOI.[61] Phenobarbital has decreased the effectiveness of coumarin anticoagulants and phenytoin in humans by stimulating the formation of hepatic microsomal enzymes necessary for the metabolism and subsequent elimination of these agents.[62] Phenobarbital reportedly has the capability of reducing the plasma concentration and enhancing the renal elimination of the tricyclic antidepressants desipramine and nortriptyline[63] and the analgesic aminopyrine.[64] These effects are also caused by stimulation of metabolic enzymes responsible for the metabolism and elimination of these agents. Phenobarbital also interacts with griseofulvin to reduce the blood levels of this antifungal agent in humans. This effect is reportedly the result of an increased metabolism of griseofulvin.[65] More recently, it has been reported that the intestinal absorption of griseofulvin was inhibited when phenobarbital was administered simultaneously in humans[66] and that the metabolic breakdown of phenobarbital was inhibited when administered simultaneously with valproic acid (an antiepileptic agent).[67] Codeine has been shown to stimulate the onset and duration of sleep induced by secobarbital in humans—an interaction that results in synergism.[68] Caffeine is able to counteract the hypnotic effect of pentobarbital when administered concomitantly. The effects induced by 250 mg caffeine plus 100 mg pentobarbital were indistinguishable from placebo.[69]

An interaction of potential clinical significance has been reported concerning the potentiation of the hypnotic effects of pentobarbital by quinine in animals. Apparently, quinine acts to inhibit the metabolism and subsequent elimination of pentobarbital from the body.[70] Magnesium and aluminum hydroxides retard gastrointestinal absorption of sodium pentobarbital in rats.[71] This effect resulted in a lowering of blood levels of the barbiturate, which caused a prevention or delay in the onset of sleep. Long-term administration of diazepam has reduced sleep time and serum levels of pentobarbital in rats and humans—an effect attributed to the stimulation of enzymes responsible for the deactivation of the latter.[72]

The concurrent use of any of the benzodiazepine tranquilizers with MAOIs or tricyclic antidepressants (imipramine-like drugs) may increase the effects of these two families of drugs, leading to adverse reactions. Chlordiazepoxide has been shown to potentiate the side effects of amitriptyline, which results in a condition resembling brain damage.[73] The administration of chlordiazepoxide with antacids reduces the rate of its absorption. Specifically, magnesium and aluminum hydroxide mixture prolonged the mean chlordiazepoxide absorption half-time from the gastrointestinal tract from 11 to 24 minutes and delayed achievement of peak blood concentration by 0.5 to 3.0 hours.[74] Patients receiving diazepam and phenytoin (an antiepileptic agent) or chlordiazepoxide and phenytoin may have higher blood levels of the antiepileptic than patients receiving phenytoin therapy without either of the other two drugs.[75] Also, a case of phenytoin toxicity has been reported in which a diazepam derivative, nitrazepam, might have contributed to the high phenytoin plasma levels.[76] Antacids apparently reduce the rate of absorption of diazepam from the gastrointestinal tract, resulting in a lower peak plasma concentration of the drug.[77] Disulfiram (Antabuse) decreases the plasma clearance of chlordiazepoxide, diazepam, and its active metabolites when administered simultaneously.[78] The administration of clorazepate with magnesium-aluminum hydroxide (Maalox) reduces the rate and extent of appearance in blood of the metabolites of clorazepate responsible for its therapeutic effect.[79] Chloral hydrate and glutethimide promote the metabolism of coumarins in humans, thus decreasing their effectiveness.[80]

Sympathomimetics and miscellaneous agents

Sympathomimetics are commonly used as additives to local anesthetic in an attempt to prolong the duration of action of these agents. These vasoconstrictors can interact with a number of drugs that patients can be receiving from their physicians.

When epinephrine is administered to patients on

tricyclic antidepressants, there is a potentiation of the vasopressor effect or hypertension. Patients with pre-existing hypertension or cardiovascular disease, or those who require large amounts of vasoconstrictor, would be more at risk to this effect. The administration of epinephrine, an alpha and beta agonist, in the presence of a beta blocker can result in a predominence of alpha (vasoconstricting) effects. The effect is to produce hypertension and, indirectly, reflex bradycardia. Epinephrine should be administered with caution to diabetic patients because it increases blood glucose by inhibiting absorption in peripheral tissues and promoting glycogenolysis. It could necessitate an increase in the dosage of either insulin or sulfonylurea, an oral hypoglycemic agent, to counter this effect.

Norepinephrine should be used with caution in patients taking tricyclic antidepressants because they enhance the pressor response, which can cause hypertension. Patients receiving guanethidine, methyldopa, or MAOIs who are given norepinephrine can experience an increase in blood pressure.

Atropine exerts an additive effect when administered simultaneously with various agents. It was shown to potentiate the phenothiazine sedation in humans by an additive CNS depressant effect and to elicit an additive anticholinergic effect with isoniazid.[22,81] Nasal bleeding, acute dryness of the mouth, fissures of the tongue, and cracked lips occurred when diphenhydramine in combination with methaqualone was administered to a patient previously medicated with the antipsychotic agent thioridazine.[82] It was also reported that diphenhydramine in combination with the anticholinergic drugs trihexyphenidyl and imipramine caused a loss of dentition in a patient as a result of prolonged xerostomia.[83] Pyridoxine (vitamin B_6) reportedly reduces the clinical benefits of the antiparkinsonian agent levodopa.[84] Patients taking B-complex vitamins simultaneously with levodopa should be sure that vitamin B_6 is not present. Two cases have been reported in which ascorbic acid (vitamin C) impaired the response to warfarin, an oral anticoagulant.[85,80] A subsequent study in several patients revealed no evidence of this interaction, however,[87] and more evidence is needed to determine the clinical significance of this interaction. The simultaneous administration of two aspirin tablets with ascorbic acid inhibits the uptake of the vitamin into leukocytic storage sites. It is suggested that the administration of aspirin on a chronic basis should be

accompanied by simultaneous administration of ascorbic acid to prevent hypovitaminosis.[88] Finally, replacement of folic acid in folate-deficient patients receiving phenytoin may increase the metabolism of the latter with a resultant decrease in serum phenytoin levels.[89,90]

ALCOHOL-DRUG INTERACTIONS

Alcohol interacts adversely with ingredients contained in more than half of the 100 most frequently prescribed drugs,[91] and these interactions can occur in the occasional drinker and chronic alcoholic. It is estimated that alcohol-drug interactions account for 2,500 deaths and 47,000 emergency room admissions a year.[92] This section will discuss the interactions with alcohol and several classes of drugs widely prescribed in dentistry and medicine.

Narcotic analgesics are frequently involved in deaths caused by alcohol-drug combinations. This is undoubtedly caused by the fact that alcohol potentiates the CNS depressant effects of the narcotic analgesics such as morphine, meperidine, codeine, and propoxyphene. Repeated exposure to alcohol has been shown to significantly increase the sensitivity of CNS to depression by morphine and probably other narcotic drugs.[93] Chronic alcohol use is associated with alterations in red blood cells, granulocytes, and platelets. Salicylates cause delayed clotting, and alcohol-salicylate combinations have predisposed patients to delayed clotting with possible hemorrhage. Also, chronic alcohol consumption may increase the susceptibility to liver damage from large doses of acetaminophen.[94]

Any combination of alcohol with the benzodiazepine tranquilizers should be considered extremely dangerous. These agents are the most frequently used minor tranquilizers, and many serious reactions have occurred in combination with alcohol. Diazepam has been specifically implicated in road traffic accidents and deaths.[95] Of particular importance is the fact that active metabolites of these drugs remain in the body after dosing, and alcohol consumption may be dangerous even long after the last dose of medication. Alcohol also acts synergistically with meprobamate to depress performance tasks and driving-related skills such as time estimation, reaction time, and alertness.[96] Alcohol also interacts with the major tranquilizers, phenothiazines. This combination produces severe and possibly fatal depression of the respiratory center and impaired hepatic functions that result in toxic manifestations. In addition, their side effect of hypotension is exacerbated by alcohol. Alcohol in combination with the phenothiazines probably impairs driving skills.

Combinations of alcohol with any barbiturate are contraindicated. It has been reported that the lethal dose for these hypnotics is 50% lower in the presence of alcohol.[97] Alcohol-barbiturate intoxication has resulted in vomiting, severe motor impairment, unconsciousness, coma, and death. Alcohol can potentiate the actions of antihypertensives to cause postural hypotension, syncope, and loss of consciousness. These effects have been implicated with reserpine, methyldopa, hydralazine, guanethidine, ganglionic blockers, and nitroglycerin.[98] The additive depressant effects resulting from alcohol and antihistamines in combination are well known. The prominent sedative effects of antihistamines, experienced as drowsiness, is increased to such an extent that it is dangerous to perform any hazardous task while taking the combination. In view of the fact that antihistamines are purchased over the counter for self-medication, particular attention should be given to counsel the patent to avoid alcohol in these circumstances.

CONCLUSION

Available to the dentist are extensive compilations of drug interaction information that can be used in preventing possible interactions that could occur through drug prescribing,[99-105] and practitioners are encouraged to maintain up-to-date drug interaction information such as that discussed in this chapter. The dentist's responsibility to his or her patients must include predicting possible adverse situations from potential interactions between prescribed drugs and medication the patient has previously taken. The dentist also should not neglect to look for possible adverse situations already present from previous multiple-drug therapy.

In conclusion, it should be noted that a known potential for interaction between two drugs is not an absolute contraindication to their concomitant use. As has been previously noted, some interactions serve therapeutic purposes. Additionally, one must recognize that drug interactions are dose related. One aspirin tablet is unlikely to cause severe hemorrhagic episodes in a patient taking a coumarin anticoagulant. However, the intended use of a course of aspirin in a patient taking these anticoagulants is best discussed with the physician maintaining the anticoagulant dos-

age. Similarly, the usual dosages of aspirin are unlikely to upset the blood glucose balance of a patient taking hypoglycemics. However, both the dentist and the patient must be aware of this potentiality, and intended high or prolonged doses of aspirin in the patient with poorly controlled diabetes should be discussed with the patient's physician.

When is a potential interaction an absolute contraindication to the use of a specific drug? If not absolutely contraindicated, what doses can be safely used? Answers to these questions can be determined only by (1) knowing the potentialities of the interaction, (2) being aware of the patient's overall health and medical status, and (3) an ability and willingness to discuss intended therapy with the other practitioner (physician or dentist) who has instituted earlier therapy.

REFERENCES

1. Cluff, L.E., Thornton, G.F., and Seidle, L.G.: Studies on the epidemiology of adverse drug reactions, J.A.M.A. **188:**976-983, 1964.
2. Stuart, D.M.: Drug metabolism, Pharm. Index, **10,** 1968.
3. Kristensen, M., and Hansen, J.M.: Potentiation of the tolbutamide effect by Dicumarol, Diabetes **16:**211, 1967.
4. Zubrod, C.G., Kennedy, T.J., and Shannon, J.A.: Studies on the chemotherapy of the human malarias. VIII. The physiological disposition of pamaquine, J. Clin. Invest. **27:**114-120, 1948.
5. Burns, J.J., and Conney, A.H.: Enzyme stimulation and inhibition in the metabolism of drugs, Proc. R. Soc. Med. **58:**955-960, 1965.
6. Shee, J.C.: Dangerous potentiation of pethidine by iproniazid and its treatment, Br. Med. J. **2:**507-509, 1960.
7. Vigran, I.M.: Potentiation of meperidine by pargyline, J.A.M.A. **187:**953-954, 1964.
8. Eade, N.R., and Renton, K.W.: The effect of phenelzine and tranylcypromine on the degradation of meperidine, J. Pharmacol. Exp. Ther. **173:**31-36, 1970.
9. Hoffman, J.C., and Smith, J.C.: The respiratory effects of meperidine and propiomazine in man, Anesthesiology **32**(4):325-331, 1970.
10. Lambertsen, C.T., Wendel, H., and Longenhagen, J.B.: The separate and combined respiratory effects of chlorpromazine and meperidine in normal men controlled at 46 mm Hg alveolar P_{CO_2}, J. Pharmacol. Exp. Ther. **131:**381-393, 1961.
11. Morton, W.R., and Turnbull, W.: Promazine and meperidine (Sparidol-50), an efficient combination for preoperative medication, Can. Med. Assoc. J. **90:**1257-1259, 1964.
12. Goodman, L.S., and Gilman, A.: The pharmacological basis of therapeutics, ed. 4, New York, 1970, The Macmillan Co., pp. 250-251.
13. Goodman, L.S., and Gilman, A.: The pharmacologic basis of therapeutics, ed. 4, New York, 1970, The Macmillan Co., p. 258.
14. Niswander, K.R.: Effect of diazepam on meperidine required of patients during labor, Obstet. Gynecol. **34:**62-67, 1969.

15. Christensen, E.M., and Gross, E.G.: Analgesic effects in human subjects of morphine, meperidine and methadone, J.A.M.A. **137:**594-597, 1948.

16. Stambaugh, J.E., Wainer, I.W., and Schwartz, I.: The effect of phenobarbital on the metabolism of meperidine in normal volunteers, J. Clin. Pharmacol. **18:**482-490, 1978.

17. Houde, R.W., Wallenstein, S.L., and Beaver, W.T.: Clinical measurement of pain. In deStevens, G., editor: Analgetics, New York, 1965, Academic Press, Inc., pp. 75-122.

18. Herz, A.: The effect of central inhibiting and stimulating actions of morphine by anticholinergic, nicotinolytic and antihistaminics in the rat, Arch. Exp. Pathol. Pharmakol. **241:**253-263, 1961.

19. Eerola, R.: The combined action of morphine and atropine: an experimental study with mice, Ann. Med. Exp. Biol. Fenn. **40:**83-90, 1962.

20. Gupta, G.P., and Dhawan, B.N.: Potentiation of morphine analgesia by mecamylamine, Arch. Int. Pharmacodyn. Ther. **134:**54-60, 1961.

21. Sethy, V.H., et al.: Role of brain amines in the analgesic action of meperidine hydrochloride, Psychopharmacologia **17:**320-326, 1970.

22. Hartshorn, E.A. In Franke, D.E., editor: Handbook of drug interactions, Cincinnati, 1970, D.E. Franke.

23. Dunphy, T.W.: The pharmacist's role in the prevention of adverse drug interactions, Am. J. Hosp. Pharm. **26:**366-377, 1969.

24. Weiner, M.: Effect of centrally active drugs on the action of coumarin anticoagulants, Nature **212:**1599-1600, 1966.

25. Anticoagulant therapy—a selected bibliography, 1968, Endo Laboratories, p. 49.

26. Widerholt, I.C.: Recurrent episodes of hypoglycemia induced by propoxyphene, Neurology **17:**703-706, 1967.

27. Buckle, R.M., and Guillebaud, J.: Hypoglycaemic coma occurring during treatment with chlorpromazine and orphenadrine, Br. Med. J. **4:**599-600, 1967.

28. Sunshine, A., Slafta, R.N., and Gruber, C.: A comparative analgesic study of propoxyphene, fenoprofen, aspirin, and placebo, J. Clin. Pharmacol. **18:**556-563, 1978.

29. Roos, J., and van Joost, H.E.: The cause of bleeding during anticoagulant treatment, Acta Med. Scand. **178:**129-131, 1965.

30. Sandler, A.I.: Interactions of oral coumarin anticoagulants. In Franke, D.E., editor: Handbook of drug interactions, Cincinnati, 1970, D.E. Franke, pp. 72-74.

31. Krakoff, I.H.: Clinical pharmacology of drugs which influence uric acid production and excretion, Clin. Pharmacol. Ther. **8:**124-138, 1967.

32. Hussar, D.A.: Therapeutic incompatibilities: drug interactions, Hosp. Pharm. **3**(8):14-24, 1968.

33. Peaston, M.J.T., and Finnegan, P.: A case of combined poisoning with chlorpropamide, aspirin and paracetamol, Br. J. Clin. Pract. **22:**30-31, 1968.

34. Wishinsky, H.: Protein interactions of sulfonylurea compounds, Diabetes **2**(suppl.):18-25, 1962.

35. Klinenburg, J.R., and Miller, F.: Effect of corticosteroids on blood salicylate concentrations, J.A.M.A. **194:**601-604, 1965.

36. Tobert, J.A., et al.: The effect of antacids on the bioavailability of diflunisal, Clin. Pharmacol. Ther. **25:**251, 1979.

37. Fraser, D.G., et al.: Displacement of phenytoin from plasma binding sites by salicylate, Clin. Pharmacol. Ther. **27:**165-170, 1980.

38. Schnell, R.C., and Miya, T.S.: Increased ileal absorption of salicylic acid induced by carbonic anhydrase inhibition, Biochem. Pharmacol. **19:**303-305, 1970.

39. Lunde, P.K.M.: Plasma protein binding of diphenylhydantoin in man: interaction with other drugs and the effect of temperature and plasma dilution, Clin. Pharmacol. Ther. **11:**846, 1970.

40. Toakley, J.G.: "Dilantin" overdosage, Med. J. Aust. **2:**639-640, 1968.

41. McDougal, M.R.: Interaction of drugs with aspirin, J. Am. Pharm. Assoc. **10:**83-85, 1970.

42. Antlitz, A.M., Mead, J.A., and Tolentino, M.A.: Potentiation of oral anticoagulant therapy by acetaminophen, Curr. Ther. Res. **10:**501-508, 1968.

43. Antlitz, A.M., and Awalt, L.F.: A double-blind study of acetaminophen used in conjunction with oral anticoagulant therapy, Curr. Ther. Res. **11:**360, 1969.

44. Segre, E.: Interaction of naproxen and aspirin in the rat and man, Scand. J. Rheumatol. Suppl. **2:**37-45, 1973.

45. Rubin, A., et al.: Interactions of aspirin with nonsteroidal anti-inflammatory drugs in man, Arthritis Rheum. **16:**635-641, 1973.

46. Runkel, R., et al.: Naproxen-probenecid interaction, Clin. Pharmacol. Ther. **24:**706-713, 1978.

47. Hussar, D.A.: Oral anticoagulants—their interactions, J. Am. Pharm. Assoc. **10:**78-82, 1970.

48. Kunin, C.M., and Finland, M.: Clinical pharmacology of the tetracycline antibiotics, Clin. Pharmacol. Ther. **2:**51-69, 1961.

49. Risk of drug interaction may exist in 1 of 13 prescriptions, J.A.M.A. **220:**1287, 1972.

50. Neuvonen, P.J., et al.: Interference of iron with the absorption of tetracyclines in man, Br. Med. J. **4:**532-534, 1970.

51. Barr, W.H., Adir, J., and Garrettson, L.: Decrease of tetracycline absorption in man by sodium bicarbonate, Clin. Pharmacol. Ther. **12:**779-784, 1971.

52. Elliott, G.R., and Armstrong, M.F.: Sodium bicarbonate and oral tetracycline, Clin. Pharmacol. Therap. **13:**459, 1972.

53. Francis, L., and Kutscher, A.H.: Why teach pharmacology to dental students—multidisciplinary commentary, J. Dent. Educ. **34:**51-58, 1970.

54. Lepper, M.H., and Dowling, H.F.: Treatment of pneumococcic meningitis with penicillin compared with penicillin plus aureomycin: studies including observations on an apparent antagonism between penicillin and aureomycin, Arch. Intern. Med. **88:**489-494, 1951.

55. Jawetz, E.: The use of combinations of antimicrobial drugs, Ann. Rev. Pharmacol. **8:**151, 1968.

56. Ritschel, W.A.: Therapeutic incompatibilities between penicillin and other antibiotics administered intravenously, Drug Intelligence **3:**355, 1969.

57. A second look at lincomycin (Lincocin), Med. Letter **11:**107, 1969.

58. Gibaldi, M., and Schwartz, M.A.: Apparent effect of probenecid on the distribution of penicillins in man, Clin. Pharmacol. Ther. **9:**345-349, 1968.

59. Kunin, C.M.: Clinical pharmacology of the new penicillins. II. Effect of drugs which interfere with binding to serum proteins, Clin. Pharmacol. Ther. **7:**180-188, 1966.

60. Kabins, S.A.: Interactions among antibiotics and other drugs, J.A.M.A. **219**:206-212, 1972.

61. Domino, E.F., Sullivan, T.S., and Luby, E.D.: Barbiturate intoxication in a patient treated with MAO inhibitor, Am. J. Psychiatry **118**:941-943, 1962.

62. Cucinell, S.A., et al.: Drug interaction in man. I. Lowering effect of phenobarbital on plasma levels of bishydroxycoumarin (Dicumarol) and diphenylhydantoin (Dilantin), Clin. Pharmacol. Ther. **6**:420-429, 1965.

63. Hammer, W., and Sjoqvist, F.: Plasma levels of monomethylated tricyclic antidepressants during treatment with imipramine-like compounds, Life Sci. **6**:1895-1902, 1967.

64. Kampffmeyer, H.G.: Failure to detect increased elimination rate of phenacetin in man after treatment with phenobarbital, Klin. Wochenschr. **42**:1237, 1238, 1969.

65. Bushfield, D., Child, K.J., and Atkinson, R.M.: An effect of phenobarbitone on blood levels of griseofulvin in man, Lancet **2**:1042-1043, 1963.

66. Riegelman, S., Rowland, M., and Epstein, W.L.: Griseofulvin-phenobarbital interaction in man, J.A.M.A. **213**:426-431, 1970.

67. Patel, I.H., Levy, R.H., and Cutler, R.E.: Phenobarbital–valproic acid interaction, Clin. Pharmacol. Ther. **27**:515-532, 1980.

68. Bellville, J.W., et al.: The hypnotic effects of codeine and secobarbital and their interaction in man, Clin. Pharmacol. Ther. **12**:607-612, 1971.

69. Forrest, W.H., Bellville, J.W., and Brown, B.W.: The interaction of caffeine with pentobarbital as a nighttime hypnotic, Anesthesiology **36**:37-41, 1972.

70. Boulos, B.M., Short, C.R., and Davis, L.E.: Quinine and quinidine inhibition of pentobarbital metabolism, Biochem. Pharmacol. **9**:723-732, 1970.

71. Hurwitz, A., and Sheehan, M.B.: The effects of antacids on the absorption of orally administered pentobarbital in the rat, J. Pharmacol. Exp. Ther. **179**:124-131, 1972.

72. Heubel, F.: Interferenz von diazepam und pentobarbital an der ratte und am menschen, Arch. Exp. Pathol. Pharmakol. **264**:246-247, 1969.

73. Kane, F.J., and Taylor, T.W.: A toxic reaction to combine Elavil-Librium therapy, Am. J. Psychiatry **119**:1179-1180, 1963.

74. Greenblatt, D.J., et al.: Influence of magnesium and aluminum hydroxide mixture on chlordiazepoxide absorption, Clin. Pharmacol. Ther. **19**:234-239, 1976.

75. Vajda, F.J.E.: Interaction between phenytoin and the benzodiazepines, Br. Med. J. **1**:346, 1971.

76. Treasure, T., and Toseland, P.A.: Hyperglycaemia due to phenytoin toxicity, Arch. Dis. Child. **46**:563, 1971.

77. Greenblatt, D.J., et al.: Diazepam absorption: effect of antacids and food, Clin. Pharmacol. Ther. **24**:600-609, 1978.

78. MacLeod, S.M., et al.: Interaction of disulfiram with benzodiazepines, Clin. Pharmacol. Ther. **24**:583-588, 1978.

79. Shader, R.I.: Impaired absorption of desmethyl-diazepam from clorazepate by magnesium aluminum hydroxide, Clin. Pharmacol. Ther. **24**:308-315, 1978.

80. Cucinell, S.A., et al.: The effect of chloral hydrate on bishydroxycoumarin metabolism, J.A.M.A. **197**:366-368, 1966.

81. Gershon, C., Neubauer, H., and Sundland, D.M.: Interaction between some anticholinergic agents and phenothiazines: potentiation of phenothiazine sedation and its antagonisms, Clin. Pharmacol. Ther. **6**:749-754, 1965.

82. Kessell, A., et al.: Side effects of a new hypnotic: drug potentiation, Med. J. Aust. **2**:1194-1195, 1967.

83. Winer, J.A., and Bahn, S.: Loss of teeth with antipressant drug therapy, Arch. Gen. Psychiatry **16**:239-240, 1967.

84. Cotzias, G.C.: Metabolic modification of some neurologic disorders, J.A.M.A. **210**:1255-1262, 1969.

85. Rosenthal, G.: Interaction of ascorbic acid and warfarin, J.A.M.A. **215**:1671, 1971.

86. Smith, E.C.: Interaction of ascorbic acid and warfarin, J.A.M.A. **221**:1166, 1972.

87. Hume, R.: Interaction of ascorbic acid and warfarin, J.A.M.A. **219**:1479, 1972.

88. Loh, H.S., and Wilson, C.W.M.: The interactions of aspirin and ascorbic acid in normal men, Clin. Pharmacol. **15**:36-45, 1975.

89. Baylis, E.M.: Influence of folic acid on blood-phenytoin levels, Lancet **1**:62, 1971.

90. Furlanut, M., et al.: Effects of folic acid on phenytoin kinetics in healthy subjects, Clin. Pharmacol. Ther. **24**:294-297, 1978.

91. Alcohol-drug interactions. FDA Drug Bulletin **9**(2), June, 1979.

92. Secretary of HEW: Third special report to the U.S. Congress on alcohol and health: technical support document, Washington, D.C., June, 1978, Alcohol, Drug Abuse and Mental Health Association, National Institute of Alcohol Abuse.

93. Kissin, B.: Interactions of ethyl alcohol and other drugs. In Kissin, B. and Begleiter, H., editors: The biology of alcoholism, vol. III; Clinical pathology, New York, 1974, Plenum Press, pp. 109-161.

94. Barker, J.D., De-Carle, D.J., and Anuras, S.: Chronic excessive acetaminophen use and liver damage, Ann. Inter. Med. **87**:299-301, 1977.

95. Bo, O., et al.: Ethanol and diazepam as causative agents in road traffic accidents. In Israelstam, S., and Lambert, S., editors, Alcohol, drugs, and traffic safety, Toronto, 1975, Addiction Research Foundation of Ontario, pp. 439-448.

96. Forney, R.R., and Hughes, F.W.: Meprobamate, ethanol or meprobamate-ethanol combinations on performance of human subjects under delayed audiofeedback (DAF), J. Psychol. **57**:431-436, 1964.

97. Bogan, J., and Smith, H.: Analytical investigation of barbiturate poisoning: description of methods and a survey of results, J. Forensic Sci. **7**:37-45, 1967.

98. Coleman, J.H., and Evans, W.E.: Drug interactions with alcohol, Alcohol Health Rec. World **14**:16-19, 1975.

99. Hansten, P.D.: Drug interactions, ed. 2, Philadelphia, 1973, Lea & Febiger.

100. Evaluation of drug interactions, ed. 2, Washington, D.C., 1976, American Pharmaceutical Association.

101. Swidler, G.: Handbook of drug interactions, New York, 1971, John Wiley & Sons, Inc.

102. Garb, S.: Clinical guide to undesirable drug interactions and interferences, New York, 1971, Springer Publishing Co., Inc.

103. Cohon, M.S.: Therapeutic drug interactions, Madison, Wis., 1970, The University of Wisconsin Medical Center.

104. Carson, J.A.: Drug interaction manual, Danville, Ill., 1970, Danville Pharmaceutical Publishing Co.

105. The United States Pharmacopeial Convention: United States pharmacopeia dispensing information, Easton, Penn., 1980, Mack Publishing Co.

CHAPTER 34

Drug abuse

MARK S. ARTHUR
BARBARA F. ROTH-SCHECHTER

The concept of using drugs to produce profound effects on mood, thought, and feeling is as old as civilization itself. Alcohol has always had the distinction of being the most abused drug; 1 out of every 10 adult drinkers in the United States is an alcoholic.[1] However, because of the vast increase in the number of drugs made available to clinicians in recent history, the amounts and kinds of abused substances have increased. It is estimated that in the United States, in addition to the alcohol abusers, there are two million nonopiate polydrug abusers as well as 500,000 heroin abusers.[2]

The purpose of this chapter is to provide information that will assist dentists and dental auxiliaries in understanding the drug abuser and the drug abuse problems that may affect dental treatment. First, concepts necessary for the understanding of the field of drug (substance) abuse will be discussed. Second, patterns of abuse, overdose, withdrawal, and management of overdose and withdrawal relevant to specific drug classes are discussed. Finally, signs and symptoms of drug abuse in the dental patient are presented. For the pharmacologic properties and therapeutic usefulness of the drugs discussed, the reader is referred to the respective chapters in this text. The legal aspects covering dispensing are presented in Chapter 4.

CONCEPTS IN DRUG ABUSE
Use, abuse, and addiction

Use. People *use* drugs because they desire to change a perceived undesirable physiologic, psychologic, or sociologic situation into one that is desirable. Acceptable drug use is determined in any given period of history by the interaction between society's attitudes, governmental and economic pressures, and the state of medical knowledge regarding the agent.

Thus therapeutic use, dosage, and methods of administration and dispensing are defined for any given drug.

Certain drugs have, in addition to their therapeutic value, the ability to alter mood and produce a sense of well-being (euphoria). Such agents are said to be psychoactive and are the most frequently abused. Based on common characteristics, they can be divided into the following classes: narcotics, sedatives, stimulants, psychedelics, and cannabinoids. The psychoactive effect of a drug may be its primary therapeutic effect at normal doses (e.g., diazepam's tranquilizing action), or a secondary side effect occurring concurrently with its primary function (e.g., the production of euphoria by oxycodone, which primarily has an analgesic action).

Abuse. The term *drug abuse* indicates the use of a drug other than for its established purpose or in doses greater than those considered appropriate for that purpose. Since the determination of abuse is predicated on variable social and legal attitudes and constantly changing medical findings, there can be great variation in the assessment of abuse by different cultures and generations. For example, the degree and frequency of ethyl alcohol consumption is mainly a function of social values and is not consistently or objectively defined; what one group may find to be acceptable use another may find to be unacceptable and therefore abuse. However, for most agents, especially those used therapeutically in a dental setting, a more clear distinction is possible. For example, if a dentist prescribes 30 tablets of oxycodone for relief of severe pain for a patient who is undergoing endodontic therapy, he is using the drug responsibly. However, if he were to prescribe 500 tablets for the same patient, even though legally permitted to do so, he would be guilty of drug abuse as a practitioner;

411

prescribing such quantities is well beyond the accepted purpose and method of use for the agent as an analgesic. When the patient takes the drug as prescribed by the dentist, one tablet every 6 hours as needed for pain, the patient is using the drug, but if the patient triples the dose to attain euphoria, he or she is abusing the drug because it was not prescribed for this purpose. Likewise, if the same patient uses the drug as prescribed but gives a friend a few for analgesic purposes, the patient and friend are both guilty of drug abuse since the method of the agent's use has been circumvented by both. The patient is not licensed to dispense the drug, the pharmacist is, and the friend has consumed a drug in the absence of the licensed professional supervision deemed necessary by law.

Addiction. The term *addiction* encompasses several definitions and concepts; thus many health care providers and researchers in the drug abuse field prefer the term *chemical dependence.* In either case, within the context of this chapter, both addiction and chemical dependence are defined as a disease characterized by continued administration of a drug despite recurring negative consequences in the person's life (i.e., health, social or marital situation, or legal and employment status). These negative consequences are a constant finding in all cases of chemical dependence, regardless of the agent's pharmacologic nature, the quantity or pattern of use, the person's psychologic make-up, or the social environment.

The relationship between abuse and chemical dependence deserves comment. A person may use or abuse drugs throughout his life and never be diagnostically definable as having the illness of chemical dependence; therefore abuse does not inevitably lead to chemical dependence. Once chemical dependence occurs, it is characteristically a progressive and chronic condition, and although episodes of abuse are typical, periods of abstinence also occur. The disease is incurable but highly treatable.[3]

Drug factors, set, and setting

Psychoactive agents are abused to escape from reality, for recreational purposes, or to prevent withdrawal symptoms. The exact reason or reasons why a person chooses to abuse drugs or falls victim to chemical dependence are unknown. However, one may gain an understanding of the person and his condition by being able to place into perspective the influence exerted on such situations by (1) the drug's charac-teristics (drug factors); (2) the person's attitudes, prior experiences, and personality traits (set); and (3) the person's sociologic/environmental factors (setting).

Drug factors. Common but not necessary characteristics of psychoactive drugs that are abused are an ability to produce psychologic dependence, tolerance to repeated doses and cross tolerance within drug classes, and physical dependence, cross dependence, and associated withdrawal syndrome.[4]

Drug-induced euphoria is a psychologic state of physical and emotional well-being and relief from anxiety, subjectively described as a ''high.'' The desire to attain this feeling is the basis for *psychologic dependence,* defined here as that mental state in which the individual believes he must take the drug to maintain well-being or to avoid discomfort. Psychologic dependence varies in severity from mild desire to compulsive obsession.

Substance abuse is commonly but not consistently associated with the development of tolerance and/or physical dependence. *Tolerance* to a psychoactive drug is characterized by a decrease in the effect obtained when the same dose is repeatedly administered; thus the tendency is to increase the dosage to achieve the desired effect. In this discussion of abuse of psychoactive drugs, the type of tolerance referred to is primarily cellular tolerance, a decreased responsiveness of brain tissue to constantly increasing amounts of drug. Tolerance of metabolic origin, that is, tolerance attributable to an accelerated rate of metabolism of the drug, is not a significant factor contributing to the tolerance to most of the psychoactive drugs observed in humans.

Physical dependence refers to the altered physiologic state resulting from constantly increasing drug concentrations in tissues. The presence of physical dependence is established by the occurrence of a *withdrawal syndrome,* that is, the combination of many drug-specific symptoms that occur after acute discontinuance of drug administration. Physical dependence and the illness of chemical dependence are two distinct entities. The former is a pharmacologic phenomenon, the latter an illness that may or may not be accompanied by physical dependence. It is generally agreed that physical dependence and withdrawal syndromes are caused by drug-induced changes at the cellular level. The most widely investigated changes have been those occurring in the CNS. Changes include alterations in neurotransmitter levels, various

Table 34-1. Comparison of abuse effects by drug class

Drug class	Example agent	Euphoria	Psychologic dependency	Tolerance	Withdrawal syndrome
Narcotics	Heroin	+++	+++	+++	+++
Sedatives	Barbiturates	++	+++	++	+++
	Alcohol	++	+++	++	+++
Stimulants	Amphetamine	+++	+++	++	+
	Cocaine	+++	+++	0	0
Psychedelics	LSD	++	+	+++	0
Cannabinoids	Thiocarbarsone (THC)	++	++	++	0

Modified from Cohen, S. The substance abuse problems, New York, 1981, Haworth Press.
+, Effect is present; *0*, effect is absent.

enzyme levels and activities, membrane permeability, and excitability characteristics, all of which can be considered secondary to drug-induced changes in number or affinities of various drug receptors. However, any definite cause-effect relationship remains to be established.

Drugs that produce tolerance and physical dependence can be grouped according to their ability to produce cross tolerance and cross dependence. *Cross tolerance* is defined as the observation of a reduced effect of a second drug after acquisition of tolerance to the first drug of the same group of drugs. *Cross dependence* occurs whenever one drug can substitute for another by maintaining the state of physical dependence induced by the first drug and suppressing the associated withdrawal symptoms. For example, if narcotic A is administered in amounts sufficient to produce both tolerance and physical dependency, one can conclude that higher than normal doses are now required to produce the original effect and that if the drug is withheld, the person will exhibit withdrawal symptoms. If narcotic B is substituted for A, and B likewise requires higher than normal doses to give the same effect as A, cross tolerance is said to exist between the drugs. Also, if when narcotic B is given, it maintains the physically dependent state existing with A, cross dependence is achieved. Cross dependence and cross tolerance may be partial or complete, can develop at different rates, and appear to be determined more by the pharmacologic action of the drug than by its chemical structure.

Thus within a group of drugs having the same pharmacologic action, any member can be substituted for another, causing maintainance of tolerance and dependence. This is not possible with a drug of another group, that is, a benzodiazepine cannot substitute for a narcotic.

Two additional generalizations can be made regarding dependence and withdrawal. When drugs of the same group are compared, the time required to produce physical dependence as well as for withdrawal symptoms to begin and subside is shortest with a rapidly metabolized drug and longest with a slowly metabolized drug. Likewise, the intensity of withdrawal reactions can be related to a large extent to the $t_{\frac{1}{2}}$ of the drug. Those with the longest $t_{\frac{1}{2}}$ tend to produce milder symptoms; those with the shortest tend to produce more intense reactions.

During drug abuse or the illness of chemical dependence, any or all of the above drug-related characteristics may exist. However, their presence and influence are not sufficient to totally explain a person's continued drug consumption in the presence of recurring problems in that person's life related to such agents. For example, a person may volunteer in a laboratory setting to consume larger and larger doses of alcohol over several days to maintain a high state of intoxication. Upon withdrawal, involving alcohol hallucination, delirium tremens, and seizures, the person will clearly demonstrate tolerance to its effects as well as psychologic and physiologic dependence. It is unlikely that this person would revolunteer to endure the profound negative consequences such as discomfort and personal danger. However the alcoholic, a person ill with the disease of chemical dependence involving the drug ethanol, "volunteers" repeatedly. Presently abused drugs and their relative ability to produce euphoria, psychologic dependence, tolerance, and a withdrawal syndrome are summarized in Table 34-1.

Set and setting. Set and setting do not entirely predict or explain why some people choose to abuse drugs or involuntarily progress from abuse to chemical dependence. However, certain family and individual psychologic traits and social correlates tend to appear with greater regularity.[5,6] It has been claimed that the family traits fostering the greatest risk factors are characterized by having less rigid convictions and more permissive parental attitudes toward drugs. Also it has been suggested that a single parent, or a dominant female influence if both parents are present, are additional risk factors.

Several psychologic traits have been observed consistently in drug abusers. The individual is unable to cope with frustrations, becomes aggressive when dealing with frustration,[7] and desires immediate gratification.[8] Sexual identity problems are common, such people tend to be norm breakers and appear likely to assume inappropriate risks, and depression appears to be consistent.[9] Finally, low self-esteem and associated guilt, emotional instability, and a lack of open communication have been observed.[10] It is beyond the scope of this presentation to evaluate whether these personality traits are predisposing for drug abuse or in fact a consequence thereof. Undoubtedly, the person's community, peer pressure, drug availability, and social occasion will also influence drug abuse. In conclusion suffice it to say that in addition to the drug factors, social set and setting are appreciated to play a significant role in any individual's predisposition to drug abuse.

ABUSE AND WITHDRAWAL BY DRUG CLASS

In this section, the specific pharmacologic effects of an agent in each drug group is presented with associated behavioral modifications. These responses depend on the amount of the agent administered, the frequency of the doses, the nature of the drug, and the organ systems affected. Therefore for each drug the effect of a therapeutic dose in a new or occasional abuser and a chronic abuser is described. Acute overdose and withdrawal, as well as techniques for managing each, are also described. Comments pertaining to polydrug abuse are interspersed. For a thorough discussion of the possible drug interactions the reader is referred to Chapter 33.

Narcotic analgesics

Heroin, methadone (Dolophine), morphine, hydromorphone (Dilaudid), meperidine (Demerol), oxyco-done (Percodan), and pentazocine (Talwin) are presently the most popular but not the only members of the narcotic analgesics abused. If obtained illegally on the street, they may be adulterated with quinine, lidocaine, mannitol, or almost anything else imaginable. The present discussion will focus only on the effects of the nonadulterated narcotics, using morphine as the representative drug.

Pattern of abuse. An initial dose of morphine will produce sedation, analgesia, miosis, and a state described as complete satiation of all drives. The mood is also elevated, causing euphoria; there is relief from fear and apprehension; and a sense of well-being prevails. Hunger and sexual desires are depressed and the individual's responses to provocation are reduced. However, routine function and productive work are not incompatible with the sporadic or regular abuse of these drugs. Thus, in the presence of morphine-like drugs, the abuser is a satisfied, complacent, and highly cooperative individual. (This is in stark contrast to the alcohol abuser, who when intoxicated is generally quarrelsome, dissatisfied, highly uncooperative, and unproductive in society.) Undoubtedly, initial abuse of morphine is reinforced by these positive experiences. Other effects of morphine are constipation, depressed respiration, urinary retention, and peripheral vasodilation.

The most common route of administration when narcotics are abused is intravenous ("mainlining"), undoubtedly favored because of the rapid and reliable effects produced and because absorption from the gastrointestinal tract is erratic. Opium, which comes from poppies and contains morphine, can also be smoked, that is, heated and its vapor inhaled ("chasing the dragon"). Morphine and heroin are sometimes injected subcutaneously ("skinpopping") by occasional abusers ("chippers"). The desire for instant gratification, a personality trait commonly identified in abusers, may account in part for heroin's popularity even though heroin is broken down to morphine in the brain. This choice of heroin is based on the fact that the diacetyl substitution on the morphine molecule enhances the rate at which the heroin (and hence morphine) enters the brain to produce its effects.[11]

Narcotics are metabolized by the liver microsomal enzyme systems and excreted in the kidney as the glucuronide conjugate. The presence of the metabolite in urine provides a means of screening for drugs, particularly significant in methadone maintenance programs.[12] Because of the presence of tolerance, many but not all of the responses are diminished in the chronic abuser who receives a therapeutic dose. Those effects to which tolerance develops are euphoria, analgesia, sedation, and respiratory depression. The responses of miosis, urinary retention, and constipation are rarely influenced. It is significant that, with the development of tolerance, the lethal dose is greatly increased. Thus, as long as intake is maintained, excessively large doses can eventually be tolerated without any respiratory or cardiovascular complications. Cross tolerance with all other narcotic analgesics is a common finding and is apparently independent of the chemical structure of the narcotic. There is no cross tolerance between the narcotics and the other classes of abused drugs. The poor quality of street narcotics and the development of tolerance are undoubtedly contributing factors to the use of more than one drug (i.e., heroin and cocaine, the "speed ball") to maintain some degree of pleasant effects.

Acute overdose. The effects of an overdose are the same for almost all members of this group. They consist of fixed pinpoint pupils, cyanosis or depressed respiration, hypotension and shock, slow or absent reflexes, drowsiness, or coma. Heroin overdose, a highly publicized hazard of its abuse, is less likely to be the result of too much drug than the result of a heroin-alcohol or heroin-barbiturate interaction.[13,14] Such interactions are characterized by sudden massive pulmonary edema, which occurs so rapidly that the syringe is frequently found still imbedded in the vein.[15]

Withdrawal. Discontinuation of drug administration to a chronic, physically dependent abuser will result in the appearance of a withdrawal syndrome. The syndrome begins at the time of the abuser's next scheduled dose, or it can be precipitated within minutes by the administration of a narcotic antagonist (naloxone). In the case of morphine or heroin, the first signs of withdrawal are yawning, lacrimation, rhinorrhea, and perspiration, followed by a restless sleep (the "yen"). With awakening and further abstinence, anorexia, tremors, irritability, weakness, severe pain, and excessive gastrointestinal activity are experienced. Heart rate is rapid, blood pressure is elevated, and chills alternate with excessive sweating. The occurence of piloerection (gooseflesh) and widely dilated pupils are considered two objective signs of narcotic withdrawal. The syndrome typically begins 6 to 8 hours after the last dose of heroin or morphine and peaks 48 to 72 hours later. All of these

physiologic symptoms are accompanied by varying degrees of desperation and fear. At any point in this ordeal, the administration of a sufficient dose of narcotic would completely block all withdrawal symptoms and alleviate the misery.

Management of acute overdose and withdrawal. If apnea caused by a narcotic overdose is suspected, narcotic antagonists should be used immediately. This is a safe procedure because apnea caused by barbiturates or other drugs will not increase from treatment with naloxone (Narcan), the drug of choice. If the rate of respiration does not increase within minutes after the administration of naloxone, opiate overdose is unlikely. If no narcotic antagonist is available, manual or mechanical artificial respiration is necessary. Drugs to raise the blood pressure and plasma expanders are used for the treatment of shock; other signs and symptoms have to be treated individually and supportively.

Two current treatment modalities for patients with chemical dependence to narcotics are methadone maintenance and methadone detoxification. Both are based on the substitution of a pharmacologically equivalent drug of long duration for the person's current narcotic. Methadone will prevent the narcotic withdrawal syndrome for 24 hours as opposed to 6 hours for heroin. Participation in rehabilitation programs is usually voluntary, with the patient reporting daily to a treatment center where he receives gradually decreasing or maintainance doses as well as counseling. Once stabilized with sufficiently large doses (70 to 100 mg) the patient is unlikely to experience euphoria from other opiates or even larger doses of methadone.[16] Other than constipation and some impotency, there are no other side effects currently known to occur with the use of methadone for as long as several years.

Therapeutically, it must be noted that individuals who chronically use narcotics are tolerant to their analgesic properties. Thus they can experience pain and, when treated for it, will need higher than normal doses of a potent narcotic. Also, the use of pentazocine (Talwin) is definitely contraindicated in patients on methadone maintenance since it is both a narcotic agonist and an antagonist. This latter property can cause immediate withdrawal in a patient on methadone maintenance. Alternately, methadone may be used in detoxification from narcotic abuse. It consists of a gradual weaning from methadone and involves a withdrawal syndrome less severe but more protracted than that for heroin. Pharmacologically, it is based on the inverse relationship between the duration of drug action and the intensity of withdrawal symptoms mentioned previously.

Another congener of methadone, levo-alpha-acetylmethadol (LAAM), has recently been advocated for the same purpose.[17] It has the same set of effects as methadone, differing only in that acetylmethadol is effective for a 2- to 3-day period, in contrast to the 24-hour relief afforded by methadone.

Another approach to the long-term management of narcotic abuse is long-term blockade of the narcotic receptor. This is achieved by maintaining the patient on a specific narcotic antagonist (naloxone or cyclazocine) after the completion of withdrawal. Although these drugs do not reduce narcotic craving, they do prevent the positive reinforcement from administering the narcotic because of receptor blockade. However, cyclazocine has some agonist action and thus poses an abuse potention of its own. A discussion of advantages and disadvantages of methadone maintenance and the use of narcotic antagonists is beyond the scope of this chapter. Both approaches are presently under active clinical investigation; their impact and success in conquering opiate abuse remain to be established.

Sedative-hypnotics and antianxiety agents

Previously, this group of abused psychoactive drugs included only the barbiturates and alcohol. The introduction of many new sedatives and antianxiety agents in the past 20 years has extended the range considerably to include glutethimide (Doriden), meprobamate (Miltown), chlordiazepoxide (Librium), diazepam (Valium), ethchlorvynol (Placidyl), and methaqualone (Quaalude). Barbiturates, alcohol, and the diazepam-type tranquilizers are the most widely abused among the sedative-hypnotics, with alcoholism affecting 10 million Americans.[18]

Pattern of abuse. Initial symptoms occurring with a therapeutic dose of any of the drugs of this category resemble the well-known symptoms of alcohol intoxication: loss of inhibition, euphoria, emotional instability, quarrelsomeness, difficulty in thinking, poor memory and judgments, ataxia, and slurred speech. If the dose is increased, drowsiness and sleep will occur because of the loss of inhibitory control mechanisms on other parts of the brain. Gastrointestinal activity is diminished, respiration is depressed, urine output is reduced, and cardiac output is decreased with the CNS depressants.

When drugs in this class are abused, the most common route of administration is oral, and metabolism is in the liver, primarily by enzymes in the smooth endoplasmic reticulum. The activity of these enzymes (an example of metabolic tolerance) can be increased by agents in this group as well as by a variety of other agents: anticonvulsants, antihistamines, antirheumatics, hypoglycemic agents, and steroids.

When a person who has been taking a CNS depressant regularly (over a period of 1 to 2 months) is given a therapeutic dose, tolerance in varying degrees to its usual pharmacologic effects will be observed. However, unlike the narcotics, there is no tolerance to the minimal lethal dose. There is complete cross tolerance between all members of this group, and the sedative-hypnotics with the exception of the benzodiazepines have a slower onset of tolerance and physical dependence than the narcotic analgesics.

Tolerance to the sedative effect of some benzodiazepines has been observed after one or two nightly doses, whereas tolerance to their anxiolytic action is very slow in onset, if it occurs at all. Rebound insomnia after a single dose testifies to the existence of rapid onset of some form of physical dependence on benzodiazepines as well.

With prolonged abuse of CNS depressants, either depressive or stimulative actions may be the overriding manifestation, but several psychologic changes also occur in either situation. Emotional instability, hostile and paranoid ideations, and suicidal tendencies are common.

Acute overdose. An acute overdose of any of the sedative-hypnotics produces essentially the same responses outlined above, with major complications arising from the depression of respiration and cardiovascular functions, leading to hypotension and coma. The pupils may be unchanged or small, and lateral nystagmus is present. Confusion, slurred speech, and ataxia are always present.

Withdrawal. The withdrawal syndrome is similar for all of these drugs, but its time course depends to a great extent on the elimination $t_{\frac{1}{2}}$ of the drug in question. The benzodiazepines and the long-acting barbiturates may not produce symptoms for as long as 48 hours after withdrawal, and the reaction may be attenuated over time, with seizures not appearing until a week or more after discontinuation of the drug. Meprobamate and short-acting barbiturates, on the other hand, produce acute reactions similar to those of alcohol. The first signs of the withdrawal syndrome from sedatives are insomnia, weakness, and a tremulous restlessness. Often a high temperature and a large degree of agitation occur. Delirium and convulsions may culminate in cardiovascular collapse and loss of the temperature-regulating mechanism.

Alcohol withdrawal syndrome is clearly a sedative withdrawal syndrome, but it does have additional features worth noting. The syndrome begins within a few hours after the last drink and consists of the same initial symptoms of abstinence seen with other sedatives; nausea, vomiting, weakness, anxiety, and perspiration. Tremors follow and may be accompanied by alcohol-specific hallucinations. These can develop into the well-known delirium tremens. Without treatment, recovery from alcohol withdrawal occurs within 7 days; recovery from other sedatives varies, depending on the drug involved.

Management of acute overdose and withdrawal. The most important consideration after an acute overdose of a sedative agent is support of the cardiovascular and respiratory functions. An airway must be established and maintained. Early gastric lavage after intubation and dialysis can assist in removal of the drug. Analeptic drugs and stimulants may be harmful and are contraindicated.

In contrast to withdrawal from narcotics, withdrawal from sedative agents is more life threatening, and the patient should be hospitalized. Abrupt withdrawal of any of these agents, including alcohol, is not considered safe medically. The two major principles of treatment are (1) replacement of the abused drug with a pharmacologically or physiologically equivalent drug in the acute situation and (2) gradual withdrawal of the equivalent drug. Drugs like pentobarbital, paraldehyde, and chloral hydrate have been standard agents for substitution during acute withdrawal of sedative drugs, but sedatives with fewer respiratory depressant actions have been found to be safer.[19] Chlordiazepoxide or diazepam is considered by many to be the drug of choice. By comparison, chlorpromazine and hydroxyzine have been found to be considerably less effective, and they also pose the danger of lowering seizure threshold, thus aggravating the tendency for withdrawal seizures. Gradual withdrawal of the substitute drug with rehabilitative therapy can then be attained in a matter of weeks.

CNS stimulants

The widely abused members of this class are methamphetamine (Methedrine), dextroamphetamine (Dexedrine), diethylpropion (Tenuate), methylphenidate (Ritalin), phenmetrazine (Preludin) and cocaine. This discussion will focus on the amphetamines with comments relating to other agents interspersed as appropriate.

Pattern of abuse. A therapeutic dose produces CNS stimulation, insomnia, excitement, euphoria or a sense of elation, a decreased sense of fatigue, talkativeness, and a feeling of omnipotence and self-confidence. The nature of the "rush" experienced with intravenous administration of amphetamine is distinct from that with heroin. However, both have in common the description of being similar to a sexual orgasm. Other effects include mydriasis, increased sweating, anorexia, increased blood pressure, and tachycardia. Respiration is not significantly affected. Of special note to dentists is the occurrence of xerostomia and bruxism. Occasionally at the therapeutic dose, and nearly always when it is exceeded, symptoms of a toxic psychosis appear with stimulants, such as aggressiveness, anxiety, stereotyped repetitious behavior, auditory hallucinations, and paranoid fears.

These drugs may be taken orally, parenterally, or intranasally. Cocaine, which is typically "snorted," is also smoked in its freebase form by abusers. Freebasing, a current method of abuse, was originally developed by illicit dealers as a process designed to draw off adulterants and verify quality. The result is a more pure and potent product that must be smoked (vapor inhalation), because its nonsolubility in water precludes other means of administration. Freebasers ("baseballers") report that this method of administration and the nature of "coke" yield the "highest high of all."[20] Testing for the presence of these drugs in suspected abusers is possible via urine screening, with as much as 75% of the drug being excreted unchanged. Cocaine may be found unchanged in the urine with the metabolite benzoylecgonine.[21]

Chronic abusers soon develop tolerance to the euphoric, anorectic, and lethal actions. Hence their initial dose no longer elicits the high levels of pleasure previously experienced. No tolerance seems to develop to the induction of toxic psychosis. In fact, it is known to appear sooner with each subsequent dose.

Acute overdose. The signs and symptoms during CNS stimulant overdose are dilated and reactive pupils, elevated blood pressure and pulse, and cardiac arrhythmias. The patient has a dry mouth, is sweating, and has a slight to moderate temperature. Fine tremors may be present, and most often the patient exhibits the hyperactive stereotyped behavior of the toxic psychosis previously described.

Withdrawal. Modest levels of prolonged abuse of stimulants do not produce any withdrawal reaction of consequence, in most cases only general fatigue and prolonged sleep. Withdrawal from some of the monumental doses used (as much as 10 gm per day of methamphetamine taken intravenously) will precipitate a withdrawal syndrome consisting of muscular aches, a ravenous appetite with abdominal pain, and long periods of sleep. On awakening, the abuser will experience a profound psychologic depression that is sometimes suicidal. Definite electroencephalographic abnormalities have been observed during that period.

The effects of cocaine are similar to those observed after the intravenous administration of amphetamines. However, its action is more brief, which may account for the absence of tolerance to and withdrawal reactions from this drug.

Management of acute overdose and withdrawal. Treatment of an acute overdose of a CNS stimulant includes the administration of a phenothiazine for the CNS symptoms and mild hypertension. If hypertension is severe, alpha adrenoreceptor blocking agents such as phenoxybenzamine and phentolamine are indicated. Abrupt withdrawal without any medication is not life threatening, but individuals can be made more comfortable with sedatives or tranquilizers for a few days. If severe depression occurs, a tricyclic antidepressant is indicated. One should also keep in mind that prolonged abuse of CNS stimulants is accompanied by prolonged appetite suppression. Thus nutritional deficiencies are likely to have occurred. Part of the long-term management of withdrawal is correction of the nutritional disturbances.

The most serious sociologic problem with stimulant abuse, especially in a population of young abusers, is the induction of mental abnormalities. Although it was formerly believed that many of the reactions observed during abuse of stimulants were exaggerations of preexisting psychopathology, experimental evidence suggests that ampheatmine psychosis can be quickly induced in previously unaffected volunteer subjects.[22]

Psychedelics

Although the psychedelic drugs are usually grouped in a separate category, their central actions are not really substantially different from many other centrally active stimulant drugs. Their separate catagorization is perpetuated by two factors: (1) they are capable of inducing states of altered sensory perception; and (2) they do not have any general therapeutic usefulness or medical acceptance (i.e., no accepted method and/or purpose of use). The drugs discussed in this presentation are classified chemically into two subgroups. The indolealkylamines include LSD, found naturally as a fungus by-product on grains such as rye, psilocybin from muschrooms found in Mexico, and dimethyltryptamine (DMT). Mescaline is the prototype of the phenylethylamine subgroup and it is found in the buttonlike head of the peyote cactus. Although not a member of either of the two chemical subgroups mentioned, phencyclohexylpiperidine (PCP), an arylcyclohexylamine with dissociative anesthetic properties, is abused by itself or as an adulterant to other street concoctions.

In general, psychedelics will affect perceptions in such a way that all sensory input is perceived with heightened awareness. Sounds are perceived to be brighter and clearer, colors seem stronger and more brilliant. Flat objects seem to stand out in three dimensions. Taste, smell, hearing, sight, and touch seem to be more acute. One sensory impression may be translated or merged into another *(synesthesia)*. For example, music may appear as a color, and colors may seem to have taste. Judgment of reality and surroundings is greatly impaired. The most pronounced manifestation is the abuser's loss of sense of time and ability to delineate boundaries. Some of these agents (e.g., mescaline) produce true hallucinations (the person sees and believes something is there that really is not), and others (e.g., LSD) produce pseudohallucinations (the person sees what is really there but in a distorted way).

Psychedelic-induced dependence is psychologic rather than physical, and tolerance develops within days and disappears as rapidly on discontinuation of the drug. These two characteristics, rapid tolerance and no physical dependence, combined with the unpredictable and profound nature of the responses favor periodic rather than continuous abuse of psychedelic drugs.

Pattern of abuse. LSD is the most potent of these agents. Because responses to it and the other drugs are similar, it is discussed as the representative example for the psychedelics.

A dose of 100 μg, given orally in a saturated sugar

cube, gelatin square, or blotter paper, will produce a full blown "trip," often described as being a "mind-expanding experience." In the sense that one's mind can perceive and experience more than it can relate or explain, this connotation is not entirely inappropriate. The kind of trip experienced is primarily a function of the abuser's mind set (expectations) and environmental setting (companions, physical security) at the time. A person who is fearful and paranoid before using LSD may have an intense panic reaction (bad trip), whereas a reassured and more open individual may experience a positive response (good trip). Clearly, these agents have been shown to exacerbate latent personality disorders and psychosis.[23] *Flashbacks,* a well-publicized effect of LSD, are described as being an unexpected "reliving" of some aspect of the original trip, but whether such occurrences are actually direct sequelae of LSD ingestion is still an unsettled issue.[24,25]

LSD has additional sympathomimetic effects, manifesting themselves as a rise in blood pressure, tachycardia, hyperflexia, nausea, piloerection, and increased body temperature.

Withdrawal. Tolerance builds to LSD so that after 4 or 5 days of administration, the person will have negligible responses to further doses. Likewise, a similar period of abstinence is accompanied by the disappearance of tolerance. Cross tolerance to psilocybin and mescaline is considerable, but none is demonstrated between LSD and amphetamines, DMT, or delta-9-tetrahydrocannabinol (see section on cannabinoids). This tolerance is not accompanied by physical dependence on the drug; thus no withdrawal syndrome appears during any drug-free period.

Acute overdose. Signs and symptoms of an acute overdose include widely dilated pupils, flushed face, elevated blood pressure, visual and temporal distortions, panic reactions, paranoia, and accidental death from misperceptions. The person does not lose consciousness and is highly suggestible throughout the experiences.

Management of acute overdose and withdrawal. As mentioned, there is no withdrawal syndrome because there is no development of physical dependence. Acute overdose is best managed by reassuring the person, limiting stimulation, providing a nonthreatening atmosphere, and having someone in constant attendance. Phenothiazines antagonize LSD effects, but neither they nor the barbiturates, which will induce sleep, are deemed preferable to the above.

Cannabinoids

Marijuana has become an all-inclusive term for varying mixtures of leaves, stems, and flowers of the plant *Cannabis sativa* (the hemp plant). Although all of the plant (whether male or female) contains pharmacologically active cannabinoids (a total of 61 isomers), the flowering tops are richest in these substances, especially the ingredient suspected to be responsible for marihuana's psychoactivity, L-delta-9-tetrahydrocannabinol (THC). This isomer will be discussed as being representative of the other cannabinoids and marijuana in general.

Mixtures vary in their concentration of THC. *Hashish,* the dried exudate from the flowering tops, contains from 1.8% to 10%. *Bhang,* a mixture of dried leaves and shoots, contains 0.5% to 6%. *Hashish oil* contains 20% but is misnamed since it does not resemble hashish in appearance or in method of preparation. Hashish oil is a dark, viscous material that results from repeated extraction of plant material. Most commonly, a tobacco-like material is prepared by cutting and chopping the plant, and it is either smoked as cigarettes (joints) or in a water pipe (bong).[26]

Pattern of abuse. The effects of 20 mg THC taken orally or the effects of smoking one 2% THC cigarette are mainly confined to the CNS and cardiovascular system. CNS effects consist of the feelings of well-being, relaxation, drowsiness, intensified visual and auditory sensory perceptions, and emotional lability tending toward euphoria. In the first-time abuser, these responses are largely dependent on the person's mind set and setting. As the dose and frequency of administration increase, the person is more quickly able to identify the subjective effects described. Thus the feeling by abusers is that the effects increase with more frequent administration. The heart rate is increased and the conjunctival vessels dilate (not a direct irritant effect of the smoke); a craving for sweets is also frequently observed. It was once thought that this latter tendency was caused by hypoglycemia, but a lowering of the blood sugar is not a consistent finding.[27]

Marijuana may be either smoked or eaten, and the smoking route is three times as potent as the oral. With the best of smoking techniques, only 50% is absorbed. The effects begin immediately, peak in 30 minutes, and last for approximately 2 to 3 hours. In humans the $t_{\frac{1}{2}}$ of THC is 7 to 8 days, metabolism is nearly complete, and urine testing for metabolites is possible but currently done only through special research laboratories. Repeated administration of cannabinoids at intervals of less than 7 to 8 days results in the accumulation of THC and its metabolites in body tissues. Marijuana alters the metabolism of ethanol and barbiturates and is additive to the responses elicited by the sedative-hypnotics.[28]

Chronic intoxication with large doses of marijuana can evoke tolerance to mood changes, the impairment of psychomotor performance, and cardiac effects.[29] However, with the chronic abuse of small to moderate doses, no tolerance is produced. Thus moderate doses and moderate frequency of administration will result in increased intensity of effects, as well as impairment of ability to carry out tasks requiring several steps. This latter phenomenon is referred to as *temporal disintegration* and is defined as the loss of time perception relevant to actions. Large-dose effects include progressive impairment of motor coordination, cognitive ability, attention span, information processing, as well as emotional apathy and increased perception of all senses, especially tactile, olfactory, and gustatory. Whether large chronic doses of marijuana produce an irreversible psychosis, an amotivational syndrome characterized by apathy and reduction in active involvement, or massive damage to cellular processes is to date unresolved.[30]

A reverse tolerance is frequently described by abusers in which a chronic smoker appears to achieve more profound effects. This observation is not caused by a manifestation of tolerance; it is a function of both improved smoking technique and mind set.

Acute overdose. Acute overdose from marijuana is rare, and lethal doses are not easily attained. The main danger comes from impulsive acts, anxiety, and panic in the inexperienced abuser.

Withdrawal. Since physical dependency does not develop, the moderate abuser shows no signs on discontinuation of administration. However, after prolonged periods of intoxication with large doses, symptoms of discontinued intake can be seen, such as sleep disturbances, irritability, anorexia, and restlessness. These manifestations begin wtihin a few hours after the last dose, are relatively mild, and last 4 to 5 days.[31]

Management of acute overdose and withdrawal. Symptoms of overdose and withdrawal are best handled as with the psychedelics, that is, limiting stimulation and providing reassurance and personal supervision to avoid accidental injury.

SIGNS AND SYMPTOMS OBSERVED BY THE DENTIST

The signs and symptoms of chronic drug abuse, many of which represent pathologic sequelae, serve as indicators of the drug's effect on the person's biologic, psychologic, and sociologic well-being. Awareness of these clues can assist the dentist in clinical detection of such patients. General consideration is given to those manifestations most easily observed in a dental setting. The reader should understand that the observation and evaluation of any signs and symptoms must be considered within the context of a complete history and examination and of themselves do not constitute a definitive diagnosis of drug abuse in a patient.

The use of either alcohol or marijuana results in redness of the eyes. Constricted pupils are a consistent finding with narcotic intoxication or overdose except during the occurrence of overdose asphyxia, when mydriasis appears. During stimulant and psychedelic intoxication and narcotic withdrawal, the pupils are dilated. With narcotic and stimulant withdrawal, tearing, cold symptoms, and rhinorrhea occur. Other nasal signs in the form of septum ulcerations or perforations are associated with the "snorting" of amphetamine or cocaine. By noting breath odors, one may detect alcohol, which is excreted to a minor degree through the lungs, and the burnt rope smell of marijuana. Xerostomia is a common finding with narcotic, stimulant, and marijuana abuse, whereas alcohol and psychedelics are associated more with increased salivation. Heavy use of strong marijuana (i.e., hashish) will also produce uvular edema.[32]

Skin changes may occur as color changes or physical aberrations. Jaundice, a result of hepatitis caused by unsterile needles, is a common finding. Cyanosis is profound in opiate and sedative overdose and in convulsion states. Flushing can be seen with narcotic intoxication and overdoses of stimulants or psychedelics. Spider nevi, acne rosacea, and dilated facial venules are frequent occurrences in people chronically imbibing large amounts of alcohol. Smoking of marijuana results in a different staining pattern of the fingers than that found in the tobacco smoker. In the former, the thumb and forefinger are stained, in the latter, the forefinger and middle finger. Physical aberrations occur in the form of tracts associated with intravenous injections (mainlining) and abscesses caused by subcutaneous injections (skin popping). Sweating is common in narcotic withdrawal (cold turkey appearance) and stimulant overdose and is an occasional complaint of people on methadone maintenance. Ankle edema is also associated with methadone maintenance.

Amphetamine, cocaine, psychedelics, and marijuana administration, as well as narcotic withdrawal, will lead to tachycardia and hypertension. Bradycardia and a decreased blood pressure are observed in narcotic overdose. Although almost any drug may elicit nausea and vomiting, these are especially consistent occurrences with psychedelic intoxication, stimulant overdose, and narcotic withdrawal.

Insomnia is a response common to stimulants and psychedelics; drowsiness is produced by sedatives, narcotics, and marijuana. Large doses of sedatives can lead to stupor and coma, and during withdrawal from sedatives, convulsions are common. The hyperactivity and stereotypical actions of stimulant abusers have been noted previously. Deep tendon reflexes are increased and quickened with stimulants and psychedelics and decreased with sedatives and narcotics. Sedative intoxication is typically associated with nystagmus, ataxia, diplopia, loss of coordination, and slurred speech. After the period of intoxication, the proverbial "hangover headache" occurs.

Vitamin deficiencies as a result of poor eating habits can produce oral signs associated with scurvy and pellagra. Angular cheilosis and perleche are common findings, stemming from general systemic debilitation. If the person is severely debilitated, moniliasis may develop. Drooling is also common with these conditions. The occurrence of xerostomia in connection with narcotic, stimulant, and marijuana abuse has been noted, as has the existence of hypersalivation in the alcohol and psychedelic abuser. Bruxism and clenching may be found with any drug abuse but are especially prevalent with intoxication from stimulants and psychedelics. With any drug or drug state associated with high levels of anxiety or increased psychomotor stimulation, the tongue may become irritated because of excessive scraping against the teeth. Heavy drinking of alcohol during pregnancy is associated with the occurrence of developmental abnormalities in the offspring, the *fetal alcohol syndrome* (FAS). Such is characterized by a thinned upper vermilion border and hypoplastic maxilla and philtrum. Periodontal disease and caries are common in drug abusers, a common finding being presenile atrophy of the periodontal structures.[33] Commonly, an irregular pattern of caries is observed,

characterized by rampant cervical lesions (white and mushy) with insignificant occlusal or interproximal caries or prior restorations. However, no definite etiologic link to these conditions and the drugs discussed has been established.

REFERENCES

1. Mendelson, J.H., and Mello, N.K.: Biological concomitants of alcoholism, N. Engl. J. Med. **301**(2):912-921, 1979.
2. Lau, J., and Beavenuto, J.: National estimates of prevalence of non-opiate drug abuse. In Wesson, D., et al., editors: Polydrug abuse, New York, 1978, Academic Press, Inc., pp. 211-218.
3. Tommasello, T., and Whitfield, C.: Basic concepts of psychoactive drug use and chemical dependency. In Whitfield, C., Williams, K. and Leipman, M., editors: The patient with alcoholism and other drug problems, Chicago, 1982, Yearbook Medical Publishers, p. 7. (In press.)
4. Cohen, S.: The substance abuse problems, New York, 1981, Haworth Press, pp. 1-7.
5. Nurco, D.: Etiological aspects of drug abuse. In Dupont, R., Goldstein, A., and Odonnell, J., editors: Hand book on drug abuse, DHEW Publication No. SN-017-024-00869-9, Washington, D.C., January, 1979, U.S. Government Printing Office, pp. 316-317.
6. Nurco, D.: Etiological aspects of drug abuse. In Dupont, R., Goldstein, A., and Odonnell, J., editors: Hand book on drug abuse, DHEW Publication No. SN-017-024-00869-9, Washington, D.C., January, 1979, U.S. Government Printing Office, p. 321.
7. Dollard, J., et al.: Frustration and aggression, New Haven, Conn., 1939, Yale University Press, p. 135.
8. Nurco, D.: A choice of treatments. In Brown, C., and Savage, C., editors: The drug abuse controversy, Baltimore, 1971, National Education Consultants.
9. Woody, G.E., and Blaine, J.: Depression in narcotic addicts: quite possibly more than a chance association. In Dupont, R., Goldstein, A., and Odonnell, J., editors: Hand book on drug abuse, DHEW Publication No. SN-017-024-00869-9, Washington, D.C., January, 1979, U.S. Government Printing Office, p. 277.
10. Anderson, D.: Anxiety, conflicts and chemical dependency, Minneapolis, 1976, Hazeldon Foundation, Inc., p. 15.
11. Oldendorf, W.H.: Factors affecting passage of opiates through the blood-brain barrier. In Adler, M.W., Manara, L., and Samanin, R., editors: Factors affecting the actions of narcotics, New York, 1978, Raven Press, pp. 221-231.
12. Cohen, S.: The substance abuse problems, New York, 1981, Haworth Press, p. 222.
13. Brecher, E.M.: Licit and illicit drugs, Boston, 1972, Little, Brown, & Co., pp. 101-114.
14. Deichmann, W.B., and Gerarde, H.W.: Toxicology of drugs and chemicals, New York, 1969, Academic Press, Inc., pp. 407-408.
15. Helpern, M., and Rho, M.Y.: Death from narcotism in New York City, N.Y. State J. Med. **66**(2):2393, 1966.
16. Dole, V.P., Nyswander, M.E., and Kreek, M.J.: Narcotic blockade, Arch. Intern. Med. **118**:304-309, 1966.
17. Ling, W., and Blaine, J.D.: The use of LAAM in treatment. In Dupont, R., Goldstein, A., and Odonnell, J., editors: Hand

book on drug abuse, DHEW Publication No. SN-017-024-00869-9, Washington, D.C., January, 1979, U.S. Government Printing Office, pp. 87-96.

18. U.S. Department of Health, Education, and Welfare: Third special report to the congress: alcohol and health, Pub. No. (ADM) 78-569, Washington, D.C., 1978, U.S. Government Printing Office, pp. 1-15.

19. Kaim, S.C., Klett, C.J., and Rothfeld, B.: Treatment of the acute alcohol withdrawal state: a comparison of four drugs, Am. J. Psychiatry **125**(2):1640-1646, 1969.

20. Daltry, L.: Freebase: can you smoke cocaine without getting burnt? High Times **121**(53):73-75, 1980.

21. Cohen, S.: The substance abuse problems, New York, 1981, Haworth Press, p. 222.

22. Griffith, J.D., et al.: Experimental psychosis induced by the administration of d-amphetamine. In Costa, E., and Garrattini, S., editors: International symposium amphetamines and related compounds, New York, 1970, Raven Press, pp. 897-904.

23. Hekimian, L.J., and Gershon, S.: Characteristics of drug abusers admitted to a psychiatric hospital, J.A.M.A. **205**(3):125-130, 1968.

24. Horowitz, M.J.: "Flashbacks": recurrent intrusive images after the use of LSD, Am. J. of Psychiatry **126**(4):565-569, 1969.

25. McGluthlin, W.H., and Arnold, D.O.: LSD revisited: a ten year follow-up of medical LSD use, Arch. Gen. Psychiatry **24**:47, 1971.

26. Heath, H., editor: Drug enforcement administration. Drugs of abuse, Drug Enforcement Administration, Washington, D.C., 1980, U.S. Government Printing Office, pp. 36-37.

27. Cohen, S.: The substance abuse problems, New York, 1981, Haworth Press, p. 8.

28. Lubbe, K.E., Starner, G.A., and Teo, R.K.C.: The effect of trans-Δ^9-tetrahydrocannabinol alone and in combination with ethanol on human performance, Psychopharmacology **62**:53-60, 1979.

29. Jones, R.T., Benowitz, N., and Bachman, J.: Clinical studies of cannabis tolerance and dependence, Ann. N.Y. Acad. Sci. **282**:221-239, 1976.

30. Cohen, S.: The substance abuse problems, New York, 1981, Haworth Press, pp. 19-22.

31. Wilker, A.: Aspects of tolerance to and dependence on cannabis, Ann. N.Y. Acad. Sci. **282**:126-147, 1976.

32. Cohen, S.: The substance abuse problems, New York, 1981, Haworth Press, p. 210.

33. Glickman, I.: Glickman's clinical periodontology, Philadelphia, 1979, W.B. Saunders Co., p. 207.

CHAPTER 35

ALBERT T. BROWN

Dental plaque and control of plaque-related oral disease

Current evidence supports a central role for oral microorganisms in the etiology of both dental caries and periodontal disease through the production of a broad spectrum of bacterial metabolic products, which can either directly or indirectly destroy oral tissues. Without sufficient accumulation of oral microorganisms at various sites in the oral environment, bacterial products simply cannot be produced at levels sufficient to initiate and sustain damage to oral host tissues. Therefore a great deal of interest has focused in recent years on determining the mechanisms responsible for allowing microbial accumulation to occur and defining what aspects of oral microbial metabolism are germane to specific disease processes so that effective preventive and interventive approaches to oral disease control can be developed. Most of the current efforts in controlling oral disease are directed toward the pathogenic potential of large accumulations of oral microorganisms that reside on the hard enamel surfaces of the teeth, which are referred to as *supragingival dental plaque*. The reasons for this are (1) a great deal is now known about the mechanisms responsible for the formation of supragingival plaque, (2) much is known concerning the pathogenic potential of plaque with respect to its microbiological content and metabolism, and (3) plaque is readily accessible for sampling and study and hence for the application of preventive and control procedures. Therefore the scope of this chapter will be restricted to supragingival plaque-related oral diseases with emphasis placed on the etiology and control of multisurface enamel caries. Less emphasis will be placed on the etiology and control of gingivitis, which can be initiated by microorganisms in supragingival plaque that have close proximity to the gingival margin and gingival epithelium.

COMPOSITION OF DENTAL PLAQUE

Dental plaque may be described as a high-density population of oral microorganisms that resides on the hard enamel surfaces of the teeth and contains an intermicrobial matrix between the respective bacterial components. The number of microorganisms that have been estimated to comprise dental plaque are 2×10^{11} cells per gram (wet weight) of plaque material,[1] which is a microbial density similar to that found in a centrifuged cell pellet. Not only does dental plaque contain large numbers of oral bacteria, but also its microbial content is mixed in that it contains a broad spectrum of genera and species, although facultative gram-positive streptococcal species generally comprise the largest percentage of the cultivable microflora.[1] Some of the bacteria routinely found in dental plaque are listed in Table 35-1.

In addition to being comprised of a mixed population of oral bacteria, the microbial content of supragingival plaque is not constant or static but rather is in a continuous state of dynamic fluctuation, succession, and change.[1,2] The dynamic nature of supragingival plaque with respect to its microbial content can be seen in Fig. 35-1. For example, it is predominantly a streptococcal population at all stages of plaque maturation. In contrast, dental plaque contains few species of *Bacteroides, Veillonella,* and *Fusobacterium* in its early stages of development, whereas older, more mature plaque contains significant numbers of members of these genera. Since the microbial composition of supragingival plaque is mixed and in a dynamic state of change and succession, it is not surprising that the bacterial composition of plaque samples vary from tooth surface to tooth surface and even from site to site on the same tooth surface. The pathogenic potential of dental plaque in plaque-re-

Table 35-1. Microorganisms regularly found in supragingival dental plaque

Microorganisms*	Reaction to Gram stain	Facultative	Anaerobe
Streptococcus sanguis	+	+	
Streptococcus mitis (miteor)	+	+	
Streptococcus mutans	+	+	
Actinomyces sp.	+	+	
Rothia sp.	+	+	
Lactobacillus sp.	+		+
Peptostreptococcus sp.	+		+
Veillonella sp.	−		+
Fusobacterium sp.	−		+
Bacteroides sp.	−		+

*Supragingival dental plaque consists primarily of gram-positive facultative microorganisms. Streptococcal species, particularly *S. sanguis*, generally predominate.

lated oral diseases is dependent on the metabolic activity of its bacterial components.[1,3]

The intermicrobial matrix of dental plaque has two important functions: (1) it serves to maintain the structural integrity of the plaque matrix, and (2) it can help fulfill the nutritional needs of the plaque microflora. The intermicrobial matrix contains water and high and low molecular weight constituents.[1,4,5] Bacterial polysaccharides, such as glucans and fructans, and salivary glycoproteins comprise a large percentage of the high molecular weight content of the intermicrobial matrix. Bacterial polysaccharides and salivary glycoproteins serve to maintain the structural integrity of supragingival plaque and can fulfill the nutritional needs of the plaque microflora during periods of dietary stress through physical biologic mechanisms, which will be discussed in detail later. Generally speaking, low molecular weight constituents of the intermicrobial matrix such as amino acids and minerals do not participate in maintaining the structural integrity of supragingival plaque but probably have important nutritional roles.

DENTAL CARIES AND GINGIVITIS AS INFECTIOUS DISEASES

Current evidence supports the theory that the presence of oral microorganisms is absolutely essential for the initiation and progression of both multisurface dental caries and gingivitis.[3] Some of the epidemiologic and experimental evidence to support the

causative role of oral microorganisms in the etiology of dental caries is as follows. In the 1890s, Miller showed that extracted teeth were demineralized when they were exposed to salivary bacteria and fermentable carbohydrates.[6] More recently, antibiotics such as penicillin have reduced caries formation in experimental animals, and humans who have undergone prolonged antibiotic therapy showed a marked caries reduction when compared with individuals who did not receive antibiotic treatment.[7,8] In addition, conventional rats, but not germ-free ones, were shown to develop caries when fed a caries-conducive diet.[9,10] Also, it has been shown that dental caries can be transmitted between certain strains of both conventional hamsters and rats in a manner similar to that of other diseases of an infectious nature.[11] Finally, certain oral bacteria such as *Streptococcus mutans*, isolated from both animal and human sources, have been shown to induce dental caries when introduced as monoinfectants into conventional and germ-free animal models.[12,13] These observations, with the correlation between bacterial deposits and caries incidence in humans, collectively support the role of oral microorganisms as causative agents of dental caries.

The onset of experimental gingivitis also correlates with plaque accumulation, and experimentally induced gingivitis can be eliminated by resumption of oral hygiene aimed at removing adherent bacterial deposits from the teeth.[14] In addition, exposure to antimicrobial agents such as antibiotics and disinfectants such as chlorhexidine, which reduce the amount of dental plaque, can either reduce or prevent entirely the onset of gingivitis.[15] Finally, certain microorganisms isolated from animals and humans have been shown to cause destruction of the periodontium when introduced as monoinfectants into both conventional and gnotobiotic animal models. Thus current evidence supports that gingivitis, like dental caries, has a bacterial etiology.

Because supragingival dental plaque is comprised of a mixed bacterial population that is in a dynamic state of succession and change, two divergent points of view have developed concerning the microbial etiology of plaque-related oral diseases.[16] One of these divergent points of view is called the *nonspecific plaque hypothesis* (NSPH), and the other is called the *specific plaque hypothesis* (SPH). In the case of the NSPH, it is proposed that plaque-dependent oral diseases such as dental caries and gingivitis result from the production of bacterial products by all

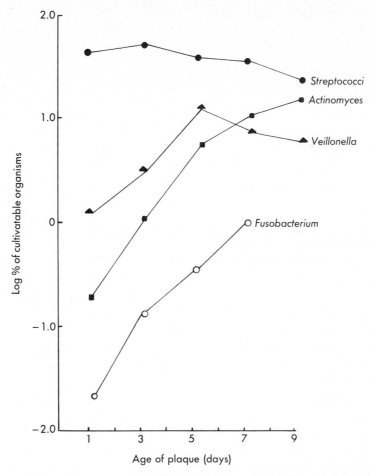

Fig. 35-1. Microbial population shifts in developing dental plaque. Diagram illustrates that facultative strepto-coccal species are the predominant organism in supragingival plaque and that its anaerobe content increases as plaque ages. (Modified from Ritz, H.L.: Arch. Oral Biol. **12:**1561-1568, 1967.)

components of the plaque microflora. The emergence of this point of view is not surprising because most oral bacteria found in dental plaque are acidogenic, and many other cytotoxic products are produced by a broad spectrum of the plaque microflora. In contrast, the SPH proposes that certain specific components of the plaque microflora are much more important in the initiation and progression of oral disease than others, and the causation of plaque-related oral diseases may be attributed to specific pathogenic components of dental plaque. It is important to consider the basic divergences between the NSPH and the SPH when therapeutic approaches are made to the prevention and control of plaque-related oral diseases. In the

case of the NSPH, therapeutic interventive proce-dures would have to be aimed at the entire spectrum of bacteria that comprise the plaque microflora, whereas in the case of the SPH, control methodolo-gies could be aimed at either specific or relatively few oral bacteria, as is the case in the treatment and pre-vention of many systemic diseases of an infectious nature.

Although current evidence does not support that a single oral bacterium causes dental caries in humans, a great deal of evidence is accumulating that specific types of oral microorganisms, such as certain strepto-coccal species, *Actinomyces,* and lactobacilli are more important than other bacterial species in the causation of certain types of dental caries.[1,8,13,17] One oral microorganism that has been the subject of extensive study in recent years concerning its central role in human dental caries is *Streptococcus mutans,* and some of the evidence to support its importance in the development of human dental caries is as follows:[1,8,13,17-21] (1) human isolates of *S. mutans* have been shown to cause multisurface dental caries when administered as monoinfectants into a variety of animal models, (2) there are up to 10 times as many *S. mutans* organisms present in pooled plaque samples obtained from caries-active individuals as compared to similar plaque samples from caries-inactive individuals, (3) *S. mutans* is present at extremely high concentrations over small localized surfaces of the teeth on which demineralization occurs, (4) tooth surfaces infected with *S. mutans* develop carious lesions and surfaces uninfected with the organism generally remain sound, and (5) *S. mutans* can be isolated from almost all human coronal carious lesions. Although much of the evidence is indirect, these observations collectively support a potentially important role for *S. mutans* in human caries, and hence this organism may serve as a "target organism" in the development of methods to control this plaque-related oral disease.

Although a great deal of evidence supports the theory that certain plaque microorganisms are more important than others in the development of dental caries, evidence to support a specific bacterial etiology of gingivitis is not nearly as strong. Indeed, many antibiotics and chemical agents useful in controlling gingivitis have a broad spectrum of antimicrobial activity.[1] However, ongoing studies may show that, as in the case of dental caries, specific components of the plaque microflora might be more important than others in the initiation of early gingivitis and alter the therapeutic approaches to the prevention and control of this disease.

FORMATION OF DENTAL PLAQUE

Central to an understanding of the pathogenesis of plaque-dependent oral diseases is information pertaining to the mechanisms that allow large numbers of oral bacteria to accumulate on the hard enamel surfaces of the teeth. Therefore this section will be devoted to a discussion of those important events and mechanisms responsible for supragingival plaque accumulation.

Acquisition of oral microflora

Since the mouth of the human fetus is sterile until immediately after birth, the first events of primary importance in plaque formation is the aquisition of a normal oral microflora. From the moment of birth, the infant is exposed to an environmental microbiologic challenge from a variety of sources but most importantly from parents and attendants.[22] Most organisms do not persist in the oral environment of the infant, but those that do must have the ability to colonize oral soft tissues because the mouth is totally edentulous at this time. *Streptococcus salivarius* and *Streptococcus mitis (miteor)* appear approximately 1 week after birth followed by the establishment of certain anaerobic forms such as *Veillonella;* all three of these organisms are also characteristic of the adult microflora.[22-24] After the teeth erupt, important changes take place in the composition of the oral microflora in that its content is similar to that of adults with a few exceptions. After tooth eruption occurs, a thin film composed primarily of salivary glycoproteins called the acquired pellicle becomes firmly attached to the surfaces of the teeth. This is followed by an increase in *Fusobacterium, Bacteroides,* and *Actinomyces* species along with an increase in other streptococcal species such as *S. mutans* and *Streptococcus sanguis,* both of which require hard tooth surfaces on which to colonize and be retained in the oral environment.[22,24-26] After puberty, the oral microbial composition of dental plaque is generally that of an adult.

Adherence and retention

For plaque microorganisms to be retained and to accumulate on the hard enamel tooth surfaces, they must possess specific adhesive properties or they will be removed by the cleansing action of salivary flow and be eliminated from the oral environment when the saliva is swallowed. The following two classes of adhesive interactions allow microorganism to be retained on the surfaces of the teeth: (1) cell–tooth surface adhesive interactions that comprise the initial colonization or attachment of bacteria to the acquired pellicle[22,26,27] and (2) cell-cell adhesive interactions, which are aggregating interactions between bacteria that are mediated in part by components of the intermicrobial plaque matrix.[22,27]

Cell–tooth surface adhesive interactions. There are three separate mechanisms that enable certain oral microorganisms to be retained on the enamel pellicle complex. One of these mechanisms is dependent on the production of adhesive bacterial polysaccharides by certain oral microorganisms, and the other two mechanisms are dependent on the glycoprotein content of the acquired pellicle and electrostatic interactions between bacterial cells and the surfaces of the teeth.

One class of adhesive bacterial polysaccharides that enable oral microorganisms, particularly *S. mutans*, to accumulate on the surfaces of the teeth are glucose-containing polymers called *glucans* produced from dietary sucrose by the action of enzymes called glucosyltransferases (GTFs).[13,22,27-30] Simply speaking, GTFs incorporate the glucose component of sucrose, which is a disaccharide containing one molecule of glucose attached covalently to one molecule of fructose, into a growing glucose polymer (glucan), giving as reaction products a glucan now containing one more glucose unit than the parent compound and free fructose. The structure of sucrose and the GTF reaction are shown below.

CH$_2$OH   CH$_2$OH

H   O   H   O   H

OH   H   O   H   OH

OH   CH$_2$OH

H   OH   OH   H

Glucose   **Fructose**

Sucrose

$$\text{Sucrose} + (\text{Glucose})_n \xrightarrow{\text{GTF}} (\text{Glucose})_{n+1} + \text{Fructose}$$

Two major classes of glucans are produced by the action of GTFs upon exogenous sucrose. One of these classes of glucans, called mutan, contains predominantly one to three linkages between its glucose monomers, is generally of high molecular weight, is water insoluble for the most part, and is produced on the cell surface of *S. mutans* through the action of cell surface associated GTFs. It is generally thought that mutan is the adhesive bacterial polysaccharide that enhances the ability of *S. mutans* to colonize the enamel pellicle complex. A second type of glucan produced by *S. mutans* contains predominantly one to six linkages between its glucose components and is structurally similar to a class of glucose polymers called dextrans. Dextrans, in contrast to mutan, are

much more water soluble, are produced extracellularly, and are probably not as important as mutan in cell–tooth surface adhesive interactions. In contrast, water-soluble extracellular glucans (dextrans) are primary determinants of cell-cell adhesive interactions within dental plaque in outer areas where the microorganisms are not in close proximity to the tooth surface. Sucrose-dependent glucan synthesis is of central importance in plaque formation and caries etiology, as evidenced by the fact that mutants of *S. mutans*, deficient in insoluble glucan synthesis cannot form plaque in vitro and do not show high caries activity in animal models fed a high-sucrose diet.[31,32]

Although they differ markedly in structure, water solubility, physical properties, and their respective roles in adherent retentive mechanisms, the two classes of glucans, mutan and dextrans, have the following four important characteristics in common: (1) both are homopolymers of glucose, (2) both are produced by the action of GTFs on sucrose, (3) their synthesis is absolutely dependent on the presence of sucrose, and (4) both are capable of being bound by specific and distinct sites on the cell surfaces of *S. mutans*. Sucrose-dependent *S. mutans* accumulation on the tooth surface is illustrated in Fig. 35-2.

Certain other microorganisms, including *S. mutans*, can synthesize another class of polysaccharides from sucrose that are called fructans. Fructans[1,8,13,30,33] are homopolymers of fructose derived from the fructose component of sucrose by the action of a class of enzymes called fructosyltransferases (FTFs). FTFs transfer the fructose component of sucrose to a fructan primer, giving as reaction products a fructan that now contains one more fructose monomer than the parent compound and a molecule of free glucose in the reaction as shown below.

$$\text{Sucrose} + (\text{Fructose})_n \xrightarrow{\text{FTF}} (\text{Fructose})_{n+1} + \text{Glucose}$$

Fructans contain predominantly two to six linkages between their fructose monomers and for the most part are highly water soluble. Fructans are not nearly as important in adhesive interactions as are glucans. However, as will be discussed later, the importance of fructans appears to be that they can serve as extracellular reserve sources of fermentable carbohydrate to be used by the plaque microflora when dietary intake is restricted.

Other oral bacteria produce polysaccharides other

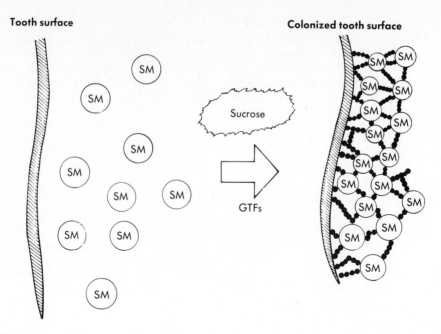

Fig. 35-2. Sucrose and glucosyltransforase-dependent glucan synthesis and plaque formation by *S. mutans*. The diagram shows the glucan (mutan and dextran)–dependent cell–tooth surface and cell-cell adhesive interactions that enable *S. mutans* to accumulate on the teeth. *SM, S. mutans; GTFs,* glucosyltransferases; ●●●● adhesive and aggregating glucans.

than glucans that are important in cell–tooth surface adhesive interactions. For example, oral strains of *Actinomyces viscosus* produce complex, cell-surface associated heteropolysaccharides, which probably enable them to colonize the enamel pellicle complex.[34–36] Unlike glucans, the synthesis of these heteropolysaccharides by *A. viscosus* is not absolutely dependent on the presence of sucrose but rather can be produced from a variety of dietary carbohydrates, including glucose and fructose.

Some oral microorganisms have the ability to colonize and be retained on the enamel pellicle complex, and their ability to do this is in no way dependent on the presence or production of either adhesive or aggregating bacterial polysaccharides. One of these organisms is *S. sanguis,* which is a predominant cultivable organism from plaque samples obtained from most individuals. Early observations indicated that *S. sanguis* had little affinity for hydroxyapatite or powdered tooth enamel. However, prior exposure of the powdered tooth enamel to human saliva greatly enhanced the adherent ability of *S. sanguis*.[37] Current evidence supports the idea that the salivary compo-

nents that are of primary importance in allowing *S. sanguis* and certain other oral microorganisms to attach to the enamel pellicle complex are the mucinous glycoprotein content of the acquired pellicle.[22,38–43] There are in all probability specific binding or receptor sites on the cell surface of these organisms that are complementary to and have a high affinity for specific mucinous glycoproteins in the acquired pellicle. These cell surface receptor site–mucinous salivary glycoprotein interactions permit microorganisms such as *S. sanguis* to be retained on the enamel pellicle complex and hence to not be washed away by salivary flow. Mucinous glycoprotein-dependent colonization of the enamel pellicle complex is shown schematically in Fig. 35-3.

A third mechanism has been proposed to explain the ability of some oral microorganisms to be retained on the enamel pellicle complex. This mechanism involves electrostatic interactions between negatively charged bacterial cell surface lipoteichoic acids and other cell surface functional groups with negatively charged, positively charged, and neutral groups occurring on components of the acquired pellicle.[44–46]

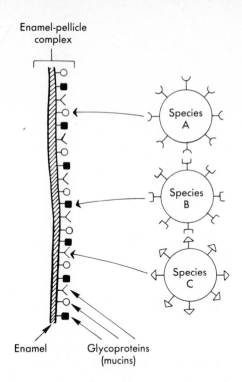

Enamel-pellicle
complex

Complementary
receptor sites

Enamel

Glycoproteins
(mucins)

Fig. 35-3. Glycoprotein-dependent colonization of enamel pellicle complex by oral microorganisms. Diagram shows three species of oral bacteria colonizing enamel pellicle complex through binding of complementary cell surface receptor sites to glycoproteins within enamel pellicle complex. One oral bacterium believed to colonize tooth surface in this manner is *S. sanguis.*

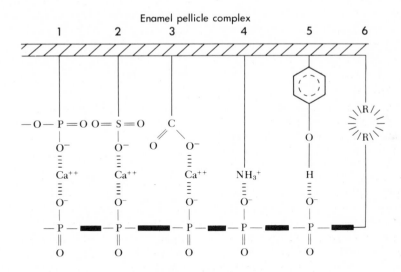

Fig. 35-4. Electrostatic interactions between bacterial cell surface and the enamel pellicle complex. The diagram shows some of the possible interactions between negatively charged lipoteichoic acids on bacterial cell surfaces with components of the enamel pellicle complex, which may be of importance in allowing certain oral bacteria to colonize the tooth surface. *1, 2,* and *3* are electrostatic interactions that are mediated by the divalent cation, calcium; *4* is an ionic type of electrostatic interaction; and *5* and *6* are hydrogen bonding and hydrophobic interactions respectively. (Modified from Rolla, G., et al. In Kleinberg, I., Ellison, S.A., and Mandel, I.D., editors: Saliva and dental caries, pp. 227-241, Microbiology Abstracts, Washington, D.C., 1979, Information Retrieval, Inc.

These interactions are represented schematically in Fig. 35-4 and are predicated on the following: (1) interactions between negatively charged groups on the bacterial cell surface and the acquired pellicle are "mediated" by calcium ions, (2) interactions between the bacterial lipoteichoic acids and positively charged components of the enamel pellicle complex are strictly electrostatic in nature, and (3) bonding between other functional groups can be mediated by alternative mechanisms such as hydrogen bonding and hydrophobic interactions. These interactions are shown in Fig. 35-4.

The three mechanisms previously discussed as being of primary importance in cell–tooth surface adhesive interactions are by no means mutually exclusive, and some may act in concert even in the case of the accumulation of single specific microorganisms. For example, some strains of *S. mutans* can colonize the enamel pellicle complex even in the absence of sucrose, presumably by binding to certain mucinous glycoproteins in the acquired pellicle.[13,38,47–52] However, sucrose greatly enhances the accumulation of these same *S. mutans* strains by serving as a precursor for the production of adhesive and aggregating glucans.[52]

Cell-cell adhesive interactions. Adhesive interactions between oral microorganisms is also important for the retention and accumulation of bacteria in dental plaque especially in its outer, developing regions that are not in close proximity to the tooth surface. Three classes of adhesive interactions are generally thought to be of primary importance in the aggregation of microorganisms within dental plaque. These adhesive, aggregating interactions are dependent on the following: (1) the production of bacterial polysaccharides, (2) the presence of salivary glycoproteins, and (3) the interaction between complementary binding sites on the respective cell surfaces of certain types of oral microorganisms.

S. mutans can synthesize a water-soluble, high molecular weight, extracellular, dextranlike glucan by the action of extracellular GTF on exogenous sucrose. When these dextrans are added to cell suspensions of *S. mutans*, they are able to rapidly aggregate the cells in these suspensions.[1,13,22,53] The reason for this is thought to be the presence of specific dextran receptor or binding sites on the *S. mutans* cell surface that enable the dextrans to form intercellular bridges between *S. mutans* cells, thus causing their aggregation. Dextrans that cause the aggregation of *S. mutans* cell suspensions have been extracted from dental

plaque, thus supporting the importance of dextran-induced aggregation *in vivo*. Although dextrans produced by *S. mutans* can also aggregate cell suspensions of *A. viscosus*,[54] they cannot aggregate other oral bacteria, even those such as certain strains of *S. sanguis*, which also produce dextranlike glucans. This is probably because of the absence of dextran receptor sites on the surfaces of the organisms that cannot undergo dextran-induced aggregation.

Other oral microorganisms such as *S. sanguis* and *S. mitis*, which are not subject to dextran-induced aggregation, can agglutinate in the presence of the glycoprotein component of human saliva.[22,27,55–59] The salivary glycoprotein content of saliva can be separated into fractions that specially aggregate *S. sanguis* but not *S. mitis* and conversely into fractions that aggregate *S. mitis* but not *S. sanguis*. These observations are probably caused by the presence of cell surface receptor sites on these organisms that bind specific salivary glycoproteins, thus forming salivary glycoprotein–containing intercellular bridges between the bacteria. Those salivary glycoproteins that aggregate *S. sanguis* cells are probably separate and distinct from those that aggregate *S. mitis* because of the specificity of these cell surface glycoprotein binding sites. Salivary glycoproteins can be extracted from dental plaque, which aggregate cell suspensions of *S. sanguis* or *S. mitis*, thus supporting their adhesive role *in vivo*. Salivary glycoprotein–induced aggregation of *S. sanguis* is depicted in Fig. 35-5.

Certain combinations of oral microorganisms are able to spontaneously aggregate in the absence of both dextrans and salivary glycoproteins.[13,27] For example, oral streptococcal species such as *S. sanguis* and *S. mitis* can coaggregate with isolates of *A. viscosus* and *A. naeslundii*,[60,61] and certain strains of *Veillonella* will attach to plaques of *A. viscosus* grown in vitro.[22] The ability of these types of oral bacteria to coaggregate is thought to be caused by the presence of complementary binding or receptor sites on their respective cell surfaces.[27] Examination of scanning electron micrographs of dental plaque shows that morphologically dissimilar bacterial cells do indeed attach to one another, thus supporting the theory that bacterial coaggregation occurs during plaque accumulation in vivo.[22,62,63] Some of the most common arrangements seen are coccal organisms such as *S. sanguis* attached to filamentous organisms such as *A. viscosus*. Coaggregation of coccal and filamentous organisms is illustrated in Fig. 35-6. All three mechanisms discussed above are probably of major impor-

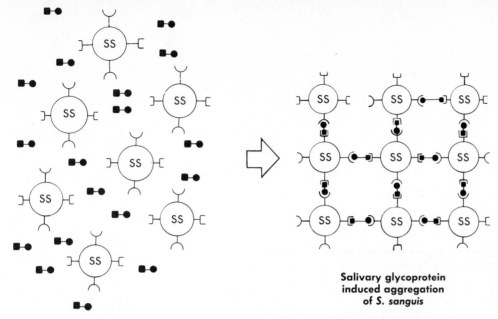

S. sanguis and salivary glycoproteins

Salivary glycoprotein induced aggregation of S. sanguis

Fig. 35-5. Salivary glycoprotein–induced aggregation of *S. sanguis*. The diagram shows glycoproteins of salivary origin causing aggregation of *S. sanguis* through formation of intercellular glycoprotein bridges, which result from the binding of salivary glycoproteins to specific complementary receptor sites, residing on bacterial cell surface. *SS, S. sanguis;* Y and Y, cell surface, glycoprotein binding or receptor sites; ▪–●, salivary glycoproteins.

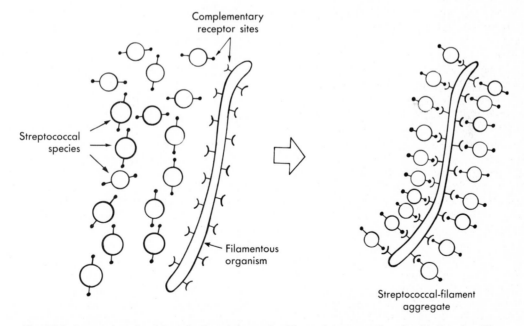

Fig. 35-6. Aggregation of oral bacteria through interaction of complementary cell surface binding sites. The diagram shows the attachment of an oral streptococcal species such as *S. sanguis* to a filamentous oral bacterium such as *Bacterionema matruchotii* or *A. visocsus* through binding of complementary cell surface sites on the respective organisms to one another.

tance concerning cell-cell adhesive interactions in vivo.

Growth and metabolism

After oral microorganisms have been retained through specific adhesive interactions on the surfaces of the teeth, an important determinant of further accumulation is their ability to increase in numbers. A broad spectrum of nutrients is essential to sustain the growth of oral bacteria, and the three primary nutritional sources from which they are derived are the diet, saliva, and metabolic products produced by the plaque microflora.

Role of the diet. The diet is an important source of nutrients for the plaque microflora, particularly with regard to its carbohydrate and protein content. The carbohydrate component of the diet is of particular importance because most of the microorganisms in dental plaque are saccharolytic and can therefore use carbohydrates as a readily available fermentable energy source to sustain growth and support their life functions.[33]

The carbohydrate content of the diet is also important for two other reasons. The total amount of dietary carbohydrate intake determines the composition of the plaque microflora. For example, high-carbohydrate intake results in an increase in lactobacilli and glycogen-amylopectin–synthesizing bacteria, whereas restriction of carbohydrate intake results in a decrease in the numbers of these same organisms.[22,26,27,64,65] Also, the type of carbohydrate in addition to the total amount determines the composition of the plaque microflora. For example, frequent ingestion of sucrose enhances the colonization of *S. mutans* and serves to increase their numbers in both rodent and human dental plaque.[1,13,17,22,26,62]

The role of salivary constituents. In addition to the diet, salivary constituents can fulfill the nutritional needs of the plaque microflora, particularly during periods of dietary stress. One important source of salivary nutrients is its glycoprotein content. Oral bacteria possess a broad spectrum of enzymes that can collectively degrade the glycoproteins of salivary origin that comprise a large proportion of the interbacterial plaque matrix.[1,22] One class of these enzymes is called glycoside hydrolases, which can collectively degrade the complex carbohydrate components of salivary glycoproteins so that they may be used as fermentable energy sources by the plaque microflora. A second class of enzymes is proteolytic

in nature, which enables plaque microorganisms to degrade and utilize the protein component of salivary glycoproteins as readily available nitrogen sources.

The role of bacterial products. Bacterial products can also serve to sustain the life functions of the plaque microflora. One important class of bacterial products is the polysaccharides, glucans and fructans, which are produced from sucrose and comprise a significant proportion of the material found in the interbacterial plaque matrix. During periods in which dietary carbohydrate intake is restricted, certain components of the plaque microflora can produce enzymes called glucan hydrolases, or glucanases, and fructan hydrolases, or fructanases, which can degrade glucans and fructans to their respective monomeric components, glucose and fructose, as shown below.[1,17,30,33,62]

$$(\text{Glucose})_n \xrightarrow{\text{Glucanases}} n \text{ Glucose}$$

$$(\text{Fructose})_n \xrightarrow{\text{Fructanases}} n \text{ Fructose}$$

The free glucose and fructose produced by the action of glucanases and fructanases, respectively, can then serve as fermentable energy sources. It should be noted that the fructan content of dental plaque is more readily metabolized than its glucan content, which is significant because glucans, more so than fructans, are determinants of certain adhesive interactions that serve to maintain the structural integrity of dental plaque. Other bacterial products in addition to polysaccharides can be utilized by bacterial components of dental plaque. *Veillonella* species for example, which cannot ferment dietary carbohydrates, can utilize lactic acid, which is an end product of carbohydrate fermentation by many plaque microorganisms, as a primary energy source.[22,66] Thus many complex nutritional interrelationships appear to exist among the plaque microflora.

Central role of sucrose

Sucrose is probably the most important dietary determinant of microbial accumulation on the surfaces of the teeth for the following reasons[1,13,17,67]: (1) it is a precursor for the synthesis of adhesive and aggregating glucans (mutan and dextran) through the action of GTF enzymes, which are of primary importance in cell–tooth surface and cell-cell adhesive retentive interactions that involve certain plaque microorganisms such as *S. mutans* and (2) sucrose is a primary determinant of microbial growth in that it can be used directly as a fermentable energy source by most components of the plaque microflora or alternatively converted to both intracellular and extracellular bacterial polysaccharides such as amylopectin-glycogen–type intracellular storage polysaccharides and extracellular glucans and fructans, all of which can be used as fermentable energy sources when the supply of dietary carbohydrates is depleted. Therefore sucrose is the only dietary constituent contributing directly to three important aspects of microbial accumulation, cell–tooth surface and cell-cell retentive interactions, and microbial growth. Because sucrose is a primary determinant of bacterial accumulation, it also plays a central role in the etiology of plaque-related oral disease, particularly dental caries.[1,13,17,67]

METABOLIC DETERMINANTS OF VIRULENCE

The production of metabolic products by the plaque microflora, which either directly or indirectly destroy oral tissues, is of central importance in the initiation and progression of dental caries and gingivitis. In the etiology of dental caries, the production of organic acids, particularly lactic acid, by oral microorganisms is of central importance because these organic acids are thought to cause demineralization of the tooth enamel. The following evidence supports the central role of acid production by plaque microorganisms in the development of dental caries[1,13,17,68,69]: (1) it has been known for some time that organic acids can initiate the in vitro dissolution of tooth enamel, (2) recent studies have shown that almost twice as much lactic acid is produced from sucrose by plaque samples taken from carious sites on human teeth as compared to samples taken from noncarious sites, (3) plaque in individuals with a high caries activity had a resting pH of approximately 5.5 before being challenged with a glucose rinse, as compared to a pH of approximately 7.2 in plaque from individuals with a low caries experience; also, the plaque of individuals with high caries activity reached a final pH of 4.5 after being challenged with a glucose rinse, as compared to a pH of approximately 5.6 in plaque from individuals with low caries activity, and (4) a mutant of the caries-conducive organism, S. mutans, which is deficient in the enzyme lactate dehydrogenase and hence cannot produce lactic acid from exogenous carbohydrates, does not cause caries in animal models as does the parent strain.

The anaerobic fermentation of dietary carbohydrates by the plaque microflora is the principal source of lactic acid in the oral environment.[1,17,33] The most important dietary carbohydrate in the initiation and progression of dental caries is sucrose, and its central roles in microbial accumulation on the surfaces of the teeth has already been discussed. In addition, most microorganisms in dental plaque, including S. mutans, can convert sucrose to large quantities of lactic acid. The significance of this is even greater when one considers that the average sucrose consumption in this country is over 100 pounds annually and therefore comprises a large percentage of an individual's intake of fermentable carbohydrates.[70] Also, sucrose appears to be a much more acidogenic substrate for the plaque microflora when compared to other dietary carbohydrates. Other sources of the lactic acid produced by the plaque microflora are intracellular and extracellular bacterial polysaccharides.[1,13,17,22,33,62] Many oral bacteria can produce intracellular glycogen-amylopectin–type storage polysaccharides from dietary carbohydrates such as sucrose. In fact, plaque samples from caries-active individuals have a higher percentage of glycogen-positive organisms than similar samples obtained from caries-inactive individuals.[1,13,17] During periods of dietary constraint or fasting, these intracellular storage polysaccharides can be mobilized for energy production and converted to lactic acid through glycolytic metabolism. The mobilization of intracellular storage polysaccharides permits lactic acid to be produced over extended periods of time, even in the absence of dietary carbohydrates. Extracellular polysaccharides in the intermicrobial plaque matrix can also serve as precursors of lactic acid production.[1,13,17,22,33] As discussed previously, two classes of extracellular polysaccharides, glucans and fructans, can be synthesized by selected components of the plaque microflora through the action of GTFs and FTFs on exogenous sucrose. When carbohydrate intake is restricted, certain plaque microorganisms produce enzymes that degrade glucans and fructans to their respective monomeric components, glucose and fructose, which can then be utilized as fermentable energy sources, resulting in lactic acid production. As discussed previously, glucan hydrolases (glucanases) degrade plaque glucans to free glucose, whereas fructan hydrolases (fructanases) serve to degrade fructans to free fructose. The relationships between dietary carbohydrates, bacterial polysaccharides, gly-

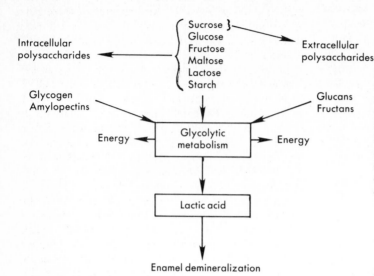

Dietary carbohydrates

Fig. 35-7. Sources of lactic acid produced by plaque microflora. The diagram shows relationships between metabolism of dietary carbohydrates and bacterial polysaccharides with glycolytic sequence, a pathway that yields biologic energy in the form of ATP and lactic acid as its fermentation end product. The lactic acid produced from dietary carbohydrates and intracellular and extracellular bacterial polysaccharides causes demineralization and dissolution of tooth enamel.

colytic metabolism, and lactic acid production is shown in Fig. 35-7.

A broad spectrum of bacterial products of both high and low molecular weight collectively produced by the microorganisms that reside in dental plaque, especially those organisms in close proximity to the gingival epithelial margin, participate in the etiology of gingivitis.[1,33,71] These bacterial products can generally be divided into the following two distinct classes or groups: (1) those products that can interact directly with oral soft tissues and initiate tissue destruction and (2) those products that interact with host factors and initiate an appropriate host response, usually of an inflammatory nature. Table 35-2 lists some of the bacterial products that comprise these two classes of bacterial cytotoxic products. A number of enzymes (Table 35-2) produced by the plaque microflora can collectively serve to disrupt the structural integrity of the oral epithelium through the destruction of its intercellular matrix. These bacterial enzymes can also alter epithelial cell surfaces and effect cellular permeability. In addition, certain low molecular weight organic compounds (Table 35-2) can also disrupt and destroy epithelial cells. After the structural integrity of the oral epithelium is disrupted, other classes of bacterial products are able to penetrate the epithelium, thus gaining access to and interacting with a variety of host factors, which results in the inflammation and edema associated with gingivitis.

Table 35-2. Bacterial metabolic products that may be of importance in the initiation and progression of gingivitis

Bacterial products causing direct tissue damage
    Enzymes
        Proteases
        Collagenase
        Neuraminidases
        Hyaluronidases
        Chondroitin sulfatases
        Glycoside hydrolases
        β-Glucuronidases
        Esterases
    Low molecular weight compounds
        Organic acids
        Indole
        Skatole
        Ammonia
        Hydrogen sulfide
        Toxic amines

Bacterial products causing indirect tissue damage through initiation of an inflammatory response
    Proteases
    Chemotactic factors (polymorphonuclear leukocyte)
    Endotoxins
    Other lipopolysaccharides
    Peptidoglycans
    Polysaccharides
    Other antigens of bacterial origin

PROSPECTS FOR DISEASE CONTROL

Because the human mouth is devoid of an endogenous microflora until immediately after birth, and because dental caries and gingivitis both have a bacterial etiology, they may be considered to be diseases of an infectious nature. Therefore approaches to the control of dental caries and gingivitis can be similar to those approaches used to control other infectious diseases and include (1) reducing the microbial challenge or burden, (2) increasing host resistance, and (3) altering an environment that is conducive to pathogenicity.[72] Increasing host resistance through the use of topical and systemic fluoridation procedures and the use of occlusal sealants have proven effective in reducing the incidence of dental caries, fluoridation programs and procedures being particularly effective. In addition, reducing the bacterial challenge through the mechanical removal of supragingival dental plaque has been shown to be effective in the control of both dental caries and gingivitis. Also, altering the composition of the oral environment through nutritional counseling aimed at reducing the intake of fermentable carbohydrates such as sucrose from the diet has been shown to reduce caries in highly motivated individuals. The remainder of this chapter will be devoted to new approaches for the control of dental caries and/or gingivitis, with emphasis placed on caries control. It should be stressed that many of these approaches to plaque-dependent disease control are controversial, and most are not in routine use in this country at the present time. However, the high level of current interest in developing new and alternative methods for oral disease control in our society merits a rather in-depth treatment of this contemporary topic area.

Reducing the microbial challenge

Microbial replacement. One novel approach to the control of plaque-related oral diseases, particularly dental caries, is the replacement or substitution of a less virulent microorganism for one that is an established pathogen. Ideally, the pair of organisms involved would be of the same genus, species, and strain so that the delicate ecologic balances that exist in dental plaque can be maintained and not shifted or disturbed. This approach to disease control is dependent on the following three essential pieces of information: (1) the identification of the components of the plaque microflora that are most important in the initiation and progression of dental disease, (2) the

identification of the important physiologic characteristics that are germane to the virulence of these particular oral microorganisms, and (3) the identification of the mechanisms that allow these organisms to be retained in the mouth. Recent studies dealing with *S. mutans* have used microbial substitution as an experimental approach to caries control in rodents.[68,69] As discussed previously, *S. mutans* is of importance in the etiology of dental caries in animals and probably also in humans, and the caries-conducive ability of this organism is caused in part by its ability to produce lactic acid from dietary carbohydrates such as sucrose. Mutants of *S. mutans* have been characterized as being deficient in lactate dehydrogenase, the enzyme that catalyzes the terminal step in lactic acid–producing glycolytic metabolism, and hence these mutants are much less acidogenic than their parent strains. However, these lactic acid–deficient mutants of *S. mutans* are still capable of producing adhesive and aggregating glucans from sucrose and can form plaque both in vivo and in vitro. Of most importance is the fact that these mutants of *S. mutans* can successfully colonize and compete with their parent counterparts in conventional rat animal models, and those animals given lactate dehydrogenase–deficient mutants in their drinking water developed fewer caries than their nonmutant counterparts when fed a caries-conducive, high-sucrose diet. Although only in the experimental stages, some current interest is being focused on microbial substitutions as an effective means for plaque control.

Antimicrobial agents. Another approach to the control of plaque-dependent oral disease has been through the use of antibiotics and other antimicrobial chemicals. Some desirable properties of an antimicrobial agent to be used for plaque control are as follows:[13,73] (1) it should remain in the mouth for long periods of time to increase its therapeutic effect, (2) it should not be readily absorbed from the gastrointestinal tract, (3) it should be nontoxic and should not elicit undesirable host side effects, (4) it should not lead to the emergence of a resistant oral microflora, (5) it should not be widely used in the treatment of systemic disease, (6) it must have patient acceptability, (7) its antimicrobial activity should be as specific as possible for the pathogens involved (for example, antimicrobial agents used for the control of dental caries should be specific for gram-positive oral microorganisms such as *S. mutans, Actinomyces,* and *Lactobacillus* because they have been proposed to perhaps be of more importance than other oral bacteria in the etiology of tooth decay), and (8) it should be effective when applied in repeated, short-term exposures.

As in the case of systemic diseases of an infectious nature, a number of antibiotics have been tested for the control of plaque-related oral diseases. Those antibiotics most thoroughly studied and tested as plaque control agents are listed in Table 35-3. For example, dietary supplements of penicillin, erythromycin, and tetracyclines have been shown to be effective in controlling plaque and dental caries in experimental rats and hamsters.[1,13,74] Although children who receive penicillin on a long-term basis as a prophylaxis for rheumatic fever have fewer caries than children not taking the antibiotic,[75,76] the long-term use of antibiotics for plaque and caries control is generally not recommended in humans for the following reasons: (1) long-term exposure to many antibiotics can lead to undesirable host side effects and in many cases induce hypersensitivity, (2) antibiotic-resistant bacteria may emerge and thus the normal ecologic relationships within dental plaque may be disturbed as reflected in population shifts among different genera and species, and (3) succession by yeast and other undesirable fungal species may occur. Although the long-term use of antibiotics as plaque control agents should be discouraged, a great deal of current interest has focused on the use of short-term exposures to a high concentration of antibiotics directed at specific pathogenic oral microorganisms such as *S. mutans* as a means for eliminating them from the oral environment. For example, 2-week exposures of hamsters that had been infected with *S. mutans* to antibiotics such as penicillin, erythromycin, or vancomycin, all of which show specificity for gram-positive organisms, resulted in the elimination of *S. mutans* and a decrease in caries incidence even when the animals were fed a diet high in sucrose.[7,8,18] A number of antibiotics are currently being studied for their ability to eliminate *S. mutans* from the teeth of humans after short-term exposures. Three of these are vancomycin, kanamycin, and actinobolin, none of which are readily absorbed from the gastrointestinal tract.[1,8,13,77-79] Short-term exposures to repeated applications of these antibiotics have resulted in a reduction in the number of *S. mutans* on the surfaces of the teeth in human clinical trials, and this reduction in *S. mutans* has been shown to last up to several months. However, the complete elimination of *S. mutans* from the human mouth has not been attained.

Table 35-3. Antibiotics tested for use as plaque control agents

Antibiotic	Spectrum	Absorbed from gastrointestinal tract
Bacitracin	Gram-positive	−
Erythromycin	Gram-positive	+
Penicillin	Gram-positive	+
Vancomycin	Gram-positive	−
Gramicidin	Gram-positive	−
Actinobolin	Broad	−
Chlortetracycline	Broad	+
Tetracycline	Broad	+
Streptomycin	Broad	−
Kanamycin	Broad	−
Neomycin	Broad	−
Niddamycin	Broad	−
Polymyxin B	Gram-negative	−

Modified from Newbrun, E.: Cariology, Baltimore, 1978, The Williams & Wilkins Co.

In addition to their effectiveness in reducing the number of *S. mutans* in humans, vancomycin and kanamycin when administered topically have also been shown to reduce total plaque scores and gingival inflammation.[15] Again, long-term use of these and other antibiotics in the control of gingivitis is contraindicated, and if used it should only be through short-term exposures. Although current interest has focused on their potential use and effectiveness with respect to plaque-related oral disease, no antibiotic is currently approved or accepted by the FDA for topical or systemic use in caries or gingivitis control.

In addition to antibiotics, other types of compounds possessing antimicrobial properties have been used and tested as plaque control agents. Most nonantibiotic antimicrobial chemicals have a broad spectrum of activity in contrast to certain antibiotics that are selective for specific components of the plaque microflora.[1] Some of these compounds are shown in Table 35-4. Generally speaking, these agents are applied through their incorporation into either mouthrinse or dentifrice preparations. The most commonly used bacteriocidal antimicrobial chemicals are quaternary ammonium compounds such as cetylpyridinium chloride, domiphen bromide, and benzethonium chloride and phenolic compounds such as phenol, betanaphthol, and hexylresorcinol. The effectiveness of many of these antimicrobial agents is limited for the following reasons: (1) they generally have an unpleasant taste, which decreases their acceptability; (2)

Table 35-4. Antimicrobial chemicals other than antibiotics that have been tested as plaque-control agents

Class of anti-bacterial agent	Specific compounds	Spectrum
bis-Biguanides	Chlorhexidine Alexidine	Broad
Quaternary ammonium compounds	Cetylpyridinium chloride Benzethonium chloride Domiphen bromide	Mostly gram-positive

Halogens	Iodine and iodophors
	  Povidone-iodine
	Chlorides
	  Oxychlorosene
	  Chloramine T
	Fluorides
		Broad

Oxygenating agents	Peroxides Perborates	Broad

Modified from Newbrun, E.: Cariology, Baltimore, 1978, The Williams & Wilkins Co.

their application via incorporation into mouthrinse preparations results in only transient exposure; and (3) many of them are rapidly degraded in the oral environment.

One class of antimicrobial chemicals, however, has received a great deal of attention in recent years and is highly effective as plaque control agents. These compounds are the bis-biguanides, specifically chlorhexidine and alexidine, whose structures are shown below.

The bis-biguanides are effective against both gram-positive and gram-negative bacteria, and they possess antifungal properties.[1] Chlorhexidine and alexidine have been shown to prevent the development of dental plaque, to decrease the incidence of experimental dental caries, and to reduce gingivitis when tested in clinical trials via their topical application in mouthrinses and gel pastes.[80-87] In addition, these agents can effectively remove large amounts of intact plaque, which accumulates in the absence of oral hygiene. Also, resistant organisms do not emerge with significant frequency even after the long-term use of these agents, nor does succession by yeast and other undesirable fungal species frequently occur.

The bis-biguanides are highly positively charged compounds at physiologic pH, and this high positive charge density may provide the basis for their effectiveness as plaque-control agents for the following reasons:[88] (1) the positively charged bis-biguanides may have a high affinity for negatively charged microbial cell surfaces and, once bound to them, serve to disrupt cellular permeability, causing cytoplasmic constituents to leak out of the cells, (2) they may have a high affinity for negatively charged groups on the enamel pellicle complex such as phosphate, sulfate, and carboxyl groups, which enable the bis-biguanides to be effective at low concentrations since the tooth surfaces serve to concentrate them and increase their substantivity in the oral environment, and (3) the high affinity of the positively charged bis-biguanides for positively charged groups within the enamel pellicle complex may compete with the binding of negatively charged bacterial cell surfaces. In addition to being highly effective plaque-control agents, studies have shown that the bis-biguanides have little local or systemic toxicity and do not induce chromosomal alterations. Use of these compounds,

$$\text{R—NH—}\overset{\overset{\displaystyle NH}{\|}}{C}\text{—NH—}\overset{\overset{\displaystyle NH}{\|}}{C}\text{—NH—}(CH_2)_6\text{—NH—}\overset{\overset{\displaystyle NH}{\|}}{C}\text{—NH—}\overset{\overset{\displaystyle NH}{\|}}{C}\text{—HN—R}$$

bis-Biguanide

R groups

Chlorhexidine

$$-CH_2-CH-(CH_2)_3-CH_3-2HCl$$
$$\underset{\displaystyle CH_2CH_3}{|}$$

Alexidine

however, has shown the following undesirable side effects[89]: (1) solutions of the bis-biguanides have an extremely unpleasant taste, (2) a brown to yellow-brown stain arises on the teeth that must be removed mechanically because it is impervious to brushing, and (3) some individuals have reported mucosal soreness after prolonged use of these compounds. Nevertheless, these compounds are effective plaque control agents and are currently experiencing widespread use in countries outside the United States through their incorporation into mouthrinses and dentifrices. However, chlorhexidine and alexidine have not been approved by the FDA thus far for use as plaque control agents in this country, although chlorhexidine has been approved as a disinfectant in certain handwashing preparations.

Interference with retention and accumulation. Specific adhesive mechanisms are responsible for the ability of plaque microorganisms to colonize the tooth surfaces and for their subsequent retention and accumulation. Theoretically, if these adhesive interactions could be eliminated, specific components of the oral microflora, particularly those that are more important in plaque-related diseases, could be selectively removed from the oral environment. Since *S. mutans* has been implicated as an important odontopathogen in the etiology of both animal and human dental caries and since a great deal is now known concerning the adherent mechanisms responsible for the retention of this organism in dental plaque, interest has focused on disrupting these adhesive interactions. Although certain *S. mutans* serotypes can colonize the enamel pellicle complex in the absence of sucrose, the production of adhesive glucans (mutan and dextran) is absolutely necessary for significant accumulation of this organism in dental plaque. Therefore, if the synthesis of adhesive glucans could be prevented or if they could be degraded or destroyed after once synthesized, the accumulation of *S. mutans* could be selectively decreased. Enzymes called glucanases or glucan hydrolases can degrade glucans; the role of these enzymes in microbial growth and acid production in caries etiology has already been discussed. Certain of these enzymes called 1,3-glucan hydrolases or mutanases degrade glucans with predominantly one to three linkages, while others called 1,6-glucan hydrolases or dextranases selectively degrade glucans with predominantly one to six cross-linkages.[1,13] In addition, low molecular weight, soluble dextran fragments have been shown to prevent the synthesis of high molecular weight adhesive glucans from sucrose.[13,90] Both glucanases and low molecular weight dextrans have been tested in vitro,[91] in animal models,[92-96] and in human clinical trials[1,97-99] for their ability to affect plaque accumulation. Dextranases and low molecular weight dextrans are both able to prevent sucrose-dependent *S. mutans* plaque formation in vitro, and long-term exposure to fungal dextranases can disperse in vitro *S. mutans* plaque formed in the presence of sucrose. In addition, the addition of dextranases or low molecular weight dextrans to the diet or drinking water of experimental animals reduced the amount of *S. mutans*–containing plaque when the animals were fed a high-sucrose diet. However, the dextranases were much more effective in preventing plaque accumulation than in removing intact plaque. Although successful in controlling plaque accumulation in animal models, both dextranases and low molecular weight dextrans have not been successful in most human clinical trials involving mouthwashes supplemented with either dextranases or low molecular weight dextrans. An exception to this general statement, however, is the observation that in one clinical study, a dextranase preparation incorporated into a chewable tablet served to markedly decrease dental plaque formation in humans.[100] The reasons for the general ineffectiveness of dextranase preparations are probably fourfold in that (1) human plaque varies in its dextran content specifically as related to frequency of sucrose intake and the relative numbers of dextran-producing organisms that reside there, (2) many components of human plaque possess adhesive-retentive mechanisms that are not dependent on dextran production, (3) dextrans produced by oral bacteria vary in their susceptibility to degradation by specific dextranases, and (4) the exposure to dextranases via mouthrinse application is probably too transient. Although mostly unsuccessful, thus far the use of dextranases represents an interesting approach to plaque control in that the therapeutic agent is directed at a specific metabolic determinant of virulence and not at the specific organism itself. Alternative approaches to the use of dextranases as plaque-control agents may be worth additional study. For example, dextranase preparations could be used that would degrade a broad spectrum of these polysaccharides. In addition, improved delivery systems for the dextranase preparations that would eliminate only transient exposure might be tested such as (1) the use of controlled or slow-release devices and (2) conjugation of dextranases with compounds such as lectin-type substances, which have affinity for the cell surfaces of certain oral microorganisms, thus enabling the conjugated dextranase to be retained within the plaque matrix for longer periods of time.

Glucan hydrolases (mutanase) that hydrolyze glucans (mutans), containing predominantly one to three cross-linkages have also been tested as plaque-control agents with some degree of success in human clinical trials. For example, mutanase preparations have been shown to reduce plaque scores in humans and also reduce the proportion of *S. mutans*.[101] Also, mutanase in a chewing gum preparation has been shown to lower plaque scores in human subjects and to decrease gingival inflammation and edema.[102]

Other enzymes in addition to glucanases have been tested for their ability to prevent plaque formation by interfering with adhesive retentive mechanisms. One of these is invertase, which hydrolyzes sucrose to equimolar quantities of glucose and fructose.[18] The rationale for the use of invertase preparations is that GTFs show absolute specificity for sucrose in that equimolar quantities of glucose and fructose will not serve as substrates for adhesive glucan synthesis. Invertase preparations prevent sucrose-dependent *S. mutans* plaque formation in vitro. In addition, invertase preparations prevent plaque formation in animal experiments in which the diet was supplemented with sucrose. However, human studies involving the use of invertase preparations are inconclusive at the present time.

Other approaches to the interference with retentive mechanisms have been aimed at blocking specific cell surface sites on *S. mutans* necessary for the adhesive interactions that enable these organisms to accumulate in dental plaque. These specific cell surface sites include, among others, those that bind GTFs, mutan, and dextrans. Binding site blocking agents that have been studied include lectin-type substances, other microorganisms, and secretory antibodies of salivary gland origin to these binding sites. The role of secretory antibodies produced by the salivary glands as potential agents for plaque control is discussed in another section of this chapter concerning an immunologic approach to caries prevention.

Increasing host resistance: immunization

Immunization, as in the case of other diseases of an infectious nature, has been proposed to be an effective way to control plaque-dependent oral diseases, particularly dental caries. An immunologic approach to caries prevention depends on (1) specific microorganisms being identified as important in the etiology of the disease, (2) the ability to stimulate the production of specific antibodies to these organisms, and (3) the ability of these antibodies to obtain access to the caries-conducive microorganisms in question. Experimental and epidemiologic evidence supports that *S. mutans* is probably more important than some other components of the oral microflora in the etiology of animal and human dental caries. Also, a class of secretory antibodies called salivary immunoglobulin A (sIgA) can be produced by the salivary glands and released into the saliva, thus gaining access to the plaque microflora. Salivary IgA differs in structure and composition from serum antibodies such as immunoglobulin G (IgG) in that it is a dimer consisting of two polypeptide subunits, which are held together by a lower molecular weight peptide called a J chain. In addition, another type of polypeptide called the secretory component is associated with sIgA molecules. This component renders sIgA molecules somewhat resistant to proteolysis. The rationale, then, for an immunologic approach to caries control is to stimulate the production of sIgA through the administration of either whole *S. mutans* cells or other immunogens derived from *S. mutans*. The interaction of specific sIgA molecules with *S. mutans* antigens would produce immunogen-sIgA complexes, resulting in a reduction in the virulence of the infectious component, *S. mutans*.

Early attempts to immunize rodents against dental caries met with varied results in that some laboratories reported success and others did not. The reasons for this were probably at least partly caused by the following: (1) it was not realized that immunologic mechanisms in the oral cavity were different than those that occur systemically, (2) the important plaque-forming mechanisms and determinants of virulence of *S. mutans* were not understood, (3) methods of caries scoring were not always described in detail and hence not standardized, (4) many times uncontrolled or noncariogenic diets were used, and (5) in some instances only mildly cariogenic microorganisms were used to illicit an immunologic response. More recently, however, studies have shown that caries scores in rodents can be significantly and consistently reduced by immunization procedures, using *S. mutans*–derived immunogens such as whole attenuated cells, certain enzymes such as GTFs, and glycoside hydrolases, and more recently with selected protein antigens.[103-109] Although the results reported are still somewhat variable from laboratory to laboratory, these types of studies with gnotobiotic and conventional rats and hamsters have collectively demonstrated the following: (1) increased levels of sIgA were detected in gnotobiotic and conventional rats immunized with *S. mutans,* (2) fewer *S. mutans* organisms were recovered from gnotobiotic rats vaccinated with *S. mutans,* (3) in many cases caries scores in the rat and hamster caries models were significantly lower in immunized animals, (4) rats immunized with *S. mutans* had a greater reduction in smooth surface caries as compared to pit and fissure caries, and (5) rats immunized with *S. mutans* will transfer immunity to *S. mutans*-induced caries to their offspring. Studies with lower primates[110-112] have also shown that these animals can be successfully immunized against *S. mutans*–induced dental caries. The monkey, although much more expensive, may be a better caries animal model than the rodent because it develops caries that resemble the disease in humans and also has a dentition and immune system similar to those of humans.[104] For example, Bowen[110] has shown that *S. mutans*–induced dental caries could be markedly decreased in monkeys immunized with *S. mutans* as compared to an unimmunized control group, and when broken cell suspensions of *S. mutans* were used to increase sIgA levels, a reduction in dental caries was maintained up to 5 years. In addition, other studies have shown that sIgA levels were increased after the monkeys were challenged with *S. mutans.* However, in many of the rodent and monkey experiments discussed above, the *S. mutans* immunogens were administered via subcutaneous inoculation and in many cases high levels of serum antibody titers were detected. Therefore the potential exists for these streptococcal antigens to stimulate cross reactions with human heart tissue similar to those found with group A streptococci. Recently, however, it has been shown that rats given *S. mutans* administered orally showed increased sIgA levels and a reduction in their caries scores.[103,104,113,114] Also, barely detectable serum levels of antibody to the organisms were found when the organisms were administered orally. Therefore, taken collectively, the immunization experiments with animal models support that there is a correlation between an increase in sIgA antibody

titers to *S. mutans* and a reduction in *S. mutans*–dependent dental caries.

Current evidence also supports the idea that the immune systems may play a role in reducing caries in humans.[103,104] Levels of agglutinating antibodies to cell walls of *S. mutans* were much higher in serum from caries-free subjects than in serum from individuals with a high caries incidence. Also it has been reported that antibodies to four serotypes of *S. mutans* were found in the serum and saliva obtained from individuals between 18 to 25 years of age. Recently, Mastecky and others have shown that human volunteers who were fed killed *S. mutans* cells over a 2-week period showed increased sIgA levels and that serum antibody levels in orally administered *S. mutans* were not increased.[115,116]

The exact mechanisms by which increased sIgA levels in response to *S. mutans*–derived immunogens affords protection against *S. mutans*–dependent dental caries is not known at this time. However, it is likely that sIgA interferes with retentive adhesive mechanisms, thus preventing the accumulation of *S. mutans* on the tooth surfaces and/or by causing the aggregation of *S. mutans* through the binding of sIgA molecules to specific antigenic sites on the cell surfaces, thus resulting in the clearance of the organism from the oral environment via salivary flow followed by swallowing (Fig. 35-8). Indeed, GTF preparations from *S. mutans* have been successfully used in immunizing both rats and hamsters against dental caries. Other *S. mutans* immunogens that may be potentially effective in inducing the production of specific sIgA molecules, which would interfere with adhesive retentive mechanisms and thus lower the number of *S. mutans* on the surfaces of the teeth, are listed in Table 35-5.

Although there is a great deal of current interest concerning immunization as a means of caries control in humans, there are several important criticisms to this approach. An immunologic approach to disease control requires the identification of the causative agent and, although *S. mutans* has been repeatedly shown to cause caries in animal model experiments, it still is not possible to absolutely state that this organism causes caries in humans. In addition, the antigenic or immunogenic determinants of many oral microorganisms are not static.[62] Therefore modification of *S. mutans* cell surface antigens via the phenomena of antigenic drift may make an immunologic

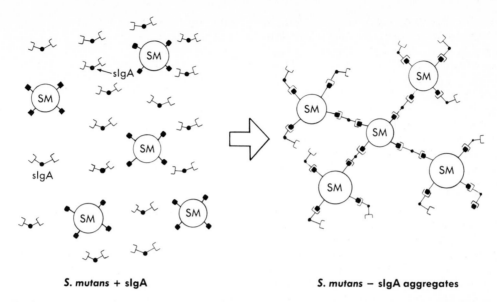

S. mutans + sIgA

S. mutans − sIgA aggregates

Fig. 35-8. Salivary immunoglobulin–induced aggregation of *S. mutans*. The diagram illustrates the ability of sIgA molecules to aggregate *S. mutans* through formation of sIgA-containing intercellular bridges. These sIgA intercellular bridges are formed through the binding of these salivary immunoglobulins to specific antigenic sites on the *S. mutans* cell surface. The *S. mutans*–sIgA aggregates are subsequently removed from the oral environment in the process of swallowing. *SM, S. mutans;* ⌁, sIgA; ◆, *S. mutans* cell surface antigenic site.

Table 35-5. Antigens involved with adherence and retentive mechanisms that may have potential significance in an immunological approach to caries control

Antigen	Role in retention
Glucosyltransferases (GTFs)	Synthesize glucans (mutan and dextran) from sucrose, which are important in cell–tooth surface and cell-cell adhesive interactions
GTF cell surface receptor sites	Permit GTF enzymes to bind to the cell surface and synthesize adhesive, cell-associated glucans
Glucan cell surface receptor sites	Allow mutan and dextran to bind to the cell surface in cell–tooth surface and cell-cell adhesive interactions

approach to caries control less feasible. Finally, in an immunologic approach to disease control, the potential always exists for harmful host side effects such as the cross reaction of serum antibodies with human heart tissue. Therefore, since dental caries is not a life-threatening disease, an immunologic approach to caries control should be approached with extreme caution.

Altering the environment

Sucrose substitutes. Because sucrose is of central importance in the etiology of multisurface dental caries, one approach to the control of dental caries has been focused on decreasing the sucrose content of the diet by replacing it with other sweet-tasting nontoxic compounds, which are more inert than sucrose with regard to their metabolism by the plaque microflora. A large number of compounds have been developed, tested, and used as substitutes for sucrose in the diet with varying degrees of success, and many of these compounds are listed in Table 35-6 with a relative sweetness rating as compared to sucrose. It should be stressed, however, that the sweetness rating of many of the compounds listed in Table 35-6 can vary from individual to individual and that figures shown in the table are maximal sweetness ratings. The sucrose substitutes listed in Table 35-6 are comprised of a broad spectrum of compounds with both simple and complex molecular structures. However, they can generally be placed into one of the four following classes or categories: (1) sugars other than sucrose, (2) reduced or hydrogenated sugars (sugar alcohols), (3) caloric and noncaloric synthetic sweeteners, and (4) naturally occurring sweetening agents. The nonsucrose sweeteners shown in Table 35-6 comprise a broad spectrum of compounds with respect to composition and structure. For example, monellin, which is approximately 300 times as sweet as sucrose, is a naturally occurring polypeptide with a molecular weight of approximately 10,000, whereas saccharin is a low molecular weight noncaloric synthetic sweetener that is approximately 700 times as sweet as sucrose.

A detailed discussion of all of the nonsucrose sweeteners listed in Table 35-6 is far beyond the scope of this chapter. However, because of a great deal of current interest, two of them, xylitol and aspartame, will be discussed in more detail. Xylitol is a five-carbon hydrogenated sugar, which is the reduced analogue of xylose and is obtained commercially from a number of natural sources. The structure of xylitol is shown below.

$$CH_2OH$$
$$|$$
$$H-C-OH$$
$$|$$
$$HO-C-H$$
$$|$$
$$H-C-OH$$
$$|$$
$$CH_2OH$$

Xylitol

Xylitol has a sweetness rating similar to that of sucrose (Table 35-6) and is less cariogenic than sucrose in animal model experiments. In addition, xylitol is much more inert than sucrose with respect to its metabolism by the plaque microflora. For example, exposure of dental plaque to xylitol does not appreciably lower the pH because of its conversion to organic acids. Of most significance pertaining to the use of xylitol are studies with human volunteers in

Table 35-6. Compounds that have been tested, evaluated, and used as sucrose substitutes

Compound	Sweetness
Sugars	
Sucrose	1.00
Lactose	0.16
Maltose	0.32
Raffinose	0.20
Galactose	0.32
Fructose	1.73
Xylose	0.40
Invert sugar (glucose and fructose)	1.30
Synthetic sweeteners	
Aspartame	200
(L-aspartyl-L-phenylalanine methyl ester)	
Noncaloric synthetic sweeteners	
Saccharin	700
Sodium cyclamate	80
Dulcin	350
Aldoximes	450
Reduced or hydrogenated sugars	
Mannitol	0.57
Sorbitol	0.54
Maltitol	0.50
Lactitol	0.84
Xylitol	1.00
Lycasin	0.58
Naturally occurring sweetening agents	
Maltol	—
Glycyrrhizin	50
Stevioside	300
Cynarin	—
Thaumatin	750
Monellin	300
Dihydrochalcones	100
Miraculin	—

Modified from Newbrun, E.: Cariology, Baltimore, 1978, The Williams & Wilkins Co.

Turku, Finland.[117] In these studies in which xylitol was substituted for sucrose in the diet of the human subjects over a 2-year period, a 90% reduction in their caries scores occurred when compared to a similar group that consumed sucrose. Xylitol is currently being used in commercial food products in northern Europe and Scandinavia.

Aspartame is a synthetically produced dipeptide that contains one molecule of aspartic acid and one molecule of phenylalanine as its methyl ester as shown below.

$$
\begin{array}{c}
\text{COOH} \\
| \\
\text{CH}_2 \qquad \text{O} \qquad\qquad \text{CH}_2 \qquad \text{O} \\
| \qquad\quad \| \qquad\qquad\quad | \qquad\quad \| \\
\text{NH}_2\!-\!\text{CH}\!-\!\text{C}\!-\!\text{NH}\!-\!\text{CH}\!-\!\text{C}\!-\!\text{OCH}_3
\end{array}
$$

L-Aspartyl-L-phenylalanine methyl ester

Aspartame

Aspartame is approximately 200 times as sweet as sucrose, and its use in this country has recently been approved by the FDA. Although approved for use, aspartame is much less stable than sucrose and may not be suitable for the processing conditions found in the food industry. In addition, concern has been expressed over the phenylalanine content of aspartame because 1 in every 10,000 individuals in this country has a genetic defect of phenylalanine metabolism called phenylketonuria. In these individuals, ingestion of phenylalanine-containing compounds causes adverse side effects such as mental retardation.

Although many of the sucrose substitutes shown in Table 35-6 are sweeter than sucrose, and animal model and human clinical studies have shown that many of them are much less cariogenic than sucrose, they collectively have certain undesirable properties that serve to decrease their acceptance and use. Many of them are expensive to produce and/or process. For example, the cost of processing xylitol is currently about 10 times that of sucrose. In addition, many of them such as monellin and aspartame are very unstable in solution and at the high temperatures found during processing procedures in the food, beverage, and confections industries. Also, long-term consumption of many sucrose substitutes leads to toxicity and adverse side effects in humans. For example, when consumed by certain individuals, sugar alcohols such as mannitol and sorbitol produce gastrointestinal distress, and the carcinogenic potential of both saccharin and sodium cyclamate has been discussed and debated at length. Concerns have also been expressed over the toxicity of the phenylalanine and aspartate components of aspartame. In addition to their expense and toxic properties, there is another potential problem associated with the long-term use of sweetening agents other than sucrose. The possibility exists that some plaque microorganisms can utilize these compounds or adapt to metabolize them after long-term

exposure to support their growth and sustain their life functions in the oral environment. This would serve to give these same microorganisms a competitive advantage within the ecologic system of dental plaque and could result in a microbial population shift away from the "normal" numbers and distribution of plaque microorganisms toward those microorganisms that possess the competitive advantage.

Although the disadvantages of sucrose substitutes discussed above are of real import and significance, perhaps the two most major problems concerning their use in the United States are of a practical nature. These practical problems are that no single sucrose substitute listed in Table 35-6 possesses all of the properties of sucrose, in addition to its sweet taste, which collectively contribute to its widespread use and acceptance in our society; also it now appears that attaining a significant level of caries reduction necessitates the elimination of virtually all sucrose from the diet. Two of the properties of sucrose that contribute to its widespread use and acceptance are that it is relatively inexpensive to process and purchase and is stable at high food processing temperatures. It also has an extremely rapid onset of the sweet taste sensation with little or no aftertaste. In addition, sucrose is an excellent flavor blender, flavor modifier, texture and bodying agent, bulking agent, and carmelizing or browning agent. In light of these properties of sucrose, it is of interest to examine the distribution of sucrose consumption in the United States. The average sucrose consumption in the United States is approximately 102 pounds per person. However, of this 102 pounds, only 24 pounds, on the average, is sold directly to the consumer for home use such as baking and canning.[70] The remaining 78 pounds of sucrose is consumed in many processed foods, beverages, and confections. Thus, given the present eating habits of many Americans, especially children in the caries-prone years, when snacking and eating prepared and processed "fast" foods is popular, the elimination of a significant amount of sucrose from the diet is highly unlikely. The major replacement of sucrose by other sweeteners is obviously a complex problem that would involve such things as major reformulation of many processed foods and would generate the need for consumers in this country to accept products that may be quite different than those to which they are accustomed. However, given the obvious contribution to the control of dental caries as well as the benefits provided for the diabetic patient and obese individuals, efforts and monies should continue to be spent in both the federal and private sectors to develop and test suitable alternatives to sucrose as sweetening agents.

Phosphates. A number of inorganic and organic phosphates have been shown to markedly reduce dental caries in experimental animal models when added as supplements to their diets.[1,118-120] Also, the topical application of certain phosphate-containing compounds has been shown to decrease the caries experience of experimental animals. More studies have been done with inorganic than with organic phosphates such as phytates and glycerophosphates. The cariostatic activity of most inorganic phosphates tested has been shown to be dependent on their anion and cation content. For example, inorganic phosphate compounds that contain magnesium and calcium are generally more cariostatic than similar compounds in which hydrogen or sodium comprise the respective cation components, and inorganic phosphate compounds that contain pyrophosphate and orthophosphate as the anion components are generally more cariostatic than compounds that contain other anionic components such as cyclic phosphate or trimetaphosphate. The relationship between cation and anion content of some inorganic phosphates to cariostatic activity is shown in Table 35-7.

The mechanism by which phosphates promote caries reduction in animals is generally not known, but their effects appear to be local rather than systemic.[1,120] Several proposed mechanisms for the cariostatic activity of phosphates in animal experiments are as follows: (1) they may interact directly with the plaque microflora and serve to decrease the rate of acid production from fermentable carbohydrates, (2) they may interact with the hydroxyapatite matrix of the tooth enamel and make it more resistant to acid-dependent demineralization, (3) they may simply serve as buffers for the acidic fermentation products produced by the plaque microflora, (4) they may remove proteins of salivary origin from the acquired pellicle and hence adversely affect the attachment of certain oral microorganisms, and (5) they may aid in the redeposition of calcium phosphate in locations where the enamel has undergone some demineralization. In all probability, no single mechanism listed above can explain the cariostatic activity of organic or inorganic phosphates.

Although they have been shown to be effective

Table 35-7. Cariostatic activity of inorganic phosphates with respect to their cation and anion content

Cation	Anion
Hydrogen	Cyclic phosphate
Sodium	Trimetaphosphate
Potassium	Tripolyphosphate
Calcium	Hexametaphosphate
Magnesium	Orthophosphate
	Pyrophosphate

Cation and anion content are listed in order of increasing cariostatic activity.

caries-reducing agents in experiments involving animal models, little success has been obtained with phosphates in the reduction of dental caries in human clinical trials in which they have been included in foodstuffs, mouthrinses, and chewable tablets. Although there are important physiologic disimilarities between humans and rodents, which may explain the differences observed in phosphate-dependent caries reduction, perhaps of most import is the manner in which the animal and human studies were done. In the case of the animal model studies, phosphate supplements were included in the entire diet, whereas in the human clinical trials phosphates have been generally incorporated into only a single portion of the diet such as in sweets and chewing gum. More extensive studies need to be performed before it can be definitely stated that inorganic and/or organic phosphates are noncariostatic or cariostatic in humans.

Trace minerals. Environmental constituents other than fluoride have been implicated as having the ability to influence the incidence of dental caries in both animals and humans, and one class of these compounds is the trace minerals.[1,121-124] Interestingly enough, certain trace minerals have been implicated as being cariostatic and others as being caries promoting. Elevated levels of strontium in the drinking water have been associated with a low caries incidence in humans, and high levels of strontium in drinking water significantly has been shown to reduce the caries experience in experimental rats. In addition to strontium, molybdenum, vanadium, and lithium have been implicated as having cariostatic properties. In contrast to the cariostatic trace minerals, selenium has been shown to promote dental caries in both human and experimental animals when taken during the

Table 35-8. Proposed effects of minerals on dental caries

Mineral	Effect
Fluorine, phosphorus	Cariostatic
Molybdenum, vanadium, copper, strontium, boron, lithium, gold, iron	Mildly cariostatic
Selenium, magnesium, cadmium, platinum, lead, silicon	Caries promoting
Barium, aluminum, nickel, palladium, titanium	Caries inert

Modified from Navia, J.M.: Int. Dent. J. **22**:427, 1972.

period of tooth development. The mechanisms that explain the cariostatic and caries-promoting activity of certain trace minerals are not definitely known. However, it has been postulated that cariostatic trace minerals may exert their effects locally by either interacting directly with the pathogenic components of dental plaque thus causing, for example, a reduction in adhesive polysaccharide synthesis, or serving to decrease the susceptibility of the tooth enamel to acid-induced demineralization. The caries-promoting effect of selenium has been attributed to its ability to affect formation of the protein matrix of enamel during tooth development. Table 35-8 shows groupings of many of the trace minerals according to their proposed role as cariostatic, caries-promoting, or caries-inert agents. A great deal of additional investigation will be necessary to determine the role of trace minerals in dental caries etiology, especially in humans.

REFERENCES

1. Newbrun, E.: Cariology, Baltimore, 1978, The Williams & Wilkins Co.
2. Ritz, H.L.: Microbial population shifts in developing human dental plaque, Arch. Oral Biol. **12**:1561, 1967.
3. Theilade, E., and Theilade, J.: Role of plaque in the etiology of periodontal disease and caries, Oral Sci. Rev. **9**:23, 1976.
4. Hotz, P., Guggenheim, B., and Schmid, R.: Carbohydrates in pooled dental plaque, Caries. Res. **6**:103, 1972.
5. Krembel, J., Frank, R.M., and Deluzarche, A.: Fractionation of human dental plaque, Arch. Oral Biol. **14**:563, 1969.
6. Miller, W.D.: Microorganisms of the human mouth: the local and general diseases which are caused by them, Philadelphia, 1890, S.S. White Publishing Co.
7. Keyes, P.H.: Present and future measures for dental caries control, J. Am. Dent. Assoc. **79**:1404, 1969.
8. Gibbons, R.J., and VanHoute, J.: Dental caries, Ann. Rev. Med. **26**:121, 1975.
9. Orland, F.J., et al.: Use of germ free animal technique in the study of experimental dental caries. I. Basic observations on rats reared free of all microorganisms, J. Dent. Res. **33**:147, 1954.
10. Orland, F.J., et al.: Experimental caries in germ free rats innoculated with enterococci, J. Am. Dent. Assoc. **50**:259, 1955.
11. Keyes, P.H.: The infectious and transmissible nature of experimental dental caries: findings and biological implications, Arch. Oral Biol. **1**:304, 1960.
12. Fitzgerald, R.J., and Keyes, P.H.: Demonstration of the etiologic role of streptococci in experimental caries in the hamster, J. Am. Dent. Assoc. **61**:9, 1960.
13. Gibbons, R.J., and VanHoute, J.: Bacteriology of dental caries. In Shaw, J.H., et al., editors: Textbook of oral biology, Philadelphia, 1978, W.B. Saunders Co.
14. Loe, H., Theilade, E., and Jensen, S.B.: Experimental gingivitis in man, J. Periodontol. **36**:177-187, 1965.
15. Mitchell, D.F., et al.: Topical antibiotic maintainence of oral health, J. Oral Ther. Pharmacol. **4**:83, 1967.
16. Loesche, W.J.: Chemotherapy of dental plaque infections, Oral Science Rev. **9**:65, 1976.
17. Miller, C.H.: Dental caries. In Roth, G.I., and Calmes, R.B., editors: Oral biology, St. Louis, 1981, The C.V. Mosby Co.
18. Scherp, H.W.: Dental caries: prospects for prevention, Science **173**:1199, 1971.
19. Gibbons, R.J., et al.: Interdental localization of *Streptococcus mutans* as related to dental caries experience, Infect. Immun. **9**:481, 1974.
20. Ikeda, T., and Sandham, H.J.: Prevalence of *Streptococcus mutans* on various tooth surfaces in Negro children, Arch. Oral Biol. **16**:1237, 1971.
21. Shklair, I.L., Keene, H.J., and Cullen, P.: The distribution of *Streptococcus mutans* on the teeth of two groups of naval recruits, Arch. Oral Biol. **19**:199, 1974.
22. Gibbons, R.J., and VanHoute, J.: Oral bacterial ecology. In Shaw, J.H., et al., editors: Textbook of oral biology, Philadelphia, 1978, W.B. Saunders Co.
23. McCarthy, C., Snyder, M.L., and Parker, R.B.: The indigenous flora of man. I. The newborn to the 1 year old infant, Arch. Oral Biol. **10**:61, 1965.
24. Carlsson, J., et al.: Establishment of *Streptococcus sanguis* in the mouths of infants, Arch. Oral Biol. **15**:1143, 1970.
25. Socransky, S.S., and Manganiello, S.D.: The oral microbiota of man from birth to senility, J. Periodontol. **42**:485, 1971.
26. Gibbons, R.J., and VanHoute, J.: Bacterial adherence in oral microbial ecology, Annu. Rev. Microbiol. **29**:19, 1975.
27. Gibbons, R.J., and VanHoute, J.: On the formation of dental plaques, J. Periodontol. **44**:347, 1973.
28. Gibbons, R.J.: Formation and significance of bacterial polysaccharides in caries etiology, Caries Res. **2**:164, 1968.
29. Guggenheim, B.: Extracellular polysaccharides and microbial plaque, Int. Dent. J. **20**:657, 1970.
30. Hamada, S., and Slade, H.D.: Biology, immunology, and cariogenicity of *Streptococcus mutans*, Microbiol. Rev. **44**:331, 1980.
31. Tanzer, J.M., et al.: Diminished virulence of glucan synthesis defective mutants of *Streptococcus mutans*, Infect. Immun. **10**:197, 1974.
32. deStoppelarr, J.D., et al.: Decreased cariogenicity of a mutant of *Streptococcus mutans*, Arch. Oral Biol. **16**:971, 1971.

33. Brown, A.T.: The role of dietary carbohydrates in plaque formation and oral disease, Nutr. Rev. **33**:353, 1975.

34. Jordan, H.V., Keyes, P.H., and Lim, S.: Plaque formation and implantation of *Odontomyces viscosus* in hamsters fed different diets, J. Dent. Res. **48**:824, 1969.

35. Hageage, G.J., Jr., Johanssen, I., and Tanzer, J.M.: In vitro plaque formation by several oral diptheroids implicated in periodontal disease, Infect. Immun. **2**:683, 1970.

36. Rosan, B., and Hammond, B.F.: Extracellular polysaccharides of *Actinomyces viscosus*, Infect. Immun. **10**:304, 1974.

37. VanHoute, J., Gibbons, R.J., and Banghart, S.B.: Adherence as a determinant of the presence of *Streptococcus salivarius* and *Streptococcus sanguis* on the human tooth surface, Arch. Oral Biol. **15**:1025, 1970.

38. Gibbons, R.J.: On the mechanisms of bacterial attachment to teeth, In Kleinberg, I., Ellison, S.A., and Mandel, I.D., editors: Saliva and dental caries, Microbiology Abstracts (sp. suppl.), Washington, D.C., 1979, Information Retrieval, Inc.

39. Clark, W.B., Bammann, L., and Gibbons, R.J.: Comparative estimates of bacterial affinities and adsorption sites on hydroxyapatite surfaces, Infect. Immun. **19**:846, 1978.

40. Gibbons, R.J.: Adherence of bacteria to host tissue, Microbiology **4**:395, 1977.

41. Liljemark, W.F., and Schauer, S.V.: Competitive binding among oral streptococci to hydroxyapatite, J. Dent. Res. **56**:157, 1977.

42. Hillman, J.D., VanHoute, J., and Gibbons, R.J.: Sorption of plaque bacteria to human enamel powder, Arch. Oral Biol. **15**:899, 1970.

43. Magnusson, I., and Ericson, T.: The effect of salivary agglutinins on reactions between hydroxyapatite and a serotype C strain of *Streptococcus mutans*, Caries Res. **10**:113, 1976.

44. Rolla, G.: Inhibition of adsorption: general considerations. In Stiles, H.M., Loesche, W.J., and O'Brien, T.C., editors: Proceedings, Microbiology Abstracts (sp. suppl.), Washington, D.C., 1976, Information Retrieval, Inc.

45. Rolla, G.: Formation of dental integuments: some basic chemical considerations, Swed. Dent. J. **1**:241, 1977.

46. Rolla, G., Bonesvoll, P., and Operman, R.: Interactions between oral streptococci and salivary glycoproteins. In Kleinberg, I., Ellison, S.A., and Mandel, I.D., editors: Saliva and dental caries, Microbiology Abstracts (sp. suppl.), Washington, D.C., 1979, Information Retrieval, Inc.

47. VanHoute, J., Burgess, R.C., and Onose, H.: Oral implantation of human strains of *Streptococcus mutans* in rats fed sucrose or glucose diets, Arch. Oral Biol. **21**:561, 1976.

48. VanHoute, J., et al.: Colonization of *Streptococcus mutans* in conventional Sprague-Dawley rats, J. Dent. Res. **55**:202, 1976.

49. VanHoute, J., and Duchin, S.: *Streptococcus mutans* in the mouths of children with congenital sucrose deficiency, Arch. Oral Biol. **20**:771, 1975.

50. Gibbons, R.J., and Qureshi, J.V.: Selective binding of blood-group reactive salivary mucins by *Streptococcus mutans* and other oral organisms, Infect. Immun. **22**:665, 1978.

51. Clark, W.B., and Gibbons, R.J.: Influence of salivary components and extracellular polysaccharide synthesis from sucrose on the attachment of *Streptococcus mutans* 6715 to hydroxyapatite surfaces, Infect. Immun. **18**:514, 1977.

52. Staat, R.H., Langley, S.D., and Doyle, R.J.: *Streptococcus mutans* adherence: presumptive evidence for protein-mediated attachment followed by glucan-dependent cellular accumulation, Infect. Immun. **27**:675, 1980.

53. Gibbons, R.J., and Fitzgerald, R.J.: Dextran-induced agglutination of *Streptococcus mutans* and its potential role in the formation of microbial dental plaque, J. Bacteriol. **98**:341, 1968.

54. McBride, B.C., and Bourgean, G.: Dextran-mediated interbacterial aggregation between dextran-synthesizing streptococci and *Actinomyces viscosus*, Infect. Immun. **13**:1228, 1976.

55. Kashet, S., and Donaldson, C.S.: Saliva-induced aggregation of oral streptococci, J. Bacteriol. **112**:1127, 1972.

56. Gibbons, R.J., and Spinell, D.M.: Salivary induced aggregation of oral streptococci. In McHugh, W.D., editor, Dental plaque, Edinburgh, 1970, E. & S. Livingstone, Ltd.

57. Williams, R.C., and Gibbons, R.J.: Inhibition of streptococcal attachment to receptors on human buccal epithelial cells by antigenically similar salivary glycoproteins, Infect. Immun. **11**:711, 1975.

58. Kashet, S., and Guilmette, K.M.: Further evidence for the nonimmunoglobulin nature of the bacterial aggregating factor in saliva, Caries Res. **12**:170, 1978.

59. Hay, D.J., Gibbons, R.J., and Spinell, D.M.: Characteristics of some high molecular weight constituents with bacterial aggregating activity from whole saliva and dental plaque, Caries Res. **5**:111, 1971.

60. Cisar, J.O., Kolenbrander, P.E., and McIntire, F.C.: Specificity of coaggregation reactions between human oral streptococci and strains of *Actinomyces viscosus* or *Actinomyces naeslundii*, Infect. Immun. **24**:742, 1979.

61. McIntire, F.C., et al.: Mechanism of coaggregation between *Actinomyces* T14V and *Streptococcus sanguis* 34, Infect. Immun. **21**:978, 1978.

62. Lillich, T.T.: Oral microbiology. In Roth, G.I., and Calmes, R.B., editors: Oral biology, St. Louis, 1981, The C.V. Mosby Co.

63. Mouton, C., Reynolds, H.S., and Genco, R.J.: Characterization of tufted streptococci isolated from the corn cob configuration of human dental plaque, Infect. Immun. **27**:235, 1980.

64. Jay, P.: The reduction of oral *Lactobacillus acidophilus* counts by periodic restriction of carbohydrate, Am. J. Orthod. **33**:162, 1947.

65. VanHoute, J.: Relationship between carbohydrate intake and polysaccharide-storing microorganisms in dental plaque, Arch. Oral Biol. **9**:91, 1964.

66. Loesche, W.J., and Gibbons, R.J.: Influence of nutrition on the ecology and cariogenicity of the oral microflora. In Nizel, A.E., editor: The science of nutrition and its application to clinical dentistry, Philadelphia, 1966, W.B. Saunders Co.

67. Newbrun, E.: Sucrose: the arch criminal of dental caries, Odontol. Rev. **18**:373, 1967.

68. Hillman, J.D.: Lactate dehydrogenase mutants of *Streptococcus mutans*: isolation and preliminary characterization, Infect. Immun. **21**:206, 1978.

69. Johnson, C.P., and Hillman, J.D.: Competitive properties of LDH-deficient mutants of *Streptococcus mutans*, J. Dent. Res. **58**(special issue A):103, 1979.

70. Shaw, J.H.: Sweeteners and dental caries, Dental Survey, p. 36, November, 1978.
71. Newman, M.G., and Calmes, R.B.: Periodontal diseases. In Roth, G.I., and Calmes, R.B., editors: Oral biology, St. Louis, 1981, The C.V. Mosby Co.
72. Bader, J.D., et al.: In Roth, G.I., and Calmes, R.B., editors: Oral biology, St. Louis, 1981, The C.V. Mosby Co.
73. Jordan, H.V.: A systematic approach to antibiotic control of dental caries, J. Can. Dent. Assoc. **39**:703, 1973.
74. Fitzgerald, R.J.: Inhibition of experimental dental caries by antibiotics, Antimicrob. Agents Chemother. **1**:296, 1972.
75. Handelman, S.L., Mills, J.R., and Hawes, R.R.: Caries incidence in subjects receiving long term antibiotic therapy, J. Oral Therap. Pharmacol. **2**:338, 1966.
76. Littleton, N.W., and White, C.L.: Dental findings from a preliminary study of children receiving extended antibiotic therapy, J. Am. Dent. Assoc. **68**:520, 1964.
77. DePaula, P.F., Jordan, H.V., and Soparker, P.M.: Inhibition of dental caries in children by topically applied vancomycin, Arch. Oral Biol. **22**:187, 1977.
78. Loesche, W.J., Bradburg, D.R., and Woolfolk, M.T.: Reduction of dental decay in rampent caries individuals following short term kanamycin treatment, J. Dent. Res. **56**:254, 1977.
79. Loesche, W.J., et al.: Effect of topical kanamycin sulfate on plaque accumulation. J. Am. Dent. Assoc. **83**:1063, 1971.
80. Schiott, R.C., et al.: The effect of chlorhexidine mouth rinses on the human oral flora, J. Periodontol. Res. **5**:84, 1970.
81. Loe, H., von der Fehr, C., and Schiott, C.R.: Inhibition of experimental caries by plaque prevention. The effect of chlorhexidine mouthrinses, Scand. J. Dent. Res. **80**:1, 1972.
82. Loe, H., et al.: Two years oral use of chlorhexidine in man. I. General design and clinical effects, J. Periodont. Res. **11**:135, 1976.
83. O'Neil, T.C.A.: The use of chlorhexidine mouthwash in the control of gingival inflammation, Br. Dent. J. **141**:276, 1976.
84. Weatherford, T.W., Finn, S.B., and Jamison, H.C.: Effects of an alexidine mouthwash on dental plaque and gingivitis in humans over a 6-month period, J. Am. Dent. Assoc. **93**:528, 1977.
85. Newcomb, G., McKellar, G., and Rawal, B.: An in vivo comparison of chlorhexidine and picoxydine mouthrinses: a possible association between chemical structure and antiplaque activity, J. Periodontol. **48**:282, 1977.
86. Carlson, H.C., Porter, K., and Alms, T.H.: The effect of an alexidine mouthwash on dental plaque and gingivitis, J. Periodontol. **48**:216, 1977.
87. Bain, M.J., and Strahan, J.D.: The effect of a 1% chlorhexidine gel in the initial therapy of chronic periodontal disease, J. Periodontol. **49**:469, 1978.
88. Rolla, G., and Melsen, B.: On the mechanism of plaque inhibition by chlorhexidine, J. Dent. Res. **54**(Special issue 13):57, 1975.
89. Foulkes, D.M.: Some toxicological observations on chlorhexidine, J. Periodont. Res. **8**(Suppl. 12):55, 1973.
90. Gibbons, R.J., and Nygaard, M.: Synthesis of insoluble dextran and its significance in the formation of gelatinous deposits by plaque-forming streptococci, Arch. Oral Biol. **11**:549, 1968.

91. Fitzgerald, R.J., Spinell, D.M., and Stoudt, T.H.: Enzymatic removal of artificial plaques, Arch. Oral Biol. **13**:125, 1968.
92. Fitzgerald, R.J., et al.: The effects of dextranase preparation on plaque and caries in hamsters, a preliminary report, J. Am. Dent. Assoc. **76**:301, 1968.
93. Block, P.L., Dooley, C.L., and Howe, E.E.: The retardation of spontaneous periodontal disease and the prevention of caries in hamsters with dextranase, J. Periodontol. **40**:105, 1969.
94. Guggenheim, B., et al.: Effect of dextranases on caries in rats harbouring an indigenous cariogenic bacterial flora, Arch. Oral Biol. **14**:555, 1969.
95. Bowen, W.H.: The effect of dextranase on caries activity in monkeys *(Macaca irus)*, Br. Dent. J. **131**:445, 1971.
96. Guggenheim, B., Regolati, B., and Muhlman, H.R.: Caries and plaque inhibition by mutanase in rats, Caries Res. **6**:253, 1972.
97. Konig, K.G., and Guggenheim, B.: In vivo effects of dextranase on plaque and caries, Helv. Odontol. Acta **12**:48, 1968.
98. Caldwell, R.C., et al.: The effect of dextranase mouthwash on dental plaque and gingivitis, J. Periodontol. **82**:124, 1971.
99. Lobene, R.R.: A clinical study of the effect of dextranase on human dental plaque, J. Am. Dent. Assoc. **82**:132, 1971.
100. Murayama, Y., et al.: Effects of dextranase from *Spicaria violaceae* (IFO 6120) on the polysaccharides produced by oral streptococci and on human dental plaque, J. Dent. Res. **52**:658, 1973.
101. Kelstrup, J., Funder-Nielsen, T.D., and Moller, E.N.: Enzymatic reduction of the colonization of *Streptococcus mutans* in human dental plaque, Acta Odontol. Scand. **31**:249, 1973.
102. Kelstrup, J., Holm-Pedersen, P., and Poulsen, S.: Reduction of the formation of dental plaque and gingivitis in humans by crude mutanase, Scand. J. Dent. Res. **86**:93, 1978.
103. Smith, D.J., and Taubman, M.A.: Immunology and dental caries. In Shaw, S.H., et al., editors: Textbook of oral biology, Philadelphia, 1978, W.B. Saunders Co.
104. Genco, R.J.: Immune response to oral organisms: implications for dental caries and periodontal disease. In Prevention of major dental disorders, J. Clin. Periodontol. **6**(7):22-31, 1979.
105. Bowen, W.H., Cohen, B., and Colman, G.: Immunization against dental caries, Br. Dent. J. **139**:45, 1975.
106. Scholler, M., Klein, J.P., and Frank, R.M.: Dental caries in gnotobiotic rats immunized with purified glucosyltransferase from *Streptococcus sanguis*, Arch. Oral Biol. **23**:501, 1978.
107. Smith, D.J., and Taubman, M.A.: Immunization experiments using rodent caries model. J. Dent. Res. **55**:C193, 1976.
108. Taubman, M.A., and Smith, D.J.: Effects of local immunization with *Streptococcus mutans* on induction of salivary IgA antibody and experimental dental caries in rats, Infect. Immun. **9**:1079, 1974.
109. Taubman, M.A., and Smith, D.J.: Effects of local immunization with glucosyltransferase fractions from *Streptococcus mutans* on dental caries in rats and hamsters, J. Immunol. **118**:710, 1977.

110. Bowen, W.H.: A vaccine against dental caries: a pilot experiment in monkeys *(Macaca irus),* Br. Dent. J. **126:**159, 1969.

111. Lehner, T., Challacombe, S., and Caldwell, J.: An immunological investigation into the prevention of caries in deciduous teeth of rhesus monkeys, Arch. Oral Biol. **20:**305, 1975.

112. Evans, R.T., Emmings, F.G., and Geneo, R.J.: Prevention of *Streptococcus mutans* infections of tooth surfaces by salivary antibody in irus monkeys, Infect. Immun. **12:**293, 1975.

113. Michalek, S.M., et al.: Effective immunity to dental caries: selective induction of secretory immunity by oral administration of *Streptococcus mutans* in rodents, Adv. Exp. Med. Biol. **107:**201, 1978.

114. McGhee, J.R., et al.: Effective immunity to dental caries: protection of gnotobiotic rats by local immunization with *Streptococcus mutans,* J. Immunol. **114:**300, 1975.

115. Mastecky, J., et al.: Selective induction of an immune response in human external secretions by ingestion of bacterial antigen, J. Clin. Invest. **61:**731, 1978.

116. McGhee, J.R., et al.: Induction of secretory antibodies in humans following ingestion of *Streptococcus mutans,* Adv. Exp. Med. Biol. **107:**184, 1978.

117. Scheinen, A., Makinen, K.K., and Ylitalo, K.: Turku sugar studies. V. Final report on the effect of sucrose, fructose, and xylitol diets on the caries incidence in man, Acta Odontol Scand. **34:**139, 1976.

118. Losee, F.L., and Ludwig, T.G.: Trace elements and caries, J. Dent. Res. **49:**1229, 1970.

119. Ericsson, Y.: Phosphates in relation to dental caries, Int. Dent. J. **15:**311, 1965.

120. Pruitt, K.M., Jamieson, A.D., and Caldwell, R.C.: Possible basis for the cariostatic effect of inorganic phosphates, Nature **225:**1249, 1970.

121. Navia, J.M.: Prevention of dental caries: agents which increase tooth resistance to dental caries, Int. Dent. J. **22:**427, 1972.

122. Curzon, M.E.J.: Strontium content of enamel and dental caries, Caries Res. **11:**321, 1977.

123. Butner, W.: Trace elements and dental caries in experiments on animals, Caries Res. **3:**1, 1969.

124. Curzon, M.E.J., and Losee, F.L.: Dental caries and trace element composition of whole human enamel: eastern United States, J. Am. Dent. Assoc. **94:**1146, 1977.

CHAPTER 36

EDWARD M. OSETEK

Endodontic medicaments and irrigating solutions

Although the overriding principle in endodontics is debridement of the root canal system, the modern practice of endodontics still demands that microbial control be achieved during treatment. Practitioners may debate the relative merits of culturing, but there is unanimity of agreement that the elimination of microorganisms from the root canal system is of paramount importance. A variety of drugs and chemicals have been employed over the years to aid in achieving this objective.

HISTORY AND RATIONALE

To help understand the role of medicaments and irrigating solutions in endodontics, it is necessary to briefly review their historical significance.

The use of potions, lotions, and a variety of other agents for the alleviation of toothache can be traced to ancient civilizations. However, the scientific and clinical basis for medicaments in root therapy began about the same time that organized dentistry evolved in the United States in the middle 1800s. The rationale for the use of medicaments at that time was based almost exclusively on pain control. It must be remembered that this era preceded the advent of anesthesia, x-ray technology, and the concept of asepsis.

The early literature is replete with formulas for the treatment of painful teeth, including chalk, pumice, charcoal, magnesia, spices, and a host of equally curious agents. Devitalization of the dental pulp was a common practice in the treatment of painful teeth. Beechwood creosote, introduced by Reichenbach in 1830, was one of the agents used for devitalization. Arsenic trioxide, phenol, and sulfuric acid were also used for this purpose.

The intracanal agents and the rationale for their use remained virtually unchanged until a series of papers were presented or published by W.D. Miller[1,2] in 1888 and 1890 and G.V. Black[3] in 1891. These papers focused attention on the significance of microorganisms in the root canal and the toxic effects of decomposed pulpal tissue. As a result, sterilization and debridement superseded pain control as the operant factor in the rationale for selection of root canal medicaments. This new concept prompted the introduction of a host of new agents and techniques for the purpose of sterilization and debridement, beginning with electrosterilization and the introduction of camphorated parachlorophenol and formocresol in the 1890s and early 1900s and continuing even today.

Throughout this entire period, little or no consideration was given to the toxic effects of the agents used, and little was known about the mode of action of these agents. It was A.H. Peck[4] who in 1898 first reported the results of a crude experiment he conducted on himself to determine the toxicity of some of the agents used at that time. He applied cotton pellets saturated with various antiseptics to the skin of his forearm and reported quite graphically the severe symptoms that developed after the pellets were allowed to remain for extended periods of time. G.V. Black[5] soon followed with similar experiments and sent out the plea to choose antiseptics ". . . not with relation to their power as a poison entirely, but with special reference to their action upon the animal tissue to which they are applied."

The final missing ingredient in the rationale was the measurement of the effectiveness of the agents used. G.V. Black[6] reported in 1889 on the effectiveness of essential oils as antiseptic agents and in 1901 T.W. Onderdonk[7] introduced the concept of root canal culture procedures to measure the effectiveness of the treatment.

The completed rationale at the beginning of the twentieth century places sterilization, debridement, and pain control as goals and provides the profession with two critical questions to be answered: (1) how toxic are the agents we use, and (2) how effective are these agents in achieving the desired result? Even the most superficial perusal of the scientific literature since that time reveals that an overwhelming amount of research has been dedicated to trying to answer these critical questions.

CLASSIFICATION

Many new and different agents have been introduced over the past 80 years in an effort to satisfy the objectives of sterilization, debridement, and pain control. Many have been discarded, but a few have withstood the test of time. It is obvious that no one agent can satisfy all criteria or help to achieve all objectives. Therefore the agents can be divided into three rather broad categories:

1. Intracanal irrigating solutions for debridement and microbial control
2. Intracanal medicaments for microbial and pain control
3. Special purpose agents

Stewart,[8] Auerbach,[9] and Ingle and Zeldow[10] have demonstrated that significant and measurable reduction in intracanal microbial population can be achieved following debridement and chemomechanical or biomechanical preparation alone. However, it has also been demonstrated that microbial growth frequently resumes between appointments (culture reversal).[11] Although no studies have been reported that demonstrate greater healing or success rates with the use of intracanal medication, nevertheless medicaments have been and are being used empirically for a variety of reasons, most notably to discourage microbial growth between appointments.

From time to time special needs arise that require the use of "special purpose agents." These agents were introduced to control interappointment pain, arrest resorptive processes, eliminate canal moisture, promote continued root formation, soften dentin for instrumentation, encourage calcific repair of fractures, and render organic tissue biochemically inert. This list is by no means inclusive, and new uses for existing agents or new agents for existing conditions are constantly being introduced through the literature. This section will concern itself only with those agents that have appeared to be successfully used in clinical

situations with some reference to agents of historical significance in the evaluation of the state of the art.

DESIRABLE QUALITIES OF INTRACANAL AGENTS

Because the objectives of root canal treatment place different demands on irrigating solutions than on intracanal medicaments, their properties would also differ.

Ideally endodontic irrigating solutions should:

1. Be bactericidal
2. Serve as a flotation and lubricating agent
3. Serve as a flushing agent
4. Be a solvent for necrotic tissue
5. Have no deleterious effect on vital tissues
6. Be readily available
7. Be inexpensive
8. Possess a reasonable shelf life
9. Be nonstaining to tooth structure
10. Not interfere with culturing procedures

As a modification of Torneck's requirements,[12] the ideal medicament should:

1. Rapidly eliminate or destroy all forms of microbial life found in the root canal
2. Neutralize or destroy toxic substances found in the root canal
3. Be effective in the presence of blood, serum, pus, or other organic matter
4. Have no deleterious effect on vital tissue
5. Not adversely alter the physiologic activities of the host tissue
6. Have good penetrating ability to be effective in inaccessible portions of the root canal system and dentinal tubules
7. Be readily available
8. Be inexpensive
9. Be stable and possess a reasonable shelf life
10. Be nonstaining to tooth structure
11. Not interfere with culturing procedures

Obviously, no agent can satisfy all the desirable properties of either an irrigating solution or a medicament. The ideal properties are listed to aid the practitioner in selecting agents for use in clinical practice.

FACTORS THAT MODIFY THE ACTIVITY OF INTRACANAL IRRIGATING SOLUTIONS AND MEDICAMENTS

It is clear from the voluminous research reported in the literature that virtually all of the agents discussed here have proved to be effective to a greater or lesser degree. Some of the modifying factors such as host resistance, bacterial virulence, microbial resistance or susceptibility, and complexity of some root canal systems are not in the control of the practitioner. Other factors, however, can be controlled or at least predicted. Those factors that fall into this latter group will be discussed here.

Concentration

Several studies relative to root canal irrigating solutions demonstrate that the tissue-dissolving ability of sodium hypochlorite is greater at a concentration of 5% than at 2.5% and least at a concentration of 0.5%.[13-15] It has also been clearly demonstrated that higher concentrations are more cytotoxic than are lower concentrations. This direct relationship of effectiveness and toxicity to concentration is generally true for all intracanal agents.

Harrison and Madonia[16] were able to demonstrate in vitro that the 35% camphorated solution of parachlorophenol was much more bactericidal than was actually necessary and that a 1% aqueous solution of parachlorophenol was significantly less toxic yet sufficiently bactericidal for use as an intracanal medicament. Straffon and Han[17] and Loos and Han[18] reported similar findings relative to tissue tolerance, using reduced concentrations of formocresol.

Contact

To be effective, the intracanal agent must contact its substrate (i.e., organic tissue or microorganisms). In the case of an irrigating solution, it could neither dissolve tissue nor physically flush out debris if not in contact with the substrate. It is critical that the canals be mechanically enlarged in the presence of irrigating solution to carry the solution to the apical extent of the root canal preparation. When the canals are sufficiently enlarged, the solution can be deposited directly in the apical area of the preparation with a fine irrigating needle. Similarly, intracanal medicaments must contact the substrate (bacteria) if they are to be effective. A dichotomy immediately becomes evident since, because of its toxicity, the medicament should not flood the entire canal system. Fortunately, debridement and chemomechanical preparation alone can free the canal of microbial activity in the majority of patients, and the medicament is used only to discourage microbial activity between appointments. Of the intracanal medicaments in popular use today, only formocresol has been demonstrated to be active by vaporization and permeation of the root canal system.[19] The other agents must rely on capillary action for diffusion through the root canal system. The once popular practice of sealing a paper point saturated with medicament into the root canal is discouraged because of the cytotoxicity of most medicaments and the subsequent danger of evoking an acute periapical inflammatory response.

Presence of organic tissue

Virtually all of the nonspecific intracanal medicaments cause protein coagulation. If organic debris is present in the root canal system, its protein content will coagulate as a result of its reaction with the medicament. This coagulum serves as a barrier to further penetration of the medicament, thus limiting its effectiveness. Therefore thorough chemomechanical preparation is essential if the intracanal medicaments are to be effective.

Quantity

Baker and coworkers,[20] in evaluating the effectiveness of low concentrations of sodium hypochlorite (1.0%) when compared to normal saline, found no significant difference in their ability to debride the root canal. However, they were able to demonstrate that the thoroughness of debridement was directly related to the quantity of irrigating solution used. Schilder[21] attributes much of his ability to debride accessory and lateral canals to thorough instrumentation and copious irrigation with sodium hypochlorite. On the other hand, increasing the quantity of an intracanal medicament to increase its effectiveness is not a prudent practice. The cytotoxicity of most medicaments has been abundantly demonstrated, and the trend today is toward minimizing dosages and decreasing concentrations to minimize host tissue damage.

Temperature

Cunningham and Balkjian[22] in 1980 and Abou-Rass and Oglesby[13] in 1981 have shown that if sodium hypochlorite is warmed before irrigation, it is much more effective as a tissue solvent. Although further studies are needed, it may well be that the most desirable irrigating technique to maximize effectiveness and minimize tissue irritation is to use reduced concentrations of sodium hypochlorite that have been warmed before use.

INTRACANAL IRRIGATING SOLUTIONS

Thorough debridement is clearly recognized as a fundamental principle in surgical procedures and wound healing. This principle is essential in root canal treatment as well because the extirpation of pulp tissue and cleansing and shaping of the root canal system are indeed a surgical procedure. Organic and inorganic debris left in the root canal system can interfere with or prevent healing after treatment is completed. The interference with healing is magnified if the residual debris is infected. Torneck[23,24] and Wenger and coworkers[25] clearly demonstrated that sterile hollow tubes implanted in connective tissue and bone, respectively, are well tolerated and exhibit no persistent inflammation. Torneck further demonstrated that when the tubes were filled with sterile autogenous organic tissue, a mild inflammatory response was observed. When he deliberately contaminated the organic tissue in the tubes before implantation, he was able to demonstrate a persistent severe inflammatory response.

Although complete debridement of complex root canal systems is seldom possible using today's techniques, the degree to which debris is removed from the system can be improved by using irrigating solutions that are bacterocidal and that dissolve necrotic tissues or enhance their physical removal.

Sodium hypochlorite (NaOCl)

Sodium hypochlorite occurs as a clear, pale, green-yellow liquid with a strong odor of chlorine. It is miscible with water and is decomposed by light. It is a strongly alkaline solution. It is commercially available in a variety of concentrations, but the 5.25% solutions of household bleach appears to be the most popular source.

Sodium hypochlorite is perhaps the most popular irrigating solution in endodontics today. Walker[26] first suggested its use in root canal therapy in 1936. Grossman and Mieman[27] demonstrated the tissue-dissolving ability of chlorinated soda when used double strength in 1941 and recommended its use as an intracanal medicament. The double strength chlorinated soda is essentially the same as a 5% solution of sodium hypochlorite. This solution exhibits a dual mode of action. Its ability to dissolve necrotic tissue is attributed to its high alkalinity. Its germicidal property is related to the formation of hypochlorous acid on release from chlorine in solution. The antibacterial action of the hypochlorous acid is by oxidation of sulfhydryl groups of bacterial enzyme systems, thereby disrupting the metabolism of the organism.

The chlorine is extremely active and readily binds

with organic debris. This combination inhibits the formation of hypochlorous acid, resulting in decreased effectiveness. Maximal germicidal potential therefore cannot be realized until debridement is completed.

In the past several years, there has been considerable interest in the toxicity of intracanal irrigating solutions and medicaments. Several studies have been reported relative to the efficacy and toxicity of sodium hypochlorite in various concentrations. Spangberg[28] reported in 1973 on the cytotoxicity and antimicrobial efficacy of a variety of endodontic antiseptics. His findings revealed that a 0.5% solution of sodium hypochlorite (modified Dakin's solution) was sufficient to provide germicidal activity but was considerably less cytotoxic to tissue culture than was the 5% solution. However, the effect of the reduced concentration on the ability to dissolve organic debris was not investigated.

In 1975 Baker and coworkers[20] reported an in vitro study relative to the thoroughness of debridement and found a reduced concentration (1.0%) of sodium hypochlorite to be no more effective in this respect than physiologic saline. However, they were able to correlate the degree of debridement to the volume of irrigating solution used.

In 1977 Trepagnier, Madden, and Lazzari,[15] comparing a 5% solution with a 2.5% solution and a 0.5% solution, found the 5% and 2.5% solutions to be significantly more effective than the 0.5% solution in dissolving organic material.

In a clinical study, Harrison, Svec, and Baumgartner[29] related postendodontic treatment pain to toxicity and found that a 5% solution caused no greater incidence of posttreatment pain when compared to physiologic saline as the control. They concluded that the toxicity of 5% sodium hypochlorite in a biologic system was clinically insignificant.

Because the primary purpose of an irrigating solution is to aid in debridement, it would appear from these studies that either a 2.5% solution or a 5% solution of sodium hypochlorite used with care and in copious amounts would satisfy both the solvent and antibacterial requirements for a root canal irrigating solution.

Urea (CH$_4$N$_2$O)

Urea occurs as a white crystalline powder that is virtually odorless. It is soluble in water in the ratio of 1 gm urea to about 1.5 ml water. Thus a saturated solution is approximately 40% urea by weight. In this concentration, it serves as a mild solvent of necrotic tissue and pus and as a mild antiseptic. Urea solution was used as a therapeutic dressing for infected wounds during World War I.

In 1951 Blechman and Cohen[30] suggested that a 30% urea solution be used as a root canal wash in patients in whom vital pulp extirpation was performed as well as in patients with necrotic pulps. They also suggested that the urea solution was an excellent vehicle for antimicrobial agents such as sulfonamides. Urea is virtually nontoxic and nonirritating to periapical tissues. It has the property of chemically debriding wounds by softening the underlying substratum of fibrin. Urea denatures protein by destroying the hydrogen bonds of the secondary structure, resulting in loss of functional activity of the protein. This mode of action is responsible for its antiseptic activity.

Although urea is not as effective an antiseptic or necrotic tissue solvent as sodium hypochlorite, its low toxicity makes it an excellent substitute for many patients in whom a vital, uninfected pulp has been extirpated or in other situations in which large areas of vital tissue are involved (e.g., wide open apices or perforative resorptive defects).

Hydrogen peroxide (H_2O_2)

Hydrogen peroxide occurs as a clear, odorless liquid. It is highly unstable and is decomposed by heat and light. It rapidly disassociates into nascent oxygen and water on contact with the tissue enzymes catalase and peroxidase. The liberated oxygen has some bactericidal effect, but this effect is transient and is rapidly diminished in the presence of organic debris. Its antibacterial action is attributed to its oxidizing action by binding neighboring sulfhydryl groups of bacterial enzyme systems, thereby interfering with bacterial metabolism.[31]

Hydrogen peroxide in a 3% solution is used extensively as a cleansing agent in wound debridement. It is also widely used as an intracanal irrigant. The rapid release of oxygen on contact with organic tissue results in an effervescence or bubbling action, which is thought to aid in mechanical debridement by dislodging particles of necrotic tissue and dentin debris and floating them to the surface. This property was confirmed by Brown and Doran[32] in 1975. This beneficial effect, however, was evidenced only when the solution is deposited in close contact with the ma-

terial to be removed. Again, it is necessary to enlarge the canal sufficiently to deposit the solution in close proximity to the apical extent of the root canal system.

Many clinicians prefer to irrigate alternately with sodium hypochlorite and hydrogen peroxide. These substances when in contact with each other speed the release of nascent oxygen from the peroxide and chlorine from the hypochlorite. The result is increased effervescence and increased germicidal activity. Although Svec and Harrison[33] demonstrated superior debridement using this technique when compared to using physiologic saline, McComb and Smith[34] found that the use of sodium hypochlorite alone was more effective in this respect than alternating irrigation with hydrogen peroxide.

A 30% aqueous solution of hydrogen peroxide is used in dentistry for bleaching of discolored vital and pulpless teeth. This solution is an extremely strong oxidizing agent. It is highly irritating to vital tissues and caution must be exercised with its use. It must *never* be used as an intracanal agent.

Urea peroxide ($CH_4N_2O \cdot H_2O_2$)

Urea peroxide is a white crystalline powder with a slight odor. It is soluble in water, alcohol, glycerine, and propylene glycol. It decomposes rapidly when exposed to heat, light, or moisture. It disassociates into urea and hydrogen peroxide. Its stability is greatly increased when placed in an anhydrous glycerol solution.

A 10% solution of urea peroxide in an anhydrous glycerol base is available commercially (Glyoxide) and has been used as an intracanal irrigating solution with considerable success.[35] This preparation provides the desirable irrigational properties of both urea and hydrogen peroxide. It is more stable and more germicidal than aqueous hydrogen peroxide alone. The anhydrous glycerol, in addition to increasing the stability of the urea peroxide, serves as an excellent lubricant and facilitates negotiation and instrumentation of thin, tortuous root canals.

Because it disassociates more slowly than aqueous hydrogen peroxide, the effervescence of urea peroxide is prolonged but not as pronounced. The effervescence can be accelerated by alternating irrigation with sodium hypochlorite. The slow release of oxygen provides for nonselective antimicrobial activity by the same mode of action as aqueous hydrogen peroxide.

A host of other agents have been used over the years for irrigation during root canal preparation. Most of them such as tincture of green soap, benzalkonium chloride, 9-aminoacridine, and sulfuric acid have been abandoned because they were ineffective or cytotoxic or they exhibited some undesirable side effects.

It must be remembered that the primary function of the irrigating solution is to aid in the physical removal of organic and inorganic debris by its flushing action and/or its necrotic tissue solvent action. Its antibacterial activity assumes a secondary albeit beneficial role.

INTRACANAL MEDICAMENTS

As already stated, the most important aspect of root canal treatment relative to success and healing is thorough debridement. Elimination of microorganisms is achieved primarily during chemomechanical preparation of the root canal system. Thorough cleansing and shaping remove the organic substrate on which microorganisms thrive. What then are the purposes of intracanal medicaments? The answer to this question has served admirably as a basis for discussion and debate. The literature is replete with studies that demonstrate the effectiveness of one or the other medicament as an antimicrobial agent. What has not been proven is that any medicament is superior to another in terms of success after root canal treatment. Indeed, many dentists have adopted the clinical practice of using *no* intracanal medicament.

Although Stewart[8] and Auerbach[9] have demonstrated that negative cultures can be achieved following chemomechanical preparation alone, about one fourth of the root canals become reinfected between appointments. The rationale for use of antimicrobial intracanal medicaments is to provide an environment in the root canal system that is unsuitable for microbial growth.

Some medicaments are used because of their ability to "fix" or "mummify" organic material that remains in the root canal system. Although this concept has some merit when the canal system is extremely complex and it is literally impossible to adequately debride the canals (as in some primary teeth), it must be remembered that this is essentially a compromise. We must guard against the temptation to do a less than thorough debridement and to rely on intracanal agents to compensate for this shortcoming.

Some intracanal medicaments are used to minimize interappointment pain. Included in this group are the antimicrobial obtundents, such as metacresyl acetate and eugenol, and the antiinflammatory steroidal agents. Here again the practitioner must be judicious. The most common causes of interappointment pain are overinstrumentation, careless irrigation, and overmedication. Extreme care must be used during root canal preparation to avoid placing instruments into the periapical tissues, to avoid forcing debris into the tissues, or to forcibly irrigate so as to injury the periapical tissues. If care is taken, there will be little reason to employ steroids to minimize the inflammatory response.

Historically, intracanal medicaments have been classified as nonspecific and specific agents. This classification was based on the antimicrobial action of the medicaments. Although many of the agents are used for reasons other than their antimicrobial action, this classification can still be used for consistency and simplicity.

Nonspecific intracanal medicaments

Nonspecific intracanal medicaments are generally classified as antiseptics. In appropriate concentrations and prolonged contact, they are effective against all forms of microbial life. Although their exact mode of action varies and is sometimes unknown, they are considered to be protoplasmic poisons, (i.e., they cause structural damage or functional disturbance to the living cell). Unfortunately, they are nonselective in their action and damage host cells as well as bacteria. Consequently, injudicious use may cause severe damage to periapical tissues and interfere with or prevent healing.

There has been considerable emphasis in recent years on using reduced concentrations and smaller dosages of many of these agents to minimize the cytotoxic effects on host tissues yet still maintain antimicrobial effectiveness.

Phenol (C_6H_5OH)

Although phenol is rarely used as an intracanal medicament in the modern practice of endodontics, it is included here because many of the agents in use today are derivatives of phenol and are similar to phenol in chemical structure (Fig. 36-1).

In high concentrations (1% or 2% aqueous solutions) phenol is a strong germicidal agent although not as effective as some of its derivatives. Phenol is obtained from the distillate of coal tar or certain petroleum products.

Phenol is a protoplasmic poison that disrupts the

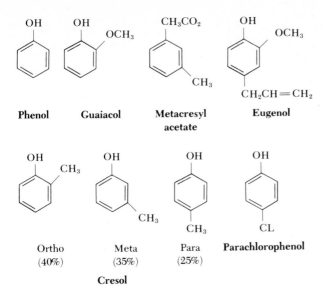

Phenol   Guaiacol   Metacresyl   Eugenol
                          acetate

Ortho   Meta   Para   Parachlorophenol
(40%)   (35%)   (25%)

Cresol

Fig. 36-1. Chemical structures of phenol and its derivatives.

cell wall and precipitates cellular protein, causing coagulation and loss of function. It is equally toxic to viable host cells and bacteria. The protein coagulum resulting from the reaction with phenol establishes a relatively impermeable barrier and limits further penetration of the drug, thus protecting the more central accumulations of microorganisms.

Because more effective medicaments have been developed and because of the high toxicity of phenol, its use in endodontics has been virtually abandoned.

Eugenol ($C_{10}H_{12}O_2$)

Eugenol occurs as a clear, colorless or pale yellow liquid, having a strong odor of cloves. It is only slightly soluble in water but is freely miscible with alcohol.

Eugenol is a phenolic compound that is classified as an essential oil and is the principal constituent of oil of cloves. Eugenol is a mild antiseptic and an anodyne. Its mode of action as an antiseptic is virtually the same as that of phenolic compounds. It is a protoplasmic poison, causing precipitation of cellular protein. Eugenol is highly irritating to vital tissue and precipitates an inflammatory response in tissues that it contacts. Its anodyne action frequently masks this inflammatory response. Because of its toxicity, it is seldom used as an intracanal medicament. It has been used, however, in pulpotomy procedures for the relief of pain. Unfortunately, when so used it often pre-

cipitates an asymptomatic inflammatory response in the remaining pulp tissue. In such tissue it is frequently difficult to achieve profound anesthesia for pulp extirpation at a subsequent appointment.

Beechwood creosote

Beechwood creosote is a mixture of phenols but is primarily (60% to 90%) guaiacol. It is a clear, colorless or pale yellow liquid with a pungent, smokey odor. It is only slightly soluble in water but is fully miscible with alcohol.

Beechwood creosote was introduced to the dental profession in 1830 by Reichenbach and was used principally to devitalize the pulps of painful teeth. It is less toxic and more germicidal than phenol; however, by today's standards its toxicity is too great. Its mode of action is the same as that of phenol (i.e., it causes protein coagulation). Attalla[36] clearly demonstrated its severe irritating potential to vital tissues. Its use as an endodontic intracanal medicament has been abandoned.

Cresol ($C_6H_4CH_3OH$)

Cresol is a mixture of orthomethylphenols, metamethylphenols, and paramethylphenols (Fig. 36-1). It occurs as a colorless, yellow or straw-colored liquid with a pungent phenolic odor. It is slightly soluble in water but is fully miscible with alcohol and glycerine. Its germicidal activity is four times as great as phenol, and it is slightly less toxic than phenol. It is obtained as a distillate from coal tar. It is a strong antiseptic with a mode of action similar to phenol but is said to be more active and less toxic than phenol. Its use as an intracanal agent has been abandoned because of its toxicity. However, it is used in combination with formalin and glycerin available commercially as formocresol (see below).

Formocresol

Formocresol, in spite of its toxicity, is a popular intracanal antiseptic and is also widely used as a "mummifying" agent in vital pulpotomies. It is a combination of orthocresol (35%) and formalin (19%) in a water-glycerin vehicle. It is a clear, slightly reddish solution with a distinctive, pungent odor.

The formaldehyde and cresol are both antiseptics and act as protoplasmic poisons. However, it appears that the ability of formaldehyde to "fix" tissue is responsible to a great degree for its popularity in clinical practice.

When formocresol is placed in the pulp chamber,

formaldehyde gas is released from the solution and readily diffuses throughout the root canal system and, if care is not taken, sometimes beyond the root canal and into the periapical tissues. It is highly toxic to viable tissues as well as to microorganisms. The action of formaldehyde is rapid and produces complex cross-linkages between proteins. This characteristic is responsible for its popularity as an agent for vital pulpotomies. Tissue thus affected has a lesser tendency to break down and act as a chronic irritant to the viable periapical tissues. There is some evidence that this ''mummified'' tissue can be phagocytosed and replaced with fibrous connective tissue.[37,38]

The mode of action of formocresol is thought to be related to its ability to bind peptide groups of side-chain amino acids and to link adjacent protein molecules by the formation of methylene bridges between their peptide groups. This binding thus prevents autolysis. Berger[37] suggests that the tissue thus affected maintains the basic overall structure of its protein, but the chemical reactivity of the protein is destroyed. He classifies formalin as an additive non-coagulation fixative, whereas Torneck[12] describes the effect of formalin on tissue as coagulation necrosis.

Berger[37] also contends that the chemical binding caused by formaldehyde is reversible, with the bond being hydrolysed by enzymatic action. He reported cases in which the ''mummified'' tissue was replaced by an ingrowth of granulation tissue and he considers this a favorable response. The implication is that the granulation tissue is eventually replaced by fibrous connective tissue.

Several studies[28,39,40] have clearly demonstrated that formocresol is an extremely cytotoxic agent and must be used judiciously and with caution.

Straffon and Han[17] and Loos and Han[18] suggest that reducing the concentration of formocresol can minimize its cytotoxic effect while sacrificing little of its effectiveness as an intracanal antiseptic.

Metacresyl acetate (Cresatin) ($C_8H_{10}CO_2$)

Metacresyl acetate is a clear, colorless, oily liquid with a strong phenolic odor. It is the acetic acid este of metacresol. It is fungicidal but only slightly antibacterial. It has a low surface tension, which allows for dissemination through the root canal system by capillary action. This feature enhances its effectiveness.

Metacresyl acetate has an anodyne effect on inflamed vital tissue and is only slightly irritating. For these reasons its use as an intracanal medicament is recommended in vital pulpectomies or preendodontic vital pulpotomies. Metacresyl acetate (Cresatin) has supplanted eugenol as the medicament of choice in these instances because it has similar obtundant qualities while being less irritating than eugenol.

The antibacterial mode of action, though not as pronounced, is similar to that of other phenolic compounds.

Parachlorophenol (C_6H_4ClOH)

Parachlorophenol is a clear, colorless or slightly pink crystalline material. It has a pungent, distinctive odor. The crystals are highly deliquescent and must be stored in a tightly sealed container. It is only slightly soluble in water but is very soluble in alcohol, metacresol acetate, and eugenol. It is soluble in camphor in the ratio of 30 to 35 parts parachlorophenol to 65 to 70 parts of gum camphor crystals. This mixture of two crystals will yield a eutectic liquid solution of camphorated parachlorophenol. Gurney[41] has stated that the substitution of a halogen atom for a hydrogen atom in the benzene ring of phenol will increase its antiseptic potential. The specific halogen and its position in the molecule will determine the extent of increased antimicrobial potency. Chlorine in the para position has proven to be one of the most effective halogenated phenols. Gurney further states that a change in polarity of the phenol molecule will alter its reactivity and germicidal effectiveness. When the chlorine ion is substituted at the para position, there is a significant decrease in polarity and increase in the reactivity and antimicrobial effectiveness. The mode of antibacterial action is not clearly understood, but it is essentially the same as that of other phenolic compounds. In addition to the protein coagulation caused by its phenolic component, the release of chlorine from the molecule reacts with sulfhydryl groups of bacterial enzymes, causing disulfide linkages resulting in metabolic interference.

Camphorated parachlorophenol (35%)

Camphorated parachlorophenol was introduced to the dental profession in 1891 by Walkoff for use as an intracanal medicament. It is a clear, slightly yellow or pink oily liquid with a pungent distinctive odor of camphor. This eutectic solution is made by mixing parachlorophenol crystals with gum camphor crystals. The eutectic phenomenon occurs only at or near the ratio of 3 or 3.5 parts of parachlorophenol to 6.5

or 7 parts of gum camphor. The commercially available camphorated parachlorophenol is usually a 35% solution.

Camphorated parachlorophenol is an extremely active antibacterial agent and, although the camphor reduces the irritation potential of parachlorophenol, it is very toxic to vital tissues. The camphor also slows the release of chlorine from the molecule thereby prolonging its antibacterial activity.

Aqueous parachlorophenol (1.0%)

Harrison and Madonia[16] in an in vitro study demonstrated that chlorophenol in a 1.0% aqueous solution was an effective antimicrobial agent. In comparing the aqueous solution with a 35% camphorated solution in a serial dilution study, they found that the camphorated solution was 350 times as powerful as what was needed as an antiseptic against microorganisms commonly found in root canals. Furthermore, the camphorated parachlorophenol was extremely irritating to vital tissues in rabbit eye and subcutaneous tests when compared to the 1.0% aqueous solutions.[29]

Avny and coworkers[42] and Taylor and coworkers[43] demonstrated that reduced aqueous concentrations (1.0% to 2.0%) of parachlorophenol penetrated further into dentinal tubules than did camphorated parachlorophenol.

The aqueous solution of parachlorophenol has the same mode of antibacterial action as the camphorated solution but is significantly less toxic.

Since it is not available commercially, the 1.0% solution must be compounded by a pharmacist on prescription.

Parachlorophenol-camphor-metacresylacetate

In 1957 Dietz[44] introduced a combination medicament that was compounded using 25% parachlorophenol, 25% metacresylacetate, and 50% gum camphor by weight. It is available commercially under a variety of proprietory names.

Dietz suggested that this medicament combined the antibacterial activity of camphorated parachlorophenol with the anodyne effect of metacresylacetate. However, there is no scientific evidence to support this rationale.

Dietz also contended that this agent remained active in the presence of pus, serum, and blood, an opinion that has not been substantiated by scientific evidence. Although the toxicity of this combination

drug has not been adequately investigated, it has been assumed to be less toxic than camphorated parachlorophenol and more toxic than metacresylacetate alone.

The mode of action is the same as that of each constituent of the mixture.

Iodine potassium iodide (IKI)

In recent years iodine potassium iodide has gained popularity as an intracanal medicament in the United States. It has long been used for this purpose in Scandinavian countries, and its rise in popularity can be attributed to the many studies relative to antimicrobial activity and toxicity reported by Spangberg, Engström, and Langeland.[45-48] In their studies they found both a 2.0% and a 5.0% solution effective against a variety of microorganisms that are found in root canals. They also found that a 2.0% solution was least toxic to tissue culture cells when compared to a variety of popularly used intracanal agents. The 5.0% solution was only slightly more toxic.

Two percent iodine potassium iodide solution is compounded by mixing 2 parts iodine, 4 parts potassium iodide, and 94 parts distilled water by weight. The resultant red-brown liquid is strongly antiseptic. Because iodine is a strong oxidizing agent, it reacts with free sulfhydryl groups of bacterial enzymes, resulting in disulfide linkages and interfering with enzyme metabolic activity.[31] The principal disadvantage to the use of iodine solutions is that occasionally patients will manifest allergic reactions.

SPECIFIC AGENTS

Antibiotics and sulfonamides are the two groups of specific antimicrobial agents that have been used as intracanal agents in endodontics. The use of antibiotics as intracanal agents enjoyed considerable popularity in the 1950s and 1960s. In recent years, however, their use in clinical practice has diminished greatly. Antibiotics have been used alone and in combination with other specific or nonspecific agents. The polyantibiotic mixtures introduced by Grossman[49] were the most widely used specific intracanal agents.

Polyantibiotic mixture
PBSC

PBSC is a polyantibiotic mixture containing potassium, penicillin G (1,000,000 units), bacitracin (10,000 units), streptomycin sulfate (1 gm), and caprylate sodium (1 gm) in 3 ml of DC200 silicone fluid.[50] The penicillin is used to destroy gram-positive microorganisms, the bacitracin is for penicillin-resistant microorganisms, the streptomycin is for gram-negative microorganisms, and the sodium caprylate is for yeasts. This mixture has been demonstrated to have a marked antimicrobial effect and to be relatively nontoxic to viable tissues.[28,51] There was some concern that the sodium caprylate was irritating to the periapical tissues, and nystatin was substituted in later formulations.

The objections to the use of polyantibiotic pastes as intracanal agents are (1) the possibility of precipitating an allergic response in sensitized patients, (2) the possibility of sensitizing the patient to penicillin, and (3) the possibility of interference with culturing by drug carryover. Although there is no definitive proof substantiating or denying the objections, the popularity of intracanal antibiotics has decreased drastically over the past several years.

Grossman, who introduced the polyantibiotic combination and reported several studies on its effectiveness, has excluded it from discussion in the most recent edition of his textbook.[52]

Discussion of PBSC is included here only because of its historic significance and because of the tendency of endodontists to continue to debate its relative merits.

Sulfonamides
Sulfathiazole

Sulfathiazole, mixed into a paste with water, has been recommended as an intracanal medicament. Ostby[53] first introduced it for this purpose in 1956. Its topical antiseptic activity has not been established, and since it is bacteriostatic rather than bactericidal, its use as an intracanal agent has been virtually abandoned. Ostby and later Frank and coworkers[54] did demonstrate, however, that the incidence of postendodontic treatment pain was reduced if a paste of sulfathiazole and water was placed into the root canal system following canal instrumentation. Its mode of action in this respect is not understood. Although no adverse effects have been reported using sulfathiazole in the root canal system, it should not be used in patients with known sulfa drug allergies.

Weisman[55] reported that tooth discoloration may occur if sodium hypochlorite solutions are used for irrigation during removal of sulfathiazole from the canal.

Sulfathiazole loses much of its antibacterial potency in the presence of pus, blood, and paraamino-benzoic acid, and therefore its effectiveness in the root canal is limited.

Paraaminotoluene sulfonamide

Paraaminotoluene sulfonamide (PATS) was introduced by Gurney and coworkers[56] in 1958. They contend that it is a highly active antibacterial agent that retains its effectiveness in the presence of paraaminobenzoic acid, pus, and necrotic tissue. It is effective against a wide range of bacteria but is ineffective against yeasts and fungi. In 1965 Sawinski and Gurney[57] combined the paraaminotoluene sulfonamide with an antifungal agent, 5-nitro-2-methylfurfuryl ether, and found that not only was the antifungal activity satisfactory but also that the antibacterial potency of the paraaminotoluene sulfonamide was enhanced.

There are no data available relative to toxicity, but the authors suggest that very little toxic effect is possible because very low concentrations are used. This combination is available commercially as Microcide A in a liquid form or as impregnated absorbent paper points. Despite the claims of its superiority as an antimicrobial agent, sulfa-containing antiseptics have lost considerable popularity mainly because readily available nonspecific agents have proven to be effective intracanal antibacterial agents and because the claims of superiority of sulfa-containing agents have not been substantiated.

SPECIAL PURPOSE AGENTS
Corticosteroids

Several agents used as intracanal dressings in endodontics fall into a separate category because their use is advocated only when special conditions warrant it. One such condition is the situation in which a patient is experiencing pain following root canal treatment. Such secondary apical periodontitis is manifested by severe pain and extreme sensitivity to touch or palpation. In many of these cases, isolation of the tooth with a rubber dam and reentry into the root canal produces immediate relief when drainage is established. However, when no relief occurs and no drainage results, further measures must be taken. It is these situations that prompted the introduction of steroidal antiinflammatory agents to endodontics.

Wolfson[58] in 1954 reported that hydrocortisone applied to the root canal could minimize posttreatment pain. He cautioned, however, that since the inflammatory response (hence the defensive response) is reduced, the periapical tissues are particularly susceptible to infection. Corticosteroids have the ability to modify the manifestations of inflammation. They do this by limiting the vascular changes associated with inflammation (i.e., they minimize capillary dilatation and permeability and stabilize lysosomal membranes, preventing the release of vasoactive kinins and enzymes). However, they also inhibit capillary proliferation, protein synthesis, and fibroplasia, thus retarding repair. Because the steroids exhibit inhibition of the natural defense of the host, extreme caution must be exercised in their use. The increased susceptibility to infection is of particular concern.

Schroeder[59] suggested the combination of a broad-spectrum antibiotic with the steroid to minimize the danger from infection.

These combination agents, like all intracanal medicaments, are essentially topical agents and act locally. There has been virtually no evidence to implicate generalized systemic steroidal or antibacterial effects with their use. Klotz, Gerstein, and Bahn[60] did, however, demonstrate that the topical application of corticosteroid to exposed pulp could result in a bacteremia and cautioned against their injudicious use.

Antibiotic-steroid combination
Triamcinolone acetonide and demeclocycline

The 1960s and 1970s experienced a resurgence of a philosophy of therapeutics in endodontics that encouraged the use of a variety of agents for vital pulp therapy. One agent that gained widespread attention in the literature is the combination of 1% triamcinolone acetonide (a synthetic corticosteroid) and 3% demeclocycline (a broad-spectrum antibiotic) suspended in a water-soluble cream base and available commercially as Ledermix. This agent was used extensively for the treatment of exposed, infected pulps in an attempt to preserve vitality and minimize pain. Success in this respect has been reported by several investigators.[59,61] In 1968 Schneider[61] reported a clinical study using this combination as an intracanal medicament following root canal preparation. He evaluated its efficacy as an antibacterial agent and found it to be as effective as camphorated parachlorophenol. He also reported that in most cases it was effective in relieving pain and discomfort.

Triamcinolone acetonide, nystatin, neomycin sulfate, and gramicidin

Another combination that has been used in endodontics for the relief and prevention of pain was reported in 1971 by VanCura and Remeikis.[62] In their clinical study, they used a combination of triamcinolone acetonide (1 mg), nystatin (100,000 units), neomycin sulfate (2.5 mg), and gramicidin (0.25 mg), available commercially as Mycolog. It is a topical preparation used for dermatologic bacterial and fungal infection. When VanCura and Remeikis used it as an intracanal medicament, they found that 86% of teeth that developed symptoms following root canal treatment exhibited relief of pain within 1 hour after application of the combination to the root canal. No adverse side effects were noted.

Calcium hydroxide ($Ca(OH)_2$)

Another special purpose agent that is accumulating an increasing number of indications for its use is calcium hydroxide. Its popularity in endodontics is growing at a phenomenal rate. In spite of the voluminous research conducted and reported on calcium hydroxide, its mode of action is unknown.

It was first introduced to dentistry as a pulp capping agent by Herman[63] in 1930. Since that time, it has been used for direct and indirect pulp capping procedures where its effect is thought to be the stimulation of reparative dentin elaboration,[64] although the calcium from calcium hydroxide does not contribute directly to dentin bridge formation.[65,66] Calcium hydroxide is also used in pulpotomy procedures as well as apexification and apexogenesis procedures.[67,68,69] More recently, its use has been suggested in the treatment of external resorptive defects resulting from traumatic injuries and to repair accidental or pathologic perforations of the root canal system into the periodontal ligament.[70]

Calcium hydroxide has also been recommended as the intracanal agent of choice in horizontal root fractures. Periradicular bone destruction is a common feature in horizontal root fractures; calcium hydroxide has been used successfully as an intracanal dressing in these cases to promote healing of the bone and in some instances fibrous or calcific reunion of the root fracture segments.

Successful treatment of all of these types of situations has been achieved to a greater or lesser degree with calcium hydroxide as the agent. As stated earlier, its mode of action is unknown, and it is unlikely that the calcium deposited during repair is provided by the dressing. Although the inductive effect of calcium hydroxide has been observed and some investigators suggest that the high pH of this material may be responsible for this effect, this hypothesis has not been substantiated and similar results have not been achieved using other materials with an equally alkaline pH.

Calcium hydroxide is bactericidal as a result of its high pH, and in some instances its routine use as an intracanal medicament has been advocated. This practice has not gained significant support in the United States, but it is widespread in some European countries.

Finally, calcium hydroxide placed as an interim root canal dressing has the ability in some instances to inhibit exudation into the prepared root canal. Frank[71] suggests that this may be caused by "the absorbency of the material"; however, its mode of action here again is unknown.

The rationale for selection of calcium hydroxide in the wide variety of conditions described is based almost completely on empiricism. Favorable results have been achieved to a greater or lesser degree in all of these instances, but by no means is the prognosis predictable.

Disodium ethylenediaminetetraacetate (disodium EDTA)

Ethylenediaminetetraacetic acid is a white, crystalline solid and is virtually insoluble in water. The disodium salt of the acid, however, is freely soluble.

Disodium EDTA is a chelating agent that was introduced to the dental profession for the purpose of facilitating root canal preparation by Ostby[72] in 1957. He recommended the use of a 15% buffered solution as an intracanal agent for softening the dentin walls of the root canals. Its action is to liberate its sodium and chelate the calcium from the dentin, resulting in partial demineralization of the canal wall. Although Patterson[73] suggested that the chelating action of disodium EDTA continues for several days after application, it is generally understood that since the agent becomes inactive when it combines with the calcium, it is essentially self-limiting. Disodium EDTA is very effective in its chelating action, and care in its use must be exercised to prevent ledging, perforation, or instrumenting a channel instead of negotiating the root canal. This agent will penetrate and soften dentin to a depth of 20 to 30 μm, following a 5-minute application.[74] Therefore it is important to discontinue use of the agent before completion of the root canal preparation. Failure to do so will result in softened dentin remaining, which could cause an inadequate seal in the final root canal filling.[75]

The buffered 15% solution of disodium EDTA is essentially nontoxic and nonirritating to periapical tissues. The solution is available commercially or can be compounded as follows:

Disodium ethylenediaminetetraacetate	17.0 gm
Distilled water	100.0 ml
5N Sodium hydroxide	9.25 ml

Disodium EDTA is also available in combination with other agents. One of the early combinations introduced for use in root canal therapy was a proprietary by the name of EDTAC. It is a 15% buffered solution of disodium EDTA to which cetavlon, a quaternary ammonium compound, was added. The quaternary ammonium compound was added to provide antibacterial activity. This combination agent is only slightly irritating to viable tissues and can be considered to be only slightly cytotoxic.

R.C. Prep. is a commercially available combination agent developed by Stewart, Kapsimalis, and Rappaport.[76] It is disodium EDTA combined with urea peroxide in a water-soluble polyethelene glycol vehicle. It combines the chelating activity of disodium EDTA and the solvent, antibacterial, and effervescent characteristics of urea peroxide. The polyethelene glycol vehicle protects the disodium EDTA from oxidation by the peroxide and also serves as an excellent lubricant.

Irrigation of this combination agent with sodium hypochlorite solution acts much the same as alternating irrigation of sodium hypochlorite and hydrogen peroxide (active effervescence and bubbling). The sodium hypochlorite inactivates the urea peroxide and disodium EDTA. The same precautions must be taken when using any agent containing disodium EDTA as when using disodium EDTA alone.

• • •

In summary, this chapter has dealt with the more commonly used intracanal agents in endodontics and some of the historic significance. No attempt has been made to be all inclusive because many of the agents are no longer used, have no current clinical significance, or have very little scientific evidence to support a rationale for their use.

Although the search for the ideal agents continues, it must be remembered that thorough mechanical debridement and instrumentation and obturation of the root canal system are critical to success in endodontics. The intracanal agents discussed here assume only secondary roles in achieving these objectives.

REFERENCES

1. Miller, W.D.: Gangrenous tooth pulps as centers of infection, Dent. Cosmos **30:**213-214, 1888.
2. Miller, W.D.: Bacteriology as an integral part of the dental curriculum, Dent. Cosmos **33:**101-105, 1891.
3. Black, G.V.: Infectious and septic matter in teeth, Dent. Items Int. **13:**663-665, 1891.
4. Peck, A.H.: Formaldehyde: its antiseptic and irritating properties, Dent. Dig. **4:**407-413, 1898.
5. Black, G.V.: Discussion on essential oils, Den. Rev. **11:**631-633, 1898.
6. Black, G.V.: Essential oils, Pract. Dent. **2:**328, 1889.
7. Onderdonk, T.W.: The treatment of unfilled root canals, Int. Dent. J. **22:**20-22, 1901.
8. Stewart, G.G.: The importance of chemomechanical preparation of the root canal, Oral Surg. **8:**993-997, 1955.
9. Auerbach, M.D.: Antibiotics vs. instrumentation in endodontics, N.Y. State Dent. J. **19:**225-228, 1953.
10. Ingle, J.I., and Zeldow, B.J.: An evaluation of mechanical instrumentation and the negative culture in endodontic therapy, J. Am. Dent. Assoc. **57:**471-476, 1958.
11. Engström, B., and Lundberg, M.: Frequency and causes of reversal from negative to positive bacteriological tests in root canal therapy, Odontol. Tidskr. **74:**189-195, 1966.
12. Torneck, C.D.: Therapeutic armamentarium. In Clark, J.W., editor: Clinical dentistry, vol. 4, New York, 1978, Harper & Row, Publishers, Inc.
13. Abou-Rass, M., and Oglesby, S.W.: The effects of temperature, concentration and tissue type on the solvent ability of sodium hypochlorite, J. Endodont. **7:**376-377, 1981.
14. Hand, R.E., Smith, M.L., and Harrison, J.W.: Analysis of the effect of dilution on necrotic tissue dissolution property of sodium hypochlorite, J. Endodont. **4:**60-64, 1978.
15. Trepagnier, C.M., Madden, R.M., and Lazzari, E.P.: Quantitative study of sodium hypochlorite as an in vitro endo irrigant, J. Endodont. **3:**194-196, 1977.
16. Harrison, J.W., and Madonia, J.V.: Antimicrobial effectiveness of parachlorophenol, Oral Surg. **30:**267-275, 1970.
17. Straffon, L.H., and Han, S.S.: The effect of formocresol on hamster connective tissue cells: a histologic and quantitative autoradiographic study with proline H3, Arch. Oral Biol. **13:**271-288, 1968.
18. Loos, P.J., and Han, S.S.: An enzyme histochemical study of the effect of various concentrations of formocresol on connective tissue, Oral Surg. **31:**571-585, 1971.
19. Cwilka, J.R.: Vaporization and capillary effect of endodontic medicaments, Oral Surg. **34:**117-121, 1972.
20. Baker, N.A., et al.: Scanning electron microscopic study of the efficacy of various irrigating solutions, J. Endodont. **1:**127-135, 1975.
21. Schilder, H., Personal communication, 1977.
22. Cunningham, W.T., and Balkjian, A.Y.: Effect of temperature on the collagen dissolving ability of sodium hypochlorite endodontic irrigant, Oral Surg. **49:**175-177, 1980.
23. Torneck, C.D.: Reaction of rat connective tissue to polyethelene tube implants. I, Oral Surg. **21:**379-387, 1966.
24. Torneck, C.D.: Reaction of rat connective tissue to polyethelene tube implants. II, Oral Surg. **24:**674-683, 1967.
25. Wenger, J.S., et al.: The effects of partially filled polyethelene tube intraosseous implants in rats, Oral Surg. **46:**88-100, 1978.
26. Walker, A.: Definite and dependable therapy for pulpless teeth, J. Am. Dent. Assoc. **23:**1418, 1936.
27. Grossman, L.I., and Mieman, B.W.: Solution of pulp tissue by chemical agents, J. Am. Dent. Assoc. **28:**223-225, 1941.
28. Spangberg, L.: Cellular reaction to intracanal medicaments. In Grossman, L.I., editor: Transactions of the fifth international conference on endodontics, Philadelphia, 1973, University of Pennsylvania Press.
29. Harrison, J.W., Svec, T.A., and Baumgartner, J.C.: Analysis of clinical toxicity of endodontic irrigants, J. Endodont. **4:**6-11, 1978.
30. Blechman, H., and Cohen, M.: Use of aqueous urea solution in the field of endodontia, J. Dent. Res. **30:**503-504, 1951.
31. Jawetz, E., Melnick, J.L., and Adelberg, E.A.: Review of medical microbiology, ed. 14, Los Altos, 1980, Lange Medical Publications.
32. Brown, J.I., and Doran, J.E.: An in vitro evaluation of the particle flotation capability of various irrigating solutions, J. Calif. Dent. Assoc. **3:**60-63, 1975.
33. Svec, T., and Harrison, J.W.: Chemomechanical removal of pulpal and dentinal debris with sodium hypochlorite and hydrogen peroxide vs. normal saline solution, J. Endodont. **3:**49-53, 1977.
34. McComb, D., and Smith, D.C.: A preliminary scanning electron microscope study of root canals after endodontic procedures, J. Endodont. **1:**238-242, 1975.
35. Stewart, G.G., Cobe, H.M., and Rappaport, H.: A study of a new medicament in the chemomechanical preparation of infected root canals, J. Am. Dent. Assoc. **63:**33-37, 1961.
36. Attalla, M.N.: Effect of beechwood creosote and chloramine on periapical tissues of dogs, Aust. Dent. J. **34:**190-195, 1968.
37. Berger, J.E.: A review of the erroneously labeled "mummification" techniques of pulp therapy, Oral Surg. **34:**131-144, 1972.
38. Langeland, K., et al.: Human pulp changes of iatrogenic origin, Oral Surg. **32:**943-980, 1971.
39. Schilder, H., and Amsterdam, M.: Inflammatory potential of root canal medicaments. A preliminary report including nonspecific drugs, Oral Surg. **12:**211-221, 1959.
40. Vanderwall, G., Dawson, J., and Shipman, C.: Antimicrobial efficacy and cytotoxicity of three endodontic drugs, Oral Surg. **33:**230-241, 1972.
41. Gurney, B.F.: Substituted phenols III: chlorophenols, hexachlorophene, Dent. Dig. **78:**368-372, 1972.
42. Avny, W.Y., et al.: Autoradiographic studies of the intracanal diffusion of aqueous and camphorated parachlorophenol in endodontics, Oral Surg. **36:**80-89, 1973.
43. Taylor, G.N., et al.: In vivo autoradiographic study of the relative penetrating abilities of aqueous 2% parachlorophenol and camphorated 35% parachlorophenol, J. Endodont. **2:**81-86, 1976.
44. Dietz, V.H.: XP-7: a universal endodontic medicament, Oral Surg. **10:**1317-1322, 1957.
45. Engström, B., and Spangberg, L.: Studies on root canal medicaments. V. Toxic and antimicrobial effects of antiseptics in vitro, Sven. Tandlak. Tidskr. **62:**543-549, 1969.
46. Spangberg, L., and Engström, B.: Studies on root canal medicaments. I. Cytotoxic effect of root canal antiseptics, Acta Odontol. Scand. **25:**77-84, 1967.
47. Spangberg, L., and Engström, B.: Studies on root canal medi-

caments. IV. Antimicrobial effect of root canal medicaments, Odontol. Revy. (Malmo) **19:**187-195, 1968.

48. Spangberg, L., Engström, B., and Langeland, K.: Biologic effects of dental materials -3- toxicity and antimicrobial effects of endodontic antiseptics in vitro, Oral Surg. **36:**856-871, 1973.

49. Grossman, L.I.: Polyantibiotic treatment of pulpless teeth, J. Am. Dent. Assoc. **43:**265-278, 1951.

50. Grossman, L.I.: Endodontic practice, ed. 9, Philadelphia, 1978, Lea & Febiger.

51. Burke, G.W., and Knighton, H.W.: Effect of local antibacterial agents on bacteria in dental pulps of rats, J. Dent. Res. **41:**1105, 1962.

52. Grossman, L.I.: Endodontic practice, ed. 10, Philadelphia, 1981, Lea & Febiger.

53. Ostby, B.N.: Introduction to endodontics, Oslo, 1971, Universitetforlaget.

54. Frank, A.L., et al.: The intracanal use of sulfathiazole in endodontics to reduce pain, J. Am. Dent. Assoc. **77:**102-106, 1968.

55. Weisman, M.I.: The interaction of sulfathiazole and sodium hypochlorite causing discoloration in endodontics, J. Ga. Dent. Assoc. **52:**17-18, 1969.

56. Gurney, B.F., et al.: Endodontic therapy with para-aminotoluene sulfonamide (Benzylog), J. Am. Dent. Assoc. **56:**329-335, 1958.

57. Sawinski, V.J., and Gurney, B.F.: Antifungal properties of a new endodontic antiseptic containing 5-nitro-2-methylfurfuryl ether, J. Dent. Res. **44:**1334-1337, 1965.

58. Wolfson, B.L.: Role of hydrocortisone in the control of apical periodontitis, Oral Surg. **7:**314-321, 1954.

59. Schroeder, A.: Corticosteroids in endodontics, J. Oral Ther. **2:**171-179, 1965.

60. Klotz, M.D., Gerstein, H., and Bahn, A.H.: Bacteremia after topical use of prednisolone in infected pulps, J. Am. Dent. Assoc. **71:**871-875, 1965.

61. Schneider, D.W.: Triamcinolone acetonide-demethylchlortetracycline HCL treatment in endodontic practice, J. Oral Med. **23:**51-55, 1968.

62. VanCura, J., and Remeikis, N.: Corticosteroid-antibiotic combination in the treatment of secondary apical periodontitis, Ill. Dent. J. **39:**307, 1970.

63. Herman, B.W.: Dentinobliteration der Wurzelkanal nach Behandlung mit Calcium, Zahnart L. Rundschau **2:**887, 1930.

64. Zander, H.A.: Reaction of the pulp to calcium hydroxide, J. Dent. Res. **18:**373-379, 1939.

65. Pisanti, S., and Sciaky, I.: Origin of calcium in the repair wall after pulp exposure in the dog, J. Dent. Res. **43:**641-644, 1964.

66. Sciaky, I., and Pisanti, S.: Localization of calcium hydroxide placed over amputated pulps in dogs, J. Dent. Res. **39:**1128-1132, 1960.

67. Steiner, J.C., and Van Hassell, H.J.: Experimental root apexification in primates, Oral Surg. **31:**409-415, 1971.

68. Frank, A.L.: Therapy for the divergent pulpless tooth by continued apical formation, J. Am. Dent. Assoc. **72:**87-93, 1966.

69. Heithersay, G.S.: Stimulation of root formation in incompletely developed pulpless teeth, Oral Surg. **29:**620-630, 1970.

70. Cvek, M.: Clinical procedures promoting apical closure and arrest of external root resorption in non-vital permanent incisors. In Grossman, L.I., editor: Transactions of the fifth international conference on endodontics, Philadelphia, 1973, University of Pennsylvania Press.

71. Frank, A.L.: Calcium hydroxide: The ultimate medicament? Dent. Clin. North Amer. **23:**691-703, 1979.

72. Ostby, B.N.: Chelation in root canal therapy: ethylenediaminetetraacetic acid for cleansing and widening of root canals, Odont. Tidskr. **65:**3-11, 1957.

73. Patterson, S.S.: In vivo and in vitro studies of the effect of the disodium salt of ethylenediaminetetraacetate on human dentin and its endodontic implications, Oral Surg. **16:**83-103, 1963.

74. von der Fehr, F.R., and Ostby, B.N.: Effect of EDTAC and sulfuric acid on root canal dentine, Oral Surg. **16:**199-205, 1963.

75. Cooke, H., Grower, M., and DelRio, C.: Effects of instrumentation with a chelating agent on the periapical seal of obturated root canals, J. Endodont. **2:**312-314, 1976.

76. Stewart, G.G., Kapsimalis, P., and Rappaport, H.: EDTA and urea peroxide for root canal preparation, J. Am. Dent. Assoc. **78:**335-338, 1969.

APPENDIX A

Top 200 prescribed drugs in 1980

It is essential that dentists know the nature of all drugs being taken by their patients. This list provides a quick reference to determine the nature of drugs patients may be taking.* Since patients usually know their drugs by trade names, drugs are listed alphabetically by trade name in the first column. The generic name/constituents, pharmacologic class, rank in frequency of use, and reference chapter of the drug are shown in the other columns.

Drug/trade name	Generic name/constituents	Pharmacologic class	Rank	Chapter
Achromycin-V	Tetracycline	Antibiotic	93	22
Actifed	Pseudoephedrine	Decongestant	14	5
	Triprolidine	Antihistamine		
Actifed-C expectorant	Pseudoephedrine	Decongestant	105	5, 16
	Triprolidine	Antihistamine		
	Codeine phosphate	Antitussive		
	Guaifenesin	Expectorant		
Aldactazide	Hydrochlorothiazide	Diuretic, antihypertensive	54	20
	Spironolactone	Diuretic, antihypertensive		
Aldactone	Spironolactone	Diuretic, antihypertensive	144	20
Aldomet	Methyldopa	Antihypertensive	13	20
Aldoril	Hydrochlorothiazide	Diuretic, antihypertensive	42	20
	Methyldopa	Antihypertensive		
Ambenyl expectorant	Bromodiphenhydramine	Antihistamine	161	12, 16
	Codeine sulfate	Antitussive		
	Potassium guaiacol-sulfonate	Expectorant		
	Ammonium chloride	Expectorant		
Aminophylline	Aminophylline	Xanthine, bronchodilator	157	13
Amoxicillin	Amoxicillin	Antibiotic	19	22
Amoxil	Amoxicillin	Antibiotic	48	22
Ampicillin	Ampicillin	Antibiotic	6	22
Antivert	Meclizine	Antihistamine, antivertigo	44	16
Anusol-HC	Hydrocortisone plus miscellaneous ingredients	Anorectal, antiinflammatory	169	18

*Modified from National Prescription Audit, Ambler, Pa., 1981, IMS America Ltd.

Continued.

Drug/trade name	Generic name/constituents	Pharmacologic class	Rank	Chapter
Apresazide	Hydrochlorothiazide Hydralazine	Diuretic, antihypertensive Antihypertensive	198	20
Apresoline	Hydralazine	Antihypertensive	85	20
Atarax	Hydroxyzine	Antihistamine, antianxiety	66	16
Ativan	Lorazepam	Antianxiety	63	9
Atromid S	Clofibrate	Lipid lowering	138	21
Bactrim	Trimethoprim Sulfisoxazole	Antibacterial Antibacterial	76	22
Bactrim DS	Trimethoprim Sulfisoxazole	Antibacterial Antibacterial	149	22
Benadryl (caps/tabs)	Diphenhydramine	Antihistamine	33	16
Benadryl elixir	Diphenhydramine	Antihistamine	106	16
Bendectin	Doxylaminesuccinate Pyridoxine Dicyclomine	Antiemetic, antihistamine Vitamin Anticholinergic	115	5, 16, 25
Bentyl	Dicyclomine	Anticholinergic	102	5
Benylin cough syrup	Diphenhydramine Alcohol	Nonnarcotic antitussive	141	10
Brethine	Terbutaline sulfate	Antiasthmatic, adrenergic	110	5
Butazolidin alka	Phenylbutazone Aluminum hydroxide gel Magnesium trisilicate	Nonsteroidal antiinflammatory Antacid Antacid	62	10, 27
Butisol	Butabarbital	Antianxiety	142	7
Catapres	Clonidine	Antihypertensive	132	20
Ceclor	Cefaclor	Antibiotic (cephalosporin)	123	22
Chlor-Trimetron	Chlorpheniramine maleate	Antihistamine	175	16
Choledyl	Oxtriphylline	Xanthine, bronchodilator	176	13
Clinoril	Sulindac	Nonsteroidal antiinflammatory	27	10
Cogentin	Benztropine mesylate	Anticholinergic (antiparkinsonism)	186	5
Combid	Isopropamide Prochlorperazine	Anticholinergic Antipsychotic, antiemetic	127	5
Compazine	Prochlorperazine	Antipsychotic, antiemetic	107	8
Cortisporin Otic	Hydrocortisone Neomycin sulfate Polymixin B sulfate	Corticosteroid Antibiotic Antibiotic	81	18, 22
Coumadin	Warfarin	Anticoagulant	92	21
Dalmane	Flurazepam	Antianxiety	12	9
Darvocet-N 100	Propoxyphene napsylate Acetaminophen	Analgesic Nonnarcotic analgesic	17	12
Darvon	Propoxyphene hydrochloride	Analgesic	190	12
Darvon Compound-65	Propoxyphene hydrochloride Aspirin Phenacetin Caffeine	Analgesic Nonnarcotic analgesic Nonnarcotic analgesic Xanthine derivative	68	10, 12, 13
Demulen-28	Ethynodiol diacetate Ethinyl estradiol	Oral contraceptive, progestin Oral contraceptive, estrogen	112	17

Drug/trade name	Generic name/constituents	Pharmacologic class	Rank	Chapter
Diabinese	Chlorpropamide	Oral hypoglycemic	39	17
Digoxin	Digoxin	Cardiac glycoside	61	21
Dilantin	Phenytoin	Anticonvulsant	35	14
Dimetane expectorant	Phenylephrine	Decongestant	151	5, 16
	Phenylpropanolamine	Decongestant		
	Brompheniramine maleate	Antihistamine		
	Guaifenesin	Expectorant		
Dimetane expectorant-DC	Phenylephrine	Decongestant	163	5, 12, 16
	Phenylpropanolamine	Decongestant		
	Brompheniramine maleate	Antihistamine		
	Codeine	Antitussive		
	Guaifenesin	Expectorant		
Dimetapp	Phenylephrine	Decongestant	10	5, 16
	Phenylpropanolamine	Decongestant		
	Brompheniramine maleate	Antihistamine		
Diuril	Chlorothiazide	Diuretic, antihypertensive	75	20
Donnatal	Atropine	Anticholinergic	28	5, 7
	Hyoscine	Anticholinergic		
	Hyoscyamine	Anticholinergic		
	Phenobarbital	Sedative		
Drixoral	Pseudoephedrine	Decongestant	45	12, 16
	Dexbrompheniramine maleate	Antihistamine		
Dyazide	Triamterene	Diuretic, antihypertensive	4	20
	Hydrochlorothiazide	Diuretic, antihypertensive		
E.E.S.	Erythromycin ethylsuccinate	Antibiotic	22	22
Elavil	Amitriptyline	Tricyclic antidepressant	37	8
Elixophyllin	Theophylline	Xanthine derivative, bronchodilator	192	13
Empirin/codeine	Aspirin	Nonnarcotic analgesic	21	10, 12
	Codeine	Narcotic analgesic		
E-mycin	Erythromycin	Antibiotic	50	22
Enduron	Methyclothiazide	Diuretic, antihypertensive	109	20
Equagesic	Aspirin	Nonnarcotic analgesic	130	9, 10, 12
	Ethoheptazine	Nonnarcotic analgesic		
	Meprobamate	Sedative		
Equanil	Meprobamate	Sedative	187	9
Erythrocin	Erythromycin stearate	Antibiotic	147	22
Erythromycin systemic	Erythromycin	Antibiotic	18	22
Esidrix	Hydrochlorothiazide	Diuretic, antihypertensive	104	20
Fastin	Phentermine	Anorexiant, adrenergic	174	5
Ferrous sulfate	Ferrous sulfate	Iron	195	26
Fiorinal	Aspirin	Nonnarcotic analgesic	38	7, 10
	Phenacetin	Nonnarcotic analgesic		
	Butalbital	Sedative		
	Caffeine	Xanthine derivative		
Fiorinal/codeine	Aspirin	Nonnarcotic analgesic	108	7, 10, 12
	Phenacetin	Nonnarcotic analgesic		

Continued.

Drug/trade name	Generic name/constituents	Pharmacologic class	Rank	Chapter
Fiorinal/codeine—cont'd	Butalbital	Sedative		
	Codeine	Narcotic analgesic		
	Caffeine	Xanthine derivative		
Flagyl Oral	Metronidazole	Trichomonacide	103	22
Flexeril	Cyclobenzaprine	Muscle relaxant	134	9
Gantrisin systemic	Sulfisoxazole	Antibacterial	139	22
Gyne-Lotrimin	Clotrimazole	Vaginal antifungal	168	22
Haldol	Haloperidol	Antipsychotic	119	8
Hydergine	Dihydroergocornine	Ergot alkaloid	160	
	Dihydroergocristine	Ergot alkaloid		
	Dihydroergocyptine	Ergot alkaloid		
Hydrochlorothi-azide	Hydrochlorothiazide	Diuretic, antihypertensive	29	20
Hydrocortisone derm.	Hydrocortisone	Corticosteroid	189	18
HydroDiuril	Hydrochlorothiazide	Diuretic, antihypertensive	20	20
Hydropres	Hydrochlorothiazide	Diuretic, antihypertensive	126	20
	Reserpine	Rauwolfia derivative, antihypertensive		
Hygroton	Chlorthalidone	Diuretic, antihypertensive	30	20
Ilosone	Erythromycin estolate	Antibiotic	84	22
Inderal	Propranolol	β-Adrenergic blocker	2	20
Indocin	Indomethacin	Nonsteroidal antiinflammatory	24	10
Insulin NPH	Insulin	Antidiabetic	122	17
Ionamin	Phentermine	Anorexiant, adrenergic	137	5
Isopto Carpine	Pilocarpine	Glaucoma, cholinergic	197	5
Isordil	Isosorbide dinitrate	Antianginal	32	21
Keflex	Cephalexin	Antibiotic (cephalosporin)	16	22
Kenalog derm.	Triamcinolone acetonide	Corticosteroid	125	18
K-Lyte	Potassium chloride	Electrolyte	150	20
Kwell	Gamma benzene hexachloride (lindane)	Antilice, antiscabies	120	
Lanoxin	Digoxin	Cardiac glycoside	7	21
Larotid	Amoxicillin	Antibiotic	129	22
Lasix (oral)	Furosemide	Diuretic, antihypertensive	5	20
Librax	Chlordiazepoxide	Antianxiety	53	5, 9
	Clidinium bromide	Anticholinergic		
Librium	Chlordiazapoxide	Antianxiety	36	9
Lidex	Fluocinonide	Corticosteroid	143	18
Limbitrol	Chlordiazepoxide	Antianxiety	166	8, 9
	Amitriptyline	Tricyclic antidepressant		
Lomotil	Diphenoxylate	Antidiarrheal	46	5, 27
	Atropine	Anticholinergic		
Lo/Ovral	Norgestrel	Progestin	65	17
	Ethinyl estradiol	Estrogen		
Lo/Ovral-28	Norgestrel	Progestin	181	17
	Ethinyl estradiol	Estrogen		
Lopressor	Metoprolol tartrate	β-Adrenergic blocker, antihypertensive	55	20
Lotrimin	Clotrimazole	Antifungal	136	22
Macrodantin	Nitrofurantoin	Antibacterial	80	22

Drug/trade name	Generic name/constituents	Pharmacologic class	Rank	Chapter
Medrol (oral)	Methylprednisolone	Glucocorticoid	162	18
Mellaril	Thioridazine	Antipsychotic	57	8
Meprobamate	Meprobamate	Antianxiety	82	9
Minipress	Prazosin	Antihypertensive	83	20
Minocin	Minocycline	Antibiotic	148	22
Monistat 7	Miconazole nitrate	Antifungal	60	22
Motrin	Ibuprofen	Nonsteroidal antiinflammatory	9	10
Mycolog	Triamcinolone acetonide	Corticosteroid	43	18, 22
	Neomycin	Antibiotic		
	Gramicidin	Antibiotic		
	Nystatin	Antifungal		
Naldecon	Phenylpropanolamine	Decongestant	72	5, 16
	Phenylephrine	Decongestant		
	Chlorpheniramine maleate	Antihistamine		
	Phenyltoloxamine citrate	Antihistamine		
Nalfon	Fenoprofen calcium	Nonsteroidal anti-inflammatory	87	10
Naprosyn	Naproxen	Nonsteroidal anti-inflammatory	52	10
Neosporin Opthalmic Solution	Polymixin B sulfate	Antibiotic	113	22
	Neomycin sulfate	Antibiotic		
	Gramicidin	Antibiotic		
Nitro-Bid	Nitroglycerin	Antianginal	89	21
Nitroglycerin	Nitroglycerin	Antianginal	90	21
Nitrostat	Nitroglycerin	Antianginal	155	21
Norgesic Forte	Aspirin	Nonnarcotic analgesic	158	9, 10
	Phenacetin	Nonnarcotic analgesic		
	Orphenadrine	Muscle relaxant		
Norinyl-1 + 50 28-Day	Norethindrone	Oral contraceptive, progestin	171	17
	Mestranol	Oral contraceptive, estrogen		
Norpace	Disopyramide	Antiarrhythmic	164	21
Omnipen	Ampicillin	Antibiotic	178	22
Orinase	Tolbutamide	Oral hypoglycemic	97	17
Ornade	Phenylpropanolamine	Decongestant	67	5, 16
	Chlorpheniramine maleate	Antihistamine		
Ortho-Novum 1/50-21	Norethindrone	Oral contraceptive, progestin	47	17
	Mestranol	Oral contraceptive, estrogen		
Ortho-Novum 1/50-28	Norethindrone	Oral contraceptive, progestin	154	17
	Mestranol	Oral contraceptive, estrogen		
Ortho-Novum 1/80-21	Norethindrone	Oral contraceptive, progestin	135	17
	Mestranol	Oral contraceptive, estrogen		
Ovral	Norgestrel	Oral contraceptive, progestin	51	17
	Ethinyl estradiol	Oral contraceptive, estrogen		
Ovral-28	Norgestrel	Oral contraceptive, progestin	200	17
	Ethinyl estradiol	Oral contraceptive, estrogen		
Ovulen-21	Ethynodiol diacetate	Oral contraceptive, estrogen	131	17
	Mestranol	Oral contraceptive, progestin		
Parafon Forte	Chlorzoxazone	Muscle relaxant	78	9, 10
	Acetaminophen	Nonnarcotic analgesic		

Continued.

Drug/trade name	Generic name/constituents	Pharmacologic class	Rank	Chapter
Pavabid	Papaverine	Vasodilator	100	12, 21
Penicillin-VK	Penicillin V potassium	Antibiotic	11	22
Pen-Vee-K	Penicillin V potassium	Antibiotic	74	22
Percodan	Oxycodone	Narcotic analgesic	56	10, 12, 13
	Aspirin	Nonnarcotic analgesic		
	Phenacetin	Nonnarcotic analgesic		
	Caffeine	Xanthine derivative		
Periactin	Cyproheptadine	Antihistamine	145	16
Persantine	Dipyridamole	Antianginal	69	21
Phenaphen/codeine	Codeine	Narcotic analgesic	91	10, 12
	Acetaminophen	Nonnarcotic analgesic		
Phenergan expectorant	Promethazine	Antihistamine	124	16
	Potassium guaiacolsulfonate	Expectorant		
Phenergan expectorant/codeine	Promethazine	Antihistamine	70	12, 16
	Codeine	Antitussive		
	Potassium guaiacolsulfonate	Expectorant		
Phenergan VC expectorant	Phenylephrine	Decongestant	167	5, 16
	Promethazine	Antihistamine		
	Potassium guaiacolsulfonate	Expectorant		
Phenergan VC expectorant/ codeine	Phenylephrine	Decongestant	96	5, 16
	Promethazine	Antihistamine		
	Codeine	Antitussive		
	Potassium guaiacolsulfonate	Expectorant		
Phenobarbital	Phenobarbital	Antianxiety	40	7
Polaramine	Dexchlorpheniramine maleate	Antihistamine	183	16
Poly-Vi-Flor chewable tablets	Vitamins A, D, E, B_1, B_2, B_3, B_6, B_{12}, C, folic acid, fluoride	Vitamins with fluoride	116	25
Potassium chloride	Potassium chloride	Electrolyte	114	20
Prednisone (oral)	Prednisone	Corticosteroid	31	18
Premarin (oral)	Conjugated estrogens	Estrogen	25	17
Proloid	Thyroglobulin	Thyroid hormone	191	17
Provera	Medroxyprogesterone	Progestin	179	17
Pyridium	Phenazopyridine	Urinary anesthetic	146	
Quibron	Theophylline	Xanthine, antiasthmatic	173	13
	Guaifenesin	Expectorant		
Quinidine sulfate	Quinidine sulfate	Antiarrhythmic	121	21
Regroton	Chlorthalidone	Diuretic, antihypertensive	170	20
	Reserpine	Rauwolfia derivative, antihypertensive		
Robaxin-750	Methocarbamol	Muscle relaxant	194	9
Salutensin	Hydroflumethiazide	Diuretic, antihypertensive	165	20
	Reserpine	Rauwolfia derivative, antihypertensive		
Septra	Sulfamethoxazole	Antibacterial	128	22
	Trimethoprim	Antibacterial		
Septra DS	Sulfamethoxazole	Antibacterial	88	22
	Trimethoprim	Antibacterial		
Ser-Ap-Es	Hydrochlorothiazide	Antihypertensive	73	20

Drug/trade name	Generic name/constituents	Pharmacologic class	Rank	Chapter
Ser-Ap-Es—cont'd	Reserpine	Antihypertensive		
	Hydralazine	Antihypertensive		
Serax	Oxazepam	Antianxiety	99	9
Sinequan	Doxepin	Antianxiety	79	9
Slo-Phyllin Gyro-cap	Theophylline	Xanthine, bronchodilator	199	13
Slow-K	Potassium chloride	Electrolyte	26	20
Sodium Sulamyd Ophthalmic drops/ointment	Sodium sulfacetamide	Sulfonamide, antiinfective	193	22
Sorbitrate	Isosorbide dinitrate	Antianginal	133	21
Stelazine	Trifluoperazine	Antipsychotic	153	8
Stuartnatal 1 + 1	Vitamins A, D, E, B_1, B_2, B_3, B_5, B_6, B_{12}, C, folic acid, Ca, Fe, I, Mg	Multivitamins with calcium and iron	180	25, 26
Sumycin	Tetracycline	Antibiotic	117	22
Synalar	Fluocinolone acetonide	Corticosteroid	184	18
Synalgos-DC	Dihydrocodeine	Narcotic analgesic	86	10, 12, 13
	Aspirin	Nonnarcotic analgesic		
	Phenacetin	Nonnarcotic analgesic		
	Caffeine	Xanthine derivative		
Synthroid	Sodium levothyroxine	Thyroid	34	17
Tagamet	Cimetidine	Antiulcer, H_2 antagonist	15	27
Talwin	Pentazocine	Narcotic analgesic	95	12
Tenuate	Diethylpropion	Anorexiant, adrenergic	98	5, 27
Tetracycline (systemic)	Tetracycline	Antibiotic	8	22
Theo-Dur	Theophylline	Xanthine, bronchodilator	118	13
Thorazine	Chloropromazine	Antipsychotic	101	8
Thyroid	Thyroid	Thyroid hormone	58	17
Tigan	Trimethobenzamide	Antiemetic, antivertigo	159	16
Timoptic	Timolol maleate	Glaucoma β-adrenergic blocker	64	5
Tofranil	Imipramine	Tricyclic antidepressant	140	8
Tolectin	Tolmetin	Nonsteroidal anti-inflammatory	196	10
Tolinase	Tolazamide	Oral hypoglycemic	111	17
Tranxene	Clorazepate dipotassium	Antianxiety	41	9
Triavil	Perphenazine	Antipsychotic	71	8
	Amitriptyline	Antidepressant		
Tri-Vi-Flor Drops	Vitamins A, D, C, fluoride	Vitamins and fluoride	177	25
Tussionex	Phenyltoloxamine	Antihistamine	185	12, 16
	Hydrocodone	Antitussive		
Tuss-Ornade	Phenylpropanolamine	Decongestant	94	5, 16
	Chloropheniramine maleate	Antihistamine		
	Caramiphen edisylate	Antitussive		
	Isopropamide iodide	Anticholinergic		
Tylenol/codeine	Acetaminophen	Nonnarcotic analgesic	3	10, 12
	Codeine	Narcotic analgesic		
Valisone	Betamethasone valerate	Corticosteroid	77	18
Valium	Diazepam	Antianxiety	1	9

Continued.

Drug/trade name	Generic name/constituents	Pharmacologic class	Rank	Chapter
Vanceril	Beclomethasone (inhaler)	Antiasthmatic (corticosteroid)	188	18
Vasodilan	Isoxsuprine	Vasodilator	156	21
V-Cillin-K	Penicillin V potassium	Antibiotic	23	22
Vibramycin	Doxycycline	Antibiotic	49	22
Vioform-Hydro-	Hydrocortisone	Corticosteroid	182	18, 22
cortisone	Iodochlorhydroxyquin	Antifungal		
	Clioquinol	Antiamebic		
Vistaril	Hydroxyzine pamoate	Antianxiety	152	9
Zaroxolyn	Metolazone	Diuretic	172	20
Zyloprim	Allopurinol	Antigout	59	31

Prevention of bacterial endocarditis

A STATEMENT PREPARED BY THE COMMITTEE ON PREVENTION OF RHEUMATIC FEVER AND BACTERIAL ENDOCARDITIS OF THE AMERICAN HEART ASSOCIATION

Bacterial endocarditis remains one of the most serious complications of cardiac disease. The morbidity and mortality remain significant despite advances in antimicrobial therapy and cardiovascular surgery. This infection occurs most often in patients with structural abnormalities of the heart or great vessels. Effective measures for prevention of this infection by physicians and dentists are highly desirable.

Dental treatment, or surgical procedures or instrumentation involving the upper respiratory tract, genitourinary tract, or lower gastrointestinal tract, may be associated with transitory bacteremia. Bacteria in the bloodstream may lodge on damaged or abnormal valves such as are found in rheumatic or congenital heart disease or on endocardium near congenital anatomic defects, causing bacterial endocarditis or endarteritis. However, it is not possible to predict specific patients with structural heart disease in whom this infection will occur, nor the specific causal event.

Prophylaxis is recommended in those situations most likely to be associated with bacteremia since bacterial endocarditis cannot occur without a preceding bacteremia. Certain patients (e.g., those with prosthetic heart valves) appear to be at higher risk to develop endocarditis than are others (e.g., those with

mitral valve prolapse syndrome). Likewise, certain dental (e.g., extractions) and surgical (e.g., genitourinary tract surgery) procedures appear to be much more likely to initiate significant bacteremia than are others. These factors, although difficult to quantitate, have been considered in developing these recommendations.

Since there have been no controlled clinical trials, adequate data for comparing various methods for prevention of endocarditis in man are not available. However, an experimental animal model permitting consistent induction of bacterial endocarditis with microorganisms which often cause the infection in man has allowed experimental evaluation of both prophylaxis and treatment. Data from these studies, although derived from animal rather than clinical investigations, represent the only direct information on the efficacy of prophylaxis that is presently available. This information has influenced formulation of the current recommendations. The significant morbidity and mortality associated with infective endocarditis and the paucity of conclusive clinical studies emphasize the need for continuing research into the epidemiology, pathogenesis, prevention, and therapy of infective endocarditis.

When selecting antibiotics for bacterial endocarditis prophylaxis one should consider both the variety of bacteria that is likely to enter the bloodstream from any given site and those organisms most likely to cause this infection. Certain species of microorganisms cause the majority of cases of infective endo-

☐ From Circulation **56:**139A, July, 1977.

Committee members: Edward L. Kaplan, M.D., Chairman; Bascom F. Anthony, M.D., Alan Bisno, M.D., David Durack, M.D., D.Phil., Harold Houser, M.D., H. Dean Millard, D.D.S., Jay Sanford, M.D., Stanford T. Shulman, M.D., Max Stillerman, M.D., Angelo Taranta, M.D., Nanette Wenger, M.D.

carditis, and their antimicrobial sensitivity patterns have been defined. The present recommendations are based on a review of available information about the organisms responsible for endocarditis including their in vivo and in vitro sensitivity to specific antibiotics and the pharmacokinetics of these drugs.

In general, *parenteral administration* of antibiotics provides more predictable blood levels and is preferred when practical, especially for patients thought to be at high risk. Optimal prophylaxis requires close cooperation between physicians, and between physicians and dentists.

Dental procedures and upper respiratory tract surgical procedures

Patients at risk to develop infective endocarditis should maintain the highest level of oral health to reduce potential sources of bacterial seeding. Even in the absence of dental procedures, poor dental hygiene or other dental disease such as periodontal or periapical infections may induce bacteremia. Patients without natural teeth are not free from the risk of bacterial endocarditis. Ulcers caused by ill-fitting dentures should be promptly cared for since they may be a source of bacteremia.

Antibiotic prophylaxis is recommended with *all* dental procedures (including routine professional cleaning) that are likely to cause gingival bleeding. Chemoprophylaxis for dental procedures in children should be managed in a similar manner to the way in which it is handled in adults. Although not a procedure, one exception to this is the spontaneous shedding of deciduous teeth; there are no data to suggest a significant risk of bacteremia accompanying this common event.

Devices which utilize water under pressure to clean between teeth and dental flossing may improve dental hygiene, but they also have been shown to cause bacteremia. However, bacterial endocarditis associated with the use of these devices has not been reported. Present data are insufficient to make firm recommendations with regard to their use in patients susceptible to endocarditis. However, caution is advised in their use by patients with cardiac defects, especially when oral hygiene is poor.

Several studies suggest that *local gingival degerming* immediately preceding a dental procedure provides some degree of protection against bacteremia. However, use of this technique is controversial, since gingival sulcus irrigation itself could theoretically induce bacteremia. If local degerming is employed, it should be used only as an adjunct to antibiotic prophylaxis.

Since alpha hemolytic streptococci (e.g., viridans streptococci) are the organisms most commonly implicated in bacterial endocarditis following dental procedures, antibiotic prophylaxis should be specifically directed toward them. Certain procedures on the upper respiratory tract (e.g., tonsillectomy or adenoidectomy, bronchoscopy—especially with a rigid bronchoscope—and surgical procedures involving respiratory mucosa) also may cause bacteremia. Since bacteria entering the bloodstream after these procedures usually have similar antibiotic sensitivities to those recovered following dental procedures, the same regimens are recommended.

The table on p. 473 contains suggested regimens for chemoprophylaxis for dental procedures or surgical procedures and instrumentation of the upper respiratory tract. The order of listing does not imply superiority of one regimen over another although parenteral administration is favored when practical. The committee also favors the combined use of penicillin and streptomycin or the use of vancomycin in the penicillin allergic patient (regimen B) in those patients felt to be at high risk (e.g., prosthetic valves).

For dental procedures and surgery of the upper respiratory tract
Regimen A —Penicillin

1. *Parenteral-oral combined:*
Adults: Aqueous crystalline penicillin G (1,000,000 units intramuscularly) <u>*mixed with*</u> *Procaine Penicillin G* (600,000 units intramuscularly). Give 30 minutes to 1 hour prior to procedure and then given penicillin V (formerly called phenoxymethyl penicillin) 500 mg orally every 6 hours for 8 doses.†

Children:* Aqueous crystalline penicillin G (30,000 units/kg intramuscularly) <u>*mixed with*</u> *Procaine Penicillin G* (600,000 units intramuscularly). Timing of doses for children is the same as for adults. For children less than 60 lbs. the dose of penicillin V is 250 mg orally every 6 hours for 8 doses.†
2. *Oral:* ‡
Adults: Penicillin V (2.0 gm orally 30 minutes to 1 hour prior to the procedure and then 500 mg orally every 6 hours for 8 doses.)†

Prophylaxis for dental procedures and surgical procedures of the upper respiratory tract

	Most congenital heart disease;[3] rheumatic or other acquired valvular heart disease; idiopathic hypertrophic subaortic stenosis; mitral valve[4] prolapse syndrome with mitral insufficiency	Prosthetic heart valves[5]
All dental procedures that are likely to result in gingival bleeding[1,2]	Regimen A or B	Regimen B
Surgery or instrumentation of the respiratory tract[6]	Regimen A or B	Regimen B

[1]Does not include shedding of deciduous teeth.

[2]Does not include simple adjustment of orthodontic appliances.

[3]E.g., ventricular septal defect, tetralogy of Fallot, aortic stenosis, pulmonic stenosis, complex cyanotic heart disease, patent ductus arteriosus or systemic to pulmonary artery shunts. Does *not* include uncomplicated secundum atrial septal defect.

[4]Although cases of infective endocarditis in patients with mitral valve prolapse syndrome have been documented, the incidence appears to be relatively low and the necessity for prophylaxis in all of these patients has not yet been established.

[5]Some patients with a prosthetic heart valve in whom a high level of oral health is being maintained may be offered oral antibiotic prophylaxis for routine dental procedures except the following: parenteral antibiotics are recommended for patients with prosthetic valves who require extensive dental procedures, especially extractions, or oral or gingival surgical procedures.

[6]E.g., tonsillectomy, adenoidectomy, bronchoscopy, and use surgical procedures of the upper respiratory tract involving disruption of the respiratory mucosa. (See text).

Children: * *Penicillin V* (2.0 gm orally 30 minutes to 1 hour prior to procedure and then 500 mg orally every 6 hours for 8 doses.† For children less than 60 lbs. use 1.0 gm orally 30 minutes to 1 hour prior to the procedure and then 250 mg orally every 6 hours for 8 doses.)†

For patients allergic to penicillin:

Use *either* Vancomycin (see Regimen B)

or use

Adults: Erythromycin (1.0 gm orally 1½-2 hours prior to the procedure and then 500 mg orally every 6 hours for 8 doses.)†

Children: Erythromycin (20 mg/kg orally 1½-2 hours prior to the procedure and then 10 mg/kg every 6 hours for 8 doses.)†

Regimen B—Penicillin plus streptomycin

Adults: Aqueous crystalline penicillin G (1,000,000 units intramuscularly)

mixed with

Procaine penicillin G (600,000 units intramuscularly)

plus

Streptomycin (1 gm intramuscularly).

Give 30 minutes to 1 hour prior to the procedure; then penicillin V 500 mg orally every 6 hours for 8 doses.†

Children: * *Aqueous crystalline penicillin G* (30,000 units/kg intramuscularly)

mixed with

Procaine penicillin G (600,000 units intramuscularly)

plus

Streptomycin (20 mg/kg intramuscularly).

Timing of doses for children is the same as for adults. For children less than 60 lbs the recommended oral dose of penicillin V is 250 mg every 6 hours for 8 doses.†

For patients allergic to penicillin:

Adults: Vancomycin (1 gm intravenously over 30 minutes to 1 hour). Start initial vancomycin infusion ½ to 1 hour prior to procedure; then *erythromycin* 500 mg orally every 6 hours for 8 doses.†

Children: * *Vancomycin* (20 mg/kg intravenously over 30 minutes to 1 hour).** Timing of doses for children is the same as for adults. *Erythromycin* dose is 10 mg/kg every 6 hours for 8 doses.†

Footnotes to regimens:

†In unusual circumstances or in the case of delayed healing, it may be prudent to provide additional doses of antibiotics even though available data suggest that bacteremia rarely persists longer than 15 minutes after the procedure. The physician or dentist may also choose to use the parenteral route of administration for all of the doses in selected situations.

*Doses for children should not exceed recommendations for adults for a single dose or for a 24-hour period.

**For vancomycin the total dose for children should not exceed 44 mg/kg/24 hours.

‡For those *patients receiving continuous oral penicillin for secondary prevention of rheumatic fever,* alpha hemolytic streptococci which are relatively resistant to penicillin are occasionally found in the oral cavity. While it is likely that the doses of penicillin recommended in Regimen A are sufficient to control these organisms, the physician or dentist may choose one of the suggestions in Regimen B or may choose oral erythromycin.

Cardiac surgery

Patients undergoing cardiac surgery utilizing extracorporeal circulation—especially those requiring placement of prosthetic heart valves or needing prosthetic intravascular or intracardiac materials—are at risk to develop infective endocarditis in the perioperative and postoperative periods. Because the morbidity and mortality of infective endocarditis in such patients are high, maximal preventive efforts are indicated, including the use of prophylactic antibiotics.

Early postoperative infective endocarditis following these surgical procedures is most often due to *Staphylococcus aureus* (coagulase positive) or *Staphylococcus epidermidis* (coagulase negative). Streptococci, gram negative bacteria, and fungi are less frequently responsible. No single antibiotic regimen is effective against all these organisms. Furthermore, the prolonged use of broad spectrum antibiotics may itself predispose to superinfection with unusual or highly resistant microorganisms. Therefore, antibiotic prophylaxis at the time of open heart surgery should be directed primarily against staphylococci and should be of short duration. The choice of antibiotic should be influenced by each individual hospital's antibiotic sensitivity data, but *penicillinase resistant penicillins* or *cephalosporin antibiotics* are most often selected. Antibiotic prophylaxis should be started shortly before the operative procedure and usually is continued for no more than three to five days postoperatively to reduce the likelihood of emergence of resistant microorganisms. The physician or surgeon should consider the effects of cardiopulmonary bypass on serum antibiotic levels and time the doses accordingly.

Careful preoperative dental evaluation is recommended so that any required dental treatment can be carried out *several weeks prior* to cardiac surgery whenever possible. Such measures may decrease the incidence of late postoperative endocarditis (occurring later than 6-8 weeks following surgery) which is often due to the same organisms which are responsible for causing infective endocarditis in the unoperated patient.

Status following cardiac surgery

Following cardiovascular surgery the same precautions should be observed that have been outlined for the unoperated patient undergoing dental, gastrointestinal, genitourinary, and other procedures. As far as is known, the risk of endocarditis probably continues indefinitely; it appears particularly significant in patients with prosthetic heart valves. Exceptions are patients with an uncomplicated secundum atrial septal defect repaired by direct suture without a prosthetic patch, and patients who have had ligation and division of a patent ductus arteriosus; these patients do not appear to be at increased risk of developing endocarditis. For these two defects, prophylaxis for prevention of infective endocarditis is not necessary following a healing period of six months after surgery. Although prophylactic antibiotics are often given intraoperatively, there is no evidence to suggest that patients who have undergone coronary artery operations are at risk to develop endocarditis in the months and years following surgery unless there is another cardiac defect present; prophylactic antibiotics to protect against endocarditis are not needed in these postoperative patients.

Other indications for antibiotic prophylaxis to prevent endocarditis

In susceptible patients chemoprophylaxis to prevent endocarditis is also indicated for surgical procedures on *any infected or contaminated tissues,* including incision and drainage of abscesses. Antibiotic prophylaxis for the indicated dental and surgical procedures should also be given to those patients who have had a documented previous episode of infective endocarditis, even in the absence of clinically detectable heart disease.

Indwelling vascular catheters, especially those which reside in one of the cardiac chambers, present a continual danger. Particular care should be given to maintaining the sterility of these catheters and to avoiding unnecessarily prolonged use.

Indwelling transvenous cardiac pacemakers appear to present a low risk of endocarditis; however, dentists and physicians may choose to employ prophylactic antibiotics to cover dental and surgical procedures in these patients. The same recommendations apply to renal dialysis patients with implanted arteriovenous shunt appliances. Although no firm recommendation can be made on the basis of current information, antibiotic prophylaxis for prevention bacteremia provoked by dental and surgical procedures also deserves consideration in patients with ventriculoatrial shunts placed to relieve hydrocephalus since there are documented cases of infective endocarditis in these patients.

Prophylactic antibiotics are *not* required in diagnostic cardiac catheterization and angiography since, with standard techniques, the occurrence of endocarditis following these procedures has proven to be extremely uncommon.

It is important to recognize that antibiotic doses used to prevent recurrences of acute rheumatic fever ("secondary" rheumatic fever prophylaxis) are *inadequate* for the prevention of bacterial endocarditis (see reference). Special attention should be paid to these patients and appropriate antibiotics should be prescribed *in addition* to the antibiotic they are receiving for prevention of group A beta hemolytic streptococcal infections (the addition of an aminoglycoside to appropriate doses of penicillin, or the use of erythromycin or vancomycin).

Warning

The committee recognizes that it is not possible to make recommendations for all possible clinical situations. Practitioners should exercise their clinical judgment in determining the duration and choice of antibiotic(s) when special circumstances apply. Furthermore, since endocarditis may occur despite antibiotic prophylaxis, physicians and dentists should maintain a high index of suspicion in the interpretation of any unusual clinical events following the above procedures. Early diagnosis is important to reduce complications, sequelae, and mortality.

SELECTED REFERENCES

1. American Heart Association Committee on Prevention of Rheumatic Fever: Prevention of Rheumatic Fever, Circulation **55**:1, 1977.
2. Durack, D.T., and Petersdorf, R.G.: Chemotherapy of experimental streptococcal endocarditis. I. Comparison of commonly recommended prophylactic regimens, J. Clin. Invest. **52**:592, 1973.
3. Durack, D.T., Starkebaum, M.S., and Petersdorf, R.G.: Chemotherapy of experimental streptococcal endocarditis. VI. Prevention of enterococcal endocarditis, J. Lab. Clin. Med. (in press), 1977.
4. Editorial: Prophylaxis of bacterial endocarditis, Faith, Hope, and Charitable Interpretations, Lancet **1**:519, 1976.
5. Everett, E.D., and Hirschman, J.V.: Transient bacteremia and endocarditis prophylaxis. A review, Medicine **56**:61, 1977.
6. Finland, M.: Current problem in infective endocarditis, Mod. Con. Cardiovasc. Dis. **41**:53, 1972.
7. Parker, M.T., and Ball, L.C.: Streptococci and aerococci associated with systemic infection in man, J. Med. Microbiol. **9**:275, 1976.
8. Pelletier, I.L., Jr., Durack, D.T., and Petersdorf, R.G.: Chemotherapy of experimental streptococcal endocarditis. IV. Further observations on prophylaxis, J. Clin. Invest. **56**:319, 1975.
9. Sande, M.A., Levison, M.E., Lukas, D.S., and Kaye, D.: Bacteremia associated with cardiac catheterization, N. Eng. J. Med. **281**:1104, 1969.
10. Sande, M.A., Johnson, W.D., Hook, E.W., and Kaye, D.: Sustained bacteremia in patients with prosthetic cardiac valves, N. Eng. J. Med. **286**:1067, 1972.
11. Scopp, I.W., and Orvieto, L.D.: Gingival degerming by povidone-iodine irrigation. Bacteremia reduction in extraction procedures, J. Am. Dent. Assoc. **83**:1294, 1971.
12. Sipes, J.N., Thompson, R.I., and Hook, E.W.: Prophylaxis of infective endocarditis: A reevaluation, Ann. Rev. Med. **28**: 371, 1977.
13. Sullivan, N.M., Sutter, V.L., Mims, M.M., Marsh, V.H., and Finegold, S.M.: Clinical aspects of bacteremia after manipulation of the genitourinary tract, J. Infect. Dis. **127**:49, 1973.

BOOKS

1. Infective Endocarditis—An American Heart Association Symposium, edited by E.L. Kaplan and A.V. Taranta. American Heart Association Monograph Series No. 52. American Heart Association, Dallas, Texas, 1977.
2. Infective Endocarditis, edited by Donald Kaye, University Park Press, Baltimore, Maryland, 1976.
3. Subacute Bacterial Endocarditis, by Andrew Kerr, Jr., Charles C Thomas, Publisher, Springfield, Illinois, 1955.

Board review questions

The purpose of these board review questions is to review key points in each chapter as a means of (1) emphasizing important points, (2) checking comprehension of what has been read, and (3) providing a review for board examination. It is suggested that you read or study each chapter and then (1) mark the answers to each question and (2) check answers in the text. For the most part, answers are in sequence within the text.

CHAPTER 1: INTRODUCTION

NOTES

1. The term *drug* may be defined as any (a) chemical substance, (b) compound that affects biologic systems, (c) substance that is effective in the treatment of disease, (d) organic chemical.
2. The dentist should be prepared to obtain the maximal advantage from available drugs while inducing minimal disadvantages. He should also know how medically prescribed drugs have altered the functions of his patients. Assume that a patient tells you that he is taking a medically prescribed drug and he only knows its proprietary name. In which of the following reference sources would you be able to locate information most conveniently about the indications and adverse effects of this drug? *(a) The United States Pharmacopeia,* (b) *Accepted Dental Therapeutics,* (c) *Physicians' Desk Reference,* (d) *Facts and Comparisons.*
3. The ''official'' name of a drug, that is, the one used in the USP-NF is the _____ name. (a) chemical, (b) trade, (c) generic, (d) proprietary.
4. A *multiple-entity drug* is one that (a) is effective against more than one disease state, (b) affects more than one organ system, (c) contains more than one ingredient, (d) contains more than one active ingredient.
5. An advantage to using trade names is that they (a) simplify drug identification, (b) allow the least expensive product to be dispensed, (c) are more familiar to the pharmacist, (d) are convenient time-savers when one writes a prescription for a multiple-entity preparation, (e) eliminate the need for learning a large number of generic names.
6. One should learn generic names because they (a) are usually shorter and easier to remember than trade names, (b) eliminate the need for learning a large number of trade names, (c) identify the manufacturer, (d) identify the chemical nature of the drug.
7. The federal control of narcotics and drugs considered to have a potential for abuse is administered by the (a) Food and Drug Administration, (b) Federal Trade Commission, (c) Department of Health and Human Services, (d) Department of Justice, (e) Internal Revenue Service.

CHAPTER 2: GENERAL PRINCIPLES OF DRUG ACTION

1-3. The log dose–effect curve is a plot of dose against effect. Questions 1 to 3 refer to the figure on p. 477.

1. What is the potency relationship between drug *A* and drug *B?* (a) *A* is more potent, (b) *B* is more potent, (c) they are of equal potency, (d) a conclusion cannot be drawn.
2. What is the potency relationship between drug *B* and drug *C?* (a) *B* is more potent, (b) *C* is more potent, (c) they are of equal potency, (d) a conclusion cannot be drawn.

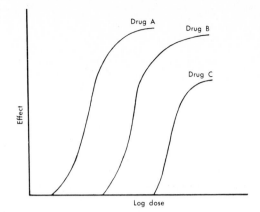

3. What is the efficacy relationship between drug *A* and drug *C*? (a) *A* is more efficacious, (b) *C* is more efficacious, (c) they are of equal efficacy, (d) a conclusion cannot be drawn.

4. The ED_{50} of a drug is (a) the effective dose of a drug in 50% of the subjects tested, (b) one half the effective or therapeutic dose, (c) the dose that gives 50% of the maximal effect.

5. Enteral routes of administration are (a) oral and rectal, (b) oral and topical, (c) topical and inhalation, (d) rectal and topical.

6. The more predictable drug response is obtained by _____ administration. (a) oral, (b) subcutaneous, (c) intramuscular, (d) intravenous.

7. The topical application of drugs to mucous membranes (a) precludes the development of systemic blood levels, (b) only allows slow absorption, (c) allows faster absorption than that obtained from skin, (d) produces only local effects.

8. Which of the following drug characteristics will *increase* the tendency of a drug to cross cell membranes? (a) nonionized and high lipid solubility, (b) nonionized and low lipid solubility, (c) ionized and high lipid solubility, (d) ionized and low lipid solubility.

9. If you inject a drug with a pH of 6.5 and a pKa of 8.1 into a tissue with a pH of 7.4, to what extent would you expect this drug to be ionized in the tissues? (a) over 50%, (b) 50%, (c) under 50%.

10. Other factors being equal, would a weakly acidic drug with a pKa of 3.4 be absorbed more readily in the stomach or in the intestine? Why? (a) stomach—because it will be more highly ionized there, (b) stomach—because it will be less highly ionized there, (c) intestine—because it will be more highly ionized there, (d) intestine—because it will be less highly ionized there.

11. A drug that is bound to plasma protein is usually inactive pharmacologically. What happens to a drug that is so bound? (a) Most protein-bound drug is metabolized before it can be released to the active form. (b) As unbound drug is distributed to the tissues, bound drug dissociates itself from protein to reestablish an equilibrium between bound and unbound fractions. (c) After most unbound drug is released from the vascular system to the tissues, the bound fraction dissociates slowly and provides a longer duration of action. (d) Protein-bound drug remains bound until it passes through capillary cell walls, at which time the protein moiety is removed and the active drug form enters the tissues.

12. Drug A characteristically becomes 50% bound to plasma protein. A patient receives a maximal dose of drug A followed by an average dose of drug B. Drug B has a greater affinity for the same protein sites that bind drug A. How will the administration of drug B alter the effects of drug A? (a) Therapeutic and adverse effects of drug A will be intensified. (b) Only the therapeutic effects of drug A will be intensified. (c) Therapeutic and adverse effects of drug A will be reduced in intensity. (d) There will be no change in the intensity of either therapeutic or adverse effects.

NOTES

13. The tissue distribution of drugs depends on both tissue affinities (guanethidine for heart and skeletal muscle, thiopental for fat) and differential passage across specialized cell membranes (blood-brain barrier, placenta). Most drugs are thought to pass the placenta by (a) active transport, (b) simple diffusion in accordance with their degree of lipid solubility, (c) simple diffusion in accordance with their degree of water solubility, (d) passage through membrane pores.

14. Tissue redistribution is particularly important in regard to (a) tetracyclines, (b) guanethidine, (c) quinine, (d) thiopental.

15. Agonists are drugs that (a) block tissue receptor sites, (b) activate tissue receptor sites, (c) reverse the effect of other drugs on tissue receptor sites.

16. To be therapeutically useful, the selective effect of drugs on cellular components must be _____ .

17. Most drugs are metabolized to products that are more easily excreted because they are _____ than the original compound. (a) less polar and more lipid soluble, (b) less polar and less lipid soluble, (c) more polar and more lipid soluble, (d) more polar and less lipid soluble.

18. Can you give an example of an inactive compound that is metabolized to an active agent?

19. Can you give an example of an active drug that is converted to another active drug before being inactivated?

20. The fact that pentobarbital can decrease the anticoagulant effect of coumarin is an example of enzyme (a) destruction, (b) binding, (c) induction, (d) inhibition.

21. What is an example of a drug that is excreted by active secretion in renal tubules? (a) phenobarbital, (b) penicillin, (c) procaine, (d) alcohol.

22. If a child's dose is calculated, the most accurate determination will be based on his (a) age, (b) weight, (c) body surface area.

23. Present evidence indicates that the fetus is probably exposed to all drugs taken by the mother. (a) True. (b) False.

24. The general concept of drug-receptor interactions holds that drugs interact with specific macromolecular components of an organism to cause a modulation in function of that organism. Drugs thus impart a new function to that organism. (a) First statement is true, second is false. (b) First statement is false, second is true. (c) Both statements are true. (d) Both statements are false.

25. Most drug receptors are (a) tissue enzymes, (b) cellular proteins, (c) neural elements, (d) cell wall mineral complexes.

26. Drugs that usually have no intrinsic activity of their own are called (a) agonists, (b) antagonists.

27. A noncompetitive antagonist prevents agonists from producing their effects, no matter what the concentration of agonist, *and* usually results from irreversible binding of antagonist to receptor. (a) First statement is true, second is false. (b) First statement is false, second is true. (c) Both statements are true. (d) Both statements are false.

28. Rates of biotransformation of drugs can vary sixfold or more between individuals, and these rates are genetically determined. (a) First statement is true, second is false. (b) First statement is false, second is true. (c) Both statements are true. (d) Both statements are false.

29. Which of the following drugs will show the least concentration in saliva relative to blood levels? (a) lithium, (b) propranolol, (c) aspirin, (d) penicillin VK, (e) ampicillin.

30. The elderly would be most likely to show exaggerated responses to drugs affecting the (a) cardiovascular system, (b) liver and kidneys, (c) autonomic nervous system, (d) CNS.

31. If the $t_{\frac{1}{2}}$ of a drug is 2 hours, you would expect that about _____ hours would be required for almost complete elimination of the drug. (a) 4, (b) 8, (c) 12, (d) 16.

CHAPTER 3: ADVERSE DRUG REACTIONS

Drug actions that are clinically desirable are termed *therapeutic effects*. Undesirable actions are termed *adverse effects*. The clinician's objective is to obtain maximal therapeutic effects while experiencing minimal adverse effects. Adverse drug effects occur frequently. Consequently, the clinician must be as concerned with a drug's adverse potentialities as with its therapeutic applicability. This chapter has only discussed definitions and general principles; adverse reactions to specific drugs are discussed in other appropriate chapters.

1. Reactions that cannot be explained by known mechanisms are termed (a) side effects, (b) idiosyncrasies, (c) allergic reactions, (d) teratogenic effects.
2. Which of the following can occur at therapeutic dosage levels in healthy patients? (a) idiosyncratic responses, (b) allergic reactions, (c) teratogenic effects, (d) all except *b*, (e) all of the above can occur.
3. The LD50 of a drug is (a) the dose (mg/kg) that kills 50% of the treated animals, (b) one half the dose that kills all of the treated animals, (c) 50% of the lethal dose in humans, (d) 50% of the lethal dose in an experimental animal.
4. The therapeutic index can be expressed (a) in mg/kg, (b) as $\dfrac{LD50}{ED50}$, (c) as $\dfrac{ED50}{LD50}$, (d) as *a* and *b*, (e) as *a* and *c*.
5. Toxic effects at therapeutic dosage levels would most likely manifest as (a) exaggerated effects on target organs or tissues, (b) effects on nontarget organs or tissues, (c) teratogenic effects.
6. Fatal anaphylaxis has never occurred after a single oral dose of penicillin. (a) True. (b) False.
7. Fatal anaphylaxis has never occurred after a single oral dose of aspirin. (a) True. (b) False.

CHAPTER 4: PRESCRIPTION WRITING

1. Approximately how many milligrams of aspirin are contained in a 5-gram tablet? (a) 200, (b) 300, (c) 400, (d) 600.
2. If a patient weighs 70 kg, what is the weight in pounds? (a) 145, (b) 155, (c) 165, (d) 170.
3. How would you abbreviate instructions if you wanted a patient to take 1 tablet every 6 hours? 1 tab. _____, (a) t.i.d., (b) q.4h., (c) q.6h., (d) q.i.d.
4. If you want a patient to start taking a drug as soon as the prescription is filled, you might use the following abbreviation: (a) stat., (b) s.o.s., (c) p.c., (d) a.c.
5. A liquid preparation of K penicillin V contains 125 mg/5 ml. If you want the patient to take 250 mg each dose you would prescribe _____ per dose. (a) 1 teaspoon, (b) 2 teaspoons, (c) 1 tablespoon, (d) 2 tablespoons.

6-11. The following drugs and doses are frequently prescribed in dental practice. Write the "bodies" of prescriptions for each of the following in the space provided and check against the text.

6. An adult has a periapical abscess. You have provided local and supportive treatment. You determine that antibiotic therapy is also indicated and wish to prescribe potassium penicillin G for 5 days. (Dose: 250 mg at bedtime and 1 hour before meals.)
℞:

7. You wish to prescribe a liquid preparation of penicillin V (125 mg/5 ml) for a child for 10 days. (Dose: 125 mg every 6 hours.)
℞:

8. You wish to prescribe an antibiotic for an adult. The bactericidal potency of penicillin is not required and you decide to prescribe tetracycline HCl tablets for 5 days. (Dose: 250 mg every 6 hours.)
℞:

9. You are prescribing 100 mg secobarbital sodium to be taken 1 hour before an appointment for preoperative sedation.
℞:

10. You are prescribing 30 mg codeine sulfate to be taken with two aspirin tablets every 4 hours. You wish coverage for 24 hours.
    ℞:

11. You are prescribing penicillin V as prophylaxis against subacute bacterial endocarditis for an adult with a history of rheumatic heart disease.
    ℞:

12. Which of the following laws required that certain drugs be sold by prescription only? (a) The Food, Drug and Cosmetic Act of 1938, (b) The Durham-Humphrey Law of 1952, (c) The Kefauver-Harris Bill of 1962, (d) The Drug Abuse Control Amendments of 1965.

13. Which of the following laws prohibited the refilling of a prescription unless directions to the contrary are indicated on the prescription? (a) The Food, Drug, and Cosmetic Act of 1938, (b) The Durham-Humphrey Law of 1952, (c) The Kefauver-Harris Bill of 1962, (d) The Drug Abuse Control Amendments of 1965.

14. Which of the following laws required that a manufacturer demonstrate a drug's *effectiveness* as well as safety before it could be marketed? (a) The Food, Drug, and Cosmetic Act of 1938, (b) The Durham-Humphrey Law of 1952, (c) The Kefauver-Harris Bill of 1962, (d) The Drug Abuse Control Amendments of 1965.

15. As established by The Controlled Substance Act of 1970, which drugs can be prescribed only by practitioners who are registered with the DEA? (a) Schedule I drugs, (b) Schedule II drugs, (c) Schedule III drugs, (d) Schedule IV drugs, (e) Schedule II, III and IV drugs.

16. Which ''schedule'' of drugs has the *lowest* potential for abuse? (a) Schedule I drugs, (b) Schedule II drugs, (c) Schedule III drugs, (d) Schedule IV drugs, (e) Schedule V drugs.

CHAPTER 5: THE PHARMACOLOGY OF THE AUTONOMIC NERVOUS SYSTEM

1-6. Indicate with P (parasympathetic) and S (sympathetic) which division of the autonomic nervous system would be stimulated to cause the effect listed.
    1. Secretion of thin, watery saliva. _____
    2. Secretion of thick, viscid saliva. _____
    3. Bradycardia. _____
    4. Constriction of pupil. _____
    5. Decrease in peristalsis. _____
    6. Increase in gastrointestinal secretions. _____

7. Nerves function to relay information not only between nerves, but also between nerves and other tissues by way of specialized junctions termed synapses. The relay of this information is controlled by which of the following? (a) type of receptor, (b) type of chemical mediator, (c) neither, (d) both *a* and *b*.

8. Acetylcholine is the specific neurotransmitter at (a) all parasympathetic synapses, (b) sympathetic preganglionic synapses, (c) neuromuscular junctions, (d) *a* and *b*, (e) *a, b,* and *c.*

9. Acetylcholine is the neurotransmitter at sympathetic postganglionic synapses that affects (a) salivary glands, (b) sweat glands, (c) the adrenal medulla, (d) the adrenal cortex, (e) all of the above.

10. Why has the attempt to use choline esters to promote salivation been unsuccessful? (a) They affect too many other body systems. (b) They cause xerostomia. (c) They are too expensive. (d) Their effect on salivation is too weak.

11. What is the mechanism of the cholinergic effects of physostigmine, neostigmine, and malathion? (a) They stimulate parasympathetic receptors directly. (b) They cause the release of acetylcholine. (c) They inhibit the enzyme that metabolizes acetylcholine. (d) They stimulate anticholinesterase.

12. Most anticholinergic drugs act by (a) destroying acetylcholine, (b) complexing with the active sites on the acetylcholine molecule, (c) activating the sympathetic division of the autonomic nervous system, (d) blocking cholinergic receptors.

NOTES

13. Atropine and scopolamine have similar pharmacologic effects. Which of the following actions does only scopolamine have? (a) reduction of salivation, (b) prevention of cardiac slowing during general anesthesia, (c) CNS depression, (d) mydriasis, (e) cycloplegia.

14. If you prescribe atropine to reduce salivary flow, you should advise the patient that the following side effects may be experienced: (a) dryness and burning of the throat, (b) vasodilation of skin capillaries with flushing, (c) blurred vision, (d) all of the above.

15. Anticholinergic drugs should be used with considerable caution in patients with cardiovascular disease and are contraindicated in patients with (a) glaucoma, (b) prostate hypertrophy, (c) intestinal obstruction, (d) any of the above.

16. Which of the following drug might you find used in the treatment of glaucoma? (a) atropine, (b) propantheline, (c) scopolamine, (d) isoflurophate.

17. Less atropine would be needed to reduce salivation in a patient who is also receiving which of the following drugs? (a) an antihistamine, (b) a tricyclic antidepressant, (c) levodopa, (d) *a* and *b* only, (e) *b* and *c* only, (f) all of these.

18. What is the effect of alpha adrenergic receptor stimulation?

19. What is the effect of beta adrenergic receptor stimulation?

20. How can epinephrine cause both vasodilation of capillaries in striated muscle and vasoconstriction in skin capillaries?

21. Both small and large doses of epinephrine cause an increase in (a) the strength of contraction, (b) heart rate, (c) cardiac output, (d) oxygen utilization, (e) all of the above, (f) all except *b*, (g) all except *d*.

22. Norepinephrine does not normally cause (a) vasoconstriction in the skin, (b) increased systolic blood pressure, (c) decreased diastolic blood pressure, (d) bradycardia.

23. Why would norepinephrine be a poor substitute for epinephrine in a severe allergic response? (a) It does not relax bronchial smooth muscle. (b) It does not increase both systolic and diastolic blood pressure. (c) It dilates pulmonary arterioles. (d) It would be a poor substitute for all of the above reasons.

24. Norepinephrine will produce significant tissue necrosis used as the vasoconstrictor in a local anesthetic solution or if injected subcutaneously. This damage results from (a) severe local vasoconstriction, (b) direct irritation to the tissues, (c) damage caused by the high pH of norepinephrine solutions, (d) thrombosis of local blood vessels.

25. Since isoproterenol (Isuprel) stimulates only beta receptors, it has all the following effects except one. Which one of these actions does it not have? (a) increases heart rate, (b) increases strength of cardiac contraction, (c) increases systolic and diastolic pressure, (d) decreases bronchial spasm.

26. The amphetamines are (a) indirect adrenergic stimulants and CNS stimulants, (b) indirect adrenergic stimulants and CNS depressants, (c) direct adrenergic stimulants and CNS stimulants, (d) direct adrenergic stimulants and CNS depressants.

27. Which of the following is *not* a true statement regarding the three drugs norepinephrine, epinephrine, and isoproterenol? (a) All three are catecholamines. (b) Only epinephrine and norepinephrine are natural neurohormones. (c) Only isoproterenol has selective beta activity. (d) All are well absorbed from the GI tract.

28. When administering adrenergic agonists for any reason, one should be alert to possible hypertensive episodes in patients (a) with hyperthyroidism, (b) with uncontrolled hypertension, (c) taking a tricyclic antidepressant, (d) *a* and *b* only, (e) *a* and *c* only, (f) all of these.

28-34. Match the following drugs with the appropriate descriptive term. (a) dopamine, (b) metaproterenol, (c) levonordefrin, (d) phentolamine, (e) timolol, (f) mecamylamine.

29. A beta adrenergic blocking agent used in the treatment of glaucoma.

30. An alpha antagonist employed in certain peripheral vascular diseases.

31. Acts via beta$_1$ receptors to stimulate heart rate, contractility and cardiac output.

32. A selective beta$_2$ agonist used in the therapy of asthma.

33. A ganglionic blocking agent used in hypertension.

34. An adrenergic agonist employed as a vasoconstrictor in local anesthetic solutions.

CHAPTER 6: GENERAL ANESTHETICS

1-3. Regarding the early history of general anesthesia, match the anesthetic agent in column B with the man responsible for its early development. Each agent will be used once.

Column A	*Column B*
1. Horace Wells	(a) Nitrous oxide
2. W.T.G. Morton	(b) Ethyl ether
3. J.Y. Simpson	(c) Chloroform

4. A balanced anesthetic technique for production of general anesthesia may include which of the following drugs? (a) an inhalation anesthetic, (b) a narcotic, (c) a muscle relaxant, (d) an intravenous barbiturate, (e) all of these.

5. According to the Meyer-Overton theory, general anesthetics (a) inhibit oxidative enzymes that are involved in glucose metabolism in neural tissue, (b) depress the transmission of nerve impulses by forming microcrystals in cerebral tissues, (c) have a potency that is roughly proportional to their oil and water solubility.

6. What stage of general anesthesia is characterized by excitement? (a) Stage I, (b) Stage II, (c) Stage III, plane 1, (d) Stage III, plane 3, (e) Stage IV.

7. If an anesthetic agent is highly soluble in both blood and tissue, then it can be predicted the anesthetic will produce (a) rapid induction, (b) slow induction, (c) slow recovery, (d) rapid recovery, (e) *a* and *c,* (d) *b* and *c,* (e) *a* and *d,* (e) *b* and *d.*

8-15. Select the characteristic that is *not* descriptive of the drug indicated.

8. Nitrous oxide: (a) nonflammable gas, (b) high patient acceptability, (c) potent anesthetic, (d) produces analgesia at 65% concentration.

9. Cyclopropane: (a) highly explosive, (b) frequently produces cardiac arrhythmias, (c) potent anesthetic, (d) stormy induction.

10. Diethyl ether: (a) irritating to mucous membranes, (b) slow induction and slow recovery, (c) explosive, (d) produces nausea and vomiting, (e) poor muscle relaxation.

11. Halothane: (a) not explosive, (b) highly potent, (c) irritating to mucous membranes, (d) produces incomplete muscle relaxation, (e) tends to produce hypotension, (f) sensitizes heart to epinephrine.

12. Methoxyflurane: (a) nonflammable liquid, (b) provides poor postoperative analgesia, (c) sensitizes myocardium to catecholamines, (d) produces metabolites that may cause renal failure.

13. Ethyl chloride: (a) nonflammable liquid, (b) principal use is anesthesia by topical refrigeration, (c) inhalation produces cardiac arrhythmias, (d) hepatotoxic.

14. Enflurane: (a) produces rapid induction, (b) potentiates nondepolarizing muscle relaxants, (c) high incidence of liver toxicity, (d) excessive motor activity with larger doses.

15. Isoflurane: (a) highly soluble in blood, (b) pungent etheral smell, (c) only slightly metabolized, (d) potent respiratory depressant.

16-17. Use the following data chart to answer the next two questions

Anesthetic	Blood/gas coefficient	Blood/tissue coefficient	MAC
(a) Nitrous oxide	0.47	1.06	100
(b) Ether	12.1	1.14	1.92
(c) Methoxyflurane	12.1	2.0	0.16
(d) Halothane	2.35	2.6	0.75

16. From the above data, the most potent general anesthetic would be _____.

17. Based on the above data, induction would be most rapid with _____.

18. Which of the following is not true of thiopental anesthesia? (a) smooth induction, (b) rapid induction, (c) moderate muscle relaxation, (d) progressive respiratory depression.

19. Anesthesia by intravenous barbiturates is contraindicated in patients with (a) asthma, (b) porphyria, (c) hyperactive cough reflexes, (d) hyperactive laryngeal reflexes, (e) all of the above conditions.

20. Which of the following is/are true of ketamine anesthesia? (a) rapid induction, (b) profound analgesia with light sleep, (c) stimulation of the cardiovascular system, (d) moderate muscle relaxation, (e) depressed laryngeal reflexes, (f) frequently induced undesirable mental effects, (g) all except *c* and *d* are true, (h) all except *d* and *e* are true, (i) all are true, (j) none is true.

21. The neuroleptic drug combination that produces a so-called wakeful anesthetic state is a combination of (a) halothane, nitrous oxide, and oxygen, (b) meperidine and diazepam, (c) atropine and ketamine, (d) droperidol and fentanyl.

22. Which of the following procedures would be useful in reducing the amount of trace anesthetic gas in the dental environment? (a) repair of leaking equipment, (b) avoiding spillage, (c) use of scavenging equipment, (d) use of monitors, (e) all of these.

CHAPTER 7: SEDATIVE-HYPNOTIC DRUGS

1. An important problem in using barbiturates is that (a) their adverse potentialities are not well known, (b) they are habit forming and addictive, (c) they are inconvenient to administer, (d) all of the above are true, (e) none of the above is true.

2. Why are the barbiturates converted to their sodium salts? (a) so that parenteral solutions can be prepared, (b) to make them less toxic, (c) to increase their stability.

3. What is a common property of methohexital, thiamylal, and thiopental? (a) all contain sulfur, (b) all are used for general anesthesia, (c) both *a* and *b*, (d) neither *a* nor *b*.

4. Which of the following barbiturates would be most likely to show a prolonged effect in a patient with renal impairment? (a) phenobarbital and secobarbital, (b) pentobarbital and amobarbital, (c) thiopental and thiamylal, (d) phenobarbital and barbital.

5. A sedative dose of a barbiturate should be expected to produce (a) respiratory depression, (b) minor analgesia, (c) decreased BMR, (d) all of the above effects, (e) none of the above effects.

6. You have a patient who is a barbiturate addict. If he continues to receive barbiturates required by his addiction, you would expect him to (a) become progressively depressed in time and to develop little tolerance to barbiturates, (b) become progressively depressed in time and to develop significant tolerance, (c) retain relative normality of function, but require increasing doses because of the rapid and extensive development of tolerance, (d) retain relative normality of function without need for increasing doses.

7. If a patient is taking dicumarol and a barbiturate, the withdrawal of the latter would _____ the effect of this coumadin anticoagulant. (a) increase, (b) decrease, (c) have no effect on.

8. In comparing the nonbarbiturate sedatives with the barbiturates, one may say that the former are (a) more potent and better known, (b) more potent, although not as well known, (c) less potent but better known, (d) less potent and not as well known.

9. Which of the following drugs is/are so highly irritating to mucosa that it (they) should not be administered to patients with ulcers or gastroenteritis? (a) bromides, (b) chloral hydrate, (c) paraldehyde, (d) ethinamate, (e) *a* and *b*, (f) *b* and *c*, (g) *c* and *d*.

10. Why would you question the use of paraldehyde in a patient with bronchopulmonary disease? (a) A significant amount is eliminated by the respiratory route. (b) It causes bronchiolar constriction. (c) Oral doses irritate the larynx. (d) It directly and extensively depresses respiration.

11. Teratogenic studies are insufficient to recommend which of the following for use in pregnant women? (a) ethinamate, (b) ethchlorvynol, (c) glutethimide, (d) none is recommended.

12. The principal adverse potential of methaqualone is (a) liver damage, (b) renal impairment, (c) hematologic depression, (d) drug abuse, (e) erratic respiratory depression.

CHAPTER 8: PSYCHOTHERAPEUTIC DRUGS
CHAPTER 9: MINOR TRANQUILIZERS AND CENTRALLY ACTING MUSCLE RELAXANTS

1. The most widely used antipsychotic drugs are the (a) *Rauwolfia* alkaloids, (b) phenothiazines, (c) butyrophenones, (d) thioxanthines.

2. The prolonged duration of action of phenothiazines results from the fact that (a) a large part of the dose enters the enterohepatic circulation and is slowly released into

general circulation, (b) they are not metabolized to any significant extent by the liver and must be eliminated by the kidney, (c) their metabolic conjugates are pharmacologically active and slowly excreted, (d) their metabolic conjugates are pharmacologically active and are retained in body fat.

3. Which of the following is one most likely to see during the long-term use of phenothiazines? (a) tolerance to antipsychotic effects, (b) euphoria, (c) ''neuroleptic syndrome,'' (d) loss of intellectual function, (e) all of the above.

4. Tolerance to the sedative effect of phenothiazines (a) develops in 1 to 2 days, (b) develops in 1 to 2 weeks, (c) develops in 2 to 4 months, (d) does not develop.

5. The time necessary to develop the full antipsychotic effect to phenothiazines is (a) 1 to 2 days, (b) 1 to 2 weeks, (c) 2 to 4 months, (d) 4 to 6 months.

6. The antiemetic effect of phenothiazines results from depression of (a) the vomiting center, (b) the chemotherapeutic trigger zone, (c) both *a* and *b*, (d) neither *a* nor *b*.

7. Chlorpromazine is not useful in controlling nausea and vomiting associated with (a) uremia, (b) gastroenteritis, (c) carcinomatosis, (d) drug therapy, (e) motion sickness.

8. The sympatholytic effect of phenothiazines accounts for the tendency of these drugs to cause (a) orthostatic hypotension with compensatory tachycardia, (b) hypertension with compensatory bradycardia, (c) increased salivation, (d) xerostomia.

9. Toxic or side effects of phenothiazines include (a) extrapyramidal stimulation, (b) antimuscarinic effects: xerostomia, urinary retention, and inhibition of sweating, (c) both *a* and *b*, (d) neither *a* nor *b*.

10. Haloperidol is sometimes a desirable alternative to chlorpromazine as an antipsychotic drug in patients with coronary or cerebrovascular disease because it produces (a) less hypotension, (b) less hypertension, (c) more sedation, (d) bradycardia.

11. When compared with phenothiazines, the thioxanthines can be described as (a) more potent and less toxic, (b) more potent and more toxic, (c) less potent and less toxic, (d) less potent and more toxic.

12. Which of the following are produced by meprobamate? (a) central tolerance and physical dependence, (b) sedation and muscle relaxation, (c) anticonvulsive effects, (d) all of the above.

13. Which of the following are produced by chlordiazepoxide? (a) central tolerance and physical dependence, (b) sedation and muscle relaxation, (c) anticonvulsive effects, (d) all of the above.

14. Diazepam (Valium) and chlordiazepoxide (Librium) have become extensively used drugs in recent years. Their pharmacologic effects are similar. What are the principal differences between these agents? (a) Only chlordiazepoxide produces muscle relaxation. (b) Diazepam is shorter acting, has a higher margin of safety, and when used intravenously, produces amnesia. (c) Only diazepam has anticonvulsant properties. (d) All the above are known differences.

15. Overdose with CNS depressants is always a problem. Which of the following has a greater potential for fatal overdose? (a) pentobarbital, (b) meprobamate, (c) chlordiazepoxide, (d) diazepam.

16. Tardive dyskinesia is known to occur after chronic use of (a) mesoridazine, (b) haloperidol, (c) molindone, (d) all of the above.

17. In a normal individual the tricyclic antidepressants have effects similar to the phenothiazines. However, the depressed patient responds with an elevation of mood and (a) increased mental and physical activity without euphoria, (b) increased mental and decreased physical activity, (c) reduced preoccupation with suicide, (d) euphoria, (e) both *a* and *c*, (f) both *b* and *d*.

18. You are least likely to see which of the following adverse effects associated with the use of the tricyclic antidepressants? (a) fine tremors and blurred vision, (b) dry mouth and constipation, (c) orthostatic hypotension and tachycardia, (d) psychologic and physical dependence.

19. Why do the effects of monoamine oxidase inhibitors (MAOIs) last for several days or even weeks after their use is discontinued? (a) Their inhibition of MAO is irreversible and new enzyme must be synthesized. (b) They conjugate with protein and consequently are very slowly excreted by the kidneys. (c) They are not metabolized by the liver and renal excretion is slow. (d) Their metabolic products are active and have a strong affinity for lipids.

20. Potentiation of cell actions of tricyclic antidepressants is known to occur with the simultaneous administration of phenylbutazone because it (a) reduces tricyclic plas-

ma binding to albumin, (b) competes for the same receptor, (c) decreases tricyclic metabolism in the liver, (d) all of the above.
21. Some MAOIs are useful in the treatment of narcolepsy since (a) they stimulate central alpha adrenoceptors, (b) they block central dopamine receptors, (c) they suppress REM sleep, (d) all of the above.

CHAPTER 10: NONNARCOTIC ANALGESICS

1. Which of the following does *not* have antipyretic effects? (a) salicylates, (b) mefenamic acid, (c) aniline derivatives, (d) propoxyphene.
2. In addition to their analgesic effects, some salicylates are used therapeutically as (a) keratolytic agents, (b) counterirritants, (c) flavoring in cooking, (d) all of the above.
3. What effects of aspirin result primarily from hypothalamic actions? (a) analgesic, (b) antipyretic, (c) antiinflammatory, (d) all of the above.
4. Large doses of aspirin (a) stimulate metabolism, (b) increase the tendency of blood platelets to adhere to endothelium, (c) do both of the above, (d) do neither of the above.
5. Buffering cannot be relied on to reduce gastrointestinal upset after the use of aspirin. The reason for this is probably because of aspirin's (a) overwhelming acidity, (b) systemic effect, (c) direct, nonacidic effects, (d) chelating tendencies.
6. Allergic reactions to aspirin are not rare. They may be characterized by (a) asthmatic symptoms, (b) angioneurotic edema, (c) anaphylactic shock, (d) only *a* and *b,* (e) all of the above.
7. The treatment of a severe toxic reaction to aspirin requires (a) immediate hospitalization and the use of intravenous fluids to correct acidosis and electrolyte imbalance, (b) intravenous cortisone and vasopressors, (c) gastric lavage, parenteral sedatives, forced fluids, and rest, (d) intravenous glucose and support of respiration.
8. An arthritic patient has been taking 20 grains/24 hr of aspirin for 3 months. You might expect to see (a) hyperprothrombinemia and electrolyte imbalance, (b) hypoprothrombinemia and inhibited platelet function, (c) acidosis and prolonged prothrombin time, (d) decreased prothrombin time and inhibited platelet function.
9. An oral dose of aspirin would normally be expected to produce a peak blood level in about (a) 15 minutes, (b) 30 minutes, (c) 1 hour, (d) 2 hours.
10. The renal excretion of aspirin would be increased by (a) acidification of the urine, (b) alkalinization of the urine, (c) diuresis, (d) *a* and *c,* (e) *b* and *c.*
11. What is a significant clinical distinction of phenylbutazone when compared with salicylates or other pyrazolones? (a) greater analgesic potency, (b) greater antipyretic potency, (c) greater antiinflammatory potency, (d) less toxicity.
12. Mefenamic acid should be administered with particular caution in (a) diabetics, (b) hypertensives, (c) asthmatics, (d) psychotics.
13. The principal pharmacologic difference among the aniline derivatives is their (a) toxicity, (b) analgesic potency, (c) antipyretic potency, (d) *a* and *b.*
14. You would not expect cross-allergy to exist between acetaminophen and (a) aspirin, (b) phenacetin, (c) acetanilid, (d) any of the above drugs.
15. Overdoses with acetaminophen have been associated with (a) anaphylactic shock and serum sickness, (b) agranulocytosis and aplastic anemia, (c) hepatic necrosis and renal failure, (d) all of the above.
16-24. Match the drug in column A with the statement in column B. Each item in both columns will be used only once.

Column A	*Column B*
16. Aspirin	(a) Methemoglobinemia
17. Aminopyrine	(b) Xerostomia
18. Phenylbutazone	(c) Agranulocytosis
19. Mefenamic acid	(d) Weak acid
20. Acetanilid	(e) Slow onset
21. Phenacetin	(f) The *P* in APC
22. Acetaminophen	(g) Popular aspirin substitute
23. Propoxyphene	
24. Ethoheptazine	

25. Large doses of aspirin (over 5 gm/24 hr) _____ uric acid secretion, and smaller doses (1 to 2 gm/24 hr) tend to _____ uric acid secretion. (a) increase, decrease, (b) decrease, increase, (c) increase, have no effect on, (d) decrease, have no effect on.

26. The most important drug interaction of the salicylates is that which occurs with (a) oral hypoglycemics, (b) antineoplastic agents, (c) oral anticoagulants, (d) thyroid drugs.

27. Acetaminophen does not (a) produce gastric bleeding, (b) affect platelet adhesiveness, (c) affect uric acid excretion, (d) do any of the above.

28. Hemolytic anemia produced by acetaminophen is usually associated with (a) acute overdose, (b) initial dosage, (c) short-term use, (d) long-term use.

29. The nonsteroidal antiinflammatory agents (NSAIAs) all have analgesic, antipyretic, and antiinflammatory properties. They may produce fetal abnormalities and delayed parturition and should be avoided during pregnancy and by nursing mothers. (a) First statement is true, second statement is false. (b) First statement is false, second statement is true. (c) Both statements are true. (d) Both statements are false.

30. The adverse effects of the proprionic acid derivatives (ibuprofen type) are _____ the indoleacetic acid derivatives (indomethacin type). (a) much more dangerous than, (b) much less dangerous than, (c) equivalent to.

31. The pyrroleacetic acid derivatives, tolmetin and zomepirac, have pharmacologic properties and adverse effects that are most equivalent to those of (a) ibuprofen, (b) indomethacin, (c) mefenamic acid.

CHAPTER 11: THE PROSTAGLANDINS, THE THROMBOXANES, AND PROSTACYCLIN

1. Prostaglandins, thromboxanes, and prostacyclin are chemically similar and have been implicated as important in a large number of biologic processes. (a) True. (b) False.

2. In humans, the prostaglandins derived from _____ are the most abundant and perhaps the most important. (a) glutathione, (b) tryptophan, (c) arachidonic acid, (d) lipoic acid, (e) any unsaturated fatty acid.

3. Only _____ can serve as a precursor for the production of the thromboxanes and prostacyclin. (a) glutathione, (b) tryptophan, (c) arachidonic acid, (d) lipoic acid, (e) any unsaturated fatty acid.

4. In contrast to many other biologically active compounds, prostaglandins are not stored in large amounts in body tissues but rather are synthesized immediately before their release. (a) True. (b) False.

5. Prostaglandin synthesis is (a) rhythmic relative to daily activity, (b) dependent on hormonal levels, (c) in response to diverse stimuli, (d) responsive to all of the above mechanisms.

6. Virtually all human tissues have the capacity to synthesize prostaglandin because _____ is found in all tissues. (a) prostaglandin synthetase, (b) prostaglandin oxidase, (c) cyclic endoperoxidase, (d) PGH-PGD isomerase, (e) all of the above enzymes.

7. It is now proposed that numerous nonsteroidal antiinflammatory drugs decrease prostaglandin synthesis by inhibiting (a) prostaglandin synthetase, (b) prostaglandin oxidase, (c) cyclic endoperoxidase, (d) PGH-PGD isomerase, (e) all of the above enzymes.

8. Prostaglandins, thromboxanes, and prostacyclin all exert their effects at extremely low concentrations and have extremely short $t_{\frac{1}{2}}$, usually less than 3 to 5 minutes (a) First statement is true, second statement is false. (b) First statement is false, second statement is true. (c) Both statements are true. (d) Both statements are false.

9. Prostaglandins cannot be categorized as hormones because they are (a) chemically distinct, (b) synthesized in virtually all tissues and exert their effects locally within these same tissues, (c) technically autocoids.

10. Different prostaglandins can have opposing or antagonistic biologic activity. (a) True. (b) False.

11. A thromboxane is a potent stimulator of platelet aggregation and constrictor of vascular smooth muscle, but prostacyclin is a powerful inhibitor of platelet aggregation and potent vasodilator (a) First statement is true, second statement is false. (b) First

statement is false, second statement is true. (c) Both statements are true. (d) Both statements are false.
12. Prostaglandins have been used therapeutically (a) to endure labor, (b) for abortive purposes, (c) to depress labor, (d) for antiabortive purposes, (e) for both *a* and *b*, (f) for both *c* and *d*.

CHAPTER 12: NARCOTIC ANALGESICS AND ANTAGONISTS

1. The principal differences between the narcotic analgesics are their (a) potencies and variety of adverse potentialities, (b) potencies, rates of onset, and durations, (c) chemical structures, (d) overall pharmacologic effects.
2. The narcotic analgesics tend to produce (a) addiction, (b) respiratory depression, (c) sedation, (d) emesis, (e) constipation, (f) only *a* and *b*, (g) only *c* and *d*, (h) all of the above.
3. All opium alkaloids (a) are obtained from the unripe seed capsules of *Papaver somniferum*, (b) are addicting, (c) are analgesics, (d) depress smooth muscle, (e) are characterized by all of the above.
4. Tolerance does *not* develop to which of the following effects of morphine? (a) analgesia, (b) sedation, (c) euphoria, (d) respiratory depression, (e) miosis.
5. Respiratory depression is an important clinical consideration relative to the use of morphine. Quantitatively, this effect generally parallels (a) analgesic potency, (b) molecular weight, (c) euphoric depth, (d) all of the above, (e) none of the above.
6. Morphine causes nausea and vomiting by (a) direct gastrointestinal effects, (b) stimulation of the emetic trigger zone, (c) stimulation of the vomiting center, (d) all of the above mechanisms.
7. Morphine and codeine produce constipation by (a) affecting specific medullary centers, (b) increasing water absorption from the gastrointestinal tract, (c) reducing gastrointestinal secretions and motility, (d) increasing the tone of the gastrointestinal musculature.
8. Which of the following series of effects can be caused by morphine? (a) urinary retention, depression of the vasomotor center, and dilation of the biliary duct, (b) bronchiolar constriction, miosis, convulsions, and urinary retention, (c) urinary retention, increased intracranial pressure, and depression of the vagus, (d) increased intracranial pressure, diuresis, and stimulation of the vagus.
9. The morphine addict may appear completely normal except for (a) sedation and dilated pupils, (b) minor disorientation and lacrimation, (c) constipation and miosis, (d) anorexia and irritability.
10. The diagnostic triad of morphine overdose consists of (a) "pinpoint" pupils, tremor, and vomiting, (b) tremor, perspiration, and chills, (c) dilated pupils, coma, and tremors, (d) coma, depressed respiration, and "pinpoint" pupils.
11. Codeine can be considered a weak morphine. However, it equals morphine as an antitussive and may have greater _____ effects. (a) constipating, (b) emetic, (c) euphoric, (d) excitatory.
12. Which of the following effects are most likely to be seen after a therapeutic dose of codeine? (a) emesis and constipation, (b) minor respiratory depression and nausea, (c) constipation and miosis, (d) euphoria and constipation, (e) all of the above.
13. Unless a patient has developed a tolerance to narcotics, maximal analgesic potency is usually obtained with _____ mg codeine. (a) 30, (b) 60, (c) 90, (d) 120.
14-18. Match the drug with the most relative characteristic given. Each characteristic will be used once.

Drug	*Characteristics*
14. Dihydrocodeinone	a. Principal current use is as an antitussive
15. Dihydromorphinone	b. More potent and more addicting than codeine; ingredient in Percodan
16. Oxymorphone	c. Cannot be legally manufactured or imported into the United States
17. Oxycodone	d. Rapid onset, rapid duration; analgesic potency about five times that of morphine
18. Heroin	e. Analgesic potency and tendency to produce undesirable effects eight to ten times greater than that of morphine

19. Which of the following effects are *not* likely to be associated with the use of meperidine? (a) sedation, (b) constipation, (c) addiction, (d) nausea, (e) relaxation of gastrointestinal musculature, (f) none of the above is associated with the use of meperidine.

20. Meperidine is most likely to be valuable in dental practice in cases where (a) the pain cannot be controlled by morphine, (b) the patient is allergic to morphine, (c) the patient has developed tolerance to morphine, (d) rapid analgesia and sedation are desirable.

21. Alphaprodine, anileridine, and piminodine are most similar to (a) meperidine, (b) morphine, (c) codeine, (d) methadone.

22. What characteristic of methadone has made it useful as a narcotic substitute for addicts? (a) It does not cause addiction. (b) Users do not suffer from mental depression. (c) Withdrawal from methadone appears to be accomplished more easily than from morphine. (d) Methadone cannot be used orally. (e) All of the above.

23. Pentazocine appears to be a more potent analgesic than codeine, but less potent than morphine. In addition to analgesia, it also (a) produces sedation, (b) reduces an elevated temperature, (c) has antiinflammatory properties, (d) does both *a* and *b*, (e) does both *b* and *c*.

24. The fact that pentazocine is classified as a schedule III drug means that it is (a) not considered to be addicting, (b) considered to be less addicting than schedule II drugs, (c) considered to be more addicting than morphine, (d) considered to be more addicting than codeine.

25. Propoxyphene produces analgesia and (a) antipyresis, (b) weak antiinflammatory effects, (c) sedation, (d) no other therapeutic effects.

26. Overdose by which of the following can be antagonized by nalorphine? (a) aspirin, (b) acetaminophen, (c) mefenamic acid, (d) propoxyphene, (e) all of the above, (f) none of the above.

27. When used alone, the analgesic potency of ethoheptazine is probably (a) inferior to that of aspirin, (b) slightly but consistently superior to a placebo, (c) more potent than mefenamic acid, (d) more potent than acetaminophen.

28. Which of the following has an antipyretic effect? (a) propoxyphene, (b) acetaminophen, (c) ethoheptazine, (d) all of the above.

29. In which of the following cases would nalorphine or levallorphan increase or initiate respiratory depression? (a) when used alone, (b) when used in a patient depressed by morphine, (c) when used in a patient depressed by a barbiturate, (d) in both *a* and *b*, (e) in both *b* and *c*, (f) in both *a* and *c*.

30. Papaverine is a benzylisoquinoline opiate that has had limited use as an (a) analgesic, (b) cough suppressant, (c) sedative, (d) peripheral vasodilator.

31. Narcotics are believed to exert their effects by copying the action of endogenous substances such as (a) prostaglandins, (b) bradykinins, (c) enkephalins, (d) endorphins, (e) both *a* and *b*, (f) both *c* and *d*.

32. The narcotic antagonist naloxone is the drug of choice to treat an overdose of propoxyphene. It counteracts the respiratory depression but not the CNS excitation, including tremors and convulsions. (a) First statement is true, second statement is false. (b) First statement is false, second statement is true. (c) Both statements are true. (d) Both statements are false.

33. The basic mechanism for the effects of narcotic agonist-antagonists and the antagonists is (a) different affinities for the different narcotic receptors, (b) affinities for nonnarcotic receptors, (c) general blockage of narcotic receptors, (d) both *b* and *c*.

34. Increasing the dose of pentazocine beyond the usual analgesic dose does not produce an equivalent increase in respiratory depression. This is characteristic of all narcotic agonist-antagonists. (a) First statement is true, second statement is false. (b) First statement is false, second statement is true. (c) Both statements are true. (d) Both statements are false.

35. Large doses of pentazocine can be expected to produce an increase in both blood pressure and heart rate. This is different from what one would expect from narcotic agonists such as morphine. (a) First statement is true, second statement is false. (b) First statement is false, second statement is true. (c) Both statements are true. (d) Both statements are false.

36. As an agonist-antagonist, pentazocine can reverse the respiratory depression secondary to morphine and precipitate withdrawal in an addict. (a) First statement is

true, second statement is false. (b) First statement is false, second statement is true. (c) Both statements are true. (d) Both statements are false.

37. Which of the lists below is the sequence of narcotic agonist-antagonists in the order of their *increasing antagonist* properties (least potent first)? (a) butorphanol, nalbuphine, pentazocine, (b) pentazocine, nalbuphine, butorphanol, (c) pentazocine, butorphanol, nalbuphine, (d) nalbuphine, butorphanol, pentazocine.

38. Which of the currently available narcotic antagonists has purely antagonist properties? (a) nalorphine, (b) levollorphan, (c) naloxone, (d) all of the above.

CHAPTER 13: CENTRAL NERVOUS SYSTEM STIMULANTS

1. The principal site of action of strychnine is the (a) cerebral cortex, (b) midbrain, (c) brain stem, (d) hindbrain, (e) spinal cord.

2. Strychnine causes excessive motor impulses that lead to heightened reflexes, stiffness of facial and cervical muscles, and possible convulsions by (a) stimulating excitatory neurons, (b) depressing inhibitory neurons, (c) both *a* and *b,* (d) neither *a* nor *b.*

3. The major site of action of picrotoxin in reversing respiratory depression caused by barbiturates is the (a) cerebral cortex, (b) midbrain, (c) medulla, (d) spinal cord.

4. The primary use(s) of pentylenetetrazol is (are) to (a) reverse respiratory depression caused by barbiturates, (b) assist in the diagnosis of epilepsy, (c) evaluate the effectiveness of anticonvulsants against petit mal epilepsy, (d) do both *a* and *b,* (e) do both *b* and *c,* (f) do all of the above.

5. Why is the effectiveness of amphetamines as anorexigenic agents limited? (a) They are not potent anorexigenic drugs. (b) Significant tolerance to the anorexigenic effect develops within 3 to 4 weeks. (c) Their effectiveness is limited because of both *a* and *b.* (d) Their effectiveness is not limited because of either *a* or *b.*

6. Which of the following signs and symptoms would you expect to see in a patient taking amphetamines? (a) increased heart rate and hypertension, (b) restlessness and irritability, (c) insomnia, (d) both *a* and *b,* (e) both *b* and *c,* (f) all of the above.

7. The xanthines allay drowsiness and fatigue and at certain doses increase the force of contraction of the heart, increase heart rate and cardiac output, and stimulate respiration. They act to a greater extent on the _____ than any of the other CNS stimulants discussed. (a) cerebral cortex, (b) midbrain, (c) medulla, (d) spinal cord.

8. In addition to action as CNS stimulants, the xanthines also have _____ properties. (a) diuretic, (b) antidiuretic, (c) histaminic, (d) antihistaminic, (e) diuretic and antihistaminic, (f) histaminic and antidiuretic.

CHAPTER 14: ANTICONVULSANT DRUGS

1. Anticonvulsants control the symptoms but do not treat the cause of the disease. Theories to explain the mechanism of action of anticonvulsants state that these drugs may prevent epileptic seizures by (a) increasing the activity of inhibitory neurons, (b) impeding the spread of discharges throughout the cortex, (c) weakening the discharge of ectopic foci, (d) any one or all of the above mechanisms.

2. When an epileptic is treated with phenobarbital, which of the following are likely to develop in time? (a) tolerance to the sedative effects, (b) tolerance to the anticonvulsant effects, (c) physical dependence, (d) only *b* and *c,* (e) none of the above, (f) all of the above.

3. Phenytoin produces gingival hyperplasia in 20% to 30% of patients. Although infrequent, phenytoin, also has caused (a) adverse hepatic and hematologic effects, (b) ataxia and hirsutism, (c) elevated blood cholesterol and phosphatase levels, (d) both *a* and *b,* (e) both *b* and *c,* (f) both *a* and *c,* (g) all of the above, (h) none of the above.

4. Why would mephenytoin *not* be selected over phenytoin as the drug of choice for prophylaxis against grand mal seizures? Mephenytoin is (a) not effective against grand mal seizures, (b) less potent than phenytoin, (c) more toxic than phenytoin, (d) both *b* and *c.*

5. Although ethosuximide is considerably less toxic than trimethadione, it has caused (a) insomnia, diarrhea, and fatigue, (b) dermatitis, headache, and liver damage, (c) blood dyscrasias, (d) all of the above except *c,* (e) all of the above.

6. Relative to structure-activity relationship, primidone is a useful anticonvulsant because it is (a) chemically related to trimethadione, (b) oxidized to phenobarbital in humans, (c) oxidized to trimethadione in humans, (d) oxidized to phenytoin in humans.

7. Phenacemide is a potent and highly toxic anticonvulsant that is used when other drugs have failed in cases of _____ seizures. (a) grand mal, (b) petit mal, (c) psychomotor, (d) all of the above.

8-18. Indicate whether the drug listed is used principally against (a) grand mal, (b) petit mal, (c) psychomotor, (d) grand mal and psychomotor, (e) grand mal, petit mal, and psychomotor.

  8. Phenobarbital
  9. Metharbital
 10. Phenytoin
 11. Mephenytoin
 12. Ethotoin
 13. Trimethadione
 14. Paramethadione
 15. Ethosuximide
 16. Methsuximide
 17. Primidone
 18. Phenacemide

CHAPTER 15: LOCAL ANESTHETICS

1. The synthesis of procaine by _____ in 1905 initiated a new era in local anesthesia. (a) Niemann, (b) Koller, (c) Halstead, (d) Einhorn.

2. The heading "Trends in Local Anesthesia in Dentistry" in this chapter indicates a movement toward (a) more potent and more toxic local anesthetics, (b) less potent and more toxic local anesthetics, (c) more potent and less toxic local anesthetics, (d) less potent and less toxic local anesthetics.

3. Local anesthetics are converted to salts for clinical use because the latter are (a) less toxic but more potent, (b) more stable and have a greater water solubility, (c) more stable and have a greater fat solubility, (d) more potent and cause less local tissue damage.

4. What is the most potent and most toxic local anesthetic in current use? (a) lidocaine, (b) mepivacaine, (c) proparacaine, (d) dibucaine.

5. Local anesthetics inhibit the propagation of nerve impulses (a) along nerve fibers, (b) at sensory endings, (c) at myoneural junctions, (d) at synapses, (e) at *a* and *b* only, (f) at all the above sites.

6. Some local anesthetics are used as cardiac antiarrhythmic agents. This is possible because they (a) depress the excitability of heart muscle, (b) reduce conduction rate, (c) increase conduction rate, (d) do both *a* and *b*, (e) do both *a* and *c*.

7. The rate at which a local anesthetic leaves the injection site and enters systemic circulation is increased by the application of (a) cold and the absence of a vasoconstrictor in the solution, (b) cold and the presence of a vasoconstrictor, (c) heat and the absence of a vasoconstrictor, (d) heat and the presence of a vasoconstrictor.

8. Severe liver disease would *least* affect the metabolism of which of the following agents? (a) procaine, (b) lidocaine, (c) mepivacaine, (d) prilocaine.

9. The presence of infection in an injection area may reduce the effectiveness of a local anesthetic because (a) the low pH of the area may inhibit the liberation of the salt from the free base form, (b) the low pH of the area may inhibit the liberation of free base, (c) the high pH of the area may inhibit the liberation of the salt from the free base form, (d) the high pH of the area may inhibit the liberation of free base.

10. Certain antihistamines, such as tripelennamine and diphenhydramine, have significant local anesthetic actions. The anesthesia produced by these drugs may be characterized as (a) potent and long acting, (b) potent and short acting, (c) weak and long acting, (d) weak and short acting.

11. Vasoconstrictors, which may be included in local anesthetic solutions, function to (a) prolong and increase the depth of anesthesia, (b) reduce the toxic effects of the drug, (c) increase the toxic effects of the drug, (d) provide both *a* and *b*, (e) provide both *a* and *c*.

12. A working conference of the American Dental Association and American Heart Association has said that the concentration of vasoconstrictors normally used in dental local anesthetics are not contraindicated in patients with cardiovascular disease when administered carefully and with preliminary aspiration. The N.Y. Heart Asso-

ciation has also stated that vasoconstrictors are *not* contraindicated in patients with cardiovascular disease but, as a guideline, recommended the following as a maximal dose of epinephrine for any one session: (a) 0.1 mg (10 ml of a 1:100,000 solution), (b) 0.2 mg (20 ml of a 1:100,000 solution), (c) 0.3 mg (30 ml of a 1:100,000 solution), (d) 0.4 mg (40 ml of a 1:100,000 solution).

13-17. According to Monheim, how many milliliters of the following 2% local anesthetic solutions represent the *maximal* recommended dose for a healthy adult?

   13. Procaine (a) 10, (b) 20, (c) 30, (d) 40
   14. Lidocaine (a) 5, (b) 10, (c) 15, (d) 20
   15. Mepivacaine (a) 5, (b) 10, (c) 15, (d) 20
   16. Prilocaine (a) 5, (b) 10, (c) 15, (d) 20
   17. Tetracaine (a) 1, (b) 1.5, (c) 2, (d) 2.5

18. The most frequent cause of a high blood level of local anesthetic after a dental injection is (a) the injection of an excessive volume, (b) the injection of an excessive concentration, (c) intravascular injection, (d) inadequate hepatic function, (e) inadequate renal function.

19. You have established that a patient had an allergic reaction to procaine 6 months ago. Which of the following would be contraindicated? (a) a topical spray containing tetracaine, (b) a topical spray containing lidocaine, (c) mepivacaine by injection, (d) prilocaine by injection, (e) all of the above, (f) none of the above.

20. Which of the following is *not* true of procaine? (a) rapid onset, (b) short duration, (c) potency one half that of lidocaine, (d) one of the safest local anesthetics, (e) effective topically.

21. Which of the following is *not* true of lidocaine? (a) rapid onset, (b) short duration, (c) spreads well through tissues, (d) effective topically, (e) neither *a* nor *b* is true of lidocaine, (f) neither *b* nor *c* is true of lidocaine.

22. Compared to lidocaine, mepivacaine is said to be (a) profoundly more potent, (b) significantly less toxic, (c) faster acting, (d) longer acting, (e) equivocal.

23. Which of the following is *least* effective topically? (a) lidocaine, (b) mepivacaine, (c) tetracaine, (d) cocaine, (e) benzocaine, (f) dyclonine.

24. Compared to lidocaine, prilocaine is (a) less potent, (b) less toxic, (c) longer acting, (d) all of the above, (e) none of the above.

25. A unique toxicity of prilocaine is that in some patients it causes (a) methemoglobinemia, (b) disorientation, (c) brain rot, (d) pregnancy, (e) all of the above.

26. Pyrrocaine is most similar therapeutically and chemically to (a) lidocaine, (b) prilocaine, (c) procaine, (d) tetracaine, (e) propoxycaine.

27. Which of the following is *not* true of tetracaine? (a) slow onset, (b) long duration, (c) low potency, (d) high toxicity, (e) rapidly absorbed topically, (f) effective topically.

28. Compared to tetracaine, propoxycaine has (a) greater potency, (b) greater toxicity, (c) a more rapid onset, (d) a lack of topical activity, (e) both *a* and *b*, (f) both *c* and *d*.

29. A patient reports an allergy to procaine. Which of the following topical agents could be most safely used? (a) benzocaine, (b) tetracaine, (c) cocaine, (d) dyclonine.

30. The relatively new long duration local anesthetics, bupivacaine and etidocaine, are _____ derivatives. (a) PABA, (b) xylidine, (c) toluidine, (d) antihistamine.

31. The protein-binding capacity of local anesthetics determines their durations. What is the relationship? (a) low degree of protein binding, short duration, high degree of protein binding, long duration; (b) high degree of protein binding, short duration, low degree of protein binding, long duration.

32. In the past, the action of local anesthetics was thought to be related to calcium ions. Now it is believed that local anesthetics block the sodium channels, thereby reducing membrane permeability to sodium. (a) First statement is true, second statement is false. (b) First statement is false, second statement is true. (c) Both statements are true. (d) Both statements are false.

33. The major advantage(s) of bupivacaine over lidocaine and mepivacaine is/are (a) lower toxicity, (b) longer duration, (c) greater potency, (d) all of the above.

34. The major advantage(s) of etidocaine over lidocaine and mepivacaine is/are (a) lower toxicity, (b) longer duration, (c) all of the above.

35. How much lidocaine is in a dental cartridge containing 2% lidocaine and 1:100,000 epinephrine?

36. How much epinephrine is in a dental cartridge containing 2% lidocaine and 1:100,000 epinephrine?

CHAPTER 16: HISTAMINE AND ANTIHISTAMINES

1. Which of the following reactions is most characteristic of histamine release in humans? (a) vasodilation, decreased capillary permeability, and stimulation of exocrine glands, (b) vasoconstriction, bronchoconstriction, and stimulation of exocrine glands, (c) increased capillary permeability, bronchoconstriction, and stimulation of exocrine glands, (d) vasodilation, bronchoconstriction, and depression of exocrine glands.
2. Tissue histamine can be released by (a) allergic reactions, (b) physical trauma, (c) infection, (d) some drugs, (e) all of the above, (f) none of the above.
3. The best method of counteracting the effects of an acute release of histamine is by (a) physiologic antagonism, (b) specific antihistaminic medication, (c) use of adrenal steroids, (d) induction of emesis.
4. Which of the following antihistamines would be expected to produce the most sedation? (a) chlorpheniramine (Chlor-Trimeton), (b) tripelennamine (Pyribenzamine), (c) chlorcyclizine (Di-Paralene), (d) promethazine (Phenergan).
5. Which one of the following actions of histamine is not blocked by H_1 antagonists? (a) vasodilation, (b) increase in gastric secretions, (c) itching, (d) increase in salivary secretions.
6. All histamine antagonists act by (a) inhibiting the release of histamine from mast cells, (b) competitively blocking histamine tissue receptor sites, (c) increasing the metabolic breakdown of histamine, (d) chelating histamine into an inactive complex.
7. The prolonged use of H_1 antagonists may produce xerostomia. This results from their (a) anticholinergic action, (b) cholinergic action, (c) inhibition of histamine-induced salivation, (d) direct depression of salivary gland cells.
8. The main therapeutic use of H_2 receptor antagonists such as cimetidine is in the treatment of (a) migraine, (b) bowel obstruction, (c) duodenal ulcer, (d) urinary retention.
9. The dental usefulness of H_1 receptor antagonists is based on their (a) sedative and antiemetic action, (b) reduction of salivary secretion, (c) reduction of dizziness, (d) postoperative reduction of swelling.

CHAPTER 17: HORMONES AND RELATED SUBSTANCES

1. Many peptide hormones produce their effects by interacting with adenylate cyclase, which acts directly to (a) increase the rate of cyclic AMP synthesis, (b) increase the rate of cyclic AMP degradation, (c) decrease the rate of cyclic AMP degradation, (d) inhibit protein kinases, (e) stimulate protein synthesis.
2. The anterior pituitary hormones that control skin pigmentation are (a) the gonadotropins, (b) thyrotropin and corticotropin, (c) beta and gamma lipotropins, (d) endorphins and enkephalins, (e) alpha and beta melanocyte-stimulating hormones.
3. Growth hormone (a) stimulates bone growth by stimulating the formation of somatomedin, (b) decreases the rate of protein synthesis, (c) is secreted by the posterior pituitary gland, (d) secretion is decreased in response to sleep, exercise, and fasting (e) deficiency causes acromegaly.
4. The following are true of antidiuretic hormone (vasopressin) *except* that (a) it is used to treat diabetes insipidus, (b) it inhibits water reabsorption by the kidney collecting ducts, (c) it is secreted by the posterior pituitary gland, (d) it has a general pressor effect on the vasculature, (e) its release is increased by pain and emotional stress.
5. The following are true of oxytocin *except* that (a) it is used to treat postpartum hemorrhage, (b) it is used to induce labor, (c) it inhibits mammary gland milk ejection, (d) it stimulates uterine contraction, (e) its release is controlled by the hypothalamus.
6. An excess of which of the following hormones is associated with increased sensitivity to epinephrine? (a) testosterone, (b) parathyroid hormone, (c) insulin, (d) thyroid hormone, (e) estrogen.
7. The following is used in the treatment of hypothyroidism (a) perchlorate ion, (b) sodium liothyronine (Cytomel), (c) Lugol's solution, (d) ^{131}I (e) propylthiouracil.
8. The following is used in the treatment of hyperthyroidism: (a) Lugol's solution, (b) thyroglobulin (Proloid), (c) liothyronine sodium (Cytomel), (d) levothyroxine sodium (Synthroid), (e) propylthiouracil.
9. Parathyroid hormone does all of the following *except* that (a) it increases the renal tubular reabsorption of calcium, (b) it increases calcium mobilization from bone, (c) it decreases the intestinal absorption of calcium, (d) it decreases calcium elimination in saliva, (e) it maintains plasma calcium above 7 mg/100 ml.

10. Calcitonin (a) is produced by the parathyroid gland, (b) production is regulated by plasma calcium levels, (c) produces hypercalcemia, (d) stimulates bone resorption, (e) is used to treat hypocalcemia.

11. Insulin (a) stimulates fat mobilization, (b) stimulates gluconeogenesis, (c) inhibits glycogen production from glucose, (d) stimulates glucose transport across cell membranes, (e) inhibits protein synthesis.

12. Treatment of a hypoglycemic reaction in an unconscious diabetic patient includes (a) intravenous glucose, (b) insulin injection, USP, (c) protamine zinc insulin suspension, USP, (d) tolbutamide (Orinase), (e) chlorpropamide (Diabinese).

13. Tolbutamide (Orinase) acts by (a) blocking the destruction of insulin, (b) stimulating the alpha cells of the pancreas, (c) stimulating the beta cells of the pancreas, (d) directly inhibiting the release of glucose from the liver, (e) increasing glucose utilization by activating the enzyme hexokinase.

14. The oral contraceptives prevent conception primarily by (a) a spermatocidal action, (b) preventing ovulation, (c) blocking implantation, (d) decreasing uterine motility, (e) stimulating FSH release from the pituitary.

15. All of the following are contraindications to the use of oral contraceptives *except* (a) hyperthyroidism, (b) thromboembolic disease, (c) breast cancer, (d) undiagnosed genital bleeding, (e) significant liver dysfunction.

CHAPTER 18: ADRENOCORTICOSTEROIDS

1. Which of the following principally affects electrolyte balance? (a) cortisone, (b) hydrocortisone, (c) deoxycorticosterone, (d) corticosterone.

2. The glucocorticoids are basically catabolic agents; consequently, they (a) increase the utilization of glucose and decrease gluconeogenesis, (b) increase gluconeogenesis and decrease the utilization of glucose, (c) increase both, (d) decrease both.

3. You would expect excessive blood levels of corticosteroids to cause (a) hyperglycemia, (b) hypoglycemia, (c) no change in blood glucose.

4. Abnormally high levels of corticoids are not likely to cause (a) negative nitrogen balance, (b) a depression of growth, (c) impaired wound healing, (d) a decrease in the deposition of fat.

5. The corticoids, particularly the mineralocorticoids, act on the renal tubules to _____ sodium retention and _____ potassium excretion. (a) increase, decrease, (b) decrease, increase, (c) decrease both, (d) increase both.

6. Excessive levels of mineralocorticoids would most likely cause (a) dehydration and hypertension, (b) dehydration and hypotension, (c) edema and hypertension, (d) edema and hypotension.

7. In Addison's disease you would expect to see a tendency toward (a) dehydration, hypotension, and hypoglycemia, (b) edema, hypotension, and hypoglycemia, (c) dehydration, hypertension, and hypoglycemia, (d) edema, hypertension, and hypoglycemia, (e) dehydration, hypotension, and hyperglycemia, (f) edema, hypertension, and hyperglycemia.

8. Which of the following effects would you expect might be induced by imbalances in corticoid levels? (a) inhibition of the activity of leukocytes, (b) altered mental function, (c) altered heart function, (d) inhibited bone formation, (e) all of the above except *b,* (f) all of the above except *d,* (g) all of the above.

9. By what mechanism can the therapeutic administration of glucocorticoids result in atrophy of the adrenal cortex? (a) by direct depression of cell growth within the cortex, (b) by causing a sclerosing effect on cortical interstitial tissues, (c) by depressing the secretion of most endogenous glucocorticoids, and some endogenous mineralocorticoids, (d) by depressing the secretion of corticotropin (ACTH), (e) by all the above mechanisms.

10. Many undesirable effects can result from the long-term use of the corticosteroids. These effects are extremely varied and occur frequently in one combination or another. Additionally, the rapid withdrawal of corticoid therapy after long-term use is most likely to cause symptoms of (a) withdrawal because of physical dependence, (b) withdrawal because of psychologic dependence, (c) adrenal insufficiency, (d) adrenal hyperactivity.

11. Fill in the blanks.
    An adrenal crisis can be precipitated by dental procedures. The basis of this crisis is that the patient is unable to make a physiologic adjustment to _____.

When used for replacement therapy, _____ is frequently used to alleviate the mineralocorticoid deficiency.

Individuals taking corticoids are likely to have a lowered resistance to _____.

The most frequently used method of administration of corticoids in dental practice is the _____ route.

CHAPTER 19: ANTINEOPLASTIC DRUGS

1. Antineoplastic agents may be used (a) as palliative therapy or as a primary treatment modality, (b) in conjunction with surgery and x-ray therapy, (c) when surgery or x-ray therapy is not curative, (d) in all of the above approaches to cancer therapy.
2. In the "cell cycle" theory (a) antimetabolites act in all phases, (b) antimetabolites act only in the mitosis stage, (c) alkylating agents act only in the synthesis stage, (d) alkylating agents act in all phases.
3. Allopurinol (Zyloprim) is sometimes prescribed with antineoplastic agents to (a) prevent hyperuricemia, (b) decrease liver toxicity, (c) inhibit alopecia, (d) accomplish all of the above.
4. An important but least common toxic manifestation of antineoplastic drug therapy is/are (a) suppression of bone marrow activity (leukopenia, thrombocytopenia, anemia), (b) gastrointestinal disturbances (nausea, stomatitis, vomiting, hemorrhagic diarrhea), (c) cutaneous reactions (erythema, exfoliative dermatitis, Stevens-Johnson syndrome), (d) hepatotoxicity and neurotoxicity, (e) renal tubular impairment, (f) immune deficiency (increased susceptibility to infection and second malignancy), (g) inhibition of spermatogenesis and oogenesis.
5. List six oral conditions often caused by the antineoplastic agents. (a) _____ (b) _____ (c) _____ (d) _____ (e) _____ (f) _____
6. The best oral rinses for patients receiving antineoplastic drug therapy are (a) pleasant-tasting commercial mouthwashes, (b) antibacterial mouthwashes, (c) 3% hydrogen peroxide, (d) warm saline rinses.

CHAPTER 20: DIURETICS AND ANTIHYPERTENSIVE DRUGS

1-6. Match the antihypertensive drug with the step in which it is usually employed in the progression of hypertension therapy. You may use the choices more than once.

1. Prazosin   (a) Step 1
2. Chlorothiazide   (b) Step 2
3. Guanethidine   (c) Step 3
4. Methyldopa   (d) Step 4
5. Propranolol
6. Hydralazine

7-10. Indicate the type of diuretic that the statement describes: (a) mercurial, (b) carbonic anhydrase inhibitor, and (c) thiazide.

7. Orally effective sulfonamides that have adverse effects, which include drowsiness, fatigue, gastrointestinal disturbances, paresthesias of the face and extremities, allergic dermatologic reactions, blood dyscrasias, and renal calculi.
8. The most potent diuretics that are usually administered intramuscularly.
9. Adverse potentialities include cardiac toxicity, allergic reactions, nephrotoxicity, stomatitis, gastric irritation, weakness, vertigo, and drowsiness.
10. Side effects are usually mild; hypokalemia is caused in some patients.

11. What is/are the principal differences between chlorothiazide and hydrochlorothiazide? Hydrochlorothiazide is (a) more potent, (b) less toxic, (c) more consistently effective, (d) more potent, less toxic, and more effective.

12-16. Select the site of action that best corresponds with the diuretic listed. You may use the choices more than once.

12. Furosemide   a. Thick cortical ascending limb of Henle's loop and distal tubule
13. Spironolactone
14. Triamterene   b. Thick medullary ascending limb of Henle's loop
15. Chlorothiazide   c. Distal tubule
16. Urea   d. Proximal tubule and Henle's loop

17-22. Match the antihypertensive drug with the best corresponding mechanism of action. You may use each choice only *one* time.

17. Nadolol   a. Alpha receptor blocker
18. Captopril   b. Beta receptor blocker
19. Prazosin   c. Blocks autonomic ganglia
20. Mecamylamine   d. A direct effect on vascular muscle
21. Minoxidil   e. Antagonist of renin-angiotensin system
22. Clonidine   f. Acts in the CNS

23. Side effects of the antihypertensive drugs that may be more prominent to the dentist would include (a) postural hypotension, (b) excessive salivation, (c) dryness of the mouth, (d) reduced renin levels, (e) *a* and *b,* (f) *c* and *d,* (g) *a* and *c,* (h) *b* and *d.*

24-28. Indicate the drug that best corresponds with each statement. (a) diazoxide, (b) methyldopa, (c) prazosin, (d) reserpine, (e) metoprolol.

   24. Established side effects include diarrhea, psychic depression leading to suicidal tendencies, and gastrointestinal upset.

   25. Selectively blocks the alpha$_1$ receptor, producing peripheral vasodilation.

   26. Is converted to alpha methylnorepinephrine in the CNS.

   27. Is a cardioselective beta$_1$ antagonist in usually employed doses.

28. Is a potent direct-acting vasodilator for use in hypertensive crisis.

CHAPTER 21: OTHER CARDIOVASCULAR DRUGS

1-6. Mark items true (T) or false (F) relative to nitroglycerin.

   1. Taken sublingually

   2. Effective prophylactically

   3. Produces vasodilation

   4. Sometimes causes sudden hypotension

   5. Sometimes causes syncope

   6. Drug of choice for relief of anginal attacks

7-13. Mark items true (T) or false (F) relative to amyl nitrite.

   7. Taken by inhalation

   8. Has a bad odor

   9. Produces vasodilation

   10. Sometimes causes sudden and severe hypotension

   11. Sometimes causes syncope

   12. Slowest acting form of nitrite

   13. Prone to produce headaches

14. Quinidine is one of the oldest and most commonly used drugs in the treatment of cardiac arrhythmias. Which of the following is/are *not* decreased by quinidine? (a) myocardial excitability, (b) conduction velocity, (c) refractory period, (d) vagal influence on myocardium.

15-18. Are the statements true (T) or false (F)?

   15. The effect of procainamide on cardiac muscle is similar to that of quinidine, including an anticholinergic effect.

   16. As an antiarrhythmic agent, the greatest use for lidocaine is in patients recovering from cardiac surgery or after myocardial infarctions.

   17. When used as an antiarrhythmic, phenytoin does not appear to depress either cardiac excitability nor automaticity.

   18. As an antiarrhythmic, digitalis is most effective against ventricular arrhythmias.

19. The cardiac glycosides differ from one another in terms of (a) potency, (b) preferred route of administration, (c) onset of action, (d) duration of action, (e) rate of excretion, (f) all of these.

20. The major action of digitalis on the failing heart is (a) increase the rate of A-V conduction, (b) decrease the force of contraction, (c) increase the force of contraction, (d) decrease atrial rhythm.

21. Which of the following is used to treat cardiac arrhythmias and angina pectoris? (a) verapamil, (b) propranolol, (c) bretylium, (d) quinidine, (e) digitalis.

22. The mechanism of the antiarrhythmic action of verapamil is best described as (a) beta$_1$ adrenergic receptor blockade, (b) coronary artery vasodilation, (c) calcium channel blockade, (d) alpha adrenergic receptor blockade.

23. Heparin is one of the most commonly used anticoagulants. It acts (a) by interfering with the interaction of thromboplastin with calcium ions, (b) as a vitamin K antimetabolite and thereby interferes with the hepatic synthesis of prothrombin, (c) as

an antithromboplastin and prevents the enzymatic conversion of prothrombin to thrombin, (d) by blocking the conversion of fibrinogen to fibrin.

24. Which of the following is not true of heparin? (a) It cannot be used orally. (b) It is expensive. (c) It has a slow onset. (d) It has a short duration of action.

25. The coumarins are commonly used oral anticoagulants. They act (a) by interfering with the interaction of thromboplastin with calcium ions, (b) as vitamin K antimetabolites and thereby interfere with the hepatic synthesis of prothrombin, (c) as an antithromboplastin and prevent the enzymatic conversion of prothrombin to thrombin, (d) by blocking the conversion of fibrinogen to fibrin.

26. Relative to heparin, the coumarins are (a) less expensive, more convenient to administer, and have a slower onset, (b) more expensive, more convenient to administer, and have a slower onset, (c) less expensive, less convenient to administer, and have a slower onset, (d) more expensive, more convenient to administer, and have a faster onset, (e) less expensive, more convenient to administer, and have a faster onset.

27. The antihyperlipidemic drug that acts through a mechanism that involves inhibition of cholesterol synthesis is (a) nicotinic acid, (b) cholestyramine, (c) clofibrate, (d) colestipol.

CHAPTER 22: ANTIMICROBIAL AGENTS

1. Antibiotic sensitivity tests (a) determine in vivo potency, (b) differentiate between bactericidal and bacteriostatic effects, (c) do neither *a* nor *b,* (d) do both *a* and *b.*

2. The culture of fluid from a periapical abscess indicates the presence of beta hemolytic streptococci. The use of an antimicrobial drug is determined to be necessary. You would continue therapy for at least (a) 48 hours after the symptoms of infection are absent, (b) 10 days, (c) 14 days after fever and tenderness are absent, (d) 20 days.

3. Sulfonamides are not considered to be antibiotics because they (a) only inhibit bacterial growth, (b) are semisynthetic chemicals, (c) are not produced by microorganisms, (d) are organic chemicals.

4. The principal difference between the potassium, procaine, and benzathine salts of penicillin G is their (a) toxicity, (b) potency, (c) duration of action, (d) antibacterial spectrum.

5. How many international units are in 125 and 250 mg of penicillin? (a) 100,000 and 200,000, (b) 200,000 and 400,000, (c) 300,000 and 600,000, (d) 400,000 and 800,000.

6. In relation to penicillin G, the penicillinase-resistant penicillins are generally (a) more effective against nonpenicillinase producers, (b) more toxic, (c) safer during pregnancy, (d) less allergenic.

7. Ampicillin differs from penicillin G in that it (a) has fewer toxic potentialities, (b) is less allergenic, (c) is resistant to penicillinase, (d) has a slightly broader spectrum.

8. Carbenicillin should be reserved for use against (a) sensitive strains of *Pseudomonas* and *Proteus,* (b) penicillinase-producing staphylococci, (c) group A beta hemolytic streptococci, (d) all the above.

9. The most common side effects of erythromycin are _____ in nature. (a) gastrointestinal, (b) dermatologic, (c) auditory, (d) hematologic.

10. Which of the following cephalosporins would be most practical for dental use on an outpatient basis? (a) cephalothin, (b) cephalexin, (c) cephaloridine, (d) cephaloglycin, (e) cephazolin.

11. Which of the following is a true comparison of lincomycin and clindamycin? (a) Clindamycin has a slightly broader antibacterial spectrum and less gastrointestinal side effects. (b) Lincomycin is absorbed faster and is more effective against osteomyelitis. (c) Clindamycin is more potent but more toxic. (d) Lincomycin causes more gastrointestinal problems but is less allergenic.

12. Tetracyclines should not be used with methoxyflurane because of (a) cross-tolerance, (b) antagonistic effects, (c) additive hepatic toxicity, (d) additive nephrotoxicity.

13. However, tetracyclines are notably ineffective for (a) acute necrotizing ulcerative gingivitis, (b) recurrent aphthous stomatitis, (c) prophylaxis against subacute bacterial endocarditis, (d) all of the above conditions.

14. The use of chloramphenicol is extremely limited because of its great toxicity. This toxicity manifests principally as serious and often fatal (a) blood dyscrasias, (b) liver damage, (c) kidney impairement, (d) cardiovascular effects.

15. Streptomycin is a toxic drug. Bacteria develop resistance to it quickly and frequently. Partly for these reasons its current use is principally in the treatment of (a) syphilis, (b) shigellosis, (c) typhoid, (d) tuberculosis.

16. Which of the following drugs has had the most significant use against staphylococcal enterocolitis? (a) gentamicin, (b) kanamycin, (c) vancomycin, (d) all three of the above are equally effective.

17. The currently important topical antibiotics are all (a) toxic systemically, (b) well absorbed orally, (c) of moderate allergenicity, (d) broad-spectrum drugs.

18. Nystatin is important in dental practice in the treatment of superficial candidiasis. What drug would be used systemically against disseminated candidiasis? (a) nystatin, (b) amphotericin B, (c) candicidin, (d) griseofulvin, (e) flucytosine.

19. Stevens-Johnson syndrome is associated with (a) most sulfonamides, (b) long-acting sulfonamides, (c) less soluble sulfonamides, (d) topical sulfonamides.

20. The following drugs are primarily used in the treatment of urinary tract infections. Which one acts by releasing formaldehyde in an acidic urine? (a) sulfisoxazole, (b) trimethoprim-sulfamethoxazole, (c) methenamine, (d) nitrofurantoin, (e) nalidixic acid.

21. Tuberculin converters and reactors exposed to tuberculosis are usually treated for one year with (a) streptomycin, (b) isoniazid, (c) ethambutol, (d) rifampin, (e) aminosalicylic acid (PAS).

22. When is streptomycin used alone in the treatment of pulmonary tuberculosis? (a) When the case is mild. (b) When the case is severe. (c) In both severe and mild cases. (d) It is seldom if ever used alone.

23-32. In questions 23 to 32, match the drug with its most appropriate description. Each drug and description will be used once.

Drug	*Description*
23. Idoxuridine	(a) An orally effective cephalosporin
24. Amatadine	(b) May produce an orange-red color in urine, saliva, and
25. Rifampin	sweat
26. Ethambutol	(c) Especially effective in the treatment of urinary tract in-
27. Nalidixic acid	fections caused by *Proteus*
28. Nitrofurantoin	(d) An antiviral agent that exerts its effect largely on DNA
29. Flucytosine	synthesis
30. Spectinomycin	(e) Has largely replaced PAS in the treatment of tuberculosis
31. Tobramycin	(f) Especially active against *Pseudomonas*
32. Cephradine	(g) A synthetic antifungal that has been used successfully against mucocutaneous candidiasis
	(h) Effective against many common urinary tract pathogens
	(i) An antiviral agent having prophylactic effects against Asian (A2) influenza
	(j) Effective against gonococci

33. Which of the following presents the least problem relative to the development of bacterial resistance? (a) penicillin G, (b) penicillin V, (c) streptomycin, (d) tetracycline.

34. Allergic reactions are a more serious concern with which of the following antimicrobial agents? (a) penicillin, (b) erythromycin, (c) tetracycline, (d) lincomycin.

35. Assume that all the following drugs "hit" the pathogen involved in a particular infection. Which agent could most likely be used safely at several times the usual dosage levels if necessary? (a) penicillin, (b) erythromycin, (c) tetracycline, (d) clindamycin.

36. Which of the following has the broadest spectrum? (a) penicillin G, (b) erythromycin, (c) tetracycline, (d) ampicillin.

37. Bacterial resistance will develop less frequently and less quickly to (a) penicillin G, (b) ampicillin, (c) tetracycline, (d) streptomycin.

38. Which of the following are bactericidal? (a) penicillins, (b) cephalosporins, (c) erythromycin, (d) clindamycin, (e) *a* and *b* only, (f) all of the above.

39. Which of the following are *not* penicillinase resistant? (a) methicillin and oxacillin, (b) ampicillin and hetacillin, (c) cloxacillin and dicloxacillin, (d) neither *a* nor *b*, (e) neither *b* nor *c*.

40. A *nonallergic* rash would most likely be seen during the use of (a) penicillin V, (b) ampicillin, (c) methicillin, (d) carbenicillin.

41. Erythromycin acts by interfering with (a) bacterial cell wall synthesis, (b) protein synthesis, (c) both *a* and *b,* (d) neither *a* nor *b.*

42. The designation of cephalosporins as first, second, or third generation is based on (a) decreasing toxicity, (b) increasing toxicity, (c) broadening antimicrobial action, (d) narrowing antimicrobial action.

43. The principal danger in using lincomycin or clindamycin is their propensity to produce (a) pseudomembranous colitis, (b) liver damage, (c) kidney damage, (d) agranulocytosis, (e) aplastic anemia.

44. For systemic effects, vancomycin is administered (a) orally, (b) intramuscularly, (c) intravenously, (d) by all of the above routes.

45. The tetracyclines are _____ drugs. (a) intermediate spectrum, bacteriostatic, (b) intermediate spectrum, bactericidal, (c) broad spectrum, bactericidal, (d) broad spectrum, bacteriostatic.

46. The main difference between the various tetracyclines is their different (a) durations of action, (b) toxicities, (c) antimicrobial spectra, (d) onset times, (e) mechanisms of action.

47. Liver damage from tetracyclines is most frequently a problem in (a) pregnant women, (b) children, (c) young adults, (d) patients with Addison's disease, (e) diabetic individuals.

48. The most significant usefulness of the aminoglycoside antimicrobials is against (a) mixed infections, (b) severe anaerobic infections, (c) severe gram-negative infections, (d) severe gram-positive infections.

49. Metronidazole is particularly useful against (a) many anaerobes, (b) trichomonal organisms, (c) penicillinase producing staphylococci, (d) only *a* and *b,* (e) only *b* and *c,* (f) all of the above.

CHAPTER 23: LOCALLY ACTING MEDICATIONS: ANTIMICROBIALS, HEMOSTATICS, AND PROTECTIVES

1. Which of the following are possible mechanisms for the bactericidal/bacteriostatic effects of antiseptics and disinfectants? (a) precipitation of bacterial cell proteins, (b) disruption of bacterial cell membranes, (c) inhibition of essential bacterial enzymes, (d) all of the above, (e) none of the above.

2. Which of the following is/are true of phenolic germicidal agents? (a) possess topical anesthetic effects, (b) used in root canal therapy to kill microorganisms in periapical infections, (c) hexachlorophene may be used as a presurgical scrub, (d) include formocresol, cresatin, eugenol, (e) all of the above.

3. Which of the following is/are true of iodine preparations? (a) povidone-iodine (Betadine) is not as irritating to mucous membranes as 10% iodine tincture, (b) combine with — SH groups on essential bacterial enzymes, (c) used to irrigate inflamed operculum in pericoronitis, (d) *a* and *c* only, (e) all of the above.

4. Which of the following statements are true? (a) antiseptics are chemicals that kill or inhibit the growth of bacteria on living tissue, (b) all disinfectants are sporocidal, (c) mercurial antiseptics such as thimersol (Merthiolate) are bactericidal, (d) oxidizing agents such as hydrogen peroxide are feeble germicides, (e) *a* and *d* only.

5. Which of the following is/are true of surface-active agents? (a) soaps inhibit the bactericidal effectiveness of benzalkonium chloride (Zephiran), (b) the cationic surface-active agents are bactericidal against most gram positive and gram negative microorganisms but are not sporocidal, (c) sodium lauryl sulphate is an anionic surface-active agent, (d) certain strains of *Pseudomonas* are resistant to benzalkonium chloride (Zephiran), (e) all of the above.

6. Silver nitrate has been used to treat or prevent (a) herpes simplex (type I), (b) recurrent aphthous ulcers, (c) ophthalmia neonatorum, (d) all of the above, (e) none of the above.

7. Hemostatic agents include (a) thrombin, (b) epinephrine, (c) aluminum chloride (Hemodent), (d) absorbable gelatin sponge (Gelfoam), (e) all of the above.

8. Which of the following is/are true of oxidized cellulose? (a) decreased pH inhibits effectiveness of thrombin, (b) inhibits bone regeneration, (c) inhibits epithelialization, (d) provides a physical matrix via combination of cellulosic acid with hemoglobin, (e) all of the above.

CHAPTER 24: FLUORIDES

1. The average plasma fluoride level in normal humans is from 0.14 to 0.19 ppm and is not elevated above this range in people consuming water with up to _____ ppm of fluoride. (a) 1, (b) 1.5, (c) 2, (d) 2.5.
2. Acute fluoride poisoning is very rare. The acute lethal dose of sodium fluoride for an adult is (a) 2 gm, (b) 3 gm, (c) 4 gm, (d) 5 gm.

3-13. Mark items true (T) or false (F).

3. Mottling of enamel associated with chronic endemic dental fluoroses is a hypo-plastic defect that results from a disturbance in the function of ameloblasts during tooth development.
4. Erupted teeth can develop mottling if exposed to sufficiently high concentrations of fluoride in drinking water.
5. People living in an area with a high mean annual temperature will have a higher fluoride intake than those in an area with a low mean annual temperature.
6. The accumulation of fluoride ions in the developing tooth occurs primarily at the external enamel surface.
7. The amount of fluoride incorporated in surface enamel can increase after eruption.
8. The surface layer of fluoroapatite is believed to impart caries resistance to teeth.
9. Fluoride levels of surface enamel increase throughout life in people who drink water containing 1 ppm or more fluoride.
10. The fact is generally conceded that neither the incidence nor the severity of gingivitis or other periodontal disease in a community is influenced by the fluoride level of its water supply.
11. The addition of sodium fluoride does not appear to have any adverse effect on the action of vitamin preparations and vice versa.
12. Part of caries reduction obtained from fluoride vitamins may result from the topical effect of chewable vitamins.
13. In a prescription for a fluoride supplement, 2.2 mg of sodium fluoride will yield _____ mg of fluoride. (a) 2.2, (b) 1.0, (c) 0.5, (d) 0.25.
14. An 18-month-old child living in an area in which the water supply contains 0.5 ppm of fluoride should receive _____ mg of fluoride supplement daily. (a) 0.25, (b) 0.5, (c) 1.0, (d) 0.
15. Why is the approach of using fluoride supplements combined with vitamins more advantageous than using fluoride tablets alone? (a) Parents are more likely to see that their children take vitamins prescribed for them than a fluoride tablet alone. (b) Vitamin preparations increase the absorption of fluoride ions. (c) Vitamin-fluoride preparations taste better. (d) All of the above are advantages of the vitamin-fluoride preparations. (e) None of the above is an advantage of the vitamin-fluoride preparations.
16. What is a disadvantage of the vitamin-fluoride tablet approach? (a) Vitamins decrease the systemic absorption of fluoride ions. (b) Vitamins decrease the topical adsorption of fluoride ions. (c) Only a small group of children who require vitamin supplementation should receive fluoride in this manner. (d) Vitamin-fluoride preparations are expensive. (e) All of the above are disadvantages.
17. Prenatal fluoride supplements should not be routinely prescribed for expectant mothers because (a) evidence of effectiveness is conflicting, (b) fluoride ions are suspected of having teratogenic effects, (c) fluoride does not cross the placental barrier, (d) all of the above reasons.
18. The most consistently beneficial results from the topical application of sodium fluoride consist of four applications of a 2% sodium fluoride solution made at 1-week intervals at 3, 7, 11, and 13 years of age. Why are these ages generally recommended? (a) They represent the times shortly after the usual eruption of groups of teeth. (b) Only because they represent adequately spaced times during critical calcification periods.
19. The first application of sodium fluoride is preceded by a prophylaxis. The teeth are thoroughly wetted with the 2% sodium fluoride solution and allowed to dry for _____ minutes. (a) 1, (b) 2, (c) 3, (d) 4.
20. How does sodium fluoride differ from stannous fluoride? (a) The taste of sodium fluoride is not unpleasant. Stannous fluoride has a most unpleasant taste. (b) Sodium

fluoride is stable in solution and does not have to be mixed for each patient. Stannous fluoride should be mixed for each patient. (c) Stannous fluoride is normally applied once annually. (d) Stannous fluoride application need not be preceded by a prophylaxis. (e) All of the above are true except *c* and *d*. (f) All of the above are true except *d*. (g) All of the above are true.

21. An 8% stannous fluoride solution is applied to air-dried and isolated teeth a quadrant or a half mouth at a time. The teeth are continually wetted for _____ minutes. (a) 1, (b) 2, (c) 3, (d) 4.

22. The topical application of stannous fluoride is generally considered to be _____ effective than (as) sodium fluoride treatment. (a) more, (b) less, (c) as equally.

23-31. Give the letter below that indicates the agent or agents that are described by the statement (a) sodium fluoride, (b) stannous fluoride, (c) acidulated phosphate fluoride, (d) agents *a* and *b* only, (e) agents *b* and *c* only, (f) agents *a* and *c* only, (g) all three agents.

23. Is effective in permanent teeth of children in nonfluoride areas.

24. *Known* to be effective in deciduous teeth in nonfluoride areas.

25. *Known* to be effective in fluoride areas.

26. *Known* to be effective in adults.

27. Requires a simple one-appointment procedure.

28. Is stable in solution.

29. Has a pleasant taste.

30. Stains teeth.

31. Can arrest existing caries.

32. What is the difference in effectiveness between stannous fluoride and sodium monofluorophosphate (SMP) dentifrices? The SMP dentifrices appear to be (a) more effective, (b) equally effective, (c) less effective, (d) ineffective.

33. The fluoride dentifrice(s) generally available that has/have the acceptance of the ADA is/are (a) stannous fluoride, (b) sodium monofluorophosphate, (c) sodium fluoride, (d) stannous fluoride and sodium monofluorophosphate, (e) sodium fluoride and stannous fluoride, (f) sodium monofluorophosphate and sodium fluoride, (g) stannous fluoride, sodium monofluorophosphate, and sodium fluoride.

34. Most fluoride rinsing programs employed by schools consist of weekly rinsing with a _____ neutral sodium fluoride solution. (a) 0.05%, (b) 0.1%, (c) 0.2%, (d) 1.0%.

35. Fluoride rinses containing 0.05% sodium fluoride and 0.1% stannous fluoride are (a) available over the counter, (b) most effective in a weekly rinsing program, (c) used in most school-based programs, (d) the only formulations accepted by the ADA, (e) all of the above.

36. In the prevention and treatment of periodontal disease, _____ seems to have potential effectiveness. (a) sodium fluoride, (b) stannous fluoride, (c) acidulated phosphate fluoride, (d) all fluoride compounds, (e) no fluoride compound.

CHAPTER 25: VITAMINS

1. A 50-year-old white woman is referred to you because of a severe glossitis characterized by a smooth-surfaced, slightly edematous tongue. The patient reports a burning sensation in the tongue. Clinical examination also reveals angular cheilosis, dermatitis, and erythema of the nasolabial folds. Dietary intake on the basis of a discussion of diet appears to be adequate. The medical history indicates that the patient is in menopause and has been taking an antihistamine and a tetracycline for 4 days to combat an acute sinusitis. The patient was exposed to tuberculosis 6 months earlier and has been taking isoniazid daily since the exposure. Just on the basis of the preceding information, you would most likely suspect (a) pyridoxine inhibition by isoniazid, (b) deficiency of vitamin K caused by tetracycline-induced reduction in intestinal bacterial flora, (c) generalized vitamin deficiency as a result of menopause, (d) a hormonal etiology not involving nutritional deficiencies.

2. Pyridoxine deficiency would most likely be seen in a (a) 16-year-old woman taking a tetracycline for acne, (b) 30-year-old, well-nourished, male narcotic addict, (c) 40-year-old woman taking an oral contraceptive, (d) 60-year-old man taking digoxin for congestive heart failure.

3. Glossitis and angular cheilitis are *least* likely to be seen in a patient with a deficiency of (a) pantothenic acid, (b) thiamine, (c) riboflavin, (d) niacin.

4. Pellagra, characterized by the "3 D's" (dermatitis, diarrhea, and dementia), is caused by a severe deficiency of (a) niacin, (b) thiamine, (c) riboflavin, (d) biotin.

5. Beriberi is caused by a severe deficiency in (a) niacin, (b) thiamine, (c) riboflavin, (d) biotin.

6. Water-soluble vitamins, except for vitamin C, function as (a) antioxidants in cellular respiration, (b) enzymes in oxidation reactions, (c) microchelating agents, (d) essential components of coenzymes.

7. Lean meats, liver, and poultry are good sources of (a) pyridoxine, (b) thiamine, (c) niacin, (d) riboflavin.

8. The amino acid tryptophan is metabolized in the body to (a) pyridoxine, (b) thiamine, (c) niacin, (d) riboflavin.

9. Why would eating uncooked egg whites reduce biotin absorption?

10. Pernicious anemia is a conditional cobalamin (B_{12}) deficiency caused by a lack of (a) extrinsic factor in the diet, (b) intrinsic factor in gastric mucosa, (c) both *a* and *b,* (d) neither *a* nor *b.*

11. Megaloblastic anemia caused by cyanocobalamin deficiency is indistinguishable from that produced by a deficiency in (a) biotin, (b) choline, (c) folic acid, (d) pantothenic acid.

12. Why cannot a deficiency of cyanocobalamin, secondary to pernicious anemia, be treated with the oral administration of cyanocobalamin?

13. Ascorbic acid is extremely important in wound healing. Its principal effect is on (a) epithelial proliferation, (b) collagen formation, (c) maturation of osteoblasts, (d) reduction of inflammation.

14. Scurvy is caused by a deficiency of vitamin (a) A, (b) B_1 and/or B_2, (c) C, (d) D.

15. The principal effect of vitamin A is in the maintenance of what tissues? (a) epithelial, (b) connective, (c) osseous, (d) vascular.

16. Nyctalopia, xerophthalmia, and keratomalacia are seen with a deficiency in vitamin (a) A, (b) B_2, (c) C, (d) D.

17. Liver disease is most likely to be related to deficiencies in vitamin (a) B complex, C, and D, (b) B complex only, (c) C, D, and folic acid, (d) A, D, E, and K.

18. The normal mineralization of bone and the homeostatic regulation of plasma calcium depends on an adequate supply of vitamin D. Its principal functions in this regard are to (a) stimulate intestinal absorption of calcium and promote mobilization of calcium from bone, (b) stimulate intestinal absorption of calcium and decrease the mobilization of calcium from bone, (c) decrease renal excretion of calcium and promote mobilization of calcium from bone, (d) decrease renal excretion of calcium and decrease mobilization of calcium from bone.

19. In children, vitamin D deficiency results in rickets, whereas in adults the disease state is _____.

20. Toxicity from excessive intake of vitamin D has been observed. This toxicity primarily manifests itself as (a) liver damage, (b) renal damage, (c) hypercalcemia, (d) all of the above.

21. Vitamin E (tocopherol) appears to prevent both the oxidation of essential cell constituents and the formation of toxic oxidation products. Severe vitamin E deficiencies in animals have been associated with degenerative changes in skeletal muscle and reproductive failure, sterility, and fetal death. The evidence that vitamin E is therapeutic against these changes in humans is (a) conclusive, (b) inconclusive.

22. Vitamin K is essential for the hepatic synthesis of prothrombin and bloodclotting factors VII, IX, and X. The usual causes of vitamin K deficiency are malabsorption syndromes and inadequate intake. Other causes include (a) liver disease, (b) prolonged use of antibiotics, (c) biliary obstruction, (d) all of the above.

23. Toxicity from hypervitaminosis will most likely be seen with vitamins (a) A and D, (b) B and C, (c) B_{12} and D, (d) E and K.

24-32. Match the vitamin deficiency with the proper deficiency state. One deficiency state will be used twice.

Vitamin deficiency	*Related deficiency state*
24. A	(a) Hypoprothrombinemia
25. B_1 (thiamine)	(b) Reproductive failure
26. B_{12} (cyanocobalamin)	(c) Hypocalcemia
27. C	(d) Defective connective tissue formation
28. D	(e) Dermatitis, dementia, diarrhea
29. E	(f) Beriberi
30. Folic acid	(g) Megaloblastic anemia
31. K	(h) Defective vision
32. Niacin	

33-44. List the three most significant clinical considerations in severe deficiencies of the vitamins indicated.

33. Pyridoxine (B_6)
34. Thiamine (B_1)
35. Pantothenic acid
36. Riboflavin (B_2)
37. Niacin
38. Biotin
39. Cyanocobalamin (B_{12})
40. Folic acid
41. Ascorbic acid
42. Vitamin A
43. Vitamin D
44. Vitamin E

CHAPTER 26: MINERALS

1. Iron is absorbed from the duodenum when (a) pH in the stomach is high, (b) the level of ferritin in the mucosal cells is high, (c) the metal is in the ferrous form, (d) oxidizing agents are present in the duodenum, (e) high concentrations of phosphate are present in the diet.

2. Potassium is one of the most important ions in mammals. Which of the following statements about potassium are correct? (a) It antagonizes some of the actions of digitalis glycosides. (b) It is the principal extracellular cation. (c) It is necessary for the normal function of muscle and nerve. (d) It is the principal intracellular cation. (e) It can be safely injected intravenously in high doses as the chloride salt.

3. The absorption of dietary calcium in the gastrointestinal tract is an active process that is (a) facilitated by vitamin E, (b) dependent on dietary sodium, (c) dependent on dietery phosphate, (d) facilitated by vitamin D.

4. Which of the following do *not* describe an action of sodium (Na$^+$) on the body or the handling of sodium (Na$^+$) by the body? (a) Excess tends to produce edema. (b) It may cause diuresis if blood levels are elevated. (c) Excess tends to produce dehydration. (d) It is readily reabsorbed from the glomerular filtrate.

5. Iodine is primarily important in the biosynthesis of (a) ACTH, (b) thyroxine, (c) adrenalin, (d) calcitonin, (e) parathyroid hormone.

6. After being absorbed from the intestine, iron is carried through the blood in the form of (a) ferritin, (b) transferrin, (c) hemosiderin, (d) apotransferrin, (e) ceruloplasmin.

7. Which of the following minerals is especially required in the blood clotting process? (a) iron (b) sodium (c) calcium (d) magnesium (e) potassium.

8. Which of the following are considered trace minerals in nutrition? (a) calcium and manganese (b) calcium, chloride, and phosphorus (c) calcium and phosphorus (d) manganese and copper (e) chloride and copper.

9. Iron is an important functional component of (a) DNA, (b) carboxypeptidase, (c) cytochromes, (d) RNA, (e) phospholipids.

10. Which of the following trace minerals is required for xanthine oxidase activity? (a) cobalt (b) molybdenum (c) copper (d) manganese (e) chromium.

CHAPTER 27: DRUGS USED FOR GASTROINTESTINAL DISORDERS

1. The side effects of therapy with aluminum hydroxide gel and methantheline might be (a) xerostomia, (b) constipation, (c) central nervous stimulation, (d) difficulty in accommodation for near vision, (e) nausea and vomiting, (f) *a, b,* and *d,* (g) *a* and *b,* only, (h) *b, c,* and *e,* (i) *c* and *d,* (j) *d* and *e.*

2. GI activity may be modified by which of the following types of drugs? (a) cathartics, (b) opiates, (c) parasympathomimetics, (d) ganglionic blocking agents, (e) *a* and *b* only, (f) *a, b,* and *d,* (g) *b, c,* and *d,* (h) all of the above, (i) none of the above.

3. A prescription for an analgesic agent for a patient with peptic ulcer should *not* include which of the following? (a) Darvon compound 65, (b) Tylenol, (c) pentazocine (Talwin), (d) meperidine, (e) aspirin, (f) *a, c,* and *d,* (g) *a* and *e,* (h) *a* and *c,* (i) *d* and *e,* (j) *b, c, d,* and *e.*

4. H₂ histamine antagonists are most useful in treating (a) asthma, (b) anaphylaxis, (c) localized allergic reactions, (d) hypertension, (e) gastric hyperacidity.

5. Which type of laxative is usually recommended if chronic use is indicated? (a) bulk forming, (b) stimulant, (c) saline, (d) lubricant.

CHAPTER 28: EMERGENCY DRUGS

1. There are only two instances in which epinephrine is indicated in dental office emergencies. These are (a) acute hypotension and respiratory arrest, (b) anaphylaxis and cardiac arrest, (c) respiratory arrest and extrapyramidal reactions to phenothiazines, (d) hypovolemia and myocardial infarction.

2. Epinephrine is *not* the drug of choice for the treatment of shock because its use may (a) further reduce venous return, (b) intensify highly undesirable renal ischemia, (c) precipitate ventricular fibrillation in the ischemic and irritable myocardium, (d) lead to all of the above.

3. The purpose of intravenous sodium bicarbonate in an emergency situation is to (a) counteract metabolic acidosis, (b) stimulate the vasopressor center, (c) increase oxygenation of hypoxic tissues, (d) all of the above.

4. Hydrocortisone sodium succinate (100 mg intravenously) is effective as a part of the management of cardiac arrest, anaphylactic shock, and acute adrenocortical insufficiency. The basis of its hemodynamic effects in these emergencies is that it (a) stimulates the vasopressor center, (b) stimulates the release of endogenous vasopressors, (c) potentiates vasopressors, (d) does all three of the above.

5. The intravenous use of 2 to 5 ml of 1% diphenhydramine will generally provide prompt relief from (a) severe allergic reactions, (b) minor dermatologic allergic reactions, (c) extrapyramidal reactions to phenothiazines, (d) all of the above.

6. Inhaled ammonia acts against syncope by (a) irritating the sensory endings of the trigeminal nerve, (b) direct stimulation of the vasomotor center, (c) direct stimulation of the respiratory center, (d) both *b* and *c*.

7. When glyceryl trinitrate (nitroglycerin) is used against anginal pain, relief is normally obtained within (a) 30 seconds, (b) 1 minute, (c) 2 to 3 minutes, (d) 5 to 10 minutes.

8. A disadvantage of amyl nitrite relative to nitroglycerin as a coronary vasodilator is that amyl nitrite (a) is less potent, (b) causes more nausea and vomiting, (c) has a shorter shelf life, (d) is less potent and has a shorter shelf life.

9. The principal reason for having morphine sulfate in a dental emergency kit is for early administration to a patient experiencing (a) an attack of angina pectoris, (b) acute myocardial infarction, (c) anaphylactic shock, (d) convulsions associated with severe pain.

10. An extremely important advantage of phenylephrine HCl over many other vasopressors is that it (a) has greater potency, (b) does not directly stimulate the heart, (c) is less toxic, (d) acts on both alpha and beta receptors.

CHAPTER 29: PHARMACOLOGY OF INTRAVENOUS SEDATION

1. The depressant effects of drugs on the central nervous system are caused by actions on the reticular activating system (RAS), medulla, and cerebral cortex. Barbiturates produce sedation and hypnosis by acting on the RAS to depress ascending neuronal conduction. Doses that produce anesthesia do so by depressing (a) ascending neuronal conduction in the RAS, (b) excitatory pathways within the cerebral cortex, (c) both *a* and *b,* (d) neither *a* nor *b*.

2. Hypnotic doses of barbiturates depress respiration by depressing (a) neurogenic control in the higher brain centers, (b) chemical centers responsive to changes in blood pH and Pco₂, (c) chemoreceptors responsive to hypoxic stimulation, (d) all of the above controls.

3. Higher anesthetic doses of barbiturates depress respiration by which of the mechanisms listed in question 2?

4. The effects of barbiturates on the cardiovascular system are (a) extremely serious because of the unpredictability of their effects, (b) serious because of the effects on medullary vasomotor tone, (c) mild and do not ordinarily constitute a hazard in clinical practice, (d) of no concern whatever.

5. What effect would you expect from heavy hypnotic doses of morphine or meperidine that you would not expect from thiopental? (a) euphoria and analgesia, (b) euphoria and respiratory depression, (c) analgesia and amnesia, (d) amnesia and respiratory depression.

6. The main differences between meperidine and alphaprodine are (a) chemical and physical properties, (b) potency and duration of action, (c) doses and routes of administration, (d) all of the above.

7. Fentanyl is chemically related to meperidine. It has an almost immediate onset of action and is the _____ narcotic analgesia available for use in intravenous sedation. (a) most toxic but most reliable, (b) least potent and least toxic, (c) most potent and shortest acting, (d) least toxic and longest acting.

8. The phenothiazines produce only sedation and not true hypnosis or general anesthesia because they (a) only block ascending neuronal projections in the RAS, (b) only block descending neuronal projections in the RAS, (c) affect cortical areas only, (d) affect the RAS and subcortical areas only.

9. Phenothiazines cause few side effects after single intravenous doses. The cardiovascular response to these drugs is minimal, but they are likely to cause (a) hypotension and reflex tachycardia, (b) hypertension and reflex tachycardia, (c) hypotension and reflex bradycardia, (d) hypertension and reflex bradycardia.

10. When used for intravenous sedation, diazepam produces (a) analgesia and some degree of muscle relaxation in 90% of patients, (b) tranquilization in all patients and neurolepsis in most patients, (c) euphoria in some patients and retrograde amnesia in approximately 50% of patients, (d) all of the above effects.

11. In neuroleptanalgesia, droperidol (Inapsine) is frequently used to provide the tranquilization component and fentanyl (Sublimaze) to provide the analgesic component (as in Innovar). Dissociative anesthesia is accomplished with (a) Innovar, (b) ketamine (Ketalar), (c) phencyclidine, (d) all of the above.

CHAPTER 30: PARENTERAL SEDATION AND NITROUS OXIDE ANALGESIA

1. Which of the following are *advantages of oral sedation* relative to intramuscular and intravenous administration? (a) safer, (b) provides more predictable degrees of sedation, (c) more rapid onset, (d) easier delivery, (e) greater patient acceptance, (f) cheaper, (g) *a, b, d,* and *e,* (h) *a, d, e,* and *f,* (i) all of the above.

2-7. Indicate which method of administration is more intimately related to the characteristic listed. Answer (a) for oral, (b) for intramuscular, (c) for intravenous, (d) for both intramuscular and intravenous, and (e) for all three methods.
   2. A principal hazard is overdepression of the cardiovascular, respiratory, and CNS.
   3. It is the most effective method of ensuring predictable, adequate sedation.
   4. Safest.
   5. Poor patient acceptance.
   6. There is an inability to remove the drug if overdose or overreaction has occurred.
   7. Slowest onset.

8. You have inadvertently injected a barbiturate extravascularly. Your treatment is to inject up to 10 ml of a 1% solution of procaine HCl into the area. How is the procaine injection helpful in preventing tissue damage? (a) It dilutes the agent injected. (b) It causes vasodilation and thereby speeds absorption of the agent. (c) It tends to neutralize the alkalinity of the barbiturate. (d) It is helpful by all the above mechanisms.

9. Why would lidocaine HCl *not* be a good substitute for procaine HCl in question 8? Lidocaine would not (a) dilute the barbiturate well because of its spreading tendency, (b) dilate blood vessels as well as procaine, (c) neutralize the alkalinity of the barbiturate, (d) dilute, dilate, or neutralize as well as procaine.

10. The alcoholic will usually require increased doses of a barbiturate for parenteral sedation unless (a) liver disease is present, (b) he is under 50 years of age, (c) he is over 50 years of age, (d) both *a* and *b* are true, (e) both *a* and *c* are true.

11. This text describes the use of a 15 mg/ml pentobarbital solution for intravenous seda-

tion. What is the percentage concentration of this solution? (a) 0.015%, (b) 0.0015%, (c) 0.15%, (d) 15%.

12. During intravenous sedation the patient's vital signs must be monitored at all times. The adult test dose of the solution mentioned in question 11 is 0.25 ml. If no adverse effects occur after the administration of this test dose, an additional 3.75 to 4.75 ml are injected slowly over a 30- to 45-second period. In a healthy patient, what is the minimal time you should wait before assuming that the full pharmacologic effect of the dose has manifested itself? (a) 30 seconds, (b) 60 seconds, (c) 2 minutes, (d) 4 minutes.

13. After the appropriate waiting time indicated in question 12, additional 15 mg (1 ml) doses are administered at 60-second intervals until the desired level of sedation is obtained. At this point sedative effects (a) are maintained by 15 mg doses every 15 minutes, (b) are maintained by 15 mg doses every 30 minutes, (c) may extend 30 to 60 minutes without further drug administration, (d) may extend 2 to 4 hours without further drug administration.

14. Why is a larger volume of a low concentration of the drug recommended as opposed to a smaller volume of a more concentrated solution? The larger volume at lower concentration (a) increases control over the depth of sedation obtained, (b) reduces chemical insult to the vein, (c) has the advantages of both *a* and *b*, (d) has neither of the advantages of *a* or *b*.

15. In the Jorgensen technique of using pentobarbital with meperidine, (a) the drugs are injected together to obtain "baseline" anesthesia; (b) the drugs are injected together throughout the procedure; (c) baseline sedation is obtained first with pentobarbital; (d) baseline sedation is obtained first with meperidine.

16. Which of the following effects is (are) *not* obtained with diazepam? (a) muscular relaxation, (b) amnesia, (c) analgesia, (d) respiratory depression, (e) neither *a* nor *b* is obtained, (f) neither *c* nor *d* is obtained, (g) none of the above effects is obtained.

17. Neuroleptanalgesia is a state of pronounced tranquility and profound analgesia. This is generally associated with the use of (a) meperidine, (b) diazepam, (c) diazepam and meperidine, (d) Innovar, (e) all of the above agents.

18. The objective of nitrous oxide–oxygen analgesia is to provide a relaxed but cooperative patient with adequate analgesia and some degree of amnesia with little or no depression of reflexes. This must be accomplished without entry into stage (a) II, (b) III, plane 1, (c) III, plane 2, (d) III, plane 3.

19. The use of the nitrous oxide–oxygen technique in combination with other sedative regimens (a) decreases the potential dangers, (b) increases the potential dangers.

20. Absolute contraindications to nitrous oxide–oxygen analgesia include (a) upper respiratory obstruction, (b) coryza, (c) emotional instability, (d) all of the above conditions, (e) none of the above conditions.

21. Nitrous oxide has little or no direct effect on organ systems other than the CNS. Important local effects are that it (a) stimulates nasal and pharyngeal secretions, (b) irritates mucous membranes, (c) does both *a* and *b*, (d) does neither *a* nor *b*.

22. Diffusion hypoxia after nitrous oxide analgesia is best prevented by (a) never using more than 60% nitrous oxide, (b) maintaining at least 30% oxygen in the system, (c) having the patient breathe 100% oxygen for 4 to 5 minutes after the procedure, (d) bringing the patient out of analgesia very slowly.

23. Although dental procedures cannot be accomplished while the patient is wearing a face mask, this piece of equipment should always be available (a) to obtain greater depths of analgesia, (b) for the application of positive pressure during emergency situations, (c) for use during emergence from analgesia, (d) for all of the above purposes.

24. During nitrous oxide–oxygen analgesia, at least _____% oxygen at a flow rate of no less than _____ liters per minute should be maintained at all times. (a) 25%, 2, (b) 25%, 4, (c) 50%, 2, (d) 50%, 4.

25. Which of the following statements is *false* relative to the patient under nitrous oxide–oxygen analgesia? He may (a) exhibit slurred speech, (b) relate a feeling of well-being, (c) be relaxed and cooperative, (d) have little or no response to local anesthetic injection, (e) have eyes open or easily opened by operator, (f) have pupils normal, (g) have respiration normal except if deep, (h) none of the above is false.

CHAPTER 31: PHARMACOLOGIC CONSIDERATIONS IN PATIENTS WITH SYSTEMIC DISEASE

1. Which of the following drugs is *least* likely to cause xerostomia? (a) nitroglycerin, (b) reserpine, (c) acetazolamide, (d) chlorothiazide.

2-11. Ten different patients list the conditions indicated below on their medical histories. Match their respective conditions with the drugs listed that they would be most likely taking. Each drug is used once.

Condition	Drug
2. Angina pectoris	(a) Indomethacin
3. Congestive heart failure	(b) Digitoxin
4. Hypertension	(c) Propantheline
5. Fluid retention	(d) Hydrochlorothiazide
6. Tuberculosis	(e) Nitroglycerin
7. Rheumatoid arthritis	(f) Methotrexate
8. Peptic ulcer	(g) Isoniazid
9. Hyperthyroidism	(h) Tolbutamide
10. Leukemia	(i) Deserpidine
11. Diabetes	(j) Isothiouracil

12. Orthostatic hypotension is *least* likely to occur in a patient who is taking (a) nitroglycerin, (b) digitalis, (c) reserpine, (d) hydralazine.

13. The oral manifestations of pregnancy gingivitis may be caused by (a) norethynodrel, (b) liothyronine, (c) polystyrene sulfonate, (d) salicylazosulfapyridine, (e) all of the above drugs.

14. Which of the following anticoagulants is (are) used parenterally? (a) sodium warfarin, (b) bishydroxycoumarin, (c) heparin, (d) all of the above, (e) none of the above.

15. Transplant patients would be most likely taking (a) antihistamines and bishydroxycoumarin, (b) prednisone and isothiouracil, (c) norethynodrel and levothyroxine, (d) phenylbutazone and methimazole, (e) azathioprine and corticosteroids.

16. Mercaptopurine, methotrexate, and chlorambucil are likely to cause or predispose to (a) bleeding tendencies, (b) infection, (c) oral candidiasis, (d) oral ulcers, (e) all of the above, (f) none of the above.

17. Chlorpropamide, tolbutamide, acetohexamide, and tolazamide are used in the treatment of (a) diabetes, (b) gout, (c) mental depression, (d) epilepsy.

CHAPTER 32: PHARMACOLOGIC MANAGEMENT OF CERTAIN COMMON ORAL DISEASE ENTITIES

1. Which of the following statements is (are) *false* relative to the pharmacologic management of acute necrotizing ulcerative gingivitis? (a) Oxygen-releasing mouthwashes are known to be more effective than saline rinses. (b) There is no convincing evidence that the vitamin preparations are routinely helpful. (c) Several antibiotics will improve the clinical course. (d) The routine use of antibiotics is to be condemned. (e) Topical caustics should not be used on the lesions. (f) All of the above are false. (g) None of the above is false.

2. Which of the following statements is (are) false relative to the pharmacologic management of primary herpetic gingivostomatitis? (a) Antibiotics generally have little or no effect on the clinical course of the disease. (b) Antipyretic analgesics are usually indicated. (c) Topical caustics are usually helpful. (d) Corticosteroids should not be used. (e) All of the above are false. (f) None of the above is false.

3. Which of the following antibiotic regimens was reported effective against recurrent aphthous stomatitis? One teaspoonful (a) tetracycline syrup (125 mg/5 ml) is swished in the mouth for 2 minutes and then swallowed four times daily. (b) Tetracycline syrup (250 mg/5 ml) is swished in the mouth for 2 minutes and then swallowed four times daily. (c) Tetracycline suspension (125 mg/5 ml) is swished in the mouth for 2 minutes and then swallowed four times daily. (d) Tetracycline suspension (250 mg/5 ml) is swished in the mouth for 2 minutes and then swallowed four times daily.

4. The treatment of oral candidiasis with nystatin should continue for a minimum of 14 days and not be discontinued until two successive smears are negative or at least until _____ hours after the signs of infection have disappeared. (a) 24, (b) 48, (c) 96, (d) 120.

5. You have determined that a severe case of angular cheilitis is caused by bacteria. Which of the following drugs in ointment form would you expect to be helpful? (a) nystatin, (b) bacitracin, (c) neomycin, (d) tetracycline, (e) *a, b,* and *c,* (f) *b, c,* and *d,* (g) all of the above.

6. The treatment of lichen planus is directed toward (a) obtaining a more physiologic hormonal balance, (b) determining and prescribing the antibacterial agent that will be effective against the etiologic agent, (c) improving the host response and the general nutritional state of the patient, (d) all of the above.

7. The use of a 0.5% sodium carboxymethyl cellulose aqueous solution as a rinse is effective in the treatment of (a) hypersensitive dentin, (b) xerostomia, (c) burning tongue syndrome, (d) lichen planus.

8. The use of local tetracycline prophylaxis to prevent alveolar osteitis (''dry socket'') (a) should be instituted routinely in all extraction cases, (b) should be instituted routinely in third molar extraction, (c) may be indicated in third molar extractions when factors predisposing to infection are present, (d) is never indicated.

9. Hypersensitive dentin can be completely and predictably eliminated by (a) sodium or stannous fluoride applications by the dentist, (b) adrenal steroid applications by the dentist, (c) desensitizing toothpastes, (d) none of the above.

CHAPTER 33: DRUG INTERACTIONS

1. If two drugs that have the same actions are given together, the resulting effects may be a simple addition of their individual effects. On the other hand, if the two drugs have opposing actions, such as a sedative and a stimulant, their effects may be subtractive or antagonistic. In addition to this simple arithmetic relationship, one drug may accentuate or reduce the effect of another by more complex mechanisms. Can you name these mechanisms and give an example of each?

2. Certain divalent metal ions may impair the gastrointestinal absorption of (a) penicillin, (b) tetracyclines, (c) erythromycin, (d) nystatin.

3. What is the significance of drug binding to plasma protein? (a) Bound drugs are usually inactive. (b) Bound drugs are usually more toxic. (c) Both *a* and *b* are true. (d) Neither *a* nor *b* is true.

4. How could phenobarbital decrease the effect of a specific regimen of bishydroxycoumarin? (a) by decreasing the absorption of bishydroxycoumarin, (b) by forming inactive complexes with bishydroxycoumarin, (c) by inducing the formation of enzymes that metabolize bishydroxycoumarin, (d) by displacing bishydroxycoumarin from protein-binding sites.

5. How can aspirin increase the effects of coumarin derivatives? (a) by inhibiting the enzymes that metabolize coumarins, (b) by displacing coumarins from their plasma protein-binding sites, (c) by decreasing gastric pH, thereby increasing absorption of coumarins, (d) by all of the above mechanisms.

6. How might the use of a tetracycline reduce the effectiveness of concomitantly administered penicillin? (a) by reducing its absorption, (b) by increasing its renal excretion, (c) by reducing bacterial multiplication rate, (d) by increasing bacterial multiplication rate.

7. How could the long-term use of an antihistamine and an anticholinergic cause the loss of teeth? By an additive interaction that (a) decreases the inflammatory response in the periodontium, (b) increases the inflammatory response in the periodontium, (c) accelerates the demineralization of dentin, (d) produces prolonged xerostomia.

8. Acetaminophen enhances the effect of (a) barbiturates, (b) MAOIs, (c) amphetamines, (d) coumarin anticoagulants.

9. Aspirin is antagonized by (a) phenylbutazone, (b) probenecid, (c) phenytoin, (d) orphenadrine.

10. Chloral hydrate antagonizes (a) probenecid, (b) coumarin anticoagulants, (c) chlordiazepoxide, (d) meperidine.

11. In an additive manner, propoxyphene appears to accentuate the toxic effects of (a) corticosteroids, (b) orphenadrine, (c) phenothiazines, (d) tolbutamide.

CHAPTER 34: DRUG ABUSE

1. The withdrawal syndrome is a combination of certain drug-specific symptoms that occur on sudden discontinuation of the drug. This syndrome is associated with (a)

psychologic dependence, (b) physical dependence, (c) the development of tolerance, (d) *a* and *b,* (e) *a, b,* and *c.*

2. Addiction is associated with the existence of (a) psychologic dependence, (b) physical dependence, (c) tolerance, (d) *a* and *b,* (e) *a, b,* and *c.*

3. Generally speaking, which of the following best characterizes the morphine abuser? (a) satisfied, complacent, cooperative individual with suppressed hunger and reduced sexual desires, (b) satisfied but uncooperative individual with suppressed hunger and increased sexual desires, (c) quarrelsome, uncooperative individual with increased appetite and sexual desires, (d) quarrelsome, dissatisfied, uncooperative individual with a reduced capacity to make a contribution to society.

4. Generally speaking, which of the following best characterizes the alcohol abuser? (a) satisfied, complacent, cooperative individual with suppressed hunger and reduced sexual desires, (b) satisfied but uncooperative individual with suppressed hunger and increased sexual desires, (c) quarrelsome, uncooperative individual with increased appetite and sexual desires, (d) quarrelsome, dissatisfied, uncooperative individual with a reduced capacity to make a contribution to society.

5. In the morphine addict, tolerance does *not* develop to the (a) lethal dose, (b) constipatory action, (c) sedative dose, (d) respiratory effects.

6. Crosstolerance develops between (a) morphine and heroin, (b) narcotics and sedative hypnotics, (c) sedative hypnotics and alcohol, (d) all of the above drugs.

7. Withdrawal symptoms reach peak intensity between 48 and 72 hours after the last dose of heroin or morphine and, without treatment, disappear in about _____ days after the last dose. (a) 4, (b) 8, (c) 14, (d) 30.

8. What are the most significant side effects known from the long-term use of methadone? (a) blood dyscrasias, (b) liver damage, (c) bradycardia and hypotension, (d) impotence and constipation.

9. Which sedatives are the most subject to drug abuse? (a) barbiturates, (b) nonbarbiturate sedatives, (c) minor tranquilizers, (d) major tranquilizers.

10. The initial symptoms of withdrawal from CNS depressants consist of (a) muscular rigidity, hyperreflexia, salivation, and miosis; (b) abdominal cramps, blurred vision, xerostomia and tachycardia; (c) abdominal cramps, rapid respiration, and chills; (d) nausea, vomiting, weakness, anxiety, and perspiration.

11. The most serious problem related to the abuse of CNS stimulants in young people is the (a) development of nutritional disturbances, (b) loss of sleep, (c) induction of mental abnormalities, (d) effect on the heart.

12. Certain generalizations can be made relative to the response to psychedelics. Which of the following statements is *not* true? (a) Psychedelics affect perception by increasing or exaggerating the awareness of sensory input. (b) Senses of sight, hearing, taste, and smell are made more acute. (c) One sensory impression may be translated to another; music may appear as color, etc. (d) Judgment of reality is impaired and there is a loss of the sense of time. (e) None of the above is false.

13. In addition to its hallucinogenic activity, LSD causes (a) an increase in blood pressure, tachycardia, hyperreflexia, nausea, piloerection, and an increase in body temperature; (b) a decrease in blood pressure, bradycardia, hyperreflexia, xerostomia, and a decrease in body temperature; (c) only gastrointestinal effects; (d) only other psychologic effects.

14-17. Indicate whether the statement applies more completely to LSD or to marijuana.

    14. The setting in which the drug is taken determines to a great extent the type of behavioral changes experienced.

    15. Tolerance develops within days and some physical dependence is believed to develop.

    16. Prolonged, high-level use may cause xerostomia.

    17. Produces more sympathomimetic actions.

CHAPTER 35: DENTAL PLAQUE AND THE CONTROL OF PLAQUE-RELATED ORAL DISEASE

1. Which of the following dietary carbohydrates is most important in modulating the frequency and incidence of multisurface dental caries? (a) maltose, (b) lactose, (c) sucrose, (d) starch, (e) fructose.

2. Which of the following is a secretory antibody probably of most importance and significance in controlling dental caries? (a) IgA, (b) IgM, (c) IgD, (d) IgE.

3. Which of the following polysaccharides are high molecular weight bacterial polymers comprised of glucose monomers that participate in adhesive retentive mechanisms? (a) fructans, (b) glucans, (c) mucopolysaccharides, (d) amylopectin, (e) glycogen.

4. Which of the following antimicrobial compounds contain a high positive charge and are extremely effective agents for plaque control? (a) phenolic compounds, (b) the penicillins, (c) bis-biguanides, (d) tetracyclines, (e) peroxides.

5. Which of the following microorganisms is proposed to be an important etiologic agent in animal and human dental caries? (a) *S. sanguis,* (b) *S. salivarious,* (c) *S. mitis,* (d) *S. faecalis,* (e) *S. mutans.*

6. Which of the following can serve as a precursor for the production of lactic acid? (a) sucrose, (b) glucans, (c) fructans, (d) amylopectins, (e) all of the above.

7. Dietary sucrose can serve as a precursor for the production of which of the following classes of compounds? (a) lactic acid, (b) glucans, (c) fructans, (d) amylopectins, (e) all of the above.

8. Which of the following is not a desirable quality of an antimicrobial compound to be used as an anticaries agent? (a) should act on gram-positive organisms, (b) should be substantive, (c) should not promote resistance, (d) should be readily absorbed from the gastrointestinal tract, (e) should be effective in short-term, repeated doses.

9. Which of the following bacterial polysaccharides are most important in cell-cell adhesive interactions? (a) mutan, (b) fructans, (c) dextrans, (d) mucopolysaccharides, (e) amylopectins.

10. Which of the following is a nonsucrose synthetic sweetener which has recently been approved by the FDA for use in this country? (a) xylitol, (b) saccharin, (c) maltitol, (d) aspartame, (e) monellin.

11. Sucrose markedly increases the ability of *S. mutans* to accumulate upon the tooth surfaces by serving as a precursor for (a) amylopectin synthesis, (b) glucan synthesis, (c) fructan synthesis, (d) mucopolysaccharides synthesis, (e) glycogen synthesis.

12. Which of the following is the predominant organic acid produced by the plaque microflora from the fermentation of dietary carbohydrates? (a) formic acid, (b) acetic acid, (c) succinic acid, (d) propionic acid, (e) lactic acid.

CHAPTER 36: ENDODONTIC MEDICAMENTS AND IRRIGANTS

1. Significant and measurable reduction in the microbial population of infected root canals can be achieved following (a) debridement alone, (b) debridement and chemomechanical preparation, (c) debridement and intracanal medication, (d) debridement and irrigation, (e) debridement and systemic antimicrobial therapy.

2. Which of the following intracanal irrigating solutions most nearly satisfies the requirements for an ideal endodontic irrigating solution? (a) urea, (b) hydrogen peroxide, (c) urea peroxide, (d) 5.0% sodium hypochlorite, (e) 0.1% sodium hypochlorite.

3. The tissue-dissolving ability of sodium hypochlorite is related to (a) its alkalinity, (b) its acidity, (c) the formation of hypochlorous acid, (d) the binding of chlorine with organic debris, (e) the formation of sodium chloride.

4. Harrison and coworkers, in comparing physiologic saline and 5% sodium hypochlorite used as intracanal irrigating solutions, found (a) a significantly greater incidence of posttreatment pain with the use of 5% sodium hypochlorite, (b) a significantly greater incidence of posttreatment pain using physiologic saline, (c) no significant difference in the incidence of posttreatment pain with the use of either agent, (d) that neither agent was biologically acceptable, (e) none of the above.

5. A saturated solution of urea used as an irrigating solution (a) is a mild solvent of necrotic tissue and pus, (b) is highly irritating, (c) is virtually nonirritating, (d) is mildly antiseptic, (e) causes protein coagulation, (f) *a, b,* and *d,* (g) *a, b,* and *e,* (h) *a, c,* and *d,* (i) *a, c,* and *e,* (j) *c, d,* and *e.*

6. The antibacterial activity of 3% hydrogen peroxide is (a) profound, (b) transient and rapidly diminished, (c) attributed to its ability to disrupt bacterial enzyme systems, (d) related to its effervescence, (e) limited to anaerobic microorganisms, (f) *a* and *c,* (g) *b* and *c,* (h) *b* and *d,* (i) *c* and *d,* (j) *b* and *e.*

7. Nonspecific intracanal medicaments are considered to be (a) antibiotics, (b) ineffective against most microorganisms, (c) virtually nontoxic, (d) responsible for accelerated healing, (e) protoplasmic poisons.

8. Formocresol is popular in some clinical practices because of its ability to (a) prevent tissue autolysis, (b) dissolve necrotic tissue, (c) act as a protoplasmic poison, (d) maintain tissue viability, (e) selectively destroy microorganisms.

9. Metacresyl acetate (Cresatin) enjoys some popularity in endodontic practice because it (a) is highly bactericidal, (b) is an excellent tissue fixative, (c) has a high surface tension, (d) is an anodyne, (e) effectively neutralizes necrotic tissue.

10. Liquefied camphorated parachlorophenol contains what percent parachlorophenol? (a) 10% to 15%, (b) 15% to 20%, (c) 20% to 25%, (d) 25% to 30%, (e) 30% to 35%.

11. The antimicrobial potency of a halogenated phenol is determined by the specific halogen and its position in the molecule. One of the most effective halogenated phenols has: (a) bromine in the ortho position, (b) chlorine in the meta position, (c) chlorine in the para position, (d) bromine in the para position, (e) chlorine in the ortho position.

12. Camphor in camphorated parachlorophenol serves to (a) accelerate the release of chlorine, (b) prevent the release of chlorine, (c) slow the release of chlorine, (d) inactivate the hydroxyl group, (e) cause release of the hydroxyl group.

13. A 1% aqueous solution of parachlorophenol (a) is a poor antiseptic, (b) is an adequate antiseptic, (c) is highly cytotoxic, (d) is slightly cytotoxic, (e) penetrates dentinal tubules further than a camphorated solution, (f) a, c, and e, (g) a, d, and e, (h) b, c, and e, (i) b, d, and e, (j) b and d only.

14. The principal disadvantage of the use of 2% and 5% solutions of iodine potassium iodide in root canals is that (a) they occasionally elicit an allergic response, (b) they are highly toxic, (c) they are not effective antimicrobials, (d) they cause irreversible staining of tooth structure, (e) they are not stable.

15. Strong oxidizing agents such as iodine disrupt bacterial enzymatic activity by (a) denaturing native protein, (b) causing protein coagulation, (c) causing disulfide bond formation of sulfhydryl groups, (d) interference with cell wall synthesis, (e) competitive antagonism.

16. Injudicious use of corticosteroids in root canal treatment can result in (a) capillary proliferation, (b) increased fiberoplasia, (c) release of vasoactive kinins, (d) increased susceptibility to infection, (e) increased protein synthesis.

17. The bactericidal activity of calcium hydroxide is attributed to its (a) alkalinity, (b) low pH, (c) absorbency, (d) interference with protein synthesis, (e) interference with cell wall synthesis.

18. A buffered 15% solution of disodium EDTA is normally used as a (a) intracanal antimicrobial, (b) necrotic tissue solvent, (c) bleaching agent, (d) chelating agent, (e) cavity cleanser.

19. Polyethelene glycol is used as the vehicle when disodium EDTA and urea peroxide are combined in a commercially available agent. The polyethelene glycol serves to (a) protect the disodium EDTA from oxidation, (b) protect the urea peroxide from oxidation, (c) prevent disassociation of the peroxide, (d) act as an antibacterial agent, (e) act as a necrotic tissue solvent.

20. Clinical effectiveness of intracanal medicaments can be enhanced by (a) using greater concentrations of medicament, (b) totally filling the pulp spaces with the medicament, (c) alternating medicaments, (d) administering systemic antibiotics, (e) thorough removal of organic debris.

ANSWERS TO BOARD REVIEW QUESTIONS

Chapter 1: Introduction

1-b 2-c 3-c 4-d 5-d 6-b 7-d

Chapter 2: General principles of drug action

1-a 2-a 3-a 4-c 5-a 6-d 7-c 8-a 9-c 10-b 11-b
12-a 13-b 14-d 15-b 16-reversible 17-d 18-see text
19-see text 20-c 21-b 22-c 23-a 24-a 25-b 26-b 27-c
28-c 29-e 30-d 31-b

Chapter 3: Adverse drug reactions

1-b 2-e 3-a 4-b 5-a 6-b 7-b

Chapter 4: Prescription writing

1-b 2-b 3-c 4-a 5-b 6-11-see text 12-b 13-b 14-c
15-e 16-e

Chapter 5: The pharmacology of the autonomic nervous system

1-P 2-S 3-P 4-P 5-S 6-P 7-d 8-e 9-b 10-a 11-c
12-d 13-c 14-d 15-d 16-f 17-f 18-see text 19-see text
20-see text 21-e 22-c 23-a 24-a 25-c 26-a 27-d
28-f 29-e 30-d 31-a 32-b 33-f 34-c

Chapter 6: General anesthetics

1-b 2-c 3-a 4-e 5-c 6-b 7-d 8-c 9-d 10-e 11-a
12-b 13-d 14-c 15-a 16-c 17-a 18-c 19-e 20-i
21-d 22-e

Chapter 7: Sedative-hypnotic drugs

1-b 2-a 3-b 4-d 5-e 6-a 7-a 8-d 9-f 10-a 11-d
12-d

Chapter 8: Psychotherapeutic drugs

Chapter 9: Minor tranquilizers and centrally acting muscle relaxants

1-b 2-a 3-c 4-b 5-b 6-d 7-e 8-a 9-c 10-a 11-c
12-d 13-d 14-b 15-a 16-d 17-e 18-d 19-a 20-a
21-c

Chapter 10: Nonnarcotic analgesics

1-d 2-d 3-b 4-a 5-b 6-e 7-a 8-b 9-b 10-c 11-c
12-c 13-a 14-a 15-c 16-d 17-c 18-b 19-e 20-a
21-g 22-i 23-h 24-f 25-a 26-c 27-d 28-d 29-c 30-b
31-a

Chapter 11: The prostaglandins, the thromboxanes, and prostacyclin

1-a 2-c 3-c 4-a 5-c 6-a 7-a 8-c 9-b 10-a 11-c
12-e

Chapter 12: Narcotic, analgesics and antagonists

1-b 2-h 3-a 4-e 5-a 6-b 7-c 8-b 9-c 10-d 11-d
12-a 13-b 14-a 15-d 16-e 17-b 18-c 19-e 20-d
21-a 22-c 23-a 24-b 25-d 26-d 27-a 28-b 29-f
30-d 31-f 32-d 33-a 34-c 35-c 36-b 37-b 38-c

Chapter 13: Central nervous system stimulants

1-e 2-b 3-c 4-e 5-b 6-f 7-a 8-a

Chapter 14: Anticonvulsant drugs

1-d 2-d 3-d 4-c 5-e 6-b 7-d 8-a 9-a 10-a 11-d
12-a 13-a 14-b 15-b 16-b 17-b 18-d

Chapter 15: Local anesthetics

1-d 2-a 3-b 4-d 5-f 6-d 7-c 8-a 9-b 10-d 11-d
12-b 13-b 14-c 15-c 16-d 17-b 18-c 19-a 20-e
21-b 22-e 23-b 24-d 25-a 26-a 27-c 28-f 29-d
30-b 31-a 32-c 33-b 34-b 35-36 mg 36-0.018 mg

Chapter 16: Histamine and antihistamines

1-c 2-e 3-a 4-d 5-b 6-b 7-a 8-c 9-a

Chapter 17: Hormones and related substances

1-a 2-e 3-a 4-b 5-c 6-d 7-b 8-e 9-c 10-b
11-d 12-a 13-c 14-b 15-a

Chapter 18: Adrenocorticosteroids

1-c 2-b 3-a 4-a,b,c 5-d 6-c 7-a 8-g 9-d 10-c
11-stress; desoxycorticosterone; infection; oral

Chapter 19: Antineoplastic drugs

1-d 2-d 3-a 4-c 5-sensitive oral tissues, mucosal
ulcerations, gingival hemorrhage, xerostomia, impaired taste
sensation, candidiasis 6-d

Chapter 20: Diuretics and antihypertensive drugs

1-b 2-a 3-d 4-b 5-b 6-c 7-b 8-a 9-a 10-c 11-a
12-b 13-c 14-c 15-a 16-d 17-b 18-e 19-a 20-c
21-d 22-f 23-g 24-d 25-c 26-b 27-e 28-a

Chapter 21: Other cardiovascular drugs

1-T 2-T 3-T 4-T 5-T 6-T 7-T 8-T 9-T 10-T 11-T
12-F 13-T 14-c 15-T 16-T 17-T 18-F 19-F 20-c
21-b 22-c 23-c 24-c 25-b 26-a 27-c

Chapter 22: Antimicrobial agents

1-c 2-b 3-c 4-c 5-b 6-b 7-d 8-a 9-a 10-d 11-c
12-a 13-b 14-a 15-d 16-c 17-a 18-b 19-b 20-c
21-b 22-d 23-d 24-i 25-b 26-e 27-c 28-h 29-g 30-j
31-f 32-a 33-d 34-a 35-a 36-c 37-c 38-e 39-b 40-b
41-b 42-c 43-a 44-c 45-d 46-a 47-a 48-c 49-d

Chapter 23: Locally-acting medications: antimicrobials, hemostatics and protectives

1-d 2-e 3-e 4-e 5-e 6-d 7-e 8-e

Chapter 24: Fluorides

1-d 2-d 3-T 4-F 5-T 6-T 7-T 8-T 9-T 10-T 11-T
12-T 13-b 14-c 15-a 16-c 17-a 18-a 19-d 20-f 21-d
22-a 23-g 24-d 25-b 26-b 27-e 28-f 29-f 30-b
31-b 32-b 33-f 34-c 35-a 36-b

Chapter 25: Vitamins

1-a 2-c 3-a 4-a 5-b 6-d 7-c 8-c 9-see p. 252 10-b
11-c 12-d 13-b 14-c 15-a 16-a 17-d 18-a
19-osteomalacia 20-c 21-b 22-b 23-a 24-h 25-f 26-g
27-d 28-c 29-b 30-g 31-a 32-e 33 through 44 see text

Chapter 26: Minerals

1-c 2-a,c,d 3-c,d 4-a,b,d 5-b 6-b 7-c 8-d 9-c 10-b

Chapter 27: Drugs used for gastrointestinal disorders

1-f 2-h 3-g 4-e 5-a

Chapter 28: Emergency drugs

1-b 2-d 3-a 4-c 5-c 6-a 7-c 8-b 9-b 10-b

Chapter 29: Pharmacology of intravenous sedation

1-c 2-a 3-d 4-c 5-a 6-d 7-c 8-d 9-a 10-c 11-b

Chapter 30: Parenteral sedation and nitrous oxide analgesia

1-h 2-c 3-c 4-a 5-d 6-e 7-a 8-d 9-b 10-a 11-c
12-b 13-d 14-c 15-c 16-f 17-d 18-a 19-b 20-d
21-d 22-c 23-b 24-a 25-h

Chapter 31: Pharmacologic considerations in patients with systemic disease

1-a 2-e 3-b 4-i 5-d 6-g 7-a 8-c 9-j 10-f 11-h
12-b 13-a 14-c 15-e 16-e 17-a

Chapter 32: Pharmacologic management of certain common oral disease entities

1-a 2-c 3-d 4-b 5-f 6-c 7-b 8-c 9-d

Chapter 33: Drug interactions

1-see text 2-b 3-a 4-c 5-b 6-c 7-d 8-d 9-a
10-b 11-b

Chapter 34: Drug abuse

1-b 2-e 3-a 4-d 5-b 6-a 7-b 8-d 9-a 10-d 11-c
12-e 13-a 14-M 15-M 16-M 17-L

Chapter 35: Dental plaque and the control of plaque-related oral disease

1-c 2-a 3-b 4-c 5-e 6-e 7-e 8-e 9-c 10-d 11-c
12-e

Chapter 36: Endodontic medicaments and irrigants

1-b 2-d 3-a 4-c 5-h 6-g 7-e 8-a 9-d 10-e 11-c
12-c 13-i 14-a 15-c 16-d 17-a 18-d 19-a 20-e

Index